Sixth Workshop on Noisy User-generated Text (W-NUT 2020)

Online
19 November 2020

ISBN: 978-1-7138-2006-2

W-NUT 2020

**The Sixth Workshop on
Noisy User-generated Text
(W-NUT 2020)**

Proceedings of the Workshop

Nov 19, 2020
Online

Introduction

The W-NUT 2020 workshop focuses on a core set of natural language processing tasks on top of noisy user-generated text, such as that found on social media, web forums and online reviews. Recent years have seen a significant increase of interest in these areas. The internet has democratized content creation leading to an explosion of informal user-generated text, publicly available in electronic format, motivating the need for NLP on noisy text to enable new data analytics applications.

This year, in addition to the main workshop track, we have three shared tasks: (1) Entity and relation recognition over wet-lab protocols, (2) Identification of informative COVID-19 English Tweets, and (3) COVID-19 Event Extraction from Twitter. We accepted 33 regular workshop papers and 47 shared-task papers. The workshop will be held online and live in two different time zones (GMT– and GMT++). There are two invited speakers for each time zone, Eduardo Blanco (University of North Texas) and Manaal Faruqui (Google) in time zone GMT– and Robert Munro (Machine Learning Consulting; former CTO of Figure Eight) and Irwin King (The Chinese University of Hong Kong) in time zone GMT++ with each of their talks covering a different aspect of NLP for user-generated text. We have the best paper award(s) sponsored by Twitter this year, for which we are thankful. We would like to thank the Program Committee members who reviewed the papers and the shared task organizers who enriched our workshop this year. We would also like to thank the workshop participants.

Wei Xu, Alan Ritter, Tim Baldwin and Afshin Rahimi
Co-Organizers

Organizers:

Wei Xu, Ohio State University
Alan Ritter, Ohio State University
Tim Baldwin, University of Melbourne
Afshin Rahimi, University of Melbourne

Program Committee:

Muhammad Abdul-Mageed (University of British Columbia)
Željko Agić (Corti)
Sweta Agrawal (University of Maryland)
Gustavo Aguilar (University of Houston)
Nikolaos Aletras (University of Sheffield)
Rahul Aralikatte (University of Copenhagen)
Eiji Aramaki (NAIST)
JinYeong Bak (Sungkyunkwan University)
Francesco Barbieri (Universitat Pompeu Fabra)
John Beieler (ODNI Science and Technology)
Eric Bell (PNNL)
Anya Belz (University of Brighton)
Adrian Benton (JHU)
Eduardo Blanco (University of North Texas)
Su Lin Blodgett (UMass Amherst)
Julian Brooke (University of British Columbia)
Cornelia Caragea (University of Illinois at Chicago)
Tuhin Chakrabarty (Columbia University)
Stevie Chancellor (Northwestern University)
Mingda Chen (Toyota Technological Institute at Chicago)
Sihao Chen (University of Pennsylvania)
Dhivya Chinnappa (Thomson Reuters)
Colin Cherry (Google)
Zewei Chu (University of Chicago)
Manuel R. Ciosici (IT University of Copenhagen)
Oana Cocarascu (Imperial College London)
Nigel Collier (University of Cambridge)
Çağrı Çöltekin (University of Tübingen)
Paul Cook (University of New Brunswick)
Marina Danilevsky (IBM Research)
Pradipto Das (Rakuten Institute of Technology)
Leon Derczynski (IT University of Copenhagen)
Jay DeYoung (Northeastern University)
Bhuwan Dhingra (Carnegie Mellon University)
Seza Doğruöz (Tilburg University)
Xinya Du (Cornell University)
Jacob Eisenstein (Google)
Heba Elfardy (Amazon)
Micha Elsner (Ohio State University)
Alexander Fabbri (Yale University)

Manaal Faruqui (Google)
Yansong Feng (Peking University)
Catherine Finegan-Dollak (IBM Research)
Tim Finin (UMBC)
Lucie Flek (Mainz University of Applied Sciences)
Lisheng Fu (New York University)
Yoshinari Fujinuma (University of Colorado, Boulder)
Juri Ganitkevitch (Google)
Dan Garrette (Google)
Sahil Garg (University of Southern California)
Spandana Gella (Amazon)
Debanjan Ghosh (MIT)
Kevin Gimpel (TTIC)
Amit Goyal (Amazon)
Yvette Graham (Dublin City University)
Chulaka Gunasekara (IBM Research)
Mika Hämäläinen (University of Helsinki)
William L. Hamilton (McGill University/MILA)
Xiaochuang Han (Carnegie Mellon University)
Devamanyu Hazarika (National University of Singapore)
Hua He (Amazon)
Jack Hessel (Cornell University)
Graeme Hirst (University of Toronto)
Nathan Hodas (PNNL)
Junjie Hu (Carnegie Mellon University)
Dirk Hovy (Bocconi University)
Binxuan Huang (Carnegie Mellon University)
Sarthak Jain (Northeastern University)
Nanjiang Jiang (Ohio State University)
Lifeng Jin (Ohio State University)
Ishan Jindal (IBM Research)
Kristen Johnson (Michigan State University)
Kenny Joseph (University at Buffalo)
Katharina Kann (University of Colorado, Boulder)
David Kauchak (Pomona College)
Ashique KhudaBukhsh (Carnegie Mellon University)
Roman Klinger (University of Stuttgart)
Hayato Kobayashi (Yahoo! Research)
Ekaterina Kochmar (University of Cambridge)
Reno Kriz (University of Pennsylvania)
Sachin Kumar (Carnegie Mellon University)
Vivek Kulkarni (Stanford University)
Jonathan Kummerfeld (University of Michigan)
Ophélie Lacroix (Siteimprove)
Wuwei Lan (Ohio State University)
Jiwei Li (ShannonAI)
Jessy Junyi Li (University of Texas Austin)
Jing Li (Hong Kong Polytechnic University)
Yitong Li (University of Melbourne)
Nut Limsopatham (University of Glasgow)
Zhiyuan Liu (Tsinghua University)

Fei Liu (University of Melbourne)
Nikola Ljubešić (Jožef Stefan Institute)
Wei-Yun Ma (Academia Sinica)
Mounica Maddela (Georgia Institute of Technology)
Peter Makarov (University of Zurich)
Héctor Martínez Alonso (Apple)
Aaron Masino (The Children's Hospital of Philadelphia)
Nitika Mathur (University of Melbourne)
Ahmed Mourad (RMIT University)
Yasuhide Miura (Fuji Xerox)
Hamdy Mubarak (Qatar Computing Research Institute)
Graham Mueller (Leidos)
Maria Nadejde (Grammarly)
Guenter Neumann (German Research Center for Artificial Intelligence)
Vincent Ng (University of Texas at Dallas)
Thien Huu Nguyen (University of Oregon)
Eric Nichols (Honda Research Institute)
Tong Niu (University of North Carolina at Chapel-Hill)
Benjamin Nye (Northeastern University)
Alice Oh (KAIST)
Naoaki Okazaki (Tohoku University)
Naoki Otani (CMU)
Myle Ott (Facebook AI)
Symeon Papadopoulos (CERTH-ITI)
Umashanthi Pavalanathan (Georgia Tech)
Yuval Pinter (Georgia Tech)
Christopher Potts (Stanford University)
Vinodkumar Prabhakaran (Stanford University)
Daniel Preoţiuc-Pietro (Bloomberg)
Ella Rabinovich (University of Toronto)
Dianna Radpour (University of Colorado Boulder)
Preethi Raghavan (IBM Research)
Afshin Rahimi (University of Queensland)
Revanth Rameshkumar (Microsoft Research)
Adithya Renduchintala (JHU)
Carolyn Rose (CMU)
Alla Rozovskaya (City University of New York)
Derek Ruths (McGill University)
Koustuv Saha (Georgia Tech)
Keisuke Sakaguchi (Allen Institute for Artificial Intelligence)
Maarten Sap (University of Washington)
Amirreza Shirani (University of Houston)
Dan Simonson (BlackBoiler)
Kevin Small (Amazon)
Jan Šnajder (University of Zagreb)
Xingyi Song (University of Sheffield)
Evangelia Spiliopoulou (Carnegie Mellon University)
Gabriel Stanovsky (Allen Institute for Artificial Intelligence)
Ian Stewart (Georgia Tech)
Nadiya Straton (Copenhagen Business School)
Shivashankar Subramanian (University of Melbourne)

Jeniya Tabassum (Ohio State University)
Yi Tay (Google)
Zhiyang Teng (Westlake University)
Joel Tetreault (Dataminr)
James Thorne (University of Cambridge)
Rob van der Goot (University of Groningen)
Vasudeva Varma (IIIT Hyderabad)
Daniel Varab (IT University of Copenhagen)
Olga Vechtomova (University of Waterloo)
Nikhita Vedula (Ohio State University)
Alakananda Vempala (Bloomberg)
Rob Voigt (Northwestern University)
Soroush Vosoughi (Dartmouth University)
Xiaojun Wan (Peking University)
Zeerak Waseem (University of Sheffield)
Zhongyu Wei (Fudan University)
Hong Wei (University of Maryland)
Steven Wilson (University of Edinburgh)
Zach Wood-Doughty (Johns Hopkins University)
Ning Yu (Leidos)
Marcos Zampieri (Rochester Institute of Technology)
Guido Zarrella (MITRE)
Vicky Zayats (University of Washington)
Justine Zhang (Cornell University)
Xiao Zhang (Purdue University)
Shi Zong (Ohio State University)

Invited Speakers:

Eduardo Blanco (University of North Texas)
Manaal Faruqui (Google)
Robert Munro (Machine Learning Consulting; former CTO of Figure Eight)
Irwin King (The Chinese University of Hong Kong)

Table of Contents

Conference Program

May I Ask Who's Calling? Named Entity Recognition on Call Center Transcripts for Privacy Law Compliance
Micaela Kaplan

"Did you really mean what you said?" : Sarcasm Detection in Hindi-English Code-Mixed Data using Bilingual Word Embeddings
Akshita Aggarwal, Anshul Wadhawan, Anshima Chaudhary and Kavita Maurya

Noisy Text Data: Achilles' Heel of BERT
Ankit Kumar, Piyush Makhija and Anuj Gupta

Determining Question-Answer Plausibility in Crowdsourced Datasets Using Multi-Task Learning
Rachel Gardner, Maya Varma, Clare Zhu and Ranjay Krishna

Combining BERT with Static Word Embeddings for Categorizing Social Media
Israa Alghanmi, Luis Espinosa Anke and Steven Schockaert

Enhanced Sentence Alignment Network for Efficient Short Text Matching
Zhe Hu, Zuohui Fu, Cheng Peng and Weiwei Wang

PHINC: A Parallel Hinglish Social Media Code-Mixed Corpus for Machine Translation
Vivek Srivastava and Mayank Singh

Cross-lingual sentiment classification in low-resource Bengali language
Salim Sazzed

The Non-native Speaker Aspect: Indian English in Social Media
Rupak Sarkar, Sayantan Mahinder and Ashiqur KhudaBukhsh

Sentence Boundary Detection on Line Breaks in Japanese
Yuta Hayashibe and Kensuke Mitsuzawa

Non-ingredient Detection in User-generated Recipes using the Sequence Tagging Approach
Yasuhiro Yamaguchi, Shintaro Inuzuka, Makoto Hiramatsu and Jun Harashima

Generating Fact Checking Summaries for Web Claims
Rahul Mishra, Dhruv Gupta and Markus Leippold

May I Ask Who's Calling? Named Entity Recognition on Call Center Transcripts for Privacy Law Compliance

Micaela Kaplan
Brandeis University / Waltham, MA
CallMiner Inc / Waltham, MA
`micaela@brandeis.edu`

Abstract

We investigate using Named Entity Recognition on a new type of user-generated text: a call center conversation. These conversations combine problems from spontaneous speech with problems novel to conversational Automated Speech Recognition, including incorrect recognition, alongside other common problems from noisy user-generated text. Using our own corpus with new annotations, training custom contextual string embeddings, and applying a BiLSTM-CRF, we match state-of-the-art results on our novel task.

1 Introduction

When a call center says "a call may be recorded", they are often collecting a transcript. These transcripts are the output of speech recognition systems, and while they are redacted for Payment Card Industry (PCI) compliance, they often contain other information about the caller such as their name and internal ID number. This data can be helpful for quality assurance and future customer care. New privacy laws, such as the General Data Protection Regulation (GDPR) in the EU, define rules and regulations for everything from how data is collected and stored to the rights of a person to retract their consent to the use of their data (gdp, 2019). In the face of these new laws, it is important to be able to identify non-public personal information and personally identifiable information (NPI/PII) in call transcripts in order to comply with regulations without compromising the data these companies rely on.

We use Named Entity Recognition (NER) to find instances of NPI/PII, remove them from a transcript, and replace them with a tag identifying which type of information was removed. For example, a transcript containing "This is john doe reference number 12345" would become "This is [NAME] reference number [NUMBER]". This problem is unique in a call center for a few reasons. Firstly, call transcripts are organic human conversations and present many of the common problems of user-generated data, including false starts, incomplete sentences, and novel words. Secondly, the text provided in a transcript is the output of an Automatic Speech Recognition (ASR) system, which is prone to error as described in Section 3.1. While modern ASR systems are reliable, our input audio is from phone calls, which are usually very low-quality and often contain a lot of background noise. This low-quality audio results in poor ASR, which then outputs sentences that may not be grammatical. This makes it difficult to understand the semantics of the call or to pick up on many of the features that are critical to most NER systems such as context or part of speech. Additionally, production-level call transcripts, or those that are used by Quality Assurance agents and data scientists, are missing capital letters, numeric digits, and accurate punctuation, which are features that are crucial to the classic approaches to NER. Moreover, traditional NER systems use labels for proper nouns, like people's names, but have no way to handle emails, spellings, or addresses, making bootstrapping from pretrained NER models impossible.

In this paper, we apply the current state-of-the-art neural architecture for sequence labeling, a BiLSTM-CRF, to our novel call center transcripts in search of NPI and PII as identified by a human. We match state-of-the-art performance for standard datasets on our novel problem by using our model in conjunction with annotated data and custom contextual string embeddings.

2 Previous Work

NER became popular in the NLP community at the Message Understanding Conferences (MUCs)

Proceedings of the 2020 EMNLP Workshop W-NUT: The Sixth Workshop on Noisy User-generated Text, pages 1–6
Online, Nov 19, 2020. ©2020 Association for Computational Linguistics

during the 1990s (Hirschman, 1998). In 2003, the CoNLL2003 shared task focused on language independent NER and popularized feature based systems (Tjong Kim Sang and De Meulder, 2003). The OntoNotes corpus, released in 2006, has also been fundamental to NER research (Hovy et al., 2006).

After CoNLL, the highest performing models were based on a CRF (Lafferty et al., 2001) which requires the manual generation of features. More recently, research has used neural techniques to generate these features. Huang et al. (2015) found great success using Bidirectional Long Short Term Memory models with a CRF layer (BiLSTM-CRF) on both the CoNLL2000 and CoNLL2003 shared task datasets. Ma and Hovy (2016) used a BiLSTM-CNN-CRF to do NER on the CoNLL2003 dataset, producing state-of-the-art results. Similarly, Chiu and Nichols (2015) used a BiLSTM-CNN, with features from word embeddings and the lexicon, which produced very similar results. Ghaddar and Langlais (2018) used embeddings for the words and for entity types to create a more robust model. Flair, proposed by Akbik et al. (2018), set the current state of the art by using character based embeddings, and built on this with their pooling approach in 2019 (Akbik et al., 2019). Crossweigh, a framework introduced by Wang et al. (2019), makes use of Flair embeddings to clean mishandled annotations.

In 2006, Sudoh et al. used the word confidence scores from ASR systems as a feature for NER on the recordings of Japanese newspaper articles. In 2018, Ghannay et al. (2018) conducted a similar experiment on French radio and TV audio. Unlike our data, neither of these tasks used spontaneous conversation. Additionally, the audio was probably recording-studio quality, making ASR a reliable task.

2.1 Conversations are Different: The Twitter Analogy

All of the previous work discussed was run on datasets primarily comprised of newswire data (Li et al., 2018). Typically, newswire follows the conventions of normal text, but call center transcripts have none of these conventions guaranteed and often explicitly lack them entirely. This is a problem for the traditional approaches to NER. Our low-quality audio adds to the difficulty of this task.

The closest approximation of this problem in

Speaker 1: Thank you for calling our company how may i help you today.
Speaker 2: Id like to pay my bill.

Figure 1: An example of turns of a conversation, where each person's line in the dialogue represents their turn. This output matches the format of our data described in Section 3.

the previous research is on Twitter data. Tweets, like transcripts, are generated by users and may not follow the grammar, spelling, or formatting rules that newswire is so careful to maintain. In 2011, Liu et al. (2011) used a K-nearest neighbors model combined with a CRF to begin tackling this problem. As part of the 2017 Workshop on Noisy User-generated Text (W-NUT) shared task, Aguilar et al. (2017) obtained a first place ranking using a model that combined a multi-step neural net with a CRF output layer. Akbik et al. (2019) also tested their pooled contextualized string embeddings on this data and found success. We use this previous work on tweets to inform our model creation for the call center space.

3 Data

Our dataset consists of 7,953 training, 500 validation, and 534 test samples. Each sample is a complete speaker turn from a call taken by a call center that deals with debt collection. For our purposes, a speaker turn is defined as the complete transcription of one speaker before another speaker starts talking, as illustrated in Figure 1. The training set is a random sample of turns from 4 months of call transcripts from the client, but was manually curated to contain examples of NPI/PII to compensate for its relatively rarity in call center conversation. The transcripts were made using a proprietary speech recognition system, which is set to provide all lowercase transcripts and omits punctuation and numeric digits. We used spaCy[1] to convert each turn to a document that starts with a capital letter and ends with a period. This is due to the default configurations of spaCy– in order to make use of entities, we needed to add in a Sentencizer module, which defaults to this capital letter and period set up.

3.1 Data Annotation

We created a schema to annotate the training and validation data for a variety of different categories of NPI/PII as described in Table 1. Initial annota-

---

[1] https://spaCy.io/

Entity Type	Description
NUMBERS	A sequence of numbers relating to a customer's information (e.g. phone numbers or internal ID number)
NAME	First and last name of a customer or agent
COMPANY	The name of a company
ADDRESS	A complete address, including city, state, and zip code
EMAIL	Any email address
SPELLING	Language that clarifies the spelling of a word, (e.g. "a as in apple")

Table 1: A brief description of our annotation schema.

tion was done with Doccano[2]. These annotations were converted to entities in the text with spaCy. The annotators were trained in NPI/PII recognition, and were instructed to lean towards a greater level of caution in ambiguous cases. This ambiguity was often caused by misrecognitions from the language model in the ASR system being used. With no audio to help the annotator, it wasn't always clear when "I need oak leaves" was supposed to be "Annie Oakley". The reverse problem was also true. "Brilliant and wendy jeff to process the refund" appears to be a full name, but is actually a misrecognition for "Brilliant and when did you want to process the refund". Emails also proved difficult, because misrecognitions made it difficult for annotators to discern exactly what words belonged in the email address. Another difficulty for annotation was that all of our data had been pre-redacted for PCI compliance, which requires the redaction of number strings relating to credit card numbers, birth dates, and social security numbers. This redaction occurs before any transcript can be released to a client or researcher. To minimize false negatives, PCI redaction frequently redacts numbers that are NPI/PII such as in an internal customer ID number or a phone number. Since the NUMBERS label was intended to catch these NPI/PII related numbers, we used context to include this [redacted] tag as part of a numbers sequence when possible. No steps to clean the transcripts were taken at any point. The naturally occurring noise in our data is critical to our use case and was left for the model to interpret.

Due to limitations with spaCy and the known complexity of nested entities, we opted to allow

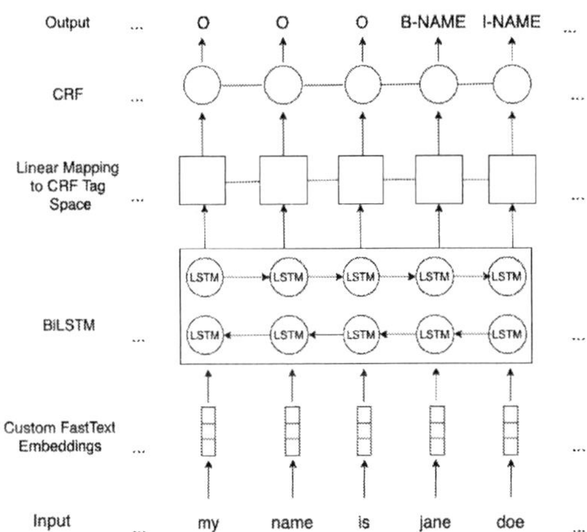

Figure 2: A schematic of our BiLSTM-CRF model. The text of each turn is passed to a word embedding layer which is followed by a BiLSTM layer, and then a linear layer that maps the word BiLSTM output into tag space. Finally, the CRF layer produces an output sequence.

only one annotation per word in our dataset. This means that "c a t as in team at gmail dot com" could only be labeled either as SPELLING[0:6] EMAIL[6:] or as EMAIL[0:] with indices that correspond to the location of the word in the text and are exclusive. This ultimately explains the much lower number of SPELLING entities in the dataset as compared to other entities, because they are often contained a part of EMAIL or ADDRESS. This will influence our analysis in Section 6.

4 Model Design

We implemented a standard BiLSTM-CRF model in PyTorch. The basic model implementation is adapted from a GitHub repository[3]. We wrote our own main.py to better allow for our spaCy preprocessing, and we also adapted the code to handle batch processing of data. After this preprocessing, we trained the model with the training set and used the validation set for any model tuning. All reported numbers are on the test set and occur after all tuning is completed. A visualization of our model is found in Figure 2.

5 Experiments

5.1 Basic Hyperparameter Tuning

We used a grid search algorithm to maximize the performance of the model. The word embedding layer uses FastText embeddings trained on the

---

[2]http://doccano.herokuapp.com/

[3]https://github.com/mtreviso/
linear-chain-crf

client's call transcripts. We find that this helps mitigate the impacts of poor ASR in other aspects of our research, and investigate this further in Sections 5.2 and 5.3. The grid search contained the following parameters: epochs (a sampled distribution between 5 and 50), the size of a dropout layer (between 0 and .5, with .1 intervals of search), the number of hidden layers (between 5 and 20 in increments of 5), and the encoding type used in the output of the CRF (BIO, BILOU, IO). The other hyperparameters in our model were learning rate .001, batch size 1, 30 nodes in each fully connected layer, and the inclusion of bias in each layer. The experiments were run in parallel using Python's multiprocessing package on a virtual machine with 16 CPUs and 128GB of memory. Each experimental configuration ran on a time scale of a few hours, relative to the configurations of the hyperparameters being used.

To better understand the performance of our model on the test set, we broke down the precision, recall, and F1 measurements by entity type. Table 2 shows these results for the best model configuration under the columns labeled "Custom". This model used 46 epochs, a dropout rate of .2, 5 hidden layers, and a BIO encoding.

5.2 Training Word Embeddings

While much of the previous research has fine-tuned existing word embeddings, the task of compensating for misrecognition seemed less straightforward than domain adaptation. We lessen the impact of the misrecognitions described in Section 3.1 by understanding that frequent misrecognitions appear in contexts similar to the intended word. For example, "why you're" is often misrecognized as "choir" which would have a totally out of context vector from a pretrained model in this data set. A custom model gives "choir" a vector that is more similar to "why" than to "chorus". Huang and Chen (2020) showed the importance of domain specific word embeddings when using ASR data.

We ran our best performing model configuration with the 300 dimensional GloVe 6b word embeddings [4]. Our embeddings, in contrast, are trained on approximately 216 million words, making them substantially smaller than other state-of-the-art embeddings used today. The results from the best epoch of this model (16) are shown in Table 2.

Entity Type	Precision		Recall		F1	
	Custom	GloVe	Custom	GloVe	Custom	GloVe
O	89.8	84.2	81.7	76.6	**85.6**	80.2
NUMBERS	95.6	88.7	85.4	82.9	**90.1**	85.7
NAME	89.6	92.1	91.1	88.7	90.3	90.3
COMPANY	98.8	99.5	72,9	64.3	**83.9**	78.1
ADDRESS	70.6	.3	75.0	18.7	**72.7**	23
EMAIL[5]	0	07.1	0	03.1	0	**04.4**
SPELLING	45.8	.34	52.4	40/5	**48.9**	37.0
Micro Average	89.2	85.6	79.6	74.0	**84**.1	79.4

Table 2: The performance by entity type of the BiLSTM-CRF model on the held out test set. This table compares the results of our custom embeddings model ("Custom") against the GloVe embeddings ("GloVe").

5.3 Using Flair

In our previous experiments, we established the importance of using custom word embeddings to accurately account for the misrecognitions, false starts, and other kinds of noise present in call center conversation transcripts. In this experiment, we test the performance of Flair[6] and its contextual string embeddings on our data.

We begin by training custom contextual string embeddings for this dataset, based on the findings in our original experiments. For training, we use the same corpus as used in Section 5.1. To do this we follow the tutorial on the Flair GitHub page using their suggested hyperparameter settings as follows: hidden_size: 1024, sequence_length: 250, mini_batch_size: 100, and otherwise use the default parameters. We use the newline to indicate a document change, and list each turn as a separate document to provide consistency with the other experiments conducted in this paper. Given the size of our corpus for word embedding training, we found that our model's validation loss stabilized after epoch 4. We use the best version of model, as given by Flair, in all of our tests.

We conduct a number of experiments using Flair's SequenceTagger with default parameters and a hidden_size of 256. We adapt the work done by Akbik et al. (2018) and Akbik et al. (2019) to explore the impact of call center data on these state-of-the-art configurations.

Flair uses only the custom trained Flair embeddings.

Flair+ FastText uses the custom trained Flair embeddings and our custom trained FastText embeddings using Flair's StackedEmbeddings.

Flair_mean pooling uses only the custom trained Flair embeddings within Flair's PooledFlairEmbedding. We use mean pooling due to the results of

[4]https://nlp.stanford.edu/projects/glove/

[5]Our custom model gets all 0s because many of its predicted EMAIL entities were off by a few words. We discuss this more in Section 6.

[6]https://github.com/flairNLP/flair

Entity	Flair	Flair$_{+ FastText}$	Flair$_{mean pooling}$	Flair$_{mean pooling + FastText}$
O	98.3	98.5	98.2	98.5
NUMBERS	83.1	**87.9**	87.7	86.2
COMPANY	**81.1**	80.7	80.7	80.3
ADDRESS	87.5	**94.1**	61.5	**94.1**
EMAIL	58.8	50.0	**73.3**	66.7
SPELLING	55.0	57.1	55.8	**57.9**
Micro Average	97.5	97.7	97.3	97.7

Table 3: The F1 scores on the test set for each entity type for each Flair embedding experiment.

Akbik et al. (2019) on the WNUT-17 shared task.

Flair$_{mean pooling + FastText}$ uses the Pooled-FlairEmbeddings with mean pooling and the custom trained FastText embeddings using Flair's StackedEmbeddings.

These results are shown in Table 3.

6 Discussion

Table 2 shows that in all cases except for EMAIL, it is beneficial to use our custom embeddings over GloVe embeddings. We explain this in the next paragraph. The Flair embeddings show a large improvement over the other word embedding varieties however in our circumstance all four varieties of Flair models have nearly identical Micro Average F1s. The best performing Flair models are those that use both the custom contextualized string embeddings and the custom FastText embeddings.

Across all of the models in this paper, EMAIL and SPELLING consistently performed worse than other categories. We believe this is due to the overlap in their occurrences as well as the variability in their appearance. In many cases the custom embeddings model identified parts of an email correctly but attributed certain aspects, like a name, as NAME followed by EMAIL instead of including them together as EMAIL. SPELLING often appears within an EMAIL entity, such as in "c as in cat a t at gmail dot com". Due to the limitations discussed in Section 3, this leads to a limited occurrence of the SPELLING entity in our training data, and many EMAIL and ADDRESS entities that contain examples SPELLING. All models, especially the custom embeddings model, frequently misidentified EMAIL as SPELLING and vice versa. Additionally, our test data contained a number of turns that consisted of only SPELLING on its own, which was poorly represented in training. The Flair$_{mean pooling}$ model outperforms the other models in EMAIL by a large margin.

The results shown in Table 3 highlight other interesting notes about our data. The NUMBERS category contains many strings that appear consistently in the text. Not only are there a finite number of NUMBER words in our corpus (those numeric words along with many instances of "[redacted]"), but the NUMBERS of interest in our dataset, such as account numbers, appear in very similar contexts and do not often get misrecognized. The COMPANY entity performs well for a similar reason. When the model was able to identify the company name correctly, it was usually in one of the very common misrecognition forms and in a known context, which furthers our claim that dataset specific embeddings give an important boost over pretrained embeddings. Where the models failed here can likely be attributed to training data. Since the name of the company is a proper noun, it is not in most standard ASR language models, including the one we use. Thus, it is a frequent candidate for misrecognition, because the language model has higher probabilities assigned to grammatically correct phrases that have nothing to do with the name of the company. This leads to high variability in appearance, which means that not every possible version of the company name was present in our training set.

Interesting variability also occurred in ADDRESS entities. With ADDRESS, both models that used Flair and FastText embeddings strongly outperformed the models that used Flair on its own, but standard Flair embeddings strongly outperformed the Pooled Flair embeddings. Neither version of the Flair only model identified addresses in which house numbers or zip codes were shown as "[redacted]" but both models that utilized FastText had no issue with these examples.

7 Conclusion and Future Work

By using a BiLSTM-CRF, in conjunction with custom-trained Flair embeddings, we match current state-of-the-art NER performance on our novel call center conversation dataset with unique entity types. We also reinforce the importance of training word embeddings that fully capture the nuances of the data being used for the task. While we cannot release any data for privacy reasons, we have shown that current state-of-the-art techniques successfully carry over to more non-traditional datasets and tasks. In the future, we'd like to assess the contribution of this model with the call transcripts from other industries. Additionally, we'd like to investigate the success of these strategies on other user-generated conversations, such as chats and emails.

Acknowledgments

Thanks to the anonymous reviewers for their invaluable feedback. Thanks to CallMiner Inc. and its research partners for providing all of the data as well as the use cases and funding. Thanks to Jamie Brandon for her help with model architecture design. Thanks to the whole CallMiner research team for their help and support throughout the process.

References

2019. What is gdpr, the eu's new data protection law?

Gustavo Aguilar, Suraj Maharjan, Adrian Pastor López Monroy, and Thamar Solorio. 2017. A multitask approach for named entity recognition in social media data. *Proceedings of the 3rd Workshop on Noisy User-generated Text.*

Alan Akbik, Tanja Bergmann, and Roland Vollgraf. 2019. Pooled contextualized embeddings for named entity recognition. In *NAACL 2019, 2019 Annual Conference of the North American Chapter of the Association for Computational Linguistics*, page 724–728.

Alan Akbik, Duncan Blythe, and Roland Vollgraf. 2018. Contextual string embeddings for sequence labeling. In *COLING 2018, 27th International Conference on Computational Linguistics*, pages 1638–1649.

Jason P. C. Chiu and Eric Nichols. 2015. Named entity recognition with bidirectional lstm-cnns.

Abbas Ghaddar and Phillippe Langlais. 2018. Robust lexical features for improved neural network named-entity recognition. In *Proceedings of the 27th International Conference on Computational Linguistics*, pages 1896–1907, Santa Fe, New Mexico, USA. Association for Computational Linguistics.

Sahar Ghannay, Antoine Caubrière, Yannick Estève, Antoine Laurent, and Emmanuel Morin. 2018. End-to-end named entity extraction from speech.

L Hirschman. 1998. The evolution of evaluation: Lessons from the message understanding conferences. *Computer Speech Language*, 12(4):281 – 305.

Eduard Hovy, Mitch Marcus, Martha Palmer, Lance Ramshaw, and Ralph Weischedel. 2006. Ontonotes: the 90% solution. In *Proceedings of the human language technology conference of the NAACL, Companion Volume: Short Papers*, pages 57–60.

C. Huang and Y. Chen. 2020. Learning asr-robust contextualized embeddings for spoken language understanding. In *ICASSP 2020 - 2020 IEEE International Conference on Acoustics, Speech and Signal Processing (ICASSP)*, pages 8009–8013.

Zhiheng Huang, Wei Xu, and Kai Yu. 2015. Bidirectional lstm-crf models for sequence tagging.

John Lafferty, Andrew Mccallum, and Fernando Pereira. 2001. Conditional random fields: Probabilistic models for segmenting and labeling sequence data. pages 282–289.

Jing Li, Aixin Sun, Jianglei Han, and Chenliang Li. 2018. A survey on deep learning for named entity recognition.

Xiaohua Liu, Shaodian Zhang, Furu Wei, and Ming Zhou. 2011. Recognizing named entities in tweets. In *Proceedings of the 49th Annual Meeting of the Association for Computational Linguistics: Human Language Technologies*, pages 359–367, Portland, Oregon, USA. Association for Computational Linguistics.

Xuezhe Ma and Eduard Hovy. 2016. End-to-end sequence labeling via bi-directional lstm-cnns-crf.

Katsuhito Sudoh, Hajime Tsukada, and Hideki Isozaki. 2006. Incorporating speech recognition confidence into discriminative named entity recognition of speech data. In *Proceedings of the 21st International Conference on Computational Linguistics and 44th Annual Meeting of the Association for Computational Linguistics*, pages 617–624.

Erik F. Tjong Kim Sang and Fien De Meulder. 2003. Introduction to the CoNLL-2003 shared task: Language-independent named entity recognition. In *Proceedings of the Seventh Conference on Natural Language Learning at HLT-NAACL 2003*, pages 142–147.

Zihan Wang, Jingbo Shang, Liyuan Liu, Lihao Lu, Jiacheng Liu, and Jiawei Han. 2019. CrossWeigh: Training named entity tagger from imperfect annotations. In *Proceedings of the 2019 Conference on Empirical Methods in Natural Language Processing and the 9th International Joint Conference on Natural Language Processing (EMNLP-IJCNLP)*, pages 5154–5163, Hong Kong, China. Association for Computational Linguistics.

"Did you really mean what you said?" : Sarcasm Detection in Hindi-English Code-Mixed Data using Bilingual Word Embeddings

Akshita Aggarwal, Anshul Wadhawan, Anshima Chaudhary and Kavita Maurya
Department of Computer Engineering
Netaji Subhas University of Technology
Dwarka, New Delhi
`{akshitaa, anshulw, anshimac, kavitam}.co.16@nsit.net.in`

Abstract

With the increased use of social media platforms by people across the world, many new interesting NLP problems have come into existence. One such being the detection of sarcasm in the social media texts. We present a corpus of tweets for training custom word embeddings and a Hinglish dataset labelled for sarcasm detection. We propose a deep learning based approach to address the issue of sarcasm detection in Hindi-English code mixed tweets using bilingual word embeddings derived from FastText and Word2Vec approaches. We experimented with various deep learning models, including CNNs, LSTMs, Bi-directional LSTMs (with and without attention). We were able to outperform all state-of-the-art performances with our deep learning models, with attention based Bi-directional LSTMs giving the best performance exhibiting an accuracy of 78.49%.

1 Introduction

With the advent of social media, a large part of human interaction is carried out online. This leads to generation of huge amounts of textual data that can be used to draw meaningful inferences. Social media websites like Facebook, Twitter, Reddit etc are used by people across cultures to communicate with each other and voice their opinions.

With the large amount of data available from social media, the study of various types of linguistic expressions like irony, humor, sarcasm, aggression, hate etc has become a keen research area. Especially in the field of NLP, automatic detection of these expressions is being widely explored (Joshi et al., 2017). Automatic detection involves using computational methods to detect the presence of a particular emotion.

Although English is the language most commonly used on these websites, a majority of people are not native English speakers. These people therefore prefer to communicate in languages other than English (Danet and Herring, 2007). A study on the languages that are most commonly used for exchange of information on Twitter showed that around 50% of the posts are written in languages other than English (Hong et al., 2011). This raises the opportunity of dealing with multi-lingual data generated by the social media sites. Various statistics show that around 26% of the Indian population is bilingual[1]. This gives rise to the phenomenon of code-switching and code-mixing (Gupta et al., 2016). Code mixing takes place when speakers use two or more languages below clause level in a single social context. Multilinguals use such a mixture of languages, particularly on social media (Mónica et al., 2009). There are multiple challenges of working with code-mixed data like large amount of new constructions that are a result of combining lexicons and syntax of two different languages, availability of very small amounts of annotated data and use of very different approaches when compared to mono-lingual data (Çetinoğlu et al., 2016).

In this paper, we wish to work on detecting one of the most popular linguistic constructs used across social medias, 'sarcasm'. The cambridge-dictionary[2] defines sarcasm as 'the use of remarks that clearly mean the opposite of what they say'. Example: "You have been working hard," he said with heavy sarcasm, as he looked at the empty page.

Starting with the earliest known work which focuses on sarcasm detection in speech (Tepperman et al., 2006), this domain has been widely explored in sentiment analysis. Since sarcasm is a sentiment, detection of sarcasm is important in order to predict

---

[1]`https://en.wikipedia.org/wiki/Multilingualism_in_India`

[2]`https://dictionary.cambridge.org/`

7

Proceedings of the 2020 EMNLP Workshop W-NUT: The Sixth Workshop on Noisy User-generated Text, pages 7–15
Online, Nov 19, 2020. ©2020 Association for Computational Linguistics

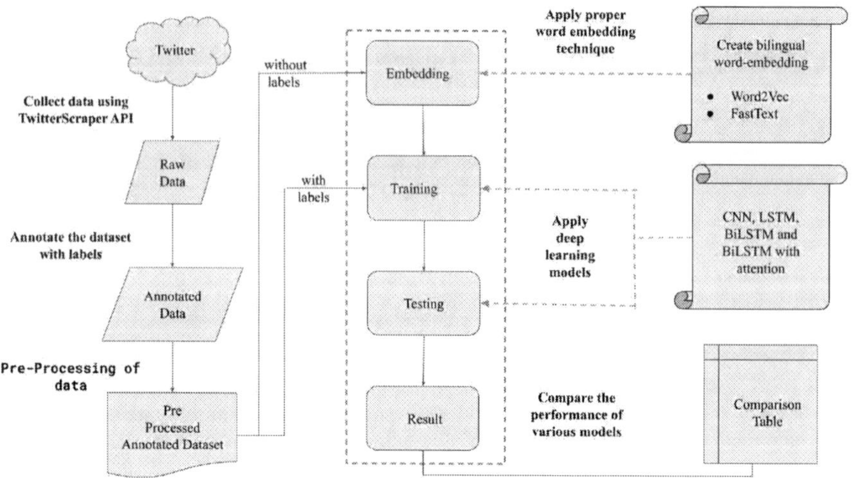

Figure 1: Proposed Methodology

the sentiment of a sentence. Being a challenging problem, automatic detection of sarcasm has been a popular area of research.

Although a lot of work has been carried out on sarcasm detection in English (Davidov et al., 2010; Bamman and Smith, 2015), the detection of sarcasm in code-mixed language like Hinglish (Hindi-English) is relatively unexplored. The current state-of-art performance is proposed via a random forest model on a dataset of 5000 Hinglish tweets (Swami et al., 2018).

The contributions of our work includes :

1. In this paper, we have experimented with deep-learning approaches to detect sarcasm in the Hindi-English code mixed dataset. The corpus prepared is released along with the paper.

2. Deep learning is being used extensively in the domain of natural language processing and has given satisfactory results (Young et al., 2018). In our work, we propose five different deep learning models namely, Series CNN, Parallel CNN, LSTM, Bi-directional LSTM and Bi-directional LSTM with attention.

3. The proposed models take self-trained bilingual word embeddings generated by Hindi-English code mixed data as input.

4. Our work present an alternate approach to the work done using traditional machine learning models like SVMs and random forests (Swami et al., 2018).

2 Proposed Methodology

2.1 Dataset Creation

The current dataset provided in paper (Swami et al., 2018) contains 5250 tweets, out of which 504 tweets are labelled as sarcastic while the remaining 4746 tweets are labelled as not sarcastic. All the deep learning models seemed to erroneously predict all tweets to be not sarcastic, since this dataset is highly skewed as well as insufficient. Therefore, to meet the model needs, we created a larger class-balanced dataset by scraping relevant tweets from twitter using TwitterScraper API[3] with search tags like #sarcasm, #irony, #humor, #bollywood, #cricket along with some common hindi words to obtain Hinglish data.

2.2 Dataset Annotation and Analysis

We were able to obtain around 427k tweets for training the proposed deep learning models. After carefully filtering out the obtained tweets for Hindi-English code mixed entries, we were successful in creating a corpus of 100k Hindi-English code mixed tweets with 49% entries being sarcastic and remaining 51% being non-sarcastic. The annotation scheme was based on the search tags(hashtags) used for scraping the tweets. We marked all examples fetched with hashtags like sarcasm, irony etc to have a positive sarcasm label, whereas all examples with generic hashtags like cricket, bollywood etc to have a negative sarcasm label. This

---

[3]`https://github.com/taspinar/twitterscraper`

Category	Tweet Count
Total Tweets	106899
Sarcastic	52587
Non-Sarcastic	54312

Table 1: Tweets per category

annotation scheme was susceptible to noise, however, as a quality check measure, we manually traversed the data and noticed that the noisy examples were meagre in proportion. Also, the noisy examples were necessary for the models to generalize well on the diverse dataset we obtained. Having a class-balanced dataset was significant to our problem to ensure that deep-learning models learn the right trends, not being biased towards a particular class. Embeddings were initally trained on solely Hinglish data, which was later on added with English data. The embedding training dataset, labelled sarcasm detection dataset and the proposed deep learning classification models are made available online [4] to facilitate further research.

Examples of some annotated data :

Tweet: Koi Rah Mushkil Nahi hain bus vo rah #bengalurutraffic se bach jaayein #sarcasm @random

Translation No path is difficult as long as it does not pass through Bangalore traffic. (Bangalore is an Indian city infamous for it's traffic)
Sarcasm : YES

Tweet : Hindustan ke tamam log chahte h ke jis trah se auraton ke upar crime bhadr rha h gang rape ke waqia ho rha iske liye central govt wali modi sarkar 1 strong law bnaye

Translation: All indians want Modi government to make strong laws on crime against women
Sarcasm: NO

2.3 Data Preprocessing

The data obtained from social media is very noisy and a lot of preprocessing is required. While creating the dataset, we removed the '#' symbols from the data, along with removing all the mentions (@). We also removed rare words (words having occurrence of less than 10 in the entire dataset) and search tags (like cricket, sarcasm) to avoid our deep learning models being biased towards certain words while learning. Further, URLs and punctuation marks were also removed.

2.4 Creation of Hindi-English Bi-lingual Word Embeddings

Being a text classification problem, it is essential for the words of the dataset to be first converted to vector representations. Word embedding is learned from unannotated plain text, useful in determining the context in which a given word is used. They provide a dense vector representation of syntactic or semantic aspects of a word (Mandelbaum and Shalev, 2016). To create a Hindi-English word embedding, we needed a huge amount of data. We used TwitterScraper API to extract 427k Hinglish tweets and 300k English tweets from Twitter for Hindi-English code-mixed data. For the Hinglish code mixed tweets, we removed the tweets obtained in pure Devnagri and kept only those which were a mixture of both Hindi and English sentences. The above obtained dataset was further processed to remove rare words, hashtags and mentions to obtain a less noisy corpus for training word embeddings.

We experimented with 2 different kinds of word embeddings for two types of datasets, one which solely consisted of Hinglish tweets, the other which consisted of 300k English along with Hinglish tweets. We chose to experiment with a mixture of Hinglish and English tweets in order to get the corelations between the words of the two languages. Each of these variations, after similar processing (removing hashtags, URLs, punctuations, user mentions and keywords used for scraping), were tried for two types of embeddings:

Word2Vec: In this embedding, words in the corpus are converted into vectors, where words that share common context are placed closed to each other in the vector-space (Mikolov et al., 2013). Since Word2Vec is pre-trained for English dataset only, we had to train our model on custom Hindi-English code mixed dataset, to obtain Hinglish word embeddings.

FastText: FastText which was given by Facebook in 2016, is an addition to the Word2Vec embeddings (Joulin et al., 2017). Rather than giving individual words to a model, FastText breaks down the words into multiple sub-words, also known as n-grams (Bojanowski et al., 2017). During the training of the model, weights are learned for all

---

[4]https://github.com/Akshitaag/Sarcasm_Detection

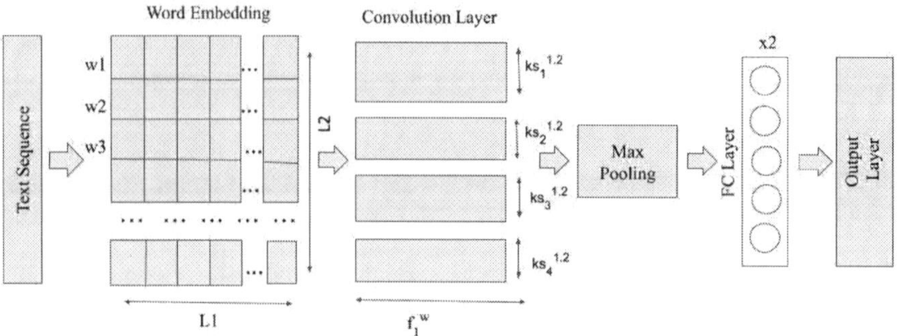

Figure 2: CNN Model 1.2 architecture

the n-grams along with the complete word. Unlike Word2vec, rare words can be appropriately featured as now it is much more likely that some of their n-grams also occur in other words. This is especially true for social media text where people use multiple spellings for the same words (amaze, amazeee, amazing, amazinggg).

2.5   Deep Learning Models

We propose 5 different models to experiment with the above problem. The models tested include Series CNN, Parallel CNN, LSTM, Bi-directional LSTM and Bi-directional LSTM with attention. Word embeddings, as generated by FastText and Word2Vec custom data trained representations, served as input to the models, generate as output a binary variable depicting the probability of the corresponding tweet being sarcastic.

2.5.1   Convolutional Neural Networks (CNN)

CNNs have the ability to extract features from data provided to it as input. In our case, the input data is a set of word vectors, over which convolution operation is performed to extract features and thereby, perform classification.

We propose 2 CNN deep learning model architectures, one which has convolution layers in series, denoted by model 1.1 and the other which has convolutional layers in parallel, denoted by model 1.2. Both the models have an embedding layer as the first one, which is used to select the word vector representations corresponding to the words of the tweet under consideration during the training session, from the word embedding matrix. In model 1.1, the embedding layer is followed by a couple sets of convolution and max pooling layers in series whereas in model 1.2, it is followed by 4 single dimensional convolution layers in parallel.

The convolution layer is responsible for the extraction of features from the word vectors provided as input. The outputs of these layers, concatenated in case of model 1.2, are fed to a global max pooling layer with a dropout activated. This layer is further followed by 3 dense fully connected layers, the final layer with a single neuron, which is responsible for the classification. We have used dropout in the the global max pooling layer so as to reduce overfitting, which already is low due to the large dataset. However, on its application, the difference between the validation accuracy and training accuracy reduced, also leading to better convergence.

2.5.2   Recurrent Neural Networks (RNN)

The meaning of a word depends on the context in which it is used. For example,

Sentence 1 : We dined at a small Mexican restaurant and spent the meal discussing general topics.
Sentence 2 : General Zod is an enemy of Superman.

The word general, in the above sentences, carries different meaning depending on the context in which it is used. Thus, in order to record the context of a particular word, i.e. the words surrounding the word under consideration, RNNs are used. There are different ways to capture the context of a particular word, each having its unique mechanism to model the meaning of the word depending on words coming before and after the word.

The RNN model equations and corresponding notation have been taken from (Yu et al., 2015). Given an input sequence $x = (x_1, x_2, ..., x_{t-1}, x_T)$, the output vector sequence $y = (y_1, y_2, ..., y_{T-1}, y_T)$ and hidden vector sequence $h = (h_1, h_2, ..., h_{T-1}, h_T)$ are computed in a standard recurrent neural network by evaluating the below equations from t = 1 to t = T:

$$h_t = \mathcal{H}\left(W_{xh}x_t + W_{hh}h_{t-1} + b_h\right)$$

$$y_t = W_{hy}h_t + b_0$$

where weight matrices are denoted by W terms, bias vectors are denoted by b terms, and hidden layer function is given by $\mathcal{H}$.

Long Short-Term Memory (LSTM): LSTMs have been successfully applied to binary text classification problems like political text classification (Rao and Spasojevic, 2016), by capturing the appropriate context. Also, the vanishing gradient problem in RNNs has been addressed successfully by LSTMs (Hochreiter and Schmidhuber, 1997). The context of a word depends on the words occurring before the word under consideration. In order to model this scenario, an LSTM based network is constructed.The LSTM design comprises of a set of repetitively associated subnets, known as memory blocks. Each block contains at least one self-associated memory cells along with three multiplicative units - the input, output and forget gates - that give regular functionality of write, read and reset operations to the cells.

A LSTM network is framed precisely like a basic RNN, other than the nonlinear units in the hidden layers being supplanted by memory blocks. The multiplicative gates permit LSTM memory cells to store and access data over extensive stretches of time, in this manner maintaining a strategic distance from the vanishing gradient issue. For instance, as long as the input gate stays shut (has an activation near 0), the activation of the cell won't be overwritten by the new inputs showing up in the network, and can in this manner be made accessible to the net a lot later in the succession, by opening the output gate. This allows the LSTM network to carry forward semantic qualities of initial parts of the sentence to the later parts. In our architecture, an LSTM layer is appended to the embedding layer in turn followed by 2 dense fully connected layers. The final output layer has a single neuron carrying out the classification depending on the extracted context based features. LSTM blocks have the structure as shown in Figure 3, and are based on the equations presented below :

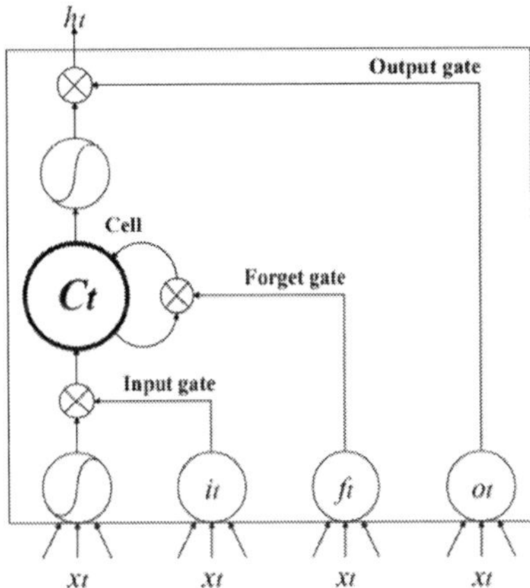

Figure 3: LSTM block structure

$$i_t = \sigma\left(W_{xi}x_t + W_{hi}h_{t-1} + W_{ci}c_{t-1} + b_i\right)$$

$$f_t = \sigma\left(W_{xf}x_t + W_{hf}h_{t-1} + W_{cf}c_{t-1} + b_f\right)$$

$$c_t = f_t c_{t-1} + i_t \tanh\left(W_{xc}x_t + W_{hc}h_{t-1} + b_c\right)$$

$$o_t = \sigma\left(W_{xo}x_t + W_{ho}h_{t-1} + W_{co}c_t + b_o\right)$$

$$h_t = o_t \tanh\left(c_t\right)$$

where logistic sigmoid function is denoted by σ, the input gate, forget gate, output gate, and cell activation vectors are denoted by i, f, o and c, all having the same size as the hidden vector h. The hidden-input gate matrix is represented by W_{hi}, and the input-output gate matrix is represented by W_{xo}.

Bi- directional LSTM: Bi-directional LSTMs have been applied and proved to be successful in capturing the context for text classification tasks (Wang et al., 2016). The context of a word not only depends on the words occurring before it, but also on the words occurring after it. Modelling this requires memory cells in the backward direction which maintain the history of words along with cells in the forward direction for the words not yet explored. To achieve this and capture the composition semantics of Hindi-English code mixed data, two LSTM layers are appended to the input embedding layer. The output features from the two layers, after concatenation ($\overrightarrow{h_t}$, $\overleftarrow{h_1}$), are flattened and fed to 2 dense fully connected layers. The classification is performed by a single neuron, as in all other models. The BiLSTM computes the forward hidden sequence $\overrightarrow{h_t}$ by traversing the

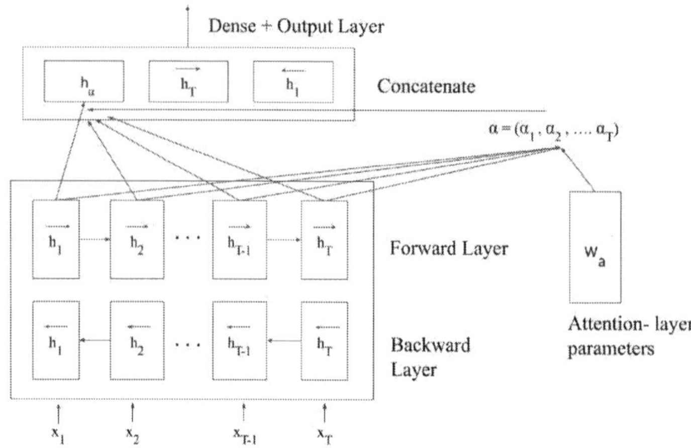

Figure 4: Attention based Bi-directional LSTM model architecture

forward layer from t = 1 to T, the backward hidden sequence $\overleftarrow{h_t}$ by traversing the backward layer from t = T to 1, and updates the output y_t as :

$$\overrightarrow{h_t} = \mathcal{H}\left(W_{x\overrightarrow{h}}x_t + W_{\overrightarrow{h}\,\overrightarrow{h}}\vec{h}_{t+1} + b_{\overrightarrow{h}}\right)$$

$$\overleftarrow{h_t} = \mathcal{H}\left(W_{x\overleftarrow{h}}x_t + W_{\overleftarrow{h}\,\overleftarrow{h}}\overleftarrow{h}_{t+1} + b_{\overleftarrow{h}}\right)$$

$$y_t = W_{\overrightarrow{h}y}\overrightarrow{h}_t + W_{\overleftarrow{h}y}\overleftarrow{h}_t + b_y$$

Attention based Bi-directional LSTM: Here, we propose a technique based on attention along with the bi-directional LSTM network. The attention based network focuses on filtering the noisy elements of a sentence by learning the words which cause the greatest effect towards deciding the final output (sarcastic or not sarcastic) of the sentence under consideration. While the bi-directional LSTM network uses concatenated $(\overrightarrow{h_T}, \overleftarrow{h_1})$ which is then fed to the dense layers, attention based bidirectional LSTM network is different in the concatenation process. Along with the above state representations, ($\overrightarrow{h_T}$ denoting the final state representation in the forward direction and $\overleftarrow{h_1}$ denoting the first state representation in the backward direction), the attention based network inculcates the weighted summation, calculated by detecting the influence of each word, of all the time steps (denoted by $\overrightarrow{h_t}, \overleftarrow{h_t}$). Thus, all these hidden states are concatenated and passed on to 2 dense fully connected layers. Final classification is performed by a single neuron, as usual.

3 Experimental Settings

For the training sessions, we made a ten percent validation split and shuffled the training dataset, so that the model does not capture sequence trends, if any, in the training data, for a total of 20 epochs. The model checkpoints were saved at every epoch and those checkpoints which were saved before the model begins to overfit and the difference between the training and validation accuracies becomes significant, were used to calculate the accuracy numbers on the ten percent test dataset split. There are many important hyper-parameters in the training script of embeddings as well as the proposed models, which are tuned to produce best training results on the validation data split. For training the word embeddings (both Word2Vec and FastText), we used an embedding size of 300, window length of 10 and negative sampling polarity. In all the models, adam optimizer along with binary cross entropy loss function has been used. All the layers have relu activation function with the exception of output layer having sigmoid activation function. We evaluated the performance of CNN models with different values for kernel_size, number_of_kernels, dropouts and strides. The best results are obtained with the following values :

stride = 1, number_of_kernels = 200, dropout = 0.5
$ks_1{}^{1.2} = 3$, $ks_2{}^{1.2} = 6$, $ks_3{}^{1.2} = 9$,
$ks_4{}^{1.2} = 12$, $ks_1{}^{1.1} = 7$

For all the proposed RNNs, the following

Traditional Models	Accuracy
Naive Bayes	54.17
Random Forest	63.37
Linear SVM	69.04
RBF Kernel SVM	71.23

Table 2: Accuracy of ML models

DL Models	Hinglish Data		Hinglish + English Data	
	Word2Vec (a)	FastText (b)	Word2Vec (a)	FastText (b)
1.1 Series CNN	72.86	72.65	74.09	73.51
1.2 Parallel CNN	74.28	73.41	75.00	74.32
2.1 LSTM	76.19	75.25	77.24	75.55
2.2 Bi-LSTM	77.12	76.25	78.28	77.12
2.3 Attention Bi-LSTM	78.19	77.11	78.40	78.06

Table 3: Accuracy of DL Models

hyper parameter combination is used :

dropout_for_recurrent_state = 0.2,
dropout_for_input_state = 0.2,
number_of_LSTM_units = 150

We used the same hyper parameter values for models 2.2 and 2.3, as in model 2.1, so as to study the impact of imposing bidirectional nature to the LSTM layer, as well as exploring the effect of attention introduction. The parameters resulted in best outputs as confirmed later by trying out different values for the same.

4   Results

The dataset, as presented in (Swami et al., 2018), being insufficient and skewed for our deep learning model architectures, we ran the state-of-the-art models on our proposed dataset to carry out unbiased accuracy comparison of state-of-the-art techniques and neural network based models.

The results for the same have been presented in Table 2. Using all features, the traditional state-of-the-art models: RBF kernel SVM, random forest and linear SVM, proposed the best accuracy of 71.23% on the proposed corpus. We tested all the deep learning models with both Word2Vec and FastText based word representations. The results of both have been presented in Table 3 where model (a) and (b) refer to application of Word2Vec and FastText generated word embeddings respectively.

To the best of our knowledge, we are the first to implement and analyze deep learning model architectures and different word representations for detection of sarcasm in Hindi-English code-mixed data with a dataset large enough for deep learning models. All the proposed deep learning models performed better than the traditional state-of-the-art models, where the attention based Bi-directional LSTM network produced the best accuracy of 78.49%. In Table 3, we present the results of our proposed deep learning models for both Word2Vec and FastText based word representations, differing in the type of datatsets being used to produce the word embeddings. Overall accuracies of all models are greater when embeddings trained on Hinglish plus English data, rather than just Hinglish data are used. One possible reason for this observation can be the additional coverage of semantics and coorelations between the word vectors of English data, which can be used for code mixed Hinglish data, thus providing additional knowledge and serving as prior information for Hinglish embeddings data. The process works analogous to a knowledge transfer step in which embeddings for English data are used as prior knowledge for embeddings of Hinglish data. Moreover, Word2Vec embeddings produce better results than FastText embeddings, for all the models. One major reason for this observation is the presence of code mixed data which does not allow character n-grams to be the primary criteria for classification, in the case of FastText embeddings, since the character n-grams belong to the constructs of two different languages. Due

to the same reason, context based word vectors i.e.
the Word2Vec representations perform better than
the character n-grams representations in case of
FastText embeddings.

The lack of clean data and linguistic complexi-
ties associated with code-mixed data are the major
challenges related to the task of sarcasm detection
in Hindi-English code mixed data. To allow the
model to accommodate the noise in textual data,
spelling errors, multiple contexts, and stemming
words, even larger data is required along with cau-
tiously labelled classes.

5   Conclusion

Social media, in recent years, has become a
medium widely used by people for expression of
thoughts and opinions, further leading to the real-
isation of tasks like emotion analysis and opinion
mining. Sarcastic content in these texts make it
even more challenging to figure out the overall sentiment of the text, thus needing proper processing
and analysis.

In this paper, we presented a class-balanced
Hindi-English code mixed dataset for the problem of sarcasm detection, by scraping relevant
tweets from twitter. We compared two representations, FastText and Word2Vec, both based on different word representation learning mechanisms and
trained on custom scraped data from scratch. We
created two versions of embeddings, one trained
with purely Hinglish data, the other with a mixture
of Hinglish and English data, and compared the
performance in each case. We analyzed the performance of different deep learning models, which
take as input the generated word embeddings, to
solve the problem of sarcasm detection. As future work, we plan to compare the vectors aligned
with multilingual word embeddings after generation using MUSE with FastText pre aligned word
embeddings. We can also explore BERT embeddings and evaluate their performance on the same
task.

References

David Bamman and Noah Smith. 2015. Contextualized
sarcasm detection on twitter.

Piotr Bojanowski, Edouard Grave, Armand Joulin, and
Tomas Mikolov. 2017. Enriching word vectors with
subword information. *Transactions of the Association for Computational Linguistics*, 5:135–146.

Özlem Çetinoğlu, Sarah Schulz, and Ngoc Thang Vu.
2016. Challenges of computational processing of
code-switching. In *Proceedings of the Second Workshop on Computational Approaches to Code Switching*, pages 1–11, Austin, Texas. Association for
Computational Linguistics.

Brenda Danet and Susan Herring. 2007. *The Multilingual Internet: Language, Culture, and Communication Online*.

Dmitry Davidov, Oren Tsur, and Ari Rappoport. 2010.
Semi-supervised recognition of sarcastic sentences
in twitter and amazon. In *Proceedings of the Fourteenth Conference on Computational Natural Language Learning*, CoNLL '10, page 107–116, USA.
Association for Computational Linguistics.

Sakshi Gupta, Piyush Bansal, and Radhika Mamidi.
2016. Resource creation for hindi-english code
mixed social media text.

Sepp Hochreiter and Jürgen Schmidhuber. 1997.
Long short-term memory. *Neural Comput.*,
9(8):1735–1780.

Lichan Hong, Gregorio Convertino, and Ed Huai hsin
Chi. 2011. Language matters in twitter: A large
scale study. In *ICWSM*.

Aditya Joshi, Pushpak Bhattacharyya, and Mark J. Carman. 2017. Automatic sarcasm detection: A survey.
ACM Comput. Surv., 50(5).

Armand Joulin, Edouard Grave, Piotr Bojanowski, and
Tomas Mikolov. 2017. Bag of tricks for efficient
text classification. In *Proceedings of the 15th Conference of the European Chapter of the Association
for Computational Linguistics: Volume 2, Short Papers*, pages 427–431, Valencia, Spain. Association
for Computational Linguistics.

Amit Mandelbaum and Adi Shalev. 2016. Word embeddings and their use in sentence classification
tasks.

Tomas Mikolov, Ilya Sutskever, Kai Chen, Greg Corrado, and Jeffrey Dean. 2013. Distributed representations of words and phrases and their compositionality. In *Proceedings of the 26th International Conference on Neural Information Processing Systems
- Volume 2*, NIPS'13, page 3111–3119, Red Hook,
NY, USA. Curran Associates Inc.

Stella Mónica, Mónica Cárdenas-Claros, and Neny
Isharyanti. 2009. Code switching and code mixing
in internet chating: betwen "yes", "ya", and "si" a
case study. *The jaltcall Journal*, Vol 5:67–78.

Adithya Rao and Nemanja Spasojevic. 2016. Actionable and political text classification using word embeddings and lstm. *ArXiv*, abs/1607.02501.

Sahil Swami, Ankush Khandelwal, Vinay Singh,
Syed Sarfaraz Akhtar, and Manish Shrivastava. 2018.
A corpus of english-hindi code-mixed tweets for sar-
casm detection.

Joseph Tepperman, David R. Traum, and Shrikanth S. Narayanan. 2006. "yeah right": sarcasm recognition for spoken dialogue systems. In (Joshi et al., 2017).

Yequan Wang, Minlie Huang, Xiaoyan Zhu, and Li Zhao. 2016. Attention-based LSTM for aspect-level sentiment classification. In *Proceedings of the 2016 Conference on Empirical Methods in Natural Language Processing*, pages 606–615, Austin, Texas. Association for Computational Linguistics.

T. Young, D. Hazarika, S. Poria, and E. Cambria. 2018. Recent trends in deep learning based natural language processing [review article]. *IEEE Computational Intelligence Magazine*, 13(3):55–75.

Zhou Yu, Vikram Ramanarayanan, David Suendermann-Oeft, Xinhao Wang, Klaus Zechner, Lei Chen, Jidong Tao, Aliaksei Ivanou, and Yao Qian. 2015. Using bidirectional lstm recurrent neural networks to learn high-level abstractions of sequential features for automated scoring of non-native spontaneous speech. pages 338–345.

Noisy Text Data: Achilles' Heel of BERT

Ankit Kumar, Piyush Makhija, Anuj Gupta
Vahan Inc.
{ankit, piyush, anuj}@vahan.co

Abstract

Owing to the phenomenal success of BERT on various NLP tasks and benchmark datasets, industry practitioners are actively experimenting with fine-tuning BERT to build NLP applications for solving industry use cases. For most datasets that are used by practitioners to build industrial NLP applications, it is hard to guarantee absence of any noise in the data. While BERT has performed exceedingly well for transferring the learnings from one use case to another, it remains unclear how BERT performs when fine-tuned on noisy text. In this work, we explore the sensitivity of BERT to noise in the data. We work with most commonly occurring noise (spelling mistakes, typos) and show that this results in significant degradation in the performance of BERT. We present experimental results to show that BERT's performance on fundamental NLP tasks like sentiment analysis and textual similarity drops significantly in the presence of (simulated) noise on benchmark datasets viz. IMDB Movie Review, STS-B, SST-2. Further, we identify shortcomings in the existing BERT pipeline that are responsible for this drop in performance. Our findings suggest that practitioners need to be vary of presence of noise in their datasets while fine-tuning BERT to solve industry use cases.

1 Introduction

Pre-trained contextualized language models such as BERT (Bidirectional Encoder Representations from Transformers) (Devlin et al., 2018), which is the focus of this work, has led to improvement in performance on many Natural Language Processing (NLP) tasks. Without listing down all the tasks, BERT has improved the state-of-the-art for a number of tasks including tasks such as summarization, Name-Entity Recognition, Question Answering and Machine Translation (Devlin et al., 2018).

Buoyed by this success, machine learning teams in industry are actively experimenting with fine-tuning BERT on their data to solve various industry use cases. These include use cases such as chatbots, sentiment analysis systems, automatically routing and prioritizing customer support tickets, NER systems, machine translation systems to name a few. Many of these use cases require practitioners to build training and test datasets by collecting text data from data sources & applications such as chats, emails, discussions from user forums, social media conversations, output of machine translation systems, automatically transcribing text from speech data, automatically recognized text from printed or handwritten material, etc. Owing to these sources & applications, the text data is known to be noisy. In some sources such discussions from user forums & social media conversations, the noise in the data can be significantly high. *It is not very clear how the pre-trained BERT performs when fine-tuned with noisy text data and if the performance degrades then why so.* These two questions are the focus of this paper.

Though the datasets used in industry are varied, many of them have a common characteristic - noisy text. This includes spelling mistakes, typographic errors, colloquialisms, abbreviations, slang, internet jargon, emojis, embedded metadata (such as hashtags, URLs, mentions), non standard syntactic constructions and spelling variations, grammatically incorrect text, mixture of two or more languages (a.k.a code mix) to name a few. This makes cleaning and preprocessing text data a key component of NLP pipeline for industrial applications. However, despite extensive cleaning and preprocessing, some degree of noise often remains. Owing to this residual noise, a common issue that NLP models have to deal with is out of vocabulary (OOV) words. These are words that are found in test and production data but are not part of train-

Proceedings of the 2020 EMNLP Workshop W-NUT: The Sixth Workshop on Noisy User-generated Text, pages 16–21
Online, Nov 19, 2020. ©2020 Association for Computational Linguistics

ing data. In this work we find that BERT fails to properly handle OOV words (due to noise). We show that this negatively impacts the performance of BERT on fundamental tasks in NLP when fine-tuned over noisy text data.

This work is motivated from the business use case where we are building a dialogue system over WhatsApp to screen candidates for blue collar jobs. Our candidate user base often comes from under-privileged backgrounds, many of them are not even college graduates. This coupled with fat finger problem[1] over a mobile keypad leads to a lot of typos and spelling mistakes in the responses sent to our dialogue system. Hence, for the purpose of this work, we focus on spelling mistakes as the noise in the data. While this work is motivated from our business use case, our findings are applicable to other use cases that deal with noisy text data.

2   Previous Work

We now present some of the relevant work viz the following related areas viz. (1) robustness of BERT, (2) degradation in performance of NLP models due to noise in text data.

Robustness of BERT: There has been some work on testing the robustness of BERT in different scenarios. Jin et al. (2019) introduce TEXTFOOLER, a system to generate adversarial text and apply it to text classification and textual entailment to successfully attack the pre-trained BERT among other models. Aspillaga et al. (2020) evaluate robustness of three models - RoBERTa, XLNet, and BERT in Natural Language Inference (NLI) and Question Answering (QA) tasks. They show that while RoBERTa, XLNet and BERT are more robust than Recurrent Neural Network (RNN) models to stress tests on tasks such as NLI and QA, these models are still very fragile and show many unexpected behaviors. Pal and Tople (2020) present novel attack techniques that utilize the unintended features learnt in the teacher (public) model to generate adversarial examples for student (downstream) models. They show that using length-based and sentence-based misclassification attacks for the Fake News Detection task trained using a context-aware BERT model, one gets misclassification accuracy of 78% and 39% respectively for the adversarial examples. Sun et al. (2020) show the BERT under-performs on sentiment analysis and question answering in

presence of typos and spelling mistakes. While our work has an overlap with their work, our work is independent (and parallel in terms of timeline) to their work.

We not only experimented with more datasets, we also pin down the exact reason for degradation in BERT's performance. We demonstrate our findings viz-a-viz two most fundamental NLP tasks - sentence classification (sentiment analysis) and textual similarity. For these, we chose the most popular benchmark datasets - for sentiment analysis we work with SST-2 and IMDB datasets and for textual similarity we use STS-B dataset. Further, Sun et al. (2020) show that mistakes/typos in the most informative words cause maximum damage. In contrast, our work shows stronger results - mistakes/typos in words chosen at random is good enough to cause substantial drop in BERT's performance. We discuss the reason for performance degradation. Last but not the least, we tried various tokenizers during the fine-tuning phase to see if there is a simple fix for the problem.

Degradation in performance of NLP models due to Noise: There has been a lot of work around understanding the effect of noise on the performance of NLP models.Taghva et al. (2000) evaluate the effect of OCR errors on text categorization. Wu et al. (2016) introduced ISSAC, a system to clean dirty text from online sources. Agarwal et al. (2007) studied the effect of different kinds of noise on automatic text classification. Subramaniam et al. (2009) presented a survey of types of text noise and techniques to handle noisy text. Newer communication mediums such as SMS, chats, twitter, messaging apps encourage brevity and informalism, leading to non-canonical text. This presents significant challenges to the known NLP techniques. Belinkov and Bisk (2017) show that character based neural machine translation (NMT) models are also prone to synthetic and natural noise even though these model do better job to handle out-of-vocabulary issues and learn better morphological representation. Ribeiro et al. (2018) develop a technique, called semantically equivalent adversarial rules (SEARs) to debug NLP models. SEAR generate adversial examples to penetrate NLP models. Author experimented this techniques for three domains: machine comprehension, visual question answering, and sentiment analysis.

There exists a vast literature that tries to understand the sensitivity of NLP models to noise and

---

[1]https://en.wikipedia.org/wiki/Fat-finger_error

develop techniques to tackle these challenges. It is beyond the scope of this paper to give a comprehensive list of papers on this topic. One can look at the work published in conferences such as 'Workshop on Noisy User-generated Text, ACL', 'Workshop on Analytics for Noisy Unstructured Text Data, IJCAI-2007' that have dedicated tracks on these issues.

3 Experiments

We evaluate the state-of-the-art model BERT[2] on two fundamental NLP tasks: sentiment analysis and textual similarity. For sentiment analysis we use popular datasets of IMDB movie reviews (Maas et al., 2011) and Stanford Sentiment Treebank (SST-2) (Socher et al., 2013); for textual similarity we use Semantic Textual Similarity (STS-B) (Cer et al., 2017). Both STS-B and SST-2 datasets are a part of GLUE benchmark (Wang et al., 2018) tasks. On these benchmark datasets we report the system's performance both - with and without noise.

3.1 Noise

As mentioned in Section 1 of the paper, we focus on the noise introduced by spelling mistakes and typos. All the benchmark datasets we work with consists of examples $X \rightarrow Y$ where X are the text inputs and Y are the corresponding labels. We call the original dataset as D_0. From D_0 we create new datasets $D_{2.5}, D_5, D_{7.5}, D_{10}, D_{12.5}, D_{15}, D_{17.5}, D_{20}$ and $D_{22.5}$. Here, D_k is a variant of D_0 with k% noise in each datapoint in D_0.

To create D_k, we take i^{th} data point $x_i \in D_k$, and introduce noise in it. We represent the modified datapoint by $x_{i,k}^{noise}$. Then, D_k is simply the collection $(x_{i,k}^{noise}, y_i), \forall i$. To create $x_{i,k}^{noise}$ from x_i, we randomly choose k% characters from the text of x_i and replace them with nearby characters in a qwerty keyboard. For example, if character *d* is chosen, then it is replaced by a character randomly chosen from *e, s, x, c, f,* or *r*. This is because in a qwerty keyboard, these keys surround the key *d*. We inject noise in the complete dataset. Later we split D_i into *train* and *test* chunks.

We believe a systematic study should be done to understand how the performance of SOTA models is impacted when fine-tuned on noisy text data. To motivate the community for this, we suggest a simple framework for the study. The framework uses four variables - SOTA model, task, dataset, and the

degree of noise in the data. For such a study it is imperative to have a scalable way to create variants of a dataset that differ in the degree of noise in them. The method for creating noisy datasets as described in the previous paragraph does exactly this. Creating datasets at scale with varying degree of natural noise is very human intensive task. Despite our method introducing synthetic noise, owing to mobile penetration across the globe, and fat finger problem, our noise model is very realistic. Also, unlike Sun et al. (2020), we introduce noise randomly rather than targeting the most informative words. This helps us model the average case setting rather than the worst case. For these reasons we stick to synthetic noise introduced randomly.

3.2 Sentiment Analysis

For sentiment analysis we use IMDB movie reviews (Maas et al., 2011) and Stanford Sentiment Treebank (SST-2) (Socher et al., 2013) datasets in binary prediction settings. IMDB datasets consist of 25000 training and 25000 test sentences. We represent the original IMDB dataset (one with no noise) as $IMDB_0$. Using the process of introducing noise (as described in section 3.1), we create 9 variants of $IMDB_0$ namely $IMDB_{2.5}, \ldots, IMDB_{22.5}$ with varying degrees of noise.

SST-2 dataset consists of 67349 training and 872 test sentences. Here too we we add noise as described in Section 3.1 to create 9 variants of $SST-2_0$ - $SST-2_{2.5}, \ldots, SST-2_{22.5}$. To measure the performance of the model for sentiment analysis task we use F1 score.

3.3 Textual Similarity

For textual similarity task, we use Semantic Textual Similarity (STS-B) (Cer et al., 2017) dataset. The dataset consists of 5749 training and 1500 test data points. Each data point consists of 2 sentences and a score between 0-5 representing the similarity between the two sentences. We represent the original data set by $STS-B_0$ and create 9 noisy variants like we mentioned in section 3.1 Here, we use Pearson-Spearman correlation to measure model's performance.

3.4 Results

Table 1 and figure 1 lists the performance of BERT on various variants (noiseless and noisy) of IMDB and STS-2 for sentiment analysis and SST-B for sentence similarity. From the numbers it is very clear that noise adversely affects the performance

---

[2] $BERT_{Base}$ uncased model

	Sentiment Analysis		Textual Similarity
% error	IMDB	SST-2	STS-B
0.0	0.93	0.89	0.89
2.5	0.85	0.86	0.84
5.0	0.79	0.80	0.75
7.5	0.67	0.76	0.65
10.0	0.62	0.70	0.65
12.5	0.53	0.67	0.49
15.0	0.51	0.60	0.40
17.5	0.46	0.59	0.39
20.0	0.44	0.54	0.29
22.5	0.41	0.49	0.31

Table 1: Results of experiments on both clean and noisy data.

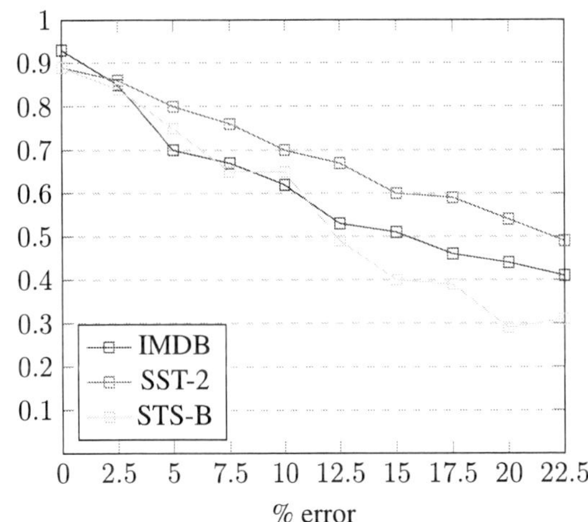

Figure 1: Accuracy vs Error

of BERT. Further, as we gradually increase the noise, the performance keeps going down. For sentiment analysis, by the time 15-17% of characters are replaced, the performance drops to almost the chance-level accuracy (i.e., around 50%). This decline is much more rapid for sentence similarity.

4   Analysis

To understand the reason behind the drop in BERT's performance in presence of noise, we need to understand how BERT processes input text data. A key component of BERT's pipeline is tokenization of input text. It first performs whitespace tokenization followed by WordPiece tokenization (Wu et al., 2016). While whitespace tokenizer breaks the input text into tokens around the whitespace boundary, the wordPiece tokenizer uses longest prefix match to further break the tokens[3]. The resultant tokens are then fed as input to the BERT model.

When it comes to tokenizing the noisy text data, we see a very interesting behaviour from BERT's pipeline. First whitespace tokenization is applied. Now, when the WordPiece tokenizer encounters these words, owing to the spelling mistakes, these words are not directly found in BERT's dictionary. So, WordPiece tokenizer tries to tokenize these (noisy) words into subwords. However, *it ends up breaking the words into subwords whose meaning can be very different from the meaning of the original word. This can change the meaning of the sentence completely, therefore leading to substan-*

tial dip in the performance.

To understand this better let us look at two examples - one each from the IMDB and STS-B datasets respectively, as shown in Example 1 and Example 2. In each Example, (a) is the sentence as it appears in $IMDB_0$ (i.e. original dataset) while (b) is the corresponding sentence after adding 5% noise ($IMDB_5$). For legibility the misspelled characters are highlighted with italics. The sentences are followed by their corresponding output after applying whitespace and WordPiece tokenizer on them. In the output, ## represents subwords.

Example 1 (from IMDB):
(a) that loves its characters and communicates something rather beautiful about human nature. (0% error)
(b) that loves *8*ts characters a*b*d communicates something rathe*e* beautiful about human natu*ee*. (5% error)
Corresponding output of tokenization:
(a) 'that', 'loves', 'its', 'characters', 'and', 'communicate', '##s', 'something', 'rather', 'beautiful', 'about', 'human', 'nature'
(b) 'that', 'loves', '8', '##ts', 'characters', 'abd', 'communicate', '##s', 'something', 'rat', '##hee', 'beautiful', 'about', 'human', 'nat', '##ue', '##e'

Example 2 (from STS-2):
(a) poor ben bratt could n't find stardom if mapquest emailed him point-to-point driving directions. (0% error)
(b) poor ben bratt could n't find stardom if

---

[3]https://github.com/google-research/bert/blob/master/tokenization.py

% error	WordPiece	WhiteSpace	n-gram
			(n=6)
0	0.89	0.69	0.73
5	0.75	0.59	0.60
10	0.65	0.41	0.46
15	0.40	0.33	0.36
20	0.39	0.22	0.25

Table 2: Comparative results on STS-B dataset with different tokenizers

mapquest emailed him point-to-point drivi*bg* dir*sctioje*. (5% error)

Output of tokenization:

(a) 'poor', 'ben', 'brat', '##t', 'could', 'n', ''', 't', 'find', 'star', '##dom', 'if', 'map', '##quest', 'email', '##ed', 'him', 'point', '-', 'to', '-', 'point', 'driving', 'directions', '.'

(b) 'poor', 'ben', 'brat', '##t', 'could', 'n', ''', 't', 'find', 'star', '##dom', 'if', 'map', '##quest', 'email', '##ed', 'him', 'point', '-', 'to', '-', 'point', 'dr', '##iv', '##ib', '##g', 'dir', '##sc', '##ti', '##oge', '.'

In Example 1(a), BERT's tokenization splits *communicates* into *communicate* and *##s* based on longest prefix matching because there is no exact match for *communicates* in pre-trained BERT's vocabulary. This results in two tokens *communicate* and *s*, both of which are present in BERT's vocabulary. We have contextual embeddings for both *communicate* and *##s*. By using these two embeddings, one can get an approximate embedding for *communicates*.

However, this approach goes for a complete toss when the word gets misspelled. In example 1(b), the word *natuee*('nature' is misspelled) is split into tokens *nat, ##ue, ##e* (based on the longest prefix match). By combining the embeddings for these three tokens, one cannot approximate the embedding of 'nature'. This is because the word *nat* has a very different meaning (it means 'a person who advocates political independence for a particular country'). This misrepresentation in turn impacts the performance of downstream sub-components of BERT bringing down the overall performance of BERT model. This is why as we introduce more errors, the quality of output of the tokenizer degrades further, resulting in the overall drop in performance.

We further experimented with different tokenizers other than WordPiece tokenizer. For this we used Character N-gram tokenizer (Mcnamee and Mayfield, 2004) and stanfordNLP whitespace tokenizer (Manning et al., 2014). For Character N-gram tokenizer, we work with N=6[4]. The results of these experiments on STS-B dataset are given in Table 2. It is clear that replacing WordPiece by whitespace or N-gram further degrades the performance. The reasons are as follows:

(1) **Replace WordPiece by whitespace**: In this case every misspelled word (say, natuee) is directly fed to BERT model. Since, these words are not present in BERT's vocabulary, they are treated as UNK[5] token. In presence of even 5-10% noise, there is a significant drop in accuracy.

(2) **Replace WordPiece by Character N-gram tokenizer**: Here, every misspelled word is broken into character n-grams of length atmost 6. It is high unlikely to find these subwords in BERT's vocabulary. Hence, they get treated as UNK.

Please note that in our experimental setup, we are not training BERT from scratch. Instead, we simply replaced the existing WordPiece tokenizer with other tokenizers while feeding tokens to BERT's embedding layer during the fine-tuning and testing phases.

5 Conclusion and Future Work

We studied the effect of synthetic noise (spelling mistakes) in text data on the performance of BERT. We demonstrated that as the noise increases, BERT's performance drops drastically. We further show that the reason for the performance drop is how BERT's tokenizer (WordPiece) handles the misspelled words.

Our results suggest that one needs to conduct a large number of experiments to see if the findings hold across other datasets and popular NLP tasks such as information extraction, text summarization, machine translation, question answering, etc. It will also be interesting to see how BERT performs in presence of other types of noise. One also needs to investigate how other models such as ELMo, RoBERTa, and XLNet which use character-based, byte-level BPE, and SentencePiece tokenizers respectively. It also remains to be seen if the results will hold if the noise was restricted to only frequent

---

[4]longer N-grams such as 6-grams are recommended for capturing semantic information (Bojanowski et al., 2016)

[5]Unknown tokens

misspellings.

To address the problem of drop in performance, there are 2 ways - (i) preprocess the data to correct spelling mistakes in the dataset before fine-tuning BERT on it (ii) make changes in BERT's architecture to make it robust to noise. From a practitioner's perspective, the problem with (i) is that in most industrial settings this becomes a separate project in itself. We leave (ii) as future work.

References

Sumeet Agarwal, Shantanu Godbole, Diwakar Punjani, and Shourya Roy. 2007. How much noise is too much: A study in automatic text classification. In *Seventh IEEE International Conference on Data Mining (ICDM 2007)*, pages 3–12. IEEE.

Carlos Aspillaga, Andrés Carvallo, and Vladimir Araujo. 2020. Stress test evaluation of transformer-based models in natural language understanding tasks. *arXiv preprint arXiv:2002.06261.*

Yonatan Belinkov and Yonatan Bisk. 2017. Synthetic and natural noise both break neural machine translation. *arXiv preprint arXiv:1711.02173.*

Piotr Bojanowski, Edouard Grave, Armand Joulin, and Tomas Mikolov. 2016. Enriching word vectors with subword information. *Transactions of the Association for Computational Linguistics*, 5.

Daniel Cer, Mona Diab, Eneko Agirre, Inigo Lopez-Gazpio, and Lucia Specia. 2017. Semeval-2017 task 1: Semantic textual similarity-multilingual and cross-lingual focused evaluation. *arXiv preprint arXiv:1708.00055.*

Jacob Devlin, Ming-Wei Chang, Kenton Lee, and Kristina Toutanova. 2018. Bert: Pre-training of deep bidirectional transformers for language understanding. *arXiv preprint arXiv:1810.04805.*

Di Jin, Zhijing Jin, Joey Tianyi Zhou, and Peter Szolovits. 2019. Is bert really robust. *A Strong Baseline for Natural Language Attack on Text Classification and Entailment.*

Andrew L Maas, Raymond E Daly, Peter T Pham, Dan Huang, Andrew Y Ng, and Christopher Potts. 2011. Learning word vectors for sentiment analysis. In *Proceedings of the 49th annual meeting of the association for computational linguistics: Human language technologies-volume 1*, pages 142–150. Association for Computational Linguistics.

Christopher D Manning, Mihai Surdeanu, John Bauer, Jenny Rose Finkel, Steven Bethard, and David McClosky. 2014. The stanford corenlp natural language processing toolkit. In *Proceedings of 52nd annual meeting of the association for computational linguistics: system demonstrations*, pages 55–60.

Paul Mcnamee and James Mayfield. 2004. Character n-gram tokenization for european language text retrieval. *Information retrieval*, 7(1-2):73–97.

Bijeeta Pal and Shruti Tople. 2020. To transfer or not to transfer: Misclassification attacks against transfer learned text classifiers. *arXiv preprint arXiv:2001.02438.*

Marco Tulio Ribeiro, Sameer Singh, and Carlos Guestrin. 2018. Semantically equivalent adversarial rules for debugging nlp models. In *Proceedings of the 56th Annual Meeting of the Association for Computational Linguistics (Volume 1: Long Papers)*, pages 856–865.

Richard Socher, Alex Perelygin, Jean Wu, Jason Chuang, Christopher D Manning, Andrew Y Ng, and Christopher Potts. 2013. Recursive deep models for semantic compositionality over a sentiment treebank. In *Proceedings of the 2013 conference on empirical methods in natural language processing*, pages 1631–1642.

L. Venkata Subramaniam, Shourya Roy, Tanveer A. Faruquie, and Sumit Negi. 2009. A survey of types of text noise and techniques to handle noisy text. In *Proceedings of The Third Workshop on Analytics for Noisy Unstructured Text Data*, AND '09, page 115–122, New York, NY, USA. Association for Computing Machinery.

Lichao Sun, Kazuma Hashimoto, Wenpeng Yin, Akari Asai, Jiugang Li, Philip S. Yu, and Caiming Xiong. 2020. Adv-bert: Bert is not robust on misspellings! generating nature adversarial samples on bert. *ArXiv*, abs/2003.04985.

Kazem Taghva, Thomas A Nartker, Julie Borsack, Steven Lumos, Allen Condit, and Ron Young. 2000. Evaluating text categorization in the presence of ocr errors. In *Document Recognition and Retrieval VIII*, volume 4307, pages 68–74. International Society for Optics and Photonics.

Alex Wang, Amanpreet Singh, Julian Michael, Felix Hill, Omer Levy, and Samuel R Bowman. 2018. Glue: A multi-task benchmark and analysis platform for natural language understanding. *arXiv preprint arXiv:1804.07461.*

Yonghui Wu, Mike Schuster, Zhifeng Chen, Quoc V Le, Mohammad Norouzi, Wolfgang Macherey, Maxim Krikun, Yuan Cao, Qin Gao, Klaus Macherey, et al. 2016. Google's neural machine translation system: Bridging the gap between human and machine translation. *arXiv preprint arXiv:1609.08144.*

Determining Question-Answer Plausibility in Crowdsourced Datasets Using Multi-Task Learning

Rachel Gardner   **Maya Varma**   **Clare Zhu**   **Ranjay Krishna**
Department of Computer Science, Stanford University, CA
`{rachel0, mvarma2, clarezhu, ranjaykrishna}@cs.stanford.edu`

Abstract

Datasets extracted from social networks and online forums are often prone to the pitfalls of natural language, namely the presence of unstructured and noisy data. In this work, we seek to enable the collection of high-quality question-answer datasets from social media by proposing a novel task for automated quality analysis and data cleaning: *question-answer (QA) plausibility*. Given a machine or user-generated question and a crowd-sourced response from a social media user, we determine if the question and response are valid; if so, we identify the answer within the free-form response.

We design BERT-based models to perform the QA plausibility task, and we evaluate the ability of our models to generate a clean, usable question-answer dataset. Our highest-performing approach consists of a single-task model which determines the plausibility of the question, followed by a multi-task model which evaluates the plausibility of the response as well as extracts answers (Question Plausibility AUROC=0.75, Response Plausibility AUROC=0.78, Answer Extraction F1=0.665).

1 Introduction

Large, densely-labeled datasets are a critical requirement for the creation of effective supervised learning models. The pressing need for high quantities of labeled data has led many researchers to collect data from social media platforms and online forums (Abu-El-Haija et al., 2016; Thomee et al., 2016; Go et al., 2009). Due to the presence of noise and the lack of structure that exist in these data sources, manual quality analysis (usually performed by paid crowdworkers) is necessary to extract structured labels, filter irrelevant examples, standardize language, and perform other preprocessing tasks before the data can be used. However,

obtaining dataset annotations in this manner is a time-consuming and expensive process that is often prone to errors.

In this work, we develop automated data cleaning and verification mechanisms for extracting high-quality data from social media platforms[1]. We specifically focus on the creation of question-answer datasets, in which each data instance consists of a question about a topic and the corresponding answer. In order to filter noise and improve data quality, we propose the task of *question-answer (QA) plausibility*, which includes the following three steps:

- *Determine question plausibility:* Depending on the type of dataset being constructed, the question posed to respondents may be generated by a machine or a human. We determine the likelihood that the question is both relevant and answerable.

- *Determine response plausibility:* We predict whether the user's response contains a reasonable answer to the question.

- *Extract answer from free-form response:* If the response is deemed to be plausible, we identify and extract the segment of the response that directly answers the question.

Because we assume social media users generally answer questions in good faith (and are posed questions which they can answer), we can assume plausible answers are correct ones (Park et al., 2019). Necessarily, if this property were not satisfied, then any adequate solutions would require the very domain knowledge of interest. Therefore, we look to apply this approach toward data with this property.

In this study, we demonstrate an application of QA plausibility in the context of visual question

---

[1]All code is available at `github.com/rachel-1/qa_plausibility`.

Proceedings of the 2020 EMNLP Workshop W-NUT: The Sixth Workshop on Noisy User-generated Text, pages 22–27
Online, Nov 19, 2020. ©2020 Association for Computational Linguistics

answering (VQA), a well-studied problem in the field of computer vision (Antol et al., 2015). We assemble a large VQA dataset with images collected from an image-sharing social network, machine-generated questions related to the content of the image, and responses from social media users. We then train a multitask BERT-based model and evaluate the ability of the model to perform the three subtasks associated with QA plausibility. The methods presented in this work hold potential for reducing the need for manual quality analysis of crowd-sourced data as well as enabling the use of question-answer data from unstructured environments such as social media platforms.

2 Related Work

Prior studies on the automated labeling task for datasets derived from social media typically focus on the generation of noisy labels; models trained on such datasets often rely on weak supervision to learn relevant patterns. However, approaches for noisy label generation, such as Snorkel (Ratner et al., 2017) and CurriculumNet (Guo et al., 2018), often use functions or other heuristics to generate labels. One such example is the Sentiment140 dataset, which consists of 1.6 million tweets labeled with corresponding sentiments based on the emojis present in the tweet (Go et al., 2009). In this case, the presence of just three category labels (positive, neutral, negative) simplifies the labeling task and reduces the effects of incorrect labels on trained models; however, this problem becomes increasingly more complex and difficult to automate as the number of annotation categories increases.

Previous researchers have studied question relevance by reasoning explicitly about the information available to answer the question. Several VQA studies have explicitly extracted premises, or assumptions made by questions, to determine if the original question is relevant to the provided image (Mahendru et al., 2017; Prabhakar et al., 2018). A number of machine comprehension models have been devised to determine the answerability of a question given a passage of text (Rajpurkar et al., 2018; Back et al., 2020). In contrast, we are able to leverage the user's freeform response to determine if the original question was valid. Our model is also tasked with supporting machine-generated questions, which may be unanswerable and lead to noisy user-generated responses.

While the concept of answer plausibility in user

responses has also been previously explored, existing approaches use hand-crafted rules and knowledge sources (Smith et al., 2005). By using a learned approach, we give our system the flexibility to adapt with the data and cover a wider variety of cases.

3 Dataset

The dataset consists of questions and responses collected from an image-sharing social media platform. We utilize an automated question-generation bot in order to access public image posts, generate a question based on image features, and record data from users that replied to the question, as shown in Figure 1 (Krishna et al., 2019). Because the question-generation bot was designed to maximize information gain, it generates questions across a wide variety of categories, including objects, attributes, spatial relationships, and activities (among others). For the sake of space, we refer readers to the original paper for more information on the method of question generation and diversity of the resulting questions asked. All users that contributed to the construction of this dataset were informed that they were participating in a research study, and IRB approval was obtained for this work. For the privacy of our users, the dataset will not be released at this time. Rather than focus on the specific dataset, we wish to instead present a general method for cleaning user-generated datasets and argue its generality even to tasks such as visual-question-answering.

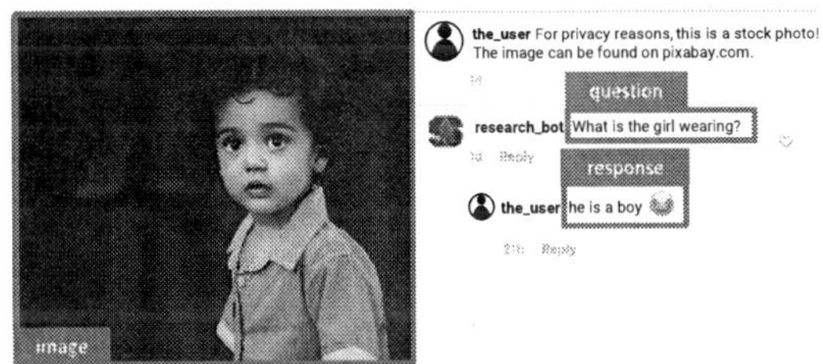

Figure 1: *An example question and response pair collected from social media.* Note that since the questions are generated by a bot, the question may not always be relevant to the image, as demonstrated here.

The dataset was labeled by crowdworkers on Amazon Mechanical Turk (AMT), who performed three annotation tasks, as shown in Table 1: (1) determine if the question was plausible, (2) deter-

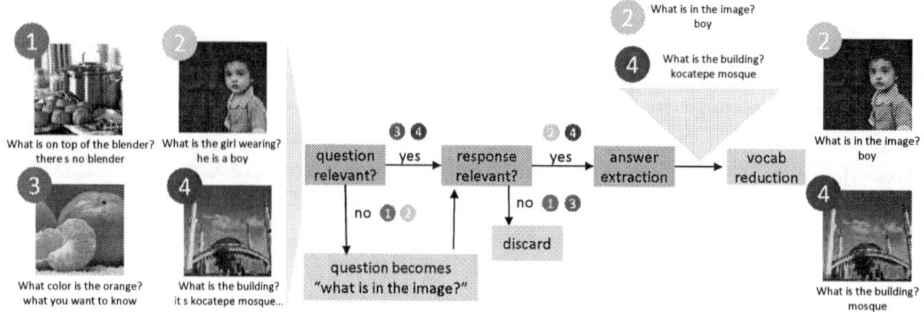

Figure 2: *Overview of the QA plausibility task, with representative examples.* Given a question and user response, we determine if the question and response are plausible given the image. If so, we then extract a structured answer label from the response.

#		Example Question/Response	Plausible?	%
1.	Q	What is on the table?	Y	50.6
	R	beet and carrot juice☺☺	Y	
2.	Q	What is the person doing?	Y	22.8
	R	not much lol	N	
3.	Q	What is on top of the cake?	N	11.4
	R	that is not cake that's chicken	Y	
4.	Q	What is the hamster doing?	N	15.3
	R	that is not a hamster	N	

Table 1: *Representative examples of cases present in the data, and the percentage of examples represented by each class in our dataset.* Examples (1) and (2) have valid questions that accurately refer to the corresponding images, while (3) and (4) do not correctly refer to objects in the image. However, in example (3), the user identifies the error made by the bot and correctly refers to the object in the image; as a result, this response is classified as valid.

mine if the response was plausible, and (3) if the response was deemed to be plausible, extract an answer span. Plausible questions and answers are defined as those that accurately refer to the content of the image.

It is important to note that since the question-generation process is automated, the question could be unrelated to the image due to bot errors; however, in such situations where the question is deemed to be implausible, the response may still be valid if it accurately refers to the content of the image. If the response is judged to be plausible, the AMT crowdworker must then extract the answer span from the user's response. In order to capture the level of detail we required (while discouraging AMT crowdworkers from simply copy/pasting the entire response), we set the maximum length of an answer span to be five words for the labeling step. However, the final model itself is not limited to answers of any particular length.

For cost reasons, each example was labeled by only one annotator. While we could have averaged labels across annotators, we found that the majority of the labeling errors were due to misunderstandings of the non-standard task, meaning that errors were localized to particular annotators rather than randomly spread across examples. This issue was mitigated by adding a qualifying task and manually reviewing a subset of labels per worker for the final data collection.

While one might expect images to be necessary (or at least helpful) for determining question and response plausibility, we found that human annotators were able to determine the validity of the inputs based solely on text without the need for the accompanying image. In our manual analysis of several hundred examples (approximately 5% of the dataset), we found that every example which required the image to label properly could be categorized as a "where" question. When the bot asked questions of the general form "where is the X" or "where was this taken," users assumed our bot had basic visual knowledge and was therefore asking a question not already answered by the image (such as "where is the dog now" or "what part of the world was this photo taken in"). This led to valid responses that did not pertain to image features and were therefore not helpful for training downstream models. Table 2 gives one such example. Once we removed these questions from the dataset, we could not find a single remaining example that required image data to label properly. As a result, we were able to explore the QA plausibility task in a VQA setting, despite not examining image features.

Our preprocessing steps and annotation procedure resulted in a total of 7200 question-response

	Example Question/Response		Valid?
	Q	Where is the dog?	Y
	R	sitting next to me on the sofa	N

Table 2: *Example requiring analysis of the original image (removed from dataset along with other "where" questions which often lead to confusion).*

pairs with answer labels. We use a standard split of 80% of the dataset for training, 10% for validation, and 10% for testing.

4   Models and Experiments

Model Architecture: As shown in Figure 3, we utilized a modified BERT model to perform the three sub-tasks associated with QA plausibility. The model accepts a concatenation of the machine-generated question and user response as input, with the [CLS] token inserted at the start of the sentence and the [SEP] token inserted to separate the question and response.

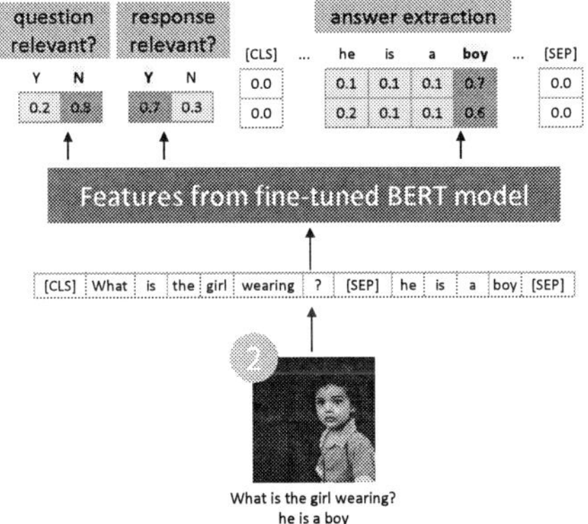

Figure 3: *Model architecture.* The question and user response serve as input to a modified BERT model, which will output question plausibility, response plausibility, and an answer label.

In order to perform the question plausibility classification task, the pooled transformer output is passed through a dropout layer (p=0.5), fully connected layer, and a softmax activation function. An identical approach is used for response plausibility classification. To extract the answer span, encoded hidden states corresponding to the last attention block are passed through a single fully connected layer and softmax activation; this yields two probability distributions over tokens, with the first representing the start token and the second representing the end token. The final model output includes the probability that the question and response are plausible, with each expressed as a score between 0 and 1; if the response is deemed to be plausible, the model also provides the answer label, which is expressed as a substring of the user response.

Experiments: We utilized a pretrained BERT Base Uncased model, which has 12 layers, 110 million parameters, a hidden layer size of 768, and a vocabulary size of 30,522. We trained several single-task and multi-task variants of our model in order to measure performance on the three subtasks associated with QA plausibility. In the multi-task setting, loss values from the separate tasks are combined; however, an exception to this exists if the user's response is classified as implausible. In these cases, the answer span extraction loss is manually set to zero and the answer extraction head is not updated.

We evaluated performance on question and response plausibilities by computing accuracy and AUC-ROC scores. Performance on the answer span extraction task was evaluated with F1 scores, which measure overlap between the predicted answer label and the true answer (Rajpurkar et al., 2018).

5   Results

We investigated performance of our BERT model on the various subtasks associated with QA plausibility. Results are summarized in Table 3. Single-task models trained individually on the subtasks achieved an AUC-ROC score of 0.75 on the question plausibility task, an AUC-ROC score of 0.77 on the response plausibility task, and an F1 score of 0.568 on the answer extraction task. A multi-task model trained simultaneously on all three tasks demonstrated decreased performance on the question and response plausibility tasks when compared to the single-task models. We found that the highest performance was achieved when a single-task model trained on the question plausibility task was followed by a multi-task model trained on both the response plausibility and answer extraction tasks; this model achieved an AUC-ROC score of 0.75 on question plausibility, an AUC-ROC score of 0.79 on response plausibility, and an F1 score of 0.665 on answer extraction.

Our results suggest that multi-task learning is most effective when the tasks are closely related, such as with response plausibility and answer extraction. Since the BERT architecture is extremely quick for both training and evaluation, we found that the increase in performance afforded by using a single-task model and multi-task model in series

Combined Task	Question Plausibility		Response Plausibility		Answer Extraction
	Acc	AUROC	Acc	AUROC	F1
Question Plausibility (QP) only	**65.51%**	**0.7488**	-	-	-
Response Plausibility (RP) only	-	-	64.62%	0.7674	-
Answer Extraction only	-	-	-	-	0.568
RP and Answer Extraction	-	-	**70.13%**	**0.7870**	**0.665**
QP, RP and Answer Extraction	63.90%	0.6803	60.91%	0.6881	0.6160

Table 3: *Model Evaluation Metrics.* Performance metrics of our model are shown here. Multi-task learning helps improve performance when the model is simultaneously trained on the response plausibility and answer extraction subtasks, but decreases performance when the model is simultaneously trained on all three subtasks.

was worth the overhead of training two separate models. It is worth noting that a more complicated model architecture might have been able to better accommodate the loss terms from all three subtasks, but we leave such efforts to future work.

6 Discussion

Deep learning studies are often hindered by lack of access to large datasets with accurate labels. In this paper, we introduced the question-answer plausibility task in an effort to automate the data cleaning process for question-answer datasets collected from social media. We then presented a multi-task deep learning model based on BERT, which accurately identified the plausibility of machine-generated questions and user responses as well as extracted structured answer labels. Although we specifically focused on the visual question answering problem in this paper, we expect that our results will be useful for other question-answer scenarios, such as in settings where questions are user-generated or images are not available.

Overall, our approach can help improve the deep learning workflow by processing and cleaning the noisy and unstructured natural language text available on social media platforms. Ultimately, our work can enable the generation of large-scale, high-quality datasets for artificial intelligence models.

References

Sami Abu-El-Haija, Nisarg Kothari, Joonseok Lee, Paul Natsev, George Toderici, Balakrishnan Varadarajan, and Sudheendra Vijayanarasimhan. 2016. Youtube-8m: A large-scale video classification benchmark.

Stanislaw Antol, Aishwarya Agrawal, Jiasen Lu, Margaret Mitchell, Dhruv Batra, C. Lawrence Zitnick, and Devi Parikh. 2015. VQA: Visual Question Answering.

Seohyun Back, Sai Chetan Chinthakindi, Akhil Kedia, Haejun Lee, and J. Choo. 2020. Neurquri: Neural question requirement inspector for answerability prediction in machine reading comprehension. In *ICLR*.

Alec Go, Richa Bhayani, and Lei Huang. 2009. Twitter sentiment classification using distant supervision.

Sheng Guo, Weilin Huang, Haozhi Zhang, Chenfan Zhuang, Dengke Dong, Matthew R. Scott, and Dinglong Huang. 2018. Curriculumnet: Weakly supervised learning from large-scale web images. *CoRR*, abs/1808.01097.

Ranjay Krishna, Michael Bernstein, and Li Fei-Fei. 2019. Information maximizing visual question generation. *CoRR*, abs/1903.11207.

Aroma Mahendru, Viraj Prabhu, Akrit Mohapatra, Dhruv Batra, and Stefan Lee. 2017. The promise of premise: Harnessing question premises in visual question answering. *EMNLP 2017*, abs/1705.00601.

Junwon Park, Ranjay Krishna, Pranav Khadpe, Li Fei-Fei, and Michael Bernstein. 2019. Ai-based request augmentation to increase crowdsourcing participation. *Proceedings of the Seventh AAAI Conference on Human Computation and Crowdsourcing*.

Prakruthi Prabhakar, Nitish Kulkarni, and Linghao Zhang. 2018. Question relevance in visual question answering. *arXiv preprint abs/1807.08435*.

Pranav Rajpurkar, Robin Jia, and Percy Liang. 2018. Know what you don't know: Unanswerable questions for squad. *Association for Computational Linguistics (ACL)*, abs/1806.03822.

Alexander Ratner, Stephen H. Bach, Henry R. Ehrenberg, Jason Alan Fries, Sen Wu, and Christopher Ré. 2017. Snorkel: Rapid training data creation with weak supervision. *CoRR*, abs/1711.10160.

Troy Smith, Thomas M. Repede, and Steven L. Lytinen. 2005. Determining the plausibility of answers to questions. *American Association for Artificial Intelligence*.

Bart Thomee, David A. Shamma, Gerald Friedland, Benjamin Elizalde, Karl Ni, Douglas Poland, Damian Borth, and Li-Jia Li. 2016. Yfcc100m. *Communications of the ACM*, 59(2):64–73.

Combining BERT with Static Word Embeddings
for Categorizing Social Media

Israa Alghanmi, Luis Espinosa-Anke, Steven Schockaert
Cardiff University, UK
{alghanmiia,espinosa-ankel,schockaerts1}@cardiff.ac.uk

Abstract

Pre-trained neural language models (LMs) have achieved impressive results in various natural language processing tasks, across different languages. Surprisingly, this extends to the social media genre, despite the fact that social media often has very different characteristics from the language that LMs have seen during training. A particularly striking example is the performance of AraBERT, an LM for the Arabic language, which is successful in categorizing social media posts in Arabic dialects, despite only having been trained on Modern Standard Arabic. Our hypothesis in this paper is that the performance of LMs for social media can nonetheless be improved by incorporating static word vectors that have been specifically trained on social media. We show that a simple method for incorporating such word vectors is indeed successful in several Arabic and English benchmarks. Curiously, however, we also find that similar improvements are possible with word vectors that have been trained on traditional text sources (e.g. Wikipedia).

1 Introduction

Social media has become an important source of information across numerous disciplines (Jaffali et al., 2020). For instance, it allows extracting and analyzing people's opinions, emotions and attitudes towards particular subjects, in a way which is difficult to achieve using other information sources. However, social media posts tend to be short and often contain abbreviations, slang words, misspellings, emoticons and dialect (Baly et al., 2017). For language models (LMs) such as BERT (Devlin et al., 2019), which have been primarily trained on Wikipedia, this poses a number of clear challenges. In the case of Arabic, the challenge is even greater, since social media posts are mostly written in regional dialects, which can be different from the language that is found in resources such

as Wikipedia (Alali et al., 2019). In particular, the Arabic language can be divided into Classical Arabic, Modern Standard Arabic, and Dialectal Arabic (Alotaibi et al., 2019). The latter differs between Arabic countries, and sometimes among regions and cities. Social Media acts as the primary source where Arabic dialects appear as written text, due to the informality of these platforms.

Similar as for English, the best results in many Arabic NLP tasks are currently obtained with LMs. In particular, the AraBERT model (Antoun et al., 2020) has achieved state-of-the-art results in sentiment analysis, named entity recognition and question answering, among others. However, AraBERT was trained on Wikipedia and news stories. It has thus not seen the Arabic dialects in which most social media posts are written. Surprisingly, however, Antoun et al. (2020) found that AraBERT is nonetheless able to outperform other methods on social media tasks. This includes methods that use the AraVec (Soliman et al., 2017) embeddings, which are word2vec vectors trained on Twitter, and have a wide coverage of dialect words.

Our hypothesis is that AraBERT and AraVec have complementary strengths, and that better results can thus be obtained by combining these two resources. Similarly, for English tasks, we would expect that the performance of BERT on social media can be improved by incorporating word embeddings that have been trained on social media. However, for English we would expect to see a smaller effect, since compared to Arabic, the vocabulary of English social media is more similar to the vocabulary in traditional sources. To test these hypotheses, we propose and evaluate a simple classifier which combines language models with static word embeddings. Our main findings are that incorporating word vectors can indeed boost performance. Surprisingly, this even holds for word embeddings that have been trained on standard sources.

Proceedings of the 2020 EMNLP Workshop W-NUT: The Sixth Workshop on Noisy User-generated Text, pages 28–33
Online, Nov 19, 2020. ©2020 Association for Computational Linguistics

2 Related Work

While there is a large literature on NLP for social media, more efforts that focus on the Arabic language are needed. A notable work is Heikal et al. (2018), which developed a CNN and LSTM ensemble model for Arabic sentiment analysis. They used AraVec pre-trained word embeddings for the word embedding representation. Recently, Kaibi et al. (2020) proposed an approach that relies on the concatenation of pre-trained AraVec and fastText vectors. However, the best results on most datasets are currently achieved by fine-tuning AraBERT (Antoun et al., 2020), as already mentioned in the introduction. For the English language, Nguyen et al. (2020) recently introduced BERTweet, a BERT-based language model that was trained on a large corpus of English tweets. Their experiments show that utilising this model led to improved results on different tasks involving Twitter posts, such as named entity recognition, part-of-speech tagging and text classification.

In this work, we investigate the effectiveness of combining pre-trained language models with static word embeddings. For earlier language models, most notably ELMo (Peters et al., 2018), it was common practice to combine contextual embeddings, predicted by the language model, with static word embeddings. However, the introduction of BERT has essentially eliminated the need for static word vectors in standard settings. On the other hand, several authors have shown that it can be beneficial to incorporate entity vectors with BERT, allowing the model to exploit factual or common-sense knowledge from structured sources (Lin et al., 2019; Poerner et al., 2019).

3 Proposed Approach

There are various ways in which BERT-based models can be combined with static word vectors. Note, however, that we cannot simply concatenate the contextualised word vectors predicted by BERT with the corresponding static word vectors, due to the fact that the tokenization strategy used by BERT means that many words are split into two or more word-piece tokens. One possible solution, adopted by Zhang et al. (2020) in a different setting, is to combine the word-piece tokens from the same word into a single vector, using a convolutional or recurrent neural network. The resulting word-level vector can then be concatenated with the corresponding static word vector. However,

without a large training set, there is a risk that the representations predicted by BERT are degraded by this aggregation step. As a simpler solution, we instead combine representations obtained from BERT and from the static word vectors at sentence level. In particular, to obtain a sentence vector from the fine-tuned BERT model, we simply take the average of the predicted contextualised vectors. To obtain a sentence vector from the static word embeddings, we use either a Convolutional Neural Network (CNN) or a Long Short Term Memory network (LSTM). After concatenating the two types of sentence vectors, we apply dropout, followed by a softmax classification layer. A diagram illustrating the model is shown in Figure 1. Rather than jointly training the combined model, we first fine-tune the BERT model on its own. After this fine-tuning step, we freeze the BERT model and train the CNN and combined classification layer. We found this strategy to be more robust against over-fitting.

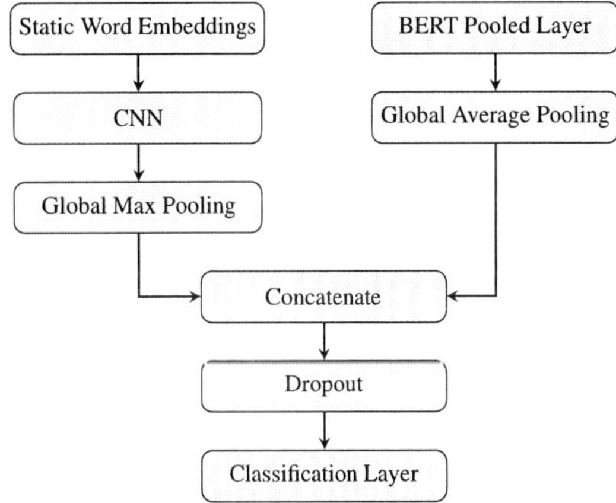

Figure 1: The CNN based proposed architecture

4 Experimental Results

We experimentally analyze the benefit of incorporating static word vectors, in both Arabic and English. For Arabic, we used the following datasets:

AJGT Arabic Jordanian General Tweets (Alomari et al., 2017) is a sentiment classification dataset. It consists of 1,800 tweets annotated with positive and negative labels.

SemEval-2017 Task 4 (Rosenthal et al., 2017) We use the Arabic subtask A dataset from SemEval 2017 Task 4. This dataset contains 10,126 tweets, annotated with negative, neutral, and positive labels.

L-HSAB A dataset for hate speech and abusive language in Arabic Levantine dialect (Mulki et al., 2019). It consists of 5846 tweets, which are annotated as normal, abusive or hate.

ArsenTD-Lev An Arabic Levantine dataset for sentiment analysis that discusses multiple topics (Baly et al., 2019). It contains 4000 tweets, labelled as a very negative, negative, neutral, positive, or very positive.

For English, we used the following datasets:

Irony Detection We use Semeval-2018 Task 3 dataset (Van Hee et al., 2018), containing 4,618 tweets that are annotated as ironic or not.

Semeval-2019 Task 6: OffensEval An offensive language identification dataset for social media (Zampieri et al., 2019). It consist of 14,100 tweets that are labeled as offensive or not.

Stance Detection We use the climate change Semeval-2016 Task 6 subtask A dataset (Mohammad et al., 2016). It contains 564 tweets, annotated as in favour, against or neutral towards the target.

Hate Speech Detection We utilize the English SemEval-2019 Task 5 dataset (Basile et al., 2019). It contains 13,000 tweets labeled as hateful or not.

For datasets without standard splits, we randomly split the data into 80% for training and 20% for testing. We removed emojis, hashtag signs (#), numbers, special characters and punctuation. We replace user mentions with [user], URLs with [link], and email addresses with [email], written in Arabic or English depending on the language of the dataset. For Arabic tweets, we also removed diacritics, elongation and English letters, besides shallow normalization. For English, we removed non-ASCII characters, convert emoticons to text, and common contractions to their full form.

Word Embeddings. For the Arabic dataset, we use AraVec word vectors (Soliman et al., 2017), which are based on the word2vec model (Mikolov et al., 2013). Pre-trained models are available for two Arabic content domains: Wikipedia and Twitter. For each domain, Skip-gram and CBOW versions with 100 and 300 dimension vector sizes were provided. In our experiments, for both domains, we have used the 300-dimensional CBOW vectors (**AraVec-twi** and **AraVec-wiki**). For English, we have used GloVe vectors provided by (Pennington et al., 2014). We have used the 100 dimensional word vectors that have been pre-trained on Twitter data (**GloVe-twi**), as well as the 100-dimensional GloVe vectors that have been trained on Wikipedia (**GloVe-wiki**).

Language Models. We use the pre-trained AraBERTv0.1 model[1] (Antoun et al., 2020) for Arabic and the $BERT_{base}$ uncased (Devlin et al., 2018) model for English.

Baselines and Methodology. As a baseline, we show the performance of a standard CNN, using only the static word vectors as input. We use 100 convolutional filters, a kernel size of 3, and a ReLU activation function. A global max-pooling layer follows the convolution layer. A dropout layer with a 0.5 drop rate is applied to the max-pooled output to avoid over-fitting. We use SGD with a batch size of 16 for 15 epochs with early stopping callback.

We also show results for BERT and AraBERT alone. We followed the BERT TensorFlow implementation for sequence classification provided by Hugging Face (Wolf et al., 2019). Both AraBERT and the English $BERT_{base}$ pre-trained language models share the same architecture, which consists of 12 layers. We utilize the Adamax optimizer and batch size of 8. The hyper-parameters search for the fine-tuning process involves the number of epochs (3 to 6) and the learning rates [2e-5, 5e-5]. We chose the best performing hyper-parameters based on a validation split. We use the standard validation split for datasets where one is provided, and use 20% of the training data as validation otherwise. We fine-tune BERT on the whole training data once the best hyper-parameters are chosen.

For the CNN variant of our proposed hybrid approach, we use the same configuration as for the CNN baseline, i.e. we use a convolution layer with a filter size of 100, a kernel size of 3, and the ReLU activation function, followed by global max-pooling. For the LSTM variant, we use 100-dimensional units. In both variants, the dropout rate is set to 0.5, and we use SGD with a batch size of 16, for 15 epochs, with the usage of early stopping callback.

---

[1] There are two versions of AraBERT, called AraBERTv0.1 and AraBERTv1. The only difference is that a Farasa Segmenter is used for the latter.

Model	Embeddings	AJGT	SemEval-2017	L-HSAB	ArsenTD-Lev
CNN	AraVec-twi	89.9	55.6	60.9	47.5
AraBERT	-	93.3	63.1	71.0	51.8
CNN + AraBERT	AraVec-twi	**93.4** (93.0, 93.9)	64.1 (63.5, 64.4)	**72.1** (71.7, 72.3)	49.2 (47.1, 51.5)
LSTM + AraBERT	AraVec-twi	93.1 (92.8, 93.6)	63.7 (63.3, 64.1)	72.0 (71.5, 72.5)	**52.2** (51.7, 52.7)
CNN + AraBERT	AraVec-wiki	**93.4** (92.8, 93.6)	**64.3** (63.9, 64.5)	71.8 (71.6, 72.1)	50.9 (48.0, 53.1)
LSTM + AraBERT	AraVec-wiki	93.1 (92.8, 93.6)	63.7 (63.4, 63.9)	71.9 (71.5, 72.5)	51.9 (51.5, 52.5)

Table 1: F1 scores (%) for Arabic datasets. We report the average result from five runs for CNN, CNN+AraBERT and LSTM+AraBERT, as well as the minimum and maximum results between parentheses. The fine-tuned AraBERT model is fixed across all variants.

Model	Embeddings	Irony	OffensEval	Hate	Stance
CNN	GloVe-twi	57.2	75.1	47.0	29.0
BERT	-	67.3	78.5	**50.6**	52.9
CNN + BERT	GloVe-twi	**68.4** (67.4, 69.7)	79.4 (79.2, 79.7)	48.1 (47.6, 48.5)	54.3 (52.9, 56.0)
LSTM+ BERT	GloVe-twi	68.3 (67.6, 68.9)	79.5 (79.2, 79.8)	47.7 (47.5, 47.8)	54.1 (53.1, 55.5)
CNN + BERT	GloVe-wiki	67.7 (66.5, 68.7)	79.4 (79.0, 79.6)	48.1 (47.8, 48.3)	**54.6** (53.6, 55.5)
LSTM+ BERT	GloVe-wiki	68.3 (67.6, 68.9)	**79.6** (79.2, 79.8)	47.7 (47.5, 47.8)	54.1 (53.1, 55.5)

Table 2: F1 scores (%) for English datasets. We report the average result from five runs for CNN, CNN+BERT and LSTM+BERT, as well as the minimum and maximum results between parentheses. The fine-tuned BERT model is fixed across all variants.

Results. Table 1 summarizes the performance of the baseline models and the proposed strategy for the Arabic language, while Table 2 shows the results for English. The results for AraBERT and BERT are the best results that were obtained over three runs. We then fix this model and combine it with the CNN and LSTM models. The results of these combined models (and the CNN baseline) are averaged over 5 runs. We use this approach since the focus is on assessing whether the performance of BERT and AraBERT can be improved.

Overall, the proposed combined model improves the results across almost all datasets, with the CNN and LSTM variants performing broadly similarly. One exception for Arabic is the **ArsenTD-Lev** dataset, where the LSTM variant performs substantially better than the CNN variant. and the English **Hate** dataset, where neither of the two variants outperforms the fine-tuned BERT model. The underperformance on the **Hate** dataset is likely related to over-fitting, as there is a clear mismatch between training and test data in this dataset (e.g. in terms of annotation strategy and average tweet length). The most surprising finding is that the AraVec-twi and AraVec-wiki word embeddings achieve comparable performance for Arabic, and similarly, the GloVe-twi and GloVe-wiki embeddings achieve comparable performance for English. This suggests that the main improvements are not due to the fact that the word embeddings are specialized towards the social media genre, but rather because they capture complementary facets of word mean-

ing. We conjecture that word vectors can, in particular, provide valuable complementary information for rare words. Schick and Schütze (2020) found that BERT struggles with rare words and we can indeed expect social media texts to contain a larger proportion of rare words than documents in other genres.

5   Conclusions

In this paper, we have presented a simple approach to combine static word embeddings with BERT-based language models. Intuitively, the reason why this hybrid approach can outperform the BERT-based models themselves is because the latter were not trained on Wikipedia. The alternative solution would be to train language models on a relevant social media corpus, as in the BERTweet model (Nguyen et al., 2020). While such a strategy is likely to lead to a better overall performance, in principle, this is not always feasible in practice. For instance, using static word vectors could play an important role in dealing with emerging terms, such as trending hashtags, as continuously updating language models (for many different languages) would be too expensive. Similarly, incorporating static word vectors seems to be a promising strategy for improving language models for low-resource languages, as specialized language models (e.g. trained on social media) are unlikely to become available for such languages.

References

Muath Alali, Nurfadhlina Mohd Sharef, Masrah Azrifah Azmi Murad, Hazlina Hamdan, and Nor Azura Husin. 2019. Narrow convolutional neural network for arabic dialects polarity classification. *IEEE Access*, 7:96272–96283.

Khaled Mohammad Alomari, Hatem M ElSherif, and Khaled Shaalan. 2017. Arabic tweets sentimental analysis using machine learning. In *International Conference on Industrial, Engineering and Other Applications of Applied Intelligent Systems*, pages 602–610. Springer.

Shoayee Alotaibi, Rashid Mehmood, and Iyad Katib. 2019. Sentiment analysis of arabic tweets in smart cities: A review of saudi dialect. In *2019 Fourth International Conference on Fog and Mobile Edge Computing (FMEC)*, pages 330–335. IEEE.

Wissam Antoun, Fady Baly, and Hazem Hajj. 2020. Arabert: Transformer-based model for arabic language understanding.

Ramy Baly, Gilbert Badaro, Georges El-Khoury, Rawan Moukalled, Rita Aoun, Hazem Hajj, Wassim El-Hajj, Nizar Habash, and Khaled Shaban. 2017. A characterization study of arabic twitter data with a benchmarking for state-of-the-art opinion mining models. In *Proceedings of the third Arabic natural language processing workshop*, pages 110–118.

Ramy Baly, Alaa Khaddaj, Hazem Hajj, Wassim El-Hajj, and Khaled Bashir Shaban. 2019. Arsentdlev: A multi-topic corpus for target-based sentiment analysis in arabic levantine tweets. *arXiv preprint arXiv:1906.01830*.

Valerio Basile, Cristina Bosco, Elisabetta Fersini, Nozza Debora, Viviana Patti, Francisco Manuel Rangel Pardo, Paolo Rosso, Manuela Sanguinetti, et al. 2019. Semeval-2019 task 5: Multilingual detection of hate speech against immigrants and women in twitter. In *13th International Workshop on Semantic Evaluation*, pages 54–63. Association for Computational Linguistics.

Jacob Devlin, Ming-Wei Chang, Kenton Lee, and Kristina Toutanova. 2018. Bert: Pre-training of deep bidirectional transformers for language understanding. *arXiv preprint arXiv:1810.04805*.

Jacob Devlin, Ming-Wei Chang, Kenton Lee, and Kristina Toutanova. 2019. BERT: pre-training of deep bidirectional transformers for language understanding. In *Proceedings of the 2019 Conference of the North American Chapter of the Association for Computational Linguistics: Human Language Technologies*, pages 4171–4186.

Maha Heikal, Marwan Torki, and Nagwa El-Makky. 2018. Sentiment analysis of arabic tweets using deep learning. *Procedia Computer Science*, 142:114–122.

Soufien Jaffali, Salma Jamoussi, Nesrine Khelifi, and Abdelmajid Ben Hamadou. 2020. Survey on social networks data analysis. In *International Conference on Innovations for Community Services*, pages 100–119. Springer.

Ibrahim Kaibi, Hassan Satori, et al. 2020. Sentiment analysis approach based on combination of word embedding techniques. In *Embedded Systems and Artificial Intelligence*, pages 805–813. Springer.

Bill Yuchen Lin et al. 2019. KagNet: Knowledge-aware graph networks for commonsense reasoning. In *EMNLP*.

Tomas Mikolov, Ilya Sutskever, Kai Chen, Greg S Corrado, and Jeff Dean. 2013. Distributed representations of words and phrases and their compositionality. In *Advances in neural information processing systems*, pages 3111–3119.

Saif Mohammad, Svetlana Kiritchenko, Parinaz Sobhani, Xiaodan Zhu, and Colin Cherry. 2016. Semeval-2016 task 6: Detecting stance in tweets. In *Proceedings of the 10th International Workshop on Semantic Evaluation (SemEval-2016)*, pages 31–41.

Hala Mulki, Hatem Haddad, Chedi Bechikh Ali, and Halima Alshabani. 2019. L-hsab: A levantine twitter dataset for hate speech and abusive language. In *Proceedings of the Third Workshop on Abusive Language Online*, pages 111–118.

Dat Quoc Nguyen, Thanh Vu, and Anh Tuan Nguyen. 2020. Bertweet: A pre-trained language model for english tweets. *arXiv preprint arXiv:2005.10200*.

Jeffrey Pennington, Richard Socher, and Christopher D Manning. 2014. Glove: Global vectors for word representation. In *Proceedings of the 2014 conference on empirical methods in natural language processing (EMNLP)*, pages 1532–1543.

Matthew Peters, Mark Neumann, Mohit Iyyer, Matt Gardner, Christopher Clark, Kenton Lee, and Luke Zettlemoyer. 2018. Deep contextualized word representations. In *Proceedings of the 2018 Conference of the North American Chapter of the Association for Computational Linguistics: Human Language Technologies*, pages 2227–2237.

Nina Poerner, Ulli Waltinger, and Hinrich Schütze. 2019. E-bert: Efficient-yet-effective entity embeddings for bert.

Sara Rosenthal, Noura Farra, and Preslav Nakov. 2017. SemEval-2017 task 4: Sentiment analysis in Twitter. In *Proceedings of the 11th International Workshop on Semantic Evaluation*, SemEval '17, Vancouver, Canada. Association for Computational Linguistics.

Timo Schick and Hinrich Schütze. 2020. Rare words: A major problem for contextualized embeddings and how to fix it by attentive mimicking. In *Proceedings of the Thirty-Fourth AAAI Conference on Artificial Intelligence*, pages 8766–8774.

Abu Bakr Soliman, Kareem Eissa, and Samhaa R El-Beltagy. 2017. Aravec: A set of arabic word embedding models for use in arabic nlp. *Procedia Computer Science*, 117:256–265.

Cynthia Van Hee, Els Lefever, and Véronique Hoste. 2018. Semeval-2018 task 3: Irony detection in english tweets. In *Proceedings of The 12th International Workshop on Semantic Evaluation*, pages 39–50.

Thomas Wolf, Lysandre Debut, Victor Sanh, Julien Chaumond, Clement Delangue, Anthony Moi, Pierric Cistac, Tim Rault, R'emi Louf, Morgan Funtowicz, and Jamie Brew. 2019. Huggingface's transformers: State-of-the-art natural language processing. *ArXiv*, abs/1910.03771.

Marcos Zampieri, Shervin Malmasi, Preslav Nakov, Sara Rosenthal, Noura Farra, and Ritesh Kumar. 2019. Semeval-2019 task 6: Identifying and categorizing offensive language in social media (offenseval). *arXiv preprint arXiv:1903.08983*.

Zhuosheng Zhang, Yuwei Wu, Hai Zhao, Zuchao Li, Shuailiang Zhang, Xi Zhou, and Xiang Zhou. 2020. Semantics-aware BERT for language understanding. In *Proceedings of the Thirty-Fourth AAAI Conference on Artificial Intelligence*, pages 9628–9635.

Enhanced Sentence Alignment Network for Efficient Short Text Matching

Zhe Hu[1]   **Zuohui Fu**[2]   **Cheng Peng**[1]   **Weiwei Wang**[1]

[1]Baidu Inc., Beijing, China
[2]Rutgers University, NJ, USA
[1]{huzhe01, pengcheng06}@baidu.com, elegate@qq.com
[2]zuohui.fu@rutgers.edu

Abstract

Cross-sentence attention has been widely applied in text matching, in which model learns the aligned information between two intermediate sequence representations to capture their semantic relationship. However, commonly the intermediate representations are generated solely based on the preceding layers and the models may suffer from error propagation and unstable matching, especially when multiple attention layers are used. In this paper, we propose an enhanced sentence alignment network with simple gated feature augmentation, where the model is able to flexibly integrate both original word and contextual features to improve the cross-sentence attention. Moreover, our model is less complex with fewer parameters compared to many state-of-the-art structures. Experiments on three benchmark datasets validate our model capacity for text matching.

1 Introduction

Modeling the semantic relationship of a sentence pair is a long standing task in natural language processing, which can be applied in many scenarios such as paraphrase detection and natural language inference (Wang et al., 2017; Bowman et al., 2015; Lan and Xu, 2018). Neural network approaches have achieved impressive results on solving text matching tasks for the good representation learning ability and benefiting from large datasets (Rocktäschel et al., 2015; Wang et al., 2017; Gong et al., 2017).

One of the major paradigms is attention based neural approach which adopts matching and fusion method (Chen et al., 2017; Wang and Jiang, 2016; Duan et al., 2018). Specifically, attention mechanism is used as a key component to compute word or phrase alignments between the two parallel sequences, and then the aligned information is fused to update the sentence representations. Recent work also adopts multiple matching processes

to equip model with power on gradually refining the attention results (Yang et al., 2019; Liang et al., 2019; Kim et al., 2019).

Unfortunately, conducting cross-sentence attention between two intermediate sentence representations may lead to unstable matching since different layers aim at capturing different semantic information (Liu et al., 2019a). Also, each intermediate representation is highly correlated to the previous layers, and error propagation would affect the following representations and lead to incorrect alignments since model is unable to amend the information without recalling the original semantic features. Furthermore, in case of multiple alignment blocks are used, models may suffer from difficulty of training such as vanishing gradients, and low-level features are inefficient to be fully trained. Different connection methods are adopted by some recent models to overcome this problem (Tay et al., 2018a; Yang et al., 2019; Nie and Bansal, 2017).

Recently pre-trained language models such as BERT have achieved impressive improvements on text matching tasks (Devlin et al., 2019; Liu et al., 2019b). Despite the promising results, the large parameter size and growing computational requirements make it hard to directly deploy these models to real-time applications (Sanh et al., 2019). Thus designing efficient and effective models to tackle text matching has been of increasing importance.

In this work, we introduce an **Enhanced Sentence Alignment Network with Gated Feature Augmentation (ESAN)**, in which our model integrates the word features (embedding outputs) and contextual features (encoding outputs) to the intermediate representations for each cross-sentence attention, as shown in Figure 1. The embedding outputs contain the original word information, and the encoding outputs represent each token with the aggregated contexts, which are helpful to guide the attention layer to properly capture the aligned

Proceedings of the 2020 EMNLP Workshop W-NUT: The Sixth Workshop on Noisy User-generated Text, pages 34–40
Online, Nov 19, 2020. ©2020 Association for Computational Linguistics

information. A gate operation is used to flexibly control how much these two features to be added. Also, incorporating the original semantic features directly to the different levels of representation layers can be viewed as a shortcut connection, which is helpful to reduce the training difficulty on low-level features. We then apply a simple but effective fusion layer to fuse the aligned features and update the sentence representations gradually. Different from previous work (Yang et al., 2019; Kim et al., 2019), we do not apply residual connections between alignment layers or use multiple encoders in alignment layers, and our architecture is *more efficient and less complex* compared with many strong baselines, indicating the feasibility to be deployed in real applications.

To demonstrate the effectiveness of our method, we conduct experiments on three text matching datasets: SNLI, MultiNLI and Quora Question Pairs. The results show our model outperforms strong baselines with fast inference speed. We also conduct model analysis including an ablation study and a case study on attention visualization.

2 Method

2.1 Encoding Layer

Given inputs S_a and S_b, the model first passes each sequence to an embedding layer to get word representations. We use pre-trained word vectors as word embeddings and keep it fixed during training. Character-based word representations is also leveraged, in which we use 1D convolutional network on the character embeddings, and then apply max pooling over the time dimension of each token. The word vectors and character-based vectors are concatenated. Following Chen et al. (2018), we further concatenate syntactical features including part-of-speech (POS) tagging feature and binary exact match feature for the NLI task. The embedding outputs are regarded as the final word features: $E_a = \{e_{a_i}\} \in \mathbb{R}^{m \times d}$ and $E_b = \{e_{b_j}\} \in \mathbb{R}^{n \times d}$, where m, n are the sequence lengths. We then pass E_a and E_b to a Bidirectional LSTM encoder to obtain the contextual features $H_a = \{h_{a_i}\}$ and $H_b = \{h_{b_j}\}$, with the same dimension size of d.

Intuitively, the word features contain the original information of each token, and the contextual features represent each word with aggregated context information. They will be used as additional features to enhance the following alignment process.

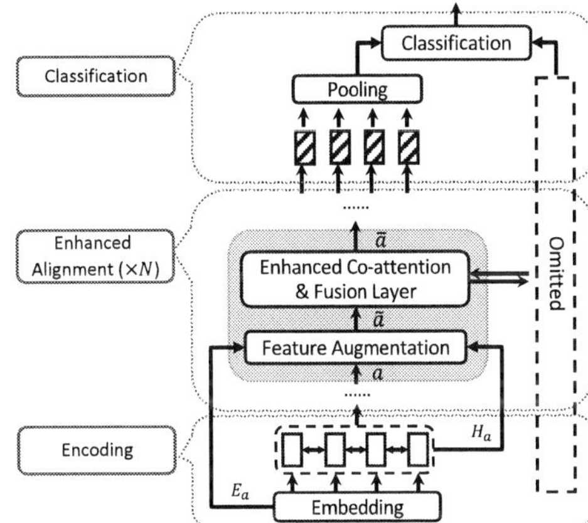

Figure 1: The overview of our model. Word features (E_a) and contextual features (H_a) are used for the enhanced sentence alignment layer, and multiple alignments are stacked with independent parameters. Symmetric structure is applied, and we omit the right part for space limitation.

2.2 Enhanced Sentence Alignment Layer

The proposed enhanced sentence alignment layer takes the intermediate representations a and b as inputs. As shown in Figure 1, the enhanced alignment layer consists of: (1) gated feature augmentation, (2) co-attention and (3) fusion layer. Multiple enhanced sentence alignment layers are stacked to enable the model to gradually refine the alignments.

2.2.1 Gated Feature Augmentation.

Given two intermediate sequence representations a and b, which are the inputs of the current alignment layer, we first augment the word and contextual features to each representation as different levels of the original semantic features. Specifically, for sequence representation $a = \{a_i | a_i \in \mathbb{R}^d, i = 1, 2, ..., m\}$, we augment the word feature E_a and contextual feature H_a with a gate operation to enable the model to selectively keep the features from different parts, which is formally defined as:

$$g_{e_i} = \sigma(W_g a_i + W_e e_{a_i} + z_e) \tag{1}$$
$$g_{h_i} = \sigma(W_g a_i + W_h h_{a_i} + z_h) \tag{2}$$
$$\widetilde{a}_i = a_i + g_{e_i} \circ e_{a_i} + g_{h_i} \circ h_{a_i} \tag{3}$$

where $W_* \in \mathbb{R}^{d \times d}$ and $z_* \in \mathbb{R}^d$ are trainable parameters. The same operation is performed for sequence b. For the first alignment inputs (the encoding outputs), we only augment the word features. Inspired by residual connections (He et al., 2016), we also try a simplified version of augmentation without gate operation:

$$\widetilde{a}_i = a_i + e_{a_i} + h_{a_i} \tag{4}$$

2.2.2 Co-attention.

We then apply the co-attention between two enhanced sequence representations $\widetilde{a}$ and $\widetilde{b}$ to capture their relationship. We first calculate similarity score e_{ij} of token $\widetilde{a}_i$ and token $\widetilde{b}_j$:

$$e_{ij} = \mathrm{ReLU}(W_c\widetilde{a}_i)^{\mathrm{T}} \cdot \mathrm{ReLU}(W_c\widetilde{b}_j) \qquad (5)$$

where W_c is a trainable parameter, and the bias term is omitted. Then the attentive representations of each sequence are computed by the weighted sum of the other sequence to highlight the relevant elements:

$$a'_i = \sum_{j=1}^{n} \frac{\exp(e_{ij})}{\sum_{k=1}^{n} \exp(e_{ik})} \widetilde{b}_j \qquad (6)$$

$$b'_j = \sum_{i=1}^{m} \frac{\exp(e_{ij})}{\sum_{k=1}^{m} \exp(e_{kj})} \widetilde{a}_i \qquad (7)$$

where m, n are the lengths of sequence $\widetilde{a}$ and $\widetilde{b}$.

2.2.3 Fusion Layer

We apply a simple yet effective fusion layer to fuse the aligned features to the original representations. The output of fusion layer $\bar{a}$ is computed as follows:

$$\bar{a}_i = \mathrm{ReLU}(W_f[\widetilde{a}_i; a'_i; \widetilde{a}_i - a'_i; \widetilde{a}_i \circ a'_i] + z_f) \qquad (8)$$

where W_f and z_f are trainable parameters, $[;]$ represents concatenation, and $\circ$ is element-wise product. The output has the same dimension size as $\widetilde{a}$ and a'.

2.3 Pooling and Classification Layer

We use both mean and max pooling on each sequence to get the corresponding vector representations, as inputs of the classification layer. Mean pooling aggregates global semantics and max pooling represents the import semantic features. Then we apply an MLP with softmax to get the final distributions. Formally, assume the outputs of the last fusion layer is V_a and V_b, we first compute the feature vector:

$$V'_a = [\frac{1}{m}\sum_{i=1}^{m} v_{a_i}; \max_{i=1}^{m} v_{a_i}] \qquad (9)$$

$$V'_b = [\frac{1}{m}\sum_{i=1}^{m} v_{b_i}; \max_{i=1}^{m} v_{b_i}] \qquad (10)$$

$$V = [V'_a; V'_b; V'_a - V'_b; V'_a \circ V'_b] \qquad (11)$$

Then a multi-layer perceptron (MLP) is used to calculate the final target:

$$\hat{y} = \mathrm{softmax}(W_2\mathrm{ReLU}(W_1V + z_1) + z_2) \qquad (12)$$

where W_* and z_* are trainable parameters.

Model	Test Accuracy (%)
ESIM (Chen et al., 2017)	88.0
BiMPM (Wang et al., 2017)	87.5
DIIN (Gong et al., 2017)	88.0
CAFE (Tay et al., 2018b)	88.5
CSRAN (Tay et al., 2018a)	88.7
ADIN (Liang et al., 2019)	88.8
RE2 (Yang et al., 2019)	88.9
OSOA-DFN (Liu et al., 2019a)	88.8
ESAN	**89.0**

Table 1: Experiment results on SNLI dataset. Our model yields better results (in bold).

3 Experimental Setups

Datasets and Preprocessing. We evaluate our model on three large-scale benchmark datasets: SNLI dataset (Bowman et al., 2015), MultiNLI dataset (Williams et al., 2018) and Quora Question Pairs (Quora) dataset. We follow the same data splits as provided in the original papers for SNLI and MultiNLI. For Quora, we use the same split as Wang et al. (2017)[1]. Accuracy is used to evaluate the model performance for all three datasets.

Training Details and Parameters. We tune the number of enhanced alignment layers from 2 to 3 in all experiments, which can be easily extended to more layers. We apply 300D-840B Glove (Pennington et al., 2014) as pre-trained word vectors. The 1D convolutional network is used for char embedding with kernel size 5 and 100 filters. We tune the number of recurrent layers from 1 to 2, and the dimension of feed-forward layers from 150 to 300 with ReLU (Glorot et al., 2011) as activation function. Adam optimizer (Kingma and Ba, 2014) is used with β_1 to be 0.9 and β_2 to be 0.999 during training. We use cropping or padding to limit each token to have 16 characters in char embedding. Dropout with dropout rate of 0.2 is applied to prevent overfitting. We set initial learning rate as 0.001 with exponential decay. The batch size is tuned from 64 to 256. More details are in Supplementary.

4 Results

4.1 Quantitative Results

Our model outperforms strong baselines with competitive results on all three datasets. For a fair comparison, we do not include the methods with pre-trained language models such as BERT (Devlin et al., 2019) or ensemble systems.

---

[1]Data statistics are in Supplementary.

Model	Test Accuracy (%)
BiMPM (Wang et al., 2017)	88.2
DIIN (Gong et al., 2017)	89.1
CAFE (Tay et al., 2018b)	88.7
CSRAN (Tay et al., 2018a)	89.2
RE2 (Yang et al., 2019)	89.2
OSOA-DFN (Liu et al., 2019a)	89.0
Enhanced-RCNN (Peng et al., 2020)	**89.3**
ESAN	**89.3**

Table 2: Experiment results on Quora datasets. Our model yields better results than all comparisons (in bold).

Model	Test Accuracy (%)	
	Matched	Mismatched
DIIN (Gong et al., 2017)	78.8	77.8
CAFE (Tay et al., 2018b)	78.7	77.9
AF-DMN (Duan et al., 2018)	76.9	76.3
MwAN (Tan et al., 2018)	78.5	77.7
ADIN (Liang et al., 2019)	78.8	77.9
ESAN	**79.3**	**78.4**

Table 3: Experiment results on MultiNLI dataset. Our model yields better results than all comparisons (in bold).

The results for SNLI and Quora are shown in Table 1 and Table 2. For SNLI, our model achieves 89.0% test accuracy, which is higher than all comparisons including some strong state-of-the-art models. For Quora, our model also achieves the best performance, with 89.3% test accuracy. Table 3 presents the results on MultiNLI, and our model produces higher accuracy on both in-domain (matched) and out-domain (mismatched) test sets, which further proves the model ability for natural language inference task. Above all, the results on the challenging datasets verify our model effectiveness for solving text matching tasks.

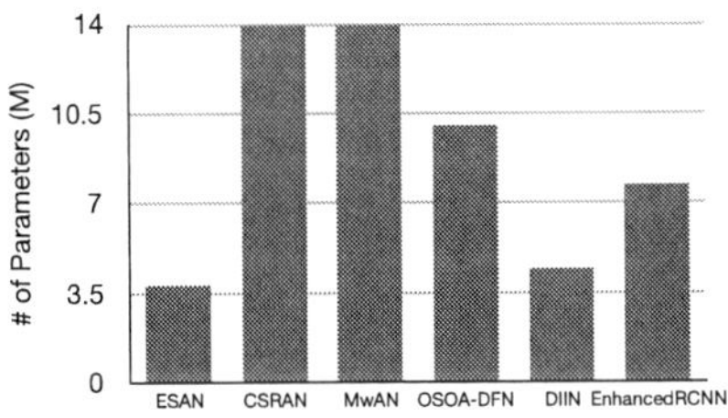

Figure 2: Total number of parameters for different models on Quora dataset.

4.2 Model Analysis

Ablation Study. To verify the effectiveness of our model components, we conduct an ablation study on Quora as shown in Table 4. The first line represents the model variant without feature augmentation (using original co-attention between intermediate representations) and the result drops dramatically. It shows that feature augmentation plays

Models	Acc. (%)
ESAN	**89.4**
(w/o Feat. Augment.)	88.1
(w/o Word Feat.)	89.0
(w/o Contextual Feat.)	88.9
(w/ Simple Augment.)	89.1

Table 4: Analysis of model components on Quora dev set.

a key role to enhance the alignment process. In the next two settings, after removing word features and contextual features respectively, both the results drop, and removing contextual features brings more decrease to the final performance. These two features are complementary to each other to improve the following cross-sentence attention. For the last ablation study, we apply simple augmentation without gate as Equation 4, and the performance decreases by 0.3 percentage point, which indicates the usefulness of the gate operation.

Models	parameter size	time (s/batch)
ESAN	3.9M	0.04 ± 0.01
BERT	109.5M	0.88 ± 0.06

Table 5: Paramter size and inference time for ESAN and BERT on Quora Question Pairs.

Model Efficiency. Figure 2 presents the comparison of total number of parameters for our model and baselines. Some strong comparisons such as CSRAN and MwAN contain more than 10M parameters, while our model has less parameters (3.9M) and achieves better results. We also compare the inference time with BERT to show the efficiency of our model in Table 5. Specifically, we set the sentence lengths as 20. Both models are required to make predictions for a batch of 8 sentence pairs on a MacBook Pro with Intel Core i7 CPUs. For BERT, we add a linear layer on top of the [CLS] token for classification as the original paper did (Devlin et al., 2019). We report the average and the standard deviation of processing 1000 batches. From the results we can see ESAN has a higher inference speed than BERT with less model complexity, which further indicates ESAN is more efficient and can be applied in many real scenarios.

4.3 Attention Visualization.

We present a case study through the attention visualization to investigate what our model learns in cross-sentence attention. We take an instance from SNLI, where sentence 1 is "police officer with riot shield stands in front of crowd" and sentence 2 is "a police officer stands in front of a crowd". The

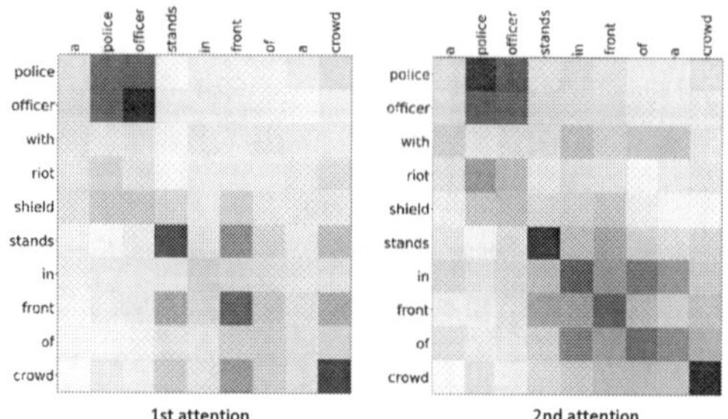

Figure 3: Visualization of attention results for a natural language inference case.

attention results are shown in Figure 3.

In the first attention, the model tends to align elements mostly in word-level. For example, "stands" and "crowd" in two sequences are successfully connected. Also, the model correctly aligns phrase "police officer" together which is one of the key components. In the second attention, the model tries to refine the attention distribution and gives "stands" and "crowd" larger weights. Also, the model tends to align longer phrases together instead of individual words. For example, phrases "in front of" in two sequences are connected. Notably, "riot shield" is also aligned to "police officer". We hypothesis that the model learns this phrase is used to describe entity "police officer", thus correctly aligning these two would help to make the final decision. With the proper alignments, the model correctly classifies their relationship as "entailment".

5 Related Work

Text matching is a key technique for many NLP tasks such as natural language inference (Bowman et al., 2015), paraphrase identification (Wang et al., 2017) and machine reading comprehension (Rajpurkar et al., 2016; Wang et al., 2018). As a long standing problem, this area has been in the center of attention and investigated widely.

Benefiting from large-scale datasets, neural networks have achieved much success for solving this problem. One of the paradigms uses sentence encoding structure, in which two sentences are encoded into vector representations, and then the vectors are combined to make the final prediction (Conneau et al., 2017; Yin and Schütze, 2015; Mueller and Thyagarajan, 2016). However, the interaction of the two input sequences is not directly considered during the encoding process, which makes the model difficult to capture complex relationship.

Later work adopts matching and aggregation method to model the alignments of the two sentences. Wang and Jiang (2016) uses a match-LSTM to conduct word-level matching of the two sequences. Parikh et al. (2016) propose a simple attention operation and use a feed-forward network to integrate the aligned representations. BiMPM (Wang et al., 2017) uses multi-perspective matching operation to compare two sequences, and applies a Bi-LSTM network for aggregation. Gong et al. (2017) uses DensNet as feature extractor to extract the semantic feature from the interaction tensor.

To better capture the sentence alignments in different levels, multiple attention operations can be stacked together. Yang et al. (2019) propose a simple but effective framework with richer alignment features. Tay et al. (2018a) leverages multi-level attention refinement component to conduct more extensive matching and improve the results. ADIN (Liang et al., 2019) stacks asynchronous inference layers for a multi-step reasoning process.

Recently the pre-trained language models have achieved state-of-the-art results on text matching tasks with pre-training and finetuning procedure (Devlin et al., 2019). Nevertheless, large parameter size and slow inference speed make it hard to directly deploy these structures to the real applications. Different from above methods, we propose a simple but effective gated augmentation layer to enrich the intermediate representations with the original word features and contextual features, and thus guide model to produce better alignments.

6 Conclusions

In this work, we present ESAN, an enhanced sentence alignment network for text matching. We flexibly integrate both word and contextual features to the intermediate representations with a gate operation to conduct better co-attention between two sequences. Our model outperforms strong baselines on three datasets and contains fewer parameters, which indicates the model capacity on producing proper alignments for text matching. In the future, we also plan to apply our methods to some other scenarios such as question answering.

Acknowledgements

This work is done when Weiwei Wang was at Baidu. We thank the anonymous reviewers for their constructive suggestions. We also thank Yu Yin for the helpful discussion and suggestions, and Zizhe Xie for proofreading the paper.

References

Samuel R. Bowman, Gabor Angeli, Christopher Potts, and Christopher D. Manning. 2015. A large annotated corpus for learning natural language inference. In *Proceedings of the 2015 Conference on Empirical Methods in Natural Language Processing*, pages 632–642, Lisbon, Portugal. Association for Computational Linguistics.

Qian Chen, Xiaodan Zhu, Zhen-Hua Ling, Diana Inkpen, and Si Wei. 2018. Neural natural language inference models enhanced with external knowledge. In *Proceedings of the 56th Annual Meeting of the Association for Computational Linguistics (Volume 1: Long Papers)*, pages 2406–2417, Melbourne, Australia. Association for Computational Linguistics.

Qian Chen, Xiaodan Zhu, Zhen-Hua Ling, Si Wei, Hui Jiang, and Diana Inkpen. 2017. Enhanced LSTM for natural language inference. In *Proceedings of the 55th Annual Meeting of the Association for Computational Linguistics (Volume 1: Long Papers)*, pages 1657–1668, Vancouver, Canada. Association for Computational Linguistics.

Alexis Conneau, Douwe Kiela, Holger Schwenk, Loïc Barrault, and Antoine Bordes. 2017. Supervised learning of universal sentence representations from natural language inference data. In *Proceedings of the 2017 Conference on Empirical Methods in Natural Language Processing*, pages 670–680, Copenhagen, Denmark. Association for Computational Linguistics.

Jacob Devlin, Ming-Wei Chang, Kenton Lee, and Kristina Toutanova. 2019. BERT: Pre-training of deep bidirectional transformers for language understanding. In *Proceedings of the 2019 Conference of the North American Chapter of the Association for Computational Linguistics: Human Language Technologies, Volume 1 (Long and Short Papers)*, pages 4171–4186, Minneapolis, Minnesota. Association for Computational Linguistics.

Chaoqun Duan, Lei Cui, Xinchi Chen, Furu Wei, Conghui Zhu, and Tiejun Zhao. 2018. Attention-fused deep matching network for natural language inference. In *IJCAI*, pages 4033–4040.

Xavier Glorot, Antoine Bordes, and Yoshua Bengio. 2011. Deep sparse rectifier neural networks. In *Proceedings of the Fourteenth International Conference on Artificial Intelligence and Statistics*, volume 15 of *Proceedings of Machine Learning Research*, pages 315–323, Fort Lauderdale, FL, USA. PMLR.

Yichen Gong, Heng Luo, and Jian Zhang. 2017. Natural language inference over interaction space. *arXiv preprint arXiv:1709.04348*.

Kaiming He, Xiangyu Zhang, Shaoqing Ren, and Jian Sun. 2016. Deep residual learning for image recognition. In *Proceedings of the IEEE conference on computer vision and pattern recognition*, pages 770–778.

Seonhoon Kim, Inho Kang, and Nojun Kwak. 2019. Semantic sentence matching with densely-connected recurrent and co-attentive information. In *Proceedings of the AAAI conference on artificial intelligence*, volume 33, pages 6586–6593.

Diederik P Kingma and Jimmy Ba. 2014. Adam: A method for stochastic optimization. *arXiv preprint arXiv:1412.6980*.

Wuwei Lan and Wei Xu. 2018. Neural network models for paraphrase identification, semantic textual similarity, natural language inference, and question answering. In *Proceedings of the 27th International Conference on Computational Linguistics (COLING)*.

Di Liang, Fubao Zhang, Qi Zhang, and Xuanjing Huang. 2019. Asynchronous deep interaction network for natural language inference. In *Proceedings of the 2019 Conference on Empirical Methods in Natural Language Processing and the 9th International Joint Conference on Natural Language Processing (EMNLP-IJCNLP)*, pages 2692–2700, Hong Kong, China. Association for Computational Linguistics.

Mingtong Liu, Yujie Zhang, Jinan Xu, and Yufeng Chen. 2019a. Original semantics-oriented attention and deep fusion network for sentence matching. In *Proceedings of the 2019 Conference on Empirical Methods in Natural Language Processing and the 9th International Joint Conference on Natural Language Processing (EMNLP-IJCNLP)*, pages 2652–2661, Hong Kong, China. Association for Computational Linguistics.

Yinhan Liu, Myle Ott, Naman Goyal, Jingfei Du, Mandar Joshi, Danqi Chen, Omer Levy, Mike Lewis, Luke Zettlemoyer, and Veselin Stoyanov. 2019b. Roberta: A robustly optimized bert pretraining approach. *arXiv preprint arXiv:1907.11692*.

Jonas Mueller and Aditya Thyagarajan. 2016. Siamese recurrent architectures for learning sentence similarity. In *thirtieth AAAI conference on artificial intelligence*.

Yixin Nie and Mohit Bansal. 2017. Shortcut-stacked sentence encoders for multi-domain inference. In *Proceedings of the 2nd Workshop on Evaluating Vector Space Representations for NLP*, pages 41–45, Copenhagen, Denmark. Association for Computational Linguistics.

Ankur Parikh, Oscar Täckström, Dipanjan Das, and Jakob Uszkoreit. 2016. A decomposable attention model for natural language inference. In *Proceedings of the 2016 Conference on Empirical Methods in Natural Language Processing*, pages 2249–2255, Austin, Texas. Association for Computational Linguistics.

Shuang Peng, Hengbin Cui, Niantao Xie, Sujian Li, Jiaxing Zhang, and Xiaolong Li. 2020. Enhanced-rcnn: An efficient method for learning sentence similarity. In *Proceedings of The Web Conference 2020*, pages 2500–2506.

Jeffrey Pennington, Richard Socher, and Christopher Manning. 2014. Glove: Global vectors for word representation. In *Proceedings of the 2014 Conference on Empirical Methods in Natural Language Processing (EMNLP)*, pages 1532–1543, Doha, Qatar. Association for Computational Linguistics.

Pranav Rajpurkar, Jian Zhang, Konstantin Lopyrev, and Percy Liang. 2016. SQuAD: 100,000+ questions for machine comprehension of text. In *Proceedings of the 2016 Conference on Empirical Methods in Natural Language Processing*, pages 2383–2392, Austin, Texas. Association for Computational Linguistics.

Tim Rocktäschel, Edward Grefenstette, Karl Moritz Hermann, Tomáš Kočiskỳ, and Phil Blunsom. 2015. Reasoning about entailment with neural attention. *arXiv preprint arXiv:1509.06664.*

Victor Sanh, Lysandre Debut, Julien Chaumond, and Thomas Wolf. 2019. Distilbert, a distilled version of bert: smaller, faster, cheaper and lighter. *arXiv preprint arXiv:1910.01108.*

Chuanqi Tan, Furu Wei, Wenhui Wang, Weifeng Lv, and Ming Zhou. 2018. Multiway attention networks for modeling sentence pairs. In *IJCAI*, pages 4411–4417.

Yi Tay, Anh Tuan Luu, and Siu Cheung Hui. 2018a. Co-stack residual affinity networks with multi-level attention refinement for matching text sequences. In *Proceedings of the 2018 Conference on Empirical Methods in Natural Language Processing*, pages 4492–4502, Brussels, Belgium. Association for Computational Linguistics.

Yi Tay, Anh Tuan Luu, and Siu Cheung Hui. 2018b. Compare, compress and propagate: Enhancing neural architectures with alignment factorization for natural language inference. In *Proceedings of the 2018 Conference on Empirical Methods in Natural Language Processing*, pages 1565–1575, Brussels, Belgium. Association for Computational Linguistics.

Shuohang Wang and Jing Jiang. 2016. Learning natural language inference with LSTM. In *Proceedings of the 2016 Conference of the North American Chapter of the Association for Computational Linguistics: Human Language Technologies*, pages 1442–1451, San Diego, California. Association for Computational Linguistics.

Wei Wang, Ming Yan, and Chen Wu. 2018. Multigranularity hierarchical attention fusion networks for reading comprehension and question answering. In *Proceedings of the 56th Annual Meeting of the Association for Computational Linguistics (Volume 1: Long Papers)*, pages 1705–1714, Melbourne, Australia. Association for Computational Linguistics.

Zhiguo Wang, Wael Hamza, and Radu Florian. 2017. Bilateral multi-perspective matching for natural language sentences. *arXiv preprint arXiv:1702.03814.*

Adina Williams, Nikita Nangia, and Samuel Bowman. 2018. A broad-coverage challenge corpus for sentence understanding through inference. In *Proceedings of the 2018 Conference of the North American Chapter of the Association for Computational Linguistics: Human Language Technologies, Volume 1 (Long Papers)*, pages 1112–1122, New Orleans, Louisiana. Association for Computational Linguistics.

Runqi Yang, Jianhai Zhang, Xing Gao, Feng Ji, and Haiqing Chen. 2019. Simple and effective text matching with richer alignment features. In *Proceedings of the 57th Annual Meeting of the Association for Computational Linguistics*, pages 4699–4709, Florence, Italy. Association for Computational Linguistics.

Wenpeng Yin and Hinrich Schütze. 2015. Convolutional neural network for paraphrase identification. In *Proceedings of the 2015 Conference of the North American Chapter of the Association for Computational Linguistics: Human Language Technologies*, pages 901–911, Denver, Colorado. Association for Computational Linguistics.

PHINC: A Parallel Hinglish Social Media Code-Mixed Corpus for Machine Translation

Vivek Srivastava*
TCS Research and Innovation
Pune, India
srivastava.vivek2@tcs.com

Mayank Singh
Indian Institute of Technology, Gandhinagar
Gujarat, India
singh.mayank@iitgn.ac.in

Abstract

Code-mixing is the phenomenon of using more than one language in a sentence. In the multilingual communities, it is a very frequently observed pattern of communication on social media platforms. Flexibility to use multiple languages in one text message might help to communicate efficiently with the target audience. But, the noisy user-generated code-mixed text adds to the challenge of processing and understanding natural language to a much larger extent. Machine translation from monolingual source to the target language is a well-studied research problem. Here, we demonstrate that widely popular and sophisticated translation systems such as Google Translate fail at times to translate code-mixed text effectively. To address this challenge, we present a parallel corpus of the 13,738 code-mixed Hindi-English sentences and their corresponding human translation in English. In addition, we also propose a translation pipeline build on top of Google Translate. The evaluation of the proposed pipeline on $PHINC$ demonstrates an increase in the performance of the underlying system. With minimal effort, we can extend the dataset and the proposed approach to other code-mixing language pairs.

1 Introduction

Code-mixing is the phenomenon of switching between two or more languages by the speaker in a single sentence of a text or speech. It is a frequently observed pattern of communication in linguistically diverse countries such as India with 23 official languages and 122 major languages. With more than 300 million native speakers each, English and Hindi are among the top five most frequently used languages across the world. With the increase in the number of English speakers in Hindi speaking communities in India, the popularity

of *Hinglish* (code-mixing in English-Hindi languages) is seeking a boom. Lambert (2018) first introduced the word Hinglish in 1967. David Crystal (Baldauf, 2004) projected in 2004 that the number of Hinglish speakers may soon outrun the number of native English speakers in the world. Other than Hinglish, multiple other bilingual code-mixed languages are popular in multilingual communities in India, such as Bengali-English, Telugu-English, etc. Lack of a standard for writing code-mixed text presents several challenges (see Section 2 for details) to natural language understanding tasks. Due to the source of origin (social media, online gaming, etc.), the code-mixed text is inherently noisy. We frequently observe code-mixing on social media platforms such as Twitter, Facebook, etc., in contrast to the formal literary sources such as books, poems, and newspapers. We, therefore, use social media platforms like Twitter and Facebook as the primary data source for our purpose.

The recent thrust on user engagement on social media platforms has led to several research directions, particularly in resource-constraint noisy user-generated content. Barman et al. (2014) discussed the language identification task for the code-mixed data involving Bengali-Hindi-English. Das and Gambäck (2014) presented various techniques to identify languages at the token-level for the Bengali-English and Hindi-English code-mixed corpus. Singh et al. (2018) discussed various techniques to identify the named-entities in the code-mixed Hindi-English corpora consisting of 3,638 tweets. Vyas et al. (2014) proposed various experiment to identify POS tags of the 1,062 code-mixed Hindi-English Facebook posts. They collected data from three popular celebrity Facebook public pages of Mr. Amitabh Bachchan (well-known actor), Mr. Shahrukh Khan (well-known actor), and Mr. Narendra Modi (current Indian Prime Minister). Besides, they leverage the BBC Hindi

---

*Work done during author's stay at IIT Gandhinagar

41

Proceedings of the 2020 EMNLP Workshop W-NUT: The Sixth Workshop on Noisy User-generated Text, pages 41–49
Online, Nov 19, 2020. ©2020 Association for Computational Linguistics

news articles. Sinha and Thakur (2005) presented a rule-based machine translation system to translate the code-mixed Hindi-English sentence to monolingual Hindi and English forms. Khanuja et al. (2020) presented an evaluation benchmark for the two code-mixed language pairs (English-Hindi and English-Spanish). The proposed evaluation benchmark has six NLP tasks, i.e., language identification, POS tagging, named entity recognition, sentiment analysis, question answering, and natural language inference. These tasks have been part of the recently shared tasks co-located with various NLP conferences or the latest research works. Even so, it presents two significant challenges and opportunities. First, most of the datasets available for various tasks are significantly less extensive to build robust standalone systems. Second, the comparatively less studied task for the code-mixed machine translation presents an opportunity to build datasets and translation systems. Dhar et al. (2018) propose a machine translation augmentation pipeline to use on top of the standard machine translation systems. They also create a parallel corpus of 6,096 English-Hindi code-mixed sentences and their corresponding translation in English.

In this paper, we present a good quality large-scale parallel corpus[1] for code-mixed English-Hindi noisy social media text messages. The main contributions are:

- We present a parallel corpus of 13,738 Hindi-English code-mixed sentences and their corresponding English translations by the human annotators.
- We discuss various challenges faced by machine translation systems in translating code-mixed sentences. Translation systems addressing these challenges could help mitigate the limitations of these systems.
- As a baseline, we propose a translation pipeline and compare the results with two widely popular translation systems (Google Translate and Bing Translate) on various evaluation metrics.
- We also discuss various limitations of the corpus and the research opportunities.

2 Code-Mixing and Challenges in Machine Translation

Code-mixing is the informal style of communication where words from two (in general) or more languages are part of the same utterance of a text or speech. An example code-mixed

Hinglish sentence is, *"Hamare paas fully autonomous vaahan hai"*. This style of writing presents several challenges to almost all monolingual natural language processing tasks such as sentiment analysis, POS tagging, dependency parsing, etc. The widely-used machine translation systems, e.g., Google Translate, Bing Translate, etc., perform reasonably well on the monolingual translation task, but they fail to perform well on the code-mixed data (see Section 4 for details). We identify six potential causes for the failure of the standard machine translations systems on the code-mixed text are:

- **C1 (Ambiguity in language identification)**: Hindi words written in the Roman script present some significant challenges to identify the language of the text at the token level. Words like *'is', 'me', 'to'*, exists in both Hindi and English, leading to ambiguity in classification as English and Hindi without proper knowledge of context. Similarly, hashtags are often used on social media platforms, and code-mixed hashtags make it challenging to identify the boundaries of code-switching.
- **C2 (Spelling variations)**: Romanized Hindi also presents a challenge with no standard spelling of the words. Various spellings for the same word is used based on the user's pronunciation of the word, emotions, etc. For example, *'jaldi', 'jldi'*, and *"jldiii',* are some of variations for the word *'hurry'* in English. At times, people use repeated instances of some particular character to emphasize emotion, such as in *'jaldiii'*.
- **C3 (Named entity recognition)**: Recognition of named entities in the code-mixed data is also a challenging task. E.g., *'Bhartiya Janta Party'* is a code-mixed named entity (name of a political party in India). In translation, the unrecognized code-mixed entity might make the translation semantically incorrect.
- **C4 (Informal style of writing)**: We largely witness an informal style of writing on social media platforms. At times, we do not follow the standard rules of sentence structure on these platforms. This presents a challenge to translate the sentence in a monolingual style where we need the formal sentence structure for semantic correctness. For example, *'Sad kabhi dekha h usko.. me never'*, when translates to English becomes, *'Have you ever seen her sad? I have never seen her sad'*.
- **C5 (Misplaced/skipped punctuation)**: In

the informal writing style on social media platforms, punctuations are usually skipped, misplaced, or repeatedly used to express an opinion, and that makes it difficult for the machine translation system to translate such sentences. For example, *'Aap kb se cricket khelne lage..never saw u bfr'* misses a question mark(?) apart from other necessary modifications to make the structure of the sentence correct.

- **C6 (Missing context)**: Lack of knowledge of the context makes the machine translation task significantly difficult and challenging. Hidden sarcasm might get unnoticed while translating the sentence with missing context. For example, *'Note kr lijiye.. Bandi chal rahi h'* is a code-mixed sentence, and demonetization (*'notebandi'*) is the hidden context.

Figure 1 shows three example code-mixed Hinglish sentences and the corresponding translations by Google Translate and the human annotator. In all the examples, we observe various associated challenges (C1 through C6) with an effective translation by Google Translate.

We posit that the above challenges can be addressed to a large extent with the higher availability of a good-quality, manually annotated parallel corpus. However, as discussed in the previous section, the only available code-mixed Hinglish dataset (Dhar et al., 2018) is significantly small and less topically diverse. Some of the major differences with the previous work (Dhar et al., 2018) (*'PW'*, hereafter) are:

- **Spelling variations:** The annotation policy in our experiment (see Section 3 for details) explicitly ask the annotators to use the correct spellings in the translated sentences. E.g., the annotators provide the correct spelling for the words *'u'*, *'coz'*, and *'plz'* as *'you'*, *'because'*, and *'please'*, respectively. In PW, we observe large traces of incorrect spellings of the words in the translated sentence, such as 78 instances of the word *u*, 37 instances of the word *pls*, and 83 instances of the word *plz*.
- **Short sentences:** We remove the sentences that are less than five tokens. It helps to remove the monolingual sentences or sentences with less code-mixing. In PW, we find 747 (12.25%) sentences with length less than or equal to 3 tokens and 1,537 (25.21%) sentences with length less than or equal to 5 tokens.
- **Ambiguous sentences:** We refrain annota-

tors to provide translation for the ambiguous sentences. In PW, we observe a few ambiguous code-mixed sentences and their corresponding translations. E.g., *"Tamil teri yadda Nai .. Har pal Teri yadda yadda wich h tu Tamil kaha aya game me ?"* is a code-mixed sentence with the English translation *"you don't rememeber Tamil .. every moment your memory memory which you in tamil where is it in game?"*.

- **Abusive sentences:** We prefilter the abusive sentences as well as refrain the annotators to translate them. In PW, we observe multiple sentences with abusive words.
- **English sentences:** We refrain the annotators to translate the sentences already in the English language. In PW, we find multiple instances of sentences in the code-mixed data which are already in English. For eg., *"my salman khan"*, *"luv u salman khan"*, *"Hallo salman sir"*, etc.

Example I

SENTENCE: Phone ka wallpaper dekhte dekhte zindagi kat rahi hai.
GOOGLE TRANSLATION: Life is cut off while watching the wallpaper of the phone.
HUMAN TRANSLATION: I'm spending my life seeing my phones wallpaper
ASSOCIATED CHALLENGES: C4 and C6

Example II

SENTENCE: Is shaher ko ye Hua kya hai.. Kahi rakh hai to kahi dhua dhua.. Play interrupted due to bad weather
GOOGLE TRANSLATION: What has happened to this city .. If there is smoke somewhere, then smoke somewhere .. Play interrupted payable then bad weather
HUMAN TRANSLATION: What has happened to this city. there is ash and smoke everywhere. play interrupted due to bad weather
ASSOCIATED CHALLENGES: C1, C4, and C5

Example III

SENTENCE: Bhai IIT wale hai pehle relationship toh bane laundon ki. break up par nacha rahe ho.
GOOGLE TRANSLATION: Brother-in-law is the first relationship to be made of laundries. you are dancing on the brake sub.
HUMAN TRANSLATION: Brother, you are an IITian. First get in to a relation. Then you can worry about break up.
ASSOCIATED CHALLENGES: C1, C2, C3, and C4

Figure 1: Comparison of translation of code-mixed sentences by Google translate and human annotators. The ineffective translation by Google Translate has various associated challenges.

3 Dataset

In India, Hinglish is a commonly observed pattern of communication on various platforms such as social media, online gaming, product reviews, discussion forums, etc. As outlined in the previous sections, multiple works have explored the various nuances of the code-mixed Hinglish text, such as language identification, sentiment analysis, etc. However, curating the code-mixed Hinglish dataset for these tasks requires a significant amount of human efforts due to the identification and filtering of noise from the useful content. In this work, we initially curated Hinglish sentences from six already existing works ((Singh et al., 2018), (Swami et al., 2018), (Joshi et al., 2016), (Barman et al., 2014), (Vrishank Shete and Mittal, 2016), and (Khandelwal, 2018)). One major advantage of using these datasets is the availability of high-quality code-mixed sentences without considerable manual filtering. Also, it offers diversity in terms of the source of the data collection as the major social networking platforms (Twitter and Facebook) are present. Additionally, the proposed curation process mitigates the topical bias, as we consider multiple topics in social-media discussions. Table 1 shows the statistics of the previous code-mixed datasets and $PHINC$. We select these datasets across various tasks, platforms, and topics/focus areas.

3.1 Description, Collection, and Pre-processing

We collect a total of 52,234 Hinglish sentences from multiple sources, as described above. We then shuffle, pre-process, and share these sentences with the annotators to provide the corresponding English translation. The script used in writing each sentence in the corpus is Roman. Pre-processing of the dataset involves the following steps:

- We remove sentences with less than five or more than 40 tokens. We introduce the upper limit on the sentence length to speed up the annotation process.
- We remove sentences having a percentage of out of vocabulary (OOV) words less than 50% or more than 90%. Lower limit (i.e., 50%) helps to filter out the sentences with the majority of English words whereas the upper limit (i.e., 90%) filter out the sentences containing a high percentage of Hindi words. We consider alphanumeric tokens as part of the vocabulary. We are using

the English dictionary of the Natural Language Toolkit (NLTK) to identify OOV.
- We filter the sentences containing abusive words in English or the Romanized Hindi.

After pre-processing, we obtain a total of 25,346 code-mixed sentences.

3.2 Annotation

The objective of the annotation process is to produce the English translation of the corresponding code-mixed Hinglish sentence. We employ 54 annotators in the annotation task. Each annotator has expert level proficiency in writing, speaking, and understanding English and Hindi languages. We assign randomly selected 400 unique samples to each annotator, and the annotator has to provide the translation of each sentence in English. Each sentence in the final dataset is annotated by a single annotator. We provide a set of guidelines for each annotator for the annotation task. The annotation guidelines are listed below:

- **Special characters and emoticons:** Use the best understanding to include or skip these symbols and characters in the translated English sentences.
- **URLs, mentions, and hashtags:** Keep the same URLs, mentions, and hashtags in the translated sentence.
- **Incorrect spellings (u, hm, pls, coz, etc.):** Translated sentence should have the correct spelling for each word.
- **Lower casing:** Write the translated sentence in lowercase.
- **Proper English sentence:** If the input sentence is already in English and also grammatically correct with no spelling mistakes, then its translation will only be "&" (without quotes). E.g., "I can translate the sentence quickly", do not require any modification.
- **Ambiguous sentence:** Do not translate an ambiguous sentence. If the sentence is unclear to translate in English, mark it as "#" (without quotes).
- **Abusive words:** Do not translate sentences containing abusive/cuss words. Mark it as "#" (without quotes).

We provide the same label to ambiguous and abusive sentences because, at times, the annotator is unaware of the abusive word used in the sentence, and the sentence appears ambiguous. Post annotation, we obtain 21,597 sentences. It also includes sentences that are refrained from the translation (i.e., proper English sentence, ambiguous sentence, and sen-

"

Dataset Source	Task	Platform	Dataset Size	Topics/Focus areas
Singh et al. (2018)	Named-entity recognition	Twitter	3,638	Politics, social events, sports, etc.
Swami et al. (2018)	Sarcasm detection	Twitter	5,250	Bollywood, cricket, and politics
Joshi et al. (2016)	Sentiment analysis	Facebook	3,879	Bollywood and politics
Barman et al. (2014)	Language identification	Facebook	771	Not available
Vrishank Shete and Mittal (2016)	Sentiment analysis	Facebook	7,663	Politics, news articles, etc.
Khandelwal (2018)	Humor detection	Twitter	31,033	Not available
PHINC	Machine translation	Twitter & Facebook	13,738	Sports, politics, Bollywood, etc.

Table 1: Statistics of the previous Hinglish code-mixed datasets and *PHINC*. Dataset size shows the number of sentences in the dataset. We select the topics/focus area of the dataset as mentioned in the corresponding dataset source.

tences containing abusive words). We then filter sentences with no human translation. Finally, we obtain 13,738 code-mixed sentences with the corresponding English translation.

Figure 2 shows three examples of the sentences that come under the refrain category of sentences for translation. Example I is a proper English sentence and requires no translation. The sentence in example II contains the abusive word, whereas the sentence in example III is ambiguous to translate. Figure 3 shows two code-mixed sentences and their corresponding translation in the corpus. Example I show a high-quality translation by the annotator that does not require any changes, whereas the translation in the example II is of poor quality, as it is semantically incorrect and requires modification. Note that we are not making any changes to the poor quality translation of the code-mixed sentences. We discuss the quality of translations in detail in Section 3.3.

3.3 Exploratory Analysis

In this section, we conduct the exploratory analysis of the sentence pairs in the corpus.

1. **Out of vocabulary (OOV) words**: Figure 4 shows the distribution of the OOV words in the code-mixed sentences. We are using the NLTK English dictionary for this study. Apart from the Romanized Hindi words, hashtags and mentions also fall into the category of OOV words. We consider alphanumeric tokens as part of the vocabulary. The code-mixed dataset contains sentences with the percentage of OOV words greater than 50% and less than 90%. A large number of sentences comprise a higher proportion of OOV words, illustrate the non-standard writing style of the users while using code-mixed languages on various platforms. Also, on manual inspection, we observe that while writing Hinglish, people often use Hindi as the matrix language and embed the words from the English lan-

Example I

CODE-MIXED SENTENCE: RT: Today is the birth anniversary of Maharana Pratap, whose bravery & indomitable spirit doesn't fail to inspire even today.
LABEL: &
REASON FOR NO TRANSLATION: Sentence already in English

Example II

CODE-MIXED SENTENCE: sach bolu ? Aap Cuss hai
LABEL: #
REASON FOR NO TRANSLATION: Presence of abusive/cuss word in sentence.

Example III

CODE-MIXED SENTENCE: yuhi kat jaayega safar sath tweetne se . ki manzil aayegi nazar sath tweetne se . Hum raahi Twitter ke
LABEL: #
REASON FOR NO TRANSLATION: Ambiguous sentence.

Figure 2: Example of the code-mixed sentences with no translation by the annotators. We replace the cuss word in Example II with the word "Cuss".

guage. We posit that usage of a high percentage of OOV words makes the text noisy and challenging to perform various natural language processing tasks such as named-entity recognition, machine translation, sentiment analysis, etc.

2. **Degree of Code-mixing**: To evaluate the degree of code-mixing in the corpus, we use Code-Mixing Index (CMI) (Das and Gambäck, 2014). CMI value range from 0 to 100. A value close to 0 suggests monolingualism in the corpus, whereas high CMI values indicate a high degree of code-mixing. To calculate the value of CMI, we randomly sample 100 code-mixed sentences from the corpus and annotate them at the token level with three language tags English, Hindi, and others. The CMI cal-

Example I

CODE-MIXED SENTENCE: Thnks buds! Kabhi kabhi aajate hai achhe photos
ENGLISH TRANSLATION: Thank you buddy, sometime good photos are captured.
REQUIRE CHANGES IN THE ENGLISH TRANSLATION?: No

Example II

CODE-MIXED SENTENCE: Australia ke saath abhi jeete nahi hai, magar NZ ke saath final kaise jeetenge iss soch mein bhartiya yuvak on twitter.
ENGLISH TRANSLATION: Indian youth on twitter thinking that - We have not won against Australia yet, but how would we win final with NZ?
REQUIRE CHANGES IN THE ENGLISH TRANSLATION?: Yes

Figure 3: Example translation of the code-mixed sentences in the corpus. The annotators provide translations to the code-mixed sentences. A change in the translation is required if the translation is semantically incorrect.

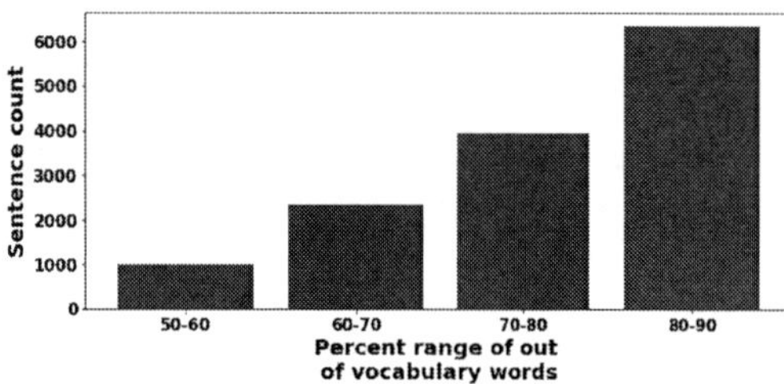

Figure 4: Distribution of out of vocabulary words in the code-mixed sentences. Large number of sentences comprise higher proportion of OOV words.

culated for this set of sentences is 75.76, which indicates a significantly higher usage of code-mixing in the text.

3. **Frequent words**: Figure 5 shows the word clouds of the code-mixed and English translated sentences. It is evident from the word cloud that words from multiple domains such as politics, entertainment, sports, etc., are very frequently used. The list of top-15 most occurring words having character length greater than six[2] are *salman, chahiye, alllahdin, krishna, meetuunnglee, atheist, kejriwal, tomorrow, mahashivratri, pakistan, narendramodi, tumhare, shaadi, gandhi,* and *indvspak*. This list contain words from multiple domains such as politics (*kejriwal, gandhi,* and *narendramodi*),

---

[2]We set the threshold to length six to remove the Romanized Hindi stopwords.

entertainment (*salman* and *allahdin*), social events/festivals (*mahashivratri* and *shaadi*), sports (*indvspak*), etc.

4. **Message Length**: Figure 6 shows the distribution of the message length for the code-mixed and the translated sentences. Distribution of message length for code-mixed and the translated sentences follows a similar trend.

5. **Quality of Translations (QT)**: To evaluate the quality of the translations by the annotators, we randomly sample 1000 sentences from the corpus. We provide two labels to each of the translation *correct translation* and *require change*. The correct translation should be syntactically and semantically correct. We calculate the quality of translation as follows

$$QT = \frac{Count\ of\ correct\ translations}{Sample\ size}$$

822 samples out of 1000 do not require any changes. Thus, the quality of translation is *0.822*. The ambiguity and the noise in the code-mixed text make the text challenging to translate even for the highly familiar and expert code-mixed language speakers.

(a)   (b)

Figure 5: Word cloud of the (a) code-mixed and (b) translated sentences.

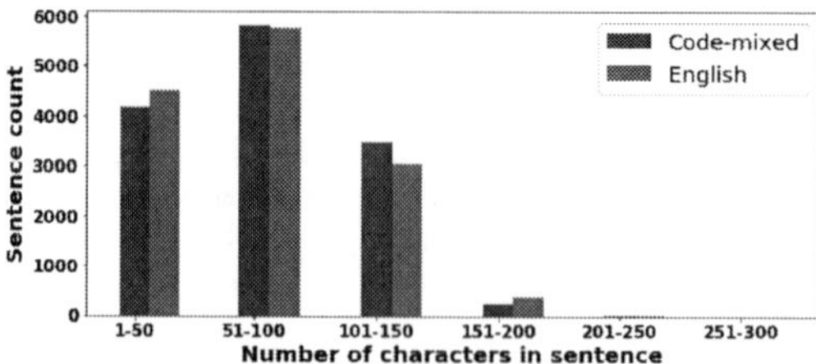

Figure 6: Distribution of message length for the code-mixed and English messages.

4 Evaluation of Machine Translation Systems

Here, we demonstrate the performance of the widely used machine translation systems on the code-mixed text. We experiment with two popular machine translation systems (Google

Translate and Bing Translate) and evaluate their performance on our proposed corpus. We use three different metrics to evaluate system performance. Bilingual Evaluation Understudy (BLEU) (Papineni et al., 2002), Word Error Rate (WER), and Translation Error Rate (TER). The values of these three metrics lie between 0 and 1.

To the best of our knowledge, we do not find translation systems build especially for the code-mixed sentences. The majority of the machine translation systems perform well for the monolingual translation tasks. However, these systems demonstrate severe limitations in translating code-mixed text. For the code-mixed text, the current machine translation systems assume input text to be in a single source language. Next, we describe the two translation systems and our proposed approach.

1. **Bing Translate (BT)**: BT is a translation service provided by Microsoft. It supports translation in 60 different languages[3] with neural machine translation capability in almost all the most frequently used languages. For translation, we set the language of the code-mixed input sentence as Hindi.

2. **Google Translate (GT)**: Next, we evaluate the performance of the GT on the code-mixed corpus. GT is a translation service provided by Google with the translation capability in 109 languages. It is the most widely used translation service with over 500 million total users, with more than 100 billion words translated daily[4]. We set GT to auto-detect the language of the code-mixed input sentence.

3. **Proposed Pipeline + Google Translate (PPGT)**: In addition to BT and GT, we propose a simple pipeline to use translation capabilities of already existing machine translation systems. In this paper, we specifically use GT. However, we can perform similar experiments with any machine translation system. The pipeline fragments the input sentence into multiple chunks before feeding it to GT. The steps of $PPGT$-based translation pipeline are:
   - We provide a label for each token of the code-mixed sentence based on the language (*English, Hindi, and other*).
   - We create chunks of Type-I using Hindi tokens with at most two English/other token allowed to be part of any chunk. A

chunk of Type-I starts with a Hindi token.
   - We create chunks of Type-II using the tokens that are labeled as English/others and not part of any Type-I chunk.
   - We only translate the Type-I chunks using GT. We keep the chunks of Type-II as it is.

Figure 7 shows example translations of code-mixed sentences from two machine translation systems namely, BT and GT, and our proposed approach $PPGT$. In $PPGT$, we maintain the original order of the chunks as that of the code-mixed sentence while translating. For instance, the order of the chunks in Example II in Figure 7 is *[[par if its], [possible and any other guest needs a room ,], [mera room de de kisi ko bhi]]*.

Additionally, we randomly sample 100 code-mixed sentences from the corpus. We use human translated sentences as reference. Table 2 shows the performance evaluation of all the three systems. $PPGT$ outperforms both the other systems on all three evaluation metrics.

	BLEU-1	**WER**	**TER**
BT	0.146	0.751	0.885
GT	0.151	0.600	0.718
PPGT	**0.153**	**0.566**	**0.685**

Table 2: Evaluation of machine translation systems on various metrics. We prefer the high value of the BLEU-1 score and the low values of WER and TER.

As most of the machine translation systems do not perform well on the code-mixed data, we can build augmentation pipelines, similar to $PPGT$, on top of these systems that can preprocess and enhance the quality of the input to these systems. We posit that these pipelines can significantly address the challenges to code-mixed machine translation, as outlined in Section 2.

5   Limitations and Opportunities

The data collection, preprocessing, annotation, and resource expansion of $PHINC$ presents several limitations and opportunities. Some of the major insights and the future research prospects of the proposed dataset are:

- Human annotation of the code-mixed parallel corpus is a challenging task which demands significant effort and time. Building a large scale code-mixed parallel corpus solely with human annotators is infeasible. We can extend the proposed dataset using

---

[3]https://www.microsoft.com/en-us/translator/business/languages/

[4]https://www.blog.google/products/translate/ten-years-of-google-translate/

Example I

CODE-MIXED SENTENCE: @Prankoholic tumko matlab kya time hai din ka, kuch samaj nahi aata na

TYPE-I CHUNKS: [tumko matlab kya time hai din ka. kuch samaj nahi aata na]

TYPE-II CHUNKS: [@Prankoholic]

ENGLISH TRANSLATION USING BT: @prankoholic what time do you mean of the day, some society does not come.

ENGLISH TRANSLATION USING GT: @Prankoholic you mean what is the time of day, don't understand anything

ENGLISH TRANSLATION USING PPGT: @Prankoholic Do you mean what is the time of day, no sense

---

Example II

CODE-MIXED SENTENCE: par if its possible and any other guest needs a room , mera room de de kisi ko bhi

TYPE-I CHUNKS: [par], [mera room de de kisi ko bhi]

TYPE-II CHUNKS: [if its possible and any other guest needs a room .]

ENGLISH TRANSLATION USING BT: On if its possible egg any other guest needs coming room , my room day to anyone

ENGLISH TRANSLATION USING GT: par if its possible and any other guest needs a room , mera room de de kisi ko bhi

ENGLISH TRANSLATION USING PPGT: par if its possible and any other guest needs a room , Give my room to anyone

---

Example III

CODE-MIXED SENTENCE: ab voh bola jisne kisi bhi party ko support karne se mana kardiya tha . . a flop show annaji

TYPE-I CHUNKS: [ab voh bola jisne kisi bhi party ko support karne se mana kardiya tha]

TYPE-II CHUNKS: [. . a flop show annaji]

ENGLISH TRANSLATION USING BT: Now Woh spoke , which was considered to support any party . . Come Flop Show Annaji

ENGLISH TRANSLATION USING GT: Now say that he had a desire to support any party. . A flop show Anna

ENGLISH TRANSLATION USING PPGT: Now speak that who had refused to support any party . . a flop show annaji

---

Figure 7: Example translation of code-mixed sentences using BT, GT, and PPGT.

various learning paradigms such as semi-supervised learning, active learning, etc.

- As machine translation systems require a large amount of data to build efficient systems, the dataset presented here alone will not be sufficient for traditional supervised methods. But, we can improve the perfor-

mance of current SOTA machine translation systems by leveraging the proposed dataset. We can also develop systems with other techniques such as meta-learning, transfer learning, etc., which shows exciting results (Gu et al., 2018; Dabre et al., 2019) with other low resource languages.

- India is a highly diverse country with 23 official languages, and we observe multiple code-mixing pairs (Bengali-English, Telugu-English, etc.) very frequently on various platforms. We can extend the proposed technique for data collection and the translation pipeline to other code-mixed language pairs.

- As the syntactic and semantic structure of the code-mixed sentences is different from the monolingual sentences, the evaluation of the quality of code-mixed data for various tasks such as text summarization, neural machine translation, text generation, etc., requires advanced metrics. $PHINC$ can help in developing such evaluation metrics.

- We observe gender and racial bias in the code-mixed text. We can use the good-quality Hinglish sentences in $PHINC$ to identify and mitigate such biases.

6 Conclusion and Future Work

In this paper, we present a parallel corpus for the English-Hindi code-mixed machine translation task. We discuss various challenges in understanding and processing code-mixed text for various natural language understanding tasks. We also show limitations of the widely popular machine translation system build for monolingual corpus in dealing with code-mixed corpora. We evaluate the performance of the various translation systems on our parallel corpus. We present a translation pipeline that outperforms the various translation systems on our proposed code-mixed $PHINC$ dataset, demonstrating the opportunities in building efficient translation systems.

In the future, we plan to explore other code-mixed languages, especially those that are low-resource and endangered. We also plan to extend the corpus for various other code-mixing tasks such as word-embedding, language identification, named-entity recognition, etc. In addition, we can extend the dataset with more annotation using semi-supervised techniques. As the dataset size is significantly small to train a traditional supervised neural machine translation system, we can build the translation systems using few-shots learning techniques.

References

Scott Baldauf. 2004. A hindi-english jumble, spoken by 350 million. [Online; accessed 23-May-2020].

Utsab Barman, Amitava Das, Joachim Wagner, and Jennifer Foster. 2014. Code mixing: A challenge for language identification in the language of social media. In *Proceedings of the First Workshop on Computational Approaches to Code Switching*, pages 13–23, Doha, Qatar. Association for Computational Linguistics.

Raj Dabre, Atsushi Fujita, and Chenhui Chu. 2019. Exploiting multilingualism through multistage fine-tuning for low-resource neural machine translation. In *Proceedings of the 2019 Conference on Empirical Methods in Natural Language Processing and the 9th International Joint Conference on Natural Language Processing (EMNLP-IJCNLP)*, pages 1410–1416.

Amitava Das and Björn Gambäck. 2014. Identifying languages at the word level in code-mixed indian social media text. In *Proceedings of the 11th International Conference on Natural Language Processing*, pages 378–387.

Mrinal Dhar, Vaibhav Kumar, and Manish Shrivastava. 2018. Enabling code-mixed translation: Parallel corpus creation and mt augmentation approach. In *Proceedings of the First Workshop on Linguistic Resources for Natural Language Processing*, pages 131–140.

Jiatao Gu, Yong Wang, Yun Chen, Victor OK Li, and Kyunghyun Cho. 2018. Meta-learning for low-resource neural machine translation. In *Proceedings of the 2018 Conference on Empirical Methods in Natural Language Processing*, pages 3622–3631.

Aditya Joshi, Ameya Prabhu, Manish Shrivastava, and Vasudeva Varma. 2016. Towards subword level compositions for sentiment analysis of hindi-english code mixed text. In *Proceedings of COLING 2016, the 26th International Conference on Computational Linguistics: Technical Papers*, pages 2482–2491.

Ankush Khandelwal. 2018. Humor detection corpus. [Online; accessed 08-Jan-2020].

Simran Khanuja, Sandipan Dandapat, Anirudh Srinivasan, Sunayana Sitaram, and Monojit Choudhury. 2020. Gluecos: An evaluation benchmark for code-switched nlp. *arXiv preprint arXiv:2004.12376*.

James Lambert. 2018. A multitude of "lishes": The nomenclature of hybridity. *English Worldwide*, 39(1):1–33.

Kishore Papineni, Salim Roukos, Todd Ward, and Wei-Jing Zhu. 2002. Bleu: a method for automatic evaluation of machine translation. In *Proceedings of the 40th annual meeting on association for computational linguistics*, pages 311–318. Association for Computational Linguistics.

Vinay Singh, Deepanshu Vijay, Syed Sarfaraz Akhtar, and Manish Shrivastava. 2018. Named entity recognition for hindi-english code-mixed social media text. In *Proceedings of the Seventh Named Entities Workshop*, pages 27–35.

R Mahesh K Sinha and Anil Thakur. 2005. Machine translation of bi-lingual hindi-english (hinglish) text. *10th Machine Translation summit (MT Summit X), Phuket, Thailand*, pages 149–156.

Sahil Swami, Ankush Khandelwal, Vinay Singh, Syed Sarfaraz Akhtar, and Manish Shrivastava. 2018. A corpus of english-hindi code-mixed tweets for sarcasm detection. *arXiv preprint arXiv:1805.11869*.

GaganDeep Singh Chhabra Vrishank Shete and Lokesh Mittal. 2016. Sentiment analysis on hindi-english code mixed data using svm. [Online; accessed 08-Jan-2020].

Yogarshi Vyas, Spandana Gella, Jatin Sharma, Kalika Bali, and Monojit Choudhury. 2014. Pos tagging of english-hindi code-mixed social media content. In *Proceedings of the 2014 Conference on Empirical Methods in Natural Language Processing (EMNLP)*, pages 974–979.

Cross-lingual Sentiment Analysis in Bengali Utilizing A New Benchmark Corpus

Salim Sazzed

Department of Computer Science
Old Dominion University
Norfolk, VA 23529, USA
ssazz001@odu.edu

Abstract

Sentiment analysis research in low-resource languages such as Bengali is still unexplored due to the scarcity of annotated data and the lack of text processing tools. Therefore, in this work, we focus on generating resources and showing the applicability of the cross-lingual sentiment analysis approach in Bengali. For benchmarking, we created and annotated a comprehensive corpus of around 12000 Bengali reviews. To address the lack of standard text-processing tools in Bengali, we leverage resources from English utilizing machine translation. We determine the performance of supervised machine learning (ML) classifiers in machine-translated English corpus and compare it with the original Bengali corpus. Besides, we examine sentiment preservation in the machine-translated corpus utilizing Cohen's Kappa and Gwet's AC1. To circumvent the laborious data labeling process, we explore lexicon-based methods and study the applicability of utilizing cross-domain labeled data from the resource-rich language. We find that supervised ML classifiers show comparable performances in Bengali and machine-translated English corpus. By utilizing labeled data, they achieve 15%-20% higher F1 scores compared to both lexicon-based and transfer learning-based methods. Besides, we observe that machine translation does not alter the sentiment polarity of the review for most of the cases. Our experimental results demonstrate that the machine translation based cross-lingual approach can be an effective way for sentiment classification in Bengali.

1 Introduction

Sentiment analysis classifies the semantic orientation of a text. With the rapid growth of user-generated content, nowadays, it is essential to determine user opinions, attitudes, and feelings from the textual data. In literature, researchers identified sentiment orientations of the text in various levels, such as document, sentence, or aspect. Researchers employed both the machine learning-based and lexicon-based approaches for sentiment analysis. Utilizing labeled data, supervised ML classifiers such as Naive Bayes (NB), Maximum Entropy (ME), Support Vector Machines (SVM), etc. (Pang et al., 2002; Gamon, 2004) and deep learning-based classifiers (Abdi et al., 2019; Araque et al., 2017) have been employed by the researchers for sentiment classification. Though the lexicon-based methods (Turney, 2002) do not require labeled data, they suffer from the lexicon coverage problem and are not robust to deal with the ambiguity and linguistic variations of natural languages.

Though English and few other languages enjoy ample resources for sentiment analysis, such resources are not available in many other languages. Cross-lingual sentiment classification aims to leverage resources like labeled data, polarity lexicons, contextual valence shifters, modifiers, etc. from resource-rich languages (typically English) to classify the sentiment polarity of the text written in a low-resource language (such as Bengali). For language mapping, several approaches such as machine translation (Banea et al., 2008a; Wan, 2009; Demirtas and Pechenizkiy, 2013; Zhou et al., 2016a,b; Abdalla and Hirst, 2017; Balahur and Turchi, 2014), cross-lingual word embedding (Barnes et al., 2018; Xu and Yang, 2017; Tang et al., 2014; AP et al., 2014), etc. have been used by the researchers.

1.1 Motivation

A limited amount of research in sentiment analysis has been conducted in Bengali in the last few decades; however, still, there is no benchmark dataset. Researchers used their curated datasets in various literatures that are not publicly available. The absence of publicly available datasets made

Proceedings of the 2020 EMNLP Workshop W-NUT: The Sixth Workshop on Noisy User-generated Text, pages 50–60
Online, Nov 19, 2020. ©2020 Association for Computational Linguistics

the research findings non-reproducible. Moreover, without a benchmark dataset, it is challenging to compare the performance of various approaches.

Though cross-lingual approaches have been successfully applied to several low-resource languages (Meng et al., 2012; Banea et al., 2008b), in Bengali only a few works utilized it for tasks like sentiment lexicon creation (Das and Bandyopadhyay, 2010a; Sazzed, 2020) and sentiment classification (Sazzed and Jayarathna, 2019). However, until now, no comprehensive study has been performed to explore the applicability of the cross-lingual sentiment classification approach in Bengali.

Therefore, in this work, we created and annotated a large Bengali review dataset for binary-level sentiment analysis. This corpus consists of around 12000 Bengali reviews collected from Youtube. We present a comprehensive study of the machine-translation based cross-lingual approach of sentiment analysis in Bengali.

Using a large and well-annotated dataset, we compare and provide detailed analysis regarding the performance of ML classifiers in the Bengali and machine-translated datasets. Besides, using Cohen's kappa and ML classifiers, we examine sentiment preservation in the machine-translated corpus.

As annotated data are not always obtainable, especially in low-resource languages, we investigate the performance of unsupervised lexicon-based methods in the machine-translated corpus. Popular lexicon-based sentiment analysis methods, VADER (Hutto and Gilbert, 2014), TextBlob[1], and SentiStrength (Thelwall et al., 2010) are applied and their relative performances are compared.

We investigate the applicability of the simple transfer learning-based approach to the machine-translated corpus. Resource-rich language such as English contains copious labeled data, which are not available in Bengali. Utilizing machine-translation and cross-domain labeled data, we show the performance of supervised ML classifiers in the translated corpus.

1.2 Contribution

Our major contributions can be summarized as follows:

- We introduce a large well-annotated benchmark dataset for sentiment analysis in Bengali.

- We perform a comparative evaluation of supervised ML classifiers in Bengali and machine-translated English corpus and provide a rigorous analysis of the results.

- We investigate cross-lingual lexicon-based methods, as well as a transfer learning-based approach to deal with the lack of labeled data in Bengali.

2 Literature Review

2.1 Sentiment Analysis in Bengali

English is the dominant language for sentiment analysis research due to commercial interest and a large research community. In recent years, with the popularity of e-commerce and social networking sites, review data is becoming available in other languages.

In Bengali, limited research has been performed using corpora collected from various sources such as Microblogs, Facebook, and other social media sources (Patra et al., 2015; Das and Bandyopadhyay, 2010b). Various supervised classifiers have been employed for Bengali sentiment analysis such as SVM with maximum entropy (Chowdhury and Chowdhury, 2014), Naive Bayes (NB) (Islam et al., 2016b), Deep Neural Network (Tripto and Eunus Ali, 2018), Convolutional Neural Network (CNN) (Sarkar, 2019). In (Al-Amin et al., 2017), the authors utilized word2vec and polarity score for the binary sentiment analysis problem. A word-embedding based approach was proposed by Islam et al. (2016a). Hassan et al. (2016) predicted sentiment orientation of Bengali and Romanized Bengali text using Long Short-Term Memory (LSTM).

2.2 Cross-lingual Sentiment Analysis

The cross-lingual sentiment analysis approaches have been studied in many languages. Mihalcea et al. (2007) leveraged the tools and resources available in English to generate subjectivity analysis resources in Romanian. They created a Romanian subjectivity lexicon translated from the English lexicon and utilized a corpus-based approach. Balamurali et al. (2012) presented an alternative approach to cross-lingual sentiment analysis (CLSA) using WordNet senses as features for supervised sentiment classification. They used the linked Word-Nets of two languages to bridge the language gap. They reported their results on two Indian languages, Hindi and Marathi. Balahur and Turchi (2014) in-

---

[1] https:textblob.readthedocs.io/

vestigated the performance and effectiveness of machine translation systems and supervised methods for multilingual sentiment analysis. In their experiment, they used four languages, English, German, Spanish, and French; three machine translation systems Google, Bing, and Moses; several supervised algorithms and various types of features. Yan et al. (2014) utilizing the SVM algorithm proposed a bilingual approach for sentiment analysis in the Chinese social media dataset. In (Meng et al., 2012), the authors proposed a cross-lingual mixture model (CLMM) to exploit unlabeled bilingual parallel corpus. In (Banea et al., 2008b), authors utilized a machine translation system for projecting resources from English to Romanian and Spanish and provided a comparative performance. Chen et al. (2015) proposed a semi-supervised learning model, CredBoost, to address cross-lingual sentiment analysis in English and Chinese. They introduced a knowledge validation step during transfer learning to reduce the noisy data caused by machine translation errors. Feng and Wan (2019) proposed a cross-lingual sentiment analysis (CLSA) model by leveraging unlabeled data in multiple languages and domains. Without using any supervised cross-lingual word embedding (CLWE), their model outperformed baseline methods on multilingual Amazon review datasets. Xu et al. (2018) proposed a learning approach that does not require any cross-lingual labeled data. Their algorithm optimizes the transformation functions of monolingual word-embedding space and uses a neural network. They evaluated their proposed approach on benchmark datasets for cross-lingual word similarity prediction and found competitive performance to other methods. Chen et al. (2018) introduced an Adversarial Deep Averaging Network (ADAN) to transfer the knowledge learned from source languages labeled data to the target language. Their experiments on Chinese and Arabic sentiment classification demonstrated the superior performance of ADAN. Rasooli et al. (2018) used multiple source languages to learn a robust sentiment transfer model. They explored the potential of using both the annotation projection approach and a direct transfer approach using cross-lingual word representations and neural networks.

The cross-lingual approach of sentiment analysis in Bengali is still largely unexplored, only a few works investigated it (Das and Bandyopadhyay, 2010a; Sazzed and Jayarathna, 2019; Sazzed, 2020). Das and Bandyopadhyay (2010a) translated English polarity lexicon to Bengali to create a Bengali sentiment dictionary. Sazzed and Jayarathna (2019) utilized two small datasets and n-gram (i.e.,unigram and bigram) feature vectors to compare the performance of supervised ML algorithms in Bengali and machine-translated English corpus. They found supervised ML algorithms showed better performance in the model trained on the translated corpus; however, they did not provide a thorough analysis of the results they reported.

Contrast to previous studies, we perform a comprehensive analysis of various cross-lingual sentiment analysis approaches in Bengali. We created a Benchmark dataset, explored several classification approaches utilizing labeled and unlabeled data, examine the applicability of transfer learning, investigate the sentiment preservation in the translated corpus, and finally provide the direction for future research. To best of our knowledge, this is the first extensive attempt to investigate the applicability of the cross-lingual approach in Bengali sentiment analysis.

3   Dataset

One of the barriers of sentiment analysis research in Bengali is the lack of publicly available review datasets. In literature, researchers reported results using their curated datasets that are not publicly available. The few publicly available datasets are either small in size or not well-annotated. Therefore, here, we have prepared a well-annotated Bengali review dataset that we made publicly available.[2]

3.1   Data Collection

We collected and manually labeled a large review dataset for sentiment analysis in Bengali. This dataset contains viewer opinions towards several Bengali dramas. Using a web scraping tool, we first downloaded the raw JSON data from Youtube that contains information such as user name, id, timestamp, comments, and like/dislike, etc. We use a parsing script to extract the viewer's comments from the JSON data. The comments are written in Bengali, English, Romanized Bengali, or use code-mixing. As we are only interested in reviews written in Bengali text, we excluded non-Bengali comments. We utilized a language detection li-

---

[2]https://github.com/sazzadcsedu/BN-Dataset.git

Bengali Reviews	**Machine Translation**	**Polarity**
এই ধরনের নাটক সমাজের কোন কাজে লাগবে।এই গুলো আর নীলছবি তো একি কথা।সাময়িক উত্তেজনা তৈরি করে,আর হিতাহিত জ্ঞান শূণ্য করে।	Such plays will be of no use to society. These blue and blue are the same thing. Creates temporary tension, and empties knowledge	Negative
শামিম ভাইয়ের কাছে এমন নাটক আশা করি নি!!	I did not expect such a drama from Shamim Bhai !!	Negative
ফালতু নাটক কবির সিং মুভির ট্রেইলার কপি করে সাওয়ার নাটক বানায়।	False drama Kabir Singh copied movie trailer and made Sawar drama.	Negative
যখন মন খুব থারাপ থাকে,তখন আপনাদের নাটক দেখি।তখন মনটা আরো থারাপ হয়ে যায়,আর একটা সময়ে মন থারাপে, মন থারাপে কাটাকাটি।সত্যি অনেক ভাল লাগে আপনাদের অভিনয় গুলা। দোয়া রইলো চালিয়ে যান ভাই।।।।।	When the mind is very bad, then I watch your dramas. The prayer continued, brother	Positive
আফরান নিশো ভাই আমাদের টাংগাইলের অহংকার	Afran Nisho Bhai is the pride of our Tangail	Positive
অসাধারণ একটা জুটির অসাধারণ একটা নাটক ছিল ।।।। শেষ ৫ মিনিট ভীষণ কষ্ট লাগলো।।।। বারবার দেখতে ইচ্ছে করছে ।।।।	An extraordinary pair had an extraordinary drama ... The last 5 minutes were very difficult ... Wanting to see again and again ...	Positive
পরিচালক একটা গাঁজা থোর ছাগলের বাচ্চা এইসব কী	The director is a cannabis-eating goat kid	Negative
অসাধারন আমার কাছে সেই লাকছে~	Extraordinary That Looks To Me	Positive

Figure 1: Example of Bengali and machine translated reviews

brary[3] to identify Bengali comments. After removing the non-Bengali comments, the corpus contains around 15000 reviews, which are labeled using the procedure described in the next section.

3.2 Data Annotation

Two native Bengali speakers classified these 15000 reviews into three categories, *positive, negative, and non-subjective*. From the annotator ratings, we observe an inter-rater agreement of around 0.83 using Cohen's kappa. We exclude all the reviews, which are marked as non-subjective by either of the annotators.

For each subjective reviews, we only include it to the corpus if both annotators assign it to the same category (i.e., *positive or negative*). Therefore, our dataset contains only highly polarized reviews. Reviews that are ambiguous or contain mixed sentiment are not included in the dataset.

The final labeled corpus consists of 11807 annotated reviews, where each review contains around 2-300 Bengali words. This corpus is class-imbalanced, comprised of 3307 *negative* and 8500 *positive* reviews. Figure 1 shows some examples of *negative* and *positive* reviews. We made this corpus publicly available for the researchers.

4 Cross-lingual Sentiment Analysis in Bengali

As Bengali is a resource-poor language, we leverage sentiment lexicon and labeled data from English for sentiment analysis in Bengali. We investigate the performances of various approaches (i.e., supervised, unsupervised, and transfer-learning based approaches) of sentiment analysis utilizing resources from English. Figure 2 shows the overview of various approaches we studied.

4.1 Language Mapping

The machine translation (MT) service is one of the most common ways to build the language connection (Wan, 2008a, 2009; Wei and Pal, 2010). Bautin et al. (2008) discussed the use of various Spanish translation systems, Wan (2008b) compared various Chinese machine translators and found Google Translate provided the best performance. Here, we use Google Translate[4] to translate our Bengali corpus into English.

4.2 Supervised Classification Approach

Supervised ML-based approaches have been successfully applied in English and other languages for sentiment classification. Since supervised ML classifiers do not rely on language resources such as sentiment lexicon, part-of-speech (POS) tagger,

---

[3]https://github.com/Mimino666/langdetect

[4]https://translate.google.com

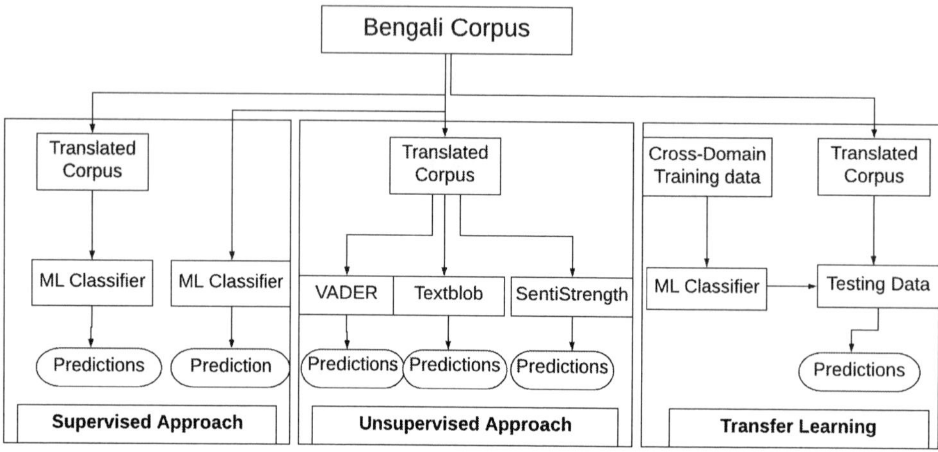

Figure 2: Various approaches of cross-lingual sentiment analysis in Bengali

etc., they can be applied to any language. In contrast to the rigid rule-based method, supervised ML algorithms learn hidden patterns from the training data; therefore, they can be more robust against noisy machine-translated English corpus.

Utilizing the annotated data, we employ four supervised ML classifiers: Logistic Regression (LR), Support Vector Machine (SVM), Random Forest (RF), and Extremely Randomized Trees (ET) on Bengali and its machine-translated English corpus. We use the scikit-learn (Pedregosa et al., 2011) implementation of the aforementioned ML classifiers. For all the ML classifiers, we utilize the default parameter settings. To deal with the class imbalance problem, we set the weight of a class inversely proportional to the number of instances it contains. Both the unigram and bi-grams features are used as input for the ML classifiers. We perform 10-fold cross-validation in both Bengali and translated English corpus.

4.3 Lexicon-based Approach

To deal with the scenario when annotated data are not available, we study the performances of lexicon-based methods in machine-translated English corpus. In Bengali, no standard lexicon-based tool is publicly available for sentiment analysis; therefore, we could not compare the performance with the English counterpart.

Three popular lexicon-based methods from English: VADER, TextBlob, and SentiStrength are employed to find the effectiveness of the cross-lingual unsupervised approach.

4.4 Transfer Learning-based Approach

Annotated data are hard to achieve in low-resource languages such as Bengali. But resource-rich languages like English owns a vast amount of labeled data. Hence, we explore the applicability of a transfer learning-based approach to the machine-translated corpus. However, in this work, we did not introduce any new transfer learning method. We examine whether utilizing existing cross-domain labeled data assist in achieving an acceptable performance of sentiment classification in Bengali when labeled data are not available.

In the transfer setting, a classifier is trained on one distribution while applied to a different distribution. The idea is to leverage labeled data from distinct domains but use in a similar task, as annotated in-domain data are not always available.

We employ multiple cross-domain datasets from the English language, IMDB (Maas et al., 2011), Yelp[5], TripAdvisor (Thelwall, 2018), Clothing[6], UCI Drug[7], WebMD[8] as shown in Table 1. We train the Logistic Regression (LR) classifier using cross-domain datasets and use the trained model to predict the semantic orientations of reviews in our machine-translated corpus. The default parameter settings of the LR classifier of scikit-learn (Pedregosa et al., 2011) library is used with a class-balanced weight.

---

[5]https://kaggle.com/omkarsabnis/yelp-reviews-dataset

[6]https://kaggle.com/nicapotato/womens-ecommerce-clothing-reviews

[7]https://kaggle.com/jessicali9530/kuc-hackathon-winter-2018

[8]https://kaggle.com/nataliele/webmd-contraceptives-reviews-file

Dataset	Domain	Positive	Negative	Total
IMDB	Movie	12500	12500	25000
YELP	Restaurant	6860	1676	8536
TripAdvisor	Hotel	9520	9520	19040
Clothing	Clothing	18540	4101	22641
UCI Drug	Drug	35437	11838	47275
WebMD	Drug	7461	1808	9269

Table 1: Cross-domain review datasets from English

Classifier	Precision	Recall	Macro F1	Accuracy
	BN/EN	BN/EN	BN/EN	BN/EN
SVM	0.908/0.912	0.924/0.934	0.916/0.923	93.0/93.5%
LR	0.889/0.893	0.922/0.927	0.905/0.910	91.8/92.2%
ET	0.893/0.882	0.882/0.865	0.888/0.874	91.0/90.0%
RF	0.878/0.889	0.870/0.881	0.874/0.885	89.9/90.8%

BN= Bengali,   EN= English

Table 2: Performances of supervised ML classifiers in Bengali and machine-translated English corpus

5 Experimental Results

5.1 Evaluation Criteria

To compare the performances of various classifiers, we compute precision, recall, macro F1 score, and accuracy. As our dataset is class-imbalanced, the macro F1 score the better metric than the accuracy for the evaluation.

Besides, we assess the agreement of the predictions of various supervised ML classifiers in Bengali and machine-translated English corpus utilizing Cohen's kappa and Gwet's AC1 statistics. Cohen's kappa and Gwet's AC1 are statistical measures used to gauge inter-rater reliability, where a score of 1 refers to perfect agreement. The purpose of evaluating the agreement is to determine the sentiment preservation in the machine-translated English corpus. .

5.2 Supervised Approach

In this section, we provide the comparative performances of ML classifiers in Bengali and machine-translated English corpus and agreement of the predictions.

5.2.1 Performance Comparison

Supervised ML classifiers show similar performance in both Bengali and translated English corpus, as shown in Table 2. The best macro F1 score and accuracy are obtained using the SVM classifier, which is 0.923 and 93.5% for English and 0.916 and 93.0% for Bengali. A similar performance is

Classifier	Cohen-kappa	AC1
SVM	0.819	0.868
LR	0.820	0.860
RF	0.694	0.800
ET	0.703	0.809

Table 3: The Cohen's kappa and AC1 scores of various ML classifiers in Bengali and translated corpus

observed when the LR classifier is applied to the English and Bengali corpus. The decision tree-based methods, RF and ET show lower F1 scores and accuracies compared to SVM and LR.

5.2.2 Agreement of Predictions

We compute the agreement of the predictions of ML classifiers in Bengali and machine-translated English corpus. The purpose is to examine whether the noise induced by machine translation changes the sentiment orientations of the translated reviews. When the sentiment orientation is maintained in the translated corpus, we can expect a high agreement between the predictions of an ML classifier in Bengali and its machine-translated version.

Table 3 provides the Cohen's kappa and AC1 scores applying various ML algorithms. SVM and LR show kappa scores above 0.80 and AC1 score above 0.85, while RF and ET provide around 0.70 kappa score and 0.80 AC1 scores.

Method	Precison	Recall	Macro F1	Accuracy
VADER	0.846	0.707	0.771	82.56%
TextBlob	0.863	0.705	0.776	82.79%
SentiStength	0.787	0.645	0.708	78.61%

Table 4: The performances of lexicon-based methods in the machine-translated corpus

5.3 Lexicon and Transfer learning-based Approaches

Table 4 shows the results of the lexicon-based methods in the translated corpus. VADER and TextBlob exhibit similar F1 scores and accuracies, while SentiStrength performs relatively worse. Using VADER, we achieve an F1 score of 0.771 and an accuracy of 82.56%, while TextBlob obtains 0.776 and 82.79%, respectively.

Table 5 provides the results of LR classifier utilizing cross-domain data. The best performance is obtained by combining all cross-domain datasets, which is 0.78 for the F1 score and 82% for the accuracy.

6 Discussion

6.1 Supervised Approach

Table 2 shows that supervised ML classifiers provide similar performance in the translated corpus and the original Bengali corpus. We found that several factors influence the comparable performance on the machine-translated corpus.

6.1.1 Error Correction

Misspelling is a common scenario in online Bengali content due to the complexity of the Bengali writing system and the education level of most of the internet users. Modern machine translation tools are trained on a huge amount of data and are capable of correcting misspelling. Although the Bengali-English machine translation system is not that sophisticated compared to some major language pairs, occasionally, it can identify misspelled words in Bengali text, and translate to correct English word. For those cases, machine translation improves the quality of data, so the classifier performance is improved.

6.1.2 Word Mapping

The current Bengali-English machine translation system still lacks enough coverage. We observed in some cases, Bengali synonym words are mapped to the same English word. This word-mapping assists supervised ML classifiers to perform well in the machine-translated corpus.

6.1.3 Regional Variety of Bengali

The Bengali language contains a large variety of dialects that are widely used on the web, especially in social media. The machine translation service that is trained on thousands of corpora can identify them as a variant of the same words and translate them to the same English word that positively impacts the performances of ML classifiers in the translated corpus.

6.1.4 Feature Importance and Sentiment Preservation

Supervised ML algorithms utilize the bag-of-words model to train the classifiers. The term frequency-inverse document frequency (tf-idf) score is calculated and used as an input feature vector. tf-idf is a numerical statistic that reflects the importance of a word considering a collection of documents.

tf-idf score refers that not all the words in a document are equally important for classification. (Abdalla and Hirst, 2017) showed that sentiment is highly preserved even in the face of poor translation accuracy. Therefore, low-quality translation does not always affect classifier accuracy.

The Cohen's kappa and AC1 scores reveal the sentiment consistency between original Bengali reviews and its machine translated version as shown in Table 3. The Cohen-kappa and AC1 scores from SVM and LR show nearly perfect agreements on the results from Bengali and translated English corpus. For RF and DT, Cohen's kappa and AC1 statistics are a bit lower compared to SVM and LR, which could be affected by the inferior performance of those classifiers, however, still, agreements are substantial.

6.2 Lexicon-based Approach

TextBlob and VADER exhibit similar accuracy, precision, recall, and F1-scores, while SentiStrength performs worse. The results demonstrate that lexical-rule based methods are not as robust as supervised ML approaches, exhibited by the lower

Training Dataset	#Reviews	Precision	Recall	Macro F1	Accuracy
IMDB	25000	0.73	0.71	0.72	78.0%
Clothing	22641	0.62	0.64	0.63	67.0%
TripAdvisor	19040	0.68	0.72	0.70	66.0%
UCI Drug	47275	0.71	0.70	0.71	76.7%
WebMD	9269	0.61	0.64	0.62	63.7%
Yelp	8536	0.67	0.65	0.66	73.6%
Aggregated Dataset	135121	0.78	0.77	0.78	82.0%

Table 5: The performance of LR classifier in the translated corpus utilizing the multi-domain training datasets

scores in all categories. Particularly, the recall scores, due to the non-comprehensive coverage of lexicon, are quite low. The poor performance of the rule-based approach mainly comes from the intrinsic nature (e.g., lexicon/rule coverage) of lexicon-based methods.

6.3 Transfer Learning with Cross-domain Datasets

The results obtained using the LR classifier and the cross-domain datasets indicate that the classifier's performance depends on both the-

- Data distribution and

- Size of the training dataset

The IMDB movie review dataset is the most similar to our translated drama review dataset considering the essence of the reviews. However, still, they differ in the aspects of data, languages used in the reviews, and the presence of noise due to machine translation. The translated drama reviews are much shorter in length and contain simple English words compared to IMDB reviews, which are written mostly by native English speakers. Utilizing 25000 reviews from IMDB, we achieve the best performance among all the cross-domain datasets used. Leveraging data from different domains, such as clothing or drug, yields worse performance despite using similar or larger size training dataset, which demonstrates the domain specificity in the sentiment analysis dataset.

We consolidate all the six cross-domain datasets to create a large corpus of over 130k reviews. The supervised LR classifier exhibits performance improvement utilizing this aggregated dataset. The results indicate that though datasets from the different domains show poor performance in isolation when aggregated, they can enhance the classifier performance.

With over 130k consolidated cross-domain reviews, the transfer learning-based approach shows noticeably worse performance compared to in-domain data, an F1 score of 0.773 compared to 0.910 using the LR classifier. It provides similar performance to the best lexicon-based method, VADER, which yields an F1 score of 0.771. Word level polarity is heavily influenced by context and domain, which was reflected in the classifier's performance when cross-domain data are used.

6.4 Findings and Implications

- We find that online content in Bengali consists of lots of misspelled and regional words, which affects the performance of sentiment classifiers. Therefore, it is necessary to build sophisticated tools that can fix misspellings and recognize regional variants of Bengali words.

- Although the existing Bengali-to-English machine translation system is still far from perfect, it is capable of preserving sentiment information; hence can be utilized for cross-lingual sentiment analysis.

- We find that the lexicon-based method performs poorly compared to the supervised ML methods in the machine-translated corpus. Therefore, it is imperative to develop an automatic or semi-automatic data annotation method.

- We find that a large number of cross-domain labeled data provides similar performance of the lexicon-based approach. Therefore, transfer learning can help when in-domain labeled data are unavailable.

- Our study reveals that the cross-lingual approach can be effective in Bengali sentiment analysis. Therefore, future research should focus on exploring and developing new methods for the cross-lingual sentiment analysis in Bengali.

7 Conclusion

To facilitate sentiment analysis research in Bengali, in this work, we introduce a benchmark dataset and explore the adaptation of resources and tools from English. We notice that due to misspellings, usage of regional varieties of Bengali, and advancement of the machine translation system, supervised ML algorithms perform comparably in the Bengali and machine-translated corpus. The agreements of the predictions suggest that Bengali-English machine translation can preserve the sentiment information. The mediocre performances of the lexicon-based methods infer that annotated data are essential to achieve better classification accuracy.

We present the performance of simple transfer learning utilizing cross-domain data. We note that with enough cross-domain training data, supervised ML classifiers provide a comparable performance of the lexicon-based methods, though lag behind the performance achieved through in-domain data. We report our findings regarding cross-lingual sentiment classification approaches in Bengali, which provide directions for future research.

References

Mohamed Abdalla and Graeme Hirst. 2017. Cross-lingual sentiment analysis without (good) translation. In *Proceedings of the Eighth International Joint Conference on Natural Language Processing (Volume 1: Long Papers)*, pages 506–515, Taipei, Taiwan. Asian Federation of Natural Language Processing.

Asad Abdi, Siti Mariyam Shamsuddin, Shafaatunnur Hasan, and Jalil Piran. 2019. Deep learning-based sentiment classification of evaluative text based on multi-feature fusion. *Information Processing & Management*, 56(4):1245–1259.

M. Al-Amin, M. S. Islam, and S. Das Uzzal. 2017. Sentiment analysis of bengali comments with word2vec and sentiment information of words. In *2017 International Conference on Electrical, Computer and Communication Engineering (ECCE)*, pages 186–190.

Sarath Chandar AP, Stanislas Lauly, Hugo Larochelle, Mitesh Khapra, Balaraman Ravindran, Vikas C Raykar, and Amrita Saha. 2014. An autoencoder approach to learning bilingual word representations. In *Advances in neural information processing systems*, pages 1853–1861.

Oscar Araque, Ignacio Corcuera-Platas, J Fernando Sánchez-Rada, and Carlos A Iglesias. 2017. Enhancing deep learning sentiment analysis with ensemble techniques in social applications. *Expert Systems with Applications*, 77:236–246.

Alexandra Balahur and Marco Turchi. 2014. Comparative experiments using supervised learning and machine translation for multilingual sentiment analysis. *Computer Speech Language*, 28(1):56 – 75.

Aiswarya Balamurali, Aditya Joshi, and Pushpak Bhattacharyya. 2012. Cross-lingual sentiment analysis for indian languages using linked wordnets. In *COLING*.

Carmen Banea, Rada Mihalcea, Janyce Wiebe, and Samer Hassan. 2008a. Multilingual subjectivity analysis using machine translation. In *Proceedings of the 2008 Conference on Empirical Methods in Natural Language Processing*, pages 127–135.

Carmen Banea, Rada Mihalcea, Janyce Wiebe, and Samer Hassan. 2008b. Multilingual subjectivity analysis using machine translation. In *2008 Conference on Empirical Methods in Natural Language Processing, EMNLP 2008, Proceedings of the Conference, 25-27 October 2008, Honolulu, Hawaii, USA, A meeting of SIGDAT, a Special Interest Group of the ACL*, pages 127–135.

Jeremy Barnes, Roman Klinger, and Sabine Schulte im Walde. 2018. Bilingual sentiment embeddings: Joint projection of sentiment across languages. In *Proceedings of the 56th Annual Meeting of the Association for Computational Linguistics (Volume 1: Long Papers)*, pages 2483–2493, Melbourne, Australia. Association for Computational Linguistics.

Mikhail Bautin, Lohit Vijayarenu, and Steven Skiena. 2008. International sentiment analysis for news and blogs. In *ICWSM*.

Qiang Chen, Wenjie Li, Yu Lei, Xule Liu, and Yanxiang He. 2015. Learning to adapt credible knowledge in cross-lingual sentiment analysis. In *Proceedings of the 53rd Annual Meeting of the Association for Computational Linguistics and the 7th International Joint Conference on Natural Language Processing (Volume 1: Long Papers)*, pages 419–429.

Xilun Chen, Yu Sun, Ben Athiwaratkun, Claire Cardie, and Kilian Weinberger. 2018. Adversarial deep averaging networks for cross-lingual sentiment classification. *Transactions of the Association for Computational Linguistics*, 6:557–570.

S. Chowdhury and W. Chowdhury. 2014. Performing sentiment analysis in bangla microblog posts. In *2014 International Conference on Informatics, Electronics Vision (ICIEV)*, pages 1–6.

Amitava Das and Sivaji Bandyopadhyay. 2010a. Sentiwordnet for bangla. *Knowledge Sharing Event-4: Task*, 2:1–8.

Amitava Das and Sivaji Bandyopadhyay. 2010b. Topic-based bengali opinion summarization. In *Proceedings of the 23rd International Conference on Computational Linguistics: Posters*, pages 232–240. Association for Computational Linguistics.

Erkin Demirtas and Mykola Pechenizkiy. 2013. Cross-lingual polarity detection with machine translation. In *Proceedings of the Second International Workshop on Issues of Sentiment Discovery and Opinion Mining*, pages 1–8.

Yanlin Feng and Xiaojun Wan. 2019. Towards a unified end-to-end approach for fully unsupervised cross-lingual sentiment analysis. In *Proceedings of the 23rd Conference on Computational Natural Language Learning (CoNLL)*, pages 1035–1044, Hong Kong, China. Association for Computational Linguistics.

Michael Gamon. 2004. Sentiment classification on customer feedback data: noisy data, large feature vectors, and the role of linguistic analysis. In *Proceedings of the 20th international conference on Computational Linguistics*, page 841. Association for Computational Linguistics.

Asif Hassan, Mohammad Rashedul Amin, Abul Kalam Al Azad, and Nabeel Mohammed. 2016. Sentiment analysis on bangla and romanized bangla text using deep recurrent models. In *2016 International Workshop on Computational Intelligence (IWCI)*, pages 51–56. IEEE.

Clayton J Hutto and Eric Gilbert. 2014. Vader: A parsimonious rule-based model for sentiment analysis of social media text. In *Eighth international AAAI conference on weblogs and social media*.

M. S. Islam, M. A. Amin, and S. Das Uzzal. 2016a. Word embedding with hellinger pca to detect the sentiment of bengali text. In *2016 19th International Conference on Computer and Information Technology (ICCIT)*, pages 363–366.

M. S. Islam, M. A. Islam, M. A. Hossain, and J. J. Dey. 2016b. Supervised approach of sentimentality extraction from bengali facebook status. In *2016 19th International Conference on Computer and Information Technology (ICCIT)*, pages 383–387.

Andrew L Maas, Raymond E Daly, Peter T Pham, Dan Huang, Andrew Y Ng, and Christopher Potts. 2011. Learning word vectors for sentiment analysis. In *Proceedings of the 49th annual meeting of the association for computational linguistics: Human language technologies-volume 1*, pages 142–150. Association for Computational Linguistics.

Xinfan Meng, Furu Wei, Xiaohua Liu, Ming Zhou, Ge Xu, and Houfeng Wang. 2012. Cross-lingual mixture model for sentiment classification. In *Proceedings of the 50th Annual Meeting of the Association for Computational Linguistics: Long Papers - Volume 1*, ACL '12, pages 572–581, Stroudsburg, PA, USA. Association for Computational Linguistics.

Rada Mihalcea, Carmen Banea, and Janyce Wiebe. 2007. Learning multilingual subjective language via cross-lingual projections. In *Proceedings of the 45th Annual Meeting of the Association of Computational Linguistics*, pages 976–983, Prague, Czech Republic. Association for Computational Linguistics.

Bo Pang, Lillian Lee, and Shivakumar Vaithyanathan. 2002. Thumbs up?: sentiment classification using machine learning techniques. In *Proceedings of the ACL-02 conference on Empirical methods in natural language processing-Volume 10*, pages 79–86. Association for Computational Linguistics.

Braja Gopal Patra, Dipankar Das, Amitava Das, and Rajendra Prasath. 2015. Shared task on sentiment analysis in indian languages (sail) tweets-an overview. In *International Conference on Mining Intelligence and Knowledge Exploration*, pages 650–655. Springer.

F. Pedregosa, G. Varoquaux, A. Gramfort, V. Michel, B. Thirion, O. Grisel, M. Blondel, P. Prettenhofer, R. Weiss, V. Dubourg, J. Vanderplas, A. Passos, D. Cournapeau, M. Brucher, M. Perrot, and E. Duchesnay. 2011. Scikit-learn: Machine learning in Python. *Journal of Machine Learning Research*, 12:2825–2830.

Mohammad Sadegh Rasooli, Noura Farra, Axinia Radeva, Tao Yu, and Kathleen McKeown. 2018. Cross-lingual sentiment transfer with limited resources. *Machine Translation*, 32(1-2):143–165.

Kamal Sarkar. 2019. Sentiment polarity detection in bengali tweets using deep convolutional neural networks. *Journal of Intelligent Systems*, 28(3):377–386.

Salim Sazzed. 2020. Development of sentiment lexicon in bengali utilizing corpus and cross-lingual resources. In *2020 IEEE 21st International Conference on Information Reuse and Integration for Data Science (IRI)*, pages 237–244. IEEE.

Salim Sazzed and Sampath Jayarathna. 2019. A sentiment classification in bengali and machine translated english corpus. *2019 IEEE 20th International Conference on Information Reuse and Integration for Data Science (IRI)*, pages 107–114.

Duyu Tang, Furu Wei, Nan Yang, Ming Zhou, Ting Liu, and Bing Qin. 2014. Learning sentiment-specific word embedding for twitter sentiment classification. In *Proceedings of the 52nd Annual Meeting of the Association for Computational Linguistics (Volume 1: Long Papers)*, pages 1555–1565, Baltimore, Maryland. Association for Computational Linguistics.

Mike Thelwall. 2018. Gender bias in machine learning for sentiment analysis. *Online Information Review*, 42:343–354.

Mike Thelwall, Kevan Buckley, Georgios Paltoglou, Di Cai, and Arvid Kappas. 2010. Sentiment strength detection in short informal text. *Journal of the American society for information science and technology*, 61(12):2544–2558.

Nafis Tripto and Mohammed Eunus Ali. 2018. Detecting multilabel sentiment and emotions from bangla youtube comments. In *2018 International Conference on Bangla Speech and Language Processing (ICBSLP)*, pages 1–6.

Peter D Turney. 2002. Thumbs up or thumbs down?: semantic orientation applied to unsupervised classification of reviews. In *Proceedings of the 40th annual meeting on association for computational linguistics*, pages 417–424. Association for Computational Linguistics.

Xiaojun Wan. 2008a. Using bilingual knowledge and ensemble techniques for unsupervised chinese sentiment analysis. In *Proceedings of the 2008 Conference on Empirical Methods in Natural Language Processing*, pages 553–561.

Xiaojun Wan. 2008b. Using bilingual knowledge and ensemble techniques for unsupervised chinese sentiment analysis. In *Proceedings of the Conference on Empirical Methods in Natural Language Processing*, EMNLP '08, pages 553–561, Stroudsburg, PA, USA. Association for Computational Linguistics.

Xiaojun Wan. 2009. Co-training for cross-lingual sentiment classification. In *Proceedings of the Joint Conference of the 47th Annual Meeting of the ACL and the 4th International Joint Conference on Natural Language Processing of the AFNLP: Volume 1-volume 1*, pages 235–243. Association for Computational Linguistics.

Bin Wei and Christopher Pal. 2010. Cross lingual adaptation: an experiment on sentiment classifications. In *Proceedings of the ACL 2010 conference short papers*, pages 258–262. Association for Computational Linguistics.

Ruochen Xu and Yiming Yang. 2017. Cross-lingual distillation for text classification. In *Proceedings of the 55th Annual Meeting of the Association for Computational Linguistics, ACL 2017, Vancouver, Canada, July 30 - August 4, Volume 1: Long Papers*, pages 1415–1425. Association for Computational Linguistics.

Ruochen Xu, Yiming Yang, Naoki Otani, and Yuexin Wu. 2018. Unsupervised cross-lingual transfer of word embedding spaces. In *Proceedings of the 2018 Conference on Empirical Methods in Natural Language Processing*, pages 2465–2474, Brussels, Belgium. Association for Computational Linguistics.

Gongjun Yan, Wu He, Jiancheng Shen, and Chuanyi Tang. 2014. A bilingual approach for conducting chinese and english social media sentiment analysis. *Comput. Netw.*, 75(PB):491–503.

Xinjie Zhou, Xiaojun Wan, and Jianguo Xiao. 2016a. Attention-based lstm network for cross-lingual sentiment classification. In *Proceedings of the 2016 conference on empirical methods in natural language processing*, pages 247–256.

Xinjie Zhou, Xiaojun Wan, and Jianguo Xiao. 2016b. Cross-lingual sentiment classification with bilingual document representation learning. In *Proceedings of the 54th Annual Meeting of the Association for Computational Linguistics (Volume 1: Long Papers)*, pages 1403–1412, Berlin, Germany. Association for Computational Linguistics.

The Non-native Speaker Aspect: *Indian English* in Social Media

Rupak Sarkar♣   **Sayantan Mahinder**♡   **Ashiqur R. KhudaBukhsh**♠*
♣Maulana Abul Kalam Azad University of Technology
♡Independent Researcher
♠Carnegie Mellon University
rupaksarkar.cs@gmail.com, sayantan.mahinder@gmail.com,
akhudabu@cs.cmu.edu

Abstract

As the largest institutionalized second language variety of English, *Indian English* has received a sustained focus from linguists for decades. However, to the best of our knowledge, no prior study has contrasted web-expressions of *Indian English* in noisy social media with English generated by a social media user base that are predominantly native speakers. In this paper, we address this gap in the literature through conducting a comprehensive analysis considering multiple structural and semantic aspects. In addition, we propose a novel application of language models to perform automatic linguistic quality assessment.

1 Introduction

Analyzing important issues through the lens of social media is a thriving field in computational social science (CSS) research. From policy debates (Demszky et al., 2019) to modern conflicts (Palakodety et al., 2020a), web-scale analyses of social media content present an opportunity to aggregate and analyze opinions at a massive scale. English being one of the widely-spoken pluricentric languages (Leitner, 1992), a considerable fraction of current CSS research primarily analyzes content authored in English. Several recent lines of CSS research on Indian sub-continental issues (Palakodety et al., 2020a; Tyagi et al., 2020; Palakodety et al., 2020c) dealt with *Indian English* (Mehrotra, 1998), a regional variant of English spoken in India and among the Indian diaspora.

As the largest institutionalized second language variety of English, *Indian English* has received sustained attention from linguists (Kachru, 1965; Shastri, 1996; Gramley and Pätzold, 2004; Sedlatschek,

2009) delineating multiple aspects in which Indian English is distinct from US or British English. However, these studies are largely confined to well-formed English written in formal settings (e.g., newspaper Dubey, 1989; Sedlatschek, 2009. The efforts so far in characterizing web-expressions of *Indian English* are somewhat scattered with isolated focus areas (e.g., code switching (Gella et al., 2014; Rudra et al., 2019; Khanuja et al., 2020; KhudaBukhsh et al., 2020a), use of swear words Agarwal et al., 2017, and word usage Kulkarni et al., 2016) and little attention given to analyzing the range of spelling, grammar and structural characteristics observed in web-scale *Indian English* corpora. Due to the deep penetration of cellphone technologies into Indian society and availability of inexpensive data (HuffPost, 2017), a user base with a wide range of English proficiency has access to the social media. Hence, understanding to what extent spelling and grammar issues affect *Indian English* found on the social web and how does that compare and contrast with typical noisy social media content generated by predominantly native English speakers is an important yet underexplored research question.

In this paper, via two substantial contemporaneous corpora constructed from comments on YouTube videos from major news networks in the US and India, we address the above research question. To the best of our knowledge, no prior study has contrasted any *Indian English* social media corpus with the variety of English observed in social media platforms frequented by native English speakers. We further use two existing corpora of news articles from India and the US to demonstrate that while college-educated, well-formed English across these two language centers does not differ by

---

*Ashiqur R. KhudaBukhsh is the corresponding author.

61

Proceedings of the 2020 EMNLP Workshop W-NUT: The Sixth Workshop on Noisy User-generated Text, pages 61–70
Online, Nov 19, 2020. ©2020 Association for Computational Linguistics

much, social media *Indian English* is different from social media *US English* on certain aspects, hence may pose a greater challenge to conduct meaningful analysis. Apart from using standard tools to assess linguistic quality, we present a novel finding that recent advances in language models can be leveraged to perform automated linguistic quality assessment of human-generated text.

2 Data Sets

We consider two social media (denoted by the superscript *sm*) data sets and two news article (denoted by the superscript *na*) data sets. We denote *Indian English* and *US English* as *en-in* and *en-us*, respectively. In order to keep our vocabulary statistics comparable, we sub-sample from our *en-us* social media data set and ensure that both social media corpora have nearly equal number of tokens. Detailed description of preprocessing steps are presented in the Appendix.

Why YouTube? Both of our social media corpora are comments on YouTube videos posted within an identical date range (30th January, 2020 to 7th May, 2020). As of January 2020, YouTube is the second-most popular social media platform in the world drawing 2 billion active users (Statista, 2020b). It is the most popular social media platform in India with 265 million monthly active users, accounting for 80% of the population with internet access (HindustanTimes, 2019; YourStory, 2018).

- $\mathcal{D}^{sm}_{en\text{-}in}$: We consider a subset of a data set first introduced in (KhudaBukhsh et al., 2020b). The original data set consists of 4,511,355 comments by 1,359,638 users on 71,969 YouTube videos from fourteen Indian news outlets posted between 30th January, 2020 and 7th May, 2020. Next, language is detected using $\hat{\mathcal{L}}_{polyglot}$, a polyglot embedding based language identifier first proposed in (Palakodety et al., 2020a) and successfully used in other multi-lingual contexts (Palakodety et al., 2020c). This yields 1,352,698 English comments (23,124,682 tokens, 2,107,233 sentences). In order to minimize the effects of code switching (Gumperz, 1982; Myers-Scotton, 1993), only sentences with low CMI (code mixing index) (Das and Gambäck, 2014) are considered. We estimate CMI using the same method presented in KhudaBukhsh et al. 2020a and set a threshold of 0.1. Upon removal of code switched sentences, our final data set, $\mathcal{D}^{sm}_{en\text{-}in}$, consists of 1,923,292 sentences (20,591,213 tokens).

- $\mathcal{D}^{sm}_{en\text{-}us}$: We consider a subset of a data set first introduced in (KhudaBukhsh et al., 2020c). We first obtain 10,245,348 comments posted by 1,690,589 users[1] on 8,593 YouTube videos from three popular US news channels (Fox news, CNN and MSNBC) (Statista, 2020a) in the same time period. We subsampled the data to make the number of tokens comparable to that of $\mathcal{D}^{sm}_{en\text{-}in}$. This resulted in $\mathcal{D}^{sm}_{en\text{-}us}$ having 1,573,355 sentences (20,591,220 tokens).

- $\mathcal{D}^{na}_{en\text{-}in}$ consists of 398,960 sentences (9,016,255 tokens) from news articles that appeared in highly circulated Indian news outlets (e.g., The Quint, Hindustan Times, Deccan Herald) (Dai, 2017).

- $\mathcal{D}^{na}_{en\text{-}us}$ consists of 94,463 sentences (2,042,024 tokens) from news articles that appeared in highly circulated US news outlets (e.g., HuffPost, Washington post, New York Times).

3 Analysis

3.1 Vocabulary and Grammar

We conduct a detailed study comparing and contrasting $\mathcal{D}^{sm}_{en\text{-}in}$ and $\mathcal{D}^{sm}_{en\text{-}us}$. In what follows, we summarize our observations (see, Appendix for details).

- *Vocabulary*: In the context of social media, US English exhibits a richer overlap with standard English dictionary as compared to Indian English.

  Let $\mathcal{V}_{dict}$ denote the English vocabulary obtained from a standard English dictionary (Kelly, 2016)[2]. Let $\mathcal{V}^{sm}_{en\text{-}in}$ and $\mathcal{V}^{sm}_{en\text{-}us}$ denote the vocabularies of $\mathcal{D}^{sm}_{en\text{-}in}$ and $\mathcal{D}^{sm}_{en\text{-}us}$, respectively. We now compute the following overlaps: $|\mathcal{V}^{sm}_{en\text{-}us} \cap \mathcal{V}^{dict}| = 43,826$ and $|\mathcal{V}^{sm}_{en\text{-}in} \cap \mathcal{V}^{dict}| = 38,260$. Also, with a list of 6,000 important words for US SAT exam[3], we find that $\mathcal{V}^{sm}_{en\text{-}us}$ has considerably larger overlap (4,349 words) than $\mathcal{V}^{sm}_{en\text{-}in}$ (3,956 words).

- *Spelling deviations*: Indian English exhibits larger spelling deviations as compared to US English. Phonetic spelling errors (i.e., spelling a word as it sounds) are common in Indian English. This observation aligns with (KhudaBukhsh et al., 2020a).

- *Loanwords*: Borrowed words, also known as loanwords, are lexical items borrowed from a donor language (Holden, 1976; Calabrese and

---

[1] The Jaccard similarity between the two social media user bases of $\mathcal{D}^{sm}_{en\text{-}in}$ and $\mathcal{D}^{sm}_{en\text{-}us}$ is 0.01 indicating minimal overlap between the two user bases.

[2] We take the union of *en-us* and *en-gb*.

[3] `https://satvocabulary.us/INDEX.ASP?CATEGORY=6000LIST`

Wetzels, 2009; Van Coetsem, 2016) . For example, the English word avatar or yoga is borrowed from Hindi. We observe that loanwords (e.g., `sadhus`, `begum`, `burqa`, `imams` and `gully`) borrowed from Hindi heavily feature in Indian English.

- ***Article and pronoun usage***: Indian English uses considerably fewer articles and pronouns as compared to US English. Pronoun and article omissions in ESL (English as Second Language) are well-studied phenomena (Ferguson, 1975). Our observation also aligns with a previous field study (Agnihotri et al., 1984) that reported even college-educated Indians make substantial errors in article usage.

- ***Preposition usage***: Indian English uses considerably fewer prepositions as compared to US English (11.48% in *en-us* and 10.84% in *en-in*).

- ***Verb usage***: Indian English uses fewer verbs than US English. Of the different verb forms (see, Figure 1), Indian English uses the root form relatively more than US English indicating (possible) poorer understanding of subject-verb agreement and tense (later verified in Section 3.2).

- ***Sentence length***: We observe shorter sentences in Indian as compared to US English (average *en-in* sentence length: 10.71 ± 12.37; average *en-us* sentence length: 13.09 ± 20.17). We acknowledge that device variability may influence this observation.

- ***Sentence validity evaluated by a parser***: A standard parser evaluates fewer Indian English sentences as valid as compared to US English (see, Table 1). However, no such discrepancy was observed in news article English from both language centers.

- ***Constituency parser depth***: For a given sentence length, Indian English exhibits lesser average constituency parser tree depth (Joshi et al., 2018) indicating (possible) structural issues. Intuitively, length of a sentence is likely to be positively correlated with its structural complexity; a long sentence is likely to have more complex (and nested) sub-structures than a shorter one. A parser's ability to correctly identify such sub-structures depends on the sentence's syntactic correctness. To tease apart the relationship between sentence-length and constituency parser's depth, in Figure 2, we present the average tree depth for a given sentence length. We observe that between well-formed English, the difference is almost imperceptible. However, as the sentence

length grows, the gap between tree depth obtained in social media *en-in* and the rest widens indicating possible structural issues. A few example long sentences with small parse-tree depth are presented in the Appendix.

- ***Generalizability across other native English variants***: Our results are consistent when compared against a British English (*en-gb*) social media corpus.

Measure	$\mathcal{D}^{na}_{en\text{-}in}$	$\mathcal{D}^{na}_{en\text{-}us}$	$\mathcal{D}^{sm}_{en\text{-}in}$	$\mathcal{D}^{sm}_{en\text{-}us}$
Valid sentences	96.93	96.61	83.88	88.30

Table 1: Percentage of sentences determined valid by a constituency parser (Joshi et al., 2018).

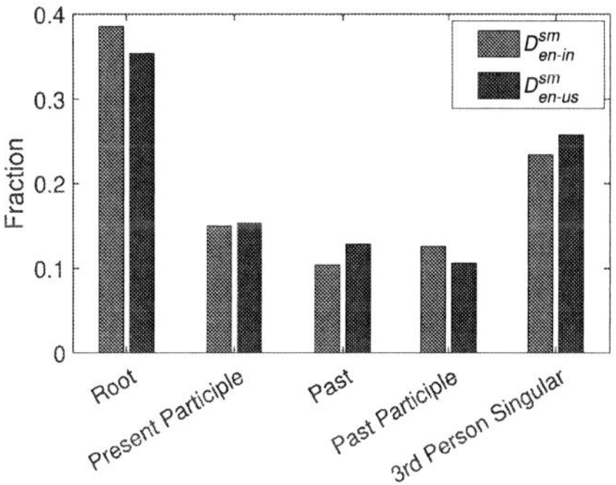

Figure 1: Distribution of different verb forms. We compute the relative occurrence of different morphological forms of a verb using a standard library (Honnibal and Montani, 2017).

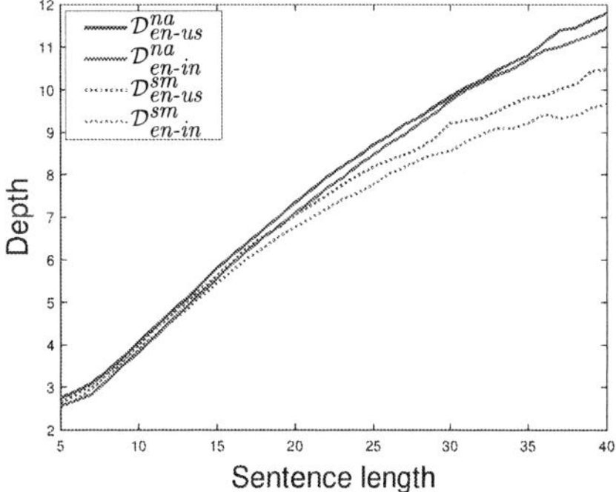

Figure 2: Constituency parser depth. A well-known parser (Joshi et al., 2018) is run on 10K sentences from each corpus. Average parse tree depth is presented for a given sentence length.

3.2 Cloze Test

Recent advances in Language Models (LMs) such as BERT (Devlin et al., 2019) have led to a substantial improvement in several downstream NLP tasks. While obtaining task-specific performance gain has been a key focus area (see, e.g., Liu and Lapata, 2019; Lee et al., 2020), several recent studies attempted to further the understanding of what exactly about language these models learn that results in these performance gains. LMs' ability to solve long-distance agreement problem and general syntactic abilities have been previously explored (Gulordava et al., 2018; Marvin and Linzen, 2018; Goldberg, 2019).

BERT's masked word prediction has a direct parallel in human psycholinguistics literature (Smith and Levy, 2011). When presented with a sentence (or a sentence stem) with a missing word, a cloze task is essentially a fill-in-the-blank task. For instance, in the following cloze task: *In the* [MASK]*, it snows a lot*, winter is a likely completion for the missing word. In fact, when given this cloze task to BERT, BERT outputs the following five seasons ranked by decreasing probability: winter, summer, fall, spring and autumn. Word prediction as a test of LM's language understanding has been explored in Paperno et al. (2016); Ettinger (2020) and recent studies leveraged it in novel applications such as relation extraction (Petroni et al., 2019) and political insight mining (Palakodety et al., 2020b). Bolstered by these findings and another recent result that uses BERT to evaluate the quality of translations (Zhang* et al., 2020), we propose an approach to estimate language quality using BERT. Our hypothesis is if a sentence is syntactically consistent and semantically coherent, BERT will be able to predict a masked word in that sentence with higher accuracy than a syntactically inconsistent or semantically incoherent sentence.

We first motivate our method with two examples. Consider the following classic syntactically correct yet semantically incoherent sentence (Chomsky, 1957): *Colorless green ideas sleep furiously.* BERT's top five predictions for a cloze task *Colorless green MASK sleep furiously* are the following: (1) eyes (2) . (3) , (4) they and (5) I. In fact, none of these words when masked, features in BERT's top 100 predictions. However, for another iconic sentence (King, 1968) when presented in the following cloze form: *I have a MASK that my four*

little children will one day live in a nation where they will not be judged by the color of their skin, but by the content of their character, BERT's top five predictions (feeling, hope, belief, vision, and dream) correctly include *dream*. Notice that, in our semantically coherent example sentence, all of the predicted words have (Part-Of-Speech) POS agreement with the masked word while the semantically incoherent sentence produced a wide variety of completion choices that include punctuation, pronouns and noun.

We randomly sample 10k sentences from each corpus. For each sentence, we mask a randomly chosen word in the sentence such that $w \in \mathcal{V}_{dict}$ and construct an input cloze statement. Following standard practice (Petroni et al., 2019), we report p@1, p@5 and p@10 performance. p@K is defined as the top-K accuracy, i.e., an accurate completion of the masked word is present in the retrieved top K words ranked by probability.

Table 2 summarizes BERT's performance in predicting masked words. We were surprised to notice that on well-formed sentences, BERT achieved higher than 80% accuracy indicating that well-formed sentences leave enough cues for an LM to predict a masked word with high accuracy. We further observe that prediction accuracy is possibly correlated with linguistic quality; the performance on well-formed text corpora is substantially better than that of on social media text corpora. Finally, among the two social media text corpora, the performance on Indian English is substantially worse possibly indicating larger prevalence of grammar, spelling or semantic disfluencies. A few randomly sampled examples are listed in Table 4.

Measure	$\mathcal{D}_{en\text{-}in}^{na}$	$\mathcal{D}_{en\text{-}us}^{na}$	$\mathcal{D}_{en\text{-}in}^{sm}$	$\mathcal{D}_{en\text{-}us}^{sm}$
p@1	53.53	55.53	33.49	42.31
p@5	75.69	77.30	55.91	65.07
p@10	81.03	82.93	62.69	71.36

Table 2: BERT's masked word prediction performance on 10k randomly sampled sentences from each corpus. For each sentence, a word belonging to a standard English dictionary is randomly chosen for masking. Appendix contains additional results on a social media corpus of British English.

We next compute the fraction of instances where the POS tags of the masked word and the predicted word agree. As shown in Table 3, the POS agreements on well-formed text corpora are substantially higher than that of on the social media corpora.

Once again, we observe that of the two social media corpora, POS agreement on $\mathcal{D}^{sm}_{en\text{-}in}$ corpus is lower than that of on $\mathcal{D}^{sm}_{en\text{-}us}$. Our results inform that masked word prediction accuracy can be an effective measure in evaluating linguistic quality. Additional results with a British English corpus is presented in the Appendix.

	$\mathcal{D}^{na}_{en\text{-}in}$	$\mathcal{D}^{na}_{en\text{-}us}$	$\mathcal{D}^{sm}_{en\text{-}in}$	$\mathcal{D}^{sm}_{en\text{-}us}$
Overall	84.27	83.68	66.56	71.72
VERB	90.17	89.72	79.47	82.76
NOUN	86.20	85.95	62.03	67.96
ADP	89.78	89.24	75.96	75.88
ADJ	68.88	70.54	48.55	61.06
ADV	74.40	73.06	47.09	58.01

Table 3: POS agreement between the masked word and BERT's top prediction. Results are computed on 10K randomly sampled sentences from each corpus. Results on social media corpora are highlighted with blue. Adposition (ADP) is a cover term for prepositions and postpositions. ADJ and ADV denote adjective and adverb, respectively. Appendix contains additional results on a social media corpus of British English.

4 Conclusions

In this paper, we present a comprehensive comparative analysis between Indian English and US English in social media. Our analyses reveal that compared to native English, social media Indian English exhibits certain differences that may add to the challenges of navigating noisy, social media texts generated in the Indian sub-continent and thus present an opportunity to the NLP community to address these challenges. Recent lines of computational social science (CSS) research focusing on Indian sub-continental issues emphasized on the challenges faced while processing Indian social media data. However, no prior work contrasted social media *Indian English* with social media native English. We believe our work will help the research community identify focus areas to facilitate CSS research in this domain. We present a novel approach to perform automated linguistic quality assessment using BERT, a well-known high-performance language model. To the best of our knowledge, our work first tests BERT's masked word prediction accuracy on human-generated texts obtained from noisy social media. World variants of English spoken and written form have been widely studied for several decades. However, limited literature exists on characterizing their social media expressions.

Error type	Comment
SVD	The goons needs to be severely punished.
SVD	They play victim card, like they too suffering from virus.
SVD	every dogs come thier own day, you get what u deserves.
IVF	I am live in Assam.
IVF	these people will be never change.

Table 4: Random sample of sentences in $\mathcal{D}^{sm}_{en\text{-}in}$ with grammatical issues. SVD denotes subject-verb disagreement. IVF denotes incorrect verb forms

Our study makes a small step towards characterizing a broad range of aspects of Indian English observed in social media.

References

Prabhat Agarwal, Ashish Sharma, Jeenu Grover, Mayank Sikka, Koustav Rudra, and Monojit Choudhury. 2017. I may talk in english but gaali toh hindi mein hi denge: A study of english-hindi code-switching and swearing pattern on social networks. In *2017 9th International Conference on Communication Systems and Networks (COMSNETS)*, pages 554–557. IEEE.

Rama Kant Agnihotri, Amrit Lal Khanna, and Aditi Mukherjee. 1984. The use of articles in indian english: Errors and pedagogical implications. *IRAL: International Review of Applied Linguistics in Language Teaching*, 22(2):115.

Edward Loper Bird, Steven and Ewan Klein. 2009. *Natural Language Processing with Python*. O'Reilly Media Inc.

Andrea Calabrese and Leo Wetzels. 2009. *Loan phonology*. John Benjamins Publishing Company.

Noam Chomsky. 1957. Syntactic structures. the hague: Mouton.. 1965. aspects of the theory of syntax. *Cambridge, Mass.: MIT Press.(1981) Lectures on Government and Binding, Dordrecht: Foris.(1982) Some Concepts and Consequences of the Theory of Government and Binding. LI Monographs*, 6:1–52.

Tianru Dai. 2017. News Articles.

Amitava Das and Björn Gambäck. 2014. Identifying languages at the word level in code-mixed indian social media text. In *Proceedings of the 11th International Conference on Natural Language Processing*, pages 378–387.

Dorottya Demszky, Nikhil Garg, Rob Voigt, James Zou, Jesse Shapiro, Matthew Gentzkow, and Dan Jurafsky. 2019. Analyzing polarization in social media: Method and application to tweets on 21 mass shootings. In *Proceedings of the 2019 Conference of the North American Chapter of the Association for Computational Linguistics: Human Language*

Technologies, Volume 1 (Long and Short Papers), pages 2970–3005, Minneapolis, Minnesota. Association for Computational Linguistics.

Jacob Devlin, Ming-Wei Chang, Kenton Lee, and Kristina Toutanova. 2019. BERT: Pre-training of deep bidirectional transformers for language understanding. In Proceedings of the 2019 Conference of the North American Chapter of the Association for Computational Linguistics: Human Language Technologies, Volume 1 (Long and Short Papers), pages 4171–4186, Minneapolis, Minnesota. Association for Computational Linguistics.

Vinod S Dubey. 1989. Newspaper English in India, volume 13. Bahri Publications.

Allyson Ettinger. 2020. What BERT is not: Lessons from a new suite of psycholinguistic diagnostics for language models. Trans. Assoc. Comput. Linguistics, 8:34–48.

Charles A Ferguson. 1975. Toward a characterization of english foreigner talk. Anthropological linguistics, pages 1–14.

Spandana Gella, Kalika Bali, and Monojit Choudhury. 2014. "ye word kis lang ka hai bhai?" testing the limits of word level language identification. In Proceedings of the 11th International Conference on Natural Language Processing, pages 368–377.

Yoav Goldberg. 2019. Assessing bert's syntactic abilities. arXiv preprint arXiv:1901.05287.

Stephan Gramley and Kurt-Michael Pätzold. 2004. A survey of modern English. Routledge.

Kristina Gulordava, Piotr Bojanowski, Edouard Grave, Tal Linzen, and Marco Baroni. 2018. Colorless green recurrent networks dream hierarchically. In Proceedings of the 2018 Conference of the North American Chapter of the Association for Computational Linguistics: Human Language Technologies, Volume 1 (Long Papers), pages 1195–1205, New Orleans, Louisiana. Association for Computational Linguistics.

John J Gumperz. 1982. Discourse strategies, volume 1. Cambridge University Press.

HindustanTimes. 2019. Youtube now has 265 million users in india. Online; accessed 20-April-2020.

Kyril Holden. 1976. Assimilation rates of borrowings and phonological productivity. Language, pages 131–147.

Matthew Honnibal and Ines Montani. 2017. spaCy 2: Natural language understanding with Bloom embeddings, convolutional neural networks and incremental parsing. To appear.

HuffPost. 2017. Youtube monthly user base touches 265 million in india, reaches 80 pc of internet population. Online; accessed 3-June-2020.

Vidur Joshi, Matthew Peters, and Mark Hopkins. 2018. Extending a parser to distant domains using a few dozen partially annotated examples. In Proceedings of the 56th Annual Meeting of the Association for Computational Linguistics (Volume 1: Long Papers), pages 1190–1199, Melbourne, Australia. Association for Computational Linguistics.

Braj B Kachru. 1965. The indianness in indian english. Word, 21(3):391–410.

Ryan Kelly. 2016. Pyenchant a spellchecking library for python. Ηλεκτρονικό]. Available: https://pythonhosted. org/pyenchant.

Simran Khanuja, Sandipan Dandapat, Anirudh Srinivasan, Sunayana Sitaram, and Monojit Choudhury. 2020. Gluecos: An evaluation benchmark for code-switched NLP. In Proceedings of the 58th Annual Meeting of the Association for Computational Linguistics, ACL 2020, Online, July 5-10, 2020, pages 3575–3585. Association for Computational Linguistics.

Ashiqur R. KhudaBukhsh, Shriphani Palakodety, and Jaime G. Carbonell. 2020a. Harnessing code switching to transcend the linguistic barrier. In Proceedings of the Twenty-Ninth International Joint Conference on Artificial Intelligence, IJCAI 2020, pages 4366–4374. ijcai.org.

Ashiqur R. KhudaBukhsh, Shriphani Palakodety, and Tom M. Mitchell. 2020b. Discovering bilingual lexicons in polyglot word embeddings.

Ashiqur R. KhudaBukhsh, Rupak Sarkar, Mark S. Kamlet, and Tom M. Mitchell. 2020c. We don't speak the same language: Interpreting polarization through machine translation.

Martin Luther King. 1968. I have a dream. Negro History Bulletin, 31(5):16.

Vivek Kulkarni, Bryan Perozzi, Steven Skiena, et al. 2016. Freshman or fresher? quantifying the geographic variation of language in online social media. In ICWSM, pages 615–618.

J Lee, W Yoon, S Kim, D Kim, S Kim, CH So, and J Kang. 2020. Biobert: Pre-trained biomedical language representation model for biomedical text mining. arxiv 2019. arXiv preprint arXiv:1901.08746.

Gerhard Leitner. 1992. English as a pluricentric language. Pluricentric languages: Differing norms in different nations, 62:178–237.

Yang Liu and Mirella Lapata. 2019. Text summarization with pretrained encoders. In Proceedings of the 2019 Conference on Empirical Methods in Natural Language Processing and the 9th International Joint Conference on Natural Language Processing (EMNLP-IJCNLP), pages 3730–3740, Hong Kong, China. Association for Computational Linguistics.

Rebecca Marvin and Tal Linzen. 2018. Targeted syntactic evaluation of language models. In *Proceedings of the 2018 Conference on Empirical Methods in Natural Language Processing*, pages 1192–1202, Brussels, Belgium. Association for Computational Linguistics.

Raja Ram Mehrotra. 1998. Indian english. *Texts and Interpretation. Amsterdam: Benjamins.*

Carol Myers-Scotton. 1993. Dueling languages: Grammatical structure in code-switching. claredon.

Shriphani Palakodety, Ashiqur R. KhudaBukhsh, and Jaime G. Carbonell. 2020a. Hope speech detection: A computational analysis of the voice of peace. In *ECAI 2020 - 24th European Conference on Artificial Intelligence*, volume 325 of *Frontiers in Artificial Intelligence and Applications*, pages 1881–1889. IOS Press.

Shriphani Palakodety, Ashiqur R. KhudaBukhsh, and Jaime G. Carbonell. 2020b. Mining insights from large-scale corpora using fine-tuned language models. In *ECAI 2020 - 24th European Conference on Artificial Intelligence*, volume 325 of *Frontiers in Artificial Intelligence and Applications*, pages 1890–1897. IOS Press.

Shriphani Palakodety, Ashiqur R. KhudaBukhsh, and Jaime G. Carbonell. 2020c. Voice for the voiceless: Active sampling to detect comments supporting the rohingyas. In *The Thirty-Fourth AAAI Conference on Artificial Intelligence, AAAI 2020, The Thirty-Second Innovative Applications of Artificial Intelligence Conference, IAAI 2020, The Tenth AAAI Symposium on Educational Advances in Artificial Intelligence, EAAI 2020, New York, NY, USA, February 7-12, 2020*, pages 454–462.

Denis Paperno, Germán Kruszewski, Angeliki Lazaridou, Ngoc Quan Pham, Raffaella Bernardi, Sandro Pezzelle, Marco Baroni, Gemma Boleda, and Raquel Fernández. 2016. The LAMBADA dataset: Word prediction requiring a broad discourse context. In *Proceedings of the 54th Annual Meeting of the Association for Computational Linguistics (Volume 1: Long Papers)*, pages 1525–1534, Berlin, Germany. Association for Computational Linguistics.

Fabio Petroni, Tim Rocktäschel, Sebastian Riedel, Patrick Lewis, Anton Bakhtin, Yuxiang Wu, and Alexander Miller. 2019. Language models as knowledge bases? In *Proceedings of the 2019 Conference on Empirical Methods in Natural Language Processing and the 9th International Joint Conference on Natural Language Processing (EMNLP-IJCNLP)*, pages 2463–2473, Hong Kong, China. Association for Computational Linguistics.

Koustav Rudra, Ashish Sharma, Kalika Bali, Monojit Choudhury, and Niloy Ganguly. 2019. Identifying and analyzing different aspects of english-hindi code-switching in twitter. *ACM Trans. Asian Low Resour. Lang. Inf. Process.*, 18(3):29:1–29:28.

Andreas Sedlatschek. 2009. Contemporary indian english. *Variation and change. Amsterdam, Philadelphia.*

SV Shastri. 1996. Using computer corpora in the description of language with special reference to complementation in indian english. *South Asian English: structure, use, and users*, 2(4):70–81.

Nathaniel Smith and Roger Levy. 2011. Cloze but no cigar: The complex relationship between cloze, corpus, and subjective probabilities in language processing. In *Proceedings of the Annual Meeting of the Cognitive Science Society*, volume 33.

Statista. 2020a. Leading cable news networks in the united states in april 2020, by number of primetime viewers. Online; accessed 3-June-2020.

Statista. 2020b. Most popular social networks worldwide as of january 2020, ranked by number of active users. Online; accessed 3-June-2020.

Aman Tyagi, Anjalie Field, Priyank Lathwal, Yulia Tsvetkov, and Kathleen M. Carley. 2020. A computational analysis of polarization on indian and pakistani social media. *arXiv preprint arXiv:2005.09803.*

Frans Van Coetsem. 2016. *Loan phonology and the two transfer types in language contact*, volume 27. Walter de Gruyter GmbH & Co KG.

YourStory. 2018. Youtube monthly user base touches 265 million in india, reaches 80 pc of internet population. Online; accessed 3-June-2020.

Tianyi Zhang*, Varsha Kishore*, Felix Wu*, Kilian Q. Weinberger, and Yoav Artzi. 2020. Bertscore: Evaluating text generation with bert. In *International Conference on Learning Representations*.

5 Appendix

5.1 Data Sets

Preprocessing: We apply the following standard preprocessing steps on the raw comments.

- We convert all comments to lowercase and remove all emojis and junk characters.

- We replace multiple occurrences of punctuation with a single occurrence. For example, `they got trapped!!!!!!!` is converted into `they got trapped!`.

- We use an off-the-shelf sentence tokenizer from NLTK (Bird and Klein, 2009) to break up the comments into sentences.

YouTube channels: Table 5 lists the Indian YouTube channels we considered for $\mathcal{D}^{sm}_{en\text{-}in}$.

IndiaTV, NDTV India, Republic World, The Times of India, Zee News, Aaj Tak, ABP NEWS, CNN-News18, News18 India, NDTV, TIMES NOW, India Today, The Economic Times, Hindustan Times

Table 5: National channels.

5.2 Vocabulary and Grammar

Observation: *In the context of social media, US English exhibits a richer overlap with standard English dictionary as compared to Indian English.*
Analysis: Let $\mathcal{V}_{dict}$ denote the English vocabulary obtained from a standard English dictionary (Kelly, 2016)[4]. Let $\mathcal{V}^{sm}_{en\text{-}in}$ and $\mathcal{V}^{sm}_{en\text{-}us}$ denote the vocabularies of $\mathcal{D}^{sm}_{en\text{-}in}$ and $\mathcal{D}^{sm}_{en\text{-}us}$, respectively. We now compute the following overlaps: $|\mathcal{V}^{sm}_{en\text{-}us} \cap \mathcal{V}^{dict}| = 43,826$ and $|\mathcal{V}^{sm}_{en\text{-}in} \cap \mathcal{V}^{dict}| = 38,260$. Also, with a list of 6,000 important words for US SAT exam[5], $\mathcal{V}^{sm}_{en\text{-}us}$ has considerably larger overlap (4,349 words) than $\mathcal{V}^{sm}_{en\text{-}in}$ (3,956 words).

Observation: *In the context of social media, Indian English exhibits larger deviation from standard spellings as compared to US English.*
Analysis: We compute the extent of spelling deviations in the following way. For each out-of-vocabulary (OOV) word that has appeared at least 5 or more times in a given corpus, we use a standard spell-checker [6] to map it to a dictionary word

---

[4]We take the union of *en-us* and *en-gb*.
[5]`https://satvocabulary.us/INDEX.ASP?CATEGORY=6000LIST`
[6]`https://norvig.com/spell-correct.html`

present that also has appeared 5 or more times in the corpus. We observe that, overall, 9,653 *en-in* words had at least one or more spelling variations (or errors) while 5,436 *en-us* words had at least one or more spelling variations (or errors). The average number of variations (or errors) per word are 2.15 and 1.42 for *en-in* and *en-us*, respectively, indicating that Indian English exhibit larger deviation from standard spellings. Qualitatively, we notice that words with a large number of vowels are particularly prone to spelling variations (or errors), for instance, the word `violence` has the following misspellings in *en-in*: `voilence`, `voilance`, and `violance`. In *en-us*, `violence` did not have any high-frequent (occurring 5 or more times in the corpus) misspelling. We further observe that phonetic spelling errors are highly common in *en-in*. For instance, the word `liar` is often misspelled as `lier` and the word `people` is often misspelled as `peaple`.

Observation: *Loanwords borrowed from Hindi heavily feature in Indian English.*

Analysis: Table 6 lists highly frequent words that belong to one social media corpus but absent in the other. We observe that loanwords (Holden, 1976; Calabrese and Wetzels, 2009; Van Coetsem, 2016) (e.g., `sadhus`, `begum`, `burqa`, `imams` and `gully`) feature in Indian English. Few nouns are actually used in different proper noun contexts. For example, `raga`, originally a Hindi loanword that means a musical construct, is actually used to refer to **Rahul Gandhi**, a famous Indian politician. Similarly, `newt` (a salamander species) and `tapper` refer to American politician Newt Gingrich and American journalist Jake Tapper, respectively. We note that terms specific to US politics (e.g., `gerrymandering`, `caucuses`, `senates`) and specific Indian political discourse (e.g., `demonetization`, `secularists`) solely appear in the relevant corpus. Words specific to Indian sports culture (e.g., `cricketers`) only appear in Indian English while US healthcare-specific words (e.g., `deductibles`) never appear in Indian English.

Observation: *Indian English uses considerably fewer articles and pronouns as compared to US English.*

Analysis: We next compute the respective unigram distributions $\mathcal{P}_{en\text{-}in}$ and $\mathcal{P}_{en\text{-}us}$. For each token

Solely present in $\mathcal{V}^{sm}_{en\text{-}in}$	Solely present in $\mathcal{V}^{sm}_{en\text{-}us}$
sadhus, pelting, raga, begum, bole, indigo, demonetization, defaulters, bade, burqa, secularists, demonetisation, rioter, labourer, madrasas, rickshaw, gully, introspect, cricketers, defaulter, imams	tapper, impeachable, newt, caucuses, electable, subpoenas, jurors, mittens, clapper, brokered, reassigned, munchkin, gaffe, buybacks, senates, gerrymandering, impeachments, felonies, blowhard, centrists, deductibles

Table 6: Dictionary words solely present in one corpus but absent in the other corpus.

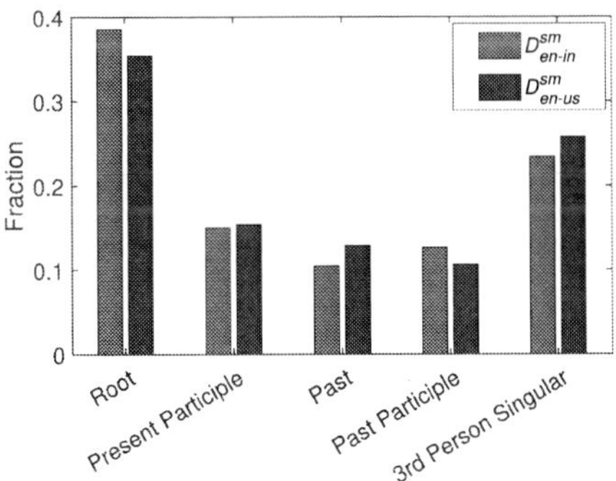

Figure 3: Distribution of different verb forms. We compute the relative occurrence of different morphological forms of a verb using a standard library (Honnibal and Montani, 2017).

$t \in \mathcal{V}_{dict} \cap \mathcal{V}^{sm}_{en\text{-}us} \cap \mathcal{V}^{sm}_{en\text{-}in}$, we compute the scores $\mathcal{P}_{en\text{-}in}(t) - \mathcal{P}_{en\text{-}us}(t)$, and $\mathcal{P}_{en\text{-}us}(t) - \mathcal{P}_{en\text{-}in}(t)$ and obtain the top tokens ranked by these scores (indicating increased usage in the respective corpus). Table 7 captures few examples with highest difference in unigram distribution. Overall, we notice that considerably fewer articles are used in *en-in*. Pronoun and article omissions in ESL (English as Second Language) are well-studied phenomena (Ferguson, 1975). This also aligns with a previous field study (Agnihotri et al., 1984) that reported even college-educated Indians make substantial errors in article usage.

Top tokens in $\mathcal{P}_{en\text{-}us}(t) - \mathcal{P}_{en\text{-}in}(t)$	Top tokens in $\mathcal{P}_{en\text{-}in}(t) - \mathcal{P}_{en\text{-}us}(t)$
the, a, trump, that, he, to, president, and, I, you, his, it, get, democrats, just, out, up, was, would, about	should, sir, u, police, good, are, in, govt, corona, very, please, is, these, them, congress, government, by, shame, only, pm

Table 7: Words with relatively more presence in one corpus over the other. Left column lists words that have relatively more presence in $\mathcal{D}^{sm}_{en\text{-}us}$ as compared to $\mathcal{D}^{sm}_{en\text{-}in}$ indicating that Indian English uses fewer articles and pronouns. Right column lists words that have relatively more presence in $\mathcal{D}^{sm}_{en\text{-}in}$ as compared to $\mathcal{D}^{sm}_{en\text{-}us}$.

Observation: *In the context of social media, Indian English uses considerably fewer prepositions as compared to US English.*

Analysis: We consider a list of highly frequent prepositions and find that *Indian English* uses fewer prepositions than US English (11.48% in *en-us* and 10.84% in *en-in*). We manually inspect usage of 100 randomly sampled sentences with the preposition `in`. 97 of such instances are evaluated correct by our annotators.

Observation: *In the context of social media, Indian English uses fewer verbs than US English.*

Analysis: In Figure 3, we summarize the relative occurrence of different verb forms. Of the different verb forms, Indian English uses the root form relatively more than US English indicating (possible) poorer understanding of subject-verb agreement and tense.

Observation: *In the context of social media, Indian English typically uses shorter sentences as compared to US English.*

Analysis: We use the recommended sentence tokenizer from NLTK (Bird and Klein, 2009) parser to obtain 1,923,292 and 1,573,355 sentences from $\mathcal{D}^{sm}_{en\text{-}in}$ and $\mathcal{D}^{sm}_{en\text{-}us}$, respectively. The average sentence length (by number of tokens) of $\mathcal{D}^{sm}_{en\text{-}in}$ and $\mathcal{D}^{sm}_{en\text{-}us}$ are 10.71 and 13.09, respectively. We acknowledge that device variability may influence this observation.

Observation: *A standard parser evaluates fewer Indian English sentences as valid as compared to US English.*

Analysis: We consider the same randomly sampled 10k sentences from each data set, and run a well-known constituency parser (Joshi et al., 2018). We first measure the fraction of sentences that are labeled as valid sentences by the parser. Table 8 shows that more than 96% sentences of both news article corpora are determined valid by the parser. Understandably, the fraction of valid sentences in the social media corpora is less with $\mathcal{D}^{sm}_{en\text{-}in}$ having few valid sentences than $\mathcal{D}^{sm}_{en\text{-}us}$.

Measure	$\mathcal{D}^{na}_{en\text{-}in}$	$\mathcal{D}^{na}_{en\text{-}us}$	$\mathcal{D}^{sm}_{en\text{-}in}$	$\mathcal{D}^{sm}_{en\text{-}us}$
Valid sentences	96.93	96.61	83.88	88.30

Table 8: Percentage of sentences determined valid by a constituency parser (Joshi et al., 2018).

Observation: *For a given sentence length, Indian*

y another pm help fund what is the need of that coz there is already a pm relief fund and its has a committee with opposition party memeber too .

thanks to god that we have priminster like a modi ji he is our great mister i salute my priminister may god bless him always he has be long life

i request news reporter to use mask, plz do this, bcoz you are facing more dangerous situation only for public sake, plz sir i request to inform our reporter,they help ussssss

if sibal and singhvi becomes enjoy similar positions den its ok for dem kapilbsibal is ant national a gunda good for u sir dey r sour grapes and crook of sonia gandhi

Table 9: Random sample of long sentences in $\mathcal{D}_{en\text{-}in}^{sm}$ with low parse tree depth.

English exhibits lesser average constituency parser tree depth (Joshi et al., 2018) indicating (possible) structural issues.

Analysis: Intuitively, length of a sentence is likely to be positively correlated with its structural complexity; a long sentence is likely to have more complex (and nested) sub-structures than a shorter one. A parser's ability to correctly identify such sub-structures depends on the sentence's syntactic correctness. To tease apart the relationship between sentence-length and constituency parser's depth, in Figure 4, we present the average tree depth for a given sentence length. We observe that between well-formed English, the difference is almost imperceptible. However, as the sentence length grows, the gap between tree depth obtained in social media *en-in* and the rest widens indicating possible structural issues. A few example long sentences with small parse-tree depth are presented in Table 9.

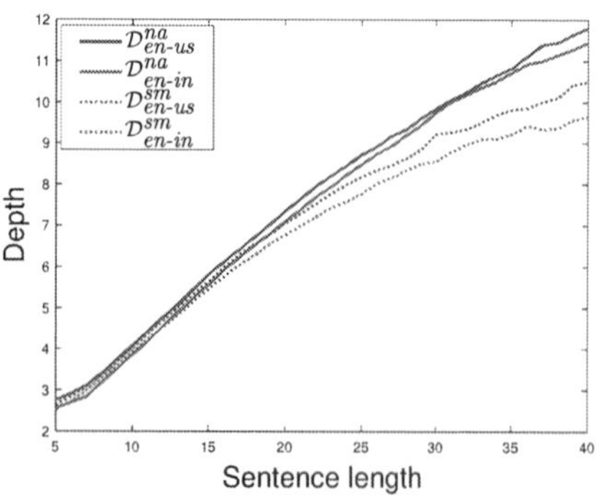

Figure 4: Constituency parser depth. A well-known parser is run on 10K sentences from each corpus. Average parse tree depth is presented for a given sentence length.

Observation: *Our results are consistent when compared against a British English (en-gb) social media corpus.*

Analysis: We construct an additional contemporaneous corpus of 4,034,513 comments from 57,019 videos from two highly popular British news outlets (BBC and Channel 4). In Table 10, 11 and 12, we present the results on British English and show that the results are very similar to US English.

	$\mathcal{D}_{en\text{-}in}^{na}$	$\mathcal{D}_{en\text{-}us}^{na}$	$\mathcal{D}_{en\text{-}in}^{sm}$	$\mathcal{D}_{en\text{-}us}^{sm}$	$\mathcal{D}_{en\text{-}gb}^{sm}$
Overall	84.27	83.68	66.56	71.72	71.41
VERB	90.17	89.72	79.47	82.76	78.30
NOUN	86.20	85.95	62.03	67.96	69.09
ADP	89.78	89.24	75.96	75.88	78.08
ADJ	68.88	70.54	48.55	61.06	58.17
ADV	74.40	73.06	47.09	58.01	62.25

Table 10: POS agreement between the masked word and BERT's top prediction. Results on social media corpora are highlighted with blue. Adposition (ADP) is a cover term for prepositions and postpositions.

Measure	$\mathcal{D}_{en\text{-}in}^{na}$	$\mathcal{D}_{en\text{-}us}^{na}$	$\mathcal{D}_{en\text{-}in}^{sm}$	$\mathcal{D}_{en\text{-}us}^{sm}$	$\mathcal{D}_{en\text{-}gb}^{sm}$
p@1	53.53	55.53	33.49	42.31	40.80
p@5	75.69	77.30	55.91	65.07	62.33
p@10	81.03	82.93	62.69	71.36	68.70

Table 11: BERT's masked word prediction performance on 10k randomly sampled sentences from each corpus.

Measure	$\mathcal{D}_{en\text{-}in}^{na}$	$\mathcal{D}_{en\text{-}us}^{na}$	$\mathcal{D}_{en\text{-}in}^{sm}$	$\mathcal{D}_{en\text{-}us}^{sm}$	$\mathcal{D}_{en\text{-}gb}^{sm}$
Valid sentences	96.93	96.61	83.88	88.30	84.17

Table 12: Percentage of sentences determined valid by a constituency parser.

70

Sentence Boundary Detection on Line Breaks in Japanese

Yuta Hayashibe[*]
hayashibe@megagon.ai
Megagon Labs, Tokyo, Japan, Recruit Co., Ltd.
7-3-5 Ginza Chuo-ku, Tokyo,
104-8227, Japan

Kensuke Mitsuzawa[*]
kensuke-mi@megagon.ai
Freelance
7-3-5 Ginza Chuo-ku, Tokyo,
104-8227, Japan

Abstract

For NLP, sentence boundary detection (SBD) is an essential task to decompose a text into sentences. Most of the previous studies have used a simple rule that uses only typical characters as sentence boundaries. However, some characters may or may not be sentence boundaries depending on the context. We focused on line breaks in them. We newly constructed annotated corpora, implemented sentence boundary detectors, and analyzed performance of SBD in several settings.

1 Introduction

Many NLP tasks treat a sentence as a unit of processing. The task for decomposing a text into sentences is called sentence boundary detection (SBD). In Japanese, periods (e.g. "。", "."), exclamation marks, and question marks are delimiters to segment sentences in most cases. For this reason, the SBD in most studies takes only the positions of these typical delimiters as sentence boundaries. For example, in the construction of the "Web Japanese N-gram database[1]" provided by Google, Inc., they extracted sentences by segmenting on their positions.

However, line breaks can also indicate sentence boundaries without periods as the following text[2].

オアシズの大久保さんが最近気になり
ます⏎</s>テレビはどの番組によく
出るんですか？(Ms. Okubo of "Oa-
siz" has been on my mind lately ⏎
</s>What TV shows does she often ap-
pear on?) (1)

Many line breaks do not follow the typical delimiters. For example, 33.4% of line breaks in the balanced corpus of contemporary written Japanese (BCCWJ) (Maekawa, 2008) were not followed by them. On the other hand, line breaks may be placed in the middle of a sentence. Therefore, we can not simply treat the positions of line breaks as sentence boundaries.

最近の映画で⏎ゲイリー・オールドマ
ンが出演している映画ってあります
か？(Among recent movies ⏎ are there
any with Gary Oldman?) (2)

This type of line break is used to make long sentences easy to read. Shinmori et al. (2003) performed a structural analysis of Japanese patent documents. They reported that 48.5% of the first claim in the 59,968 patent documents contain line breaks in the sentence. They explain it is common that claims written in Japanese are described in one sentence and the use of line breaks is intended to improve readability.

There can be more sentence boundaries than these. Nishimura (2003) showed that there are more than six variations of Japanese sentence boundaries in an online forum: Description of actions (e.g. "(照)": embarrassment, "(涙)": tears), "Smiley" Icons (e.g. "（＊＾∇＾＊）", "§ ＾。＾ §"), and so on. Sakai (2013) conducted a linguistic analysis of Japanese emails written by young people on their mobile phones and found that about 63% of the emails used emoticons instead of punctuation marks for sentence boundaries.

In this paper, we focus on SBD on line breaks in Japanese. We newly construct annotated corpora to answer the following three research questions:

1. Is it possible to train a sentence boundary detector on line breaks with annotated corpora? (Section 4.2)

---

[*]Both authors contributed equally.
[1]https://www.gsk.or.jp/files/catalog/
GSK2007-C/GSK2007C_README.utf8.txt

[2]In this paper, we use "⏎" to show line breaks and "</s>" to show sentence boundaries.

Proceedings of the 2020 EMNLP Workshop W-NUT: The Sixth Workshop on Noisy User-generated Text, pages 71–75
Online, Nov 19, 2020. ©2020 Association for Computational Linguistics

2. Is a trained model accurate enough to work with data in another writing style? (Section 4.3)

3. Is it possible to train a sentence boundary detector with unannotated corpora? (Section 4.4)

2 Related Work

Zhu et al. (2007) removed noise in English email text by removing extra lines and spaces and restoring wrong cases of characters. They show that 49.5% of the noise in about 5,000 texts is due to line breaks. Three labels for line breaks were trained and predicted by the Conditional Random Fields (CRF) algorithm (Lafferty et al., 2001): PRV (Preserve line break), RPA (Replace line break by space), DEL (Delete line break). The accuracy is reported as F-measure 93.75.

Huang and Chen (2011) insist that the concept of "sentences" is fuzzier and less-defined in Chinese, and Native Chinese writers seldom follow the usage guidelines of punctuation marks. They listed the symbols used as sentence boundaries, such as whitespaces, commas, periods, line breaks. They reported F1 of manual SBD is 81.18 and one of CRF is 77.48.

Stanza[3] (Qi et al., 2020) is a language-agnostic fully neural pipeline for text analysis, including tokenization, multiword token expansion, lemmatization, part-of-speech and morphological feature tagging, dependency parsing, and named entity recognition. Unlike most existing toolkits, it does tokenization and SBD at the same time by using a bidirectional long short-term memory network (Graves and Schmidhuber, 2005) (Bi-LSTM) for characters in texts. It provides models for 66 languages including Japanese. The Japanese model is trained with with UD Japanese GSD[4]. Its architecture enables SBD on any characters, including line breaks. However the training corpus does not contain line breaks. Therefore the model can not perform SBD on line breaks.

3 Corpus Preparation

3.1 BCCWJ

The balanced corpus of contemporary written Japanese (BCCWJ) is a corpus annotated with sen-

Corpus	Documents	Sentences	LBs	LBs w/o SB
BCCWJ	2,918	44,760	23,099	1,702
(PN)	340	8,747	3,069	0
(PB)	83	8,956	3,290	0
(PM)	86	9,424	3,890	0
(OW)	62	3,751	2,223	0
(OC)	*1,876	6,413	4,055	818
(OY)	471	7,469	6,572	884
Jalan-F	500	3,290	1,484	170
Jalan-A	298	?	1,193	153

Table 1: Statistics of corpus. LB means "line break," and SB means "sentence boundary." Each two letters for BCCWJ reperesents newspaper articles (PN), books (PB), magazines (PM), white papers (OW), QA texts in the Internet (OC) and blog texts (OY). * In OC, we regarded an answer setcion for a question section is in a different document in the question.

tence boundaries (Konishi et al., 2015) and morphological information. It covers a wide range of genres such as books, magazines, newspapers, business reports, blogs, internet forums, and textbooks. Some of them contain line breaks. Table 1 shows the statistics of the corpus[5,6] It consists 44,770 sentences in 2,918 documents. They contain 1,721 line breaks that do not segment sentences out of 26,056 line breaks. Such line breaks are contained only limited domains: QA texts and blog texts on the web.

3.2 Jalan Corpora

We create two kinds of Japanese corpora with sentence boundary annotation: Jalan-F and Jalan-A, in order to perform experiments in another domain and another writing style. Both of them are composed of a part of hotel reviews posted on Jalan[7], which is a popular travel information web site. Table 1 shows the statistics of the corpora. All annotations are performed by one worker and confirmed by another worker.

Jalan-F[8] comprises 500 reviews. We fully anno-

---

[3] https://stanfordnlp.github.io/stanza/

[4] https://universaldependencies.org/treebanks/ja_gsd/

[5] In this paper, we removed all line breaks at the end of documents because they are obvious sentence boundaries. Additionally, if there is a series of line breaks or a space before or after a line break, we replaced it with a single line break.

[6] We only used the "core" in BCCWJ. Its annotation is manual while no manual correction is performed for "non-core."

[7] https://www.jalan.net

[8] The "F" is an abbreviation for "full annotation."

tated sentence boundaries for all texts. As a result, we found 3,290 sentences. It contains 1,484 line breaks. Out of them, 170 line breaks do not segment sentences.

Jalan-A[9] comprises 298 reviews in an atypical writing style. They do not contain typical Japanese periods ("。"). This is an example.

$$
\begin{array}{l}
個室を利用させていただきました↵ \\
</s>清潔感があり↵お部屋も広く↵ \\
またお邪魔させていただきますね↵ \\
</s>スタッフの対応も最高でした \\
\text{(We stayed in a private room ↵</s>} \\
\text{The room was clean ↵ and spacious,} \\
\text{↵ so we'll be back again ↵</s> The} \\
\text{staffs were great)}
\end{array} \tag{3}
$$

Some line breaks segment sentences and some do not. We only annotated sentence boundaries on line breaks. While the number of boundaries is 1,374, there may be more sentences. It contains 1,983 line breaks. Out of them, 153 line breaks do not segment sentences.

3.3 Pseudo Annotation Corpora

To answer the third research question, we created two pseudo annotation corpora: P-BCCWJ and P-Jalan. First, we removed all line breaks from BCCWJ and 10,000 reviews additionally extracted from Jalan. Then, we replaced typical Japanese sentence boundaries "。" into line breaks and regard all of them as sentence boundaries. Finally, we replaced ideographic commas "、" into line breaks with 50% probability. This is an example.

$$
\begin{array}{l}
\text{Original: } 眺めのよいところで、遠くを \\
見ることですよ。\text{ (It is to look into the} \\
\text{distance from a good view.)} \\
\text{Pseudo annotation: } 眺めのよいところ \\
で↵遠くを見ることですよ↵</s>
\end{array} \tag{4}
$$

4 Experiments

4.1 Experiment Settings

We create sentence boundary detectors by fine-turning the BERT (Devlin et al., 2019) model[10] pre-trained on Japanese Wikipedia by Tohoku

---

Token	Gold	Prediction	Evaluation
ます (is)	O	SB	(ignored)
↵	SB	SB	TP
テレビ (TV)	O	O	(ignored)
↵	NSB	SB	FP
は (is)	O	NSB	(ignored)

Table 2: An example of input, output, and evaluation for sentence boundary detectors

University. Texts are first tokenized with MeCab[11] morphological parser and then spitted into subwords by WordPiece. Its vocabulary size is 32,000. We exploit implementations of sequence labeling in "transformers"[12] by Hugging Face with three labels[13]: "Sentence boundary" (SB) and "Not sentence boundary" (NSB) for line breaks, and "Others" (O) for tokens that are not line breaks. We only use predictions for line breaks. Table 2 shows an example of input, output, and evaluation for detectors. In training, all tokens are labeled "O" except for line breaks. Whatever predictions are output for them, we do not consider them in the evaluation. Line breaks are labeled "SB" or "NSB" for training. We recognize sentence boundaries only on the tokens whose predictions are "SB."

We set the maximum sequence length 320, the training batch size 32, and the number of epochs five. If the maximum number of input tokens is exceeded, we divide them into multiple inputs. We perform the Unicode NFKC normalization for all inputs.

For training and evaluation, we exclude 663 documents from BCCWJ and 164 documents from Jalan-F that do not contain line breaks. Each corpus of BCCWJ, Jalan-F, and Jalan-A is divided into 8:2 for learning and training. We built four models by using the three training sources and the data from the combination of Jalan-F and Jalan-A.

4.2 Experiments 1: Impact of Domains

First, we investigate the impact of domains. As shown in Table 3, In BCCWJ test data, the F_1 score of the model Jalan-F+A (96.8) is not very

---

[9]The "A" is an abbreviation for "atypical."

[10]https://huggingface.co/cl-tohoku/bert-base-japanese-whole-word-masking

[11]https://github.com/taku910/mecab

[12]https://github.com/huggingface/transformers

[13]We did a preliminary experiment with binary labels "Sentence boundary" (SB) and "Not sentence boundary" (NSB), but it was low performance.

Test	Train	TP	TN	FP	FN	F_1
BCCWJ	BCCWJ	4,029	568	50	96	**98.2**
	Jalan-F	3,749	520	98	376	94.1
	Jalan-A	4,014	325	293	111	95.2
	Jalan-F+A	3,921	559	59	204	96.8
Jalan-F	BCCWJ	258	18	0	0	**100.0**
	Jalan-F	258	15	3	0	99.4
	Jalan-A	258	7	11	0	97.9
	Jalan-F+A	258	17	1	0	99.8

Table 3: SBD Performance on line breaks by models traied with annotated copora

Test	Train	TP	TN	FP	FN	F_1
Jalan-A	BCCWJ	210	46	1	11	**97.2**
	Jalan-F	188	39	8	33	90.2
	Jalan-A	204	27	20	17	91.7
	Jalan-F+A	202	45	2	19	95.1

Table 4: SBD Performance on line breaks in atypical writing style by models traied with annotated copora

Test	Train	TP	TN	FP	FN	F_1
P-BCCWJ	P-BCCWJ	2,715	570	48	1,410	78.8
	P-Jalan	1,868	575	43	2,257	61.9
Jalan-A	P-BCCWJ	200	46	1	21	94.8
	P-Jalan	192	46	1	29	92.8

Table 5: SBD Performance on line breaks by models traied with pseudo copora

bad compared to one of the model BCCWJ (98.2). This shows that we can make reasonably accurate models using training data even from different domains. On the other hand, F_1 scores for Jalan-F test data are close to 100 for all models. Therefore, we consider Jalan-F only contains simple cases.

4.3 Experiments 2: Impact of Writing Styles

Second, we investigate the impact of writing styles. As shown in Table 4, the F_1 score of the model BCCWJ is the best (97.2) among the four models. This shows that models trained on a large amount of data are more accurate, even if the writing styles are different.

4.4 Experiments 3: Effect of Pseudo Corpora

Third, we investigate the effect of pseudo corpora. Table 5 shows the result. The F_1 scores

of the model P-BCCWJ for BCCWJ is 78.8. It is much worse than one of the model BCCWJ (98.2). This is an example of a false negative (FN) by the model P-BCCWJ.

防災対策を構築する必要がある。↵
</s>消防庁においては、…
(It is necessary to build disaster pre-   (5)
vention measures. ↵</s>In the fire and
disaster management agency, …)

They were often wrong even in the almost obvious cases where periods "。" were just before line breaks.

The F_1 scores of the models P-BCCWJ and P-Jalan are respectively 94.8 and 92.8. Though they are better than one of the model Jalan-F (90.2), worse than one of the model Jalan-F+A (95.1).

These results suggest that although a sentence boundary detector with pseudo-corpus could achieve moderate performance, we can obtain better detectors by training with annotated corpora.

5 Conclusion

We implemented sentence boundary detectors by using BERT and revealed the following facts:

- It is possible to train a sentence boundary detector on line breaks with annotated corpora.

- Training with much annotation data is effective even for texts in another writing style.

- Although it is possible to train a sentence boundary detector even with pseudo-corpus to some extent, more performance will be gained by training with annotated corpora.

There are two main issues that we need to address in the future. The first issue is to do is to use active learning to increase the number of learning examples and improve accuracy. The second issue is to perform SBD for other atypical sentence boundary expressions other than line breaks.

Acknowledgements

We recognize Dr. Yuki Arase at Osaka University for the many discussions and insightful comments. Furthermore, we thank the anonymous reviewers for their careful reading and valuable comments.

References

Jacob Devlin, Ming-Wei Chang, et al. 2019. BERT: Pre-training of Deep Bidirectional Transformers for Language Understanding. In *Proceedings of the 2019 Conference of the North American Chapter of the Association for Computational Linguistics: Human Language Technologies, Volume 1*, pages 4171–4186.

Alex Graves and Jürgen Schmidhuber. 2005. Framewise Phoneme Classification with Bidirectional LSTM and Other Neural Network Architectures. *Neural Networks*, 18(5):602–610.

Hen-Hsen Huang and Hsin-Hsi Chen. 2011. Pause and Stop Labeling for Chinese Sentence Boundary Detection. In *Proceedings of the International Conference Recent Advances in Natural Language Processing 2011*, pages 146–153.

Hikari Konishi, Takenori Nakamura, et al. 2015. Correction of Sentence Boundaries in the Balanced Corpus of Contemporary Written Japanese DVD Version 1.0. *NINJAL Research Papers*, (9):81–100.

John Lafferty, Andrew McCallum, et al. 2001. Conditional Random Fields: Probabilistic Models for Segmenting and Labeling Sequence Data. In *Proceedings of the 18th International Conference on Machine Learning*, pages 282–289.

Kikuo Maekawa. 2008. Balanced Corpus of Contemporary Written Japanese. In *Proceedings of the 6th Workshop on Asian Language Resources*.

Yukiko Nishimura. 2003. Linguistic Innovations and Interactional Features of Casual Online Communication in Japanese. *Journal of Computer-Mediated Communication*, 9(1).

Peng Qi, Yuhao Zhang, et al. 2020. Stanza: A Python Natural Language Processing Toolkit for Many Human Languages. In *Proceedings of the 58th Annual Meeting of the Association for Computational Linguistics: System Demonstrations*, pages 101–108.

Noboru Sakai. 2013. The role of sentence closing as an emotional marker: A case of Japanese mobile phone e-mail. *Discourse, Context & Media*, 2(3):149–155.

Akihiro Shinmori, Manabu Okumura, et al. 2003. Patent Claim Processing for Readability: Structure Analysis and Term Explanation. In *Proceedings of the ACL-2003 Workshop on Patent Corpus Processing*, pages 56–65.

Conghui Zhu, Jie Tang, et al. 2007. A Unified Tagging Approach to Text Normalization. In *Proceedings of the 45th Annual Meeting of the Association of Computational Linguistics*, pages 688–695.

Non-ingredient Detection in User-generated Recipes using the Sequence Tagging Approach

Yasuhiro Yamaguchi, Shintaro Inuzuka, Makoto Hiramatsu, and Jun Harashima
Cookpad Inc.
Yebisu Garden Place Tower 12F, 4-20-3 Ebisu, Shibuya-ku, Tokyo, 150-6012, Japan
{yasuhiro-yamaguchi, shintaro-inuzuka, makoto-hiramatsu, jun-harashima}@cookpad.com

Abstract

Recently, the number of user-generated recipes on the Internet has increased. In such recipes, users are generally supposed to write a title, an ingredient list, and steps to create a dish. However, some items in an ingredient list in a user-generated recipe are not actually edible ingredients. For example, headings, comments, and kitchenware sometimes appear in an ingredient list because users can freely write the list in their recipes. Such noise makes it difficult for computers to use recipes for a variety of tasks, such as calorie estimation. To address this issue, we propose a non-ingredient detection method inspired by a neural sequence tagging model. In our experiment, we annotated $6,675$ ingredients in 600 user-generated recipes and showed that our proposed method achieved a 93.3 F1 score.

1 Introduction

At the present time, many people upload their recipes to the Internet. For example, over 6.7 million recipes have been uploaded to Cookpad,[1] one of the largest recipe sharing services in the world. Most of the recipes on the service are posted by ordinary users.

Figure 1 shows an example of a recipe. Note that we use Japanese examples in this study because approximately half of the recipes on Cookpad are written in Japanese. As seen in the figure, a recipe generally consists of a title, ingredient list, and steps. An ingredient list is a set of items that have an ingredient name and quantity.

However, some items in an ingredient list in a user-generated recipe are not actually edible ingredients in a user-generated recipe. For example, the third item 調味料 (seasoning) in Figure 1 is

---

[1]https://cookpad.com

Title	
ナスとピーマンの味噌炒め (Eggplant and Green Pepper Miso Stir-fry)	
Ingredient list	
ナス (eggplant)	5 個 (5 pieces)
ピーマン (green pepper)	5 個 (5 pieces)
調味料 (seasoning)	N/A
味噌 (miso)	大さじ 3 (3 tbs)
砂糖 (sugar)	大さじ 2 (2 tbs)
酒 (sake)	大さじ 2 (2 tbs)
Steps	
1. ナスを輪切りにする (cut eggplants into round slices) 2. ...	

Figure 1: Example of a recipe. The N/A means that the user (i.e., recipe author) has not written the information.

not an ingredient but the heading for the following ingredients. In a user-generated recipe, people freely use the ingredients field to describe ingredients. This noise makes it difficult for computers to use recipes for a variety of tasks, such as calorie estimation.

In this paper, we propose a method to detect non-ingredient items from an ingredient list in a user-generated recipe. Inspired by a sequence tagging approach, our method solves the problem by predicting a label (ingredient or non-ingredient) for each item in an ingredient list sequentially. In our experiment, we annotated $6,675$ ingredients in 600 recipes from Cookpad and investigated the performance of our method using the recipes.

2 Related Work

The increase in the number of recipes on the Internet has led to an increase in studies on these data, such as recipe analysis (Sasada et al., 2015; Hiramatsu et al., 2019), recipe organization (Kiddon et al., 2015; Jermsurawong and Habash, 2015), and recipe

Proceedings of the 2020 EMNLP Workshop W-NUT: The Sixth Workshop on Noisy User-generated Text, pages 76–80
Online, Nov 19, 2020. ©2020 Association for Computational Linguistics

generation (Salvador et al., 2019; Kiddon et al., 2016). Additionally, many recipe-related corpora and datasets have been published recently to promote studies on recipes (Mori et al., 2014; Harashima et al., 2016; Salvador et al., 2017; Yagcioglu et al., 2018).

Among such recipe-related studies, the following two previous works focused on informal text in user-generated recipes, like our study. Harashima and Yamada (2018) converted ingredients written in an user-generated recipe into their canonical forms in an ingredient dictionary. However, in that study, there was no assumption that non-ingredients appear in a recipe, unlike our study.

By contrast, Inuzuka et al. (2018) distinguished non-steps written in a user-generated recipe from actual steps, such as an advertisement for the author's recipe books, which are not related to cooking. Our study focuses on ingredients in a recipe, unlike their work; that is, we distinguish non-ingredients written in a user-generated recipe from actual ingredients.

Our study is the first to pay attention to non-ingredients in a user-generated recipe. This contributes to a variety of recipe-related studies, particularly based on ingredients in a recipe, such as calorie estimation (Harashima et al., 2020), recipe clustering (Nadamoto et al., 2016), and recipe-related term detection (Chung, 2012).

3 Task Definition

The primary task in this study is to classify an item in an ingredient list as an ingredient or non-ingredient. In this work, we define non-ingredient items based on edibility. Figure 2 shows examples of ingredient lists in user-generated recipes. "ホワイトソース" (white sauce) in Figure 2(a) is not an ingredient but a heading. The items below it are ingredients for white sauce. An item without a quantity is likely to be a non-ingredient. By contrast, "お好みの野菜" (favorite vegetables) in Figure 2(b) is an actual ingredient. As shown by this example, an item without a quantity is not always a non-ingredient. "(↑バターでもいいです)" ((↑ you can use butter)) in Figure 2(c) is used as a comment, which mentions the previous ingredient "マーガリン" (margarine). "竹串" (bamboo skewers) in Figure 2(d) is a non-ingredient because it is not edible. In some recipes, kitchenware appears on the ingredient list, like this example. The goal

Ingredient list	
...	...
ローリエ (bay leaf)	2 枚 (2 pieces)
ホワイトソース (white sauce)	N/A
バター (butter)	30g (30 grams)
...	...

(a) Example of a cream stew recipe.

Ingredient list	
...	...
にんじん (carrot)	1 本 (1 piece)
お好みの野菜 (favorite vegetables)	N/A
水 (water)	1000cc (1000 cc)
...	...

(b) Example of a hot pot recipe.

Ingredient list	
...	...
マーガリン (margarine)	60g (60 grams)
(↑バターでもいいです) ((↑ you can use butter))	N/A
砂糖 (sugar)	40g (40 grams)
...	...

(c) Example of a cookie recipe.

Ingredient list	
...	...
サラダ油 (vegetable oil)	小さじ 1 (1 tsp)
竹串 (bamboo skewers)	3 本 (3 pieces)
岩塩 (rock salt)	適量 (desired amount)
...	...

(d) Example of a meat roll recipe.

Figure 2: Examples of ingredient lists.

of this study is to detect these inedible items as non-ingredients.

4 Proposed Method

In this study, we detect non-ingredient items in an ingredient list using a neural sequence tagging model, shown in Figure 3.

4.1 Ingredient Representations

First, we convert each item in the ingredient list into its ingredient representation, which consists of an ingredient name representation and additional features. The former is obtained as follows:

TF-IDF: We compute TF-IDF vectors for each item in the ingredient list. The term frequency and inverse document frequency are given as

$$\text{tf}(i, j) = \frac{n_{i,j}}{\sum_k n_{k,j}} \qquad (1)$$

$$\text{idf}(j, D) = \log \frac{|D|}{|\{d \in D : t_i \in d\}|}, \qquad (2)$$

where $n_{i,j}$ is the number of words t_i in the j th ingredient name, d is the set of tokenized words in the ingredient name, and D is the set of all ingredient names in the recipe dataset. We tokenize each

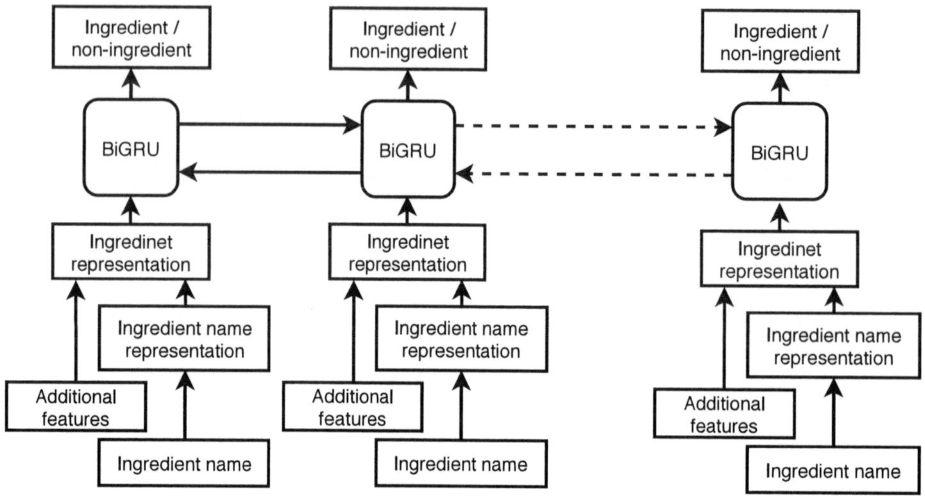

Figure 3: Overview of our method.

ingredient name and compute the TF-IDF values for each token.

char-CNN: Instead of TF-IDF, we can also use a CNN-based sequence encoder (Zhang and Wallace, 2017) to obtain the character-level features of ingredient names. We compute the features using different kernel sizes (2, 3, 4, 5) and concatenate them.

Note that we do not use pre-trained embeddings such as GloVe or fastText for the ingredient name representation because these embeddings did not show a good performance in our preliminary expemriments.

In addition to the ingredient name representation, we use additional features of the ingredient name and quantity: character count and ingredient name frequency. The ingredient name frequency is computed from the recipe dataset, which is also used for the TF-IDF calculations. We count the ingredients with the same name and use the log-scaled value as the name frequency.

Finally, we concatenate the ingredient name representation and additional features into one vector to create the ingredient representation.

4.2 Model

We use the sequence tagging model shown in Figure 3. Each time step corresponds to each item in the ingredient list. The model takes all items in the ingredient list as its inputs in the order that they appear in the recipe. Whereas the inputs of our model are ingredient representations described in the previous section, the outputs of our model are

# of recipes	600
# of ingredients	5,829
# of non-ingredients	846

Table 1: Statistics of our dataset.

binary predictions, each of which represents an ingredient or non-ingredient.

By performing a non-ingredient detection task as a sequence tagging problem, the model can make predictions by taking items before and after the target item into account. In many recipes, related ingredients are usually written close to each other. As shown in Figure 2(a), if an item in an ingredient list is used as a heading, related ingredients are listed below it.

5 Experiment

5.1 Dataset

In our experiment, we chose 600 recipes from Cookpad. More precisely, we collected recipes whose ingredient lists contained items without quantity information because such items tended to be non-ingredients in our preliminary investigation. Each ingredient in the recipes was labeled as an ingredient or non-ingredient by three domain-expert annotators. The gold labels were decided by majority vote. Table 1 shows the statistics of our dataset.

5.2 Methods

In our experiment, we compared the performance of the following methods using 10-fold cross vali-

Model	F1	Precision	Recall
Random Forest	87.2 ± 5.1	82.8 ± 8.3	92.8 ± 4.5
+ ingredient freq.	88.8 ± 4.1	86.8 ± 6.6	91.4 ± 4.8
BiGRU + TF-IDF	90.8 ± 3.1	90.1 ± 3.7	91.2 ± 3.6
+ ingredient freq.	91.6 ± 3.4	89.4 ± 4.8	94.1 ± 3.6
BiGRU + char-CNN	91.2 ± 2.7	91.3 ± 4.8	91.4 ± 3.5
+ ingredient freq.	$\mathbf{93.3 \pm 2.3}$	$\mathbf{93.2 \pm 3.7}$	$\mathbf{94.1 \pm 3.1}$

Table 2: Experimental results.

Name	Frequency
砂糖 (sugar)	524,647
塩 (salt)	507,766
水 (water)	450,370
卵 (egg)	400,572
醤油 (soy sauce)	320,834

Table 3: Top 5 ingredient names in our dataset.

dation:

Random forest (baseline model): We used *RandomForestClassifier* included in scikit-learn as a baseline model. The input of the random forest model was the ingredient representation described in the previous section. This model predicted a label for each item in an ingredient list independently.

BiGRU model (our model): We used two-layer bidirectional GRU (BiGRU) (Cho et al., 2014). The dimension of the BiGRU hidden layer was 128. We trained the BiGRU model for 50 epochs using the Adam optimizer.

5.3 Results and Discussion

Table 2 shows the experimental results. We evaluated the methods using F1, precision, and recall. As shown in Table 2, the BiGRU + char-CNN model with the ingredient frequency achieved the highest F1 score of 93.3. The BiGRU-based model was better than the random forest, so this result suggests that a sequence labeling approach is effective for the non-ingredient detection task.

The ingredient frequency improved the F1 scores for both the random forest and BiGRU models. Table 3 shows the most frequent ingredient names, which were calculated from approximately 3 million recipes from Cookpad. As shown in Table 3, many ingredient names that occurred frequently in recipes were actual ingredients, so ingredient name frequency is important for ingredient detection. The ingredient frequency can be an alternative feature of an ingredient dictionary which is usually rarely available.

In most cases, an item without a quantity in the ingredient list was used as a heading or comment, as described in Section 3. When we predicted an item without a quantity as a non-ingredient, the F1 score was 85.3 in our further investigation. However, some items such as vegetables or fruits, had no quantities although they were actually ingredients. Using the ingredient name frequency, it became possible to predict such items as ingredients properly because names of vegetables or fruits frequently occurred in our recipe dataset.

6 Conclusion

In this paper, we introduced a non-ingredient detection task for user-generated recipes and proposed a neural model based on the sequence tagging approach. We used a BiGRU-based model to predict a label for each ingredient over an ingredient sequence. To evaluate our method, we constructed a dataset that contained 6,675 ingredients of 600 recipes from Cookpad. Our experimental results showed that the proposed method achieved a 93.3 F1 score in the task. In future work, we plan to verify the effectiveness of our method for downstream tasks, such as calorie estimation.

References

Kyunghyun Cho, Bart van Merriënboer, Caglar Gulcehre, Dzmitry Bahdanau, Fethi Bougares, Holger Schwenk, and Yoshua Bengio. 2014. Learning Phrase Representations using RNN Encoder-Decoder for Statistical Machine Translation. In *Proceedings of the 2014 Conference on Empirical Methods in Natural Language Processing (EMNLP 2014)*, pages 1724–1734.

Young-joo Chung. 2012. Finding Food Entity Relationships using User-generated Data in Recipe Service. In *Proceedings of the 21th ACM International on Conference on Information and Knowledge Management (CIKM 2012)*, pages 2611–2614.

Jun Harashima, Michiaki Ariga, Kenta Murata, and Masayuki Ioki. 2016. A Large-scale Recipe and Meal Data Collection as Infrastructure for Food Research. In *Proceedings of the 10th International*

Conference on Language Resources and Evaluation (LREC 2016), pages 2455–2459.

Jun Harashima, Makoto Hiramatsu, and Satoshi Snajo. 2020. Calorie Estimation in a Real-World Recipe Service. In *Proceedings of the 32th Annual Conference on Innovative Applications of Artificial Intelligence (IAAI-20)*.

Jun Harashima and Yoshiaki Yamada. 2018. Two-Step Validation in Character-based Ingredient Normalization. In *Proceedings of the 10th Workshop on Multimedia for Cooking and Eating Activities (CEA 2018)*, pages 29–32.

Makoto Hiramatsu, Kei Wakabayashi, and Jun Harashima. 2019. Named Entity Recognition by Character-based Word Classification using a Domain Specific Dictionary. In *Proceedings of the 20th International Conference on Computational Linguistics and Intelligent Text Processing (CICLing 2019)*.

Shintaro Inuzuka, Takahiko Ito, and Jun Harashima. 2018. Step or Not: Discriminator for The Real Instructions in User-generated Recipes. In *Proceedings of the 4th Workshop on Noisy User-generated Text (W-NUT 2018)*, page 214.

Jermsak Jermsurawong and Nizar Habash. 2015. Predicting the Structure of Cooking Recipes. In *Proceedings of the 2015 Conference on Empirical Methods in Natural Language Processing (EMNLP 2015)*, pages 781–786.

Chloé Kiddon, Ganesa Thandavam Ponnuraj, Luke Zettlemoyer, and Yejin Choi. 2015. Mise en Place: Unsupervised Interpretation of Instructional Recipes. In *Proceedings of the 2015 Conference on Empirical Methods in Natural Language Processing (EMNLP 2015)*, pages 982–992.

Chloé Kiddon, Luke Zettlemoyer, and Yejin Choi. 2016. Globally Coherent Text Generation with Neural Checklist Models. In *Proceedings of the 2016 Conference on Empirical Methods in Natural Language Processing (EMNLP 2016)*, pages 329–339.

Shinsuke Mori, Hirokuni Maeta, Yoko Yamakata, and Tetsuro Sasada. 2014. Flow Graph Corpus from Recipe Texts. In *Proceedings of the 9th International Conference on Language Resources and Evaluation (LREC 2014)*, pages 2370–2377.

Akiyo Nadamoto, Shunsuke Hanai, and Hidetsugu Nanba. 2016. Clustering for Similar Recipes in User-generated Recipe Sites based on Main Ingredients and Main Seasoning. In *Proceedings of the 19th International Conference on Network-Based Information Systems (NBiS-2016)*, pages 336–341.

Amaia Salvador, Michal Drozdzal, Xavier Giro i Nieto, and Adriana Romero. 2019. Inverse Cooking: Recipe Generation from Food Images. In *Proceedings of the 2019 IEEE Conference on Computer Vision and Pattern Recognition (CVPR 2019)*.

Amaia Salvador, Nicholas Hynes, Yusuf Aytar, Javier Marin, Ferda Ofli, Ingmar Weber, and Antonio Torralba. 2017. Learning Cross-modal Embeddings for Cooking Recipes and Food Images. In *Proceedings of the 2017 IEEE Conference on Computer Vision and Pattern Recognition (CVPR 2017)*, pages 3020–3028.

Tetsuro Sasada, Shinsuke Mori, Tatsuya Kawahara, and Yoko Yamakata. 2015. Named Entity Recognizer Trainable from Partially Annotated Data. In *Proceedings of the 14th International Conference of the Pacific Association for Computational Linguistics (PACLING 2015)*, pages 148–160.

Semih Yagcioglu, Aykut Erdem, Erkut Erdem, and Nazli Ikizler-Cinbis. 2018. RecipeQA: A Challenge Dataset for Multimodal Comprehension of Cooking Recipes. In *Proceedings of the 2018 Conference on Empirical Methods in Natural Language Processing (EMNLP 2018)*, pages 1358–1368.

Ye Zhang and Byron C. Wallace. 2017. A Sensitivity Analysis of (and Practitioners' Guide to) Convolutional Neural Networks for Sentence Classification. In *Proceedings of the 8th International Joint Conference on Natural Language Processing (IJCNLP 2017)*, pages 253–263.

Generating Fact Checking Summaries for Web Claims

Rahul Mishra[1], Dhruv Gupta[2], Markus Leippold[3]

[1]University of Stavanger, Norway
[1]rahul.mishra@uis.no
[2]Max Planck Institute for Informatics, Germany
[2]dhgupta@mpi-inf.mpg.de
[3]University of Zurich, Switzerland
[3]markus.leippold@bf.uzh.ch

Abstract

We present SUMO, a neural attention-based approach that learns to establish the correctness of textual claims based on evidence in the form of text documents (e.g., news articles or Web documents). SUMO further generates an extractive summary by presenting a diversified set of sentences from the documents that explain its decision on the correctness of the textual claim. Prior approaches to address the problem of fact checking and evidence extraction have relied on simple concatenation of claim and document word embeddings as an input to claim driven attention weight computation. This is done so as to extract salient words and sentences from the documents that help establish the correctness of the claim. However, this design of claim-driven attention does not capture the contextual information in documents properly. We improve on the prior art by using improved claim and title guided hierarchical attention to model effective contextual cues. We show the efficacy of our approach on datasets concerning political, healthcare, and environmental issues.

1 Introduction

Most of the information consumed by the world is in the form of digital news, blogs, and social media posts available on the Web. However, most of this information is written in the absence of facts and evidences. Our ever-increasing reliance on information from the Web is becoming a severe problem as we base our personal decisions relating to politics, environment, and health on unverified information available online. For example, consider the following unverified claim on the Web:

> *"Smoking may protect*
> *against COVID-19."*

A user attempting to verify the correctness of the above claim will often take the following steps: issue keyword queries to search engines for the claim; going through the top reliable news articles; and finally making an informed decision based on the gathered information. Clearly, this approach is laborious, takes time, and is error-prone. In this work, we present SUMO, a neural approach that assists the user in establishing the correctness of claims by automatically generating explainable summaries for fact checking. Example summaries generated by SUMO for couple of Web claims are given in Figure 1.

Prior approaches to automatic fact checking rely on predicting the credibility of facts (Popat et al., 2017), instance detection (Ma et al., 2018; Xu et al., 2018), and fact entailment in supporting documents (Parikh et al., 2016). The majority of these methods rely on linguistic features (Popat et al., 2017; Potthast et al., 2018; Qazvinian et al., 2011), social contexts, or user responses (Ma et al., 2015) and comments. However, these approaches do not help explain the decisions generated by the machine learning models. Recent works such as (Atanasova et al., 2019; Mishra and Setty, 2019; Popat et al., 2018) overcome the explainability gap by extracting snippets from text documents that support or refute the claim. (Mishra and Setty, 2019; Popat et al., 2018) apply claim-based and latent aspect-based attention to model the context of text documents. (Mishra and Setty, 2019) model latent aspects such as the speaker or author of the claim, topic of the claim, and domains of retrieved Web documents for the claim. We observe in our experiments that in prior works (Mishra and Setty, 2019; Popat et al., 2018), the design of claim guided attention in these methods is not effective and latent aspects such as the topic and speaker of claims are not always available. The snippets extracted by such models are not comprehensive or topically diverse. To overcome these limitations, we propose a novel design of claim and document

Proceedings of the 2020 EMNLP Workshop W-NUT: The Sixth Workshop on Noisy User-generated Text, pages 81–90
Online, Nov 19, 2020. ©2020 Association for Computational Linguistics

Claim: *Smoking may protect against COVID-19*	Label: False	Verdict: False
Summary: The current evidence suggests that the severity of COVID is higher among smokers, prevent the health risk linked to the excessive consumption or misuse" of nicotine products by people hoping to protect themselves from COVID-19. Evidence from China, where COVID-19 originated, shows that people who have cardiovascular and respiratory conditions caused by tobacco use, or otherwise, are at higher risk of developing severe COVID-19 symptoms. HO urges researchers, scientists and the media to be cautious about amplifying unproven claims that tobacco or nicotine could reduce the risk of COVID-19. Smoking is also associated with increased development of acute respiratory distress syndrome, a key complication for severe cases of COVID-19.		
Claim: *Deforestation has made humans more vulnerable to pandemics*	Label: True	Verdict: True
Summary: Deforestation can directly increase the likelihood that a pathogen will be transferred from wildlife species to humans through the creation of suitable habitats for vector species. Climate change, including deforestation which drives it, is a key driver of cross-species transmission which is where zoonotic emerging diseases come from . There is a correlation between deforestation and the rise in the spread of infectious diseases affecting humans. Deforestation forces various species into smaller, shared habitats and increases encounters between wildlife and humans. Habitat destruction and fragmentation due to deforestation can also increase the frequency of contact between humans, wildlife species, and the pathogens they carry . This can occur through direct transfer of pathogens from animals to humans or indirectly through cross-species transfer of pathogens from wildlife to domesticated species . Deforestation could be to blame for the rise of infectious diseases like the novel coronavirus.		

Figure 1: Example summaries generated by SUMO for unverified claims on the Web.

title driven attention, which better captures the contextual cues in relation to the claim. In addition to this, we propose an approach for generating summaries for fact-checking that are non-redundant and topically diverse.

Contributions. Contributions made in this work are as follows. First, we introduce SUMO, a method that improves upon the previously used claim guided attention to model effective contextual representation. Second, we propose a novel attention on top of attention (Atop) method to improve the overall attention effectiveness. Third, we present an approach to generate topically diverse multi-document summaries, which help in explaining the decision SUMO makes for establishing the correctness of claims. Fourth, we provide a novel testbed for the task of fact checking in the domain of climate change and health care.

Outline. The outline for the rest of the article is as follows. In Section 2, we describe prior work in relation to our problem setting. In Section 3, we formalize the problem definition and describe our approach, SUMO, to generate explainable summaries for fact checking of textual claims. In Sections 4 and 5, we describe the experimental setup that includes a description of the novel datasets that we make available to the research community and an analysis of the results we have obtained. In Section 6, we present the concluding remarks of our study.

2 Related work

We now describe prior work related to our problem setting. First, we describe works that rely only on features derived from documents that support the input textual claim. Second, we describe works that additionally include features derived from social media posts in connection to the claim. Third and finally, we describe works that rely on extracting textual snippets from text documents to explain a model's decision on the claim's correctness.

2.1 Content Based Approaches

Prior approaches for fact checking vary from simple machine learning methods such as SVM and decision trees to highly sophisticated deep learning methods. These works largely utilize features that model the linguistic and stylistic content of the facts to learn a classifier (Castillo et al., 2011; Ma et al., 2016; Qazvinian et al., 2011; Rashkin et al., 2017). The key shortcomings of these approaches are as follows. First, classifiers trained on linguistic and stylistic features perform poorly as they can be misguided by the writing style of the false claims, which are deliberately made to look similar to true claims but are factually false. Second, these methods lack in terms of user response and social context pertaining to the claims, which is very helpful in establishing the correctness of facts.

2.2 Social Media Based Approaches

Works such as (Qian et al., 2018; Shu et al., 2019; Yang et al., 2019) overcome the issue of user feedback by using a combination of content-based and context-based features derived from related social media posts. Specifically, the features derived from social media include propagation patterns of claim related posts on social media and user responses in the form of replies, likes, sentiments, and shares. These methods outperform content-based methods significantly. In (Yang et al., 2019), the authors propose a probabilistic graphical model for causal mappings among the post's credibility, user's opinions, and user's credibility. In (Qian et al., 2018), the authors introduce a user response generator based on a deep neural network that leverages the user's past actions such as comments, replies, and posts to generate a synthetic response for new social media posts.

2.3 Model Explainability

Explaining a machine learning model's decision is becoming an important problem. This is because modern neural network based methods are increasingly being used as black-boxes. There exist few machine learning models for fact checking that explain this decision via summaries. Related works (Mishra and Setty, 2019; Popat et al., 2018) achieve significant improvement in establishing the credibility of textual claims by using external evidences from the Web. They additionally extract snippets from evidences that explain their model's decision. However, we find that the claim-driven attention design used in these methods is inadequate, and does not capture sufficient context of the documents in relation to the input claim. The snippets extracted by these methods are often redundant and lack topical diversity offered by Web evidences. In contrast, our method enhances the claim-driven attention mechanism and generates a topically diverse, coherent multi-document summary for explaining the correctness of claims.

3 SUMO

We now formally describe the task of fact checking and explain SUMO in detail. SUMO works in two stages. In the first stage, it predicts the correctness of the claim. In the second stage, it generates a topically diverse summary for the claims. As input, we are provided with a Web claim $c \in C$, where C is a collection of Web claims and a pseudo-relevant set of documents $D = \{d_1, d_2, \ldots, d_m\}$, where m is the number of results retrieved for claim c. The documents $d \in D$ are retrieved from the Web as potential evidences, using claim c as a query. Each retrieved document d is accompanied by its title t and text body bd, i.e. ($d = \langle t, bd \rangle$). We define the representation of each document's body as a collection of k sentences as $bd = \{s_1, s_2, ..., s_k\}$ and each sentence as the collection of l words as $\{w_1, w_2, ..., w_l\} \in \mathbb{W}$, where $\mathbb{W}$ is the overall word vocabulary of the corpus. By k and l, we denote the maximum numbers of sentences in a document and the maximum number of words in a sentence, respectively. We use both WORD2VEC and pre-trained GloVe embeddings to obtain the vector representations for each claim, title, and document body. The objective is to classify the claim as either true or false and automatically generate a topically diverse summary pieced together from D for establishing the correctness of the claim.

3.1 Predicting Claim Correctness by Neural Attention

We now describe SUMO's neural architecture (see Figure 2) that helps in predicting the correctness of the input claim along with its pseudo-relevant set of documents. The model additionally learns the weights to words and sentences in the document's body that help ascertain the claim's correctness. First, we need to encode the pseudo-relevant documents that support a claim. To this end, as a **sequence encoder**, we use a Gated Recurrent Unit (GRU) to encode the document's body content. Claim and document's title are not encoded using sequence encoder; we explain the method to represent them in detail in upcoming sections.

Claim-driven Hierarchical Attention., aims to attend salient words that are significant and have relevance to the content of the claim. Similarly, we aim to attend the salient sentences at the sentence level attention. Recent works have used claim guided attention to model the contextual representation of the retrieved documents from the Web. These approaches provide claim-guided attention by first concatenating the claim word embeddings with document word embeddings and then applying a dense softmax layer to learn the attention weights as follows:

$$r_i = c_i \parallel d_i \ \& \ a_i = \tanh(W_a r_i + b_a)$$
$$\alpha = \text{softmax}(a_i), \tag{1}$$

where c_i and d_i are the ith claim and document

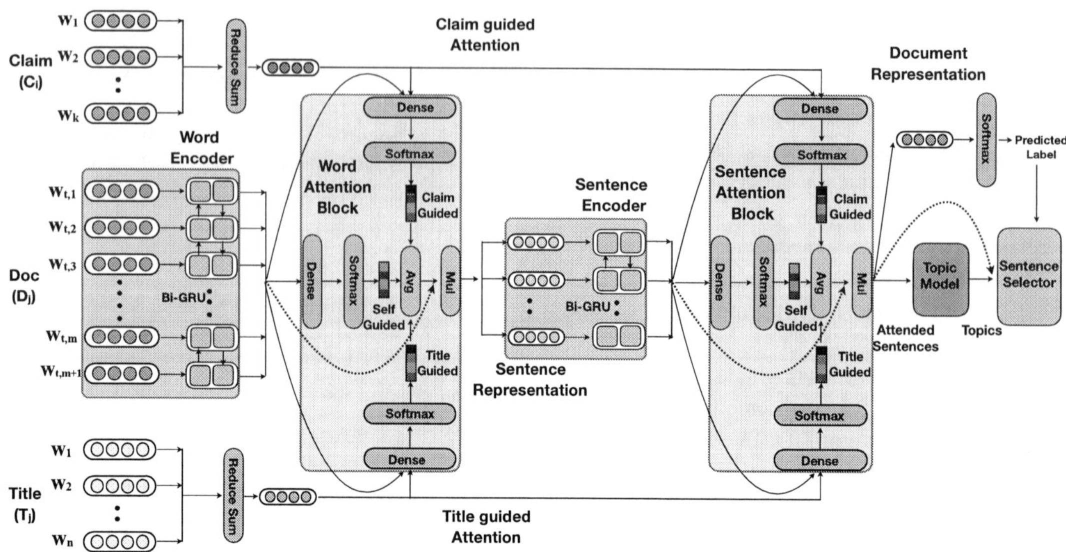

Figure 2: SUMO's neural network architecture for establishing the correctness of Web claims.

embeddings. W_a and b_a are the weight matrix and bias and α is the learned attention weight. However, during experiments, we observe that applying claim-based attention provides an inferior overall document representation. Therefore, we do not concatenate the claim and document embeddings before attention weight computation.

Each claim c_i is consists of l maximum number of words as $\{w_1, w_2, \ldots\ldots, w_l\}$. We represent each claim c_i as the summation of embeddings of all the words contained in it as: $Cl_i = \sum_{j=1}^{l} f(w_j)$, where $f(w_j)$ is the word embedding of the j_{th} word of claim c_i. Claim representation Cl_i and hidden states h_j from the GRU are used to **compute word-level claim-driven attention weights** as:

$$u_{j,i} = \tanh(W_{j,i} h_j + b_{j,i})$$
$$\alpha_{j,i}^{C} = \text{softmax}(u_{j,i}^{\top} Cl_i), \qquad (2)$$

where $W_{j,i}$ and $b_{j,i}$ are the weight matrix and bias, $\alpha_{j,i}^{C}$ is the word level claim driven attention weight vector, and $h_j = (h_{j,1}, h_{j,2}, ..., h_{j,l})^{\top}$ represents the tuple of all the hidden states of the words contained in the jth sentence. To **compute sentence level claim-driven attention weights**, we use claim representation Cl_i and hidden states h_j^S from the sentence level GRU units as concatenations of both forward and backward hidden states

$h_j^S = \overrightarrow{h_j^S} \parallel \overleftarrow{h_j^S}$ as follows:

$$u_j = \tanh(W_j h^S + b_{j,i})$$
$$\alpha_j^{C} = \text{softmax}(u_j^{\top} Cl_i), \qquad (3)$$

where W_j and b_j are the weight matrix and bias, $h^S = (h_1^S, h_2^S, ..., h_l^S)^{\top}$ is the combination of all hidden states from sentences, and $\alpha_j^{C} = (\alpha_{j,1}, \alpha_{j,2}, ..., \alpha_{j,k})^{\top}$ is the sentence level claim-driven attention weight vector for the jth document.

Title-driven Hierarchical Attention. The objective of using the document title is to guide the attention in capturing sections in the document that are more critical and relevant for the title. Articles convey multiple perspectives, often reflected in their titles. By title-driven attention, we attend to those words and sentences that are not covered in claim-driven attention. Title-driven attention at both word and sentence level can be computed in a similar fashion as claim-driven attention. Each title t_i is comprised of l maximum number of words as $\{w_1, w_2, \ldots, w_l\}$. We represent each claim t_i as the summation of embeddings of all the words contained in it as: $T_i = \sum_{j=1}^{l} f(w_j)$. Title-driven attention weights for both words and sentence level can be computed as follows:

$$
\begin{aligned}
u_{j,i} &= \tanh(W_{j,i}h_j + b_{j,i}) \\
\alpha_{j,i}^{T} &= \text{softmax}(u_{j,i}^{\top}T_i) \\
u_j &= \tanh(W_j h^S + b_{j,i}) \\
\alpha_j^{T} &= \text{softmax}(u_j^{\top}T_i).
\end{aligned}
\tag{4}
$$

Hierarchical Self-Attention. Self-attention is a simplistic form of attention. It tries to attend salient words in a sequence of words and salient sentences in a collection of sentences based on the self context of a sequence of words or a collection of sentences. In addition to claim-driven and title-driven attention, we apply self-attention to capture the unattended words and sentences which are not related to claim or title directly but are very useful for classification and summarization. Self-attention weights for both words and sentence level can be computed as follows:

$$
\begin{aligned}
u_{j,i} &= \tanh(W_{j,i}h_j + b_{j,i}) \\
\alpha_{j,i}^{Sl} &= \text{softmax}(u_{j,i}^{\top}) \\
u_j &= \tanh(W_j h^S + b_{j,i}) \\
\alpha_j^{Sl} &= \text{softmax}(u_j^{\top}),
\end{aligned}
\tag{5}
$$

where $\alpha_{j,i}^{Sl}$ and α_j^{Sl} are the self-attention weight vectors at word and sentence levels respectively.

Fusion of Attention Weights. We combine the attention weights from the three kinds of attention mechanisms: claim-driven, title-driven, and self-attention at both the word and sentence levels. At the word level, we set:

$$
\alpha_j = (\alpha_{j,i}^C + \alpha_{j,i}^T + \alpha_{j,i}^{Sl})/3
\tag{6}
$$

$$
S_j = \alpha_j^{\top}h_j,
\tag{7}
$$

where $\alpha_{j,i}^C$, $\alpha_{j,i}^T$, and $\alpha_{j,i}^{Sl}$ are the attention weight vectors from claim, title and self-attention at the word level. S_j is the formed sentence representation after overall attention for the jth sentence. At the sentence level, we set:

$$
\alpha_j^S = (\alpha_j^C + \alpha_j^T + \alpha_j^{Sl})/3
\tag{8}
$$

$$
doc = \alpha_j^{\top}h^S,
\tag{9}
$$

where α_j^C, α_j^T, and α_j^{Sl} are the attention weight vectors from claim, title, and self-attention at the sentence level, and doc is the formed document representation after overall attention.

Attention on top of Attention (Atop). Although the fusion of the three kinds of attention weights as an average of them works well, we realize that we lose some context by averaging. To deal with this issue, we use a novel attention on top of attention (Atop) method. We concatenate all three kinds of attentions α_{con} and α_{con}^S at both the word and sentence levels correspondingly. We apply a tanh activation based dense layer as a scoring function and subsequently, a softmax layer to compute attention weights for each of three kinds of attention:

$$
\begin{aligned}
\text{At word level:} \quad \alpha_{con} &= (\alpha_{j,i}^C \parallel \alpha_{j,i}^T \parallel \alpha_{j,i}^{Sl}) \\
u_{wa} &= \tanh(W_{wa}\alpha_{con} + b_{wa}) \\
\beta^w &= \text{softmax}(u_{wa}) \\
S_j &= \beta_1^w \alpha_{j,i}^C + \beta_2^w \alpha_{j,i}^T + \beta_3^w \alpha_{j,i}^{Sl} \\
\text{At sentence level:} \quad \alpha_{con}^S &= (\alpha_j^C \parallel \alpha_j^T \parallel \alpha_j^{Sl}) \\
u_{sa} &= \tanh(W_{sa}\alpha_{con}^S + b_{sa}) \\
\beta^s &= \text{softmax}(u_{sa}) \\
doc &= \beta_1^s \alpha_j^C + \beta_2^s \alpha_j^T + \beta_3^s \alpha_j^{Sl},
\end{aligned}
\tag{10}
$$

where β^w and β^s are the learned attention weight vectors for three kinds of attentions at the word and sentence levels, and doc is the formed document representation after Atop attention.

Prediction and Optimization. We use the overall document representation doc in a softmax layer for the classification. To train the model, we use standard softmax cross-entropy with logits as a loss function, we compute $\hat{y}$, the predicted label as:

$$
\hat{y} = \text{softmax}(W_{cl}doc + b_{cl}).
\tag{11}
$$

3.2 Generating Explainable Summary

Recent works retrieve documents from the Web as external evidence to support or refute the claims and thereafter extract snippets as explanations to model's decision (Mishra and Setty, 2019; Popat et al., 2018). However, the extracted snippets from these methods are often redundant and lack topical diversity. The objective of our summarization algorithm is to provide ranked list of sentences that are: novel, non-redundant, and diverse across the topics identified from the text of the documents. In this section, we outline the method we utilize for achieving this objective.

Multi-topic Sentence Model: Each sentence in the document that is retrieved against the claim is modeled as a collection of topics: $s =$

$\langle a^{(1)}, a^{(2)}, \ldots a^{(k)} \rangle$. Let $\mathcal{A}$ be the set of topics $a_i \in \mathcal{A}$ across all candidate sentences from all the pseudo relevant set of documents D for the claim.

Objective. We formulate the summarization task as a diversification objective. Given a set of relevant sentences $\mathcal{R}$ which are attended by Atop attention in SUMO while establishing the claim's correctness. We have to find the *smallest* subset of sentences $\mathcal{S} \subseteq \mathcal{R}$ such that *all* topics $a_i \in \mathcal{A}$ are covered. This is a variation of the Set Cover problem (Agrawal et al., 2009; Korte and Vygen, 2002; Vazirani, 2001; Williamson and Shmoys, 2011; Johnson, 1974; Lovász, 1975; Chvátal, 1979). However, unlike IA-Select (Agrawal et al., 2009) we do not choose to utilize the Max Coverage variation of the Set Cover problem. Instead, we formulate it as Set Cover itself (Korte and Vygen, 2002; Vazirani, 2001). That is, given a set of topics $\mathcal{A}$, find a minimal set of sentences $\mathcal{S} \subseteq \mathcal{R}$ that cover those topics (Vazirani, 2001). Additionally, the inclusion of each sentence in the subset $\mathcal{S}$ has a *cost* associated with it, given by:

$$cost(s) = (Score)^{-1}$$
$$Score = (\lambda \theta_s + (1 - \lambda)(W_{wa} + W_{sa})), \quad (12)$$

where θ_s is the topic distribution score for sentence s computed using a topic model (e.g., Latent Dirichlet Allocation (Blei et al., 2003)), $W_{wa} = \sum_{i=1}^{l} W_{wa}(i)$ is the average of attention weights of the words contained in sentence s, W_{sa} is the attention weight of the sentence s, and λ is a parameter to be tuned. We briefly describe our adaptation of the Greedy algorithm, which provides an approximate solution to the Set Cover problem, based on the discussion in (Korte and Vygen, 2002; Vazirani, 2001; Williamson and Shmoys, 2011; Johnson, 1974; Lovász, 1975; Chvátal, 1979).

4 Evaluation

Datasets. We use two publicly available datasets, namely PolitiFact political claims dataset and Snopes political claims dataset (Popat et al., 2018) for evaluating SUMO's capability for fact checking. Dataset statistics for both the datasets are shown in Table 1. In the case of Politifact, claims have one of the following labels, namely: 'true', 'mostly true', 'half true', 'mostly false', 'false', and 'pants-on-fire,'. We convert 'true', 'mostly true', and 'half true' labels to the 'true' and the rest of them to

---

Algorithm 1: Adaption of the approximate Greedy algorithm for Set Cover problem from (Korte and Vygen, 2002; Vazirani, 2001; Williamson and Shmoys, 2011; Johnson, 1974; Lovász, 1975; Chvátal, 1979) to our topical diversification problem setting. At each iteration, a sentence is chosen that covers the most number of topics reflected by topic distribution score and has the highest attention weights. As an output, we are assured a non-redundant, novel, and a diversified set of sentences.

```
Input:  A: Set of topics learned from the topic model
        for diversification.
        R: Set of sentences, attended by Atop.
Output: S ⊆ R: Diversified set of sentences over A
S ← φ        // S contains diversified
  sentences
A' ← φ // A' contains topics covered
  by S
while A' ≠ A do
    /* identify the sentence that
       covers the most topics and is
       highly relevant for
       fact-checking           */
    s* ← arg min  cost(s)/|A−T'|
         s∈R\S
    A' ← A' ∪ {a_s*}        // a_s* is the
      dominant topic of sentence s*
    S ← S ∪ s*
end
```

Table 1: Dataset Statistics

PUBLIC DATASETS		
STATISTICS	POLITIFACT	SNOPES
#CLAIMS	3568	4341
#DOCUMENTS	29556	29242
#DOMAINS	3028	3267
NEW DATASETS		
STATISTICS	CLIMATE	HEALTH
#CLAIMS	104	100
#DOCUMENTS	1050	978
#DOMAINS	97	83

'false' label. For the Snopes dataset, each claim has either 'true' or 'false' as a label.

We evaluate SUMO for the task of summarization on PolitiFact, Snopes, Climate, and Health datasets. The two new datasets, Climate and Health, are about climate change and health care respectively. We test SUMO only on the PolitiFact and Snopes dataset for the task of fact checking as they are magnitudes larger than the new datasets that we release. The climate change dataset contains claims broadly related to climate change and global warming from `climatefeedback.org`. We use each claim as a query using Google API to search the Web and retrieve external evidences in the form of search results. Similarly, we create a dataset related to health

The figure box contains the following examples:

Figure 3: Examples from climate change and health care dataset

care that additionally contains claims pertaining to the current global COVID-19 pandemic from `healthfeedback.org`. Examples of claims from these two datasets are shown in Figure 3. We make the new datasets, publicly available to the research community at the following URL: `https://github.com/rahul0mishra/SUMO/`.

SUMO Implementation. We use TensorFlow to implement SUMO. We use per class accuracy and macro F_1 scores as performance metrics for evaluation. We use bi-directional Gated Recurrent Unit (GRU) with a hidden size of 200, word2vec (Mikolov et al., 2013), and GloVe (Pennington et al., 2014) embeddings with embedding size of 200 and softmax cross-entropy with logits as the loss function. We keep the learning rate as 0.001, batch size as 64, and gradient clipping as 5. All the parameters are tuned using a grid search. We use 50 epochs for each model and apply early stopping if validation loss does not change for more than 5 epochs. We keep maximum sentence length as 45 and maximum number of sentences in a document as 35. For the task of summarization, we use Latent Dirichlet Allocation (LDA) (Blei et al., 2003) as a topic model to compute topic distribution scores and the dominant topic for each candidate sentence.

5 Results

5.1 Setup for the Task of Claim Correctness

We experiment with five variants of our proposed SUMO model and compare with six state-of-the-art methods. The six state-of-the-art methods are as follows. First, we have the basic Long Short Term Memory (LSTM) (Hochreiter and Schmidhuber, 1997)) unit which is used with claim and document contents for classification. Second, we have a convolutional neural network (CNN) (Kim, 2014) for document classification. Third, we compare against the model proposed in (Tang et al., 2015) that uses a hierarchical representation of the documents using hierarchical LSTM units (Hi-LSTM). Fourth, we compare against the model proposed in (Yang et al., 2016) that uses a hierarchical neural attention on top of hierarchical LSTMs (HAN) to learn better representations of documents for classification. Fifth, we compare against the model proposed in (Popat et al., 2018) that uses a claim guided attention method (DeClarE) for correctness prediction of claims in the presence of external evidences. Sixth and finally, we compare against the recent work (Mishra and Setty, 2019) that improves on DeClarE method by using latent aspects (speaker, topic, or domain) based attention.

The proposed five variants of our method SUMO are as follows. First, we have the SUMO-AW2V variant that corresponds to the basic SUMO model with word2vec embeddings. Second, we have SUMO-AtopW2V variant consists of the SUMO model with WORD2VEC embeddings. Furthermore, in SUMO-AtopW2V we use Atop method of attention fusion rather than a simple average. Third, we have the SUMO-AGlove variant, which is the basic SUMO model that uses GloVe embeddings. Fourth, we have the SUMO-AtopGlove variant, that consists of the SUMO model with GloVe embeddings. Moreover, in SUMO-AtopGlove, we use Atop method of attention fusion rather than a simple average. Fifth and finally, we have the SUMO-AtopGlove+source-Emb variant that is similar to SUMO-AtopGlove however with additional source embeddings (domains of retrieved documents).

5.2 Claim Correctness Task Results

The results for establishing claim correctness are shown in Table 2. We observe that the basic LSTM based model achieves 57.89% and 69.89% in terms of macro F_1 accuracy in prediction of claim correctness for POLITIFACT and SNOPES, respec-

Table 2: Comparison of the proposed models with various state of the art baseline models for two publicly available datasets.

POLITIFACT				SNOPES			
Model	**True Accuracy**	**False Accuracy**	**Macro F_1**	**Model**	**True Accuracy**	**False Accuracy**	**Macro F_1**
LSTM	53.51	56.32	57.89	LSTM	69.23	70.67	69.89
CNN	55.92	57.33	59.39	CNN	72.05	74.29	72.63
HAN	60.13	65.78	63.44	HAN	72.89	76.25	73.84
DeClarE (full)	68.18	66.01	67.10	DeClarE (full)	60.16	80.78	70.47
SADHAN-agg	68.37	78.23	75.69	SADHAN-agg	79.47	84.26	80.09
SUMO-AW2V	67.30	69.22	70.74	SUMO-AW2V	77.32	80.67	75.56
SUMO-AtopW2V	67.81	70.09	71.15	SUMO-AtopW2V	78.02	81.66	76.86
SUMO-AGlove	68.03	72.57	72.39	SUMO-AGlove	78.74	82.03	77.22
SUMO-AtopGlove	68.93	73.43	72.79	SUMO-AtopGlove	78.89	82.46	78.45
SUMO-AtopGlove+source-Emb	**69.33**	**80.08**	**77.69**	SUMO-AtopGlove+source-Emb	**81.29**	**86.82**	**82.93**

tively. The CNN model performs slightly better than LSTM as it captures the local contextual features better. The hierarchical attention network outperforms CNN with macro F_1 accuracy of 63.4% and 73.84%. The reason for this improvement is hierarchical representation using word and sentence level attention. The state of the art DeClarE model provides significant improvements on baseline methods with macro F_1 accuracy of 67.10% and 70.47%. This gain can be attributed to claim guided attention and source embeddings. However, we observe that this design of claim based attention is not very effective. The more recent work, SADHAN improves on DeClarE, which uses a similar design for claim-oriented attention and incorporates a more comprehensive structure by using several latent aspects to guide attention.

SADHAN outperforms DeClarE with macro F_1 accuracy of 75.69% and 80.09%, respectively. Interestingly, we observe that the basic SUMO model with word2vec embeddings performs better than DeClarE with source embeddings. This observation is a clear indication of the superiority of our claim- and title-driven attention design. The SUMO with Atop attention fusion is more effective than a simple average fusion of attention weights, which becomes apparent from the gain in macro F_1 accuracy in both the datasets. SUMO with pertained GloVe embeddings outperforms the word2vec versions of SUMO as the GloVe embeddings are trained on a large corpus and therefore captures better context for the words. SUMO-AtopGlove+source-Emb outperforms all the other models and it is statistically significant with a p-value of 2.79×10^{-3} for POLITIFACT and 3.09×10^{-4} for SNOPES. The statistical significance values were computed using a two sample Student's t-test. We notice that SUMO could not outperform SADHAN without source embeddings, as SADHAN uses the very complex structure, having three parallel models with hier-

archical latent aspects guide attention. However, SADHAN has many drawbacks. First, it is challenging to train and requires more hardware resources and time. Second, the latent aspects are not available for all the Web claims. Therefore, it is not generalizable. Third, it fails to accommodate new values of latent variables at the test time.

5.3 Setup for the Task of Summarization

For the evaluation of the summarization capability of SUMO, we create gold reference summaries for claims. For creating the gold reference summaries, we include all the facts related to the claim, which are important for the claim correctness prediction, non-redundant, and topically diverse. We find that the descriptions provided for a claim on fact-checking websites such as `snopes.com` and `politifact.com` are suitable for this purpose. We use cosine similarity score of 0.4 between claims and sentences of description to filter out irrelevant or noisy sentences. As evaluation metrics, we use ROUGE-1, ROUGE-2, and ROUGE-L scores. The ROUGE-1 score represents the overlap of unigrams, while the ROUGE-2 score represents the overlap of bigrams between the summaries generated by the SUMO system and gold reference summaries. The ROUGE-L score measures the longest matching sequence of words using Longest Common Sub-sequence algorithm.

Standard summarization techniques are not useful in such a scenario as the objective of summarization with standard techniques is usually not fact-checking. Hence, we compare the SUMO results with an information retrieval (BM25) and a natural language processing based method (Query-Sum). BM25 is a ranking function, which uses a probabilistic retrieval framework and ranks the documents based on their relevance to a given search query. We use Web claims as a query and apply BM25 to get the most relevant sentences from all

Table 3: Results for the Task of Summarization.

Model	ROUGE-1	ROUGE-2	ROUGE-L
BM25	26.08	14.78	29.98
QuerySum	29.78	16.49	30.16
SUMO	**33.89**	**19.21**	**35.92**

the documents retrieved for the claim. We also compare the results with the query-driven attention based abstractive summarization method Query-Sum (Nema et al., 2017), which also uses a diversity objective to create a diverse summary. We use ROUGE metrics with a gold reference summary to evaluate the generated summaries.

5.4 Comparison of Summarization Results

Results for the task of summarization are shown in Table 3, the QuerySum method performs significantly better than BM25 with a ROUGE-L score of 30.16 as it uses query-driven attention and diversity objective, which results in a diverse and query oriented summary. The proposed model SUMO outperforms QuerySum with a ROUGE-L score of 35.92. We attribute this gain to the use of word and sentence level weights, which are trained using back-propagation with correctness label. We also notice that in QuerySum some sentences are related to the claim but are not useful for fact checking. Therefore, they are absent in the gold reference summary. The results for SUMO are statistically significant (p-value $= 1.39 \times 10^{-4}$) using a pairwise Student's t-test.

6 Conclusion

We presented SUMO, a neural network based approach to generate explainable and topically diverse summaries for verifying Web claims. SUMO uses an improved version of hierarchical claim-driven attention along with title-driven and self-attention to learn an effective representation of the external evidences retrieved from the Web. Learning this effective representation in turn assists us in establishing the correctness of textual claims. Using the overall attention weights from the novel Atop attention method and topical distributions of the sentences, we generate extractive summaries for the claims. In addition to this, we release two important datasets pertaining to climate change and healthcare claims.

In future, we plan to investigate the BERT (Devlin et al., 2019) and other Transformer (Vaswani et al., 2017) architecture based embedding meth-ods in place of GloVe (Pennington et al., 2014) embeddings for better contextual representation of words.

References

Rakesh Agrawal, Sreenivas Gollapudi, Alan Halverson, and Samuel Ieong. 2009. Diversifying search results. In *Proceedings of the Second ACM International Conference on Web Search and Data Mining*, WSDM '09, page 5–14, New York, NY, USA. Association for Computing Machinery.

Pepa Atanasova, Jakob Grue, Simonsen Christina, and Lioma Isabelle. 2019. Generating Fact Checking Explanations.

David M. Blei, Andrew Y. Ng, and Michael I. Jordan. 2003. Latent dirichlet allocation. *J. Mach. Learn. Res.*, 3(null):993–1022.

Carlos Castillo, Marcelo Mendoza, and Barbara Poblete. 2011. Information credibility on twitter. In *WWW*.

Vasek Chvátal. 1979. A greedy heuristic for the set-covering problem. *Math. Oper. Res.*, 4(3):233–235.

Jacob Devlin, Ming-Wei Chang, Kenton Lee, and Kristina Toutanova. 2019. BERT: Pre-training of deep bidirectional transformers for language understanding. pages 4171–4186, Minneapolis, Minnesota. Association for Computational Linguistics.

Sepp Hochreiter and Schmidhuber. 1997. Long short-term memory. volume 9, page 1735–1780, Cambridge, MA, USA. MIT Press.

David S. Johnson. 1974. Approximation algorithms for combinatorial problems. *J. Comput. Syst. Sci.*, 9(3):256–278.

Yoon Kim. 2014. Convolutional neural networks for sentence classification. In *Proceedings of the 2014 Conference on Empirical Methods in Natural Language Processing (EMNLP)*, pages 1746–1751, Doha, Qatar. Association for Computational Linguistics.

Bernhard Korte and Jens Vygen. 2002. Approximation algorithms. In *Combinatorial Optimization: Theory and Algorithms*, pages 361–396, Berlin, Heidelberg. Springer Berlin Heidelberg.

László Lovász. 1975. On the ratio of optimal integral and fractional covers. *Discret. Math.*, 13(4):383–390.

Jing Ma, Wei Gao, Prasenjit Mitra, Sejeong Kwon, Bernard J. Jansen, Kam-Fai Wong, and Meeyoung Cha. 2016. Detecting rumors from microblogs with recurrent neural networks. In *Proceedings of the Twenty-Fifth International Joint Conference on Artificial Intelligence*, IJCAI'16, page 3818–3824. AAAI Press.

Jing Ma, Wei Gao, Zhongyu Wei, Yueming Lu, and Kam-Fai Wong. 2015. Detect rumors using time series of social context information on microblogging websites. CIKM '15, page 1751–1754.

Jing Ma, Wei Gao, and Kam-Fai Wong. 2018. Detect rumor and stance jointly by neural multi-task learning. WWW '18, page 585–593, Republic and Canton of Geneva, CHE. International World Wide Web Conferences Steering Committee.

Tomas Mikolov, Ilya Sutskever, Kai Chen, Greg Corrado, and Jeffrey Dean. 2013. Distributed representations of words and phrases and their compositionality. In *Proceedings of the 26th International Conference on Neural Information Processing Systems - Volume 2*, NIPS'13, page 3111–3119, Red Hook, NY, USA. Curran Associates Inc.

Rahul Mishra and Vinay Setty. 2019. Sadhan: Hierarchical attention networks to learn latent aspect embeddings for fake news detection. ICTIR '19, page 197–204.

Preksha Nema, Mitesh M. Khapra, Anirban Laha, and Balaraman Ravindran. 2017. Diversity driven attention model for query-based abstractive summarization. In *Proceedings of the 55th Annual Meeting of the Association for Computational Linguistics (Volume 1: Long Papers)*, pages 1063–1072, Vancouver, Canada. Association for Computational Linguistics.

Ankur P. Parikh, Oscar Täckström, Dipanjan Das, and Jakob Uszkoreit. 2016. A Decomposable Attention Model for Natural Language Inference.

Jeffrey Pennington, Richard Socher, and Christopher D. Manning. 2014. Glove: Global vectors for word representation. In *EMNLP*.

Kashyap Popat, Subhabrata Mukherjee, Jannik Strötgen, and Gerhard Weikum. 2017. Where the truth lies: Explaining the credibility of emerging claims on the web and social media. In *WWW*, pages 1003–1012.

Kashyap Popat, Subhabrata Mukherjee, Andrew Yates, and Gerhard Weikum. 2018. Declare: Debunking fake news and false claims using evidence-aware deep learning. In *EMNLP*, pages 22–32.

Martin Potthast, Johannes Kiesel, Kevin Reinartz, Janek Bevendorff, and Benno Stein. 2018. A stylometric inquiry into hyperpartisan and fake news. In *ACL*, volume 1, pages 231–240.

Vahed Qazvinian, Emily Rosengren, Dragomir R. Radev, and Qiaozhu Mei. 2011. Rumor has it: Identifying misinformation in microblogs. EMNLP '11.

Feng Qian, Chengyue Gong, Karishma Sharma, and Yan Liu. 2018. Neural user response generator: Fake news detection with collective user intelligence. IJCAI '18, pages 3834–3840.

Hannah Rashkin, Eunsol Choi, Jin Yea Jang, Svitlana Volkova, and Yejin Choi. 2017. Truth of varying shades: Analyzing language in fake news and political fact-checking. In *Proceedings of the 2017 Conference on Empirical Methods in Natural Language Processing*, pages 2931–2937, Copenhagen, Denmark. Association for Computational Linguistics.

Kai Shu, Suhang Wang, and Huan Liu. 2019. Beyond news contents: The role of social context for fake news detection. In *Proceedings of the Twelfth ACM International Conference on Web Search and Data Mining*, WSDM '19, page 312–320, New York, NY, USA. Association for Computing Machinery.

Duyu Tang, Bing Qin, and Ting Liu. 2015. Document modeling with gated recurrent neural network for sentiment classification. In *Proceedings of the 2015 Conference on Empirical Methods in Natural Language Processing*, pages 1422–1432, Lisbon, Portugal. Association for Computational Linguistics.

Ashish Vaswani, Noam Shazeer, Niki Parmar, Jakob Uszkoreit, Llion Jones, Aidan N. Gomez, Lukasz Kaiser, and Illia Polosukhin. 2017. Attention is all you need. abs/1706.03762.

Vijay V. Vazirani. 2001. Approximation algorithms. New York, NY, USA. Springer-Verlag New York, Inc.

David P. Williamson and David B. Shmoys. 2011. The design of approximation algorithms. New York, NY, USA. Cambridge University Press.

Brian Xu, Mitra Mohtarami, and James Glass. 2018. Adversarial Domain Adaptation for Stance Detection. (Nips):1–6.

Shuo Yang, Kai Shu, Suhang Wang, Renjie Gu, Fan Wu, and Huan Liu. 2019. Unsupervised fake news detection on social media: A generative approach.

Zichao Yang, Diyi Yang, Chris Dyer, Xiaodong He, Alex Smola, and Eduard Hovy. 2016. Hierarchical attention networks for document classification. In *NAACL: HLT*, pages 1480–1489.

Intelligent Analyses on Storytelling for Impact Measurement

Koen Kicken
KU Leuven
kicken.koen@gmail.com

Tessa De Maesschalck
KU Leuven
tessa.dema@telenet.be

Bart Vanrumste
KU Leuven
bart.vanrumste@kuleuven.be

Tom De Keyser
Kunlabora
tom.dekeyser@kunlabora.be

Hee Reen Shim
KU Leuven
heereen.shim@kuleuven.be

Abstract

This paper explores how Dutch diary fragments, written by family coaches in the social sector, can be analysed automatically using machine learning techniques to quantitatively measure the impact of social coaching. The focus lays on two tasks: determining which sentiment a fragment contains (sentiment analysis) and investigating which fundamental social rights (education, employment, legal aid, etc.) are addressed in the fragment. To train and test the new algorithms, a dataset consisting of 1715 Dutch diary fragments is used. These fragments are manually labelled on sentiment and on the applicable fundamental social rights. The sentiment analysis models were trained to classify the fragments into three classes: negative, neutral or positive. Fine-tuning the Dutch pre-trained Bidirectional Encoder Representations from Transformers (BERTje) (de Vries et al., 2019) language model surpassed the more classic algorithms by correctly classifying 79.6% of the fragments on the sentiment analysis, which is considered as a good result. This technique also achieved the best results in the identification of the fundamental rights, where for every fragment the three most likely fundamental rights were given as output. In this way, 93% of the present fundamental rights were correctly recognised. To our knowledge, we are the first to try to extract social rights from written text with the help of Natural Language Processing techniques.

1 Introduction

In Leuven, Belgium, there are many charitable organisations that support socially vulnerable people. For evaluating the progress of their work, each of them has their own system, mostly handwritten on paper. In 2018, the local community organisation *vzw Buurtwerk 't Lampeke* started a cooperation with software company *Kunlabora*. They wanted to obtain qualitative insights in their coaching, since they were lumbered with a lot of administration. The result was a tailor-made software tool named *Mezuri*[1], a Java application for organisations supporting socially vulnerable people to understand and measure the impact of their coaching tracks. In this tool, collaborators called *bridging coaches* can keep diary fragments (written in Dutch) for different families. In this way, the bridging coaches can, with the help of intelligent analyses, keep track of how the family is doing and which fundamental social rights (regarding education, work, etc.) are acquired. The most important aspect of Mezuri is that these diaries have open-ended instead of closed-ended inputs. This allows the coaches of the organisations to write free text and focus on the family instead of having to tick boxes or fill in scales. It is then the task of the Mezuri programme itself to get more objective, scale-like information out of these text fragments with the help of intelligent analyses.

In this paper, there is a focus on improving the following two algorithms important for the bridging coaches:

1. **Sentiment analysis:** To find out how a family is doing, Mezuri determines how positive or how negative a diary fragment is.

2. **Extracting the social rights:** Social rights are basic rights every human should have, for example legal assistance, healthcare and education. There are eight of them (see Table 2) and the bridging coaches strive to accomplish them for every family. To this end, it is important to know on which rights they have already focused.

---

[1] https://www.kunlabora.be/blog/2018/11/15/mezuri-1.0-is-live/

Proceedings of the 2020 EMNLP Workshop W-NUT: The Sixth Workshop on Noisy User-generated Text, pages 91–100
Online, Nov 19, 2020. ©2020 Association for Computational Linguistics

This paper investigates which algorithms obtain the most accurate analysis on these Dutch text fragments. This involves several challenges. Firstly, little data exists and the available data are private. Secondly, the diary fragments consist of subjective information which is also not always 100% correct: sometimes, a family does not immediately tell the truth or perhaps glosses over reality. This make it even more difficult to objectify and quantify the information written in the diary fragments.

Contributions   1) We show that by fine-tuning the existing BERTje language model on classifying a Dutch diary fragment into three classes (negative, neutral, positive) an accuracy of 80% can be reached. 2) We show that this technique can also be used to fine-tune the model to recognise fundamental rights: when for every fragment the three most likely rights are given as output, 93% of the present rights are correctly recognised.

2   Background and Related work

Sentiment Analysis (SA) is a hot topic in Natural Language Processing (NLP). It is often used on reviews or social media posts to monitor the reputation of a service, person or product. A text fragment is then classified as positive or negative (i.e. binary classification) or, in case of a ternary classification, as neutral.

In the past, often lexicon-based (Aaldering and Vliegenthart, 2016) or machine learning with bag-of-words (Pang et al., 2002) approaches were used for sentiment analysis. More recently, the use of embeddings (Rudkowsky et al., 2018) and neural networks became more popular (Prabha and Umarani Srikanth, 2019) in NLP. However, a disadvantage of using neural networks is the large amount of training data they require, which can be limited by using transfer learning. In NLP, this is often done using pre-trained language models. BERT (Bidirectional Encoder Representations from Transformers) is such a language model made available by Google (Devlin et al., 2018). BERT has proven to achieve state-of-the-art results on various tasks including sentiment analysis, as in the study of Munikar et al. (2019) where English 1-sentence movie reviews were classified into 5 classes, reaching accuracies of up to 84%. Therefore, it is investigated whether this approach can also achieve high performance on sentiment analysis with the Mezuri dataset. However, the dataset of this paper contains Dutch text fragments and mostly longer than one

sentence, making the task more complex.

Since December 2019, there also exists a Dutch BERT model *BERTje* (de Vries et al., 2019). Trained on 2.4 billion Dutch tokens, this monolingual model outperforms BERT's equally-sized multilingual model in various tasks, including sentiment analysis. To this end, BERTje will be used instead of the multi-language version of BERT.

There is a lot of research done on SA in other use-cases. For example, Gräbner et al. (2012) classified customer reviews of hotels as *good* or *bad* (i.e. binary classification) with a Lexicon-based approach yielding an accuracy of 90%. Bouazizi and Ohtsuki (2016) uses machine learning algorithms to classify tweets into 3 different classes achieving an accuracy equal to 70%. However, the task in Mezuri is more difficult than the task in Gräbner et al. (2012) in several ways. Firstly, in Mezuri, a fragment is classified into three classes instead of two. Secondly, the fragments in Mezuri are written in Dutch, a language on which less research has been done than on English. Lastly, assigning labels to the fragments of Mezuri is a subjective task, while when two people label reviews or social media posts, they will probably reach a higher agreement score.

To our knowledge, we are the first to try to extract social rights from written text. This is considered a multi-label problem, as a single fragment can contain multiple social rights. The task is then to predict the *set* of correct labels. This is different from the sentiment analysis task, where a fragment belongs to a single class. According to Madjarov et al. (2012), there are three ways to tackle the multi-label classification problem: adapt the method, transform the problem and ensembles.

As described by Szymański and Kajdanowicz (2017), the first method is based on the idea to adapt the single-label methods in a way they can cope with multi-labelled data. A method that uses this principal is *Multi-label k Nearest Neighbours (MLkNN)* (Szymański and Kajdanowicz, 2017). An advantage of this method is that the correlations between the labels are taken into account.

The second idea is to transform the multi-label problem into multiple single-label problems. *Binary Relevance*, *Classifier Chains* and *Label Powerset* (Szymański and Kajdanowicz, 2017) use this approach.

A third manner of extracting social rights in a supervised way is with ensemble methods. An example is *RAkEL (Szymański and Kajdanowicz, 2017)*, where random k-labelsets are given to the Label Powerset method.

3 Dataset

About ten bridging coaches of *CAW Oost-Brabant* and *Werfgezinscoach* wrote the diary fragments in which they reflect on a meeting with a family. Together they coached nineteen families, from which they made 460 high-quality, Dutch text fragments available. For this project, they anonimysed these text fragments by replacing the names with initials. The original diary fragments have an average of about 188 words per diary fragment with a standard deviation of 198.

3.1 Splitting the dataset

First, the diary fragments are split into smaller fragments since it enlarges the number of fragments, as more training examples generally means better performance of machine learning models. Moreover, it makes it easier to label a fragment since a longer fragment often consists of multiple parts talking about different subjects, making it more complex. This splitting is done automatically on every new line character (\n). This splitting enlarged the dataset from 460 to 1715 fragments. Figure 1 shows the variation in length of this new dataset, with a new average length of 50 words and standard deviation of 47.5.

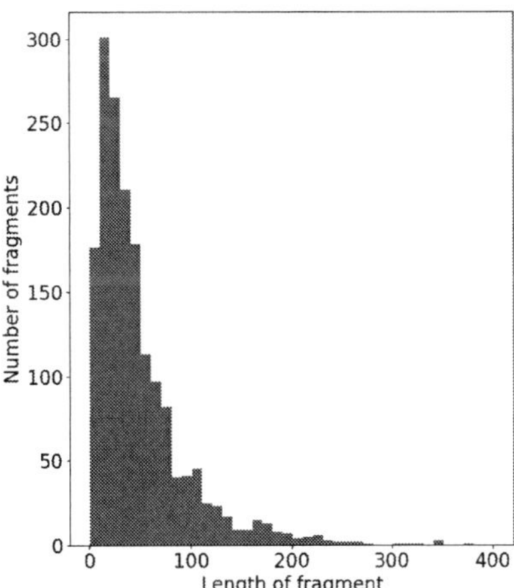

Figure 1: Distribution of the length of the fragments (in words) after splitting the original dataset

3.2 Labelling the dataset

Sentiment labels Every fragment is manually labelled (-1, 0 or 1) describing the sentiment going from negative (-1) to positive (1), with 0 representing a neutral fragment. However, assigning a label to each fragment is a subjective task: different people label some fragments differently than others. To quantify and inspect these differences, two people labelled the dataset. When analysing the labels, 16.4% (i.e. 271 fragments) were found to be labelled differently. 1.6% was even labelled inversely: a fragment once labelled as being positive, once as being negative. For determining the final label, these differences were discussed to come to a consensus on the best suitable label. Table 1 shows some examples of fragments that were labelled differently. This shows that capturing the overall sentiment of a diary fragment is a rather complex and subjective task. When splitting in a training and a test set, all fragments are shuffled and divided randomly.

The result is a dataset with 1715 fragments labelled on their sentiment. Figure 2 shows the distribution among the different labels. This makes clear that this dataset has more negative than positive fragments.

Pauze. Iets gezellig gaan drinken in café X. Het is één van de weinige cafés waar X nog binnen mag. Hoe lang zou dat nog duren?   *(Break. Going for a cozy drink in bar x. It is one of the few places where x is still welcome. But for how long?)*
Schriftelijk is inderdaad moeilijker. Hij schrijft zeer onbeholpen, een beetje op het niveau van de lagere school. Spelling is ook erg moeilijk voor hem. Hij maakt wel vooruitgang, mede omdat hij zo gemotiveerd is. Zijn handschrift wordt met de week leesbaarder en hij begint de juiste strategieën toe te passen voor spelling   *(Writing is indeed more difficult. Spelling is also very hard for him. He does make progress, partly because he is so motivated. His handwriting is becoming more readable and he starts to apply the right strategies.)*
De ouders hebben al veel samen gepraat en gehuild. Ze hebben veel verdriet. Ik benoem deze sterkte want emotie tonen is geen evidentie voor papa   *(The parents have already talked and cried a lot together. They are very sad. I mention this strength because showing emotion is not obvious for dad.)*
Het valt me op hoe vaak er iemand ziek is van het gezin. Gelukkig kan er steeds beroep gedaan worden op de huisarts.   *(I notice how often someone is sick in the family. Fortunately, the doctor can always be called upon.)*
In de auto vraag hij nog even het Frans te oefenen met hem. Het gaat echter nog altijd heel moeizaam.   *(In the car, he asks to practice French with him. However, it is still very difficult for him.)*
De ouders hadden veel problemen veroorzaakt op de school. Maar de school heeft deze ondertussen kunnen oplossen.   *(The parents had caused many problems at the school. But the school has now been able to solve these.)*

Table 1: Examples of fragments that are labelled differently

Social right labels In addition to the sentiment label, the social rights are labelled in every fragment. There are eight social rights defined (see

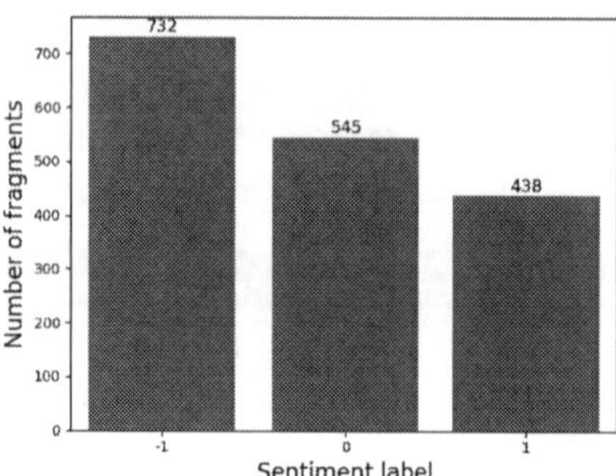

Figure 2: Distribution among the sentiment labels

ID	Social right
0	legal assistance
1	sports, games, leisure, culture
2	belonging, network reinforcement
3	health
4	financial and material support
5	education and training
6	work, internship
7	healthy and affordable home
8	not applicable / miscellaneous

Table 2: The possible social rights

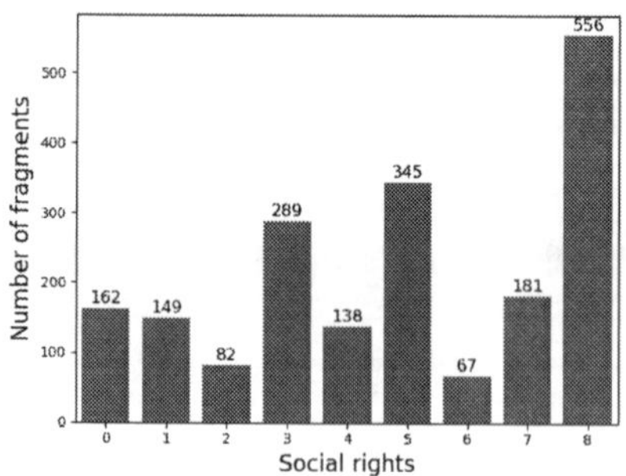

Figure 3: Chart showing in how many fragments the different social rights occur

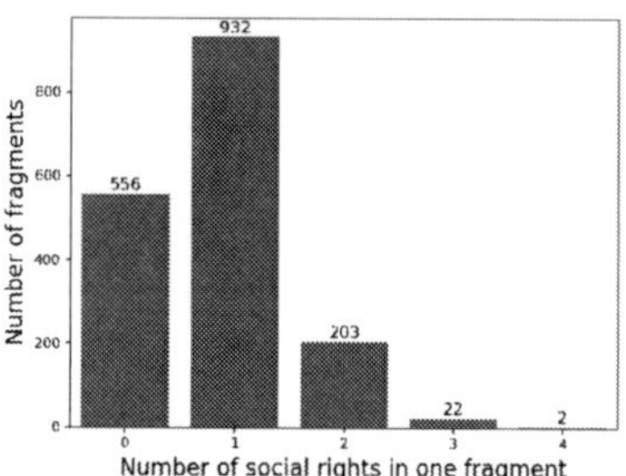

Figure 4: Distribution of the number of social rights in a fragment (one fragment can contain several social rights)

Table 2). This task was considered as less subjective than labelling the sentiment of a fragment, and hence it was not investigated what the agreement would be between different people labelling the same fragments. Figure 3 shows how many fragments there are for each social right. In this figure, one can see that the distribution among these social rights is not balanced.

Every fragment may contain none, one or several social rights. A fragment may, for example, contain some sentences about school and some sentences about health, which are 2 different social rights. Figure 4 shows that in most fragments there is only one right present and that there are 215 fragments in which there are 2 social rights mentioned. On the other hand, it is also possible that a fragment does not contain any social right. The fragment is then labelled as category 8: not applicable or miscellaneous. This is the case for 556 fragments.

4 Methods

Before feeding the data to the Machine Learning model, the data needs to be standardised. This can be done by removing the special characters and the unnecessary blank spaces. Furthermore, the replacement of capital letters by lowercase letters, the removal of stop words and stemming or lemmatisation (Jurafsky and Martin, 2014) is investigated. To avoid bias (i.e. assigning a sentiment to gender specific pronouns), personal pronouns and names

(i.e. initials) of persons are replaced by the words *persoon* (*person*) and *naam* (*name*) respectively.

Next, the text fragments need to be vectorised (i.e. transformed into a numerical representation). In this paper, this is performed in two ways. Firstly, with a bag-of-words (BOW) approach (Jurafsky and Martin, 2014) and secondly, with word embeddings (Levy and Goldberg, 2014).

4.1 Algorithms for sentiment analysis

Previously used algorithm - Pattern In the past, Pattern (De Smedt and Daelemans, 2012) was used to perform the sentiment analysis in Mezuri. It returns a continuous score between -1 (very negative) and +1 (very positive). The algorithm is based on a lexicon of adjectives and then calculates a score based on the presence of certain adjectives, as mentioned by De Smedt and Daelemans (2012).

Fine-tuning BERTje In this paper, the Dutch pre-trained language model BERTje (de Vries et al., 2019), which has the same architecture as BERT (Devlin et al., 2018), is used. To fine-tune BERTje on this specific task (classifying a diary fragment as being negative, neutral or positive), first the data is standardised as mentioned above. Then, every fragment is split into tokens and to the start of every fragment and to the end of each sentence, the tokens *[CLS]* and *[SEP]* are added respectively. Finally, the tokens are mapped to their vector representation. For more information on how this is performed, consult the paper of Devlin et al. (2018).

Next, all fragments are truncated so that they have the same length. In case the fragment consists of too many tokens, the last ones are ignored, in case the fragment is too short, it is padded with zeros. The ideal length for this is examined by varying it, see section 6.1.

For fine-tuning, an additional pooler layer (with a linear layer and a $tanh$ as activation function) and an extra single linear layer are added on top of BERTje for classification, as Figure 5 shows. These linear layers apply a linear transformation on the data ($y = xA^T + b$, with x the input vector of dimension 768, and y the output vector of dimension 768 for the pooler layer, and dimension 3 for the classification layer). For these layers, only the vector corresponding to the *[CLS]* token is used, since BERT is trained to use this vector for classification tasks (Devlin et al., 2018). This is possible thanks to the transformer encoder layers where the whole fragment gets encoded in this single 768-wide vector. The activation and classification layers are added using a model named *BertForSequenceClassification* from Transformers (a package from Hugging Face which provides an interface to efficiently work with pre-trained language models, provided by Wolf et al. (2019)).

Then, the network is trained using the AdamW optimisation algorithm (Kingma and Ba, 2017). For training, the data is divided in batches of size 16. To find the optimal number of epochs, this number is varied. The learning rate is set to 2e-5, which was found by Sun et al. (2019) to be a good number to avoid catastrophic forgetting. Another method to avoid this is to *freeze* certain layers of the model. The parameters of a frozen layer then no longer change when fine-tuning on a specific task. Often, the lower layers are frozen, as also performed by Lee et al. (2019). Therefore, in this paper it is investigated what the influence is of freezing the first N layers.

4.2 Algorithms for extracting social rights

Extracting socials rights is considered as a multi-label problem as a single fragment can contain multiple social rights (see Figure 4). To solve this prob-lem, MLkNN, Binary Relevance, Classifier Chains, Label Powerset and RAkEL are used (Szymański and Kajdanowicz, 2017), as explained in section 2.

However, apart from all these methods, BERTje is also fine-tuned on the task of extracting the social rights. This is done using Simple Transformers[2], a library built on top of the Huggingface Transformers library. This library is used since it offers a framework that directly accepts multi-labelled data. The used BERT model (BERTje) is the same as used for the sentiment analysis. However, now the linear fully connected classifier layer added to the network has eight outputs (one for every social right) instead of the three used for sentiment analysis. In addition, instead of applying a softmax function to the outputs of the classifier layer, a sigmoid function is used because the probabilities do not have to sum to one as it is a multi-label problem.

Bridging coaches have indicated that it is interesting to output the n most probable social rights. In this way, the coach can manually select the correct social rights out of the n most probable given by the model. To accomplish this, an array containing a probability for every right indicating how likely it is to be present in the fragment is used.

5 Experiments

5.1 Evaluation metric

The models for sentiment analysis and extracting the social rights are evaluated using the accuracy score. This approach is valid since the data is not very skewed. The accuracies are calculated using 5-fold cross validation (cv) by splitting the fragments into a training set (80%) and a test set (20%) for every fold, which results in a test set of 343 fragments in every fold. A 1% increase in accuracy corresponds to 17 extra fragments classified correctly.

5.2 Experiments for sentiment analysis

BOW-based The results of the BOW approach strongly depend on which classifier is used. Several machine learning classifiers from scikit-learn (Pedregosa et al., 2011) are tested out. To see which one works best, all classifiers are tested in the same conditions: all on the same (shuffled) lemmatised dataset with the same pre-processing steps and using 5-fold cv.

---

[2]https://github.com/ThilinaRajapakse/
simpletransformers

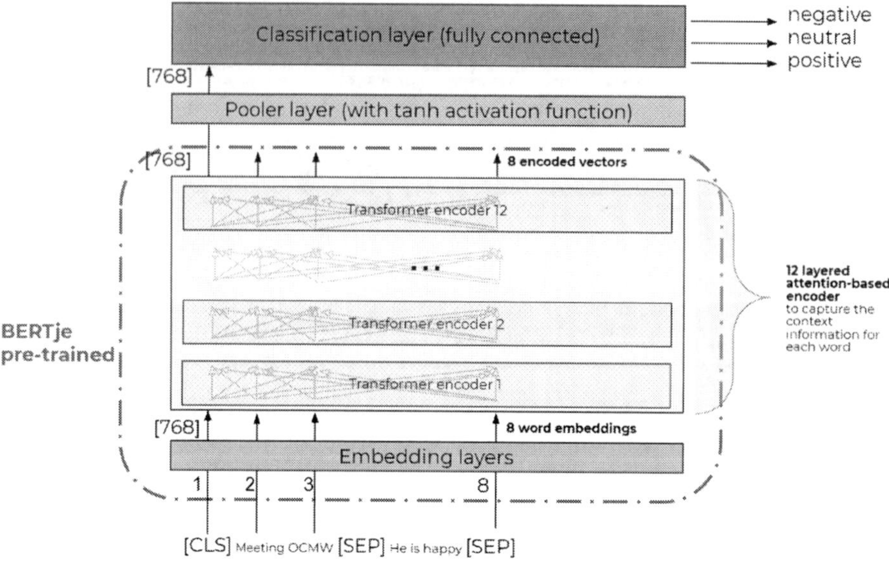

Figure 5: A simplified illustration of the complete architecture of the used model based on BERT, with a pooler layer and a classification layer on top

Embeddings-based When using embeddings, the accuracy heavily depends on which tool is used to generate these embeddings. To identify the best tool, different vectorising tools such as fastText (Bojanowski et al., 2017), spaCy [3], Dutch embeddings from CLiPS (Tulkens et al., 2016), Wikipedia2Vec (Yamada et al., 2020), NLPL (Fares et al., 2017), Dutch Word2Vec [4] are tested with the same classifier. In addition, the data is pre-processed in the same way for every tool: removing special characters, spaces and upper cases and tokenising the sentences. The Doc2Vec tools (fast-Text and spaCy) generate a single embedding vector for the whole fragment, while the other tools generate an embedding for every word, which are averaged element-wise afterwards.

Fine-tuning BERTje The results of the model created by fine-tuning BERTje depend on which setup is used. To identify the best setup, several parameters are varied, such as the number of epochs, the maximum length to which a fragment is truncated and the number of frozen layers.

5.3 Experiments for extracting social rights

To examine whether a BOW or an embedding approach works best when doing multi-label classification, both methods are compared. The accura-

cies (obtained using 5-fold cv) are defined as the number of correct predictions divided by the total number of predictions, where one prediction is considered as correct if the set of predicted social rights exactly matches the corresponding set of social rights as manually labelled.

Next, when giving the n most probable social rights as output, the accuracy is calculated by dividing the number of correctly predicted social rights by the number of rights manually labelled, using 5-fold cv. The discussed methods LabelPowerset, BinaryRelevance, ClassifierChain, RAkEL (all using logistic regression) and BERTje are compared when using varying number of outputs.

6 Results

6.1 Sentiment Analysis

The previously used algorithm Pattern (De Smedt and Daelemans, 2012) reaches an accuracy of 48% on the dataset of this paper.

BOW-based Table 3 shows the results of the BOW approach obtained with different classifiers, with Logistic Regression as best result reaching an accuracy of **68%**.

Embeddings-based To investigate which tool suits best, different embeddings generators are tested with the same classifier, being logistic regression since this one gave best results when using

---

[3]`https://spacy.io/models/nl`
[4]`https://github.com/coosto/`
`dutch-word-embeddings`

		Accuracy (%)
Linear Models	SGDClassifier	66.8
	PassiveAggressiveClassifier	67.0
	RidgeClassifier	67.3
	LogisticRegression	**68.4**
SVM	SVC	66.8
	NuSVC	67.2
	LinearSVC	67.6
Naive Bayes	ComplementNB	66.7
Ensemble	ExtraTreesClassifier	67.0

Table 3: The results of the different classifiers on the SA task. The accuracy is obtained by using 5-fold cv. All classifiers are obtained from the scikit-learn library (Pedregosa et al., 2011).

BOW. Table 4 shows that only when using embeddings generated with the Dutch Word2Vec tool, a higher accuracy of **71%** is reached than with BOW.

Category	Embedding generator	Accuracy (%)
Doc2Vec	fastText	46.1
	spaCy	52.1
Word2Vec	Dutch Embed. CLiPS	55.0
	Wikipedia2Vec	63.6
	NLPL	64.4
	Dutch Word2Vec	**71.4**

Table 4: Results of the different embedding generators on the SA task.

BERTje-based   Table 5 shows the influence of the maximum length when using 3 epochs and without freezing. Table 6 shows the influence of freezing layer 0 until layer N, with varying number of epochs.

maximum length	accuracy (%)
225	78.5
250	79.3
275	78.3
300	79.0
350	78.7

Table 5: The influence of the maximum length of a fragment (in tokens) on the SA accuracy with BERTje. These results are obtained by fine-tuning for 3 epochs without freezing, using 5-fold cross validation.

When using BERTje with the best settings (i.e. maximum length of 350, freezing layers 0-6 and training for 6 epochs), the sentiment analysis reaches an accuracy of **79.6%**.

frozen layers	accuracy (%)		
	3 epochs	6 epochs	10 epochs
0	78.8	79.0	78.9
0-4	78.3	78.7	78.8
0-6	77.8	**79.6**	78.3
0-8	74.2	77.7	78.3
0-10	65.3	72.2	74.3
0-11	65.8	67.3	68.1

Table 6: The influence of freezing layers of the pre-trained BERTje on the SA accuracy. The column *frozen layers* indicates which layers are frozen (i.e. not fine-tuned), then for every case the accuracy (obtained using 5-fold cross validation) is determined after training for 3, 6 or 10 epochs.

6.2   Extracting Social Rights

Table 7 shows the results when comparing whether an embedding (generated with the Dutch Word2Vec since this gave the best result for the sentiment analysis) or a BOW approach works best when doing multi-label classification. For the techniques requiring a BaseEstimator, logistic regression is used. When fine-tuning BERTje, it was found that training for 5 epochs instead of 3 and restricting the input to 350 tokens was slightly beneficial for the results.

Table 8 shows the results when giving the n most probable social rights as output of LabelPowerset, BinaryRelevance, ClassifierChain, RAkEL (all using logistic regression) and BERTje when using varying number of outputs.

97

	Binary-Relevance (LogReg)	Classifier-Chain (LogReg)	Label-Powerset (LogReg)	RAkEL (LogReg)	mLkNN	BERTje
BOW	37%	39%	46%	42%	32%	/
Embeddings	51%	51%	53%	51%	40%	**66%**

Table 7: The results using different multi-label classification techniques to extract the social rights using a BOW and an embedding approach.

	accuracy (%)			
	Number of social rights in output			
	3	**4**	**5**	**6**
LabelPowerset	84.6	89.3	93.3	97.1
BinaryRelevance	87.1	91.3	94.7	97.6
ClassifierChain	86.2	91.2	94.6	97.5
RAkEL	86.0	90.3	94.2	97.6
BERTje	93.0	96.0	97.7	98.9

Table 8: The results when a certain number of social rights are given as output based on the highest probabilities of the social rights, using the different multi-label classification approaches with embeddings.

7 Discussion

7.1 Sentiment Analysis

When compared to the manually given labels, the previously used algorithm for sentiment analysis reaches an accuracy of about **48%**, serving as baseline. This low accuracy can be explained by the fact that the sentiment analysis tool from CLiPS is not developed specifically for data from the social context, which is typically more complex.

With an accuracy of **79.6%**, fine-tuning BERTje outperforms the BOW and embeddings-based approaches.

This accuracy (79.6%) is considered as a good result if compared to other use-cases which also perform ternary classification. As mentioned in section 2, Bouazizi and Ohtsuki (2016), for example, achieves an accuracy equal to 70.1% when classifying tweets into 3 different classes.

Moreover, the influence of a few hyperparameters on the performance of this model is investigated. Table 5 does not show a trend in the length of a fragment (i.e. increasing the length does not increase the accuracy or vice versa). As the influence on the performance is not clear, the maximum length was set to 350, as most fragments (99.5%) are shorter than this number and will thus be taken completely as input.

Next, Table 6 shows that the accuracy depends on whether layers are frozen or not. The last row of this table shows that when freezing all encoder layers, the accuracy drops significantly since the more epochs and the less frozen layers, the higher the risk to overfit. When freezing fewer layers, the accuracy rises, reaching a maximum when freezing about half of the model. Besides this, the table shows that when more layers are frozen, the differences between the accuracy when training for three, six or ten epochs is much larger than when fewer layers are frozen. This could be explained by the fact that when freezing more layers, overfitting occurs only after extensive training with more epochs, and it is then beneficial to train longer. Therefore, it may also be possible that a high accuracy can also be achieved when freezing many layers, but that in that case more than ten epochs would be required. However, table 6 shows freezing layers 0-6 and training for six epochs yields the best result.

7.2 Extracting Social Rights

Table 7 also shows that for recognising social rights, embeddings are more suitable than BOW. This can be explained by the fact that for extracting the social rights, the model has to understand the topics of the fragments and embeddings are made to capture this meaning in a vector. This table also shows that fine-tuning BERTje yields the best results with an accuracy of 66%.

Since the user is interested in seeing the most probable social rights instead of the exact prediction of the model, the probability-based results (i.e. selecting top-k outputs based on their probability value) are considered as the most important measures. When giving the three most probable rights as output, the BERTje-based model detects 93% of all social rights. It is remarkable that BERTje with n social rights as output reaches a higher accuracy than all the other methods with $n + 1$ social rights as output. From this can be concluded that

BERTje is superior to LabelPowerset, BinaryRelevance, ClassifierChain and RakelD and thus should be used to predict the social rights.

8 Conclusion

In this paper, we investigate the best way to perform sentiment analysis and extract social rights from subjective Dutch text fragments with the help of manually given labels. The results demonstrate that fine-tuning BERTje outperforms other techniques with an accuracy of 80% on sentiment analysis and 93% on extracting social rights when using the 3 most probable rights as output.

Further research directions could explore other pre-trained language models or exploit automatic data augmentation.

References

L Aaldering and R Vliegenthart. 2016. Political leaders and the media: can we measure political leadership images in newspapers using computer-assisted content analysis? *Quality & quantity*, 50(5):1871–1905.

Piotr Bojanowski, Edouard Grave, Armand Joulin, and Tomas Mikolov. 2017. Enriching word vectors with subword information. *Transactions of the Association for Computational Linguistics*, 5:135–146.

Mondher Bouazizi and Tomoaki Ohtsuki. 2016. Sentiment analysis: From binary to multi-class classification: A pattern-based approach for multi-class sentiment analysis in twitter. In *2016 IEEE International Conference on Communications (ICC)*, pages 1–6. IEEE.

T De Smedt and W Daelemans. 2012. Pattern for python. *Journal Of Machine Learning Research*, 13:2063–2067.

Jacob Devlin, Ming-Wei Chang, Kenton Lee, and Kristina Toutanova. 2018. Bert: Pre-training of deep bidirectional transformers for language understanding.

Murhaf Fares, Andrey Kutuzov, Stephan Oepen, and Erik Velldal. 2017. Word vectors, reuse, and replicability: Towards a community repository of large-text resources. In *Proceedings of the 21st Nordic Conference on Computational Linguistics, NoDaLiDa, 22-24 May 2017, Gothenburg, Sweden*, 131, pages 271–276. Linköping University Electronic Press, Linköpings universitet.

Dietmar Gräbner, Markus Zanker, Günther Fliedl, Matthias Fuchs, et al. 2012. Classification of customer reviews based on sentiment analysis. In *ENTER*, pages 460–470. Citeseer.

Daniel Jurafsky and James H Martin. 2014. *Speech and language processing: an introduction to natural language processing, computational linguistics, and speech recognition*, new international ed., 2nd ed. edition. Pearson, Harlow.

Diederik Kingma and Jimmy Ba. 2017. Adam: A method for stochastic optimization. *arXiv.org*.

Jaejun Lee, Raphael Tang, and Jimmy Lin. 2019. What would elsa do? freezing layers during transformer fine-tuning. *arXiv.org*.

Omer Levy and Yoav Goldberg. 2014. Dependency-based word embeddings. In *Proceedings of the 52nd Annual Meeting of the Association for Computational Linguistics (Volume 2: Short Papers)*, pages 302–308.

Gjorgji Madjarov, Dragi Kocev, Dejan Gjorgjevikj, and Sašo Džeroski. 2012. An extensive experimental comparison of methods for multi-label learning. *Pattern recognition*, 45(9):3084–3104.

Manish Munikar, Sushil Shakya, and Aakash Shrestha. 2019. Fine-grained sentiment classification using bert. *arXiv.org*.

Bo Pang, Lillian Lee, and Shivakumar Vaithyanathan. 2002. Thumbs up? sentiment classification using machine learning techniques. *arXiv preprint cs/0205070*.

F. Pedregosa, G. Varoquaux, A. Gramfort, V. Michel, B. Thirion, O. Grisel, M. Blondel, P. Prettenhofer, R. Weiss, V. Dubourg, J. Vanderplas, A. Passos, D. Cournapeau, M. Brucher, M. Perrot, and E. Duchesnay. 2011. Scikit-learn: Machine learning in Python. *Journal of Machine Learning Research*, 12:2825–2830.

M. Indhraom Prabha and G Umarani Srikanth. 2019. Survey of sentiment analysis using deep learning techniques. pages 1–9. IEEE.

Elena Rudkowsky, Martin Haselmayer, Matthias Wastian, Marcelo Jenny, Štefan Emrich, and Michael Sedlmair. 2018. More than bags of words: Sentiment analysis with word embeddings. *Communication methods and measures*, 12(2-3):140–157.

C. Sun, X. Qiu, Y. Xu, and X. Huang. 2019. How to fine-tune bert for text classification? volume 11856, pages 194–206. Springer.

Piotr Szymański and Tomasz Kajdanowicz. 2017. A scikit-based python environment for performing multi-label classification. *arXiv preprint arXiv:1702.01460*.

Stephan Tulkens, Chris Emmery, and Walter Daelemans. 2016. Evaluating unsupervised dutch word embeddings as a linguistic resource. In *Proceedings of the Tenth International Conference on Language Resources and Evaluation (LREC 2016)*, Paris, France. European Language Resources Association (ELRA).

Wietse de Vries, Andreas van Cranenburgh, Arianna Bisazza, Tommaso Caselli, Gertjan van Noord, and Malvina Nissim. 2019. Bertje: A dutch bert model.

Thomas Wolf, Lysandre Debut, Victor Sanh, Julien Chaumond, Clement Delangue, Anthony Moi, Pierric Cistac, Tim Rault, R'emi Louf, Morgan Funtowicz, and Jamie Brew. 2019. Huggingface's transformers: State-of-the-art natural language processing. *ArXiv*, abs/1910.03771.

Ikuya Yamada, Akari Asai, Jin Sakuma, Hiroyuki Shindo, Hideaki Takeda, Yoshiyasu Takefuji, and Yuji Matsumoto. 2020. Wikipedia2vec: An efficient toolkit for learning and visualizing the embeddings of words and entities from wikipedia. *arXiv preprint 1812.06280v3*.

An Empirical Analysis of Human-Bot Interaction on Reddit

Ming-Cheng Ma, John P. Lalor
Department of IT, Analytics, and Operations
University of Notre Dame
mma4@alumni.nd.edu, john.lalor@nd.edu

Abstract

Automated agents ("bots") have emerged as an ubiquitous and influential presence on social media. Bots engage on social media platforms by posting content and replying to other users on the platform. In this work we conduct an empirical analysis of the activity of a single bot on Reddit. Our goal is to determine whether bot activity (in the form of posted comments on the website) has an effect on how humans engage on Reddit. We find that (1) the sentiment of a bot comment has a significant, positive effect on the subsequent human reply, and (2) human Reddit users modify their comment behaviors to overlap with the text of the bot, similar to how humans modify their text to mimic other humans in conversation. Understanding human-bot interactions on social media with relatively simple bots is important for preparing for more advanced bots in the future.

1 Introduction

People across the world engage with each other on social media sites for personal, professional, and entertainment-related reasons. In recent years automated agents ("bots") have become more prevalent on social media (Ferrara et al., 2016). Bots engage with human users on social media platforms via the platforms' application programming interfaces (APIs). By listening to content using the API, bots are coded to engage based on specific keywords or phrases that are used by human users.

As bots become more prevalent on social media, more and more humans find themselves engaging with these bots. These humans may or may not be aware of the fact that the bots are not humans. There is a need to study how humans and bots interact with each other, and to analyze how bots influence the way humans engage on the platforms. On certain platforms bots are opaque (that is, you do not know if a user is a bot). For example, on

Twitter most bots are opaque, and there is a steady stream of research on detecting bots and analyzing the effect they have on the behavior of human Twitter users e.g., (Wang, 2010; Chu et al., 2012; Clark et al., 2016). However, on Reddit many bots are open and explicit about their botness. Reddit users engage with each other on topic-focused communities ("subreddits"). If users are knowingly interacting with a bot, does the bot influence what the users will comment? More specifically, our research question for this work is: *How does engagement with a known bot influence human behavior on social media?*

In this work we present a case study of a bot that engages frequently on a small number of subreddits to do a deep dive into the way the bot interacts with humans on the subreddits. The bot's comments are pre-defined and randomly selected, so there is no true "interaction" per-se with respect to how the bot replies to human users. We are interested in seeing if humans reply to this simple bot in interesting ways. As bots become more advanced with improving NLP technologies, the effect on human-bot interaction will become more pronounced. Therefore, it is important to understand interaction dynamics with simple bots to theorize about how these interactions may change with more advanced bots.

As a result of our analyses we identify two interesting findings. First, we find that the sentiment of the (randomly generated) bot comment has a significant effect on the sentiment of the human reply comment. Second, we compare the text content of the bot comments and human replies and find evidence of *lexical entrainment*, where humans overlap with bots in terms of their text comments, consistent with known patterns of conversation between humans (Beňuš et al., 2014).

Proceedings of the 2020 EMNLP Workshop W-NUT: The Sixth Workshop on Noisy User-generated Text, pages 101–106
Online, Nov 19, 2020. ©2020 Association for Computational Linguistics

Variable	M1	M2	M3
Parent Sentiment	-0.008 (0.011)	0.077 (0.012)***	-0.008 (0.011)
Bot Sentiment	0.039 (0.009)***	0.084 (0.009)***	0.039 (0.008)***
Parent Child Same User	0.036 (0.006)***	-	-
Parent Sentiment x Bot Sentiment	-0.022 (0.023)	-0.042 (0.023)*	-0.022 (0.022)
Parent Sentiment x PC Same	0.085 (0.016)***	-	-
Bot Sentiment x PC Same	0.046 (0.013)***	-	-
PS x BS x PC Same	-0.020 (0.032)	-	-

Table 1: Regression results. Standard errors in parentheses. $*p < 0.1$, $***p < 0.001$

2   Data Collection

In this work we focus on interactions between humans and a single-purpose Reddit entertainment bot. We analyze interactions between Reddit users and bobby-b-bot, a Reddit bot inspired by the Game of Thrones books and TV series.[1] Bobby-b-bot posts are randomly selected quotes from a Game of Thrones character, Robert Baratheon.

We selected the bobby-b-bot for our analyses because the bot is a purely "entertainment" bot, in contrast to many Reddit bots that perform some utility (e.g., text summarization or subreddit moderation). The bot source code is open-sourced and available, so we can see how the bot identifies comments on Reddit that it should reply to. To activate bobby-b-bot, a Reddit user posting on one of the specified subreddits[2] must include some variation of the bot's name in their comment. Once activated, the bot will reply to the comment with a randomly selected quote from the GoT books.

To collect all bobby-b-bot comments from Reddit, we pulled the bot comment data as comment triples from the Pushshift Reddit API[3]. In each triple, there is a human post ("parent"), followed by the bobby-b-bot reply, and finally another human post ("child"). We extracted 126,329 bot comments, spanning from 2017/10/23 GMT-4 to 2020/06/14 GMT-4. There are 95,206 (75%) positive parent comments and 31,123 (25%) negative parent comments. For bot comments, there are 75,634 (55%) positive bot comments and 50,695 (45%) comments. When accounting for those bots comments where another user replied, we were left with 16,124 parent-bot-child comment triples. Among these child comments, we identified 12,109 (75%) positive comments and 4,015 (25%) negative comments.

3   Sentiment Analysis

We first analyze the Reddit comment data using sentiment analysis (Liu et al., 2010). In particular, our goal is to determine whether the sentiment of a bot's comment has an effect on the sentiment of comments made in reply. We use the VADER (Valence Aware Dictionary and sEntiment Reasoner) lexicon as our sentiment tool (Hutto and Gilbert, 2014). VADER is a specific tool that is designed for analyzing social media texts. It can generate the sentiment score based on the unlabeled given texts showing the polarity of sentiment (how positive or negative). We fit a linear regression model to predict the VADER sentiment score of the child comments in our data set. Our three independent variables were: the parent sentiment score, the bot sentiment score, and an indicator variable for whether the parent and child in the triple are the same user. We included all interactions between independent variables in our model.

The regression results provide some interesting observations (Table 1, M1). Parent sentiment does not have a significant effect on the child sentiment, whereas bot sentiment has a significant positive effect on child sentiment. The indicator variable has a significant positive effect on child sentiment as well. The interaction between parent sentiment and the indicator variable is significant. Because the parent sentiment is by itself not significant, there is potentially a crossover interaction. Therefore, we ran two additional regression models, splitting the data based on whether the parent and child were the same user (M2) or different users (M3).

When the parent and child users are the same, both parent and bot sentiment have a significant positive effect on the child comment sentiment (Table 1, M2). That the parent comment sentiment affects child comment sentiment is intuitive, as the same user will be more likely to be consistent in terms of sentiment in the conversation with the bot. However, it is interesting that the bot sentiment has

---

[1] https://github.com/bobby-b-bot/reddit
[2] https://github.com/bobby-b-bot/reddit/blob/master/subs.json
[3] https://pushshift.io/

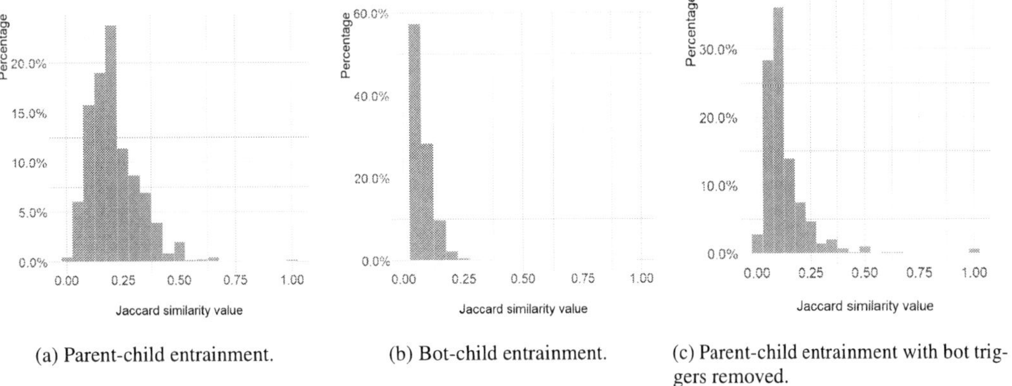

(a) Parent-child entrainment.   (b) Bot-child entrainment.   (c) Parent-child entrainment with bot triggers removed.

Figure 1: Histograms of Jaccard scores for the three comment pairs in our analyses.

a positive affect as well. When the parent and child users are different, there is no longer a significant effect from the parent comment sentiment, but the bot comment sentiment is still significant (Table 1, M3). That a randomly generated quote can affect the sentiment of a comment written by a human is interesting. This result is consistent with prior work on bots influencing human behavior, but here there is no incentive or end goal for which the bot was built (Nass et al., 1995; Bell et al., 2003; Coulston et al., 2002). The human influence is only based on the entertainment value.

4 Textual Overlap

We next consider how Reddit users modify the text of their comments in response to the bot (*lexical entrainment*). Lexical entrainment is when speakers use words that overlap with words of their conversational partner (Beňuš et al., 2014). Prior work has shown that humans will adapt their speech when interacting with computers (Nass et al., 1995; Bell et al., 2003; Coulston et al., 2002). Computer agents have been designed to encourage individuals to adapt their speaking rate or amplitude (Bell et al., 2003; Coulston et al., 2002). However, here the bot presents randomly selected text, and the only aim of the bot, insofar as it has an aim, is to entertain. Will humans adjust their comments when interacting with the bot?

For our entrainment metric we use Jaccard similarity (Levandowsky and Winter, 1971). Jaccard similarity is a ratio of overlapping tokens to total tokens between two comments, and from 0 (no overlap) to 1 (perfect overlap). Entrainment metrics in prior work are token-focused, where entrainment

for specific keywords are measured (Beňuš et al., 2014). Here we are interested in a global measure, and we therefore use Jaccard similarity to that end.

We measure entrainment in our comment triples across three comment pairs: (1) between parent and child comments, (2) between bot and child comments, (3) and between parent and child comments where the trigger phrase has been removed. For cases 1 and 2 we can compare human-human entrainment with bot-human entrainment. However, we include case 3 so that we can remove examples that may artificially inflate our entrainment results. Recall that the bobby-b-bot is activated by a user including the bot name in a comment. Therefore the phrase "bobby b" (or a variation) appears in all parent comments. In certain cases the child comment also includes the phrase, as the child user also wants to summon the bot. To avoid counting these we remove all instances of "bobby b" from the parent and child comments for our case 3 analysis. In all cases we remove stop words before calculation.

In each case we plot a histogram showing, of those triples where there is some overlap, the Jaccard scores of the relevant pair in the triple (Figure 1). For parent-child entrainment there are 10,723 comment pairs with overlap, for bot-child entrainment there are 4,527 pairs, and for parent-child entrainment with the bot triggers removed there are 2,728 pairs. First, the vast majority of overlap between humans (i.e., the parent-child comment pairs) is a result of the child comment user calling the bot again via the "bobby b" keyword. Once this is removed the number of instances with overlap drops significantly. However, we still observe some positive amounts of overlap between humans. That this overlap occurs with another conversant

	Parent comment	Bot Comment	Child comment
1	Bobby B is our true savior, he helped us cope with *season 8*.	CAREFUL, NED! CAREFUL NOW!	That's right, Bobby B, we have to be careful when watching *Season 8* or we might lose braincells.
2	I'm usually always for more but I actually re-watched a clip from e2 the other day (when it's decided Lady will be killed in Nymeria's place) and forgot how disappointed I was in how Bobby B handled it when Ned questioned the order. Been sad about it	SURROUNDED BY LANNISTERS! EVERY TIME I CLOSE MY EYES I SEE THEIR BLONDE HAIR AND THEIR SMUG, SATIS-FIED FACES!	I suppose you were surrounded at that time and couldn't do much else, I get it. This bot is alive Rip Lady
3	*Bobby B*, c'mon man, you have to admit it's pretty similar to something you say all the time.	GODS WHAT A STUPID NAME!	'What? Ros? Well it's probably short for something like Roselyn, or knowing GRRM, maybe like Rosmallysyn or some moderately real sounding anglo name that isn't actually a name. I'm surprised he went with something as normal as Robert for you. Handy nicknames like *Bobby B* are pretty common though. Like Ned. Ned is a normal name, but I don't think Eddard is a name in real life. Thoughts?
4	*Why do you keep calling me Ned Bobby B?*	A DOTHRAKI HORDE ON AN OPEN FIELD, NED!	*Why do you keep calling me Ned Bobby B?*

Table 2: Examples of comment triples from the data set. Parent-child comment overlaps are *italicized*, and bot-child overlaps are underlined.

(the bot) in between suggests that the human users are conversing between themselves even though the bot is in the middle. This could be due to the fact that the bot randomly generates text, and is not contributing to the conversation per se. We found that some of the human-human entrainment occurs when the parent and child user are the same, suggesting that the individual has the bot as a conversant but is in effect speaking with herself.

That there are positive amounts of overlap between humans is interesting but not surprising. More surprising is the presence of entrainment between the bot and the child comment user. While evidence of human-machine entrainment has been found in prior work (Bell et al., 2003; Brennan, 1996; Coulston et al., 2002), such research involved bots that were programmed with a purpose, so the bots were designed to generate relevant content to interact with humans. However, here the text for the bobby-b-bot is randomly sampled from a list of pre-existing scripts. People still overlap with bot texts to some positive degree even though there is no need for them to modify their speaking behavior in the conversations.

We sampled instances where there is evidence of entrainment to see why human users are interacting with bobby-b-bot (Table 2). In certain cases users will address the bot directly, but even in doing so will entrain with the bot as well, if only in a small way (e.g., a word or two, Table 2 line 1). However, there are times when a user will engage with the bot as part of the flow of conversation (Table 2, lines 2 and 3). Here the user takes the randomly-generated bot response as an actual response and continues the conversation. Finally, in certain cases it seems that users simply want to engage with the bot to see what comments the bot will post, and therefore repeat themselves to re-trigger the bot in an extended conversation thread (Table 2, line 4).

It is intriguing to see that the child comment adopts words both from the parent comment and the bot comment. Even though the humans are interacting with a bot, and a simple bot at that, they still will try to behave like they are talking to other human beings. Even when the overlaps are just one or two words within the text, those words serve as an important role for human referencing. By mentioning the key common words, humans can still efficiently keep the conversation going.

5   Related Work

Much of the recent work regarding bots has been in the area of bot detection, in particular bots on Twitter (Chu et al., 2012; Clark et al., 2016; Ferrara et al., 2016). On Reddit there are some opaque bots (Hurtado et al., 2019), however in many cases bots are transparent, typically by including the word "bot" in the username. Prior work has looked at human-bot cooperation for subreddit moderation (Jhaver et al., 2019), but to the best of our knowledge this is the first work to study human-bot interaction and comment pattern effects on Reddit. This work also diverges from prior work on human-bot interaction (Bell et al., 2003; Brennan, 1996; Coulston et al., 2002). In most work where the influence of bots is investigated, the bot is purposefully programmed or designed to elicit some response or interaction. However, bobby-b-bot comments are randomly selected snippets of text, and the bot's purpose is to entertain.

6   Conclusion

In this work we present a detailed analysis of the effects of a single social media bot on human communication. While our sample is limited, the number of such social entertainment bots is only going to increase with more advanced text generation capabilities. The bobby-b bot we studied uses a simple random text selection algorithm to "interact" with users on Reddit. We have shown that even a simple bot can have an effect on the way individuals communicate on the platform. Understanding human-bot interaction when bots are simple is key for building theories of interaction for when the bot technology improves (e.g., a bot that is built on top of GPT-3, Brown et al. 2020).

In this work we consider a single Reddit bot as a case study. Our goal was to determine whether a bot built for entertainment, and not meaningful back and forth with human users, had an effect on human user sentiment and word selection. Certain details of how the bobby-b-bot is implemented (e.g., randomly selecting what text will be posted) are not consistent with the normal flow of conversation. However, we see that in response to the bot's post, humans are matching keywords that the bot used. So in the context of short, discrete interactions on social media, it would be interesting to see if this behavior holds with other bots. An important direction for future work would be to extend this further and conduct similar studies on a wider range of human-bot interactions to see if the results are more broadly applicable. In particular, is this effect more prevalent in goal-driven bots (i.e., bots that seek to change opinion or raise awareness) than in bots that exist for entertainment purposes?

Typically, lexical entrainment is *targeted*, that is, specific keywords are investigated to see if there is overlap (Brandstetter et al., 2017; Iio et al., 2015). However in this work we consider global entrainment, where any overlap (stop words excluded) is tracked. Because the interactions are short, we consider all overlap meaningful. While Jaccard similarity is an appropriate metric in terms of calculating the overall token overlap, more sensitive metrics could also be considered to incorporate weights for different types of tokens (e.g., rare words).

Prior work on human-machine lexical entrainment looked at conversations between humans and physical robots in a shared space, or conversational agents (Hoegen et al., 2019). More generally, the entrainment phenomenon is usually studied over the course of a conversation, to determine if conversation participants imitate each other's conversation styles. However in this work we look at discrete human-bot interactions on social media.

We find evidence of entrainment in short interactions with a technically simple bot. That humans are imitating the bots in these discrete interactions is an interesting result. Future work to investigate this on a larger bot data set is needed to determine if this behavior is wide-spread on Reddit. Even beyond Reddit, bots on other social media platforms such as Twitter may be able to influence human responses without an extended back-and-forth to establish trust.

Acknowledgments

This work supported in part by the University of Notre Dame Center for Research Computing.

References

Linda Bell, Joakim Gustafson, and Mattias Heldner. 2003. Prosodic Adaptation in Human-Computer Interaction. page 4.

Štefan Beňuš, Agustín Gravano, Rivka Levitan, Sarah Ita Levitan, Laura Willson, and Julia Hirschberg. 2014. Entrainment, dominance and alliance in supreme court hearings. *Knowledge-Based Systems*, 71:3–14.

Jürgen Brandstetter, Clay Beckner, Eduardo Benitez Sandoval, and Christoph Bartneck. 2017. Persistent lexical entrainment in hri. In *Proceedings of the 2017 ACM/IEEE International Conference on Human-Robot Interaction*, pages 63–72.

Susan E Brennan. 1996. Lexical Entrainment in Spontaneous Dialog. page 4.

Tom B Brown, Benjamin Mann, Nick Ryder, Melanie Subbiah, Jared Kaplan, Prafulla Dhariwal, Arvind Neelakantan, Pranav Shyam, Girish Sastry, Amanda Askell, et al. 2020. Language models are few-shot learners. *arXiv preprint arXiv:2005.14165*.

Zi Chu, Steven Gianvecchio, Haining Wang, and Sushil Jajodia. 2012. Detecting automation of twitter accounts: Are you a human, bot, or cyborg? *IEEE Transactions on Dependable and Secure Computing*, 9(6):811–824.

Eric M Clark, Jake Ryland Williams, Chris A Jones, Richard A Galbraith, Christopher M Danforth, and Peter Sheridan Dodds. 2016. Sifting robotic from organic text: a natural language approach for detecting automation on twitter. *Journal of computational science*, 16:1–7.

Rachel Coulston, Sharon Oviatt, and Courtney Darves. 2002. Amplitude Convergence in Children's Conversational Speech with Animated Personas. page 4.

Emilio Ferrara, Onur Varol, Clayton Davis, Filippo Menczer, and Alessandro Flammini. 2016. The rise of social bots. *Communications of the ACM*, 59(7):96–104.

Rens Hoegen, Deepali Aneja, Daniel McDuff, and Mary Czerwinski. 2019. An end-to-end conversational style matching agent. In *Proceedings of the 19th ACM International Conference on Intelligent Virtual Agents*, pages 111–118.

Sofia Hurtado, Poushali Ray, and Radu Marculescu. 2019. Bot detection in reddit political discussion. In *Proceedings of the Fourth International Workshop on Social Sensing*, pages 30–35.

Clayton J Hutto and Eric Gilbert. 2014. Vader: A parsimonious rule-based model for sentiment analysis of social media text. In *Eighth international AAAI conference on weblogs and social media*.

Takamasa Iio, Masahiro Shiomi, Kazuhiko Shinozawa, Katsunori Shimohara, Mitsunori Miki, and Norihiro Hagita. 2015. Lexical entrainment in human robot interaction. *International Journal of Social Robotics*, 7(2):253–263.

Shagun Jhaver, Iris Birman, Eric Gilbert, and Amy Bruckman. 2019. Human-machine collaboration for content regulation: The case of reddit automoderator. *ACM Transactions on Computer-Human Interaction (TOCHI)*, 26(5):1–35.

Michael Levandowsky and David Winter. 1971. Distance between sets. *Nature*, 234(5323):34–35.

Bing Liu et al. 2010. Sentiment analysis and subjectivity. *Handbook of natural language processing*, 2(2010):627–666.

Clifford Nass, Youngme Moon, B. J. Fogg, Byron Reeves, and D. Christopher Dryer. 1995. Can computer personalities be human personalities? *International Journal of Human-Computer Studies*, 43(2):223–239.

Alex Hai Wang. 2010. Don't follow me: Spam detection in twitter. In *2010 international conference on security and cryptography (SECRYPT)*, pages 1–10. IEEE.

Detecting Trending Terms in Cybersecurity Forum Discussions

Jack Hughes[1]   Seth Aycock[2]   Andrew Caines[1]   Paula Buttery[1]   Alice Hutchings[1]

[1] Computer Laboratory, University of Cambridge, U.K.
`firstname.lastname@cl.cam.ac.uk`
[2] Theoretical & Applied Linguistics, University of Cambridge, U.K.
`seth@manx.net`

Abstract

We present a lightweight method for identifying currently trending terms in relation to a known prior of terms, using a weighted log-odds ratio with an informative prior. We apply this method to a dataset of posts from an English-language underground hacking forum, spanning over ten years of activity, with posts containing misspellings, orthographic variation, acronyms, and slang. Our statistical approach supports analysis of linguistic change and discussion topics over time, without a requirement to train a topic model for each time interval for analysis. We evaluate the approach by comparing the results to TF-IDF using the discounted cumulative gain metric with human annotations, finding our method outperforms TF-IDF on information retrieval.

1   Introduction

Underground hacking forums contain a large collection of noisy text data around various topics, with misspellings, changing lexicons, and slang phrases. The evolving domain-specific lexicon includes homonyms, where "rat" may be identified as an animal by off-the-shelf tools, but is typically defined as a "remote access trojan" in this context, a type of malware used to gain access to a victim's computer.

We work with texts from the HackForums site[1], the largest English-language hacking forum, with multiple bulletin boards arranged around various topics, and many active users submitting thousands of new posts every day. The dataset contains over a decade of text data, but detecting trends is non-trivial, due to the informal language used by members, not only technical terms such as "rat", but also misspellings, slang, orthographic variation, and acronyms.

For instance, the following texts demonstrate how posts are structured into threads on given top-

ics, and how users both deliberately and accidentally use noisy language[2]:

User1	Ransomware infects hospitals all over UK: `link`
User2	anyone think they made some money from this?
User1	They might of done but idk they'll get caught eventually, it's stupid to commit crimes like this
User3	Who tf targets hospitals for ransomeware
User1	I dont believe they actually went for the nhs.. the ransom would be more \$\$\$ lol
User4	I looked up a few btc addresses and can confirm they made money

Researchers interested in analysing hot topics on the forum will find it hard to gain a clear perspective on this due to the volume of data going through the forum every day. Therefore, an overview of trending topics with natural language processing and statistical techniques is useful for identifying what may be of interest to security researchers. We propose a tool to identify tokens from trending topics, by pre-tokenising post data, followed by adapting a statistical technique for measuring changes, which can be used to scan across the dataset.

The tool builds upon a weighted log-odds ratio (Monroe et al., 2008) with an informative Bayesian prior (Silge et al., 2020), used to compare differences in two corpora. In our case the corpora represents two distinct time periods of interest within the same subforum[3]. For known events, one period can be a set of texts preceding the event (the

---

[2] The texts are fabricated so as to preserve user anonymity, but they are based on real ones we have encountered in the database.

[3] A forum is the whole site, and a subforum or bulletin board is a page on the site, dedicated to a given general topic and created by the administrators. Subforums contain member–created threads consisting of an ordered set of posts typically focused on a single topic.

---

[1] `https://hackforums.net`

Proceedings of the 2020 EMNLP Workshop W-NUT: The Sixth Workshop on Noisy User-generated Text, pages 107–115
Online, Nov 19, 2020. ©2020 Association for Computational Linguistics

prior) and the other period can be texts following the event (the target). Also, the tool can be used for live listings of trending terms in the present day, by comparing new posts against some fixed prior.

Our method identifies the relative importance of tokens to each time period. The log-odds ratio indicates whether terms are more likely to appear in a given corpus over others. A log-odds score is higher for terms that are both unique and more frequent to a given period. Other NLP methods require the removal of pre-defined stopwords. However, for our approach, as stopwords have a similar distribution across both time periods, they will have a low log-odds score and rank.

The tool looks at "bursty" events: for a token to be trending, frequency of the token should be significantly different between the prior and target periods, and be more frequent than other terms in the target period. For identifying topics, our method uses a feature-pivot approach (a topic is a cluster of keywords) over a document-pivot approach (a topic is a cluster of documents). The latter may struggle with documents about multiple topics, whereas the former may incorrectly identify correlations between words as topics.

A major challenge in developing the tool is that it is to be used on a large dataset of noisy data, for exploring the evolution of underground hacking forums. We take mitigating steps such as storing the pre-tokenised and part-of-speech tagged text, to decrease computation time for longitudinal analysis. While we focus on a cybercrime context, we note this type of data has similarities to Twitter data: short posts, and informal language. However, while Twitter data has some minimal inter-tweet connections through hashtags, quoting comments and replies, forums have a rigid discussion-based structure set by the forum administrators.

Our contributions are:

- We adapt a technique used for capturing the linguistic changes between two corpora, to be used as a trending topics tool for temporal analysis of data.

- We show the application of this trending topics tool in the context of cybercrime research.

2 Related work

2.1 TF-IDF

Term-frequency inverse-document-frequency (TF-IDF) (Spärck Jones, 1972) identifies common terms in a document, but not common across all documents. This technique provides a mechanism for ranking tokens which are "important" to a document. However, forum text is noisy, with varying spelling of words and creative use of punctuation. While TF-IDF is a popular NLP technique, use on forum data would require stemming or lemmatisation, and defining a document either as individual posts, or a thread of posts, for best performance.

2.2 LDA

TF-IDF assumes each document is based on a single topic, although with forum data, posts and threads may discuss several topics. LDA (Blei et al., 2003) takes a different approach by assuming each document is built from a number of topics, with one primary topic, by learning a distribution of terms in topics. Similar to TF-IDF, this method also requires finding a suitable tokenisation approach and representation of a document. Also, while LDA learns a distribution of terms in topics, this is not as lightweight computationally as TF-IDF.

2.3 Trending Topic Techniques

TF-IDF and LDA are both commonly used, but these both have limitations, and improved models have been proposed.

Burst and dynamic topic models have been used for detecting trending topics, including a burst model proposed by Kleinberg (2003), and Takahashi et al. (2012); Koike et al. (2013) who combine Kleinberg's burst model with a dynamic topic model. While these approaches measure frequency changes over time to detect bursts, we use a different approach similar to "two-point trends" discussed by Kleinberg (2016) with "rising" and "falling" words. In addition, we use a Bayesian approach instead of measuring absolute change.

Aiello et al. (2013) explored common NLP methods for detecting trending topics on Twitter, related to major events which differ in time scale and topic churn rates, and suggest later work should look at topics evolving in parallel. They found n-gram co-occurrence (groups of words typically appearing in the same document), and DF-IDF$_t$ topic ranking (an adaptation of TF-IDF to look for common topics unique to a given time period in comparison to prior time periods) to perform the best. They also boosted the score of proper nouns in their approach, finding these are useful keywords for trending topics.

Follow-up work by Martin et al. (2015) detected bursts of phrases for a topic detection system, using DF-IDF$_t$ to group co-occurring bursty phrases, followed by topic ranking, using the apriori algorithm. They also look at windowing, where events which are focused on real-time activity (e.g sports) have a smaller window of activity, with greater topic recall than longer topics (e.g. politics) with discussions continuing after events. Super Tuesday (the Tuesday in which many US states hold their primary elections) performed better with fewer prior tweets as this was a longer event, than others which performed better with a longer window.

Previous research has focused on static snapshots of events, whereas Shamma et al. (2011) used temporal analysis to identify both peaky and persistent topics. Trending topics tools which are sensitive to noise may only detect peaky topics over persistent topics. They used normalised term frequency, with the number of tweets containing the word, rather than the number of times a word is used, and the peaks look at terms particular to an exact window of time. Persistence looks at peaks of normalised term frequency, assuming these terms have not been used before, and have been used more frequently afterwards.

While much of the literature focuses on detecting English-language trending topics, many cybercrime forums are not English-speaking, which can add complexity into analysis. Also, there are some cases where topic modelling may produce poor quality results, and could be refined with user feedback, which is explored by Hu et al. (2014) with iterating models (hierarchical-LDA trees).

2.4   Fightin' Words paper

Monroe et al. (2008) introduced a method for comparing lexical tokens used by two political parties. This uses a model-based approach, modelling terms as a function of political party, to compute the likelihood of terms used by a political party as log likelihoods ("log-odds"). They used an uninformative Dirichlet prior.

We adapt this method to time-based analysis, modelling terms as a function of time. We use an informative Bayes prior, which was used in the R tidylo library by Silge et al. (2020). While this method was initially used to compare two distinctly different political party news corpora, we adapt this to examine a longitudinal dataset to explore how a particular corpus has changed over time.

2.5   Named Entity Recognition

Our method uses a Bayesian approach to identifying trending topics, with filtering by noun phrases using a part-of-speech (PoS) tagger. However, an alternative approach may use named entity recognition to detect trending topics, and later, for extracting events from text. However, Caines et al. (2018) note named entity recognisers are trained on well-formed English text, and their performance is degraded with noisy text.

There has been prior work in using NER on noisy text, including with a shared challenge at W-NUT 2017 (Derczynski et al., 2017). One approach by Aguilar et al. (2017) used a convolutional neural network with both character-level and word-level features combined with contextual information, input into a bidirectional LSTM, for this task. Jansson and Liu (2017) also used a bidirectional LSTM for word and character embeddings, but combined these with an LDA topic model.

Additionally, contextual data can be used to assist with this task. Xing and Paul (2017) combined word embeddings with Twitter network and geolocation data to improve the accuracy of NER. While we do not have access to this type of data about HackForums users, the forum structure provides hierarchy with administrator defined subforums, which could be used as a feature to combine with embeddings.

2.6   Cybercrime trending topics

Work into trending topics in cybercrime has focused on identifying new threats, using data from tweets, blogs, and underground forums. This includes the creation of large-scale frameworks, such as Sapienza et al. (2018) who detect emerging threats across datasets, although this depends on annotations of known keywords. This is problematic for cybercrime research, due to the constantly changing lexicon.

Behzadan et al. (2018) released a tool to assist annotators in exploring Twitter data, with an annotated dataset of 21,000 tweets on cyber threats. However, this still requires manual identification of new terms.

Once a trending topic is identified, topic ranking is needed, to avoid overwhelming a user. This is used to highlight current important topics, including Bose et al. (2019) who use this to detect and flag known serious threats.

Also, other approaches such as PoS-tagging

and sentiment analysis have been used to identify threats, such as work by Macdonald et al. (2015), however there is a range of jargon used on the forum, with spelling variations and changes to meaning over time, which models would need to handle. There have been other approaches to look at trends on forums and marketplaces, including Tavabi et al. (2019) who use a large topic model to map the evolution of different forums as they evolve.

These communities also evolve over time, with changing meanings of words, and an evolving lexicon, which should be taken into account with longitudinal topic modelling. Bhandari and Armstrong (2019) have looked at subforums of Reddit to explore the use of high affinity terms used by communities, looking at how the semantics of these have changed.

3 Method

3.1 Data

For our method, we use the CrimeBB dataset from the Cambridge Cybercrime Centre (Pastrana et al., 2018b), available for researcher use from the Cambridge Cybercrime Centre[4]. CrimeBB contains posts scraped from 27 underground and dark web forums related to cybercrime, with over 13 years of post data. The database contains English, Russian, and German-language forums. Each forum is structured by subforums, which are based on general topics e.g. hacking methods or marketplace, and are defined by the forum administrators. Each subforum contains threads, which are an ordered collection of posts focusing on a defined topic set by the first post in the thread, such as a particular tutorial the author is sharing. Later posts can be providing a reply to the original first post, a reply to a later post by another user, or new information on the topic. While threads are typically focused on a particular topic, longer threads may become off-topic.

We selected HackForums from this dataset for our evaluation, which is an underground hacking forum discussing various aspects of hacking techniques. Our dataset contains over 190 administrator–curated subforums, with 4 million threads, and 42 million posts, created by over 630,000 members of the forum.

The method is selected due to the focus of the dataset: the data is "noisy", containing variations

of spelling (e.g., "ransomeware" instead of "ransomware"), orthography (e.g., "NK" and "nk" for North Korea), and length of posts (ranging from short replies "pm me" to longer in-depth tutorials). In addition, due to the size of the dataset, our method requires a lightweight approach in order to measure the evolution of trends and topics over time.

3.2 Ethics

Ethics approval was granted from the department's ethics committee for this work. We used data collected from a publicly available forum, and could not gain informed consent from all members as this would be considered to be spamming. As we only analyse posts as a collective whole, rather than identifying individual posts, under the British Society of Criminology's Statement of Ethics, this falls outside of the requirement of informed consent. We also avoid publishing details that could identify individuals, including usernames and original post contents.

3.3 Tokenisation and pre-processing

We first remove chunks of the forum post text which are not the main content of posts, including quote, link, and code blocks. These are identified by using regular expressions to identify relevant markup blocks. This approach is specific to the dataset we use.

Secondly, we tokenise the lowercased forum post text, using TweetTokeniser in NLTK (Bird et al., 2009). This is suited to handling URLs and punctuation based emoticons in text. Note we do not remove a pre-defined list of stop words, however our Bayesian approach will decrease the relevance of a large number of very frequent words which appear equivalently in the prior and target texts.

Following this, we carry out PoS-tagging using spaCy (Honnibal and Montani, 2017) to identify nouns and noun phrases in posts, which we filter results by. Note that we do not apply this step before calculating log-odds, as this would change the distribution of tokens used in a period, affecting the quality of results.

We store both the token counts and set of nouns for each post in the forum. These are stored separately for each subforum in HackForums. Note that we do not attempt to merge terms which may vary in their orthographic form – for instance acronyms or abbreviations with their full forms, spelling errors, and casing differences. It remains a matter

---

[4]https://www.cambridgecybercrime.uk

for future investigation whether acronyms and abbreviations should always be associated with fully spelled-out forms, or whether they should be kept distinct because they represent different uses of the term. Secondly, we can introduce a spell-checker in future work to cluster misspelled words with their intended form, but this will need adaptation to the vocabulary of the cybersecurity domain. Finally, we do capture casing differences (e.g., "WannaCry" and "wannacry", and "NHS" and "nhs") because all texts are lower-cased before tokenisation.

3.4 Windowing: Prior and Target

The method requires the selection of two time windows: a prior and target period. The prior period is used to learn a distribution of terms used, as a comparator for the target period. The size and placement of windows can be varied depending on the desired results: long-term trend detection would have a longer, and more distant, target window than for short-term trend detection.

These windows should be selected depending on the dataset used and research questions. If the prior window and target window overlap the same event, then these terms will appear in both windows with a similar frequency, and will therefore have low log-odds. If the prior and target window are too far apart, then the prior may not be representative, leading to poor quality results. Also, if a topic is re-trending, and the previous trending period falls in the prior, then this may affect whether a term appears to be trending.

3.5 Overview of the log-odds method

Our approach uses a method implemented in the tidylo R library by Silge et al. (2020), which we have re-implemented in Python for compatibility with other tools. The tidylo R library uses an informative prior Bayesian approach, instead of the Dirichlet uninformative prior used by Monroe et al. (2008). A later version of the tidylo library added support for the uninformative prior. However, we chose to continue using the Bayesian approach as our time-based application of the tool is suited to using an informative prior.

We adapt this approach, created for comparing two corpora, to detect trending tokens. Instead of selecting corpora by pre-existing classes, we choose prior and target time windows, to find terms which are more likely to appear in the prior or target period. Each period is represented as a "bag-of-words", for all posts in the selected period.

This Bayesian approach is shown in the following series of equations, based upon the tidylo implementation.

For the corpus (combined set of posts in both periods) y, we define y_w as the frequency of token w, and y_{wi} as the frequency of the token w in period i. n is the sum of frequencies of tokens across all periods, and n_i is the sum of frequencies of tokens in the period i.

First, we calculate ω_{wi}, the odds of each token appearing in period i, and ω_w, the odds of each token appearing the corpus:

$$\omega_{wi} = \frac{y_{wi}}{n_i - y_{wi}} \tag{1}$$

$$\omega_w = \frac{y_w}{n - y_w} \tag{2}$$

Secondly, we calculate δ_{wi}, the log odds ratio to compare the usage of the token w in period i to the whole corpus:

$$\delta_{wi} = \log \omega_{wi} - \log \omega_w \tag{3}$$

Thirdly, we calculate the variance of our estimate, σ^2_{wi}:

$$\sigma^2_{wi} = \frac{1}{y_{wi}} + \frac{1}{y_w} \tag{4}$$

Finally, we calculate the log odds score ζ_{wi} for each token w in period i:

$$\zeta_{wi} = \frac{\delta_{wi}}{\sqrt{\sigma^2_{wi}}} \tag{5}$$

Depending on when the prior and target time windows occur, the tool will either pick up short or long term trending tokens.

4 Evaluation

We evaluate the results of the tool by carrying out an information retrieval task with human annotators. We compare the log-odds approach with TF-IDF using discounted cumulative gain and the human annotations as a ground-truth ranking of identified terms. We use both a known cybersecurity event to define our target window, as well as a randomly-selected target window.

4.1 Trending Event Selection

Within CrimeBB, we selected HackForums, as this is widely studied in prior cybercrime literature (Pastrana et al., 2018a,b; Bhalerao et al., 2019).

First, for the known event we selected the spread of WannaCry in the year 2017. WannaCry is a type of ransomware, which encrypts data until the victim pays a ransom. WannaCry spreads through vulnerable computer systems, instead of directly targeting specific entities, where these systems have not previously updated their systems to patch this issue. One of the largest organisations affected by this attack was the National Health Service (NHS), the universal public healthcare system in the UK. We selected this event as we anticipated it would have been extensively covered on the forum. Indeed, it was later revealed that the individual who was instrumental in stopping the spread of WannaCry had formerly been an active forum member (Krebs, 2017).

The incident within the NHS began on Friday 12 May 2017 (Smart, 2018), which we select as the start of the 7 day window for our analysis. We selected the "News and Happenings" subforum with a prior period of 2017-04-12 to 2017-04-18 and a target period of 2017-05-12 to 2017-05-18. The prior contains 404 posts, and the target contains 470 posts.

Secondly, we randomly selected a subforum, "Monetizing Techniques", and a random date range for the target (2016-12-23 to 2016-12-29 for the target, and a week in the previous month for the prior: 2016-11-23 to 2016-11-29). The prior contains 195 posts and the target contains 295 posts.

4.2 Log-odds and TF-IDF Results

We compare our approach to TF-IDF for topic ranking, using a similar approach to log-odds. This includes creating two TF-IDF "documents" as the set of posts for a given period (e.g. prior or target), as this is similar to the current method (frequent terms in the period but not frequent across all periods). We use the same tokenisation and pre-processing approach as the log-odds tool, to provide direct comparison. We selected TF-IDF, as it is a lightweight technique for topic ranking and detection.

For each event and technique, we plotted the top 10 tokens for the prior and target periods. For the "WannaCry" event, Figures 1 and 2 show the top tokens and scores for the prior and target periods. The results of the log-odds tool for the target period all contain tokens related to the WannaCry ransomware event. While TF-IDF also includes tokens related to the WannaCry ransomware event,

it additionally contains terms related to different events (e.g., "notebook", "pirates", and "sharing"). Figures 3 and 4 show the top tokens and scores for the randomly selected event.

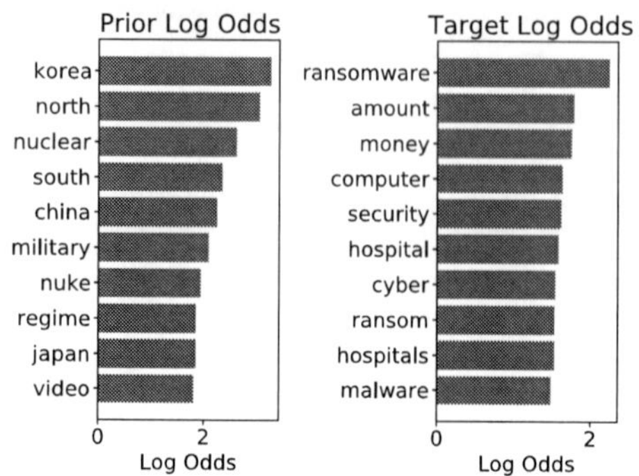

Figure 1: WannaCry Event with log-odds

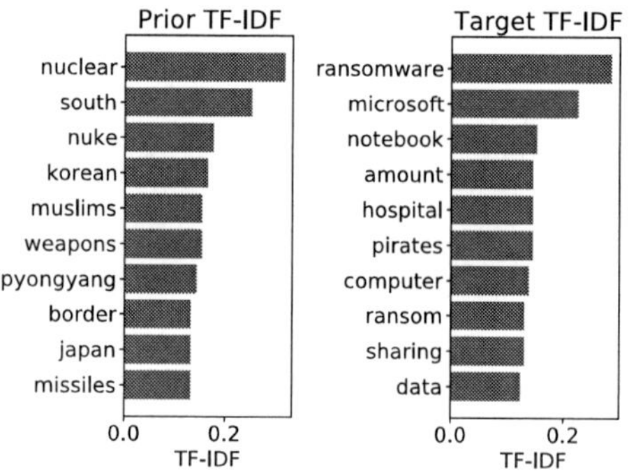

Figure 2: WannaCry Event with TF-IDF

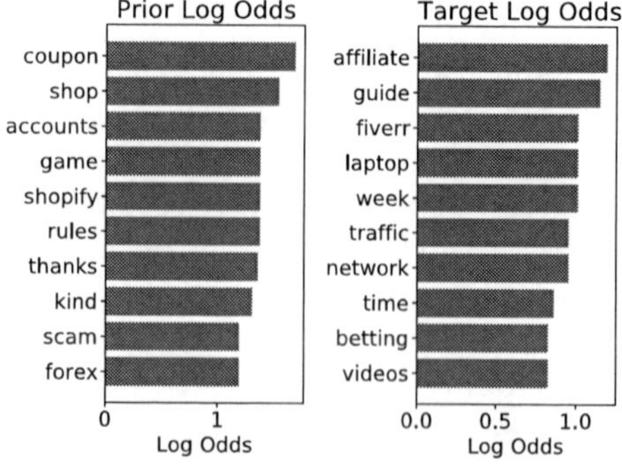

Figure 3: Random Event with log-odds

4.3 Annotation Task

First, we generated a list of ranked terms from both the tool and from TF-IDF, selecting the union of

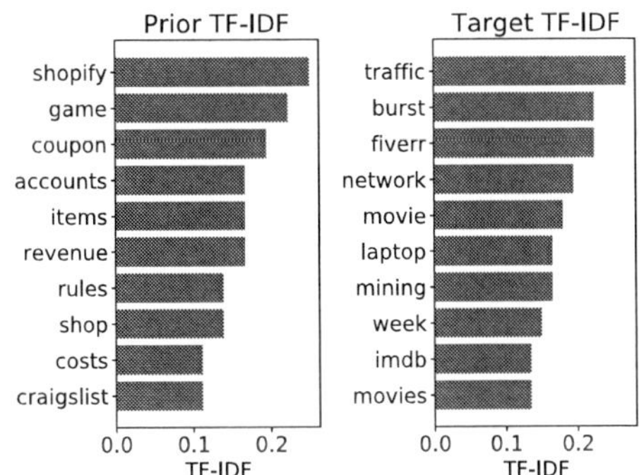

Figure 4: Random Event with TF-IDF

the top 10 terms of each event.

For the WannaCry event, these were: `amount`, `computer`, `cyber`, `data`, `hospital`, `hospitals`, `malware`, `microsoft`, `money`, `notebook`, `pirates`, `ransom`, `ransomware`, `security`, `sharing`.

For the randomly selected event, these were: `affiliate`, `betting`, `burst`, `fiverr`, `guide`, `imdb`, `laptop`, `mining`, `movie`, `movies`, `network`, `time`, `traffic`, `videos`, `week`.

For each event, we presented the three annotators with each post from the prior and target periods with the accompanying tags. The annotators selected the most salient tags for each post, leaving posts not annotated if there were no suitable salient tags. We measured inter-annotator agreement using multinomial Krippendorff's alpha with the MASI distance metric of sets (Passonneau, 2006) for comparison, finding an overall agreement of 0.833.

4.4 Discounted Cumulative Gain

Using our annotations combined using majority voting, we compared the ranking of the log-odds tool against TF-IDF, using normalised discounted cumulative gain (Järvelin and Kekäläinen, 2002). This is a metric used to evaluate the usefulness of a ranking of a list, by measuring the quality (salience) of tokens returned from the tool. We use discounted cumulative gain with the annotations of salient tokens, as the metric increases the weight of errors towards the top of the ranked list, compared to other rank correlation measures, such as Kendall's tau. Additionally, we do not have ground truth information on the ordering of all tokens.

For the WannaCry event, our log-odds tool scored 0.979 compared to TF-IDF of 0.877. For the random event, the log-odds tool scored 0.978 compared to TF-IDF of 0.753.

For both events, the log-odds tool had a greater discounted cumulative gain score than the TF-IDF approach, finding the ranking of terms provided by the log-odds tool produced more relevant salient terms than the TF-IDF method, for our forum dataset.

5   Discussion

Detecting trending topics on noisy social media data is not a new problem for information retrieval and NLP. However, we believe our application of an existing statistical method onto a longitudinal dataset provides a novel lightweight approach to detecting trending terms, which returns terms of more relevance than TF-IDF, and remains computationally less expensive than topic modelling such as LDA.

This work provided an initial step towards detecting temporal linguistic changes over time, by preprocessing text data, followed by using a Bayesian approach with a moving prior and target window depending on whether a user is observing short or long term trends. While our method does not identify the relevant windows itself, the tool can be combined with trending topic detection techniques to identify lexically distinct events, where some terms may re-trend.

Having shown that the statistical model is strong, and using a Bayesian approach can support new and evolving slang in the dataset without fine tuning a language model, we recognise that there are ways to further improve the NLP of cybersecurity forum texts. For instance, we can improve preprocessing in order to better deal with noisy texts: this includes the detection of misspellings, orthographic variation, acronyms and abbreviation, and deliberate obfuscation such as leetspeak. In addition, we can start to incorporate the detection of multiword expressions and named entity recognition techniques for noisy language, since both are likely to be of interest to researchers analysing language use in cybersecurity forums.

In future work we aim to increase understanding of the evolution of forums, changing language over time, and the changing topics of discussion by forum members. We also aim to automatically detect and extract events in the CrimeBB dataset. Although we have focused on analysing forum data, the tool can be used to explore trends in other corpora. In future work, we plan to use this approach to analyse how spam emails have changed following the COVID-19 pandemic.

6 Conclusion

In this work, we presented a new use-case for the log-odds tool introduced by Monroe et al. (2008) and implemented in the tidylo R library by Silge et al. (2020), for detecting trending terms in longitudinal historical noisy text data of an underground hacking forum. The tool can be used for both detecting short term and long term trends depending on the time windowing and separation of windows selected. Using annotations of salient terms during both discussion of WannaCry, and a randomly chosen duration, we found our approach to produce more relevant salient terms over TF-IDF.

Acknowledgments

We thank the Cambridge Cybercrime Centre for access to the CrimeBB dataset. We also thank our colleagues at the Cambridge Cybercrime Centre. This work was supported by the Economic and Social Research Council (ESRC), grant number ES/T008466/1. The third and fourth authors are supported by Cambridge Assessment, University of Cambridge.

References

Gustavo Aguilar, Suraj Maharjan, Adrian Pastor López-Monroy, and Thamar Solorio. 2017. A multi-task approach for named entity recognition in social media data. In *Proceedings of the 3rd Workshop on Noisy User-generated Text*, pages 148–153, Copenhagen, Denmark. Association for Computational Linguistics.

Luca Maria Aiello, Georgios Petkos, Carlos Martin, David Corney, Symeon Papadopoulos, Ryan Skraba, Ayse Goker, Ioannis Kompatsiaris, and Alejandro Jaimes. 2013. Sensing Trending Topics in Twitter. *IEEE Transactions on Multimedia*, 15(6):1268–1282.

Vahid Behzadan, Carlos Aguirre, Avishek Bose, and William Hsu. 2018. Corpus and Deep Learning Classifier for Collection of Cyber Threat Indicators in Twitter Stream. In *2018 IEEE International Conference on Big Data (Big Data)*, pages 5002–5007, Seattle, WA, USA. IEEE.

R. Bhalerao, M. Aliapoulios, I. Shumailov, S. Afroz, and D. McCoy. 2019. Mapping the underground: Supervised discovery of cybercrime supply chains. In *2019 APWG Symposium on Electronic Crime Research (eCrime)*, pages 1–16.

Abhinav Bhandari and Caitrin Armstrong. 2019. Tkol, httt, and r/radiohead: High affinity terms in Reddit communities. In *Proceedings of the 5th Workshop on Noisy User-generated Text (W-NUT 2019)*, pages 57–67, Hong Kong, China. Association for Computational Linguistics.

Steven Bird, Edward Loper, and Ewan Klein. 2009. *Natural Language Processing with Python*. O'Reilly Media Inc.

David M. Blei, Andrew Y. Ng, and Michael I. Jordan. 2003. Latent dirichlet allocation. *J. Mach. Learn. Res.*, 3:993–1022.

Avishek Bose, Vahid Behzadan, Carlos Aguirre, and William H. Hsu. 2019. A novel approach for detection and ranking of trendy and emerging cyber threat events in twitter streams. In *Proceedings of the 2019 IEEE/ACM International Conference on Advances in Social Networks Analysis and Mining*, ASONAM '19, page 871–878, New York, NY, USA. Association for Computing Machinery.

Andrew Caines, Sergio Pastrana, Alice Hutchings, and Paula J. Buttery. 2018. Automatically identifying the function and intent of posts in underground forums. *Crime Science*, 7(1):19.

Leon Derczynski, Eric Nichols, Marieke van Erp, and Nut Limsopatham. 2017. Results of the WNUT2017 shared task on novel and emerging entity recognition. In *Proceedings of the 3rd Workshop on Noisy User-generated Text*, pages 140–147, Copenhagen, Denmark. Association for Computational Linguistics.

Matthew Honnibal and Ines Montani. 2017. spaCy 2: Natural language understanding with Bloom embeddings, convolutional neural networks and incremental parsing.

Yuening Hu, Jordan Boyd-Graber, Brianna Satinoff, and Alison Smith. 2014. Interactive topic modeling. *Machine Learning*, 95(3):423–469.

Patrick Jansson and Shuhua Liu. 2017. Distributed representation, LDA topic modelling and deep learning for emerging named entity recognition from social media. In *Proceedings of the 3rd Workshop on Noisy User-generated Text*, pages 154–159, Copenhagen, Denmark. Association for Computational Linguistics.

Kalervo Järvelin and Jaana Kekäläinen. 2002. Cumulated gain-based evaluation of ir techniques. *ACM Trans. Inf. Syst.*, 20(4):422–446.

Jon Kleinberg. 2003. Bursty and Hierarchical Structure in Streams. *Data Mining and Knowledge Discovery*, 7(4):373–397.

Jon Kleinberg. 2016. *Temporal Dynamics of On-Line Information Streams*, pages 221–238. Springer Berlin Heidelberg, Berlin, Heidelberg.

Daichi Koike, Yusuke Takahashi, Takehito Utsuro, Masaharu Yoshioka, and Noriko Kando. 2013. Time series topic modeling and bursty topic detection of correlated news and twitter. In *Proceedings of the Sixth International Joint Conference on Natural Language Processing*, pages 917–921, Nagoya, Japan. Asian Federation of Natural Language Processing.

Brian Krebs. 2017. Who Is Marcus Hutchins? `https://krebsonsecurity.com/2017/09/who-is-marcus-hutchins/`.

Mitch Macdonald, Richard Frank, Joseph Mei, and Bryan Monk. 2015. Identifying Digital Threats in a Hacker Web Forum. In *Proceedings of the 2015 IEEE/ACM International Conference on Advances in Social Networks Analysis and Mining 2015 - ASONAM '15*, pages 926–933, Paris, France. ACM Press.

Carlos Martin, David Corney, and Ayse Goker. 2015. Mining Newsworthy Topics from Social Media. In *Advances in Social Media Analysis*, volume 602 of *Studies in Computational Intelligence*, pages 21–43. Springer International Publishing, Cham.

Burt L. Monroe, Michael P. Colaresi, and Kevin M. Quinn. 2008. Fightin' Words: Lexical Feature Selection and Evaluation for Identifying the Content of Political Conflict. *Political Analysis*, 16(4):372–403.

Rebecca Passonneau. 2006. Measuring agreement on set-valued items (MASI) for semantic and pragmatic annotation. In *Proceedings of the Fifth International Conference on Language Resources and Evaluation (LREC'06)*, Genoa, Italy. European Language Resources Association (ELRA).

Sergio Pastrana, Alice Hutchings, Andrew Caines, and Paula Buttery. 2018a. Characterizing Eve: Analysing Cybercrime Actors in a Large Underground Forum. In *Research in Attacks, Intrusions, and Defenses*, volume 11050, pages 207–227. Springer International Publishing, Cham.

Sergio Pastrana, Daniel R. Thomas, Alice Hutchings, and Richard Clayton. 2018b. CrimeBB: Enabling Cybercrime Research on Underground Forums at Scale. In *Proceedings of The Web Conference 2018*, Lyon, France.

Anna Sapienza, Sindhu Kiranmai Ernala, Alessandro Bessi, Kristina Lerman, and Emilio Ferrara. 2018. DISCOVER: Mining Online Chatter for Emerging Cyber Threats. In *Companion of the The Web Conference 2018 on The Web Conference 2018 - WWW '18*, pages 983–990, Lyon, France. ACM Press.

David A. Shamma, Lyndon Kennedy, and Elizabeth F. Churchill. 2011. Peaks and persistence: modeling the shape of microblog conversations. In *Proceedings of the ACM 2011 conference on Computer supported cooperative work - CSCW '11*, page 355, Hangzhou, China. ACM Press.

Julia Silge, Alex Hayes, and Tyler Schnoebelen. 2020. tidylo: Weighted Tidy Log Odds Ratio. `https://github.com/juliasilge/tidylo`.

William Smart. 2018. Lessons learned review of the WannaCry Ransomware Cyber Attack. Technical report, Department of Health and Social Care.

Karen Spärck Jones. 1972. A statistical interpretation of term specificity and its application in retrieval. *Journal of Documentation*, 28:11–21.

Yusuke Takahashi, Takehito Utsuro, Masaharu Yoshioka, Noriko Kando, Tomohiro Fukuhara, Hiroshi Nakagawa, and Yoji Kiyota. 2012. Applying a burst model to detect bursty topics in a topic model. In *Advances in Natural Language Processing*, pages 239–249, Berlin, Heidelberg. Springer Berlin Heidelberg.

Nazgol Tavabi, Nathan Bartley, Andres Abeliuk, Sandeep Soni, Emilio Ferrara, and Kristina Lerman. 2019. Characterizing activity on the deep and dark web. In *Companion Proceedings of The 2019 World Wide Web Conference*, WWW '19, page 206–213, New York, NY, USA. Association for Computing Machinery.

Linzi Xing and Michael J. Paul. 2017. Incorporating metadata into content-based user embeddings. In *Proceedings of the 3rd Workshop on Noisy User-generated Text*, pages 45–49, Copenhagen, Denmark. Association for Computational Linguistics.

Service registration chatbot: collecting and comparing dialogues from AMT workers and service's users

Luca Molteni   **Mittul Singh**   **Juho Leinonen**   **Katri Leino**   **Mikko Kurimo**
Department of Signal Processing and Acoustics, Aalto University, Finland
`firstname.lastname@aalto.fi`
Emanuele Della Valle
Department of Electronics, Information and Bioengineering, Politecnico of Milano, Italy
`emanuele.dellavalle@polimi.it`

Abstract

Crowdsourcing is the go-to solution for data collection and annotation in the context of NLP tasks. Nevertheless, crowdsourced data is noisy by nature; the source is often unknown and additional validation work is performed to guarantee the dataset's quality. In this article, we compare two crowdsourcing sources on a dialogue paraphrasing task revolving around a chatbot service. We observe that workers hired on crowdsourcing platforms produce lexically poorer and less diverse rewrites than service users engaged voluntarily. Notably enough, on dialogue clarity and optimality, the two paraphrase sources' human-perceived quality does not differ significantly. Furthermore, for the chatbot service, the combined crowdsourced data is enough to train a transformer-based Natural Language Generation (NLG) system. To enable similar services, we also release tools for collecting data and training the dialogue-act-based transformer-based NLG module[1].

1 Introduction

Task-specific neural dialogue models demand high-quality annotated dialogue data. Unfortunately, gathering human-generated and annotated dialogues is a costly and time-consuming task. Easily accessible sources, like social-network feeds and online forums, are cursed by systematic problems such as extra-linguistic annotations, irregular turn-taking, and the lack of a standard format leading to an intense pre-processing phase. Even so, models trained with this type of data might not work well in a more natural domain (Leino et al., 2020). In recent times, thanks to online platforms like Amazon Mechanical Turk (AMT) [2], crowdsourcing has become the most popular solution to tackle

the problem of manually generating and annotating written dialogues.

However, as a small business, minimizing such added costs while automating user-based workflows is essential. In this work, we consider leveraging voluntary submissions by business users for creating a chatbot.

For the chatbot service, we consider a new class of broadly diffused tasks that we name Service Registration Tasks (SRTs), which involves the domain-agnostic act of registering to an online service. As a use case, we work with SiirtoSoitto[3] to provide users with a chatbot for service registration. SiirtoSoitto is a free online service offered to the city of Helsinki that notifies users about scheduled roadworks and imminent car towings. We employ a dialogue templating method called Machine Talking to Machines (M2M) (Shah et al., 2018b,a). It simulates the interaction between a user and system to automatically generate templates, which are then paraphrased by AMT and service users.

In this work, we make the following contributions. **1)** We release the data collection tools to the public, including an integration with popular instant messaging platforms to engage with service's users (Section 4). **2)** We analyze and compare the data collected via AMT workers and service's users in an empirical and human evaluation (Section 5). **3)** We show the usefulness of collected data by training a dialogue act induced transformer-based language generation module (Section 6). We also release the module's code publicly.

2 Service Registration Task (SRT)

Here, we focus on a class of tasks named Service Registration Tasks that consists of registering to a general online service. This human-machine interaction is characterized by the collection and val-

---

[1] `https://github.com/Molteh/M2M`
[2] `https://www.mturk.com/`

[3] `https://www.siirtosoitto.com`

Proceedings of the 2020 EMNLP Workshop W-NUT: The Sixth Workshop on Noisy User-generated Text, pages 116–121
Online, Nov 19, 2020. ©2020 Association for Computational Linguistics

idation of information and preferences from the user. As a specific instance of this class of tasks, we picked the use case of SiirtoSoitto, an online service that warns and notifies vehicle owners in the city of Helsinki about road maintenance and imminent towings.

3 Machines Talking to Machines (M2M)

For chatbot development, we employ the Machine Talking to Machines (M2M) framework (Shah et al., 2018b,a) to setup the annotated data collection. Conceived as being domain-independent, M2M generates dialogues centered on completing a specific task.

The M2M consists of four major steps. **1)**, the developer provides the task-specific knowledge used by the system. It can be seen as a collection of all the units of information exchanged during the dialogue. **2)** Given a task specification, a simulated interaction of a user and the system generates sequences of dialogue acts exhaustively. The output sequences enclose the semantic content of the dialogue. The user is modeled as an agenda-based user simulator (Schatzmann et al., 2007) while the system is designed as a *Mealy* machine. This process is also called *self-play*, where a simulated user interacts with the system. A generated example is shown in the first row of Table 1. **3)** Using the semantic parses, we can then build dialogue templates using a simple domain grammar. The templates are slightly unnatural computer-generated dialogue utterances paired with their semantic representation in the form of dialogue acts (second row of Table 1). **4)** Finally, the dialogue templates enter a paraphrasing phase where crowdsource workers provide natural and contextual rewrites of the machine-generated sentences (last row of Table 1).

4 Applying M2M to SRT

Our SRT is characterized by exchanging information such as telephone numbers, license plates, areas of interest, and the acceptance of terms and conditions. These characteristics form the task-specification used to initialize the M2M's first step. A dialogue scenario is sampled by assigning a valid or invalid value to each entity.

Through self-play, we can generate sequences of dialogue acts until the goal of registering is reached or some invalid state is encountered (e.g., the user provides invalid values). Next, we build a simple rule-based domain grammar that converts the anno-

Self-play annotations	request(license_plate), request (phone_number)
Template utterance	provide reference for: License plate and Phone number
Paraphrase	please list your license plates and your phone number

Table 1: A single-turn sample showcasing the M2M generation process.

tated sequences into templates, first turning them into syntactic skeletons with proper punctuation and conjunctions, and then substituting the entity values with custom terms to increase readability.

In the next step, the same dialogues are used to set up a paraphrasing task on AMT and on the rule-based chatbot that makes SiirtoSoitto available to the public. Chatbot users are asked to participate voluntarily in an experimental task. They are presented with dialogue turns to rewrite sequentially on their preferred instant messaging application. A quick manual quality check removed roughly 25% of all AMT feedback due to a lack of compliance with the instructions. In contrast only 10% of SiirtoSoitto users failed to understand their task and produced unusable data.

In the above process, instead of annotating natural utterances, we are building dialogues upon annotations. The automatic generation of the outlines guarantees greater diversity and explores all the relevant paths conceived by the task designer. Finally, employing human writers ensures the *naturalness* of the utterances, and the variety is boosted by asking them to rephrase highly generic machine-generated sentences. This reverse processing guarantees the quality of the semantic annotations.

In Table 4, we present the statistics of the data collected by employing AMT and service users (SiirtoSoitto). In each case, we ran the paraphrasing step over multiple sessions across five days. We presented the same dialogue set to both the groups to improve the comparability among generated paraphrases. Then, we performed a human evaluation to validate paraphrase quality and removed any spurious paraphrases. We were able to collect 98 and 83 dialogues via AMT and SiirtoSoitto users, respectively. With a larger number of dialogues and turns, AMT workers produced more data than SiirtoSoitto users.

In terms of effort, we set up the paraphrasing task on AMT and the chatbot service in similar

Metric	AMT	SiirtoSoitto
Dialogues	98	83
#Turns	898	718
#Tokens	7723	5069
Lexical richness (#Unique *n-grams*/ #Tokens)		
Unigrams	0.104	**0.161**
Bigrams	0.103	**0.122**
Trigrams	0.28	**0.387**
Diversity		
Tdiv	155	**270**
Jaccard distance	0.432	**0.490**

Table 2: Summary of the quantitative evaluation.

amounts of time. For the chatbot service, we introduced some additional conversational interaction and integrated the M2M-generated templates into the service. For the AMT setup, we had to design and implement the paraphrasing task in AMT task's single HTML page and import batches of dialogue templates by hand. From a monetary standpoint, as we recruited users voluntarily, paraphrasing with chatbot users did not lead to any costs. On AMT, we spent a total of 63$ which includes the cost for each single task (0.5$) and the platform fees.

5   Evaluation

In this section, we compare the data collected via the two different crowdsourcing sources. We compare them quantitatively based on the lexical richness and language diversity. We also ask human evaluators to grade dialogues qualitatively.

5.1   Lexical Richness and Diversity

Lexical rich and diverse paraphrases can allow the chatbot to feel more real and natural. In effect, it helps the users to have a more satisfying experience even in a simple task. Hence, having lexical rich and diverse data is desirable.

Lexical richness is calculated as the ratio between unique *n-grams* and total tokens per collection source (Hout and Vermeer, 2007). Interestingly, even with a lower dialogue count, the SiirtoSoitto dataset presents a higher lexical richness than the AMT dataset. This effect indicates greater language variety associated with expert user rewrites. Moreover, higher bigram and trigram lexical richness for SiirtoSoitto dataset than AMT datasets highlights a greater construct variety in SiirtoSoitto dataset. Table 3 displays an example this effect

Dialogue template	provide reference for: Phone number
AMT rewrite	please provide phone number.
SiirtoSoitto rewrite	can you still give me your phone number please?

Table 3: Example of rewrite collected from AMT and SiirtoSoitto chatbot service users.

where the SiirtoSoitto users rewrite with more constructs than AMT workers.

Diversity is measured by using two metrics: Term Frequency - Inverse Document Frequency (TF-IDF) diversity metric (Tdiv) (Liu et al., 2019) and Jaccard distance.

Tdiv is the sum of TF-IDF scores over *n-grams* ($n \leq 3$) in a document (D), as defined below. TF-IDF reflects the importance of an *n-gram*. *n-grams* with lower frequency in the collected data have higher IDFs. Thus, the Tdiv metric denotes the extent of diversity of an expression in the dataset.

$$Tdiv(R) = \sum_{n=1}^{N} \frac{\sum_{n\text{-}gram \in R} TF\text{-}IDF(n\text{-}gram)}{V_n}$$

$$V_n = \frac{1}{|D|} \sum_{R \in D} \sum_{n\text{-}gram \in R} TF\text{-}IDF(n\text{-}gram)$$

The Tdiv score for a sentence has little meaning, as it needs to be compared with Tdiv scores of sentences that entail the same semantic content. Given two rewrites for the same turn, one from the AMT dataset and one from SiirtoSoitto, if the latter has a higher Tdiv score, it is considered having more vibrant expressions than the former. For an overall comparison, we keep track these *wins* for each type of dataset per turn. We observe that SiirtoSoitto wins almost two out of three times, thus having paraphrases with richer expressions.

The Jaccard distance is a metric based on the Jaccard similarity coefficient that measures the dissimilarity between two finite sets of elements, in this case, the words that make up a sentence. This coefficient has been used as a proxy of the effort put in by the crowdsource to write paraphrases with different wordings from the proposed templates. In terms of average Jaccard distance, SiirtoSoitto (0.490) users outperform Amazon Turkers (0.432). This effect is exemplified by the example shown in

	AMT	SiirtoSoitto
Naturalness	4.05 (0.74)	4.15 (0.65)
Clearness	4.30 (0.71)	4.05 (0.80)
Grammaticality	3.85 (0.65)	4.20 (0.67)
Optimality	4.05 (0.49)	4.00 (0.63)

Table 4: Results of human evaluation on the collected dialogues. Numbers shows average scores of per dialogue grading. Standard deviation in brackets.

Table 3, where SiirtoSoitto users use more words than AMT workers.

5.2 Qualitative evaluation

Human evaluators assessed the perceived quality of the generated and paraphrased dialogues. Each dialogue was judged for four qualities: naturalness, clearness, grammaticality, and optimality. Naturalness indicates how well the sentences resemble typical human expressions. Clearness refers to the extent to which the meaning conveyed by the dialogue turns is easily understandable. Grammaticality reflects the absence of misspellings or badly formatted sentences. Finally, optimality refers to how quickly the proposed rewrites seem to go straight to the point. The scores were provided on a scale of one to five, with one representing the lowest quality and five being the highest. Table 4 details the score average across the twenty evaluators. Both AMT- and SiirtoSoitto-based datasets were judged to be similar from a human standpoint, as their differences were not significant. Also, both datasets scored highly on the four dimensions attesting the quality of the data collected.

6 Transformer-based language generator

We train a neural model for Natural Language Generation (NLG) to observe the effectiveness of the collected data. The neural model is a Transformer network (Vaswani et al., 2017) that converts the next dialogue acts into an output sentence. For the NLG use case, our Transformer architecture includes two separate encoders. The first encoder inputs a sequence of dialogue acts capturing the semantic meaning of the sentence that needs to be generated. The second encoder inputs the user's turn. As a single person writes each paraphrase of an entire dialogue, the person's style is reflected in both user and system turns. Intuitively, the second encoder employs the user's style to adapt the generated utterance to the user's persona. Our trans-

```
> hi ! EOS
> act greeting slot none value none  act propose
slot registration value none EOS
< hello ! would you like to register to this
service ? EOS

> hi EOS
> act greeting slot none value none act propose
slot registration value none EOS
< hello would you like to register to SiirtoSoitto
EOS

> my area is Helsinki Central EOS
> act request slot terms and conditions value
none EOS
< please accept the terms and conditions EOS
```

Figure 1: Examples of some test set sentences generated with the NLG module.

former implementation is trained with the Noam optimizer on negative log-likelihood loss (Vaswani et al., 2017). Encoders and decoder are characterized by three identical replicated blocks, 16 attention heads and a dropout rate of 0.1. Both the first encoder and decoder have 1024 hidden nodes while the second encoder uses 256 hidden nodes. We release our dialogue-act based transformer implementation with this work[4].

Figure 1 showcases some of the sentences generated with the NLG module. It also includes an instance in which the same sequence of input dialogue acts results in different system output sentences given the different user's utterances.

7 Related work

In our work, we applied M2M via two types of crowdsourcing methods. Earlier work (Kittur et al., 2008) has shown that AMT workers achieve significantly lower performances when the degree of experience and contextual knowledge is important. However, their performance improves with a more guided task structure. In our experiment, the service's users already had the background knowledge necessary for the task. Moreover, considering the generated dialogue's lexical richness and diversity, their paraphrases were ranked higher than AMT workers. However, at a qualitative level, both types of paraphrase ranked similarly.

Prior work (Walker et al., 2018; Budzianowski et al., 2018) has been concerned about the *unnatural* process of dialogue generation in the M2M approach. In our perspective, this issue affects scenarios where a simulated user cannot model the ambiguities of a real user, but for a simplistic SRT

---

[4]https://github.com/Molteh/M2M

use case, we disregard this issue.

For creating the NLG module, we focus on the generation of surface expression based on sequences of dialogue acts. Similarly, quite a few prior work (Stent, 2001; Wen et al., 2015; Liu and Liu, 2019; Varshney et al., 2020; Chen et al., 2019; Nayak et al., 2017) have employed semantic structures to generate dialogue utterances. Stent (2001) leveraged custom dialogue acts to implement a rule-based utterance generator as part of a bigger modular conversational system. Recently, LSTM-based machine translation models (Wen et al., 2015; Nayak et al., 2017) and Transformers (Liu and Liu, 2019; Varshney et al., 2020; Chen et al., 2019) have also been successfully explored in NLG tasks for open-domain and task-specific dialogue systems. For both open-domain and task-specific modules, large corpora of annotations are required for training the modules. In contrast, our work considers a simple SRT where even small amounts of crowd-sourced data can help build good models. Additionally, unlike most of the prior work, we release our NLG module code to the public.

8 Conclusions

Collecting annotated datasets for NLG is a challenging task which sees crowdsourcing as the preferred solution to balance costs and time. In this work, we considered voluntarily engaging SiirtoSoitto's users to contribute towards a paraphrasing task for building a chatbot. Our findings suggest that engaging SiirtoSoitto users might produce more diverse and lexically rich results than engaging AMT workers empirically whereas, from a qualitative standpoint, both the datasets are similar for a simple service registration task. We can obtain similar amounts of data while running the data collection effort employing both sets of users for a comparable time. More importantly, through this process, we were able to reduce our costs of collecting data.

Additionally, in simple use cases like the SRT, this data are enough to build a transformer-based NLG module conditioned on dialogue acts. To support other small businesses, we make our data collection pipeline and code to train the transformer-based NLG module public.

Acknowledgments

We thank Twenty Hexagons Oy, the company behind SiirtoSoitto service, which provided us the opportunity to work with their infrastructure and engage with their user base. We also thank anonymous reviewers for their helpful comments.

References

Paweł Budzianowski, Tsung-Hsien Wen, Bo-Hsiang Tseng, Iñigo Casanueva, Stefan Ultes, Osman Ramadan, and Milica Gašić. 2018. MultiWOZ - a large-scale multi-domain wizard-of-Oz dataset for task-oriented dialogue modelling. In *Proceedings of the 2018 Conference on Empirical Methods in Natural Language Processing*, pages 5016–5026, Brussels, Belgium. Association for Computational Linguistics.

Wenhu Chen, Jianshu Chen, Pengda Qin, Xifeng Yan, and William Yang Wang. 2019. Semantically conditioned dialog response generation via hierarchical disentangled self-attention.

Roeland Hout and Anne Vermeer. 2007. Comparing measures of lexical richness. *In: H. Daller, J. Milton J. Treffers-Daller (eds.), Modelling and assessing vocabulary knowledge (93-116). Cambridge: Cambridge University Press.*

Aniket Kittur, Ed H. Chi, and Bongwon Suh. 2008. Crowdsourcing user studies with mechanical turk. In *Proceedings of the SIGCHI Conference on Human Factors in Computing Systems*, CHI '08, page 453–456, New York, NY, USA. Association for Computing Machinery.

Katri Leino, Juho Leinonen, Mittul Singh, Sami Virpioja, and Mikko Kurimo. 2020. Finchat: Corpus and evaluation setup for finnish chat conversations on everyday topics. *arXiv preprint arXiv:2008.08315.*

D. Liu and G. Liu. 2019. A transformer-based variational autoencoder for sentence generation. In *2019 International Joint Conference on Neural Networks (IJCNN)*, pages 1–7.

L. Liu, J. Tang, X. Wan, and Z. Guo. 2019. Generating diverse and descriptive image captions using visual paraphrases. In *2019 IEEE/CVF International Conference on Computer Vision (ICCV)*, pages 4239–4248.

Neha Nayak, Dilek Hakkani-Tur, Marilyn Walker, and Larry Heck. 2017. To plan or not to plan? discourse planning in slot-value informed sequence to sequence models for language generation. pages 3339–3343.

Jost Schatzmann, Blaise Thomson, Karl Weilhammer, Hui Ye, and Steve Young. 2007. Agenda-based user simulation for bootstrapping a POMDP dialogue system. In *Human Language Technologies 2007: The Conference of the North American Chapter of the Association for Computational Linguistics; Companion Volume, Short Papers*, pages 149–152, Rochester, New York. Association for Computational Linguistics.

Pararth Shah, Dilek Hakkani-Tür, Bing Liu, and Gokhan Tür. 2018a. Bootstrapping a neural conversational agent with dialogue self-play, crowdsourcing and on-line reinforcement learning. In *Proceedings of the 2018 Conference of the North American Chapter of the Association for Computational Linguistics: Human Language Technologies, Volume 3 (Industry Papers)*, pages 41–51, New Orleans - Louisiana. Association for Computational Linguistics.

Pararth Shah, Dilek Hakkani-Tür, Gökhan Tür, Abhinav Rastogi, Ankur Bapna, Neha Nayak, and Larry P. Heck. 2018b. Building a conversational agent overnight with dialogue self-play. *CoRR*, abs/1801.04871.

Amanda Stent. 2001. *Dialogue Systems as Conversational Partners: Applying conversation acts theory to natural language generation for task-oriented mixed-initiative spoken dialogue*. Ph.D. thesis.

Deeksha Varshney, Asif Ekbal, Ganesh Prasad Nagaraja, Mrigank Tiwari, Abhijith Athreya Mysore Gopinath, and Pushpak Bhattacharyya. 2020. Natural language generation using transformer network in an open-domain setting. In *Natural Language Processing and Information Systems*, pages 82–93, Cham. Springer International Publishing.

Ashish Vaswani, Noam Shazeer, Niki Parmar, Jakob Uszkoreit, Llion Jones, Aidan N Gomez, Ł ukasz Kaiser, and Illia Polosukhin. 2017. Attention is all you need. In I. Guyon, U. V. Luxburg, S. Bengio, H. Wallach, R. Fergus, S. Vishwanathan, and R. Garnett, editors, *Advances in Neural Information Processing Systems 30*, pages 5998–6008. Curran Associates, Inc.

Marilyn Walker, Albry Smither, Shereen Oraby, Vrindavan Harrison, and Hadar Shemtov. 2018. Exploring conversational language generation for rich content about hotels. In *Proceedings of the Eleventh International Conference on Language Resources and Evaluation (LREC-2018)*, Miyazaki, Japan. European Languages Resources Association (ELRA).

Tsung-Hsien Wen, Milica Gašić, Nikola Mrkšić, Pei-Hao Su, David Vandyke, and Steve Young. 2015. Semantically conditioned LSTM-based natural language generation for spoken dialogue systems. In *Proceedings of the 2015 Conference on Empirical Methods in Natural Language Processing*, pages 1711–1721, Lisbon, Portugal. Association for Computational Linguistics.

Automated Assessment of Noisy Crowdsourced Free-text Answers for Hindi in Low Resource Setting

Dolly Agarwal[1], Somya Gupta[2], Nishant Baghel[1]

[1]Pratham Education Foundation
[2]Pratham Volunteer*
[1]{dolly.agarwal, nishant.baghel}@pratham.org, [2]somya.gupta1@gmail.com

Abstract

The requirement of performing assessments continually on a larger scale necessitates the implementation of automated systems for evaluation of the learners' responses to free-text questions. We target children of age group 8-14 years and use an ASR integrated assessment app to crowdsource learners' responses to free text questions in Hindi. The app helped collect 39641 user answers to 35 different questions of Science topics. Since the users are young children from rural India and may not be well-equipped with technology, it brings in various noise types in the answers. We describe these noise types and propose a preprocessing pipeline to denoise user's answers. We showcase the performance of different similarity metrics on the noisy and denoised versions of user and model answers. Our findings have large-scale applications for automated answer assessment for school children in India in low resource settings.

1 Introduction

Posing and assessing open-ended descriptive questions to children is crucial to evaluating their learning levels and improving their understanding of concepts. Unfortunately, this puts an enormous load on the classroom teacher who is faced with assessing and providing feedback to every child. As a result, teachers are not able to give writing assignments or do oral evaluation as often as they would wish. The problem is even more important in rural areas where availability of teachers is low, and children seldom get access to quality assessments. This highlights the importance of developing applications that automate assessments for children. Free-text questions allow a respondent to answer in open text format such that they can answer based on their complete knowledge and understanding. This means that response to this question is not limited to a set of options.

Though the evaluation of multiple-choice questions is straightforward and can be scaled, we need robust systems to assess the free text questions as well. This presents an interesting challenge for automated assessments as there are multiple versions of correct answers for the same question in free-text format. We show some examples in Table 1. Extracting information from the text in low resource languages such as Hindi is even more challenging for the NLP community. Further, crowdsourcing such free-text answers at scale brings another challenge of noise in the collected data.

This paper presents our experience with automated assessment of free-text answers by developing an automated assessment system for one of the low resource languages - Hindi which is the medium of instruction in government schools in Rajasthan and Uttar Pradesh states of India. The children were of age group 8-14 years from rural areas of India, and hence were not well equipped with technology like their urban counterparts. We developed an Android assessment app for these children to give assessments at any time they wanted to. One assessment has a mix of question types including

---

* Currently affiliated with LinkedIn. This work was done as a Pratham volunteer and is not connected with LinkedIn.

Proceedings of the 2020 EMNLP Workshop W-NUT: The Sixth Workshop on Noisy User-generated Text, pages 122–131
Online, Nov 19, 2020. ©2020 Association for Computational Linguistics

Question (Hindi / ETL)	Varieties of correct answers (Original / ETL)
आंखों में धूल चली जाने पर आंसू क्यों आ जाते हैं? / Why do we tear up when dirt enters our eyes?	aansu nikalne se dhul ke kan bahar aa jate hai / dust particles get released due to tears
	आंखों से धूल बाहर निकलने के लिए / to remove dirt from eyes
उत्तोलक कितने प्रकार के होते हैं? / How many types of levers are there?	तीन / three
	तीन प्रकार का / of three types
	3
	three
	प्रथम श्रेणी दितीय श्रेणी तृतीय श्रेणी यह तीन प्रकार के होते हैं / first class, second class, third class, these three types
	Teen / three

Table 1: Varieties of correct answers for the same question

MCQ and free-text questions. To facilitate the answer to free-text questions, we allowed the children to type the answers. We also enabled automated speech recognition services where the child could speak out the answer and then edit it. It also reinforced our objective to test the knowledge and understanding of a child in a particular subject and not their writing ability. The assessment app helped collect 39641 user answers to 35 different questions of Science topics.

We manually went through various user answers and found different varieties of noise that needed cleaning before it could be evaluated. With these noise types in answers, it is a challenging task even for a human evaluator to assess children's answers. It is also critical to enable assessment through denoising, as we do not wish to incorrectly mark an answer that can lead to a child getting discouraged from using the platform altogether. For example, a noisy answer which is correct is shown below:

User Answer: tan,k.g\n
Model Answer: १० किग्रा (ETL: 10 kg)

Though the test was in Hindi, we also found that around ~60% of the answers contained English alphabets. This may be for two reasons:

i. The child is not comfortable using Indic Keyboard and hence typed in English

ii. Language pack was not downloaded for Hindi in the phone and hence the Hindi text was transliterated to English while using Speech-To-Text (STT).

Following are two examples of correct answers which are in English alphabets:

Question: हड्डियों के बीच जोड़ नहीं होते तो क्या होता? (ETL: What would have happened if there were no joints between the bones?)
User Answer:
a. ham hil nahi pate (Transliterated to English)
b. We cannot be move and do action (English Translation)

In this paper, we describe various noise types identified in detail and propose a preprocessing pipeline for answers collected through automated speech recognition (ASR) enabled assessment app.

After the preprocessing, we compute similarity scores between user answers with their reference answer. We test different similarity metrics for both original noisy answers and their denoised versions. The idea is to measure the significance of denoising the answer before passing through assessment. Interestingly we find that denoising enables a simple word-matching based metric to perform as good as semantic similarity measures. This finding has promising implications for deployment of such solutions in low resource settings.

It is important to note that the focus of our study is for the rural children in remote areas of India with limited internet access. Hence, we need to find a solution which could be integrated with a system in low resource setting i.e., with low computing, memory and battery capacity. Thus, while more complex state-of the-art models like LSTMs, BERT may give higher performance for sentence similarity measurement, we choose similarity measures as our assessment methodology as the primary requirement we have is to keep the assessment model as simple as possible to ensure it does not add a lot of memory requirement to the app.

The main contributions in this paper are (1) listing the types of noise possible in a text-based ASR enabled assessment tool, (2) a preprocessing pipeline to handle those noises and transform the user answer to a format consumable by NLP systems, (3) comparison of various semantic similarity measures on noisy and denoised answers.

2   Previous Work

Research in the area of evaluation of descriptive free text answers has been in progress since a decade and a half. Burrows et al., (2015) did a comprehensive review of Automatic Short Answer Grading (ASAG) research and systems according to history and components. Their historical analysis identifies 35 ASAG systems within 5 temporal themes that mark advancement in methodology or evaluation.

Butcher et al., (2010) compared the marking accuracy of three separate computerized systems, one system (Intelligent Assessment Technologies FreeText Author) is based on computational linguistics whilst two (Regular Expressions and OpenMark) are based on the algorithmic manipulation of keywords. Patil et al. (2018) experimented with training a Naive Bayes classifier based on three parameters: Keywords, Grammar and Question Specific things. They proposed a system where students will have a certain degree of freedom while writing the answer as the system checks for the presence of keywords, synonyms, right word context and coverage of all concepts. But the experiment was conducted with only 20 students and 3 questions to each student.

Perez et al., (2005) presented a comparative evaluation between BLEU-inspired algorithm and a system based on Latent Semantic Analysis and proposed a combination schema. Despite the simplicity of these shallow NLP methods, they achieved state-of-the-art correlations to the teachers' scores while keeping the language-independence and without requiring any domain specific knowledge

Lun et al., (2020) proposed multiple data augmentation strategies for improving performance on automatic short answer scoring. They combined it with the latest fine-tuned BERT model for the short answer scoring task, and show significant gain.

Bonadiman et al., (2019) discuss a new Question Paraphrase Retrieval (QPR) system that can be used to understand and answer rare and noisy reformulations of common questions by mapping them to a set of canonical forms.

To the best of our knowledge, this is the first study which handles noises in user answers while evaluating the short answers typed in by the children in Indian language. Also, focus is in a method with less computing and memory needs, so that it can be used for large scale implementation in Android devices.

3   Data and Attributes

We conducted our assessment in the Hybrid Learning program of Pratham which reaches more than 1000 villages and over 109,560 children. Every group of 5-6 children have one tablet provided by Pratham with digital learning content. An Android Assessment app (Figure 1) was developed and loaded in these tablets for children to give assessments anytime they wanted to. The assessment app helped collect 39641 user answers to 35 different questions of Science topics. Each answer was then manually evaluated as correct/incorrect by two different raters and their agreement score as calculated by Cohen's Kappa κ score is 0.74. Total Average number of unique correct answers per question is 34.

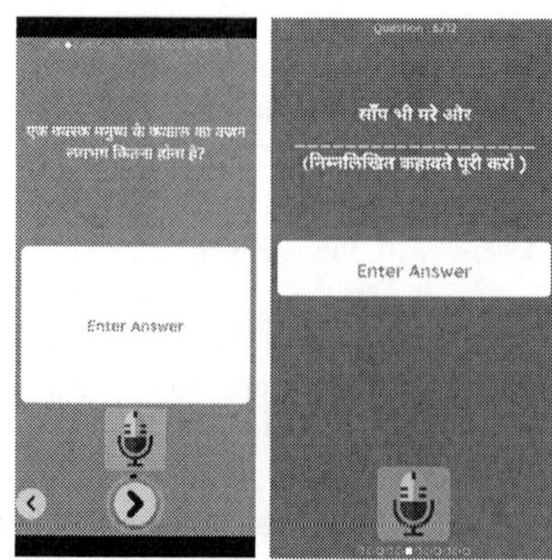

Figure 1: UI for free text question (space to type in the answer and a mic to use STT)

3.1 Challenges

Since any child could give the assessment whenever they like in an unsupervised way, this increased the chances of gibberish in the dataset as the child could use the app just for fun. Furthermore, the option to enter the answer through a speech recognition system was helpful for the child but also bought in its own unique challenges. Listed in Table 2 are the various types of noise we found in the data. Additionally, when we checked the evaluated data, the level of agreement between two annotators calculated by Cohen's Kappa κ score is 0.74. We can see that even with human raters there is a mismatch between the ratings. This puts a spotlight on the requirement of a standardized mechanism to evaluate children on the same scoring model. Another important finding from the evaluated dataset is that the same question can have many varieties of correct answers, a sample of such answers are highlighted in Table 1. On average, there are 34 unique correct answers per question in our crowdsourced dataset.

3.2 Noise Types in Crowdsourced Data

We begin by highlighting different types of noise and their prevalence in the data (Table 2) which we came across in the answers submitted by children. We have discussed them in detail below as it gives a fair idea about the noise types to expect in a text-based speech recognition enabled assessment app. This list is not exhaustive, but it covers the vast majority of cases observed in this paper's datasets.

Type of Noise	Percentage (%)
Punctuators	14.80
URL	0.12
Emoji	0.53
Subscripts/Superscripts	0.015
English Alphabets	59.4

Table 2: Different types of noise

1. **Punctuations:** Since our focus is on the semantic similarity of short answer questions, the significance of punctuation is less. We observed that there are unnecessary punctuations due to typos in ~15% of user answers. We removed the punctuators, and replaced comma with spaces. Example of such answers:

10,kg
हम,हिल,डुल,नही,सकते / ETL: we can't move
Hilana,dulana,asmbhav,ho,jata

These answers are correct but have unnecessary commas after every word. We replaced these commas with space. Also, we removed all other punctuations observed in the answers.

2. **Emojis:** Though Emoji can express an emotion for sentiment analysis it is irrelevant in our use case because our aim is to analyze knowledge of a child on a particular concept. Only 0.53% of user answers had some form of emoji and it seemed to be typo and thus can safely be removed. For example,
😄रक्त का थक्का नही जमेगा (ETL: *There would be no blood clotting*) is a correct answer but has emoji as noise.

3. **Translated Text:** The assessment test was in Hindi and expected answers from children were in the same language. But we see that there are instances (~60%) where the answer is in English and some of which are correct too. Since, our main objective is to assess how well acquainted the child is with the concept irrespective of the language, we need to consider these answers and handle it accordingly. So, we used Google translate library to convert the answers back to Hindi before it can be used by the NLP systems. For example, BONES was converted to हड्डियों

4. **Transliterated Text:** We also found some scenarios where the answer was in native language (Hindi) but was transliterated in English. This happens when the device that the child is using to give assessment does not have the Language pack downloaded for their native language. In such scenarios, the Hindi text is transliterated to English while using STT. To handle the transliterated text, we use Indic Transliteration library to transliterate it back to Hindi for evaluation.

For example, *haddi* was converted to *हड्डी* (ETL: Bone)

5. **Digits:** While working on the solution, we realized there is a performance drop in the similarity metrics because of numbers. We need to ensure that both the ideal answer and user answer either specify numbers as digits or number names. Our ideal answers have numbers present as number names; hence, we converted the numbers to their corresponding word lexemes. For example, *4561* was converted to *चार हज़ार पांच सौ इकसठ* (ETL: *Four Thousand Five Hundred and Sixty-One*).

6. **URL:** There were answers which contained urls in them and are irrelevant in our context. These urls were also present sometimes along with the correct answers. Since, these urls are insignificant, they are considered noise and removed from the answers. Here's an example of a correct answer that has a url at the end which can safely be removed: *हड्डियोंसेhttps://faq.whatsapp.com/general/26000015?lg=en&lc=IN&eea=0* (Ideal answer here is *हड्डियों से*, ETL: *with bones*)

7. **Subscript & Superscript characters:** A few user answers had subscript and superscript characters in the answers. Although these subscripts and superscripts might be significant in Science answers, the question-answer set in our dataset had none. We were facing issues with these characters while using Google Translate and hence we considered this as noise and removed them from the answers. Going ahead, we will look into ways to handle them instead of removing.

8. **Human Reasoning:** Apart from the cases mentioned above, there are few other types of noise which require human reasoning to decode. For example,

   a. Missing space between words, ex: *हमहिलनहिसकते* (should have been *हम हिल नहि सकते* (ETL: *we cannot move*)

   b. Words replaced with phonetically similar sounding ones but with a completely different meaning. These might occur due to STT dialect/child speech issue.

   Example 1:
   Reference answer: '*ऊर्जा*' (ETL: energy)
   Child's answer: '*उड जा*' (ETL: fly)

   Example 2:
   Reference answer: *das gram hota hai*
   Child's answer: *that's gram hita hai*

   c. Answer hidden among other meaningful words which are irrelevant to the answer present, ex: *हड्डियों का बोल हड्डियों का*(ETL: *bones say with bones*)

4 Descriptive Answer Assessment

While including questions with descriptive answers is an important aspect of learning, it brings unique challenges in terms of assessment. In this section we describe our methodology for assessment of such descriptive free-text answers and the challenges that are unique to it, thus emphasizing the importance of more research in this area. One major challenge as described previously is the presence of various noise types in the crowdsourced answers data. In this section we describe a preprocessing pipeline to denoise the answers. We also provide description of the semantic similarity measures we use to assess the user answers at scale in low resource setting.

4.1 Data Preprocessing

The purpose of data preprocessing is to improve text quality for downstream evaluation methodologies. The quality of data can have a significant influence on assessment methods hence, removing the noise in the crowdsourced free-text data is essential. Our proposed preprocessing pipeline is shown in Figure 2.

First, we denoise the text data by removing the unwanted elements like the emoji, url, superscript/subscript characters and replace punctuations with space. For example,

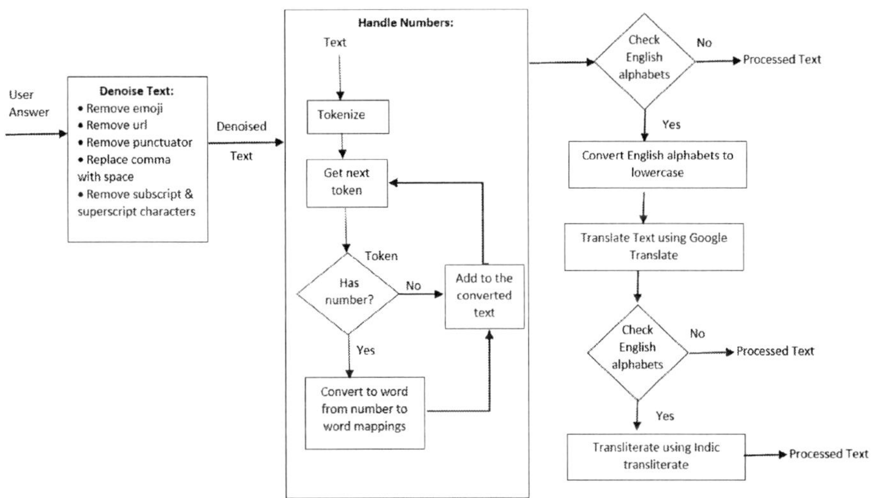

Figure 2: Data Preprocessing pipeline

User Answer: रक्त का थक्का नही जमेगा\n\ n😃 😃😃😃😃😃 \n
Processed Text: रक्त का थक्का नही जमेगा (ETL: blood clots will not form)

Next, this text is processed to convert numbers to their corresponding word lexemes. For example,

User Answer: 5 किलो ग्राम (ETL: *5 Kilogram*)
Processed Text: पांच किलो ग्राम (ETL: *Five Kilogram*)

We then check for presence of English alphabets in the processed text, which we identify and then pass through Google Translate service to convert it to Hindi. For example,

User Answer: We can not move , we can not work
Processed Text: हम हिल नहीं सकते हम काम नहीं कर सकते (ETL: *We can't move, we can't work*)

As mentioned before there are additionally a few instances where the Hindi text is transliterated to English which needs to be converted back to Hindi. These are not converted by the Google translation service and hence we check for English alphabets again and transliterate them to Hindi. We use the Indic Transliteration library to do the same. For example,

User Answer: hilna dulna asmbhav

Processed Text: हिलना दुलना असम्भव (ETL: *impossible to move*)

This final denoised data is now ready for assessment, methods for which are described in next section.

4.2 Answer Assessment Methodology

We model the assessment of user answers against ideal answers as a similarity task. It is important to note that the focus of our study is for the rural children in remote areas of India with limited internet access. Hence, we need to find a solution which could be integrated with a system in low resource setting. Thus, we choose similarity measures instead of paraphrase detection as our assessment methodology to ensure it does not add a lot of memory requirement or internet connectivity to the app. Additionally, training robust Paraphrase identification systems requires availability of large amounts of corpus that we do not have the luxury of for Hindi language, and education data. We thus lean towards using word embedding based similarity measures to capture semantic similarity among user and ideal answers. To compare performance of these similarity measures on our dataset, we need ground truth dataset of manually evaluated actual vs user answer pairs. The methodology used for creation of this ground truth is described below.

Ground Truth using Human Evaluation: A web portal was created to evaluate the answers of

127

children with respect to questions and model answers. Every answer contains three options for the evaluator - correct, incorrect, can't say. An additional optional field Remarks was given to highlight any comments/irregularities that were seen in the data. The answers were evaluated by corporate volunteers of Pratham. Each answer was evaluated by two people, and we collect human evaluations on a total of 15479 user answers.

4.3 Semantic Similarity Measures

Each user answer is assigned a similarity score with ideal answer using the various scores described in this section. The intent is to measure semantic similarity and not syntactic similarity for the purpose of this task. Since this task is for Science subject, ensuring the user answer matches semantically to the ideal is more important than ensuring syntactic correctness. We use the following similarity scores to provide a benchmark on the dataset.

1. **Baseline:** We compare random score assignment with the described scores as baseline. This is generated as by marking the user answer as correct based on a coin toss.

2. **Jaccard Similarity:** It calculates the number of words from user answer appearing in the ideal answer sentence. This is normalized w.r.t the total number of words present in the given answers as described in equation (1), where J is the jaccard similarity score between C, the set of words in user answer and I, the set of words in ideal answer.

$$J = \frac{(C \cap I)}{(C \cup I)} \tag{1}$$

3. **Semantic Similarity Scores:** We segment the user and ideal answer into their constituent words. We then retrieve word embeddings for each of these words. User and ideal answer are represented as vectors by taking the average of these word embeddings. We then calculate the cosine similarity score between the answers. The Hindi word embeddings used are:

IndicNLP: Pre-trained word embeddings available for 1.1B Hindi tokens trained using fastText on corpus crawled from news websites (Kunchukuttan et al., 2020).

fastText: Pre-trained word embeddings for Hindi, trained on Wikipedia and Common Crawl datasets consisting of 1.8B tokens (Grave et al., 2018).

5 Results and Analysis

We now compare the performance of various similarity scores on the human evaluated ground truth on answer assessment. We study the performance of these similarity measures before and after denoising and observe that denoising leads to considerable improvements in their performance.

5.1 Results

The results have been measured on 9055 user answer, ideal answer pairs out of 15479 answers where both human evaluators matched in their markings. Among these 9055 evaluated and matched answer pairs, 30% are correct and 70% are incorrect answers. The marking is converted to binary where we assign label 1 if the human evaluators marked the user answer as correct, and 0 if the human evaluator marked the answer as wrong.

We compare the performance of various similarity measures described earlier on this evaluation data. Figure 3 and Figure 4 show the ROC curves for each of these similarity measures along with the area under the ROC curve (ROC AUC). In Figure 3, we plot the performance of similarity scores on the original noisy user data. In Figure 4, we plot the performance of similarity scores on denoised user data (output from our preprocessing pipeline). It can be observed that embeddings based semantic similarity scores have similar performance on our answer assessment dataset and considerably outperform the simple jaccard similarity method on noisy data.

It is very interesting to observe that though the performance of embedding based methods sees an ~8.9% lift upon denoising, the performance of Jaccard Similarity improves considerably with a 23.1% lift making it comparable to the embedding based semantic similarity scores, fastText and indicNLP on this dataset.

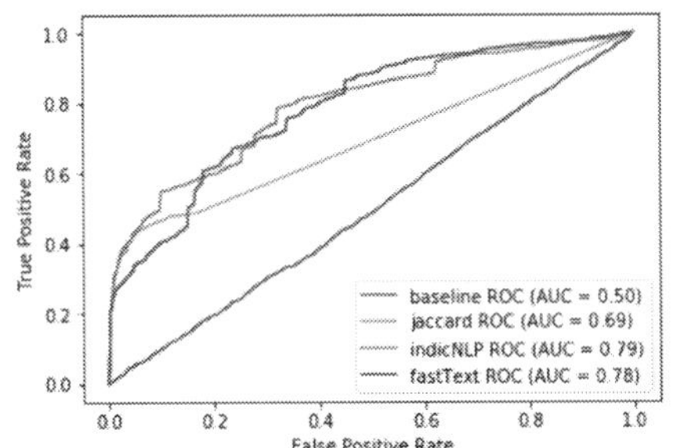

Figure 3: ROC Curves for various similarity scores on original noisy data

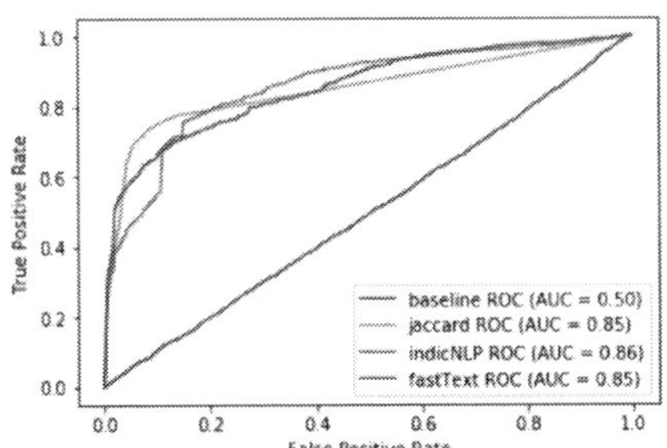

Figure 4: ROC Curves for various similarity scores on denoised data

Since we want to focus on the errors made by these similarity measures, we additionally evaluate the model based on cost, i.e. the number of wrong assessments the similarity scores result in as compared to the actual ground truth. We select the threshold to convert a given similarity score to binary that minimizes this cost. In the equation below, FP is false positives, FN is false negatives, TP is the number of true positives and TN, the number of true negatives in evaluation data.

$$cost = (FP + FN) / (TP + FN + FP + TN) \qquad (2)$$

Table 3 and 4 show the comparison of various metrics for similarity scores and the minimum cost associated with each on noisy and denoised data respectively.

Similarity	Cost	Precision	Recall	F1 Score
baseline	0.267	0.43	0.00	0.00
jaccard	**0.185**	**0.86**	**0.36**	**0.51**
indicNLP	**0.183**	**0.85**	**0.37**	**0.52**
fastText	0.205	0.86	0.27	0.41

Table 3: Performance of similarity measures on original noisy user answers

Similarity	Cost	Precision	Recall	F1 Score
baseline	0.281	0.27	0.00	0.00
jaccard	**0.126**	**0.82**	**0.69**	**0.75**
indicNLP	0.169	0.70	0.69	0.69
fastText	0.149	0.87	0.54	0.67

Table 4: Performance of similarity measures on denoised user answers

5.2 Error Analysis

We show a few examples comparing Jaccard Similarity errors and indicNLP Similarity errors on the denoised data. Row 1 in Table 5 shows an example where the answer is incorrect, but Jaccard Similarity assigns it a high score due to matching word "तरंग / waves". Row 2 shows error made by indicNLP as it assigns a high similarity score to word pair ("वायुमंडल / atmosphere", "गुरुत्वाकर्षण / gravitation") perhaps because they appear in similar context often. Additionally, row 3 shows error made by indicNLP as it assigns a high similarity score among numbers and number names.

User Answer / ETL	Ideal Answer / ETL	Ideal	Jaccard	indic NLP
मुखिया तरंग / Head waves	विद्युत् चुम्बकीय तरंग / electromagnetic waves	0	1	0
क्योंकि वहां पर गुरुत्वाकर्षण कम होना है / Because there's less gravitation	वायुमंडल ना होने के कारण / Due the absence of atmosphere	0	0	1
तीन / three	पांच प्रकार / five types	0	0	1

Table 5: Errors by Jaccard and indicNLP in assessment

5.3 Ablation Study

We have demonstrated performance of various similarity measures on both original (noisy) and denoised evaluation data. In this section, we perform an ablation study of different noise types and effect of their removal on the performance of each of these similarity measures to get a better understanding of their relative importance.

We consider three buckets of noise types: (1) Punctuations, urls and emojis (2) Presence of numbers (3) Translated or transliterated text. These buckets are created based on prevalence from Table 2.

Table 6 shows the performance of similarity measures on removing each of these noise buckets individually and compared with the original (noisy) answers plus the fully denoised answers. We observe that while removal of each noise type leads to improvement in the similarity measure AUCs, it is the cumulative effect of removing all the noise types that boosts their performance overall.

Similarity Score →	jaccard	indicNLP	fastText
Original Answers	0.69	0.79	0.78
Punctuations, urls, emojis removed	0.69	0.80	0.79
Numbers processed	0.84	0.82	0.83
Translated, Transliterated Answers	0.70	0.82	0.80
Fully Denoised Answers	**0.85**	**0.86**	**0.85**

Table 6: ROC AUC of similarity measures upon each individual noise type removal

5.4 Discussion

Even though Jaccard similarity is a crude measure of similarity, it outperformed other semantic similarity scores for answer assessment task upon denoising. Lift of 23.1% in performance of a simple, feasible measure like Jaccard due to denoising is promising for us as our requirement is to deploy the solution in low resource setting where fast and accurate computation of a similarity score for assessment is very critical in absence of internet connectivity. Jaccard similarity, however, fails to capture the synonym relations between words, and while intuitively it seems that it would underperform compared to embeddings, this benchmark shows that in order to outperform a simple score, there is considerable scope for improvement in embeddings, especially for education domain. We also observed that embeddings for words like ऑक्सिज़न (ETL: *Oxygen*), *भारहीनता (ETL: Weightlessness), तारत्व(ETL: String), रक्तकणिका (ETL: Blood cell)* etc. are absent from fastText embeddings leaving scope for improvement through fine tuning. We believe that using science textbook data for fine tuning the word embeddings (trained on generic data), can help alleviate some of the mentioned concerns.

6 Conclusion

In this paper we have described various noise types and proposed a preprocessing pipeline to denoise crowdsourced free-text answers provided by children for grade 8 level Science topics in Hindi. This work is intended to facilitate research in automatic assessment of student's free text answers in regional India languages in low resource settings. We have compared the performance of various semantic similarity scores using human evaluated ground truth on their original noisy and denoised versions. We see that denoising helps Jaccard Similarity outperform semantic similarity measures thus presenting a strong case for feasibility of automated assessment in low resource settings. In the next phase of this work, we will fine tune the existing embeddings on education domain. With Pratham's reach into 22 states and up to 15 million children in India, we can scale our crowdsourcing easily to include more responses in other regional languages. We hope that our findings mutually benefit the research community working in the area of descriptive answer assessments for regional languages meanwhile solving a very practical problem for society at scale.

Acknowledgements

This work has been supported by the Pratham Education Foundation. We are thankful to the corporate volunteers who helped us create the evaluation data for this work. We are also thankful to the web and android application team of Pratham for enabling the collection and recording of this data.

References

Anoop Kunchukuttan, Divyanshu Kakwani, Satish Golla, Avik Bhattacharyya, Mitesh M. Khapra, and Pratyush Kumar, 2020. AI4Bharat-IndicNLP Corpus: Monolingual Corpora and Word Embeddings for Indic Languages. *arXiv preprint* arXiv:2005.00085.

Daniele Bonadiman, Anjishnu Kumar, and Arpit Mittal, 2019. Large Scale Question Paraphrase Retrieval with Smoothed Deep Metric Learning. *arXiv preprint* arXiv:1905.12786.

Diana Pérez, Alfio Massimiliano Gliozzo, Carlo Strapparava, Enrique Alfonseca, Pilar Rodríguez, and Bernardo Magnini, 2005. Automatic Assessment of Students' Free-Text Answers Underpinned by the Combination of a BLEU-Inspired Algorithm and Latent Semantic Analysis. In *FLAIRS conference*, pp. 358-363.

Edouard Grave, Piotr Bojanowski, Prakhar Gupta, Armand Joulin, and Tomas Mikolov, 2018. Learning word vectors for 157 languages. *arXiv preprint* arXiv:1802.06893.

Jiaqi Lun, Jia Zhu, Yong Tang, and Min Yang, 2020. Multiple Data Augmentation Strategies for Improving Performance on Automatic Short Answer Scoring. *In AAAI*, pp. 13389-13396.

Philip G. Butcher, and Sally E. Jordan, 2010. A comparison of human and computer marking of short free-text student responses. In *Computers & Education* 55, no. 2 (2010): 489-499.

Piyush Patil, Sachin Patil, Vaibhav Miniyar, and Amol Bandal. 2018. Subjective Answer Evaluation Using Machine Learning. In *International Journal of Pure and Applied Mathematics* 118, no. 24.

Steven Burrows, Iryna Gurevych, and Benno Stein, 2015. The eras and trends of automatic short answer grading. In *International Journal of Artificial Intelligence in Education* 25, no. 1 (2015): 60-117.

T. Kwiatkowski, J. Palomaki, O. Redfield, M. Collins, A. Parikh, C. Alberti, D. Epstein, I. Polosukhin, J. Devlin, K. Lee, and K. Toutanova, 2019. Natural questions: a benchmark for question answering research. In *Transactions of the Association for Computational Linguistics*, 7, pp.453-466.

Transliteration tools to convert text in one indic script encoding to another.
https://pypi.org/project/indic-transliteration/

Translator: Google Translate API for Python.

https://pypi.org/project/googletrans/

Punctuation Restoration using Transformer Models
for High-and Low-Resource Languages

Tanvirul Alam[1]　　**Akib Khan[1]**　　**Firoj Alam[2]**

`{tanvirul.alam, akib.khan}@bjitgroup.com, fialam@hbku.edu.qa`
[1] BJIT Limited, Dhaka, Bangladesh
[2] Qatar Computing Research Institute, HBKU, Qatar

Abstract

Punctuation restoration is a common post-processing problem for Automatic Speech Recognition (ASR) systems. It is important to improve the readability of the transcribed text for the human reader and facilitate NLP tasks. Current state-of-art address this problem using different deep learning models. Recently, transformer models have proven their success in downstream NLP tasks, and these models have been explored very little for the punctuation restoration problem. In this work, we explore different transformer based models and propose an augmentation strategy for this task, focusing on high-resource (English) and low-resource (Bangla) languages. For English, we obtain comparable state-of-the-art results, while for Bangla, it is the first reported work, which can serve as a strong baseline for future work. We have made our developed Bangla dataset publicly available for the research community.

1 Introduction

Due to the recent advances in deep learning methods, the accuracy of Automatic Speech Recognition (ASR) systems has increased significantly (e.g., 3.4% WER on LibriSpeech noisy test set (Park et al., 2020)). The improved performance of ASR enabled the development of voice assistants (e.g., Siri, Cortana, Bixby, Alexa, and Google Assistant) and their wider use at the user end. Among different components (e.g., acoustic, language model), pre- and post-processing steps, the punctuation restoration is one of the post-processing steps that also needs to be dealt with to improve the readability and utilize the transcriptions in the subsequent NLP applications (Jones et al., 2003; Matusov et al., 2007).[1] This is because state-of-the-art NLP models are mostly trained using punctuated texts (e.g.,

texts from newspaper articles, Wikipedia). Hence, the lack of punctuation significantly degrades performance. For example, there is a performance difference of more than $\sim 10\%$ when the model is trained with newspaper texts and tested with transcriptions for the Named Entity Recognition system (Alam et al., 2015).

To address this issue, most of the earlier efforts on the punctuation restoration task have been done using lexical, acoustic, prosodic, or a combination of these features (Gravano et al., 2009; Levy et al., 2012; Zhang et al., 2013; Xu et al., 2014; Szaszák and Tündik, 2019; Che et al., 2016a). For the punctuation restoration task, lexical features have been widely used because the model can be trained using any punctuated text (i.e., publicly available newspaper articles or content from Wikipedia) and because of the availability of such large-scale text. This is a reasonable choice as developing punctuated transcribed text is a costly procedure.

In terms of machine learning models, conditional random field (CRF) has been widely used in earlier studies (Lu and Ng, 2010; Zhang et al., 2013). Lately, the use of deep learning models, such as Long Short-Term Memory (LSTM), Convolutional Neural Network (CNN), and transformers have also been used (Che et al., 2016b; Gale and Parthasarathy, 2017; Zelasko et al., 2018; Wang et al., 2018) for this task.

There has been a variant of transformer based language models (e.g., BERT (Devlin et al., 2019a), RoBERTa (Liu et al., 2019)), which have not been explored widely to address this problem. Hence, we aimed to explore different architectures and fine-tune pre-trained models for this task focusing on English and Bangla. Punctuation restoration models are usually trained on clean texts but used on noisy ASR texts. As such, the performance may degrade due to errors introduced by ASR models which are not present in the training data. We design an augmentation strategy (see Section 4.1.2)

---

[1] Example of downstream NLP applications include question answering, information extraction, named entity recognition (Makhoul et al., 2005), text summarization, etc.

Proceedings of the 2020 EMNLP Workshop W-NUT: The Sixth Workshop on Noisy User-generated Text, pages 132–142
Online, Nov 19, 2020. ©2020 Association for Computational Linguistics

to address this issue. For English, we train and evaluate the models using IWSLT reference and ASR test datasets. We report that our proposed augmentation strategy yields a 3.8% relative improvement in the F1 score on ASR transcriptions for English and obtains state-of-the-art results. For Bangla, there has not been any prior reported work for punctuation restoration. In addition, no resource has been found. Therefore, we prepare a training dataset from a news corpus and provide strong baselines for news, reference, and ASR transcriptions. To shade light in the current state-of-the-art on punctuation restoration task, our contributions in this study are as follows:

1. Explore transformer based language models for the punctuation restoration task.
2. Propose an augmentation strategy.
3. Prepare training and evaluation datasets for Bangla and provide strong benchmark results.
4. We have made our source code and datasets publicly available.[2]

We organize the rest of the paper as follows. In Section 2, we discuss recent works based on lexical features. We describe English and Bangla datasets used in this study in Section 3. Experimental details are provided in Section 4. We compare our results against other published results on the IWSLT dataset and provide benchmark results on the Bangla dataset in Section 5. We conclude the paper in Section 6.

2   Related Work

Recent lexical features based approaches for punctuation restoration tasks are predominantly based on deep neural networks. Che et al. (2016b) used pre-trained word embeddings to train feedforward deep neural network and CNN. Their result showed improvements over a CRF based approach that uses purely text data.

Since context is important for this type of task, several studies explored the recurrent neural network (RNN) based architectures combined with CRF and pre-trained word vectors. For instance, Tilk and Alumäe (2016) used a bidirectional recurrent neural network (RNN) with an attention mechanism to improve performance over DNN and CNN models. In another study, Gale and Parthasarathy (2017) used character-level LSTM architecture to

achieve results that are competitive with the word-level CRF based approach. Yi et al. (2017) combined bidirectional LSTM with a CRF layer and an ensemble of three networks. They further used knowledge distillation to transfer knowledge from the ensemble of networks to a single DNN network.

Transformer based approaches have been explored in several studies (Yi and Tao, 2019; Nguyen et al., 2019). Yi and Tao (2019) combined pre-trained word and speech embeddings that improves performance compared to only word embedding based model. Nguyen et al. (2019) used transformer architecture to restore both punctuation and capitalization. Punctuation restoration is also important for machine translation. The study by Wang et al. (2018) used a transformer based model for spoken language translation. They achieved significant improvements over CNN and RNN baselines, especially on joint punctuation prediction task.

More recent approaches are based on pre-trained transformer based models. Makhija et al. (2019) used pre-trained BERT (Devlin et al., 2019a) model with bidirectional LSTM and a CRF layer to achieve state-of-the-art result on reference transcriptions. Yi et al. (2020) used adversarial multi-task learning with auxiliary parts of speech tagging task using a pre-trained BERT model.

In this study, we also explore transformer based models; however, unlike prior works that solely studied one architecture (BERT), we experiment with different models. We also propose a novel augmentation scheme that improves the performance. Our augmentation is closely related to the augmentation techniques proposed in (Wei and Zou, 2019b) where the authors consider synonym replacement, random insertion, random swap, and random deletion. While their work is intended for the text classification tasks, we propose a different version of it for this study, which is a sequence labeling task. We do not use synonym replacement and random swap as they do not usually appear in speech transcription.

3   Datasets

3.1   English Dataset

We use IWSLT dataset for English punctuation restoration, which consists of transcriptions from TED Talks.[3] Though this dataset was originally released in the IWSLT evaluation campaign in 2012

---

[2]`https://github.com/xashru/punctuation-restoration`

[3]`http://hltc.cs.ust.hk/iwslt/index.php/evaluation-campaign/ted-task.html`

Dataset	Total	Period	Comma	Question	Other (O)
English					
Train	2102417	132393 (6.3%)	158392 (7.53%)	9905 (0.47%)	1801727 (85.7%)
Dev	295800	18910 (6.39%)	22451 (7.59%)	1517 (0.51%)	252922 (85.5%)
Test (Ref.)	12626	807 (6.39%)	830 (6.57%)	46 (0.36%)	10943 (86.67%)
Test (ASR)	12822	809 (6.31%)	798 (6.22%)	35 (0.27%)	11180 (87.19%)
Bangla					
Train	1379986	98791 (7.16%)	65235 (4.73%)	4555 (0.33%)	1211405 (87.78%)
Dev	179371	13161 (7.34%)	7544 (4.21%)	534 (0.3%)	158132 (88.16%)
Test (news)	87721	6263 (7.14%)	4102 (4.68%)	305 (0.35%)	77051 (87.84%)
Test (Ref.)	6821	996 (14.6%)	279 (4.09%)	170 (2.49%)	5376 (78.82%)
Test (ASR)	6417	887 (13.82%)	253 (3.94%)	125 (1.95%)	5152 (80.29%)

Table 1: Distributions of English and Bangla datasets. The number in parenthesis represents percentage.

Dataset	English		Bangla	
	Avg.	Std	Avg.	Std
Train	13.8	10.8	12.4	7.6
Dev	13.5	10.7	12.1	7.2
Test: News	-	-	12.4	7.2
Test: Ref.	13.8	9.6	4.8	3.2
Test: ASR	14.2	9.7	5.3	3.6

Table 2: Average sentence length (Avg.) with standard deviation (Std.) for each language.

(Cettolo et al., 2013; Federico et al., 2012), later, Che et al. (2016b) prepared and released a refined version of the IWSLT dataset publicly. For this study, we use the same train, development, and test splits released by Che et al. (2016b). The training and development set consist of 2.1M and 296K words, respectively. Two test sets are provided with manual and ASR transcriptions, each containing 12626 and 12822 words, respectively. These are taken from the test data of IWSLT2011 ASR dataset.[3] A detailed description of the dataset can be found in (Che et al., 2016b). There are four labels including three punctuation marks: *(i) Comma:* includes commas, colons and dashes, *(ii) Period:* includes full stops, exclamation marks and semicolons, *(iii) Question:* only question mark, and *(iv) O:* for any other token.

3.2 Bangla Dataset

To the best of our knowledge, there are no publicly available resources for the Bangla punctuation restoration task. Hence, we prepare a dataset using a publicly available corpus of Bangla newspaper articles (Khatun et al., 2019). This dataset is available in train and test splits. For our task, we selected 4000 and 500 articles respectively for preparing training and development sets from their train split, and 200 articles for test from their test split. Training, development, and test sets consist of 1.38M, 180K, and 88K words respectively.

Additionally, we prepare two test datasets consisting of manual and ASR transcriptions to evaluate the performance. We collected 65 minutes of speech excerpts extracted from four Bangla short stories (i.e., monologue read speech).[4] These are manually transcribed with punctuation. We obtained ASR transcriptions for the same audios using Google Cloud speech API.[5] Note that the Google speech API does not provide punctuation for Bangla. The obtained ASR transcriptions from Google speech API are then manually annotated with punctuation. We computed the Word Error Rate (WER) of the ASR transcriptions by comparing against our manual transcriptions, which results in 14.8% WER. The number of words in manual and ASR transcriptions consists of 6821 and 6417 words respectively. Similar to English, we consider four punctuation marks for Bangla i.e., *Period, Comma, Question, and O*.

In Table 1, we present the distributions of the labels for both English and Bangla. In parenthesis, we provide the percentage of the punctuation. In general, the distribution of questions is low (less than 1%), which we observe both in English and Bangla news data. However, this is much higher in the Bangla manual and ASR transcriptions. This is due to the fact that these texts are selected from short stories where people often engage in conversation and ask each other questions. The literary style of the stories is different from news and as a result, the distribution of *Period* is also higher in the Bangla manual and ASR transcriptions. This results in a much smaller average sentence length in these datasets, as can be seen in Table 2. We can compare these numbers with English as reported

---

[4]Due to the limited annotation resources we could not collect more data, and this could be a future effort.

[5]https://cloud.google.com/speech-to-text

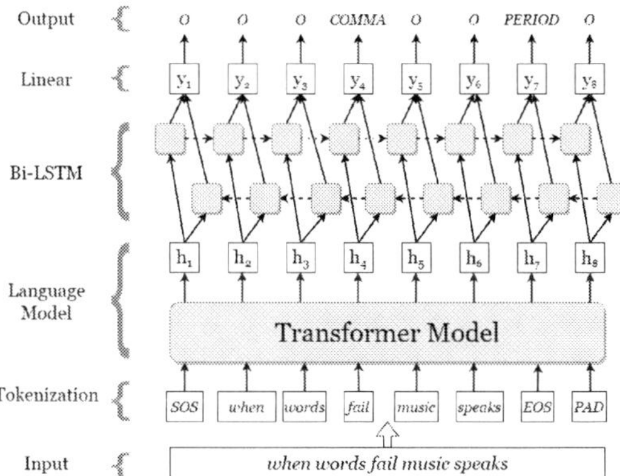

Figure 1: A general model architecture for our experiments.

in (Zelasko et al., 2018). The authors reported 79.1% O token on the training data collected from conversational speech. We have 78.82% O token on our reference test data. This suggests that our transcribed data are more similar in distribution to natural conversations.

4 Experiments

For this study, we explored different transformer based models for both English and Bangla. In addition, we used bidirectional LSTM (BiLSTM) on top of the pre-trained transformer network, and an augmentation method to improve the performance of the models.

4.1 Models and Architectures

In Figure 1, we report a general network architecture that we used in our experiments. We obtained d dimensional embedding vector from the pre-trained language model for each token. This is used as input for a BiLSTM layer, consisting of h hidden units. This allows the network to make effective use of both past and future contexts for prediction. The outputs from the forward and backward LSTM layers are concatenated at each time step and fed to a fully connected layer with four output neurons, which correspond to 3 punctuation marks and one O token.

As can be seen in the Figure, the input sentence *"when words fail music speaks"* does not have any punctuation, and the task of the model is to predict a *Comma* after the word "fail" and *Period* after the word "speaks" to produce the output sentence *"when words fail, music speaks."*

We measure the performance of the models in terms of precision (P), recall (R), and F1-score (F_1).

4.1.1 Pretrained Language Model

Transfer learning has been popular in computer vision, and the emergence of the transformers (Vaswani et al., 2017) has shown the light to use transfer learning in NLP applications. The models are trained on a large text corpus (e.g., BERT is trained on 800M words from Book Corpus and 2,500M words from Wikipedia) and their success has been proven by fine-tuning downstream NLP applications. In our experiment, we used such pre-trained language models for the punctuation restoration task. We briefly discuss the monolingual language models for English and multi-lingual language models used in this study.

BERT (Devlin et al., 2019a) is designed to learn deep bidirectional representation from unlabeled texts by jointly conditioning the left and right contexts in all layers. It uses a multi-layer bidirectional transformer encoder architecture (Vaswani et al., 2017) and makes use of two objectives during pretraining: masked language model (MLM) and next sentence prediction (NSP) task.

RoBERTa (Liu et al., 2019) performs a replication study of BERT pretraining and shows that improvements can be made using larger datasets, vocabulary, and training on longer sequences with bigger batches. It uses dynamic masking of the tokens i.e., the masking pattern is generated every time a sequence is fed to the model instead of generating them beforehand. They also remove the NSP task and use only MLM loss for pretraining.

ALBERT (Lan et al., 2020) incorporates a couple of parameter reduction techniques to design an architecture with significantly fewer parameters than a traditional BERT architecture. The *first improvement* is factorizing embedding parameters by decomposing the embedding matrix $V \times H$ into two smaller matrices $V \times E$ and $E \times H$, where V is the vocabulary size, E is the word piece embedding size, and H is hidden layer size. This reduces embedding parameters from $O(V \times H)$ to $O(V \times E + E \times H)$, which can be significant when $E << H$. The *second improvement* is parameter sharing across layers. This prevents the parameter from growing as the depth is increased. The NSP task introduced in BERT is replaced by a sentence-order prediction (SOP) task in ALBERT.

DistilBERT (Sanh et al., 2019) uses knowledge distillation from BERT to train a model that has 40% fewer parameters and is 60% faster while retaining 97% of language understanding capabilities of the BERT model. The training objective is a linear combination of distillation loss, supervised training loss, and cosine distance loss.

Multilingual Models MLM has also been utilized for learning language models from large scale multi-lingual corpora. BERT multilingual model (mBERT) is trained on more than 100 languages with the largest Wikipedia dataset. To account for the variation among Wikipedia sizes of different languages, data is sampled using an exponentially smoothed weighting (with a factor 0.7) so that high-resource languages like English are under-sampled compared to low resource languages. Word counts are weighted the same way as the data so that low-resource language vocabularies are up weighted by some factor.

Cross-lingual models (XLM) (Conneau and Lample, 2019) use MLM in multiple language settings, similar to BERT. Instead of using a pair of sentences, an arbitrary number of sentences are used with text length truncated at 256 tokens.

XLM-RoBERTa (Conneau et al., 2020) is trained with a multilingual MLM objective similar to XLM but on a larger dataset. It is trained in one hundred languages, using more than two terabytes of filtered Common Crawl data (Wenzek et al., 2020).

4.1.2 Augmentation

For this study, we propose an augmentation method inspired by the study of Wei and Zou (2019a), as discussed earlier. Our augmentation method is based on the types of error ASR makes during recognition, which include *insertion*, *substitution*, and *deletion*.

Due to the lack of large-scale manual transcriptions, punctuation restoration models are typically trained using written text, which is well-formatted and correctly punctuated. Hence, the trained model lacks the knowledge of the typical errors that ASR makes. To train the model with such characteristics, we use an augmentation technique that simulates such errors and dynamically creates a new sequence on the fly in a batch. Dynamic augmentation is different from the traditional augmentation approach widely used in NLP (Wei and Zou, 2019a); however, it is widely used in computer vision for image classification tasks (Cubuk et al.,

2020).

The three different kinds of augmentation corresponding to three possible errors are as follows.

1. *First* (i.e., substitution), we replace a token by another token. In our experiment, we randomly replace a token with the special *unknown* token.
2. *Second* (i.e., deletion), we delete some tokens randomly from the processed input sequence.
3. *Finally*, we add (i.e., insertion) the *unknown* token at some random position of the input.

We hypothesize that not all three errors are equally prevalent, hence, different augmentation will have a different effect on performance. Keeping this in mind, to process input text, we used three tunable parameters: *(i)* a parameter to determine token change probability, α, *(ii)* a parameter, α_{sub}, to control the probability of substitution, *(iii)* a parameter, α_{del}, to control the probability of deletion. Probability of insertion is given by $1 - (\alpha_{sub} + \alpha_{del})$.

When applying substitution, we replaced the token in that position with the *unknown* token and left the target punctuation mark unchanged. For deletion, both the token and the punctuation mark in that position are deleted. For insertion, we inserted the *unknown* token and *O* token, in that position.

Since deletion and insertion operation may make the sequence smaller or longer than the fixed sequence length we used during training, we added padding or truncated as necessary.

4.2 Experimental Settings

We used pre-trained models available in the HuggingFace's Transformers library (Wolf et al., 2019). More details about different architectures can be found on HuggingFace website.[6] For tokenization, we used model-specific tokenizers.

During training, we used a maximum sequence length of 256. Each sequence starts with a special *start of sequence* token and ends with a special *end of sequence* token. Since the tokenizers use byte-pair encoding (Sennrich et al., 2016), a word may be tokenized into subword units.[7] If adding the subword tokens of a word results in sequence length exceeding 256, we excluded those tokens

---

[6] `https://huggingface.co/transformers/pretrained_models.html`

[7] If the model predicts punctuation in the middle of a word, these are ignored.

Test	Model	Comma			Period			Question			Overall		
		P	R	F_1	P	R	F_1	P	R	F_1	P	R	F_1
Ref.	SAPR (Wang et al., 2018)	57.2	50.8	55.9	96.7	97.3	**96.8**	70.6	69.2	70.3	78.2	74.4	77.4
	DRNN-LWMA-pre (Kim, 2019)	62.9	60.8	61.9	77.3	73.7	75.5	69.6	69.6	69.6	69.9	67.2	68.6
	Self-attention (Yi and Tao, 2019)	67.4	61.1	64.1	82.5	77.4	79.9	80.1	70.2	74.8	76.7	69.6	72.9
	BERT-Transfer (Makhija et al., 2019)	70.8	74.3	72.5	84.9	83.3	84.1	82.7	93.5	**87.8**	**79.5**	**83.7**	**81.4**
	BERT-Adversarial (Yi et al., 2020)	76.2	71.2	**73.6**	87.3	81.1	84.1	79.1	72.7	75.8	80.9	75.0	77.8
	BERT-base-uncased	71.7	70.1	70.9	82.5	83.1	82.8	75.0	84.8	79.6	77.0	76.8	76.9
	BERT-large-uncased	72.6	72.8	72.7	84.8	84.6	84.7	70.0	91.3	79.2	78.3	79.0	78.6
	RoBERTa-base	73.6	75.1	74.3	84.9	87.6	86.2	77.4	89.1	82.8	79.2	81.5	80.3
	RoBERTa-large	76.9	75.8	76.3	86.8	90.5	88.6	72.9	93.5	81.9	81.6	83.3	82.4
	ALBERT-base-v2	70.1	75.5	72.7	84.9	84.1	84.5	79.5	76.1	77.8	77.2	79.7	78.4
	ALBERT-large-v2	75.1	72.4	73.7	82.0	88.0	84.9	77.6	82.6	80.0	78.7	80.2	79.4
	DistilBERT-base-uncased	67.0	65.5	66.3	77.1	81.0	79.0	69.2	78.3	73.5	72.1	73.3	72.7
	BERT-base-multilingual-uncased	70.4	68.1	69.2	80.1	85.4	82.7	62.7	80.4	70.5	75.0	76.7	75.9
	XLM-RoBERTa-base	75.1	70.5	72.7	81.2	89.3	85.1	71.7	82.6	76.8	78.1	79.9	79.0
	XLM-RoBERTa-large	73.3	80.4	76.7	87.9	86.4	87.1	82.0	89.1	85.4	80.1	**83.5**	81.8
	DistilBERT-base-multilingual-cased	65.5	58.0	61.5	74.8	79.2	76.9	58.2	69.6	63.4	70.1	68.4	69.3
	RoBERTa-large + augmentation	76.8	76.6	**76.7**	88.6	89.2	**88.9**	82.7	93.5	**87.8**	**82.6**	83.1	**82.9**
ASR	Self-attention (Yi and Tao, 2019)	64.0	59.6	61.7	75.5	75.8	75.6	72.6	65.9	69.1	70.7	67.1	68.8
	BERT-Adversarial (Yi et al., 2020)	72.4	69.3	**70.8**	80.0	79.1	**79.5**	71.2	68.0	**69.6**	**74.5**	**72.1**	**73.3**
	BERT-base-uncased	49.3	64.2	55.8	75.3	76.3	75.8	44.7	60.0	51.2	60.4	70.0	64.9
	BERT-large-uncased	49.9	67.0	57.2	77.0	78.9	77.9	50.0	74.3	59.8	61.4	73.0	66.7
	RoBERTa-base	51.9	69.3	59.3	77.5	80.3	78.9	50.0	65.7	56.8	62.8	74.7	68.2
	RoBERTa-large	56.6	67.9	61.8	78.7	85.3	81.9	46.6	77.1	58.1	66.5	76.7	71.3
	ALBERT-base-v2	48.7	66.0	56.1	75.7	79.9	77.7	59.3	45.7	51.6	60.6	72.4	66.0
	ALBERT-large-v2	52.1	64.4	57.6	73.8	82.7	78.0	53.3	68.6	60.0	62.2	73.5	67.4
	DistilBERT-base-uncased	46.8	59.1	52.2	70.0	74.8	72.3	48.9	65.7	56.1	57.3	67.0	61.8
	BERT-base-multilingual-uncased	49.8	62.4	55.4	72.0	78.2	75.0	47.8	62.9	54.3	59.9	70.2	64.6
	XLM-RoBERTa-base	54.7	61.7	58.0	73.2	83.3	77.9	47.7	60.0	53.2	63.6	72.3	67.7
	XLM-RoBERTa-large	53.2	71.4	61.0	82.0	81.8	81.9	62.5	71.4	**66.7**	65.5	76.6	70.6
	DistilBERT-base-multilingual-cased	47.5	52.8	50.0	66.7	71.9	69.2	41.3	54.3	46.9	56.7	62.2	59.3
	RoBERTa-large + augmentation	64.1	68.8	**66.3**	81.0	83.7	**82.3**	55.3	74.3	63.4	**72.0**	**76.2**	**74.0**

Table 3: Results on IWSLT2011 manual (Ref.) and ASR transcriptions of test sets. Highlighted rows are the comparable results between ours and previous study. For overall best results we use bold form, and for the best F1 of individual punctuation we use a combination of bold and italic form.

5 Results and Discussions

5.1 Results on English Dataset

from the current sequence and start the next sequence from them. We use *padding* token after the *end of sequence* token to fill the remaining slots of the sequence. Padding tokens are masked to avoid performing attention on them. We use a batch size of 8 and shuffle the sequences before each epoch. Our chosen learning rates are 5e-6 for large models, and 1e-5 for base models, which are optimized using the development set. LSTM dimension h is set to the token embedding dimension d. All models are trained with Adam (Kingma and Ba, 2015) optimization algorithm for 10 epochs. Other parameters are kept as the default settings, discussed in (Devlin et al., 2019b). The model with the best performance on the development set is used for evaluating the test datasets.

For the augmentation experiments, we used $\alpha \in \{0.05, 0.1, 0.15, 0.2\}$, $\alpha_{sub} \in \{0.2, 0.3, 0.4, 0.5\}$, $\alpha_{del} \in \{0.2, 0.3, 0.4, 0.5\}$ with additional constraint $0.5 \leq (\alpha_{sub} + \alpha_{del}) \leq 0.8$. Optimum values for these were obtained using the development set.

In Table 3, we report our experimental results with a comparison from previous results on the same dataset. We provide the results obtained using BERT, RoBERTa, ALBERT, DistilBERT, mBERT, XLM-RoBERTa models without augmentation. *Large* variants of the models perform better than the *Base* models. Monolingual models perform better than their multilingual counterparts. RoBERTa achieves a better result than other models as it was trained on a larger corpus and has a larger vocabulary. Our best result is obtained using the RoBERTa model with augmentation in which the parameters were $\alpha = 0.15, \alpha_{sub} = 0.4, \alpha_{del} = 0.4$. Performance gain from augmentation comes from improved precision.

We obtained the state of the art result on both test sets in terms of the overall F_1 score (rows are highlighted). On Ref. test set, we obtained the best result on *Comma*, and comparable results for

Test	Model	Comma			Period			Question			Overall		
		P	R	F_1	P	R	F_1	P	R	F_1	P	R	F_1
News	BERT-base-multilingual-uncased	79.8	68.2	73.5	80.4	85.4	82.8	72.1	77.0	74.5	79.9	78.5	79.2
	DistilBERT-base-multilingual-cased	72.1	60.8	66.0	74.5	71.6	73.0	56.9	67.5	61.8	73.0	67.3	70.1
	XLM-MLM-100-1280	76.9	71.2	73.9	82.0	83.4	82.9	70.2	76.4	73.2	80.0	78.5	79.3
	XLM-RoBERTa-large	86.0	77.0	81.2	89.4	92.3	*90.8*	77.4	85.6	81.3	**87.8**	86.2	87.0
	XLM-RoBERTa-large + augmentation	85.8	77.5	*81.4*	88.8	92.5	90.6	77.9	86.6	*82.0*	87.4	**86.6**	**87.0**
Ref.	BERT-base-multilingual-uncased	35.6	34.4	35.0	67.4	64.7	66.0	39.8	28.8	33.4	58.5	54.6	56.5
	DistilBERT-base-multilingual-cased	32.6	31.5	32.1	64.0	50.2	56.3	32.5	14.7	20.2	54.3	42.4	47.6
	XLM-MLM-100-1280	33.4	39.8	36.3	70.3	64.0	67.0	42.4	22.9	29.8	59.2	54.5	56.7
	XLM-RoBERTa-large	39.3	36.9	38.1	76.9	81.4	79.1	54.3	58.8	*56.5*	67.6	70.2	68.8
	XLM-RoBERTa-large + augmentation	43.3	37.3	*40.1*	76.5	82.6	*79.4*	53.0	56.5	54.7	**68.3**	**70.8**	**69.5**
ASR	BERT-base-multilingual-uncased	29.3	30.0	29.7	60.6	60.2	60.4	36.1	38.4	37.2	51.7	52.0	51.9
	DistilBERT-base-multilingual-cased	29.0	33.6	31.1	62.6	50.6	56.0	31.3	20.8	25.0	51.2	44.3	47.5
	XLM-MLM-100-1280	31.2	38.7	34.6	63.4	59.5	61.4	32.0	24.8	27.9	52.8	51.9	52.4
	XLM-RoBERTa-large	38.3	35.6	*36.9*	69.2	77.2	73.0	38.5	52.0	44.2	60.3	66.4	63.2
	XLM-RoBERTa-large + augmentation	37.2	33.2	35.1	69.1	77.8	*73.2*	45.5	60.8	**52.1**	**61.1**	**67.2**	**64.0**

Table 4: Result on Bangla test datasets.

Question (highlighted using a combination of the bold and italic form). However, SAPR (Wang et al., 2018) method performed much better compared to others for *Period* on this data. On ASR test set, our result is marginally better than Yi et al. (2020) for overall F_1 score. Our model performed better for *Period* but comparatively lower for *Comma* and *Question*. Overall, our model has better recall than precision on this dataset.

5.2 Results on Bangla Dataset

In Table 4, we report results on the Bangla test set comprised of news, manual, and ASR transcriptions. Since no monolingual transformer model is publicly available for Bangla, we explored different multilingual models. We obtained the best result using XLM-RoBERTa (large) model as it is trained with more texts for low-resource languages like Bangla and has larger vocabulary for them. This is consistent with the findings reported in (Liu et al., 2019), where the authors report improvement over multi-lingual BERT and XLM models in cross-lingual understanding tasks for low-resource languages. We apply augmentation on XLM-RoBERTa model and best result is obtained using augmentation parameters $\alpha = 0.15$, $\alpha_{sub} = 0.4$, and $\alpha_{del} = 0.4$. However, the performance gain from augmentation is marginal on the Bangla dataset. Overall, performance on the news test set is better compared to the manual and ASR data. Performance for *Comma* is lower than *Period* and *Question*. Compared to English, we notice a performance drop of about 10% for *Period* and *Question*, but for *Comma*, this is more than 30% on the ASR test set.

For many applications (e.g., semi-automated subtitles generation), it is of utmost importance to facilitate human labelers to reduce their time and effort and make the manual annotation process faster. In such cases, identifying the correct position of the punctuations is important, as reported in (Che et al., 2016b). For Bangla, we wanted to understand what we can gain while merging the punctuation and identifying their position. For this purpose, we evaluate performance on 3-Classes and 2-Classes test sets. We combine *Period* and *Question* together to form the 3-classes test sets. *Comma* is further combined with those to form the 2-Classes test sets, i.e., punctuation or no punctuation. In Table 5, we report the results with binary and multiclass settings using XLM-RoBERTa (large) model coupled with augmentation. As can be seen, the model performs well for predicting punctuation positions. For manual (Ref.) and ASR transcriptions, we have a significant gain while merging the number of classes from four towards two. It could be because–as the number of classes reduces, the classifier's complexity reduces, which leads to an increase in the model's performance. The performance gain is comparatively lower for news while merging four classes into three classes; however, it increased significantly when reduced to two. Considering these findings, we believe this type of model can help

Dataset	4-Classes			3-Classes			2-Classes		
	P	R	F_1	P	R	F_1	P	R	F_1
News	87.4	86.6	**87.0**	88.0	87.2	**87.6**	94.1	93.3	**93.7**
Ref.	68.3	70.8	**69.5**	72.9	75.6	**74.2**	83.6	86.6	**85.1**
ASR	61.1	67.2	**64.0**	65.1	71.5	**68.1**	77.0	84.7	**80.6**

Table 5: Result on Bangla test datasets by merging classes.

Test	Type	Comma			Period			Question			Overall		
		P	R	F_1	P	R	F_1	P	R	F_1	P	R	F_1
Ref.	Linear	76.9	75.8	**76.3**	86.8	90.5	**88.6**	72.9	93.5	81.9	81.6	**83.3**	**82.4**
	CRF	75.7	76.9	76.3	88.1	89.0	88.5	77.8	91.3	**84.0**	**81.7**	83.1	82.4
ASR	Linear	56.6	67.9	61.8	78.7	85.3	**81.9**	46.6	77.1	58.1	**66.5**	**76.7**	**71.3**
	CRF	56.7	69.0	**62.3**	78.5	82.8	80.6	50.9	80.0	**62.2**	66.4	76.1	70.9

Table 6: Results of CRF on IWSLT2011 Ref. and ASR test data with RoBERTa-large model

Test	Augmentation	Comma			Period			Question			Overall		
		P	R	F_1	P	R	F_1	P	R	F_1	P	R	F_1
Ref.	None	76.9	75.8	76.3	86.8	90.5	88.6	72.9	93.5	81.9	81.6	83.3	82.4
	Substitution ($\alpha = 0.1$)	77.6	77.6	**77.6**	87.7	90.7	**89.2**	76.4	91.3	83.2	82.4	**84.3**	**83.3**
	Substitution ($\alpha = 0.15$, random)	76.5	76.4	76.4	87.2	90.6	88.9	86.3	95.7	**90.7**	82.0	83.7	82.9
	Delete ($\alpha = 0.1$)	75.0	76.0	75.5	88.6	88.4	88.5	84.3	93.5	88.7	81.7	82.4	82.1
	Insert($\alpha = 0.05$)	77.6	75.5	76.6	87.1	90.6	88.8	82.7	93.5	87.8	82.5	83.2	82.9
	All($\alpha = 0.15, \alpha_{sub} = 0.4, \alpha_{del} = 0.4$)	76.8	76.6	76.7	88.6	89.2	88.9	82.7	93.5	87.8	**82.6**	83.1	82.9
ASR	None	56.6	67.9	61.8	78.7	85.3	81.9	46.6	77.1	58.1	66.5	76.7	71.3
	Substitution ($\alpha = 0.1$)	57.0	70.8	63.1	80.8	85.4	**83.1**	50.9	77.1	61.4	67.5	**78.1**	72.4
	Substitution ($\alpha = 0.15$, random)	57.2	69.3	62.7	79.2	83.9	81.5	56.3	77.1	**65.1**	67.3	76.7	71.7
	Delete ($\alpha = 0.1$)	60.0	70.4	64.8	82.7	82.8	82.8	52.1	71.4	60.2	70.0	76.6	73.1
	Insert($\alpha = 0.05$)	57.4	67.2	61.9	79.6	84.8	82.1	49.2	82.9	61.7	67.5	76.2	71.6
	All($\alpha = 0.15, \alpha_{sub} = 0.4, \alpha_{del} = 0.4$)	64.1	68.8	**66.3**	81.0	83.7	82.3	55.3	74.3	63.4	**72.0**	76.2	**74.0**

Table 7: Results of Augmentation IWSLT2011 Ref. and ASR test data with RoBERTa-large model

human annotators in such applications.

5.3 Ablation Studies

We experimented with using CRF after the linear layer for predicting the most probable tag sequence instead of using the softmax layer. However, we did not notice any performance improvement and even a slight decrease in ASR test data performance. The results using RoBERTa large model are reported in Table 6.

We also analyzed the effect on performance when substitution, insert and delete augmentations are applied in isolation. These results are reported in table 7 for RoBERTa large model. We explored substitution with a random token from vocabulary (reported in row Substitution ($\alpha = 0.15$, random). However, it performed worse compared to substituting with the *unknown* token. We notice that the performance gain from different augmentations is larger on the ASR test set than the reference test set.

5.4 Discussion

For English, we obtained state-of-art results for manual and ASR transcriptions using our augmentation technique coupled with the RoBERTa-large model. There is still a large difference between manual and ASR transcriptions results. In Figure 2, we report the confusion matrix (in percentage), for manual and ASR transcriptions. From the figure, we observe that for ASR transcriptions, a high proportion of cases *Question* and *Comma* are predicted as *O* and *Period*. We will investigate this finding further in our future study.

Compared to English, the performance of Bangla is relatively low. We hypothesize several factors are responsible for this. *First*, the pre-trained monolingual language models for English usually perform better than multilingual models. Even in the case of multilingual models, the content of the English language is higher in the training data, and as a result, the models are expected to perform better for English. *Second* and perhaps a more important factor is the nature of training data. For Bangla, due to the lack of punctuated transcribed data, we used a news corpus for training. Hence, the trained model does not learn the nuances of transcriptions, which reduces prediction accuracy. *Third*, our ASR transcriptions are taken from some story excerpts, containing monologue and a significant amount of conversations (dialogue), which varies in terms of complexity (e.g., the dialogue has interruptions and overlap, short *vs* long utterance). An aspect of such a complexity is also evident in Table 1, where we see that the distribution of *Period* is almost double compared to news data and the distribution of *Question* is more than six times greater. On the other hand, for English, both train and test data are taken

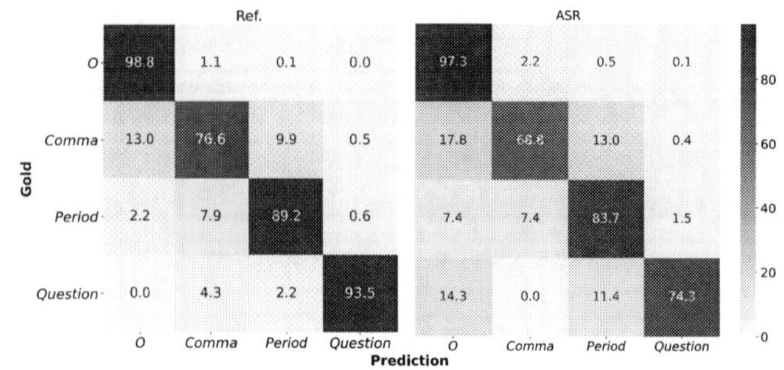

Figure 2: Confusion matrix (in percentage) for English test datasets.

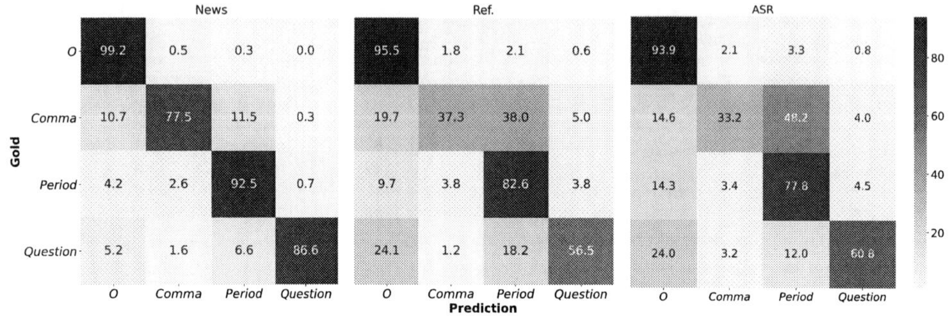

Figure 3: Confusion matrix (in percentage) for Bangla test datasets.

from TED talks, and there is no such discrepancy between the data distributions.

Similarly to English, we also wanted to see error cases for Bangla. In Figure 3, we report the confusion matrix. We observed similar phenomenon as English for Bangla, comparatively much higher in proportion, i.e., *Question* and *Comma* are predicted as *O* and *Period* for news, manual and ASR transcriptions.

6 Conclusion

In this study, we explore different transformer models for high-and low-Resource languages (i.e., English and Bangla). In addition, we propose an augmentation technique, which improves performance on noisy ASR texts. There has not been any reported result and resources for punctuation restoration on Bangla. Our study, findings, and developed resources will enrich and push the current state-of-art for this low-resource language. We have released the created Bangla dataset and code for the research community.

References

Firoj Alam, Bernardo Magnini, and Roberto Zanoli. 2015. Comparing named entity recognition on transcriptions and written texts. In *Harmonization and Development of Resources and Tools for Italian Natural Language Processing within the PARLI Project*, pages 71–89. Springer.

Mauro Cettolo, Jan Niehues, Sebastian Stüker, Luisa Bentivogli, and Marcello Federico. 2013. Report on the 10th iwslt evaluation campaign. In *Proceedings of the International Workshop on Spoken Language Translation, Heidelberg, Germany*.

Xiaoyin Che, Sheng Luo, Haojin Yang, and Christoph Meinel. 2016a. Sentence boundary detection based on parallel lexical and acoustic models. In *Interspeech*, pages 2528–2532.

Xiaoyin Che, Cheng Wang, Haojin Yang, and Christoph Meinel. 2016b. Punctuation prediction for unsegmented transcript based on word vector. In *Proceedings of the Tenth International Conference on Language Resources and Evaluation LREC 2016, Portorož, Slovenia, May 23-28, 2016*. European Language Resources Association (ELRA).

Alexis Conneau, Kartikay Khandelwal, Naman Goyal, Vishrav Chaudhary, Guillaume Wenzek, Francisco Guzmán, Edouard Grave, Myle Ott, Luke Zettlemoyer, and Veselin Stoyanov. 2020. Unsupervised cross-lingual representation learning at scale. In *Proceedings of the 58th Annual Meeting of the Association for Computational Linguistics, ACL 2020, Online, July 5-10, 2020*, pages 8440–8451. Association for Computational Linguistics.

Alexis Conneau and Guillaume Lample. 2019. Cross-lingual language model pretraining. In *Advances in Neural Information Processing Systems 32: Annual Conference on Neural Information Processing Systems 2019, NeurIPS 2019, 8-14 December 2019, Vancouver, BC, Canada*, pages 7057–7067.

Ekin D Cubuk, Barret Zoph, Jonathon Shlens, and Quoc V Le. 2020. Randaugment: Practical automated data augmentation with a reduced search space. In *Proceedings of the IEEE/CVF Conference on Computer Vision and Pattern Recognition Workshops*, pages 702–703.

Jacob Devlin, Ming-Wei Chang, Kenton Lee, and Kristina Toutanova. 2019a. BERT: pre-training of deep bidirectional transformers for language understanding. In *Proceedings of the 2019 Conference of the North American Chapter of the Association for Computational Linguistics: Human Language Technologies, NAACL-HLT 2019, Minneapolis, MN, USA, June 2-7, 2019, Volume 1 (Long and Short Papers)*, pages 4171–4186. Association for Computational Linguistics.

Jacob Devlin, Ming-Wei Chang, Kenton Lee, and Kristina Toutanova. 2019b. BERT: Pre-training of deep bidirectional transformers for language understanding. In *Proc. of the 2019 Conference of the NAACL*, pages 4171–4186, Minneapolis, Minnesota. ACL.

Marcello Federico, Mauro Cettolo, Luisa Bentivogli, Paul Michael, and Stüker Sebastian. 2012. Overview of the iwslt 2012 evaluation campaign. In *IWSLT-International Workshop on Spoken Language Translation*, pages 12–33.

William Gale and Sarangarajan Parthasarathy. 2017. Experiments in character-level neural network models for punctuation. In *INTERSPEECH*, pages 2794–2798.

Agustin Gravano, Martin Jansche, and Michiel Bacchiani. 2009. Restoring punctuation and capitalization in transcribed speech. In *2009 IEEE International Conference on Acoustics, Speech and Signal Processing*, pages 4741–4744. IEEE.

Douglas A. Jones, Florian Wolf, Edward Gibson, Elliott Williams, Evelina Fedorenko, Douglas A. Reynolds, and Marc A. Zissman. 2003. Measuring the readability of automatic speech-to-text transcripts. In *8th European Conference on Speech Communication and Technology, EUROSPEECH 2003 - INTERSPEECH 2003, Geneva, Switzerland, September 1-4, 2003*. ISCA.

Aisha Khatun, Anisur Rahman, Hemayet Ahmed Chowdhury, Md. Saiful Islam, and Ayesha Tasnim. 2019. A subword level language model for bangla language. *CoRR*, abs/1911.07613.

Seokhwan Kim. 2019. Deep recurrent neural networks with layer-wise multi-head attentions for punctuation restoration. In *IEEE International Conference on Acoustics, Speech and Signal Processing, ICASSP 2019, Brighton, United Kingdom, May 12-17, 2019*, pages 7280–7284. IEEE.

Diederik P. Kingma and Jimmy Ba. 2015. Adam: A method for stochastic optimization. In *3rd International Conference on Learning Representations, ICLR 2015, San Diego, CA, USA, May 7-9, 2015, Conference Track Proceedings*.

Zhenzhong Lan, Mingda Chen, Sebastian Goodman, Kevin Gimpel, Piyush Sharma, and Radu Soricut. 2020. ALBERT: A lite BERT for self-supervised learning of language representations. In *8th International Conference on Learning Representations, ICLR 2020, Addis Ababa, Ethiopia, April 26-30, 2020*. OpenReview.net.

Tal Levy, Vered Silber-Varod, and Ami Moyal. 2012. The effect of pitch, intensity and pause duration in punctuation detection. In *2012 IEEE 27th Convention of Electrical and Electronics Engineers in Israel*, pages 1–4. IEEE.

Yinhan Liu, Myle Ott, Naman Goyal, Jingfei Du, Mandar Joshi, Danqi Chen, Omer Levy, Mike Lewis, Luke Zettlemoyer, and Veselin Stoyanov. 2019. Roberta: A robustly optimized BERT pretraining approach. *CoRR*, abs/1907.11692.

Wei Lu and Hwee Tou Ng. 2010. Better punctuation prediction with dynamic conditional random fields. In *Proceedings of the 2010 conference on empirical methods in natural language processing*, pages 177–186.

Karan Makhija, Thi-Nga Ho, and Eng Siong Chng. 2019. Transfer learning for punctuation prediction. In *2019 Asia-Pacific Signal and Information Processing Association Annual Summit and Conference, APSIPA ASC 2019, Lanzhou, China, November 18-21, 2019*, pages 268–273. IEEE.

John Makhoul, Alex Baron, Ivan Bulyko, Long Nguyen, Lance Ramshaw, David Stallard, Richard Schwartz, and Bing Xiang. 2005. The effects of speech recognition and punctuation on information extraction performance. In *Ninth European Conference on Speech Communication and Technology*.

Evgeny Matusov, Dustin Hillard, Mathew Magimai-Doss, Dilek Hakkani-Tür, Mari Ostendorf, and Hermann Ney. 2007. Improving speech translation with automatic boundary prediction. In *Eighth Annual Conference of the International Speech Communication Association*.

Binh Nguyen, Vu Bao Hung Nguyen, Hien Nguyen, Pham Ngoc Phuong, The-Loc Nguyen, Quoc Truong Do, and Luong Chi Mai. 2019. Fast and accurate capitalization and punctuation for automatic speech recognition using transformer and chunk merging. In *2019 22nd Conference of the Oriental COCOSDA International Committee for the Co-ordination and Standardisation of Speech Databases and Assessment Techniques (O-COCOSDA)*, pages 1–5. IEEE.

Daniel S. Park, Yu Zhang, Ye Jia, Wei Han, Chung-Cheng Chiu, Bo Li, Yonghui Wu, and Quoc V. Le. 2020. Improved noisy student training for automatic speech recognition.

Victor Sanh, Lysandre Debut, Julien Chaumond, and Thomas Wolf. 2019. Distilbert, a distilled version of BERT: smaller, faster, cheaper and lighter. *CoRR*, abs/1910.01108.

Rico Sennrich, Barry Haddow, and Alexandra Birch. 2016. Neural machine translation of rare words with subword units. In *Proceedings of the 54th Annual Meeting of the Association for Computational Linguistics, ACL 2016, August 7-12, 2016, Berlin, Germany, Volume 1: Long Papers*. The Association for Computer Linguistics.

György Szaszák and Máté Ákos Tündik. 2019. Leveraging a character, word and prosody triplet for an asr error robust and agglutination friendly punctuation approach. In *INTERSPEECH*, pages 2988–2992.

Ottokar Tilk and Tanel Alumäe. 2016. Bidirectional recurrent neural network with attention mechanism for punctuation restoration. In *Interspeech 2016, 17th Annual Conference of the International Speech Communication Association, San Francisco, CA, USA, September 8-12, 2016*, pages 3047–3051. ISCA.

Ashish Vaswani, Noam Shazeer, Niki Parmar, Jakob Uszkoreit, Llion Jones, Aidan N. Gomez, Lukasz Kaiser, and Illia Polosukhin. 2017. Attention is all you need. In *Advances in Neural Information Processing Systems 30: Annual Conference on Neural Information Processing Systems 2017, 4-9 December 2017, Long Beach, CA, USA*, pages 5998–6008.

Feng Wang, Wei Chen, Zhen Yang, and Bo Xu. 2018. Self-attention based network for punctuation restoration. In *2018 24th International Conference on Pattern Recognition (ICPR)*, pages 2803–2808. IEEE.

Jason Wei and Kai Zou. 2019a. Eda: Easy data augmentation techniques for boosting performance on text classification tasks. *ArXiv*, abs/1901.11196.

Jason W. Wei and Kai Zou. 2019b. EDA: easy data augmentation techniques for boosting performance on text classification tasks. In *Proceedings of the 2019 Conference on Empirical Methods in Natural Language Processing and the 9th International Joint Conference on Natural Language Processing, EMNLP-IJCNLP 2019, Hong Kong, China, November 3-7, 2019*, pages 6381–6387. Association for Computational Linguistics.

Guillaume Wenzek, Marie-Anne Lachaux, Alexis Conneau, Vishrav Chaudhary, Francisco Guzmán, Armand Joulin, and Edouard Grave. 2020. Ccnet: Extracting high quality monolingual datasets from web crawl data. In *Proceedings of The 12th Language Resources and Evaluation Conference, LREC 2020, Marseille, France, May 11-16, 2020*, pages 4003–4012. European Language Resources Association.

Thomas Wolf, Lysandre Debut, Victor Sanh, Julien Chaumond, Clement Delangue, Anthony Moi, Pierric Cistac, Tim Rault, R'emi Louf, Morgan Funtowicz, and Jamie Brew. 2019. Huggingface's transformers: State-of-the-art natural language processing. *ArXiv*, abs/1910.03771.

Chenglin Xu, Lei Xie, Guangpu Huang, Xiong Xiao, Eng Siong Chng, and Haizhou Li. 2014. A deep neural network approach for sentence boundary detection in broadcast news. In *Fifteenth annual conference of the international speech communication association*.

Jiangyan Yi and Jianhua Tao. 2019. Self-attention based model for punctuation prediction using word and speech embeddings. In *IEEE International Conference on Acoustics, Speech and Signal Processing, ICASSP 2019, Brighton, United Kingdom, May 12-17, 2019*, pages 7270–7274. IEEE.

Jiangyan Yi, Jianhua Tao, Ye Bai, Zhengkun Tian, and Cunhang Fan. 2020. Adversarial transfer learning for punctuation restoration. *CoRR*, abs/2004.00248.

Jiangyan Yi, Jianhua Tao, Zhengqi Wen, and Ya Li. 2017. Distilling knowledge from an ensemble of models for punctuation prediction. In *Interspeech 2017, 18th Annual Conference of the International Speech Communication Association, Stockholm, Sweden, August 20-24, 2017*, pages 2779–2783. ISCA.

Piotr Zelasko, Piotr Szymanski, Jan Mizgajski, Adrian Szymczak, Yishay Carmiel, and Najim Dehak. 2018. Punctuation prediction model for conversational speech. In *Interspeech 2018, 19th Annual Conference of the International Speech Communication Association, Hyderabad, India, 2-6 September 2018*, pages 2633–2637. ISCA.

Dongdong Zhang, Shuangzhi Wu, Nan Yang, and Mu Li. 2013. Punctuation prediction with transition-based parsing. In *Proceedings of the 51st Annual Meeting of the Association for Computational Linguistics (Volume 1: Long Papers)*, pages 752–760.

Truecasing German user-generated conversational text

Yulia Grishina   **Thomas Gueudré**   **Ralf Winkler**
Amazon Alexa
{yuliag,tgueudre,rwinkle}@amazon.com

Abstract

True-casing, the task of restoring proper case to (generally) lower case input, is important in downstream tasks and for screen display. In this paper, we investigate truecasing as an intrinsic task and present several experiments on noisy user queries to a voice-controlled dialog system. In particular, we compare a rule-based, an n-gram language model (LM) and a recurrent neural network (RNN) approaches, evaluating the results on a German Q&A corpus and reporting accuracy for different case categories. We show that while RNNs reach higher accuracy especially on large datasets, character n-gram models with interpolation are still competitive, in particular on mixed-case words where their fall-back mechanisms come into play.

1 Introduction

Truecasing is a natural language processing task that consists of assigning proper case to all words within a text where such information is not available. For many natural language applications, it is an important pre-processing step, shown to be useful in downstream tasks such as named entity recognition (Bodapati et al., 2019), automatic content extraction (Cucerzan, 2010) and machine translation (Etchegoyhen and Gete, 2020). For languages with complex casing rules (e.g., German), determining part of speech (POS) or named entity becomes almost impossible without casing information:

(1) Was fressen **Fliegen**?
     what eat   flies

(2) Wie hoch **fliegen** Vögel?
     how high fly   birds

In this example, the token 'fliegen' in (1) is a noun and therefore should begin with a capital letter, while in (2) it is a verb and is hence lowercased.

Truecasing is particularly hard in the German language, as it follows multiple capitalization rules, some of which we describe below. For instance, all nouns (including both common nouns and proper nouns) and nominalized verbs must be capitalized. Furthermore, German adjectives should be capitalized when used as substantive (e.g., *bei Grün*), while not being confused with their true adjective form (which is not capitalized). Another common ambiguity is the formal pronoun *Sie*, capitalized in all of its form (as opposed to informal *sie* which must be lowercased).

Truecasing becomes particularly important in dialog systems that aim to correctly interpret the natural language of user queries. Such systems often rely on automatic speech recognition (ASR) output, often quite noisy and non-grammatical as users frequently engage with their devices using highly colloquial speech. This output is used by downstream modules such as spoken language understanding (SLU) or entity resolution (ER). Another use case is displaying such output, e.g., on a device with screen, where casing information is necessary for readability and customer experience.

In this paper, we investigate different approaches to truecasing German user queries in the context of a voice-controlled dialog agent. We focus on informational and world knowledge queries, in which the users ask the device questions about, e.g., recent events, famous people, general world knowledge etc. In particular, we pit a rule-based approach against two learnt models, a character n-gram one and a neural one. We report the results across different case categories and discuss the benefits and the drawbacks for each of the approaches.

This paper is organized as follows: In Section 2, we provide an overview of related work on text truecasing. Next, we describe our experiment (Section 3), giving the overview of the truecasing approaches and datasets used. In Section 4, we

Proceedings of the 2020 EMNLP Workshop W-NUT: The Sixth Workshop on Noisy User-generated Text, pages 143–148
Online, Nov 19, 2020. ©2020 Association for Computational Linguistics

present the results of the experiment and provide a detailed error analysis. Finally, we discuss the results and outline future directions of research (Section 5).

2 Related work

The simplest approach to truecasing is to use unigram tagging, converting all tokens to their most frequent form in the training data. It is typically used as a baseline in capitalisation experiments which improve over this straightforward approach (e.g. (Lita et al., 2003; Chelba and Acero, 2006)).

Most of the earlier approaches to truecasing rely on statistical modeling and work mostly at word level. For instance, one of such approaches was proposed by Lita et al. (2003) who used a trigram language model and sentence level context to predict the most probable case sequence in a sentence. Next, Wang et al. (2006) proposed a CRF-based probabilistic model, which exploited bilingual information and was able to improve over monolingual methods on machine translation output, while Chelba and Acero (2006), Batista et al. (2008) used an approach based on maximum entropy models. Benefiting from larger computational power, the more recent approaches advocate modelling at character level. Susanto et al. (2016) first proposed to use a character-level RNN for truecasing, demonstrating the superiority of a character-level approach to word-based approaches. They show that the benefits of such approaches over word-based are that they are able to better generalise on "unseen" words and they also perform better on mixed-case[1]. Following this argument, we compare their architecture with based large character n-gram models with various smoothing.

3 Experiments

3.1 Dataset

For our experiments, we rely on two different datasets: (a) an internal German Q&A dataset, and (b) the German part of the Leipzig corpus collection[2] (Goldhahn et al., 2012). The Q&A dataset is a corpus that consists of frequent questions coming from a spoken dialog system users and answers provided by the same system[3]. It contains 30K

sentences, or 410K tokens, covering mostly the Information domain. All of the data used in this paper was anonymized prior to the experiment, to make sure that it does not include any user identifying information. A typical example from the corpus would be the following query:

(3) [User:] Welche Farben hat der Regenbogen? ('What is the color of the rainbow?')

[Device]: Die Regenbogenfarben sind Rot, Orange, Gelb, Grün, Hellblau, Dunkelblau und Violett. ('The rainbow colors are Red, Orange, Yellow, Green, Blue, Indigo, and Violet.')

Leipzig Corpus collection is a freely available corpus of newspaper articles. For our experiment, we have taken a cleaned dataset consisting of newspaper texts of 2015[4], from which we have randomly selected 100K sentences (around 2M tokens) for the experiment.

For both datasets, we used a 80/20 random split for training and test purposes, and use the same split for both the n-gram and neural language modelling approaches. A small portion (5%) of the train set was kept as development set, to tune the hyper-parameters of each model.

3.2 Truecasing approaches

3.2.1 Majority rule with tagged LM as baseline

We provide a simple baseline, using the majority rule and a tag-based model. The majority rule consists in turning each token of the test-set into the most common capitalized form in the training set. Words that have not been seen in the training corpora are left untouched and tallies are broken by lexicographic order (therefore picking the lowercased form first).

As a standard way of taking into account sequence correlations, we tag each training example with the case category (upper, lower, mixed and punct)[5] and train a 10-gram LM over the tags sequences, built with Kneser-Ney interpolation method. Finally, we compose this LM with the above majority baseline.

---

[1] Mixed-case words are those that contain upper-cased characters in the middle of a word, such as 'Rheinland-Pfalz'.

[2] https://corpora.uni-leipzig.de?corpusId=deu_newscrawl-public_2018

[3] The Q&A data is a subset of the questions and answers that can be accessed via https://alexaanswers.amazon.de.

[4] https://www.kaggle.com/rtatman/3-million-german-sentences

[5] "Upper" contains tokens that have a capital letter only at the beginning, while "lower" means that all letters in a token are lowercased. "Mixed" category includes tokens that have capital letters in the middle of a token as well as acronyms (e.g., *NASA*).

	Q&A				Leipzig			
	ΔAcc	ΔP	ΔR	$\Delta F1$	ΔAcc	ΔP	ΔR	$\Delta F1$
Baseline Majority rule	-8,98	-0,03	-26,47	-17,08	-3,50	+0,28	-11,13	-6,78
Rule-based	-2.43	-8.74	+0.62	-3.82	-4.31	-18.07	+3.88	-6.76
Kneser-Ney 5-gram leipz	-1.24	-7.74	+2.37	-2.45	+0.07	-7.31	+7.80	+0.78
Kneser-Ney 10-gram leipz	+0.11	-5.90	+4.30	-0.56	+3.00	-2.14	+11.93	+5.44
Kneser-Ney 15-gram leipz	+0.19	-5.81	+4.35	-0.49	+3.15	-2.01	+12.29	+5.68
Kneser-Ney 5-gram q&a	+2.08	-2.37	+8.08	+3.09				
Kneser-Ney 10-gram q&a	+4.09	+1.15	+10.4	+6.01				
Kneser-Ney 15-gram q&a	+4.20	+1.25	+10.64	+6.19				
char-rnn LSTM leipz	+1.43	-3.15	+5.21	+1.27	+4.29	+0.18	+13.52	**+7.39**
char-rnn GRU leipz	+1.26	-3.76	+5.13	+0.92	+4.13	-0.33	+13.27	+7.01
char-rnn LSTM q&a	+4.28	+1.22	+10.58	+6.14				
char-rnn GRU q&a	+3.79	+0.56	+9.39	+5.21				
Kneser-Ney 15-gram q&a + leipz	+4.58	+1.85	+11.04	+6.68	+3.14	-1.99	+12.26	+5.67
char-rnn LSTM q&a + leipz	+4.81	+2.17	+11.28	**+6.96**	+3.55	-1.21	+12.21	+6.04

Table 1: Truecasing results (%) relative to the tag-based LM baseline: Accuracy, Precision, Recall and F1 across all approaches evaluated on two datasets - the Q&A corpus (column 2) and the Leipzig corpus (column 3). For the n-gram LM and the RNN approaches, we also specify the corpus used for training. Majority rule baseline was trained and evaluated on the same dataset (no cross-domain evaluation). Models trained on the Q&A corpus were not evaluated on the Leipzig corpus.

3.2.2 Rule-based approach

For this approach we compiled grammars based on regular expressions into weighted finite-state transducers (FSTs) using OpenGrm and Thrax libraries (Roark et al., 2012). The system consists of token lists, each associated with a POS (e.g., pronouns, adjectives, verbs, etc.) and several rules containing POS patterns frequently preceding tokens in uppercase. If an input token matches one of the lists, a path with decreased local weight is generated and the following token, if not in one of the lists, is uppercased. Each additional match within a rule adds a further decreased local weight, reflecting the assumption, that the probability for an token in uppercase increases with the number of known predecessors. By applying these rules on input text, we end up with several possible paths for each sentence, and select the path with lowest global weight as best candidate. Rules were hand-tuned on a development subset of the Q&A dataset.

3.2.3 N-gram language modelling with FSTs

This approach also relies on the FST machinery, but makes use of a trained language model (LM) to re-rank the possible hypothesis. The approach is standard (Manning et al. (2008)), except from the fact we employ it with characters rather than words.

We first build an FST that, when composed with a lower-cased input, returns a lattice of all possible capitalized variants (for example, "hi" being transformed to "Hi", "hI" and "HI").

To estimate the probability of each hypothesis produced by the above lattice, we collect N-gram counts from the capitalized training corpus and re-normalize them into probabilities. Especially for high N values, N-gram models are sparse (as some sequences of characters are seen only a few times) and require some back-off or smoothing strategies. We pick the Kneser-Ney interpolation scheme (using the OpenGrm library), a widely used scheme which estimates the probability of a given N-gram based on lower order statistics (Ney et al. (1994)).

Finally, model prediction is obtained by composing the lattice of capitalized variant with the LM, and extracting the path of lowest cost.

We tried models with various smoothing schemes (Katz, Witten-Bell and Kneser-Ney) on the dev set, and kept the interpolated Kneser-Ney for its superior accuracy. For completeness, we also report the results for different n-gram sizes (5, 10 and 15) and observe that larger values lead to higher accuracy, albeit greatly increasing the required memory (1Gb for the largest models).

	Rule	KN 15-gram q&a	KN 15-gram leipz	char-rnn q&a	char-rnn leipz
Upper	90.2	97.0	95.3	97.3	96.9
Lower	92.6	98.6	97.8	98.6	98.9
Mixed	68.1	94.0	84.9	89.6	75.6

Table 2: Token accuracy per case category (upper, lower, mixed case)

	q&a	leipz
Upper	21 691	101 177
Lower	46 171	245 225
Mixed	6947	23 957

Table 3: Number of tokens with upper, lower, mixed case per test set

3.2.4 Recurrent neural networks

We used the approach of Susanto et al. (2016) to train a character-level RNN language model. We use the provided implementation[6] to train a small RNN model with 2 layers and 300 hidden states, varying the type of the hidden unit (LSTM/GRU). It uses truncated backpropagation for 50 time steps. After training, the model with the smallest validation loss after 30 epochs is chosen.

4 Results and error analysis

In the following, we present a comparison of the approaches on the the Q&A corpus and the Leipzig corpus. Improvements for each of the approaches relative to the tag-based LM baseline are presented in Table 1. We are also reporting results on a mixed dataset, i.e., taking all available Q&A training data, and adding a similar amount of the Leipzig corpus training data. While we are reporting relative improvement results due to privacy concerns on the Q&A dataset, baselines on this task are known to be quite strong (over 90% accuracy, e.g. (Lita et al., 2003)) and state-of-the art approaches such as the neural networks used in this paper reach accuracy of the order of 96-98% (Susanto et al., 2016).

4.1 Case categories and mixed-case words

First, we look at accuracy per case category (upper, lower, mixed), which can be seen in Table 2. The overall number of tokens belonging to each of the categories are presented in Table 3.

As one can see from Table 2, mixed case words are best handled by the n-gram LMs, while the rule-based approach shows the lowest accuracy on those. Low scores on mixed case words for the Leipzig corpus are due to a large portion of proper names coming from newspaper articles (e.g., "NewVoiceMedia" or "TecDAX") that were not capitalized properly. The success of n-gram LMs for mixed cases is naturally explained by the back-off smoothing mechanism in interpolated n-gram models, where subwords found capitalized in the corpora largely contribute to the final cost.

4.2 Unseen words

From the test/train splits, there are 16048 unseen words in the Leipzig corpora, and 3494 in the Q&A corpora. Accuracy percentages for those unseen words are presented in Table 4 (we do not evaluate unseen words on the rule-based approach, as we used automatically created POS lists which therefore may have contained unseen words). The RNN approach in this case is the most accurate, following the conclusion of Susanto et al. (2016).

We attribute the bulk of the mistakes of the n-gram model to its inability to capture longer dependencies. Despite a large n-gram value (15), the model is often unable to implicitly obtain the POS of the token when the information is contained in the suffix. The model then defaults to the most common occurrence. For example, the noun "Gleichstrom" ("direct current") is normalized as "gleichstrom" because of the commonly seen adjective "gleich" ("equal"), without considering the suffix "strom".

4.3 Accuracy by Part of Speech

We used spacy[7] German model to PoS tag our test corpus, and subsequently extracted most common categories of errors. Unsurprisingly, common nouns, adjectives and proper nouns constituted the highest proportion of errors in all approaches. We inspected the most frequent failing tokens for each

---

[6]https://gitlab.com/raymondhs/char-rnn-truecase

[7]https://spacy.io/

	Unseen words
KN 15-gram q&a	76.00
KN 15-gram leipz	78.06
char-rnn LSTM q&a	86.10
char-rnn LSTM leipz	83.20

Table 4: Token accuracy for unseen words on the Q&A corpus

	Sentence-based accuracy
KN 15-gram leipz	65.45
char-rnn LSTM leipz	72.60
char-rnn GRU leipz	70.00

Table 5: Sentence-based accuracy on Leipzig corpus

of the approaches on the Q&A dataset, but the models show no major difference there. For all of them, the failing tokens belong to the class of frequent pronouns or prepositions, whose capitalization is particularly ambiguous and context dependent, such as "Sie" or "die".

4.4 Sentence-based accuracy

We report the sentence accuracy for the LM and RNN approaches as well, in Table 5. Sentence-based accuracy is computed as the ratio of the number of sentences where all tokens were predicted correctly to the overall number of sentences in the test set. Sentence-based accuracy for the majority rule baseline is extremely low (<15.0) which is mostly due to the fact that the initial letter in a sentence is frequently left lowercased.

We distinctly observe that RNNs outperform simple n-gram LMs on this conservative metric. This implies that RNNs often perform a flawless normalization of the whole sentence, while n-gram approaches scatter mistakes more uniformly across sentences. However, a more detailed analysis shows that mistakes done by RNN are more critical. For instance, it sometimes tends to overgenerate, which results in hardly readable mixed-cased (e.g., "KAffeMaschine") or conversational words (e.g., capitalizing the colloquial form 'ne' of the indefinite article 'eine').

5 Conclusion and future work

In this paper, we presented a study on truecasing, a common task in natural language processing, either as a pre-processing step in a larger pipeline (f.e. in MT), or as a post-processing one (f.e. when displaying the output of an spoken language system on screen). Comparing rule-based, n-gram and neural models, we showed that, while state of the art methods such as DNNs unsurprisingly reach the highest accuracy, standard n-gram models are still competitive, in particular on mixed-case words, where their fall-back mechanisms come into play. They also fair well in noisier corpora (such as the Q&A corpora).

Truecasing, as a part of text normalization, is peculiar in that its bulk can be solved simply by a few hand-written rules, with however a long tail of very difficult cases such as acronyms, unseen words. Finding a proper balance between the flexibility of neural approaches, and the controlled, more interpretable behaviour of FST-based systems, remains an open and challenging problem (Mansfield et al. (2019), Sproat and Jaitly (2016), Zhang et al. (2019)).

Acknowledgements

We thank Fernando Koch and Saskia Schuster from Amazon Alexa for providing the Q&A data, and Spyros Matsoukas for his valuable feedback on an earlier draft of this paper. We also thank anonymous reviewers for their helpful comments.

References

Fernando Batista, Nuno Mamede, and Isabel Trancoso. 2008. Language dynamics and capitalization using maximum entropy. In *Proceedings of ACL-08: HLT, Short Papers*, pages 1–4.

Sravan Bodapati, Hyokun Yun, and Yaser Al-Onaizan. 2019. Robustness to capitalization errors in named entity recognition. *arXiv preprint arXiv:1911.05241*.

Ciprian Chelba and Alex Acero. 2006. Adaptation of maximum entropy capitalizer: Little data can help a lot. *Computer Speech & Language*, 20(4):382–399.

Silviu Cucerzan. 2010. Does capitalization matter in web search? In *KDIR*, pages 302–306.

Thierry Etchegoyhen and Harritxu Gete. 2020. To case or not to case: Evaluating casing methods for neural machine translation. In *Proceedings of The 12th Language Resources and Evaluation Conference*, pages 3752–3760.

Dirk Goldhahn, Thomas Eckart, and Uwe Quasthoff. 2012. Building large monolingual dictionaries at the Leipzig corpora collection: From 100 to 200 languages. In *LREC*, volume 29, pages 31–43.

Lucian Vlad Lita, Abe Ittycheriah, Salim Roukos, and Nanda Kambhatla. 2003. Truecasing. In *Proceedings of the 41st Annual Meeting of the Association for Computational Linguistics*, pages 152–159.

Christopher D. Manning, Prabhakar Raghavan, and Hinrich Schütze. 2008. *Introduction to Information Retrieval*. Cambridge University Press, USA.

Courtney Mansfield, Ming Sun, Yuzong Liu, Ankur Gandhe, and Björn Hoffmeister. 2019. Neural text normalization with subword units. In *Proceedings of the 2019 Conference of the North American Chapter of the Association for Computational Linguistics: Human Language Technologies, Volume 2 (Industry Papers)*, pages 190–196, Minneapolis, Minnesota. Association for Computational Linguistics.

Hermann Ney, Ute Essen, and Reinhard Kneser. 1994. On structuring probabilistic dependences in stochastic language modelling. *Computer Speech and Language*, 8(1):1–38.

Brian Roark, Richard Sproat, Cyril Allauzen, Michael Riley, Jeffrey Sorensen, and Terry Tai. 2012. The OpenGrm open-source finite-state grammar software libraries. In *Proceedings of the ACL 2012 System Demonstrations*, pages 61–66, Jeju Island, Korea. Association for Computational Linguistics.

Richard Sproat and Navdeep Jaitly. 2016. RNN approaches to text normalization: A challenge. *CoRR*, abs/1611.00068.

Raymond Hendy Susanto, Hai Leong Chieu, and Wei Lu. 2016. Learning to capitalize with character-level recurrent neural networks: an empirical study. In *Proceedings of the 2016 Conference on Empirical Methods in Natural Language Processing*, pages 2090–2095.

Wei Wang, Kevin Knight, and Daniel Marcu. 2006. Capitalizing machine translation. In *Proceedings of the Human Language Technology Conference of the NAACL, Main Conference*, pages 1–8.

Hao Zhang, Richard Sproat, Axel H Ng, Felix Stahlberg, Xiaochang Peng, Kyle Gorman, and Brian Roark. 2019. Neural models of text normalization for speech applications. *Computational Linguistics*, 45(2):293–337.

Fine-Tuning MT systems for Robustness to Second-Language Speaker Variations

Md Mahfuz Ibn Alam and Antonios Anastasopoulos
Department of Computer Science, George Mason University
{malam21,antonis}@gmu.edu

Abstract

The performance of neural machine translation (NMT) systems only trained on a single language variant degrades when confronted with even slightly different language variations. With this work, we build upon previous work to explore how to mitigate this issue. We show that fine-tuning using *naturally occurring* noise along with pseudo-references (i.e. "corrected" non-native inputs translated using the baseline NMT system) is a promising solution towards systems robust to such type of input variations. We focus on four translation pairs, from English to Spanish, Italian, French, and Portuguese, with our system achieving improvements of up to 3.1 BLEU points compared to the baselines, establishing a new state-of-the-art on the JFLEG-ES dataset.[1]

1 Introduction

Neural machine translation (NMT) approaches have aided the machine translation field in achieving great advances in the recent years, starting with encoder-decoder models with attention (Bahdanau et al., 2014; Luong et al., 2015), to transformers using self-attention (Vaswani et al., 2018), to massively multilingual models that yield large improvements even in low-resource settings (Aharoni et al., 2019; Zhang et al., 2020).

Despite these very encouraging developments, the list of shortcomings of NMT is also quite vast (Koehn and Knowles, 2017), and one of the most crucial shortcomings is the lack of robustness to source-side noise.[2] When confronted with inputs that are even slightly different from the inputs that the models were trained on, the quality of the outputs significantly degrades. This observation has

been confirmed for noise due to typos or character scrambling (Belinkov and Bisk, 2018), due to faulty speech recognition (Heigold et al., 2018), or due to naturally-occurring errors by second-language non-native speakers (Anastasopoulos et al., 2019).

However, this issue can particularly degrade the user experience for millions of potential users. For example, the number of non-native English speakers is three times larger than the number of native English speakers (c.f. around 1 billion for the former and about 300 million for the latter). Had one had access to large amounts of data for all different language varieties, it would be straightforward to train variety-specific MT models. Such data, though, are of course scarce.

In this paper we work on addressing this particular shortcoming, in an attempt to make NMT systems more robust to source-side variations that non-native speakers produce. Since English is the language with the largest amount of second-language learners and non-native speakers, we only focus on MT systems translating out of English, but we point out that such work is urgently needed for other colonial languages (i.e. French, Spanish) or majority languages (such as Russian, Mandarin, or Hindi) that are taking over minority ones.[3]

The main difference of our approach compared to previous work is that we do not attempt to synthesize different types of noise, but rather use *naturally-occurring* texts, as produced by non-native speakers. We utilize grammar error correction corpora and produce pseudo-references, which we then use to fine-tune a NMT system with a goal of increasing its robustness to such source-side noise. In our view, our approach has two main advantages and a single disadvantage over previous

---

[1]All datasets and code are publicly available here: `https://github.com/mahfuzibnalam/finetuning_for_robustness`.

[2]This is not to say that non-neural statistical approaches did not suffer from the same drawbacks.

[3]That is also not to say that robustness is not necessary for low-resource languages; to the contrary! We just focus on high-resource settings first as they are the ones that have the potential to affect a larger number of downstream users.

Proceedings of the 2020 EMNLP Workshop W-NUT: The Sixth Workshop on Noisy User-generated Text, pages 149–158
Online, Nov 19, 2020. ©2020 Association for Computational Linguistics

works. First, the types of *realistic* "non-native-like" noise that can be synthesized are limited, covering among others typos or simple morphological or syntactic mistakes (Belinkov and Bisk, 2018; Cheng et al., 2018; Anastasopoulos et al., 2019; Tan et al., 2020, et alia) but not covering the interplay between all these or any other higher level issues (e.g. word choice). Our approach has the potential to handle a larger spectrum of language variation, as it appears in naturally occurring data. Second, our choice of fine-tuning, rather than training from scratch as previous works have opted for, leads to lower training times and lower compute needed for similar improvements on robustness. The main drawback of our approach lies in the need for corrected (or "normalized") versions of "noisy" non-native sentences, but we take solace in the fact that at least for the majority of the high-resource languages (such as English, French, German, Russian, or Chinese) such datasets already exist. Very briefly, our contributions are summarized here:

- We show that fine-tuning a pre-trained system on noisy source-side data along with pseudo-references is a viable approach towards NMT robustness to grammar errors and input from non-native speakers.

- We show that fine-tuning of a multilingual NMT system on several languages is also advisable, yielding better performance for a subset of the languages.

- We also discuss the potential of achieving zero-shot robustness, as long as catastrophic forgetting issues can be overcome.

2   Related Work

Our work is inspired by and combines two lines of research: (1) robustness studies in NMT and (2) data augmentation.

Robust NMT   Making robust models for NMT has recently gained popularity, with Shared Tasks organized in the Conference of Machine Translation (Li et al., 2019) and several solutions put forth (Berard et al., 2019; Helcl et al., 2019; Post and Duh, 2019; Zhou et al., 2019; Zheng et al., 2019, et alia). Liu et al. (2018); Karpukhin et al. (2019) focus on creating black-box methods for making synthetic or natural noises. Ebrahimi et al. (2018) use white-box methods and creates adversarial examples for character-level NMT. Anastasopoulos et al. (2019) show that including noisy

synthetic data in the training data can increase the model's robustness without sacrificing performance on clean data, an approach that Tan et al. (2020) extend to more NLP tasks.

While these approaches are indeed meritorious and indeed improve a model's robustness, we argue that one needs to use *natural* noise instead, on account of two phenomena. The first is language change: the different variations that the models will have to contend with are not static, but rather constantly changing at an ever-increasing pace. Second, and perhaps a partial direct consequence of the first point, one cannot rely on synthetic examples to properly capture the wide variety of naturally-occurring variations. Besides, if one could properly model noise creation, they could also similarly model the inverse problem adequately, namely remove said noise, in which case a noise-removing preprocessing step would be most likely suffiecient to tackle the issue.

On working with real-world noise, the approach of Michel and Neubig (2018) is the most similar to ours. They collected "noisy" English, French, and Japanese sentences from Reddit, created translations, and split their dataset (MTNT) into train, development, and test, ranging from 5 to 36 thousand training examples. To build robust NMT systems, they first train a model on standard clean data and then fine-tune it on the training portion of MTNT using techniques from domain adaptation. The main difference between this worthy effort and our approach is two-fold. First, our approach does not require gold translations of the noisy inputs, which can be expensive and hard to collect, but we instead rely on the abundance of corrected second-language learner data (which we use to create pseudo-references, see §3). Second, we attest that Reddit language translation is much closer to a domain adaptation scenario, and includes additional noise types that are not pertinent to non-native language translation such as emoji, Reddit jargon such us "upvote" or "gild", and internet slang such as "tbh" and "smh".[4]

On working with pseudo-references, the approach of Cheng et al. (2019a) is the most similar to ours. They use ASR corpora to create synthetic ASR-induced noise and try to make NMT system more robust to this type of noise. As speech-to-transcription-to-translation datasets are

---

[4]"tbh" stands for "to be honest" and "smh" for "shake my head".

very costly to produce, they use standard speech-to-transcription datasets instead. They translate the gold transcription data set to get translation pseudo-references. Then they jointly train the model on noisy source transcription using the pseudo-reference translations as the target.

Data Augmentation Data augmentation techniques have become increasingly popular for MT and other NLP tasks, from back-translation of monolingual data (Sennrich et al., 2016) to counterfactual augmentation to address gender bias issues (Zmigrod et al., 2019, et alia). For our purposes, we will focus on data augmentation techniques aimed at increasing NMT robustness.

Simple perturbations typically used include the infusion of character-level noise (e.g. character scrambling (Heigold et al., 2018) or typos (Belinkov and Bisk, 2018)) or word order scrambling (Sperber et al., 2017). Cheng et al. (2018, 2019b) propose a gradient based method to attack the translation model with adversarial source examples, but there's not guarantee that the adversarial attack results in realistic noise (Michel et al., 2019a). Anastasopoulos et al. (2019) add specific types of errors (such as subject-verb agreement or determiner errors) on the source-side of parallel data, while Tan et al. (2020) specifically perturb the inflectional morphology of words to create adversarial examples and show that adversarial fine-tuning them for a single epoch significantly improves robustness. Our work is highly motivated from these last two works, but instead of creating synthetic perturbed adversarial examples we use real noisy examples.

3 Fine-tuning for Robustness

Our goal is to achieve robustness to source-side variations that are similar to the mistakes that non-native English speakers make. To do so, we will utilize state-of-the-art pretrained systems and fine-tune them using pseudo-references over corpora that include *real-world* noise. The general outline of our approach is straightforward:

1. Start with a English-to-X NMT system pretrained on any available data.
2. Obtain an English Grammar Error Correction dataset, which provides tuples $(\mathbf{x}, \tilde{\mathbf{x}})$ of original and corrected sentences.
3. Translate the corrected sentences obtaining pseudo-references $\tilde{\mathbf{y}} = \text{NMT}(\tilde{\mathbf{x}})$.

4. Fine-tune the NMT system on $(\mathbf{x}, \tilde{\mathbf{y}})$ pairs.

Notation Throughout this work, we use the notation of Anastasopoulos (2019) to denote different types of data:

- $\mathbf{x}$: the original, noisy, potentially ungrammatical English sentence. Its tokens will be denoted as x_i.
- $\tilde{\mathbf{x}}$: the English sentence with the correction annotations applied to the original sentence $\mathbf{x}$, which is deemed fluent and grammatical. Again, its tokens will be denoted as $\tilde{x}_i$.
- $\tilde{\mathbf{y}}$: the output of the NMT system when $\tilde{\mathbf{x}}$ is provided as input (tokens: $\tilde{y}_j$). This will be our pseudo-reference for fine-tuning or evaluation.

For the sake of readability, we use the terms grammatical errors, noise, or edits interchangeably. In the context of this work, they will all denote the annotated grammatical errors in the source sentences ($\mathbf{x}$).

Data There are many publicly available corpora for non-native English that are annotated with corrections, which have been widely used for the Grammar Error Correction tasks (Bryant et al., 2019). We specifically use NUCLE (Dahlmeier et al., 2013), FCE (Yannakoudakis et al., 2011), and Lang-8 (Tajiri et al., 2012) for creating the pseudo-references. For evaluation we use the JFLEG dataset (Napoles et al., 2017) and its accompanying Spanish translations in the JFLEG-ES dataset (Anastasopoulos et al., 2019).

The NUS Corpus of Learner English (**NUCLE**) contains essays written by Singaporean students. It is generally considered the main benchmark for GEC. This dataset consists of 21.3K sentences. The First Certificate in English corpus (**FCE**) is also made of essays, written by learners who were sitting the English as Second or Other Language (ESOL) examinations. We use the publicly available version, which includes 17.6K sentences.

Lang-8 is a slightly different dataset than the previous two datasets. This dataset was built from user-provided corrections in an online learner forum. In comparison to the others, this dataset is much larger, consisting of 149.5K sentences. However, this datasets' error domain is very versatile. It does not consist any test and validation set.

The JHU FLuency-Extended GUG corpus (**JFLEG**) is a small corpus of only 1.3K sentences, intended only for evaluation. It has an unique character that is different from other datasets, as it contains correction annotations that include extended fluency edits rather than just minimal grammatical ones.

The JFLEG corpus was translated into Spanish by Anastasopoulos et al. (2019) to create the **JFLEG-ES** corpus, which provides gold-standard Spanish translations for every JFLEG sentence.

Evaluation   In cases where we have access to human references, we can simply evaluate with reference-based metrics (e.g. BLEU (Papineni et al., 2002)). Unfortunately, we only have references for the JFLEG-ES dataset in Spanish.

For all other datasets and languages, we treat the translations of the corrected clean English sources as pseudo-references, and use the metrics from (Anastasopoulos, 2019): Robustness Score (RB), f-BLEU, f-METEOR, and Noise Ratio (NR).

Robustness Score (RB) is defined as the percentage of translations of noisy sentences that are *exactly the same* as the translation of the respective corrected sentence.

f-BLEU and **f-METEOR** are slight modification of the popular BLEU and METEOR metrics. The only difference is that they use pseudo-references instead of true human-created ones, and hence are referred to as faux BLEU and faux METEOR. In our case, the pseudo-references are the translations of the corrected sentence.

Target-Source Noise Ratio (NR) is the ratio between the target- and source-side BLEU score between noisy and corrected sentences. All other measures do not take into consideration how large are the source-side differences. The intuition behind this metric is that if there is minimal perturbation $d(\mathbf{x}, \tilde{\mathbf{x}})$ on the input side then there should be minimal reflection on the target side perturbation $d(\mathbf{y}, \tilde{\mathbf{y}})$ as well. NR is computed as:

$$\text{NR}(\mathbf{x}, \tilde{\mathbf{x}}, \mathbf{y}, \tilde{\mathbf{y}}) = \frac{d(\mathbf{y}, \tilde{\mathbf{y}})}{d(\mathbf{x}, \tilde{\mathbf{x}})} = \frac{100 - \text{BLEU}(\mathbf{y}, \tilde{\mathbf{y}})}{100 - \text{BLEU}(\mathbf{x}, \tilde{\mathbf{x}})}$$

4   Experiments and Results

We name our models in a way that is convenient to understand. Our models are named as such: dataset_language; e.g. the NUCLE_ES model will refer to the model fine-tuned on the NUCLE dataset for Spanish language. We will overload the naming convention to also refer to datasets in the same way, e.g. the NUCLE_ES dataset.

Experimental Details   All data are tokenized and true-cased using the Moses tools (Koehn et al., 2007).We use the SentencePiece (Kudo and Richardson, 2018) toolkit to split the sentences into sub-words. We use the unigram language model algorithm of the toolkit with 65,000 operations. We filter the fine-tuning dataset so that sentence length is capped at 80 words.

Target Side Creation   Given the recent success and promise of massively multilingual systems (Johnson et al., 2016; Firat et al., 2016), we use as our original model the OPUS-MT multilingual Romance model[5] (Tiedemann and Thottingal, 2020), trained using Marian NMT (Junczys-Dowmunt et al., 2018) within the HuggingFace's Transformers library (Wolf et al., 2019). For every dataset we pass source sentences (both original and corrected versions) and obtain target side sentences. Then we use the corrected target side sentences as our ground truth for fine-tuning the same model.

Transformer Model Details   We use a transformer architecture as they have shown to be much superior to recurrent architectures. We use HugginFace's Transformers' BartForConditionalGeneration as our model and tokenizer. This model uses 12 layers, 16 attention heads, the embedding dimension is 1024, and positional feed-forward dimension is 4096. Dropout is set to 0.1. We use the same learning rate schedule as in (Vaswani et al., 2017) with 500 warm-up steps but only decay the learning rate until it reaches $3 * 10^{-5}$. We fine-tune our models on a V100 GPU for a maximum of 100 epochs (although best validation set performance is reached around 20 to 25 epochs). For testing we use the model with the best performance on the validation dataset. Our validation check interval is set to 0.2.

Evaluation   We use METEOR (Denkowski and Lavie, 2014) to calculate the f-METEOR scores. We calculate BLEU and f-BLEU scores using Sacrebleu (Post, 2018). We compute statistical significance with paired bootstrap resampling (Koehn, 2004).

Results on English-Spanish   We first discuss the results on the JFLEG-ES test set, which is the only dataset with human gold references.

The performance of our systems on the JFLEG-ES test set, as measured by detokenized BLEU is

---

[5]name: Helsinki-NLP/opus-mt-en-ROMANCE

System	en→es BLEU		
	Clean[†]	Noisy	Δ
(Anastasopoulos et al., 2019)	27.80	26.80	-1.00
Helsinki-NLP/opus-mt-en-ROMANCE	30.14	28.04	-2.10
-fine-tuned on:			
NUCLE	27.89	26.62	-1.27
FCE	26.93	25.54	-1.39
Lang-8	28.85	28.20	-0.65
all noisy in Spanish	29.37	**31.14***	1.77
all noisy in all four languages	28.16	29.04	0.88
all clean in Spanish	**30.39**	27.83	-2.56

Table 1: Translation quality (BLEU scores) on the JFLEG_ES data-set. †: average over 4 corrected sentences as input to the translation model. *statistically significantly better than the baseline, with $p < 0.05$.

System	Sentence	BLEU
Source (original)	it has some problems that *it* can effect *to humens*.	
OPUS-MT output	tiene algunos problemas que *puede* afectar a los *humens*.	47
Finetuned output	tiene algunos problemas que pueden afectar a los humanos.	89
Reference	esto tiene algunos problemas que pueden afectar a los humanos.	
Source (original)	last month, I needed to buy *digtal-camera*.	
OPUS-MT output	el mes pasado, necesitaba comprar *digtal-camera*.	26
Finetuned output	el mes pasado, necesitaba comprar una cámara digital.	66
Reference	el mes pasado necesitaba comprar una cámara digital.	

Table 2: Examples (cherry-picked) of sentences with high BLEU improvement after fine-tuning (English-Spanish on the the JFLEG-ES dataset).

summarized in Table 1. The "Clean" column refers to an average BLEU score over the four versions of source-side corrections provided by the JFLEG dataset, the "Noisy" column reports results with the original sentences as input, and the last column presents the difference (Δ) between the two.

The first thing to note is that the multilingual OPUS-MT model outperforms the previously published results of Anastasopoulos et al. (2019) by more than 2 BLEU points on both clean and noisy settings. This is unsurprising, if one considers that the OPUS-MT model has been trained on an order of magnitude more English-Spanish data (about 25x), and it has in addition been trained on other related Romance languages. However, we should also note that the difference of the two models is imbalanced: the improvement from all these additional data is +2.3 BLEU points when evaluated on clean data, but only +1.2 BLEU points when evaluated on the noisy pairs. This outlines the importance of evaluating MT systems not only on clean data but also on other language variants. Although imbalanced these improvements are significant and hence we treat our multilingual OPUS-MT model as the baseline in all following discussions.

Fine-tuning on individual datasets yields inconsistent results, with the BLEU score changing from -2.5 to +0.16. The highest drop is observed when fine-tuning on FCE; this is reasonable as JFLEG and FCE include errors on quite different domains (Napoles et al., 2017). This ablation allows us to identify Lang-8 as perhaps the most appropriate single dataset for this kind of tasks, most likely due to its size and diversity of errors and domains.

Using all available datasets, however, is significantly better. We find that our model performs particularly well when fine-tuned on pseudo-references from all corpora (the "all noisy in Spanish" model (sixth row) that is a concatenation of all the datasets in Spanish). We observe a 3.1 BLEU improvement for noisy data, while suffering a small decrease (0.8 BLEU points) on clean data. The dif-

en→x	system	RB	f-BLEU noisy (clean)	f-METEOR	NR
Spanish	original	9.56	62.61 (99.1)	0.79	0.99
	adapted on es	24.45	69.88* (81.76)	**0.84**	0.69
	adapted on all	**24.76**	**69.92*** (75.81)	0.83	**0.68**
Italian	original	9.40	59.06 (99.32)	0.70	1.08
	adapted on it	**34.48**	**84.64*** (81.54)	**0.87**	**0.46**
	adapted on all	23.35	67.71* (75.14)	0.76	0.72
French	original	10.32	61.96 (99.16)	0.77	1.00
	adapted on fr	**43.02**	**87.30*** (83.12)	**0.90**	**0.31**
	adapted on all	22.22	67.80* (74.38)	0.78	0.73
Portuguese	original	9.20	61.12 (99.01)	0.72	1.02
	adapted on pt	**24.29**	68.61* (81.60)	**0.77**	0.70
	adapted on all	24.00	**69.36*** (76.47)	**0.77**	**0.69**

Table 3: Translation robustness evaluation (multiple metrics) for English to four Romance language translation. Adaptation significantly increases the Robustness percentage as well as f-BLEU. *statistically significantly better than the "original" baseline, with $p < 0.05$.

ferent datasets cover different types of errors and domains, and as a result the fine-tuning process does not get biased by a single type of domain.

The second-to-last row ("all noisy in all four languages") reports results when pseudo-references in all four experimental MT directions (EN to ES,FR,IT,PT) are used in the fine-tuning process of our multilingual model. In this case, we still observe 1 BLEU improvement over the noisy data, compared to the baseline, but the performance on clean data is further degraded.

Last, it was crucial to examine whether the improvements we obtained are due to our fine-tuned models becoming indeed more robust to errors, as opposed to adapting to the domain and other characteristics of the datasets we train and evaluate on. In the last row ("all clean in Spanish") we present the results following fine-tuning the models with the *corrected* sentences as inputs.[6] We confirm that indeed our model improves slightly on the clean data, but its performance does not improve on the noisy inputs. Hence, we can conclude that the effect of domain adaptation is minimal, and our fine-tuned model has indeed learn to deal with non-standard inputs.

Table 2 displays a couple of sentences where our fine-tuned system produces more fluent outputs that then pre-trained system, properly han-

dling the source-side noise. The mistakes in the English source sentence and the MT outputs are highlighted with *red italics*. In the first example (top) our system can handle the typo "digtal" and correctly translate it as "digital." In the second example (bottom) our system, in addition to handling the typo "humens", it also correctly inflects the verb "pueden" (third person, plural) to agree with its subject, while the pretrained model produces an ungrammatical Spanish output (the verb "puede" is in third person singular and does not agree with its subject).

Results on other ROMANCE language In this section we report results obtained with the model fine-tuned on pseudo-references from all datasets for each of the four languages, as they were consistently better than any single-dataset fine-tuning approach. Table 3 presents the scores with all four evaluation metrics on all four En-to-X translation directions. For each language, we compare three models: the pre-trained one, one fine-tuned on pseudo-references for the respective language only, and one fine-tuned on all four languages simultaneously.

As we don't have human references for the other languages except Spanish, we use the Robustness Score, faux-BLEU, faux-METEOR, and Target-Source Noise Ratio metrics. As showcased by Table 3, in every language our approach yields a minimum of 7 f-BLEU points improvement over

---

[6]This would amount to a straightforward case of self-training, since it the target outputs were produced by the model itself prior to fine-tuning.

the original system when trained on that single language. In Italian and French, the improvement is particularly significant of at least 25 f-BLEU points. We have also listed the f-BLEU for clean test set which shows that the f-BLEU score decreased giving us assurance that the model is learning to be robust on noisy data. Also 75-80 BLEU score is still very significant.

The f-METEOR scores indicate similar trends. It is worth noting, though, that the differences between the original and the fine-tuned systems are less pronounced. We attribute this difference to the fact that most output differences are generally small local changes (e.g. on the inflection of a verb or a noun), which METEOR's paraphrase matching considers to be quite similar.

The Robustness Scores (RB) are also revealing: when the original system only returned the same output for the potentially noisy original sentence and the corrected one about 10% of the time, after fine-tuning all systems return the same outputs more than 24% of the time, reaching a RB score of more than 43% for French.

The Noise Ratio (NR) allows us to inspect if we actually manage to create a system that reduces the noise or not. An NR of less than 1 means that indeed our system reduces the source-side noise in its output, while a NR higher than one implies that the system amplifies the source-side differences (the lower NR the better). The pre-trained system consistently produces an NR of around 1, meaning that even though it does not amplify noise, it also does not reduce it. In comparison, our adapted models manage to reduce the source-side noise, with scores significantly lower than 1.

Can we achieve zero-shot robustness? An intriguing question that arose during our experiments, was whether one could fine-tune a multilingual system for robustness on only one language (e.g. Spanish) and consequently make the system more robust not only in that language but also in the other languages supported by the system. This avenue would significantly increase the value of not only our approach but also of the original multilingual systems: perhaps the community might eventually have access to large collections of true reference translations of non-native English, which would allow us to train systems robust to such source-side variations. Such datasets are unlikely to be available in multiple languages, though, hence the need for a way to improve a multilingual system's

Finetune on:	en→es BLEU
Italian	5.04
French	10.02
Portuguese	3.86

Table 4: Simple finetuning on only a single language leads to catastrophic forgetting of the other languages, as the low translation quality (BLEU scores) on the JF-LEG_ES data-set show.

robustness using single-language data.

We attempt a first step towards this direction, by evaluating on English-Spanish the systems that we fine-tuned solely on English-Italian, English-French, and English-Portuguese. Unfortunately, as outlined in Table 4, this simple approach does not work out-of-the-box. Fine-tuning on a single language pair leads to catastrophic forgetting (French, 1999) of the multilingual abilities of the system. This is a phenomenon commonly observed in continued learning or fine-tuning scenarios (Goodfellow et al., 2013) as well as on MT domain adaptation scenarios in particular (Freitag and Al-Onaizan, 2016), for the mitigation of which several approaches have been proposed (Lopez-Paz and Ranzato, 2017; Thompson et al., 2019; Michel et al., 2019b, et alia). As this research direction is beyond the scope of this paper, we leave the application of such approaches for future work.

5 Conclusion

In this work, we studied the effect of fine-tuning a NMT model using *real* source-side noise paired with pseudo-references obtained by translating Grammar Error Correction corpora. We confirmed previous works on the utility of training with source-side noise, as it leads to models more robust to non-native English inputs, but also showed that instead of using synthetically-induced noise, we can (a) use real-user data with pseudo-references and (b) fine-tune a pre-trained system, rather than training from scratch. We will release all pseudo-references and our code upon acceptance. Our approach of fine-tuning a pre-trained system with pseudo-references approach has particular appealing advantages (less training time, no need for costly translation references) and it improves the robustness of MT systems significantly on all language pairs we tested.

For future work, we will explore ways to integrate strategies for avoiding catastrophic forgetting, in order to achieve *multilingual* robustness without needing to fine-tune a multilingual model on all interested languages, as well as incorporating robustness rewards through reinforcement learning in the fine-tuning process. In addition, we will investigate how the quality of the pseudo-references affects the downstream results, and we also plan to explore the trade-off between language-specific and multilingual fine-tuning.

Acknowledgements

The authors want to thank the reviewers for their insightful comments. The first author was funded by a George Mason Computer Science Department's 2020 PhD Research Initiation Award.

References

Roee Aharoni, Melvin Johnson, and Orhan Firat. 2019. Massively multilingual neural machine translation. In *Proceedings of the 2019 Conference of the North American Chapter of the Association for Computational Linguistics: Human Language Technologies, Volume 1 (Long and Short Papers)*, pages 3874–3884, Minneapolis, Minnesota. Association for Computational Linguistics.

Antonios Anastasopoulos. 2019. An analysis of source-side grammatical errors in NMT. In *Proceedings of the 2019 ACL Workshop BlackboxNLP: Analyzing and Interpreting Neural Networks for NLP*, pages 213–223, Florence, Italy. Association for Computational Linguistics.

Antonios Anastasopoulos, Alison Lui, Toan Q. Nguyen, and David Chiang. 2019. Neural machine translation of text from non-native speakers. In *Proceedings of the 2019 Conference of the North American Chapter of the Association for Computational Linguistics: Human Language Technologies, Volume 1 (Long and Short Papers)*, pages 3070–3080, Minneapolis, Minnesota. Association for Computational Linguistics.

Dzmitry Bahdanau, Kyunghyun Cho, and Yoshua Bengio. 2014. Neural machine translation by jointly learning to align and translate. Cite arxiv:1409.0473Comment: Accepted at ICLR 2015 as oral presentation.

Yonatan Belinkov and Yonatan Bisk. 2018. Synthetic and natural noise both break neural machine translation. In *Proc. ICLR*.

Alexandre Berard, Ioan Calapodescu, and Claude Roux. 2019. Naver labs Europe's systems for the WMT19 machine translation robustness task. In *Proceedings of the Fourth Conference on Machine Translation (Volume 2: Shared Task Papers, Day 1)*, pages 526–532, Florence, Italy. Association for Computational Linguistics.

Christopher Bryant, Mariano Felice, Øistein E. Andersen, and Ted Briscoe. 2019. The BEA-2019 shared task on grammatical error correction. In *Proceedings of the Fourteenth Workshop on Innovative Use of NLP for Building Educational Applications*, pages 52–75, Florence, Italy. Association for Computational Linguistics.

Qiao Cheng, Meiyuan Fang, Yaqian Han, Jin Huang, and Yitao Duan. 2019a. Breaking the data barrier: Towards robust speech translation via adversarial stability training.

Yong Cheng, Lu Jiang, and Wolfgang Macherey. 2019b. Robust neural machine translation with doubly adversarial inputs. *CoRR*, abs/1906.02443.

Yong Cheng, Zhaopeng Tu, Fandong Meng, Junjie Zhai, and Yang Liu. 2018. Towards robust neural machine translation. In *Proceedings of the 56th Annual Meeting of the Association for Computational Linguistics (Volume 1: Long Papers)*, pages 1756–1766, Melbourne, Australia. Association for Computational Linguistics.

Daniel Dahlmeier, Hwee Tou Ng, and Siew Mei Wu. 2013. Building a large annotated corpus of learner English: The NUS corpus of learner English. In *Proceedings of the Eighth Workshop on Innovative Use of NLP for Building Educational Applications*, pages 22–31, Atlanta, Georgia. Association for Computational Linguistics.

Michael Denkowski and Alon Lavie. 2014. Meteor universal: Language specific translation evaluation for any target language. In *Proceedings of the Ninth Workshop on Statistical Machine Translation*, pages 376–380, Baltimore, Maryland, USA. Association for Computational Linguistics.

Javid Ebrahimi, Daniel Lowd, and Dejing Dou. 2018. On adversarial examples for character-level neural machine translation. *CoRR*, abs/1806.09030.

Orhan Firat, Kyunghyun Cho, and Yoshua Bengio. 2016. Multi-way, multilingual neural machine translation with a shared attention mechanism. In *Proceedings of the 2016 Conference of the North American Chapter of the Association for Computational Linguistics: Human Language Technologies*, pages 866–875, San Diego, California. Association for Computational Linguistics.

Markus Freitag and Yaser Al-Onaizan. 2016. Fast domain adaptation for neural machine translation. arXiv:1612.06897.

Robert M French. 1999. Catastrophic forgetting in connectionist networks. *Trends in cognitive sciences*, 3(4):128–135.

Ian J Goodfellow, Mehdi Mirza, Da Xiao, Aaron Courville, and Yoshua Bengio. 2013. An empirical investigation of catastrophic forgetting in gradient-based neural networks.

Georg Heigold, Stalin Varanasi, Günter Neumann, and Josef van Genabith. 2018. How robust are character-based word embeddings in tagging and MT against wrod scramlbing or randdm nouse? In *Proceedings of the 13th Conference of the Association for Machine Translation in the Americas (Volume 1: Research Papers)*, pages 68–80, Boston, MA. Association for Machine Translation in the Americas.

Jindřich Helcl, Jindřich Libovický, and Martin Popel. 2019. CUNI system for the WMT19 robustness task. In *Proceedings of the Fourth Conference on Machine Translation (Volume 2: Shared Task Papers, Day 1)*, pages 539–543, Florence, Italy. Association for Computational Linguistics.

Melvin Johnson, Mike Schuster, Quoc V. Le, Maxim Krikun, Yonghui Wu, Zhifeng Chen, Nikhil Thorat, Fernanda B. Viégas, Martin Wattenberg, Greg Corrado, Macduff Hughes, and Jeffrey Dean. 2016. Google's multilingual neural machine translation system: Enabling zero-shot translation. *CoRR*, abs/1611.04558.

Marcin Junczys-Dowmunt, Roman Grundkiewicz, Tomasz Dwojak, Hieu Hoang, Kenneth Heafield, Tom Neckermann, Frank Seide, Ulrich Germann, Alham Fikri Aji, Nikolay Bogoychev, et al. 2018. Marian: Fast neural machine translation in c++. arXiv:1804.00344.

Vladimir Karpukhin, Omer Levy, Jacob Eisenstein, and Marjan Ghazvininejad. 2019. Training on synthetic noise improves robustness to natural noise in machine translation. *CoRR*, abs/1902.01509.

Philipp Koehn. 2004. Statistical significance tests for machine translation evaluation. In *Proceedings of the 2004 Conference on Empirical Methods in Natural Language Processing*, pages 388–395, Barcelona, Spain. Association for Computational Linguistics.

Philipp Koehn, Hieu Hoang, Alexandra Birch, Chris Callison-Burch, Marcello Federico, Nicola Bertoldi, Brooke Cowan, Wade Shen, Christine Moran, Richard Zens, Chris Dyer, Ondřej Bojar, Alexandra Constantin, and Evan Herbst. 2007. Moses: Open source toolkit for statistical machine translation. In *Proceedings of the 45th Annual Meeting of the Association for Computational Linguistics Companion Volume Proceedings of the Demo and Poster Sessions*, pages 177–180, Prague, Czech Republic. Association for Computational Linguistics.

Philipp Koehn and Rebecca Knowles. 2017. Six challenges for neural machine translation. In *Proceedings of the First Workshop on Neural Machine Translation*, pages 28–39, Vancouver. Association for Computational Linguistics.

Taku Kudo and John Richardson. 2018. SentencePiece: A simple and language independent subword tokenizer and detokenizer for neural text processing. In *Proceedings of the 2018 Conference on Empirical Methods in Natural Language Processing: System Demonstrations*, pages 66–71, Brussels, Belgium. Association for Computational Linguistics.

Xian Li, Paul Michel, Antonios Anastasopoulos, Yonatan Belinkov, Nadir Durrani, Orhan Firat, Philipp Koehn, Graham Neubig, Juan Pino, and Hassan Sajjad. 2019. Findings of the first shared task on machine translation robustness. In *Proceedings of the Fourth Conference on Machine Translation (Volume 2: Shared Task Papers, Day 1)*, pages 91–102, Florence, Italy. Association for Computational Linguistics.

Hairong Liu, Mingbo Ma, Liang Huang, Hao Xiong, and Zhongjun He. 2018. Robust neural machine translation with joint textual and phonetic embedding. *CoRR*, abs/1810.06729.

David Lopez-Paz and Marc'Aurelio Ranzato. 2017. Gradient episodic memory for continual learning. In *Advances in neural information processing systems*, pages 6467–6476.

Minh-Thang Luong, Hieu Pham, and Christopher D. Manning. 2015. Effective approaches to attention-based neural machine translation. *CoRR*, abs/1508.04025.

Paul Michel, Xian Li, Graham Neubig, and Juan Pino. 2019a. On evaluation of adversarial perturbations for sequence-to-sequence models. In *Proceedings of the 2019 Conference of the North American Chapter of the Association for Computational Linguistics: Human Language Technologies, Volume 1 (Long and Short Papers)*, pages 3103–3114, Minneapolis, Minnesota. Association for Computational Linguistics.

Paul Michel and Graham Neubig. 2018. MTNT: A testbed for machine translation of noisy text. *CoRR*, abs/1809.00388.

Paul Michel, Elisabeth Salesky, and Graham Neubig. 2019b. Regularizing trajectories to mitigate catastrophic forgetting. Preprint.

Courtney Napoles, Keisuke Sakaguchi, and Joel Tetreault. 2017. JFLEG: A fluency corpus and benchmark for grammatical error correction. In *Proceedings of the 15th Conference of the European Chapter of the Association for Computational Linguistics: Volume 2, Short Papers*, pages 229–234, Valencia, Spain. Association for Computational Linguistics.

Kishore Papineni, Salim Roukos, Todd Ward, and Wei-Jing Zhu. 2002. Bleu: a method for automatic evaluation of machine translation. In *Proceedings of the 40th Annual Meeting of the Association for Computational Linguistics*, pages 311–318, Philadelphia, Pennsylvania, USA. Association for Computational Linguistics.

Matt Post. 2018. A call for clarity in reporting BLEU scores. In *Proceedings of the Third Conference on Machine Translation: Research Papers*, pages 186–191, Brussels, Belgium. Association for Computational Linguistics.

Matt Post and Kevin Duh. 2019. JHU 2019 robustness task system description. In *Proceedings of the Fourth Conference on Machine Translation (Volume 2: Shared Task Papers, Day 1)*, pages 552–558, Florence, Italy. Association for Computational Linguistics.

Rico Sennrich, Barry Haddow, and Alexandra Birch. 2016. Improving neural machine translation models with monolingual data. In *Proceedings of the 54th Annual Meeting of the Association for Computational Linguistics (Volume 1: Long Papers)*, pages 86–96, Berlin, Germany. Association for Computational Linguistics.

Matthias Sperber, Jan Niehues, and Alex Waibel. 2017. Toward robust neural machine translation for noisy input sequences. In *Proc. IWSLT*.

Toshikazu Tajiri, Mamoru Komachi, and Yuji Matsumoto. 2012. Tense and aspect error correction for ESL learners using global context. In *Proceedings of the 50th Annual Meeting of the Association for Computational Linguistics (Volume 2: Short Papers)*, pages 198–202, Jeju Island, Korea. Association for Computational Linguistics.

Samson Tan, Shafiq Joty, Min-Yen Kan, and Richard Socher. 2020. It's morphin' time! Combating linguistic discrimination with inflectional perturbations. In *Proceedings of the 58th Annual Meeting of the Association for Computational Linguistics*, pages 2920–2935, Online. Association for Computational Linguistics.

Brian Thompson, Jeremy Gwinnup, Huda Khayrallah, Kevin Duh, and Philipp Koehn. 2019. Overcoming catastrophic forgetting during domain adaptation of neural machine translation. In *Proceedings of the 2019 Conference of the North American Chapter of the Association for Computational Linguistics: Human Language Technologies, Volume 1 (Long and Short Papers)*, pages 2062–2068, Minneapolis, Minnesota. Association for Computational Linguistics.

Jörg Tiedemann and Santhosh Thottingal. 2020. OPUS-MT — Building open translation services for the World. In *Proceedings of the 22nd Annual Conferenec of the European Association for Machine Translation (EAMT)*, Lisbon, Portugal.

Ashish Vaswani, Samy Bengio, Eugene Brevdo, Francois Chollet, Aidan Gomez, Stephan Gouws, Llion Jones, Łukasz Kaiser, Nal Kalchbrenner, Niki Parmar, Ryan Sepassi, Noam Shazeer, and Jakob Uszkoreit. 2018. Tensor2Tensor for neural machine translation. In *Proceedings of the 13th Conference of the Association for Machine Translation in the Americas (Volume 1: Research Papers)*, pages 193–199, Boston, MA. Association for Machine Translation in the Americas.

Ashish Vaswani, Noam Shazeer, Niki Parmar, Jakob Uszkoreit, Llion Jones, Aidan N. Gomez, Lukasz Kaiser, and Illia Polosukhin. 2017. Attention is all you need. *CoRR*, abs/1706.03762.

Thomas Wolf, Lysandre Debut, Victor Sanh, Julien Chaumond, Clement Delangue, Anthony Moi, Pierric Cistac, Tim Rault, R'emi Louf, Morgan Funtowicz, and Jamie Brew. 2019. Huggingface's transformers: State-of-the-art natural language processing. arXiv:1910.03771.

Helen Yannakoudakis, Ted Briscoe, and Ben Medlock. 2011. A new dataset and method for automatically grading ESOL texts. In *Proceedings of the 49th Annual Meeting of the Association for Computational Linguistics: Human Language Technologies*, pages 180–189, Portland, Oregon, USA. Association for Computational Linguistics.

Biao Zhang, Philip Williams, Ivan Titov, and Rico Sennrich. 2020. Improving massively multilingual neural machine translation and zero-shot translation. In *Proceedings of the 58th Annual Meeting of the Association for Computational Linguistics*, pages 1628–1639, Online. Association for Computational Linguistics.

Renjie Zheng, Hairong Liu, Mingbo Ma, Baigong Zheng, and Liang Huang. 2019. Robust machine translation with domain sensitive pseudo-sources: Baidu-OSU WMT19 MT robustness shared task system report. In *Proceedings of the Fourth Conference on Machine Translation (Volume 2: Shared Task Papers, Day 1)*, pages 559–564, Florence, Italy. Association for Computational Linguistics.

Shuyan Zhou, Xiangkai Zeng, Yingqi Zhou, Antonios Anastasopoulos, and Graham Neubig. 2019. Improving robustness of neural machine translation with multi-task learning. In *Proceedings of the Fourth Conference on Machine Translation (Volume 2: Shared Task Papers, Day 1)*, pages 565–571, Florence, Italy. Association for Computational Linguistics.

Ran Zmigrod, Sabrina J. Mielke, Hanna Wallach, and Ryan Cotterell. 2019. Counterfactual data augmentation for mitigating gender stereotypes in languages with rich morphology. In *Proceedings of the 57th Annual Meeting of the Association for Computational Linguistics*, pages 1651–1661, Florence, Italy. Association for Computational Linguistics.

Impact of ASR on Alzheimer's Disease Detection:
All Errors are Equal, but Deletions are More Equal than Others

Aparna Balagopalan
Winterlight Labs
Toronto, Canada
aparna@winterlightlabs.com

Ksenia Shkaruta
Georgia Tech
Atlanta, USA
k.shkaruta@gatech.edu

Jekaterina Novikova
Winterlight Labs
Toronto, Canada
jekaterina@winterlightlabs.com

Abstract

Automatic Speech Recognition (ASR) is a critical component of any fully-automated speech-based dementia detection model. However, despite years of speech recognition research, little is known about the impact of ASR accuracy on dementia detection. In this paper, we experiment with controlled amounts of artificially generated ASR errors and investigate their influence on dementia detection. We find that deletion errors affect detection performance the most, due to their impact on the features of syntactic complexity and discourse representation in speech. We show the trend to be generalisable across two different datasets for cognitive impairment detection. As a conclusion, we propose optimising the ASR to reflect a higher penalty for deletion errors in order to improve dementia detection performance.

1 Introduction

There is a rapid growth in the number of people living with Alzheimer's disease (AD) (Alzheimer's Association, 2018). Clinical research has shown that quantifiable signs of cognitive decline associated with AD and mild cognitive impairment (MCI) are detectable in spontaneous speech (Bucks et al., 2000; Sajjadi et al., 2012). Machine learning (ML) models have proved to be successful in detecting AD using speech and language variables, such as syntactic and lexical complexity of language extracted from the transcripts of the speech (Fraser et al., 2016; Meilán et al., 2012; Rentoumi et al., 2014). Since transcripts should be accurate enough to properly represent syntactic and linguistic characteristics, current approaches (Fraser et al., 2013; Zhu et al., 2019) frequently rely on 100% accurate human-created transcripts produced by trained transcriptionists. However in real-life speech-based applications of AD detection, ASR is used and it produces noisy, error-prone transcripts (Yousaf

et al., 2019). To our best knowledge, while the importance of well-performing ASR in speech classification has been studied in depth (Zhou et al., 2016), no prior research was done to understand what patterns of speech are influenced the most by ASR errors such as word deletions and substitutions, and how this impacts performance of AD detection using ML models.

In this paper, we focus on this issue and study the *effect of deletion, insertion and substitution errors on lexico-syntactic language features* and their resulting *effect on classification performance*. The effect of these errors on binary AD-healthy classification performance is studied and suggestions are provided on how to improve ASR in order to maintain reasonable AD classification performance.

We identify that deletion errors affect the classification more than substitution and insertion errors on two datasets of spontaneous impaired speech. The effect of these deletion errors are most profound on features related to syntactic complexity and discourse representations in speech, such as production rules, word-level structure and repetitions. These features are also identified as being the most important for the classification task using a feature gradient-based importance metric.

2 Data and Setup

2.1 Datasets

DementiaBank (DB) The DementiaBank[1] dataset is a large dataset of pathological speech. It consists of narrative picture descriptions from participants aged between 45 to 90 (Becker et al., 1994). Out of the 210 participants in the study, 117 were diagnosed with AD (180 samples of speech) and 93 were healthy (HC, 229 samples). Voice recordings and manual transcriptions (following CHAT protocol (MacWhinney, 2000)) are available for all

---

[1] https://dementia.talkbank.org

159

Proceedings of the 2020 EMNLP Workshop W-NUT: The Sixth Workshop on Noisy User-generated Text, pages 159–164
Online, Nov 19, 2020. ©2020 Association for Computational Linguistics

Dataset		Del (%)	Ins (%)	Sub (%)
DB	HC	54.14	4.27	41.59
	AD	56.98	3.89	39.13
HA	HC	24.37	13.11	62.52
	MCI	21.78	14.81	63.40

Table 1: Rates of ASR errors on DB and HA datasets.

samples. This dataset is used for the experiments in Section 4, 5, and 6.

Healthy Aging (HA) The Healthy Aging dataset (Balagopalan et al., 2018) consists of speech samples of 97 participants with no cognitive impairment diagnosis, all older than 50 years. Every participant describes a picture, analogous to the DB dataset. The dataset constitutes 8.5 hours of audio with manual transcriptions. Each speech sample is associated with a score on the Montreal Cognitive Assessment (MoCA) (Nasreddine et al., 2005). Based on published cut-off scores (Nasreddine et al., 2005) for presence of MCI (minimum score for healthy participants is 26), we obtain class-labels for this dataset.

2.2 ASR Setup

The Automatic Speech Recognition (ASR) system we use for this work is based on the open-source Kaldi toolkit (Povey et al., 2011). ASR uses ASPiRE chain model trained on multi-condition Fisher English corpus as a 3-gram language model.

Rates of ASR errors for healthy and impaired speakers for DB and HA datasets are in Table 1. Majority of errors arise from deletions and substitutions for both datasets and groups.

3 Methodology

3.1 Feature Extraction and Aggregation

Following previous studies (Fraser et al., 2016; Balagopalan et al., 2018), we automatically extract 507 lexico-syntactic and acoustic features. To simplify the presentation, the extracted features are aggregated into the following major groups:

Syntactic Complexity: features to analyze the syntactic complexity of speech, such as number of occurrence of various production rules, mean length of clause (in words) etc.

Lexical Complexity and Richness : measures of lexical density and variation, such as average familiarity scores of all nouns, age of word acquisition, frequency of POS tags etc.

Discourse mapping: features that help identify cohesion in speech using a *speech graph*-based representation of message organization in speech

(Mota et al., 2012). Examples of features include the number of edges in the graph, number of self-loops, cosine-distance across unique utterances etc.

Additionally, we extract features quantifying difficulty in finding the right words (e.g. filled pauses), measures related to description of content in the picture (e.g. number of content units), coherence in speaking at local and global level, and acoustic measures. such as MFCC and Zero Crossing Rate related voice representations (full list in App.A.1).

3.2 Error and Noise Addition

3.2.1 Artificial ASR Errors

We introduce artificial ASR errors to understand if any specific error type influences the classification performance more than others. In previous research it was shown that lexical and syntactic groups of features extracted from transcripts of speech have different predictive power in dementia classification (Novikova et al., 2019). As such, we hypothesize that different ASR error types may influence the features differently and would cause different effects on classification performance. The non-artificial output of ASR combines the errors of deletion, insertion and substitution in some proportion, thus not allowing analysis of the individual effects of each error type separately. This is why we generate each type of errors artificially.

3.3 Error Addition Method

We follow a method similar to the one used by Fraser et al. (2013) to artificially add errors to manual transcripts at predefined 20%, 40% and 60% WER rates. All altered words w, where w refers to a word in gold-standard manual transcripts, are selected at random. The following modifications are done: a) *deletion* - word instance w is deleted, b) *insertion* - new word w_1 is added after the word w, c) *substitution* - word w is replaced with a new word w_1.

For *deletion* we simply delete random words from manual transcript at a specified rate.

To *substitute* word w, we select a unigram from 2,000 most used unigrams from Fisher language model that has the smallest Levenshtein distance with word w based on the phonemic model from The Carnegie Mellon Pronouncing on Pronouncing Dictionary (Weide, 1998). If word w is not found in the Fisher language model a random unigram from the top 2,000 is used for substitution.

For *insertion*, we select a word from the bigram

list from the language model that has the highest probability to follow after word w and insert it if it does not match the following word in transcript. In case of a match, the next most probable word is inserted. If word w is not found in bigram list a random unigram is used for insertion.

To verify if simulated errors are a fair approximation of what is seen on a true ASR output, we have calculated the BLEU score (Papineni et al., 2002) between the manual and ASR-generated transcripts and compared them to the BLEU score between the manual transcripts and the transcripts with artificially simulated errors. The correlation between these two BLEU scores is strong and significant for both datasets (Spearman $\rho = 0.72, p < 0.001$ for DB; $\rho = 0.66, p < 0.001$ for HA), i.e. transcripts with simulated errors are corrupted with respect to the manual transcripts in a similar manner as the ASR-generated transcripts are.

3.3.1 Noise Addition

We perturb all lexico-syntactic features or equivalently features that could be affected by ASR errors such as deletions, insertions, and/or substitutions, to mimic random sources of errors using Gaussian noise. We do this to compare and differentiate from the consequences of ASR errors. This modification is implemented by adding a randomized number to the extracted feature values where the mean of the number added to a given feature is zero and the standard deviation varies depending on the amount of noise we add (see App.A.2 for details).

3.4 Classification Setup

Model: All our experiments are based on predictions obtained from a 2-hidden layer neural network (see App.A.3 for details). We chose this model type and parameter-setting since it attained performance on-par with previously published results (Fraser et al., 2016) with 10-fold cross-validation on gold-standard manual DB transcripts.

4 Changes in Classification Performance Due to Simulated Errors

We evaluate performance of classifying samples of speech to two classes - AD or healthy - using the DB dataset.

Figure 1 shows that deletion errors affect classification performance significantly more than insertion and substitution errors do. 40% of deletions reduce F1 score by more than 10%, while 40% of

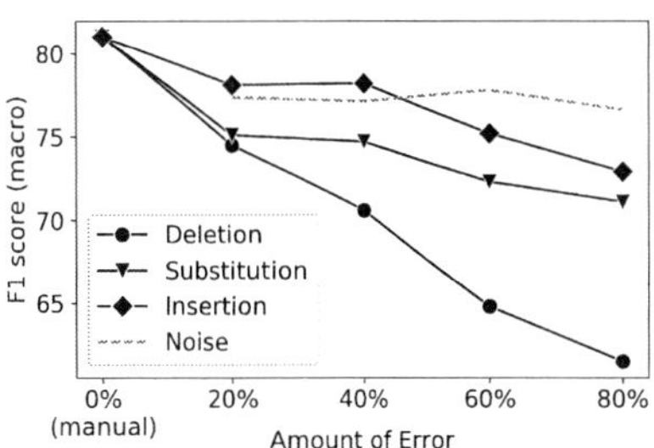

Figure 1: Effect of a controlled amount of ASR errors and random noise on classification performance.

Transcript	Accuracy	F1 (macro)	Sensitivity	Specificity
Manual	80.20	79.76	79.29	80.83
ASR-based	74.96	73.97	76.01	74.36

Table 2: Effect of original ASR on classification performance with the DB dataset.

insertions only result in 2.8%, and 40% of substitutions - in 6.3% of F1 score reduction. These differences become even more pronounced with adding a bigger amount of errors. Trajectory of F1 score with varying levels of noise is substantially different from that with varying deletion errors but not that with insertions or substitutions, showing that insertion and substitution errors influence classification performance in a way that is similar to a random noise. Deletion errors, however, have a significantly stronger effect on classification. It is also interesting to note that the model utilizing automatic transcripts from ASR retains a level of performance at 74.96% (Table 2), which is comparable to the potential decrease in performance due to the rate of ASR deletion errors.

Different effects of errors on classification performance suggest that some features, extracted from the speech samples and used as an input for the classification algorithm, are affected far more substantially by deletions rather than any other type of errors. This leads us to inspect the correlation of feature values and the amount of deletions.

5 Distinctive Effects of Deletion Errors

In order to understand why deletions errors influence the classification performance significantly more than other error types, we identify features maintaining higher correlation with the amount of deletions than that with the amount of insertions and substitutions. We observe 18 features in total that distinctively correlate with deletions. Out of these, the absolute majority of 15 features (83.33%

of all selected) are associated with syntactic complexity (production rules of a constituency parser) and discourse phenomena (graph self-loop with 3 edges) and 3 (16.7%) - with lexical richness in speech. Other feature groups, such as acoustic features or those associated with word finding difficulty, do not meet the required conditions. Such results show that syntactic structure of language is much more vulnerable to deletions than to other ASR errors. This can be explained by the fact that insertions and substitutions use words from the language model (i.e. most probable words) for the modifications, which to some extent helps maintain basic syntactic rules and structure.

Correlation between the number of deletions and features of syntactic structure shows the vulnerability of the feature group representing syntactic complexity and discourse phenomena to ASR deletion errors. However, it does not explain a decrease in classification performance when adding deletion errors. In Section 6 we inspect if features of syntactic complexity are more influential in AD detection than other characteristics of speech.

6 Model-based Analysis of Feature Importance

In order to quantify the importance of input features for classification, we obtain the gradient of the output prediction loss with respect to input features on a manually-transcribed version of the DB dataset.

We define gradient-based importance for feature k for an input, $X_{i,j}$, in the training set for a classification model as:

$$imp^{i,j,k} = \frac{\partial L(y_{i,j}, p_{i,j})}{\partial X_{i,j,k}} \quad (1)$$

where L denotes the loss criterion (binary cross-entropy loss), $y_{i,j}$ is the ground-truth label, $p_{i,j} \subset [0,1]$ is the prediction probability; $p_{i,j} > 0.5$ denotes an AD prediction, k is a given feature (1 to D), and i is a number of samples (1 to N_j) in the training set in fold j of the DB dataset classification setup. Hence, to obtain the average importance for feature k in a single fold, we compute:

$$imp^{j,k} = 1/N_j \sum_{i=1}^{N_j} \frac{\partial L(y_{i,j}, p_{i,j})}{\partial X_{i,j,k}} \quad (2)$$

This importance is then averaged across the 10-

Feature group	Importance of top-10 features HC	AD	#features	Group rank
Syntactic complexity and Discourse phenomena	0.94	0.95	37	1
Lexical richness	0.91	0.92	18	2

Table 3: Importance of the two feature groups, summarised as the mean value of the top-10 most important features selected for HC and AD components, number of features having significant Spearman correlation with deletion errors, and the rank of each group.

folds to obtain the final importance, i.e.:

$$imp^k = 1/10 \sum_{j=1}^{10} imp^{j,k} \quad (3)$$

In order to interpret high-level patterns of input importance, we aggregate the feature importances into the groups defined in Section 3.1, where aggregation of importances involves averaging the absolute gradient-importance, $|imp^k|$, of features belonging to that group.

Results provided in Table 3 show that the average normalised importance of the features associated with syntactic complexity and discourse is higher than the average importance of lexical richness features, when top-10 most important features across all the groups are selected for comparison.

To conclude, the feature group of syntactic complexity and discourse phenomena is affected significantly and distinctively the most by deletion errors as seen in Section 5. This group is also important for classification as seen in Table 3, indicating why classification is affected significantly by deletion errors. Hence, we track the effects from the initial step of adding artificial errors of different amounts to obtaining the final predictions in this manner.

7 Generalisability Evaluation

In order to test how well our conclusions generalise to a different dataset of impaired speech, we repeat the same experiments performed on DB on the HA dataset (Section 2.1).

We follow the same method, as described in Section 3 to extract the features and classify samples. Similarly to the results obtained on DB data, with HA deletion errors affect classification performance the most. Furthermore, deletion errors differentiate the same feature group of syntactic complexity and discourse phenomena: with HA dataset, 39 features correlate with deletions stronger than with insertions or substitutions, with 79.49% of features belonging to the aggregate group of syntactic complexity and discourse, and 20.51% - to the group of lexical richness. The rank of feature groups, based on the average absolute Spearman correlation of all the features included in the groups, correspond to the rank observed with DB dataset, with a stronger significant correlation corresponding to the group of syntactic complexity, rather than lexical richness.

8 Conclusions

We observe that simulated deletion errors have a strong effect on classification performance when detecting cognitive impairment from speech and language, which can be traced back to their effect on syntactic complexity and discourse representations. With this observation in mind, the practical suggestion would be to optimise the ASR to reflect a higher penalty for deletion errors to improve dementia detection performance. For example, the decoder can be parametrised to find a balance between insertions and deletions, so that the number of deletion errors is minimised.

However, dealing with deletions in training time is not trivial, so in future work, we will focus on the optimisation of ASR performance and its effect on AD detection. Careful ASR error management, following previous work by Simonnet et al. (2017), could help enable strong fully-automated speech-based predictive models for dementia detection.

References

Alzheimer's Association. 2018. 2018 Alzheimer's disease facts and figures. *Alzheimer's & Dementia*, 14(3):367–429.

Aparna Balagopalan, Jekaterina Novikova, Frank Rudzicz, and Marzyeh Ghassemi. 2018. The Effect of Heterogeneous Data for Alzheimer's Disease Detection from Speech. In *NIPS Workshop on Machine Learning for Health ML4H*.

James T Becker, François Boiler, Oscar L Lopez, Judith Saxton, and Karen L McGonigle. 1994. The natural history of Alzheimer's disease: description of study cohort and accuracy of diagnosis. *Archives of Neurology*, 51(6):585–594.

Romola S Bucks, Sameer Singh, Joanne M Cuerden, and Gordon K Wilcock. 2000. Analysis of spontaneous, conversational speech in dementia of Alzheimer type: Evaluation of an objective technique for analysing lexical performance. *Aphasiology*, 14(1):71–91.

Kathleen Fraser, Frank Rudzicz, Naida Graham, and Elizabeth Rochon. 2013. Automatic speech recognition in the diagnosis of primary progressive aphasia. In *Proceedings of the fourth workshop on speech and language processing for assistive technologies*, pages 47–54.

Kathleen C Fraser, Jed A Meltzer, and Frank Rudzicz. 2016. Linguistic features identify Alzheimer's disease in narrative speech. *Journal of Alzheimer's Disease*, 49(2):407–422.

Diederik P Kingma and Jimmy Ba. 2014. Adam: A method for stochastic optimization. *arXiv preprint arXiv:1412.6980*.

Xiaofei Lu. 2010. Automatic analysis of syntactic complexity in second language writing. *International journal of corpus linguistics*, 15(4):474–496.

Brian MacWhinney. 2000. *The Childes Project: Tools for Analyzing Talk: Vol. II: The Database*. Mahwah.

Juan JG Meilán, Francisco Martínez-Sánchez, Juan Carro, José A Sánchez, and Enrique Pérez. 2012. Acoustic markers associated with impairment in language processing in Alzheimer's disease. *The Spanish journal of psychology*, 15(2):487–494.

Tomas Mikolov, Ilya Sutskever, Kai Chen, Greg S Corrado, and Jeff Dean. 2013. Distributed representations of words and phrases and their compositionality. In *Advances in neural information processing systems*, pages 3111–3119.

Natalia B Mota, Nivaldo AP Vasconcelos, Nathalia Lemos, Ana C Pieretti, Osame Kinouchi, Guillermo A Cecchi, Mauro Copelli, and Sidarta Ribeiro. 2012. Speech graphs provide a quantitative measure of thought disorder in psychosis. *PloS one*, 7(4):e34928.

Ziad S Nasreddine, Natalie A Phillips, Valérie Bédirian, Simon Charbonneau, Victor Whitehead, Isabelle Collin, Jeffrey L Cummings, and Howard Chertkow. 2005. The montreal cognitive assessment, moca: a brief screening tool for mild cognitive impairment. *Journal of the American Geriatrics Society*, 53(4):695–699.

Jekaterina Novikova, Aparna Balagopalan, Ksenia Shkaruta, and Frank Rudzicz. 2019. Lexical Features Are More Vulnerable, Syntactic Features Have More Predictive Power. In *EMNLP Workshop on on Noisy User-generated Text*.

Kishore Papineni, Salim Roukos, Todd Ward, and Wei-Jing Zhu. 2002. Bleu: a method for automatic evaluation of machine translation. In *Proceedings of the 40th annual meeting on association for computational linguistics*, pages 311–318. Association for Computational Linguistics.

Fabian Pedregosa, Gaël Varoquaux, Alexandre Gramfort, Vincent Michel, Bertrand Thirion, Olivier Grisel, Mathieu Blondel, Peter Prettenhofer, Ron

Weiss, Vincent Dubourg, et al. 2011. Scikit-learn: Machine learning in python. *Journal of machine learning research*, 12(Oct):2825–2830.

Daniel Povey, Arnab Ghoshal, Gilles Boulianne, Lukas Burget, Ondrej Glembek, Nagendra Goel, Mirko Hannemann, Petr Motlicek, Yanmin Qian, Petr Schwarz, et al. 2011. The Kaldi speech recognition toolkit. Technical report, IEEE Signal Processing Society.

Vassiliki Rentoumi, Ladan Raoufian, Samrah Ahmed, Celeste A de Jager, and Peter Garrard. 2014. Features and machine learning classification of connected speech samples from patients with autopsy proven Alzheimer's disease with and without additional vascular pathology. *Journal of Alzheimer's Disease*, 42(s3):S3–S17.

Seyed Ahmad Sajjadi, Karalyn Patterson, Michal Tomek, and Peter J Nestor. 2012. Abnormalities of connected speech in semantic dementia vs Alzheimer's disease. *Aphasiology*, 26(6):847–866.

Edwin Simonnet, Sahar Ghannay, Nathalie Camelin, Yannick Estève, and Renato de Mori. 2017. Asr error management for improving spoken language understanding. In *Interspeech 2017*.

Robert L Weide. 1998. The CMU pronouncing dictionary. *URL: http://www. speech. cs. cmu. edu/cgibin/cmudict.*

Kanwal Yousaf, Zahid Mehmood, Israr Ahmad Awan, Tanzila Saba, Riad Alharbey, Talal Qadah, and Mayda Abdullateef Alrige. 2019. A comprehensive study of mobile-health based assistive technology for the healthcare of dementia and alzheimer's disease (ad). *Health Care Management Science*, pages 1–23.

Luke Zhou, Kathleen C Fraser, and Frank Rudzicz. 2016. Speech Recognition in Alzheimer's Disease and in its Assessment. In *INTERSPEECH*, pages 1948–1952.

Zining Zhu, Jekaterina Novikova, and Frank Rudzicz. 2019. Detecting cognitive impairments by agreeing on interpretations of linguistic features. *NAACL*.

Detecting Entailment in Code-Mixed Hindi-English Conversations

Sharanya Chakravarthy[*]   **Anjana Umapathy**[*]   **Alan W Black**
Language Technologies Institute
Carnegie Mellon University
{sharanyc, aumapath, awb}@cs.cmu.edu

Abstract

The presence of large-scale corpora for Natural Language Inference (NLI) has spurred deep learning research in this area, though much of this research has focused solely on monolingual data. Code-mixing is the intertwined usage of multiple languages, and is commonly seen in informal conversations among polyglots. Given the rising importance of dialogue agents, it is imperative that they understand code-mixing, but the scarcity of code-mixed Natural Language Understanding (NLU) datasets has precluded research in this area. The dataset by Khanuja et al. (2020a) for detecting conversational entailment in code-mixed Hindi-English text is the first of its kind. We investigate the effectiveness of language modeling, data augmentation, translation, and architectural approaches to address the code-mixed, conversational, and low-resource aspects of this dataset. We obtain +8.09% test set accuracy over the current state of the art.

1 Introduction

Natural Language Inference (NLI) is a widely researched NLP task which involves determining if a premise entails or contradicts a hypothesis. The performance of machine learning models on this task has important implications for other Natural Language Understanding tasks such as Question Answering, Semantic Search and Text Summarization. While large corpora such as SNLI (Bowman et al., 2015) and MultiNLI (Williams et al., 2018) are available for monolingual and cross-lingual NLI, Khanuja et al. (2020a) introduce the first NLI dataset with Hindi-English (Hinglish) text. We refer to this dataset as CS-NLI.

Code-mixing is a phenomenon prevalent in multilingual communities (Claros and Isharianty, 2009). It poses a number of interesting challenges for NLP applications, such as the mixing of units from multiple grammar systems, morphological

differences between monolingual and code-mixed text due to the intermixing of affixes, and non-standard transliteration between the writing systems involved. In CS-NLI, Hindi is present in a non-standard Romanized form. Multilingual speakers most often code-mix in informal settings such as social media, in-person, and telephonic conversations, due to which there is a dearth of clean, large-scale code-mixed corpora such as Wikipedia articles and books that can be used for pre-training, making this a low-resource task.

Khanuja et al. (2020a) leverage Bollywood movie scripts containing Hinglish text to create CS-NLI, with conversations as premises. The creation of hypotheses based on dialogue-like premises transforms the task from one of textual entailment to one of conversational entailment. The inclusion of scripts from multiple movies makes this data inherently noisy due to non-standard Romanization of Hindi, the variation in dialects across movies and differing grammar styles among Hinglish speakers.

In this work, we explore and analyze a variety of techniques to leverage existing pre-trained models such as BERT (Devlin et al., 2019) for processing code-mixed and conversational text. We present a comparison of linguistic, data augmentation and architectural approaches to conversational entailment in code-mixed text. We show multiple techniques that interestingly give similar results, while also beating the current state of the art[1]. The code for the approaches described in this paper will be made available on GitHub [2].

2 Related Work

NLI for monolingual and cross-lingual text is a well-researched task that has been addressed using a variety of techniques including neural networks, symbolic logic and knowledge bases (Bowman

---

[*]Equal contribution

[1]https://microsoft.github.io/GLUECoS/
[2]https://github.com/sharanyarc96/
HinglishNLI

Proceedings of the 2020 EMNLP Workshop W-NUT: The Sixth Workshop on Noisy User-generated Text, pages 165–170
Online, Nov 19, 2020. ©2020 Association for Computational Linguistics

et al., 2015). The use of transformer models such as BERT and RoBERTa (Liu et al., 2019), pre-trained on large monolingual corpora, has advanced the state of the art on the SNLI and MultiNLI datasets. While unsupervised pre-training of deep learning models has been shown to improve performance on a variety of NLP tasks, the limited amount of data available precludes large-scale pre-training on code-mixed text. Multilingual BERT (mBERT) (Devlin et al., 2019) is pre-trained on monolingual Wikipedia corpora from 104 languages, including Hindi in its original Devanagari script. XLM-RoBERTa (XLM-R) (Conneau et al., 2020) is trained on the CommonCrawl corpus, which includes Romanized Hindi text, making this model the closest one to being pre-trained on Hinglish.

3 Task Definition

Khanuja et al. (2020a) introduce a dataset spurring two challenging directions of research - NLI for code-mixing, and conversational entailment. The dataset contains 2,240 unique code-mixed premise-hypothesis pairs and their corresponding labels, with an 80:20 train-test split. We tackle the binary classification task of assigning an ENTAILMENT label if the premise entails the hypothesis and a CONTRADICTION label if the premise contradicts the hypothesis. Premises are in the form of multiple utterances from a conversation, with each utterance preceded by the name of the speaker. For example-

Premise (Code-Mixed): RAHUL : Tumhara scooter aur ek joota security guard ko lobby mein mila . ## RIANA : Thank god !!

Premise (Translation): RAHUL : The security guard found your scooter and one shoe in the lobby. ## RIANA : Thank god !!

4 Methodology

Given the success of pre-trained models on other NLI tasks, we tackle this task by fine-tuning BERT, mBERT and XLM-R for sentence-pair classification. Due to the scarcity of examples in CS-NLI, we focus our efforts on the modification and augmentation of the data used to fine-tune these models. In this section, we describe techniques to address the code-mixed, low-resource, and conversational aspects of the task.

4.1 Addressing Code-Mixing

We use approaches such as language modeling, transliteration, and translation to alleviate the ab-sence of code-mixing in the data used to pre-train transformer models.

Masked Language Modeling: We fine-tune mBERT on the masked language modeling objective, following Khanuja et al. (2020b), on a combination of in-domain code-mixed movie scripts and publicly available datasets by Roy et al. (2013) and Bhat et al. (2018) to obtain modified mBERT (mod-mBERT) to be fine-tuned on the sentence-pair classification task.

Transliteration: We perform token-level language identification and transliterate the detected Romanized Hindi words in CS-NLI to Devanagari script using the approach in Singh et al. (2018), to enable mBERT to better understand them.

Translation: Due to the difficulty in training code-mixed to monolingual translation models, we follow the approach in Dhar et al. (2018) to obtain translations. We first transliterate the Romanized Hindi words, and then translate English phrases to Hindi using the Google Cloud translation API. [3].

4.2 Addressing the Low-Resource Aspect

Due to the limited amount of code-mixed NLI data available for fine-tuning, we augment CS-NLI with 4000 monolingual entailment and contradiction examples sampled from the SNLI, XNLI (Conneau et al., 2018), and MPE (Lai et al., 2017) datasets. Transliterations of Devanagari Hindi sentence-pairs from the XNLI dataset provide additional NLI data in Romanized Hindi while SNLI examples do the same in English. The MPE dataset adds examples requiring aggregation of information across sentences (Lai et al., 2017).

4.3 Approaches to Conversational NLI

Each premise in CS-NLI contains turns in the form "Speaker Name: Utterance". Khanuja et al. (2020a) show that a number of hypotheses require an understanding of the transition between speakers, in addition to the meaning of the utterance itself. In order to estimate whether BERT understands the role of speakers, we remove speaker names occurring before each utterance, and fine-tune the models on CS-NLI. We find that the accuracy does not deteriorate, indicating that the BERT models may benefit from reinforcing speaker roles.

Data Augmentation with Speaker Names: Khanuja et al. (2020a) present a set of examples that involve swapping roles. We generate additional CONTRADICTION examples for role

---

[3] https://cloud.google.com/translate/docs/quickstarts

Example	Premise	Hypothesis	Label
Original	KRITI: VIKAS pad raha hai ## VARUN: Which subject? ## VIKAS: Physics	VIKAS pad raha hai	Entailment
Translation	KRITI: VIKAS is studying ## VARUN: Which subject? ## VIKAS: Physics	VIKAS is studying	Entailment
Contradiction Augmentation	KRITI: VIKAS pad raha hai ## VARUN: Which subject? ## VIKAS: Physics	VARUN pad raha hai	Contradiction
Speaker Name Augmentation	VEENA: MADAN pad raha hai ## ARJUN: Which subject? ## MADAN: Physics	MADAN pad raha hai	Entailment

Table 1: Example of augmentation of CS-NLI by modifying speaker names. Original: Example from CS-NLI, Contradiction Augmentation: Adding a contradiction example by modifying a name in a hypothesis from an entailment hypothesis, Speaker Name Augmentation: Adding an entailment example by modifying all the names in an entailment example

swapping by modifying speaker names found in the hypotheses of ENTAILMENT examples. We augment the existing dataset with examples which differ only in the names of the speakers, with the goal of helping the model to focus on the role of speaker names in detecting entailment. Examples of these augmentation techniques are shown in Table-1.

Utterance Representations using BERT: The premises in CS-NLI contain multiple turns of a conversation. Since BERT is commonly used for single-sentence representations, we encode each turn separately using mod-mBERT. We obtain utterance representations from mod-mBERT and pass them through a bidirectional LSTM (biLSTM). We concatenate the initial and final hidden states of the biLSTM with the mod-mBERT encoding of the hypothesis, and pass them through an MLP with two linear layers to obtain a classification output.

5 Experimental Setup

In the majority of our approaches, we fine-tune BERT, mBERT, mod-mBERT (110M parameters), and XLM-R (550M parameters) for 1 to 6 epochs on an Nvidia GeForce GTX 1070 GPU. We experiment with batch sizes of 8,16, and 32, and learning rates between 1e-5 and 5e-5, and report results using a batch size of 8 and learning rate of 1e-5.

6 Results and Analysis

On fine-tuning the BERT models on CS-NLI, we observe a large variation in the results based on the subset of data used for evaluating the model, as demonstrated in Table-2. To address this variation, we perform eight-fold cross validation with early stopping, and report the mean and standard deviation of the accuracies across eight splits. These

results are shown in Table-3. We evaluate the models with the highest cross-validation accuracy on the test set and report these results in Table-4.

Split	Accuracy	Split	Accuracy
1	65.91%	5	60.09%
2	56.50%	6	62.78%
3	57.85%	7	61.71%
4	64.57%	8	58.10%

Table 2: mBERT - Cross-validation accuracy variation

In this section, we provide qualitative and quantitative analysis of our approaches. The qualitative analysis is performed on the cross-validation splits.

6.1 Comparison of Pre-Trained Models

The majority of Hindi words in the NLI dataset are out of vocabulary for BERT. Nevertheless, it obtains a high cross-validation accuracy of 61.11%. We believe it achieves this by tuning the embeddings of WordPiece tokens of both Hindi and English text present in the dataset. To verify that it does not learn only from in-vocabulary English words, we fine-tune BERT after removing the words identified as Hindi, and find that its performance deteriorates sharply.

The benefit of mBERT's multilingual pre-training seems to be lost in CS-NLI due to the script mismatch between Devanagari Hindi used to pre-train mBERT, and Romanized Hindi in CS-NLI.

mod-mBERT performs better than BERT and mBERT due to its enhanced understanding of Hinglish. We believe that fine-tuning on in-domain movie scripts increases mBERT's understanding of conversational code-mixed text, while the inclusion of code-mixed text from other sources enables it to better understand non-standard Romanization.

Model Name	Mean Acc.	Std. Dev.
FINE-TUNING PRE-TRAINED MODELS		
BERT	61.11%	3.38
mBERT	60.94%	3.16
mod-mBERT	61.28%	2.08
TRANSLITERATION & TRANSLATION (MBERT)		
Transliteration of CS-NLI	62.17%	2.00
Hi translation of CS-NLI	60.04%	3.71
CS-NLI & its Hi translation	63.30%	3.05
AUGMENTATION OF CS-NLI		
mod-mBERT on 3k XNLI	**63.69%**	**1.58**
mod-mBERT on 4k SNLI & 4k XNLI	63.35%	2.53
mod-mBERT on 4k MPE	62.19%	3.11
XLM-R on 4k SNLI & 4k XNLI	63.52%	1.85
CONVERSATIONAL APPROACHES (MOD-MBERT)		
CS-NLI & Speaker Name Augmentation	62.85%	2.00
CS-NLI & Speaker Name, Contradiction Augmentation	61.39%	1.87
biLSTM	54.83%	1.72

Table 3: Results on 8-fold cross validation. Hi: Hindi

Although XLM-R is the only model which contains Romanized Hindi in its pre-training data, the model does not converge when fine-tuned on just CS-NLI. However, on augmentation with monolingual NLI examples, there is a large improvement in performance as shown in Table-3. The output of XLM-R's tokenizer shows that many of the Romanized Hindi words are in the model's vocabulary, in contrast to BERT and mBERT where the words get broken into multiple WordPiece tokens. Despite this fact, the model is unable to fit the training data even with an extensive hyper-parameter search, leading us to hypothesize that larger amounts of data are required for fine-tuning XLM-R. However, the performance of this model on code-mixed datasets bears further investigation.

6.2 Transliteration and Translation

Manual inspection shows that errors in language identification and transliteration result in noisy translated and transliterated versions of the data, deterring the performance. However, we find that augmenting the original training set with its translations allows the model to learn from code-mixed and monolingual forms of the same examples.

Model	Acc.
mBERT for 5 epochs i.e. w/o early stopping (baseline)	54.32%
BERT	58.83%
mBERT	60.85%
mod-mBERT	**62.41%**
mBERT on CS-NLI, Hi translation of CS-NLI	56.37%
mod-mBERT on CS-NLI, XNLI	56.82%
mod-mBERT on CS-NLI, SNLI, XNLI	58.16%
XLM-R on CS-NLI, SNLI, XNLI	57.49%

Table 4: Results on the test set. We perform early-stopping while fine-tuning our models. Since we have 8 cross-validation splits, we stop on the epoch that most frequently gives the highest accuracy across these splits.

6.3 Data Augmentation

Although the SNLI, XNLI and MPE datasets contain monolingual examples of textual, non-conversational entailment, augmenting the data with examples from these datasets improves the performance of the models. We believe this is because the addition of these examples aids their general understanding of entailment. The mismatch between the nature of the entailment tasks poses the question of whether there exists an optimal subset and quantity of external data for augmentation. We were unable to find a correlation between the performance and number of external examples added. Finding the categories, if any exist, of examples that are most helpful to the model is challenging. Possible strategies include selection based on length, language complexity, dialect, and domain similarity in the case of Hindi XNLI data. In this work, however, we take a random sample of examples from these corpora.

Since each of these augmentation techniques improve the performance of the model, we augment CS-NLI with different combinations of the datasets, shown in Table-3. We observe an improvement, although it is not proportional to that of the individual augmentations.

6.4 Utterance Representations Using BERT

Separating utterance representations performs worse than the majority of our approaches. The addition of biLSTM layers over the BERT model introduces a large number of uninitialized parameters. We believe that the scarcity of data available to train these parameters leads to its poor performance. Further, the lack of an attention mechanism between utterances and the hypothesis may also pose a problem.

6.5 Qualitative Analysis

Khanuja et al. (2020a) provide an analysis of the various kinds of examples present in CS-NLI. We attempt to discern similarities in the examples that the various models predict incorrectly in order to better address these classes of examples. We analyze various statistical properties of the premises such as their length, the number of turns in the conversation, and the number of distinct speakers, and observe no correlation between these properties and the correctness of the model's predictions. While the complexity of the Hindi and English vocabulary used may make some code-mixed examples more difficult than others, automatically identifying such differences is difficult.

McCoy et al. (2019) show that most neural models including BERT are expected to accurately predict examples involving negation, role swapping, paraphrasing and numerical changes, such as those shown in Khanuja et al. (2020a). However, cross-lingual paraphrasing and negation in CS-NLI make it hard to detect these otherwise simple examples in code-mixed settings.

We evaluate the ability of BERT models to recognize role-swapping by generating examples of this nature. We find that mod-mBERT trained on CS-NLI only predicts 19% of these examples correctly, whereas a model trained using the speaker name data augmentation technique described in Section-4.3, with weighted cross-entropy loss, gets an accuracy of 87% on these examples, substantiating this approach.

6.6 Performance on the Test Set

The accuracy of mBERT with early stopping is 6% higher than the baseline. mod-mBERT shows the best performance with an accuracy that is 8% higher than the baseline, while the augmentation and modification approaches seem to reduce the performance of the model. We attribute the large difference between the test set and cross-validation accuracies to the sensitivity of models to different splits in the dataset, as shown in Table-2.

7 Conclusion

Our results show that there is a long way to go in NLP for code-mixed language tasks. Even using standard techniques such as multilingual language modeling and data augmentation, our results are still behind an equivalent task in a high resource environment.

Although this dataset contains higher level challenges such as sarcasm detection that are not yet solved even in high-resource languages, even phenomena such as negation, role swapping and paraphrasing become challenging due to code-mixing.

Code-mixed language pairs can be thought of as a separate language (Sitaram et al., 2019), and perhaps large-scale pre-training on code-mixed data would be able to push the boundaries of code-mixed interpretation, as has been the case with high-resource languages.

References

Irshad Bhat, Riyaz A. Bhat, Manish Shrivastava, and Dipti Sharma. 2018. Universal dependency parsing for Hindi-English code-switching. In *Proceedings of the 2018 Conference of the North American Chapter of the Association for Computational Linguistics: Human Language Technologies, Volume 1 (Long Papers)*, pages 987–998, New Orleans, Louisiana. Association for Computational Linguistics.

Samuel Bowman, Gabor Angeli, Christopher Potts, and Christopher D Manning. 2015. A large annotated corpus for learning natural language inference. In *Proceedings of the 2015 Conference on Empirical Methods in Natural Language Processing*, pages 632–642.

Monica Stella Cardenas Claros and Neny Isharianty. 2009. Code-switching and code-mixing in internet chatting: between 'yes,' 'ya', and 'si': a case study. *Jaltcall*, 5:67–78.

Alexis Conneau, Kartikay Khandelwal, Naman Goyal, Vishrav Chaudhary, Guillaume Wenzek, Francisco Guzmán, Edouard Grave, Myle Ott, Luke Zettlemoyer, and Veselin Stoyanov. 2020. Unsupervised cross-lingual representation learning at scale. In *Proceedings of the 58th Annual Meeting of the Association for Computational Linguistics*, pages 8440–8451, Online. Association for Computational Linguistics.

Alexis Conneau, Ruty Rinott, Guillaume Lample, Adina Williams, Samuel Bowman, Holger Schwenk, and Veselin Stoyanov. 2018. XNLI: Evaluating cross-lingual sentence representations. In *Proceedings of the 2018 Conference on Empirical Methods in Natural Language Processing*, pages 2475–2485, Brussels, Belgium. Association for Computational Linguistics.

Jacob Devlin, Ming-Wei Chang, Kenton Lee, and Kristina Toutanova. 2019. BERT: Pre-training of deep bidirectional transformers for language understanding. In *Proceedings of the 2019 Conference of the North American Chapter of the Association for Computational Linguistics: Human Language Technologies, Volume 1 (Long and Short Papers)*, pages 4171–4186, Minneapolis, Minnesota. Association for Computational Linguistics.

Mrinal Dhar, Vaibhav Kumar, and Manish Shrivastava. 2018. Enabling code-mixed translation: Parallel corpus creation and mt augmentation approach. In *Proceedings of the First Workshop on Linguistic Resources for Natural Language Processing*, pages 131–140.

Simran Khanuja, Sandipan Dandapat, Sunayana Sitaram, and Monojit Choudhury. 2020a. A new dataset for natural language inference from code-mixed conversations. *arXiv preprint arXiv:2004.05051*.

Simran Khanuja, Sandipan Dandapat, Anirudh Srinivasan, Sunayana Sitaram, and Monojit Choudhury. 2020b. GLUECoS: An evaluation benchmark for code-switched NLP. In *Proceedings of the 58th Annual Meeting of the Association for Computational Linguistics*, pages 3575–3585, Online. Association for Computational Linguistics.

Alice Lai, Yonatan Bisk, and Julia Hockenmaier. 2017. Natural language inference from multiple premises. In *Proceedings of the Eighth International Joint Conference on Natural Language Processing (Volume 1: Long Papers)*, pages 100–109, Taipei, Taiwan. Asian Federation of Natural Language Processing.

Yinhan Liu, Myle Ott, Naman Goyal, Jingfei Du, Mandar Joshi, Danqi Chen, Omer Levy, Mike Lewis, Luke Zettlemoyer, and Veselin Stoyanov. 2019. Roberta: A robustly optimized bert pretraining approach.

R Thomas McCoy, Ellie Pavlick, and Tal Linzen. 2019. Right for the wrong reasons: Diagnosing syntactic heuristics in natural language inference. *arXiv preprint arXiv:1902.01007*.

Rishiraj Saha Roy, Monojit Choudhury, Prasenjit Majumder, and Komal Agarwal. 2013. Overview of the fire 2013 track on transliterated search. In *Post-Proceedings of the 4th and 5th Workshops of the Forum for Information Retrieval Evaluation*, pages 1–7.

Kushagra Singh, Indira Sen, and Ponnurangam Kumaraguru. 2018. Language identification and named entity recognition in hinglish code mixed tweets. In *Proceedings of ACL 2018, Student Research Workshop*, pages 52–58.

Sunayana Sitaram, Khyathi Raghavi Chandu, Sai Krishna Rallabandi, and Alan W Black. 2019. A survey of code-switched speech and language processing. *arXiv preprint arXiv:1904.00784*.

Adina Williams, Nikita Nangia, and Samuel Bowman. 2018. A broad-coverage challenge corpus for sentence understanding through inference. In *Proceedings of the 2018 Conference of the North American*

Chapter of the Association for Computational Linguistics: Human Language Technologies, Volume 1 (Long Papers), pages 1112–1122. Association for Computational Linguistics.

Detecting Objectifying Language in Online Professor Reviews

Angie Waller and Kyle Gorman
Graduate Center, City University of New York

Abstract

Student reviews often make reference to professors' physical appearances. Until recently RateMyProfessors.com, the website of this study's focus, used a design feature to encourage a "hot or not" rating of college professors. In the wake of recent #MeToo and #TimesUp movements, social awareness of the inappropriateness of these reviews has grown; however, objectifying comments remain and continue to be posted in this online context. We describe two supervised text classifiers for detecting objectifying commentary in professor reviews. We then ensemble these classifiers and use the resulting model to track objectifying commentary at scale. We measure correlations between objectifying commentary, changes to the review website interface, and teacher gender across a ten-year period.

1 Introduction

Natural language processing techniques have long been used to study subjectivity and sentiment in media and product reviews. In this study, we employ these technologies to study objectifying language in reviews of professors using archival data from RateMyProfessors.com (RMP). Detecting such language is difficult because it is somewhat rare, making up a small part of a small proportion of reviews (Davison and Price, 2009), and references to physical appearance show enormous linguistic variation (discussed in Section 2.2), making them difficult to detect accurately using simple text features.

This study provides insights into bias in professor reviews and their interaction with the design of the web user interface. We propose two models— a chunk tagger and a document classifier—used to build an ensemble to detect objectifying reviews at scale. This approach could be applied to many other domains where noisy user-generated reviews may contain harassment or exhibit harm.

We focus on the RMP website because it has been active for over twenty years, giving us ample data to study trends across time. The website has long been associated with students commenting on their professors' appearances (Lagorio, 2006) and has been the subject of many prior studies on bias in course reviews. Recent changes to the website interface allow us to consider how text reviews may have been influenced by its design feature for rating professor "hotness".

1.1 Prior work

We look to previous work on bias in professor reviews, effects of interface design on internet discourse, and detecting subjectivity and opinions in online reviews.

1.1.1 Bias and student reviews

Prior studies address bias among students' reviews of teachers. Freng and Webber (2009) find a positive correlation between "hotness" and quality scores of professors on RMP, accounting for 8% of variance. Chang and McKeown (2019) report gendered differences in students' descriptions of computer science professors on RMP which is also reflected in visualizations by Schmidt (2015) showing that words like *genius* are more frequently attributed to male professors and words like *nurturing* to female professors. This is supported in work by Boring et al. (2016) and Boring (2017) where in-class reviews show higher ratings for leadership skills among male professors and "being warm" among female professors. Noting that perceptions of "easiness" predict overall ratings, Davison and Price (2009) recommend an RMP interface change replacing the site's "easiness" rating with better-defined terms such as "amount learned".

Proceedings of the 2020 EMNLP Workshop W-NUT: The Sixth Workshop on Noisy User-generated Text, pages 171–180
Online, Nov 19, 2020. ©2020 Association for Computational Linguistics

1.1.2 Interface design and online discourse

The interaction between interface design and online discourse is a central focus in computer-mediated discourse analysis (Herring, 2004; Herring and Androutsopoulos, 2015) and critical technocultural discourse analysis (Brock, 2018). Both consider not only how people express themselves in online environments, but also how elements like interface design of a website shape people into "users", affecting how they express themselves. Because we are interested in the relationship between attractiveness commentary and interface design, we constrain this study to the RMP website and its interface elements, including its professor rating form (Appendix, Figure 3), featuring the "hot or not" chili pepper rating.

Interface design is also considered quantitatively, and at scale, in company-led user experience studies. For example, Facebook found that by curating users' News Feeds to positive or negative posts, they influenced the emotional tenor of the users' own posts (Kramer et al., 2014). NextDoor, a popular neighborhood classifieds website, made their web form for reporting suspicious activity more detailed and inadvertently arduous, successfully decreasing suspicious activity posts and therefore decreasing posts with racial profiling (Hempel, 2017). In an effort to combat online harassment, Twitter introduced interface elements to warn users before posting tweets with inflammatory language (Statt, 2020). These interventions suggest that small interface changes may produce measurable effects in online discourse.

1.1.3 Subjectivity in workplace reviews

Like all genres of review, professor reviews interweave subjective and objective statements (e.g., "the class was poorly attended"). We consider commentary on a professor's physical attractiveness, which we refer to as objectifying or attractiveness commentary, to be subjective content.

Wiebe et al. (2001) discuss a method of labeling spans of subjective text within news corpora so that opinion phrases, even those that occur infrequently, can be detected using collocation clues. To determine review sentiment, Pang and Lee (2004) automatically segment movie reviews into subjective and objective portions, discarding the objective portions before attempting to determine the overall sentiment. Here we are also interested primarily in a subjective portion of reviews, but whereas subjectivity is an expected feature in other genres of reviews, comments about a professor's "hotness" may constitute workplace harassment (Flaherty, 2018) among other harms. To our knowledge, this is the first study to target objectifying commentary in professor reviews and its relationship to website design.

1.2 Our approach

Our classification scheme is tailored for a low-resource setting with a limited amount of labeled data. The goal is to construct classifiers which achieve sufficient accuracy to allow extrapolation to a much larger set of unlabeled reviews. To achieve our goal of analyzing large-scale trends, we train two models for identifying objectifying commentary in RMP reviews: (1) a token-level chunk tagger similar to those used for named entity recognition; and (2) a review-level text classifier similar to those used for document classification. Unlike the chunk tagger, the document classifier can take into account more variety in features and account for attractiveness commentary that occurs multiple times in a document. Multiple spans can "gang up", allowing them to be more easily detected at document level. In contrast, the chunk tagger considers objectifying language as a highly-local phenomena and is therefore more able to detect attractiveness commentary in the context of longer reviews covering a range of topics.

We then build ensembles of these models. We anticipate that ensembling will be useful because we hypothesize that the two classifiers' patterns of errors will be only weakly correlated (van Halteren et al., 1998), and because labeled data is limited, high-variance, and class-imbalanced (Brill and Wu, 1998) for this task.

2 Data

For this study, anonymous RMP reviews of professors were scraped on two occasions.[1] The first scrape, in July 2018, paired textual data with the professor's "hotness" rating, defined by the number of times a student rated the professor as "hot" minus the number times they rated them as "not hot" (Felton et al., 2008). In the web interface, the names of professors receiving positive attractiveness scores are marked with a chili pepper emoji (see Appendix, Figure 5). The second scrape, in August 2019, targeted a broader set of regions and

---

[1] Scraping was seeded using a list of professors and their chili pepper scores (http://morph.io/chrisguags).

schools. Test data was drawn from this latter data set, which was also used for trend analysis.

By this latter date, the chili pepper emoji had been removed from the website in response to public criticism (McLaughlin, 2018), so it was no longer possible to extract hotness scores. In addition to text, both scrapes also collected the names of professors, student-reported quality and difficulty scores (averaged by professor, on a five-point scale), subject area, and the name of the school. See Table 8 and Table 9 in the Appendix for the full list of schools.

2.1 Defining objectifying language

We define objectifying or attractiveness commentary as reviews that describe a professor's physical appearance, demeanor, clothing style, or resemblance. In contrast to prior work (e.g., Felton et al., 2008), we also include language disparaging a professor's appearance. Although previous work has considered objectifying comments in limited RMP datasets (Davison and Price, 2009; Kindred and Mohammed, 2017), there are no previous annotation guidelines to follow for labeling these expressions. Kindred and Mohammed (2017) find out of 788 RMP ratings in their sample, only 3.6% describe teacher attractiveness. Given the low frequency of these reviews and their informal qualities, creating instructions that cover attractiveness commentary in all of its variations is not possible. We acknowledge some reviews like ones described in Section 2.3 will be more subjective than others.

2.2 Review characteristics

RMP reviews contain stylistic flourishes common to online discourse: slang and non-standard language, typographical errors, expressive punctuation and capitalization, and emoticons. The examples below are fragments from 30-to-50-word reviews representing attractiveness commentary. See Figure 4 in the Appendix for additional examples in screen-capture format.

- *Everyone LOOOOOVES sexy Jeff!*

- *...he doesn't assume students understand complex stuff like other math teachers do. Plus, hello, HOT!*

- *He's also pretty cute which helps. :)*

- *...when he talked about vector space he almost saw my O-face.*

2.3 Fuzzy samples

This section describes reviews that pose challenges in labeling attractiveness spans and the process behind how distinctions are made. Annotators were instructed that, when in doubt, reviews that imply romantic interest, or lack thereof, are considered objectifying.

Flirtation but no attractiveness commentary Examples where the review may be flirtatious but not directly describing professor appearance present a grey area.

- *Damn, I love that man.* **None**

Referring to a professor as "that man" borders on objectifying, but without additional context it is not considered attractiveness commentary.

- *I love him so much, I would totally marry him if I could.* **Obj.**

However, we consider references to marriage or dating the professor like the above example to be objectifying commentary. We decide this because the element of fantasy in samples like these is taken to be indicative of an attraction to the professor.

- *He is a math god!* **None**

Reviews that compare the professor to a deity are also difficult to distinguish. If the focus could be the professor's expertise, the review is not considered attractiveness commentary.

Accents The most common challenging examples refer to the professor's voice or accent. These types of reviews primarily fall into two categories: (1) the accent is sexy, charming, or appealing; and (2) denoting professors who are non-native English speakers described as difficult to understand. Reviews in the latter category can be considered denigrating of the professor but are not necessarily attractiveness commentary. We consider the intent of the student. If the comment is personally derogatory, such as "horrible accent", it is considered objectifying. The following examples illustrate these distinctions:

- *And he's British, such a charmer! Love his accent!* **Obj.**

- *He has the cutest accent.* **Obj.**

- *His accent was difficult to understand.* **None**

	He	is	CUT	for	a	Stanford	professor
word-lower	he	is	cut	for	a	stanford	professor
lemma	he	is	cut	for	a	stanford	professor
pos	PRON	AUX	NOUN	NOUN	DET	PROPN	NOUN
has-hot	false	false	false	false	false	false	false
next-word	is	CUT	for	a	stanford	professor	[END]
next-pos	AUX	NOUN	ADP	DET	PROPN	NOUN	[END]
prev-word	[START]	He	is	cut	for	a	stanford
prev-pos	[START]	PRON	AUX	NOUN	ADP	DET	PROPN
prev-iob	O	O	O	B	O	O	O
all-caps	false	false	true	false	false	false	false
prev-all-caps	false	false	false	true	false	false	false
next-all-caps	false	true	false	false	false	false	false

Table 1: Example feature vector for chunk tagger using review snippet commenting on professor's physique.

3 Methods

We implement classification techniques with unique strengths for capturing the qualities and contexts of objectifying comments. The first, a chunk tagger, represents a bottom-up strategy, whereas the second, a document classifier, uses top-down processing and a richer feature set.

3.1 Chunk tagger

Because discussion of a professor's attractiveness may only be a small portion of any given review, we annotate spans of tokens which refer to attractiveness. These labels can then be automatically propagated from spans to the document level. That is, if a review contains any spans tagged as containing objectifying language, the whole review is labeled objectifying. We employ a chunk tagger customized to identify these spans within reviews. During preprocessing, labeled data is tagged for part of speech (POS) using the spaCy tagger (Honnibal and Montani, 2017). Text spans that refer to attractiveness are tagged using the CoNLL-2003 IOB format (Tjong Kim Sang and De Meulder, 2003). The chunker is built using the nltk.chunk library (Bird et al., 2009, ch. 7); it uses a multinomial logistic regression classifier and a greedy left-to-right decoding strategy.

Attractiveness features In addition to token features, we develop a dictionary of words describing attractiveness (see Appendix, Table 10); these are matched using regular expressions so alternative spellings (e.g., *hoooottt*, *hottttt*) are also captured. See Table 1 for an example token feature vector.

3.2 Document classifier

We also develop a model that can take advantage of features extracted from the entire review. The document classifier is built using a linear-kernel support vector machine classifier from sklearn (Pedregosa et al., 2011). The primary features used are term frequency-inverse document frequency weighted unigrams and bigrams. Several other types of features, described below, are used to improve classifier accuracy.

Formality Impressionistically, RMP reviews that discuss teacher appearance tend to be less formal than those that focus on the quality of instruction. To capture this distinction, we use features proposed by Pavlick and Tetreault (2016) to measure textual formality. These include average word and sentence length, the ratio of nouns to verbs, and the proportion of words over 4 characters. We also add one-hot features for the use of non-standard punctuation and capitalization. Finally, we also extract features tracking the use of titles such as *Dr., Professor, Mrs.*, and *Mr.*

Gender We extract professor gender by tracking third-person singular pronouns (e.g., *he, his, she, her*) in reviews; gender-non-specific pronouns like *they* and neo-pronouns like *ze* were not present in

	Reviews	Tokens	Words
Labeled	4,050	12,209	139,091
Unlabeled	358,970	71,700	15m

Table 2: Summary statistics for datasets.

the labeled data and therefore not tracked. We also do not track gender of the reviewers as all reviews are submitted anonymously.

Subjectivity Davison and Price (2009) and Ritter (2008) argue that student reviews largely follow a transactional consumerist discourse similar to customer service reviews. We hypothesize that this would be reflected in the ratio of first-person to third-person pronouns; a greater proportion of first-person pronouns may indicate a review about personal opinions and feelings (*consumerist*) rather than instruction. We also reuse the attractiveness dictionary regular expression patterns from the chunk tagger, expanding this to include common idioms such as *easy on the eyes* and *good looking*. Additionally, each review is scored for its sentiment and subjectivity using the `textblob`[2] sentiment classifier.

Style We consider features measuring the use of text properties characteristic of internet discourse, including the use of emoticons, repeated exclamation points, and words in all uppercase letters.

3.3 Feature ablation

For the document classifier, a feature ablation study on the development data (Appendix, Table 11) shows accuracy scores rely on the custom dictionaries for "hotness" including pattern matching for idiomatic expressions. However, omitting formality and stylistic features does not impact performance.

3.4 Ensembling

After training the chunk tagger and document classifier on the labeled data, a simple document-level ensemble of these models is applied to the unlabeled data. Since there are only two weak classifiers available, we use two forms of voting: in ensemble 1 we consider reviews with disagreement as non-objectifying reviews; in ensemble 2, we completely discard reviews when the classifiers disagree to achieve higher accuracy.

4 Results

4.1 Experiment setup

The labeled data of 4,050 reviews is randomly split into training (80%) and development sets (20%), the latter used for feature ablation (Appendix, Table 11). During annotation, professors labeled

[2]`https://textblob.readthedocs.org`

Chunk tagger	Doc. classifier	
	Targeted	None
Targeted	8,573	9,858
None	4,295	336,242

Table 3: Confusion matrix for chunk tagger and document classifier models; Targeted: reviews which contain attractiveness commentary.

"hot" were deliberately oversampled. Review and token counts can be found in Table 2.

4.2 Annotation

To estimate interannotator agreement, a subset of the labeled data was independently labeled by a second annotator, a graduate student in linguistics, according to the authors' guidelines. This gave a span-level Cohen's $\varkappa = .785$ and a document-level $\varkappa = .801$; both correspond to "substantial" agreement according to the Landis and Koch (1977) qualitative guidelines.

4.3 Performance

After applying the chunk tagger and document classifier to the unlabeled data, we find the classifiers disagree on 4.1% of the reviews (see Table 3). This is roughly what one might expect given the overall low proportion of true positive samples. We determine accuracy by creating a test set from 600 of these reviews. This set includes reviews with classifier agreement on 150 documents predicted to contain, and 150 documents predicted not to contain, objectifying language. We also sample 300 reviews in which the chunk tagger and document classifier disagree.[3] These 600 samples are randomly sorted and then adjudicated by a human judge to create the test set.

The results for the chunk tagger and document classifier are shown in Table 4. As can be seen, both classifiers have relatively high accuracy but significantly lower precision and recall. Table 5

[3]We oversample from recent date ranges to better capture any new trends in reviews.

Classifier	Prec.	Rec.	$F1$	Acc.	$\varkappa$
Chunk tag.	.42	.21	.28	.89	.23
Doc. class.	.44	.23	.30	.93	.26

Table 4: Weak classifier results.

Review	Chunk tagger	Doc. class.
Not a great teacher (in fact pretty awful) but she's looking GOOD.	FN	TP
he is now bald, but he still has the look ;)	FN	TP
His classes are worthwhile because he's a good teacher, but mostly because he has the most awesome accent in the world. Rawr.	FN	TP
*the WORST ****ING TEACHER EVER. WORST CLASS, WORST PERSON. NOT PROFESSIONAL AT ANYTHING, DOES NOT KNOW PHYSICS FROM THE HOLE IN HIS ASS. AVOID!*	FP	TN
My experience with this professor was awful. He wasn't helpful and I ended up learning everything on my own without his help. I should have just stared at the wall rather than wasting my time in this class. He did not BUMP my grade up!	FP	TN
Probably the BEST Org Chem prof out of all the ones I've had. His slides are actually notes, not just pictures with lines on the side for you to write on. The exam is based onthe notes, but you also need to read the book. Def didn't mind looking at him for 1 hour 25 mins either.	TP	FN
not a bad prof. has a nice smile. class discussions were pretty interesting. grades are based on ur attendance, and ur blog entries (they are not hard, but be careful, cuz her way of grading is kinda picky). overall, not a hard class. kinda interesting. take it if u want, but if u cant stand reading don't. TONS of reading.	TP	FN
Jason's a fantastic section leader–some of the best classes I've had here were in section for this class. Plus, he knows his stuff, is super eloquent, and kicks ass in suits (just sayin'). I will say that he can come off as cold and intimidating at first, but he actually cares and is really willing to help you.	TP	FN
I can't understand her heavy accent. I found her subject boring.	TN	FP
Jenny is an extraordinary professor- she truly cares about how you do in her class, and does her best to help you in whatever fashion she can.	TN	FP
Very easy going. Knows what he is doing from lived experience. The power-points are very good. You can skip class and just follow along on the slides and get the idea of things (although probably not a good grade). Hot daughter.	FP	FP
worst prof ever, and i really mean that. she's not even a professor, just some plant biologist hired as a lecturer. she is completely inept as a lab manager and universally hated by the students. oh, and very not hot	TP	TP

Table 5: Examples with classifier disagreement; reviews have been modified to reflect their original format while protecting the identity of professors.

shows example reviews where the classifiers disagree. The chunk tagger performs better in reviews with higher word counts. In some cases, the chunk tagger avoids false positives of the document classifier where keywords from custom dictionaries appear but are in a context that is not objectifying. The document classifier performed well on lower word count reviews and where words from custom dictionaries and regular expression patterns are present. In Table 6, we show the same results for the two ensembles; note that results for ensemble 2 do not include the 300 samples from the test data on which the two weak models disagree.

We see that both ensemble classifiers achieve greatly improved results compared to either the chunk tagger or the document classifier alone, and as expected, error can be further reduced in ensemble 2 by discarding data on which they disagree.

We conclude that ensemble methods are effective for detecting objectifying commentary in student reviews in the face of unbalanced data. In what follows, the ensemble 2 classifier is used to to analyze trends in attractiveness commentary on 344,815 reviews.

5 Analysis

Building on previous RMP research studying bias in student reviews, we continue this inquiry focusing on how attractiveness commentary is distributed based on teacher gender, and quality and

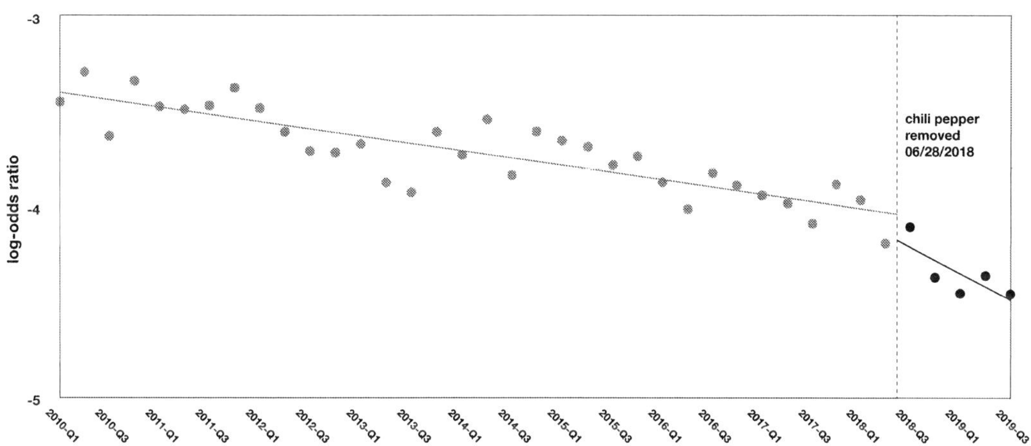

Figure 1: Log-odds of attractiveness commentary in reviews from 2010 to August 2019.

Classifier	Prec.	Rec.	$F1$	Acc.	$\varkappa$
Ensemble 1	.72	.44	.55	.93	.50
Ensemble 2	.72	1.00	.84	.99	.83

Table 6: Ensemble classifier results.

difficulty scores. We then focus on a logistic regression analysis using generalized estimating equations (GEE) to determine if there was a decrease in attractiveness commentary following the removal of the chili pepper feature from the web interface.

5.1 Teacher gender

Our dataset contains 39.7% female professors $(11,192)$ compared to 60.2% male professors $(16,967)$. This proportion is similar to those found in U.S. higher education where women make up only 31% of full-time faculty (Kelly, 2019). Since this breakdown leads to more reviews for male professors overall, we consider each professor and whether or not they have at least one objectifying comment. In our dataset, 21.0% of male professors have at least one attractiveness review compared to 18.4% of female professors. We find in a chi-square test of independence that this difference is significant ($\chi^2 = 17.75, p < .01$). In contrast, Rosen (2018) found that women were more likely to have the chili pepper rating (27.8%) than men (22.7%). We believe this difference could be attributed to the distinction between the low effort act of clicking "hot" on the review form versus actually writing commentary on the teacher's appear-

ance. Also, unlike chili pepper ratings, our counts include reviews with negative commentary.

5.2 Logistic regression

We deploy logistic generalized estimating equations (GEE; Liang and Zeger 1986), an extension of the generalized linear modeling that takes into account the correlation between observations. A logistic GEE accommodates the unequal number of earlier observations across professors and conditions as well as the variation in review activity volume over quarterly time intervals. This is optimal for the noise in the dataset and allows utilization of the entire collection of reviews. The final model parameters are determined by the best goodness-of-fit score computed using the full log quasi-likelihood function. School size and tuition did not have significant outcomes in the results and were discarded. The final model includes presence or absence of the chili pepper interface feature, teacher quality and difficulty scores, and professor gender. Time is input as an interval covariate by quarter, while chili pepper condition is a binary factor; final parameters and their outcomes are given in Table 7.

Chili pepper and time interval First, we focus on our primary question concerning the proportion of objectifying comments and the removal of the chili pepper. We observe a downward trend over the time period prior to the interface change; however, the log-odds of attractiveness commentary after the chili pepper was removed on June 28, 2018 is lower than the time variable can account for

	Estimate (log-odds)	Std. err.	Wald χ^2	$p(\chi^2)$
(Intercept)	-3.111	.143	476.18	$< .001$
pepperAbsent	$-.428$	.136	9.93	.002
timeInQuarters	$-.020$	.002	79.44	$< .001$
difficultyHigh	$-.075$	.022	11.49	$< .001$
qualityHigh	.051	.026	3.76	.053
genderFemale	$-.528$	.174	9.19	.002
qualityHigh:genderFemale	.097	.043	5.09	.024

Table 7: GEE model parameter estimates with attractiveness commentary as dependent variable. The intercept represents pepperPresent, timeInQuarters = 0, difficultyLow, qualityLow, genderMale. $N = 344,815$.

alone (see Table 7). Our analysis finds a significant effect of time and condition (with vs. without the chili pepper). These findings support our hypothesis: RMP's removal of the chili pepper coincides with a decline in reviews mentioning professor attractiveness.

Quality and teacher gender We compare the proportions for attractiveness commentary in relation to quality and difficulty rating scales (Figure 2). There is a significant interaction between teacher quality and gender, female professors rated high quality are significantly more likely to receive attractiveness commentary than male professors rated high quality (see Table 7). Difficulty was also a significant factor, the higher the difficulty score, the less likely the reviews for the professor will contain attractiveness commentary.

6   Discussion

While our work has focused on the text contents of reviews, our analysis of objectifying comments follows previous findings about biases of the original chili pepper rating, correlating with teacher gender, quality, and difficulty ratings. This is the first study to find a correlation between attractiveness commentary and the website interface.

More research is needed to understand the observed steady eight-year decline. As this was an observational study rather than a controlled experiment, there are many uncontrolled variables. For instance, we cannot compare attractiveness commentary by size of professor's class or attributes of the reviewer. We tried to estimate these factors with proxies such as university size, geographic area, and tuition amounts, but these only provide rough estimates and did not have significant effect on the presence of attractiveness commentary. Mc-

Neil (2020) reflects on how users' perceptions of anonymity have changed, from posting to online bulletin boards in the late 1990s, to present-day "sharing" on corporate-owned, heavily surveilled social network sites like Facebook. This turn from anonymity to self-awareness is observed by Marwick and boyd (2011) in their study of Twitter users. These users describe their own self-censoring behaviors by imagining their audiences to include not only friends but also parents and employers. The decline in attractiveness commentary on RMP may reflect broader internet trends, corresponding with internet users being more conscious of their perceived audience and realizing that true online anonymity is impossible.

7   Conclusion

We find that a small change to the RMP website, removal of the chili pepper rating, is associated with a lower likelihood of comments on professor attractiveness. Our experiments show that an ensemble of classifiers can accurately detect objectifying language in online professor reviews and can allow us to analyze trends in a large unlabeled dataset.

One area where classifiers disagreed was in the "fuzzy samples" such as accents and godliness discussed in Section 2.3. Breitfeller et al. (2019) describe similar challenges in classifying microaggressions and label themes within their dataset to better define these utterances. Based on our classifier's success in pulling out objectifying comments from large datasets, we can identify enough examples to consider labeling categories such as accent criticism and comments about unattractiveness. Finally, one could apply an active learning approach (Yarowsky, 1995) to label and train on examples where the classifiers disagreed.

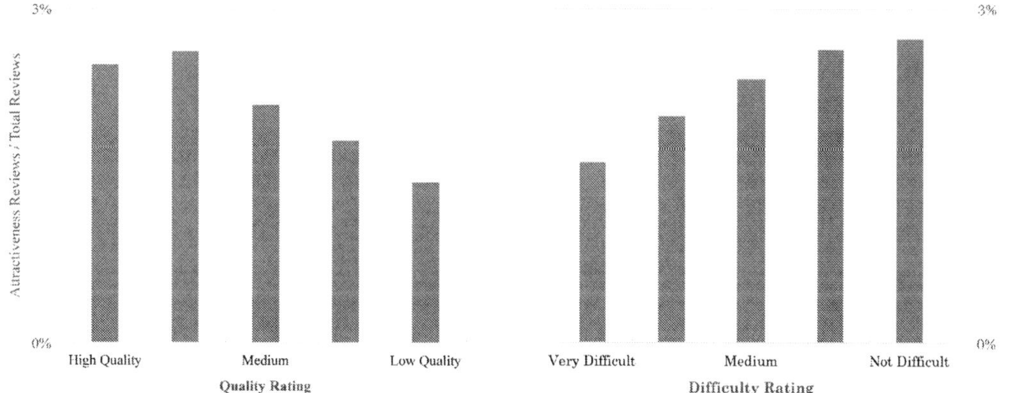

Figure 2: Proportion of reviews with attractiveness commentary by quality and difficulty ratings.

With further exploration it is hoped these techniques could be applied to detecting other forms of abusive language in online reviews. Insofar as the removal of the chili pepper feature correlated with a significant decrease in attractiveness commentary, we suggest that web interface design may positively influence online discourse. As the scope of the gig economy continues to expand and more workers find themselves evaluated by anonymous online reviews, we hope these findings will inspire future research around potential biases in online reviews based on gender, appearance, and the design of the online interface used.

8 Acknowledgments

We would like to thank Martin Chodorow for his guidance in statistical analysis and Deepali Advani for her assistance with data preparation. We appreciate Jonathan Butterick for helping with data collection. We would also like to acknowledge Sara Morini for her assistance with the data annotation, William Jordan for proofreading, and anonymous reviewers for their helpful feedback.

References

Steven Bird, Ewan Klein, and Edward Loper. 2009. *Natural language processing with Python*. O'Reilly.

Anne Boring. 2017. Gender biases in student evaluations of teaching. *Journal of Public Economics*, 145:27–41.

Anne Boring, Kellie Ottoboni, and Philip B. Stark. 2016. Student evaluations of teaching (mostly) do not measure teaching effectiveness. *ScienceOpen Research*, 1:1–11.

Luke Breitfeller, Emily Ahn, David Jurgens, and Yulia Tsvetkov. 2019. Finding microaggressions in the wild: A case for locating elusive phenomena in social media posts. In *Proceedings of the 2019 Conference on Empirical Methods in Natural Language Processing and the 9th International Joint Conference on Natural Language Processing (EMNLP-IJCNLP)*, pages 1664–1674.

Eric Brill and Jun Wu. 1998. Classifier combination for improved lexical disambiguation. In *36th Annual Meeting of the Association for Computational Linguistics and 17th International Conference on Computational Linguistics, Volume 1*, pages 191–195.

André Brock. 2018. Critical technocultural discourse analysis. *New Media & Society*, 20(3):1012–1030.

Serina Chang and Kathy McKeown. 2019. Automatically inferring gender associations from language. In *Proceedings of the 2019 Conference on Empirical Methods in Natural Language Processing and the 9th International Joint Conference on Natural Language Processing*, pages 5746–5752.

Elizabeth Davison and Jammie Price. 2009. How do we rate? An evaluation of online student evaluations. *Assessment & Evaluation in Higher Education*, 34(1):51–65.

James Felton, Peter T. Koper, John Mitchell, and Michael Stinson. 2008. Attractiveness, easiness and other issues: student evaluations of professors on ratemyprofessors.com. *Assessment & Evaluation in Higher Education*, 33(1):45–61.

Colleen Flaherty. 2018. Bye, bye, chili pepper: Rate My Professors ditches its chili pepper "hotness" quotient. Accessed 10/28/2018.

Scott Freng and David Webber. 2009. Turning up the heat on online teaching evaluations: Does "hotness" matter? *Teaching of Psychology*, 36(3):189–193.

Hans van Halteren, Jakub Zavrel, and Walter Daelemans. 1998. Improving data driven wordclass tagging by system combination. In *36th Annual Meeting of the Association for Computational Linguistics and 17th International Conference on Computational Linguistics, Volume 1*, pages 491–497.

Jessi Hempel. 2017. For Nextdoor, Eliminating Racism Is No Quick Fix. *Wired.*

Susan C. Herring. 2004. Computer-mediated discourse analysis. In Sasha Barab, Rob Kling, and James H.Editors Gray, editors, *Designing for Virtual Communities in the Service of Learning*, page 338–376. Cambridge University Press.

Susan C. Herring and Jannis Androutsopoulos. 2015. Computer-mediated discourse 2.0. In Deborah Tannen, Heidi E. Hamilton, and Deborah Schiffrin, editors, *The Handbook of Discourse Analysis*, pages 127–151. John Wiley & Sons.

Matthew Honnibal and Ines Montani. 2017. spaCy 2: natural language understanding with Bloom embeddings, convolutional neural networks and incremental parsing. Accessed 1/4/20.

Bridget Turner Kelly. 2019. Though more women are on college campuses, climbing the professor ladder remains a challenge.

Jeannette Kindred and Shaheed N. Mohammed. 2017. "he will crush you like an academic ninja!": Exploring teacher ratings on RateMyProfessors.com. *Journal of Computer-Mediated Communication*, 10(3).

Adam D. I. Kramer, Jamie E. Guillory, and Jeffrey T. Hancock. 2014. Experimental evidence of massivescale emotional contagion through social networks. *Proceedings of the National Academy of Sciences*, 111(24):8788–8790.

Christine Lagorio. 2006. Hot for teacher. *The Village Voice.*

J. Richard Landis and Gary G. Koch. 1977. The measurement of observer agreement for categorical data. *Biometrics*, 33(1):159–174.

Kung-Yee Liang and Scott L. Zeger. 1986. Longitudinal data analysis using generalized linear models. *Biometrika*, 73(1):13–22.

Alice E. Marwick and danah boyd. 2011. I tweet honestly, i tweet passionately: Twitter users, context collapse, and the imagined audience. *New Media & Society*, 13(1):114–133.

BethAnn McLaughlin. 2018. I killed the chili pepper on Rate My Professors. Accessed 1/4/2020.

Joanne McNeil. 2020. *Lurking: How a Person Became a User.* Macmillan.

Bo Pang and Lillian Lee. 2004. A sentimental education: sentiment analysis using subjectivity summarization based on minimum cuts. In *Proceedings of the 42nd Annual Meeting on Association for Computational Linguistics*, page 271–278.

Ellie Pavlick and Joel Tetreault. 2016. An empirical analysis of formality in online communication. *Transactions of the Association for Computational Linguistics*, 4:61–74.

Fabian Pedregosa, Gaël Varoquaux, Alexandre Gramfort, Vincent Michel, Bertrand Thirion, Olivier Grisel, Mathieu Blondel, Peter Prettenhofer, Ron Weiss, Vincent Dubourg, Jake Vanderplas, Alexandre Passos, David Cournapeau, Matthieu Brucher, Matthieu Perrot, and Édouard Duchesnay. 2011. Scikit-learn: machine learning in Python. *Journal of Machine Learning Research*, 12:2825–2830.

Kelly Ritter. 2008. E-valuating learning: Rate My Professors and public rhetorics of pedagogy. *Rhetoric Review*, 27(3):259–280.

Andrew S. Rosen. 2018. Correlations, trends and potential biases among publicly accessible web-based student evaluations of teaching: a large-scale study of ratemyprofessors.com data. *Assessment & Evaluation in Higher Education*, 43(1):31–44.

Ben Schmidt. 2015. Gendered language in teacher reviews. Accessed 7/13/19.

Nick Statt. 2020. Twitter tests a warning message that tells users to rethink offensive replies. *The Verge.*

TextBlob. 2018. TextBlob: simplified text processing. Accessed 1/8/2020.

Erik F. Tjong Kim Sang and Fien De Meulder. 2003. Introduction to the CoNLL-2003 shared task: language-independent named entity recognition. In *Proceedings of the Seventh Conference on Natural Language Learning at HLT-NAACL 2003*, pages 142–147.

Janyce Wiebe, Theresa Wilson, and Matthew Bell. 2001. Identifying collocations for recognizing opinions. In *Proceedings of the ACL-01 Workshop on Collocation: Computational Extraction, Analysis, and Exploitation*, pages 24–31.

David Yarowsky. 1995. Unsupervised word sense disambiguation rivaling supervised methods. In *33rd Annual Meeting of the Association for Computational Linguistics*, pages 189–196.

Annotation Efficient Language Identification from Weak Labels

Shriphani Palakodety[*]
Onai
spalakod@onai.com

Ashiqur R. KhudaBukhsh[*]
Carnegie Mellon University
akhudabu@cs.cmu.edu

Abstract

India is home to several languages with more than 30m speakers. These languages exhibit significant presence on social media platforms. However, several of these widely-used languages are under-addressed by current Natural Language Processing (NLP) models and resources. User generated social media content in these languages is also typically authored in the Roman script as opposed to the traditional native script further contributing to resource scarcity. In this paper, we leverage a minimally supervised NLP technique to obtain weak language labels from a large-scale Indian social media corpus leading to a robust and annotation-efficient language-identification technique spanning nine Romanized Indian languages. In fast-spreading pandemic situations such as the current COVID-19 situation, information processing objectives might be heavily tilted towards under-served languages in densely populated regions. We release our models to facilitate downstream analyses in these low-resource languages[1]. Experiments across multiple social media corpora demonstrate the model's robustness and provide several interesting insights on Indian language usage patterns on social media. We release an annotated data set of 1,000 comments in ten Romanized languages as a social media evaluation benchmark[1].

1 Introduction

Much of the current NLP research focuses on a handful of world languages (e.g., English, French, Spanish etc.). They enjoy substantially larger computational linguistic resources as compared to their low-resource counterparts (e.g., Bengali, Odia etc.). However, in the midst of global-scale events like the ongoing COVID-19 pandemic, demand for linguistic resources might get recalibrated; information processing objectives might be heavily tilted towards under-served languages that are prevalent in many densely populated regions.

In this paper, we focus on *language identification* in noisy, social media settings - a basic and highly critical linguistic resource prerequisite for downstream analysis in a multilingual environment. Our solution extends support for nine major Indian languages (see, Table 1) spanning the native tongues of 85% of India's population (Census, 2011). These under-resourced languages are heavily used in several densely populated travel hubs and on social media. User generated web content in these languages is typically authored in the Roman script as opposed to the traditional native script leading to scarcer linguistic resources (Virga and Khudanpur, 2003; Choudhury et al., 2010; Gella et al., 2014; Barman et al., 2014; Palakodety et al., 2020a). Existing large-scale language identification tools prioritize the languages' native scripts (e.g., (FastText; Google)) over the Romanized variants. Our solution focuses on the these Romanized variants and is integrated with a widely used existing language-identification system (FastText) supporting 355 languages. We **release our open-source language identification system**[1]. to facilitate Indian social media analysis.

Annotator availability is a major concern that may constrain data acquisition efforts in low resource settings (Joshi et al., 2019). Our proposed solution is extremely **annotation efficient**; it utilizes a recent result (Palakodety et al., 2020a) to automatically group a multilingual corpus into largely monolingual clusters that can be extracted with minimal supervision. Using a mere 260 annotated short documents (YouTube video comments), we

---

[*] Shriphani Palakodety and Ashiqur R. KhudaBukhsh are equal-contribution first authors. Ashiqur R. KhudaBukhsh is the corresponding author.

[1] Resources are available at: https://www.cs.cmu.edu/~akhudabu/IndicLanguage.html.

Proceedings of the 2020 EMNLP Workshop W-NUT: The Sixth Workshop on Noisy User-generated Text, pages 181–192
Online, Nov 19, 2020. ©2020 Association for Computational Linguistics

assign *weak labels* to a data set of 2.8 million comments spanning the aforementioned languages. Our model performs favorably when compared against an existing commercial solution.

While census data and surveys can provide useful information about linguistic diversity and spread, analyses of user-generated multi-lingual corpora can complement these surveys with additional useful insights of their own. We conduct a focused analysis to explore if the (estimated) distribution of web-usage of Hindi across different Indian states aligns with common knowledge. Our analysis indicates that Hindi's web-presence is considerably higher in a cluster of North Indian states referred to as the Hindi belt (Jaffrelot, 2000) as compared to the South Indian states. We further analyze similar research questions concerning the relative usage of the Roman script and the native script for Hindi. We finally conclude with a small exploratory study on our method's effectiveness in detecting languages with trace presence in multiple corpora and outline some of the possible utilities.

Contributions: Our main contributions of the paper are the following:

• *Resource*: We release an important linguistic resource to detect nine heavily-spoken Indic languages expressed in Roman script.

• *Method*: We propose an annotation efficient method to construct this language identifier and demonstrate extensibility.

• *Linguistic*: We conduct a web-scale analysis of Hindi usage shedding light on multilinguality, geographic spread, and usage patterns.

• *Social*: We outline how our tool can detect trace presence of other languages that can aid in constructing data sets for humanitarian challenges.

2 Data Set: YouTube Video Comments

In order to construct our language identification system, we would require a web-scale Indian social media data set that (i) has considerable presence of the nine languages we are interested in, and (ii) captures a representative fraction of the Indian web users. To achieve this two-fold goal, we consider a data set introduced in Palakodety et al. (2020b) to analyze the 2019 Indian General Election. The data set consists of comments on YouTube videos hosted by popular news outlets in India. Overall, the corpus consists of 6,182,868 comments on 130,067 videos by 1,518,077 users posted in a 100 day period leading up to the 2019

Indian General Election.

Why YouTube? As of January 2020, YouTube is the second-most popular social media platform in the world drawing 2 billion active users (Statista, 2020). YouTube is the most popular social media platform in India with 265 million monthly active users (225 million on mobile), accounting for 80% of the population with internet access (Hindustan-Times, 2019; YourStory, 2018). YouTube video comments have been used as data sources to analyze recent important events (Palakodety et al., 2020a,c; Sarkar et al., 2020; Cinelli et al., 2020).

Language	ISO code	First language speakers
Bengali	*bn*	8.03%
Gujarati	*gu*	4.58%
Hindi	*hi*	43.63%
Kannada	*kn*	3.61%
Marathi	*mr*	6.86%
Malayalam	*ml*	2.88%
Odiya	*or*	3.10%
Tamil	*ta*	5.70%
Te	*te*	6.70%

Table 1: List of languages we considered with their corresponding ISO 693-1 codes and first language speakers as percentage of Indian population. Data is collected from 2011 census (Census, 2011).

Why this data set? The data set considers two highly popular YouTube news channels for each of the 12 Indian states that contribute 20 or more seats in the lower house of the parliament. State boundaries in India were drawn along linguistic lines (Dewen, 2010). The dominant regional language in the Hindi belt (Jaffrelot, 2000) is Hindi, and the other states feature a unique dominant language written in either the Latin alphabet (in informal settings) or a native script. All the nine languages we focused on (listed in Table 1), are the dominant language in one or more of these 12 states. The regional news networks considered provide coverage in the dominant regional language. Hence, the data set exhibits strong presence of all the nine regional languages we are interested in. In addition to these 24 regional news channels, the data set considers YouTube channels for 14 highly popular national news outlets (listed in the Appendix). Overall, this implies 38 YouTube channels (24 regional, 14 national) with an average subscriber count of 3,338,628.

3 Related Work

Learning from weak labels: The role of unlabeled and weakly (or noisily) labeled data in supervised learning is a well-studied problem and has received sustained focus (Mitchell, 2004; Donmez et al., 2010), and annotation efficiency in low-resource settings is a well-established requirement (Joshi et al., 2019). Our work leverages $\hat{\mathcal{L}}_{polyglot}$ (Palakodety et al., 2020a), a recently-proposed method for noisy language identification that requires minimal supervision. We utilize it as a dependency to obtain *weak labels* and reduce annotation burden and construct a substantially more robust system.

Language identification: While language identification of well-formed text is a nearly-solved problem, the difficulty in identifying language in a noisy social media setting is well-established (Bergsma et al., 2012; Gella et al., 2014; Lui and Baldwin, 2014; Jaech et al., 2016; Jauhiainen et al., 2019). We see our work as a part of this continuing trend and as an important resource contribution to analyze Indian social media.

Romanized Indian Languages: In the context of processing Indian languages expressed on the web, challenges posed by the use of Roman script instead of the native script have been reported in several recent studies in the context of code-mixed English-Bengali (Chanda et al., 2016), and English-Hindi (Kumar et al., 2018) text. While addressing word level language identification, (Gella et al., 2014) reported that 90% of posts in Indian languages on Facebook are expressed in Roman script. Prevalence of Romanized Hindi has also been previously reported in (Barman et al., 2014). Our study takes previous findings one small step forward with a (noisy) geographical analysis of Hindi web usage.

Bridging the resource gap: We also see our work as a part of the ongoing effort in bridging the resource gap between Indian languages and world languages (Vyas et al., 2014; Vijayakrishna and Sobha, 2008; Kunchukuttan et al., 2014; Mohanty et al., 2017; Joshi et al., 2020).

4 Background

In this section, we summarize a few key NLP models and results critical to our methods.

Skip-gram embeddings: The Skip-gram model takes as input a word $w \in W$ (vocabulary), and predicts words $w_c \in W$ that are likely to occur in the context of w. The training objective (predicting an input word's context) is parameterized by real-valued word representations or embeddings (Mikolov et al., 2013). Bojanowski et al. (2017) introduced sub-word extensions to the Skip-gram model to learn robust word representations even in the presence of misspellings or spelling variations. Following (Palakodety et al., 2020a), we normalize and average a document's constituent word embeddings to yield the *document embedding*.

Monolingual cluster discovery: Palakodety et al. (2020a) introduced a minimal supervision language detection method using polyglot Skip-gram embeddings with sub-word information. These embeddings discover monolingual subsets (clusters) in a multilingual corpus which are subsequently retrieved using k-Means and a small sample per-cluster (10 documents) are annotated. We refer to this method as $\hat{\mathcal{L}}_{polyglot}$ and leverage it for constructing our data set with minimal annotation burden. For obvious reason, we do not compare $\hat{\mathcal{L}}_{polyglot}$ against our supervised solution that supports more than 300 languages. In Section 7.5, we demonstrate that our method detects languages with trace presence in a corpus ($< 1\%$), a known limitation of $\hat{\mathcal{L}}_{polyglot}$ (Palakodety et al., 2020a).

5 Method

Research question: *How to construct an annotation-efficient language identification method supporting a wide array of Indian languages?* Our method has two main components: (i) an annotation-efficient procedure to construct a substantial data set with weak labels, (ii) a supervised system trained on a data set comprising this corpus and an existing data set, $\mathcal{D}_{tatoeba}$ (Tatoeba, 2020), a well-known annotated data set supporting 355 languages (Tatoeba, 2020). For the construction of this data set, the election corpus (Palakodety et al., 2020b) is stripped of all comments containing any non English character. This maintains the focus on Romanized Indian languages with the native variants sourced from $\mathcal{D}_{tatoeba}$.

5.1 Assigning Weak Labels

Algorithm 1 outlines the steps in obtaining weak labels for nine Indian languages from multiple multilingual corpora and combining it with $\mathcal{D}_{tatoeba}$. Our training data set is denoted by
$\mathcal{D} = \{d_i, \mathcal{L}(d_i)\}_{i=1}^{N_1} \cup \{d_i, \hat{\mathcal{L}}(d_i)\}_{i=1}^{N_2}$ where d_i is a document, $\mathcal{L}(.)$ returns a label annotated by a

Algorithm 1: $\mathcal{F}_{weakLabel}(\{\mathcal{D}_1,\ldots,\mathcal{D}_n\})$

Initialization:

$\mathcal{D} \leftarrow \mathcal{D}_{tatoeba}$

foreach $\mathcal{D}_i \in \{\mathcal{D}_1,\ldots,\mathcal{D}_n\}$ **do**

    Run $\hat{\mathcal{L}}_{polyglot}$ on $\mathcal{D}_i$

    Obtain clusters $\mathcal{C}_1,\ldots,\mathcal{C}_K$ using k-means s.t. $|\mathcal{C}_1| \geq |\mathcal{C}_2|\ldots \geq |\mathcal{C}_K|$

    Identify $J \leq K$ dominant clusters

    for $(j = 1; j \leq J; j = j + 1)$ **do**

        Assign language to $\mathcal{C}_j$ (denoted by $\mathcal{L}(\mathcal{C}_j)$), (supplied by the annotator)

        Sample $\gamma|\mathcal{C}_j|$ comments from $\mathcal{C}_j$ ranked by proximity from cluster center, $0 < \gamma \leq 1$

        Add the sampled comments to $\mathcal{D}$ with *weak label* $\mathcal{L}(\mathcal{C}_j)$

    end

end

Output: Return $\mathcal{D}$

---

human, $\hat{\mathcal{L}}(.)$ returns a weak label obtained from $\hat{\mathcal{L}}_{polyglot}$.

$\mathcal{D}$ is initialized with an annotated corpus, $\mathcal{D}_{tatoeba}$ (Tatoeba, 2020), i.e., N_1 is the total number of samples present in $\mathcal{D}_{tatoeba}$. Next, using $\hat{\mathcal{L}}_{polyglot}$, our method obtains *weak labels* for N_2 documents from the election corpus and adds to $\mathcal{D}$.

Our method, $\mathcal{F}_{weakLabel}(.)$, takes an array of n multilingual corpora as inputs, runs $\hat{\mathcal{L}}_{polyglot}$ on each of them to obtain K language clusters, $\mathcal{C}_1,\ldots,\mathcal{C}_K$, such that $|\mathcal{C}_1| \geq |\mathcal{C}_2|\ldots \geq |\mathcal{C}_K|$. J largest of these clusters are selected and annotators assign a language $\mathcal{L}(\mathcal{C}_j)$, $1 \leq j \leq J$. For a given cluster $\mathcal{C}_j$, we obtain a set of pairs $\langle d, \hat{\mathcal{L}}(d)\rangle$ where $d \in \mathcal{C}_j$, and $\hat{\mathcal{L}}(d) = \mathcal{L}(\mathcal{C}_j)$, i.e., the weak label of the document is the cluster's language label. For each of these J clusters, the top γ fraction are chosen for inclusion into $\mathcal{D}$.

To summarize, for each multilingual corpus, $\hat{\mathcal{L}}_{polyglot}$ is used to obtain the top monolingual clusters, and a fraction of those are included with the cluster language label into the data set. Each cluster's language label is assigned by labeling 10 documents in the cluster and thus the vast majority of samples added to the data set is neither manually inspected nor labeled.

Recall that, each of the regional news outlets we considered presents news in one of the dominant regional languages. We group all comments obtained from the news outlets of one particular state as one distinct corpus - i.e. each $\mathcal{D}_i$ consists of comments posted in response to videos from a news outlet from a particular state. The choice of treating each individual state's corpus separately contributes further to annotation efficiency - know-

ing that a corpus is sourced from a region where a certain language is dominant allows us to select the appropriate annotators and reduces the annotation cost per document. We considered comments obtained from the 14 national outlets as a separate corpus. This led to 13 multilingual corpora (12 regional and 1 national). Hence, in our experiments, n, denoting the total number of corpora in Algorithm 1, was set to 13.

Parameter configuration: Our Algorithm has two configurable parameters: (1) j, the number of clusters selected per corpus for inclusion in the final data set, and (2) γ, the fraction of documents per cluster chosen for inclusion. We set j to 2. The choice of j was guided by the intuition that English is widely spoken in India and each state would have at least one dominant regional language. Our choice of γ was guided by an in-depth analysis of $\hat{\mathcal{L}}_{polyglot}$ in the context of code switching (Khud-aBukhsh et al., 2020). The study revealed that documents closest to the cluster centers exhibit strong monolinguality and those farther from the centers can exhibit code-switching or may even be authored in languages with trace presence. In order to obtain high quality weak labels, we set γ to 0.75.

Annotation Efficiency: $\hat{\mathcal{L}}_{polyglot}$ requires 10 annotated samples to assign a language label to a cluster (Palakodety et al., 2020a). Our method requires $10jn$ annotated samples. Hence, our method required $10 \times 2 \times 13 = 260$ annotated comments to construct a corpus of 2,793,375 comments supporting nine Indian languages. This is combined with the $\mathcal{D}_{tatoeba}$ to yield $\mathcal{D}$ consisting of 11,042,839 documents.

Predicted Label

	bn	en	gu	hi	kn	ml	mr	or	ta	te	ol
bn	100	0	0	0	0	0	0	0	0	0	0
en	0	100	0	0	0	0	0	0	0	0	0
gu	0	0	100	0	0	0	0	0	0	0	0
hi	0	0	0	100	0	0	0	0	0	0	0
kn	0	0	0	0	99	0	0	0	0	0	1
ml	0	0	0	0	0	99	0	0	1	0	0
mr	0	0	0	0	0	0	100	0	0	0	0
or	0	0	1	2	0	0	0	96	1	0	0
ta	0	0	0	0	0	0	0	0	100	0	0
te	0	0	0	0	0	0	0	0	0	100	0
ol	0	0	0	0	0	0	0	0	0	0	0

(True Label is the row-axis label for the above matrix.)

Table 2: Confusion matrix of performance evaluation of $\mathcal{F}_{end\text{-}to\text{-}end}$ on 1000 annotated comments. For a given language, better or equal performance than the baseline is highlighted with blue; *ol* denotes other languages.

Predicted Label

	bn	en	gu	hi	kn	ml	mr	or	ta	te	ol
bn	97	0	0	2	0	0	0	0	0	0	1
en	0	99	0	1	0	0	0	0	0	0	0
gu	0	0	92	4	0	0	4	0	0	0	0
hi	0	0	0	99	0	0	1	0	0	0	0
kn	1	1	2	0	86	5	0	0	0	3	2
ml	0	0	0	0	1	95	1	0	2	1	0
mr	0	0	1	0	0	0	99	0	0	0	0
or	20	0	13	18	2	3	16	0	0	4	24
ta	0	0	0	0	3	10	0	0	79	3	5
te	1	0	0	1	1	1	1	0	0	95	0
ol	0	0	0	0	0	0	0	0	0	0	0

(True Label is the row-axis label for the above matrix.)

Table 3: Confusion matrix of performance evaluation of `GoogleLandID` on 1000 annotated comments. For a given language, better or equal performance than $\mathcal{F}_{end\text{-}to\text{-}end}$ is highlighted with blue; *ol* denotes other languages.

5.2 Learning with Weak Labels

Once $\mathcal{D}$ is obtained, we train a classifier that takes as input a document, and predicts the language label. We provide an end-to-end model operating directly on the text and producing a language label. The model utilizes a highly efficient text classification framework introduced in (Joulin et al., 2017). The framework introduces a variety of optimizations and is capable of classifying billions of documents in minutes without compromising on accuracy (implementation details are presented in the Appendix). We refer to this model as $\mathcal{F}_{end\text{-}to\text{-}end}$. The model achieves comparable performance (test accuracy $> 98\%$) against a held out set that is not seen during any of the training phases.

6 Experimental Setup

Test set: We construct an Indian language test set consisting of 1,000 annotated YouTube comments (consensus labels by two proficient annotators per language) in 10 languages (Bengali, English, Gujarati, Hindi, Kannada, Malayalam, Marathi, Odia, Tamil, Telugu), and 100 documents in each language. These documents are randomly sampled from the output of $\mathcal{F}_{weakLabel}$ and are never seen during our supervised training phase with weak labels. The average number of tokens in the comments is 22.6 ± 18.7. Please see Appendix for detailed statistics of our test data set.

Baseline: We consider a commercial solution (Google) that can detect over 100 languages including the 10 mentioned above (referred to as `GoogleLangId`) as our baseline. In addition to `GoogleLangId`, Palakodety et al. (2020a) compared against `FastTextLangID`. We avoid this comparison because we feel it is unfair to compare against `FastTextLangID` given that it does

not support romanized Indic languages (achieves an overall accuracy 10% on our test set). We see our paper as a resource paper that makes a small step forward in addressing the lack of linguistic resources for Indian social media analysis.

Fairness: We first emphasize that the main purpose of comparing against `GoogleLangID` is **not to claim that our annotation-efficient solution is superior to `GoogleLangID` across the board**. Our goal is rather *to attract the research community's attention to our solution's effectiveness in this under-explored, specific domain of noisy social media texts generated in the Indian subcontinent.* A fairer performance comparison between the two methods would require the methods to be trained on identical data sets and comparable computation budget. Due to these varying levels of resources, it is not possible to claim one method's superiority over the other. We are rather highlighting our method's (1) annotation efficiency and (2) ability to extend support for newer languages (e.g., at present `GoogleLangID` has limited support for Odia (*or*) and no support for Assamese *as*).

7 Results and Analysis

Method	Overall accuracy	Excluding Odia
$\mathcal{F}_{end\text{-}to\text{-}end}$	**99.4**	**99.8**
`GoogleLangID`	84.1	93.4

Table 4: Performance comparison. Since it is unclear if `GoogleLangID` supports Odia (*or*), the left-most column presents performance excluding Odia from the test set.

Table 4 summarizes the performance comparison between our proposed classifier and the `GoogleLangID` baseline. Our results indicate that our method considerably outperforms the baseline which is a well-known commercial solution. A closer look at the individual performance of each language (confusion matrices presented in 2 and Table 3) reveals that across all languages, our method performs equal or better than `GoogleLangID`. Although the performance gap primarily stems from our method's overwhelmingly stronger performance in Odia (*or*), we perform considerably better than `GoogleLangID` even if we exclude Odia from the test data set.

Our performance comparison highlights the following two points. First, we reiterate that our goal is not to claim that our method would perform better than `GoogleLangID` across the board, but rather, to demonstrate the value our method adds in processing noisy social media texts. It is possible that our method is more attuned to noisy short social media texts while `GoogleLangID` could be (possibly) trained on cleaner corpora which explains our method's stronger performance. This is further corroborated by the fact that even our mispredictions (barring one) remain confined to the regional languages while many of `GoogleLangID`'s mispredictions are distributed across other languages (*ol*). Second, `GoogleLangID`'s weak performance in detecting Odia highlights the gap in current solutions and shows how our method can effectively and efficiently address these issues[2].

Recall that $\mathcal{D}_{tatoeba}$ contains a large set of languages (including the native script versions of the Indian languages considered in this paper). Test accuracy on a held-out set was 98.4%. Experiments reveal that introduction of the weakly labeled corpus does not impact performance on $\mathcal{D}_{tatoeba}$ (identical test accuracy of 98.4%).

7.1 Extensibility

We constructed a new data set of comments on YouTube videos from an Assamese news channel (News18 Assam/Northeast) and used the same approach of using $\hat{\mathcal{L}}_{polyglot}$ to obtain weak labels for Romanized Assamese. We do not show a direct comparison with `GoogleLangID` because `GoogleLangID` does not support Assamese (*as*). However, on an augmented test data set of 1,100 comments (100 Assamese comments with consensus labels from two annotators), we achieved a

performance of 92% accuracy on identifying Assamese while retaining our previous performance on every other language. Assam has been a center for political debates and unrest in recent times (BBC). Our resource to detect Romanized Assamese can be a vital tool which to the best of our knowledge, does not exist. Details are presented in the Appendix.

7.2 Domain-robustness

Our goal is to present an important Indian NLP resource that can perform well across multiple social media platforms. Hence, it is paramount that our system generalizes well both to *in domain* and *out of domain* instances. In the context of the task of language identification, domain adaption has received recent attention (Li et al., 2018). In this section, we present an analysis on our system's *out of domain* performance.

Data set of Hinglish tweets: We consider a data set of tweets introduced in Mathur et al. (2018). The data set consists of 3,189 tweets written in English (*en*), Romanized Hindi (*hi*) and code-mixed English-Hindi (*en-hi*). We construct a randomly sampled data set of 100 tweets with equal proportion of Hindi and English tweets (consensus labels obtained from two annotators).

As shown in Table 5, our system's *out of domain* performance was consistent with its *in domain* performance. We performed marginally better than `GoogleLangID`. We admit that a more robust test on multiple data sets comprising content from a larger set of Indian languages from other social media platforms would further validate our *out of domain* performance. However, our current experiment indicates that our system's success is not limited to YouTube comment texts, it can generalize to tweets as well.

7.3 Usage Statistics

As demonstrated, our integrated setup covers the Romanized and native script variants of the most prevalent Indian languages. This enables us to

Method	Accuracy	Language	P	R	F1
$\mathcal{F}_{end\text{-}to\text{-}end}$	**0.98**	*en*	**1.00**	**1.00**	**1.00**
		hi	0.96	**0.96**	**0.96**
`GoogleLangID`	0.95	*en*	**1.00**	**1.00**	**1.00**
		hi	**1.00**	0.90	0.95

Table 5: Performance comparison on the tweet data set. Best metric is highlighted in bold for each language. P: precision, R: recall.

---

[2]Odia is listed as one of the supported languages by `GoogleLangID`, it is unclear if this tool supports Romanized Odia. Assamese is not supported by `GoogleLangID`.

State	hi	$hi_{\mathcal{N}}$	$hi \cap hi_{\mathcal{N}}$
Andhra Pradesh	1.66%	0.05%	1.71%
Bihar	67.97%	14.29%	82.26%
Gujarat	24.23%	3.41%	27.64%
Karnataka	1.85%	0.02%	1.87%
Kerala	0.48%	0.02%	0.5%
Madhya Pradesh	76.21%	10.39%	86.60%
Maharashtra	7.46%	4.18%	11.64%
Odisha	9.20%	0.02%	9.22%
Rajasthan	58.48%	29.90%	88.38%
Tamil Nadu	0.22%	0.01%	0.23%
Uttar Pradesh	63.56%	22.23%	85.79%
West Bengal	4.72%	0.18%	4.90%

Table 6: Presence of Hindi. hi is Romanized Hindi. $hi_{\mathcal{N}}$ is Devanagari Hindi. Hindi belt states (Jaffrelot, 2000) are highlighted with blue.

explore research questions on the usage patterns of these Indian languages. This part of our analysis is conducted on the entire election corpus containing comments written in all scripts.

Weak geo-labels: Recall that, all of the 24 regional news outlets we consider present news in the dominant language of their respective states. Hence, it is reasonable to assume that a considerable fraction of users consuming the regional news and participating in the comments section have some affiliation to the region (state). Thus, a comment posted in response to a regional news outlet's video can be assigned a weak/noisy geographic label - the state targeted by the news network. For instance, we assume that a comment posted in response to a Tamil news video clip, is likely to be authored by someone who either resides in or retains strong ties to Tamil Nadu. Combining these weak/noisy geographic labels with our language identification system, we can assess the geographic distribution of language use in India. Note that, these results are only approximate estimates - YouTube comments do not contain any geographic information. Further, it is also not possible to estimate a user's knowledge of other languages through our analysis. For example, if a user comments solely in Hindi, it is not possible to assess their fluency in English or Bengali.

7.4 Hindi Web Usage

Geographic extent of Hindi usage: We label each comment with the language prediction from $\mathcal{F}_{end\text{-}to\text{-}end}$ and a geographic label corresponding to the origin state of the news outlet. All comments posted in Romanized and Devanagari Hindi (denoted by hi and $hi_{\mathcal{N}}$, respectively) are retained and

the resulting choropleth is visualized in Figure 1(b). We also provide in Figure 1(a), the region referred to as the Hindi belt (Jaffrelot, 2000) where Hindi is the first language of the bulk of the population. We observe a strong correlation of the estimated geographic extent of Hindi with the Hindi belt states.

In Table 6, we list the state-wise estimates of Hindi usage in our corpus. Our findings are consistent with existing knowledge of Hindi's geographic spread. In the Hindi belt states, more than 80% of the comments were authored in Hindi. Consistent with census data (Census, 2011) and prior literature (Ramaswamy, 1997), the fraction of Hindi comments discovered in the Tamil Nadu origin subset was minuscule.

Romanized vs Devanagari: As shown in Table 6, the ratio of hi and $hi_{\mathcal{N}}$ usage reveals that a vast majority of internet users eschew the traditional Devanagari script and instead use Roman script. However, the ratio of Roman script to Devanagari script is substantially less lopsided in the Hindi belt states than in the other states. Our studies are consistent with Gella et al. (2014).

Estimating bilinguality: We conduct a user-focused study by computing language usage statistics on a per-user basis. We assume that a user is proficient in a language, $\mathcal{L}$, if she posts two or more comments (in order to accommodate for some estimation error) in $\mathcal{L}$. If a user is estimated to be proficient in two languages, then we label her as bilingual. Romanized and native script comments are both considered to be an equal demonstration of proficiency in a given language. We acknowledge that this is at best a noisy estimate.

Out of 159,993 total users, 41,776 users (26.1%) were marked as bilinguals using $\mathcal{F}_{end\text{-}to\text{-}end}$. According to the 2011 census (Census, 2011), 26% of the Indian population are bilinguals. Hence, surprisingly, our noisy estimate was reasonably close to the ground truth. We observe that over 70% of the discovered bilinguals in our corpus used Hindi-English. A detailed plot is presented in the Appendix.

7.5 Trace Language Detection

We conclude this section with an analysis on (1) to what extent we address $\hat{\mathcal{L}}_{polyglot}$'s inability to detect trace languages, and (2) why it could be worth addressing. Our definition of trace language is corpus-specific. We consider a language $\mathcal{L}$ to be a trace language in a corpus $\mathcal{D}$ if fewer than 1%

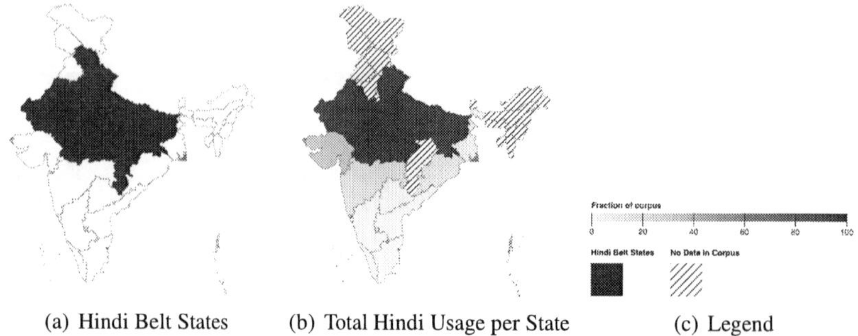

(a) Hindi Belt States   (b) Total Hindi Usage per State   (c) Legend

Figure 1: Choropleths of Hindi usage patterns in India. (a) shows the geographic region identified as the Hindi belt. (b) shows the patterns of Hindi usage. We extend the results for Andhra Pradesh to Telangana, and Bihar to Jharkhand because the same news networks cater to both states. The base maps used for this plot are sourced from the Government of India. The authors are aware that these maps include disputed territories. These maps do not constitute judgments on existing disputes.

Language	Data set	Example comment	Loose translation
bn	$\mathcal{D}_{hope}$	`Indian air force k varote ferea deoar jonno osonkho dhonnobad Pak armyke`	*Thank you Pak army for returning our Indian Air Force (pilot).*
te	$\mathcal{D}_{hope}$	`yudham vasthey manam kuda chala nastha potham...`	*We'll suffer a lot too in the event of war...*
bn	$\mathcal{D}_{help}$	`Tawhid ami rohiggha dhar help korte chai plz amaka hepl korar moto kisu opai bolo bz ami dhashar bahira thaki`	*Tawhid, I want to help the Rohingyas. Please suggest me some ways I can help them. I live outside of the country.*
te	$\mathcal{D}_{help}$	`manama hinduvulama muslim christans ani kadu manushulama aannadi kavali manamu valla paristutulalo unte telustundi`	*Are we Hindu, Muslim, Christian - this is irrelevant, are we human - this is relevant; if we were in their position, we would understand*
bn	$\mathcal{D}_{COVID}$	`Amra 500jon Lok Bangalore atkie Achi please amader Bari. Pouche din ,amader Bari west Bengal India`	*We are 500 people stuck in Bangalore. Please make some arrangements so that we can reach our home in West Bengal, India.*
te	$\mathcal{D}_{COVID}$	`Please sir twitter lo pettandi please nenoka mahilalu 2 chinna pillalu unnaru Sir mem jammikunta lo undipoyamu nijamabad cherela chudandi Sir`	*Please sir, post on Twitter, I'm a woman with 2 small kids, we're stuck in Jammikunta, please help us get to Nijambad*

Table 7: Random sample of comments in trace language detected by our system.

of the documents in $\mathcal{D}$ are authored in $\mathcal{L}$. In this section, we focus on the following three corpora one of which ($\mathcal{D}_{COVID}$) we introduce here:

1. $\mathcal{D}_{hope}$: 2.04 million YouTube comments relevant to the 2019 India-Pakistan conflict (Palakodety et al., 2020a).

2. $\mathcal{D}_{help}$: 263k YouTube comments relevant to the Rohingya refugee crisis (Palakodety et al., 2020c).

3. $\mathcal{D}_{COVID}$: 777,748 comments from 5,301 videos from two highly popular Indian news channels (NDTV and Zee News) posted between 30th January, 2020[3] and 10th April, 2020.

As reported in Palakodety et al. (2020a), $\hat{\mathcal{L}}_{polyglot}$ discovered three clusters in $\mathcal{D}_{hope}$: (1) *en*, (2) *hi* and (3) *hi$_N$*; no other languages were detected. However, in our experiments, we found presence of multiple trace languages. For instance, overall, our method $\mathcal{F}_{end-to-end}$ found 3,373 Telugu (*te*) and 205 Bengali (*bn*) comments in $\mathcal{D}_{hope}$. Human annotation of randomly sampled 100 comments in each of the two languages revealed a precision of 100% and 97% for *te* and *bn*, respectively. Similarly, we conducted a search for *bn* and *te* comments in $\mathcal{D}_{help}$, and found 1,251 and 146 comments, respectively. Human annotation on randomly sampled 100 comments from each of the two languages yielded

---

[3]First COVID-19 positive case was reported in India on this day.

188

precision of 99% for both *bn* and *te*. In Table 7, we list example peace-seeking, hostility-diffusing comments (*hope speech*) and comments indicating support for the disenfranchised Rohingyas (*help speech*).

Finally, when $\mathcal{F}_{end\text{-}to\text{-}end}$ is run on $\mathcal{D}_{COVID}$, we discover comments in several languages requesting assistance during the nationwide lockdown (BBC, 2020). Our method reveals the presence of vulnerable individuals who express themselves in low-resource languages. We hope our tool can open the gates for research in this humanitarian domain.

8   Conclusion

In this paper, we present a language identification tool with a focus on nine major Romanized Indian languages. Despite the widespread use of Romanization on social media, NLP resources and tools often focus more on the native scripts. Our tool integrates with an existing large-scale corpus and holds promise in being a valuable resource for Indian social media analysis. Our pipeline leverages a recent NLP algorithm and obtains weak labels for a large number of samples substantially reducing the annotation cost. Finally, we conduct studies on the geographic extent, bilinguality, and Romanization of Hindi and observe that these align with existing studies and surveys.

References

Utsab Barman, Amitava Das, Joachim Wagner, and Jennifer Foster. 2014. Code mixing: A challenge for language identification in the language of social media. In *Proceedings of the first workshop on computational approaches to code switching*, pages 13–23.

BBC. Why has india's assam erupted over an 'anti-muslim' law? Online; accessed 12-May-2020.

BBC. 2020. Coronavirus: India's pandemic lockdown turns into a human tragedy. Online; accessed 3-June-2020.

Shane Bergsma, Paul McNamee, Mossaab Bagdouri, Clayton Fink, and Theresa Wilson. 2012. Language identification for creating language-specific twitter collections. In *Proceedings of the second workshop on language in social media*, pages 65–74. Association for Computational Linguistics.

Piotr Bojanowski, Edouard Grave, Armand Joulin, and Tomas Mikolov. 2017. Enriching word vectors with subword information. *Transactions of the Association for Computational Linguistics*, 5:135–146.

Census. 2011. 2011 census data. Online; accessed 3-June-2020.

Arunavha Chanda, Dipankar Das, and Chandan Mazumdar. 2016. Unraveling the English-Bengali code-mixing phenomenon. In *Proceedings of the Second Workshop on Computational Approaches to Code Switching*, pages 80–89, Austin, Texas. Association for Computational Linguistics.

Monojit Choudhury, Kalika Bali, Tirthankar Dasgupta, and Anupam Basu. 2010. Resource creation for training and testing of transliteration systems for indian languages. LREC.

Matteo Cinelli, Walter Quattrociocchi, Alessandro Galeazzi, Carlo Michele Valensise, Emanuele Brugnoli, Ana Lucia Schmidt, Paola Zola, Fabiana Zollo, and Antonio Scala. 2020. The covid-19 social media infodemic.

Ma Dewen. 2010. A study on the two waves of states-reorganization in india [j]. *South Asian Studies Quarterly*, 1.

Pinar Donmez, Jaime Carbonell, and Jeff Schneider. 2010. A probabilistic framework to learn from multiple annotators with time-varying accuracy. In *Proceedings of the 2010 SIAM international conference on data mining*, pages 826–837. SIAM.

FastText. FastTextLangID. [Online; accessed 3-June-2020].

Spandana Gella, Kalika Bali, and Monojit Choudhury. 2014. "ye word kis lang ka hai bhai?" testing the limits of word level language identification. In *Proceedings of the 11th International Conference on Natural Language Processing*, pages 368–377.

Google. GoogleLangID. [Online; accessed 3-June-2020].

HindustanTimes. 2019. Youtube now has 265 million users in india. Online; accessed 3-June-2020.

Aaron Jaech, George Mulcaire, Shobhit Hathi, Mari Ostendorf, and Noah A. Smith. 2016. Hierarchical character-word models for language identification. In *Proceedings of The Fourth International Workshop on Natural Language Processing for Social Media*, pages 84–93, Austin, TX, USA. Association for Computational Linguistics.

Christophe Jaffrelot. 2000. The rise of the other backward classes in the hindi belt. *The Journal of Asian Studies*, 59(1):86–108.

Tommi Sakari Jauhiainen, Marco Lui, Marcos Zampieri, Timothy Baldwin, and Krister Lindén. 2019. Automatic language identification in texts: A survey. *Journal of Artificial Intelligence Research*, 65:675–782.

Pratik Joshi, Christain Barnes, Sebastin Santy, Simran Khanuja, Sanket Shah, Anirudh Srinivasan, Satwik Bhattamishra, Sunayana Sitaram, Monojit Choudhury, and Kalika Bali. 2019. Unsung challenges of building and deploying language technologies for low resource language communities. *arXiv preprint arXiv:1912.03457*.

Pratik Joshi, Sebastin Santy, Amar Budhiraja, Kalika Bali, and Monojit Choudhury. 2020. The state and fate of linguistic diversity and inclusion in the nlp world. *arXiv preprint arXiv:2004.09095*.

Armand Joulin, Edouard Grave, Piotr Bojanowski, and Tomas Mikolov. 2017. Bag of tricks for efficient text classification. In *Proceedings of the 15th EACL: Volume 2, Short Papers*, pages 427–431.

Ashiqur R. KhudaBukhsh, Shriphani Palakodety, and Jaime G. Carbonell. 2020. Harnessing code switching to transcend the linguistic barrier. In *Proceedings of the Twenty-Ninth International Joint Conference on Artificial Intelligence, IJCAI 2020*, pages 4366–4374. ijcai.org.

Upendra Kumar, Vishal Singh, Chris Andrew, Santhoshini Reddy, and Amitava Das. 2018. Consonant-vowel sequences as subword units for code-mixed languages. In *Thirty-Second AAAI Conference on Artificial Intelligence*.

Anoop Kunchukuttan, Abhijit Mishra, Rajen Chatterjee, Ritesh Shah, and Pushpak Bhattacharyya. 2014. Sata-anuvadak: Tackling multiway translation of indian languages. *pan*, 841(54,570):4–135.

Yitong Li, Timothy Baldwin, and Trevor Cohn. 2018. What's in a domain? learning domain-robust text representations using adversarial training. In *Proceedings of the 2018 Conference of the North American Chapter of the Association for Computational Linguistics: Human Language Technologies, Volume 2 (Short Papers)*, pages 474–479, New Orleans, Louisiana. Association for Computational Linguistics.

Marco Lui and Timothy Baldwin. 2014. Accurate language identification of twitter messages. In *Proceedings of the 5th workshop on language analysis for social media (LASM)*, pages 17–25.

Puneet Mathur, Ramit Sawhney, Meghna Ayyar, and Rajiv Shah. 2018. Did you offend me? classification of offensive tweets in Hinglish language. In *Proceedings of the 2nd Workshop on Abusive Language Online (ALW2)*, pages 138–148, Brussels, Belgium. Association for Computational Linguistics.

Tomas Mikolov, Kai Chen, Greg Corrado, and Jeffrey Dean. 2013. Efficient estimation of word representations in vector space. In *1st International Conference on Learning Representations*.

Tom M Mitchell. 2004. The role of unlabeled data in supervised learning. In *Language, Knowledge, and Representation*, pages 103–111. Springer.

Gaurav Mohanty, Abishek Kannan, and Radhika Mamidi. 2017. Building a sentiwordnet for odia. In *Proceedings of the 8th Workshop on Computational Approaches to Subjectivity, Sentiment and Social Media Analysis*, pages 143–148.

Shriphani Palakodety, Ashiqur R. KhudaBukhsh, and Jaime G. Carbonell. 2020a. Hope speech detection: A computational analysis of the voice of peace. In *ECAI 2020 - 24th European Conference on Artificial Intelligence*, volume 325 of *Frontiers in Artificial Intelligence and Applications*, pages 1881–1889. IOS Press.

Shriphani Palakodety, Ashiqur R. KhudaBukhsh, and Jaime G. Carbonell. 2020b. Mining insights from large-scale corpora using fine-tuned language models. In *ECAI 2020 - 24th European Conference on Artificial Intelligence*, volume 325 of *Frontiers in Artificial Intelligence and Applications*, pages 1890–1897. IOS Press.

Shriphani Palakodety, Ashiqur R. KhudaBukhsh, and Jaime G. Carbonell. 2020c. Voice for the voiceless: Active sampling to detect comments supporting the rohingyas. In *The Thirty-Fourth AAAI Conference on Artificial Intelligence, AAAI 2020*, pages 454–462.

Sumathi Ramaswamy. 1997. *Passions of the tongue: Language devotion in Tamil India, 1891–1970*, volume 29. Univ of California Press.

Rupak Sarkar, Sayantan Mahinder, Hirak Sarkar, and Ashiqur R. KhudaBukhsh. 2020. Social media attributions in the context of water crisis. In *Empirical Methods in Natural Language Processing (EMNLP), 2020*, page to appear.

Statista. 2020. Most popular social networks worldwide as of january 2020, ranked by number of active users. Online; accessed 3-June-2020.

Tatoeba. 2020. Tatoeba. Online; accessed 3-June-2020.

R Vijayakrishna and L Sobha. 2008. Domain focused named entity recognizer for tamil using conditional random fields. In *Proceedings of the IJCNLP-08 Workshop on Named Entity Recognition for South and South East Asian Languages*.

Paola Virga and Sanjeev Khudanpur. 2003. Transliteration of proper names in cross-lingual information retrieval. In *Proceedings of the ACL 2003 workshop on Multilingual and mixed-language named entity recognition-Volume 15*, pages 57–64. Association for Computational Linguistics.

Yogarshi Vyas, Spandana Gella, Jatin Sharma, Kalika Bali, and Monojit Choudhury. 2014. POS tagging of English-Hindi code-mixed social media content. In *Proceedings of the 2014 Conference on Empirical Methods in Natural Language Processing (EMNLP)*, pages 974–979, Doha, Qatar. Association for Computational Linguistics.

YourStory. 2018. Youtube monthly user base touches 265 million in india, reaches 80 pc of internet population. Online; accessed 3-June-2020.

9 Appendix

9.1 Annotation

All annotations are performed by two native speakers of each of the languages we considered. All labels are consensus labels.

9.2 Detailed Performance with Assamese

Our data set was crawled using publicly available YouTube API on the YouTube channel of CNN News18 Assam/Northeast. Overall, we obtained 66,923 comments from 7,170 videos of which weak labels (4,337 English and 21,411 Assamese) were obtained using $\hat{\mathcal{L}}_{polyglot}$. We augmented our previous training set with these obtained (weak labels) comments. The detailed performance is presented in Table 9.

9.3 Classification Framework

State	Channels
Andhra Pradesh	V6 News Telugu TV9 Telugu Live
Bihar	News18 Bihar Jharkhand ZeeBiharJharkhand
Gujarat	TV9 Gujarati ABP Asmita
Karnataka	TV9 Kannada Suvarna News
Kerala	Asianetnews Manorama News
Madhya Pradesh	News18 MP Chhattisgarh Zee Madhya Pradesh Chhattisgarh
Maharashtra	ABP Majha ZEE 24 TAAS
Odisha	OTV News18 Odia
Rajasthan	News18 Rajasthan ZeeRajasthanNews
Tamil Nadu	Puthiyathalaimurai TV Polimer News
Uttar Pradesh	News18 UP Uttarakhand Zee Uttarpradesh Uttarakhand
West Bengal	ABP ANANDA News18 Bangla

Table 8: Regional channels.

The classification framework we use (Joulin et al., 2017), contains a variety of optimizations focused on text classification - an architecture that enables parameter sharing, and efficient techniques to include token n-grams. The inference phase is able to process and label over 10 million documents in under five minutes (wall clock time).

9.4 Test data set details

100 comments are randomly sampled for each of the 10 languages (*bn, en, gu, hi, kn, ml, mr, or, ta, te*). The average number of tokens in the comments is 22.6 ± 18.7. A language-wise breakdown is presented in Table 10.

Predicted Label

	as	bn	en	gu	hi	kn	ml	mr	or	ta	te	ol
as	92	3	0	1	2	0	0	0	2	0	0	0
bn	0	100	0	0	0	0	0	0	0	0	0	0
en	0	0	100	0	0	0	0	0	0	0	0	0
gu	0	0	0	100	0	0	0	0	0	0	0	0
hi	0	0	0	0	100	0	0	0	0	0	0	0
kn	1	0	0	0	0	99	0	0	0	0	0	0
ml	0	0	0	0	0	0	99	0	0	1	0	0
mr	0	0	0	0	0	0	0	100	0	0	0	0
or	0	0	0	1	2	0	0	0	96	1	0	0
ta	0	0	0	0	0	0	0	0	0	100	0	0
te	0	0	0	0	0	0	0	0	0	0	100	0
ol	0	0	0	0	0	0	0	0	0	0	0	0

(True Label is the row-axis label.)

Table 9: Confusion matrix of performance evaluation of $\mathcal{F}_{end\text{-}to\text{-}end}$ on 1,100 annotated comments; *ol* denotes other languages.

9.5 Language pairs used by bilinguals

Figure 2 summarizes the relative distribution of language pairs in our bilingualism estimation experiment. Results show that Hindi-English bilingualism is the most dominant one.

State	Comment length
as	17.03 ± 19.95
bn	25.19 ± 18.33
en	31.52 ± 27.04
gu	23.82 ± 20.91
hi	24.72 ± 15.33
kn	17.85 ± 10.57
ml	19.91 ± 11.92
mr	25.73 ± 21.88
or	13.34 ± 11.72
ta	21.98 ± 14.59
te	22.05 ± 20.95

Table 10: Statistics of test data set.

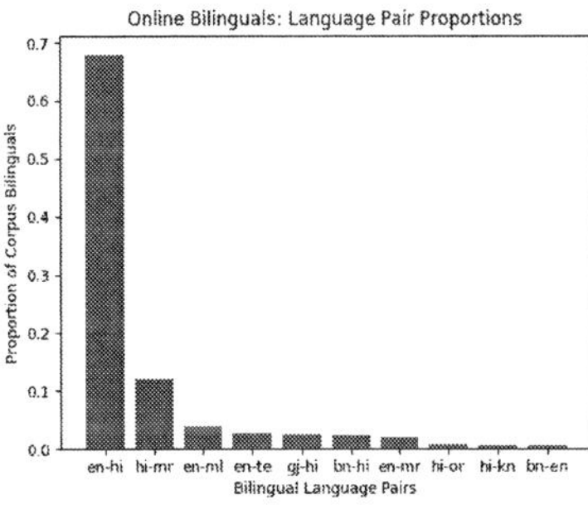

Figure 2: The top language pairs used by bilinguals in our corpus. Hindi and English feature prominently in all the language pairs.

IndiaTV, NDTV India, Republic World, The Times of India, Zee News, Aaj Tak, ABP NEWS, CNN-News18, News18 India, NDTV, TIMES NOW, India Today, The Economic Times, Hindustan Times

Table 11: National channels.

9.6 List of YouTube channels

The YouTube channels considered in Palakodety et al. (2020b) are listed in Table 8 and 11.

Fantastic Features and Where to Find Them: Detecting Cognitive Impairment with a Subsequence Classification Guided Approach

Benjamin Eyre
Winterlight Labs
Toronto, Canada

Aparna Balagopalan
Winterlight Labs
Toronto, Canada

Jekaterina Novikova
Winterlight Labs
Toronto, Canada

{benjamin, aparna, jekaterina}@winterlightlabs.com

Abstract

Despite the widely reported success of embedding-based machine learning methods on natural language processing tasks, the use of more easily interpreted engineered features remains common in fields such as cognitive impairment (CI) detection. Manually engineering features from noisy text is time and resource consuming, and can potentially result in features that do not enhance model performance. To combat this, we describe a new approach to feature engineering that leverages sequential machine learning models and domain knowledge to predict which features help enhance performance. We provide a concrete example of this method on a standard data set of CI speech and demonstrate that CI classification accuracy improves by 2.3% over a strong baseline when using features produced by this method. This demonstration provides an example of how this method can be used to assist classification in fields where interpretability is important, such as health care.

1 Introduction

In recent years, word and sentence embedding-based methods have had a significant impact on the field of NLP (Devlin et al., 2019; Mikolov et al., 2013; Pennington et al., 2014; Di Palo and Parde, 2019). These approaches stand as an alternative to classical feature engineering approaches, where carefully crafted features, such as word length or part of speech tag, are extracted from text and used as input. Despite the promise of embedding-based methods, there are still several advantages to feature engineering. Most notably, using embeddings as input can lead to issues with interpretability (Heimerl and Gleicher, 2018; Hooker et al., 2019; Kindermans et al., 2017), which is especially important in a healthcare domain (Balagopalan et al., 2020). Meanwhile, feature engineering approaches directly lend themselves to easily inter-

pretable models (Ribeiro et al., 2016). As such, feature engineering remains an important practice for fields such as health care, where interpretability is imperative. An extensive body of work has been produced where ML methods and engineered features have been applied to cognitive impairment (CI) detection (Balagopalan et al., 2018; Karlekar et al., 2018; Zhu et al., 2019).

In this work, we present a new feature engineering method that is guided by classifying subsets of a pause-centred speech sequence (subsequences), and inspired by literature suggesting that CI could be indicated by the words that subjects pause before (Calley et al., 2010; Mack et al., 2013; Seifart et al., 2018). This approach aims to extract pause-related information while minimizing the noise added from unrelated factors. This method generates interpretable and effective features, potentially saving time and resources spent on excess feature engineering. We validate this method by presenting a 2.3% accuracy increase over a strong baseline on CI vs healthy (HC) classification, matching the state of the art (Hernández-Domínguez et al., 2018).

In summary, our major contributions are:

• A method of classifying speech using only a token of interest and a small context around it, i.e. *subsequence classification* (Sec. 3.3).

• A novel *feature engineering approach* guided by subseqence classification (Sec. 4).

• Validating this approach by showing that it aids in achieving classification results comparable to the state of the art (Sec. 5.2).

2 Related work

Several authors report increases in CI detection performance by extracting acoustic features such as filled and unfilled pause counts, as well as average pause duration (Tóth et al., 2015, 2018; Pistono

Proceedings of the 2020 EMNLP Workshop W-NUT: The Sixth Workshop on Noisy User-generated Text, pages 193–199
Online, Nov 19, 2020. ©2020 Association for Computational Linguistics

Data Subset	HC	CI	Total
DB (transcripts)	229 (42%)	321 (58%)	550
DB-C1	317 (33%)	645 (67%)	962
DB-C2	511 (35%)	963 (65%)	1,474
DB-C3	529 (35%)	980 (65%)	1,509
DB-Utt	755 (42%)	1,059 (58%)	1,814

Table 1: Overview of the number of samples (subsequences or transcripts) in different subsets of DB.

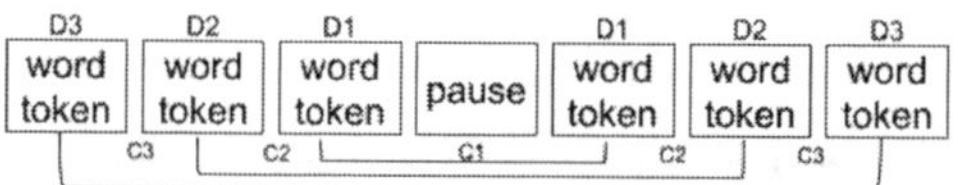

Figure 1: Visualization of the difference between contexts and distances in a pause-focussed subsequence.

et al., 2016). However, we believe further performance increases can be achieved if we focus not only on the pauses themselves, but also the linguistic context in which the pauses occur in speech.

Recently, Hernández-Domínguez et al. (2018) achieved an accuracy of 78% when classifying Dementiabank (Sec. 3.1) transcripts as CI or HC using an extended set of lexical features, which is to the best of our knowledge the state of the art (SOTA). We use their recorded performance as a benchmark when validating our approach.

Several authors have reported performance gains by using subsequences to aid with classification. These authors use subsequences only as a means to process full sequences (Phan et al., 2017), or they use the presence of common subsequences as a feature for longer text sequences (Iglesias et al., 2007; Kumar et al., 2005). To the best of our knowledge, no prior work describes using subsequence classification to guide feature engineering.

3 Experimental Method

In this section, we define the data sets and methodology used in our experimental framework.

3.1 Data Sets

Dementiabank (DB): Dementiabank[1] is a large public data set of pathological speech (Becker et al., 1994), containing audio files and transcripts of participants describing the 'Cookie Theft' image. Transcripts are created manually by trained transcriptionists following the CHAT protocol (MacWhinney, 2014). Out of the 286 participants, 193 are diagnosed with some form of CI (CI; N = 321 transcripts) and 93 are healthy controls (HC; N = 229 transcripts). Transcripts receive a CI or HC label corresponding to whether the participant who produced the transcribed speech was cognitively impaired or not.

Subsequence-based Data Subsets: To conduct subsequence classification, we extract subsequences of varying length from each transcript.

For each transcript in DB, each utterance containing a pause was extracted and labelled as positive if the sample contains CI speech, or negative otherwise. Subsequences were extracted from these utterances by taking the first one, two, or three speech tokens before and after each pause.[2] We created three data subsets by including subsequences of at most one, two, or three tokens around the pause: Context 1 (DB-C1), Context 2 (DB-C2), and Context 3 (DB-C3), respectively. We also included one data subset including full utterances that include pauses, DB-Utt (Tab.1). Identical subsequences found in both classes were removed. Furthermore, subsequences extracted from HC transcripts are labeled as HC, and subsequences extracted from CI transcripts are labeled as CI. We refer to the tokens that are next to the pause as Distance 1 (D1), the tokens that are one token away from the pause as Distance 2 (D2), and the tokens that are two tokens away from the pause as Distance 3 (D3). The differences between *context* and *distance* are shown in Fig.1. For example, for the pause sequence *"The boy is *uh* stealing a cookie"*, only the tokens *"boy"* and *"a"* would be considered the Distance 2 tokens for this sequence, while the tokens *"boy"*, *"is"*, *"*uh*"*, *"stealing"*, and *"a"* would be considered the Context 2 tokens for this sequence.

3.2 Feature Extraction

In this section, we describe how features are extracted on the transcript-level (for transcript classification) and on the token-level (for subsequence classification).

Transcript-Level Features: We extract over 500 linguistic and acoustic features from each transcript, such as part of speech counts and average word length (App.A). These features, referred to as the *Original* feature set, are used to provide a baseline to benchmark transcript-level classification performance. We also use the *Original* feature

---

[1] https://dementia.talkbank.org

[2] If there were less than two or three tokens before or after a pause, the largest possible sequence of tokens was extracted.

set as a base that we extend with newly engineered transcript-level features (Sec. 4). To produce an additional baseline, we perform feature selection on the *Original* feature set, and found $k = 85$ features led to the greatest performance.

Token-Level Features: In order to conduct subsequence classification, we extract features on the token-level for each of the subsequence-based data subsets. Of the *Original* feature set, we select a subset of features that have a clear token-level analogue (App.A). For instance, the transcript-level feature of average word length has the token-level analogue of individual word length. After feature extraction, each token is represented by a 23-dimensional input vector. Consequently, each subsequence in the DB-C1, DB-C2, DB-C3, and DB-Utt data subsets is represented as a T by 23 matrix, where T is the length of the sequence in tokens.

3.3 Classification

In this section, we describe the methodology used for subsequence and transcript classification. Subsequence classification is used to guide the engineering of new features, while transcript classification validates the new features' effectiveness.

Subsequence Classification: Our subsequence classification experiment involves performing 5-fold cross validation with each of the DB-C1, DB-C2, DB-C3, and DB-Utt data subsets. Subsequences are classified as either HC or CI. We conduct classification using GRU-based (Cho et al., 2014) models with an attention mechanism designed for document classification (Yang et al., 2016), with model parameters tuned for each of the data subsets. We report accuracy for M-C1, the model that achieved the highest accuracy on DB-C1, M-C2, the model that achieved the highest accuracy on DB-C2, M-C3, the model that achieved the highest accuracy on DB-C3, and M-Utt, the model that achieved the highest accuracy on DB-Utt (additional training details provided in App.B).

Transcript Classification: We evaluate the efficacy of our feature engineering approach (Sec.4) by performing transcript-level 10-fold cross validation with a variety of feature sets. Transcripts are classified as either HC or CI. We use the *Original* feature set, as well as the top 85 of the *Original* features, based on their ANOVA F-values, as baselines. Additionally, we extend the *Original* feature set with the k best features, based on ANOVA F-values, from each of the feature sets generated using our novel feature engineering approach (Sec. 4), separately. k is optimized for accuracy for each extending feature set separately. To classify DB transcripts, we use 5 ML models: an SVM, a gradient boosting ensemble, a 2-layer neural network (NN), a random forest, and an ensemble of the previous four models (Ens). We report the accuracy (Acc), precision (Prec), sensitivity (Sens), and specificity (Spec) for the model that achieved the greatest cross validated accuracy for each feature set, separately (training details provided in App.B).

4 Proposed Feature Engineering Approach

Our approach to engineering new transcript-level features involves three major steps:

1) Subsequences of varying length centred around a token of interest, in our case a pause, must be extracted from each of the input transcripts and grouped into subsets based on maximum length. Each of the tokens in these subsequences must have token-level features extracted. The token-level features, as well as the central token, should be chosen based on in-domain knowledge.

2) A sequential ML model must be cross validated on each of the subsequence data subsets from the previous step in a subsequence classification experiment. Here, we are specifically attempting to exploit the ability for sequential machine learning models to uncover patterns in sequential data. The mean cross validated accuracy on each of these length-based data subsets should be used as an indicator of how much distinguishing information can be extracted from tokens within the specified range of the pause.

3) Based on the recorded cross validated accuracies from the previous step, transcript-level aggregations of the token-level features must be created at various distances from the pause. We propose two methods of aggregating token-level features (DB-specific details provided in App.A):

- **Continuous features** can be aggregated simply by taking the average of a feature across each of the tokens. An example of this would be calculating the average word length for each of the tokens found at a specified distance from a pause.

- **Categorical features** can be aggregated using counts or ratios, such as the number of nouns occurring at a specified distance from a pause.

These transcript-level aggregates should only be extracted for the distances that produced the great-

Feature Set	Model	Acc	Prec	Sens	Spec
Original	Ens	74.77±0.6*	82.08±0.4*	73.1±0.5*	79.74±0.4*
Original w/ feat.sel.	Ens	75.18±1.4	83.37±1.2	72.21±1.3*	81.67±1.6
Original + F-D1	NN	74.41±1.9*	78.59±1.1*	**77.15±3.3**	72.63±1.9*
Original + F-D2	Ens	**77.09±1.0**	**84.40±0.8**	75.21±1.0	82.32±0.9
Original + F-D3	Ens	76.05±0.8	84.02±0.9	71.92±0.7*	**83.33±1.3**
Original + F-C2	NN	75.14±1.4	79.85±1.5*	76.93±0.9*	74.02±2.5*
Original + F-C3	Ens	74.82±1.2*	83.68±1.2	70.62±1.9*	82.63±1.4

Table 2: Transcript classification performance for each feature set's best performing classification model, averaged across four random seeds. Bold indicates best performance, and * indicates significance ($p < 0.05$) when compared to the model using F-D2 features.

Model	M-C1	M-C2	M-C3	M-Utt
Accuracy	59.6±2.6	**60.7±2.5**	59.8±0.9	60.3±1.0

Table 3: Subsequence classification performance. Accuracy is averaged across four random seeds.

est cross validated accuracy during subsequence classification, as the subsequence classification performance indicates that the features found in that range are the most distinguishing. For instance, if subsequences of up to two tokens around a pause produced the most accurate subsequence classifier, transcript-level aggregates should only be extracted for tokens at the D1 and D2 positions in reference to the pause, and not the D3 position.

To validate this method, we create five transcript-level feature sets: features aggregated from tokens at the D1 position in reference to a pause (*F-D1*), features aggregated from the D2 position (*F-D2*), features aggregated from the D3 position (*F-D3*), the combination of F-D1, F-D2, and F-D3 (*F-C3*), and the combination of F-D1 and F-D2 (*F-C2*).

5   Results

In this section, we report the results for the subsequence and transcript classification experiments.

5.1   Subsequence Classification

After averaging across four random seeds, M-C2 was able to achieve an accuracy of 60.7%, higher than M-C1, M-C3, or M-Utt (Tab.3). This leads us to the conclusion that using features from the two tokens preceding and succeeding a pause could enhance transcript-level classification performance.

5.2   Transcript Classification

We create the F-D1, F-D2, and F-C2 aggregate feature sets, as the highest subsequence classification accuracy was achieved by a model trained on DB-C2. Additionally, in order to validate our claims,

we create F-D3 and F-C3. The highest accuracy of 77.09% on transcript classification is achieved by an ensemble model that used the *Original* + F-D2 feature set (Tab. 2).

Using one of the four random seeds used to produce the average performance metrics presented in Tab. 2, the model using F-D2 features was able to achieve an accuracy of 78.36%, the same as the single-seed SOTA accuracy of 78% (Hernández-Domínguez et al., 2018).

6   Discussion

As shown in Tab. 3 and Tab. 2, features from tokens within 2 tokens of a pause were the most effective in enhancing both subsequence and transcript classification. To determine how these two tasks are connected, we conduct a statistical analysis on the token-level and transcript-level features. Two sided t-tests between features extracted from tokens found at D1, D2, and D3 from different classes show similar patterns for features that are significantly different between classes for both the token and transcript-level. Larger concentrations of distinguishing features are found at D1 and D2 than at D3. This could explain the effectiveness of features from the D2 position in both tasks (Tab. 4).

However, this pattern congruity does not explain why F-D3 features on their own are more effective than F-D1 features on their own. The trend that both the F-D3 and F-C3 feature sets produced greater transcript-level accuracy than the F-D1 feature set, and lower transcript-level accuracy than the F-D2 and F-C2 feature sets, is the same as the trend for the subsequence classification results reported in Tab. 3. This indicates that subsequence classification may be able to provide better insight into potential transcript classification performance than traditional statistical testing.

It is important to consider the implications of producing a model with the F-D2 feature set that

Distance	Token-Level	Transcript-Level
D1	18	12
D2	21	12
D3	7	6

Table 4: Number of features that are significantly different between classes according to two sided t-tests for each distance.

achieved significantly higher accuracy than the most accurate model produced with the F-C3 feature set. As described in Section 3.3, we perform feature selection using ANOVA F-values for each of the aggregate feature sets. Since F-D2 is a subset of F-C3, this implies that this more traditional feature selection method did not select a group of features from F-C3 that was more effective than the features from F-D2, even though it was able to select any and all of the features in F-D2. This serves as a testament to our feature engineering method, as it demonstrates that even popular feature selection methods are not able to completely remove the negative effects of engineering an excessive amount of ineffective features.

Following several other works that used the DB data set (Hernández-Domínguez et al., 2018; Pou-Prom and Rudzicz, 2018; Sarawgi et al., 2020), all of our experiments are conducted with K-fold cross validation. While the small size of the DB data set helps to justify this as a validation procedure, optimizing a cross validated performance metric (accuracy, F1, etc.) may lead results using K-fold cross validation to be an overestimate of generalization performance.

DB-C2 produced a more accurate subsequence classifier than any other data subset of DB. This suggests that the class distinguishing signal from the pause is strongest within a two token radius around the pause. Beyond that radius, the signal may be obstructed by noise from other patterns in speech. However, in different data sets, a different subsequence length may present the strongest, least noisy signal. New aggregate features should be created for tokens within whichever range produces the best subsequence classification performance.

However, our results do indicate that there is a strong link between how well features from certain token positions contribute to both subsequence and transcript classification. This may relate to the effect of noise on those token positions, which we use subsequence classification to identify.

7 Conclusion and Future Work

In this work, we present two principle contributions. First, we describe a novel method for speech classification - subsequence classification - in which speech is modelled as a token of interest, such as a pause, along with surrounding tokens of context. Secondly, we demonstrate how subsequence classification can be used to engineer features that extract distinguishing information while minimizing added noise, and consequently match SOTA performance on a standard data set of CI speech.

Future work should be done to understand why certain context lengths are more conducive for subsequence classification than others, and when that performance can transfer to effective transcript-level classification. Finally, additional work should be done to develop techniques for finding tokens of interest, such as pauses, that can be exploited using our feature engineering technique.

References

Aparna Balagopalan, Benjamin Eyre, and Jekaterina Novikova. 2020. To BERT or Not To BERT: Comparing Speech and Language-based Approaches for Alzheimer's Disease Detection. In *Proceedings of INTERSPEECH*.

Aparna Balagopalan, Jekaterina Novikova, Frank Rudzicz, and Marzyeh Ghassemi. 2018. The effect of heterogeneous data for alzheimer's disease detection from speech. In *Proceedings of the ML4H Workshop at NeurIPS*.

James T Becker, François Boiler, Oscar L Lopez, Judith Saxton, and Karen L McGonigle. 1994. The natural history of Alzheimer's disease: description of study cohort and accuracy of diagnosis. *Archives of Neurology*, 51(6):585–594.

Marc Brysbaert, Amy Beth Warriner, and Victor Kuperman. 2014. Concreteness ratings for 40 thousand generally known english word lemmas. *Behavior Research Methods*, 46(3):904–911.

Clifford S Calley, Gail D Tillman, Kyle Womack, Patricia Moore, John Hart Jr, and Michael A Kraut. 2010. Subjective report of word-finding and memory deficits in normal aging and dementia. *Cognitive and behavioral neurology: official journal of the Society for Behavioral and Cognitive Neurology*, 23(3):185.

Nitesh V Chawla, Kevin W Bowyer, Lawrence O Hall, and W Philip Kegelmeyer. 2002. Smote: synthetic minority over-sampling technique. *Journal of artificial intelligence research*, 16:321–357.

Kyunghyun Cho, Bart Van Merriënboer, Caglar Gulcehre, Dzmitry Bahdanau, Fethi Bougares, Holger Schwenk, and Yoshua Bengio. 2014. Learning phrase representations using rnn encoder-decoder for statistical machine translation. *arXiv preprint arXiv:1406.1078*.

Mark Davies. 2009. The 385+ million word corpus of contemporary american english (1990–2008+): Design, architecture, and linguistic insights. *International journal of corpus linguistics*, 14(2):159–190.

Jacob Devlin, Ming-Wei Chang, Kenton Lee, and Kristina Toutanova. 2019. Bert: Pre-training of deep bidirectional transformers for language understanding. In *Proceedings of the 2019 Conference of the North American Chapter of the Association for Computational Linguistics: Human Language Technologies, Volume 1 (Long and Short Papers)*, pages 4171–4186.

Flavio Di Palo and Natalie Parde. 2019. Enriching neural models with targeted features for dementia detection. *arXiv preprint arXiv:1906.05483*.

Kathleen C Fraser, Jed A Meltzer, and Frank Rudzicz. 2016. Linguistic features identify alzheimer's disease in narrative speech. *Journal of Alzheimer's Disease*, 49(2):407–422.

Florian Heimerl and Michael Gleicher. 2018. Interactive analysis of word vector embeddings. In *Computer Graphics Forum*, volume 37, pages 253–265. Wiley Online Library.

Laura Hernández-Domínguez, Sylvie Ratté, Gerardo Sierra-Martínez, and Andrés Roche-Bergua. 2018. Computer-based evaluation of alzheimer's disease and mild cognitive impairment patients during a picture description task. *Alzheimer's & Dementia: Diagnosis, Assessment & Disease Monitoring*, 10:260–268.

Matthew Honnibal and Ines Montani. 2017. spaCy 2: Natural language understanding with Bloom embeddings, convolutional neural networks and incremental parsing. To appear.

Sara Hooker, Dumitru Erhan, Pieter-Jan Kindermans, and Been Kim. 2019. A benchmark for interpretability methods in deep neural networks. In *Advances in Neural Information Processing Systems*, pages 9737–9748.

José Antonio Iglesias, Agapito Ledezma, and Araceli Sanchis. 2007. Sequence classification using statistical pattern recognition. In *International Symposium on Intelligent Data Analysis*, pages 207–218. Springer.

Sweta Karlekar, Tong Niu, and Mohit Bansal. 2018. Detecting linguistic characteristics of alzheimer's dementia by interpreting neural models. In *Proceedings of NAACL-HLT*, pages 701–707.

Pieter-Jan Kindermans, Sara Hooker, Julius Adebayo, Maximilian Alber, Kristof T Schütt, Sven Dähne, Dumitru Erhan, and Been Kim. 2017. The (un)reliability of saliency methods. *arXiv preprint arXiv:1711.00867*.

N Pradeep Kumar, M Venkateswara Rao, P Radha Krishna, and Raju S Bapi. 2005. Using sub-sequence information with knn for classification of sequential data. In *International Conference on Distributed Computing and Internet Technology*, pages 536–546. Springer.

Victor Kuperman, Hans Stadthagen-Gonzalez, and Marc Brysbaert. 2012. Age-of-acquisition ratings for 30,000 english words. *Behavior research methods*, 44(4):978–990.

Jennifer E Mack, Aya Meltzer-Asscher, Sarah D. Chandler, Sandra Weintraub, Marek Marsel Mesulam, and Cynthia K Thompson. 2013. Word-finding pauses in primary progressive aphasia (ppa): Effects of lexical category. *Procedia - Social and Behavioral Sciences*, 94:129–130.

Brian MacWhinney. 2014. *The CHILDES project: Tools for analyzing talk, Volume I: Transcription format and programs*. Psychology Press.

Tomas Mikolov, Kai Chen, Greg Corrado, and Jeffrey Dean. 2013. Efficient estimation of word representations in vector space. *arXiv preprint arXiv:1301.3781*.

Natalia B Mota, Nivaldo AP Vasconcelos, Nathalia Lemos, Ana C Pieretti, Osame Kinouchi, Guillermo A Cecchi, Mauro Copelli, and Sidarta Ribeiro. 2012. Speech graphs provide a quantitative measure of thought disorder in psychosis. *PloS one*, 7(4):e34928.

Adam Paszke, Sam Gross, Francisco Massa, Adam Lerer, James Bradbury, Gregory Chanan, Trevor Killeen, Zeming Lin, Natalia Gimelshein, Luca Antiga, Alban Desmaison, Andreas Kopf, Edward Yang, Zachary DeVito, Martin Raison, Alykhan Tejani, Sasank Chilamkurthy, Benoit Steiner, Lu Fang, Junjie Bai, and Soumith Chintala. 2019. Pytorch: An imperative style, high-performance deep learning library. In H. Wallach, H. Larochelle, A. Beygelzimer, F. d'Alché-Buc, E. Fox, and R. Garnett, editors, *Advances in Neural Information Processing Systems 32*, pages 8024–8035. Curran Associates, Inc.

Fabian Pedregosa, Gaël Varoquaux, Alexandre Gramfort, Vincent Michel, Bertrand Thirion, Olivier Grisel, Mathieu Blondel, Peter Prettenhofer, Ron Weiss, Vincent Dubourg, et al. 2011. Scikit-learn: Machine learning in python. *the Journal of machine Learning research*, 12:2825–2830.

Jeffrey Pennington, Richard Socher, and Christopher Manning. 2014. Glove: Global vectors for word representation. In *Proceedings of the 2014 Conference on Empirical Methods in Natural Language Processing (EMNLP)*, pages 1532–1543, Doha, Qatar. Association for Computational Linguistics.

Huy Phan, Philipp Koch, Fabrice Katzberg, Marco Maass, Radoslaw Mazur, and Alfred Mertins. 2017. Audio scene classification with deep recurrent neural networks. *arXiv preprint arXiv:1703.04770*.

Aurélie Pistono, Mélanie Jucla, Emmanuel J Barbeau, Laure Saint-Aubert, Béatrice Lemesle, Benjamin Calvet, Barbara Köpke, Michèle Puel, and Jérémie Pariente. 2016. Pauses during autobiographical discourse reflect episodic memory processes in early alzheimer's disease. *Journal of Alzheimer's Disease*, 50(3):687–698.

Chloé Pou-Prom and Frank Rudzicz. 2018. Learning multiview embeddings for assessing dementia. In *Proceedings of the 2018 Conference on Empirical Methods in Natural Language Processing*, pages 2812–2817.

Marco Tulio Ribeiro, Sameer Singh, and Carlos Guestrin. 2016. Why should i trust you?: Explaining the predictions of any classifier. In *Proceedings of the 22nd ACM SIGKDD international conference on knowledge discovery and data mining*, pages 1135–1144. ACM.

Utkarsh Sarawgi, Wazeer Zulfikar, Nouran Soliman, and Pattie Maes. 2020. Multimodal inductive transfer learning for detection of alzheimer's dementia and its severity. *arXiv preprint arXiv:2009.00700*.

Frank Seifart, Jan Strunk, Swintha Danielsen, Iren Hartmann, Brigitte Pakendorf, Søren Wichmann, Alena Witzlack-Makarevich, Nivja H de Jong, and Balthasar Bickel. 2018. Nouns slow down speech across structurally and culturally diverse languages. *Proceedings of the National Academy of Sciences*, 115(22):5720–5725.

Hans Stadthagen-Gonzalez and Colin J. Davis. 2006. The bristol norms for age of acquisition, imageability, and familiarity. *Behavior Research Methods*, 38(4):598–605.

Laszló Tóth, Gábor Gosztolya, Veronika Vincze, Ildikó Hoffmann, Gréta Szatlóczki, Edit Biró, Fruzsina Zsura, Magdolna Pákáski, and János Kálmán. 2015. Automatic detection of mild cognitive impairment from spontaneous speech using asr. In *Sixteenth Annual Conference of the International Speech Communication Association*.

László Tóth, Ildikó Hoffmann, Gábor Gosztolya, Veronika Vincze, Gréta Szatlóczki, Zoltán Bánréti, Magdolna Pákáski, and János Kálmán. 2018. A speech recognition-based solution for the automatic detection of mild cognitive impairment from spontaneous speech. *Current Alzheimer Research*, 15(2):130–138.

Amy Beth Warriner, Victor Kuperman, and Marc Brysbaert. 2013. Norms of valence, arousal, and dominance for 13,915 english lemmas. *Behavior Research Methods*, 45(4):1191–1207.

Zichao Yang, Diyi Yang, Chris Dyer, Xiodong He, Alex Smola, and Hovy. 2016. Hierarchical attention networks for document classification. In *Proceedings of NAACL-HLT*, pages 1480–1489.

Zining Zhu, Jekaterina Novikova, and Frank Rudzicz. 2019. Detecting cognitive impairments by agreeing on interpretations of linguistic features. In *Proceedings of the 2019 Conference of the North American Chapter of the Association for Computational Linguistics: Human Language Technologies, Volume 1 (Long and Short Papers)*, pages 1431–1441.

Quantifying the Evaluation of Heuristic Methods for Textual Data Augmentation

Omid Kashefi and **Rebecca Hwa**
School of Computing and information
University of Pittsburgh
{kashefi, hwa}@cs.pitt.edu

Abstract

Data augmentation has been shown to be effective in providing more training data for machine learning and resulting in more robust classifiers. However, for some problems, there may be multiple augmentation heuristics, and the choices of which one to use may significantly impact the success of the training. In this work, we propose a metric for evaluating augmentation heuristics; specifically, we quantify the extent to which an example is "hard to distinguish" by considering the difference between the distribution of the augmented samples of different classes. Experimenting with multiple heuristics in two prediction tasks (positive/negative sentiment and verbosity/conciseness) validates our claims by revealing the connection between the distribution difference of different classes and the classification accuracy.

1 Introduction

Machine learning approaches have been shown to be capable of making accurate predictions in many well-known problem domains with an abundance of training data. This heavy reliance on the availability of the data, however, may hamper the application of machine learning approaches to resource-limited problem domains, where a sizable training data are not always available.

There is a growing body of research on training under resource scarcity, and data augmentation is one of such techniques. It aims to reconcile the data requirement of the machine learning approaches by applying a general (e.g., randomly remove a word) or domain-inspired heuristic (e.g., replace an adjective with an antonym) to the (limited) existing data in order to generate more training samples.

One challenge for data augmentation is in choosing the most appropriate heuristic for the application in question. There may be many domain-independent augmentation heuristics, and a domain expert may come up with many different domain-inspired heuristics; but the choices of which examples from these heuristics to use may have a significant impact on the success of the trained model.

A straightforward approach to choose an augmentation heuristic is to actually perform the classification experiment on all possible augmented datasets and then chose the best performing one(s) based on the evaluative results. However, this approach may not be computationally practical when there are too many augmentation heuristic options.

In this paper, we propose an alternative heuristic evaluation approach based on the idea that a good heuristic should aim to generate *"hard to distinguish"* samples for different classes. We further argue that the generation quality of "hard to distinguish" examples could be quantified as the difference between the distribution of the augmented samples that a heuristic generates for different classes.

To calculate the distribution difference, we proposed to use pre-trained off-the-shelf embeddings to convert sentences into class distributions, then calculate the KL-divergence between them and used that as a metric to evaluate the "hard to distinguish" examples that a heuristic produces.

We validate our proposed heuristic evaluation approach by experimenting with multiple heuristics and augmented datasets for two classification tasks: predicting whether a sentence expresses positive or negative sentiment and predicting whether a sentence is verbose or concise. Results suggest that quantifying the "hard to distinguish" example generation quality of the heuristics as the difference between class distribution of the augmented examples, could be served as an effective metric for choosing a suitable augmented dataset for a classification task.

Proceedings of the 2020 EMNLP Workshop W-NUT: The Sixth Workshop on Noisy User-generated Text, pages 200–208
Online, Nov 19, 2020. ©2020 Association for Computational Linguistics

2 Data Augmentation

Data augmentation is a technique for generating additional training data by applying a heuristic transformation to the existing training examples. For example, an existing image could by rescaled or flipped to get more images with the same label to expand the size and diversity of the training dataset and thus train a more reliable and accurate model (Frénay and Verleysen, 2014; Hendrycks et al., 2018; Shorten and Khoshgoftaar, 2019).

In general, data augmentation could be formulated as Equation 1, where h is a heuristic function that transforms the datapoint and label pair of (x, y) to a new augmented sample $(\hat{x}, \hat{y})$.

$$(\hat{x}, \hat{y}) = h(x, y) \tag{1}$$

The majority of existing data augmentation approaches are *label-preserving*, which relaxes the Equation 1 as $(\hat{x}, y) = h(x, y) = (h(x), y)$; this means, if x belong to some class A, augmented $\hat{x}$ also belong to class A. For example, using a synonym replacement heuristic, a sentence with positive sentiment could be augmented into a new example, while preserving the overall positive sentiment. Label-preserving data augmentation requires existing labeled samples for every class that is needed to be augmented.

Data augmentation can be *non-label-preserving* as well, where the label itself might also transform using function h_y that expands Equation 1 as:

$$(\hat{x}, \hat{y}) = h(x, y) = (h_x(x), h_y(y))$$

This means, while x belongs to class A, $\hat{x}$ might not necessarily belong to class A. For example, by replacing the most positive word(s) of a sentence with positive sentiment with an antonym, the sentence's sentiment may become negative. Non-label-preserving data augmentation is not bound to the assumption of having labeled samples for instances of all classes and samples from one class may be enough to generate instances of other classes.

Given a classification task, there may be multiple heuristics and data augmentation approaches that allow us to transform existing samples to new ones, but the choice of heuristic may significantly impact the success of the task. In this paper, we aim to answer the key question: *"which heuristic and data augmentation approach is more appropriate for a classification task?"* In Section 3, we propose a low-cost approach to quantify the evaluation of different heuristics and the resulting augmented datasets for classification tasks.

We believe our proposed approach could be a contribution to the NLP community because data augmentation has been shown to be useful for many NLP applications, with researchers proposing many different approaches for text data augmentation; for example, (Zhang et al., 2015; Wei and Zou, 2019) used thesaurus-based and (Wang and Yang, 2015; Kobayashi, 2018; Jiao et al., 2019) used embedding-based lexical substitution approach, (Wei and Zou, 2019; Xie et al., 2019) used random noise injection, including random word insertion, deletion, or sentence shuffling, (Luque, 2019) used instance crossover by combining halves of tweets, (Guo et al., 2019) adapt the mixup approach (Zhang et al., 2018) to text by interpolating the distributed representation of different sentences, (Sennrich et al., 2016; Fadaee et al., 2017; Xie et al., 2019) used back-translation, and (Hu et al., 2017; Iyyer et al., 2018; Anaby-Tavor et al., 2020; Kumar et al., 2020) used (deep) generative models to augment more training examples.

However, with all these textual augmentation options, trying all of them for a (classifier) training task might be impractical, and to our best knowledge, there is not a guideline for how to choose between them for a task.

3 Quantification of Heuristics Suitability

A straightforward approach to assess which heuristic and data augmentation approach is more appropriate for the task is to try every heuristic to generate an augmented dataset, then train a classifier on each and check the final classification performance (Qiu et al., 2020; Wei and Zou, 2019). The training process in this brute-force approach, however, may be time-consuming and resource-intensive, especially in complex training scenarios.

Alternatively, we may try to identify qualities that make a heuristic effective. Intuitively, a good heuristic ought to generate augmented samples that are the most similar to the original data distribution. However, this approach may overlook the additional generalization benefit that may come from diverse augmented training examples. Moreover, this approach may not be possible for problem domains with limited resources, where original labeled data is not available for all classes, and one may have to use non-label-preserving heuristics to augment examples for all classes.

On the other hand, from the classification task perspective, a good heuristic should aim to generate near-miss examples (samples of class B hard to distinguish from A). We believe, the "hard to distinguish" samples can be quantified by finding a way to compute the difference between the samples of different classes, to sever as an guideline for choosing between different heuristic approaches.

Let us assume samples of class A are drawn from distribution A, which should be different from distribution B that samples of class B are drawn from. The difference between distribution A and B can be calculated as the KL-divergence (KLD) (Kullback and Leibler, 1951) from B to A as: $D_{KL}(A||B)$. KLD calculates how probability distribution A is different from the reference probability distribution B as the amount of information gained if samples of B are used instead of samples of A.

Thus, a lower $D_{KL}(A||B)$ means distribution A is more similar to distribution B, so samples of class A are *harder to distinguish* from samples of class B. Therefore, the extent to which "hard to distinguish" samples can be generated by heuristic h could be quantified as $D_{KL}(A_h||B_h)$, where A_h and B_h indicate the samples of class A and B augmented using heuristic h, and Equation 2 could be used to identify which heuristic is generating "harder to distinguish" samples and so more suitable for the classification task.

$$\arg \min_h D_{KL}(A_h||B_h) \qquad (2)$$

Finally, to transform sentences from their discrete word representation into a continuous distribution representation, we utilize a few of the numerous pre-trained embeddings that nowadays are the de facto approach for encoding sentences into vector space (Cho et al., 2014; Le and Mikolov, 2014; Cer et al., 2018; Devlin et al., 2019).

We examine the applicability of our proposed approach by studying two classification tasks: *sentiment analysis*, as a resource-rich problem domain that allows experimenting with both label-preserving and non-label-preserving heuristics, and *verbosity analysis*, as a resource-limited problem domain that the absence of sizable labeled data limits the options to non-label-preserving heuristics.

4 Augmented Datasets

In this section, we go over some heuristic options for augmenting training corpora for sentiment analysis and verbosity detection domains.

4.1 Augmented Sentiment Corpus

Our sentiment analysis task is to predict whether a sentence expresses *positive*, *negative*, or *neutral* sentiment? For this task, we use the sentences from the Yelp Polarity Dataset (YPD) (Zhang et al., 2015) to create the augmented dataset.

As *label-preserving* heuristics, we use following heuristics proposed by Wei and Zou (2019):

- **Synonym Replacement (SR).** Randomly pick a content word from the sentence and replace it with a synonym chosen at random.

- **Random Insertion (RI).** Randomly choose a content word from the sentence and insert one of its synonyms to a random place in the sentence.

- **Random Swap (RS).** Swap the position of two randomly chosen words in the sentence.

- **Random Deletion (RD).** Delete a randomly chosen word from the sentence.

We apply these heuristics to the positive sentences of YPD to generate more positive examples, and the other way around for generating more negative examples. For each sentence, we repeat each heuristic operation until about 20% of its words are changed ($\alpha = .2$).

Moreover, we propose the following *non-label-preserving* heuristics and apply them to the positive sentences to create the augmented negative examples, and the other way around for generating the augmented positive examples.

- **ALL.** In this heuristic, we replace all the sentiment words of a sentence with their antonyms. To find the sentiment words, we first collected a vocabulary of positive and negative unigrams by combing the labeled words of *Stanford Sentiment Treebank* (Socher et al., 2013) and the *Opinion Lexicon* (Hu and Liu, 2004). This results in a vocabulary of 3,453 positive and 6,000 negative unigrams.

  Then, for a positive sentence in YPD, we replace every word of it that appeared in the positive portion of the collected vocabulary by one of its randomly chosen antonyms, using WordNet (Miller, 1995), to create the augmented negative sentence. We perform similarly but in the opposite direction to create the augmented positive sentences.

Heuristic	Sentence	Label
None	super generous portion !	positive
SR	super generous ~~portion~~ **+slice** !	positive
RI	super **+slice** generous portion !	positive
RS	**portion**← generous →**super** !	positive
RD	super generous ~~portion~~ !	positive
ALL	~~super~~ **+lousy** ~~generous~~ **+meager** portion!	negative
ONE	super ~~generous~~ **+meager** portion !	negative

Table 1: Examples of Sentences Augmented using Label-Preserving (SR, RI, RS, and RD) and Non-Label-Preserving (ALL and ONE) Sentiment Heuristics

- **ONE.** In this heuristic, instead of replacing all sentiment words with their randomly chosen antonym, we first filtered for antonyms that match the POS and sense of the sentiment word, then we pick the antonym that makes the most fluent augmented sentences, ranked by a language model (LM) trained on YPD. Finally, for every sentence, we only replace one of its sentiment words with its POS, sense, and LM filtered antonym.

  Using this heuristic, for example, a sentence with overall positive polarity may still contain a word that expresses a negative opinion about an aspect, so intuitively, this creates "harder to distinguish" examples compared to the **ALL** heuristic.

In total, we generated 50K positive and 50K negative augmented samples using each heuristic. We removed all of the original YPD sentences so that these datasets contain only augmented samples. We refer to each dataset with the same name as the heuristic function it is augmented with. Table 1 shows examples of sentences augmented using the label-preserving and non-label-preserving sentiment heuristics.

4.2 Augmented Verbosity Corpus

The verbosity detection task is to predict whether a sentence is *verbose* or *concise*. Unlike the sentiment analysis domain, the set of existing resources for the verbosity detection problem is much more limited: NUCLE covers grammatical redundancy (Dahlmeier et al., 2013), and Kashefi et al. (2018) has a small corpus called Semantic Pleonasm Corpus (**SPC**) that contains semantic redundancy (i.e.,

verbosity) labels. Due to its small size, it is primarily suitable as a benchmark.

Since to the best of our knowledge, there is no sizable resource with explicit *verbose* and *concise* labels, to augment a dataset of concise and verbose sentences, we start by trying to identify an existing real-world data source that has verbosity or conciseness characteristics. One domain-specific feature of Yelp that we exploit is the data category called "tips." Since "tips" are very short sentences, they are likely to be concise; we sample for "tips" that contain adjectives because the evaluation corpus (i.e. SPC) mainly focuses on adjectival semantic redundancies.

Based on domain knowledge, we come up with the following *non-label-preserving* heuristics to create verbose samples based on the collected "concise" sentences by adding a superfluous adjective to the concise sentences:

- **Duplicate (DUP).** This heuristic is an obvious case for word redundancy by duplicating an adjective word of the sentence right next to itself.

- **Synonym (SYN).** This heuristic inserts a synonym next to an adjective word of the sentence. The conventional way to get synonyms of a word is to use WordNet, however, since these synonyms may express a different quality of the noun clause compared to the original adjective, augmented construction might not be semantically redundant.

  For this reason, we opt to use sense2vec (Trask et al., 2015), a contextual word-embedding fine-tuned on Yelp "tips". Since the adjective synonyms from sense2vec are matching the context and follow the same intent and emotional state of the original adjective, these two adjacent synonyms are likely to make a pleonastic construction.

- **Near-Miss Negative (NMN).** In this heuristic, we try to create **concise** examples that are "hard to distinguish" from the verbose examples. We trained a language model on the Yelp "tips" and used that to predict the most likely words that can occur right after an adjective of the sentence. Let assume for adjective w_{adj} in sentence s, using LM, we retrieved $\{w_{aug1}, w_{aug2}, ..., w_{aug5}\}$ as a sorted list of most likely words that can appear next to w_{adj} given its context s.

Heuristic	Sentence	Label
None	delicious bread !	concise
DUP	delicious **+delicious** bread !	verbose
SYN	delicious **+tasty** bread !	verbose
NMN	delicious **+redolent** bread !	concise

Table 2: Examples of Sentences Augmented using the Verbosity Heuristics

We then filter for w_{aug}s that are adjective themselves and a synonym of w_{adj}, lets assume the filtered list be $\{w_{aug2}, w_{aug5}\}$. Since LM is trained on Yelp, the w_{aug2} is already observed in the Yelp tips after the w_{adj} in some context. Taking into account that Yelp tips are considered concise, the sequence of $... w_{adj} w_{aug2} ...$ is also concise. Therefore, we can create concise examples that are containing two adjacent synonyms but are **not** verbose

For each heuristic, we generate only one augmented verbose sample from an original concise sentence. In total, we augmented 100K concise and 100K verbose samples using each heuristic. Since the verbose examples are generated from concise sentences that are included in the augmented corpus, we removed the concise sentences with odd and verbose sentences with even indexes to make sure that non of the concise are verbose sentences in the corpus are corresponding to each other. The final augmented corpus, thus, contains 50K non-parallel samples of each class. We refer to each dataset with the same name as the heuristic function that was used to augment it.

Table 2 shows examples of sentences augmented using the non-label-preserving verbosity heuristics. While duplicating the word "delicious" or adding "tasty" next to it makes the sentence verbose, adding "redolent" does not make it verbose because "redolent" and "delicious" are describing different quality of the "bread."

5 Experiments

The key questions for validating our proposed approach for quantifying the evaluation of heuristic textual data augmentation methods are:

- **Q1.** Can generating "hard to distinguish" examples be an effective way to assess whether a heuristic is generating a suitable augmented training dataset?

- **Q2.** To what extent could the notion of "hard to distinguish" examples be quantified by our proposed metric – the difference between the class distribution of the augmented samples?

- **Q3.** Is calculating the difference of class distributions computationally efficient in practice?

To measure the accuracy of sentiment and verbosity classification in answering **Q1**, we trained an **LSTM** (Liu et al., 2016) and a **CNN** (Kim, 2014) classifier on each the augmented dataset. The classification result for each task and augmented dataset is reported in Section 5.2.

The LSTM and CNN models are trained on augmented corpora separately for each task; the sentiment classifiers are evaluated on a held-out portion of the YPD, and the verbosity classifiers are evaluated on SPC. None of the sentences of the held-out YPD and SPC are used during the creation of the augmented datasets.

To answer **Q2**, we use two pre-trained encoder models: Universal Sentence Encoder (**USE**) (Cer et al., 2018) and Bidirectional Encoder Representations from Transformers (**BERT**) (Devlin et al., 2019), both of which are transformer-based encoder of greater-than-word length text, to transform the sentences into a continuous space so that we can treat them as class distributions and measure their similarity.

5.1 Classification Accuracy

If a good heuristic is the one that generates "hard to distinguish" examples, the dataset augmented using **ONE** should train a better classifier than **ALL** for the sentiment analysis task, and the verbosity classifier trained on **NMN** should outperform the classifiers trained on **SYN** and **DUP**.

Table 3 and Table 4 show the classification accuracy of the neural models trained on different augmented datasets for sentiment and verbosity prediction tasks, and as we expected, heuristics that intuitively generate "harder to distinguish" examples are more suitable for the prediction task and trained a better classifier on both tasks:

Sentiment Classification Accuracy:
$$ACC(ONE) > ACC(ALL)$$

Verbosity Classification Accuracy:
$$ACC(NMN) > ACC(SYN) > ACC(DUP)$$

Dataset		Model	ACC	KLD	
				USE	BERT
Label-Preserving	RS	LSTM	.943		
		CNN	.966	16.78	5.33
		AVG	.954		
	SR	LSTM	.941		
		CNN	.962	19.84	7.27
		AVG	.951		
	RI	LSTM	.936		
		CNN	.944	24.11	9.84
		AVG	.940		
	RD	LSTM	.930		
		CNN	.938	23.99	12.15
		AVG	.934		
Non-Label-Preserving	ALL	LSTM	.683		
		CNN	.716	26.26	13.97
		AVG	.699		
	ONE	LSTM	.808		
		CNN	.822	17.41	9.90
		AVG	.815		

Table 3: Sentiment Classification Accuracy and Difference between Augmented Positive and Negative Distributions

Dataset		Model	ACC	KLD	
				USE	BERT
Non-Label-Preserving	DUP	LSTM	.393		
		CNN	.442	14.86	15.90
		AVG	.417		
	SYN	LSTM	.526		
		CNN	.551	10.23	12.99
		AVG	.538		
	NMN	LSTM	.692		
		CNN	.738	8.91	7.77
		AVG	.715		

Table 4: Verbosity Classification Accuracy and Difference between Augmented Verbose and Concise Distributions

These observations suggest that an augmented dataset generated from a heuristic that produces "harder to distinguish" examples for different classes could train a better classifier (**Q1**).

Since label-preserving heuristics do not change the class label of the samples, the extent to which "hard to distinguish" examples can be generated rely heavily on their existence in the original data. Thus, we cannot intuitively predict which label-preserving heuristic might be a better choice, however, in Section 5.2, we further study whether our purposed heuristic evaluation approach is applicable to label-preserving heuristics.

5.2 Augmented Distribution Difference

To investigate the extent to which "hard to distinguish" examples might be quantified as a difference between the distribution of the augmented samples of different classes, we first encode the augmented sentences into a continuous high dimensional vector space; then, we computed the difference between the distribution of the augmented samples of different classes as the divergence from high dimensional representation of one class to another.

For the sentiment analysis task, we computed the difference between augmented positive and negative distribution as follow, where E is either BERT or USE encoders, and *positive* and *negative* indicate augmented positive and negative examples respectively:

$$D_{KL}(E(positive)\|E(negative))$$

The distribution difference for the verbosity analysis task is calculated as follow, where *concise* and *verbose* indicate augmented concise and verbose examples respectively:

$$D_{KL}(E(concise)\|E(verbose))$$

It must be noted that since there is no correspondence between the augmented examples of different classes, we computed the difference as the average KL-Divergence over mini-batches of the size 64 samples from the shuffled augmented dataset for 10 epochs (the same batch and epoch values used for training LSTM and CNN models).

Table 3 shows the distribution difference between augmented *positive* and *negative* samples for the sentiment analysis task. As shown, although the average classification accuracy of models trained on label-preserving heuristics are only marginally different, the divergence between distributions of augmented examples with positive and negative sentiments are following the reverse order for both

BERT and USE representations, with one exception for USE representation of RI compared to RD:

– Label-Preserving Heuristics –

Sentiment Classification Accuracy:
$$ACC(RS) > ACC(SR) > ACC(RI) > ACC(RD)$$

Positive Distribution vs. Negative Distribution:
$$KLD(RS) < KLD(SR) < KLD(RI) < KLD(RD)$$

Since the non-label-preserving heuristics apply significant semantic changes to the original samples to change its class label, it is expected that the choice of heuristic should have a more noticeable impact on the classification accuracy compared to the augmentation using label-preserving heuristics. We also observe the same results for non-label-preserving heuristics: augmented dataset with higher classification accuracy has lower divergence between distributions of their positive and negative examples:

– Non-Label-Preserving Sentiment Heuristics –

Sentiment Classification Accuracy:
$$ACC(ONE) >> ACC(ALL)$$

Positive Distribution vs. Negative Distribution:
$$KLD(ONE) < KLD(ALL)$$

Table 4 shows the distribution difference between augmented *concise* and *verbose* samples for the verbosity prediction task. Here, similar to the sentiment analysis task, we observe that the divergence between distributions of augmented concise and verbose examples are following the reverse order of classification accuracy for both BERT and USE representations:

– Non-Label-Preserving Verbosity Heuristics –

Verbosity Classification Accuracy:
$$ACC(NMN) > ACC(SYN) > ACC(DUP)$$

Verbose Distribution vs. Concise Distribution:
$$KLD(NMN) < KLD(SYN) < KLD(DUP)$$

Encoding		KLD	Classification	
USE	**BERT**		**LSTM**	**CNN**
33.2s	92.8s	13.4s	2773s	878s
AVG: 63s				
Overall: 76.4s			**AVG:** 1825.5s	

Table 5: Execution Time of Our Proposed Heuristic Suitability Evaluation Approach Compared to the Classifier Training Time

These observations may indicate that the extent to which a heuristic might generate "hard to distinguish" examples could be quantified as the difference (divergence) between the distribution of augmented examples in different classes (**Q2**).

5.3 Computational Efficiency

Now that we have investigated the role of "hard to distinguish" examples in the success of training a classifier (**Q1**) and how to quantify that (**Q2**), it is time to evaluate the computational efficiency of our purposed approach to see how practical it is compared to training a separate classifier for each augmented dataset and pick the best performing one(s) (**Q3**).

To investigate this, we calculated the time for encoding the augmented examples into continuous space and the time requires for computing the KLD and compared them with the time required for training a classifier on an augmented dataset.

Table 5 shows the average execution time of our proposed approach for evaluating the suitability of different data augmentation heuristics and training neural classifiers on augmented datasets. Reported numbers are averaged over sentiment and verbosity prediction tasks for all augmented datasets. Encoding is a one-time process for each augmented dataset, and numbers reported under KLD and Classification columns are the overall execution time after 10 epochs of training on an NVIDIA Tesla P100 GPU.

We observed that encoding and divergence calculation times only depend on the number of samples and the classification task and choice of heuristic is not affecting the execution times. We also observed that the training time for both LSTM and CNN also highly depends on the number of training samples, and changing tasks and augmented dataset only slightly change the training time (standard deviation of 9.4s and 6.8s, respectively).

Execution times are showing that our proposed heuristic evaluation approach is about 25 times faster than training a classifier; this may suggest that our proposed approach could be a low-cost alternative solution for assessing the suitability of the heuristic strategies for augmenting training dataset for different classification tasks, especially for complex training scenarios when training many classifiers on different augmented dataset might not be computationally practical (**Q3**).

6   Conclusion

This paper presents an approach for evaluating the suitability of augmentation heuristics for classifications task via "hard to distinguish" example generation capacity of the heuristics through analyzing the difference of class distribution of the augmented examples.

Experimental results suggest our proposed heuristic evaluation approach could be a low-cost yet effective way of measuring the suitability of an augmented heuristic for a classification task.

Acknowledgments

We would like to thank the anonymous reviewers for their helpful comments. This material is based upon work supported by the National Science Foundation under Grant Number 1735752.

References

Ateret Anaby-Tavor, Boaz Carmeli, Esther Goldbraich, Amir Kantor, George Kour, Segev Shlomov, Naama Tepper, and Naama Zwerdling. 2020. Not Enough Data? Deep Learning to the Rescue! In *AAAI*.

Daniel Cer, Yinfei Yang, Sheng-yi Kong, Nan Hua, Nicole Limtiaco, Rhomni St John, Noah Constant, Mario Guajardo-Céspedes, Steve Yuan, Chris Tar, Yun-Hsuan Sung, Brian Strope, and Ray Kurzweil Google Research Mountain View. 2018. Universal Sentence Encoder. *Computing Research Repository*, arXiv:1803.11175.

Kyunghyun Cho, Bart Van Merriënboer, Caglar Gulcehre, Dzmitry Bahdanau, Fethi Bougares, Holger Schwenk, and Yoshua Bengio. 2014. Learning Phrase Representations using RNN Encoder-Decoder for Statistical Machine Translation. In *EMNLP*.

Daniel Dahlmeier, Hwee Tou Ng, and Siew Mei Wu. 2013. Building a Large Annotated Corpus of Learner English: The NUS Corpus of Learner English. In *SIGEDU*.

Jacob Devlin, Ming-Wei Chang, Kenton Lee, and Kristina Toutanova. 2019. BERT: Pre-training of Deep Bidirectional Transformers for Language Understanding. In *NAACL*.

Marzieh Fadaee, Arianna Bisazza, and Christof Monz. 2017. Data Augmentation for Low-Resource Neural Machine Translation. In *NAACL*.

Benoît Frénay and Michel Verleysen. 2014. Classification in the Presence of Label Noise: a Survey. *IEEE Transactions on Neural Networks and Learning Systems*, 25(5):845.

Hongyu Guo, Yongyi Mao, and Richong Zhang. 2019. Augmenting Data with Mixup for Sentence Classification: An Empirical Study. *Computing Research Repository*, arXiv:1905.08941.

Dan Hendrycks, Mantas Mazeika, Duncan Wilson, and Kevin Gimpel. 2018. Using Trusted Data to Train Deep Networks on Labels Corrupted by Severe Noise. In *NIPS*.

Minqing Hu and Bing Liu. 2004. Mining and Summarizing Customer Reviews. In *KDD*.

Zhiting Hu, Zichao Yang, Xiaodan Liang, Ruslan Salakhutdinov, and Eric P Xing. 2017. Toward Controlled Generation of Text. In *ICML*.

Mohit Iyyer, John Wieting, Kevin Gimpel, and Luke Zettlemoyer. 2018. Adversarial Example Generation with Syntactically Controlled Paraphrase Networks. In *NAACL*.

Xiaoqi Jiao, Yichun Yin, Lifeng Shang, Xin Jiang, Xiao Chen, Linlin Li, Fang Wang, and Qun Liu. 2019. TinyBERT: Distilling BERT for Natural Language Understanding. *Computing Research Repository*, arXiv:1909.10351.

Omid Kashefi, Andrew T Lucas, and Rebecca Hwa. 2018. Semantic Pleonasm Detection. In *NAACL*.

Yoon Kim. 2014. Convolutional Neural Networks for Sentence Classification. *EMNLP*.

Sosuke Kobayashi. 2018. Contextual Augmentation: Data Augmentation by Words with Paradigmatic Relations. In *NAACL*.

S. Kullback and R. A. Leibler. 1951. On Information and Sufficiency. *The Annals of Mathematical Statistics*, 22(1):79–86.

Varun Kumar, Ashutosh Choudhary, and Eunah Cho. 2020. Data Augmentation using Pre-trained Transformer Models. *Computing Research Repository*, arXive: 2003.02245.

Quoc Le and Tomas Mikolov. 2014. Distributed Representations of Sentences and Documents. In *ICML*.

Pengfei Liu, Xipeng Qiu, and Xuanjing Huang. 2016. Recurrent Neural Network for Text Classification with Multi-Task Learning. In *IJCAI*.

Franco M. Luque. 2019. Atalaya at TASS 2019: Data Augmentation and Robust Embeddings for Sentiment Analysis. In *TASS: Workshop on Sentiment Analysis at SEPLN*.

George A. Miller. 1995. WordNet: a lexical database for English. *Communications of the ACM*, 38(11):39–41.

Siyuan Qiu, Binxia Xu, Jie Zhang, Yafang Wang, Xiaoyu Shen, Gerard de Melo, Chong Long, and Xiaolong Li. 2020. EasyAug: An Automatic Textual Data Augmentation Platform for Classification Tasks. In *The Web Conference*.

Rico Sennrich, Barry Haddow, and Alexandra Birch. 2016. Improving Neural Machine Translation Models with Monolingual Data. In *ACL*.

Connor Shorten and Taghi M. Khoshgoftaar. 2019. A survey on Image Data Augmentation for Deep Learning. *Journal of Big Data*, 6(1):1–48.

Richard Socher, Alex Perelygin, Jean Y Wu, Jason Chuang, Christopher D Manning, Andrew Y Ng, and Christopher Potts. 2013. Recursive Deep Models for Semantic Compositionality Over a Sentiment Treebank. In *EMNLP*.

Andrew Trask, Phil Michalak, and John Liu. 2015. sense2vec - A Fast and Accurate Method for Word Sense Disambiguation In Neural Word Embeddings. *Computing Research Repository*, arXiv:1511.06388.

William Yang Wang and Diyi Yang. 2015. That's So Annoying!!!: A Lexical and Frame-Semantic Embedding Based Data Augmentation Approach to Automatic Categorization of Annoying Behaviors using #petpeeve Tweets. In *EMNLP*.

Jason Wei and Kai Zou. 2019. EDA: Easy data augmentation techniques for boosting performance on text classification tasks. In *EMNLP*.

Qizhe Xie, Zihang Dai, Eduard Hovy, Minh-Thang Luong, and Quoc V. Le. 2019. Unsupervised Data Augmentation for Consistency Training. *Computing Research Repository*, arXive: 1904.12848.

Hongyi Zhang, Moustapha Cisse, Yann N. Dauphin, and David Lopez-Paz. 2018. mixup: Beyond Empirical Risk Minimization. In *ICLR*.

Xiang Zhang, Junbo Zhao, and Yann Lecun. 2015. Character-level Convolutional Networks for Text Classification. In *NIPS*.

An Empirical Survey of Unsupervised Text Representation Methods on Twitter Data

Lili Wang[1], Chongyang Gao[2], Jason Wei[3], Weicheng Ma[4], Ruibo Liu[5], and Soroush Vosoughi[6]

[1,2,4,5,6]Department of Computer Science, Dartmouth College
[3]ProtagoLabs
[1,2,4,5]`{first.last.gr}@dartmouth.edu`
[3]`jason@protagolabs.com`
[6]`soroush.vosoughi@dartmouth.edu`

Abstract

The field of NLP has seen unprecedented achievements in recent years. Most notably, with the advent of large-scale pre-trained Transformer-based language models, such as BERT, there has been a noticeable improvement in text representation. It is, however, unclear whether these improvements translate to noisy user-generated text, such as tweets. In this paper, we present an experimental survey of a wide range of well-known text representation techniques for the task of text clustering on noisy Twitter data. Our results indicate that the more advanced models do not necessarily work best on tweets and that more exploration in this area is needed.

1 Introduction

Recent years have witnessed an exponential increase in the usage of social media platforms. These platforms have become an important part of politics, business, entertainment, and general social life. Correspondingly, the amount of data generated by users on these platforms has also grown exponentially. Though data on social media includes various modalities, such as images, videos, and graphs, text is by far the largest type of data generated by users. Thus, in order to extract knowledge and insight from social media, sophisticated text processing models are needed. Luckily, in parallel to the growth of social media, there has been a rapid rise in the development of sophisticated text representation techniques, the most recent being large-scale pre-trained language models that use Transformer-based architecture (Vaswani et al., 2017)(such as BERT (Devlin et al., 2018), and XLNet(Yang et al., 2019)). These methods can generate general-purpose vector representations of documents that can be used for any downstream task (e.g., sentiment classification).

However, the representation power of these methods for data from social media is not well understood. This is especially true for tweets which are usually short, noisy, and idiosyncratic. This paper is an attempt to evaluate and catalogue the representation power of a wide range of methods for tweets, starting from very simple bag-of-words representations (or embeddings) to representations generated by recent Transformer-based models, such as BERT. Since we are interested in the general representation power of the methods and not their performance on any specific downstream tasks, we do not fine-tune any of the methods using downstream tasks and use unsupervised evaluation (i.e., clustering) for our survey.

2 Text Representation Methods

In this section, we briefly introduce the methods used in our survey, sorted from oldest to newest. For word embedding methods like word2vec, GloVe, and fastText, which dot not explicitly support sentence embeddings, we average the word embeddings to get sentence embeddings. For deep models like ELMo, BERT, ALBERT, and XLNet, we take the average of the hidden state of the last layer on the input sequence axis. Note that some other works use the hidden state of the first token ([CLS]), but in our experiments, we use the pre-trained model without fine-tuning, in this case, the hidden state of [CLS] is not a good sentence representation. Note that we use all these deep neural models without fine-tuning. This is because fine-tuning is usually based on specific downstream tasks which bias the information in the hidden states, weakening the general representation. Note that when we refer to n-gram models we mean models that capture all grams up to and including the n-gram (e.g., bigram models will include bigrams and unigrams).

Proceedings of the 2020 EMNLP Workshop W-NUT: The Sixth Workshop on Noisy User-generated Text, pages 209–214
Online, Nov 19, 2020. ©2020 Association for Computational Linguistics

1. bag-of-words (BoW). This is a representation of text that describes the occurrence of words within a document. In our experiments, we use a random sample of 5 million tweets collected from the Internet Archive Twitter dataset [1] (IAT) to create a vocabulary. We also remove stop words from the tweets. We try unigram, bigram, and trigram models.

2. TF-IDF.. Term frequency–inverse document frequency (TF-IDF) reflects how important a word is with respect to documents in a collection or corpus. We use a similar experimental setup as BoW.

3. LDA (Hoffman et al., 2010). Latent Dirichlet allocation (LDA) is a generative statistical model for capturing the topic distribution of documents in a corpus. We train this model on the IAT dataset. We also remove stop-words and train models with 5, 10, 20, and 100 topics.

4. word2vec (Mikolov et al., 2013). word2vec is a distributed representation of words based on a model trained on predicting the current word from surrounding context words (CBOW). We train unigram, bigram, and trigram word2vec models using the IAT dataset.

5. doc2vec (Le and Mikolov, 2014). This model extends word2vec by adding another document vector based on ID. Our model is trained on the IAT dataset.

6. GloVe (Pennington et al., 2014). This model combines global matrix factorization and local context window methods for training distributed representations. We use the 200-dimensional version that was pre-trained on 2 billion tweets.

7. fastText (Joulin et al., 2016). fastText is another word embedding method that extends word2vec by representing each word as an n-gram of characters. We use the 300-dimensional off-the-shelf version which was pre-trained on Wikipedia.

8. Tweet2vec (Dhingra et al., 2016). This model finds vector-space representations of whole tweets by learning complex, non-local dependencies in character sequences. In our experiments, we use the pre-trained best model provided by the authors.[2]

9. Universal Sentence Encoder (USE) (Cer et al., 2018). USE encodes sentences into high dimensional vectors. The pre-trained encoder comes in two versions, one trained with deep averaging network (DAN) (Iyyer et al., 2015) and one with Transformer. We use the DAN version of USE.

10. ELMo (Peters et al., 2018). This method provides context-dependent word representations based on bidirectional language models. We use the version pre-trained on the One Billion Word Benchmark.

11. BERT (Devlin et al., 2018). BERT is a large-scale Transformer-based language representation model (Vaswani et al., 2017). We use two off-the-shelf pre-trained versions BERT-base and BERT-large, which are pre-trained on the BooksCorpus and English Wikipedia respectively.

12. ALBERT (Lan et al., 2019). This is a lite version of BERT, with far fewer parameters. We use two off-the-shelf versions, ALBERT-base and ALBERT-large, which are pre-trained on the BooksCorpus and English Wikipedia respectively.

13. XLNet (Yang et al., 2019). This is an autoregressive Transformer-based language model. Like BERT, XLNet is a large-scale language model with millions of parameters. We use the off-the-shelf versions pre-trained on the BooksCorpus and English Wikipedia.

14. Sentence-BERT (Reimers and Gurevych, 2019). Sentence-BERT modifies BERT by using siamese and triplet network structures to derive semantically meaningful sentence embeddings. We use five off-the-shelf versions provided by the authors, Sentence-BERT-base, Sentence-BERT-large, Sentence-Distilbert, Sentence-RoBERTa-base, and Sentence-RoBERTa-large, all pre-trained on NLI data.

3 Experiments

Since we are interested in measuring the general text representation power of our methods, we use clustering as a way to evaluate the representations generated by each model (instead of any downstream supervised tasks). We use the vector representations of each tweet to run k-means clustering for different values of k. We use two tweet datasets for our evaluation. The tweets in these datasets have labels corresponding to their topic which we use as cluster ground-truth for evaluation purposes.

Dataset 1 (Zubiaga et al., 2015): This dataset includes 356,782 tweets belonging to 1,036 topics.

---

[1] https://archive.org/search.php?query=collection%3Atwitterstream&sort=-publicdate

[2] https://github.com/bdhingra/tweet2vec/tree/master/tweet2vec/best_model There is another tweet2vec model that uses a character-level cnn-lstm encoder-decoder (Vosoughi et al., 2016), but for the sake of brevity we only show the results for one of the tweet2vec models.

We use $k \in \{200, 400, 600, 800, 1000\}$, for this dataset.

Dataset 2 (Rosenthal et al., 2017): This dataset includes 35,323 tweets belonging to 374 topics. We use $k \in \{100, 200, 300, 400, 500\}$, for this dataset.

3.1 Evaluation Metrics

We use a total of six metrics for evaluating the "goodness" of our clusters, described below. Except for the Silhouette score, all other metrics rely on ground-truth labels.

Silhouette score (Rousseeuw, 1987): A good clustering will produce clusters where the elements inside the same cluster are close to each other and the elements in different clusters are far from each other. The Silhouette score takes both these factors into account. The score goes from -1.0 to 1.0, where higher values mean better clustering.

Homogeneity, Completeness, and V-measure, (Rosenberg and Hirschberg, 2007): If clusters contain only data points that are members of a single class, in other words, high homogeneity, this usually indicates good clustering. Similarly, if all members of a given class are assigned to the same cluster, in other words, high completeness, this usually indicates good clustering. The Homogeneity and Completeness scores are between 0.0 and 1.0, where higher values correspond to better clustering. The V-measure score is the harmonic mean of Homogeneity and Completeness.

Adjusted Rand Index (ARI) (Hubert and Arabie, 1985): The Rand Index can be used to compute the similarity between generated clusters and ground-truth labels. This is done by considering all pairs of samples and seeing whether their label agreement (i.e., belonging to the same ground-truth cluster or not) matches the generated cluster agreement (i.e., belonging to the same generated cluster or not). The raw RI score is then "adjusted for chance" into the ARI. score using the following formula: The ARI score can be between -1.0 and 1.0, where random clusterings have an ARI close to 0.0 and 1.0 stands for perfect clustering.

Adjusted Mutual Information (AMI) (Vinh et al., 2010): The Mutual Information (MI) score is an information-theoretic metric that measures the amount of "shared information" between two clusterings. The Adjusted Mutual Information (AMI) is an adjustment of the Mutual Information (MI) score to account for chance. It accounts for the fact that the MI is generally higher for two cluster-

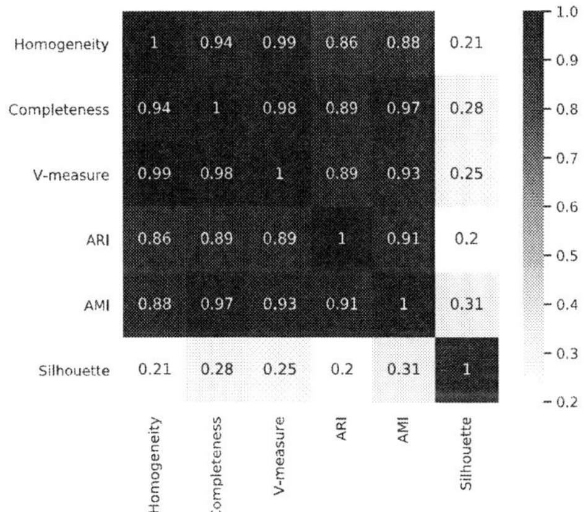

Figure 1: Confusion matrix of the correlation (Pearson's r) between each pair of methods.

ings with a larger number of clusters, regardless of whether there is actually more information shared. The AMI score can be between 0.0 and 1.0, where random clusterings have an AMI close to 0.0 and 1.0 stands for perfect clustering.

4 Results & Discussion

For each dataset, we average the scores from k-means clustering with different values of k. Though we use several metrics in our evaluations for the sake of being thorough, most of the metrics are in fact highly correlated. Fig. 1 shows the correlation between each pair of metrics (calculated based on the clustering results of our methods). We can see that all the *external* evaluation metrics (Homogeneity, Completeness, V-measure, AMI, and ARI, which need external ground-truth labels) highly agree with each other while the *internal* evaluation metric (Silhouette score, which does not need external ground-truth labels) does not.

The clustering results are shown in Fig. 2 and Fig. 3, the methods in both figures are sorted based on the date of their release to capture the advancements in NLP. Unlike conventional tasks and datasets (such as the GLUE benchmark (Wang et al., 2018)), there does not seem to be a very clear trend of improvement for capturing tweet representations. The more advanced models are not necessarily the best. Notably, the BERT family of large-scale pre-trained language models (ALBERT, Sentence-BERT, etc) do not vastly or consistently outperform much simpler methods such as bag-of-words and tf-idf. XLNet, on the other hand, seems to be the best performing method for cap-

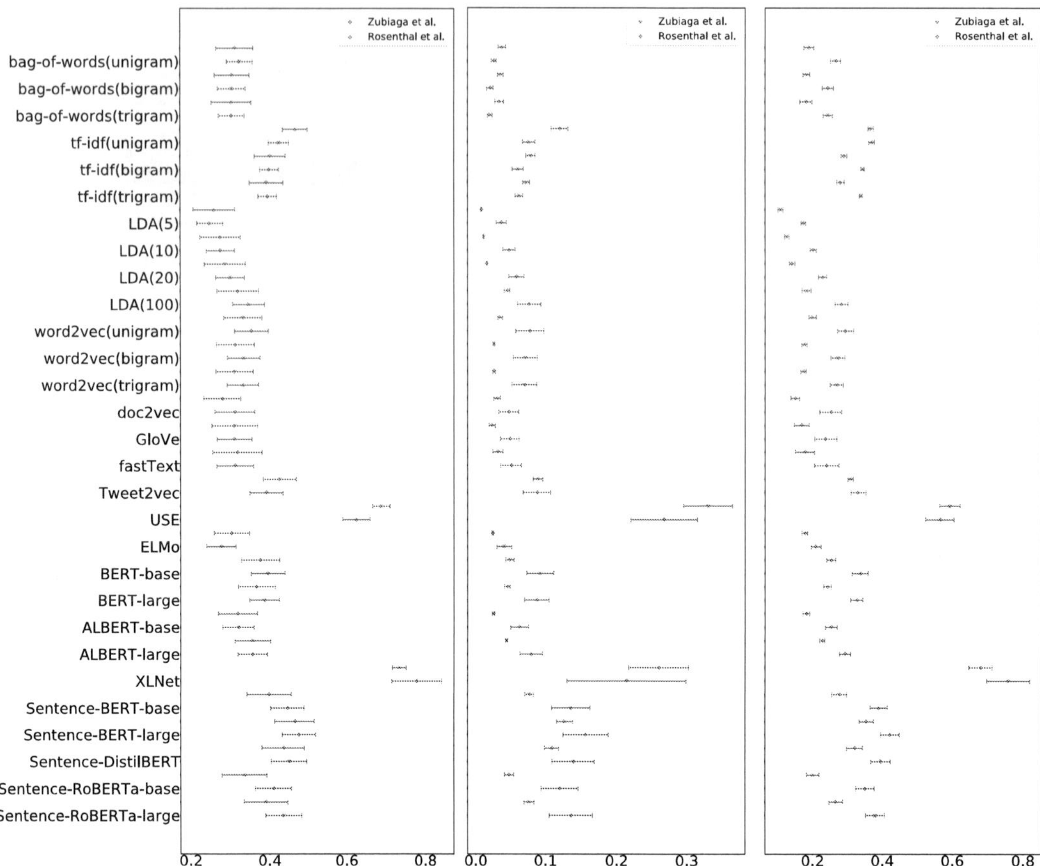

Figure 2: The V-measure (left), ARI (middle), and AMI (right) of all the methods on the two datasets. The points in the figure denote the average value across different k values and the blue lines denote the standard deviations. The methods are sorted from the oldest to the newest.

turing tweet representations, followed closely by USE. Interestingly, XLNet is also the most volatile with respect to the choice of k in our clustering. We think XLNet outperforms other comparable (in terms of complexity) models such as BERT since it uses permutation language modeling, allowing for prediction of tokens in random order. This might make it more robust to the noisy user-generated text, such as tweets. We think that our results are unexpected and inconclusive, demonstrating that much is still unknown about the performance of the most recent models on noisy and idiosyncratic user-generated text.

Very recently, a large-scale pre-trained BERT model for English Tweets was trained and released (Nguyen et al., 2020). This model was released just days before the publication of this paper and thus we did not have time to thoroughly compare its performance against the other models. However, we believe this model is a step in the right direction

as we have shown in this paper that models trained on standard English corpora do not perform well on Tweets.

5   Conclusion

In this paper, we presented an experimental survey of 14 methods for representing noisy user-generated text prevalent in tweets. These methods ranged from very simple bag-of-words representations to complex pre-trained language models with millions of parameters. Through clustering experiments, we showed that the advances in NLP do not necessarily translate to better representation of tweet data.

We believe more work is needed to better understand and potentially improve the performance of the more recent methods, such as BERT, on noisy, user-generated data.

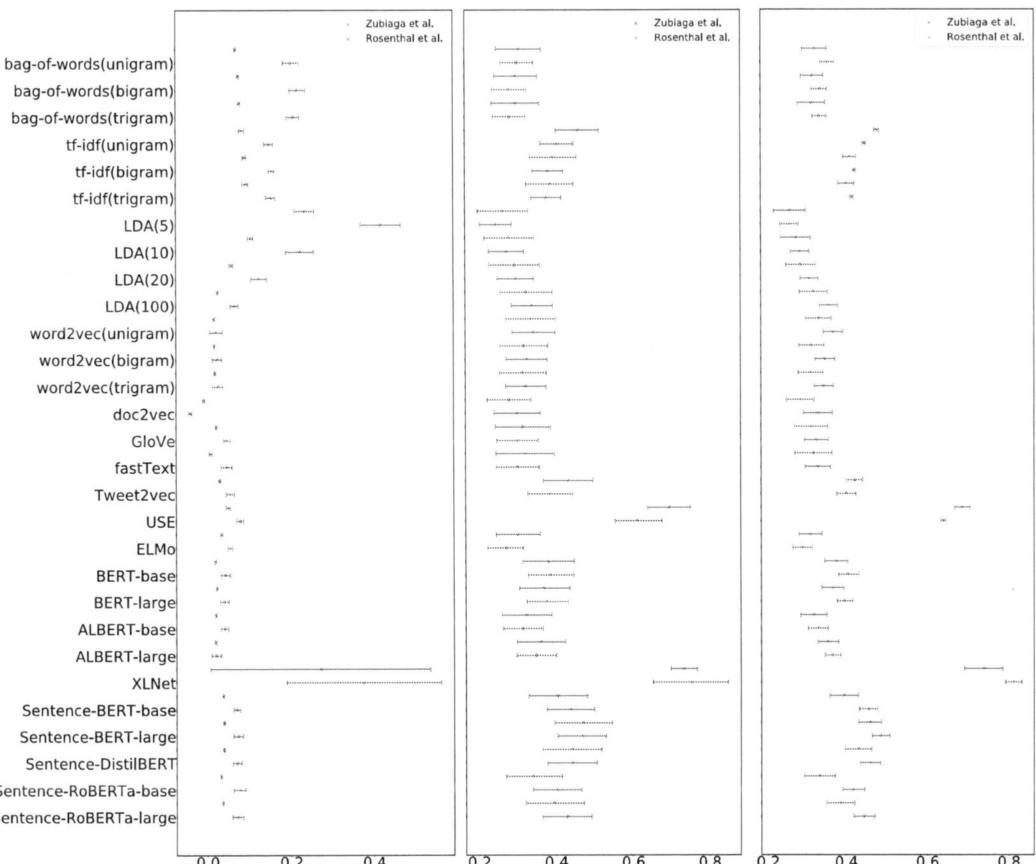

Figure 3: The Silhouette (left), Homogeneity (middle), and Completeness (right) of all the methods on the two datasets. The points in the figure denote the average value across different k values and the blue lines denote the standard deviations. The methods are sorted from the oldest to the newest.

References

Daniel Cer, Yinfei Yang, Sheng-yi Kong, Nan Hua, Nicole Limtiaco, Rhomni St John, Noah Constant, Mario Guajardo-Cespedes, Steve Yuan, Chris Tar, et al. 2018. Universal sentence encoder. *arXiv preprint arXiv:1803.11175*.

Jacob Devlin, Ming-Wei Chang, Kenton Lee, and Kristina Toutanova. 2018. Bert: Pre-training of deep bidirectional transformers for language understanding. *arXiv preprint arXiv:1810.04805*.

Bhuwan Dhingra, Zhong Zhou, Dylan Fitzpatrick, Michael Muehl, and William Cohen. 2016. Tweet2vec: Character-based distributed representations for social media. In *Proceedings of the 54th Annual Meeting of the Association for Computational Linguistics (Volume 2: Short Papers)*, pages 269–274, Berlin, Germany. Association for Computational Linguistics.

Matthew Hoffman, Francis R Bach, and David M Blei. 2010. Online learning for latent dirichlet allocation. In *advances in neural information processing systems*, pages 856–864.

Lawrence Hubert and Phipps Arabie. 1985. Comparing partitions. *Journal of classification*, 2(1):193–218.

Mohit Iyyer, Varun Manjunatha, Jordan Boyd-Graber, and Hal Daumé III. 2015. Deep unordered composition rivals syntactic methods for text classification. In *Proceedings of the 53rd annual meeting of the association for computational linguistics and the 7th international joint conference on natural language processing (volume 1: Long papers)*, pages 1681–1691.

Armand Joulin, Edouard Grave, Piotr Bojanowski, and Tomas Mikolov. 2016. Bag of tricks for efficient text classification. *arXiv preprint arXiv:1607.01759*.

Zhenzhong Lan, Mingda Chen, Sebastian Goodman, Kevin Gimpel, Piyush Sharma, and Radu Soricut. 2019. Albert: A lite bert for self-supervised learning of language representations. *arXiv preprint arXiv:1909.11942*.

Quoc Le and Tomas Mikolov. 2014. Distributed representations of sentences and documents. In *Interna-*

213

tional conference on machine learning, pages 1188–1196.

Tomas Mikolov, Kai Chen, Greg Corrado, and Jeffrey Dean. 2013. Efficient estimation of word representations in vector space. *arXiv preprint arXiv:1301.3781*.

Dat Quoc Nguyen, Thanh Vu, and Anh Tuan Nguyen. 2020. Bertweet: A pre-trained language model for english tweets. *arXiv preprint arXiv:2005.10200*.

Jeffrey Pennington, Richard Socher, and Christopher D Manning. 2014. Glove: Global vectors for word representation. In *Proceedings of the 2014 conference on empirical methods in natural language processing (EMNLP)*, pages 1532–1543.

Matthew E. Peters, Mark Neumann, Mohit Iyyer, Matt Gardner, Christopher Clark, Kenton Lee, and Luke Zettlemoyer. 2018. Deep contextualized word representations. In *Proc. of NAACL*.

Nils Reimers and Iryna Gurevych. 2019. Sentence-bert: Sentence embeddings using siamese bert-networks. In *Proceedings of the 2019 Conference on Empirical Methods in Natural Language Processing*. Association for Computational Linguistics.

Andrew Rosenberg and Julia Hirschberg. 2007. V-measure: A conditional entropy-based external cluster evaluation measure. In *Proceedings of the 2007 joint conference on empirical methods in natural language processing and computational natural language learning (EMNLP-CoNLL)*, pages 410–420.

Sara Rosenthal, Noura Farra, and Preslav Nakov. 2017. SemEval-2017 task 4: Sentiment analysis in twitter. In *Proceedings of the 11th International Workshop on Semantic Evaluation (SemEval-2017)*, pages 502–518, Vancouver, Canada. Association for Computational Linguistics.

Peter J Rousseeuw. 1987. Silhouettes: a graphical aid to the interpretation and validation of cluster analysis. *Journal of computational and applied mathematics*, 20:53–65.

Ashish Vaswani, Noam Shazeer, Niki Parmar, Jakob Uszkoreit, Llion Jones, Aidan N Gomez, Łukasz Kaiser, and Illia Polosukhin. 2017. Attention is all you need. In *Advances in neural information processing systems*, pages 5998–6008.

Nguyen Xuan Vinh, Julien Epps, and James Bailey. 2010. Information theoretic measures for clusterings comparison: Variants, properties, normalization and correction for chance. *The Journal of Machine Learning Research*, 11:2837–2854.

Soroush Vosoughi, Prashanth Vijayaraghavan, and Deb Roy. 2016. Tweet2vec: Learning tweet embeddings using character-level cnn-lstm encoder-decoder. In *Proceedings of the 39th International ACM SIGIR conference on Research and Development in Information Retrieval*, pages 1041–1044.

Alex Wang, Amanpreet Singh, Julian Michael, Felix Hill, Omer Levy, and Samuel R Bowman. 2018. Glue: A multi-task benchmark and analysis platform for natural language understanding. *arXiv preprint arXiv:1804.07461*.

Zhilin Yang, Zihang Dai, Yiming Yang, Jaime Carbonell, Russ R Salakhutdinov, and Quoc V Le. 2019. Xlnet: Generalized autoregressive pretraining for language understanding. In *Advances in neural information processing systems*, pages 5753–5763.

Arkaitz Zubiaga, Damiano Spina, Raquel Martínez, and Víctor Fresno. 2015. Real-time classification of twitter trends. *Journal of the Association for Information Science and Technology*, 66(3):462–473.

Civil Unrest on Twitter (CUT):
A Dataset of Tweets to Support Research on Civil Unrest

Justin Sech*, Alexandra DeLucia*, Mark Dredze*, Anna L Buczak[†]

*Center for Language and Speech Processing, Johns Hopkins University
[†]Johns Hopkins University Applied Physics Laboratory
{jsech1, aadelucia, mdredze}@jhu.edu, Anna.Buczak@jhuapl.edu

Abstract

We present CUT, a dataset for studying Civil Unrest on Twitter. Our dataset includes 4,381 tweets related to civil unrest, hand-annotated with information related to the study of civil unrest discussion and events. Our dataset is drawn from 42 countries from 2014 to 2019. We present baseline systems trained on this data for the identification of tweets related to civil unrest. We include a discussion of ethical issues related to research on this topic.

1 Introduction

From the tomb-builder strikes in 1159 BCE Egypt[1] to the Black Lives Matter protests in 2020 CE U.S.[2], humanity has utilized protests and other demonstrations to register grievances and affect change in government or society. While some basic elements of protest remain unchanged for thousands of years, the ability to organize and execute civil unrest activities has been transformed by social media.

Twitter has played a central role in several recent civil unrest related activities, with the most noted being the Arab Spring, a series of pro-democratic uprisings, protests, and armed rebellions from 2010 to 2012 in Tunisia, Morocco, Syria, Libya, Egypt and Bahrain, that led to regime changes[3]. Some sociologists believe that the distrust in official country press due to censorship led to civilians turning to each other on social media for independent news (Smidi and Shahin, 2017; Soengas-Pérez, 2013). In addition to spreading news, civilians also use social media to share opinions on new policies or recent events (e.g. political debates), and to share information for upcoming events (e.g. protests). The use of social media to plan protests was a key motivator for the Planned Protest module in the

---

[1] https://www.ancient.eu/article/1089/the-first-labor-strike-in-history/

[2] https://blacklivesmatter.com

[3] https://www.history.com/topics/middle-east/arab-spring

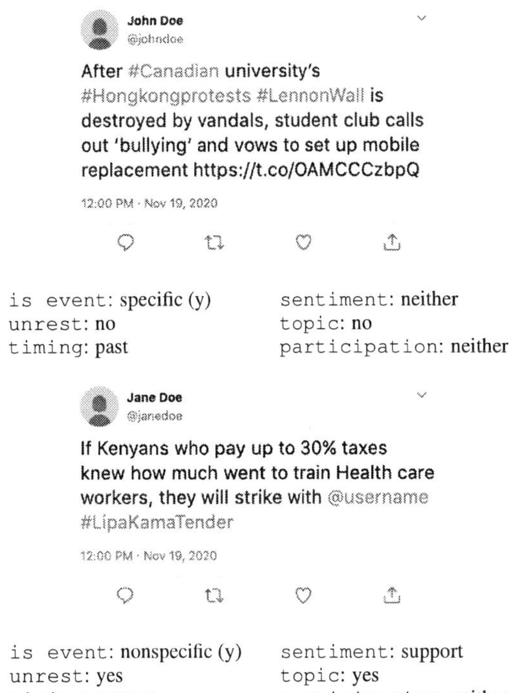

Figure 1: Example tweets and their annotations in the Civil Unrest on Twitter (CUT) dataset.

EMBERs civil unrest forecasting system (Muthiah et al., 2015; Ramakrishnan et al., 2014).

We study civil unrest discussions on Twitter for the exact same reason Tunisians turned to Twitter—we believe civilian voices are an important source of information about the state of a country. Ramakrishnan et al. (2014) hinted at this with their paper title, "Beating the News," for what is news other than reports of the people to the people? While news articles can inform about the presence of civil unrest, we (and other researchers who utilize Twitter data) seek to find information about events and opinions from Twitter before official news reports

Proceedings of the 2020 EMNLP Workshop W-NUT: The Sixth Workshop on Noisy User-generated Text, pages 215–221
Online, Nov 19, 2020. ©2020 Association for Computational Linguistics

(Osborne and Dredze, 2014).

We discuss ethical concerns of analyzing civil unrest data in §5.

A challenge to studying civil unrest in social media is finding it. Tweets cover a wide range of topics, and identifying those directly relevant to a protest can be challenging. Therefore, to support the study of civil unrest from Twitter, we present the Civil Unrest on Twitter (CUT) dataset: a collection of 4,381 tweets with annotations for a variety of information related to civil unrest. Examples of annotated tweets are shown in the appendix (Figure 1). Tweets are labeled for the following: whether a tweet refers to a protest/strike/riot, if general unrest/dissatisfaction is conveyed, the time of the tweet with respect to the event, the user's stance, whether the event topic is present, if the user intends to participate, and event-specific hashtags. These annotations are useful for a variety of tasks, such as stance detection and event extraction (Mohammad et al., 2016; Zong et al., 2020). As an example use case, we create a model that distinguishes between tweets that discuss civil unrest events from those that do not. This filtration model is a popular processing step in civil unrest detection and forecasting pipelines (Islam et al., 2020; Alsaedi et al., 2017; Edouard, 2018; Korolov et al., 2016; Ranganath et al., 2016).

We make the following contributions:

- CUT: A dataset of 4,381 English Tweets from 42 African, Middle Eastern, and Southeast Asian countries (2014-2019), annotated for a variety of information of interest with respect to civil unrest.

- Baseline classifiers that determine if a tweet is related to a civil unrest event.

Our dataset and code are available at `https://github.com/AADeLucia/JHU-CUT`.

2   Related Work

Several studies have examined specific events on social media. Examples include tracking information related to public health, such as COVID-19 (Zong et al., 2020; Paul and Dredze, 2017), and riots, such as the London Riots (Alsaedi et al., 2017).

Several studies have specifically considered building datasets related to the task of civil unrest detection. Alsaedi et al. (2017) label a sample of 5,000 tweets from the Middle East from October to November 2015, however they were labelled for general events and not only disruptive events (e.g. weather). Islam et al. (2020) use a list of keywords to filter tweets, and then manually label a sample 10,500 tweets from 178 countries from November 26, 2017 to June 25, 2018 to verify their "informative" vs "uninformative" filtration model. De Silva and Riloff (2014) incorporated profile information (i.e. organization or user) to predict protest-related tweets from a collection of 6,000 English and Spanish disease and civil-unrest keyword-filtered tweets. Edouard (2018) created an Event2012/FSD corpus with roughly 155K tweets from late 2011 and late 2012, and labelled the tweets as event/non-event related according to a list of events from Wikipedia Current Event Portal. Korolov et al. (2016) purchased third-party curated tweets related to the 2015 Baltimore protests and manually annotated those to filter related tweets in a larger set from the same time period in large U.S. cities. Ranganath et al. (2016) collected geotagged messages from Nigeria and manually labelled 2,686 tweets for their relation to the 2015 general election and Boko Haram insurgencies.

Other work collects tweets from a known event with location and hashtag filters. Wang et al. (2015) collected 6.5 million tweets from the dates and locations that were affected by Hurricane Sandy (October 22nd, 2012–November 2nd, 2012, northeastern US). Littman (2018) collected 7.6 millions tweets from the 2017 "Unite the Right" protest in Charlottesville, Virginia with event-specific hashtags (e.g. #defendCville, #HeatherHeye).

Other work uses external information from news articles and other sources to categorize groups of tweets, e.g. country and day, but not to identify individual tweets related to an event (Korkmaz et al., 2016; Chen and Neill, 2014).

A drawback of these efforts is that they focus on specific events or locations, rather than producing a more general dataset that can be used to identify civil unrest tweets from new or emerging events. Our goal is to produce a more general dataset from a large number of countries (42) over several years (2014 to 2019).

3   Dataset Creation

We present a dataset to support the study of civil unrest on Twitter. Our data set contains English tweets with annotations related to civil unrest produced through annotations from Amazon Mechanical Turk.

Twitter Data We selected a sample of tweets from 2014 to 2019 that were collected from the Twitter streaming API based on filters to collect geolocated data. Our geolocation filters included African, Middle Eastern, and Southeast Asian countries (see Table 4 in the appendix.) We filtered the data set to include English only tweets as identified by `langid` (Lui and Baldwin, 2012).[4] We excluded retweets. Geolocation is present in every tweet due to the method of collection.

We select tweets based on their inclusion of an English language keyword related to civil unrest. Using an approach similar to that of Muthiah et al. (2015) and Ramakrishnan et al. (2014), we used a combination of manual and automated methods to create a large set of 709 keywords, which include terms such as "unemployment," "police," and "extremist." The full list of keywords appears with the released dataset.

In total, we include 4,415 tweets in the dataset for annotation.[5] 34 Tweets are removed from the dataset after annotators report them as non-English, resulting in the final dataset of 4,381 Tweets.

Annotations Our goal was to collect a wide range of annotations that could potentially be helpful in the study of civil unrest on Twitter. Annotators were asked several questions about each tweet:

1. Does this Tweet discuss a protest, march, riot, or strike?

    (a) At the time of this Tweet, is the referenced event currently in progress, in the past, or an upcoming event?

    (b) Does this Tweet support or oppose the event in question?

    (c) Does this Tweet state a specific topic of the event that reflects the intent of the protesters?

    (d) Does this Tweet describe participation/intent to participate in the event?

    (e) If this Tweet contains hashtags specific to the event, list the hashtags.

---

[4] While Twitter includes language identification in tweets, this feature was introduced after the start of our data collection. For consistency, we used `langid` for all tweets.

[5] The odd number is due to the presence of pre-labeled tweets in HITs for quality control, and a handful of tweets that were sampled multiple times.

2. Does this Tweet indicate civil or political unrest, frustration, or dissatisfaction? For example, dissatisfaction with government policy, economic situation, etc.

Questions 1(b)-1(e) were only answered if the answer to (1) was 'specific' or 'nonspecific', and Question 1(a) was only answered if (1) was 'specific.' A screenshot of the survey is in the appendix (Figure 2).

Survey Setup We obtained annotations using Amazon Mechanical Turk. Our HIT contained 10 tweets, and each HIT was annotated by 3 workers.

To ensure a balanced inclusion of different countries and time periods in the annotated set, we selected tweets uniformly by country and year, i.e. each country had the same probability of having a tweet included in the annotated set.

To ensure annotation quality we release the HITs in batches and perform a quality check by inserting pre-annotated tweets into each HIT. These 100 quality check tweets were manually annotated by two annotators (one an author of this paper). Conflicting annotations were adjudicated by the author annotator. If an annotator incorrectly annotates a quality check tweet, then their work is set aside to be inspected by the author annotator. If their work is considered unsatisfactory (i.e. the author had reason to believe that the annotator was simply clicking through) then their annotations are removed[6]. Workers were paid $0.40/HIT, for 500 HITs with 3 annotators each, for a total cost of $200.

Our first batch of annotations had a very low rate of civil unrest related tweets (7%). This is likely because of the breadth of keywords used to filter tweets and polysemy (e.g. "guns" could refer to weapons or muscles). This issue was also encountered De Silva and Riloff (2014), where 80% of the tweets collected through keyword filtering alone did not discuss events. Therefore, we sought to bias future annotation rounds towards more civil unrest related tweets. We trained a Random Forest classifier on the tweets from the first round of annotations using features of unigram counts.

While the classifier only achieved an F1 of 0.502, we found that the highly scored tweets were much more likely to be about civil unrest.

We then included the keyword feature importance as weights for sampling the next batch of

---

[6] All ties were broken by author annotations or 2 volunteer annotators.

Rank	Keyword	Importance
1	protest	0.198
2	protests	0.117
3	protesters	0.077
4	strike	0.047
5	violence	0.020
6	fight	0.019
7	campaign	0.015
8	detained	0.014
9	demonstrations	0.014
10	protesting	0.013

Table 1: Top 10 important keywords for sampling tweets obtained from a random forest model.

Question (IAA)	Annotations		
1 (0.430)	yes, specific — 539	yes, non-specific — 151	no — 3,691
1(a) (0.478)	current — 381	past — 111	future — 47
1(b) (0.325)	support — 196	oppose — 69	neither — 425
1(c) (0.312)	yes — 322	no — 364	unclear — 4
1(d) (0.183)	yes — 65	no — 4	neither — 621
2 (0.168)	yes — 1,951	no — 2,446	

Table 2: Annotation results from the Mechanical Turk survey. 4,415 tweets were labelled by three annotators for a variety of civil unrest-related questions (§3). 34 tweets were labelled as "not English" and removed. The inter-annotator agreement (IAA) was calculated using Fleiss' kappa for 3 annotators, before the "unsatisfactory" workers were removed. Due to the overriding nature of our adjudications, recalculating agreement would be inaccurate.

tweets. If a tweet contained words from the top of the important keyword list, it had a higher chance of being selected. The top keywords are in Table 1. The concept of not treating all keywords as equal was also brought up in Islam et al. (2020), where they categorized their civil unrest "keyword dictionary" into ranked categories based "negative impact of an unrest event on civil life." The third and final batch was sampled the same way as batch two (using the keyword weights).

For each question we selected the majority label from the three annotators. If no majority label existed, then the answer was adjudicated by the authors[7].

Annotated Dataset Table 2 shows statistics for the final dataset. Despite efforts to increase the number of civil unrest-related tweets, only 690 of 4,381 tweets were about events, but 1,951 tweets did contain signs of general unrest. Annotators labeled 34 Tweets from the original 4,415 dataset as "not English," and we removed those from the final dataset.

After manually inspecting some of the provided hashtags, we decided that the hashtag question contained the least quality answers. The answers were mostly blank. We suspect this is due to answering the hashtag free-response question is more time consuming than the other multiple choice questions. For greater coverage, we will include all listed hashtags in the released dataset instead of the hashtags listed by at least 2 annotators.

In terms of annotator agreement, question 2 had the lowest agreement with a Fleiss' kappa of 0.168 and question 1a the highest (0.478) (See Table 2). Lower agreement rates are not uncharacteristic for labeling tweets. One potential difficulty in our setting is that our questions are very specific. While

other datasets ask about "event vs. no event," we ask for more details.

4 Civil Unrest Classification

Using our annotated dataset we created a baseline model for predicting if a tweet was related to civil unrest, i.e. predicting if the label was "yes, a specific event" or "yes, in a non-specific fashion" for question 1 (690 of 4,381 tweets or 16%). The resulting classifier can be used to identify large amounts of data around specific events for further study (Islam et al., 2020; Alsaedi et al., 2017; Edouard, 2018; Korolov et al., 2016; Ranganath et al., 2016).

We considered two logistic regression classifiers. 1) Unigram counts of all tokens in a tweet. 2) Counts of the civil unrest keywords only. Both of these methods used the scikit learn implementation of logistic regression and `CountVectorizer` (Pedregosa et al., 2011). The unigram models were regularized with L2 loss and were evaluated with 5-fold cross validation (same folds across experiments).

All methods preprocessed tweets with the `littlebird` implementation of the BERTweet tokenizer (DeLucia, 2020). This tokenizer was used to allow easy extendability and future comparison with a BERTweet-based model.

Table 3 shows that the keyword based logistic

---

[7]See footnote 6

Features	F1	Precision	Recall
Keywords	0.782	0.894	0.697
Unigrams	0.775	0.892	0.687

Table 3: Logistic regression results on predicting if a tweet is related to civil unrest. Standard deviation across 5-fold cross validation (F1) for keywords is 0.023, unigrams is 0.030. F1 is for the positive class only (i.e. events).

regression model outperformed the unigram model (0.782 F1 vs 0.775 F1). This out-performance is slight, but still worthwhile, especially since the keyword model is smaller (only 700 features instead of 15K) and converges faster (roughly 50 iterations versus 100). Additionally, since the civil unrest keywords were used to sample tweets their inclusion as features adds further information to the keyword-based model.

5   Ethical Considerations

Many studies of event detection on Twitter have explored the implications for public health (e.g. spread of infectious diseases) (Paul and Dredze, 2017) and natural disasters (Wang et al., 2015), which offer benefits in combating harmful events. However, civil unrest presents a more complex cost benefit trade off as it can yield insights into what issues are most important to a population, but can also be used to monitor or track individuals who participate in these events. Deciding what constitutes civil unrest versus unjustified violence requires a value judgement, which could easily degrade into weaponizing against dissenting opinion. Additionally, non-government actors could use predictions of unrest to squash disapproving voices. Moreover, frequently, marginalized voices have found solace and organization using social media (Xiong et al., 2019; Ince et al., 2017) and predicting civil unrest could unintentionally lead to actions such as further policing of overpoliced communities.

With this in mind, we should consider Twitter data not just as text data, but as people. Several proposals for protecting people including avoiding reverse identification (Ayers et al., 2018; Benton et al., 2017)) and data anonymization tools (Nguyen-Son et al., 2012). We believe that the numerous studies of civil unrest that further our understanding of complex societal issues are convincing evidence that there is much to be gained from developing data resources in support of this topic. At the same time, we must remain vigilant in our evaluation of research efforts to ensure they remain supportive of these goals.

6   Conclusion

We have presented the Civil Unrest on Twitter (CUT) dataset and a baseline classifier trained on the data for identifying tweets related to a civil unrest event. Future work can build on our multi-faceted annotations to expand the study of communities and how they express concern about complex societal issues through civil unrest.

Acknowledgments

The authors thank Ben Mitsunaga for testing the Twitter survey, and the Mechanical Turkers who annotated our dataset. We also thank Zach Wood-Doughty, Alicia Nobles, and Arya McCarthy for their comments and advice. We thank Arya again for assisting with annotation tie-breaking. This work relates to Department of Navy award N00014-19-1-2316 issued by the Office of Naval Research. The United States Government has a royalty-free license throughout the world in all copyrightable material contained herein. Any opinions, findings, and conclusions or recommendations expressed in this material are those of the author(s) and do not necessarily reflect the views of the Office of Naval Research.

References

Nasser Alsaedi, Pete Burnap, and Omer Rana. 2017. Can We Predict a Riot? Disruptive Event Detection Using Twitter. *ACM Transactions on Internet Technology*, 17(2):1–26.

John W. Ayers, Theodore L. Caputi, Camille Nebeker, and Mark Dredze. 2018. Don't quote me: reverse identification of research participants in social media studies. *npj Digital Medicine*, 1(1):1–2. Number: 1 Publisher: Nature Publishing Group.

Adrian Benton, Glen Coppersmith, and Mark Dredze. 2017. Ethical research protocols for social media health research. In *Proceedings of the First ACL Workshop on Ethics in Natural Language Processing*, pages 94–102, Valencia, Spain. Association for Computational Linguistics.

Feng Chen and Daniel B. Neill. 2014. Non-parametric scan statistics for event detection and forecasting in heterogeneous social media graphs. In *Proceedings of the 20th ACM SIGKDD international conference on Knowledge discovery and data mining - KDD*

'*14*, pages 1166–1175, New York, New York, USA. ACM Press.

Lalindra De Silva and Ellen Riloff. 2014. User Type Classification of Tweets with Implications for Event Recognition. In *Proceedings of the Joint Workshop on Social Dynamics and Personal Attributes in Social Media*, pages 98–108, Baltimore, Maryland. Association for Computational Linguistics.

Alexandra DeLucia. 2020. AADeLucia/littlebird. Original-date: 2020-04-24T00:15:07Z.

Amosse Edouard. 2018. *Event detection and analysis on short text messages*. Ph.D. thesis.

Jelani Ince, Fabio Rojas, and Clayton A. Davis. 2017. The social media response to black lives matter: how twitter users interact with black lives matter through hashtag use. *Ethnic and Racial Studies*, 40(11):1814–1830.

Kamrul Islam, Manjur Ahmed, Kamal Z. Zamli, and Salman Mehbub. 2020. An online framework for civil unrest prediction using tweet stream based on tweet weight and event diffusion.

Gizem Korkmaz, Jose Cadena, Chris J. Kuhlman, Achla Marathe, Anil Vullikanti, and Naren Ramakrishnan. 2016. Multi-source models for civil unrest forecasting. *Social Network Analysis and Mining*, 6(1):50.

Rostyslav Korolov, Di Lu, Jingjing Wang, Guangyu Zhou, Claire Bonial, Clare Voss, Lance Kaplan, William Wallace, Jiawei Han, and Heng Ji. 2016. On predicting social unrest using social media. In *2016 IEEE/ACM International Conference on Advances in Social Networks Analysis and Mining (ASONAM)*, pages 89–95, San Francisco, CA, USA. IEEE.

Justin Littman. 2018. Charlottesville Tweet Ids. Publisher: Harvard Dataverse type: dataset.

Marco Lui and Timothy Baldwin. 2012. langid.py: An Off-the-shelf Language Identification Tool. In *Proceedings of the ACL 2012 System Demonstrations*, pages 25–30, Jeju Island, Korea. Association for Computational Linguistics.

Saif Mohammad, Svetlana Kiritchenko, Parinaz Sobhani, Xiaodan Zhu, and Colin Cherry. 2016. SemEval-2016 task 6: Detecting stance in tweets. In *Proceedings of the 10th International Workshop on Semantic Evaluation (SemEval-2016)*, pages 31–41, San Diego, California. Association for Computational Linguistics.

Sathappan Muthiah, Bert Huang, Jaime Arredondo, David Mares, Lise Getoor, Graham Katz, and Naren Ramakrishnan. 2015. Planned Protest Modeling in News and Social Media. In *Twenty-Seventh IAAI Conference*.

H. Nguyen-Son, Q. Nguyen, M. Tran, D. Nguyen, H. Yoshiura, and I. Echizen. 2012. Automatic anonymization of natural languages texts posted on social networking services and automatic detection of disclosure. In *2012 Seventh International Conference on Availability, Reliability and Security*, pages 358–364.

Miles Osborne and Mark Dredze. 2014. Facebook, twitter and google plus for breaking news: Is there a winner? In *ICWSM*.

Michael J. Paul and Mark Dredze. 2017. Social monitoring for public health. *Synthesis Lectures on Information Concepts, Retrieval, and Services*, 9(5):1–183.

F. Pedregosa, G. Varoquaux, A. Gramfort, V. Michel, B. Thirion, O. Grisel, M. Blondel, P. Prettenhofer, R. Weiss, V. Dubourg, J. Vanderplas, A. Passos, D. Cournapeau, M. Brucher, M. Perrot, and E. Duchesnay. 2011. Scikit-learn: Machine learning in Python. *Journal of Machine Learning Research*, 12:2825–2830.

Naren Ramakrishnan, Gizem Korkmaz, Chris Kuhlman, Achla Marathe, Liang Zhao, Ting Hua, Feng Chen, Chang Tien Lu, Bert Huang, Aravind Srinivasan, Khoa Trinh, Patrick Butler, Lise Getoor, Graham Katz, Andy Doyle, Chris Ackermann, Ilya Zavorin, Jim Ford, Kristen Summers, Youssef Fayed, Jaime Arredondo, Dipak Gupta, Sathappan Muthiah, David Mares, Nathan Self, Rupinder Khandpur, Parang Saraf, Wei Wang, Jose Cadena, and Anil Vullikanti. 2014. 'Beating the news' with EMBERS: forecasting civil unrest using open source indicators. In *Proceedings of the 20th ACM SIGKDD international conference on Knowledge discovery and data mining - KDD '14*, pages 1799–1808, New York, New York, USA. ACM Press.

Suhas Ranganath, Fred Morstatter, Xia Hu, Jiliang Tang, and Huan Liu. 2016. Predicting Online Protest Participation of Social Media Users. *AAAI Press*, page 7.

Adam Smidi and Saif Shahin. 2017. Social Media and Social Mobilisation in the Middle East: A Survey of Research on the Arab Spring:. *India Quarterly*. Publisher: SAGE PublicationsSage India: New Delhi, India.

Xosé Soengas-Pérez. 2013. The role of the Internet and social networks in the arab uprisings an alternative to official press censorship. *Comunicar*, 21(41):147–155.

Haoyu Wang, E. Hovy, and Mark Dredze. 2015. The hurricane sandy twitter corpus. In *AAAI Workshop: WWW and Public Health Intelligence*.

Ying Xiong, Moonhee Cho, and Brandon Boatwright. 2019. Hashtag activism and message frames among social movement organizations: Semantic network analysis and thematic analysis of twitter during the #metoo movement. *Public Relations Review*, 45(1):10 – 23.

Shi Zong, Ashutosh Baheti, Wei Xu, and Alan Ritter. 2020. Extracting COVID-19 Events from Twitter. *arXiv:2006.02567 [cs]*. ArXiv: 2006.02567.

Tweeki: Linking Named Entities on Twitter to a Knowledge Graph

Bahareh Harandizadeh
University of California
Irvine, CA 92617
bharandi@uci.edu

Sameer Singh
University of California
Irvine, CA 92617
sameer@uci.edu

Abstract

To identify what entities are being talked about in tweets, we need to automatically link named entities that appear in tweets to structured KBs like WikiData. Existing approaches often struggle with such short, noisy texts, or their complex design and reliance on supervision make them brittle, difficult to use and maintain, and lose significance over time. Further, there is a lack of a large, linked corpus of tweets to aid researchers, along with lack of gold dataset to evaluate the accuracy of entity linking. In this paper, we introduce (1) Tweeki, an unsupervised, modular entity linking system for Twitter, (2) Tweeki-Data, a large, automatically-annotated corpus of Tweets linked to entities in WikiData, and (3) TweekiGold, a gold dataset for entity linking evaluation. Through comprehensive analysis, we show that Tweeki is comparable to the performance of recent state-of-the-art entity linkers models, the dataset is of high quality, and a use case of how the dataset can be used to improve downstream tasks in social media analysis (geolocation prediction).

1 Introduction

Popularity and steady increase in adoption of social media makes it a ripe domain for understanding and analyzing world events, with Twitter as one of the largest social media platforms. As a result, tweets now have become a rich source of information, and Twitter analysis has been widely applied for many applications such as trend detection (Lau et al., 2012), opinion mining (Pak and Paroubek, 2010), election politics (Conover et al., 2011), and many others. However, short length of the text, casual and error-prone writing style, and evolving topics over time is extremely challenging for existing text analysis tools (Derczynski et al., 2015).

One of the common approaches is to bridge the gap between unstructured text (e.g. a tweet) and

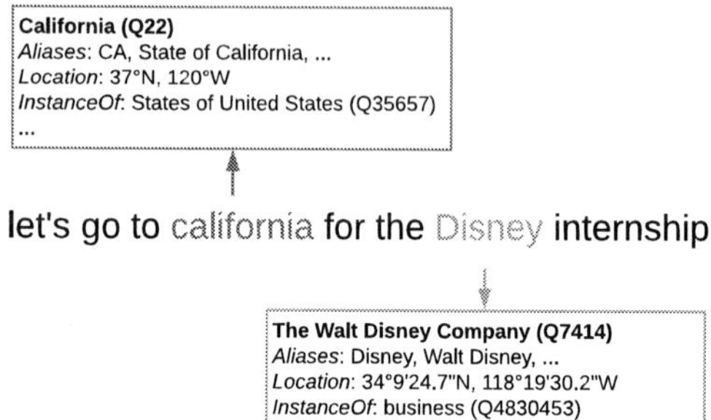

Figure 1: **Example** of an *entity-linked* tweet, containing two mentions linked to WikiData entities.

structured, machine-readable knowledge bases (e.g. Wikidata) using *entity linking* (EL) that grounds named mentions to a unique, real-world entity, i.e., an entry in the knowledge base (see Figure 1 for an example). Entity linking has been widely applied in natural language processing (Ling et al., 2015; Gupta et al., 2017; Raiman and Raiman, 2018; Radhakrishnan et al., 2018) on domains including news, biographical text, movie/show plots, amongst others. Although entity linking has been used in social media applications as well (Miyazaki et al., 2018; Dai et al., 2018), it is much less common.

There are a number of reasons by existing entity linking systems are not commonly used for social media analysis. One of the primary concerns is that many of the existing entity linking systems are supervised (Yosef et al., 2011; Ganea and Hofmann, 2017), which not only makes them suitable for the domains they are trained on (Meij et al., 2012), but also makes them excessively reliant on context around the mention. For these reasons, supervised EL systems tend to be inaccurate on noisy and short text (Cornolti et al., 2013). Even unsupervised systems are heavily-engineered and complex in nature (Kulkarni et al., 2009), containing rules, obso-

Proceedings of the 2020 EMNLP Workshop W-NUT: The Sixth Workshop on Noisy User-generated Text, pages 222–231
Online, Nov 19, 2020. ©2020 Association for Computational Linguistics

lete lexicons, low coverage KBs, heuristic scoring, etc., making them difficult to maintain, extend, and adapt. This is especially a problem for social media where relevant (and new) entities, writing styles, and vocabulary change completely and frequently. Finally, we currently lack linked datasets to use for social media analysis, such as manually annotated data to evaluate, compare, and benchmark these entity linking systems. These shortcomings need to be addressed before entity linking can be used widely for social media analysis.

In this paper, we propose *Tweeki*, a system and resource for entity linking Twitter to WikiData, that addresses the above challenges. The Tweeki entity linking pipeline is unsupervised, simple, and modular, thus mitigating the problems arising from the supervised setup and complexity design. The pipeline components are chosen based on their performance on short, noisy texts, and can be easily extended with more/new entities and improved taggers. Further, we use WikiData[1] as the KB, benefiting from regular updates and higher coverage compared to Wikipedia and other KBs. We run the Tweeki system on a large collection of tweets to provide the first large, automatically-linked corpus of tweets, that we call *TweekiData*. Finally, we also manually annotate a small set of tweets to provide *gold* annotations for entity links to create the *TweekiGold* dataset, which can be used to evaluate and compare entity linking systems on social media text. The implementation of Tweeki, and the accompanying datasets (TweekiData and TweekiGold) are available publicly[2].

We provide a comprehensive evaluation of the pipeline, using the manually annotated TweekiGold data and other tweet-based datasets. We show that Tweeki performs comparably to leading sophisticated entity linking systems and proposed models for NEEL2016 challenge (Radovanovic et al., 2016). Further, we carry out analysis on mention extraction and candidate generation for different types of mentions, and show the variety and diversity of mentions and entities that get linked. Finally, as a potential downstream application of Tweeki, we develop a preliminary model for geolocation prediction from tweet text, and show that leveraging Tweeki leads to increased the accuracy of such systems for social media analysis.

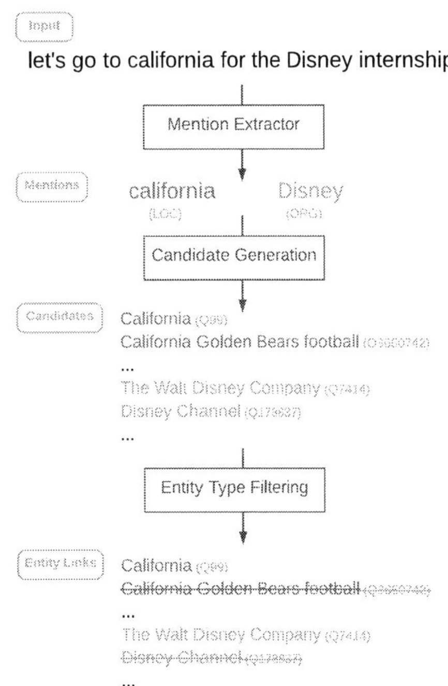

Figure 2: **Tweeki Pipeline (and example execution):** containing detection of mention spans, generation of candidates (and their probabilities, omitted for clarity), and a final entity type-based filtering.

2   Tweeki Entity Linking Pipeline

In this section we propose a simple, unsupervised entity linker called Tweeki that, as we will show later, performs similar to the state of the art. First, we introduce the task definition and some assumptions that we made to build Tweeki, then describe the pipeline components in more detail.

2.1   Task and Pipeline Overview

Given a tweet T, the *end-to-end* linking task is to provide a set of segmented mentions with their associated entities: $T \rightarrow \{(m_i, l_i)\}$. A mention (m_i) refers to a span of tokens in the tweet that refers to an entity, and an entity (l_i) refers to an item of a knowledge base (here, Wikidata unique ID). We exclude the so-called *NIL* entities in our setup, i.e. mentions of entities that do not appear in the KB.

The Tweeki pipeline consists of three modules, shown in Figure 2. Starting from taking raw text of the tweet as input, Tweeki first extracts the mentions and assigns each an entity type. Then, for each identified mention, Tweeki generates a set of candidate entities (with corresponding scores based on prior probability). Finally, after type

---

[1]https://www.wikidata.org/wiki/
[2]Code and data at https://ucinlp.github.io/tweeki.

compatibility-based filtering, a candidate entity (remaining one with the maximum score) is selected as the predicted link. Since we are primarily interested in WikiData, we make certain assumptions that are only relevant for that KB, such as existence of aliases for most of the entities, being able to infer coarse-grained entity types for them ($\mathcal{T}_{\text{NER}} = \{\text{PER}, \text{LOC}, \text{ORG}, \text{MISC}\}$), and others that we mention in text.

2.2 Mention Extraction

Extracting mentions (contiguous spans of tokens) to be linked from the tweet is the first step of any entity linking pipeline. We focus on named entity linking in this work, and thus our mentions are similar to the standard task of named entity recognition (NER) in natural language processing. To support easy extensibility and deployment, we use an off-the-shelf NER systems released as part of AllenNLP library (Gardner et al., 2017). We compare against other NER systems to make this decision, which we present in the results. Further, we were concerned about the accuracy of these newswire trained taggers on the short and noisy tweets, however, as we will see later, they were fairly accurate on the standard NER metrics. The mention extraction module thus returns a list of mentions with associated types, i.e. $\{(m_i, t_i)\}$ where $t_i \in \mathcal{T}_{\text{NER}}$. Although we do not use contextual embeddings in the rest of the pipeline (which links each mention independently), the NER model uses contextual representation to identify the mentions and types, thus provides much of their benefit.

2.3 Candidate Generation

Given a mention m_i, we use the KB itself to produce a set of candidate entities, with associated scores, that will allow us to estimate the conditional probability $p(c|m_i)$. In current literature, there are primarily two ways to generate such candidates: (1) Crosswiki links, i.e. a web crawl that aggregates anchor links to Wikipedia entities (Ling et al., 2015), and (2) Intrawiki links: i.e. doing the same within Wikipedia (Ratinov et al., 2011). We use the latter approach since it is much easier to maintain and update over time. To adapt Intrawiki links to the WikiData KB, we use the existing links between Wikipedia and WikiData entities to gather all the entity aliases and number of time each alias is used in Wikipedia for the entity. The candidate generation module thus returns a set of scored candidates for each mention, i.e. $\{(m_i, C_i)\}$ where

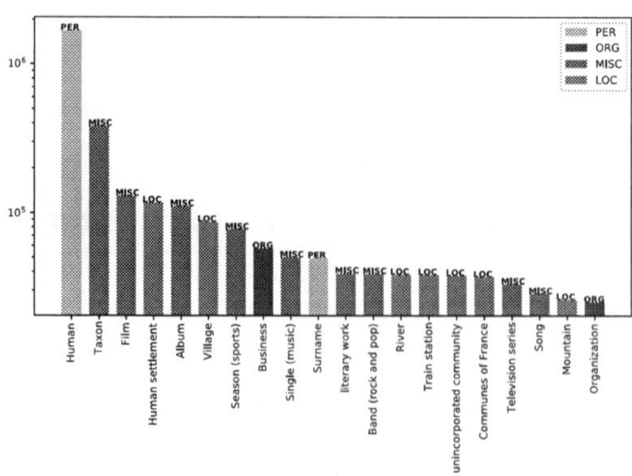

Figure 3: **Entity Type Distribution**: Distribution of the 20 most frequent objects of the *P31: Instance Of* relation from WikiData, which are manually classified into four types from $\mathcal{T}_{\text{NER}}$.

$C_i = \{(c_j, p(c_j|m_i))\}$, where c_j are candidate entities to link the mentions. See Figure 2 for an example (we omit the probabilities for clarity). Note that candidate generation ignores the context (rest of the tweet), and thus is far from optimal. However, when combined with entity type filtering (next), the "prior" probabilities often produce the correct links, as we will show in the experiments.

2.4 Incorporating Entity Types

As a motivating example, consider the following tweet: "*Syracuse and Pitt in the #ACC*". In general, "*Syracuse*" may refer to a name of a city, or a name of an American basketball team, with a lower prior probability for the latter. However, by applying contextual information(e.g "*#ACC*"), the basketball team seems more appropriate. As a result, an entity linking system should have a mechanism to promote more contextually consistent candidates, while lowering the score of the others.

We incorporate this intuition by filtering the prior probability computed during candidate generation ($p(c_j|m_i)$), the notion of entity types of the candidates ($t_j \in \mathcal{T}_{\text{NER}}$, for every c_j), and the type of each mention ($t_i \in \mathcal{T}_{\text{NER}}$ for each m_i). For extracting the entity type (t_j), we use the *P31: Instance Of* relation from the WikiData ontology to find unique entity types, and manually categorize all types that occure more than 100 times (2098 types) into the four types in $\mathcal{T}_{\text{NER}}$. We show the occurence frequency of the top-20 types in Figure 3, along with the coarse-grained types they are assigned (e.g. *Human*'s assigned type is PER, *Film* is MISC, *River* is LOC, and *Business* is ORG). For example Obama (Q76) is Instance Of (P31) *Human* and *Human*'s assigned type is PER, so Q67 entity type is PER.

Mathematically, we assume $p(c_j|m_i, t_i, T) = p(c_j|m_i, t_i)$, where T denotes the tweet containing this mention, as we assume the candidate c_j and the tweet context are conditionally independent if both the mention and the mention type are given. Then we assign zero probabilities to all candidate where $t_j \neq t_i$[3], and renormalize the probabilities of the remaining candidates to obtain the final probability $\hat{p}(c_j|m_i)$. Although we pick the entity for each mention by picking the maximum score, $l_i = \arg\max_{c_j \in C_i} \hat{p}(c_j|m_i)$, we still renormalize to produce a valid confidence in the link. Returning to the above example, if NER assigns LOC to *Syracuse*, then we filter candidates to only be LOC type (e.g Q128069-city name), and similarly restrict to MISC types if that is assigned by NER (e.g Q15718182-basketball team).

3   TweekiData and TweekiGold

In this section, we will describe TweekiData, a massive automatically-linked corpus created by running Tweeki on a number of *source* datasets (3.1). We also introduce TweekiGold, a small, manually-annotated dataset for measuring the quality of the linker and the automatically linked dataset.

3.1   TweekiData

TweekiData is a large automatically-annotated dataset, which is linked to Wikidata using Tweeki. The linking of text and KG is a valuable resource for learning representations that enable better reasoning about entities and how they are expressed in text (tweets in this case), such as pretrained language models that use such resources for better contextual modeling (Peters et al., 2019; Logan et al., 2019). Having access to the full knowledge graph can also help models that perform entity analysis using hops in the knowledge graphs, i.e. location modeling by using relations such as livesIn or headquarteredIn of the linked entities, even if the location is not mention directly.

As the source of the tweets in TweekiData, we identify two prominent datasets that are commonly used in the community, in order to ensure the resulting dataset will be useful. (1) **BTC**, or "Broad Twitter Corpus" (Derczynski et al., 2016), is seven sets of gold datasets of tweets collected over stratified times, places and social, and is widely used

	TweekiGold	TweekiData
# tweets	500	5M
# tokens/tweet	16.31	14.41
# mentions (toks)	8,155	8,010,253
# mentions (spans)	958	5,038,870
# links	852	1,954,229
# uniq entities	638	273,685

Table 1: **Statistics** of the Tweeki-linked datasets.

for Named Entities Recognition. We use section A and H of this corpus, with the size of 1000 and 2000 tweets respectively, and (2) **UT-GEO2011**, a massive Twitter dataset mainly created for tweet geolocation prediction, but also used for other purposes (Roller et al., 2012). The dataset is limited to US region and has two versions: UTGEO2011-Large containing 38M tweets belongs to almost 450K users, and UTGEO2011-Small contains 1.6M tweets with 10K users. We took a random subset of 5M tweets from UTGEO2011, to build TweekiData.

3.2   TweekiGold

As there is no gold data available linking Twitter to Wikidata, we collect a gold dataset manually. We use mention extraction on tweets from UTGEO2011-small, and select 700 random tweets to annotate. An expert manually provides the following for each tweet: correct NER tags from $\mathcal{T}_{NER}$ (in IOB2 format), a Wikidata entity ID for all applicable spans, and Wikipedia page-title for corresponding Wikidata entity. If the tweet is too ambiguous or erroneous, it is deleted by annotator. Finally 500 tweets remain as the final gold dataset that we call TweekiGold for future use.

3.3   Dataset Statistics

We present statistics of both datasets in Table 1. TweekiGold contains 500 tweets mostly about sport and social events limited to US region geographically. There are 8155 tokens in total, and the length of each tweet is 16.31 on average. The 958 mentions consist of 399 LOC, 171 MISC, 212 ORG and 176 PER entity types. We are able to link 852 of them to WikiData (the rest could not be matched to existing entities), resulting in 1.91 mentions and 1.7 links per tweet on average. The number of all tokens in the larger TweekiData dataset is 72,086,330, so on average the length of each tweet is 14.41. It also contains 5M mentions of which almost 2M are linked to Wikidata successfully (40%).

---

[3]if there are no such candidates, we ignore this filtering.

	Spacy		Stanford		AllenNLP	
	P	R	P	R	P	R
TweekiGold	43.8	57.9	71.8	65.2	81.1	80.9
BTC-A	10.8	42.4	41.1	56.5	48.1	66.6
BTC-H	7.3	14.3	40.6	19.9	74.2	54.2
Average	20.6	38.2	51.2	47.2	**67.8**	**67.2**

Table 2: **NER Performance:** Token-wise accuracy of popular frameworks on tweet-based NER datasets.

4 Experiments

In this section, we present experiments to address the following questions: (Section 4.1) what is the quality of each components in Tweeki pipeline? (Section 4.2) how does the performance of our simple Tweeki linker compare to other existing linkers? and finally, (Section 4.3) how can we use Tweeki for other use cases for NLP on Twitter?

4.1 Evaluating the Linker Components

Here we will investigate few of the individual modules and design choices of the Tweeki pipeline.

Mention Extraction To find the best NER-Tagger to use for mention extraction, we examined the accuracy of the three well-known, available NER taggers on TweekiGold and the both sections of BTC datasets. Table 2 shows precision and recall of StanfordNLP[4], AllenNLP (Gardner et al., 2017), and Spacy[5]. Based on the results, on TweekiGold, AllenNLP has 10% more precision compare to the second best (Stanford), while also superior on BTC-A (by 7%) and in BTC-B (by 30%). On average (last row), AllenNLP has around 16% more precision and 20% more recall compare to the second best option(Stanford). This consistent outstanding performance on different datasets shows AllenNLP can handle the casual and error-prone nature of tweets well, and thus is best to use for extracting mentions among popular alternatives.

Candidate Generation The primary way to evaluate the effectiveness of the candidate generation is its coverage, i.e. what fraction of the input mentions is it able to provide candidates for? We evaluate the coverage of Tweeki using the complete 5M tweets from the TweekiData described in Section 3.1. Table 3 shows the results for each $\mathcal{T}_{\text{NER}}$ types separately. LOC type has the best performance with 52% linked items. Missed locations

Type	#mentions	#entities	Coverage
PER	2.1m	550k	25%
LOC	1.8m	950k	52%
ORG	550k	200k	35%
MISC	490k	200k	40%

Table 3: **Linking Coverage of TweekiData, by Types:** Number of mentions extracted for each type, along with how many of these mentions are linked by Tweeki.

	Precision	Recall	F1
w/o Entity Types	66.6	59.6	63.4
w/ Entity Types	**69.1**	**61.2**	**65.1**

Table 4: **Entity Type Filtering:** Tweeki with entity type filtering obtains more than 2% improvement on all metrics compared to without filetring.

mainly happen due to overly specific information (e.g 2nd Street) or noisy writing style (using "la" instead of "LA" or "Los Angeles"). Also the low coverage of PER type is mostly related to the mentions started with '@', making them hard to match with any aliases in the KB. Although we use Twitter API[6] to substitute these mentions to their real name (e.g change "@MittRomney" to "Mitt Romney"), the source dataset was gathered in 2011, and many of these are not valid anymore.

Need for Entity Types Finally, to show how incorporating entity types can be helpful in linking process, Tweeki was tested on TweekiGold dataset, with and without considering the third module of the pipeline. As shown in Table 4, using entity types can improves all metrics more than 2%, justifying its inclusion in the entity linking pipeline.

4.2 Comparison to Existing Linkers

In this section, we analyze the overall performance of Tweeki by comparing it with other linkers on TweekiGold, NEEL2016 (Rizzo et al., 2015), and Derczynski datasets (Derczynski et al., 2015). For the linkers to compare against, we include TagMe (Ferragina and Scaiella, 2010) as it is designed for short and noisy text. AIDA (Yosef et al., 2011) and Babelfly (Moro et al., 2014) both use graph building and dense subgraph algorithms to tackle entity linking and usually provide a good baseline for many previous studies. We also compare more recent EL models, End-to-End Neural

---

[4]https://nlp.stanford.edu/software/CRF-NER.html
[5]https://spacy.io/usage/linguistic-features

[6]https://developer.twitter.com/en

	NEEL2016			Derczynski			TweekiGold		
	P	R	F1	P	R	F1	P	R	F1
TagMe	19.1	**30.0**	24.1	18.2	**50.1**	26.3	38.1	56.1	45.0
Babelfy	8.08	10.6	9.06	9.0	41.1	15.2	17.1	47.2	25.1
AIDA	-	-	-	-	-	-	53.2	32.1	38.5
End-to-End	**87.9**	13.1	22.8	**57.05**	29.2	**39.0**	**79.1**	35.2	49.4
OpenTapioca	11.0	19.1	14.8	9.1	36.0	14.0	20.2	50.4	29.1
Tweeki	58.0	15.2	**24.8**	41.1	34.2	37.1	69.0	**61.0**	**65.0**

Table 5: **Entity Linking Performance** of existing linkers, using *strong matching* metric on three datasets.

	Derczynski			TweekiGold		
	P	R	F1	P	R	F1
Tw-Stanford	36.4	29.4	32.5	56.7	44.6	49.9
Tw-AllenNLP	41.1	34.2	37.1	69.0	61.0	65.0

Table 6: **Choice of Mention Extraction:** using Stanford for mention extraction and NER, compared to using AllenNLP, in the first module of the pipeline.

	ORG		PER		LOC	
	P	R	P	R	P	R
TweekiGold	68.1	66.8	53.4	84.4	82.3	77.1
BTC-A	34.5	27.2	40.2	62.1	56.8	49.0
BTC-H	31.3	10.0	60.9	21.0	63.4	50.8
Average	44.6	34.6	51.5	55.8	67.5	58.9

Table 7: **Span-based accuracy** for each mention type on different datasets annotated with gold NER.

Entity Linking (Kolitsas et al., 2018) and OpenTapioca (Delpeuch, 2019).

Table 5 compares these models on different datasets using precision/recall/F1 based on *EL strong matching*. TagMe has acceptable performance on all datasets and the best Recall for NEEL2016, while Babelfy performs the worst, specifically on NEEL2016. While End-to-End is not specifically designed for short, noisy text, it is the winner of all three datasets in terms of precision. OpenTapioca has average performance on all datasets, with low accuracy on NEEL2016. Our proposed system, Tweeki, has the best F1 on NEEL2016 and TweekiGold, while being quite close to the best on Derczynski. Tweeki also has provides a relative high precision on all datasets.

We also compare Tweeki to the best submissions for the NEEL2016 challenge. Even though Tweeki is unsupervised and not specifically designed for this challenge (i.e. the prominent entities in that dataset), it would place third in the challenge, obtaining 24.8 F1 behind 39.6 F1 from Greenfield et al. (2016) and 50.1 F1 from KEA (Waitelonis and Sack, 2016)), both of which are supervised.

Finally, to emphasize how selecting NER tagger effects the pipeline, we substitute AllenNLP with Stanford for *Mention Extraction* in Tweeki and tested it on Derczynski and TweekiGold. As shown in Table 6, this choice has a significant effect. By using AllenNLP in mention extraction, not only desired spans are selected and passed to the next module properly, but also more accurate entity types improve the filtering of candidates.

4.3 Use Case: Geolocating Tweets

We can use the links of named mentions to a knowledge base for a number of interesting applications in social media analysis. Prediction the location of tweets, for instances, has been a popular task for understanding the geographic trends and behaviors (Cheng et al., 2010; Chang et al., 2012; Miura et al., 2017), since users do not provide this information accurately (Chang et al., 2012). Some recent models have even used KBs for geolocation (Miyazaki et al., 2018). We will study a use case of Tweeki for geolocation prediction.

Using UTGEO2011-small dataset (see Section 3.1 for more details), we want to predict the location of each tweet. Each tweet in the dataset has a *true* label (longitude, latitude), which is framed as a supervised classification problem of which US city (of 378 most popular ones) and state the tweet originated from. Our main intuition is to incorporate the locations mentioned in the tweet explicitly as part of the input to the classifier, since people likely talk about nearby locations.

As our focus is on LOC mentions, we analyze AllenNLP mention extraction capability on different mention types, and show, in Table 7, that it achieves a 67% accuracy on average for LOC mentions, the best accuracy among other types. We also show how often these mentions are linked in Table 8, indicating most of the LOC mentions actually get linked to entities in the KB. For all the linked mentions, we can extract the relevant data from the KB,

	Size	#LOC	#Links	Coverage
Train	544,667	385,295	219,167	**56%**
Test	527,783	322,852	201,563	**62%**

Table 8: **Statistics of UTGEO2011-small**, with number of all LOC mentions, number of mentions that are linked to KB, and fraction of tweets with at least 1 link.

	State prediction		City prediction	
	Base	+Tweeki	Base	+Tweeki
Tweet-level	18.0	**19.3**	9.1	**11.0**
User-level	24.3	**26.1**	13.0	**15.2**

Table 9: **City and State Prediction** using base model (without any extra information) and when combined with locations from Tweeki preprocessing.

in this case the actual geographical *coordinates* of each mentioned entity (using WikiData as the KG makes this much easier as it is structured, compared to linking to Wikipedia as is common). We convert these coordinates to their nearest US state and city, and append these locations to the tweet (a simple form of feature engineering). For example the tweet: *"Duran Duran Concert (@Nokia Theatre w/ others)"* will change to *"Duran Duran Concert (@Nokia Theater w/ others) Los Angeles, California"*. We apply above to the whole dataset, and train a simple deep learning model (BiLSTM).

Based on the results in Table 9, using Tweeki and appending Wikidata information to tweets increases accuracy for the both tweet and user-level (for user-level prediction we aggregate output probabilities of all tweets from the user, then choose the most probable label). This demonstrates that even such a simple approach to incorporating KB information can provide improvements to existing problems, suggesting many applications of entity linking to tweets and other social media text.

5   Related Work

Entity Linking Systems   Entity linking (EL) of tweets has attracted a lot of attention recently (Liu et al., 2013; Huang et al., 2014; Sikdar and Gambäck, 2016; Nie et al., 2018). Similar to entity linking systems for general text, EL for tweets is primarily composed of two major steps: 1) the identification of the mentions, similar to tasks such as term expansion (Zou et al., 2014), and 2) identifying the candidate entities to the identified mentions. For the latter step, roughly two types of features are used. Local features identify one mention at the time and disambiguate it separately such

as using prior probability in Liu et al. (2013) or temporal relevance mention in Tran et al. (2015). Global features take a more comprehensive view and consider the relations between the entity candidates for the different mentions of the tweet (Huang et al., 2014; Feng et al., 2018). However, global approaches are more challenging in noisy domains like tweets, and unlikely to provide significant benefits for short texts. Some approaches use a graph-based representation to combine of local and global features (Huang et al., 2014). Moreover, recently, neural network methods have been applied to entity linking to model the local contextual information, such as (Nie et al., 2018) that captures semantic information between the local context and the candidate entity via representation-based and interaction-based neural semantic matching models.

Among all the proposed models, in this paper, we chose TagMe (Ferragina and Scaiella, 2010) that uses global features in an unsupervised manner, and Babelfy (Moro et al., 2014) that uses random walks and a densest subgraph algorithm for jointly disambiguating word senses and entity linking. Although Tag-Me is specifically designed for short text, Babelfy is a general purpose entity linker which also suitable for short and highly ambiguous text disambiguation (Moro et al., 2014). We also consider other popular linking approaches from outside of social media such as AIDA (Hoffart et al., 2011b), which uses Stanford NER Tagger and adopts the YAGO2 knowledge base (Hoffart et al., 2011a). From recent state-of-the-art models, we select End-to-End Neural Entity Linking (Kolitsas et al., 2018) that uses context-aware compatibility score based on word and entity embeddings, coupled with a neural attention and a global voting mechanisms, and OpenTapioca (Delpeuch, 2019) as an end to end EL approach to Wikidata that relies on topic similarities and local entity context. Although these models are not specifically designed for noisy and short text, but they are sophisticated general purpose EL proposed recently and tested on different data types including Twitter.

Twitter-related datasets   Many Twitter-based datasets have been introduced for different research goals. Related to EL task, we can divide the datasets into two categories: named entity recognition (NER) datasets and named entity linking (NEL) datasets. NER datasets focus on identifying mentions and their types, such as dataset by Ritter et al. (2011) or BTC (Derczynski et al., 2016), with gold dataset published for concept extraction challenge in #MSM2013 (Cano Basave et al., 2013).

Based on GERBIL benchmark report (Röder et al., 2018), for the A2KB (NER and NEL) task in tweets, the most commonly used datasets have been introduced in "Making Sense of Microposts" challenge (#Microposts) from 2014 till 2016. Among them, Named Entity Extraction and Linking Challenge2016 (NEEL2016) is the most popular one to use, consisting of 296 tweets in testset with 3.4 mentions in each tweet on average. It is also valuable to mention that 384 out of 1022 mentions in this dataset refer to three topics: *"Donald Trump"*, *"StarWars"* and *"StarWars (The Force Awakens)"*(Nie et al., 2018). Another dataset designed for A2KB task is Derczynski et al. (2015), consist of 183 tweets with 1.57 entities per tweet on avg. As these datasets links are not provided in Wikidata ID, we designed a converter to map each link to its corresponding Wikidata ID.

6 Conclusions

Although entity linking for social media text has many potential applications, it has not been widely adopted by the community due to presence of supervised and complex entity linking systems that are hard to maintain, extend, and apply to new entities and different writing styles. Further, there is no large-scale linked corpus of tweets available for researchers to use for social media analysis, and very few *gold* annotated tweet datasets to evaluate and compare different entity linking systems. Our proposed work, collectively called Tweeki, consists of an unsupervised, extensible entity linking pipeline, a massive automatically-linked dataset of tweets (TweekiData), and a small, manually annotated dataset of gold links (TweekiGold). Our experiments show that the linker is accurate, and the dataset can be used to obtain improvements in downstream applications. We have released the source code and datasets from this paper at https://ucinlp.github.io/tweeki.

Acknowledgements

We would like to thank the anonymous reviewers for their feedback. We are also grateful for authors of End-to-End Neural Entity Linking, OpenTapioca, Spacy, and AllenNLP for making their code available. This work was funded in part by National Science Foundation award #IIS-1817183.

References

Amparo Elizabeth Cano Basave, Andrea Varga, Matthew Rowe, Milan Stankovic, and Aba-Sah Dadzie. 2013. Making sense of microposts (# msm2013) concept extraction challenge.

H. Chang, D. Lee, M. Eltaher, and J. Lee. 2012. @phillies tweeting from philly? predicting twitter user locations with spatial word usage. In *2012 IEEE/ACM International Conference on Advances in Social Networks Analysis and Mining*, pages 111–118.

Zhiyuan Cheng, James Caverlee, and Kyumin Lee. 2010. You are where you tweet: A content-based approach to geo-locating twitter users. In *Proceedings of the 19th ACM International Conference on Information and Knowledge Management*, CIKM 10, page 759768, New York, NY, USA. Association for Computing Machinery.

M. D. Conover, B. Goncalves, J. Ratkiewicz, A. Flammini, and F. Menczer. 2011. Predicting the political alignment of twitter users. In *2011 IEEE Third International Conference on Privacy, Security, Risk and Trust and 2011 IEEE Third International Conference on Social Computing*, pages 192–199.

Marco Cornolti, Paolo Ferragina, and Massimiliano Ciaramita. 2013. A framework for benchmarking entity-annotation systems. In *Proceedings of the International World Wide Web Conference (WWW) (Practice & Experience Track)*.

Hongliang Dai, Yangqiu Song, Liwei Qiu, and Rijia Liu. 2018. Entity linking within a social media platform: A case study on yelp. In *Proceedings of the 2018 Conference on Empirical Methods in Natural Language Processing*, pages 2023–2032, Brussels, Belgium. Association for Computational Linguistics.

Antonin Delpeuch. 2019. Opentapioca: Lightweight entity linking for wikidata. *ArXiv*, abs/1904.09131.

Leon Derczynski, Kalina Bontcheva, and Ian Roberts. 2016. Broad twitter corpus: A diverse named entity recognition resource. In *Proceedings of COLING 2016, the 26th International Conference on Computational Linguistics: Technical Papers*, pages 1169–1179, Osaka, Japan. The COLING 2016 Organizing Committee.

Leon Derczynski, Diana Maynard, Giuseppe Rizzo, Marieke van Erp, Genevieve Gorrell, Raphal Troncy, Johann Petrak, and Kalina Bontcheva. 2015. Analysis of named entity recognition and linking for tweets. *Information Processing & Management*, 51(2):32 – 49.

Yue Feng, Fattane Zarrinkalam, Ebrahim Bagheri, Hossein Fani, and Feras Al-Obeidat. 2018. Entity linking of tweets based on dominant entity candidates. *Social Network Analysis and Mining*, 8:1–16.

Paolo Ferragina and Ugo Scaiella. 2010. Tagme: on-the-fly annotation of short text fragments (by wikipedia entities). In *CIKM '10*.

Octavian-Eugen Ganea and Thomas Hofmann. 2017. Deep joint entity disambiguation with local neural attention. In *Proceedings of the 2017 Conference on Empirical Methods in Natural Language Processing*, pages 2619–2629, Copenhagen, Denmark. Association for Computational Linguistics.

Matt Gardner, Joel Grus, Mark Neumann, Oyvind Tafjord, Pradeep Dasigi, Nelson F. Liu, Matthew Peters, Michael Schmitz, and Luke S. Zettlemoyer. 2017. Allennlp: A deep semantic natural language processing platform.

K. Greenfield, Rajmonda S. Caceres, M. Coury, K. Geyer, Youngjune Gwon, J. Matterer, A. Mensch, C. Sahin, and Olga Simek. 2016. A reverse approach to named entity extraction and linking in microposts. In *#Microposts*.

Nitish Gupta, Sameer Singh, and Dan Roth. 2017. Entity linking via joint encoding of types, descriptions, and context. In *Empirical Methods in Natural Language Processing (EMNLP)*.

Johannes Hoffart, Fabian M. Suchanek, Klaus Berberich, Edwin Lewis-Kelham, Gerard de Melo, and Gerhard Weikum. 2011a. Yago2: Exploring and querying world knowledge in time, space, context, and many languages. In *Proceedings of the 20th International Conference Companion on World Wide Web*, WWW 11, page 229232, New York, NY, USA. Association for Computing Machinery.

Johannes Hoffart, Mohamed Amir Yosef, Ilaria Bordino, Hagen Fürstenau, Manfred Pinkal, Marc Spaniol, Bilyana Taneva, Stefan Thater, and Gerhard Weikum. 2011b. Robust disambiguation of named entities in text. In *Proceedings of the 2011 Conference on Empirical Methods in Natural Language Processing*, pages 782–792, Edinburgh, Scotland, UK. Association for Computational Linguistics.

Hongzhao Huang, Yunbo Cao, Xiaojiang Huang, Heng Ji, and Chin-Yew Lin. 2014. Collective tweet wikification based on semi-supervised graph regularization. In *Proceedings of the 52nd Annual Meeting of the Association for Computational Linguistics (Volume 1: Long Papers)*, pages 380–390, Baltimore, Maryland. Association for Computational Linguistics.

Nikolaos Kolitsas, Octavian-Eugen Ganea, and Thomas Hofmann. 2018. End-to-end neural entity linking. In *Proceedings of the 22nd Conference on Computational Natural Language Learning*, pages 519–529, Brussels, Belgium. Association for Computational Linguistics.

Sayali Kulkarni, Amit Singh, Ganesh Ramakrishnan, and Soumen Chakrabarti. 2009. Collective annotation of wikipedia entities in web text. In *Proceedings of the 15th ACM SIGKDD International Conference on Knowledge Discovery and Data Mining*, KDD 09, page 457466, New York, NY, USA. Association for Computing Machinery.

Jey Han Lau, Nigel Collier, and Timothy Baldwin. 2012. On-line trend analysis with topic models: #twitter trends detection topic model online. In *Proceedings of COLING 2012*, pages 1519–1534, Mumbai, India. The COLING 2012 Organizing Committee.

Xiao Ling, Sameer Singh, and Daniel S. Weld. 2015. Design challenges for entity linking. *Transactions of the Association for Computational Linguistics*, 3:315–328.

Xiaohua Liu, Yitong Li, Haocheng Wu, Ming Zhou, Furu Wei, and Yi Lu. 2013. Entity linking for tweets. In *Proceedings of the 51st Annual Meeting of the Association for Computational Linguistics (Volume 1: Long Papers)*, pages 1304–1311.

Robert L. Logan, Nelson F. Liu, Matthew E. Peters, Matt Gardner, and Sameer Singh. 2019. Barack's Wife Hillary: Using Knowledge Graphs for Fact-Aware Language Modeling. In *Association for Computational Linguistics (ACL)*, pages 5962–5971.

Edgar Meij, Wouter Weerkamp, and Maarten de Rijke. 2012. Adding semantics to microblog posts. In *Proceedings of the Fifth ACM International Conference on Web Search and Data Mining*, WSDM 12, page 563572, New York, NY, USA. Association for Computing Machinery.

Yasuhide Miura, Motoki Taniguchi, Tomoki Taniguchi, and Tomoko Ohkuma. 2017. Unifying text, metadata, and user network representations with a neural network for geolocation prediction. In *Proceedings of the 55th Annual Meeting of the Association for Computational Linguistics (Volume 1: Long Papers)*, pages 1260–1272, Vancouver, Canada. Association for Computational Linguistics.

Taro Miyazaki, Afshin Rahimi, Trevor Cohn, and Timothy Baldwin. 2018. Twitter geolocation using knowledge-based methods. In *Proceedings of the 2018 EMNLP Workshop W-NUT: The 4th Workshop on Noisy User-generated Text*, pages 7–16, Brussels, Belgium. Association for Computational Linguistics.

Andrea Moro, Alessandro Raganato, and Roberto Navigli. 2014. Entity linking meets word sense disambiguation: a unified approach. *Transactions of the Association for Computational Linguistics*, 2:231–244.

F. Nie, Shuyan Zhou, Jing Liu, Jinpeng Wang, Chin-Yew Lin, and R. Pan. 2018. Aggregated semantic matching for short text entity linking. In *CoNLL*.

Alexander Pak and Patrick Paroubek. 2010. Twitter as a corpus for sentiment analysis and opinion mining. In *Proceedings of the Seventh International Conference on Language Resources and Evaluation (LREC'10)*, Valletta, Malta. European Language Resources Association (ELRA).

Matthew E. Peters, Mark Neumann, Robert L. Logan, Roy Schwartz, Vidur Joshi, Sameer Singh, and Noah A. Smith. 2019. Knowledge enhanced contextual word representations. In *Empirical Methods in Natural Language Processing (EMNLP)*.

Priya Radhakrishnan, Partha Talukdar, and Vasudeva Varma. 2018. ELDEN: Improved entity linking using densified knowledge graphs. In *Proceedings of the 2018 Conference of the North American Chapter of the Association for Computational Linguistics: Human Language Technologies, Volume 1 (Long Papers)*, pages 1844–1853, New Orleans, Louisiana. Association for Computational Linguistics.

Danica Radovanovic, Katrin Weller, and Aba-Sah Dadzie. 2016. Making sense of microposts (#microposts2016) social sciences track. In *#Microposts*.

Jonathan Raiman and Olivier Raiman. 2018. Deeptype: Multilingual entity linking by neural type system evolution. In *AAAI*.

Lev Ratinov, Dan Roth, Doug Downey, and Mike Anderson. 2011. Local and global algorithms for disambiguation to Wikipedia. In *Proceedings of the 49th Annual Meeting of the Association for Computational Linguistics: Human Language Technologies*, pages 1375–1384, Portland, Oregon, USA. Association for Computational Linguistics.

Alan Ritter, Sam Clark, Mausam, and Oren Etzioni. 2011. Named entity recognition in tweets: An experimental study. In *Proceedings of the 2011 Conference on Empirical Methods in Natural Language Processing*, pages 1524–1534, Edinburgh, Scotland, UK. Association for Computational Linguistics.

G. Rizzo, M. V. Erp, J. Plu, and Raphaël Troncy. 2015. Making sense of microposts (#microposts2016) named entity recognition and linking (neel) challenge. In *#Microposts*.

Michael Röder, Ricardo Usbeck, and Axel-Cyrille Ngonga Ngomo. 2018. GERBIL - benchmarking named entity recognition and linking consistently. *Semantic Web*, 9(5):605–625.

Stephen Roller, Michael Speriosu, Sarat Rallapalli, Benjamin Wing, and Jason Baldridge. 2012. Supervised text-based geolocation using language models on an adaptive grid. In *EMNLP-CoNLL*.

Utpal Kumar Sikdar and Björn Gambäck. 2016. Twitter named entity extraction and linking using differential evolution. In *ICON*.

Tuan Tran, Nam Khanh Tran, Asmelash Teka Hadgu, and Robert Jäschke. 2015. Semantic annotation for microblog topics using Wikipedia temporal information. In *Proceedings of the 2015 Conference on Empirical Methods in Natural Language Processing*, pages 97–106, Lisbon, Portugal. Association for Computational Linguistics.

Jörg Waitelonis and H. Sack. 2016. Named entity linking in #tweets with kea. In *#Microposts*.

Mohamed Amir Yosef, Johannes Hoffart, Ilaria Bordino, Marc Spaniol, and Gerhard Weikum. 2011. Aida: An online tool for accurate disambiguation of named entities in text and tables. *PVLDB*, 4:1450–1453.

Xianqi Zou, Chengjie Sun, Yaming Sun, Bingquan Liu, and Lei Lin. 2014. Linking entities in tweets to wikipedia knowledge base. In *Natural Language Processing and Chinese Computing*, pages 368–378, Berlin, Heidelberg. Springer Berlin Heidelberg.

Representation learning of writing style

Julien Hay[1,2,3], **Bich-Liên Doan**[2,3], **Fabrice Popineau**[2,3] **and Ouassim Ait Elhara**[1]

[1]Octopeek SAS, 95880 Enghien-les-Bains, France
[2]Laboratoire de Recherche en Informatique, Paris-Saclay University, 91190 Gif-sur-Yvette, France
[3]CentraleSupélec, Paris-Saclay University, 91190 Gif-sur-Yvette, France
{julien.hay, ouassim.aitelhara}@octopeek.com
{bich-lien.doan, fabrice.popineau}@centralesupelec.fr

Abstract

In this paper, we introduce a new method of representation learning that aims to embed documents in a stylometric space. Previous studies in the field of authorship analysis focused on feature engineering techniques in order to represent document styles and to enhance model performance in specific tasks. Instead, we directly embed documents in a stylometric space by relying on a reference set of authors and the *intra-author consistency* property which is one of two components in our definition of writing style. The main intuition of this paper is that we can define a general stylometric space from a set of reference authors such that, in this space, the coordinates of different documents will be close when the documents are by the same author, and spread away when they are by different authors, even for documents by authors who are not in the set of reference authors. The method we propose allows for the clustering of documents based on stylistic clues reflecting the authorship of documents. For the empirical validation of the method, we train a deep neural network model to predict authors of a large reference dataset consisting of news and blog articles. Albeit the learning process is supervised, it does not require a dedicated labeling of the data but it relies only on the metadata of the articles which are available in huge amounts. We evaluate the model on multiple datasets, on both the authorship clustering and the authorship attribution tasks.

1 Introduction

Authorship analysis is an ensemble of methods that aims to extract useful authorship information of a text by analyzing writing style. The most commonly addressed tasks in this field are classification tasks such as authorship attribution (Stamatatos, 2017), authorship verification (Boumber et al., 2019) and authorship characterization. The authorship attribution is the process of inferring the author of documents among known authors while the authorship verification is the process of deciding whether or not a given document was written by a given author. To this end, most studies rely on feature engineering to represent the input documents in order to improve the performance of machine learning algorithms. Feature engineering consists in transforming raw input data into new input data by using domain knowledge with the expectation that the new features will be more suitable for learning an efficient model. For the two aforementioned tasks, the process consists in selecting textual characteristics of documents, then, either use a classifier to predict the author of a document based on these characteristics, or calculate similarities between document representations.

One common way to choose these document representation features is by assessing whether or not they can enhance the prediction accuracy. Sometimes these features intuitively belong to style such as function words (Goldstein-Stewart et al., 2009; Menon and Choi, 2011), sometimes they just correspond to common NLP features such as distributional representations of documents (Chen et al., 2017; Gupta et al., 2019; Bagnall, 2015). Few studies attempt to directly produce unsupervised representations of style in order to project unseen documents in a low dimensional stylometric space (Ding et al., 2019; Jasper et al., 2018; Boumber et al., 2019). Feature engineering is designed by humans based on heuristics, a labor-intensive process. However, recent studies show that automatically learning a representation of raw data is useful for many reasons described in Bengio et al. (2013). Learned representations are suitable in classification and clustering tasks since these representations manage to select discriminating information from raw data and represent them in a low dimensional vector space (Arora and Risteski, 2017). Moreover,

Proceedings of the 2020 EMNLP Workshop W-NUT: The Sixth Workshop on Noisy User-generated Text, pages 232–243
Online, Nov 19, 2020. ©2020 Association for Computational Linguistics

this discriminating information is not necessarily captured by humans through heuristics.

Documents belonging to same authors are generally consistent in their writing style (Karlgren, 2004) even for authors covering a large range of topics (Patchala and Bhatnagar, 2018). The method we propose relies on this observation. In this paper, we validate the *style-generalization* assumption which is based on two propositions. First, it states that we can represent unseen documents of unseen authors by generalizing stylometric features from a set of known authors and known documents. Second, documents that belong to the same author tend to have similar representations in the stylometric space (given a standard similarity function). In order to validate this assumption, we exploit recent advances in text and sentence representation with deep neural network (DNN) architectures, especially transformers (Devlin et al., 2019; Yang et al., 2019). We propose a transformer-based DNN model fine-tuned on the authorship attribution task using a large dataset of documents whose authors are known (the reference set). Then we assess the model in its ability to capture the similarity between documents of the same authors in a clustering experiment.

In this paper, we first give an overview of related work on authorship analysis in Section 2. In Section 3, we propose a definition of the style and the motivations behind our representation learning method. In Section 4, we explain our method and introduce the *style-generalization* assumption. Section 5 presents the experimentation on the main task which is the authorship clustering and on a second, the authorship attribution task. Finally, in Section 6, we deepen our analysis by studying the second property of our definition of style.

2 Related work

Neal et al. (2017) and Stamatatos (2009) gave an overview of features used for authorship analysis. Categories of features for stylometry are lexical (e.g. sentences length, vocabulary richness), syntactic (e.g. punctuation, *Part-of-Speech* tags), semantic (e.g. synonyms, semantic dependencies), structural (e.g. average paragraph length, presence of quotes) and application-specific (presence of words in a specific lexicon). Authors also consider additional features which are hard to classify such as topic modeling based features and readability metrics. For instance, Bayesian methods such as

LDA was shown to be efficient in the e-mails and blog content authorship attribution (Seroussi et al., 2014) and the research paper authorship attribution (Rosen-Zvi et al., 2004). Most experiments in authorship analysis involve training machine learning models that take as input different features of these categories (Houvardas and Stamatatos, 2006; Yang et al., 2018; Tausczik and Pennebaker, 2010).

Recent studies tackle issues of the feature engineering process for authorship analysis by exploiting raw text samples using deep neural networks. Chen et al. (2017) proposed a gated recurrent unit (GRU) DNN trained on article and sentences for the authorship verification task. Other studies demonstrated the relevance of recurrent neural networks such as GRU and long short-term memory (LSTM) DNNs on the authorship attribution task (Gupta et al., 2019; Bagnall, 2015). More recently, Boumber et al. (2018) proposed a convolutional neural network-based model for the multi-label authorship attribution of scientific publications.

Besides the use of DNN for classification, very few studies attempt to automatically embed stylometric features from a corpus of documents. Qian et al. (2015) are the first to rely on an external dataset of known authors to pretrain a general model which can compute stylometric similaries between documents. They proposed training a support vector machine-based (SVM) model that was re-used for a test dataset containing unseen authors. As far as we know, this study is the first attempt at generalizing a stylometric similarity space while still relying on handcrafted stylometric features. Ding et al. (2019) proposed a model that jointly learns topical and lexical distributional representation of documents in an unsupervised manner to help authorship analysis. Jasper et al. (2018) proposed a model that embeds the writing style of English novels. The model is composed of *fast-Text* word embeddings and a stacked LSTM. The authors demonstrated that their model performed well on a subset of the PAN14 dataset for the authorship verification task. In order to verify authorship of social networks posts, they designed their experiments so that model inputs were short text samples. Boumber et al. (2019) recently used a recurrent neural network-based architecture and adversarial learning to tackle the authorship verification task. The model was trained to embed pairs of documents and was assessed on authorship verification task in transfer learning settings, when authors of the test set do not exist in the train set.

Instead, we propose a representation learning method that aims to embed documents in a stylometric space relative to a large dataset of well-known authors. We use a modification of a pre-trained BERT model (Sanh et al., 2019) in a classification task as proposed in several recent works (Sun et al., 2019; Reimers and Gurevych, 2019). To the best of our knowledge, this paper is the first to propose an authorship attribution-training driven model generalizing stylometric features so that documents of unseen authors can be clustered without fine-tuning. Additionally, our method relies on a large dedicated dataset that can be extended. We trained our models on a large amount of data by using news and blog articles benefiting from the wide availability of such data on the web.

3 Motivation

An author can adopt several styles, and one of them can be similar to the writing style of another author. Karlgren (2004) defined the style as "a consistent and distinguishable tendency to make [some of these] linguistic choices". Moreover, Karlgren (2004) explained that "texts are much more than what they are about". Any textual characteristic that is not semantic or topical belongs to stylistic choices of the author. Different expressions can have a common meaning, and can refer to the same objects and the same events, but still be made up of different words and different syntax, corresponding to the author's willingness to let a context, an orientation, sometimes an emotion be shown through (Argamon et al., 2005).

News articles showed to have specific writing style by using, for instance, date as adverb in "The governor Thursday announced..." or anthropomorphization in "The 1990s saw an increase in crime...". It is called journalese (Dickson and Skole, 2012). Headlines of newspapers also have their own style, called headlinese, such as articles drop (Weir, 2009). Today's trend towards clickbait also has an influence on headlines (Chakraborty et al., 2016). Finally, let's mention style guides of newspapers that not only influence typography (e.g. paragraph structure, quotation, italic) but also the usage of the language (Cameron, 1996). For instance, a style guide can more or less encourage the use of the active voice against the passive voice. Some of the newspapers can have their own style guide that their writers follow, allowing the text to be consistent for the reader while any variation having no purpose could be distracting (Hicks, 2002).

Style appears more or less pronounced depending on the text passages, it is difficult to define it precisely and, given a document, to find a set of words (or sequence of words) that will strictly define the style of its author. The text is the combination of a shape – its style – and a content which are intertwinned thanks to the choice of specific words. Words or sequence of words in the text can rarely be denoted as belonging specifically to the style or to the content. This is why extracting style features is hard. From documents of a reference corpus, we aim to extract latent structures falling within the scope of writing style. We argue that these latent structures can be identified by DNNs, typically RNN models with attention layers which will focus on style-related terms. From a linguistic point of view these latent structures map to lexical, syntactic or structural fragment of sentences or paragraphs. Intuitively, when extracting a style representation of a document, we seek to focus on latent structures that will satisfy these two properties :

Intra-author consistency the property of being consistent in documents belonging to the same author.

Semantic undistinguishness the property of carrying very little information on what makes the document semantically (e.g. topics, named entities) distinguishable in the corpus.

Thus, this definition, inspired by Karlgren (2004); Holmes (1998), means that the style of a document is represented by linguistic structures which are consistent for individual authors (allowing their identification) but more likely semantically poor regarding the content of the document (e.g. topic, named entities). Indeed, what the document is about is a constraint that imposes on the author to use a specific vocabulary. The terms that belong to this specific vocabulary have a strong semantic value with respect to the theme of the document, and on the contrary, are less likely to convey the author's style. The representation learning method is based on identifying consistent latent structures following the *intra-author consistency* property. Next to that, the *semantic undistinguishness* is a property which can be verified by studying attention weights of a trained DNN models.

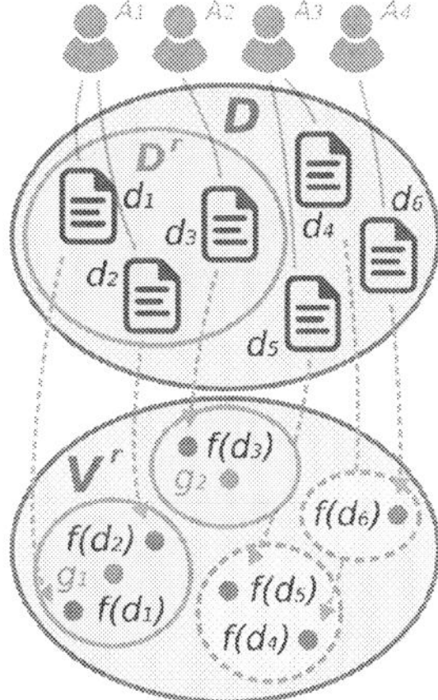

Figure 1: The *style-generalization* assumption

4 Method

Let's denote $D = \{d_1, ..., d_n\}$ a set of documents and $A = \{a_1, ..., a_m\}$ a set of authors so that each document belongs to one and only one author and each author wrote at least one document.

Let's denote $R\text{-}set = (D^r, A^r)$ the reference set with $D^r \subset D$, $A^r \subset A$, $|D^r| = n^r$, $|A^r| = m^r$ and A^r is the set of all the authors of the documents in D^r. Sizes n^r and m^r are typically large and $n^r \geq m^r$.

Let's denote $V^r \in [0, 1]^{m^r}$ a vector space so that $\forall v \in V^r, \sum_{i=1}^{m^r} v_i = 1$. Thus, softmax vectors for A^r belong to V^r. We denote $G^r = \{g_1^r, ..., g_{m^r}^r\}$ the set of one-hot vectors that correspond to the ground-truth vectors of each author in A^r. Thus, vectors from G^r also belong to V^r. Each document in D^r is associated with one and only one vector from G^r.

Let $f^r : \mathbb{R}^l \times \mathbb{R}^w \rightarrow V^r$ a function that projects input documents, represented by word vectors, from D^r into V^r with l the size of the documents (truncated or padded) and w the dimension of the word vectors. The purpose of f^r is to project each document $d_i^r, i \in \{1, ..., n^r\}$ closer to its corresponding vector in G^r than to any other ground-truth vector.

The main assumption of this paper, the *style-generalization* assumption, is that two representations defined by f^r of two unseen documents are more likely to be similar if they belong to the same author than if they do not. Intuitively, we assume that any unseen document belonging to an unknown author is similar, in terms of style, to documents belonging to a subset of known authors and that another document of the same unknown author is likely to be similar, in terms of style, to documents belonging to this same subset of known authors. Figure 1 illustrates the *style-generalization* assumption. Blue sets in V^r correspond to representations of documents from D^r. f^r allows to project documents from D^r to V^r such that the representation of a document is close to its corresponding ground truth vector (in red color). Green sets correspond to unseen document representations in V^r. The assumption states that close representations (green sets) likely belong to the same author.

More formally, let's denote $U\text{-}set = (D^u, A^u)$ a set of unseen documents and authors with $D^u \subset D$, $A^u \subset A$, $|D^u| = n^u$, $|A^u| = m^u$ and A^u is the set of all the authors of the documents in D^u. $A^r \cap A^u = \emptyset$ and $D^r \cap D^u = \emptyset$. The *style-generalization* assumption states that the projection of documents from D^u (the $U\text{-}set$) into V^r using f^r allows to compute similarities such that similar documents from D_u are likely written by the same author. Thus, learning f^r on a reference set allows authorship clustering in the general stylometric space that it defines.

This method, which can be called the *style-generalization* learning method, aims to calculate stylometric similarities of documents without considering the author of the document, i.e. without fine-tuning. In Section 5, we propose to use a DNN model as the function f^r. We train the model on the reference set and generate vector representations of unseen documents by using intermediate weights representation in the DNN.

5 Experimentation

5.1 Dataset

Since it is important to have heterogeneous documents in the dataset to generalize representations, we relied on a large amount of English news and blog articles. We merged all documents from The Blog Authorship Corpus (Schler et al., 2006), ICWSM datasets (Burton et al., 2009, 2011) and news collected for this study[1].

All documents have at least one domain name such as *nytimes.com*. Authors were extracted from the HTML content. In cases when an author is found, we consider the label of the document to be the concatenation of the domain and the author, or else the label is the domain alone. Domains correspond, in most cases, to online newspapers or blogs.

---

[1] Datasets, code and pretrained models are available at `https://github.com/hayj/DeepStyle`

We made the final dataset, named *NewsID* (*News Source Identification*), by only keeping documents longer than 20 words. We also removed documents having a class (the author) that is sub-represented, i.e. a class with less than 200 documents.

Finally, we randomly generated a *R-set* gathering ~3.3 millions of documents and 1 200 different classes. We set a limit of 3 0000 documents per class. The average number of documents per class is 3 000. The *R-set* is large which is a requirement for our method. It is composed of reference authors with balanced numbers of documents to avoid having majority classes and majority "reference styles". We also randomly generated ~500 *U-sets* having 50 classes and 50 documents per class. *U-sets* does not contain any authors or documents of the *R-set*. Each *U-sets* is specific to an online newspaper or a blog (e.g. *blogger.com, livejournal.com, washingtonpost.com, breitbart.com, cnn.com, theguardian.com* and *nytimes.com*) and gather documents of different authors from the given websites. For example, the *U-set nytimes.com* has 2 500 news articles of *nytimes.com*. The articles were written by authors of this online newspaper. Each author wrote 50 articles in the *U-set*. The same goes with other online newspaper and blogs.

In the *NewsID* dataset, we concatenated the authors of the articles with the domain name of online newspapers and blogs. After studying the labels of our dataset, we noticed that a large majority (approximately 99%) of the authors common to several journals are actually namesakes because they use short pseudonyms (*Alex, Erik, Lucy,* etc.). Thus, we have not differentiated the rare cases where an author appears to have written for several newspapers (e.g. *Andrew Restuccia* for *politico.com* and *thehill.com*) by manual labeling. Authors are consistent in their writings, and as we have seen, so are online newspapers, especially because their writers have to follow a style guide. But even in cases where it is difficult to distinguish the articles of an author who has written for two different newspapers, we argue that the existence of two labels for the same author will have little impact on the learning of our models and the stylometric representation of the documents. Indeed, if the model fails to capture the differences between the documents of this author, the consequence will be that the internal representations of the deep neural network will be close for the documents of one or the other of the two labels it has to predict. The

similarity of the internal representations of the deep neural network for these two reference authors will not necessarily imply the addition of noise in the projection of unseen documents from the *U-sets*.

5.2 Models for learning f^r

In order to validate the *style-generalization* assumption, we need to learn the function f^r. To fulfill this objective, we propose to train two DNNs on the *R-set* following the authorship attribution task, a classification task. Data are documents of the *R-set* and labels are those described in Section 5.1. By relying on the *intra-author consistency* property, we train the models to capture consistent lexical clues of each author. Then we rely on the trained model to embed documents of the *U-set* by selecting weights in an intermediate layer.

First we implemented the *SNA* model (*Stylometric Neural Attention*) which is a bi-directionnal LSTM with attentions mainly based on the architecture proposed by Zhou et al. (2016) with two fully connected layers of 500 units and of softmax layer of 1 200 units. The loss function is the multiclass log loss. We set dropouts of each layer to 0.2. Inputs of the DNN are the *GloVe 840B* word vectors of firsts 1 200 words (Pennington et al., 2014) of a document. Documents are padded or truncated so that each has a size of 1 200 words.

Second, we implemented a model based on the BERT transformer architecture (Devlin et al., 2019) which is a bidirectional attention model with the use of masked words and next sentence prediction for the unsupervised pre-training phase. We use a variant of BERT, called DistilBERT, which uses the knowledge distillation principle reducing the size of the final DNN model (Sanh et al., 2019). We used DistilBERT because its training is less time-consuming. The DistilBERT base model was trained on an English corpus of books and Wikipedia pages. The *DBert-ft* model corresponds to an authorship attribution fine-tuning of the DistilBERT base model (uncased) on the *R-set*. We used a linear layer on top of the base model and a multi-class log loss as the loss function. The size of the last layer is 1 200 and corresponds to the number of classes in the *R-set*. We let all layers trainable. Dropouts are set to 0.1.

When training the *DBert-ft* model, input documents are split into multiple parts of 512 *wordpieces*. Each part has the same label. This allows to increase the number of samples in the *R-set*. Inputs of the DNN take the form of 512 indexes from a common *wordpieces* vocabulary. In the next sections of this paper, when generating the representation of a single document, we compute the mean vector of all its parts. By doing so, we capture more information that can be used in the representation of the authorship of the document than if we only considered the first or last part of the document. Vector representations are outputs of the last layer before the classification layer on top of the model.

Intermediate layer choice for representation of documents in both models as well as the mean of document parts have been experimentally validated on a validation *U-set*. Both models are implemented with *TensorFlow* (Abadi et al., 2015). For both models, the learning time was about one week on a *NVIDIA TITAN V* GPU (12GB memory).

5.3 Baselines

In order to compare representations of our models in the authorship clustering experiment, we use several baselines. We generate random vectors of different dimensions and variances. **Stylo** corresponds to stylometric handcrafted features commonly used in authorship analysis such as readability scores, vocabulary richness, sentences count. **TFIDF** corresponds to TFIDF weights of documents reduced to 100 dimensions using SVD. **LDA** (Blei et al., 2003) corresponds to topics vectors (100 topics) of documents. **Doc2Vec** corresponds to vectors representations of a *Doc2Vec* (Le and Mikolov, 2014) model trained in an unsupervised manner on documents of the *NewsID R-set*. **USent** corresponds to vectors of the *Universal Sentence Encoder* model trained on English Wikipedia and news data (Cer et al., 2018). **InferSent** corresponds to vectors of an InferSent model trained on natural language inference data (Conneau et al., 2017). **BERT** corresponds to vectors of BERT trained on large English books and wikipedia articles dataset (Devlin et al., 2019). We used the large and uncased version of BERT. **DBert** corresponds to vectors of the non fine-tuned DistilBERT uncased model (Sanh et al., 2019). For models producing sentence representations (*USent, InferSent, BERT*), inputs are the mean of sentences representations.

5.4 Metrics

In order to evaluate each model, we first generated vector representations $V = \{v_1, ..., v_p\}$ of all $d_p^u \in D^u$ (the *U-set*) using a given model such that $\forall v \in V, |v| = k, k > 0$. Then, we assessed the ability

of these representations to cluster the documents well according to a similarity measure and ground truth labels (internal clustering evaluation). We use labels $L = \{L_1, ..., L_p\}$ such that $L_i = L_j$ if and only if d_i^u has the same author as d_j^u. We rely on a standard clustering metric: the *Davies-Bouldin index* (*DavB*) (Davies and Bouldin, 1979). *DavB* takes V and L and returns a clustering quality score greater than 0. It is defined as the average similarity between each cluster and its most similar one. The lower the *DavB* is, the better is the quality of clusters.

In this experiment, we also want to assess, on average, how well documents are ranked in relation to each other, given their vector representation and a similarity measure. Thus we introduce a new clustering metric, called *SimRank*, based on a commonly used metric assessing the ranking quality: the *nDCG* (Järvelin and Kekäläinen, 2002).

$$\text{SimRank}(REL) = \frac{\sum_{p=1}^{|REL|} \text{nDCG}'(REL_p)}{|REL|} \tag{1}$$

Equation 1 gives the *SimRank* with REL a set of ranking vectors. A ranking vector (or graded relevance vector) rel is a vector such that $|rel| = k$ with k the number of documents in the *U-set* and $rel_i \in \{0, 1\}$. rel_i indicates whether the corresponding document in the ordered set of documents is relevant ($rel_i = 1$) or not ($rel_i = 0$). Documents are ordered by the cosine similarity between their vector representations and the vector representation of a target document. In this experiment, a document is relevant if it belongs to the same author as the target document. Thus, in our case, each rel vector corresponds to a ranking vector of each document in the *U-set* ordered by similarity with a target document in the *U-set*. REL is a square matrix corresponding to the all ranking vectors given each of documents in the *U-set* as the target document.

$$\text{DCG}(rel) = \sum_{i=1}^{k} \frac{2^{rel_i} - 1}{\log_2(i+1)} \tag{2}$$

$nDCG$ is the DCG given in equation 2 normalized between 0 and the DCG of the ideal ranking (namely the $iDCG$). In Eq. 1, we use $nDCG'$ which is the DCG normalized between the DCG of the worst ranking and the DCG of the ideal ranking. We normalized $nDCG$ using the worst ranking because, in our case, we always rank every

Id	Clusters	SimRank (±2σ)	DavB (±2σ)
1		1.0 (±0)	0.25 (±0.01)
2		0.69 (±0.01)	170 (±393)
3		0.66 (±0)	1.27 (±0.05)
4		0.53 (±0)	38 (±109)

Figure 2: Average *SimRank* and *DavB* scores of 1 000 randomly generated sets of 600 samples in four different cluster configurations

document according to a target document, while $nDCG$ is usually computed on a subset of documents that are returned by a search engine. Thus, the minimal value if we had used the original $nDCG$ would not be zero.

Figure 2 shows the advantages of *SimRank* compared to *DavB*. It shows the average *SimRank* and *DavB* scores of 1 000 randomly generated sets of 600 samples in four different cluster configurations. For the same cluster configuration, *SimRank* has less variance than *DavB*. In addition, some clusters such as those in the second configuration will be considered of lower quality than those in the last two configurations by the *DavB* metric.

However, as we discussed in section 3, an author can adopt several styles. For example, an author writing on political topics may sometimes write articles in a factual and descriptive style, and occasionally write in a completely different style: e.g. humorous, satirical. Thus, the articles of this author will be divided into two distinct clusters in a stylometric space as in the second configuration in the Figure 2. By using *SimRank*, we do not want to penalize these cases. Taking into account the order of the examples and not the distances, as well as the fact that the weights attributed to the samples decrease with the use of *nDCG*, allows us to minimize the effects of this multi-partitioning.

The *DavB* and the *SimRank* metric will give an insight of models performance regarding external tasks such as classification tasks. After the evaluation of models using both clustering metrics, we will evaluate models on the authorship attribution task which consist in predicting right author labels in *U-sets* (classification task). We will use the accuracy metric.

5.5 Results

Table 1 shows the performance of all models and baselines for the *SimRank* and *DavB* metrics. Scores are the mean on 22 *U-sets*. DBert-ft and

SNA score higher on the *SimRank* metric following by *TFIDF* and *Doc2Vec*. DBert-ft, *SNA* and *TFIDF* also perform well for the *DavB* metric with close scores. In this experiment, all documents and authors of test sets (*U-sets*) are unknown for all evaluated models.

Model	SimRk	DavB
Random	0.185	14.81
TFIDF	0.455	**4.683**
LDA	0.309	8.353
Stylo	0.276	65.71
Doc2Vec	0.430	6.194
USent	0.416	5.328
InferSent	0.374	5.625
BERT	0.378	5.469
SNA	0.463	4.785
DBert	0.339	7.058
DBert-ft	**0.474**	4.777

Table 1: Authorship clustering on 22 *U-sets*

All parameters, such as dimensions, number of topics and window size of *Doc2Vec*, were grid-searched on a validation *U-set*. In this experiment, we also generated *Sent2Vec* vectors (Pagliardini et al., 2018) but we didn't add it in results since the others sentences representation models score higher. The same goes for the non-negative matrix factorization on TFIDF weighting, which scores lower compared to *LDA*. Regarding the *SNA* model, we implemented a version without an attention layer and another with an unidirectional LSTM. We obtained lower scores for each of them. The difference in scores of *DBert* and *DBert-ft* indicates that the proposed *style-generalization* learning method allows to train a model generating better authorship clusters.

In addition to the authorship clustering, we propose to compare all these models on the authorship attribution task. Table 2 shows the mean accuracy of all combinations of models on the same 22 *U-sets*. The diagonal gives scores of models alone. In order to evaluate each of these combinations on a given *U-set*, we trained a linear SVM classifier model on 80% of the *U-set* with the concatenation of vector representations as input data. The score corresponds to the accuracy of predicting the right author label on the 20% remaining data. The model choice and its hyperparameters were grid-searched on another validation *U-set*.

Results show that the *DBert-ft* model obtains the

Model	TFIDF	LDA	Stylo	Doc2Vec	USent	InferSent	BERT	SNA	DBert	DBert-ft
TFIDF	0.514	0.525	0.096	0.475	0.599	0.629	0.553	0.581	0.547	0.598
LDA		0.163	0.098	0.477	0.518	0.590	0.541	0.555	0.541	0.600
Stylo			0.098	0.108	0.103	0.097	0.102	0.101	0.097	0.191
Doc2Vec				0.472	0.474	0.491	0.526	0.543	0.519	**0.641**
USent					0.499	0.612	0.538	0.579	0.550	0.598
InferSent						0.594	0.560	0.598	0.578	0.604
BERT							0.536	0.621	0.571	0.616
SNA								0.552	0.598	0.614
DBert									0.522	0.610
DBert-ft										**0.597**

Table 2: Mean accuracy (22 *U-sets*) of models combinations for the authorship attribution task

best accuracy when used alone. Its combination with *Doc2Vec* vectors obtain the highest scores, showing that these two representations are complementary and are able to capture different clues for the classification of authors. Note that *InferSent*, despite its low scores on the authorship clustering, obtains scores close to those of *DBert-ft* when used alone. Its combination with *TFIDF* vectors also obtains scores near the best combination. We tested the same combinations of models on the authorship clustering task with the *SimRank* metric and obtained the same results, i.e. *DBert-ft* got the highest scores when combined with the other models, and the best combination was *DBert-ft* with *Doc2Vec*. All these results validate the *style-generalization* assumption and prove the benefit of the method.

6   In-depth analysis

In this section, we intend to assess how well the trained models can, by using the *style-generalization* learning method, focus on terms exposing the second property of our definition of writing style: the *semantic undistinguishness*. For this purpose, we propose to analyze attention weights of the *SNA* model. In this experiment, our main concern was not the performance in the authorship attribution task but on the use of the attention layer trained with the method described in Section 4. Thus, we used *SNA* since its training phase is less time-consuming.

The *semantic undistinguishness* suggests that style-related linguistic structures tend to carry little information on content, topics, entities, etc. These style-related structures are often referred to as function words which are frequent in a corpus (Keste-

mont, 2014; Argamon et al., 2007). On the other hand, terms with a high semantic value that will identify, for instance, a topic, are those allowing the document to be distinguishable in a corpus. The TFIDF weighting is a well established method to estimate how important a word is to a document in a corpus. Thus, in order to quantitatively assess the *undistinguishness* of the *SNA* model, we propose a measure based on the TFIDF weighting. The *TFIDF focus* measure allows to compute how well attentions of the model focus on words having lower TFIDF weights:

$$\text{TFIDFFocus}(A, T) = \frac{\sum_{i=1}^{d} \sum_{j=1}^{w} A_{ij} \cdot T_{ij}}{d} \quad (3)$$

A is the attention matrix of size $w \times d$. w is the number of words in a document that we set to 1200 and d is the number of documents. Each line of the matrix corresponds to the attention weights in the *SNA* model for a document in a given *U-set*. An attention vector of a single document is normalized so that the weights sum to 1. The same goes with the normalized TFIDF matrix T of size $w \times d$. Thus, we defined the *TFIDF focus* as the mean of the attention weight times the TFIDF weight of each word. This measure is high when high values of TFIDF are in line with high values of attention and low when these high values of TFIDF are in line with low values of attention.

Given a pretrained *SNA* model and a *U-set*, we generate the matrix A using the model, the matrix T using the TFIDF weighting on the target *U-set* and, finally, the *TFIDF focus* score. Table 3 reports *TFIDF focus* scores on five *U-sets* composed of news articles and five *U-sets* composed of blog arti-

U-set **type**	*SNA* **trained on**	*U-set 1*	*U-set 2*	*U-set 3*	*U-set 4*	*U-set 5*	*Mean*
News	*Target U-sets*	0.642	0.650	0.606	0.601	0.661	0.632
	Other U-set	0.611	0.591	0.576	0.559	0.623	0.592
	R-set	**0.497**	**0.479**	**0.477**	**0.459**	**0.507**	**0.483**
Blog	*Target U-sets*	0.668	0.722	0.734	0.645	0.702	0.694
	Other U-set	0.637	0.670	0.670	0.606	0.648	0.646
	R-set	**0.547**	**0.579**	**0.575**	**0.526**	**0.560**	**0.557**

Table 3: *TFIDF focus* of *SNA* models on 5 news *U-sets* and 5 blog *U-sets*.

cles. For news articles, the third line shows *TFIDF focus* scores of the original *SNA* model trained in Section 5 following the *style-generalization* learning method. The first line shows *TFIDF focus* scores computed by a *SNA* model trained on the target *U-set*. Thus, these models learn to focus on words specific to authors in the target *U-set* to perform well in the authorship attribution. Scores show that these words have higher TFIDF weights. The second line shows *TFIDF focus* scores computed by a *SNA* model trained on an external *U-set* that we randomly chose. The external *U-set* acts as a short *R-set* with fewer documents and authors. As we can see, the use of a short *R-set* is not sufficient for the model to focus on words with lower TFIDF weights. The same goes for the three last lines but for blog articles.

In this experiment, we quantitatively showed that the original *SNA* model focuses its attention on function words having lower TFIDF weights (10% less on average), thus it is more able to capture stylometric features related to specific words exposing the *semantic undistinguishness* property than other models trained on smaller *U-sets*. The method proposed in Section 4 as well as the use of a large reference corpus have an impact on the results.

Note that, in the clustering experiment in Section 5, good performances of standard baselines such as *TFIDF* can be explained by the fact that documents of same authors have a topic bias (they share same semantic/topic words) because an author generally write on a few topics. This bias helps representations of vocabulary-based models to be close. However, such features fail to identify authors in cross-domain scenarios (Stamatatos, 2018), while our model focuses less on topic- and semantic-related words but achieves comparable performance (even better for *SimRank* and the authorship attribution task).

7 Conclusion

In this paper, we proposed a new method for the representation learning of writing style. We have shown that it is possible to generalize the writing style on the basis of a set of reference authors. The method follows a property of the style that we call *intra-author consistency*. We sought to validate two underlying propositions of the *style-generalization* assumption. First, we can represent unseen documents of unseen authors by using a model generalizing stylometric features from a set of known authors and known documents. Second, if two unseen documents have close representations using this model, they are likely to belong to the same author. Results show that the DNN model that was trained following our method succeeded in the authorship clustering of unseen documents belonging to unseen authors. It also performs well on the authorship attribution task. Moreover, we showed that a model trained with the *style-generalization* learning method is more able to capture stylometric structures exposing the *semantic undistinguishness* property.

From a practical point of view, our method does not require a tedious labeling effort but relies only on the metadata of a large dataset of articles. We believe that this work provides new perspectives in the field of authorship analysis by proposing a definition of writing style based on distributional properties, as well as a new method aiming to learn stylometric representations. In further studies, we intend to exploit style features in external tasks such as news recommendation. We already have promising results showing that style representations of news articles allow to diversify recommendation lists and to recommend "novel" news articles without loosing prediction accuracy.

References

Martín Abadi, Ashish Agarwal, Paul Barham, Eugene Brevdo, Zhifeng Chen, Craig Citro, Greg S. Corrado, Andy Davis, Jeffrey Dean, Matthieu Devin, Sanjay Ghemawat, Ian Goodfellow, Andrew Harp, Geoffrey Irving, Michael Isard, Yangqing Jia, Rafal Jozefowicz, Lukasz Kaiser, Manjunath Kudlur, Josh Levenberg, Dan Mané, Rajat Monga, Sherry Moore, Derek Murray, Chris Olah, Mike Schuster, Jonathon Shlens, Benoit Steiner, Ilya Sutskever, Kunal Talwar, Paul Tucker, Vincent Vanhoucke, Vijay Vasudevan, Fernanda Viégas, Oriol Vinyals, Pete Warden, Martin Wattenberg, Martin Wicke, Yuan Yu, and Xiaoqiang Zheng. 2015. TensorFlow: Large-scale machine learning on heterogeneous systems. Software available from tensorflow.org.

Shlomo Argamon, Sushant Dhawle, Moshe Koppel, and James W. Pennebaker. 2005. Lexical predictors of personality type. In *Proceedings of the Joint Annual Meeting of the Interface and the Classification Society of North America*.

Shlomo Argamon, Casey Whitelaw, Paul Chase, Sobhan Raj Hota, Navendu Garg, and Shlomo Levitan. 2007. Stylistic text classification using functional lexical features. *Journal of the American Society for Information Science and Technology*, 58(6):802–822.

Sanjeev Arora and Andrej Risteski. 2017. Provable benefits of representation learning. *CoRR*, abs/1706.04601.

Douglas Bagnall. 2015. Author identification using multi-headed recurrent neural networks. *CoRR*, abs/1506.04891.

Y. Bengio, A. Courville, and P. Vincent. 2013. Representation learning: A review and new perspectives. *IEEE Transactions on Pattern Analysis and Machine Intelligence*, 35(8):1798–1828.

David M. Blei, Andrew Y. Ng, and Michael I. Jordan. 2003. Latent dirichlet allocation. *Journal of Machine Learning Research*, 3:993–1022.

Dainis Boumber, Yifan Zhang, Marjan Hosseinia, Arjun Mukherjee, and Ricardo Vilalta. 2019. Robust authorship verification with transfer learning. EasyChair Preprint no. 865.

Dainis Boumber, Yifan Zhang, and Arjun Mukherjee. 2018. Experiments with convolutional neural networks for multi-label authorship attribution. In *Proceedings of the Eleventh International Conference on Language Resources and Evaluation (LREC-2018)*, Miyazaki, Japan. European Languages Resources Association (ELRA).

Kevin Burton, Akshay Java, Ian Soboroff, et al. 2009. The icwsm 2009 spinn3r dataset. In *Third Annual Conference on Weblogs and Social Media (ICWSM 2009)*.

Kevin Burton, Niels Kasch, and Ian Soboroff. 2011. The icwsm 2011 spinn3r dataset. In *Proceedings of the Annual Conference on Weblogs and Social Media (ICWSM 2011)*.

Deborah Cameron. 1996. Style policy and style politics: a neglected aspect of the language of the news. *Media, Culture & Society*, 18(2):315–333.

Daniel Cer, Yinfei Yang, Sheng-yi Kong, Nan Hua, Nicole Limtiaco, Rhomni St. John, Noah Constant, Mario Guajardo-Cespedes, Steve Yuan, Chris Tar, Yun-Hsuan Sung, Brian Strope, and Ray Kurzweil. 2018. Universal sentence encoder. *CoRR*, abs/1803.11175.

A. Chakraborty, B. Paranjape, S. Kakarla, and N. Ganguly. 2016. Stop clickbait: Detecting and preventing clickbaits in online news media. In *2016 IEEE/ACM International Conference on Advances in Social Networks Analysis and Mining (ASONAM)*, pages 9–16.

Qian Chen, Ting He, and Rao Zhang. 2017. Deep learning based authorship identification.

Alexis Conneau, Douwe Kiela, Holger Schwenk, Loïc Barrault, and Antoine Bordes. 2017. Supervised learning of universal sentence representations from natural language inference data. In *Proceedings of the 2017 Conference on Empirical Methods in Natural Language Processing*, pages 670–680, Copenhagen, Denmark. Association for Computational Linguistics.

D. L. Davies and D. W. Bouldin. 1979. A cluster separation measure. *IEEE Transactions on Pattern Analysis and Machine Intelligence*, PAMI-1(2):224–227.

J. Devlin, Ming-Wei Chang, Kenton Lee, and Kristina Toutanova. 2019. Bert: Pre-training of deep bidirectional transformers for language understanding. In *NAACL-HLT*.

Paul Dickson and Robert Skole. 2012. *Journalese: A Dictionary for Deciphering the News*. Marion Street Press.

S. H. H. Ding, B. C. M. Fung, F. Iqbal, and W. K. Cheung. 2019. Learning stylometric representations for authorship analysis. *IEEE Transactions on Cybernetics*, 49(1):107–121.

Jade Goldstein-Stewart, Ransom Winder, and Roberta Sabin. 2009. Person identification from text and speech genre samples. In *Proceedings of the 12th Conference of the European Chapter of the ACL (EACL 2009)*, pages 336–344, Athens, Greece. Association for Computational Linguistics.

Shriya TP Gupta, Jajati Keshari Sahoo, and Rajendra Kumar Roul. 2019. Authorship identification using recurrent neural networks. In *Proceedings of the 2019 3rd International Conference on Information System and Data Mining*, ICISDM 2019, pages 133–137, New York, NY, USA. ACM.

Wynford Hicks. 2002. *Subediting for Journalists (Media Skills)*. Routledge.

David I. Holmes. 1998. The Evolution of Stylometry in Humanities Scholarship. *Literary and Linguistic Computing*, 13(3):111–117.

John Houvardas and Efstathios Stamatatos. 2006. N-gram feature selection for authorship identification. In *Artificial Intelligence: Methodology, Systems, and Applications*, pages 77–86, Berlin, Heidelberg. Springer Berlin Heidelberg.

Kalervo Järvelin and Jaana Kekäläinen. 2002. Cumulated gain-based evaluation of ir techniques. *ACM Transactions on Information Systems*, 20(4):422–446.

Johannes Jasper, Philipp Berger, Patrick Hennig, and Christoph Meinel. 2018. Authorship verification on short text samples using stylometric embeddings. In *Analysis of Images, Social Networks and Texts*, pages 64–75, Cham. Springer International Publishing.

Jussi Karlgren. 2004. The wheres and whyfores for studying text genre computationally. In *Workshop on Style and Meaning in Languange, Art, Music and Design. National Conference on Artificial Intelligence*.

Mike Kestemont. 2014. Function words in authorship attribution. from black magic to theory? In *Proceedings of the 3rd Workshop on Computational Linguistics for Literature (CLFL)*, pages 59–66, Gothenburg, Sweden. Association for Computational Linguistics.

Quoc Le and Tomas Mikolov. 2014. Distributed representations of sentences and documents. In *Proceedings of the 31st International Conference on International Conference on Machine Learning - Volume 32*, ICML'14, page II–1188–II–1196. JMLR.org.

Rohith Menon and Yejin Choi. 2011. Domain independent authorship attribution without domain adaptation. In *Proceedings of the International Conference Recent Advances in Natural Language Processing 2011*, pages 309–315, Hissar, Bulgaria. Association for Computational Linguistics.

Tempestt Neal, Kalaivani Sundararajan, Aneez Fatima, Yiming Yan, Yingfei Xiang, and Damon Woodard. 2017. Surveying stylometry techniques and applications. *ACM Comput. Surv.*, 50(6):86:1–86:36.

Matteo Pagliardini, Prakhar Gupta, and Martin Jaggi. 2018. Unsupervised learning of sentence embeddings using compositional n-gram features. In *Proceedings of the 2018 Conference of the North American Chapter of the Association for Computational Linguistics: Human Language Technologies, Volume 1 (Long Papers)*, pages 528–540, New Orleans, Louisiana. Association for Computational Linguistics.

Jagadeesh Patchala and Raj Bhatnagar. 2018. Authorship attribution by consensus among multiple features. In *Proceedings of the 27th International Conference on Computational Linguistics*, pages 2766–2777, Santa Fe, New Mexico, USA. Association for Computational Linguistics.

Jeffrey Pennington, Richard Socher, and Christopher D. Manning. 2014. Glove: Global vectors for word representation. In *Empirical Methods in Natural Language Processing (EMNLP)*, pages 1532–1543.

Tie-Yun Qian, Bing Liu, Qing Li, and Jianfeng Si. 2015. Review authorship attribution in a similarity space. *Journal of Computer Science and Technology*, 30(1):200–213.

Nils Reimers and Iryna Gurevych. 2019. Sentence-bert: Sentence embeddings using siamese bert-networks. In *Proceedings of the 2019 Conference on Empirical Methods in Natural Language Processing*. Association for Computational Linguistics.

Michal Rosen-Zvi, Thomas Griffiths, Mark Steyvers, and Padhraic Smyth. 2004. The author-topic model for authors and documents. In *Proceedings of the 20th Conference on Uncertainty in Artificial Intelligence*, UAI '04, page 487–494, Arlington, Virginia, USA. AUAI Press.

Victor Sanh, Lysandre Debut, Julien Chaumond, and Thomas Wolf. 2019. Distilbert, a distilled version of bert: smaller, faster, cheaper and lighter.

Jonathan Schler, Moshe Koppel, Shlomo Argamon, and James Pennebaker. 2006. Effects of age and gender on blogging. In *Computational Approaches to Analyzing Weblogs - Papers from the AAAI Spring Symposium, Technical Report*, volume SS-06-03, pages 191–197.

Yanir Seroussi, Ingrid Zukerman, and Fabian Bohnert. 2014. Authorship attribution with topic models. *Computational Linguistics*, 40(2):269–310.

Efstathios Stamatatos. 2009. A survey of modern authorship attribution methods. *Journal of the American Society for Information Science and Technology*, 60(3):538–556.

Efstathios Stamatatos. 2017. Authorship attribution using text distortion. In *Proceedings of the 15th Conference of the European Chapter of the Association for Computational Linguistics: Volume 1, Long Papers*, pages 1138–1149, Valencia, Spain. Association for Computational Linguistics.

Efstathios Stamatatos. 2018. Masking topic-related information to enhance authorship attribution. *Journal of the Association for Information Science and Technology*, 69(3):461–473.

Chi Sun, Xipeng Qiu, Yige Xu, and Xuanjing Huang. 2019. How to fine-tune bert for text classification? In *Chinese Computational Linguistics*, pages 194–206, Cham. Springer International Publishing.

Yla R. Tausczik and James W. Pennebaker. 2010. The psychological meaning of words: LIWC and computerized text analysis methods. *Journal of Language and Social Psychology*, 29(1):24–54.

Andrew Weir. 2009. Article drop in english headlinese. *London: University College MA thesis.*

Min Yang, Xiaojun Chen, Wenting Tu, Ziyu Lu, Jia Zhu, and Qiang Qu. 2018. A topic drift model for authorship attribution. *Neurocomput.*, 273(C):133–140.

Zhilin Yang, Zihang Dai, Yiming Yang, Jaime Carbonell, Russ R Salakhutdinov, and Quoc V Le. 2019. Xlnet: Generalized autoregressive pretraining for language understanding. In *Advances in Neural Information Processing Systems 32*, pages 5753–5763. Curran Associates, Inc.

Peng Zhou, Wei Shi, Jun Tian, Zhenyu Qi, Bingchen Li, Hongwei Hao, and Bo Xu. 2016. Attention-based bidirectional long short-term memory networks for relation classification. In *Proceedings of the 54th Annual Meeting of the Association for Computational Linguistics (Volume 2: Short Papers)*, pages 207–212, Berlin, Germany. Association for Computational Linguistics.

"A Little Birdie Told Me ... " - Inductive Biases for Rumour Stance Detection on Social Media

Karthik Radhakrishnan[*] **Tushar Kanakagiri**[*] **Sharanya Chakravarthy**[*]
Vidhisha Balachandran

Language Technologies Institute

Carnegie Mellon University

{kradhak2, tkanakag, sharanyc, vbalacha}@cs.cmu.edu

Abstract

The rise in the usage of social media has placed it in a central position for news dissemination and consumption. This greatly increases the potential for proliferation of rumours and misinformation. In an effort to mitigate the spread of rumours, we tackle the related task of identifying the stance (Support, Deny, Query, Comment) of a social media post. Unlike previous works (Fajcik et al., 2019; Yang et al., 2019), we impose inductive biases that capture platform specific user behavior. These biases, coupled with social media fine-tuning of BERT allow for better language understanding, thus yielding an F_1 score of 58.7 on the SemEval 2019 task on rumour stance detection.

1 Introduction

Social media has seen an exponential growth, replacing traditional news sources as the primary news source. The apparent value of interesting truth-like news and the ease of access to such news jointly make social media a hotbed for rumours, misinformation and fake news. In the absence of an authority to verify or debunk a rumour, social media users often share their own thoughts on its veracity, creating a collaborative inter-subjective sense-making to determine the veracity of the rumour. Hence, an important step in achieving the objective of veracity detection is tracking how other users opine on the accuracy of the rumourous story (Zubiaga et al., 2018).

The content on these social media platforms vary in their topics, style, sentiments, and structure (Manikonda et al.). Reddit, for example, is used for gathering a comprehensive view of opinions from users in a short period of time. On the other hand, an event on Twitter is alive for a longer duration and is used for following the development and evolution of an event (Priya et al., 2019).

It is also important to effectively utilize the context surrounding a particular tweet and model the exchanges in a conversation as they often contain crucial background information.

Given the extensive usage of sarcasm and rhetoric in expressing opinions (Carvalho et al.), understanding 'social media' style of text is also essential for effective stance identification.

In this work, we impose inductive biases accounting for the underlying social media platform, conversational context, and noisy social media style of text to improve on the task of rumour detection. To the best extent of our knowledge, this is the first work that applies inductive biases inspired from a deep analysis of communities and their usage patterns to the task of stance identification. We achieve a Macro F_1 score of 58.7 on the 2019 SemEval RumourEval task with novel techniques that surpass state of the art models (non-ensemble) by $2\ F_1$. The code for our approaches will be made available on GitHub[1].

2 Task Definition

To judge the veracity of a social media post, it is useful to analyze the surrounding discourse (comments/replies) by other users. The discourse is initiated by a SOURCE post and followed by tree-structured threads. Each post in a thread is made in response to a PARENT post that immediately precedes it. This problem was modeled as a SemEval shared task - RUMOUREVAL (Gorrell et al., 2019), consisting of two subtasks.

A. Stance Classification - Given a source post introducing a rumour and the ensuing conversation thread, classify the source and each post in the thread into one of 4 categories.

- **SUPPORT** : The author of the response supports the veracity of the rumour.

---

[*]Equal contribution

[1]https://github.com/sharanyarc96/
SocialMediaRumorStanceDetection

Proceedings of the 2020 EMNLP Workshop W-NUT: The Sixth Workshop on Noisy User-generated Text, pages 244–248
Online, Nov 19, 2020. ©2020 Association for Computational Linguistics

- **DENY** : The author of the response denies the veracity of the rumour.
- **QUERY** : The author of the response asks for additional evidence in relation to the veracity of the rumour.
- **COMMENT** : The author of the response makes their own comment without a clear contribution to assessing the veracity of the rumour.

B. Veracity Prediction - Classify the rumour as TRUE, UNVERIFIED, or FALSE.

In this work, we focus on the Stance Classification (highlighted in Appendix A). The heavy class imbalance (highlighted in Appendix B) coupled with the low inter-annotator agreement ($\sim$63 %) (Derczynski et al., 2017) makes this a challenging task.

3 Related Work

This section highlights prior work on the RumourEval dataset. Table 1 provides a short summary of each of the models analysed below.

Model	Description
BranchLSTM (Kochkina et al., 2017)	LSTM-based stance prediction using tweet branches
BLCU (Yang et al., 2019)	Inference-chain based GPT with word and tweet features
BUT-FIT (Fajcik et al., 2019)	BERT ensemble for stance classification, without hand-crafted features
EventAI (Li et al., 2019)	Ensemble of ML and Rule-based models with extensive feature engineering

Table 1: Related Work

3.1 Feature Engineering

EventAI, BranchLSTM and BLCU employed extensive feature engineering as described below.

- **Lexicon Based:** BranchLSTM utilized the count of negation words and swear words. BLCU made more extensive use of lexicons and looked for the presence of positive and negative words, swear words, query words and different classes of verbs.
- **Relation To Other Posts:** BranchLSTM and EventAI used cosine similarity between source and target embeddings. BLCU used the depth of the post in the thread.
- **Content Based:** BLCU checked for the presence of punctuations, hashtags, URLs and "RT". EventAI used similar features along with mentions of special accounts and hashtags (@cnn, #fakenews etc).
- **Tweet Role:** BranchLSTM and EventAI had features indicating whether the tweet was a source or a reply.
- **Tweet and User Metadata:** BLCU used tweet and user features such as favorite and retweet counts, follower and friend counts etc.

3.2 Pre-training

Since unsupervised pre-training for word representations has demonstrated success on a large variety of NLP tasks, the top performing models use pre-trained contextual word representations. BUT-FIT uses BERT (Devlin et al., 2019), BLCU uses GPT (Radford, 2018) and CLEARumor (Baris et al., 2019) uses ELMo (Peters et al., 2018). However, since none of these models are trained on Twitter/Reddit data, fine-tuning on social media data might help capture its idiosyncrasies such as usage of emoticons, opinion-centric text as opposed to fact-centric text, shorter sentences etc.

3.2.1 Intra-thread context

BranchLSTM and EventAI used similarity of the target post with other parts of the thread as features. Additionally, BranchLSTM treated a conversation thread as a set of linear branches. They defined a branch as a chain of tweets that included a leaf post and all its parents all the way to the source post.

BLCU utilized the entire conversation thread by concatenating it with the target post.

BUT-FIT made the assumption that the stance of the target post depends only on itself, the source post, and the previous post in the thread.

4 System Description

Our system (Figure 1) utilizes the content from the SOURCE and PARENT tweets as additional context following previous work (Fajcik et al.,2019;Yang et al.,2019) which noted that the above two tweets mostly contain sufficient information to classify a TARGET tweet correctly. In this work, we leverage various inductive biases and propose late fusion in §4.1, social media fine-tuning to better leverage BERT in §4.2, discrimination between social media platforms in §4.3, domain-specific features over generic textual features in §4.4, and transition priors to better capture conversation dynamics in §4.5.

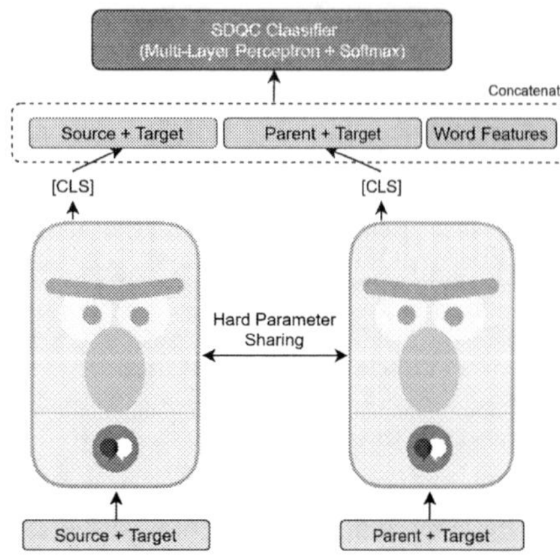

Figure 1: Model Architecture showcasing Late Fusion of SOURCE + TARGET and PARENT + TARGET representations along with additional features. BERT Input is of the form - [CLS] CONTEXT [SEP] TARGET. SOURCE is the post initiating the conversation. The TARGET post is made in response to the PARENT.

4.1 Late Fusion

We attend over the SOURCE and PARENT tweets separately followed by a late fusion of their [CLS] representations. This architecture allows for the TARGET tweets to independently attend over the SOURCE and the PARENT tweet, ensuring the capture of complementary information. This avoids the dilution of context that occurs through the combination of SOURCE and PARENT as context.

4.2 Understanding conversational constructs

One pattern of errors exhibited by the previous models is due to their lack of ability to understand the 'social media' style of text. Common conversational constructs like sarcasm / rhetoric (usually intended to attack / refute someone as opposed to being a genuine question seeking more information) were wrongly labelled as QUERY due to the text containing symbols like "?" or interrogative words.

To combat this, we use Conversational BERT [2] which is trained on social media and dialogue data. We further fine-tune this model on tweets from the RumourEval dataset and the larger PHEME dataset

to incorporate additional background knowledge about rumourous tweets.

4.3 Domain Separation

Our rumours originate from two different social media domains - Twitter and Reddit. Though all prior work has trained models on a combination of data from both sources, we argue for domain separation owing to the fundamental differences in the type of content and interactions on these platforms.

Twitter rumours are concerned with breaking news (Charlie Hebdo shooting, Ferguson unrest) while Reddit rumours are around long-standing conspiracy theories (Flat earth, benefits of Nicotine etc). Reddit discussion threads are shorter and converge sooner i.e. it takes fewer replies to collect the required information. But in case of Twitter, obtaining information that resolves a rumour is a more continuous and a longer process (Priya et al., 2019).

Hence, we train separate models on the Twitter and Reddit data and later aggregate the results.

4.4 Additional Features

Prior work has experimented with inclusion of lexical, sentiment, and emotional features but report little to no improvement (likely because BERT already captures these features). We instead run a TF-IDF vectorizer to extract most discriminatory features for each class and use a subset along with BERT. It also worth noting that these features varied between Twitter and Reddit, further corroborating our hypothesis for domain separation.

4.5 Incorporating a prior

Upon deeper analysis of our training data, we observed that social media conversations tend to follow certain patterns - a QUERY stance is less likely to follow another QUERY stance (questions are usually followed by answers) while SUPPORT stance is highly likely to follow another SUPPORT stance (users espousing the same opinion). We incorporate this inductive bias via a post-processing module where we linearly interpolate the confidence scores from our model and the prior.

5   Experimental Setup

We use the HuggingFace Transformers library [3] to fine-tune $BERT_{base}$ on the Sequence Classification task. We use the Adam optimizer (Kingma and Ba,

---

[2] docs.deeppavlov.ai/en/master/
features/models/bert.html

[3] https://github.com/huggingface/
transformers

ID	Example	Prediction	Comments
1	So multiple doctors don't count but only Hillary's do? Do you even understand her conditions?	SUPPORT	Conversational Pre-training helps differentiate between genuine queries and rhetorical questions
2	Necessary precaution? Isn't it better to close shop for some hours than to risk lives?	COMMENT	It isn't obvious that this reply is rhetorical, but since its parent was tagged as QUERY and queries don't normally follow each other, prior guides the model (Before priors, scores - 0.35 QUERY & 0.33 COMMENT)
3	**Tweet 1** - "WERE YOU THERE THOUGH" **Tweet 2** - "Your mind just can't fathom that can it?"	COMMENT	The gold label is QUERY though these questions are rhetorical
4	**Source** -"At least 10 killed in shooting" **Tweet 1** - "11 Killed now" *in reply to* **Source** **Tweet 2** - "11 Killed" *in reply to* **Source**	-	Gold labels are different {Tweet 1: SUPPORT, Tweet 2: DENY} though the texts have the same meaning

Table 2: Qualitative examples from our model

2014), with a learning rate of 1.5e-6 and batch size of 32 and train on an NVIDIA Tesla T4 GPU.

6 Results and Error Analysis

Our approach achieves an F_1 of 58.7, outperforming non-ensemble approaches by 2 F_1 as shown in Table 3. Though ensembles from BUT-FIT and BLCU achieve a higher F_1 score, we do not ensemble our model owing to high computational cost for training and inference (for ex. BUT-FIT ensembles over 100 BERT$_{large}$ models). We report our best and average (over 5 random seeds) on the RumourEval 2019 dev dataset. Table 2 shows some qualitative examples from our model.

Model	Macro-F1
BUT-FIT BERT$_{base}$ (Average)	51.4
BranchLSTM	49.3
BUT-FIT BERT$_{large}$ (Average)	56.2
BLCU (Best Reported)	56.6
Ours (Average)	56.7
Ours (Best)	**58.7**

Table 3: Comparison with state of the art models Ensembles from BUT-FIT and BLCU produce scores that are higher than those presented here. We show results of comparable non-ensemble versions of state of the art models.

6.1 Ablation Study

In this section, we analyze individual components of our contribution and report incremental improvements in Table 4.

Model	Macro-F1
Base Model	51.2
+ Conversational Pre-Training	53.7 (**+2.5**)
+ TF-IDF features	55.2 (**+1.5**)
+ Domain Sep. and Late Fusion	56.4 (**+1.2**)
+ Transition Priors	58.7 (**+2.3**)

Table 4: Effect of each of our inductive biases

Conversational Pre-Training allows the model to correctly interpret social media constructs like sarcasm, rhetoric (Table 2, Ex. 1) and yields a boost of 2.5 F_1.

TF-IDF features improve the score by 1.5 F_1 by biasing the model based on frequently used words/phrases for each stance.

Domain Separation and Late Fusion provide further gains, increasing the F_1 by 1.2. In addition to improving the score, domain separation is also essential for using TF-IDF features and prior as they are platform dependant.

Transition Priors increase the performance by 2.3 F_1 by guiding the prediction based on stance transition priors in cases where the model makes uncertain predictions (Table 2, Ex. 2).

7 Unsolvable Examples

The RumourEval dataset contains examples with noisy annotations (Table 2, Ex. 3) where the ground truth is mislabeled, thus penalizing our model for correct predictions. Additionally, few examples which have the same hierarchy and similar text (Table 2, Ex. 4) are assigned different labels (Possibly due to different interpretations among annotators) resulting in noisy training examples.

Another class of unsolvable examples stemmed from deleted tweets. If a particular tweet was deleted, the dataset attaches its children to their GRANDPARENT tweet. This presents issues as the children express opinions towards a deleted tweet. A potential solution would be to remove tweets where the '@' mention is towards an unseen author but we would risk further reducing the small number of training examples in our dataset.

8 Conclusion and Future Work

In this work, we showcased the efficacy of inductive biases to the task of stance classification and achieved a score of 58.7 F_1, surpassing existing approaches. We hope to utilize this model in other downstream tasks like veracity detection (Task B) and expand our inductive biases to other social media tasks such as fact verification and conversation derailment detection.

References

Ipek Baris, Lukas Schmelzeisen, and Steffen Staab. 2019. CLEARumor at SemEval-2019 Task 7: ConvoLving ELMo Against Rumors. *arXiv preprint arXiv:1904.03084*.

Paula Carvalho, Luís Sarmento, Mário J. Silva, and Eugénio de Oliveira. Clues for Detecting Irony in User-Generated Contents: Oh...!! It's "so Easy";-), year = 2009, isbn = 9781605588056, publisher = Association for Computing Machinery, address = New York, NY, USA, url = https://doi.org/10.1145/1651461.1651471,.

Leon Derczynski, Kalina Bontcheva, Maria Liakata, Rob Procter, Geraldine Wong Sak Hoi, and Arkaitz Zubiaga. 2017. SemEval-2017 Task 8: RumourEval: Determining rumour veracity and support for rumours. In *Proceedings of the 11th International Workshop on Semantic Evaluation (SemEval-2017)*, pages 69–76, Vancouver, Canada. Association for Computational Linguistics.

Jacob Devlin, Ming-Wei Chang, Kenton Lee, and Kristina Toutanova. 2019. BERT: Pre-training of Deep Bidirectional Transformers for Language Understanding. In *NAACL-HLT*.

Martin Fajcik, Lukáš Burget, and Pavel Smrz. 2019. BUT-FIT at SemEval-2019 Task 7: Determining the Rumour Stance with Pre-Trained Deep Bidirectional Transformers. *arXiv preprint arXiv:1902.10126*.

Genevieve Gorrell, Elena Kochkina, Maria Liakata, Ahmet Aker, Arkaitz Zubiaga, Kalina Bontcheva, and Leon Derczynski. 2019. SemEval-2019 Task 7: RumourEval, Determining Rumour Veracity and Support for Rumours. In *Proceedings of the 13th International Workshop on Semantic Evaluation*, pages 845–854, Minneapolis, Minnesota, USA. Association for Computational Linguistics.

Diederik P. Kingma and Jimmy Ba. 2014. Adam: A Method for Stochastic Optimization. *CoRR*, abs/1412.6980.

Elena Kochkina, Maria Liakata, and Isabelle Augenstein. 2017. Turing at semeval-2017 task 8: Sequential approach to rumour stance classification with branch-lstm. *arXiv preprint arXiv:1704.07221*.

Quanzhi Li, Qiong Zhang, and Luo Si. 2019. eventAI at SemEval-2019 Task 7: Rumor Detection on Social Media by Exploiting Content, User Credibility and Propagation Information. In *Proceedings of the 13th International Workshop on Semantic Evaluation*, pages 855–859.

Lydia Manikonda, Ghazaleh Beigi, Huan Liu, and Subbarao Kambhampati. Twitter for Sparking a Movement, Reddit for Sharing the Moment: #metoo.

Matthew E. Peters, Mark Neumann, Mohit Iyyer, Matt Gardner, Christopher Clark, Kenton Lee, and Luke Zettlemoyer. 2018. Deep contextualized word representations. *ArXiv*, abs/1802.05365.

Shalini Priya, Ryan Sequeira, Joydeep Chandra, and Sourav Kumar Dandapat. 2019. Where should one get news updates: Twitter or reddit. *Online Social Networks and Media*, 9:17–29.

Alec Radford. 2018. Improving Language Understanding by Generative Pre-Training.

Ruoyao Yang, Wanying Xie, Chunhua Liu, and Dong Yu. 2019. BLCU_NLP at SemEval-2019 Task 7: An Inference Chain-based GPT Model for Rumour Evaluation. In *Proceedings of the 13th International Workshop on Semantic Evaluation*, pages 1090–1096.

Arkaitz Zubiaga, Ahmet Aker, Kalina Bontcheva, Maria Liakata, and Rob Procter. 2018. Detection and Resolution of Rumours in Social Media: A Survey. *ACM Comput. Surv.*, 51:32:1–32:36.

Paraphrase Generation via Adversarial Penalizations

Gerson Vizcarra and **José Ochoa-Luna**
Department of Computer Science
Universidad Católica San Pablo
Arequipa, Perú
{gerson.vizcarra, jeochoa}@ucsp.edu.pe

Abstract

Paraphrase generation is an important problem in Natural Language Processing (NLP) that has been addressed with neural network-based approaches recently. This paper presents an adversarial framework to address the paraphrase generation problem in English. Unlike previous methods, we employ the discriminator output as penalization instead of using policy gradients, and we propose a global discriminator to avoid the Monte-Carlo search. In addition, this work use and compare different settings of input representation. We compare our methods to some baselines in the Quora question pairs dataset. The results show that our framework is competitive against the previous benchmarks.

1 Introduction

Paraphrase generation is a task in NLP which aims to transform a given sentence in another with the same meaning. This task is challenging because of the complexity of semantic and syntactic relationships in language. Moreover, the capacity to generate paraphrases automatically is an opportunity to use data augmentation in NLP. However, one of the main problems of paraphrase generation is that the meaning of a sentence can be changed radically by modifying a word.

Paraphrase generation is a hot task and recent neural-approaches have addressed the problem. We organize previous works of paraphrase generation into two groups: task-support and task-based. The task-support paraphrase generation works create paraphrases to add training data or adversarial-examples. Paraphrases have been created to augment data in question answering (Dong et al., 2017; Gan and Ng, 2019). Some techniques are substitution of words (Jiao et al., 2019; Xie et al., 2019), make syntactic changes to the original sentences (Coulombe, 2018; Iyyer et al., 2018; Sennrich et al.,

2016), and back-translation (Mallinson et al., 2017; Xie et al., 2019). Other works apply rule-based generative models to perform multiple changes (Samanta and Mehta, 2017; Li et al., 2017).

On the other hand, task-based paraphrase generation works aim to benchmark their results on specific paired datasets. In this paper, we focus on task-based works. Prakash et al. (2016) use a stacked residual Long-Short Term Memory (LSTM) network that outperforms a vanilla LSTM. Gupta et al. (2018) apply a Variational Autoencoder (VAE) to get better results than the stacked LSTM. Huang et al. (2018) use a Seq2Seq-based model with a dictionary-based attention mechanism. The dictionary search guides the insertion or deletion of a word. Li et al. (2018b) generate paraphrases using a deep reinforcement learning framework. Ma et al. (2018) propose an attention network using word embeddings information. Yang et al. (2019) present an adversarial setup over latent space using a conditional VAE as a generator. Chen et al. (2019) propose a VAE to make syntactically and semantically changed paraphrases. Wang et al. (2019) propose a transformer (Vaswani et al., 2017) with multiple encoders to process extra semantic information of the input. The work of Egonmwan and Chali (2019) shows a hybrid model between a transformer and a Recurrent Neural Network (RNN). Li et al. (2019) design a transformer-based model that can generate paraphrases at different levels of granularity.

From the prior works on paraphrase generation, most of them learn by conditional Maximum Likelihood Estimation (MLE). However, Yang et al. (2019) highlight the exposure bias problem (Bengio et al., 2015; Ranzato et al., 2015) in paraphrase generation. Some works address the problem by applying REINFORCE (Williams, 1992) to generate text in their adversarial setups (Yu et al., 2017; Fedus et al., 2018; Li et al., 2018a; Liu et al., 2018; de Masson d'Autume et al., 2019). However, simi-

Proceedings of the 2020 EMNLP Workshop W-NUT: The Sixth Workshop on Noisy User-generated Text, pages 249–259
Online, Nov 19, 2020. ©2020 Association for Computational Linguistics

lar to prior works (He et al., 2019; Lu et al., 2019), we observe that REINFORCE has a high variance and is difficult to tune.

At the same time, pre-trained Language Models (LMs) (Devlin et al., 2019; Peters et al., 2018; Radford et al., 2019) have outperformed previous works in many NLP tasks. An important reason is that they provide contextual representations of words, which are more specific than static word embeddings (Pennington et al., 2014; Mikolov et al., 2013, 2018). However, static word embeddings consume fewer resources and are faster than pre-trained LMs. Ethayarajh (2019) shows that the static embeddings extracted from pre-trained LMs outperform Glove (Pennington et al., 2014) and FastText (Bojanowski et al., 2017) in many word vector benchmarks.

In this paper, we propose an adversarial model (generator-discriminator) to address the English paraphrase generation task. Unlike previous approaches, we train our model using a weighted conditional maximum likelihood by a "penalization" score given by the discriminator. Also, we test variations of our setup by changing the input representations and the Monte-Carlo search. Overall, our contributions are as follows.

- We propose the use of penalizations (discriminator outputs) in supervised adversarial setups as an alternative to the REINFORCE algorithm.

- We evaluate the substitution of the Monte-Carlo search by using a discriminator that outputs a score for each word.

- We provide an experimental analysis of the impact of input representations over a paraphrase generation model. Further, we include the use of the first-layer embeddings from pre-trained language models.

- Our experiments show that our setup can generate feasible paraphrases. Furthermore, our results are competitive against prior benchmarks in the Quora question pairs dataset.

2 Preliminaries

Before presenting our model, we provide some preliminaries about the MLE training and REINFORCE algorithm in sequential problems.

2.1 Conditional Maximum Likelihood Estimation

The conditional MLE training for sequence to sequence tasks aims to learn the probability distribution of the estimated token $\hat{y}_t$ constrained by an input sequence $X_{1:T} = \{x_1, ..., x_T\}$ and a list of previous tokens $\hat{Y}_{1:t-1} = \{\hat{y}_1, ..., \hat{y}_{t-1}\}$. We consider the sets of tokens X and $\hat{Y}$ in a finite vocabulary V. Given a dataset D with pairs of sequences of tokens $X_{1:T}, Y_{1:T}$ with length T (due to truncation and padding), the objective function J_{MLE} of conditional MLE is

$$J_{MLE} = \mathbb{E}_{\hat{Y} \sim Y}[\sum_{t=1}^{T} \log G(\hat{y}_t|X, \hat{Y}_{1:t-1})] \quad (1)$$

Where $G(\hat{y}_t|\hat{Y}_{1:t-1}, X)$ is the neural network that generates the word $\hat{y}_t$. Most works use teacher forcing (Williams and Zipser, 1989) by using the correct tokens Y instead of $\hat{Y}$ to improve the results. In that way, the "exposure" of the network to the target words could "bias" the inference process.

2.2 REINFORCE

REINFORCE (Williams, 1992) in sequence to sequence tasks aims to maximize the reward r of a policy (neural network) received due to the generation of the word $\hat{y}_t$. In similar dataset conditions, the objective function J_R of REINFORCE is

$$J_R = \sum_{t=1}^{T} [\log G(\hat{y}_t|X, \hat{Y}_{1:t-1})] \cdot r(t) \quad (2)$$

Instead of calculating the reward using the likelihood, most works rely on a discriminator (Yu et al., 2017; Li et al., 2018a; Liu et al., 2018; Guo et al., 2018) or an evaluator (Li et al., 2018b).

In REINFORCE, the discriminator/evaluator D outputs a single scalar for a whole sentence. D learns using the cross-entropy of the dataset distribution Y and the generated distribution $\hat{Y}$. The objective function J_D of the discriminator/evaluator is

$$J_D = -\log D(X, Y) - \log(1 - D(X, \hat{Y})) \quad (3)$$

So, the reward function for a complete sequence is $r(T) = D(X, \hat{Y}_{1:T})$. However, the discriminator is trained with only completed sequences. REINFORCE establishes the use of Monte-Carlo search with roll-out to sample possible sequences starting from incomplete ones. We define the Monte-Carlo search MC as

$$MC^G(\hat{Y}_{1:t}; N) = \left\{ \hat{Y}^1_{1:T}, ..., \hat{Y}^N_{1:T} \right\} \quad (4)$$

In that way, the reward function for all timesteps is

$$r(t) =$$

$$\begin{cases} \dfrac{1}{N} \sum_{n=1}^{N} D(X, \hat{Y}^n_{1:T}), \hat{Y}^n_{1:T} \in MC^G(\hat{Y}_{1:t}; N) & \\ & \text{for } t < T \\ D(X, \hat{Y}_{1:T}) & \text{for } t = T \end{cases}$$

$$(5)$$

3 Methodology

Our adversarial setup is composed of two neural networks like previous works: a generator and a discriminator. We make some observations of prior approaches to propose our model. On the one hand, MLE could suffer exposure bias when switching from train to inference. On the other hand, we observe that the REINFORCE algorithm is very fluctuating when training because it relies only on the discriminator. Furthermore, it is slow to train due to the Monte-Carlo search.

We propose a weighted conditional maximum likelihood objective to train our generator. In consequence, we take advantage of the conditional MLE principle and, also, we can guide the training using a penalization function. The penalization function is similar to the reward in REINFORCE. The conditional MLE part let us reduce the variance of training. In addition, we substitute the Monte-Carlo search by using a discriminator that outputs a score for each token.

3.1 Model Architecture

We first define two sequences of tokens $X_{1:T} = \{x_1, ..., x_T\}$, $Y_{1:T} = \{y_1, ..., y_T\}$ of length T that represent a paraphrase. Let G_θ and D_ϕ be a θ-parameterized generator and a ϕ-parameterized discriminator.

Given X we train G_θ to produce a sequence of tokens $\hat{Y}_{1:T} = (\hat{y}_1, ..., \hat{y}_T)$ that is similar to Y. Given X we train D_ϕ to distinguish between Y and $\hat{Y}$.

In the following sections we also call X, Y, and $\hat{Y}$ as the *condition sentence*, *target sentence*, and *generated sentence* respectively.

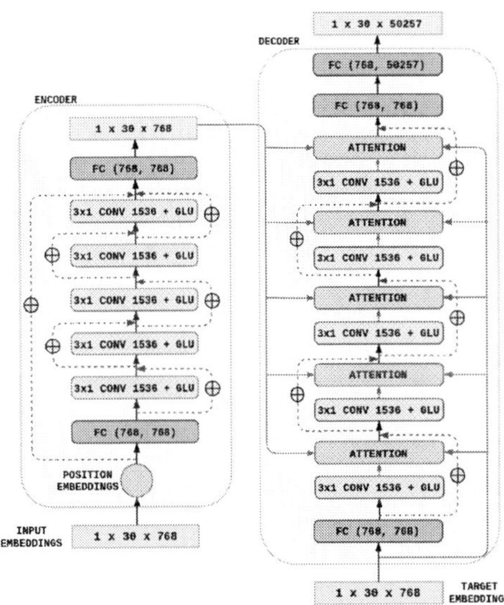

Figure 1: Architecture of generator network

3.1.1 Generator (G_θ)

Our generator is a Convolutional Sequence to Sequence (ConvS2S) model (Gehring et al., 2017). We choose this architecture over a Seq2Seq (Sutskever et al., 2014) and Transformer (Vaswani et al., 2017) because the ConvS2S needs fewer number of parameters to achieve similar results. That let us train our framework using large batch sizes to reduce the generator variance (de Masson d'Autume et al., 2019). Furthermore, the model performs parallel convolutions to speed up the training time. That feature allows us to conduct more experiments.

Figure 1 shows the overall architecture of G_θ. We feed G_θ encoder with the condition sentence embeddings (input embeddings). We add position embeddings on the encoder side. The first encoder layer is a fully connected. Then, each following layer performs iteratively: (a) one-dimensional convolutions without padding and (b) a gated linear unit over the previous layer result. We also add residual connections between non-adjacent layers.

The decoder has convolutional and attention layers interleaved. However, the decoder performs temporal convolutions to avoid leakage of future information. We achieve that by padding the input vector on the left side. There are no position embeddings on the decoder side because they produce a negative impact on the generation. At training time, we feed the decoder with the target sentence to perform convolutions in parallel. At inference

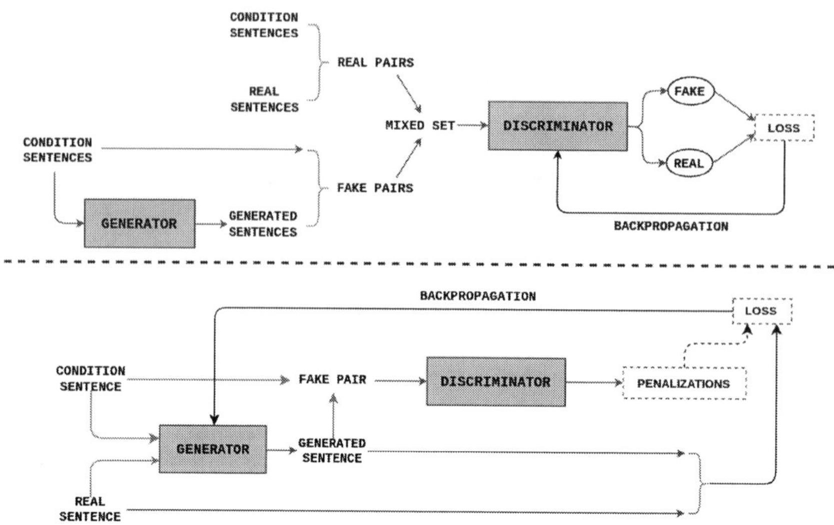

Figure 2: Our model training. Up: Discriminator process. Down: Generator process

time, the decoder is sequential. First, we feed the decoder with our initial token. Then, we repeat two procedures until G_θ generates all words: the decoder performs a forward pass and output a new token; we concatenate the new token to the previous input in order to feed the decoder. Finally, the result vector passes through two dense layers to output the vocabulary probabilities.

3.1.2 Discriminator (D_ϕ)

The architecture of the discriminator is similar to that of the generator. We change the last fully connected layer of D_ϕ decoder to output one number. So, D_ϕ output one score per token. Then, we pass the result to a sigmoid layer that outputs the probability that the tokens belong to the *fake* category.

We feed the encoder with the *condition* sentence, and the decoder with either the *generated* or *target* sentence.

3.2 Training

The training process of D_ϕ and G_θ are different. Figure 2 shows the overall training procedure.

We first generate paraphrases for all condition sentences. We build a mixed set of sentence pairs using the *condition-target (real pairs)* and *condition-generated (fake pairs)*. In that way, we feed the discriminator with a pair of sentences. D_ϕ outputs a score for each generated / target word. So, each pair of sentences is classified as a set of zeros and ones in the *real* or *fake* case, respectively.

D_ϕ learns using the following function

$$J(\phi) = -\log D_\phi(X, Y) - \log(1 - D_\phi(X, \hat{Y})) \quad (6)$$

We train G_θ using a unified learning objective. We multiply the negative log-likelihood loss of each word by the result of our penalization function. The objective function $J(\theta)$ of G_θ is

$$J(\theta) = -\sum_{t=1}^{T} \mathbb{E}_{\hat{Y}_{1:T} \sim Y_{1:T}} \Big[\sum_{\hat{y}_t \in \hat{Y}} \log G_\theta(\hat{y}_t | \hat{Y}_{1:T}, X) \cdot P_{D_\phi}^{G_\theta} \Big] \quad (7)$$

We calculate the G_θ log-likelihood loss using the *real* sentence as decoder input. Nevertheless, we estimate the penalization function $P_{D_\phi}^{G_\theta}(t)$ with the decoding inference result. Thus, we increase the loss value of tokens that tend to yield infeasible paraphrases.

$P_{D_\phi}^{G_\theta}(t)$ is the discriminator output multiplied by a constant k. The discriminator outputs scores in the interval $[0, 1]$ according to the probability that a token is classified as *fake*. That is, tokens classified as fake receive higher penalizations.

$$P_{D_\phi}^{G_\theta}(t) = k \cdot D_\phi(X, \hat{Y}_{1:T}) \quad (8)$$

We avoid the Monte-Carlo search using our discriminator score per word. We update D_ϕ at each training round to improve the quality of our generated sentences.

Algorithm 1 presents the overall procedure to train our model. As first step, we pre-train G_θ using conditional maximum likelihood with the *condition* and *target* samples. Also we pre-train D_ϕ using supervised learning using pairs composed of *condition-real* or *condition-generated*. Then, we start the adversarial training phase for several rounds. First, we sample and calculate $P_{D_\phi}^{G_\theta}$ to train G_θ using equation 7. After updating the parameters, we output a *generated* sample per *condition* sentence using G_θ. That results in a balanced set of fake and real pairs to feed D_ϕ. Finally, we train D_ϕ with Equation 6.

Algorithm 1: Training of the model

Result: Trained G_θ
Pre-train G_θ.
Generate samples using G_θ.
Pre-train $D\phi$ with fake and real pairs.
for *n rounds* **do**
    for *examples* **do**
        Generate a sequence using G_θ.
        Calculate $P_{D_\phi}^{G_\theta}$.
        Train G_θ using 7
    end
    Generate samples using G_θ.
    for *examples$*$2* **do**
        Train D_ϕ using 6
    end
end

---

4 Experiments

In this section, we evaluate our model and compare it with prior methods. We describe the dataset used, experimental setup, baseline methods, and results of our experiments.

4.1 Dataset

To test our model, we used the Quora question pairs dataset. This dataset contains paired questions associated with a label. The pairs are labeled with *1* whether they express the same idea and *0* otherwise. For this work, we decided to use only the duplicated ones. There are around *155K* duplicated questions. We observed that some questions appear in more than one pair.

We built three sets: Quora I, Quora II, and Quora III to evaluate our framework. In Quora I, we randomly selected *133K* pairs: *100K* for training, *30K* for testing, and *3K* for validation. In Quora III, we sampled *83K* pairs: *50K* for training, *30K* for testing, and *3K* for validation. In Quora II, we sampled *30K* pairs for testing which questions do not appear in the training (*50K*) and validation (*3K*) sets. That makes Quora II the most challenging

set. It is worth to notice that there are some overlaps of input questions between the training and testing sets in Quora I and III. Table 1 shows the distribution of quantities of our sets.

Dataset	Train	Test	Validation
Quora I	100K	30K	3K
Quora II	50K	30K (Unique)	3K
Quora III	50K	30K	3K

Table 1: Dataset distribution.

4.2 Experimental setup

G and D are 5-layer ConvS2S in the encoder and decoder side. The value of k in the penalization function is 2. For all models, we use the negative log-likelihood as the loss function. We adopted the optimization algorithm Adam (Kingma and Ba, 2014) for pre-training the generator and to train the discriminator. We use $1e-4$ as the learning rate for G_θ and $1e-6$ for D_ϕ without modifying the default betas. Model parameters have been initialized using uniform distribution values, as described in (He et al., 2015). We pre-trained the generator and discriminator for 20 epochs. In the adversarial training phase, we changed the learning rate to $2e-4$ performing 40 rounds of adversarial training. In Monte-Carlo and REINFORCE baselines, a roll-out of size four has been used. The batch size to feed our generator and discriminator is *250*. All samples were generated using greedy decoding. We tuned our hyperparameters manually. We run our experiments in a PC with Intel 9900K and Nvidia Titan RTX for two hours on average for each model. The framework used for implementation has been Pytorch 1.3 (Paszke et al., 2019).

4.3 Input representations

The input representation for deep learning models is important because it is their unique information before solving a task. We tested the influence of the input representations in our results by changing the source of the embedding. In our experiments, we consider three recent methods: The Byte-level BPE extracted from the OpenAI GPT-2 (Radford et al., 2019) with 50257 tokens, the pre-trained wordpiece embeddings from BERT proposed by (Devlin et al., 2019) with 30522 tokens, and the 1 million FastText embeddings trained on 16 billion tokens (Mikolov et al., 2018) considering the

Target Sentence	GPT-2 embeddings	BERT embeddings	Fasttext embeddings
who is best indian hacker?	who are the best hackers in india?	who is the best seo company in india?	who are the best [UNK] in india ?
how can we earn from youtube?	how can i make money from youtube?	how can i make money on youtube?	how can we make money from gmail ?
how can i grow tall?	how can i grow taller?	how can i become taller?	how do i become tall ?
which is best tv series you have seen? and way?	what are the best tv series you have watched?	what are the best tv movies in all time?	what are the best [UNK] movies you have seen ?

Table 2: Generated Sentences by changing the input representation.

100000 most common tokens in their vocabulary. We used ConvS2S architecture in all cases. We only change the input to lowercase and truncate in 30 tokens as preprocessing. Table 3 shows the BLEU-2 score of the testing sets. Table 2 presents some generated sentences using different input representations.

Input Representation	BLEU-2		
	Quora I	Quora II	Quora III
GPT-2 embeddings	**44.84**	**33.48**	**42.48**
BERT embeddings	39.03	19.18	29.28
Fasttext embeddings	31.20	17.37	28.19

Table 3: Comparative results by changing the input representation.

As can be seen in Table 3, the ConvS2S architecture that uses the Byte level BPE embeddings surpasses the BERT embeddings in 11.13 points in the BLEU score in average, and in 14.68 to the Fast-Text. Also, the generated texts of Table 2 presents a correlation with the BLEU scores. The results confirm the superiority of embeddings extracted from contextualizing environments against traditional embeddings. Overall, the presented results indicate that the byte-level BPE embeddings from GPT-2 are the most suitable input representation for our framework.

4.4 Automatic evaluation

We used some automatic metrics to evaluate our framework and compare it with other methods. We use BLEU (Papineni et al., 2002) which evaluates similarities between n-grams, ROUGE (Lin, 2004) which is a common metric in text summarization, METEOR (Denkowski and Lavie, 2014) that considers synonyms, and iBleu (Sun and Zhou, 2012) which penalizes similarities with the source sentence (parroting), as Li et al. (2019); Mao and Lee (2019); Qian et al. (2019) suggest. We consider the

following methods as baselines of our research. In all cases, we extracted directly the results reported from their publications.

VAE-SVG and VAE-SVG-eq from Gupta et al. (2018): A variational autoencoder and its modification with fewer parameters. RbM-SL and RbM-IRL from Li et al. (2018b): Reinforcement learning method with an evaluator trained with supervised learning and another with inverse reinforcement learning. DNPG from Li et al. (2019): Multi-granularity encoder and decoder framework using multi-head attention. GAP from Yang et al. (2019): Generative model using REINFORCE with two losses per word. TranSEQ from Egonmwan and Chali (2019): Model with a transformer encoder and an RNN decoder. Our implementation of ConvS2S from Gehring et al. (2017) using byte-level BPE. Our implementation of Transformer from Vaswani et al. (2017) using byte-level BPE as initial embeddings. Our model setup using REIN-FORCE and another with only Monte-Carlo search.

We compared our results using similar configurations of prior works to make a fair comparison. Quora I and III are identical to the sets of Gupta et al. (2018); Yang et al. (2019); Egonmwan and Chali (2019). Quora I and II are analogous to the sets proposed by Li et al. (2018b). Also, the Quora I set is similar to the set of Li et al. (2019).

Table 4, 5, and 6 show the results for Quora I, II, and III corpora respectively. The results presented refer to the scores of testing sets. Conv-Adv-MC refers to the method with Monte-Carlo discriminator and Conv-Adv-S, to our discriminator. The best results in each metric are in **bold**.

The automatic evaluation results show that our models are competitive against the state of the art baselines. Moreover, the Conv-Adv-S has slightly higher scores than previous methods in Quora I and III. However, RBM-SL is still the best method for generating paraphrases that are completely differ-

Proposed Model	Quora I					
	BLEU-2	BLEU-4	iBLEU	ROUGE-1	ROUGE-2	METEOR
VAE-SVG	-	22.50	-	-	-	25.50
VAE-SVG-eq	-	22.90	-	-	-	25.50
RbM-SL	43.54	-	-	**64.39**	38.11	32.84
RbM-IRL	43.09	-	-	64.02	37.72	31.97
DNPG	-	25.03	18.01	63.73	37.75	-
GAP	44.83	-	-	-	-	32.48
TranSEQ	38.75	-	-	-	-	**35.84**
Transformer	42.03	26.56	20.17	57.80	34.25	29.06
ConvS2S	**44.84**	29.44	21.20	61.72	**38.48**	31.28
REINFORCE	43.96	28.87	20.86	60.43	37.53	31.12
Conv-Adv-MC	44.65	**29.48**	21.08	61.18	38.03	31.01
Conv-Adv-S (ours)	**44.84**	29.07	**21.40**	60.34	37.09	31.27

Table 4: Comparative results on Quora I.

Proposed Model	Quora II			
	BLEU-2	ROUGE-1	ROUGE-2	METEOR
RbM-SL	**35.81**	**57.34**	**31.09**	**28.12**
RbM-IRL	34.79	56.86	29.90	26.67
Transformer	25.45	38.57	18.22	17.71
ConvS2S	33.48	48.30	26.83	23.07
REINFORCE	32.41	47.58	26.19	22.15
Conv-Adv-MC	32.73	47.76	26.63	22.58
Conv-Adv-S	33.27	47.73	26.25	23.03

Table 5: Comparative results on Quora II.

Proposed Model	Quora III		
	BLEU-2	BLEU-4	METEOR
VAE-SVG	-	17.1	22.20
VAE-SVG-eq	-	17.4	22.20
GAP	37.18	-	22.24
TranSEQ	38.75	-	**33.73**
Transformer	35.74	16.48	24.73
ConvS2S	42.48	27.02	29.52
REINFORCE	42.05	26.73	29.20
Conv-Adv-MC	41.98	26.84	29.45
Conv-Adv-S	**42.81**	**27.33**	29.70

Table 6: Comparative results on Quora III.

ent than the training set (Quora II).

The scores on BLEU and ROUGE indicate that our model produces paraphrases that are more similar to the targets. Also, the iBLEU scores suggest that our model generates more diverse paraphrases than some of the prior works. However, the METEOR scores indicate that some of the previous baselines use more synonyms when generating paraphrases than our model does.

4.5 Human evaluation

We make a human evaluation of the generated models because we believe that the automatic evaluation is not always accurate. We randomly select 120 condition-target questions and the generated of two methods of the Quora I testing set, and we distribute them to 4 evaluators using a form. We ask the evaluators to verify three main aspects in scores from 1 to 5:

- **Relevance**: Whether the paraphrase has the same meaning of the original sentence and does not lose information.

- **Fluency**: Whether the paraphrase has a correct grammar and use of vocabulary.

- **Diversity**: Whether the paraphrase varies syntactically and semantically.

Table 7 presents the average ratings given by human evaluators. It is worth to notice that all appraisals are from 1 to 5, being five the highest score.

Model	Relevance	Fluency	Diversity
Reference	3.97	4.42	3.22
ConvS2S	3.98	4.32	2.65
Conv-Adv-S (ours)	3.97	4.24	2.77

Table 7: Results of human evaluation.

From the results, we analyze each evaluated aspect: The three paraphrases have equivalent Relevance scores. We infer that this is due to some reference examples that lose some extra information in the paraphrase and for the random sampling. Overall, the scores indicate that our model can produce paraphrases that are highly related to the original input questions.

Although the ConvS2S model has a better fluency than our method with non-statistical significant differences (paired t-test, p-value$\sim$0.21), both are near the reference examples. We believe that the process of correcting some specific words could cause disorder when decoding some sentences. Besides, we assume that another decoding algorithm

Input Sentence	ConvS2S	Conv-Adv-S (ours)	Target sentence
what is the difference between militants and terrorists?	what is the difference between terrorists and terrorists?	what is the difference between a person and terrorists?	what is the difference between terrorists and militants?
who is going to win, trump or hillary?	who will win the election, trump or clinton?	who will win, trump or clinton?	who will win, trump or clinton?
is it possible to advertise on quora?	is it possible to advertise on quora?	is promotion allowed on quora?	can we advertise our business on quora?
how do you train your memory to memorize things fast?	how do i memorize my memory?	how can i memorize things faster?	how can i memorize things faster?
what are the top 5 mobile app development companies in india?	what are the top 5 mobile app development companies in india?	which is the best mobile app development company in india?	what is the best mobile app development company in india?
how can i persuade my parents to let me wear makeup?	how do i convince my parents to let me wear makeup?	how do i let my parents to let me wear makeup?	how do i convince my parents to let me wear makeup?
why doesn't germany pursues indigenous jet engine development?	why doesn't germany angulic in the world?	why doesn't the germany always a bit of it's limited/2.2.2.50 & sandys have been fired in the	why doesn't germany produce jet engines?

Table 8: Generated sentences on Quora I testing set.

could benefit the generation of fluent paraphrases.

Our model produces more diverse sentences than ConvS2S does. However, the difference is not statistical significant (p-value~0.19). Also, the reference sentences are still more diverse than the outputs of our model. We believe that a penalization function for similarity with the source sentence could help to improve the results.

Overall, human evaluation shows that our model produces relevant and fluent paraphrases, which indicates that our model works properly. Although we improved the diversity factor of the ConvS2S, it is still non-comparable with the variety of the original distribution.

As a case study, Table 8 presents some of the sentences that our model and the ConvS2S generated in the test set of Quora I. We color the cells depending on our criterion of the quality of each paraphrase. The red color represents a bad paraphrase (a repetition from the source question, a nonsense sentence, or a not related question). The yellow color represents a paraphrase with some missing information. The green color represents a correct paraphrase.

4.6 Discussion

The presented results on the experimentation of the representations of the input show that the embeddings of pre-trained models are better input representations than the ones provided by classic algorithms of word-embeddings. The results concur with the study of (Ethayarajh, 2019). Furthermore, we found that the input representation has a high impact on the framework results (difference up to 14.68). Also, the results indicate that the GPT-2 has more robust embeddings in the first layer than the ones provided by BERT. We infer that BERT relies more on its contextual similarities calculated in its higher layers than GPT-2 does, as is suggested in previous studies (Ethayarajh, 2019; Hoover et al., 2019).

The comparison with previous baselines indicates that our framework achieves competitive results against the state-of-the-art methods considering all automatic metrics. Further, we improved some benchmarks on BLEU, ROUGE, and METEOR. The results indicate that the weighted adversarial loss is a suitable option to REINFORCE, and it provides generation diversity to our ConvS2S implementation (improvement of 0.12 in human evaluation). The BLEU and ROUGE scores indicate that our model has similarities with the target questions. However, it also has a lack of diversity as the METEOR score shows. Similar to (Qian et al., 2019; Banerjee and Lavie, 2005), the results from the automatic evaluation concur with the human evaluation, especially on diversity.

5 Conclusions

We propose an adversarial setup to address the paraphrase generation task. The automatic evaluation results show some improvements over previous baselines. The human evaluation suggests a trade-off between the fluency and diversity of the generated paraphrases of the fine-tuned model. We conclude that our setup is a suitable option to RE-

INFORCE and MLE training. In addition, the case study shows that our method helps to improve the quality of paraphrases in general.

Acknowledgments

This work was supported by grant 234-2015-FONDECYT (Master Program) from Cienciactiva of the National Council for Science, Technology and Technological Innovation (CONCYTEC-PERU).

References

Satanjeev Banerjee and Alon Lavie. 2005. Meteor: An automatic metric for mt evaluation with improved correlation with human judgments. In *Proceedings of the acl workshop on intrinsic and extrinsic evaluation measures for machine translation and/or summarization*, pages 65–72.

Samy Bengio, Oriol Vinyals, Navdeep Jaitly, and Noam Shazeer. 2015. Scheduled sampling for sequence prediction with recurrent neural networks. In *Advances in Neural Information Processing Systems*, pages 1171–1179.

Piotr Bojanowski, Edouard Grave, Armand Joulin, and Tomas Mikolov. 2017. Enriching word vectors with subword information. *Transactions of the Association for Computational Linguistics*, 5:135–146.

Mingda Chen, Qingming Tang, Sam Wiseman, and Kevin Gimpel. 2019. Controllable paraphrase generation with a syntactic exemplar. In *Proceedings of the 57th Annual Meeting of the Association for Computational Linguistics*, pages 5972–5984.

Claude Coulombe. 2018. Text data augmentation made simple by leveraging nlp cloud apis. *arXiv preprint arXiv:1812.04718*.

Michael Denkowski and Alon Lavie. 2014. Meteor universal: Language specific translation evaluation for any target language. In *Proceedings of the EACL 2014 Workshop on Statistical Machine Translation*.

Jacob Devlin, Ming-Wei Chang, Kenton Lee, and Kristina Toutanova. 2019. BERT: Pre-training of deep bidirectional transformers for language understanding. In *Proceedings of the 2019 Conference of the North American Chapter of the Association for Computational Linguistics: Human Language Technologies, Volume 1 (Long and Short Papers)*, pages 4171–4186, Minneapolis, Minnesota. Association for Computational Linguistics.

Li Dong, Jonathan Mallinson, Siva Reddy, and Mirella Lapata. 2017. Learning to paraphrase for question answering. In *Proceedings of the 2017 Conference on Empirical Methods in Natural Language Processing*, pages 875–886.

Elozino Egonmwan and Yllias Chali. 2019. Transformer and seq2seq model for paraphrase generation. In *Proceedings of the 3rd Workshop on Neural Generation and Translation*, pages 249–255.

Kawin Ethayarajh. 2019. How contextual are contextualized word representations? comparing the geometry of bert, elmo, and gpt-2 embeddings. In *Proceedings of the 2019 Conference on Empirical Methods in Natural Language Processing and the 9th International Joint Conference on Natural Language Processing (EMNLP-IJCNLP)*, pages 55–65.

William Fedus, Ian Goodfellow, and Andrew M Dai. 2018. Maskgan: Better text generation via filling in the _. *arXiv preprint arXiv:1801.07736*.

Wee Chung Gan and Hwee Tou Ng. 2019. Improving the robustness of question answering systems to question paraphrasing. In *Proceedings of the 57th Annual Meeting of the Association for Computational Linguistics*, pages 6065–6075.

Jonas Gehring, Michael Auli, David Grangier, Denis Yarats, and Yann N Dauphin. 2017. Convolutional sequence to sequence learning. In *Proceedings of the 34th International Conference on Machine Learning-Volume 70*, pages 1243–1252. JMLR. org.

Jiaxian Guo, Sidi Lu, Han Cai, Weinan Zhang, Yong Yu, and Jun Wang. 2018. Long text generation via adversarial training with leaked information. In *Thirty-Second AAAI Conference on Artificial Intelligence*.

Ankush Gupta, Arvind Agarwal, Prawaan Singh, and Piyush Rai. 2018. A deep generative framework for paraphrase generation. In *Thirty-Second AAAI Conference on Artificial Intelligence*.

Kaiming He, Xiangyu Zhang, Shaoqing Ren, and Jian Sun. 2015. Delving deep into rectifiers: Surpassing human-level performance on imagenet classification. In *Proceedings of the IEEE international conference on computer vision*, pages 1026–1034.

Tianxing He, Jingzhao Zhang, Zhiming Zhou, and James Glass. 2019. Quantifying exposure bias for neural language generation. *arXiv preprint arXiv:1905.10617*.

Benjamin Hoover, Hendrik Strobelt, and Sebastian Gehrmann. 2019. exbert: A visual analysis tool to explore learned representations in transformers models. *arXiv preprint arXiv:1910.05276*.

Shaohan Huang, Yu Wu, Furu Wei, and Ming Zhou. 2018. Dictionary-guided editing networks for paraphrase generation. *arXiv preprint arXiv:1806.08077*.

Mohit Iyyer, John Wieting, Kevin Gimpel, and Luke Zettlemoyer. 2018. Adversarial example generation with syntactically controlled paraphrase networks. In *Proceedings of the 2018 Conference of the North*

American Chapter of the Association for Computational Linguistics: Human Language Technologies, Volume 1 (Long Papers)*, volume 1, pages 1875–1885.

Xiaoqi Jiao, Yichun Yin, Lifeng Shang, Xin Jiang, Xiao Chen, Linlin Li, Fang Wang, and Qun Liu. 2019. Tinybert: Distilling bert for natural language understanding. *arXiv preprint arXiv:1909.10351*.

Diederik P Kingma and Jimmy Ba. 2014. Adam: A method for stochastic optimization. *arXiv preprint arXiv:1412.6980*.

Yang Li, Quan Pan, Suhang Wang, Tao Yang, and Erik Cambria. 2018a. A generative model for category text generation. *Information Sciences*, 450:301–315.

Yitong Li, Trevor Cohn, and Timothy Baldwin. 2017. Robust training under linguistic adversity. In *Proceedings of the 15th Conference of the European Chapter of the Association for Computational Linguistics: Volume 2, Short Papers*, volume 2, pages 21–27.

Zichao Li, Xin Jiang, Lifeng Shang, and Hang Li. 2018b. Paraphrase generation with deep reinforcement learning. In *Proceedings of the 2018 Conference on Empirical Methods in Natural Language Processing*, pages 3865–3878.

Zichao Li, Xin Jiang, Lifeng Shang, and Qun Liu. 2019. Decomposable neural paraphrase generation. In *Proceedings of the 57th Annual Meeting of the Association for Computational Linguistics*, pages 3403–3414.

Chin-Yew Lin. 2004. ROUGE: A package for automatic evaluation of summaries. In *Text Summarization Branches Out*, pages 74–81, Barcelona, Spain. Association for Computational Linguistics.

Xinyue Liu, Xiangnan Kong, Lei Liu, and Kuorong Chiang. 2018. Treegan: Syntax-aware sequence generation with generative adversarial networks. *arXiv preprint arXiv:1808.07582*.

Sidi Lu, Lantao Yu, Siyuan Feng, Yaoming Zhu, and Weinan Zhang. 2019. Cot: Cooperative training for generative modeling of discrete data. In *International Conference on Machine Learning*, pages 4164–4172.

Shuming Ma, Xu Sun, Wei Li, Sujian Li, Wenjie Li, and Xuancheng Ren. 2018. Query and output: Generating words by querying distributed word representations for paraphrase generation. In *Proceedings of the 2018 Conference of the North American Chapter of the Association for Computational Linguistics: Human Language Technologies, Volume 1 (Long Papers)*, pages 196–206.

Jonathan Mallinson, Rico Sennrich, and Mirella Lapata. 2017. Paraphrasing revisited with neural machine translation. In *Proceedings of the 15th Conference of the European Chapter of the Association for Computational Linguistics: Volume 1, Long Papers*, volume 1, pages 881–893.

Hong-Ren Mao and Hung-Yi Lee. 2019. Polly want a cracker: Analyzing performance of parroting on paraphrase generation datasets. In *Proceedings of the 2019 Conference on Empirical Methods in Natural Language Processing and the 9th International Joint Conference on Natural Language Processing (EMNLP-IJCNLP)*, pages 5962–5970.

Cyprien de Masson d'Autume, Shakir Mohamed, Mihaela Rosca, and Jack Rae. 2019. Training language gans from scratch. In *Advances in Neural Information Processing Systems*, pages 4302–4313.

Tomas Mikolov, Edouard Grave, Piotr Bojanowski, Christian Puhrsch, and Armand Joulin. 2018. Advances in pre-training distributed word representations. In *Proceedings of the Eleventh International Conference on Language Resources and Evaluation (LREC-2018)*, Miyazaki, Japan. European Languages Resources Association (ELRA).

Tomas Mikolov, Ilya Sutskever, Kai Chen, Greg S Corrado, and Jeff Dean. 2013. Distributed representations of words and phrases and their compositionality. In *Advances in neural information processing systems*, pages 3111–3119.

Kishore Papineni, Salim Roukos, Todd Ward, and Wei-Jing Zhu. 2002. Bleu: a method for automatic evaluation of machine translation. In *Proceedings of the 40th annual meeting on association for computational linguistics*, pages 311–318. Association for Computational Linguistics.

Adam Paszke, Sam Gross, Francisco Massa, Adam Lerer, James Bradbury, Gregory Chanan, Trevor Killeen, Zeming Lin, Natalia Gimelshein, Luca Antiga, Alban Desmaison, Andreas Kopf, Edward Yang, Zachary DeVito, Martin Raison, Alykhan Tejani, Sasank Chilamkurthy, Benoit Steiner, Lu Fang, Junjie Bai, and Soumith Chintala. 2019. Pytorch: An imperative style, high-performance deep learning library. In *Advances in Neural Information Processing Systems 32*, pages 8024–8035. Curran Associates, Inc.

Jeffrey Pennington, Richard Socher, and Christopher Manning. 2014. Glove: Global vectors for word representation. In *Proceedings of the 2014 Conference on Empirical Methods in Natural Language Processing (EMNLP)*, pages 1532–1543, Doha, Qatar. Association for Computational Linguistics.

Matthew Peters, Mark Neumann, Mohit Iyyer, Matt Gardner, Christopher Clark, Kenton Lee, and Luke Zettlemoyer. 2018. Deep contextualized word representations. In *Proceedings of the 2018 Conference of the North American Chapter of the Association for Computational Linguistics: Human Language Technologies, Volume 1 (Long Papers)*, pages 2227–2237, New Orleans, Louisiana. Association for Computational Linguistics.

Aaditya Prakash, Sadid A Hasan, Kathy Lee, Vivek Datla, Ashequl Qadir, Joey Liu, and Oladimeji Farri. 2016. Neural paraphrase generation with stacked residual lstm networks. *arXiv preprint arXiv:1610.03098*.

Lihua Qian, Lin Qiu, Weinan Zhang, Xin Jiang, and Yong Yu. 2019. Exploring diverse expressions for paraphrase generation. In *Proceedings of the 2019 Conference on Empirical Methods in Natural Language Processing and the 9th International Joint Conference on Natural Language Processing (EMNLP-IJCNLP)*, pages 3164–3173.

Alec Radford, Jeffrey Wu, Rewon Child, David Luan, Dario Amodei, and Ilya Sutskever. 2019. Language models are unsupervised multitask learners. *OpenAI Blog*, 1(8):9.

Marc'Aurelio Ranzato, Sumit Chopra, Michael Auli, and Wojciech Zaremba. 2015. Sequence level training with recurrent neural networks. *arXiv preprint arXiv:1511.06732*.

Suranjana Samanta and Sameep Mehta. 2017. Towards crafting text adversarial samples. *arXiv preprint arXiv:1707.02812*.

Rico Sennrich, Barry Haddow, and Alexandra Birch. 2016. Improving neural machine translation models with monolingual data. In *Proceedings of the 54th Annual Meeting of the Association for Computational Linguistics (Volume 1: Long Papers)*, pages 86–96, Berlin, Germany. Association for Computational Linguistics.

Hong Sun and Ming Zhou. 2012. Joint learning of a dual smt system for paraphrase generation. In *Proceedings of the 50th Annual Meeting of the Association for Computational Linguistics: Short Papers- Volume 2*, pages 38–42. Association for Computational Linguistics.

Ilya Sutskever, Oriol Vinyals, and Quoc V Le. 2014. Sequence to sequence learning with neural networks. In *Advances in neural information processing systems*, pages 3104–3112.

Ashish Vaswani, Noam Shazeer, Niki Parmar, Jakob Uszkoreit, Llion Jones, Aidan N Gomez, Łukasz Kaiser, and Illia Polosukhin. 2017. Attention is all you need. In *Advances in neural information processing systems*, pages 5998–6008.

Su Wang, Rahul Gupta, Nancy Chang, and Jason Baldridge. 2019. A task in a suit and a tie: paraphrase generation with semantic augmentation. In *Proceedings of the AAAI Conference on Artificial Intelligence*, volume 33, pages 7176–7183.

Ronald J Williams. 1992. Simple statistical gradient-following algorithms for connectionist reinforcement learning. *Machine learning*, 8(3-4):229–256.

Ronald J Williams and David Zipser. 1989. A learning algorithm for continually running fully recurrent neural networks. *Neural computation*, 1(2):270–280.

Qizhe Xie, Zihang Dai, Eduard Hovy, Minh-Thang Luong, and Quoc V Le. 2019. Unsupervised data augmentation for consistency training.

Qian Yang, Dinghan Shen, Yong Cheng, Wenlin Wang, Guoyin Wang, Lawrence Carin, et al. 2019. An end-to-end generative architecture for paraphrase generation. In *Proceedings of the 2019 Conference on Empirical Methods in Natural Language Processing and the 9th International Joint Conference on Natural Language Processing (EMNLP-IJCNLP)*, pages 3123–3133.

Lantao Yu, Weinan Zhang, Jun Wang, and Yong Yu. 2017. Seqgan: Sequence generative adversarial nets with policy gradient. In *AAAI*, pages 2852–2858.

WNUT-2020 Task 1 Overview: Extracting Entities and Relations from Wet Lab Protocols

Jeniya Tabassum[1], Sydney Lee[1], Wei Xu[2], Alan Ritter[2]
[1] Department of Computer Science and Engineering, The Ohio State University
[2] School of Interactive Computing, Georgia Institute of Technology
{bintejafar.1, lee.7509}@osu.edu   {wei.xu, alan.ritter}@cc.gatech.edu

Abstract

This paper presents the results of the wet lab information extraction task at WNUT 2020. This task consisted of two sub tasks: (1) a Named Entity Recognition (NER) task with 13 participants and (2) a Relation Extraction (RE) task with 2 participants. We outline the task, data annotation process, corpus statistics, and provide a high-level overview of the participating systems for each sub task.

1 Introduction

Wet Lab protocols consist of natural language instructions for carrying out chemistry or biology experiments (for an example, see Figure 1). While there have been efforts to develop domain-specific formal languages in order to support robotic automation[1] of experimental procedures (Bates et al., 2017), the vast majority of knowledge about how to carry out biological experiments or chemical synthesis procedures is only documented in natural language texts, including in scientific papers, electronic lab notebooks, and so on.

Recent research has begun to apply human language technologies to extract structured representations of procedures from natural language protocols (Kuniyoshi et al., 2020; Vaucher et al., 2020; Kulkarni et al., 2018; Soldatova et al., 2014; Vasilev et al., 2011; Ananthanarayanan and Thies, 2010). Extraction of named entities and relations from these protocols is an important first step towards machine reading systems that can interpret the meaning of these noisy human generated instructions.

However, performance of state-of-the-art tools for extracting named entity and relations from wet lab protocols still lags behind well edited text genres (Jiang et al., 2020). This motivates the need for continued research, in addition to new datasets and tools adapted to this noisy text genre.

---

[1] https://autoprotocol.org/

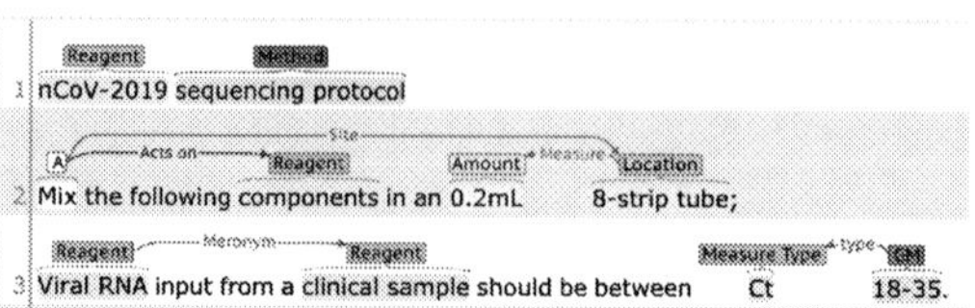

Figure 1: Examples of named entities and relations in a wet lab protocol

In this overview paper, we describe the development and findings of a shared task on named entity and relation extraction from the noisy wet lab protocols, which was held at the 6-th Workshop on Noisy User-generated Text (WNUT 2020) and attracted 15 participating teams.

In the following sections, we describe details of the task including training and development datasets in addition to the newly annotated test data. We briefly summarize the systems developed by selected teams, and conclude with results.

2 Wet Lab Protocols

Wet lab protocols consist of the guidelines from different lab procedures which involve chemicals, drugs, or other materials in liquid solutions or volatile phases. The protocols contain a sequence of steps that are followed to perform a desired task. These protocols also include general guidelines or warnings about the materials being used. The publicly available archive of `protocol.io` contains such guidelines of wet lab experiments, written by researchers and lab technicians around the world. This protocol archive covers a large spectrum of experimental procedures including neurology, epigenetics, metabolomics, stem cell biology, etc. Figure 1 shows a representative wet lab protocol.

The wet lab protocols, written by users from all over the worlds, contain domain specific jargon as well as numerous nonstandard spellings, abbreviations, unreliable capitalization. Such diverse and

Proceedings of the 2020 EMNLP Workshop W-NUT: The Sixth Workshop on Noisy User-generated Text, pages 260–267
Online, Nov 19, 2020. ©2020 Association for Computational Linguistics

	Train	Dev	Test-18	Test-20	Total			per Protocol	per Sentence
#protocols	370	122	123	111	726	avg. #sentences	24.32	-
#sentences	8444	2839	2813	3562	17658	avg. #tokens	318.77	13.11
#tokens	107038	36106	36597	51688	231429	avg. #entities	255.25	10.49
#entities	48197	15972	16490	104654	185313	avg. #relation	171.90	7.07
#relations	32158	10812	11242	70591	124803			

Table 1: Statistics of the Wet Lab Protocol corpus.

noisy style of user created protocols imposed crucial challenges for the entity and relation extraction systems. Hence, off-the-shelf named entity recognition and relation extraction tools, tuned for well edited texts, suffer a severe performance degradation when applied to noisy protocol texts (Kulkarni et al., 2018).

To address these challenges, there has been an increasing body of work on adapting entity and relation extraction recognition tools for noisy wet lab texts (Jiang et al., 2020; Luan et al., 2019; Kulkarni et al., 2018). However, different research groups have used different evaluation setups (e.g., training / test splits) making it challenging to perform direct comparisons across systems. By organizing a shared evaluation, we hope to help establish a common evaluation methodology (for at least one dataset) and also promote research and development of NLP tools for user generated wet-lab text genres.

2.1 Annotated Corpus

Our annotated wet lab corpus includes 726 experimental protocols from the 8-year archive of ProtocolIO (April 2012 to March 2020). These protocols are manually annotated with 15 types of relations among the 18 entity types[2]. The fine-grained entities can be broadly classified into 5 categories: ACTION, CONSTITUENTS, QUANTIFIERS, SPECIFIERS, and MODIFIERS. The CONSTITUENTS category includes mentions of REAGENT, LOCATION, DEVICE, MENTION, and SEAL. The QUANTIFIERS category includes mentions of AMOUNT, CONCENTRATION, SIZE, TIME, TEMPERATURE, pH, SPEED, GENERIC-MEASURE and NUMERICAL. The SPECIFIERS category includes mentions of MODIFIER, MEASURE-TYPE and METHOD. The ACTION entity refers to the phrases denoting tasks that are performed to complete a step in the protocol. The mentions of these entities contain different types of relations, including– SITE, SETTING, CREATES, MEASURE-

TYPE-LINK, CO-REFERENCE-LINK, MOD-LINK, COUNT, MERONYM, USING, MEASURE, COMMANDS, OF-TYPE, OR, PRODUCT, and ACTS-ON.

2.1.1 Train and Development data

The training and development dataset for our task was taken from previous work on wet lab corpus (Kulkarni et al., 2018) that consists of from the 623 protocols. We excluded the eight duplicate protocols from this dataset and then re-annotated the 615 unique protocols in BRAT (Stenetorp et al., 2012). This re-annotation process aided us to add the previously missing 20,613 missing entities along with 10,824 previously missing relations and also to facilitate removing the inconsistent annotations. The updated corpus statics is provided in Table 1. This full dataset (Train, Dev, Test-18) was provided to the participants at the beginning of the task and they were allowed to use any of part of this dataset to train their final model.

2.1.2 Test Data

For this shared task we added 111 new protocols (Test-20) which were used to evaluate the submitted models. Test-20 dataset consists of 100 randomly sampled general protocols and 11 manually selected covid-related protocols from ProtocolIO (https://www.protocols.io/). This 111 protocols were double annotated by three annotators using a web-based annotation tool, BRAT (Stenetorp et al., 2012). Figure 1 presents a screenshot of our annotation interface. We also provided the annotators a set of guidelines containing the entity and relation type definitions. The annotation task was split in multiple iterations. In each iteration, an annotator was given a set of 10 protocols. An adjudicator then went through all the entity and relation annotations in these protocols and resolved the disagreements. Before adjudication, the inter-annotator agreement is 0.75 , measured by Cohen's Kappa (Cohen, 1960).

2.2 Baseline Model

We provided the participants baseline model for both of the subtasks. The baseline model for named

---

entity recognition task utilized a feature-based CRF tagger developed using the CRF-Suite[3] with a standard set of contextual, lexical and gazetteer features. The baseline relation extraction system employed a feature-based logistic regression model developed using the Scikit-Learn[4] with a standard set of contextual, lexical and gazetteer features.

2.3 NER Systems

Thirteen teams (Table 3) participated in the named entity recognition sub-task. A wide variety of approaches were taken to tackle this task. Table 2 summarizes the word representations, features and the machine learning approaches taken by each team. Majority of the teams (11 out of 13) utilized contextual word representations. Four teams combined the contextual word representations with global word vectors. Only two teams did not use any type of word representations and relied entirely on hand-engineered features and a CRF taggers. The best performing teams utilized a combination of contextual word representation with ensemble of learning. Below we provide a brief description of the approach taken by each team.

B-NLP (Lange et al., 2020) modeled the NER as a parsing task and uses a biaffine classifier. The second classifier of their system used the predictions from the first classifier and then updated the labels of the predicted entities. Both of the classifiers utilized word2vec (Mikolov et al., 2013) and SciBERT (Lee et al., 2019) word representations.

BIO-BIO (Kecheng et al., 2020) implemented a BiLSTM-CRF tagger that utilized BioBERT (Lee et al., 2020) word representation.

BiTeM (Knafou et al., 2020) developed a voting based ensemble classifier containing 14 transformer models, and utilized 7 different word representations including BERT (Devlin et al., 2019), ClinicalBERT (Huang et al., 2019), PubMedBERT$_{base}$ (Gu et al., 2020), BioBERT (Lee et al., 2020), RoBERTa (Liu et al., 2019), Biomed-RoBERTa$_{base}$ (Gururangan et al., 2020) and XLNet (Yang et al., 2019).

DSC-IITISM (Gupta et al., 2020) developed a BiLSTM-CRF model that utilized a concatenation of CamemBERT$_{base}$ (Martin et al., 2020), Flair(PubMed) (Akbik et al., 2018), and GloVe(en) (Pennington et al., 2014) word representations.

Fancy Man (Zeng et al., 2020) fine-tuned the BERT$_{base}$ (Devlin et al., 2019) model with an additional linear layer.

IBS (Sikdar et al., 2020) utilized an ensemble classifier with 4 feature based on CRF taggers.

Kabir (Khan, 2020) employed an RNN-CRF model that utilized concatenation of Flair(PubMed) (Akbik et al., 2018) and ELMo(PubMed) (Peters et al., 2018) word representations.

KaushikAcharya (Acharya, 2020) employed a linear CRF with hand-crafted features.

mahab (Pour and Farinnia, 2020) fine-tuned the BERT$_{base}$ (Devlin et al., 2019) sequence tagging model.

mgsohrab (Sohrab et al., 2020) fine-tuned the SciBERT (Beltagy et al., 2019) model.

PublishInCovid19 (Singh and Wadhawan, 2020) employed a structured ensemble classifier (Nguyen and Guo, 2007) consisting of 11 BiLSTM-CRF taggers, that utilized the PubMedBERT (Gu et al., 2020) word representation.

SudeshnaTCS (Jana, 2020) fine-tuned XLNet (Yang et al., 2019) model.

IITKGP (Kaushal and Vaidhya, 2020) fine-tuned the Bio-BERT (Lee et al., 2020) model.

2.4 RE Systems

Two teams (Table 3) participated in the relation extraction sub-task. Both of the teams followed fine-tuning of contextual word representation and did not use any hand-crafted features. Table 5 summarizes the word representations and the machine learning approaches followed by each team. Below we provide a brief description of the model developed by taken by each team.

Big Green (Miller and Vosoughi, 2020) considered the protocols as a knowledge graph, in which relationships between entities are edges in the knowledge graph. They trained a BERT (Devlin et al., 2019) based system to classify edge presence and type between two entities, given entity text, label, and local context.

---

[3]http://www.chokkan.org/software/crfsuite/

[4]https://scikit-learn.org/

262

Team	Word Representation	Features	Approach
BiTeM	BERT, BioBERT, RoBERTa, XLNet	-	Ensemble of Transformers
PublishInCovid19	PubMedBERT	-	Ensemble of BiLSTM-CRFs
Fancy Man	BERT	-	BERT fine tuning
mahab	BERT	Lexical	BERT fine tuning
mgsohrab	SciBERT	Lexical	SciBERT fine tuning
SudeshnaTCS	XLNet	Rules	XLNet fine tuning
IITKGP	BioBERT	-	BioBERT fine tuning
B-NLP	SciBERT, word2vec	-	Biaffine Classifier
BIO-BIO	BioBERT	-	BiLSTM-CRF
DSC-IITISM	GLoVe, CamemBERT, Flair	-	BiLSTM-CRF
Kabir	GLoVe, ELMo, BERT, Flair	Gazetteers	RNN-CRF
IBS	-	Gazetteers, POS Tagger	Ensemble of CRFs
KaushikAcharya	-	POS Tagger, Dependency Parser	CRF
Baseline	-	Gazetteers, Lexical, Contextual	CRF

Table 2: Summary of NER systems designed by each team.

Team Name	Affiliation
B-NLP	Bosch Center for Artificial Intelligence
Big Green	Dartmouth College
BIO-BIO	Harbin Institute of technology, Shenzhen
BiTeM	University of Applied Sciences and Arts of Western Switzerland, Swiss Institute of Bioinformatics, University of Geneva
DSC-IITISM	IIT(ISM) Dhanbad
Fancy Man	University of Manchester, Xian Jiaotong University, East China University of Science and Technology, Zhejiang University
IBS	IBS Software Pvt. Ltd, NTNU
IITKGP	IIT, Kharagpur
Kabir	Microsoft
KaushikAcharya	Philips
mahab	Amirkabir University of Technology
mgsohrab	National Institute of Advanced Industrial Science and Technology
PublishInCovid19	Flipkart Private Limited
SudeshnaTCS	TCS Research & Innovation Lab

Table 3: Team Name and affiliation of the participant.

	P	R	F_1
Exact Match			
BiTeM	**84.73**	72.25	**77.99**
PublishInCovid19	81.36	**74.12**	77.57
Fancy Man	76.21	71.76	73.92
mahab	50.19	52.96	51.54
mgsohrab	83.69	70.62	76.60
SudeshnaTCS	74.99	71.43	73.16
IITKGP	77.00	72.93	74.91
B-NLP	77.95	63.93	70.25
BIO-BIO	78.49	71.06	74.59
DSC-IITISM	64.20	57.07	60.42
Kabir	78.79	72.20	75.35
IBS	74.26	62.55	67.90
KaushikAcharya	73.68	63.98	68.48
Baseline	70.06	61.91	65.73
Partial Match			
BiTeM	**88.72**	75.66	81.67
PublishInCovid19	85.74	**78.11**	**81.75**
Fancy Man	81.15	76.41	78.71
mahab	55.09	58.14	56.57
mgsohrab	87.95	74.22	80.50
SudeshnaTCS	79.73	75.95	77.80
IITKGP	81.76	77.43	79.54
B-NLP	84.85	69.59	76.46
BIO-BIO	83.16	75.29	79.03
DSC-IITISM	68.52	60.90	64.49
Kabir	83.73	76.73	80.08
IBS	79.72	67.15	72.89
KaushikAcharya	79.31	68.87	73.73
Baseline	75.66	66.85	70.98

Table 4: Results on extraction of 18 Named Entity types from the *Test-20* dataset. **Exact Match** reports the performance when the predicted entity type is same as the gold entity and the predicted entity boundary is the exact same as the gold entity boundary. **Partial Match** reports the performance when the predicted entity type is same as the gold entity and the predicted entity boundary has some overlap with gold entity boundary.

mgsohrab (Sohrab et al., 2020) utilized PubMedBERT (Gu et al., 2020) as input to the relation extraction model that enumerates all possible pairs of arguments using deep exhaustive span representation approach.

3 Evaluation

In this section, we present the performance of each participating systems along with a description of the errors made by the model types.

3.1 NER Errors Analysis

Table 4 shows the comparison of precision (**P**), recall (**R**) and F_1 score among different teams, evaluated on the *Test-20* corpus. Here the exact match refers to the cases where a predicted entity is considered correct, only if the predicted type and boundary is exactly same as the gold entity. Whereas, in partial match, a predicted entity is considered correct if the predicted type is the same as the gold entity type and predicted entity boundary

Team	Word Representation	Features	Approach
mgsohrab	PubMedBERT	-	PubMedBERT fine-tuning
Big Green	BERT	-	BERT fine-tuning
Baseline	-	Gazetteers, Lexical, Contextual	Logistic Regression

Table 5: Summary of relation extraction systems designed by each team.

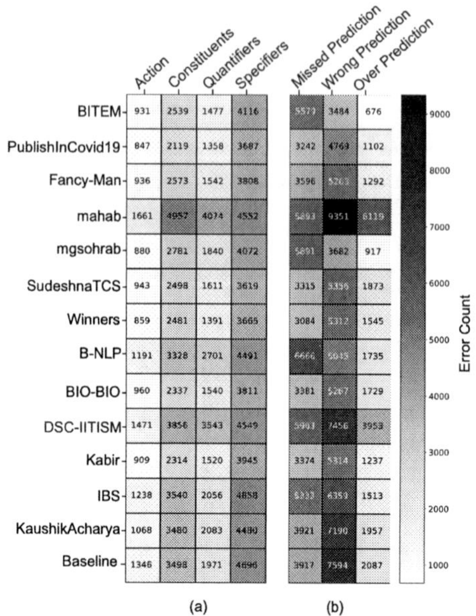

Figure 2: Summary of incorrectly classified entity tokens by each submitted systems.

has some overlap with the gold entity boundary.

We observe that ensemble models with contextual word representations outperforms all other approaches by achieving 77.99 F_1 score in exact match (Team:BiTeM) and 81.75 F_1 score in partial match (Team:PublishInCovid19). Fine tuning of contextual word representation systems demonstrated quite competent performance with SciBERT-fine tuning being the best (Team:mgsohrab).

In Figure 2, we present an error analysis. Among the best performing models, the ensemble of transformer (Team:BiTeM) had significantly lower amount of 'over prediction' error (i.e., tagging a non-entity token as entity), compared to the system with ensemble of BiLSTM-CRFs (Team:PublishInCovid19).

3.2 RE Errors Analysis

Table 6 shows the comparison of precision (**P**), recall (**R**) and F_1 score among the participant teams, evaluated on the *Test-20* corpus. Both of the teams utilized the gold entities and then predict the relations among these entities by fine-tuning con-

textual word representations. We observed that fine-tuning of domain related PubMedBERT, provides significantly higher performance compared to the general domain BERT. While examining the relation predictions from both of these systems, we found that model with fine-tuned PubMedBERT (Team:mgsohrab) resulted in significantly less amount of errors in every category (Figure 3).

	P	**R**	**F_1**
mgsohrab	**80.86**	80.07	**80.46**
Big Green	45.42	**86.54**	59.57
Baseline	80.10	66.21	72.50

Table 6: Results on extraction of 15 relation types from the *Test-20* dataset.

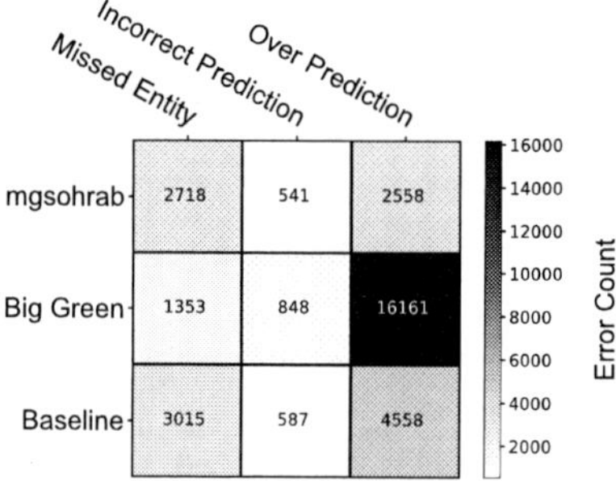

Figure 3: Summary of incorrectly predicted relations in each submitted systems.

4   Related Work

The task of information extraction from wet lab protocols is closely related to the event trigger extraction task. The event trigger task has been studied extensively, mostly using ACE data (Doddington et al., 2004) and the BioNLP data (Nédellec et al., 2013). Broadly, there are two ways to classify various event trigger detection models: (1) *Rule-based* methods using pattern matching and regular expression to identify triggers (Vlachos et al., 2009) and (2) *Machine Learning based* methods focusing on generation of high-end hand-crafted features to be used in classification models like SVMs or maxent classifiers (Pyysalo et al., 2012). Kernel based learning methods have also been utilized with embedded features from the syntactic and semantic contexts to identify and extract the biomedical event entities (Zhou et al., 2014). In order to counteract highly sparse representations, different neural models were proposed. These neural models utilized the dependency based word embeddings with feed forward neural networks (Wang et al., 2016b), CNNs (Wang et al., 2016a) and Bidirectional RNNs (Rahul et al., 2017).

Previous work has experimented on datasets of well-edited biomedical publications with a small number of entity types. For example, the JNLPBA corpus (Kim et al., 2004) with 5 entity types (CELL LINE, CELL TYPE, DNA, RNA, and PROTEIN) and the BC2GM corpus (Hirschman et al., 2005) with a single entity class for genes/proteins. In contrast, our dataset addresses the challenges of recognizing 18 fine-grained named entities along with 15 types of relations from the user-created wet lab protocols.

5 Summary

In this paper, we presented a shared task for consisting of two sub-tasks: named entity recognition and relation extraction from the wet lab protocols. We described the task setup and datasets details, and also outlined the approach taken by the participating systems. The shared task included larger and improvised dataset compared to the prior literature (Kulkarni et al., 2018). This improvised dataset enables us to draw stronger conclusions about the true potential of different approaches. It also facilitates us in analyzing the results of the participating systems, which aids us in suggesting potential research directions for both future shared tasks and noisy text processing in user generated lab protocols.

Acknowledgement

We would like to thank Ethan Lee and Jaewook Lee for helping with data annotation. This material is based upon work supported by the Defense Advanced Research Projects Agency (DARPA) under Contract No. HR001119C0108. The views, opinions, and/or findings expressed are those of the author(s) and should not be interpreted as representing the official views or policies of the Department of Defense or the U.S. Government.

References

Kaushik Acharya. 2020. KaushikAcharya at WNUT 2020 Shared Task-1: Conditional Random Field(CRF) based Named Entity Recognition(NER) for Wet Lab Protocols. In *Proceedings of EMNLP 2020 Workshop on Noisy User-generated Text (WNUT)*.

Alan Akbik, Duncan Blythe, and Roland Vollgraf. 2018. Contextual String Embeddings for Sequence Labeling. In *COLING 2018, 27th International Conference on Computational Linguistics*.

Vaishnavi Ananthanarayanan and William Thies. 2010. Biocoder: A programming language for standardizing and automating biology protocols. *Journal of biological engineering*.

Maxwell Bates, Aaron J Berliner, Joe Lachoff, Paul R Jaschke, and Eli S Groban. 2017. Wet lab accelerator: a web-based application democratizing laboratory automation for synthetic biology. *ACS synthetic biology*.

Iz Beltagy, Arman Cohan, and Kyle Lo. 2019. SciBERT: Pretrained Contextualized Embeddings for Scientific Text. In *Proceedings of the 2019 Conference on Empirical Methods in Natural Language Processing (EMNLP)*.

Jacob Cohen. 1960. A Coefficient of Agreement for Nominal Scales. *Educational and Psychological Measurement*.

Jacob Devlin, Ming-Wei Chang, Kenton Lee, and Kristina Toutanova. 2019. BERT: Pre-training of Deep Bidirectional Transformers for Language Understanding. In *Proceedings of the 2019 Annual Conference of the North American Chapter of the Association for Computational Linguistics (NAACL)*.

George R Doddington, Alexis Mitchell, Mark A Przybocki, Lance A Ramshaw, Stephanie Strassel, and Ralph M Weischedel. 2004. The automatic content extraction (ace) program-tasks, data, and evaluation. In *LREC*.

Yu Gu, Robert Tinn, Hao Cheng, Michael Lucas, Naoto Usuyama, Xiaodong Liu, Tristan Naumann, Jianfeng Gao, and Hoifung Poon. 2020. Domain-Specific Language Model Pretraining for Biomedical Natural Language Processing. *arXiv preprint arXiv:2007.15779*.

Saket Gupta, Aman Sinha, and Rohit Agarwal. 2020. DSC-IITISM at WNUT 2020 Shared Task-1: Name Entity Extraction from Wet Lab Protocol. In *Proceedings of EMNLP 2020 Workshop on Noisy User-generated Text (WNUT)*.

Suchin Gururangan, Ana Marasović, Swabha Swayamdipta, Kyle Lo, Iz Beltagy, Doug Downey, and Noah A Smith. 2020. Don't Stop Pretraining: Adapt Language Models to Domains and Tasks. *arXiv preprint arXiv:2004.10964*.

Lynette Hirschman, Alexander Yeh, Christian Blaschke, and Alfonso Valencia. 2005. Overview of biocreative: critical assessment of information extraction for biology.

Kexin Huang, Jaan Altosaar, and Rajesh Ranganath. 2019. Clinicalbert: Modeling clinical notes and predicting hospital readmission. *arXiv preprint arXiv:1904.05342*.

Sudeshna Jana. 2020. SudeshnaTCS at WNUT 2020 Shared Task-1: Name Entity Extraction from Wet Lab Protocol. In *Proceedings of EMNLP 2020 Workshop on Noisy User-generated Text (WNUT)*.

Zhengbao Jiang, Wei Xu, Jun Araki, and Graham Neubig. 2020. Generalizing Natural Language Analysis through Span-relation Representations. In *Proceedings of the 2020 Conference of the Association for Computational Linguistics*.

Ayush Kaushal and Tejas Vaidhya. 2020. IITKGP at WNUT 2020 Shared Task-1: Domain specific BERT representation for Named Entity Recognition of lab protocol. In *Proceedings of EMNLP 2020 Workshop on Noisy User-generated Text (WNUT)*.

Zhan Kecheng, Xiong Ying, Peng Hao, Yao, and LiQing Yao. 2020. BIO-BIO at WNUT 2020 Shared Task-1: Name Entity Extraction from Wet Lab Protocol.

Kabir Khan. 2020. kabir at WNUT 2020 Shared Task-1: Name Entity Extraction from Wet Lab Protocol. In *Proceedings of EMNLP 2020 Workshop on Noisy User-generated Text (WNUT)*.

Jin-Dong Kim, Tomoko Ohta, Yoshimasa Tsuruoka, Yuka Tateisi, and Nigel Collier. 2004. Introduction to the bio-entity recognition task at jnlpba. In *Proceedings of the international joint workshop on natural language processing in biomedicine and its applications*.

Julien Knafou, Nona Naderi, Jenny Copara, Douglas Teodoro, and Patrick Ruch. 2020. BiTeM at WNUT 2020 Shared Task-1: Named Entity Recognition over Wet Lab Protocols using an Ensemble of Contextual Language Models. In *Proceedings of EMNLP 2020 Workshop on Noisy User-generated Text (WNUT)*.

Chaitanya Kulkarni, Wei Xu, Alan Ritter, and Raghu Machiraju. 2018. An Annotated Corpus for Machine Reading of Instructions in Wet Lab Protocols. In *Proceedings of the 2018 Conference of the North American Chapter of the Association for Computational Linguistics: Human Language Technologies*.

Fusataka Kuniyoshi, Kohei Makino, Jun Ozawa, and Makoto Miwa. 2020. Annotating and Extracting Synthesis Process of All-Solid-State Batteries from Scientific Literature. *arXiv preprint arXiv:2002.07339*.

Lukas Lange, Xiang Dai, Heike Adel, and Jannik Strötgen. 2020. B-NLP at WNUT 2020 Shared Task-1: Name Entity Extraction from Wet Lab Protocol. In *Proceedings of EMNLP 2020 Workshop on Noisy User-generated Text (WNUT)*.

Jinhyuk Lee, Wonjin Yoon, Sungdong Kim, Donghyeon Kim, Sunkyu Kim, Chan Ho So, and Jaewoo Kang. 2019. BioBERT: a pre-trained biomedical language representation model for biomedical text mining. *Bioinformatics*.

Jinhyuk Lee, Wonjin Yoon, Sungdong Kim, Donghyeon Kim, Sunkyu Kim, Chan Ho So, and Jaewoo Kang. 2020. BioBERT: a pre-trained biomedical language representation model for biomedical text mining. *Bioinformatics*.

Y Liu, M Ott, N Goyal, J Du, M Joshi, D Chen, O Levy, M Lewis, L Zettlemoyer, and V Stoyanov. 2019. RoBERTa: A robustly optimized BERT pretraining approach. *arXiv preprint arXiv:1907.11692*.

Yi Luan, Dave Wadden, Luheng He, Amy Shah, Mari Ostendorf, and Hannaneh Hajishirzi. 2019. A general framework for information extraction using dynamic span graphs. In *Proceedings of the 2019 Conference of the North American Chapter of the Association for Computational Linguistics: Human Language Technologies*.

Louis Martin, Benjamin Muller, Pedro Javier Ortiz Suárez, Yoann Dupont, Laurent Romary, Éric de la Clergerie, Djamé Seddah, and Benoît Sagot. 2020. CamemBERT: a Tasty French Language Model. In *Proceedings of the 58th Annual Meeting of the Association for Computational Linguistics*.

Tomas Mikolov, Kai Chen, Greg Corrado, and Jeffrey Dean. 2013. Efficient estimation of word representations in vector space. *arXiv preprint arXiv:1301.3781*.

Chris Miller and Soroush Vosoughi. 2020. Big Green at WNUT 2020 Shared Task-1: Relation Extraction as Contextualized Sequence Classification. In *Proceedings of EMNLP 2020 Workshop on Noisy User-generated Text (WNUT)*.

Claire Nédellec, Robert Bossy, Jin-Dong Kim, Jung-Jae Kim, Tomoko Ohta, Sampo Pyysalo, and Pierre Zweigenbaum. 2013. Overview of bionlp shared task 2013. In *Proceedings of the BioNLP Shared Task 2013 Workshop*. Association for Computational Linguistics Sofia, Bulgaria.

Nam Nguyen and Yunsong Guo. 2007. Comparisons of sequence labeling algorithms and extensions. In *Proceedings of the 24th international conference on Machine learning*.

Jeffrey Pennington, Richard Socher, and Christopher D. Manning. 2014. GloVe: Global Vectors for Word Representation. In *Proceedings of the Empirical Methods in Natural Language Processing (EMNLP)*.

Matthew E. Peters, Mark Neumann, Mohit Iyyer, Matt Gardner, Christopher Clark, Kenton Lee, and Luke Zettlemoyer. 2018. Deep Contextualized Word Representations. In *Proceedings of the of Conference of the North American Chapter of the Association for Computational Linguistics (NAACL)*.

Mohammad Mahdi Abdollah Pour and Parsa Farinnia. 2020. mahab at WNUT 2020 Shared Task-1: Name Entity Extraction from Wet Lab Protocol. In *Proceedings of EMNLP 2020 Workshop on Noisy User-generated Text (WNUT)*.

Sampo Pyysalo, Tomoko Ohta, Makoto Miwa, Han-Cheol Cho, Jun'ichi Tsujii, and Sophia Ananiadou. 2012. Event extraction across multiple levels of biological organization. *Bioinformatics*.

Patchigolla VSS Rahul, Sunil Kumar Sahu, and Ashish Anand. 2017. Biomedical event trigger identification using bidirectional recurrent neural network based models. *arXiv preprint arXiv:1705.09516*.

Utpal Kumar Sikdar, Bjorn Gamback, and M Krishana Kumar. 2020. IBS at WNUT 2020 Shared Task-1: Name Entity Extraction from Wet Lab Protocol. In *Proceedings of EMNLP 2020 Workshop on Noisy User-generated Text (WNUT)*.

Janvijay Singh and Anshul Wadhawan. 2020. PublishInCovid19 at WNUT 2020 Shared Task-1: Entity Recognition in Wet Lab Protocols using Structured Learning Ensemble and Contextualised Embeddings. In *Proceedings of EMNLP 2020 Workshop on Noisy User-generated Text (WNUT)*.

Mohammad Golam Sohrab, Khoa Duong, Makoto Miwa, and Hiroya Takamura. 2020. mgsohrab at WNUT 2020 Shared Task-1: Neural Exhaustive Approach for Entity and Relation Recognition Over Wet Lab Protocols. In *Proceedings of EMNLP 2020 Workshop on Noisy User-generated Text (WNUT)*.

Larisa N Soldatova, Daniel Nadis, Ross D King, Piyali S Basu, Emma Haddi, Véronique Baumlé, Nigel J Saunders, Wolfgang Marwan, and Brian B Rudkin. 2014. EXACT2: the semantics of biomedical protocols. *BMC bioinformatics*.

Pontus Stenetorp, Sampo Pyysalo, Goran Topić, Tomoko Ohta, Sophia Ananiadou, and Jun'ichi Tsujii. 2012. brat: a Web-based Tool for NLP-Assisted Text Annotation. In *Proceedings of the Demonstrations at the 13th Conference of the European Chapter of the Association for Computational Linguistics (EACL)*.

Viktor Vasilev, Chenkai Liu, Traci Haddock, Swapnil Bhatia, Aaron Adler, Fusun Yaman, Jacob Beal, Jonathan Babb, Ron Weiss, Douglas Densmore, et al. 2011. A software stack for specification and robotic execution of protocols for synthetic biological engineering. In *3rd international workshop on bio-design automation*.

Alain C Vaucher, Federico Zipoli, Joppe Geluykens, Vishnu H Nair, Philippe Schwaller, and Teodoro Laino. 2020. Automated extraction of chemical synthesis actions from experimental procedures.

Andreas Vlachos, Paula Buttery, Diarmuid O Séaghdha, and Ted Briscoe. 2009. Biomedical event extraction without training data. In *Proceedings of the Workshop on Current Trends in Biomedical Natural Language Processing: Shared Task*. Association for Computational Linguistics.

Jian Wang, Honglei Li, Yuan An, Hongfei Lin, and Zhihao Yang. 2016a. Biomedical event trigger detection based on convolutional neural network. *International Journal of Data Mining and Bioinformatics*.

Jian Wang, Jianhai Zhang, Yuan An, Hongfei Lin, Zhihao Yang, Yijia Zhang, and Yuanyuan Sun. 2016b. Biomedical event trigger detection by dependency-based word embedding. *BMC medical genomics*.

Zhilin Yang, Zihang Dai, Yiming Yang, Jaime Carbonell, Russ R Salakhutdinov, and Quoc V Le. 2019. Xlnet: Generalized autoregressive pretraining for language understanding. In *Advances in neural information processing systems*.

Qingcheng Zeng, Haoding Meng, Xiaoyang Fang, and Zhexin Liang. 2020. Fancy Man Launches Zippo at WNUT 2020 Shared Task-1: A Bert Case Model for Wet Lab Entity Extraction. In *Proceedings of EMNLP 2020 Workshop on Noisy User-generated Text (WNUT)*.

Deyu Zhou, Dayou Zhong, and Yulan He. 2014. Event trigger identification for biomedical events extraction using domain knowledge. *Bioinformatics*.

IITKGP at W-NUT 2020 Shared Task-1: Domain specific BERT representation for Named Entity Recognition of lab protocol

Tejas Vaidhya and **Ayush Kaushal**
Indian Institute of Technology, Kharagpur
`iamtejasvaidhya@gmail.com, ayushk4@gmail.com`

Abstract

Supervised models trained to predict properties from representations, have been achieving high accuracy on a variety of tasks. For instance, the BERT family seems to work exceptionally well on the downstream task from NER tagging to the range of other linguistic tasks. But the vocabulary used in the medical field contains a lot of different tokens used only in the medical industry such as the name of different diseases, devices, organisms, medicines, etc. that makes it difficult for traditional BERT model to create contextualized embedding. In this paper, we are going to illustrate the **System for Named Entity Tagging based on Bio-Bert**. Experimental results show that our model gives substantial improvements over the baseline and stood the **fourth runner up** in terms of F1 score, and **first runner up** in terms of Recall with just 2.21 *F1* score behind the best one.[1]

1 Introduction

A large amount of data is generated every year in the medical field. One of the most important generated data is the documentation of protocols. It provides individual sets of instructions that allow scientists to recreate experiments in their own laboratory. Most of them are written in Natural language which reduces its machine readability. The protocol gives a concise overview of the project which reduces its pre-processing needs but also make it less informative syntactically that eventually results in less accuracy.

Recent progress in Named Entity Recognition was made possible by the advancements of deep learning techniques used in natural language processing (NLP). For instance, Long Short-Term Memory (LSTM) (Hochreiter and Schmidhuber, 1997) and Conditional Random Field (CRF) (Namikoshi et al., 2017) have greatly improved performance in biomedical named entity recognition (NER) over the last few years. Bio-BERT(Lee et al., 2019) outperform all the other previous approaches with the help of BERT (Devlin et al., 2018) architecture pre-trained on Bio-medical texts (Giorgi and Bader, 2018; Habibi et al., 2017; Wang et al., 2018; Yoon et al., 2019).

In this paper, we are introducing our system for the NER tagging on the WLP dataset (Kulkarni et al., 2018). We use a variant of Bio-Bert (Lee et al., 2019). The primary motivation to use the model is it's medical vocabulary and features encoded in the pre-trained model.

2 Task Description and Data Set

Formally, the WNUT 2020 Shared Task-1 Named Entity Recognition, organized within, the 6th Workshop on Noisy User-generated Text (WNUT), 2020 (Tabassum et al., 2020) is a NER prediction task. It can be expressed as 'tokens-level' classification task mathematically as:

Let the sentence S be defined as:
$$S = \{s_1, s_2, ..., s_n\}$$
n is the number words in the sentences can be classified into the following label set
$$y = \{l_1, l_2, l_3, ..., l_m\}$$
where m is labels.

Given named entity of type XXX. Whenever two entities of type XXX are immediately next to each other, the first word of the second entity will be tagged B-XXX in order to show that it starts another entity and the entities inside B-XXX will be represented as I-XXX. For example, the sentence {nCoV-2019, sequencing, protocol} have the following labels {B-Reagent, B-Method, I-Method}.

DataSet: All of the protocols (Kulkarni et al., 2018) were collected from protocols.io using their public APIs by organising team. For the shared

---

[1] `https://github.com/tejasvaidhyadev/ NER_Lab_Protocols`

Proceedings of the 2020 EMNLP Workshop W-NUT: The Sixth Workshop on Noisy User-generated Text, pages 268–272
Online, Nov 19, 2020. ©2020 Association for Computational Linguistics

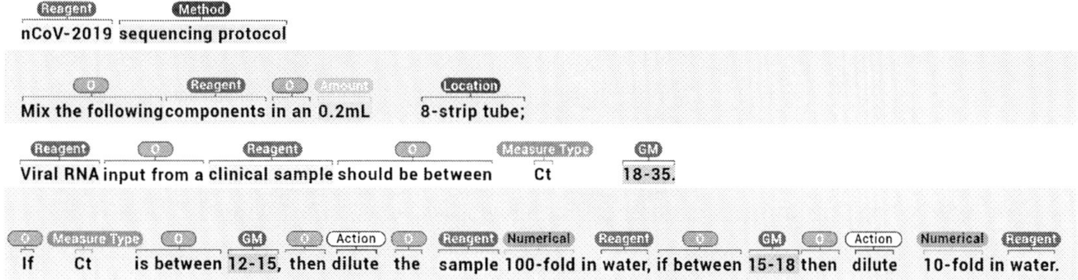

Figure 1: Visualisation of annotated dataset [2]

Task-1 W-NUT 2020: Named Entity Extraction, the annotation of 615 protocols are re-annotated using BART styled annotated protocols by 3 annotators with 0.75 inter-annotator agreement, measured by span-level Cohen's Kappa. The re-annotators incorporate missing entity-relations and also corrected the inconsistencies.

The task aims to create the system for Protocol-Named Entities Recognition (NER). The main difference that makes it difficult for traditional NER taggers is the vast vocabulary in medical filed and use of limited syntactic information. For instances "QIAprep Spin Miniprep" is device used in medical industry, but not present in our regular vocabulary that also makes it difficult for traditional NER tagger to learn.

Figure 1 provides the visualization of annotated datasets provided by WNUT 2020 Shared Task-1 .

3 Approach

In the section 3.1 we are going to define our proposed architecture and in section 3.2 briefly review the Bio-BERT (Lee et al., 2019) used for final submission and also different Domain specific BERT based model used for experiment as shown in the Table 1.

Baseline The organiser provided a simple Linear CRF model[3]. It utilized simple gazetteers and hand-crafted feature to predict the entities from the test data. We replaced it with our proposed BERT based Architecture as describe in the section below.

3.1 Architecture

As described in figure 2, we first sub-word tokenize each token of sentences, using BERT's word-piece tokenizer of Huggingface library and pass it through different domain specific BERT models or BERT Transformer stacks (scibert, biobert, bert-based, bert-large etc) to extract contextualised representation (Beltagy et al., 2019; Lee et al., 2019; Devlin et al., 2018). We then select the representation of first sub-word token for each word and use simple Linear or Dense layer with the softmax activation function as classifier to get probability on the labels from the contextualised representation.

3.2 Bio-BERT

Bio-BERT (Lee et al., 2019) is a contextualized language representation model, based on BERT, a pre-trained model that is trained on different combinations of general & biomedical domain corpora. According to Lee et al. (2019), just like its parental model BERT, it is also capable of capturing contextualized bidirectional representations. Thus it has outperformed existing architectures in most of the Named Entity Recognition tasks within the biomedical domain by using a limited amount of dataset. We hypothesize that such domain-specific bidirectional representations are also critical for our task. Bio-BERT are pre-trained on the following different datasets {*Wiki + Books, Wiki + Books + PubMed, Wiki + Books + PMC, Wiki + Books + PubMed + PMC*}.

we again hypothesize to achieved best performance in *PubMed*(comprises more than 30 million citations for biomedical literature from MEDLINE, life science journals, and online books.) trained dataset because of its linguistic similarity with protocols. For instance both of them contains medical procedure to reproduce medical experiment.

Other Models used in Experiment We also used other domain specific BERT for experimentation using the same architecture as discussed in section 3.1 with replacement of BERT Models in place of BioBERT (as shown in figure 2)

---

[2]Image Source: Github repository of WNUT 2020 Shared Task-1 NER.

[3]https://github.com/jeniyat/WNUT_2020_NER/tree/master/code/baseline_CRF

Models	F1-score	Recall	Precision
`biobert_v1.1_pubmed`	79.10	79.72	78.61
`biobert_v1.0_pubmed_pmc`	79.02	79.51	79.02
`scibert_uncased`	77.66	79.60	76.00
`bert-large-cased`	77.79	78.74	77.10
`bert-large-uncased`	75.50	77.39	73.79
`bert-base-cased`	78.05	79.29	76.87
`Baseline`	74.39	73.32	75.49

Table 1: Shows the results of test set provided by shared task organisers during experimental and details of the experimental setting is describe in section 4

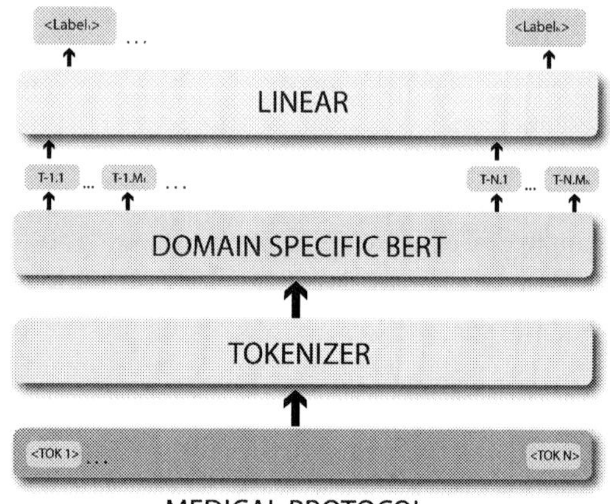

Figure 2: The TOK X represents the token of sentence where $X \in N$ and N is the length of sentence. T-I.J represents the Ith tokens and J^{th} subtokens and we used WordPiece tokenizer for all of our models.

- Sci-BERT (Beltagy et al., 2019) : A pretrained contextualized embedding model based on BERT to address the lack of high-quality, large-scale labeled scientific data.

- BERT$_{\{large/base,cased/uncased\}}$:BERT (Devlin et al., 2018) It is designed to train deep bidirectional representations by jointly conditioning on both left and right context in all layers. Language models have demonstrated that rich, unsupervised pre-training is an integral part of many language understanding systems. Hence, we try fine-tuning BERT to obtain better results on this task.

4 Comparison and Discussion

We experimented with different BERT models as shown in Table 1. We avoid any preprocessing other than the Bert specific tokenization, as it may result in loss of crucial semantic information in text.

We also assumed protocols are relatively less noisy compare to other crowd source data with compact sentences.

4.1 Experimental setting

We keep maximum length of input sentence to 512 to consider Long sentences in protocols. For all the base models (12-layer, 768-hidden, 12-heads, 110M parameters) including our Bio-BERT model, we train all for 8 epoch with batch size 16. Large models(24-layer, 1024-hidden, 16-heads, 340M parameters.) are trained for 4 epochs with batch size 16. We early stop the models using the valid set. The dropout probability was set to 0.1 for all layers. Optimization is done using Adam(Kingma and Ba, 2014) with a learning rate of 1e-5. The remaining hyperparameters were kept same as Devlin et al. (2018). We used the PyTorch (Paszke et al., 2019) implementation of BERT from Huggingfaces tranformers (Wolf et al., 2019) library.

For selecting best models in experimental phase (i.e. before release of test set) we use split of 60/20/20 for train, dev and test respectively. Our final submission, used a 70/30 split for train/valid set of initial data and Bio-BERT(Lee et al., 2019) model and split sentence with more than 512 tokens to two more sentence to get desired model's input sentence length. To evaluate the performance of the system, an evaluation script along with the dataset was provided by the organizers[4].

4.2 Results and Inferences

Our Bio-Bert(Lee et al., 2019) based model performed best of all the models because of domain specific knowledge. Our model performed extremely well on final test set as shown in Table 2 and stood *4th runner* up in term of F1 score and

---

[4]`https://github.com/jeniyat/WNUT_2020_`
`NER/tree/master/code/eval`

Models	F1-score	Recall	Precision
`biobert_v1.1_pubmed (partial match)`	79.54	77.43	81.76
`biobert_v1.0_pubmed_pmc (complete match)`	74.91	72.93	77

Table 2: Results on the held-out test set provided by shared task organisers on final submission

Tokens	correct labels	predicted labels
standard	B-Reagent	B-Reagent
T4	I-Reagent	B-Device
DNA	I-Reagent	I-Reagent
Ligase	I-Reagent	I-Reagent

Table 3: Error arises due to consideration of token level classification

Bio-Med Terms	subword-tokenized
acetyltransferase	['ace','ty','lt','ran','s', 'fer','ase']
Hematoxylin	['He','mat','ox','yl','in']
sulfanilamide	['su','lf','ani','lam','ide']
ddH2O	['d','d','H','2','O']
lBiotin-16-UTP	['l','B','iot','in','-','16', '-','U','TP']

Table 4: Illustration of inefficient sub-tokenization of Bio-Med words

1st runner up in term of recall out of 13 teams participated in the competition.

Inferences: Use of uncased large BERT results in significant loss of about 2.29 F1 score in comparison of cased-large BERT (Devlin et al., 2018), clearly shows importance of syntactic nature of protocols. We observed better performance, after increase in both training and validation set for our final submissions indicating inability of model to fully capture the representation due to fine tuning on limited data.

5   Error Analysis

1. BERT tokenizer is not efficient on Bio-Medical text as illustrated in Table 4 . Its vocabulary does not consists of Bio-medical words and it is not trained on domain specific setting. Hence makes it difficult for BERT model to learn the encoding based on poorly sub tokenized word. The possible solution will be training tokenizers on both biomedical and general text sets.

2. Treatment of task as token level classification problem results in incorrect detection of intermediate Entity as illustrated in Table 3. Hence evidenced in decrease of F1 score in complete match compare to partial match in our submission provided by organisers.

3. Use of Nomenclature, Scientific formula, abbreviations makes it difficult for Pre-trained language models to generalised with limited fine tuning data. Though with the help of contextual details it is observed that the BERT was able to correctly predict scientific formula

at some places. For instance, in the sentence {Add, 5gm, SDS}, *SDS* was correctly labelled as *Reagent* by our model.

6   Conclusion and Future Work

In this paper, we present our system for the Named Entity recognition for Bio-medical protocols a for Shared Task at W-NUT Task-1 2020. We built upon the recent success of Pre-trained language models and apply them for protocols. Our System achieves close to state-of-art performance on this task.

As future work, we will try to experiment with XLNet(Yang et al., 2019) and different ensembling between the models and would like to extend the work of Clark et al. (2019) by performing layer by layer Analysis of BERT.

Acknowledgments

We would like to thank the Computer Science and Engineering Department of Indian Institute of Technology, Kharagpur for providing us the computational resources required for performing various experiments.We are very grateful for the invaluable suggestions given by T.Y.S.S. santosh[5] and Aarushi Gupta. We also thank the organizers of the Shared Task-1 at WNUT, EMNLP-2020.

References

Iz Beltagy, Kyle Lo, and Arman Cohan. 2019. Scibert: Pretrained language model for scientific text. In *EMNLP*.

---

[5] `https://www.linkedin.com/in/ santosh-t-y-s-s-39227b116/`

Kevin Clark, Urvashi Khandelwal, Omer Levy, and Christopher D. Manning. 2019. What does bert look at? an analysis of bert's attention. In *BlackBoxNLP@ACL*.

Jacob Devlin, Ming-Wei Chang, Kenton Lee, and Kristina Toutanova. 2018. Bert: Pre-training of deep bidirectional transformers for language understanding. Cite arxiv:1810.04805Comment: 13 pages.

John M Giorgi and Gary D Bader. 2018. Transfer learning for biomedical named entity recognition with neural networks. *Bioinformatics*, 34(23):4087–4094.

Maryam Habibi, Leon Weber, Mariana Neves, David Luis Wiegandt, and Ulf Leser. 2017. Deep learning with word embeddings improves biomedical named entity recognition. *Bioinformatics*, 33(14):i37–i48.

Sepp Hochreiter and Jürgen Schmidhuber. 1997. Long short-term memory. *Neural Comput.*, 9(8):1735–1780.

Diederik Kingma and Jimmy Ba. 2014. Adam: A method for stochastic optimization. *International Conference on Learning Representations*.

Chaitanya Kulkarni, Wei Xu, Alan Ritter, and Raghu Machiraju. 2018. An annotated corpus for machine reading of instructions in wet lab protocols. In *Proceedings of the 2018 Conference of the North American Chapter of the Association for Computational Linguistics: Human Language Technologies (NAACL)*.

Jinhyuk Lee, Wonjin Yoon, Sungdong Kim, Donghyeon Kim, Sunkyu Kim, Chan Ho So, and Jaewoo Kang. 2019. BioBERT: a pretrained biomedical language representation model for biomedical text mining. *Bioinformatics*, 36(4):1234–1240.

D. Namikoshi, M. Ohta, A. Takasu, and J. Adachi. 2017. Crf-based bibliography extraction from reference strings using a small amount of training data. In *2017 Twelfth International Conference on Digital Information Management (ICDIM)*, pages 59–64.

Adam Paszke, Sam Gross, Francisco Massa, Adam Lerer, James Bradbury, Gregory Chanan, Trevor Killeen, Zeming Lin, Natalia Gimelshein, Luca Antiga, Alban Desmaison, Andreas Kopf, Edward Yang, Zachary DeVito, Martin Raison, Alykhan Tejani, Sasank Chilamkurthy, Benoit Steiner, Lu Fang, Junjie Bai, and Soumith Chintala. 2019. Pytorch: An imperative style, high-performance deep learning library. In *Advances in Neural Information Processing Systems 32*, pages 8024–8035. Curran Associates, Inc.

Jeniya Tabassum, Wei Xu, and Alan Ritter. 2020. WNUT-2020 Task 1: Extracting Entities and Relations from Wet Lab Protocols. In *Proceedings of EMNLP 2020 Workshop on Noisy User-generated Text (WNUT)*.

Xuan Wang, Yu Zhang, Xiang Ren, Yuhao Zhang, Marinka Zitnik, Jingbo Shang, Curtis Langlotz, and Jiawei Han. 2018. Cross-type biomedical named entity recognition with deep multi-task learning. *Bioinformatics*, 35(10):1745–1752.

Thomas Wolf, Lysandre Debut, Victor Sanh, Julien Chaumond, Clement Delangue, Anthony Moi, Pierric Cistac, Tim Rault, Rémi Louf, Morgan Funtowicz, Joe Davison, Sam Shleifer, Patrick von Platen, Clara Ma, Yacine Jernite, Julien Plu, Canwen Xu, Teven Le Scao, Sylvain Gugger, Mariama Drame, Quentin Lhoest, and Alexander M. Rush. 2019. Huggingface's transformers: State-of-the-art natural language processing. *ArXiv*, abs/1910.03771.

Zhilin Yang, Zihang Dai, Yiming Yang, Jaime Carbonell, Ruslan Salakhutdinov, and Quoc V. Le. 2019. Xlnet: Generalized autoregressive pretraining for language understanding.

Wonjin Yoon, Chan So, Jinhyuk Lee, and Jaewoo Kang. 2019. Collabonet: collaboration of deep neural networks for biomedical named entity recognition. *BMC Bioinformatics*, 20:249.

PublishInCovid19 at WNUT 2020 Shared Task-1: Entity Recognition in Wet Lab Protocols using Structured Learning Ensemble and Contextualised Embeddings

Janvijay Singh and Anshul Wadhawan
Flipkart Private Limited
`{janvijay.singh,anshul.wadhawan}@flipkart.com`

Abstract

In this paper, we describe the approach that we employed to address the task of Entity Recognition over Wet Lab Protocols - a shared task in EMNLP WNUT-2020 Workshop. Our approach is composed of two phases. In the first phase, we experiment with various contextualised word embeddings (like Flair, BERT-based) and a BiLSTM-CRF model to arrive at the best-performing architecture. In the second phase, we create an ensemble composed of eleven BiLSTM-CRF models. The individual models are trained on random train-validation splits of the complete dataset. Here, we also experiment with different output merging schemes, including Majority Voting and Structured Learning Ensembling (SLE). Our final submission achieved a micro F1-score of 0.8175 and 0.7757 for the partial and exact match of the entity spans, respectively. We were ranked first and second, in terms of partial and exact match, respectively.

1 Introduction

Entity Recognition (aka entity extraction or chunking) involves detection (begin and end boundaries) and classification of entities mentioned in unstructured text into pre-defined categories. It is one of the foundational sub-task of several Information Extraction (Hanafiah and Quix, 2014) (IE) and Natural Language Processing (NLP) pipelines. Hence, errors introduced during the extraction of entities can propagate further and degrade the performance of the complete IE or NLP pipeline. In the domains of experimental biology, the growing complexity of experiments has resulted in a need to automate wet laboratory procedures. Such an automation will be useful in avoiding human errors introduced in the wet lab protocols and thereby will enhance the reproducibility of experimental biological research.

To achieve this reproducibility, some of the previous research works have focussed on defining machine-readable formats for writing wet lab protocols (King et al., 2009; Ananthanarayanan and Thies, 2010; Vasilev et al., 2011). However, the vast majority of today's protocols are written in natural language with jargon and colloquial language constructs that emerge as a byproduct of ad-hoc protocol documentation. This motivates the need for machine reading systems that can interpret the meaning of these natural language instructions, to enhance reproducibility via semantic protocols (e.g. the Aquarium project) and enable robotic automation (Bates et al., 2017) by mapping natural language instructions to executable actions. In order to enable research on interpreting natural language instructions, with practical applications in biology and life sciences, an annotated database (Kulkarni et al., 2018) of wet lab protocols was introduced.

The first step in interpreting natural language lab protocols is to extract entities, followed by identification of relations between them. To address the research focussing on entity recognition over Wet Lab Protocols a shared task (Tabassum et al., 2020) was introduced at EMNLP WNUT-2020 Workshop. The task was based on the annotated database (Kulkarni et al., 2018) of wet lab protocols. We tackle this task in two phases. In the first phase, we experiment with various contextualised word embeddings (like Flair, BERT-based) and a BiLSTM-CRF model to arrive at the best-performing architecture. In the second phase, we create an ensemble composed of eleven BiLSTM-CRF models. The individual models are trained on random train-validation splits of the complete dataset. Here, we also experiment with different output merging schemes, including Majority Voting and SLE.

The rest of the paper is structured as follows: Section 2 states the task definition. Section 3 describes the specifics of our methodology. Section 4 explains the experimental setup and the results,

273

Proceedings of the 2020 EMNLP Workshop W-NUT: The Sixth Workshop on Noisy User-generated Text, pages 273–280
Online, Nov 19, 2020. ©2020 Association for Computational Linguistics

and Section 5 concludes the paper.

2   Task Definition

The steps involved in any lab procedure are specified by lab protocols. These protocols have several characteristics like noise, density and domain specificity. Any process that can automatically or semi-automatically convert protocols into a format that machine recognizes advantages biological research. In this task, system entries for entity recognition on a dataset of lab protocols are invited. Since the protocols are written manually by lab technicians and researchers, they are subject to spelling errors and non standard language.

The data provided in the task is made available in two formats:

2.1   CoNLL format

In this format, each line represents the named entity in the following manner:

$$< word >+ "\backslash t"+ <NE >$$

An empty line denotes the end of a sentence.

2.2   Standoff format

The standoff format contains each protocol represented by two separate files. One file, with .txt extension, contains protocols in text format, while the other file, with .ann extension, contains protocol annotations. The two files are linked by using a simple file naming convention wherein their base name is the same, i.e. the file name without the extension is the same. For example, the annotation file named as protocol_17.ann contains annotations for the file protocol_17.txt.

Within each annotation file, individual annotations connect to different parts of text through character offsets. For example, in the document starting as "Put 3.68 g of NaCl", the text "Put" is denoted by the offset range 0..3. It is evident from the above example that all offsets are 0 indexed and include the character at the start offset and exclude the character at the end offset. All text files have the file extension .txt and contain the text of original documents provided as inputs to the system. The encoding used in the protocol text files which are stored as plain text files is UTF-8 (an extension of ASCII). Each line in the protocol text file denotes a single step in the protocol. Hence, all steps in the entire protocol are separated by newline characters. The first line in every file indicates the protocol's name/title.

3   Methodology

This section talks about the core methodology we adopted to tackle the given problem. The process pipeline involves providing contextualised word embeddings as input to the BiLSTM-CRF model, followed by a Structured learning Ensemble approach. Each of the these modules have been described in detail in the below subsections.

3.1   Embeddings

We experiment with two types of contextualised word embeddings, BERT and Flair based, which we discuss in detail in the below subsections.

3.1.1   BERT

Neural models based on transformers (Vaswani et al., 2017) have excelled in most NLP tasks. The primary components in their architecture being the self attention blocks and feed forward layers, these models have been proven successful in providing a significant boost to state-of-the-art results. The major difference between transformers and RNN based models (Li et al., 2018) is that transformers do not rely on recurrence mechanisms to establish relations and dependencies in the input sequence, by making use of self attention at each input time step instead. Attention can be interpreted as a technique to map a query and a set of key-value pairs to an output, where the query, keys, values and output are all vectors. As far as self attention is concerned, a separate feed forward layer is used to formulate the query, key and value vectors for each vector in the input sequence. For every input vector, the score for attention is calculated using a compatibility function which takes as input the input keys and query vector. These attention scores are used to denote the weights of a weighted sum of value vectors, which is the output of self attention technique. Another technique widely used is the multi headed attention technique in which several modules of these self attention blocks work over the input sequence. The encoder module in the transformer's architecture contains 6 identical layers each having two sublayers - position wise densely connected feed forward network and multi headed self attention layers. These sublayers are wrapped around with residual connections. Layer normalisation follows the above module. BERT pre-trains bidirectional representations by jointly utilizing both right and left contexts across all layers with the help of a multi layer encoder module.

These pre-trained BERT representations are then fine tuned as per the required task by appending a separate output layer depending on the task to be performed.

For every token, the summation of the corresponding token, segment and position embeddings is carried out to produce BERT's input representation. The training process for BERT involves Masked Language Modelling (Nozza et al., 2020) and Next Sentence Prediction (Shi and Demberg, 2019), both of which are unsupervised prediction tasks. BERT representation for each token in the input text is then fed to the appended densely connected layers to produce the output labels for the token as part of the fine tuning process. The predictions produced are independent of the surrounding predictions produced.

We experimented with different variations of BERT models (Devlin et al., 2018) for generating word embeddings. All the listed model types have 12 layers, 12 attention heads and 110M parameters.

BERT-base-cased : This model is trained on cased English text of general domain like Wikipedia text and BooksCorpus.

BioBERT (Lee et al., 2019) : BioBERT is a language representation model pre-trained on the domain of biomedical data. The pre-training process for BioBERT involves initializing weights with those of BERT which is pre-trained on general domain corpora, followed by pre-training BioBERT with biomedical data corpora like PMC full-text articles and PubMed abstracts.

PubMedBERT (Gu et al., 2020) : The base architecture of PubMedBERT is the same as an uncased BERT base model. The model is pre-trained on full PubMed Central articles and PubMed abstracts. The pre-training process for this model involves direct pre-training on biomedical text from scratch. Thus, the weights are not initialized with those of BERT as was in the case of BioBERT. The pre-training corpus contains 14 million PubMed abstracts with 3 billion words, 21 GB of textual data in total. Another version of the same model is pre-trained on additional data of full text PubMed Central articles, with the total textual data containing 16.8 billion words and 107 GB in size.

3.1.2 Flair

[1] Flair embeddings are pre-trained Contextualised Word Embeddings (CWE) provided in the Flair NLP framework. In contrast to classical work embeddings like GloVe, the Flair CWE concatenate two context vectors based on the left and right sentence context of the word to it. These context vectors are computed using two recurrent neural models. One of the character language model is trained from left to right while the other is trained from right to left. Flair CWEs have been applied successfully to sequence tagging tasks such as Named Entity Recognition and Part of Speech Tagging. Since this shared task is closely related to Bio-medical domain, we have used "pubmed" variant of Flair CWEs in all our experiments.

3.2 BiLSTM-CRF Model

The ability of Recurrent Neural Networks (RNNs) (Yadav and Bethard, 2018) to execute the same function at each time step, allowing parameters to be shared across the input sequence, make them highly suitable for sequential input data . Useful information from each time step is forwarded to further time steps in the form of a hidden vector, which is utilized to make a prediction at each of the future steps. However, RNNs face the issue of vanishing gradients in case of large input sequences. To solve this issue of vanishing gradients, (Long Short Term Memory) LSTM (Hochreiter and Schmidhuber, 1997) was introduced. The presence of gating mechanisms in LSTMs makes sure that long range dependencies are captured appropriately. While LSTMs utilize only past time steps to make a prediction, Bidirectional LSTM (BiLSTM) (Schuster and Paliwal, 1997) utilizes information from past as well as future time steps. In our case, the output embeddings are fed to the BiLSTM layer, which outputs a vector for each word in the input sequence. Since the task under consideration has labels which have dependencies among themselves, such as an intermediate_label following a start_label, we need to consider these dependencies in our modelling approach. For this, a linear chain (Conditional Random Fields) CRF layer (Sutton and McCallum, 2010) is appended to the BiLSTM layer. Due to utilization of transition matrices for output labels, a linear chain CRF is able to learn inter label dependencies, if any, among the output labels.

3.3 Ensemble Process

We created eleven randomly shuffled splits of training and validation data, and fine tuned our final model on these eleven splits to produce eleven sets

---

[1] https://github.com/flairNLP/flair

of predictions. We then merged these predictions following two merging techniques, Majority Voting and Structured Learning Ensemble (SLE), thus comparing the performance of the two merging functions. In our experiments, we provide a fair comparison of the above two combination techniques, i.e. Majority Voting technique and SLE.

Given N number of ensembles and x as the input example, $\{y_1 , y_2 , ..., y_N\}$ being the predictions from N different models are merged to produce the final prediction y. The ensemble methods for structured output classification and multiclass classification differ in the way they merge the predicted results of the base models.

The merging techniques have been described below:

3.3.1 Majority voting

For every entity predicted, we choose the mode i.e. the most frequently occurring entity among the eleven predictions (Adejo and Connolly, 2017). Thus, the entity which has the maximum number of votes wins.

Mathematically, the above process of majority voting scheme to produce the final predictions can be denoted in the below manner :

$$\mathbf{y} = \langle majority\,\{(\mathbf{y}_1)_1 , (\mathbf{y}_2)_1 , \ldots , (\mathbf{y}_N)_1\}\rangle$$
$$\ldots\ldots\ldots\ majority\,\{(\mathbf{y}_1)_L , (\mathbf{y}_2)_L , \ldots , (\mathbf{y}_N)_L\}\rangle$$

where L is the length of all predictions.

3.3.2 Structured Learning Ensemble (SLE)

Due to the presence of correlations and intrinsic structures in the output labels, we speculated that the majority voting scheme would not suffice for our problem. (Nguyen and Guo, 2007) proposed a technique to combine the predictions considering the correlations of the output labels. Named as weighted transition combination, the algorithm involves construction of (L-1) transition matrices of size ($|\Sigma|$ x $|\Sigma|$) , where Σ is the set of all possible labels. Apart from this, it also involves construction of a transition matrix T^k which provides the number of transitions at the kth position as follows:

$$T^k\,(t_i, t_j) = count_k\,(t_i, t_j)\,,\forall 1 \leq k \leq (L-1)$$

where $count_k(t_i, t_j)$ denotes the number of times the label t_j occurs after t_i at the kth position in the set of predicted sequences $\{y_1 , y_2 , ..., y_N\}$. Also, a stateweight vector is constructed that denotes the

number of times label t_j occurs at position k in the predicted sequences.

$$U^k\,(t_i) = count_k\,(t_i)\,,\forall 1 \leq k \leq L$$

The predicted sequence of SLE is given by:

$$\mathbf{y} = argmax_\mathbf{y} \prod_{k=1}^{L-1} T^k\,(y_k, y_{k+1}) \prod_{k=1}^{L} U^k\,(y_k)$$

The computation involved in the argmax calculation of the above equation is similar to Viterbi dynamic programming approach.

4 Experiments

Our experimentation strategy is distributed in two phases. In the first phase, we experiment with various architectures and their specifications by varying the type of pre-trained model, deciding layers to freeze i.e. complete fine-tuning or contextual word embeddings, varying type and size of final layer in order to arrive at the best performing model. We trained each of our model architectures on the train split and identified the checkpoint which worked best using the validation split. We reported the final numbers on the test split. For each model, we train three different models with random seed values and then report averaged f1 scores to ensure that improvements are not the result of randomisation. A configuration of concatenated contextual word embeddings from PubmedBERT and Flair, followed by 2 BiLSTM layers with 512 dimensional hidden size and a CRF layer in the end worked best. In the second phase, we train individual models on random splits of train + validation sets. In order to merge the outputs of individual models, we experiment with two output merging schemes namely Majority Voting and Structured Learning Ensemble (SLE). Finally, we report the results on the test dataset.

In the following sub-sections, we describe the dataset, system settings, evaluation metrics, results and a brief error analysis for our final submitted system.

4.1 Dataset

Wet Lab Protocol (WLP) dataset consists of 615 unique protocols from 623 protocols released by (Kulkarni et al., 2018). It excludes the following 8 duplicate protocols:

protocol 45 (duplicate of protocol 441)
protocol 459 (duplicate of protocol 310)

	train_data	dev_data	test_data	test_data_2020
Measure-Type	857	329	272	731
Numerical	838	262	231	520
Size	262	124	114	238
Seal	210	92	64	119
Speed	626	241	167	240
Location	3929	1407	1327	1670
Temperature	1594	492	532	760
Amount	3438	1102	1193	1238
Method	1605	545	582	1077
pH	67	37	62	66
Generic-Measure	487	136	143	176
O	53690	18454	17925	26012
Action	12368	4057	4140	5439
Mention	257	84	56	145
Concentration	1333	427	537	705
Reagent	11142	3646	4004	5079
Time	2399	751	870	959
Modifier	4593	1554	1601	3476
Device	1752	618	468	911

Table 1: Frequency of various entity-types in different dataset splits.

	#protocols	#sentences
train_data	370	8444
dev_data	122	2839
test_data	123	2862
test_data_2020	111	3562

Table 2: Statistics of different dataset splits.

	Vocabulary	OOV (wrt ref)
train_data	7397	-
dev_data	4082	1148
test_data	3946	982
test_data_2020	5718	2461

Table 3: Out-of-Vocabulary statistics.

protocol 464 (duplicate of protocol 46)
protocol 480 (duplicate of protocol 473)
protocol 482 (duplicate of protocol 474)
protocol 483 (duplicate of protocol 475)
protocol 484 (duplicate of protocol 476)
protocol 621 (duplicate of protocol 570)

After discarding the duplicate protocols, the remaining 615 unique protocols are re-annotated in brat by 3 annotators with 0.75 inter-annotator agreement, measured by span-level Krippendorff's α. The annotators not only added the missing entity-relations but also rectified the inconsistencies.

The detailed class-wise statistics pertaining to each of the dataset splits provided in the task are shown in Table 1. Corresponding number of protocols and sentences are provided in Table 2. Here, train_data denotes the training dataset, dev_data denotes the validation dataset, test_data denotes the test dataset and test_data_2020 denotes the surprise test dataset. The surprise dataset was not revealed before the evaluation window.

Table 3 presents the total number of words, words absent in reference and words present in reference for each dataset. Reference varies according to the dataset being considered. For validation dataset and test dataset, training dataset is the reference. For surprise dataset, all data i.e. the union of training dataset, validation dataset and test dataset is considered as the reference. There is no reference in case of training dataset.

4.2 System Settings

While training individual models of our final ensemble, we rely on concatenated word representations from PubMedBERT and Flair. We train the BiLSTM-CRF based model with 3 BiLSTM layer each of hidden size 512 using a patience-based strategy. With this strategy, after every epoch of

Hyperparameter	Value
Embedding	Flair + PubMedBERT
Final layer type	BiLSTM
Final layer hidden size	512
# Final layers	2
CRF	✓
Patience epochs	3
max epochs	30
Initial learning rate	0.1
Mini batch size	32
Merging scheme	SLE

Table 4: System Settings for the final model.

training, we compute the F1-score on validation split and if the metric doesn't improve continuously for "patience" number of epochs, we reduce the learning rate by half. We ultimately stop the training when either the learning rate diminishes to 0.0001 or the epoch number reaches a maximum limit. We have utilised hugging-face[2] BERT APIs and Flair Framework(Akbik et al., 2019) to train our model. We ran our experiments on a single NVIDIA V100 GPU. It took around 2.5 hours to train each individual model of our final submitted ensemble. Table 4 summarises the hyperparameters which we employed to train our models.

4.3 Evaluation Metrics

Assuming that P and T represent the set of predicted and ground-truth entities for a particular word in the protocol text. Then, precision, recall and F1-score for the entity prediction of the considered word is defined as follows:

$$Precision = \frac{|P \cap T|}{|P|}$$

$$Recall = \frac{|P \cap T|}{|T|}$$

$$F1 = \frac{2 * Precision * Recall}{Precision + Recall}$$

There were two criteria for evaluation metrics in the task, partial match and exact match. In case of partial match, P intersection T will include all entities whose types match and boundaries match partially, i.e. there is some overlap in the boundaries. However, in case of exact match, for an entity to be included in the intersection set, it must have the same type as well as exact same boundaries.

---

[2]https://huggingface.co/transformers/

4.4 Results and Error Analysis

Our approach involved working in two phases, first in which we experiment with different model architectures and the second in which we experiment with two output merging schemes. The results of our experiments in Phases 1 and 2 are summarised in Table 5 and 6 respectively. In Table 5, we present the micro-F1 and macro-F1 scores for different model architectures we experiment with by varying the base model, fine tuning implementation, type and specifications of final layer and CRF layer addition. Table 6 presents the micro-F1 scores on the test set when we experiment with the number of ensembles, i.e. on merging different number of prediction sets.

For our final submission to WNUT Shared Task-1, we employed an ensemble of eleven individual models. Each of these models was trained on a random train-validation split of original train + validation + test dataset. Our ensemble achieved a micro-F1 score of 0.8175 and 0.7757 for the partial and exact match of entity boundaries, respectively. We achieved highest micro-recall score among all the participating teams. In Table 7, we report the top-10 confusions which our model makes while assigning entity type to different words. Results of the final submission on surprise test set are summarised in Table 8. Upon close inspection of predicted outputs on test split, we identified the following error patterns in the model predictions:

- From Table 7, we can see that model dominantly gets confused while identifying the begin and intermediate tags for class Reagent. Upon inspection of the predictions, we identified that such errors were more common when the Reagent class in validation/test set was unseen in training examples. We can come up with a dictionary based approach to improve the precision of tags specifically for the Reagent class.

- Modifier entity type modifies the semantics of some other entity type, so for a word to be Modifier or not is highly dependent on context and modified entity. But since our model fails to over-rely on context for recognition of certain entities, Modifier entity-type often gets confused with Other type.

- For the entities corresponding to numerical values like Concentration, Amount, Size and

Base Model	Finetuning	Final Layer			CRF	micro-F1	macro-F1
		Type	#layers	#dim			
Bert-base-cased	✓	Dense	1	-	✗	78.78	71.06
Bert-base-cased	✗	BiLSTM	1	128	✓	80.56	73.41
BioBERT	✗	BiLSTM	1	128	✓	81.01	73.81
PubmedBERT	✗	BiLSTM	1	128	✓	81.36	73.67
Flair	✗	BiLSTM	1	128	✓	81.63	74.84
PubmedBERT + Flair	✗	BiLSTM	1	128	✓	81.71	75.22
PubmedBERT + Flair	✗	BiLSTM	2	374	✓	82.06	75.18
PubmedBERT + Flair	✗	BiLSTM	2	512	✓	82.28	75.57

Table 5: Results of experiments to identity the best architecture specification.

#ensembles	MajV	SLE
3	82.32	82.50
5	82.52	82.68
7	82.52	82.58
9	82.55	82.64
11	82.60	82.74

Table 6: micro-F1 on test-set after ensembling.

P_Label	T_Label	Count
O	B-Modifier	324
B-Modifier	O	287
O	I-Modifier	247
B-Reagent	I-Reagent	180
I-Reagent	B-Reagent	112
B-Modifier	B-Reagent	122
O	B-Action	137
O	I-Reagent	115
O	I-Method	112
B-Action	O	190

Table 7: Top-10 errors occurring in model predictions.

	Exact Match	Partial Match
Precision	81.36	85.74
Recall	74.12	78.11
Micro-F1	77.57	81.75

Table 8: Final results on surprise-test dataset.

Numerical, model often gets confused among such entities. The main reason which we suspect is that to classify these entities, the model should over-rely on context and not on the token corresponding to the entity itself. Since tokens can be shared across different classes. e.g. 1.5 ml microcentrifuge tube; Preds: B-Amount I-Amount B-Location I-Location; True Label: B-Size I-Size B-Location I-Location;

5 Conclusion and Future Work

Through this paper, we showcased our approach to tackle the Shared Task 1 in EMNLP WNUT-2020 Workshop which involved Entity Recognition over Wet Lab Protocols. We solved the task in two phases. The first phase involved experimenting with different contextualised word embeddings like BERT and Flair, and a BiLSTM-CRF model to find the best performing model configuration for the problem at hand. In the second phase, we create an ensemble consisting of eleven BiLSTM-CRF models. We train individual models on randomly shuffled train-validation splits of the complete dataset. Also, we experiment with different merging techniques like Majority Voting and Structured Learning Ensemble (SLE). Our end solution achieved a micro F1-score of 0.8175 and 0.7757 in the partial and exact match categories, respectively. We were ranked first and second in partial and exact match categories respectively. In the future, we wish to explore the idea of employing rule-based approach to overcome the shortcomings of current solution.

References

Olugbenga Adejo and Thomas Connolly. 2017. Predicting student academic performance using multi-model heterogeneous ensemble approach. *Journal of Applied Research in Higher Education*, 10:00–00.

Alan Akbik, Tanja Bergmann, Duncan Blythe, Kashif Rasul, Stefan Schweter, and Roland Vollgraf. 2019. FLAIR: An easy-to-use framework for state-of-the-art NLP. In *Proceedings of the 2019 Conference of the North American Chapter of the Association for Computational Linguistics (Demonstrations)*, pages 54–59, Minneapolis, Minnesota. Association for Computational Linguistics.

Vaishnavi Ananthanarayanan and William Thies. 2010. Biocoder: A programming language for standardizing and automating biology protocols. *Journal of biological engineering*, 4(1):1–13.

Maxwell Bates, Aaron J Berliner, Joe Lachoff, Paul R Jaschke, and Eli S Groban. 2017. Wet lab accelerator: a web-based application democratizing laboratory automation for synthetic biology. *ACS synthetic biology*, 6(1):167–171.

Jacob Devlin, Ming-Wei Chang, Kenton Lee, and Kristina Toutanova. 2018. Bert: Pre-training of deep bidirectional transformers for language understanding.

Yu Gu, Robert Tinn, Hao Cheng, Michael Lucas, Naoto Usuyama, Xiaodong Liu, Tristan Naumann, Jianfeng Gao, and Hoifung Poon. 2020. Domain-specific language model pretraining for biomedical natural language processing.

Novita Hanafiah and Christoph Quix. 2014. Entity recognition in information extraction. In *Intelligent Information and Database Systems*, pages 113–122, Cham. Springer International Publishing.

S. Hochreiter and J. Schmidhuber. 1997. Long short-term memory. *Neural Computation*, 9:1735–1780.

Ross D King, Jem Rowland, Stephen G Oliver, Michael Young, Wayne Aubrey, Emma Byrne, Maria Liakata, Magdalena Markham, Pinar Pir, Larisa N Soldatova, et al. 2009. The automation of science. *Science*, 324(5923):85–89.

Chaitanya Kulkarni, Wei Xu, Alan Ritter, and Raghu Machiraju. 2018. An annotated corpus for machine reading of instructions in wet lab protocols. In *Proceedings of the 2018 Conference of the North American Chapter of the Association for Computational Linguistics: Human Language Technologies (NAACL)*.

Jinhyuk Lee, Wonjin Yoon, Sungdong Kim, Donghyeon Kim, Sunkyu Kim, Chan Ho So, and Jaewoo Kang. 2019. Biobert: a pre-trained biomedical language representation model for biomedical text mining. *Bioinformatics*.

Jing Li, Aixin Sun, Jianglei Han, and Chenliang Li. 2018. A survey on deep learning for named entity recognition.

Nam Nguyen and Yunsong Guo. 2007. Comparisons of sequence labeling algorithms and extensions. In *Proceedings of the 24th International Conference on Machine Learning*, ICML '07, page 681–688, New York, NY, USA. Association for Computing Machinery.

Debora Nozza, Federico Bianchi, and Dirk Hovy. 2020. What the [mask]? making sense of language-specific bert models.

M. Schuster and K.K. Paliwal. 1997. Bidirectional recurrent neural networks. *Trans. Sig. Proc.*, 45(11):2673–2681.

Wei Shi and Vera Demberg. 2019. Next sentence prediction helps implicit discourse relation classification within and across domains. In *Proceedings of the 2019 Conference on Empirical Methods in Natural Language Processing and the 9th International Joint Conference on Natural Language Processing (EMNLP-IJCNLP)*, pages 5790–5796, Hong Kong, China. Association for Computational Linguistics.

Charles Sutton and Andrew McCallum. 2010. An introduction to conditional random fields.

Jeniya Tabassum, Wei Xu, and Alan Ritter. 2020. WNUT-2020 Task 1: Extracting Entities and Relations from Wet Lab Protocols. In *Proceedings of EMNLP 2020 Workshop on Noisy User-generated Text (WNUT)*.

Viktor Vasilev, Chenkai Liu, Traci Haddock, Swapnil Bhatia, Aaron Adler, Fusun Yaman, Jacob Beal, Jonathan Babb, Ron Weiss, and Douglas Densmore. 2011. A software stack for specification and robotic execution of protocols for synthetic biological engineering.

Ashish Vaswani, Noam Shazeer, Niki Parmar, Jakob Uszkoreit, Llion Jones, Aidan N. Gomez, Lukasz Kaiser, and Illia Polosukhin. 2017. Attention is all you need.

Vikas Yadav and Steven Bethard. 2018. A survey on recent advances in named entity recognition from deep learning models. In *Proceedings of the 27th International Conference on Computational Linguistics*, pages 2145–2158, Santa Fe, New Mexico, USA. Association for Computational Linguistics.

Big Green at WNUT 2020 Shared Task-1: Relation Extraction as Contextualized Sequence Classification

Chris Miller
Department of Computer Science
Dartmouth College, Hanover, NH
chris.20@dartmouth.edu

Soroush Vosoughi
Department of Computer Science
Dartmouth College, Hanover, NH
soroush.vosoughi@dartmouth.edu

Abstract

Relation and event extraction is an important task in natural language processing. We introduce a system which uses contextualized knowledge graph completion to classify relations and events between known entities in a noisy text environment. We report results which show that our system is able to effectively extract relations and events from a dataset of wet lab protocols.

1 Introduction

Wet lab protocols specify the steps and ingredients required to synthesize chemical and biological products. The majority of wet lab protocols are formatted as natural language, designed for human lab workers to interpret and carry out. Protocols are formatted differently depending on lab norms and the author writing them, and may include spelling mistakes, nonstandard abbreviations, colloquial phrasing, and assumptions that may not be obvious to readers from outside of the author's lab or field.

Automated extraction of events, relations, and entities from this noisy language data enables standardized tracking of lab protocols, and is an important step forward for the automated reproduction of scientific results. We examine the problem of automatically identifying and classifying events and relations between entities as part of Shared Task 1 at WNUT 2020 (Tabassum et al., 2020). This shared task works with the Wet Lab Protocol Corpus (WLPC) introduced by Kulkarni et al. (2018). The WLPC dataset consists of wet lab protocols drawn from an open-source database and annotated by a group of human annotators which included subject matter experts.

2 Prior Work

Past approaches to relation and event extraction from wet lab data have included systems based on propagating information across graphs. Jiang et al. (2019) introduce an end-to-end system, called SpanRel, for identifying and labeling text spans and the relations between them using any text embedding model. The DyGIE and DyGIE++ systems, meanwhile, learn to propagate useful information across graphs of coreferences, relations, and events, allowing long-distance contextual information to support relation and event extraction tasks based on sliding window BERT embeddings of the text (Luan et al., 2019; Wadden et al., 2019).

3 Knowledge Graphs

Knowledge graphs are graph representations of the relations between entities (Schneider, 1973). In a typical knowledge graph construction, graph nodes represent entities, while edges of different types represent relations between entities. As an example, a knowledge graph may contain nodes for "United Kingdom" and "United Nations" with an edge of type "Member-Of" between "United Kingdom" and "United Nations."

Because knowledge graphs are generated from imperfect information, they represent a subset of information about their component nodes and thus suffer from incompleteness. Incompleteness means that edges representing relations which exist between nodes in reality are not present in the graph (for example, if the knowledge graph contains the "United Kingdom" and "United Nations" nodes but does not contain the "Member-Of" relation between them). This property of knowledge graphs has given rise to efforts to identify missing relations between entities, a task referred to as knowledge graph completion (Lin et al., 2017).

There are obvious parallels between knowledge graph completion and relation extraction from text given prelabeled entities; namely that both tasks require identifying a relation (if one exists) between

Proceedings of the 2020 EMNLP Workshop W-NUT: The Sixth Workshop on Noisy User-generated Text, pages 281–285
Online, Nov 19, 2020. ©2020 Association for Computational Linguistics

a given pair of entities. We therefore develop a model which represents the task of extracting relations from wet lab protocols as a knowledge graph completion problem.

4 Methodology

4.1 Representing relation extraction as sequence classification

Relation classification requires the input of two target entities to predict a relation between them. Therefore, to formulate relation extraction as relation classification, we must identify target entity pairs. A basic approach might be to simply sample each possible pair of entities in both possible orders (bidirectional sampling is required because relations are order-dependent).

This sampling strategy, however, ignores structural information about the data. Protocols are separated into lines with one line for each step, and relations and events typically occur between entities which are close together.

This naïve approach also introduces computational problems. The number of possible entity pairs for n entities is $n^2 - n$, which produces a high number of entity pairs as the number of entities grows. We find that real relations represent just 0.37% of the possible relations in the WLPC training data, indicating that a system which enumerates all possible entity pairs would have to be exceptionally accurate to be effective.

The structural features of the data enable us to reduce the scope of our evaluation by focusing only on entities which are close to each other. We initially evaluated based on only considering entity pairs in the same step. By analyzing the training data, we find that 99% of true relations are between entities which contain less than 14 tokens between them. We thus restrict our analysis to entity pairs which are less than 14 tokens apart. Using this method (based on training data statistics) we are able to maintain 99% of true relations while reducing the total number of relations evaluated by 41% over a sentence based approach and improving our precision substantially.

4.2 Contextualization

One distinction between knowledge graph completion and relation extraction is important to consider. In a knowledge graph, nodes are unique and any given relation between two nodes always exists. In relation extraction from text, nodes are not unique. Consider the following protocol instruction:

"Separate 5mL of the solution and add 5mL water to replace the removed volume."

In this protocol, the "5mL" entity of type measurement which refers to the solution is distinct from the "5mL" entity of type measurement which refers to the water. The action "Separate" acts on the former, but not on the latter, while the action "combine" acts on the latter, but not on the former. We handle this discrepancy by adding a local context sequence, identifying the targeted entities in-text.

We generate this context sequence by taking the tokens corresponding to the n sentences surrounding the target entity tokens as contextual information. We find empirically that $n = 1$ provides the best performance, and that higher values of n tend to cause overfitting.

To resolve the issue of ambiguous entity reference in a sequence where multiple entities share the same text (as above), we identify entities in-context. To do this, we add entity label tokens ([EntA] and [EntB]) surrounding the referenced entities in the context, tagging them for easy identification.

4.3 Relation Classification

Once we have extracted a set of viable entity pair candidates, given two labeled candidate entities E_a and E_b, and surrounding context C we attempt to achieve two tasks: identifying whether or not a relationship is present between the two entities, and if there is, to classify the relationship between the entities using a knowledge graph completion approach.

Prior work has introduced the idea of using language models to formulate relation prediction between entities in a knowledge graph as a sequence classification task (Yao et al., 2019). Pre-trained language models such as ELMo and BERT have seen widespread success when fine-tuned for use in sequence classification tasks (Devlin et al., 2019; Vaswani et al., 2017; Peters et al., 2018).

We finetune a BERT model provided by the HuggingFace library to perform relation prediction based on multi-sequence classification (Wolf et al., 2019). We finetune for 15 epochs, using an initial learning rate of 5×10^{-5} and an input size of 100 tokens. Hyperparameters were determined via grid search over the development set.

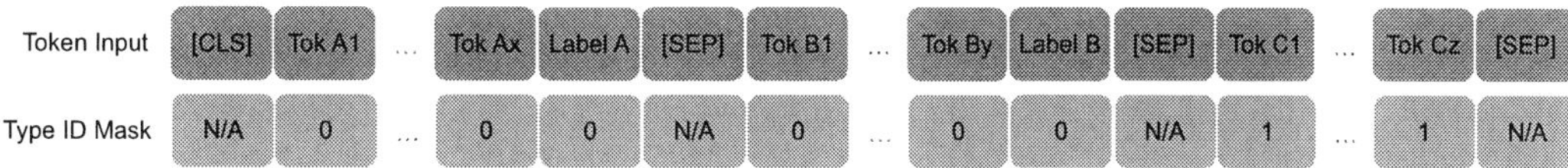

Figure 1: Input tokens and type ID masks for BERT pretraining.

4.4 Sequence Parameters

We formulate our input sequence as shown in Figure 1. Token Input indicates the actual tokens which are passed into the model. For this field, [CLS] represents the start of the sequence, Tok An represents the nth token of entity A, and Tok Bn and Tok Cn represent the equivalent tokens for entity B and the context sequence, Label A and Label B are the labels for entities A and B, and [SEP] indicates separators between different sequence sources.

Type ID Mask represents the token type IDs passed to the BERT model. These binary type IDs indicate different sequence sources for multi-sequence problems such as this one. For example, when performing a classification task with two sequences, tokens from the first sequence would have a type ID of 0, and tokens from the second sequence would have a type ID of 1. The type IDs improve learning stability for BERT, ensuring that the model is able to distinguish between different sources of data.

Typically, three-sequence classification tasks in BERT are handled by masking in a 0-1-0 style (ie, the type ID mask for sequence 1 is 0, the type ID mask for sequence 2 is 1, and the type ID mask for sequence 3 is 0 again). We find that the distinct information types of entity information and contextual information mean that labeling a sequence of Entity-Entity-Context sequences as 0-1-0 is ineffective, as BERT is not able to effectively learn the difference between context and entity information. We instead use the type-mask format 0-0-1, labeling labeled entity tokens 0 and context tokens 1. This method improves training stability and increases model performance substantially. We suggest that differences in sequence information type is the most important metric for determining type ID mask.

5 Results & Discussion

Our results, shown in Table 1, show that our system is able to effectively identify many types of relations even given this noisy data format. More specifically, this approach is able to identify relations and events with extremely high recall (as high as .95 for Measure and Measure-Type-Link relations).

Our approach is relatively weak in precision. This is likely due to our formulation of the task as an evaluation of potential entity pairs. We find that our system classifies relations with an accuracy of 93% on the development set, but because there are many more possible pairings between entities in a given protocol than there are actual pairings, even a system with high accuracy can incorrectly predict nonexistent relations.

We reduce the number of possible entity pairings generated by applying a distance heuristic discussed in Section 4. We found that tuning the amount of entity pair candidates evaluated impacted results significantly (for example, our development set F1-score rose almost 20% when using a token-based distance metric rather than a sentence-based distance metric for selecting candidate entity pairs). The recall of our results suggests that our distance heuristic is effective at dramatically reducing the number of evaluated entity combinations without removing too many valid combinations, but the precision indicates that it may be valuable to modify or find an alternative method for producing candidate entity pairs. This could include a method which considers contextual information, instead of focusing only on the token distance between a pair of entities.

Class-specific result analysis allows us to identify where our system struggles. One such area is classes which occur less frequently in the data. Our macro-average F1-score is 0.69 for the seven most frequent relation classes (each of these has over 1000 examples in the training data), versus a macro-average of 0.43 for the seven least frequent relation classes (each of which has less than 1000 examples in the training data). BERT and similar language-embedding models rely on large quantities of training data, and class performance suffering due to lack of training data is not unex-

Table 1: Results by relation type on withheld WLPC test data.

Relation Type	Precision	Recall	F1-Score	Support
Site	0.72	0.82	0.77	1622
Setting	0.70	0.86	0.77	2034
Measure-Type-Link	0.50	0.95	0.65	275
Coreference-Link	0.42	0.53	0.47	286
Mod-Link	0.66	0.88	0.75	3429
Count	0.62	0.80	0.70	183
Meronym	0.22	0.72	0.34	558
Using	0.52	0.74	0.61	1120
Measure	0.69	0.95	0.80	2370
Commands	0.03	0.50	0.05	12
Of-Type	0.56	0.62	0.58	193
Or	0.22	0.66	0.33	193
Product	0.13	0.55	0.21	42
Acts-On	0.68	0.89	0.77	4072
Micro-Avg	0.61	0.86	0.71	16354
Macro-Avg	0.44	0.70	0.52	16354

pected here. We expect that collection of more data for imbalanced classes could improve performance of predictions for those classes substantially.

Recent prior work has shown that BERT and other language embedding models can become overly reliant on simple patterns in the data. Chauhan (2020) showed that the addition of the text "10 deaths" to uninformative tweets about COVID-19 caused a BERT based system to mistakenly label them as informative. We anticipate that this effect may make our system more prone to failure in edge cases, where basic clues that the model has learned in terms of entity type patterns or contextual patterns are not present. A potential solution for this problem is to augment the training data using examples which do not have certain attributes (for example, masking entity labels). This may reduce the model's tendency to learn from basic patterns rather than true relationships between text and a relation or event class.

6   Conclusion & Future Work

We show that contextualized knowledge graph completion using sequence classification can perform effectively on a relation extraction task in a noisy and specialized domain. Our model effectively identifies relations and events in the data, and our work leaves open many avenues for future work.

As discussed in Section 5, our system is sensitive to how candidate entity pairs are selected. We use a distance heuristic based on statistics of the training data to achieve our results, but we anticipate that more sophisticated methods for identifying promising candidate entity pairs could improve our results. We also suggest that our results could be improved by using a domain-specific model such as SciBERT or BioBERT (models trained on scientific papers and abstracts respectively). Prior work shows that these models often outperform standard BERT models on scientific data (Beltagy et al., 2019; Lee et al., 2020).

We believe that our results and the results of any systems which require training or fine-tuning large models would be improved by increasing available training data. Finding an effective method for augmenting existing training data and generating or collecting new training data (artificial or real) is a valuable route for further study.

Finally, we are interested in further investigation of representing relation and event identification as graph completion. Link prediction systems which support a variety of edge labels could allow us to leverage structural data from a protocol relation graph. This could enable the identification of relations which are improbable or those which may be missing from the predictions.

References

Iz Beltagy, Kyle Lo, and Arman Cohan. 2019. Scibert: A pretrained language model for scientific text. In *Proceedings of the 2019 Conference on Empirical Methods in Natural Language Processing and the 9th International Joint Conference on Natural Language Processing (EMNLP-IJCNLP)*, pages 3606–3611.

Kumud Chauhan. 2020. Neu at wnut-2020 task 2: Data augmentation to tell bert that death is not necessarily informative. *arXiv preprint arXiv:2009.08590*.

Jacob Devlin, Ming-Wei Chang, Kenton Lee, and Kristina Toutanova. 2019. Bert: Pre-training of deep bidirectional transformers for language understanding. In *HLT-NAACL*.

Zhengbao Jiang, Wei Xu, Jun Araki, and Graham Neubig. 2019. Generalizing natural language analysis through span-relation representations. *arXiv*, pages arXiv–1911.

Chaitanya Kulkarni, Wei Xu, Alan Ritter, and Raghu Machiraju. 2018. An annotated corpus for machine reading of instructions in wet lab protocols. In *HLT-NAACL*, pages 97–106.

Jinhyuk Lee, Wonjin Yoon, Sungdong Kim, Donghyeon Kim, Sunkyu Kim, Chan Ho So, and Jaewoo Kang. 2020. Biobert: a pre-trained biomedical language representation model for biomedical text mining. *Bioinformatics*, 36(4):1234–1240.

Hailun Lin, Yong Liu, Weiping Wang, Yinliang Yue, and Zheng Lin. 2017. Learning entity and relation embeddings for knowledge resolution. *Procedia Computer Science*, 108:345–354.

Yi Luan, Dave Wadden, Luheng He, Amy Shah, Mari Ostendorf, and Hannaneh Hajishirzi. 2019. A general framework for information extraction using dynamic span graphs. In *HLT-NAACL*, pages 3036–3046.

Matthew E Peters, Mark Neumann, Mohit Iyyer, Matt Gardner, Christopher Clark, Kenton Lee, and Luke Zettlemoyer. 2018. Deep contextualized word representations. *arXiv preprint arXiv:1802.05365*.

Edward W Schneider. 1973. Course modularization applied: The interface system and its implications for sequence control and data analysis.

Jeniya Tabassum, Wei Xu, and Alan Ritter. 2020. WNUT-2020 Task 1: Extracting Entities and Relations from Wet Lab Protocols. In *Proceedings of EMNLP 2020 Workshop on Noisy User-generated Text (WNUT)*.

Ashish Vaswani, Noam Shazeer, Niki Parmar, Jakob Uszkoreit, Llion Jones, Aidan N Gomez, Łukasz Kaiser, and Illia Polosukhin. 2017. Attention is all you need. In *Advances in Neural Information Processing Systems (NeurIPS)*, pages 5998–6008.

David Wadden, Ulme Wennberg, Yi Luan, and Hannaneh Hajishirzi. 2019. Entity, relation, and event extraction with contextualized span representations. In *EMNLP*, pages 5788–5793.

Thomas Wolf, Lysandre Debut, Victor Sanh, Julien Chaumond, Clement Delangue, Anthony Moi, Pierric Cistac, Tim Rault, Rémi Louf, Morgan Funtowicz, Joe Davison, Sam Shleifer, Patrick von Platen, Clara Ma, Yacine Jernite, Julien Plu, Canwen Xu, Teven Le Scao, Sylvain Gugger, Mariama Drame, Quentin Lhoest, and Alexander M. Rush. 2019. Huggingface's transformers: State-of-the-art natural language processing. *ArXiv*, abs/1910.03771.

Liang Yao, Chengsheng Mao, and Yuan Luo. 2019. Kg-bert: Bert for knowledge graph completion. *arXiv preprint arXiv:1909.03193*.

KaushikAcharya at WNUT 2020 Shared Task-1: Conditional Random Field(CRF) based Named Entity Recognition(NER) for Wet Lab Protocols

Kaushik Acharya

Philips India Ltd. / Bangalore, India

acharya.kaushik@gmail.com

Abstract

Detecting named entities in user generated text is a challenging task. Lab protocols specify steps in performing a lab procedure. The majority of wet lab protocols are written in noisy, dense, and domain-specific natural language. There is a growing need of automatic or semi-automatic conversion of protocols into machine-readable format to benefit biological research.

The paper describes how a classifier model built using Conditional Random Field[1] detects named entities in wet lab protocols. The model[1] trained on the training data showed precision, recall and F1-score of 0.762, 0.743 and 0.752 respectively on the development set. When applied to unseen test data, the model showed 0.737, 0.640 and 0.685 respectively.

1 Introduction

Wet laboratories are laboratories for conducting biology and chemistry experiments. These require handling of various types of chemicals and potential "wet" hazards. These experiments are guided by a sequence of instructions collectively referred as wet lab protocols.

The instructions are mostly composed of imperative statements which are meant to describe an action. Figure 1 shows a representative wet lab protocol. Figure 2 shows BRAT annotations (entities and relations) on two sentences from the representative protocol. For each protocol, annotators had identified and marked every span of text corresponding to action or one of the 17 types of entities. Table 1 shows a few typical examples for each of these classes. For detailed description of entities please refer Kulkarni et al's [2] Annotation Guidelines.

Standard RNA Synthesis (E2050)
Thaw the necessary kit components.
Mix and pulse-spin in microfuge to collect solutions to the bottoms of tubes. Keep on ice.
Assemble the reaction at room temperature in the following order:.
Mix thoroughly and pulse-spin in a microfuge.
Incubate at 37C for 2 hours.
Optional step: DNase treatment to remove DNA template.
To remove template DNA, add 30 l nuclease-free water to each 20 l reaction,
followed by 2 l of DNase I (RNase-free), mix and incubate for 15 minutes at 37C.
Proceed with purification of synthesized RNA or analysis of transcription products by gel electrophoresis.

Figure 1: An example wet lab protocol

Named Entity Recognition (NER) aims at identifying these entities within a given protocol.

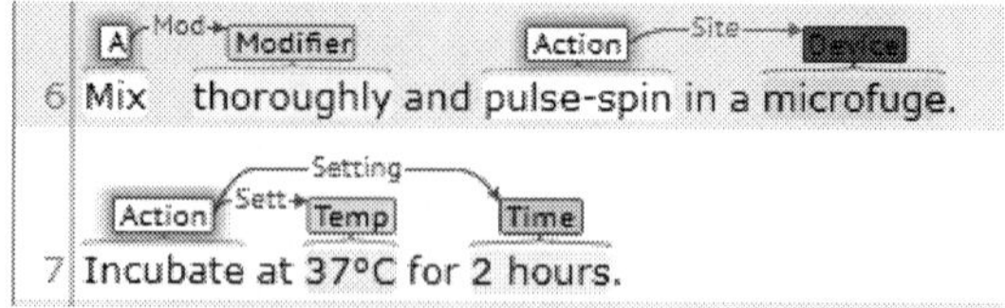

Figure 2: Example sentences from the wet lab protocol example shown in figure 1 as shown in the BRAT annotation interface.

2 Named Entity Recognition Methodology

A Conditional Random Fields (CRF) classifier was trained to recognize named entities. The CRF NER model was implemented using sklearn-crfsuite [2]

---

[1]https://github.com/kaushikacharya/ wet_lab_protocols

[2]https://sklearn-crfsuite.readthedocs. io/en/latest/

Proceedings of the 2020 EMNLP Workshop W-NUT: The Sixth Workshop on Noisy User-generated Text, pages 286–289
Online, Nov 19, 2020. ©2020 Association for Computational Linguistics

which is a Python wrapper over C++ based CRF-suite [3]. It utilized L-BFGS [3], a limited memory quasi-Newton algorithm for large scale numerical optimization. The classifier was trained with both L1 and L2 regularization.

2.1 Features

Three types of features have been extracted using Python library spaCy [4].

- Lexical features
    - Unigrams
    - Lemmas

- Parts of speech (POS) features
    - Current word's POS
    - Prev and Next word's POS
    - Governor word's POS

- Dependency parse features
    - Governor words
    - Dependency type
    - Dependency type of Governor word

As an example, **microfuge** in the sentence shown in Figure 3 produces the following features:

- **current word POS**: NOUN

- **dependency tag**: pobj

- **parent dependency tag**: prep

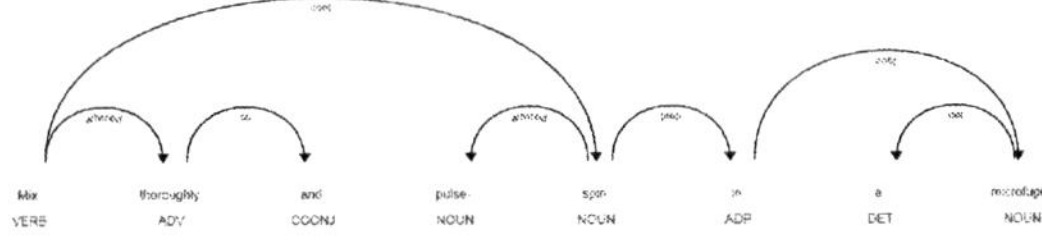

Figure 3: POS and dependency parse for the sentence shown in figure 2. Dependency parse tree visualized using spaCy's displaCy.

3 Experiments

The experiments were based on the datasets provided by the organizers of W-NUT 2020 shared task on Entity and Relation Recognition over Wet Lab Protocols [5]. The dataset (Table 2) was annotated in both StandOff and CoNLL formats. Entities and relations of 615 protocols were annotated in brat with 3 annotators with 0.75 inter-annotator agreement, measured by span-level Cohen's Kappa.

---

³`http://www.chokkan.org/software/crfsuite/`

Tag	Examples
Action	add, incubate, mix
Amount	50 l, equal volume
Concentration	1x
Device	filter, vacuum, microfuge
Generic-Measure	30-kd, several times, 100v
Location	tube, plate, well
Measure-Type	volume, concentration
Mention	It, them, this
Method	up and down, extraction
Modifier	each, gently, at least
Numerical	one, 3, several, several times
pH	ph 8.0, ph8.0
Reagent	cells, supernatant
Seal	Lid, cap, aluminum foil
Size	0.02 m, 12 x 75 mm
Speed	14,000xg, 10,000 rpm
Temperature	room temperature, overnight
Time	5 minutes

Table 1: Top frequent examples of Action and Entities

Dataset	Protocols	Sentences
Training	370	8444
Development	122	2839
Test	123	2813

Table 2: Wet Lab Protocols dataset statistics

3.1 Results

For the experiments, the classifier was trained on the training data and evaluated on development and test data.

The reported averages are defined as follows:

- **Macro average**: averaging the unweighted mean per label.

- **Micro average**: averaging the total true positives, false negatives and false positives.

- **Weighted average**: averaging the support-weighted mean per label

Table 3 and Table 4 show results at token and entity level respectively.

Table 5 compares my results (**KaushikAcharya**) to the other systems participating in the shared task on the unseen test data.

Dataset	Average	P	R	F1
Dev	Macro	0.677	0.633	0.651
Dev	Weighted	0.809	0.817	0.812
Test	Macro	0.691	0.646	0.666
Test	Weighted	0.833	0.839	0.835

Table 3: Token level metrics on development and test sets(P: Precision, R: Recall, F1: F1 score). This includes non-entity tokens also as one of the classes.

Dataset	Average	P	R	F1
Dev	Micro	0.762	0.743	0.752
Dev	Macro	0.755	0.743	0.748
Test	Micro	0.782	0.766	0.774
Test	Macro	0.777	0.766	0.771

Table 4: Entity level metrics on development and test sets (P: Precision, R: Recall, F1: F1 score).

Team	Exact	Partial
BITEM	77.99	81.67
PublishInCovid19	77.57	81.75
mgsohrab	76.6	80.5
Kabir	75.35	80.08
Winners	74.91	79.54
BIO-BIO	74.59	79.03
Fancy Man Launches Zippo	73.92	78.71
SudeshnaTCS	73.16	77.8
B-NLP	70.25	76.46
KaushikAcharya	68.48	73.73
IBS	67.9	72.89
DSC-IITISM	60.42	64.49
mahab	51.54	56.57

Table 5: Comparison of system results on both exact and partial match (F1 score)

3.2 Error Analysis

Entity type wise performance metrics on development dataset are available in Table 6. This is based on strict evaluation mode of matching as defined in SemEval'13 [6]. As per strict evaluation, a predicted entity is correct only if it matches with gold-standard in both exact boundary and type. Used seqeval [4] for the evaluation.

Table 7 shows the poorly performing entity classes along with their frequent confusers.

Errors are of primarily two types:

[4] https://github.com/chakki-works/seqeval

Entity	Precision	Recall	F1 score
Action	0.871	0.885	0.878
Amount	0.865	0.824	0.844
Concentration	0.688	0.730	0.708
Device	0.613	0.584	0.598
Generic-Measure	0.255	0.205	0.227
Location	0.726	0.678	0.701
Measure-Type	0.562	0.502	0.530
Mention	0.662	0.589	0.623
Method	0.473	0.395	0.430
Modifier	0.588	0.502	0.541
Numerical	0.544	0.480	0.510
pH	0.853	0.784	0.817
Reagent	0.742	0.781	0.761
Seal	0.769	0.778	0.773
Size	0.625	0.385	0.476
Speed	0.881	0.784	0.830
Temperature	0.919	0.919	0.919
Time	0.919	0.907	0.913

Table 6: Entity level classification metrics per entity type

Truth	Confusers
Generic-Measure	Concentration, Numerical
Method	Action, Reagent
Modifier	Reagent, Location, Action
Numerical	Amount, Generic-Measure
Size	Concentration, Location

Table 7: Frequent confuser entity classes

- Predicted entity text span matches truth but entity class is incorrect.

- Entity text span mismatches.

  - Partial match: Example shown in Table 8.
  - Complete mis-match: Example shown in Table 9.

Table 8 and Table 9 show examples of misclassification for the highlighted text portion of the corresponding sentences.

Table 8: Expected: Two entities for the highlighted phrase: a) Modifier: *lab grade* b) Reagent: *water*. Whereas the system predicted a single entity(Reagent) over the entire text span.

Table 9: Expected: Entity(Method) for the highlighted phrase. Whereas the system predicted two entities: a) Action: *without lysing* b) Reagent: *erythrocytes*.

Text	Entity	Truth/Predicted
lab grade	**Modifier**	**Truth**
water	**Reagent**	**Truth**
lab grade water	Reagent	Predicted

Table 8: Mis-classification #1:
Sentence: Rinse slides with **lab grade water**.

Text	Entity	Truth/Predicted
without lysing erythrocytes	**Method**	**Truth**
without lysing	Action	Predicted
erythrocytes	Reagent	Predicted

Table 9: Mis-classification #2:
Sentence: Prepare cells from your tissue of interest **without lysing erythrocytes**.

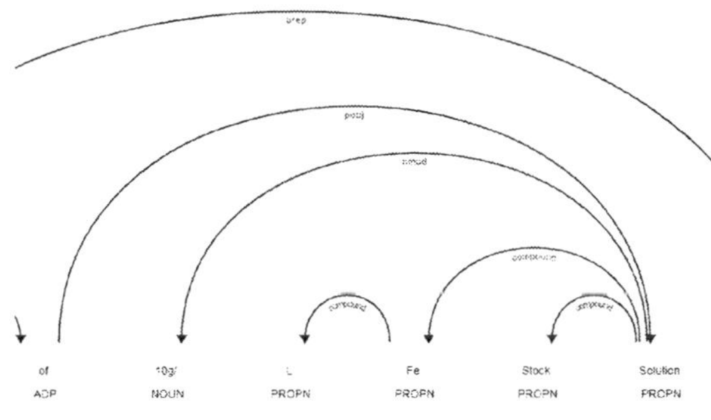

Figure 4: Global structured information in the dependency tree. The figure shows the dependency sub-tree for the **Reagent** entity: **10g/L Fe Stock Solution**. The entity's text span is covered by the subtree having **Solution** as its root and **of** as its head.

4   Conclusion

This paper has proposed a CRF-based named entity extraction system to extract Action and 17 Entities of wet lab protocols.

Future plan:

- Analyse the errors in more detail and extract richer features.

- Extract global structured information features of the dependency trees[7] as shown in Figure 4. Currently as the system only uses local

dependency features, it predicts **Fe Stock Solution** as Reagent entity and misses **10g/L**.

- Develop Long Short-Term Memory (LSTM) recurrent neural network model [8].

References

[1] John Lafferty, Andrew Mccallum, and Fernando Pereira. Conditional random fields: Probabilistic models for segmenting and labeling sequence data. pages 282–289, 01 2001.

[2] Alan Ritter Raghu Machiraju Chaitanya Kulkarni, Wei Xu. An Annotated Corpus for Machine Reading of Instructions in Wet Lab Protocols. *In Proceedings of NAACL-HLT*, 2018.

[3] Dong C. Liu and Jorge Nocedal. On the limited memory BFGS method for large scale optimization. *Mathematical Programming*, 45:503–528, 1989.

[4] Matthew Honnibal and Ines Montani. spaCy 2: Natural language understanding with Bloom embeddings, convolutional neural networks and incremental parsing. To appear, 2017.

[5] Jeniya Tabassum, Sydney Lee, Wei Xu, and Alan Ritter. WNUT-2020 Task 1 Overview: Extracting Entities and Relations from Wet Lab Protocols. In *Proceedings of EMNLP 2020 Workshop on Noisy User-generated Text (WNUT)*, 2020.

[6] Isabel Segura-Bedmar, Paloma Martínez, and María Herrero-Zazo. SemEval-2013 task 9 : Extraction of drug-drug interactions from biomedical texts (DDIExtraction 2013). In *Second Joint Conference on Lexical and Computational Semantics (*SEM), Volume 2: Proceedings of the Seventh International Workshop on Semantic Evaluation (SemEval 2013)*, pages 341–350, Atlanta, Georgia, USA, June 2013. Association for Computational Linguistics.

[7] Zhanming Jie, Aldrian Obaja Muis, and Wei Lu. Efficient dependency-guided named entity recognition, 2018.

[8] Guillaume Lample, Miguel Ballesteros, Sandeep Subramanian, Kazuya Kawakami, and Chris Dyer. Neural architectures for named entity recognition. In *Proceedings of the 2016 Conference of the North American Chapter of the Association for Computational Linguistics: Human Language Technologies*, pages 260–270, San Diego, California, June 2016. Association for Computational Linguistics.

mgsohrab at WNUT 2020 Shared Task-1: Neural Exhaustive Approach for Entity and Relation Recognition Over Wet Lab Protocols

Mohammad Golam Sohrab[†]**, Khoa N. A. Duong**[†]**,**
Makoto Miwa[†, ‡]**, and Hiroya Takamura**[†]

[†]Artificial Intelligence Research Center (AIRC)
National Institute of Advanced Industrial Science and Technology (AIST),
2-4-7 Aomi, Koto-ku, Tokyo, 135-0064, Japan
[‡]Toyota Technological Institute, Japan
{sohrab.mohammad, khoa.duong, takamura.hiroya}@aist.go.jp,
makoto-miwa@toyota-ti.ac.jp

Abstract

We present a neural exhaustive approach that addresses named entity recognition (NER) and relation recognition (RE), for the entity and relation recognition over the wet-lab protocols shared task. We introduce BERT-based neural exhaustive approach that enumerates all possible spans as potential entity mentions and classifies them into entity types or no entity with deep neural networks to address NER. To solve relation extraction task, based on the NER predictions or given gold mentions we create all possible trigger-argument pairs and classify them into relation types or no relation. In NER task, we achieved 76.60% in terms of F-score as third rank system among the participated systems. In relation extraction task, we achieved 80.46% in terms of F-score as the top system in the relation extraction or recognition task. Besides we compare our model based on the wet lab protocols corpus (WLPC) with the WLPC baseline and dynamic graph-based information extraction (DyGIE) systems.

1 Introduction

The entity and relation recognition over wet-lab protocol (Tabassum et al., 2020) shared task[1] is an open challenge that allows participants to use any methodology and knowledge sources for the wet lab protocols that specify the steps in performing a lab procedure. The task aims at two sub-tasks in wet lab protocols domain: named entity recognition (NER), and relation recognition or extraction (RE). In NER, the task is to detect mentions and classify them into entity types or no entity. NER has drawn considerable attentions as the first step towards many natural language processing (NLP) applications including relation extraction (Miwa and Bansal, 2016), event extraction (Feng et al.,

2016), and co-reference resolution (Fragkou, 2017). In contrast, relation extraction (RE) is a task to identify relation types between known or predicted entity mentions in a sentence.

In this paper, we present a BERT-based neural exhaustive approach that addresses both NER and RE tasks. We employ a neural exhaustive model (Sohrab and Miwa, 2018; Sohrab et al., 2019b) for NER and the extended model that addresses RE task. The model detects flat and nested entities by reasoning over all the spans within a specified maximum span length. Unlike the existing models that rely on token-level labels, our model directly employs an entity type as the label of a span. The spans with the representations are classified into their entity types or non-entity. With the mentions predicted by the NER module, we then feed the detected or known mentions to the RE layer that enumerates all trigger-argument pairs as trigger-trigger or trigger-entity pairs and assigns a role type or no role type to each pair.

The best run for each sub-task achieved the F-score of 76.60% on entity recognition task that stands third rank system and the F-scores of 80.46% on relation extraction task as the top system. Besides, we also compare our model with the state-of-the-art models over the wet lab protocols corpus (WLPC). We compare the WLPC baseline model based on LSTM-CRF and maximum-entropy-based approaches to address NER and RE tasks respectfully. We also compare our model with dynamic graph-based information extraction (DyGIE) system. Our model outperforms by 4.81% for NER and 7.79% for RE over the WLPC baseline and 3.61% for NER over the DyGIE system.

2 Related Work

Most NER work focus on flat entities. Lample et al. (2016) proposed a LSTM-CRF (conditional ran-

---

[1]http://noisy-text.github.io/2020/wlp-task.html

Proceedings of the 2020 EMNLP Workshop W-NUT: The Sixth Workshop on Noisy User-generated Text, pages 290–298
Online, Nov 19, 2020. ©2020 Association for Computational Linguistics

dom fields) model and this has been widely used and extended for the flat NER, e.g., Akbik et al. (2018). In recent studies of neural network based flat NER, Gungor et al. (2018, 2019) have shown that morphological analysis using additional word representations based on linguistic properties of the words, especially for morphologically rich languages such as Turkish and Finnish, improves the NER performances further compared with using only representations based on the surface forms of words.

Recently, nested NER has been widely interested in NLP. Zhou et al. (2004) detected nested entities in a bottom-up way. They detected the innermost flat entities and then found other NEs containing the flat entities as sub-strings using rules on the detected entities. The authors reported an improvement of around 3% in the F-score under certain conditions on the GENIA data set (Collier et al., 1999). Recent studies show that the conditional random fields (CRFs) can produce significantly higher tagging accuracy in flat or nested (stacking flat NER to nested representation) NERs (Son and Minh, 2017). Ju et al. (2018) proposed a novel neural model to address nested entities by dynamically stacking flat NER layers until no outer entities are extracted. A cascaded CRF layer is used after the LSTM output in each flat layer. The authors reported that the model outperforms state-of-the-art results by achieving 74.5% in F-score on the GENIA data set. Sohrab and Miwa (2018) proposed a neural model that detects nested entities using exhaustive approach that outperforms the state-of-the-art results in terms of F-score on the GENIA data set. Sohrab et al. (2019b) further extended the span representations for entity recognition and addressed sensitive span detection tasks in the MED-DOCAN (MEDical DOCument ANonymization) shared task[2], and the system achieved 93.12% and 93.52% in terms of F-score for NER and sensitive span detection, respectively.

Recent successes in neural networks have shown impressive performance on coupling information extraction (IE) tasks as in joint modeling of entities and relations (Miwa and Bansal, 2016). Yi et al. (2019) proposed a dynamic graph information extraction (DyGIE) system for coupling multiple IE tasks, a multi-task learning approach to entity, relation, and coreference extraction. DyGIE uses dynamic graph propagation to explicitly incorporate rich contextual information into the span representations, and the system achieved significant F1 score improvement on the different datasets. Kulkarni et al. (2018) establised a baseline for IE on the wet lab protocols corpus (WLPC). They employ an LSTM-CRF for entity recognition approach. For relation extraction, they assume the presence of gold entities and train a maximum-entropy classifier using features from the labeled entities.

3 Neural Exhaustive Approach for NER and Relation Extraction

Our BERT-based neural exhaustive approach is built upon a pipeline approach of two modules:

- Named entity recognition that uses a contextual neural exhaustive approach

- Relation extraction that aims to predict relations from detected/given mentions.

To solve entity and relation recognition tasks, the pipeline approach can be presented as three layers: BERT layer, entity recognition layer, and relation recognition layer. Figure 1 shows the system architecture of entity and relation recognition.

3.1 BERT Layer

For a given sequence, the BERT layer receives sub-word sequences and assigns contextual representations to the sub-words via BERT. We assume each sentence S has n words and the i-th word, represented by S_i, is split into sub-words. This layer assigns a vector $v_{i,j}$ to the j-th sub-word of the i-th word. It also produces the representation v_S as a local context for the sentence S, which corresponds to the embedding of [CLS] token.

3.2 Entity Recognition layer

We build mention detection layer, a.k.a named entity recognition (NER) on top of the BERT. This layer assigns entity or trigger types to overlapping text spans, or word sequences, in a sentence. We firstly generate mention candidates based on the same idea as the span-based model (Lee et al., 2017; Sohrab and Miwa, 2018; Sohrab et al., 2019a), in which all continuous word sequences are generated given a maximum span length L_x. Since BERT layer works only on sub-words, we choose the embedding of the first sub-word $v_{i,1}$ as word embedding v_i of i-th word. The representation $x_{b,e} \in R^{d_x}$ for the span from the b-th word to the e-th word in a sentence is calculated from the

---

[2]http://temu.bsc.es/meddocan/

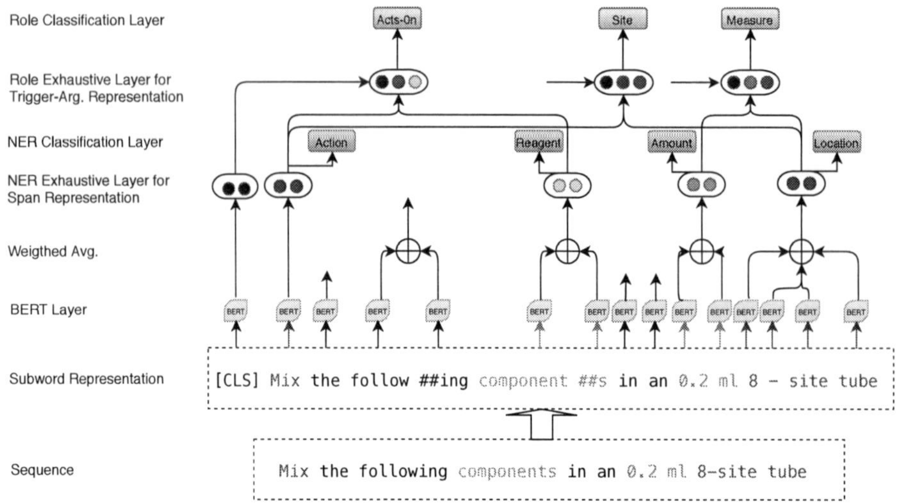

Figure 1: System Architecture for Neural Exhaustive Approach for NER and Relation Extraction. The example sequence is taken from Wet Lab Protocols Data set

embeddings of the first word, the last word, and the weighted average of all words in the span as follows:

$$x_{b,e} = \left[v_b; \sum_{i=b}^{e} \alpha_{b,e,i} v_i; v_e \right], \quad (1)$$

where $\alpha_{b,e,i}$ denotes the attention value of the i-th word in a span from the b-th word to the e-th word, and $[;;]$ denotes concatenation.

3.3 Relation Recognition Layer

The relation recognition layer enumerates all trigger-argument pairs (trigger-trigger and trigger-entity pairs) given triggers and entities detected by the entity recognition layer and assigns a role type or no role to each pair. We generate relation representation based on the same idea as the deep event extraction system (Trieu et al., 2020).

Since each role is constructed by a trigger and an argument, we firstly compute representations of all triggers and arguments detected by the entity recognition layer. The representations of a trigger and an argument are calculated in the same way. A trigger t ranging from the starting t_s-th word to the ending t_e-th word is represented with the concatenation of its span representation x_t (from Equation 1) and a 300-dimensional entity type embedding s_t, as follows:

$$v_t = [x_t; s_t], \quad (2)$$

Similarly, the representation of an argument a can

be calculated as

$$v_a = [x_a; s_a]. \quad (3)$$

The representation $r_i \in R^{d_r}$ for a relation pair i is then calculated from its trigger representation v_t, argument representation v_a, and the context representation v_S which is obtained from the sentence representation of the BERT layer:

$$r_i = GELU\left(w_r [v_t; v_a; v_S] + b_r\right), \quad (4)$$

where W_r and b_r are learnable weights and biases respectively and GELU is the Gaussian Error Linear Unit activation function. After obtaining the pair representation r_i, we classify it with a softmax function to predict the corresponding role type.

4 Experimental Settings

We provide empirical evidence on the effectiveness of the pipeline architecture in both NER and relation extraction over the wet lab protocols[3] task of the W-NUT 2020[4]. The wet lab protocols corpus with eighteen entity types[5] and fifteen relation types[6] are randomly split into four subsets: train,

[3] http://noisy-text.github.io/2020/wlp-task.html
[4] http://noisy-text.github.io/2020/
[5] Entity Type: Action, Seal, Numerical, Concentration, Size, Modifier, Measure-Type, Generic-Measure, Time, Speed, Action, Location, Method, Temperature, Mention, pH, Device, Amount, Reagent
[6] Relation Type: Coreference-Link, Measure, Site, Meronym, Measure-Type-Link, Product, Commands, Mod-Link, Count, Acts-on, Using, Creates, Setting, Of-Type, Or

development, test, and test release (unlabeled) sets, which contain 370, 122, 123 and 111 lab protocols respectively. In our experiments, we merge the train and development as train-set, test-set use as development-set, and predict the annotations for test release set which is used as test-set.

Our model is implemented in the PyTorch[7] framework. We employed the official wet lab protocols evaluation script for NER[8] and relation extraction[9] to evaluate our system's performances on both tasks.

4.1 Data Preprocessing

Each text and the corresponding annotation file were preprocessed by several simple rules[10] only for tokenization[11]. After tokenization, each text with mapping annotation files were directly passed to the deep neural approach for mention detection and relation extraction. Note that the offsets were restored to the original offsets in evaluation.

4.2 Training Settings

We train the model in a pipeline manner based on the pre-trained BERT model. We employed the pre-trained PubmedBERT (Gu et al., 2020) model which is an uncased BERT Base model that was pretrained over PubMed abstracts and full PubMed central articles. Besides, we also employed SciBERT (Beltagy et al., 2019) model that is pre-trained based on large-scale biomedical text. Moreover, we also employed original pre-trained BERT (Devlin et al., 2019) model which is a uncased BERT base model to judge the performances of our model among the PubmedBERT, SciBERT and BERT.

According to our investigation, we choose 10 as the maximum span length of mention candidates. We also truncate every sentences at 256 sub-words without losing any gold entities or relations (we maintain a 100% recall of gold entities and relations in the training set).

NER and RE models are trained on 100 epochs with learning rate of 0.00003.

---

[7]https://pytorch.org

[8]https://github.com/jeniyat/WNUT_2020_NER/tree/master/code/eval

[9]https://github.com/jeniyat/WNUT_2020_RE/blob/master/code/evaluation.py

[10]We also published our preprocessing script at https://github.com/dnanhkhoa/WNUT-2020

[11]Unlike the traditional NER models, our model is independent from traditional 'BIO' tagging scheme, where 'B', 'I', and 'O' stand for 'Begin', 'Inside', and 'Outside' of named entities respectively, so we do not need to assign such tags to the tokens.

5 Results and Discussions

In order to evaluate the performance of NER, we conduct experiments on different sets of BERT-based learning representations, including PubmedBERT with merging training- and dev-set (PubmedBERT-Merge), PubmedBERT along with training (PubmedBERT-Train), SciBERT with merging training- and dev-set (SciBERT-Merge), and SciBERT along with training (SciBERT-Train).

In contrast to relation extraction, as based on our primary results of NER with PubmedBERT and SciBERT where PubmedBERT is outperforming to SciBERT. Therefore, we conduct all our relation extraction experiments using PubmedBERT. For relation extraction task, we learn our model on two data scenarios. First, we perform a clustering approach on training- and dev-set to find the similar or duplicate text files in wet-lab data set. We found that many similar text files with inconsistent annotations exist in the train- and dev-set. The similarity approach with a setting threshold is applied on the train and dev-set to cluster the similar or duplicate text protocols. We then eliminate those text and its corresponding annotation files which appear in the training set to avoid model learning confusion and data leakage. We also applied the predefined relation rules (Kulkarni et al., 2018) to filter out any invalid relations appearing in the system output. We conduct experiments on different sets of PubmedBERT based learning representations, including PubmedBERT using finetune with filtering approach (PubmedBERT-Finetune-Filter), PubmedBERT along with finetune (PubmedBERT-Finetune), PubmedBERT along with filter approach (PubmedBERT-Filter) and PubmedBERT without finetune and filtering approaches (PubmedBERT).

In second data scenario, we learn our model by keeping all the original training set, development set, and test set. Based on original data setting, the PubmedBERT-based learning representations are PubmedBERT-Original-Finetune-Filter, PubmedBERT-Original-Finetune, PubmedBERT-Original-Filter and PubmedBERT-Original.

We also report the result of ensemble learning that combines the predictions using different span representations to reduce the variance of predictions and the generalization error.

5.1 NER Performances

Table 1 shows the results of NER on the dev- and test-set. Here, the PubmedBERT-Merge, SciBERT-

	Dev: NER			Test: NER		
Learning Approach	P	R	F	P	R	F(%)
Ensemble	**83.14**	83.28	**83.21**	83.69	70.62	76.60
PubmedBERT-Merge (Train+dev)	82.04	**83.51**	82.77	80.59	71.57	75.81
SciBERT-Merge (Train+Dev)	82.47	82.80	82.64	80.79	70.40	75.24
PubmedBERT-Train	82.46	79.23	80.81	83.66	69.59	75.98
SciBERT-Train	80.68	80.46	80.57	80.78	71.70	75.97

Table 1: Performance of NER on the dev- and test-set

	Exact Match			Partial Match		
Team Name	P	R	F	P	R	F(%)
BITEM	**84.73**	72.25	**77.99**	**88.72**	75.66	81.67
PublishInCovid19	81.36	**74.12**	77.57	85.74	**78.11**	**81.75**
mgsohrab	83.69	70.62	76.60	87.95	74.22	80.50
Kabir	78.79	72.20	75.35	83.73	76.73	80.08
IITKGP	77.00	72.93	74.91	81.76	77.43	79.54
BIO-BIO	78.49	71.06	74.59	83.16	75.29	79.03
Fancy Man Launches Zippo	76.21	71.76	73.92	81.15	76.41	78.71
SudeshnaTCS	74.99	71.43	73.16	79.73	75.95	77.80
B-NLP	77.95	63.93	70.25	84.85	69.59	76.46
KaushikAcharya	73.68	63.98	68.48	79.31	68.87	73.73
IBS	74.26	62.55	67.90	79.72	67.15	72.89
DSC-IITISM	64.20	57.07	60.42	68.52	60.90	64.49
mahab	50.19	52.96	51.54	55.09	58.14	56.57

Table 2: Team performances of NER on the test-set

	Dev: RE			Test: RE		
Learning Approach	P	R	F	P	R	F(%)
Ensemble	88.16	**86.91**	**87.53**	80.86	**80.07**	**80.46**
PubmedBERT-Finetune-Filter	**88.59**	85.47	87.00	**83.03**	77.35	80.09
PubmedBERT-Finetune	88.55	85.47	86.99	82.93	77.36	80.05
PubmedBERT-Filter	88.54	84.84	86.65	81.96	75.96	78.84
PubmedBERT	88.50	84.84	86.63	81.92	75.97	78.83
PubmedBERT-Original-Finetune-Filter	87.85	86.36	87.10	78.67	79.03	78.85
PubmedBERT-Original-Finetune	87.85	86.36	87.10	78.59	79.03	78.81
PubmedBERT-Original-Filter	88.09	85.15	86.60	80.36	77.48	78.89
PubmedBERT-Original	88.04	85.15	86.57	80.30	77.48	78.87

Table 3: Performance of relation extraction (RE) on the dev- and test-set

	Relation Extraction		
Team Name	P	R	F(%)
mgsohrab	**80.86**	80.07	**80.46**
Big Green	45.42	**86.54**	59.57

Table 4: Team performances of relation extraction (RE) on the test-set

Merge, PubmedBERT-Train, and SciBERT-Train are used for ensemble approach. In this table, it is shown that the ensemble approach using maximum voting of all the approaches is effective to improve the NER system performance with achieving 83.21% and 76.60% in terms of F-score over the dev- and test-set respectfully. In contrast, the PubmedBERT-Merge shows the best performance as an individual learning on NER with achieving

	NER Test-set			RE Test-set		
Entity Level	P	R	F	P	R	F(%)
All	82.70	71.25	76.55	80.96	80.05	80.50
Single-token	**85.43**	**72.05**	**78.17**	**82.95**	78.97	**80.91**
Multi-token	77.73	69.70	73.50	79.01	**81.20**	80.09

Table 5: Performances of NER and RE of our model on different entity level on the test-set

	NER			RE		
Model	P	R	F	P	R	F(%)
WLPC Baseline (Kulkarni et al., 2018)	–	–	78.30	80.98	77.04	78.96
DyGIE (Yi et al., 2019)	–	–	79.50	–	–	*64.10
Our Model	82.83	83.40	**83.11**	**88.75**	84.86	**86.75**

Table 6: Performance comparison of NER and RE based on different models on the wet lab protocols dataset. '-' denotes results are not reported in the original paper. '*' indicates the performance of relation extraction system is based on predicted entity boundary as input.

Label	P	R	F(%)	Prediction	Annotation	Correct
Action	90.71	92.92	91.80	4239	4138	3845
Concentration	85.45	85.61	85.53	536	535	458
Reagent	85.20	86.43	85.81	4053	3995	3453
Amount	91.78	91.93	91.86	1192	1190	1094
Location	79.27	78.43	78.85	1312	1326	1040
Method	65.36	54.56	59.47	485	581	317
Time	91.77	91.03	91.40	863	870	792
Temperature	93.63	91.17	92.38	518	532	485
Device	69.92	70.51	70.21	472	468	330
Modifier	64.68	66.58	65.62	1648	1601	1066
Size	75.70	71.68	73.64	107	113	81
Mention	64.29	80.36	71.43	70	56	45
Ph	83.64	74.19	78.63	55	62	46
Numerical	65.06	70.13	67.50	249	231	162
Seal	70.00	65.62	67.74	60	64	42
Measure-type	65.53	56.62	60.75	235	272	154
Speed	90.75	94.01	92.35	173	167	157
Generic-measure	41.90	30.77	35.48	105	143	44
Overall (micro)	83.14	83.28	83.21	16372	16344	13611

Table 7: Categorical performances of NER on the dev-set

82.77% in terms of F-score.

Table 2 shows the NER task results on the participated teams. In this table results are listed in descending order in terms of exact match-based F-score. The top system achieves 77.99% where our team achieves 76.60% in terms of F-score for NER task.

5.2 Relation Extraction Performances

Table 3 shows the results of relation extraction task on the dev- and test-set. Here, all the reported learning approaches in this table are used for ensemble approach. In this table, it is shown that the ensemble approach using maximum voting of all the approaches is also effective to improve the relation extraction system performance with achieving 87.53% and 80.46% in terms of F-score over the dev- and test-set respectfully. In contrast, the PubmedBERT-Original-Finetune-Filter and PubmedBERT-Finetune-Filter are showing the best performances as an individual learning on relation extraction with achieving 87.10% and 80.09%

Label	P	R	F(%)	Prediction	Annotation	Correct
Coreference-Link	69.64	46.43	55.71	56	84	39
Measure	92.66	91.20	91.93	1880	1910	1742
Site	81.61	87.82	84.61	1202	1117	981
Meronym	73.97	65.98	69.74	388	435	287
Measure-Type-Link	87.90	88.62	88.26	124	123	109
Product	43.18	20.00	27.34	44	95	19
Commands	07.14	05.00	05.88	14	20	1
Mod-Link	92.52	91.85	92.18	1510	1521	1397
Count	87.37	83.84	85.57	95	99	830
Acts-On	91.44	89.82	90.63	3050	3105	2789
Using	77.04	75.50	76.26	832	849	641
Creates	00.00	00.00	00.00	0	0	0
Setting	91.13	92.48	91.80	1713	1688	1561
Of-Type	75.00	54.55	63.16	16	22	12
Or	68.99	62.64	65.66	158	174	109
Overall (micro)	88.16	86.91	87.53	11082	11242	9770

Table 8: Categorical performances of relation extraction (RE) on the dev-set

	RE		
Training Strategy	P	R	F(%)
Not pre-finetune NER layer	**88.09**	85.15	86.60
Pre-finetune NER layer using gold entities	87.85	**86.36**	**87.10**

Table 9: Performance of relation extraction (RE) using different training strategies on the dev-set

	NER			RE		
Entity	P	R	F	P	R	F(%)
BERT-base-uncased	84.18	83.19	83.68	87.84	85.55	86.83
PubmedBERT-full-uncased	**84.50**	**83.70**	**84.10**	**87.85**	**86.36**	**87.10**

Table 10: Performance of NER and relation extraction (RE) using different BERT-based learning on the dev-set

Span Length	P	R	F(%)
8	82.65	82.55	82.60
10	**82.83**	82.89	**82.86**
12	81.95	**83.71**	82.82

Table 11: Performance of our model with different spans on the dev-set

in terms of F-score over the dev- and test-set respectively.

Table 4 shows the relation extraction task results on the participated teams. Our relation extraction system achieves 80.56% in terms of F-score as a top system in this task. We outperformed the second best system by 20.89% in terms of F-score.

Our system is based on span-based representation, therefore we also investigate the performances for all vs single-token vs multi-token entities. Table 5 shows the break down performances of our model on different entity levels over the NER and relation extraction on the test set.

In contrast, we also compare our model with the state-of-the-art models over the wet lab protocols corpus (WLPC). Table 6 shows the comparison of our model with the WLPC baseline and Dy-GIE systems. In NER, our model outperforms the WLPC baseline and DyGIE systems by 4.81% and 3.61% respectively in terms of F-score. In RE, our model outperforms the WLPC baseline by 7.79% in terms of F-score. In compare the RE task for DyGIE, NER predictions are given as input in Dy-GIE where gold data boundary is given as input in our and WLPC baseline models. We report the DyGIE RE performance without comparing with our RE performance. In these comparisons, we use the same train-, dev-, test-set, and evaluation script that reported in the WLPC baseline (Kulkarni et al., 2018) for fair comparisons.

5.3 Ablation Study

We show the performances of different BERT-based learning models for NER and relation extraction tasks on the development column in Table 1 and Table 3 to compare the possible scenarios of the given solutions and to report the best system submissions for NER and relation extraction. For NER and relation extraction tasks, all the results in Table 1 and Table 3 in development column window show that almost all the results in different approaches are close to each other to solve the NER and relation extraction tasks.

Table 7 shows the categorical performances using ensemble learning of NER on the dev-set. In this table, we also break down the number of predicted and correct mentions among the gold annotations of each category. Here, prediction can be denoted as number of predicted entities, annotation as number of gold entities of each category, and correct as number of true positive outcomes where the model correctly predicts the positive category. In this table, it can be observed that for the frequent classes (e.g. Action, Reagent, Amount etc.), the model shows high performance because there are a reasonable number of training instances for the classes. In contrast, for the rare classes (e.g. Size, Mention, Ph, numerical etc.), the performances are also consistence. Table 8 shows the categorical performances using ensemble learning of relation extraction on the dev-set. In this table, it shows the categorical performances using ensemble learning of relation extraction on the development set. In this table, it seems that the model is well generalized to classify the relation types that leads to achieve the top system in the shared task.

Since we provided gold entities in the RE task, therefore, we also examine two different strategies for training the RE model that present in the Table 9. In this table, it shows that we can significantly boost the RE performance just by pre-finetuning the NER layer using gold entities. Table 10 shows the performances of NER and RE based on the original BERT base in compare to the Pubmed-BERT. The results show that PubmedBERT is outperformed both in NER and RE tasks. In Table 11, we compared our model in different span length.

We chose the maximum span size from 8, 10, and 12 that covers more than 99% mentions to judge the sensitivity of our approach in different span length. In ths table, it can be observed that the performances of our model are consistence even with different span lengths.

6 Conclusion

This paper presented a BERT-based neural exhaustive approach that addresses both named entity recognition (NER) and relation extraction (RE) tasks. This neural approach consider all possible spans exhaustively, for NER which is capable to detect flat and nested entities from the generated mention candidates.

Several enhancements, namely PubmedBERT, SciBERT, BERT-base-uncased, filtering, clustering, and ensembling are investigated for the wet-lab protocol data set to enhance the system performance. In NER task, we achieved 76.60% in terms of F-score as third rank system among the participated systems. In relation extraction task, we achieved 80.46% in terms of F-score as the top system that participated in the relation extraction task. Moreover, our model outperforms by 4.81% for NER and 7.79% for RE over the WLPC baseline and 3.61% for NER over the DyGIE system.

In the future direction, we will implement a joint modeling that addresses NER and relation extraction in an end-to-end manner.

Acknowledgments

This work is based on results obtained from a project commissioned by the Public/Private R&D Investment Strategic Expansion PrograM (PRISM).

References

Alan Akbik, Duncan Blythe, and Roland Vollgraf. 2018. Contextual string embeddings for sequence labeling. In *COLING 2018, 27th International Conference on Computational Linguistics*, pages 1638–1649.

Iz Beltagy, Kyle Lo, and Arman Cohan. 2019. Scibert: A pretrained language model for scientific text. In *Proceedings of the 2019 Conference on Empirical Methods in Natural Language Processing and the 9th International Joint Conference on Natural Language Processing (EMNLP-IJCNLP)*, pages 3606–3611.

N. Collier, H. S. Park, N. Ogata, Y. Tateisi, C. Nobata, T. Ohta, T. Sekimizu, H. Imai, K. Ibushi, and

Jun'ichi Tsujii. 1999. The GENIA Project: Corpus-based Knowledge Acquisition and Information Extraction from Genome Research Papers. In *Proceedings of EACL*, pages 171–172. ACL.

Jacob Devlin, Ming-Wei Chang, Kenton Lee, and Kristina Toutanova. 2019. BERT: Pre-training of deep bidirectional transformers for language understanding. In *Proceedings of the 2019 Conference of the North American Chapter of the Association for Computational Linguistics: Human Language Technologies, Volume 1 (Long and Short Papers)*, pages 4171–4186.

Xiaocheng Feng, Lifu Huang, Duyu Tang, Heng Ji, Bing Qin, and Ting Liu. 2016. A Language-Independent Neural Network for Event Detection. In *Proceedings of the 54th Annual Meeting of the ACL (Volume 2: Short Papers)*, pages 66—71, Berlin, Germany.

Pavlina Fragkou. 2017. Applying named entity recognition and co-reference resolution for segmenting english texts. *Progress in Artificial Intelligence*, 6(4):325—346.

Yu Gu, Robert Tinn, Hao Cheng, Michael Lucas, Naoto Usuyama, Xiaodong Liu, Tristan Naumann, Jianfeng Gao, and Hoifung Poon. 2020. Domain-specific language model pretraining for biomedical natural language processing. *arXiv preprint arXiv:2007.15779*.

Onur Gungor, Tunga Gungor, and Suzan Uskudarli. 2019. The effect of morphology in named entity recognition with sequence tagging. *Natural Language Engineering*, 25(1):147–169.

Onur Gungor, Suzan Uskudarli, and Tunga Gungor. 2018. Improving named entity recognition by jointly learning to disambiguate morphological tags. In *COLING 2018, 27th International Conference on Computational Linguistics*, pages 2082–2092.

Meizhi Ju, Makoto Miwa, and Sophia Ananiadou. 2018. A Neural Layered Model for Nested Named Entity Recognition. In *Proceedings of the 2018 Conference of the North American Chapter of the Association for Computational Linguistics: Human Language Technologies, Volume 1 (Long Papers)*, pages 1446—1459, New Orleans, Louisiana. ACL.

Chaitanya Kulkarni, Wei Xu, Alan Ritter, and Raghu MachirajuYi. 2018. An annotated corpus for machine reading of instructions in wet lab protocols. In *Proceedings of NAACL-HLT 2018*.

Guillaume Lample, Miguel Ballesteros, Sandeep Subramanian, Kazuya Kawakami, and Chris Dyer. 2016. Neural Architectures for Named Entity Recognition. In *Proceedings of the 2016 Conference of the North American Chapter of the ACL: Human Language Technologies. ACL*, volume 1, pages 260—-270, San Diego, California. ACL.

Kenton Lee, Luheng He, Mike Lewis, and Luke Zettlemoyer. 2017. End-to-end neural coreference resolution. In *Proceedings of the 2017 Conference on Empirical Methods in Natural Language Processing*, pages 188–197, Copenhagen, Denmark. Association for Computational Linguistics.

Makoto Miwa and Mohit Bansal. 2016. End-to-End Relation Extraction using LSTMs on Sequences and Tree Structures. In *Proceedings of the 54th Annual Meeting of the ACL*, pages 1105—1116, Berlin, Germany. ACL.

Mohammad Golam Sohrab and Makoto Miwa. 2018. Deep exhaustive model for nested named entity recognition. In *Proceedings of the 2018 Conference on Empirical Methods in Natural Language Processing*, pages 2843–2849, Brussels, Belgium. Association for Computational Linguistics.

Mohammad Golam Sohrab, Minh Thang Pham, Makoto Miwa, and Hiroya Takamura. 2019a. A neural pipeline approach for the pharmaconer shared task using contextual exhaustive models. In *Proceedings of The 5th Workshop on BioNLP Open Shared Tasks*, pages 47–55.

Mohammad Golam Sohrab, Pham Minh Thang, and Makoto Miwa. 2019b. A generic neural exhaustive approach for entity recognition and sensitive span detect. In *Proceedings of the Iberian Languages Evaluation Forum (IberLEF 2019)*, pages 735–743, Span. IberLEF 2019.

Nguyen Truong Son and Nguyen Le Minh. 2017. Nested Named Entity Recognition Using Multilayer Recurrent Neural Networks. In *Proceedings of PACLING 2017*, pages 16–18, Sedona Hotel, Yangon, Myanmar.

Jeniya Tabassum, Sydney Lee, Wei Xu, and Alan Ritter. 2020. WNUT-2020 Task 1 Overview: Extracting Entities and Relations from Wet Lab Protocols. In *Proceedings of EMNLP 2020 Workshop on Noisy User-generated Text (WNUT)*.

Hai-Long Trieu, Thy Tran, Khoa N A Duong, Anh Nguyen, Makoto Miwa, and Sophia Ananiadou. 2020. DeepEventMine: End-to-end Neural Nested Event Extraction from Biomedical Texts. *Bioinformatics*. Btaa540.

Luan Yi, Wadden Dave, He Luheng, Shah Amy, Ostendorf Mari, and Hajishirzi Hannaneh. 2019. A general framework for information extraction using dynamic span graphs. In *Proceedings of NAACL-HLT 2019*.

Guodong Zhou, Jie Zhang, Jian Su, Dan Shen, and Chewlim Tan. 2004. Recognizing Names in Biomedical Texts: a Machine Learning Approach. *Bioinformatics*, 20(7):1178—1190.

Fancy Man Launches Zippo at WNUT 2020 Shared Task-1: A Bert Case Model for Wet Lab Entity Extraction

Haoding Meng
Xian Jiaotong University
menghd@stu.xjtu.edu.cn

Qingcheng Zeng
The University of Manchester
qingcheng.zeng@student.manchester.ac.uk

Xiaoyang Fang
East China University of Science and Technology
10182412@mail.ecust.edu.cn

Zhexin Liang
Zhejiang University
3170103561@zju.edu.cn

Abstract

Automatic or semi-automatic conversion of protocols specifying steps in performing a lab procedure into machine-readable format benefits biological research a lot. These noisy, dense, and domain-specific lab protocols processing draws more and more interests with the development of deep learning. This paper presents our teamwork on WNUT 2020 shared task-1: wet lab entity extract, that we conducted studies in several models, including a BiLSTM CRF model and a Bert case model which can be used to complete wet lab entity extraction. And we mainly discussed the performance differences of **Bert case** under different situations such as *transformers* versions, case sensitivity that may don't get enough attention before.

1 Introduction

The task of named entity recognition (NER) was first put forward in 1991, after which it gradually became an essential part of natural language processing (NLP). The methods for NER is generally classified into four kinds: rule-based approaches, unsupervised learning approaches, feature-based supervised learning approaches and deep-learning based approaches. The previous methods are mainly rule-based, performing well on small dataset, like the LaSIE-II system provided by Humphreys et al.. Under the rapid development of deep learning since 2013, methods like **BiLSTM CRF** has been a hot spot in recent years. Even now, most of the deep learning methods for NER are based on this framework. But lately, some new research based on the concept of "pre-training" has attracted more and more attention, for example, Bert, which stands for bidirectional encoder representations from transformers (Devlin et al., 2018). It both pushed the GLUE score to 80.5 % , which got 7.7 % point absolute improvement and

Isolation of temperate phages by plaque agar overlay
1. Melt soft agar overlay tubes in boiling water and place in the 47C water bath.
2. Remove one tube of soft agar from the water bath.
3. Add 1.0 mL host culture and either 1.0 or 0.1 mL viral concentrate.
4. Mix the contents of the tube well by rolling back and forth between two hands, and immediately empty the tube contents onto an agar plate.
5. Sit RT for 5 min.
6. Gently spread the top agar over the agar surface by sliding the plate on the bench surface using a circular motion.
7. Harden the top agar by not disturbing the plates for 30 min.
8. Incubate the plates (top agar side down) overnight to 48h.
9. Temperate phage plaques will appear as turbid or cloudy plaques, whereas purely lytic phage will appear as shaply defined, clear plaques.

Figure 1: An example wet lab protocol (Kulkarni et al., 2018)

created a new paradigm of natural language processing task method: using the model pre-trained on a large corpus to complete downstream tasks through fine-tuning.

2 Task

For WNUT 2020 shared task-1 (Tabassum et al., 2020), participants were asked to develop a system that automatically identify entities from the provided lab instructions dataset. The dataset is from wet lab protocols, which usually refer to the experiment instructions in biology or chemistry experiments, involving substances like chemicals, proteins, drugs and other materials. Figure 1 shows one representative example of the wet lab protocols. In this shared task, the data was divided into three parts, training data with 370 protocols, development data with 122 protocols and test data with 123 protocols. The data was given in CoNLL format. To sum up, this was a small dataset in

Proceedings of the 2020 EMNLP Workshop W-NUT: The Sixth Workshop on Noisy User-generated Text, pages 299–304
Online, Nov 19, 2020. ©2020 Association for Computational Linguistics

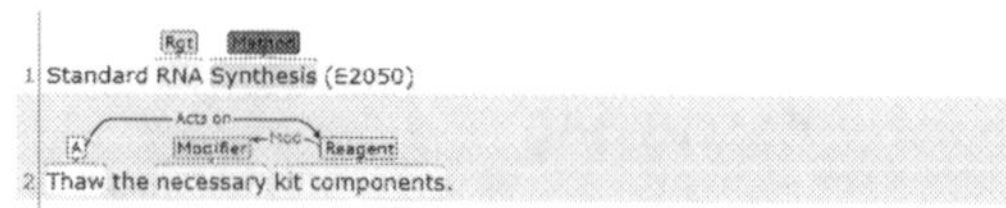

Figure 2: A visualization of the BRAT style annotation

	Type	Example
1	Method	Extraction
2	Modifier	High Quality Genomic
3	Reagent	DNA
4	Action	dissect
5	Amount	1-10mg
6	Device	Flow Cytometer
7	Time	5 minutes
8	Speed	350xg
9	Mention	ethanol wash
10	Location	tube
11	Numerical	10 times
12	Temperature	60C
13	Size	0.45m
14	Concentration	4%
15	Measure-Type	volume
16	Generic-Measure	TFSC=40
17	Seal	bottle cap
18	pH	pH 8.0

Table 1: Named entity types in WNUT 2020 shared task-1

size, and specialized in laboratory settings. The dataset is annotated by the researchers in Ohio State University (Kulkarni et al., 2018) with BRAT (Stenetorp et al., 2012). It could be visualized via `http://bit.ly/WNUT2020platform`. Figure 2 shows a visualization result of the protocol 3 in our training dataset. And there are 18 kinds of entities as shown in table 1.

In order to facilitate narration and comparison, we merged all the files of *test* provided into one during training and verification, and separated and saved the prediction results of corresponding files by using dictionary when submitting verification.

3 Model

3.1 Baseline

The provided baseline model is a linear conditional random field (CRF) tagger, which is one of the traditional machine learning ways to complete the named entity recognition task (Finkel et al., 2005). This tagger does the NER task with feature engineering, taking word features, context features and gazatteer features into consideration.

3.2 BiLSTM CRF

BiLSTM CRF is a deep learning oriented tagger to complete the NER task (Huang et al., 2015). The long-short term memory (LSTM) unit (Hochreiter and Schmidhuber, 1997) is a kind of specifically designed recurrent neural network (RNN) to process the timing sequential information. Here, LSTM units are adopted to collect the information in the context. Additionally, they are bidirectional so that they can take information from both sides into consideration.

One more CRF layer is added into this model because it will help the model to standardizing output results. For example, a sequence like "B-Action I-Mention" will never be possible in real world. However, a pure BiLSTM model is possibly giving this kind of errors.

The basic architecture of **BiLSTM CRF** is shown in figure 3.

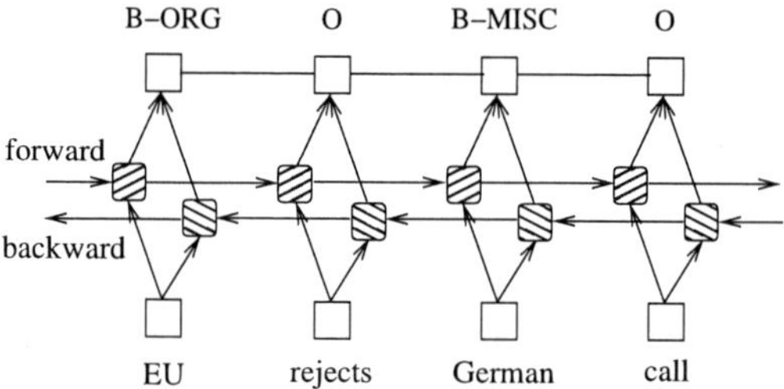

Figure 3: The architecture of a BiLSTM CRF model (Huang et al., 2015)

3.3 Bert

Bidirectional encoder representations from transformers (Bert) was first proposed by Google AI researchers in 2018 (Devlin et al., 2018). It achieved quite a few new records in NLP field and the concept of "pre-training" has been popular since then.

In this shared task, we also adopted Bert pre-training model to do the NER task and to compare the results with **BiLSTM CRF** to explore the performance of different techniques.

Our **Bert case** adopted *BertforTokenClassification* class in *transformers* (Wolf et al., 2019) and added one more fine-tuning layer to complete the task. The architecture is shown in the following figure 4.

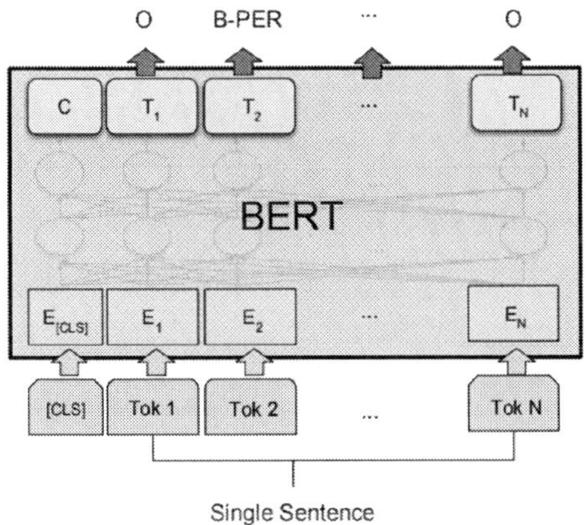

Figure 4: Bert fine-tuning for token classification (Devlin et al., 2018)

4 Experiment

In this shared task, we tried to compare the relatively traditional deep learning method, **BiLSTM CRF**, and pre-training Bert based, including Bert base cased model and Bert base uncased model. The former needs to train static word vector from dataset, while the latter is equivalent to using dynamic word vector and we can directly conduct fine-tuning experiments on NER by connecting *BertforTokenClassification* after pre-training model. It can be seen that from table 2 that the performance of **BiLSTM CRF** without careful training of word vector is not as good as the baseline model provided, **Linear CRF**. Therefore, our follow-up experiments will focus on training Bert in different situations and carry out exploration and discussion.

	precision	recall	F1
Linear CRF	0.7549	0.7332	0.7439
BiLSTM CRF	0.7208	0.6605	0.7101

Table 2: Results of **BiLSTM CRF** and baseline

4.1 Stipulate

For the sake of simplicity, we will use wd and η represent weight decay and learning rate respectively and **cased/uncased with/without** to abbreviate the corresponding model with lowercase processing or not in subsequent trials. In addition, v means importing the required classes like *BertModel* from *pytorch-transformers*, and V means importing from *transformers*, and classes are imported from the lat-

ter by default. In general, the precision and recall of the model are considered comprehensively in f1-score, so the performance of the model is often evaluated using f1-score (micro avg). And the numbers underlined in the chart represent possible anomalies, while the numbers highlighted in bold represent the best results.

The model doesn't converge when it's trained only once, but it may face problems of over fitting and CUDA out of memory if it is more than 4, for only 8G memory in RTX 2060 Super and RTX 2080. After several trials, 3 is selected as the optimal default epoch number. For alleviating over fitting, weight decay technique (or L2 regularization) is usually adopted and wd is empirically set between 0.001 and 0.01. If there is no special explanation, the default value of weight decay value in this paper is 0.005.

4.2 Train

4.2.1 Learning Rate

Named entity recognition is one of downstream tasks of Bert. Since it has been trained on a large scale corpus, the recommended learning rate is generally small, such as $2e-5, 3e-5, 5e-5$ (Devlin et al., 2018). But this needs to be considering with the specific application scenarios. By using the default Bert model: **cased without** and **uncased with**, we trained on both 2060s and 2080 with different learning rates.

As shown in table 3, all recommended learning rates did not perform well in this task, and we thought that the dataset provided this time are not common in daily life, so we were ought to increase the learning rate appropriately. At the same time, we noticed that the uncased model is better than the cased model on 2060s, but it is opposite in 2080. Although the best model is obtained by training on 2080, the model training on 2060s is more stable.

4.2.2 Case Sensitivity and Version

Generally speaking, the uncased model is better than the cased model, however, the cased model performs better when there are obvious case differences in specific aspects such as named entity recognition. But we also noticed that we could train an uncased model after processing the text in lowercase.

During testing, we also found that different versions of classes imported will lead to differing results. To better explore the influence of case sensitivity and version, we further trained three pos-

	learning rate	2e-5	3e-5	5e-5	8e-5	9e-5	1e-4	2e-4	3e-4	4e-4	5e-4
2060s	**cased without**	0.7776	0.7848	0.7909	0.7949	0.7961	0.7965	**0.7980**	0.7963	0.7956	0.7911
	uncased with	0.7797	0.7900	0.7974	0.7987	**0.7993**	**0.7993**	0.7972	0.7968	0.7970	0.7928
2080	**cased without**	0.7775	0.7844	0.7907	0.7951	0.7973	0.7994	**0.8008**	0.7946	0.7917	0.7876
	uncased with	0.7775	0.7881	0.7948	0.7974	0.7956	0.7962	**0.7988**	0.7948	0.7974	0.7903

Table 3: Bert case default model performances at differing learning rates

sible casing methods, including: **cased without**, **cased with** and **uncased with** (by the way, **uncased without** should perform the worst, because it can't actually distinguish case information, and the experimental results are exactly the same, so we omit this possible combination) and two different versions of the combination model. Record the performance of each model and take the top two to get table 4.

Except for some models with slight performance decrease, in most cases, the model can be further improved by using *pytorch-transformers* to import the required classes. Moreover, we noticed that **uncased with** is the best model on both 2060s and 2080 when considering the use of previous versions of classes (**uncased with** *V*), however, when only the latest version of *transformers* is used, the cased model works best. But the relationship between whether to use lowercase processing and the final performance is not obvious from our experiments.

Theoretically, words with different case could represent the same named entity, while using lowercase processing can increase the number of training samples but reduce the number of types. So we suggest that when using the updated *transformers* training, please use **cased without**, and when using the previous version training, consider using **uncased with**. What's more, **cased with** is also an option worth considering.

4.2.3 Weight Decay

We used 0.005 as our default weight decay value before, which based on several simple attempts. Here, we selected the best four models on 2060s and 2080 respectively to adjust the weight decay under the condition of using previous version classes or not, and sorted them out as figure 5.

In theory, the increase of weight decay will make the performance of the model increase to the maximum firstly and then decrease. This is because at the beginning, the model performs poorly in the test set due to over fitting. With the increase of penalty term, the performance of the model is improved and the best value is generated. If the penalty term continues to increase, the model will tend to be more simple model, so the performance of the model drops. However, the actual situation in the evaluation is that the performance of the model firstly increases and then decreases with the increase of weight decay, and then increases to the maximum value and then decreases according to the theory. It is worth noting that the f1-score of **case without** when weight decay value is 0.009 is the same as that is 0.005, which is difficult to explain according to the classical theory (more specifically, the recall of the former is higher, but the precision of the latter is higher). Though it's true that the best performance of most models is achieved at 0.005, the final selected model in this experiment is **uncased with** *V* on 2080 when the weight decay value is 0.007. The specific index comparison table between this Base case model and baseline is shown in table 5.

Bert case based on Transformer has achieved better results in the recognition of most entity categories than **Linear CRF** combined with traditional feature engineering. It can be seen that using a large corpus for pre-training combined with specific downstream task fine-tuning strategies is a very effective and operational model paradigm. However, for the output results of **Bert case** without CRF standardizing, we could find that many unreasonable annotation results are generated in the test set, and on some indicators, the model does not perform as well as the baseline, especially in the prediction results on Temperature and Measure. All in all, Bert can be used as a relatively good benchmark, but there is still much room for improvement. We planned to replace it with other pre-trained models such as Roberta, Albert, XLNet, and connected it with CRF to observe the effect of the experiment, but it finally failed to achieve due to limited time and capacity.

4.3 Test

The classification results of each group participating in this task can be accessed from results. As the

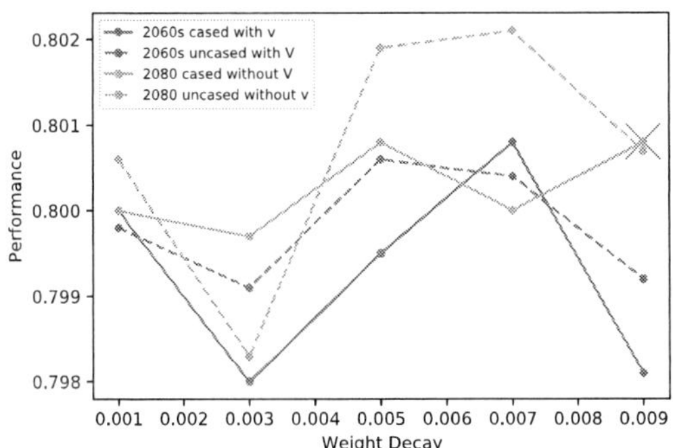

Figure 5: The tendency comparisons under different weight decay and experimental conditions

		cased without		uncased with		cased with	
transformers	2080	0.8008	0.7994	0.7988	0.7974	0.7979	0.7956
	2060s	0.7980	0.7965	0.7993	0.7993	0.7995	0.7960
pytorch-transformers	2080	0.8004	0.7997	0.8019	0.7992	0.7975	0.7975
	2060s	0.7990	0.7982	0.8006	0.7994	0.7993	0.7997
avg		+0.03%	+0.12%	+0.28%	+0.11%	-0.03%	+0.35%

Table 4: The performance change under different versions and case sensitivity

final test model was submitted before, it could not be trained from aspects proposed in this paper, and the model could only be trained on RTX 2060 Super, so the final model is **uncased with** with lower f1-score. In addition to these influencing factors shown above, we also noted that on different operating systems (Ubuntu and Windows), whether or not to enable X service and perform other tasks during training may also change the performance of the model with the same other conditions. However, due to its complexity, we have not got the results temporarily and we hope further research could carry on in the future.

5 Conclusion

This article introduces our relevant experimental research based on this WNUT 2020 shared task-1. By trying **BiLSTM CRF**, we learn about that the method based on static word vector needs to be trained on a specific dataset, so its transferability is relatively low. And we mainly focused on the fine-tuning experiments based on Bert under different conditions, including learning rate, GPU, *transformers* version, case sensitivity and weight decay, and conducted discussions, so as to understand that the possible influencing factors in actual model training. It is quite necessary to unify and clarify experimental conditions while evaluating

	Linear CRF			Bert case		
	precision	recall	F1	precision	recall	F1
Action	0.8456	0.8423	0.8440	0.8889	0.9179	0.9031
Amount	0.8521	0.8319	0.8419	0.8798	0.9078	0.8936
Concentration	0.7770	0.7929	0.7849	0.8230	0.8659	0.8439
Device	0.6125	0.5629	0.5867	0.6455	0.6966	0.6701
Measure	0.3600	0.2553	0.2988	0.3119	0.2378	0.2698
Location	0.6883	0.6951	0.6917	0.7525	0.7882	0.7700
Type	0.5164	0.4649	0.4893	0.4713	0.5735	0.5174
Mention	0.5965	0.6071	0.6018	0.6567	0.7857	0.7154
Method	0.5069	0.3830	0.4363	0.5080	0.4914	0.4996
Modifier	0.5682	0.5134	0.5394	0.5968	0.6140	0.6053
Numerical	0.5636	0.5758	0.5696	0.6000	0.6623	0.6296
Reagent	0.7475	0.7522	0.7498	0.8161	0.8412	0.8284
Seal	0.6825	0.6719	0.6772	0.6712	0.7656	0.7153
Size	0.6667	0.5000	0.5714	0.7805	0.5614	0.6531
Speed	0.8421	0.8675	0.8546	0.8908	0.9281	0.9091
Temperature	0.9385	0.8975	0.9176	0.9130	0.9079	0.9105
Time	0.8969	0.8762	0.8864	0.8857	0.9080	0.8967
pH	0.7255	0.5968	0.6549	0.7273	0.7742	0.7500
avg	0.7549	0.7332	0.7439	0.7897	0.8148	0.8021

Table 5: Comparison of classification results between **Bert case** and **Linear CRF**

the performance of related models in the future, because even the class imported matters.

We noted that recently, several papers presented NER studies using convolutional neural network (CNN) (Li and Guo, 2018; Zhai et al., 2018). This may imply that more work combining pre-trained model and CNN will be a new direction for NER studies. Additionally, although more and more attention has been focused on deep learning nowadays, the methods based on traditional machine learning still get attention and continue to develop with its interpretability and robustness in specific domain tasks.

References

Jacob Devlin, Ming Wei Chang, Kenton Lee, and Kristina Toutanova. 2018. Bert: Pre-training of deep bidirectional transformers for language understanding.

Jenny Rose Finkel, Trond Grenager, and Christopher Manning. 2005. Incorporating non-local information into information extraction systems by gibbs sampling. In *Proceedings of the 43rd Annual Meeting on Association for Computational Linguistics*, ACL '05, page 363–370, USA. Association for Computational Linguistics.

Sepp Hochreiter and JüRgen A Schmidhuber. 1997. Long short-term memory. *Neural Computation*.

Zhiheng Huang, Wei Xu, and Kai Yu. 2015. Bidirectional lstm-crf models for sequence tagging. *arXiv: Computation and Language*.

K. Humphreys, R. Gaizauskas, S. Azzam, C. Huyck, and Y. Wilks. 1995. *University of Sheffield: Descrip-*

tion of the LaSIE-II system as used for MUC-7. Association for Computational Linguistics.

Chaitanya Kulkarni, Wei Xu, Alan Ritter, and Raghu Machiraju. 2018. An annotated corpus for machine reading of instructions in wet lab protocols. 2:97–106.

SL Li and YK Guo. 2018. Biomedical named entity recognition with cnn-blstm-crf [j]. *Journal of chinese information processing*, 32(1):116–122.

Lisa F Rau. 1991. Extracting company names from text. In *Proceedings The Seventh IEEE Conference on Artificial Intelligence Application*, pages 29–30. IEEE Computer Society.

Pontus Stenetorp, Sampo Pyysalo, Goran Topic, Tomoko Ohta, Sophia Ananiadou, and Junichi Tsujii. 2012. brat: a web-based tool for nlp-assisted text annotation. pages 102–107.

Jeniya Tabassum, Wei Xu, and Alan Ritter. 2020. WNUT-2020 Task 1: Extracting Entities and Relations from Wet Lab Protocols. In *Proceedings of EMNLP 2020 Workshop on Noisy User-generated Text (WNUT)*.

Thomas Wolf, Lysandre Debut, Victor Sanh, Julien Chaumond, Clement Delangue, Anthony Moi, Pierric Cistac, Tim Rault, Rémi Louf, and Morgan and Funtowicz. 2019. Huggingface's transformers: State-of-the-art natural language processing.

Zenan Zhai, Dat Quoc Nguyen, and Karin Verspoor. 2018. Comparing cnn and lstm character-level embeddings in bilstm-crf models for chemical and disease named entity recognition. *arXiv preprint arXiv:1808.08450*.

BiTeM at WNUT 2020 Shared Task-1: Named Entity Recognition over Wet Lab Protocols using an Ensemble of Contextual Language Models

Julien Knafou[1,2,3], Nona Naderi[1,2], Jenny Copara[1,2,3], Douglas Teodoro[1,2], and Patrick Ruch[1,2]

Emails : {firstname.lastname}@hesge.ch
[1]University of Applied Sciences and Arts of Western Switzerland
[2]Swiss Institute of Bioinformatics, Geneva, Switzerland
[3]University of Geneva, Switzerland

Abstract

Recent improvements in machine-reading technologies attracted much attention to automation problems and their possibilities. In this context, WNUT 2020 introduces a Name Entity Recognition (NER) task based on wet laboratory procedures. In this paper, we present a 3-step method based on deep neural language models that reported the best overall exact match F_1-score (77.99%) of the competition. By fine-tuning 10 times, 10 different pretrained language models, this work shows the advantage of having more models in an ensemble based on a majority of votes strategy. On top of that, having 100 different models allowed us to analyse the combinations of ensemble that demonstrated the impact of having multiple pretrained models versus fine-tuning a pretrained model multiple times.

1 Introduction

The last decades have seen both the amount and the complexity of biological experiments grow. Coupling this phenomenon with the improvement in machine-reading technologies seem to have led researchers to look for ways to automate wet laboratory procedures. Such technologies should allow reproducibility while reducing human errors in the process. However, as current protocols are usually written in a natural language, a collection of wet laboratory protocols annotated with entities and relations would help assess current machine-reading performances in this specific setting (Kulkarni et al., 2018).

In this context, WNUT (Workshop on Noisy User-generated Text[1]) 2020 (Tabassum et al., 2020) proposes two tasks, a Named Entity Recognition (NER) task and a Relation Extraction (RE) task. In this paper, we present a 3-step method we used for the NER task. Our approach is essentially

based on a deep neural language models supported by transformer-like architectures (Vaswani et al., 2017). First, we fine-tuned 10 different pretrained language models on the downstream task. Then, we generated 10 instances of those pretrained models, each time with a new random initialization of the last layer, namely the classifier. Finally, we used an ensemble strategy based on a majority of votes. Our approach achieves the exact-match F_1-score of 77.99% that ranks first in the shared task.

2 Related work

Deep learning approaches trained on large unstructured data have shown considerable success in NLP problems, including NER (Devlin et al., 2019; Liu et al., 2019; Lample et al., 2016; Beltagy et al., 2019; Jin et al., 2019). These models use the learned representations over the large data and reuse them in a supervised setting for a downstream task. For domain-specific tasks, the models that are trained on large general text can be further trained on domain specific large data and then adapted for a downstream task (Lee et al., 2019; Gururangan et al., 2020; Alsentzer et al., 2019) or the models can be trained only on domain-specific data and then adapted for a specific task (Beltagy et al., 2019).

3 Data

The data provided for this task is a subset of Kulkarni *et al.*'s corpus (Kulkarni et al., 2018). The dataset consists of 615 unique protocols annotated with 17 types of entities and *action* (an example is shown in Figure 1).

The organizers provided a set of protocols for training, development, and test. They further released a final set of unlabelled protocols for test during the competition (called test 2020). Table 1 shows the way the dataset has been split into a

---

[1]`http://noisy-text.github.io/2020/wlp-task.html`

Proceedings of the 2020 EMNLP Workshop W-NUT: The Sixth Workshop on Noisy User-generated Text, pages 305–313
Online, Nov 19, 2020. ©2020 Association for Computational Linguistics

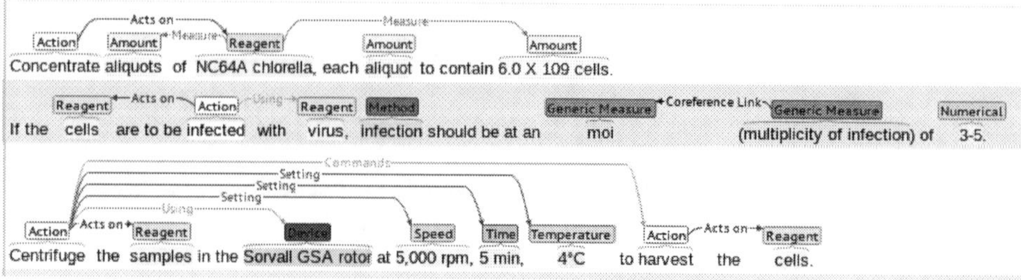

Figure 1: An example of the data.

Split	# of protocols
Train	370
Dev	123
Test	123
Test 2020	111
Total	727

Table 1: Number of protocols in WNUT-NER dataset.

Entity	Train		Dev		Test		Test 2020	
	Count	%	Count	%	Count	%	Count	%
Action	12,355	25.91	4,011	25.49	4,138	25.32	5,346	23.04
Amount	3,432	7.20	1,090	6.93	1,190	7.28	1,223	5.27
Concentration	1,330	2.79	422	2.68	535	3.27	701	3.02
Device	1,752	3.67	616	3.92	468	2.86	888	3.83
Generic-Measure	484	1.02	132	0.84	143	0.87	173	0.75
Location	3,921	8.23	1,396	8.87	1,326	8.11	1,657	7.14
Measure-Type	857	1.79	324	2.06	272	1.66	720	3.10
Mention	257	0.54	83	0.53	56	0.34	142	0.61
Method	1,597	3.36	538	3.43	581	3.56	1,059	4.56
Modifier	4,588	9.62	1,547	9.83	1,601	9.79	3,416	14.72
Numerical	832	1.75	259	1.65	231	1.41	513	2.21
Reagent	11,121	23.33	3,594	22.93	3,995	24.44	5,012	21.60
Seal	210	0.44	92	0.58	64	0.39	119	0.51
Size	262	0.55	123	0.78	113	0.69	232	1.00
Speed	626	1.31	239	1.52	167	1.02	238	1.03
Temperature	1,592	3.34	486	3.09	532	3.25	744	3.21
Time	2,396	5.02	745	4.74	870	5.32	951	4.10
pH	67	0.14	37	0.23	62	0.38	66	0.28
Total	47,679		15,734		16,344		23,200	

Table 2: Entity distribution across the dataset (based on the Standoff format).

training set, a development set,[2] a test set, and the competition test (test 2020).

In Table 2, we see the distribution of all the entities by each subset. As we can see, we have 18 entities and only two of them (*Action* and *Reagent*) represent about 50% of annotations. This table also shows us that entities' proportions are fairly similar across all the subsets.

4 Method

Our models essentially focused on transformers-like (Vaswani et al., 2017) language models that we fine-tuned on the NER task by adding a fully

connected layer on top of the token representations. The models include BERT (cased) (Devlin et al., 2019), BioBERT (BERT trained on PubMed abstracts and PMC full-text articles) (Lee et al., 2019), Bio+ClinicalBERT (BioBERT trained on notes in the MIMIC-III v1.4 database) (Alsentzer et al., 2019), PubMedBERT (Gu et al., 2020), RoBERTa (Liu et al., 2019), BioMed RoBERTa (Gururangan et al., 2020), and XLNet (Yang et al., 2019).

Our method has been driven in 3 steps. First, we chose 10 different pretrained models and fine-tuned them on the downstream task. Then, using a voting strategy, we created ensemble models. Finally, we fine-tuned 9 more times each model, each time with a new random initialization of the fully connected layer, to see if sampling ensemble models from this set of models would improve the results even more.

4.1 Transformers with a fully connected layer on top of the token representations

In order to use transformers as a NER model, the only preprocessing we had to do was to break each protocol into sentences. Those sentences will then be the sequences that are fed into our model. As there were no overlapping entities in the text, we used a $softmax$ function which allowed us to classify each token to only one entity.

As transformers usually use tokenizers that work on word bits (or sub-tokens), we had to deal with it by assigning a dummy entity to each sub-token that was part of a word. In such cases, at training time, we only assign the true entity to the first sub-token. This allowed us to build back the original text quite easily. Indeed, during prediction, a word will get the highest probable entity label among all the sub-tokens' predictions of that word. In other words, the highest probable entity label will be assigned to all the sub-tokens of the word and the sub-tokens will be merged to build back the original word with the respective assigned label. Finally, in a given

---

[2]Protocol 621 (in the development set) is a duplicate of protocol 570 (in the train set), but their labels do not totally match.

Pretrained Models		Corpus type	# Parameters
BERT (Devlin et al., 2019)	base large	General	110M 340M
BioBERT (Lee et al., 2019)		Bio	110M
Bio+ClinicalBERT (Alsentzer et al., 2019)		Bio	110M
PubMedBERT (Gu et al., 2020)		Bio	110M
RoBERTa (Liu et al., 2019)	base large	General	110M 340M
BioMed RoBERTa (Gururangan et al., 2020)		Bio	110M
XLNet (Yang et al., 2019)	base large	General	110M 340M

Table 3: Pretrained models features

sequence, if two adjacent words were given the same entity prediction, we would consider the two words as a passage related to that entity.

Using the above setup, we fine-tuned 10 pretrained transformers for 10 epochs using an Adam optimizer (Kingma and Ba, 2014), a learning rate of $3e^{-5}$, a batch size of 24 and a maximum sequence length of 256 tokens. We used 1x T4 GPU for all base models and 2x T4 GPUs for the large ones. For a given model, it took in average roughly 16 minutes per epoch to train, thus about 2.67 hours for the 10 epochs. After each epoch, we predicted the development set, computed the F_1-score and saved the model if it improved the previous epoch score. Table 3 shows more information about all the pretrained models that we fine-tuned on the NER task. Indeed, 4 models out of 10 were trained on Biomedical corpus, such as PubMed and/or BioMed whereas the others were trained on general corpora, such as Wikipedia. Another key difference is the model type which defines the way a given model has been trained. This includes the training task (e.g., MLM, next sentence prediction, . . .), the tokenizer algorithm, the optimizer and more. We used 5 different kinds of BERT-based, 3 of RoBERTa-based and 2 of XLNet-based models. For more details regarding the specifics of the architectures, please refer directly to their respective papers.

4.2 An ensemble based on a voting strategy

As implemented in (Copara et al., 2020b,a), our ensemble model strategy is based on a majority of votes. This means that for a given ensemble model composition, each composing model has the right to vote. In other words, for a given protocol and a given sequence, each model will return its predictions which can be interpreted as passage/entity combinations. Once we collected all models' predictions, we then counted all the passage/entity combinations and validated only those that had cast a majority of votes.

4.3 Sampling

Once we had all the models trained and ready, we were wondering if we could improve efficiency by adding more voters. The idea is to repeat the first step where each time we have a new random initialization on the fully connected layer. We ended up with 100 different models, corresponding to 10 different pretrained models fine-tuned 10 times.

With only a few models to choose from, we would have been able to predict all the possible model compositions; however, as using 50 models out of 100 would have resulted in about 10^{29} possible ensembles, we had to sample randomly ensemble model compositions. For each number of models taken into account in a given ensemble, we took a sample size of 1000 combinations. This will later allow us to show the results distribution of our ensemble models and examine how it will behave in certain circumstances.

The ensemble model we chose to use for the submission was the one that gave us the best F_1-score on the test set. It is a composition of 14 models that were fine-tuned on the task. It contained the following pretrained models: $2\times$ BioBERT (BioBERT models with two different random initializations or seeds), $2\times$ BioClinicalBERT (2 random seeds), $3\times$ PubMedBERT (3 random seeds), $2\times$ RoBERTa$_{base}$ (2 random seeds), $1\times$ RoBERTa$_{large}$ $1\times$ BioMed RoBERTa and $3\times$ XLNet$_{large}$ (3 random seeds).

5   Results and Discussions

In Table 4, we see the F_1-score for all the 10 models we fine-tuned across all the 18 entities. The reported baseline is the CRF baseline[3] that was provided for the shared task. First, we can see that the ensemble model outperforms the baseline by far. When comparing all the models (ensemble apart), we also notice that PubMedBERT is quite consistent as it often outperforms all the other models, including the ensemble for a few entities, namely *Mention*, *Seal*, *Temperature* and *pH*. Additionally, when compared to its peers, it clearly shows the best micro and macro F_1-scores.

However, when looking at *Speed*, it seems that the transformers-based models we used are not able to do a better job than the baseline. A closer look at the errors should be done in order to see what caused such a difference with the baseline (see Section 5.4).

---

[3] https://github.com/jeniyat/WNUT_2020_NER/tree/master/code/baseline_CRF

Entity	BERT (cased)		BioClinical BERT	BioBERT	RoBERTa		BioMed RoBERTa	PubMed BERT	XLNet		Ensemble	Baseline
	base	*large*			*base*	*large*			*base*	*large*		
Action	$88.98_{0.2}$	$88.51_{0.2}$	$88.87_{0.2}$	$89.06_{0.2}$	$88.78_{0.3}$	$88.75_{0.2}$	$88.70_{0.2}$	$89.29_{0.3}$	$89.32_{0.1}$	$89.11_{0.3}$	**90.00** (0.68↑)	84.40
Amount	$85.73_{0.2}$	$85.14_{0.3}$	$85.21_{0.4}$	$85.96_{0.5}$	$85.59_{0.3}$	$85.53_{0.7}$	$85.99_{0.4}$	$85.66_{0.2}$	$85.00_{0.3}$	$84.47_{0.6}$	**86.41** (0.42↑)	84.19
Concentration	$82.61_{0.7}$	$81.83_{0.7}$	$82.31_{0.6}$	$83.14_{0.4}$	$82.68_{0.5}$	$82.14_{1.0}$	$83.34_{0.5}$	$83.81_{0.4}$	$82.25_{0.7}$	$82.40_{1.1}$	**84.64** (0.83↑)	78.49
Device	$62.96_{1.1}$	$62.18_{0.8}$	$63.57_{0.6}$	$64.24_{1.2}$	$63.39_{0.8}$	$64.21_{1.0}$	$63.44_{0.9}$	$64.17_{1.0}$	$63.27_{0.9}$	$63.65_{1.2}$	**67.11** (2.87↑)	58.67
Generic-Measure	$30.44_{1.6}$	$29.73_{1.9}$	$26.37_{1.8}$	$30.40_{1.7}$	$32.12_{1.1}$	$32.23_{2.0}$	$30.54_{1.7}$	$31.57_{1.8}$	$30.33_{1.3}$	$31.10_{2.1}$	**33.17** (0.94↑)	29.88
Location	$75.53_{0.4}$	$75.05_{0.4}$	$75.54_{0.3}$	$76.06_{0.7}$	$75.85_{0.5}$	$76.10_{0.6}$	$75.32_{0.6}$	$76.24_{0.3}$	$75.62_{0.3}$	$75.53_{1.0}$	**77.50** (1.26↑)	69.17
Measure-Type	$52.75_{1.4}$	$53.32_{1.4}$	$52.42_{1.7}$	$54.23_{1.1}$	$53.89_{1.6}$	$52.62_{1.1}$	$53.61_{0.9}$	$52.47_{0.6}$	$54.61_{1.3}$	$55.35_{2.0}$	**55.36** (0.01↑)	48.93
Mention	$71.00_{3.0}$	$67.15_{2.5}$	$68.40_{1.9}$	$68.18_{1.7}$	$68.70_{1.0}$	$70.35_{2.2}$	$68.44_{2.1}$	$\mathbf{72.35}_{0.9}$	$68.66_{2.8}$	$63.02_{11.1}$	71.79 (0.56↓)	60.18
Method	$48.70_{1.3}$	$48.40_{1.0}$	$47.22_{0.8}$	$47.01_{1.3}$	$49.64_{1.6}$	$48.86_{1.1}$	$47.85_{1.5}$	$47.58_{1.9}$	$49.89_{1.4}$	$49.89_{1.0}$	**53.19** (3.30↑)	43.63
Modifier	$58.83_{0.8}$	$57.93_{0.7}$	$58.80_{0.6}$	$59.07_{0.6}$	$58.68_{0.8}$	$59.56_{0.8}$	$58.45_{0.6}$	$59.72_{0.6}$	$59.47_{0.6}$	$58.44_{1.2}$	**60.27** (0.55↑)	53.94
Numerical	$62.56_{3.6}$	$64.73_{2.2}$	$63.10_{2.7}$	$61.40_{4.5}$	$59.88_{2.6}$	$62.51_{3.2}$	$61.53_{2.7}$	$64.83_{4.0}$	$63.41_{3.8}$	$63.05_{3.7}$	**66.98** (2.15↑)	56.96
Reagent	$80.38_{0.2}$	$80.34_{0.3}$	$80.60_{0.2}$	$80.94_{0.2}$	$80.51_{0.3}$	$80.84_{0.2}$	$80.35_{0.2}$	$81.24_{0.3}$	$81.19_{0.1}$	$80.68_{0.3}$	**82.59** (1.35↑)	74.98
Seal	$65.56_{5.1}$	$59.90_{1.9}$	$62.46_{2.7}$	$63.07_{2.6}$	$64.13_{2.8}$	$66.42_{3.4}$	$63.95_{2.7}$	$\mathbf{69.51}_{3.9}$	$62.65_{3.3}$	$62.83_{3.7}$	69.42 (0.09↓)	67.72
Size	$58.36_{1.8}$	$60.16_{0.9}$	$60.07_{1.8}$	$61.65_{1.5}$	$59.79_{1.8}$	$56.47_{2.1}$	$59.30_{2.1}$	$62.48_{2.1}$	$61.12_{1.3}$	$59.63_{3.0}$	**62.56** (0.08↑)	57.14
Speed	$83.92_{0.8}$	$83.64_{1.0}$	$82.21_{0.8}$	$83.06_{0.8}$	$84.71_{0.7}$	$83.67_{1.0}$	$84.33_{0.6}$	$84.13_{1.0}$	$84.45_{0.7}$	$83.43_{2.3}$	84.24 (0.47↓)	**85.46**
Temperature	$91.47_{0.5}$	$90.20_{0.6}$	$91.36_{0.5}$	$90.84_{0.8}$	$91.32_{0.6}$	$90.70_{0.6}$	$91.39_{0.7}$	$\mathbf{92.20}_{0.5}$	$91.49_{0.5}$	$90.20_{1.4}$	92.11 (0.09↓)	91.76
Time	$88.75_{0.3}$	$88.92_{0.7}$	$88.78_{0.4}$	$88.85_{0.5}$	$88.70_{0.6}$	$89.02_{0.7}$	$89.28_{0.4}$	$88.49_{0.6}$	$88.87_{0.4}$	$88.20_{1.5}$	**89.49** (0.21↑)	88.64
pH	$72.56_{2.3}$	$67.07_{3.0}$	$72.47_{1.4}$	$72.41_{2.3}$	$71.27_{2.8}$	$66.78_{2.2}$	$72.50_{4.1}$	$\mathbf{78.04}_{1.7}$	$69.35_{2.8}$	$70.77_{2.9}$	77.59 (0.45↓)	65.49
micro F_1-score	$78.38_{0.2}$	$77.94_{0.2}$	$78.27_{0.1}$	$78.56_{0.2}$	$78.42_{0.2}$	$78.52_{0.2}$	$78.31_{0.1}$	$79.00_{0.2}$	$78.76_{0.1}$	$78.34_{0.3}$	**80.42** (1.42↑)	74.39
macro F_1-score	$70.06_{0.7}$	$69.12_{0.3}$	$69.43_{0.3}$	$69.98_{0.5}$	$69.98_{0.4}$	$69.82_{0.3}$	$69.91_{0.3}$	$71.32_{0.3}$	$70.05_{0.4}$	$69.54_{0.8}$	**72.47** (1.15↑)	66.65

Table 4: F_1-score by model on the test set. We reported averages across the 10 random seeds for all the pretrained model results, for those, subscripts represents the standard deviations. The improvements of the ensemble model over the best performing transformer model is shown in parentheses in the ensemble column.

When comparing the micro to the macro F_1-score standard deviations across all the models, we can see that the macro F_1-score standard deviations are systematically higher. This is probably due to the fact that some entities, namely *Generic-Measure*, *Mention*, *Seal*, *Size* and *pH*, which account for less than 1% of the test set each (see Table 2), seem to have a relatively high F_1-score standard deviations level. The same applies to *Measure-Type*, *Numerical* and *Speed* that are less than 2% of the test set each. This is in line with the results reported by Dodge et al. (2020) which shows that results can vary a lot across the seeds when a small amount of data is available. Indeed, as these entities are quite rare, a simple misclassification can have a high impact on the macro F_1-score. That being said, the micro F_1-scores seem relatively stable across all the pretrained models.

5.1 Ensemble results analysis

In this section, we will try to analyse the results we observe when sampling on different ensemble model compositions. These results are exclusively computed on the test set. The idea behind this experiment is to try to understand the behaviour of some metrics when adding more models.

Figures 2 to 4 show the F_1-score, the recall and precision distributions with respect to the number of models taken in a given ensemble, respectively.

The first thing we notice from Figures 2 to 4 is that the more the number of models taken into account in an ensemble grows, the more the metrics variance tends to be smaller and steadier.

When looking at Figure 3 and 4, we clearly see that odd number of voters has a positive impact on

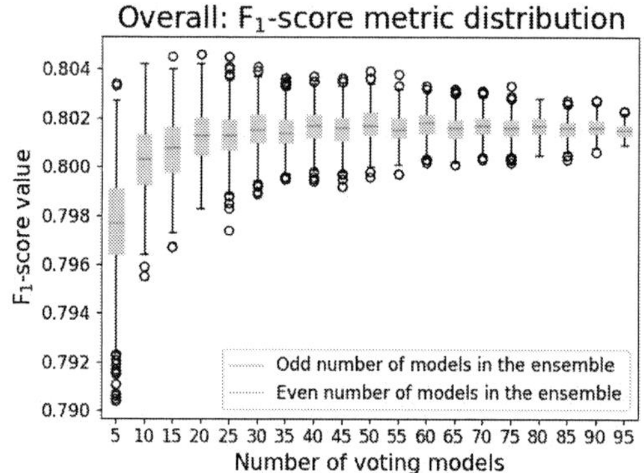

Figure 2: Micro F_1-score distribution by number of models used in an ensemble (sample size of 1000) on the test set.

the recall while it looks like it has a negative impact on the precision. For the moment, this is unclear to us why this behaviour can be observed; however, we think it could be linked to the majority rule we introduced in our voting strategy where majority is easier to reach in an odd system. When looking closely at Figure 2, it appears that the "odd/even number effect" tends to cancel out when the number of voters increases and even number of voter getting slightly better results.

In Figure 3, there is clearly a positive slope that seems to flatten at the end, which means that the more models we have in our ensemble, the higher recall we should expect. Conversely, this trend doesn't seem that clear for precision (Figure 4) where it looks like we have a positive relation with odd numbers of voters, a negative one with even number of voters which at the end seem to converge

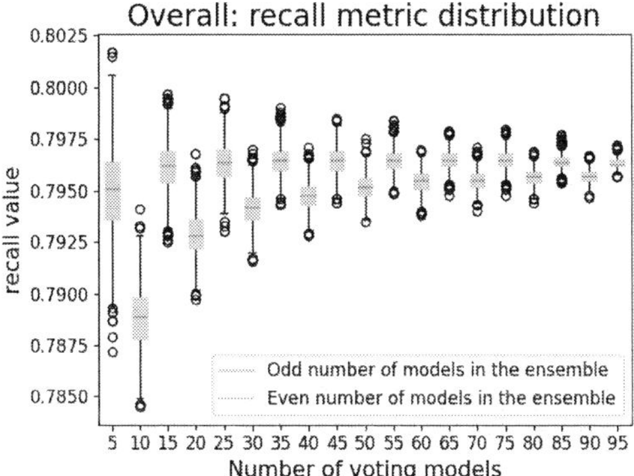

Figure 3: Micro recall distribution by number of models used in an ensemble (sample size of 1000) on the test set.

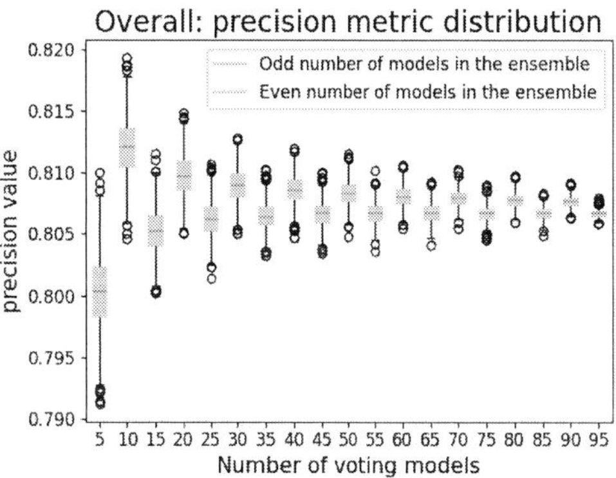

Figure 4: Micro precision distribution by number of models used in an ensemble (sample size of 1000) on the test set.

into a flat trend for both of them. However, in both figures, as already mentioned, the variance of their respective metrics seems to get steadier and smaller when adding more models in the ensemble composition.

Figures 6 to 8 show the same metrics while trying to isolate the effect of adding a new pretrained model versus the effect of adding an already taken pretrained model with a new random fully connected layer initialization.

In order to understand the setting of this experiment, we first build a matrix (see Figure 5) where each column is a pretrained model and each row is a fine-tuned version of it. We then compare the performances of ensemble models based on combinations of columns to those of the ensemble models based on combinations of rows. In Figures 6 to 8, the x−axis represents the number of row or columns taken into account.

For instance, the first two boxplots are computing metrics distributions of ensembles taking either one row or one column as an ensemble, the following two boxplots will take a combination of either two rows or two columns as ensemble and so on up to 9 rows/columns combinations.

More precisely, the first pink boxplot will compose an ensemble taking one column of models, namely, all the BERT_{base} models to begin with, then all the BERT_{large} models and so on until it computes the metrics for an ensemble composed with all the XLNet_{large} models. Then, the second pink boxplot will take the composition of 2 columns, for example, it will first compute an ensemble with all the BERT_{base} models and all the BERT_{large} models, then another with all the

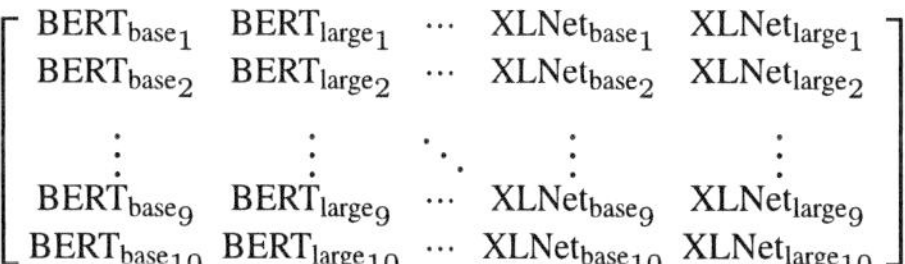

$$\begin{bmatrix} \text{BERT}_{base_1} & \text{BERT}_{large_1} & \cdots & \text{XLNet}_{base_1} & \text{XLNet}_{large_1} \\ \text{BERT}_{base_2} & \text{BERT}_{large_2} & \cdots & \text{XLNet}_{base_2} & \text{XLNet}_{large_2} \\ \vdots & \vdots & \ddots & \vdots & \vdots \\ \text{BERT}_{base_9} & \text{BERT}_{large_9} & \cdots & \text{XLNet}_{base_9} & \text{XLNet}_{large_9} \\ \text{BERT}_{base_{10}} & \text{BERT}_{large_{10}} & \cdots & \text{XLNet}_{base_{10}} & \text{XLNet}_{large_{10}} \end{bmatrix}$$

Figure 5: Matrix where each column represents a pretrained model and each row represents a fine-tuned model with a new random initialization of the fully connected layer.

BERT_{base} models and all XLNet_{base} models and so on until it computes an ensemble containing all the XLNet_{base} and XLNet_{large} models.

On the other hand, the blue boxplots will compose ensembles with combination of rows. This means that the first blue boxplot will first compute an ensemble composed of the first row (BERT_{base_1}, BERT_{large_1}, ..., XLNet_{base_1}, XLNet_{large_1}), then of the second row (BERT_{base_2}, BERT_{large_2}, ..., XLNet_{base_2}, XLNet_{large_2}) and so on until it computes an ensemble with the last row ($\text{BERT}_{base_{10}}$, $\text{BERT}_{large_{10}}$, ..., $\text{XLNet}_{base_{10}}$, $\text{XLNet}_{large_{10}}$). In the same manner, the second blue boxplot will compute ensembles composed by the combinations of two rows. First, all the models in the first and second rows, then, all the models in the first and third rows and so on until it computes an ensemble composed with all the models of the last two rows.

In this setting, as the maximum number of possible combinations of row is $252 = \binom{10}{5}$, we were able to compute all the possible combinations instead of sampling them. As we have the same number of pretrained models as fine-tuned versions, we end up with the same number of possible com-

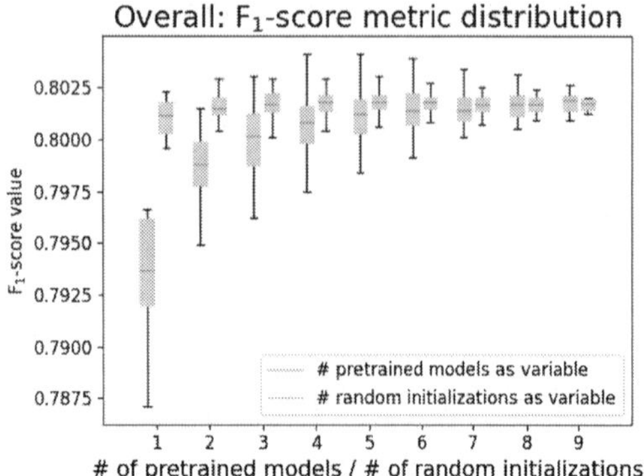
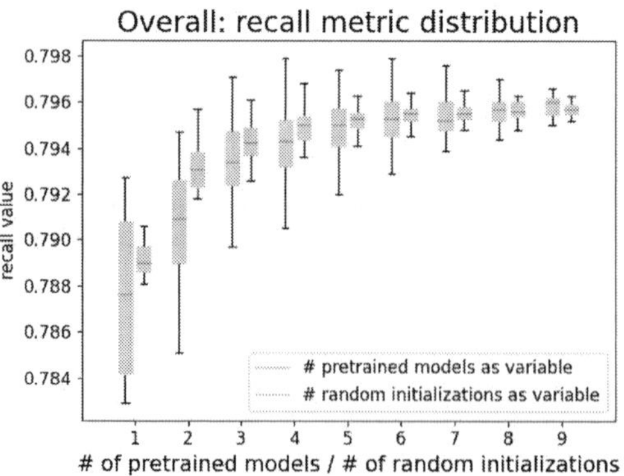

Figure 6: Micro F_1-score distribution using ensemble composed of either 1 to 9 different pretrained models (each time with 10 different fine-tuning) vs. 1 to 9 different fine-tuning using all the pretrained models.

Figure 7: Micro recall distribution using ensemble composed of either 1 to 9 different pretrained models (each time with 10 different fine-tuning) vs. 1 to 9 different fine-tuning using all the pretrained models.

binations of ensemble. That being said, for each number of models taken into account in an ensemble, this allows us to compare the pink boxplot with the blue one in a more convenient manner.

It is worth noting that the more we increase the number of columns and rows present in an ensemble model, the more they share a certain number of models. For example, at 9, the pink boxplot shows the distribution of the metrics for all the possible ensemble models containing 9 columns of models (90 models out of 100), while the blue boxplot shows the same metrics for 9 rows of models (also 90 models out of 100). At this point, it is expected to see both boxplots converging as they both share 64 models predictions out of 90.

Focusing on the left part of Figure 6, we clearly see the benefits of using more pretrained models. First, it shows better results with only an ensemble of 10 different pretrained models. Then, it really looks steadier as the F_1-score distribution is much narrower than the ensemble composed of multiple fine-tuning of the same pretrained model.

When looking at Figure 7, we see that the major difference between both distributions are the variances of the recall distributions, indeed, taking different pretrained models tends to retrieve important passages more systematically. The trend of both selection strategies seems to be increasing, in other words, in both cases, the more we add models, the more we retrieve important passages.

Finally, it is interesting to see in Figure 8 that the precision begins quite high and tends to decrease when we add more fine-tuned models. Conversely, when taking more pretrained models, it seems the

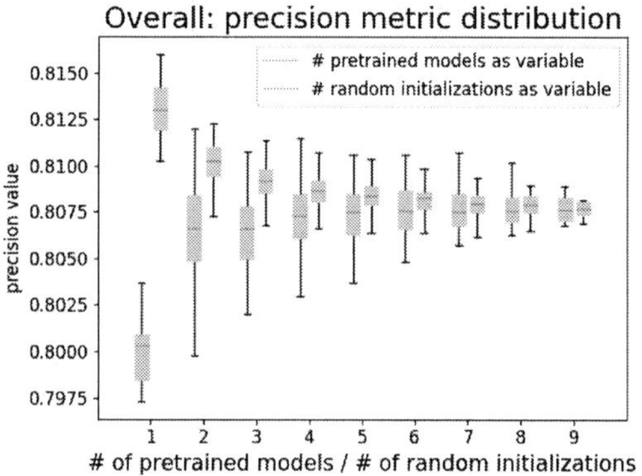

Figure 8: Micro precision distribution using ensemble composed of either 1 to 9 different pretrained models (each time with 10 different fine-tuning) vs. 1 to 9 different fine-tuning using all the pretrained models.

precision has a positive relation to the number of models we use. As explained before, this relation is also due to the fact that we share more and more models in both ensemble selection strategies.

This analysis helped us to understand a bit more about what was happening behind our majority of votes strategy, it would be interesting to take notes of some of the observed behaviours and try to devise new strategies accordingly.

5.2 Official results

The official results in terms of Precision, Recall, and F_1 on the test 2020 set is shown in Table 5. Each team was allowed to submit only one run. Our submitted run was based on the ensemble model described in sections 4.2 and 4.3. Our BiTeM team achieved the highest precision score in both ex-

Team Name	Exact Match			Partial Match		
	P	R	F_1	P	R	F_1
B-NLP	77.95	63.93	70.25	84.85	69.59	76.46
BIO-BIO	78.49	71.06	74.59	83.16	75.29	79.03
BiTeM	**84.73**	72.25	**77.99**	**88.72**	75.66	81.67
DSC-IITISM	64.20	57.07	60.42	68.52	60.90	64.49
Fancy Man	76.21	71.76	73.92	81.15	76.41	78.71
IBS	74.26	62.55	67.90	79.72	67.15	72.89
Kabir	78.79	72.20	75.35	83.73	76.73	80.08
KaushikAcharya	73.68	63.98	68.48	79.31	68.87	73.73
mahab	50.19	52.96	51.54	55.09	58.14	56.57
mgsohrab	83.69	70.62	76.60	87.95	74.22	80.50
PublishInCovid19	81.36	**74.12**	77.57	85.74	**78.11**	**81.75**
SudeshnaTCS	74.99	71.43	73.16	79.73	75.95	77.80
IITKGP	77.00	72.93	74.91	81.76	77.43	79.54

Table 5: Official results on Test 2020.

act match and partial match evaluation reaching 84.73% and 88.72%, respectively, and F_1-score in exact match evaluation reaching 77.99% among 13 teams. The F_1-score of our model in partial match (81.67%) was slightly lower than the best F_1-score (81.75%).

5.3 Results of the ensemble model on test 2020 data

The precision, recall, and F_1-score results of all entities and *Action* on the test 2020 in the exact match evaluation is represented in Table 6. The best F_1-score was achieved for *pH*. *Size* was the most difficult entity for detection.

5.4 Error analysis

Figure 9 shows the normalized confusion matrix for the predictions (exact match) of the ensemble model on the test 2020 data. As we can see, more than 78% of *Size* predictions are mislabelled as *Amount*. This can be due to the few number of training instances of *Size* entity. As we can see in the following examples, *50 mL* can refer to both *Size* and *Amount* depending on the context. In the first example, *50 mL* refers to *Amount* and in the second example, it refers to *Size*.

Example 5.4.1 *Add more NEB —no β—mercaptoethanol to final volume of 50 mL.*

Example 5.4.2 *Transfer the aqueous phase to a.new 50 mL Falcon tube.*

About 17% of the *Device* predictions are mislabelled as *Location* that can be due to the inconsistencies in the annotation process, for example *magnetic rack* is annotated as *Device* in a few protocols (protocol 0680, protocol 0683, protocol 0685), and as *Location* in others (protocol 32148, protocol

Entity	Precision	Recall	F_1
Action	90.09	82.29	86.01
Amount	77.09	89.47	82.82
Concentration	86.76	88.16	87.45
Device	80.38	56.00	66.01
Generic-Measure	55.65	37.87	45.07
Location	69.59	68.98	69.28
Measure-Type	73.87	46.00	56.70
Mention	67.32	74.10	70.55
Method	61.49	35.77	45.23
Modifier	83.02	42.66	56.36
Numerical	65.32	38.49	48.44
Reagent	82.58	82.54	82.56
Seal	81.58	78.15	79.83
Size	63.64	17.80	27.81
Speed	86.38	86.38	86.38
Temperature	91.68	83.27	87.27
Time	92.58	87.66	90.05
pH	96.72	90.77	93.65

Table 6: The precision, recall, and F_1-score of the ensemble model for all the entities and *action* on the test 2020.

33630). Here are two examples of *magnetic rack* annotated as *Location* and *Device*, respectively.

Example 5.4.3 *Place samples on magnetic rack, and incubate for 5 mins on the rack. Remove supernatant.*

Example 5.4.4 *Place the tube on a magnetic rack.*

Similarly *freezer* is annotated interchangeably as *Location* and *Device*. *Generic-Measure* is mostly confused with *Concentration* label (20.4%), and *Method* is mostly confused by *Action*. About 12% of *Numerical* is annotated as *Concentration*.

6 Conclusion

With almost no preprocessing, we have seen that current pretrained language models seem to be quite efficient in any NER task (Copara et al., 2020a,b). By analysing our voting strategy, we have also demonstrated the strengths as well as the weaknesses of such ensemble models. For instance, it looks like the more models we use, the more the performances tend to be high and stable, however, it appears that new pretrained model brings more information than fine-tuning again a pretrained model with a new fully connected weights random initialization.

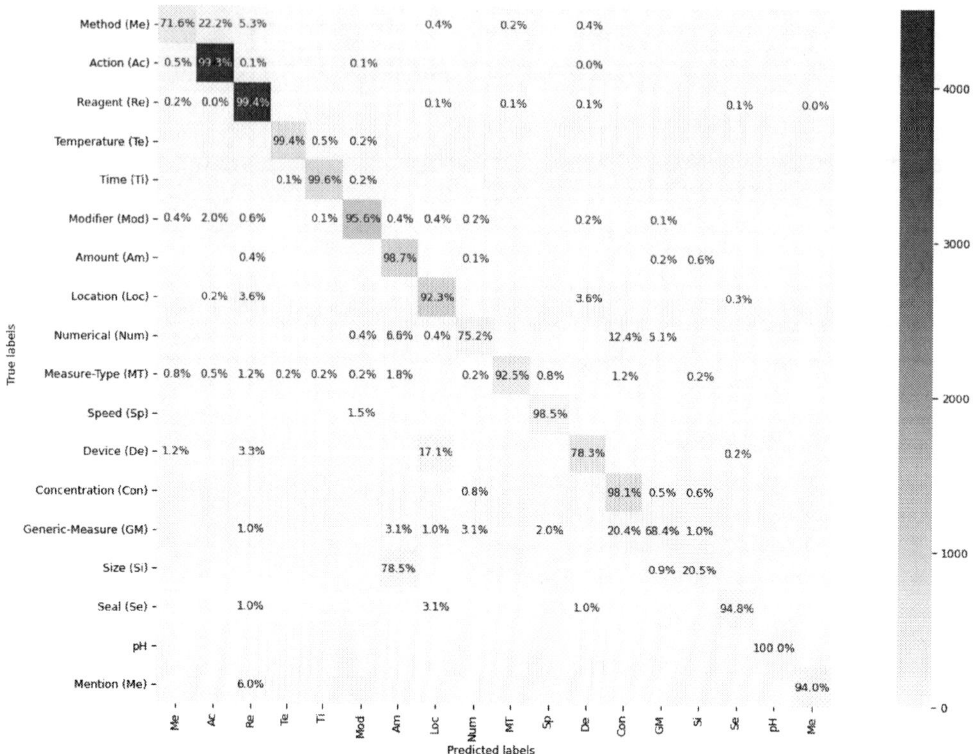

Figure 9: Normalized Confusion matrix for the ensemble model on the test 2020 data.

With this voting strategy, our submission achieved the best exact match overall F_1-score of the competition. This clearly shows the power of such models. With almost no knowledge on the topic of wet laboratory protocols required, we think that those models open opportunity to out-of-field researchers.

In future work, it would be interesting to improve the number of pretrained models selection and explore bootstrapping instead of fine-tuning multiple times the same pretrained model. It would also be interesting to see if some preprocessing tweaks could help us to improve the detection performance of *Speed* where our models were outperformed by the baseline.

References

Emily Alsentzer, John Murphy, William Boag, Wei-Hung Weng, Di Jindi, Tristan Naumann, and Matthew McDermott. 2019. Publicly Available Clinical BERT Embeddings. In *Proceedings of the 2nd Clinical Natural Language Processing Workshop*, pages 72–78.

Iz Beltagy, Kyle Lo, and Arman Cohan. 2019. SciB-ERT: A Pretrained Language Model for Scientific Text. In *Proceedings of the 2019 Conference on Empirical Methods in Natural Language Processing and the 9th International Joint Conference on Natural Language Processing (EMNLP-IJCNLP)*, pages 3606–3611.

Jenny Copara, Julien Knafou, Nona Naderi, Claudia Moro, Patrick Ruch, and Douglas Teodoro. 2020a. Contextualized French language models for biomedical named entity recognition. In *Actes de la 6e conférence conjointe Journées d'Études sur la Parole (JEP, 33e édition), Traitement Automatique des Langues Naturelles (TALN, 27e édition), Rencontre des Étudiants Chercheurs en Informatique pour le Traitement Automatique des Langues (RÉCITAL, 22e édition). Atelier DÉfi Fouille de Textes*, pages 36–48, Nancy, France. ATALA et AFCP.

Jenny Copara, Nona Naderi, Julien Knafou, Patrick Ruch, and Douglas Teodoro. 2020b. Named entity recognition in chemical patents using ensemble of contextual language models. *arXiv preprint arXiv:2007.12569*.

Jacob Devlin, Ming-Wei Chang, Kenton Lee, and Kristina Toutanova. 2019. BERT: Pre-training of Deep Bidirectional Transformers for Language Understanding. In *Proceedings of the 2019 Conference of the North American Chapter of the Association for Computational Linguistics: Human Language*

Technologies, Volume 1 (Long and Short Papers), pages 4171–4186.

Jesse Dodge, Gabriel Ilharco, Roy Schwartz, Ali Farhadi, Hannaneh Hajishirzi, and Noah Smith. 2020. Fine-tuning pretrained language models: Weight initializations, data orders, and early stopping. *arXiv preprint arXiv:2002.06305.*

Yu Gu, Robert Tinn, Hao Cheng, Michael Lucas, Naoto Usuyama, Xiaodong Liu, Tristan Naumann, Jianfeng Gao, and Hoifung Poon. 2020. Domain-specific language model pretraining for biomedical natural language processing.

Suchin Gururangan, Ana Marasović, Swabha Swayamdipta, Kyle Lo, Iz Beltagy, Doug Downey, and Noah A. Smith. 2020. Don't stop pretraining: Adapt language models to domains and tasks. In *Proceedings of ACL.*

Qiao Jin, Bhuwan Dhingra, William Cohen, and Xinghua Lu. 2019. Probing biomedical embeddings from language models. In *Proceedings of the 3rd Workshop on Evaluating Vector Space Representations for NLP*, pages 82–89.

Diederik P. Kingma and Jimmy Ba. 2014. Adam: A method for stochastic optimization. *arXiv preprint arXiv:1412.6980.*

Chaitanya Kulkarni, Wei Xu, Alan Ritter, and Raghu Machiraju. 2018. An annotated corpus for machine reading of instructions in wet lab protocols. In *Proceedings of the 2018 Conference of the North American Chapter of the Association for Computational Linguistics: Human Language Technologies, Volume 2 (Short Papers)*, pages 97–106, New Orleans, Louisiana. Association for Computational Linguistics.

Guillaume Lample, Miguel Ballesteros, Sandeep Subramanian, Kazuya Kawakami, and Chris Dyer. 2016. Neural architectures for named entity recognition. In *Proceedings of the 2016 Conference of the North American Chapter of the Association for Computational Linguistics: Human Language Technologies*, pages 260–270.

Jinhyuk Lee, Wonjin Yoon, Sungdong Kim, Donghyeon Kim, Sunkyu Kim, Chan Ho So, and Jaewoo Kang. 2019. BioBERT: a pretrained biomedical language representation model for biomedical text mining. *Bioinformatics*, 36(4):1234–1240.

Yinhan Liu, Myle Ott, Naman Goyal, Jingfei Du, Mandar Joshi, Danqi Chen, Omer Levy, Mike Lewis, Luke Zettlemoyer, and Veselin Stoyanov. 2019. Roberta: A robustly optimized BERT pretraining approach. *CoRR*, abs/1907.11692.

Jeniya Tabassum, Sydney Lee, Wei Xu, and Alan Ritter. 2020. WNUT-2020 Task 1 Overview: Extracting Entities and Relations from Wet Lab Protocols. In *Proceedings of EMNLP 2020 Workshop on Noisy User-generated Text (WNUT).*

Ashish Vaswani, Noam Shazeer, Niki Parmar, Jakob Uszkoreit, Llion Jones, Aidan N. Gomez, Lukasz Kaiser, and Illia Polosukhin. 2017. Attention is all you need. In *Proceedings of the 31st International Conference on Neural Information Processing Systems*, pages 6000–6010.

Zhilin Yang, Zihang Dai, Yiming Yang, Jaime G. Carbonell, Ruslan Salakhutdinov, and Quoc V. Le. 2019. XLNet: Generalized Autoregressive Pretraining for Language Understanding. In *Advances in neural information processing systems*, pages 5753–5763.

WNUT-2020 Task 2:
Identification of Informative COVID-19 English Tweets

Dat Quoc Nguyen[1,*]**, Thanh Vu**[2,*]**, Afshin Rahimi**[3]**, Mai Hoang Dao**[1]**,**
Linh The Nguyen[1] **and Long Doan**[1]

[1]VinAI Research, Vietnam; [2]Oracle Digital Assistant, Oracle, Australia;
[3]The University of Queensland, Australia

```
v.datnq9@vinai.io; thanh.v.vu@oracle.com; a.rahimi@uq.edu.au
{v.maidh3, v.linhnt140, v.longdct}@vinai.io
```


Abstract

In this paper, we provide an overview of the WNUT-2020 shared task on the identification of informative COVID-19 English Tweets. We describe how we construct a corpus of 10K Tweets and organize the development and evaluation phases for this task. In addition, we also present a brief summary of results obtained from the final system evaluation submissions of 55 teams, finding that (i) many systems obtain very high performance, up to 0.91 F_1 score, (ii) the majority of the submissions achieve substantially higher results than the baseline fastText (Joulin et al., 2017), and (iii) fine-tuning pre-trained language models on relevant language data followed by supervised training performs well in this task.

1 Introduction

As of late-September 2020, the COVID-19 Coronavirus pandemic has led to about 1M deaths and 33M infected patients from 213 countries and territories, creating fear and panic for people all around the world.[1] Recently, much attention has been paid to building monitoring systems (e.g. The Johns Hopkins Coronavirus Dashboard) to track the development of the pandemic and to provide users the information related to the virus,[2] e.g. any new suspicious/confirmed cases near/in the users' regions.

It is worth noting that most of the "official" sources used in the tracking tools are not frequently kept up to date with the current pandemic situation, e.g. WHO updates the pandemic information only once a day. Those monitoring systems thus use social network data, e.g. from Twit-

ter, as a real-time alternative source for updating the pandemic information, generally by crowd-sourcing or searching for related information manually. However, the pandemic has been spreading rapidly; we observe a massive amount of data on social networks, e.g. about 3.5M of COVID-19 English Tweets posted daily on the Twitter platform (Lamsal, 2020) in which the majority are uninformative. Thus, it is important to be able to select the informative Tweets (e.g. COVID-19 Tweets related to new cases or suspicious cases) for downstream applications. However, manual approaches to identify the informative Tweets require significant human efforts, do not scale with rapid developments, and are costly.

To help handle the problem, *we propose a shared task which is to automatically identify whether a COVID-19 English Tweet is informative or not.* Our task is defined as a binary classification problem: Given an English Tweet related to COVID-19, decide whether it should be classified as INFORMATIVE or UNINFORMATIVE. Here, informative Tweets provide information about suspected, confirmed, recovered and death cases as well as the location or travel history of the cases. The following example presents an informative Tweet:

> **INFORMATIVE**
>
> Update: Uganda Health Minister Jane Ruth Aceng has confirmed the first #coronavirus case in Uganda. The patient is a 36-year-old Ugandan male who arrived from Dubai today aboard Ethiopian Airlines. Patient travelled to Dubai 4 days ago. #CoronavirusPandemic

The goals of our shared task are: (i) To develop a language processing task that potentially impacts research and downstream applications, and

---

* The first two authors contributed equally to this work. Most of the work was done when Thanh Vu was at the Australian e-Health Research Centre, CSIRO, Australia.

[1]`https://www.worldometers.info/coronavirus/`

[2]`https://coronavirus.jhu.edu/map.html`

Proceedings of the 2020 EMNLP Workshop W-NUT: The Sixth Workshop on Noisy User-generated Text, pages 314–318
Online, Nov 19, 2020. ©2020 Association for Computational Linguistics

(ii) To provide the research community with a new dataset for identifying informative COVID-19 English Tweets. To achieve the goals, we manually construct a dataset of 10K COVID-19 English Tweets with INFORMATIVE and UNINFORMATIVE labels. We believe that the dataset and systems developed for our task will be beneficial for the development of COVID-19 monitoring systems. All practical information, data download links and the final evaluation results can be found at the CodaLab website of our shared task: `https://competitions.codalab.org/competitions/25845`.

2 The WNUT-2020 Task 2 dataset

2.1 Annotation guideline

We define the guideline to annotate a COVID-19 related Tweet with the "INFORMATIVE" label if the Tweet mentions suspected cases, confirmed cases, recovered cases, deaths, number of tests performed as well as location or travel history associated with the confirmed/suspected cases.

In addition, we also set further requirements in which the "INFORMATIVE" Tweet has to satisfy. In particular, the "INFORMATIVE" Tweet should not present a rumor or prediction. Furthermore, quantities mentioned in the Tweet have to be specific (e.g. *"two new cases"* or *"about 125 tested positives"*) or could be inferred directly (e.g. *"120 coronavirus tests done so far, 40% tested positive"*), but not purely in percentages or rates (e.g. *"20%"*, *"1000 per million"*, or *"a third"*).

The COVID-19 related Tweets not satisfying the "INFORMATIVE" annotation guideline are annotated with the "UNINFORMATIVE" label. An uninformative Tweet example is as follows:

> **UNINFORMATIVE**
>
> Indonesia frees 18,000 inmates, as it records highest #coronavirus death toll in Asia behind China HTTPURL

2.2 COVID-19 related Tweet collection

To be able to construct a dataset used in our shared task, we first have to crawl the COVID-19 related Tweets. We collect a general Tweet corpus related to the COVID-19 pandemic based on a predefined list of 10 keywords, including: "coronavirus", "covid-19", "covid_19", "covid_2019", "covid19", "covid2019", "covid-2019", "CoronaVirusUpdate", "Coronavid19" and "SARS-CoV-2". We utilize the Twitter streaming API to download real-time English Tweets containing at least one keyword from the predefined list.[3]

We stream the Tweet data for four months using the API from 01st March 2020 to 30th June 2020. We then filter out Tweets containing less than 10 words (including hashtags and user mentions) as well as Tweets from users with less than five hundred followers. This is to help reduce the rate of Tweets with fake news (our manual annotation process does not involve in verifying fake news) with a rather strong assumption that reliable information is more likely to be propagated by users with a large number of followers.[4] To handle the duplication problem: (i) we remove Retweets starting with the "RT" token, and (ii) in cases where two Tweets are the same after lowercasing as well as removing hashtags and user mentions, the earlier Tweet is kept and the subsequent Tweet will be filtered out as it tends to be a Retweet. Applying these filtering steps results in a final corpus of about 23M COVID-19 English Tweets.

2.3 Annotation process

From the corpus of 23M Tweets, we select Tweets which are potentially informative, containing predefined strings relevant to the annotation guideline such as "confirm", "positive", "suspected", "death", "discharge", "test" and "travel history". We then remove similar Tweets with the token-based cosine similarity score (Wang et al., 2011) that is equal or greater than 0.7, resulting in a dataset of "INFORMATIVE" candidates. We then randomly sample 2K Tweets from this dataset for the first phase of annotation.

Three annotators are employed to independently annotate each of the 2K Tweets with one of the two labels "INFORMATIVE" and "UNINFORMATIVE". We use the "docanno" toolkit for handling the annotations (Nakayama et al., 2018). We measure the inter-annotator agreement to assess the quality of annotations and to see whether the guideline allows to carry out the task consistently. In particular, we use the Fleiss'

---

[3] `https://developer.twitter.com/en/docs/twitter-api/v1/tweets/filter-realtime/overview`

[4] We acknowledge that there are accounts with a large number of followers, who participate in publication and propagation of misinformation.

Item	Training	Validation	Test	Total
#INFOR	3,303	472	944	4,719
#UNINF	3,697	528	1,056	5,281
Total	7,000	1,000	2,000	10,000

Table 1: Basic statistics of our dataset. #INFOR and #UNINF denote the numbers of "INFORMATIVE" and "UNINFORMATIVE" Tweets, respectively.

Kappa coefficient to assess the annotator agreement (Fleiss, 1971). For this first phase, the Kappa score is 0.797 which can be interpreted as substantial (Landis and Koch, 1977). We further run a discussion for Tweets where there is a disagreement in the assigned labels among the annotators. The discussion is to determine the final labels of the Tweets as well as to improve the quality of the annotation guideline.

For the second phase, we employ the 2K annotated Tweets from the first phase to train a binary fastText classifier (Joulin et al., 2017) to classify a COVID-19 related Tweet into either "INFORMATIVE" or "UNINFORMATIVE". We utilize the trained classifier to predict the probability of "INFORMATIVE" for each of all remaining Tweets in the dataset of "INFORMATIVE" candidates from the first phase. Then we randomly sample 8K Tweets from the candidate dataset, including 3K, 2K and 3K Tweets associated with the probability $\in$ [0.0, 0.3), [0.3, 0.7) and [0.7, 1.0], respectively (here, we do not sample from the existing 2K annotated Tweets). The goal here is to select Tweets with varying degree of detection difficulty (with respect to the baseline) in both labels.

The three annotators then independently assign the "INFORMATIVE" or "UNINFORMATIVE" label to each of the 8K Tweets. The Kappa score is obtained at 0.818 which can be interpreted as almost perfect (Landis and Koch, 1977). Similar to the first phase, for each Tweet with a disagreement among the annotators, we also run a further discussion to decide its final label annotation.

We merge the two datasets from the first and second phases to formulate the final gold standard corpus of 10K annotated Tweets, consisting of 4,719 "INFORMATIVE" Tweets and 5,281 "UN-INFORMATIVE" Tweets.

2.4 Data partitions

To split the gold standard corpus into training, validation and test sets, we first categorize its Tweets into two categories of "easy" and "not-easy", in which the "not-easy" category contains Tweets with a label disagreement among annotators before participating in the annotation discussions. We then randomly select 7K Tweets for training, 1K Tweets for validation and 2K Tweets for test with a constraint that ensures the number of the "not-easy" Tweets in the training is equal to that in the validation and test sets. Table 1 describes the basic statistics of our corpus.

3 Task organization

Development phase: Both the training and validation sets with gold labels are released publicly to all participants for system development. Although we provide a default training and validation split of the released data, participants are free to use this data in any way they find useful when training and tuning their systems, e.g. using a different split or performing cross-validation.

Evaluation phase: The raw test set is released when the final phase of system evaluation starts. To keep fairness among participants, the raw test set is a relatively large set of 12K Tweets, and the actual 2K test Tweets by which the participants' system outputs are evaluated are hidden in this large test set. We allow each participant to upload at most 2 submissions during this final evaluation phase, in which the submission obtaining higher F_1 score is ranked higher in the leaderboard.

Metrics: Systems are evaluated using standard evaluation metrics, including Accuracy, Precision, Recall and F_1 score. Note that the latter three metrics of Precision, Recall and F_1 will be calculated for the "INFORMATIVE" label only. The system evaluation submissions are ranked by the F_1 score.

Baseline: fastText (Joulin et al., 2017) is used as our baseline, employing the default data split.

4 Results

In total, 121 teams spreading across 20 different countries registered to participate in our WNUT-2020 Task 2 during the system development phase. Of those 121 teams, 55 teams uploaded their submissions for the final evaluation phase.[5]

We report results obtained for each team in Table 2. The baseline fastText achieves 0.7503 in

<hr>

[5]CXP949 is not shown on our CodaLab leaderboard because this team unfortunately makes an incorrectly-formatted submission file name, resulting in a fail for our CodaLab automatic evaluation program. We manually re-evaluate their submission and include its obtained results in Table 2.

Team	F_1	P	R	Acc.	Team	F_1	P	R	Acc.
NutCracker	**0.9096**	0.9135	0.9057	**0.9150**	CUBoulder-UBC	0.8841	0.8606	0.9089	0.8875
NLP_North	**0.9096**	0.9029	0.9163	0.9140	Sic Mundus	0.8823	0.8832	0.8814	0.8890
UIT-HSE	0.9094	0.9046	0.9142	0.9140	LynyrdSkynyrd	0.8805	0.8567	0.9057	0.8840
#GCDH	0.9091	0.8919	0.9269	0.9125	Dartmouth CS	0.8757	0.8818	0.8697	0.8835
Loner	0.9085	0.8918	0.9258	0.9120	L3STeam	0.8754	0.8654	0.8856	0.8810
Phonemer	0.9037	0.8934	0.9142	0.9080	XSellResearch	0.8739	0.8857	0.8623	0.8825
EdinburghNLP	0.9011	0.8768	0.9269	0.9040	Linguist Geeks	0.8715	0.9130	0.8337	0.8840
TATL	0.9008	0.8588	**0.9470**	0.9015	DSC-IITISM	0.8715	0.8343	0.9121	0.8730
SunBear	0.9005	0.8728	0.9301	0.9030	AmazingAI	0.8714	0.8637	0.8792	0.8775
InfoMiner	0.9004	0.9102	0.8909	0.9070	Siva	0.8527	0.8115	0.8983	0.8535
NEU	0.8992	0.8959	0.9025	0.9045	CSECU-DSG	0.8198	0.8155	0.8242	0.8290
Not-NUTs	0.8991	0.8787	0.9206	0.9025	IIITBH	0.7979	0.7991	0.7966	0.8095
UET	0.8989	0.8891	0.9089	0.9035	NLPRL	0.7854	0.8335	0.7426	0.8085
Emory	0.8974	0.8744	0.9216	0.9005	Kai	0.7772	0.7540	0.8019	0.7830
NJU ConvAI	0.8973	0.8751	0.9206	0.9005	IBS	0.7765	0.7692	0.7839	0.7870
IDSOU	0.8964	0.8988	0.8941	0.9025	MrRobot	0.7648	0.7515	0.7786	0.7740
ComplexDataLab	0.8945	**0.9195**	0.8708	0.9030	ISWARA	0.7631	0.8073	0.7235	0.7880
UPennHLP	0.8941	0.9028	0.8856	0.9010	TheWalkingBy	0.7614	0.7709	0.7521	0.7775
DATAMAFIA	0.8940	0.8857	0.9025	0.8990	KZhu	0.7580	0.7788	0.7383	0.7775
NIT_COVID-19	0.8914	0.8594	0.9258	0.8935	IRLab@IITBHU	0.7508	0.7904	0.7150	0.7760
CXP949	0.8910	0.8698	0.9131	0.8945	Baseline–fastText	0.7503	0.7730	0.7288	0.7710
NHK_STRL	0.8898	0.8985	0.8814	0.8970	Amrita_CEN_NLP	0.7496	0.8078	0.6992	0.7795
COVCOR20	0.8887	0.8655	0.9131	0.8920	intelligentCyborgs	0.7417	0.6507	0.8623	0.7165
CIA_NITT	0.8887	0.8772	0.9004	0.8935	BhagwanBharose	0.7269	0.7723	0.6864	0.7565
honeybee	0.8884	0.8956	0.8814	0.8955	IITKGPPHD	0.7132	0.7535	0.6769	0.7430
BANANA	0.8881	0.8853	0.8909	0.8940	NITK_NLP	0.6826	0.7581	0.6208	0.7275
SU-NLP	0.8881	0.8895	0.8867	0.8945	36H102	0.5800	0.5015	0.6875	0.5300
VT	0.8846	0.8723	0.8972	0.8895	TMU-COVID19	0.5789	0.5000	0.6875	0.5280

Table 2: Final results on the test set. **P**, **R** and **Acc.** denote the Precision, Recall and Accuracy, respectively. Teams are ranked by their highest F_1 score.

F_1 score. In particular, 48 teams outperform the baseline in terms of F_1. There are 39 teams with an F_1 greater than 0.80, in which 10 teams are with an F_1 greater than 0.90. Both NutCracker (Kumar and Singh, 2020) and NLP_North (Møller et al., 2020) obtain the highest F_1 score at 0.9096, in which NutCracker obtains the highest Accuracy at 91.50% that is 0.1% absolute higher than NLP_North's.

Of the 55 teams, 36 teams submitted their system paper, in which 34 teams' papers are finally included in the Proceedings. All of the 36 teams with paper submissions employ pre-trained language models to extract latent features for learning classifiers. The majority of pre-trained language models employed include BERT (Devlin et al., 2019), XLNet (Yang et al., 2019), RoBERTa (Liu et al., 2019), BERTweet (Nguyen et al., 2020) and especially CT-BERT (Müller et al., 2020).

Not surprisingly, CT-BERT, resulted in by continuing pre-training from the pre-trained BERT-large model on a corpus of 22.5M COVID-19 related Tweets, is utilized in a large number of the highly-ranked systems. In particular, all of top 6 teams including NutCracker, NLP_North, UIT-HSE (Tran et al., 2020), #GCDH (Varachkina et al., 2020), Loner and Phonemer (Wadhawan, 2020) utilize CT-BERT. That is why we find slight differences in their obtained F_1 scores. In addition, ensemble techniques are also used in a large proportion (61%) of the participating teams. Specifically, to obtain the best performance, the top 10 teams, except NLP_North, #GCDH and Loner, all employ ensemble techniques.

5 Conclusion

In this paper, we have presented an overview of the WNUT-2020 Task 2 "Identification of Informative COVID-19 English Tweets": (i) Provide details of the task, data preparation process, and the task organization, and (ii) Report the results obtained by participating teams and outline their commonly adopted approaches.

We receive registrations from 121 teams and final system evaluation submissions from 55 teams, in which 34/55 teams contribute detailed system descriptions. The evaluation results show that many systems obtain a very high performance of up to 0.91 F_1 score on the task, using pre-trained language models which are fine-tuned on unlabelled COVID-19 related Tweets (CT-BERT) and are subsequently trained on this task.

References

Jacob Devlin, Ming-Wei Chang, Kenton Lee, and Kristina Toutanova. 2019. BERT: Pre-training of deep bidirectional transformers for language understanding. In *Proceedings of the 2019 Conference of the North American Chapter of the Association for Computational Linguistics: Human Language Technologies, Volume 1 (Long and Short Papers)*, pages 4171–4186.

Joseph L Fleiss. 1971. Measuring nominal scale agreement among many raters. *Psychological bulletin*, 76(5):378–382.

Armand Joulin, Edouard Grave, Piotr Bojanowski, and Tomas Mikolov. 2017. Bag of Tricks for Efficient Text Classification. In *Proceedings of the 15th Conference of the European Chapter of the Association for Computational Linguistics: Volume 2, Short Papers*, pages 427–431.

Priyanshu Kumar and Aadarsh Singh. 2020. NutCracker at WNUT-2020 Task 2: Robustly Identifying Informative COVID-19 Tweets using Ensembling and Adversarial Training . In *Proceedings of the 6th Workshop on Noisy User-generated Text*.

Rabindra Lamsal. 2020. CORONAVIRUS (COVID-19) TWEETS DATASET. *IEEE Dataport*.

J Richard Landis and Gary G Koch. 1977. The measurement of observer agreement for categorical data. *Biometrics*, 33(1):159–174.

Yinhan Liu, Myle Ott, Naman Goyal, Jingfei Du, Mandar Joshi, Danqi Chen, Omer Levy, Mike Lewis, Luke Zettlemoyer, and Veselin Stoyanov. 2019. RoBERTa: A Robustly Optimized BERT Pretraining Approach. *arXiv preprint*, arXiv:1907.11692.

Anders Giovanni Møller, Rob van der Goot, and Barbara Plank. 2020. NLP North at WNUT-2020 Task 2: Pre-training versus Ensembling for Detection of Informative COVID-19 English Tweets. In *Proceedings of the 6th Workshop on Noisy User-generated Text*.

Martin Müller, Marcel Salathé, and Per E Kummervold. 2020. COVID-Twitter-BERT: A Natural Language Processing Model to Analyse COVID-19 Content on Twitter. *arXiv preprint arXiv:2005.07503*.

Hiroki Nakayama, Takahiro Kubo, Junya Kamura, Yasufumi Taniguchi, and Xu Liang. 2018. doccano: Text Annotation Tool for Human. Software available from https://github.com/doccano/doccano.

Dat Quoc Nguyen, Thanh Vu, and Anh Tuan Nguyen. 2020. BERTweet: A pre-trained language model for English Tweets. In *Proceedings of the 2020 Conference on Empirical Methods in Natural Language Processing: System Demonstrations*.

Khiem Tran, Hao Phan, Kiet Nguyen, and Ngan Luu Thuy Nguyen. 2020. UIT-HSE at WNUT-2020 Task 2: Exploiting CT-BERT for Identifying COVID-19 Information on the Twitter Social Network. In *Proceedings of the 6th Workshop on Noisy User-generated Text*.

Hanna Varachkina, Stefan Ziehe, Tillmann Dońicke, and Franziska Pannach. 2020. #GCDH at WNUT-2020 Task 2: BERT-Based Models for the Detection of Informativeness in English COVID-19 Related Tweets. In *Proceedings of the 6th Workshop on Noisy User-generated Text*.

Anshul Wadhawan. 2020. Phonemer at WNUT-2020 Task 2: Sequence Classification Using COVID Twitter BERT and Bagging Ensemble Technique based on Plurality Voting. In *Proceedings of the 6th Workshop on Noisy User-generated Text*.

J. Wang, G. Li, and J. Fe. 2011. Fast-join: An efficient method for fuzzy token matching based string similarity join. In *Proceedings of the 27th IEEE International Conference on Data Engineering*, pages 458–469.

Zhilin Yang, Zihang Dai, Yiming Yang, Jaime Carbonell, Russ R Salakhutdinov, and Quoc V Le. 2019. XLNet: Generalized Autoregressive Pretraining for Language Understanding. In *Advances in Neural Information Processing Systems 32*, pages 5753–5763.

TATL at WNUT-2020 Task 2: A Transformer-based Baseline System for Identification of Informative COVID-19 English Tweets

Anh Tuan Nguyen

NVIDIA, Santa Clara, USA

tuananhn@nvidia.com

Abstract

As the COVID-19 outbreak continues to spread throughout the world, more and more information about the pandemic has been shared publicly on social media. For example, there are a huge number of COVID-19 English Tweets daily on Twitter. However, the majority of those Tweets are uninformative, and hence it is important to be able to automatically select only the informative ones for downstream applications. In this short paper, we present our participation in the W-NUT 2020 Shared Task 2: Identification of Informative COVID-19 English Tweets. Inspired by the recent advances in pretrained Transformer language models, we propose a simple yet effective baseline for the task. Despite its simplicity, our proposed approach shows very competitive results in the leaderboard as we ranked 8 over 55 teams participated in total.

1 Introduction

The COVID-19 pandemic has been spreading rapidly across the globe and has infected more than 20 millions men and women. As a result, more and more people have been sharing a wide variety of information related to COVID-19 publicly on social media. For example, there are a huge number of COVID-19 English Tweets daily on Twitter. However, the majority of those Tweets are uninformative and do not contain useful information, therefore, systems which can automatically filter out uninformative tweets are needed by the community. Tweets are generally different from traditional written-text such as Wikipedia or news articles due to its short length and informal use of words and grammars (e.g abbreviations, hashtags, marker). These special characteristics of Tweets may pose a challenge for many NLP techniques that focus solely on formally written texts.

In this paper, we present our participation in the W-NUT 2020 Shared Task 2: Identification of

category	#training	#valid	#test
informative	3303	472	944
uninformative	3697	528	1056

Table 1: Statistics of Shared task 2 dataset. "#training", "#valid" and "#test" denote the size of the training, validation and test sets, listed by categories, respectively.

Informative COVID-19 English Tweets (Nguyen et al., 2020b). Inspired by the recent success of Transformer-based pre-trained language models in many NLP tasks (Devlin et al., 2019; Lai et al., 2019; Chen et al., 2019; Nguyen and Nguyen, 2020; Lai et al., 2020), we propose a simple yet effective baseline for the task. Despite its simplicity, our proposed approach shows very competitive results.

In the following sections, we first describe the task definitions in Section 2 and proposed methods in Section 3. We then describe the experiments and their results in Section 4. Finally, in Section 5, we conclude this work and discuss potential future research directions.

2 Task Definitions

The goal of Shared task 2 is to identify whether a COVID 19 English Tweet is informative or not. Such informative Tweet provides information about recovered, suspected, confirmed and death cases as well as location and history of each case. The dataset introduced in this Shared task consists of 10K COVID 19 English Tweets. Dataset statistics can be found in Table 1

3 Method

3.1 Baseline Model

The task is formulated as a binary classification of Tweets into informative or uninformative classes. Figure 1 gives a high-level overview of our proposed approach. Given a Tweet consisting of n

Proceedings of the 2020 EMNLP Workshop W-NUT: The Sixth Workshop on Noisy User-generated Text, pages 319–323
Online, Nov 19, 2020. ©2020 Association for Computational Linguistics

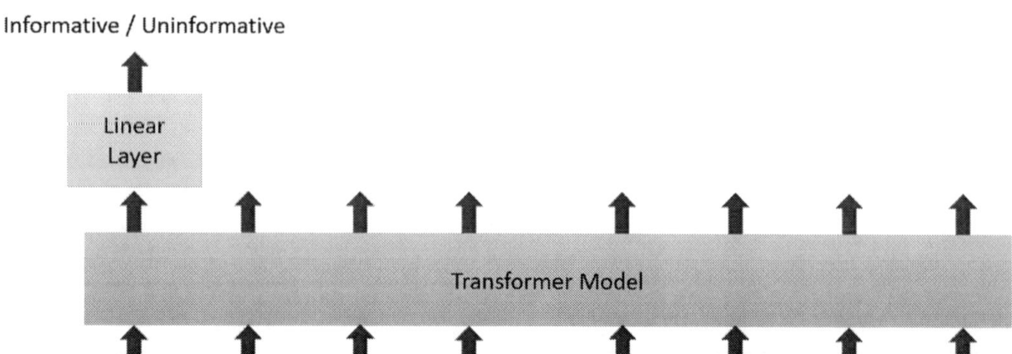

Figure 1: A high level overview of our proposed model for the task.

tokens $\mathbf{x} = \{x_1, x_2, ..., x_n\}$, we first form a contextualized representation for each token using a Transformer-based encoder such as BERT (Devlin et al., 2019). Following common conventions, we append special tokens to the beginning and end of the input Tweet before feeding it to the Transformer model. For example, if we use BERT, x_1 will be the special [CLS] token and x_n will be the special [SEP] token. Let $\mathbf{H} = \{\mathbf{h}_1, \mathbf{h}_2, ..., \mathbf{h}_n\}$ denote the contextualized representations produced by the Transformer model. We then use $\mathbf{h}_1$ as an aggregate representation of the original input and feed it to a linear layer to calculate the final output:

$$y = \sigma(\mathbf{W}\mathbf{h}_1 + \mathbf{b}) \in \mathbb{R} \qquad (1)$$

where the transformation matrix $\mathbf{W}$ and the bias term $\mathbf{b}$ are model parameters. σ denotes the sigmoid function. It squashes the score to a probability between 0 and 1. y is the predicted probability of the input Tweet being informative.

In this work, we experiment with various state-of-the-art Transformer models including BERTweet (Nguyen et al., 2020a), XLM-RoBERTa (Conneau et al., 2020), RoBERTa (Liu et al., 2019), and ELECTRA (Clark et al., 2020). In the following subsections, we will briefly describe these Transformer models.

3.1.1 RoBERTa

RoBERTa (Liu et al., 2019) improved over BERT (Devlin et al., 2019) by leveraging different training objectives which leads to more robust optimization i.e removing next sentence prediction and using dynamic masking for masked language modelling.

Liu et al. (2019) also shows that training the language model longer and with more data hugely benefits the performance on downstream tasks.

3.1.2 XLM-RoBERTa

Inspired by the success of multilingual language model (Devlin et al., 2019; Lample and Conneau, 2019), XLM-RoBERTa (Conneau et al., 2020) significantly scaled up the amount of multilingual training data used in unsupervised MLM pre-training compares to previous work (Lample and Conneau, 2019) and achieved state-of-the-art performance in both monolingual and cross-lingual benchmarks.

3.1.3 BERTweet

BERTweet (Nguyen et al., 2020a) is a domain-specific language model pre-trained on a large corpus of English Tweets. Similar to the success of BioBERT (Lee et al., 2019) in BioNLP domain and the success of SciBERT (Beltagy et al., 2019) in ScientificNLP domain, BERTweet achieved state-of-the-art performance across many TweetNLP tasks, outperformed its counterparts RoBERTa (Liu et al., 2019) and XLM-RoBERTa (Conneau et al., 2020).

3.1.4 ELECTRA

ELECTRA (Clark et al., 2020) proposed a new pre-training objective which is different from Masked Language Modelling (Devlin et al., 2019; Liu et al., 2019). Instead of masking input tokens, ELECTRA corrupts the tokens using a small generator network to produces distribution over tokens, while the discriminator tries to guess which tokens are actually corrupted by the generator. ELECTRA achieved state-of-the-art results across many tasks in the GLUE benchmark (Wang et al., 2019) while using much less compute resources compared to other pre-training methods (Devlin et al., 2019; Liu et al., 2019).

3.2 Ensemble Learning

To further boost the performance of our baseline models, we leverage ensemble learning technique. We performed ensemble learning over all of the Transformer models mentioned in the previous section and employed two different ensemble schemes, namely Unweighted Averaging and Majority Voting.

3.2.1 Unweighted Averaging

In this approach, the final prediction is estimated from the unweighted average of the posterior probability from all of our models. Thus, the final prediction is given by:

$$p = \arg\max_{c} \frac{1}{M} \sum_{n=1}^{M} p_i, \quad p_i \in \mathbb{R}^{\mathbb{C}} \qquad (2)$$

where C is the number of classed, M is the number of models, and p_i is the probability vector computed using the softmax function of model i.

3.2.2 Majority Voting

Majority Voting counts the votes of all the models and select the class with most votes as prediction. Formally, the final prediction is given by:

$$v_c = \sum_{n=1}^{M} F_i(c), \quad p = \arg\max_{c} v_c \qquad (3)$$

where v_c denotes the votes of class c from all different models, F_i is the binary decision of model i, which is either 0 or 1.

4 Experiments

4.1 Finetuning

To fine-tune our baseline models, we employ `transformers` library (Wolf et al., 2019). We use AdamW optimizer (Loshchilov and Hutter, 2019) with a fixed batch size of 32 and learning rates in the set $\{1e-5, 2e-5, 5e-5\}$. We fine-tune the models for 30 epochs and select the best checkpoint based on performance of the model on the validation set.

Model	Dev F1
XLM-RoBERTa (base)	0.905
XLM-RoBERTa (large)	0.906
RoBERTa (base)	0.911
RoBERTa (large)	**0.918**
BERTweet	0.909
ELECTRA (base)	0.907
ELECTRA (large)	0.914
Ensemble (averaging)	**0.927**
Ensemble (voting)	0.922

Table 2: Performance of individual models as well as ensemble models on the validation set.

Model	Test F1
Ensemble (averaging)	0.8988
Ensemble (voting)	**0.9008**

Table 3: Performance of our system on the test set.

4.2 Performance of our baselines

Table 2 shows the overall results on the validation set. The large version of RoBERTa achieves the highest F1 score on the validation set (compared to other individual models). To our surprise, we find that BERTweet does not outperform the base version of RoBERTa on the validation set, even though BERTweet was trained on English Tweets using the same training procedure of RoBERTa. Finally, XLM-RoBERTa achieves lower F1 score than both RoBERTa and ELECTRA, suggesting that using a multilingual pretrained language models may not improve the performance since the shared task is mainly about English Tweets. We also evaluate the performance of our ensemble models. The results show that ensemble learning improves the F1 score compare to each individual model and Unweighted Averaging perform better than Majority Voting on the validation set. We also submitted the predictions of both ensemble scheme to the competition and final results on the leaderboard are shown in table 3. We notice that Majority Voting slightly performs better than Unweighted Averaging on the hidden test set.

5 Conclusion

In this paper, we introduce a simple but effective approach for identifying informative COVID-19 English Tweets. Despite the simplicity of our approach, it achieves very competitive results in the leaderboard as we ranked 8 over 56 teams participated in total. In future work, we will conduct thorough error analysis and apply visualization techniques to gain more understandings of our models (Murugesan et al., 2019). Furthermore, we will also extend our approach to other languages. Finally, we will investigate the use of advanced techniques such as transfer learning, few-shot learning, and self-training to improve the performance of our system further (Pan et al., 2017; Huang et al., 2018; Lai et al., 2018; Yoon et al., 2019; Xie et al., 2020).

References

Iz Beltagy, Kyle Lo, and Arman Cohan. 2019. Scibert: Pretrained language model for scientific text. In *EMNLP*.

Qian Chen, Zhu Zhuo, and W. Wang. 2019. Bert for joint intent classification and slot filling. *ArXiv*, abs/1902.10909.

K. Clark, Minh-Thang Luong, Quoc V. Le, and Christopher D. Manning. 2020. Electra: Pre-training text encoders as discriminators rather than generators. *ArXiv*, abs/2003.10555.

Alexis Conneau, Kartikay Khandelwal, Naman Goyal, Vishrav Chaudhary, Guillaume Wenzek, Francisco Guzmán, Edouard Grave, Myle Ott, Luke Zettlemoyer, and Veselin Stoyanov. 2020. Unsupervised cross-lingual representation learning at scale. In *Proceedings of the 58th Annual Meeting of the Association for Computational Linguistics*, pages 8440–8451, Online. Association for Computational Linguistics.

Jacob Devlin, Ming-Wei Chang, Kenton Lee, and Kristina Toutanova. 2019. BERT: Pre-training of deep bidirectional transformers for language understanding. In *Proceedings of NAACL*, pages 4171–4186.

Lifu Huang, Heng Ji, Kyunghyun Cho, Ido Dagan, Sebastian Riedel, and Clare Voss. 2018. Zero-shot transfer learning for event extraction. In *Proceedings of the 56th Annual Meeting of the Association for Computational Linguistics (Volume 1: Long Papers)*, pages 2160–2170, Melbourne, Australia. Association for Computational Linguistics.

Tuan Lai, Trung Bui, Nedim Lipka, and Sheng Li. 2018. Supervised transfer learning for product information question answering. In *2018 17th IEEE International Conference on Machine Learning and Applications (ICMLA)*, pages 1109–1114. IEEE.

Tuan Lai, Quan Hung Tran, Trung Bui, and Daisuke Kihara. 2019. A gated self-attention memory network for answer selection. In *Proceedings of the 2019 Conference on Empirical Methods in Natural Language Processing and the 9th International Joint Conference on Natural Language Processing (EMNLP-IJCNLP)*, pages 5953–5959, Hong Kong, China. Association for Computational Linguistics.

Tuan Manh Lai, Quan Hung Tran, Trung Bui, and Daisuke Kihara. 2020. A simple but effective bert model for dialog state tracking on resource-limited systems. In *ICASSP 2020-2020 IEEE International Conference on Acoustics, Speech and Signal Processing (ICASSP)*, pages 8034–8038. IEEE.

Guillaume Lample and Alexis Conneau. 2019. Cross-lingual language model pretraining. *Advances in Neural Information Processing Systems (NeurIPS)*.

Jinhyuk Lee, Wonjin Yoon, Sungdong Kim, Donghyeon Kim, Sunkyu Kim, Chan Ho So, and Jaewoo Kang. 2019. BioBERT: a pre-trained biomedical language representation model for biomedical text mining. *Bioinformatics*.

Yinhan Liu, Myle Ott, Naman Goyal, Jingfei Du, Mandar Joshi, Danqi Chen, Omer Levy, Mike Lewis, Luke Zettlemoyer, and Veselin Stoyanov. 2019. RoBERTa: A Robustly Optimized BERT Pretraining Approach. *arXiv preprint*, arXiv:1907.11692.

Ilya Loshchilov and Frank Hutter. 2019. Decoupled Weight Decay Regularization. In *Proceedings of ICLR*.

Sugeerth Murugesan, Sana Malik, Fan Du, Eunyee Koh, and Tuan Manh Lai. 2019. Deepcompare: Visual and interactive comparison of deep learning model performance. *IEEE computer graphics and applications*, 39(5):47–59.

Dat Quoc Nguyen and Anh Tuan Nguyen. 2020. PhoBERT: Pre-trained language models for Vietnamese. *Findings of EMNLP*.

Dat Quoc Nguyen, Thanh Vu, and A. Nguyen. 2020a. Bertweet: A pre-trained language model for english tweets. *EMNLP 2020*.

Dat Quoc Nguyen, Thanh Vu, Afshin Rahimi, Mai Hoang Dao, Linh The Nguyen, and Long Doan. 2020b. WNUT-2020 Task 2: Identification of Informative COVID-19 English Tweets. In *Proceedings of the 6th Workshop on Noisy User-generated Text*.

Xiaoman Pan, Boliang Zhang, Jonathan May, Joel Nothman, Kevin Knight, and Heng Ji. 2017. Cross-lingual name tagging and linking for 282 languages. In *Proceedings of the 55th Annual Meeting of the Association for Computational Linguistics (Volume 1: Long Papers)*, pages 1946–1958, Vancouver, Canada. Association for Computational Linguistics.

Alex Wang, Amanpreet Singh, Julian Michael, Felix Hill, Omer Levy, and Samuel R. Bowman. 2019. GLUE: A multi-task benchmark and analysis platform for natural language understanding. In *7th International Conference on Learning Representations, ICLR 2019, New Orleans, LA, USA, May 6-9, 2019*. OpenReview.net.

Thomas Wolf, Lysandre Debut, Victor Sanh, Julien
Chaumond, Clement Delangue, Anthony Moi, Pierric Cistac, Tim Rault, R'emi Louf, Morgan Funtowicz, and Jamie Brew. 2019. HuggingFace's Transformers: State-of-the-art Natural Language Processing. *arXiv preprint*, arXiv:1910.03771.

Qizhe Xie, E. Hovy, Minh-Thang Luong, and Quoc V.
Le. 2020. Self-training with noisy student improves
imagenet classification. *2020 IEEE/CVF Conference on Computer Vision and Pattern Recognition
(CVPR)*, pages 10684–10695.

Seunghyun Yoon, Franck Dernoncourt, Doo Soon Kim,
Trung Bui, and Kyomin Jung. 2019. A compare-
aggregate model with latent clustering for answer
selection. In *Proceedings of the 28th ACM International Conference on Information and Knowledge
Management*, pages 2093–2096.

NHK_STRL at WNUT-2020 Task 2: GATs with Syntactic Dependencies as Edges and CTC-based Loss for Text Classification

Yuki Yasuda*   Taichi Ishiwatari*   Taro Miyazaki*   Jun Goto

NHK Science and Technology Research Laboratories

{yasuda.y-hk,ishiwatari.t-fa,miyazaki.t-jw,goto.j-fw}@nhk.or.jp

Abstract

The outbreak of COVID-19 has greatly impacted our daily lives. In these circumstances, it is important to grasp the latest information to avoid causing too much fear and panic. To help grasp new information, extracting information from social networking sites is one of the effective ways. In this paper, we describe a method to identify whether a tweet related to COVID-19 is informative or not, which can help to grasp new information. The key features of our method are its use of graph attention networks to encode syntactic dependencies and word positions in the sentence, and a loss function based on connectionist temporal classification that can learn a label for each token without reference data for each token. Experimental results show that the proposed method achieved an F1 score of 0.9175, outperforming baseline methods.

1 Introduction

The outbreak of COVID-19 that has occurred since the end of 2019 has greatly impacted our daily lives. In these circumstances, it is important for everyone to understand the situation and grasp the latest information to avoid causing too much fear and panic. Nowadays, social networking sites (SNSs) such as Twitter and Facebook are important information sources because users post information regarding their personal events—including that related to COVID-19—in real time. For this reason, many monitoring systems for COVID-19 have been developed such as The Johns Hopkins Coronavirus Dashboard[1] and the COVID-19 Health System Response Monitor[2]. Many systems use SNSs as resources, but largely depend on manual work such as using cloud sourcing to extract informative posts from massive numbers of uninformative ones. Generally, SNSs contain too much information on miscellaneous topics, so extracting important information is difficult. Therefore, we attempted to develop a method to extract important information.

Our method first embeds each token in the input sentence using BERT (Devlin et al., 2019). Then, the vectors are fed into graph attention networks (GATs) (Veličković et al., 2018) to encode token-to-token relations. Finally, our method classifies each vector into labels using feed-forward neural networks (FFNNs). In the training process, we use a loss function based on connectionist temporal classification (CTC) (Graves et al., 2006). Experimental results show that our method using GATs and the CTC-based loss function achieved an F1 score of 0.9175, outperforming baseline methods.

Our contributions are as follows: (1) We propose a GAT-based network to embed syntactic dependencies and positional features of tokens in an input sentence. (2) We also propose a loss function, which enables to train labels for each token. (3) We confirmed the effectiveness of our proposed methods using the identification of informative COVID-19 English Tweets shared task dataset.

2 Identifying Informative COVID-19 Tweets Shared Task

The identification of informative COVID-19 English Tweets[3] is a shared task held at W-NUT (Workshop on Noisy User-generated Text) 2020 (Nguyen et al., 2020b). The purpose of the task is to identify whether English tweets related to COVID-19 are informative or not. The dataset for the task contains 7,000 tweets for training, 1,000 for validating, and 2,000 for testing. Each tweet in the data, excluding those in the testing data are labelled informative or uninformative. The target metric of the task is the F1 score for informative tweets.

---

*These authors are equally contributed to this work.

[1] https://coronavirus.jhu.edu/map.html

[2] https://www.covid19healthsystem.org

[3] http://noisy-text.github.io/2020/covid19tweet-task.html

Proceedings of the 2020 EMNLP Workshop W-NUT: The Sixth Workshop on Noisy User-generated Text, pages 324–330

Online, Nov 19, 2020. ©2020 Association for Computational Linguistics

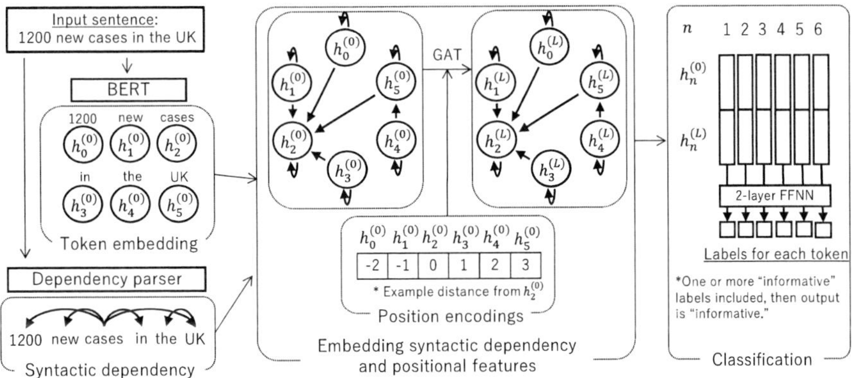

Figure 1: Overview of our method. Our method first embeds each token in an input sentence using BERT. Also, syntactic dependencies are obtained using a dependency parser. Then, our method embeds syntactic features using GATs, by using a graph that has nodes of token-embedding vectors and edges of syntactic dependencies and self-loops. Positional features are also added to the graph. The output vectors of the GATs are concatenated with BERT output vectors, and then fed into 2-layer FFNNs, which classifies each vector into labels. If one or more vectors are labelled as informative, the output class is informative. Note that the arrows in the the dependency parser example connect the head word to the dependent word as to follow a convention. On the other hand, arrows in the GAT example connect the dependent word to the head word, as used in our proposed method.

3 Methods

The overview of our method is illustrated in Figure 1. The key features of our method are embedding syntactic dependencies and positional features using GATs (Veličković et al., 2018), and calculating loss in the training process using a loss function based on CTC (Graves et al., 2006).

We use masked-token estimation as multi-task learning to help improve the generalization capability. We use word-dropout (Sennrich et al., 2016) before BERT, and the "dropped" tokens are used as masked words to be estimated in the training process as a multi-task.

3.1 GATs for encoding token-to-token relations

The BERT model, which we use for token embedding, uses position encoding to consider the position of tokens in the model, but its ability to capture global information including syntactic features is limited (Lu et al., 2020). Therefore, we use GATs with syntactic dependencies as edges of the graph, which enables our method to handle syntactic dependency explicitly. This is inspired from the work of Huang and Carley (2019).

We use all of the universal dependency (McDonald et al., 2013) as a directional edge regardless of dependency type[4]. The tokenizer used in BERT

---

[4]We attempted to use each type separately with the GAT, but the results were worse regardless of dependency types.

often separates a single word into many tokens. We connect edges from all tokens of a word to all tokens of the head word. For example, if there is a relation between the two words *COVID-19* and *tweet*, and the former word is divided into two tokens *COVID* and *##-19*, our method connects the two edges, *COVID* to *tweet* and *##-19* to *tweet*.

The GAT is based on multi-head attention (Vaswani et al., 2017) among neighbor nodes, with all the connected nodes used as the keys and values of the attention calculation. In many cases, the number of incoming edges for a node is only zero or one if syntactic dependencies are used as edges. Nodes that have no incoming edges cannot update the vector in the GATs. Also, for nodes that have only one incoming edge, the attention weight in the multi-head attention is 1.0, which leads to poor results. To overcome this problem, a self-loop for each node was proposed (Huang and Carley, 2019; Xu and Yang, 2019). Following that, we use a self-loop for each node in the GATs.

Positional features

Many edges are concentrated on the root word of a sentence, so the GATs treats all nodes equally. On the other hand, nearby and distant words are generally more and less related to the root word, respectively. To simulate this, we use positional encoding to our GATs. We use the relative distance between tokens as a parameter, then embed them along with the attention coefficient between nodes

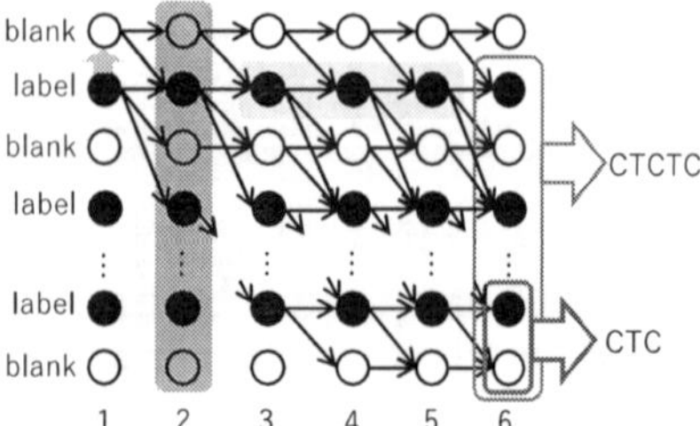

Figure 2: CTC is calculated as the sum of two probabilities in the blue box, while CTCTC is the sum of all probabilities except for the all-blank path as shown in the red box. Green and yellow boxes and orange arrow show the direction of label smoothing, token smoothing, and leaking, respectively.

when calculating the multi-head attention on the basis of the work from Ingraham et al. (2019) and Ishiwatari et al. (2020).

Following the work of Ishiwatari et al. (2020), we compared two types of positional embedding in our experiments, fixed and learned.

For fixed, we use the following representation as a positional embedding between the i-th and j-th tokens of the sentence:

$$PE^{ij}_{\text{fixed}} = L - (i - j) , \qquad (1)$$

where L is the number of tokens in the sentence.

For learned, we use a 1-layer FFNN with an input of PE^{ij}_{fixed} as a positional embedding as follows:

$$PE^{ij}_{\text{learned}} = \mathbf{W}_{PE} PE^{ij}_{\text{fixed}} + \mathbf{b}_{PE} , \qquad (2)$$

where $\mathbf{W}_{PE} \in \mathbb{R}^{|1 \times 1|}$ and $\mathbf{b}_{PE} \in \mathbb{1}^{|d|}$ are a learnable weight and bias, respectively.

The positional features are then broadcasted into $PE^{ij} \in |1 \times d|$ where d is the dimension of a GAT layer, and added after calculating the multi-head attention along the edges in the graph.

3.2 CTC for Text Classification (CTCTC)

Most tweets that were labelled as informative contain not only informative phrases but also uninformative parts. To consider this, we propose a new loss function—CTC for Text Classification (CTCTC).

The basis of CTC

Let us consider the input sequence of probabilities $\mathbf{x} \in \mathbb{R}^{|T| \times |L|}$ where $|T|$ denotes the length of the sequence and $|L|$ denotes the number of labels to classify. Note that L includes *blank*, which is a special symbol for CTC labelled for the data in which no labels are aligned. The probability $p_{ctc}(\mathbf{y}|\mathbf{x})$ for input $\mathbf{x}$ and reference data $\mathbf{y} \in \mathbb{1}^{\leq |T|}$ is calculated as follows:

$$p_{ctc}(\mathbf{y}|\mathbf{x}) \;=\; \sum_{\pi \in \mathcal{B}^{-1}(\mathbf{y})} p(\pi|\mathbf{x}) , \qquad (3)$$

where $\mathcal{B}^{-1}$ is the inverse of the many-to-one map $\mathcal{B}$ of all possible labellings from the input to reference data. In generating $\mathcal{B}$, *blanks* are inserted between each label in $\mathbf{y}$, i.e., for $\mathbf{y} = \{y_1, y_2, \cdots, y_{|\mathbf{y}|}\}$, a modified reference $\mathbf{y}' = \{blank, y_1, blank, y_2, \cdots, y_{|\mathbf{y}|}, blank\}$ is used to generate $\mathcal{B}$. In Figure 2, $\mathcal{B}$ is equal to the set of the paths of black arrows that finally reach one of the two dots in the blue box. Then, p_{ctc} represents the probability of the sum of all probabilities of paths that pass all labels with the given order as reference data, which is shown as the sum of two probabiliuties in the blue box in Figure 2.

CTCTC loss

We use a CTC-based loss function that is utilized for text classification. Our loss function accepts the reference data $\bar{y}$, which is a single label for an "informative" or "uninformative" sentence in the task, and assign a label or *blank* for all tokens in the sentence. It works by handling the uninformative parts in informative tweets as *blank* automatically.

Calculating CTCTC is almost the same as CTC, differing only in the construction of the many-to-one map. First, CTCTC arranges a sufficient number of the given reference label $\bar{y}$ and blank, i.e., $\bar{\mathbf{y}}' = \{blank, \bar{y}, blank, \bar{y}, \cdots, \bar{y}, blank\}$. Then, $\bar{\mathcal{B}}$ is generated, which is the set of all possible labellings from the input $\mathbf{x}$ to modified reference data $\bar{\mathbf{y}}'$ regardless of the number of passed labels in $\bar{\mathbf{y}}'$. In Figure 2, $\bar{\mathcal{B}}$ is equal to the set of the paths of black arrows that finally reach one of the dots in the red box. To calculate a CTCTC loss, $\bar{\mathcal{B}}$ is used instead of $\mathcal{B}$ in Equation (3). As a result, the probability p_{ctctc} represents the probability of at least one token in the input sequence being aligned to the label $\bar{y}$, which is illustrated as the sum of all dots in the red box in Figure 2.

Smoothing for CTCTC

CTCTC tends to align most tokens to *blank*, and only one token to the reference label. This is because the probability for *blank* is learned for every sentence in the training data regardless of its label, so the probability tends to be high for all data. To avoid the probabilities of all data being learned as blank, we prepare three types of smoothing.

Label smoothing We use label smoothing (Szegedy et al., 2016), which is a regularization technique to avoid overfitting and overconfidence. This replaces the one-hot reference label l with the smoothed label $l'(k)$ as follows:

$$l'(k) = (1 - \epsilon)\delta_{k,l} + \frac{\epsilon}{K} , \qquad (4)$$

where $\delta_{k,l}$ is the Dirac delta function, which equals 1 when $k = l$ and 0 otherwise, K is the set of labels to classify, and ϵ is the smoothing rate. The label-wise smoothing is illustrated as a green box in Figure 2.

Token smoothing This is almost the same as label smoothing but differs in the direction of the smoothing—token-wise. It works on the basis that words close together often have similar meanings. We set the max width to 5 to consider this smoothing in the experiments. The token-wise smoothing is illustrated as a yellow box in Figure 2.

Leaking To enable learning the probability for labels instead of *blank*, we use the one-direction smoothing named "leaking." This is calculated as follows:

$$p'_{i,blank} = (1 - \epsilon')p_{i,blank} + \epsilon'p_{i,\bar{y}} , \qquad (5)$$

where ϵ' is the smoothing rate, $p_{i,blank}$ and $p_{i,\bar{y}}$ are the probabilities for *blank* and the reference label $\bar{y}$ of i-th data of the input sequence, respectively. This is calculated only for the probability of *blank*, and is illustrated as an orange arrow in Figure 2.

4   Experiments

4.1   Experimental settings

Our experiments were based on the identification of informative COVID-19 English Tweets dataset mentioned in Section 2. We conducted two experiments on the basis of the validation and testing data, respectively. For the validation data-based experiment, we used training data contains 7,000 tweets and validating data contains 1,000 tweets for training and testing, respectively. For the testing data-based experiment, we used 8,000 tweets mixed from the training and validating data for 4-fold cross validation. Then, an ensemble of the best model of each fold data were used for testing data.

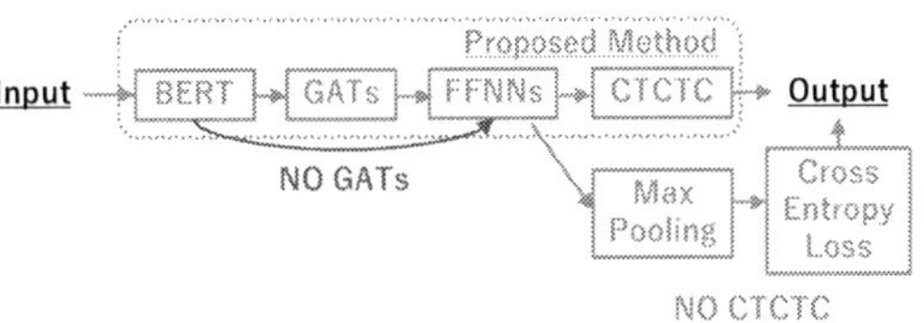

Figure 3: Overview of baseline methods. Green elements show the process of our proposed method. The blue arrow and orange elements show the process of a baseline method that does not use GATs and does not use CTCTC, respectively.

We added the output scores of each model for the model ensemble.

The models were implemented in PyTorch (Paszke et al., 2019), with Transformers (Wolf et al., 2019) and Deep Graph Library (Wang et al., 2019), and learned with the RAdam optimizer (Liu et al., 2020) with a learning rate of 0.0001. We used BERT-base, uncased (Devlin et al., 2019) as a pretrained model, with fine-tuning and a learning rate of 0.00002. We used spaCy (Honnibal and Montani, 2017) for dependency parsing.

The following hyperparameters were used: number of GATs layers was 2; a mini-batch size of 16; L2 regularization coefficient of 0.1; dropout rate of 0.1; word dropout rate of 0.2; 50 training iterations, with early stopping on the validating data on the basis of the F1 score for the informative class; and smoothing ratio for the three smoothing methods of CTCTC of 0.2.

4.2   Baseline methods

We prepared baseline methods as shown in Figure 3. To confirm the effectiveness of the GATs, a baseline method of "no GATs" that does not use GATs but the output vectors of BERT is directly fed into the FFNNs. Also, to confirm the effectiveness of CTCTC, a baseline of "no CTCTC" that does not use CTCTC but cross entropy loss is used.

4.3   Results

Table 1 shows the results for the validation data-based experiment. The rows in which Use GATs and Use CTCTC are not checked indicate the baselines shown in Section 4.2. F1 score shows the F1 score for the informative class with the mean and standard deviation of five-time trials of the same settings. Our methods using both GATs and CTCTC (# 9 and 10) achieved the top-2 results in the table.

Table 2 shows the results on the test data, which

Table 1: Experimental results on validation data-based experiments.

#	GATs parameters		CTCTC parameters				F1 score
	Use GATs	Positional feature	Use CTCTC	Label smoothing	Token smoothing	Leaking	
1							0.9154 ± 0.0041
2	✓						0.9134 ± 0.0015
3	✓	Fixed					0.9151 ± 0.0026
4	✓	Learned					0.9151 ± 0.0009
5			✓				0.0000 ± 0.0000
6			✓	✓			0.9128 ± 0.0026
7			✓	✓	✓		0.9133 ± 0.0052
8			✓	✓	✓	✓	0.9153 ± 0.0024
9	✓	Fixed	✓	✓	✓	✓	0.9172 ± 0.0027
10	✓	Learned	✓	✓	✓	✓	$\mathbf{0.9175 \pm 0.0044}$

Table 2: Results on the test data.

Team / Method	F1 score
Ours (#9 in Table 1)	0.8898
Ours (#10 in Table 1)	0.8885
NutCracker	0.9096
NLP_North	0.9096
UIT-HSE	0.9094

are the official results of the shared task and we ranked 21st out of 55 participants[5]. The table also shows the results of the top-3 teams in the shared task.

4.4 Discussion

The results for the methods using GATs with CTCTC (#9 and 10) are better than the others. This is because our CTCTC uses vectors of each token so the performance depends on the quality of the vector of each token. Our GATs work to improve the quality of the vector of each token by using token-to-token relations. Therefore, we believe our GATs and CTCTC work well in combination. On the other hand, GATs without CTCTC cannot make the best use of the improved vectors because they are mixed up vectors of tokens into one vector using max-pooling, so some of the details of the vectors are lost. Also, in using CTCTC without GATs, we observed that the output vectors of each token in the sentence are almost the same. This means that token-level information is lost, so accuracy may be lower for methods using CTCTC in these cases. By using GATs with CTCTC, we can avoid losing the information, which leads to good results.

5 Related Work

There are a number of methods that use GATs with a pre-trained language model. Lu et al. (2020) use a network on a vocabulary graph, which is based on word co-occurrence information, and Huang and Carley (2019) and Xu and Yang (2019) use syntactic features as a graph. Also, there are several methods that use positional encoding into GATs (Ingraham et al., 2019; Ishiwatari et al., 2020). Our method uses GATs to consider syntactic features with positional features in combination, which is distinguishable from conventional methods.

The CTC loss function is widely used for long data sequence with not-one-to-one-aligned reference data such as speech recognition (Graves et al., 2013; Kim et al., 2017), but to the best of our knowledge, no method that uses CTC for text classification tasks exists.

6 Conclusion and Future Work

In this paper, we proposed a GATs-based model that embeds token-to-token relations, and a loss function that can learn classes for each tokens. We conducted evaluations using the identification of informative COVID-19 English Tweets dataset, and confirmed that our proposed methods are effective.

To determine whether CTCTC can work for other tasks especially for the classification into large amount of classes and to exploit pre-trained models other than BERT, especially for tweet-specific models such as BERTweet (Nguyen et al., 2020a) and CT-BERT (Müller et al., 2020), are subjects of as our future work.

Acknowledgement

We would like to thank the identification of informative COVID-19 English Tweets shared task organizers for providing the dataset and opportunity for discussion. We also thank the anonymous reviewers for their helpful comments.

---

[5]https://competitions.codalab.org/
competitions/25845#results

References

Jacob Devlin, Ming-Wei Chang, Kenton Lee, and Kristina Toutanova. 2019. BERT: Pre-training of deep bidirectional transformers for language understanding. In *Proceedings of the 2019 Conference of the North American Chapter of the Association for Computational Linguistics: Human Language Technologies, Volume 1 (Long and Short Papers)*, pages 4171–4186, Minneapolis, Minnesota. Association for Computational Linguistics.

Alex Graves, Santiago Fernández, Faustino Gomez, and Jürgen Schmidhuber. 2006. Connectionist temporal classification: labelling unsegmented sequence data with recurrent neural networks. In *Proceedings of the 23rd international conference on Machine learning*, pages 369–376.

Alex Graves, Abdel-rahman Mohamed, and Geoffrey Hinton. 2013. Speech recognition with deep recurrent neural networks. In *2013 IEEE international conference on acoustics, speech and signal processing*, pages 6645–6649. IEEE.

Matthew Honnibal and Ines Montani. 2017. spaCy 2: Natural language understanding with Bloom embeddings, convolutional neural networks and incremental parsing. To appear.

Binxuan Huang and Kathleen M Carley. 2019. Syntax-aware aspect level sentiment classification with graph attention networks. In *Proceedings of the 2019 Conference on Empirical Methods in Natural Language Processing and the 9th International Joint Conference on Natural Language Processing (EMNLP-IJCNLP)*, pages 5472–5480.

John Ingraham, Vikas Garg, Regina Barzilay, and Tommi Jaakkola. 2019. Generative models for graph-based protein design. In *Advances in Neural Information Processing Systems*, pages 15820–15831.

Taichi Ishiwatari, Yuki Yasuda, Taro Miyazaki, and Jun Goto. 2020. Relation-aware graph attention networks with relational position encodings for emotion recognition in conversations. In *Proceedings of the 2019 Conference on Empirical Methods in Natural Language Processing (EMNLP 2020)*.

Suyoun Kim, Takaaki Hori, and Shinji Watanabe. 2017. Joint CTC-attention based end-to-end speech recognition using multi-task learning. In *2017 IEEE international conference on acoustics, speech and signal processing (ICASSP)*, pages 4835–4839. IEEE.

Liyuan Liu, Haoming Jiang, Pengcheng He, Weizhu Chen, Xiaodong Liu, Jianfeng Gao, and Jiawei Han. 2020. On the variance of the adaptive learning rate and beyond. In *Proceedings of the Eighth International Conference on Learning Representations (ICLR 2020)*.

Zhibin Lu, Pan Du, and Jian-Yun Nie. 2020. VGCN-BERT: Augmenting BERT with graph embedding for text classification. In *European Conference on Information Retrieval*, pages 369–382. Springer.

Ryan McDonald, Joakim Nivre, Yvonne Quirmbach-Brundage, Yoav Goldberg, Dipanjan Das, Kuzman Ganchev, Keith Hall, Slav Petrov, Hao Zhang, Oscar Täckström, et al. 2013. Universal dependency annotation for multilingual parsing. In *Proceedings of the 51st Annual Meeting of the Association for Computational Linguistics (Volume 2: Short Papers)*, pages 92–97.

Martin Müller, Marcel Salathé, and Per E Kummervold. 2020. Covid-twitter-bert: A natural language processing model to analyse covid-19 content on twitter. *arXiv preprint arXiv:2005.07503*.

Dat Quoc Nguyen, Thanh Vu, and Anh Tuan Nguyen. 2020a. BERTweet: A pre-trained language model for English Tweets. In *Proceedings of the 2020 Conference on Empirical Methods in Natural Language Processing: System Demonstrations*.

Dat Quoc Nguyen, Thanh Vu, Afshin Rahimi, Mai Hoang Dao, Linh The Nguyen, and Long Doan. 2020b. WNUT-2020 Task 2: Identification of Informative COVID-19 English Tweets. In *Proceedings of the 6th Workshop on Noisy User-generated Text*.

Adam Paszke, Sam Gross, Francisco Massa, Adam Lerer, James Bradbury, Gregory Chanan, Trevor Killeen, Zeming Lin, Natalia Gimelshein, Luca Antiga, Alban Desmaison, Andreas Kopf, Edward Yang, Zachary DeVito, Martin Raison, Alykhan Tejani, Sasank Chilamkurthy, Benoit Steiner, Lu Fang, Junjie Bai, and Soumith Chintala. 2019. PyTorch: An imperative style, high-performance deep learning library. In H. Wallach, H. Larochelle, A. Beygelzimer, F. d'Alché-Buc, E. Fox, and R. Garnett, editors, *Advances in Neural Information Processing Systems 32*, pages 8024–8035. Curran Associates, Inc.

Rico Sennrich, Barry Haddow, and Alexandra Birch. 2016. Edinburgh neural machine translation systems for WMT 16. In *Proceedings of the First Conference on Machine Translation: Volume 2, Shared Task Papers*, pages 371–376, Berlin, Germany. Association for Computational Linguistics.

Christian Szegedy, Vincent Vanhoucke, Sergey Ioffe, Jon Shlens, and Zbigniew Wojna. 2016. Rethinking the inception architecture for computer vision. In *Proceedings of the IEEE conference on computer vision and pattern recognition*, pages 2818–2826.

Ashish Vaswani, Noam Shazeer, Niki Parmar, Jakob Uszkoreit, Llion Jones, Aidan N Gomez, Łukasz Kaiser, and Illia Polosukhin. 2017. Attention is all you need. In *Advances in neural information processing systems*, pages 5998–6008.

Petar Veličković, Guillem Cucurull, Arantxa Casanova, Adriana Romero, Pietro Liò, and Yoshua Bengio. 2018. Graph Attention Networks. *International Conference on Learning Representations*.

Minjie Wang, Lingfan Yu, Da Zheng, Quan Gan, Yu Gai, Zihao Ye, Mufei Li, Jinjing Zhou, Qi Huang, Chao Ma, et al. 2019. Deep graph library: Towards efficient and scalable deep learning on graphs. *arXiv preprint arXiv:1909.01315*.

Thomas Wolf, Lysandre Debut, Victor Sanh, Julien Chaumond, Clement Delangue, Anthony Moi, Pierric Cistac, Tim Rault, R'emi Louf, Morgan Funtowicz, and Jamie Brew. 2019. HuggingFace's transformers: State-of-the-art natural language processing. *ArXiv*, abs/1910.03771.

Yinchuan Xu and Junlin Yang. 2019. Look again at the syntax: Relational graph convolutional network for gendered ambiguous pronoun resolution. *GeBNLP 2019*, page 96.

NLP North at WNUT-2020 Task 2: Pre-training versus Ensembling for Detection of Informative COVID-19 English Tweets

Anders Giovanni Møller
IT University of Copenhagen
Rued Langgaards Vej 7
2300 Copenhagen
`agmo@itu.dk`

Rob van der Goot
IT University of Copenhagen
Rued Langgaards Vej 7
2300 Copenhagen
`robv@itu.dk`

Barbara Plank
IT University of Copenhagen
Rued Langgaards Vej 7
2300 Copenhagen
`bapl@itu.dk`

Abstract

With the COVID-19 pandemic raging world-wide since the beginning of the 2020 decade, the need for monitoring systems to track relevant information on social media is vitally important. This paper describes our submission to the WNUT-2020 Task 2: Identification of informative COVID-19 English Tweets. We investigate the effectiveness for a variety of classification models, and found that domain-specific pre-trained BERT models lead to the best performance. On top of this, we attempt a variety of ensembling strategies, but these attempts did not lead to further improvements. Our final best model, the standalone CT-BERT model, proved to be highly competitive, leading to a shared first place in the shared task. Our results emphasize the importance of domain and task-related pre-training.[1]

1 Introduction

The amount of COVID-19 pandemic cases is rapidly approaching 25M world wide, with almost 1M people who have lost their life to the merciless disease, according to worldometer.[2] This paper exploits the capabilities of Natural Language Processing (NLP) techniques to extract informative tweets, and is a participation in the WNUT-2020 Task 2: Identification of informative COVID-19 English Tweets (Nguyen et al., 2020).

Social media is a useful medium for rapid access to information about the pandemic - but along with all the informative tweets comes an even larger amount of non-informative information. Being able to extract what is informative, and hereby leave out all the non-informative posts, is vital in monitoring and tracking the development of COVID-19. In the

---

[1] source code is available on: `https://github.com/AGMoller/noisy_text/`

[2] `https://www.worldometers.info/coronavirus/`

> **Informative**
> Oklahoma's first confirmed case of coronavirus is in Tulsa County
> <URL>#SmartNews
> **Uninformative**
> Trump could cure Coronavirus 19, AIDS, and Cancer in the same day and the media would say he wasn't doing anything.

Figure 1: Examples of INFORMATIVE and UNINFORMATIVE tweets from the training data.

shared task, informative tweets were defined as to contain information about COVID-19 cases such as statistics, locations or travel history. Figure 1 shows two examples from the training data.

The introduction of neural networks has led to an increase in performance for many natural language processing tasks (Manning, 2015). However, previous work on classification showed that SVMs with character and/or word n-grams often still outperform neural networks (Zampieri et al., 2017; Medvedeva et al., 2017; Çöltekin and Rama, 2018; Basile et al., 2018). Neural network approaches can elegantly exploit raw data, by pre-training word embeddings using a language modeling objective. Recently, more powerful contextual embeddings were introduced (Peters et al., 2018; Devlin et al., 2019), which base each word embedding on its context. These contextual embeddings are generally pre-trained on huge amounts of raw data, and then fine-tuned on the target task. This leads to the question: *How do the three types of classification models viz. SVM, neural models with pre-trained embeddings and various contextual models compare and perform in this classification task?* (**RQ1**)

Neural networks as well as transformer-based models can directly exploit additional raw data by

Proceedings of the 2020 EMNLP Workshop W-NUT: The Sixth Workshop on Noisy User-generated Text, pages 331–336
Online, Nov 19, 2020. ©2020 Association for Computational Linguistics

pre-training. This pre-training often leads to superior performance, depending mainly on the size and distribution of the pre-training data. Although no additional annotation effort is necessary for pre-training, it often comes with huge computational cost and exhaustive training time. Recent work has shown that selecting data which matches the target domain better (domain-specific or task-specific) is important for transformer-based pre-training (Gururangan et al., 2020; Gu et al., 2020). This leads to the question: *How important is task-specific pre-training for detection of informative COVID-19 tweets?* (**RQ2**)

Finally, we are interested in the supplementary of the three different architectures. Even though one model outperforms the other two models, it can still be that they have different strengths, and combining them can thus lead to superior performance. Our last question is: *Can we ensemble SVM, neural network and BERT-based models to improve robustness?* (**RQ3**)

2 Methodology

Below we will discuss our implementations of each of the classifiers and the ensemble models.

2.1 SVM

We used the linear SVM classifier with default parameters from Scikit-learn (Pedregosa et al., 2011) as basis for our implementation. We experimented with n-grams on a variety of levels. Besides the standard word and character n-grams, we also evaluate wordpiece n-grams (Schuster and Nakajima, 2012).[3] For each granularity (character, word piece, word), we systematically evaluated each range of n between 1-7. We found the optimal range of n to be 1-2 for words, 5-6 for characters, and 1-2 for word pieces. When combining all features, and ablating one group, we found that the highest score was obtained with word and character n-grams which was used in the final model. We found that adding word pieces led to a small performance decrease.

2.2 Neural Networks

We experimented with two different neural architectures, a multi-layer perceptron (MLP) and a 1-dimensional convolutional neural network (Conv1d). The text input was embedded using GloVe embeddings (Pennington et al., 2014), pre-trained on 2B English tweets with 27B tokens and a vocabulary of 1.2M words. These embeddings are chosen, because they are trained on Twitter data, even though this data was sampled before the COVID-19 pandemic. The embeddings were not further tuned during training but were kept static.

The MLP is a two-layer neural net using ReLU as activation in the hidden layers. The layers consist of 1024 and 512 neurons respectively. Between the two layers a dropout with a rate of 0.5 is applied. The Conv1d model consists of a single layer of 1-dimensional convolution with 64 filters and a kernel size of 5, max-pooling with a pool-size of 2, and a dropout layer with a rate of 0.5. Both architectures apply a sigmoid function in the final output layer.

2.3 BERT

Three different pre-trained transformer models were used and evaluated to investigate the impact of diverse pre-training domains and task-specific fine-tuning. All transformer models were fine-tuned on 4 epochs and optimized using the AdamW optimizer (Loshchilov and Hutter, 2017) with a learning rate of 2×10^{-5} and an epsilon value of 1×10^{-8}. We used the following transformers:

- BERT base (uncased) (Devlin et al., 2019): pre-trained on the BookCorpus dataset (Zhu et al., 2015) consisting of 800M words and English Wikipedia with 2.5B words.

- RoBERTa base (Liu et al., 2019): similar to BERT base, but has extended the training data with CC-News (Nagel, 2016), OpenWebText (Gokaslan and Cohen, 2019) and Stories (Trinh and Le, 2018), a total amount of 160GB of text.

- Covid-Twitter BERT (CT-BERT) (Müller et al., 2020): based on BERT-Large, but has been trained further on a collection of 22.5M corona related tweets collected from January 12 to April 16, 2020. The data consisted of 40.7M sentences and 633M tokens.

Where BERT-base is trained on ∼3B words unrelated to COVID-19, RoBERTa is trained on much more data, and the CT-BERT training data is similar in size as BERT-base, but matches the domain of our task.

2.4 Ensembling

In an attempt to achieve better performance, different ensembling experiments were carried out,

---

[3] We used the mBERT word piece vocabulary.

Model	F1	Note
SVM	83.64	word 1-2 grams, char 5-6 grams
SVM	83.54	word 1-2 grams, char 5-6 grams, word-piece 1-2
MLP	78.05	200d Twitter GloVe embeddings
Conv1d	75.52	200d Twitter GloVe embeddings
BERT-base	89.86	
RoBERTa-base	89.59	
CT-BERT	**92.19**	

Ensemble Model	F1	Note
CT-BERT, RoBERTa, BERT-base	88.19	Soft voting
CT-BERT, RoBERTa, BERT-base	89.99	Hard voting
CT-BERT, SVM	92.19	Thresholding
Random Forest Classifier	**91.67**	Stacking

Table 1: Model results evaluated on the development data using weighted F1 score as metric.

which included majority voting, stacking and thresholding.

Majority: Majority voting was used among the BERT-models, both with hard and soft voting. In hard voting classification, each transformer model would provide a predicted label, and the majority label would be the final prediction. In soft voting, each model produces a probability for each class using a sigmoid function. The final prediction is the class with the highest average probability. All three models were weighted equally.

Stacking: Our second ensembling approach is stacked generalization (Wolpert, 1992), where we trained a meta-classifier which takes the predictions of all other models as input as well as their confidence. Confidence being the probability for each class. We tuned this step in a 10-fold setup on the development data. As classifier, we chose a random forest classifier (Breiman, 2001), because it can model different types of features (binary and continuous), and can model feature interactions intrinsically.

Thresholding: We test whether CT-BERT outputs can be replaced with SVM predictions whenever the confidence score of CT-BERT is below a certain threshold. Here, we use SVM as second system instead of the better performing BERT models because SVM in nature is very different compared to CT-BERT, and is thus more likely to give a complementary perspective.

3 Evaluation

3.1 Data

The data used in this work is provided in connection with the shared task (Nguyen et al., 2020) of the 2020 W-NUT workshop. The training data consists of 7,000 tweets, the validation data 1,000 tweets and the final test data of 12,000 tweets of which 2,000 where annotated and used for the final scores and ranking. All the data has a close to equal class distribution being either INFORMATIVE or UNINFORMATIVE.

3.2 Individual Model Evaluation on Development Data

As found in Table 1, CT-BERT had the overall best performance on the validation data scoring a weighted F1 of 0.92185. Compared to the other transformer models, the domain-specific pre-training appears to be crucial in this specific classification task, with a relative difference in weighted F1-score of absolute 2.6% higher than BERT-base and 2.9% higher than RoBERTa (**RQ2**). When comparing BERT-base and RoBERTa one can observe that they achieve almost similar results, despite being pre-trained on datasets covering different domains. This shows that the domain on which the embeddings are trained is more important compared to the size (RoBERTA is trained on more general text compared to BERT-base, whereas CT-BERT is trained on domain-specific data).

The two neural networks using GloVe embeddings achieved the lowest scores among the tested

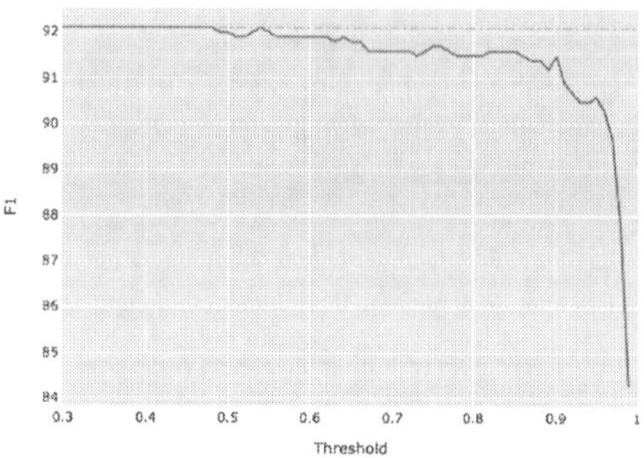

Figure 2: Thresholding: CT-BERT predictions with SVM replacement

models with an F1 of 78.05 for the MLP model, and 75.52 for the Conv1d model. They both suffered from lack of fine-tuning of parameters and non-contextualized embeddings.

The SVM achieved an F1 score of 83.64, being in the middle when comparing the three types of models. Our initial ablation study in the selection of n-gram features allowed for an increase in performance of $\sim 2\%$. This, however, shows that an SVM with sparse n-gram input can outperform neural models with pre-trained embeddings, confirming previous work (Section 1) (**RQ1**). It should be noted that an SVM does not require any pre-training, and is much faster and cheaper to train, so in specific situations it could in fact be the preferred solution.

3.3 Ensembling on Development Data

Majority: Neither hard voting nor soft voting managed to overcome the performance of standalone CT-BERT. Soft voting, which was based on the probabilities of the two labels, achieved an F1 score of 88.19. Using hard voting, where each transformer model contributes with a single predicted label, an F1 score of 89.99 was achieved.

Stacking: The stacking model proved to be the best ensemble model and was used as alternative model to our standalone CT-BERT in the official shared task submission, which allowed for two final submissions. On development data, our 10-fold development setup achieved an F1 score of 91.67. This is a relative difference of -0.55% compared to CT-BERT (**RQ3**). The standalone model is more accurate and more efficient, and hence the preferred solution over ensembling.

Model	F1
Ensemble (Random Forest)	90.54
CT-BERT (ours)	**90.96**
Highest (team NutCracker)	**90.96**

Table 2: Results on the test data, we evaluate our best individual model, best ensemble model and the highest score achieved in the shared task. According to F1, our system shares the first place with team NutCracker.

Thresholding: CT-BERT proved to perform the best compared to the other models. In an attempt to assist CT-BERT when the confidence score of a prediction was below a certain threshold, the non-neural SVM model would provide its prediction on the given input tweet and replace the CT-BERT prediction.

Figure 2 shows the F1 score when testing different confidence thresholds. The dashed line indicates standalone CT-BERT. We found that replacing CT-BERT does not at a single point obtain better F1 score than the standalone model. When the threshold surpasses a certain lower boundary, all predictions are solely from CT-BERT. This is the reason why the maximum F1 score achieved is equal to standalone CT-BERT, and why it is not considered as the best ensemble model. In the other end when the threshold approaches 1, all predictions are provided by the SVM.

3.4 Test data

Results in Table 2 confirm that ensembling is not beneficial over using the output of CT-BERT directly. It appears from the evaluated scores on both the development and test data that task-specific pre-training is crucial in this particular classification task, and that complementing CT-BERT with ensembling did not improve the performance. Furthermore, the performance of CT-BERT is confirmed by comparing to the other participants of the shared task, where it ranked 1st out of 98 submissions from 55 teams (according to official F1 score ranking; we rank 2nd if we consider both F1 and accuracy). Our CT-BERT model shares the first place with the submission by team NutCracker.

4 Conclusion

In this paper we have presented our winning participation for the shared task of WNUT-2020 on Identification of Informative COVID-19 English Tweets. We evaluated three types of models; SVM, neural networks with pre-trained embeddings, and transformer models. We found that the transformer-based covid-related CT-BERT model performed the best, achieving an F1 score of 90.96 on the hidden test data **(RQ1)**. Evaluating our models on the development data, we found that the CT-BERT model, which was pre-trained on domain and task-related data, performed better than BERT-base and RoBERTa pre-trained on data unrelated to the shared task **(RQ2)**. Different types of ensembling approaches were tested in an attempt to improve robustness. This included majority voting, stacking and thresholding. We found stacking to be most competitive, albeit it still underperformed compared to standalone CT-BERT (-0.55%) **(RQ3)**.

Acknowledgement

We would like to thank the organizers for this shared task. Part of this research is supported by a grant from Danmarks Frie Forskningsfond (9063-00077B).

References

Angelo Basile, Gareth Dwyer, Maria Medvedeva, Josine Rawee, Hessel Haagsma, and Malvina Nissim. 2018. Simply the best: Minimalist system trumps complex models in author profiling. In *Experimental IR Meets Multilinguality, Multimodality, and Interaction*, pages 143–156, Cham. Springer International Publishing.

Leo Breiman. 2001. Random forests. *Machine learning*, 45(1):5–32.

Çağrı Çöltekin and Taraka Rama. 2018. Tübingen-oslo at SemEval-2018 task 2: SVMs perform better than RNNs in emoji prediction. In *Proceedings of The 12th International Workshop on Semantic Evaluation*, pages 34–38, New Orleans, Louisiana. Association for Computational Linguistics.

Jacob Devlin, Ming-Wei Chang, Kenton Lee, and Kristina Toutanova. 2019. BERT: Pre-training of deep bidirectional transformers for language understanding. In *Proceedings of the 2019 Conference of the North American Chapter of the Association for Computational Linguistics: Human Language Technologies, Volume 1 (Long and Short Papers)*, pages 4171–4186, Minneapolis, Minnesota. Association for Computational Linguistics.

Aaron Gokaslan and Vanya Cohen. 2019. Openwebtext corpus. http://Skylion007.github.io/OpenWebTextCorpus.

Yu Gu, Robert Tinn, Hao Cheng, Michael Lucas, Naoto Usuyama, Xiaodong Liu, Tristan Naumann, Jianfeng Gao, and Hoifung Poon. 2020. Domain-specific language model pretraining for biomedical natural language processing. *arXiv preprint arXiv:2007.15779*.

Suchin Gururangan, Ana Marasović, Swabha Swayamdipta, Kyle Lo, Iz Beltagy, Doug Downey, and Noah A. Smith. 2020. Don't stop pretraining: Adapt language models to domains and tasks. In *Proceedings of the 58th Annual Meeting of the Association for Computational Linguistics*, pages 8342–8360, Online. Association for Computational Linguistics.

Yinhan Liu, Myle Ott, Naman Goyal, Jingfei Du, Mandar Joshi, Danqi Chen, Omer Levy, Mike Lewis, Luke Zettlemoyer, and Veselin Stoyanov. 2019. Roberta: A robustly optimized BERT pretraining approach. *CoRR*, abs/1907.11692.

Ilya Loshchilov and Frank Hutter. 2017. Fixing weight decay regularization in adam. *CoRR*, abs/1711.05101.

Christopher D. Manning. 2015. Computational linguistics and deep learning. *Computational Linguistics*, 41(4):701–707.

Maria Medvedeva, Martin Kroon, and Barbara Plank. 2017. When sparse traditional models outperform dense neural networks: the curious case of discriminating between similar languages. In *Proceedings of the Fourth Workshop on NLP for Similar Languages, Varieties and Dialects (VarDial)*, pages 156–163, Valencia, Spain. Association for Computational Linguistics.

M. Müller, Marcel Salathé, and P. Kummervold. 2020. Covid-twitter-bert: A natural language processing model to analyse covid-19 content on twitter. *ArXiv*, abs/2005.07503.

Sebastian Nagel. 2016. https://commoncrawl.org/2016/10/news-dataset-available/.

Dat Quoc Nguyen, Thanh Vu, Afshin Rahimi, Mai Hoang Dao, Linh The Nguyen, and Long Doan. 2020. WNUT-2020 Task 2: Identification of Informative COVID-19 English Tweets. In *Proceedings of the 6th Workshop on Noisy User-generated Text*.

F. Pedregosa, G. Varoquaux, A. Gramfort, V. Michel, B. Thirion, O. Grisel, M. Blondel, P. Prettenhofer, R. Weiss, V. Dubourg, J. Vanderplas, A. Passos, D. Cournapeau, M. Brucher, M. Perrot, and E. Duchesnay. 2011. Scikit-learn: Machine learning in Python. *Journal of Machine Learning Research*, 12:2825–2830.

Jeffrey Pennington, Richard Socher, and Christopher D. Manning. 2014. Glove: Global vectors for word representation. In *Empirical Methods in Natural Language Processing (EMNLP)*, pages 1532–1543.

Matthew Peters, Mark Neumann, Mohit Iyyer, Matt Gardner, Christopher Clark, Kenton Lee, and Luke Zettlemoyer. 2018. Deep contextualized word representations. In *Proceedings of the 2018 Conference of the North American Chapter of the Association for Computational Linguistics: Human Language Technologies, Volume 1 (Long Papers)*, pages 2227–2237, New Orleans, Louisiana. Association for Computational Linguistics.

Mike Schuster and Kaisuke Nakajima. 2012. Japanese and korean voice search. In *2012 IEEE International Conference on Acoustics, Speech and Signal Processing (ICASSP)*, pages 5149–5152. IEEE.

Trieu H. Trinh and Quoc V. Le. 2018. A simple method for commonsense reasoning. *CoRR*, abs/1806.02847.

David Wolpert. 1992. Stacked generalization. *Neural Networks*, 5:241–259.

Marcos Zampieri, Shervin Malmasi, Nikola Ljubešić, Preslav Nakov, Ahmed Ali, Jörg Tiedemann, Yves Scherrer, and Noëmi Aepli. 2017. Findings of the VarDial evaluation campaign 2017. In *Proceedings of the Fourth Workshop on NLP for Similar Languages, Varieties and Dialects (VarDial)*, pages 1–15, Valencia, Spain. Association for Computational Linguistics.

Yukun Zhu, Ryan Kiros, Richard S. Zemel, Ruslan Salakhutdinov, Raquel Urtasun, Antonio Torralba, and Sanja Fidler. 2015. Aligning books and movies: Towards story-like visual explanations by watching movies and reading books. *CoRR*, abs/1506.06724.

Siva at WNUT-2020 Task 2: Fine-tuning Transformer Neural Networks for Identification of Informative Covid-19 Tweets

Siva Sai

Birla Institute of Technology & Science, Pilani Campus

Pilani-333031

`f20170779@pilani.bits-pilani.ac.in`

Abstract

Social media witnessed vast amounts of misinformation being circulated every day during the Covid-19 pandemic so much so that the WHO Director-General termed the phenomenon as "infodemic." The ill-effects of such misinformation are multifarious. Thus, identifying and eliminating the sources of misinformation becomes very crucial, especially when mass panic can be controlled only through the right information. However, manual identification is arduous, with such large amounts of data being generated every day. This shows the importance of automatic identification of misinformative posts on social media. WNUT-2020 Task 2 aims at building systems for automatic identification of informative tweets. In this paper, I discuss my approach to WNUT-2020 Task 2. I fine-tuned eleven variants of four transformer networks - BERT, RoBERTa, XLM-RoBERTa, ELECTRA, on top of two different preprocessing techniques to reap good results. My top submission achieved an F1-score of 85.3% in the final evaluation.

1   Introduction

In today's highly connected world, social media assumes a vital role during pandemics like Covid-19. Social media platforms have been used positively by international health organizations and Governments to disseminate information about the pandemic and precautions regrading the same. Unfortunately, the world has also seen the misuse of social media for achieving cheap ends, severely damaging the physical and mental health of individuals, along with the increase in societal distrust. The false information is dangerous during a crisis when the mass panic can only be controlled with information(Lancet, 2020). A study(Wilson and Chen, 2020) identifies that panic in social media regarding Covid-19 spread faster than the Covid-19

virus spread. The proportionately large volume of misinformation compared to credible information can be seen from the very less engagement generated by posts from WHO (in several thousands) as compared to false news(over 52 million)(Mian and Khan, 2020).

The direct damage of misinformation is clearly evident. In Iran, hundreds of people died after consuming methanol, which is propagated on social media as one of the cures[1]. There is even concern from authorities that even if a vaccine is discovered, anti-vaccination groups on social media may prevent people from getting vaccinated. False and conspiracy information about leading health organizations like WHO and leading scientists can quickly decrease the public trust on the correct agents, thus causing self-damage to individuals. The ill-effects of misinformation during pandemics can reach such extremes where they can even affect governmental policies. For example,(Mian and Khan, 2020) reminds us how the rejection of AIDS by the South African government in the early 2000s cost more than 300,000 lives.

In this context, proper identification and control of misleading information on social media assume a pivotal role. However, manual identification and control of the false posts is a Herculean task. For example, a 900 percent increase of fact-checkers during Covid-19 could not handle the flow of misinformation(Shahi et al., 2020). So developing automated methods and techniques to identify misinformation is essential in the current context. The WNUT-2020 Task 2 take steps in this direction. Recently, Transformer neural architectures achieved State-of-the-art results in several NLP tasks, including text classification. In this work, I make use of eleven variants of four different Transformer archi-

---

[1] `https://www.who.int/news-room/feature-stories/detail/immunizing-the-public-against-misinformation`

Proceedings of the 2020 EMNLP Workshop W-NUT: The Sixth Workshop on Noisy User-generated Text, pages 337–341
Online, Nov 19, 2020. ©2020 Association for Computational Linguistics

tectures to reap better results on the identification of informative Covid-19 tweets.

The rest of the paper is organized as follows. Section 2 discusses work related to the Covid-19 misinformation spread. Section 3 provides a brief description of the task and dataset. Later, in section 4, I discuss the training procedure followed by my submission's internal and official results in section 5. Finally, I conclude my work in section 6.

2   Related works

(Shahi et al., 2020) performs an exploratory study on Covid-19 misinformation. Their work focuses on content, authors, and propagation of misinformation of Covid-19 related tweets. Their work shows that false claims spread more rapidly than partially false claims on Twitter. Further, they revealed that verified Twitter handles like celebrities and organizations are also involved in propagating misinformation.(Pennycook and Rand, 2020) in their work, discuss the damaging effects of misinformation regarding Covid-19. Their findings reveal that misinformation increases fear in society, creates disaccord, and can even lead to direct damage. The direct damage can be due to harmful medical advice, overreaction to the situation like hoarding and underacting such as deliberate engagement in risky behavior. However, (Gallotti et al., 2020) maintains an optimistic tone regarding the spread of misinformation. The authors claim that false information is quickly replaced with reliable information when the epidemic hits a particular area. Their analysis is based on 100 million tweets in 64 languages on the Covid-19 topic.

The quantitative analysis, done on 673 tweets by (Kouzy et al., 2020) shows that around 25% of tweets are misinformative, and 17% of the tweets have unverifiable information.The authors also report that misinformation rate is higher than informal individual accounts and that certain tags like "@2019_nconv" and "Corona" are associated with higher misinformation than tags like "COVID-19". (Yang et al., 2020) reports that most of the misinformation spreads via retweets and that social bots are involved in amplifying and posting low-credibility information. Furthermore, they analyze that the amount of misinformation on Covid-19 is more than the total volume of New York Times articles. There is no research in the automatic identification of misinformative posts on social media so far.

3   Brief description of Task and Dataset

In this section, I present a brief description about the task and the dataset provided. Interested readers can refer the task description paper(Nguyen et al., 2020) for further details.

3.1   Task

The objective of WNUT-2020 Task 2 is to develop systems that automatically identify an English tweet related to Covid-19 as informative or not informative. Hence, this is a binary classification task.

3.2   Dataset

The complete dataset provided by the organizers of the task, consists of 10K tweets related to Covid-19 of which 4719 tweets are informative and 5281 tweets are uninformative. Table 1 provide samples of informative and uninformative tweets from the dataset.

4   System Description

4.1   Preprocessing

The tweets provided by organizers are anonymized. All the user mentions are replaced with '@USER.' Basic preprocessing like URL removal is also done beforehand by. In my work, I experimented with two different preprocessing techniques to analyze the impact of preprocessing on the system's final performance. Later, I fine-tuned the models with final tweets obtained using both the preprocessing techniques. One of the techniques does minimal preprocessing, which can help preserve additional semantics in tweets. The other one does complete preprocessing along with the introduction of additional features for emojis.

4.1.1   Minimal preprocessing

In this step, I perform the following steps:

- Removal of user mentions and numbers.

- Removal of the hash symbol in hashtags. Here, I am not deleting hashtags as they can have some useful information, and removing them completely may lead to loss of information. Few examples are - "#IndiaFightsCOVID", "#SummerVibes".The first hashtag is more promising to be from an informative tweet than the second one.

- Removal of url symbol - "HTTPURL".

Text	Label
#COVID19 Updates. #SothSudan's fist positive patient is a 29 yo Dutch, who arrived in the country from Netherlands via Addis Ababa on 28 February. #SSOT HTTPURL	INFO
Democrats somehow managed to fight ebola without calling it ""the African virus."" A cluster of COVID-19 cases has emerged in New York CIty's Hassidic neighborhood, so it's only a matter of time before the local Trump Klux Klan starts talking about ""the Jew virus.""	UNINFO

Table 1: Sample tweets from the dataset.

- Removal of Emojis.

Often, proper-casing of letters and the presence of punctuation helps in improving the embeddings extracted by Transformer architectures. Few transformer architectures' versions like Bert-base-cased and Bert-large-cased are expected to perform well with this technique.

4.1.2 Complete preprocessing

In this technique,first three steps remain the same as that of minimal preprocessing. Additional steps followed are:

- Lower casing of letters.
- Conversion of emojis to text[2].
- Removal of extra white spaces, punctuation, and all non-alphabetical characters.

This kind of preprocessing is best suited for'uncased' versions of the Transformer networks like Bert-large-uncased.

4.2 Transformer architectures

Recent advancements in several NLP tasks, particularly text classification, are made possible by Transformer architectures. At their core, Transformers use attention mechanism, which helps in representing the contextual information. They have outperformed all the traditional methods like Bag of Words models, N-grams features, and dictionary-based techniques in most of the NLP domain tasks. These architectures had shown good performance in cross-lingual and multilingual contexts as well(Conneau et al., 2019). Due to these architectures' success, I focused entirely on fine-tuning transformer models in my work to identify informative Covid-19 tweets. I used the following Transformer models for fine-tuning:

- BERT based models(base uncased, base cased, large uncased, large cased).

- RoBERTa-based models(base, large).

- XLM-RoBERTa-based models(base, large).

- ELECTRA-based models(base discriminator, small discriminator, large discriminator).

A brief description of each of the architectures is provided below:

BERT BERT(Bidirectional Encoder Representations from Transformers)(Devlin et al., 2018) is a multi-layer bidirectional encoder transformer. The model is pre-trained on two tasks - Masked Language Modeling(MLM) and Next Sentence Prediction. There are two broad variants of the architecture available - BERT Base with 12 Transformer layers & 110 million parameters and BERT Large with 24 Transformer layers & 340 million parameters. This architecture is a path-breaking invention in the field of NLP, and several other variants of this are developed later. Few of them are Multilingual BERT(mBERT), A Lite BERT(ALBERT), and A Distilled version of BERT(DistilBERT).

RoBERTa RoBERTa(Liu et al., 2019) builds on BERT's masked language modeling task, and this architecture does not have the sentence prediction task in its training objectives. The authors of RoBERTa modified key hyper-parameters of BERT and trained the model with larger data and larger mini-batches.Also,the masking pattern applied to training data is changed dynamically in RoBERTa. This helped RoBERTa to perform better on MLM objective and leading to good down-stream task performance. The base version of RoBERTa has 125M parameters, and the large version has 355M parameters.

XLM-RoBERTa XLM-RoBERTa(Conneau et al., 2019) is a multilingual model trained on 2.5 TB data from CommonCrawl. This model is released by the Facebook AI team as an extension to the XLM-100 model, with the biggest update being the large amount of training data

---

used in the former. This architecture showed improved performance on several NLP tasks of low-resource languages and outperformed other transformer models like mBERT on cross-lingual benchmarks. XLM-RoBERTa's base version has 250M parameters, while its large version has 560M parameters. Both versions have a vocabulary size of 250K.

ELECTRA ELECTRA(Efficiently Learning an Encoder that Classifies Token Replacements Accurately)(Clark et al., 2020) matched the performances of its predecessor models like RoBERTa and XLNet with less than one-fourth of computational budget and achieved State-of-the-art performance on SQuAD benchmark. The general design of GANs highly inspires this architecture design. The model used a new pre-training objective - Replaced Token Detection. Three variants of ELECTRA are available: ELECTRA-Small with 14M parameters, ELECTRA-Base with 110M parameters, and ELECTRA-Large with 335M parameters.

4.3 Training

In this work, I fine-tuned all the aforementioned Transformer models using the FARM framework[3]. Minimal hyper-parameter tuning is performed. Before the test data was made available by the organizers, I have used the provided validation data as test data, and 10% of the training data for dev set. A batch size of 32 is used, and the class weights are incorporated in loss function(Binary Cross Entropy) to upweight the loss of minorities as the dataset is imbalanced. AdamW optimizer is used for optimization. Early stopping with a patience of 5 is used targeting positive-class F1-score, the evaluation metric specified by organizers. A maximum epochs of 50 are specified. Dropout of 0.2 is used to prevent over-fitting. Sequence length of 70 is used as around 90% of the tweets have fewer than 70 tokens. I have evaluated the model once for every 100 batches during fine-tuning. So, the model is evaluated once in 1.25 epochs. All the experiments are performed on Google Colaboratory.

5 Results

5.1 Internal Evaluation Results

As mentioned in 4.3, validation data is used as test data for internal evaluation, and the final evaluation is done by organizers using gold test labels.

---

[3]https://github.com/deepset-ai/FARM

Model	Prepro	F1	Acc
BERT-base-uncased	comp	0.86	0.81
BERT-base-uncased	comp	0.86	0.86
BERT-base-cased	min	0.86	0.87
BERT-large-uncased	comp	0.86	0.86
BERT-large-cased	min	0.83	0.85
RoBERTa-base	min	0.87	0.87
RoBERTa-large	min	**0.89**	**0.89**
XLM-RoBERTa-base	comp	0.85	0.85
XLM-RoBERTa-large	comp	**0.88**	**0.88**
ELECTRA-base	min	0.83	0.83
ELECTRA-small	min	0.82	0.83
ELECTRA-large	min	0.85	0.85

Table 2: Internal Evaluation Results.

Run	F1-score	Acc
Run-1	**0.85**	**0.85**
Run-2	0.83	0.83

Table 3: Official Results.

Internal evaluation results are provided in Table 2. From results, it can be inferred that minimal preprocessing, which preserves casing and punctuation achieves better results with fine-tuning.

5.2 Official Results

In the organizers' official results, my two submissions(best performing ones in internal evaluation results) obtained 85% and 83% positive class F1-score. The detailed results are provided in Table 3.

6 Conclusion

In this work, I presented my system submission details for WNUT-2020 Task 2. My submissions, using eleven variants of four different fine-tuned Transformer architectures achieved F1-score of 85.3% and 83.2% during official evaluation. The ill-effects of misinformation and the importance of automatic identification techniques regarding Covid-19 posts are also highlighted in the paper. My work also emphasizes that minimal preprocessing works better than complete preprocessing for fine-tuning State-of-the-art Transformers.

I make my source code publicly available to facilitate further experimentation in the field[4].

---

[4]https://github.com/SivaAndMe/
Fine-tuning-Transformer-architectures-for-identification-o

References

Kevin Clark, Minh-Thang Luong, Quoc V Le, and Christopher D Manning. 2020. Electra: Pre-training text encoders as discriminators rather than generators. *arXiv preprint arXiv:2003.10555.*

Alexis Conneau, Kartikay Khandelwal, Naman Goyal, Vishrav Chaudhary, Guillaume Wenzek, Francisco Guzmán, Edouard Grave, Myle Ott, Luke Zettlemoyer, and Veselin Stoyanov. 2019. Unsupervised cross-lingual representation learning at scale. *arXiv preprint arXiv:1911.02116.*

Jacob Devlin, Ming-Wei Chang, Kenton Lee, and Kristina Toutanova. 2018. Bert: Pre-training of deep bidirectional transformers for language understanding. *arXiv preprint arXiv:1810.04805.*

Riccardo Gallotti, Francesco Valle, Nicola Castaldo, Pierluigi Sacco, and Manlio De Domenico. 2020. Assessing the risks of' infodemics" in response to covid-19 epidemics. *arXiv preprint arXiv:2004.03997.*

Ramez Kouzy, Joseph Abi Jaoude, Afif Kraitem, Molly B El Alam, Basil Karam, Elio Adib, Jabra Zarka, Cindy Traboulsi, Elie W Akl, and Khalil Baddour. 2020. Coronavirus goes viral: quantifying the covid-19 misinformation epidemic on twitter. *Cureus*, 12(3).

The Lancet. 2020. Covid-19: fighting panic with information. *Lancet (London, England)*, 395(10224):537.

Yinhan Liu, Myle Ott, Naman Goyal, Jingfei Du, Mandar Joshi, Danqi Chen, Omer Levy, Mike Lewis, Luke Zettlemoyer, and Veselin Stoyanov. 2019. Roberta: A robustly optimized bert pretraining approach. *arXiv preprint arXiv:1907.11692.*

Areeb Mian and Shujhat Khan. 2020. Coronavirus: the spread of misinformation. *BMC medicine*, 18(1):1–2.

Dat Quoc Nguyen, Thanh Vu, Afshin Rahimi, Mai Hoang Dao, Linh The Nguyen, and Long Doan. 2020. WNUT-2020 Task 2: Identification of Informative COVID-19 English Tweets. In *Proceedings of the 6th Workshop on Noisy User-generated Text.*

Gordon Pennycook and David G. Rand. 2020. Who falls for fake news? the roles of bullshit receptivity, overclaiming, familiarity, and analytic thinking. *Journal of Personality*, 88(2):185–200.

Gautam Kishore Shahi, A. Dirkson, and T. A. Majchrzak. 2020. An exploratory study of covid-19 misinformation on twitter. *ArXiv*, abs/2005.05710.

Mary E Wilson and Lin H Chen. 2020. Travellers give wings to novel coronavirus (2019-ncov).

Kai-Cheng Yang, Christopher Torres-Lugo, and Filippo Menczer. 2020. Prevalence of low-credibility information on twitter during the covid-19 outbreak. *arXiv preprint arXiv:2004.14484.*

IIITBH at WNUT-2020 Task 2: Exploiting the best of both worlds

Saichethan Miriyala Reddy[*]
Dept. of Computer Science
IIIT Bhagalpur
Bihar, India
miriyala.cse.1725@iiitbh.ac.in

Pradeep Kumar Biswal
Dept. of Computer Science
IIIT Bhagalpur
Bihar, India
pkbiswal.cse@iiitbh.ac.in

Abstract

In this paper, we present IIITBH team's effort to solve the second shared task of the 6th Workshop on Noisy User-generated Text (W-NUT) i.e Identification of informative COVID-19 English Tweets. The central theme of the task is to develop a system that automatically identify whether an English Tweet related to the novel coronavirus (COVID-19) is informative or not. Our approach is based on exploiting semantic information from both max pooling and average pooling, to this end we propose two models.

1 Introduction

COVID-19 pandemic started in Wuhan, China in December 2019, caused by the infection of individuals by the severe acute respiratory syndrome coronavirus 2 (SARS-CoV-2) this dangerous virus is spreading around the world since then. The COVID-19 pandemic continues to have a devastating effect on the health and well-being of the global population. It is creating fear and panic for people all around the world, while the vaccine can hopefully brings the situation under control soon. To track the development of the outbreak and to provide users with the information related to the virus, e.g. any new cases in the user's regions. Need for building real-time monitoring system which uses social network data like Twitter is high. However, manual approaches to identify the informative Tweets require significant human efforts and thus are costly. To help handle this problem, WNUT shared task 2 (Nguyen et al., 2020) aim participants to build systems to automatically identify whether a COVID-19 English Tweet is informative or not. Such informative Tweets provide information about recovered, suspected, confirmed and death cases as well as location or travel history of the cases.

Pooling-based recurrent neural architectures consistently outperform their counterparts without pooling (Maini et al., 2020). However, the reasons for their enhanced performance are largely unexamined. In this work, we examine how two most commonly used pooling techniques (mean-pooling or average pooling, and max-pooling) perform for solving WNUT-2020 shared task 2[1] and develop two novel systems exploiting semantic features of both techniques.

2 Data

Dataset consists a total of $10,000$ tweets split into training, validation, test set in 70/10/20 ratio respectively. Detailed breakdown of data is shown in Table 1. Maximum and minimum length of tweets in test data is 64 and 8 respectively. Distribution of tweet length in test dataset is illustrated in Figure 1

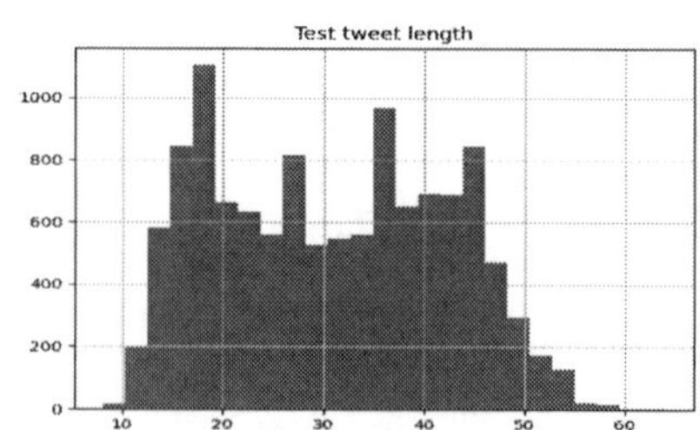

Figure 1: Frequency vs length of tweet

	Informative	Uninformative	Total
Training	3303	3697	7000
Validation	472	528	1000
Test	944	1056	2000
Total	4719	5281	10000

Table 1: Dataset Statistics

---

[*] Major Contribution and corresponding author

[1] http://noisy-text.github.io/2020/

Proceedings of the 2020 EMNLP Workshop W-NUT: The Sixth Workshop on Noisy User-generated Text, pages 342–346
Online, Nov 19, 2020. ©2020 Association for Computational Linguistics

3 Proposed Methodology

In our proposed architecture, we aim to leverage the semantic information from both pooling layers for identifying whether given tweet is informative or not. In this section, we describe our method (base model illustrated in Figure 2) and elaborate on each part with details.

3.1 Bidirectional LSTM

Recurrent neural network (RNN) is a form of neural network which maintains a memory based on history information. RNNs are good for sequential prediction, but the problem of exploding or vanishing gradients makes learning long distance dependencies very difficult for them (Hochreiter, 1998). The LSTM architecture is proposed to address this problem (Hochreiter and Schmidhuber, 1997). Bidirectional LSTM uses the features coming from both the previous hidden states as well as the future hidden states. This structure allows the networks to have both forward and backward information about the sequence at every time step. It helps the language model in understanding the context better (Schuster and Paliwal, 1997).

Formally, at time t, the memory, c_t, and the hidden state, h_t, are updated with the following equations.

$$i_t = \sigma(W_{xi}h_{t-1} + W_{ci}c_{t-1}) \qquad (1)$$

$$c_t = (1 - i_t) \odot c_{t-1} + i_t \odot tanh(W_{xc}X_{w,t}W_{hc}h_{t-1}) \quad (2)$$

$$o_t = \sigma(W_{xo}x_{w,t} + W_{ho}h_{t-1} + W_{co}c_t) \qquad (3)$$

$$h_t = o_t \odot tanh(c_t) \qquad (4)$$

where x is the input at time step t. Bidirectional LSTM contains two separate LSTMs to capture both past and future inputs. One of the LSTM networks encodes the sentence from left to right and the other one from right to left.

$$\overrightarrow{h_t} = Forward(h_t) \qquad (5)$$

$$\overleftarrow{h_t} = Backward(h_t) \qquad (6)$$

$$h_T = \overrightarrow{h_t} \bigoplus \overleftarrow{h_t} \qquad (7)$$

Thus, for each time step t, we obtain two representations, $\overrightarrow{h_t}$ and $\overleftarrow{h_t}$, finally these two representations are concatenated to form the final output, h_T.

For the purpose of simplifying the information in the output from the Bi LSTM layer (passed through the activation function), pooling layers are used. Pooling layer is a down sampling method, which reduces the number of parameters of the feature map,retaining the important information. Different pooling types like average, max, sum, etc., present. However common pooling types are Max pooling and Average Pooling.

$$S = x_1, x_2, ..., x_n \qquad (8)$$

Let S be an input tweet, where x_t is a representation of the input word at position t. A recurrent neural network such as a Bi-LSTM produces a hidden state h_T (equation 7) .

3.2 Average Pooling

Average pooling weighs down the activation by combining the nonmaximal activations (Passricha and Aggarwal, 2019)

$$y_{ap}^i = avg_{i\epsilon(1,n-w)}(h^{i:i+w}) \qquad (9)$$

$$y_{ap} = [y_{ap}^1, y_{ap}^2, ..., y_{ap}^{n-w+1}] \qquad (10)$$

where w is width of pooling window

$$\xi_{ap} = average(y_{ap}) \qquad (11)$$

The use of a global average pooling(ξ_{ap}) layer as a last layer was proposed by (Lin et al., 2013), and got its breakthrough by the well known image recognization system, the residual network (ResNet) (He et al., 2015).

3.3 Max Pooling

Max pooling extracts only the maximum activations (Passricha and Aggarwal, 2019) independent of distribution. One dimensional max pooling can be expressed as follow:

$$y_{mp}^i = max_{i\epsilon(1,n-w)}(h^{i:i+w}) \qquad (12)$$

$$y_{mp} = [y_{mp}^1, y_{mp}^2, ..., y_{mp}^{n-w+1}] \qquad (13)$$

where w is width of pooling window

$$\xi_{mp} = max(y_{mp}) \qquad (14)$$

Global max pooling(ξ_{mp}) was proposed for weakly-supervised learning (Oquab et al., 2014) and is also used in the PHOCNet for the task of word spotting. (Sudholt and Fink, 2016).

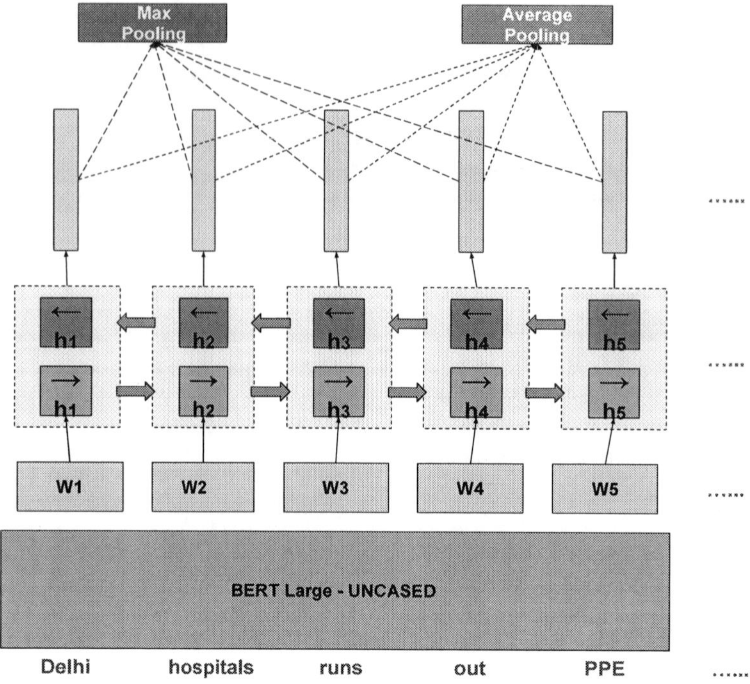

Figure 2: Base Model

From (Section 3.2 and 3.3) we know that max pooling identify only maximum activations irrespective of distribution and frequency, wheras average pooling focus on distribution, and frequency irrespective of maximum values. To leverage this both types of information we propose the following two models (Section 3.4 and 3.5)

3.4 Model I

In Model I, we simply concatenate both global max pooling and global average pooling layers (equation 15). Though this can be considered as a naive model but previous works (Nguyen et al., 2018) (Sun et al., 2018) (Tu et al., 2017) suggests that feature concatenation improves performance of systems, our results supported this intuition.

$$h^* = \xi_{mp} \bigoplus \xi_{ap} \qquad (15)$$

where ξ_{mp}, ξ_{ap} are global max pooling and global average pooling from eq 14 and eq 11 respectively.

$$\hat{y} = \sigma(h^*) \qquad (16)$$

where, $\sigma(z) = \frac{1}{1+e^{-z}}$.

3.5 Model II

In Model II, we intend to use the information such as distribution and frequency from average pooling to understand the context better. While the max-pooling layer attempts to find the most important latent semantic factors in the tweet (Lai et al., 2015). First, we compute the dot product of global average pooling and global max pooling (equation 17), and later multiply with global average pooling (equation 18)

$$o = \xi_{ap} \odot \xi_{mp} \qquad (17)$$

$$h^\dagger = o \otimes \xi_{ap} \qquad (18)$$

where ξ_{mp}, ξ_{ap} are global max pooling and global average pooling from eq 14 and eq 11 respectively.

$$\hat{y} = \sigma(h^\dagger) \qquad (19)$$

where, $\sigma(z) = \frac{1}{1+e^{-z}}$.

Note: For both models, we used binary cross entropy as our loss function. We submitted results of both systems (Model I & Model II).

4   Experimental Setup

Our model is implemented in Tensorflow[2] and Keras[3]. We use a batch size of B = 500, we train our neural network for 25 epochs with the Adam optimizer. A dropout and recurrent dropout of 0.25 is used. Complete code is made available on Github[4]. During the pre processing stage of data we removed all unwanted symbols and user mentions. Large-uncased BERT model is employed for obtaining tweet embeddings. We also analysed how accuracy and loss of max pooling and average pooling changes with number of epochs in different contextual embeddings (Devlin et al., 2019) (Peters et al., 2018) (Yang et al., 2019) complete code and plots are uploaded in our repository.

5   Results

In order to illustrate the efficacy of our proposed methods, we compare the results with simple average pooling and max pooling on validation set in Table 2. Results in Table 2 are average of 5 runs of each model. From this Table we can infer that our proposed models perform better than existing approaches. In Figure 3 and 4 we illustrated how loss vary with number of epochs on validation data.

Model	F1	Precision	Recall	Accuracy
Avg Pool	84.08	84.28	83.86	85.06
Max Pool	84.18	84.50	84.01	85.13
Model I	84.58	84.73	84.30	85.41
Model II	**84.79**[†]	85.05	84.69	86.04

Table 2: Results on Validation data

From Table 2 we can infer our proposed models (section 3.4 and section 3.5) works than simple average or max pooling. Results of our proposed models on test data are showed in Table 3, we achieved an F1 score of 0.7979 using Model II and 0.7932 using Model I.

Model	Test			
	F1 score	Precision	Recall	Accuracy
Model II	0.7979	0.7991	0.7966	0.8095
Model I	0.7932	0.7983	0.7881	0.8060

Table 3: Results on test data

[2] https://www.tensorflow.org/
[3] https://keras.io/
[4] https://github.com/Saichethan/ WNUT-2020

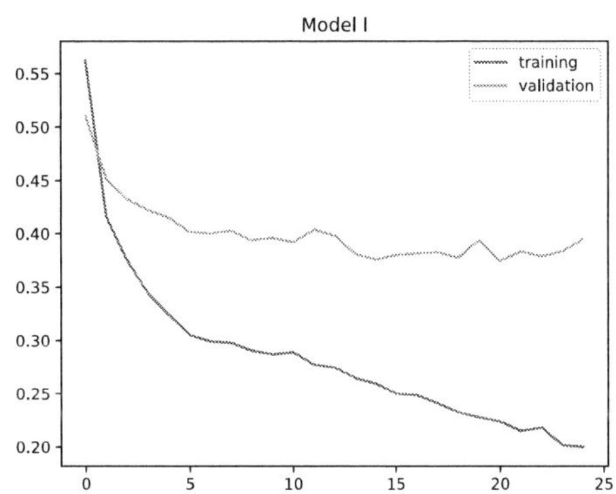

Figure 3: Model I loss on validation set

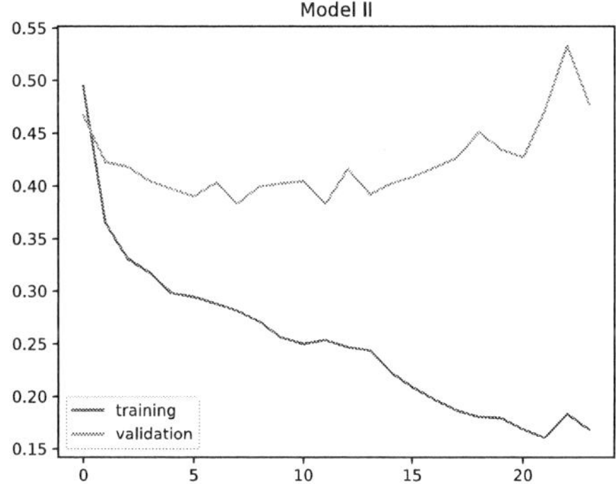

Figure 4: Model II loss on validation set

6   Conclusion

In this paper we presented our system to WNUT 2020 shared task on "Identification of informative COVID-19 English Tweets". Traditional text classification models mainly focus on three topics: feature engineering, feature selection and using different types of machine learning algorithms. Our main goal in this paper is to show how we can leverages on different pooling methods of BiLSTM, without using any human-engineered features and improve efficacy of any system. We believe performance of our system can be further improved by tweaking hyper parameters. In future we would like to explore how our models perform with different attention mechanisms (Vaswani et al., 2017) for different tasks like relation classification (Zhou et al., 2016), image captioning (Xu et al., 2015), and machine translation (Bahdanau et al., 2014).

Acknowledgments

We would like to thank anonymous reviewer for their suggestion, which helped us in improving the quality of paper further. We would also like to thank Dr. Aravind Choubey (Director), for encouraging research at Indian Institute of Information Technology, Bhagalpur[5].

References

Dzmitry Bahdanau, Kyunghyun Cho, and Yoshua Bengio. 2014. Neural machine translation by jointly learning to align and translate.

J. Devlin, Ming-Wei Chang, Kenton Lee, and Kristina Toutanova. 2019. Bert: Pre-training of deep bidirectional transformers for language understanding. In *NAACL-HLT*.

Kaiming He, Xiangyu Zhang, Shaoqing Ren, and Jian Sun. 2015. Deep residual learning for image recognition.

Sepp Hochreiter. 1998. The vanishing gradient problem during learning recurrent neural nets and problem solutions. *Int. J. Uncertain. Fuzziness Knowl.-Based Syst.*, 6(2):107–116.

Sepp Hochreiter and Jürgen Schmidhuber. 1997. Long short-term memory. *Neural Comput.*, 9(8):1735–1780.

Siwei Lai, L. Xu, Kang Liu, and Jun Zhao. 2015. Recurrent convolutional neural networks for text classification. In *AAAI*.

Min Lin, Qiang Chen, and Shuicheng Yan. 2013. Network in network.

Pratyush Maini, Keshav Kolluru, Danish Pruthi, and Mausam. 2020. Why and when should you pool? analyzing pooling in recurrent architectures.

Dat Quoc Nguyen, Thanh Vu, Afshin Rahimi, Mai Hoang Dao, Linh The Nguyen, and Long Doan. 2020. WNUT-2020 Task 2: Identification of Informative COVID-19 English Tweets. In *Proceedings of the 6th Workshop on Noisy User-generated Text*.

L. D. Nguyen, D. Lin, Z. Lin, and J. Cao. 2018. Deep cnns for microscopic image classification by exploiting transfer learning and feature concatenation. In *2018 IEEE International Symposium on Circuits and Systems (ISCAS)*, pages 1–5.

Maxime Oquab, Leon Bottou, Ivan Laptev, and Josef Sivic. 2014. Learning and transferring mid-level image representations using convolutional neural networks. In *Proceedings of the IEEE conference on computer vision and pattern recognition*, pages 1717–1724.

Vishal Passricha and Rajesh Kumar Aggarwal. 2019. End-to-end acoustic modeling using convolutional neural networks. In *Intelligent Speech Signal Processing*, pages 5–37. Elsevier.

Matthew E. Peters, Mark Neumann, Mohit Iyyer, Matt Gardner, Christopher Clark, Kenton Lee, and Luke Zettlemoyer. 2018. Deep contextualized word representations.

M. Schuster and K. K. Paliwal. 1997. Bidirectional recurrent neural networks. *IEEE Transactions on Signal Processing*, 45(11):2673–2681.

Sebastian Sudholt and Gernot A Fink. 2016. Phocnet: A deep convolutional neural network for word spotting in handwritten documents. In *2016 15th International Conference on Frontiers in Handwriting Recognition (ICFHR)*, pages 277–282. IEEE.

Xudong Sun, Pengcheng Wu, and Steven CH Hoi. 2018. Face detection using deep learning: An improved faster rcnn approach. *Neurocomputing*, 299:42–50.

Yan-Hui Tu, Jun Du, Qing Wang, Xiao Bao, Li-Rong Dai, and Chin-Hui Lee. 2017. An information fusion framework with multi-channel feature concatenation and multi-perspective system combination for the deep-learning-based robust recognition of microphone array speech. *Computer Speech & Language*, 46:517–534.

Ashish Vaswani, Noam Shazeer, Niki Parmar, Jakob Uszkoreit, Llion Jones, Aidan N Gomez, Łukasz Kaiser, and Illia Polosukhin. 2017. Attention is all you need. In *Advances in neural information processing systems*, pages 5998–6008.

Kelvin Xu, Jimmy Ba, Ryan Kiros, Kyunghyun Cho, Aaron Courville, Ruslan Salakhutdinov, Richard Zemel, and Yoshua Bengio. 2015. Show, attend and tell: Neural image caption generation with visual attention.

Z. Yang, Zihang Dai, Yiming Yang, J. Carbonell, R. Salakhutdinov, and Quoc V. Le. 2019. Xlnet: Generalized autoregressive pretraining for language understanding. In *NeurIPS*.

Peng Zhou, Wei Shi, Jun Tian, Zhenyu Qi, Bingchen Li, Hongwei Hao, and Bo Xu. 2016. Attention-based bidirectional long short-term memory networks for relation classification. In *Proceedings of the 54th Annual Meeting of the Association for Computational Linguistics (Volume 2: Short Papers)*, pages 207–212.

---

[5]https://www.iiitbh.ac.in/

Phonemer at WNUT-2020 Task 2: Sequence Classification Using COVID Twitter BERT and Bagging Ensemble Technique based on Plurality Voting

Anshul Wadhawan

Flipkart Private Limited

`anshul.wadhwan@flipkart.com`

Abstract

This paper presents the approach that we employed to tackle the EMNLP WNUT-2020 Shared Task 2 : Identification of informative COVID-19 English Tweets. The task is to develop a system that automatically identifies whether an English Tweet related to the novel coronavirus (COVID-19) is informative or not. We solve the task in three stages. The first stage involves pre-processing the dataset by filtering only relevant information. This is followed by experimenting with multiple deep learning models like CNNs, RNNs and Transformer based models. In the last stage, we propose an ensemble of the best model trained on different subsets of the provided dataset. Our final approach achieved an F1-score of 0.9037 and we were ranked sixth overall with F1-score as the evaluation criteria.

1 Introduction

Up till mid-June 2020, the coronavirus pandemic has caused 445K deaths and has infected more than 8.2M people belonging to 215 regions and countries. This has led to a surge of panic and fear among people all around the globe. Recently, there has been rapid development in building monitoring systems (e.g. The Johns Hopkins Coronavirus Dashboard) to track any news regarding the outbreak, to let users know of any information related to the coronavirus for example, new cases emerging near the user's location. Most of the official sources from where the information is released are not updated very frequently and the information reported by such organizations may be stale, for example, WHO updates the information regarding the virus only once a day. These monitoring systems tend to use social network data like posts from Facebook or tweets from Twitter as an alternative source of information relating to the pandemic, generally by scraping relevant information or by crowd sourcing. However, due to increased panic and emotions

among people, social media is flooded with massive amounts of data, e.g. about 4M COVID-19 English tweets are posted daily on twitter. But the major issue regarding this is that the majority of such tweets are uninformative and thus, do not impart useful information that can be used. Hence, any application that requires to update the news has to first filter these tweets to detect which among the tweets are actually useful. Manual approaches for this filtering task are not only cumbersome, frustrating and ineffective for vast amounts of data, but also costly. This calls for automated systems which can filter the information given huge amounts of mixed data, and thus serve as the motivation for the shared task. Although a lot of work has been done on the lines of sequence classification on general English texts (Agarwal et al., 2011; Bagheri and Islam, 2017) , since the COVID-19 outbreak has grown in a short while, not many systems which deal with COVID-19 related texts have been developed.

In this paper, we describe our approach to tackle the WNUT 2020 shared task 2. The paper is structured as follows: Section 2 talks about the problem statement and provided dataset. Section 3 describes a step-by-step methodology process that we employ. Section 4 explains the experiments that were carried out along with a detailed discussion of the dataset, system settings and results of our experiments. Section 5 provides a brief conclusion of the paper along with the future scope of our research.

2 Task Definition

The WNUT-2020 Shared Task 2 (Nguyen et al., 2020) is based on a sequence classification problem wherein the aim is to identify whether an English Tweet related to the novel coronavirus (COVID-19) is informative or not. A tweet is said to be informative if it provides information regarding recov-

Proceedings of the 2020 EMNLP Workshop W-NUT: The Sixth Workshop on Noisy User-generated Text, pages 347–351
Online, Nov 19, 2020. ©2020 Association for Computational Linguistics

	Total	Positive	Negative
Training set	7000	3303	3697
Validation set	1000	472	528
Test set	2000	944	1056

Table 1: Data Distribution

ered, suspected, confirmed, death cases, location or travel history of cases.

The goals of the shared task are:

1. To develop a language processing task that potentially impacts research and downstream applications.

2. To provide the community with a new dataset for identifying informative COVID-19 English Tweets.

To achieve the goals of the shared task, a dataset of 10K COVID-19 English tweets are provided, in which 4719 tweets are labelled INFORMATIVE and 5281 tweets are labelled UNINFORMATIVE. Each tweet is annotated by three independent annotators with an inter-annotator agreement score of Fleiss' Kappa at 0.818. The 10K dataset is divided into training/validation/test sets in the ratio 70/10/20 with distribution as shown in table 1.

Systems are evaluated using standard evaluation metrics, including accuracy, precision, recall and F1-score. However, the submissions are ranked by F1-score.

3   Methodology

We have split the proposed methodology in three steps- data preprocessing, deep learning models for sequence classification and ensemble process (bagging). The code corresponding to each of the steps has been made available online[1] to facilitate further research.

3.1   Data Pre-Processing

The dataset provided in the WNUT shared task is not suitable to be processed directly by the models we plan to implement. This is due to the fact that the texts provided are tweets which are directly fetched from the website and users from all over the world have different ways of expressing their opinions. On manually going through the dataset, we find that the texts are very diverse in the sense

that many users post non-ascii characters such as emoticons, slang words for informal tweets, and spelling errors in words, etc. The dataset contains URLs replaced by the tag HTTPURL and user mentions replaced by the tag @USER. Apart from this, newline characters are also present within tweets. All the above discrepancies add to noise and do not contribute to being appropriate features for sequence classification.

In order to clean this data, we perform the following cleaning operations :

1. Remove all non-ascii characters i.e. characters belonging to the range [\x00-\x7f]. We determined this range by parsing through the dataset and recording all non-ascii characters.

2. Remove all newline (\n) and tab (\t) characters.

3. Remove all HTTPURL and @USER tags.

3.2   Deep Learning Models

Deep learning techniques have recently shown great results in the domain of computer vision (Krizhevsky et al., 2012) and speech recognition (Graves et al., 2013). As far as natural language processing is concerned, most of the work involving deep learning makes use of word vector representations (Bengio et al., 2003; Yih et al., 2011; Mikolov et al., 2013) to carry out finer tasks like classification.

3.2.1   CNNs

(Kim, 2014) Convolutional Neural Networks are used to operate on local features with the help of convolving filters. CNNs have not only shown promising results in the domain of computer vision (Lecun et al., 1998), but they have also been utilized extensively for NLP tasks like search query retrieval (Shen et al., 2014), semantic parsing (Yih et al., 2014), sentence modeling (Kalchbrenner et al., 2014), and other traditional NLP tasks (Collobert et al., 2011).

3.2.2   RNNs

LSTM : LSTMs have shown great results in sequence classification problems like political sentiment classification (Rao and Spasojevic, 2016), by capturing the appropriate context. Also, they work towards solving the vanishing gradient problem (Hochreiter and Schmidhuber, 1997). **BiLSTM** : Bi-directional LSTMs have tackled a variety of sequence classification tasks (Wang et al., 2016) by

---

[1] https://github.com/anshulwadhawan/
BERT_for_sequence_classification_COVID

considering the fact that context of a word depends on the words occurring before it as well as those occurring after it. **Attention based BiLSTM** : By including attention to a BiLSTM, we try to find out the specific words which have the greatest impact to the overall sentiment of the sequence under consideration.

3.2.3 Transformer based models

BERT (bert-base-cased): (Devlin et al., 2018) BERT is a bidirectional transformer based model pre-trained on a huge corpus of Wikipedia and Toronto Book Corpus which uses a combination of objectives meant for the tasks of next sentence prediction and masked language modeling. **RoBERTa (roberta-base)**: (Liu et al., 2019) It is built on top of BERT by removing the next sentence prediction objective, changing key hyperparameters and training with increased learning rate values and batch sizes. **ALBERT (albert-base-v2)**: (Lan et al., 2019) This is another variation of BERT which tries to increase the training speed of BERT and lower memory utilization by repeating layers which are split among groups and splitting the embedding matrix into two. **XLNet (xlnet-base-cased)**: (Yang et al., 2019) This model extends over the Transformer-XL model by learning bidirectional contexts and maximizing the likelihood over different permutations of the input sequence factorization order after pre-training. **XLM (xlm-mlm-en-2048)**: (Lample and Conneau, 2019) This is a transformer based model with an option to choose the objective functions from the tasks of masked language modeling, casual language modeling, and translation language modeling. **COVID Twitter BERT (ct-bert)**: (Müller et al., 2020) COVID-Twitter-BERT (CT-BERT) is a transformer-based model pre-trained on a corpus of 22.5M (633M tokens) COVID-19 related tweets.

3.3 Ensemble Process - Bagging

We merge the training and validation datasets provided in the task to create a global dataset. Then, we shuffle this global dataset and split it into training and validation datasets with the same ratio. This process is repeated seven times to create seven sets of training and validation datasets, each of which have a random class distribution. The best performing model, based on validation scores on default training and validation split provided in the task, is trained from scratch on each of these seven sets of training and validation splits, and the

	Train Set		Val Set	
	Pos	Neg	Pos	Neg
Shuffle1	3285	3715	490	510
Shuffle2	3294	3706	481	519
Shuffle3	3305	3695	470	530
Shuffle4	3293	3707	482	518
Shuffle5	3313	3687	462	538
Shuffle6	3299	3701	476	524
Shuffle7	3293	3707	482	518

Table 2: Data Distribution

predictions are recorded. Once we have the seven sets of predictions, we use a max-voting algorithm that is based on calculating mode of the seven predictions for each test instance to produce the final predictions.

4 Experiments

We experiment with ten deep learning models with the provided training and validation splits. Based on the scores produced above, we evaluate the final test predictions by training the best performing model with the seven synthesised randomly shuffled versions of the dataset, followed by merging the output predictions made on the test set. In this section, we present the dataset distribution, experimental settings, evaluation metrics, results and a brief analysis of the proposed system.

4.1 Dataset

The class-wise distribution in the training and validation splits of the provided as well as the shuffled datasets are shown in Table 2.

4.2 System Settings

For training the CNN, LSTM and BiLSTMs, word vectors for english language pre-trained on Common Crawl[2] and Wikipedia[3] are downloaded[4] and used using FastText[5] library. These word vectors are used to create the embedding matrix which is further used for transforming the words of the input sentence. We use binary cross entropy loss function and adam optimizer for all the CNN and RNN models. All the layers except the last layer have relu activation function. Since the problem is a binary

---

[2]https://commoncrawl.org/
[3]https://www.wikipedia.org/
[4]https://dl.fbaipublicfiles.com/fasttext/vectors-crawl/cc.en.300.bin.gz
[5]https://fasttext.cc/docs/en/crawl-vectors.html

	F1	P	R	A
CNN	0.787	0.805	0.771	0.804
LSTM	0.807	0.850	0.769	0.827
BiLSTM	0.822	0.806	0.838	0.829
Att-BiLSTM	0.823	0.773	0.881	0.822
BERT	0.891	0.875	0.908	0.896
RoBERTa	0.899	0.886	0.913	0.904
ALBERT	0.844	0.851	0.836	0.854
XLNet	0.892	0.864	0.921	0.895
XLM	0.870	0.850	0.891	0.875
CT-BERT	**0.914**	0.869	0.963	**0.915**

Table 3: Model Scores on Validation Set

classification, we use sigmoid activation function in the last layer. The training session is run for a total of 20 epochs and early stopping was inculcated in case of successive unproductive(in terms of f1-score) iterations. For all proposed RNNs, dropout of 0.2 and number_of_units of 150 are found to be the most effective. To fine-tune the transformer based models, we use pre-trained models, namely bert-base-cased, roberta-base, albert-base-v2, xlnet-base-cased and xlm-mlm-en-2048. We use hugging-face[6] API to train all the transformer based models. We use a learning_rate of 4e-5, epsilon_parameter_for_adam_optimizer of 1e-8, maximum_sequence_length of 128 and a batch_size of 8 due to hardware limitations. We train the models for 10 epochs and evaluate the model's performance on the validation set after every epoch.

4.3 Results and Analysis

The performance results of the proposed models on the given validation dataset in terms of f1-score(F1), precision(P), recall(R) and accuracy(A) have been presented in table 3.

We can conclude the following from table 3:

1. RNN based models perform better than CNN due to their context capturing potential.

2. Transformer based models perform better than both CNN and RNN based models due to more parallelization because of the fact that they don't need to traverse the input in order.

3. The COVID Twitter BERT (CT-BERT) outperforms all the other models by a significant margin. Higher recall is one major observation in this case. This is evident from the

fact that the model is pre-trained on 22.5M COVID-19 related tweets.

From the above results, we choose CT-BERT to be the primary model to train on the seven randomly shuffled datasets as well as carry out inferences on the unseen dataset. The ensemble of produced predictions results in an F1-score of 0.9037 on the test dataset. The best performing model i.e. CT-BERT on being trained over the global dataset results in an F1-score of 0.8954 on the test dataset. This shows that by inculcating the bagging technique, a boost of 0.83% in F1-score is seen. This can be credited to the fact that by creating seven sets of randomly selected training examples, we essentially cover the entire global dataset. Although we exclude portions of the dataset by excluding randomly selected instances from the training dataset, we cover all the instances in the global dataset by selecting those labels which are predicted by majority of the seven trained CT-BERT models. This can be deduced from the assumption that a particular instance which is absent in the training set of one of the seven models is likely to be present in the training set of most of the remaining models.

5 Conclusion and Future Work

In this paper, we provide a detailed description of our approach to solve the EMNLP WNUT-2020 Shared Task 2. Our approach involves processing in three stages. In the first stage, we pre-process the provided dataset by cleaning and extracting only relevant information from the provided text. In the second stage, we experiment with several deep neural networks like CNN, RNNs and Transformer based networks like XLNet, XLM, BERT and its different variations. In the final phase, we introduce the idea of ensemble learning (bagging) to our solution which is a major improvement over the individual model. We submitted an ensemble and an individual system based on the CT-BERT model as our final entries to the shared task. The ensemble approach fetches us a private leaderboard rank of 6 with F1-score as the evaluation criteria. Our system promotes the usage of transformer based models pre-trained on relevant corpora and ensemble learning with as many candidate models as feasible. In future, we aim to explore the usage of non-ascii characters like emoticons as features for classification and imparting ensemble learning through an end-to-end deep learning solution.

---

[6]`https://huggingface.co/transformers/`

References

Apoorv Agarwal, Boyi Xie, Ilia Vovsha, Owen Rambow, and Rebecca Passonneau. 2011. Sentiment analysis of twitter data. In *Proceedings of the Workshop on Languages in Social Media*, LSM '11, page 30–38, USA. Association for Computational Linguistics.

Hamid Bagheri and Md Johirul Islam. 2017. Sentiment analysis of twitter data.

Yoshua Bengio, Réjean Ducharme, Pascal Vincent, and Christian Janvin. 2003. A neural probabilistic language model. *J. Mach. Learn. Res.*, 3(null):1137–1155.

Ronan Collobert, Jason Weston, Leon Bottou, Michael Karlen, Koray Kavukcuoglu, and Pavel Kuksa. 2011. Natural language processing (almost) from scratch.

Jacob Devlin, Ming-Wei Chang, Kenton Lee, and Kristina Toutanova. 2018. Bert: Pre-training of deep bidirectional transformers for language understanding.

Alex Graves, Abdel rahman Mohamed, and Geoffrey Hinton. 2013. Speech recognition with deep recurrent neural networks.

Sepp Hochreiter and Jürgen Schmidhuber. 1997. Long short-term memory. *Neural Comput.*, 9(8):1735–1780.

Nal Kalchbrenner, Edward Grefenstette, and Phil Blunsom. 2014. A convolutional neural network for modelling sentences. In *Proceedings of the 52nd Annual Meeting of the Association for Computational Linguistics (Volume 1: Long Papers)*, pages 655–665, Baltimore, Maryland. Association for Computational Linguistics.

Yoon Kim. 2014. Convolutional neural networks for sentence classification.

Alex Krizhevsky, Ilya Sutskever, and Geoffrey E. Hinton. 2012. Imagenet classification with deep convolutional neural networks. In *Proceedings of the 25th International Conference on Neural Information Processing Systems - Volume 1*, NIPS'12, page 1097–1105, Red Hook, NY, USA. Curran Associates Inc.

Guillaume Lample and Alexis Conneau. 2019. Crosslingual language model pretraining.

Zhenzhong Lan, Mingda Chen, Sebastian Goodman, Kevin Gimpel, Piyush Sharma, and Radu Soricut. 2019. Albert: A lite bert for self-supervised learning of language representations.

Y. Lecun, L. Bottou, Y. Bengio, and P. Haffner. 1998. Gradient-based learning applied to document recognition. *Proceedings of the IEEE*, 86(11):2278–2324.

Yinhan Liu, Myle Ott, Naman Goyal, Jingfei Du, Mandar Joshi, Danqi Chen, Omer Levy, Mike Lewis, Luke Zettlemoyer, and Veselin Stoyanov. 2019. Roberta: A robustly optimized bert pretraining approach.

Tomas Mikolov, Ilya Sutskever, Kai Chen, Greg Corrado, and Jeffrey Dean. 2013. Distributed representations of words and phrases and their compositionality. In *Proceedings of the 26th International Conference on Neural Information Processing Systems - Volume 2*, NIPS'13, page 3111–3119, Red Hook, NY, USA. Curran Associates Inc.

Martin Müller, Marcel Salathé, and Per E Kummervold. 2020. Covid-twitter-bert: A natural language processing model to analyse covid-19 content on twitter.

Dat Quoc Nguyen, Thanh Vu, Afshin Rahimi, Mai Hoang Dao, Linh The Nguyen, and Long Doan. 2020. WNUT-2020 Task 2: Identification of Informative COVID-19 English Tweets. In *Proceedings of the 6th Workshop on Noisy User-generated Text*.

Adithya Rao and Nemanja Spasojevic. 2016. Actionable and political text classification using word embeddings and lstm.

Yelong Shen, Xiaodong He, Jianfeng Gao, Li Deng, and Grégoire Mesnil. 2014. Learning semantic representations using convolutional neural networks for web search. In *Proceedings of the 23rd International Conference on World Wide Web*, WWW '14 Companion, page 373–374, New York, NY, USA. Association for Computing Machinery.

Yequan Wang, Minlie Huang, Xiaoyan Zhu, and Li Zhao. 2016. Attention-based LSTM for aspect-level sentiment classification. In *Proceedings of the 2016 Conference on Empirical Methods in Natural Language Processing*, pages 606–615, Austin, Texas. Association for Computational Linguistics.

Zhilin Yang, Zihang Dai, Yiming Yang, Jaime Carbonell, Ruslan Salakhutdinov, and Quoc V. Le. 2019. Xlnet: Generalized autoregressive pretraining for language understanding.

Scott Wen-tau Yih, Xiaodong He, and Chris Meek. 2014. Semantic parsing for single-relation question answering. In *Proceedings of ACL*. Association for Computational Linguistics.

Wen-tau Yih, Kristina Toutanova, John C. Platt, and Christopher Meek. 2011. Learning discriminative projections for text similarity measures. In *Proceedings of the Fifteenth Conference on Computational Natural Language Learning*, pages 247–256, Portland, Oregon, USA. Association for Computational Linguistics.

CXP949 at WNUT-2020 Task 2: Extracting Informative COVID-19 Tweets - RoBERTa Ensembles and The Continued Relevance of Handcrafted Features

Calum Perrio
School of Computer Science
University of Birmingham
United Kingdom
cperrio2015@gmail.com

Harish Tayyar Madabushi
School of Computer Science
University of Birmingham
United Kingdom
harish@harishtayyarmadabushi.com

Abstract

This paper presents our submission to Task 2 of the Workshop on Noisy User-generated Text. We explore improving the performance of a pre-trained transformer-based language model fine-tuned for text classification through an ensemble implementation that makes use of corpus level information and a handcrafted feature. We test the effectiveness of including the aforementioned features in accommodating the challenges of a noisy data set centred on a specific subject outside the remit of the pre-training data. We show that inclusion of additional features can improve classification results and achieve a score within 2 points of the top performing team.

1 Introduction

Identification of informative tweets in relation of coronavirus presents a text classification problem. Pre-trained bidirectional transformer-based models such as such as BERT (Devlin et al., 2018) and RoBERTa (Liu et al., 2019) have proven to be extremely successful on text classification tasks; the process of pre-training on a large corpora enables the generation of effective contextual embeddings during fine-tuning, which can be leveraged on the classification task through the addition of an output layer (Devlin et al., 2018). The progression of the state-of-the-art that these models have facilitated is clearly demonstrable on performance against the General Language Understanding Evaluation (GLUE) benchmark (Wang et al., 2019); a collection of Natural Language Understanding tasks with an associated online platform for evaluation and analysis.

The corpora utilised during pre-training of transformer-based models typically consists of documents written in formal English. Moreover, this data is highly unlikely to contain references to the coronavirus pandemic which has only just occurred.

Therefore, the noise inherent in social media data and subject specificity to coronavirus in the current data set (Nguyen et al., 2020), present challenges to conducting text classification with a pre-trained transformer-based model alone. To this regard, supplementary information may be useful to improving performance; corpus level information may potentially capture notions of relevance to words which fall outside the pre-trained vocabulary, and handcrafted features may show additional distinctions between classes. In this paper, we describe the development of a system with includes such features through the use of an ensemble, and which in the final submission to the evaluation stage achieved an F_1 Score of 0.8910.

The rest of this paper is organised as follows, firstly a discussion of related work is presented at Section 2. This is followed by a description of the methodological approach at Section 3. We present our results and analysis at Section 4 and present our conclusions in Section 5.

2 Related Work

As the 6th Workshop of Noisy User-generated Text presents the first time Task 2 has been made available, we consider research utilising pre-trained bidirectional transformer-based models from similar tasks to better enable informed decision making.

2.1 Related Tasks

SemEval-2020 Task 12: Multilingual Offensive Language Identification in Social Media (Zampieri et al., 2020), presented at sub-task A a similar binary classification problem to the present task. Many of the highest performing teams on this sub-task made use of "contextualised BERT-style Transformers" (Zampieri et al., 2020). Sub-task A specifically comprised of identifying whether a tweet presented content that contained inappropriate language, threats or insults, or was neither offensive

Proceedings of the 2020 EMNLP Workshop W-NUT: The Sixth Workshop on Noisy User-generated Text, pages 352–358
Online, Nov 19, 2020. ©2020 Association for Computational Linguistics

nor profane (Zampieri et al., 2020). Additionally, the sub-task was split based on the language of the tweet text, and to this regard we only consider relevant systems on the English data set, which present the highest degree of correlation to Task 2.

Wiedemann et al. (2020) achieved first place on SemEval-2020 Task 12 sub-task A utilising an ensemble of RoBERTa (Liu et al., 2019). Additionally, the authors leveraged the Masked Language Model pre-training objective of RoBERTa and further pre-trained on an *in-domain* data set. Domain specific pre-training is observed to be a method that is established as improving later results of supervised task-specific fine-tuning. Further pre-training is equally explored by Sotudeh et al. (2020) in their submission on SemEval-2020 Task 12 sub-task A that utilised BERT and achieved 4[th]place.

Lim and Madabushi (2020) presented an ensemble model of BERT and TF-IDF. They hypothesise that corpus level count information captured by TF-IDF can boost the performance of BERT, and the authors achieve a result within 2 points of the top scoring team. Moreover, they note this performance was achieved using only 10% of the available training data due to physical constraints. We implement a similar method of incorporating TF-IDF features described at Section 3, but differentiate from this work through our ability to incorporate the entire training data.

2.2 User-generated Content

A key aspect of the present task to consider is the nature of Twitter data, or more broadly User-generated Content. This is specifically relevant to our implementation using transformer based models, with Kumar et al. (2020) showing the reduction in the performance of BERT with the introduction of noise in the form of spelling mistakes and typos. Similar inaccuracies can be expected in the data set for the present task given the informal nature of Twitter, the distinctive character limit, and modification of words by user to indicate emotion.

In relation to overcoming the challenges of Twitter data specifically, Ying et al. (2019) leveraged a token pattern detector to obtain domain-specific features. This comprised a convolution network trained on annotated features derived from pre-processing for domain-specific features. These representations were concatenated with the [CLS] token embedding from BERT, with the resulting model producing a statistically significant improvement on multi-label emotion classification over pure BERT (Ying et al., 2019).

2.3 Leveraging Metadata

Social media's widespread use generates a vast amount of data, not just in text but additionally in metadata. In the body of work surrounding the classification of rumors on Twitter , metadata has been successfully leveraged to develop handcrafted features (Li et al., 2019b). In the classification model produced by Li et al. (2019a), metadata information specific to Twitter, such as whether the account id is verified, if the profile includes a location or a description is concatenated together to form a input of "User Information" which is passed to a classifier along with textual and other features (Li et al., 2019a). This methodology of handcrafting features which provide supplementary information to a classifier is particularly related to the models in this work where we leverage a handcrafted feature derived from the text (Section 3).

3 Methodology

The data for this work was provided by the Workshop on Noisy User-generated Text (Xu et al., 2019) and consisted of 10,000 English tweets in relation to Covid-19. A 70/10/20 rate had been used to split the 10,000 tweets into training, validation and test sets. Each tweet had been labelled either as 'uninformative' or 'informative' by three independent annotators with an inter-annotator agreement score of Fleiss' Kappa at 0.818 (Xu et al., 2019). At the onset of this work, only the training and validation data had been provided. The test set was retained as a holdout set for the Workshop to evaluate the performance of models, discussed at Section 5.

In an attempt to build upon the success of leveraging tweet metadata in a classification model (see Section 2.3) an initial exploration of the distribution of metadata and text features between the "uninformative" and "informative" classes in the training dataset was conducted. This processes highlighted little differentiation between the classes, suggesting the distinction was more nuanced and conveyed within the circumstantial and contextual meanings. However, it was found that the higher the probability any given character in tweet was a numeric character increased the probability of it being "informative". We present a visual representation of this at Figure 1.

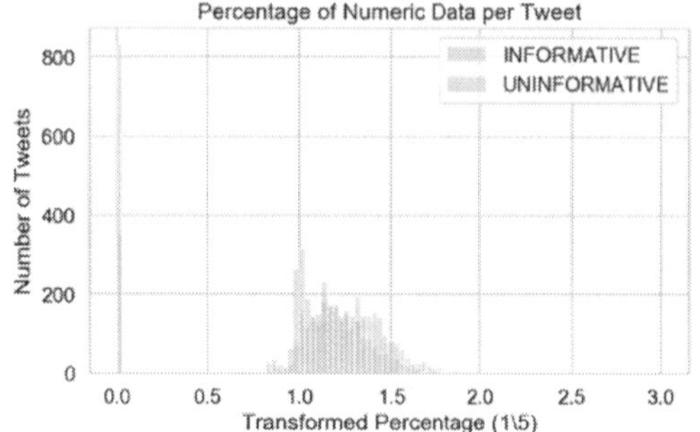

Figure 1: Probability of a character being numeric (power transformed $x^{\frac{1}{5}}$).

By virtue of the competitive element, this task presented an incentive to find the best performing model. In order to have a basis for comparison two initial models were trained on the raw training data and evaluated against the validation data: **(1)** a Linear Support Vector Machine (SVM) using TF-IDF features, and **(2)** fine-tuned BERT$_{BASE}$. As is the case with all the deep networks tested in this study, we test a range of hyperparameter values (details of which are available in the program code and model details released as part of this publication [1]), and test each combination against five different random seeds. The effect of random seed on BERT is emphasised in Dodge et al. (2020) where varying only the random seed was shown to produce substantial improvements over previously published results. We present the highest performing results of these models at Table 1.

Model	F_1 **Score**
SVM	0.8155
BERT	0.9051
RoBERTa (unprocessed)	0.9101
RoBERTa (processed)	0.9131

Table 1: Baseline results achieved by BERT and SVM, and results from RoBERTa. All tested aganist the validation data.

The SVM model was chosen due to the established high accuracy this model can achieve on the task of text classification ((Kadhim, 2019); (Shah and Patel, 2016)).

We observe that a fine-tuned BERT model achieved a good performance against the validation data. The next logical progression was to experiment with a fine-tuned RoBERTa implementation, given that the robustly optimised pre-training this

<hr>

[1] https://github.com/CalumPerrio/WNUT-2020

model employs improved performance over BERT (Liu et al., 2019). We fine-tuned a RoBERTa$_{BASE}$ model, and the results of this are presented against the BERT and SVM baselines in Table 1. We present two versions of the RoBERTa model: processed and unprocessed. The processed implementation draws inspiration from the pre-processing adopted by Nikolov and Radivchev (2019), in which we also segmented camel-cased hashtags into distinct tokens e.g. the token "#HashTag" would become "#Hash" and "Tag". Additionally, the two forms primarily used to refer to coronavirus: "covid-19" and "coronavirus" were parsed for in an extensive number of variations and standardised to "coronavirus" to ensure the token representation for this key term was consistent across inputs.

Model	False Negative	False Positive
BERT	62.16%	41.81%
RoBERTa	56.6%	43.27%

Table 2: Percentage of miss-classifications shared with the SVM. Visual representations are included in the Appendix.

An error analysis was conducted after the development and testing of RoBERTa which explored the intersection of the false negative and false positive classifications from the SVM, BERT and the processed RoBERTa implementations. We present the most interesting finding from this in Table 2: despite higher overall miss-classification, the SVM trained on TF-IDF features was able to correctly classify a significant proportion of miss-classifications from the fine-tuned BERT and RoBERTa models. This suggests, as in Lim and Madabushi (2020), that incorporation of corpus level information could improve performance.

Additionally, the error analysis noted the BPE tokenization of "coronavirus" was out-of-vocabulary, splitting into the tokens "Ġcoron, av, irus". To this regard, post submission we have tested a promising implementation that instead replaces all forms referring to "coronavirus" to "coronavirus disease". With the intention of leveraging through self-attention the context of these terms as a disease. This is explored further in the future work.

3.1 Exploration of Improving Baseline Performances

The error analysis and initial feature exploration motivated the experimentation of improving the performance of a pre-trained language model in the following three ensemble models. In all instances the RoBERTa processed implementation was used as the base pre-trained language model due to it achieving the highest F_1 score on the validation data in our initial experiments.

Three ensemble models were experimented, presented broadly below and explored in details at Section 3.2, these were: **a)** RoBERTa together with a percentage metric of the probability of a character in the text being numeric, **b)** RoBERTa with TF-IDF features, and **c)** RoBERTa with both TF-IDF features and the percentage metric.

3.2 Model Architecture

For all three ensemble models, we concatenate the additional features to the final hidden layer for the $</s>$ token, which we use as an aggregate representation of the sequence. This vector then forms the input to the fully connected output layer.

With regards to the TF-IDF features. A document-term matrix was constructed from a processed version of the training data, and a TF-IDF feature vector fit for the text for the equivalent tokenized input to the model. Processing involved removing punctuation, stopwords and emojis, and stemming. During testing, two combinations of maximum features in the document-term matrix were tested: 6000 and 9000.

The probability metric was produced by first removing emojis from the text to prevent the influence of numbers in unicode. Then returning the probability of any character in the tweet being a digit, transformed as a (1,1) tensor.

4 Results and Analysis

We present the results of the three ensemble models in comparison to the processed RoBERTa model from Table 1 in Table 3.

Model	F_1 Score
RoBERTa (baseline)	0.9131
RoBERTa+PROB	0.9141
RoBERTa+TFIDF	0.9111
RoBERTa+PROB+TFIDF	0.9151

Table 3: F1 score results of the three ensemble models presented against the baseline performance of RoBERTa.

We observe that against the baseline RoBERTa model, inclusion of the hand-crated feature improved performance. However, the increase is small, potentially reflecting that the number of

tweets in the data set for which this features is a useful indicator is equally small. We also observe that the inclusion of TF-IDF features on the validation data alone did not improve performance, however the inclusion of both the average metric and TF-IDF produced an improved result over the baseline and RoBERTa+PROB. The former result does not support our hypothesis of improving performance with the inclusion of TF-IDF features and is in contradiction to the latter result.

Between the RoBERTa+TFIDF model and RoBERTa+TFIDF+PROB models, the highest performances were found on models featuring 9000 and 6000 TF-IDF features respectively. It is notable that the total dimension of the stemmed document-term matrix was over 15,000 features. As such, due to memory constraints it was not possible to use a vector of this entire dimension. We submit an interesting experiment would be to parse for domain-specific expressions as in (Ying et al., 2019) and standardise these to dictionary representation to reduce the number of TF-IDF features. Additionally, standardisation of these expressions across the corpus could potentially enable greater accuracy in calculating the Inverse Document Frequency, and by virtue of this better capture the amount of information a term provides.

In our submission to the evaluation stage we submit the RoBERTa+PROB+TFIDF ensemble model which achieved the highest performance of all models tested against the validation data (see Table 3). Our results against the holdout test set are presented at Table 4 [2]. Our ensemble model achieves an F_1 score of 0.8910, within two points of the highest performing team.

Rank	Team	F1 Score
1	NutCracker	0.9096
2	NLP_North	0.9096
...		
21	cxp949 (this work)	0.8910
...		
55	TMU-COVID19	0.5000

Table 4: F1 score of Final Model against the holdout test set.

4.1 Error Analysis

We present at Figure 2 the confusion matrices of the baseline RoBERTa model and RoBERTa+PROB+TFIDF ensemble model. We

---

[2] Independently evaluated by organisers.

observe that inclusion of the handcrafted feature and TF-IDF features provided a net gain on true-positive "uninformative" classifications, and reduced the number of false-positive miss-classifications when compared with the baseline.

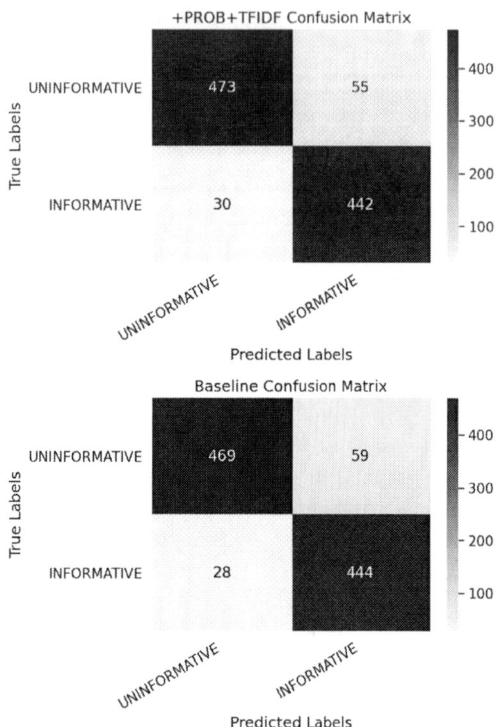

Figure 2: Confusion matrices of the RoBERTa+PROB+TFIDF ensemble model and RoBERTa baseline model respectively.

We additionally explored the intersection of false-positive and false-negative miss-classifications between the two models. We observed that the intersect between the models comprised 87% of the RoBERTa+PROB+TFIDF ensemble model's false-positive miss-classifications, and 77% of the false-negative miss-classifications. We submit that this large intersection within the miss-classifications is indicative of a large proportion of tweets with which the RoBERTa model inherently struggles. Valentini and Masulli (2002) describe how the effectiveness of an ensemble model directly relies upon the accuracy and *diversity* of the individual base learners, and to this regard we submit that more substantial improvements in performance require overcoming the limitations of the RoBERTa model in it's current form.

5 Conclusions and Further Work

We have explored with providing supplementary information to improve the performance of RoBERTa. We have observed that the addition of a handcrafted feature improved performance of a pre-trained bidirectional transformer-based language model, suggesting that for text classification tasks and noisy data sets the inclusion of additional features that distinguish the classes can be beneficial. We intend to explore this concept further, beginning with conducting a statistical test to observe whether the difference between the presence of numeric data in informative tweets is significant.

Additionally, we have experienced success with incorporating TF-IDF features with BERT to a degree, however we present that the size of the document-term matrix, the short length of tweets and domain-specific features of Twitter present potentially a challenge in utilising this optimally.

As the global coronavirus pandemic continues to develop, the nature of what becomes "informative" information will likely develop also. Therefore, in the present task, an approach with a greater level of generalisation is arguably preferable. To this regard, initial testing of parsing the tweets and replacing the terms "coronavirus" and "covid-19" to "coronavirus disease", with a view to leveraging the existing embedding for "disease" to provide contextual information has shown promising results. The application of this new parsing objective presents an opportunity for future work.

Furthermore, we observed in Section 2 that conducting additional *in-domain* pre-training was successfully utilised in relation to pre-training transformer-based models in a similar task. Additionally, in Müller et al. (2020) the authors release a BERT model pre-trained on a data set of tweets in relation to the coronavirus that shows a 10-30% marginal improvement on numerous classification data sets compared to BERT$_{\text{LARGE}}$. Exploration of these two concepts may provide insight into improving the base RoBERTa model's performance (as discussed in Section 4.1), and present further potential for future work and overcoming the challenges of a noisy data set centred around the topic of coronavirus.

Acknowledgements

We would like to thank the NVIDIA Deep Learning Institute for the provision of AWS credits which we used to access GPU resources in this work.

References

Jacob Devlin, Ming-Wei Chang, Kenton Lee, and Kristina Toutanova. 2018. BERT: pre-training of deep bidirectional transformers for language understanding. *CoRR*, abs/1810.04805.

Jesse Dodge, Gabriel Ilharco, Roy Schwartz, Ali Farhadi, Hannaneh Hajishirzi, and Noah Smith. 2020. Fine-tuning pretrained language models: Weight initializations, data orders, and early stopping.

Ammar Ismael Kadhim. 2019. Survey on supervised machine learning techniques for automatic text classification. *Artificial Intelligence Review*, 52(1):273–292.

Ankit Kumar, Piyush Makhija, and Anuj Gupta. 2020. User generated data: Achilles' heel of bert.

Quanzhi Li, Qiong Zhang, and Luo Si. 2019a. Rumor detection by exploiting user credibility information, attention and multi-task learning. In *Proceedings of the 57th Annual Meeting of the Association for Computational Linguistics*, pages 1173–1179, Florence, Italy. Association for Computational Linguistics.

Quanzhi Li, Qiong Zhang, Luo Si, and Yingchi Liu. 2019b. Rumor detection on social media: Datasets, methods and opportunities.

Wah Meng Lim and Harish Tayyar Madabushi. 2020. Uob at semeval-2020 task 12: Boosting bert with corpus level information.

Yinhan Liu, Myle Ott, Naman Goyal, Jingfei Du, Mandar Joshi, Danqi Chen, Omer Levy, Mike Lewis, Luke Zettlemoyer, and Veselin Stoyanov. 2019. Roberta: A robustly optimized bert pretraining approach.

Martin Müller, Marcel Salathé, and Per E Kummervold. 2020. Covid-twitter-bert: A natural language processing model to analyse covid-19 content on twitter.

Dat Quoc Nguyen, Thanh Vu, Afshin Rahimi, Mai Hoang Dao, Linh The Nguyen, and Long Doan. 2020. WNUT-2020 Task 2: Identification of Informative COVID-19 English Tweets. In *Proceedings of the 6th Workshop on Noisy User-generated Text*.

Alex Nikolov and Victor Radivchev. 2019. Nikolov-radivchev at SemEval-2019 task 6: Offensive tweet classification with BERT and ensembles. In *Proceedings of the 13th International Workshop on Semantic Evaluation*, pages 691–695, Minneapolis, Minnesota, USA. Association for Computational Linguistics.

F. P. Shah and V. Patel. 2016. A review on feature selection and feature extraction for text classification. In *2016 International Conference on Wireless Communications, Signal Processing and Networking (WiSPNET)*, pages 2264–2268.

Sajad Sotudeh, Tong Xiang, Hao-Ren Yao, Sean MacAvaney, Eugene Yang, Nazli Goharian, and Ophir Frieder. 2020. Guir at semeval-2020 task 12: Domain-tuned contextualized models for offensive language detection.

Giorgio Valentini and Francesco Masulli. 2002. Ensembles of learning machines. In *Neural Nets*, pages 3–20, Berlin, Heidelberg. Springer Berlin Heidelberg.

Alex Wang, Amanpreet Singh, Julian Michael, Felix Hill, Omer Levy, and Samuel Bowman. 2019. Glue: A multi-task benchmark and analysis platform for natural language understanding. In *Proceedings of the EMNLP Workshop BlackboxNLP*.

Gregor Wiedemann, Seid Muhie Yimam, and Chris Biemann. 2020. Uhh-lt at semeval-2020 task 12: Fine-tuning of pre-trained transformer networks for offensive language detection.

Wei Xu, Alan Ritter, Tim Baldwin, and Afshin Rahimi, editors. 2019. *Proceedings of the 5th Workshop on Noisy User-generated Text (W-NUT 2019)*. Association for Computational Linguistics, Hong Kong, China.

Wenhao Ying, Rong Xiang, and Qin Lu. 2019. Improving multi-label emotion classification by integrating both general and domain-specific knowledge. In *Proceedings of the 5th Workshop on Noisy User-generated Text (W-NUT 2019)*, pages 316–321, Hong Kong, China. Association for Computational Linguistics.

Marcos Zampieri, Preslav Nakov, Sara Rosenthal, Pepa Atanasova, Georgi Karadzhov, Hamdy Mubarak, Leon Derczynski, Zeses Pitenis, and Çağrı Çöltekin. 2020. Semeval-2020 task 12: Multilingual offensive language identification in social media (offenseval 2020).

A Appendix

Pie Chart Representations of the Intersection between SVM, BERT and RoBERTa

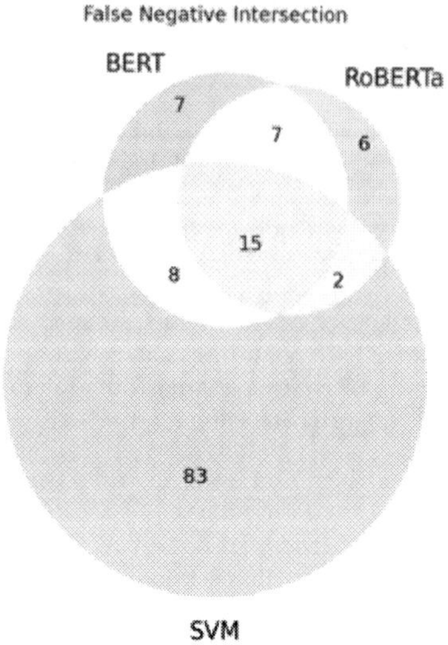

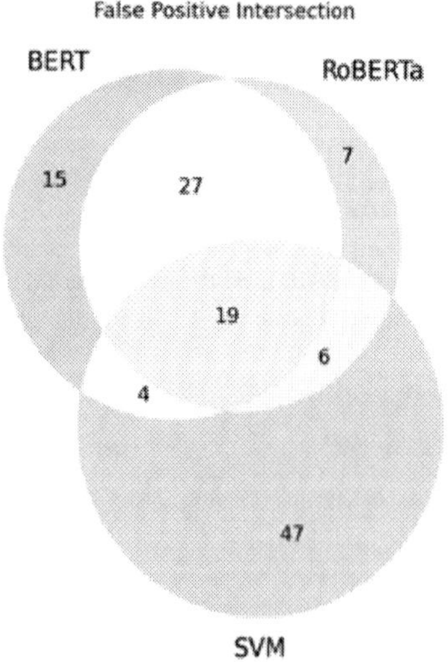

InfoMiner at WNUT-2020 Task 2: Transformer-based Covid-19 Informative Tweet Extraction

Hansi Hettiarachchi[♡], Tharindu Ranasinghe[‡]
[♡]School of Computing and Digital Technology, Birmingham City University, UK
[‡]Research Group in Computational Linguistics, University of Wolverhampton, UK
hansi.hettiarachchi@mail.bcu.ac.uk
tharindu.ranasinghe@wlv.ac.uk

Abstract

Identifying informative tweets is an important step when building information extraction systems based on social media. WNUT-2020 Task 2 was organised to recognise informative tweets from noise tweets. In this paper, we present our approach to tackle the task objective using transformers. Overall, our approach achieves 10th place in the final rankings scoring 0.9004 F1 score for the test set.

1 Introduction

By 31st August 2020, coronavirus COVID-19 is affecting 213 countries around the world infecting more than 25 million people and killing more than 800,000. Recently, much attention has been given to build monitoring systems to track the outbreaks of the virus. However, due to the fact that most of the official news sources update the outbreak information only once or twice a day, these monitoring tools have begun to use social media as the medium to get information.

There is a massive amount of data on social networks, e.g. about 4 millions of COVID-19 English tweets daily on the Twitter platform. However, majority of these tweets are uninformative. Thus it is important to be able to select the informative ones for downstream applications. Since the manual approaches to identify the informative tweets require significant human efforts, an automated technique to identify the informative tweets will be invaluable to the community.

The objective of this shared task is to automatically identify whether a COVID-19 English tweet is informative or not. Such informative Tweets provide information about recovered, suspected, confirmed and death cases as well as location or travel history of the cases. The participants of the shared task were required to provide predictions for the test set provided by the organisers whether a tweet is informative or not. Our team used recently released transformers to tackle the problem. Despite achieving 10th place out of 55 participants and getting high evaluation score, our approach is simple and efficient. In this paper we mainly present our approach that we used in this task. We also provide important resources to the community: the code, and the trained classification models will be freely available to everyone interested in working on identifying informative tweets using the same methodology [1].

2 Related Work

In the last few years, there have been several studies published on the application of computational methods in order to identify informative contents from tweets. Most of the earlier methods were based on traditional machine learning models like logistic regression and support vector machines with heavy feature engineering. Castillo et al. (2011) investigate tweet newsworthiness classification using features representing the message, user, topic and the propagation of messages. Others use features based on social influence, information propagation, syntactic and combinations of local linguistic features as well as user history and user opinion to select informative tweets (Inouye and Kalita, 2011; Yang et al., 2011; Chua and Asur, 2013). Due to the fact that training set preparation is difficult when it comes informative tweet identification, several studies suggested unsupervised methods. Sankaranarayanan et al. (2009) built a news processing system, called *TwitterStand* using an unsupervised approach to classify tweets collected from pre-determined users who frequently post news about events. Even though these traditional approaches have provided good results, they

---

[1]The GitHub repository is publicly available on https://github.com/hhansi/informative-tweet-identification

Proceedings of the 2020 EMNLP Workshop W-NUT: The Sixth Workshop on Noisy User-generated Text, pages 359–365
Online, Nov 19, 2020. ©2020 Association for Computational Linguistics

are no longer the state of the art.

Considering the recent research, there was a tendency to use deep learning-based methods to identify informative tweets since they performed better than traditional machine learning-based methods. To mention few, ALRashdi and O'Keefe (2019) suggested an approach based on Bidirectional Long Short-Term Memory (Bi-LSTM) models trained using word embeddings. Another research proposed a deep multi-modal neural network based on images and text in tweets to recognise informative tweets (Kumar et al., 2020). Among the different neural network models available, transformer models received a huge success in the area of natural language processing (NLP) recently. Since the release of BERT (Devlin et al., 2019), transformer models gained a wide attention of the community and they were successfully applied for wide range of tasks including tweet classification tasks such as offensive tweet identification (Ranasinghe et al., 2019) and topic identification (Yüksel et al., 2019). But we could not find any previous work on transformers for informative tweet classification. Hence, we decided to use transformer for our approach and this study will be important to the community.

3 Task Description and Data Set

WNUT-2020 Task 2: Identification of informative COVID-19 English Tweets (Nguyen et al., 2020) is to develop a system which can automatically categorise the tweets related to coronavirus as informative or not. A data set of 10K tweets which are labelled as *informative* and *uninformative* is released to conduct this task. The class distributions of the data set splits are mentioned in Table 1.

Data set	Informative	Uninformative
Training	3303	3697
Validation	472	528
Test	944	1056

Table 1: Class distribution of data set splits

4 Methodology

The motivation behind our methodology is the recent success that the transformers had in wide range of NLP tasks like language generation (Devlin et al., 2019), sequence classification (Ranasinghe and Hettiarachchi, 2020; Ranasinghe et al., 2019; Ranasinghe and Zampieri, 2020), word similarity

(Hettiarachchi and Ranasinghe, 2020), named entity recognition (Liang et al., 2020) and question and answering (Yang et al., 2019a). The main idea of the methodology is that we train a classification model with several transformer models in-order to identify informative tweets.

4.1 Transformers for Text Classification

Predicting whether a certain tweet is informative or not can be considered as a sequence classification task. Since the transformer architectures have shown promising results in sequence classification tasks (Ranasinghe and Hettiarachchi, 2020; Ranasinghe et al., 2019; Ranasinghe and Zampieri, 2020), the basis for our methodology was transformers. Transformer architectures have been trained on general tasks like language modelling and then can be fine-tuned for classification tasks. (Sun et al., 2019)

Transformer models take an input of a sequence and outputs the representations of the sequence. There can be one or two segments in a sequence which are separated by a special token [SEP]. In this approach we considered a tweet as a sequence and no [SEP] token is used. Another special token [CLS] is used as the first token of the sequence which contains a special classification embedding. For text classification tasks, transformer models take the final hidden state $\mathbf{h}$ of the [CLS] token as the representation of the whole sequence (Sun et al., 2019). A simple softmax classifier is added to the top of the transformer model to predict the probability of a class c as shown in Equation 1 where W is the task-specific parameter matrix. The architecture of transformer-based sequence classifier is shown in Figure 1.

$$p(c|\mathbf{h}) = softmax(W\mathbf{h}) \qquad (1)$$

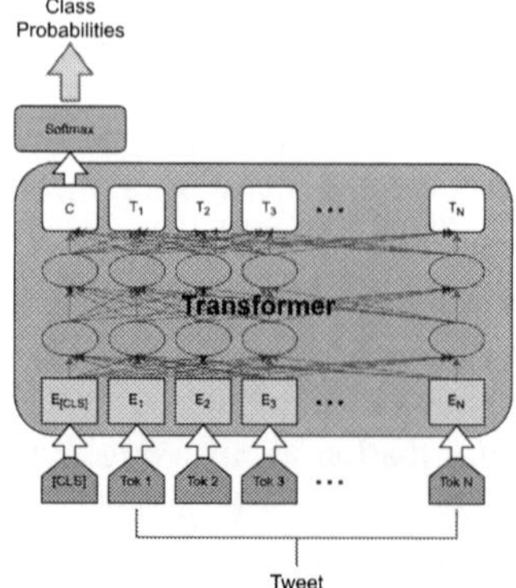

Figure 1: Text Classification Architecture

360

4.2 Transformers

We used several pre-trained transformer models in this task. These models were used mainly considering the popularity of them (e.g. BERT (Devlin et al., 2019), XLNet (Yang et al., 2019b), RoBERTa (Liu et al., 2019), ELECTRA (Clark et al., 2020), ALBERT (Lan et al., 2020)) and relatedness to the task (e.g. COVID-Twitter-BERT (CT-BERT) (Müller et al., 2020) and BERTweet (Dat Quoc Nguyen and Nguyen, 2020)).

BERT (Devlin et al., 2019) was the first transformer model that gained a wide attention of the NLP community. It proposes a masked language modelling (MLM) objective, where some of the tokens of a input sequence are randomly masked, and the objective is to predict these masked positions taking the corrupted sequence as input. As we explained before BERT uses special tokens to obtain a single contiguous sequence for each input sequence. Specifically, the first token is always a special classification token [CLS] which is used for sentence-level tasks.

RoBERTa (Liu et al., 2019), ELECTRA (Clark et al., 2020) and ALBERT (Lan et al., 2020) can all be considered as variants of BERT. They make a few changes to the BERT model and achieves substantial improvements in some NLP tasks (Liu et al., 2019; Clark et al., 2020; Lan et al., 2020). XLNet on the other hand takes a different approach to BERT (Yang et al., 2019b). XLNet proposes a new auto-regressive method based on permutation language modelling (PLM) (Uria et al., 2016) without introducing any new symbols such as [MASK] in BERT. Also there are significant changes in the XLNet architecture like adopting two-stream self-attention and Transformer-XL (Dai et al., 2019). Due to this XLNet outperforms BERT in multiple NLP downstream tasks (Yang et al., 2019b).

We also used two transformer models based on Twitter; CT-BERT and BERTweet. The CT-BERT model is based on the BERT-LARGE model and trained on a corpus of 160M tweets about the coronavirus (Müller et al., 2020) while the BERTweet model is based on BERT-BASE model and trained on general tweets (Dat Quoc Nguyen and Nguyen, 2020).

4.3 Data Preprocessing

Few general data preprocessing techniques were employed with InfoMiner to preserve the universality of this method. More specifically, used techniques can be listed as removing or filling usernames and URLs, and converting emojis to text. Further, for uncased pretrained models (e.g. *albert-xxlarge-v1*), all tokens were converted to lower case.

In WNUT-2020 Task 2 data set, mention of a user is represented by *@USER* and a URL is represented by *HTTPURL*. For all the models except CT-BERT and BERTweet, we removed those mentions. The main reason behind this step is to remove noisy text from data. CT-BERT and BERTweet models are trained on tweet corpora and usernames and URLs are introduced to the models using special fillers. CT-BERT model knows a username as *twitteruser* and URL as *twitterurl*. Likewise, BERTweet model used the filler *@USER* for usernames and *HTTPURL* for URLs. Therefore, for these two models we used the corresponding fillers to replace usernames and URLs in the data set.

Emojis are found to play a key role in expressing emotions in the context of social media (Hettiarachchi and Ranasinghe, 2019). But, we cannot assure the existence of embeddings for emojis in pretrained models. Therefore as another essential preprocessing step, we converted emojis to text. For this conversion we used the Python libraries *demoji*[2] and *emoji*[3]. *demoji* returns a normal descriptive text and *emoji* returns a specifically formatted text. For an example, the conversion of ☺ is 'slightly smiling face' using *demoji* and ':slightly_smiling_face:' using *emoji*. For all the models except CT-BERT and BERTweet, we used *demoji* supported conversion. For CT-BERT and BERTweet *emoji* supported conversion is used, because these models are trained on correspondingly converted Tweets.

4.4 Fine-tuning

To improve the models, we experimented different fine-tuning strategies: majority class self-ensemble, average self-ensemble, entity integration and language modelling, which are described below.

1. **Self-Ensemble (SE)** - Self-ensemble is found as a technique which result better performance than the performance of a single model (Xu et al., 2020). In this approach, same model architecture is trained or fine-tuned with different random seeds or train-validation splits.

[2]demoji repository - https://github.com/bsolomon1124/demojis
[3]emoji repository - https://github.com/carpedm20/emoji

Strategy	Single-model			MSE (N=3)		
Model	**P**	**R**	**F1**	**P**	**R**	**F1**
bert-large-cased	0.9031	0.8686	0.8855	0.8884	0.8941	0.8912
roberta-large	0.9056	0.8941	0.8998	0.8926	0.9153	0.9038
albert-xxlarge-v1	0.9009	0.8856	0.8932	0.9032	0.8898	0.8965
xlnet-large-cased	0.8778	0.9280	0.9022	0.8743	0.9280	0.9003
electra-large-generator	0.8297	0.8771	0.8527	0.8901	0.8750	0.8825
bertweet-base	0.8710	0.8968	0.8753	0.8741	0.8998	0.8780
covid-twitter-bert	0.8984	0.9364	0.9170	0.9002	0.9364	0.9180

Table 2: Results of different transformer models (All these experiments are executed for 3 learning epochs with $1e^{-5}$ learning rate.)

Learning R.		$1e^{-5}$			$1e^{-6}$			$2e^{-5}$		
S. 1	**S. 2**	**P**	**R**	**F1**	**P**	**R**	**F1**	**P**	**R**	**F1**
MSE (N=3)	-	0.9072	0.9322	0.9195	0.9317	0.8962	0.9136	0.9125	0.9280	0.9202
	EI	0.8864	0.9258	0.9057	0.9181	0.9025	0.9103	0.8975	0.9089	0.9032
	LM	0.8912	0.9195	0.9051	0.8987	0.9025	0.9006	0.9070	0.9301	0.9184
ASE (N=3)	-	0.9091	0.9322	0.9205	0.9295	0.8941	0.9114	0.9146	0.9301	**0.9223**
	EI	0.8960	0.9131	0.9045	0.9124	0.9047	0.9085	0.9025	0.9025	0.9025
	LM	0.9021	0.9174	0.9097	0.8971	0.9047	0.9008	0.9160	0.9237	0.9198

Table 3: Result obtained for CT-BERT model with different fine-tuning strategies (All these experiments are executed for 5 learning epochs and S. abbreviates the Strategy)

Then the output of each model is aggregated to generate the final results. As the aggregation methods, we analysed majority-class and average in this research. The number of models used with self-ensemble will be denoted by N.

- *Majority-class SE (MSE)* - As the majority class, we computed the mode of the classes predicted by each model. Given a data instance, following the softmax layer, a model predicts probabilities for each class and the class with highest probability is taken as the model predicted class.
- *Average SE (ASE)* - In average SE, final probability of class c is calculated as the average of probabilities predicted by each model as in Equation 2 where h is the final hidden state of the [CLS] token. Then the class with highest probability is selected as the final class.

$$p_{ASE}(c|h) = \frac{\sum_{k=1}^{N} p_k(c|h)}{N} \quad (2)$$

2. **Entity Integration (EI)** - Since we are using pretrained models, there can be model un-known data in the task data set such as person names, locations and organisations. As entity integration, we replaced the unknown tokens with their named entities which are known to the model, so that the familiarity of data to model can be increased. To identify the named entities, we used the pretrained models available with spaCy [4].

3. **Language Modelling (LM)** - As language modelling, we retrained the transformer model on task data set before fine-tuning it for the downstream task; text classification. This training is took place according with the model's initial trained objective. Following this technique model understanding on the task data can be improved.

5 Experiments and Results

In this section, we report the experiments we conducted and their results. As informed by task organisers, we used precision, recall and F1 score calculated for *Informative* class to measure the model performance. Results in sections 5.1 - 5.3 are computed on validation data set and results in section

---

[4]More details about spaCy are available on `https://spacy.io/`

5.4 are computed on test data set.

5.1 Impact by Transformer Model

Initially we focused on the impact by different transformer models. Selected transformer models were fine-tuned for this task using single-model (no ensemble) and MSE with 3 models, and the obtained results are summarised in Table 2. According to the results, CT-BERT model outperformed the other models. Also, all the models except XL-Net showed improved results with self-ensemble approach than single-model approach. Following these results and considering time and resource constraints, we limited the further experiments only to CT-BERT model.

5.2 Impact by Epoch Count

We experimented that increasing the epoch count from 3 to 5 increases the results. However, increasing it more than 5 did not further improved the results. Therefore, we used an epoch count of 5 in our experiments. To monitor the evaluation scores against the epoch count we used Wandb app [5]. As shown in the Figure 2 evaluation f1 score does not likely to change when trained with more than five epochs.

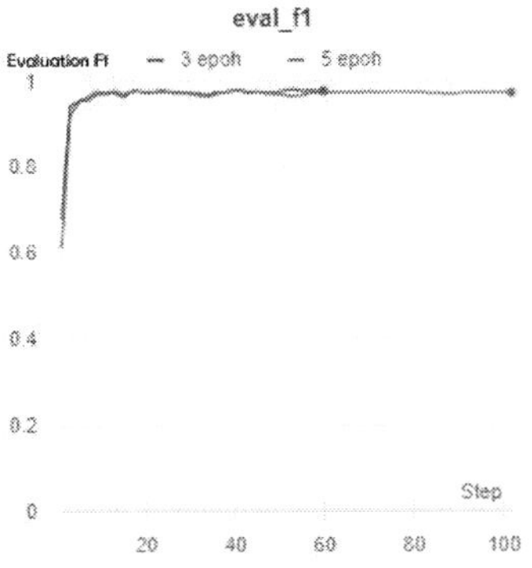

Figure 2: Evaluation F1 score against the epoch count

5.3 Impact by Fine-tuning

The fine-tuning strategies mentioned in Section 4.4 were experimented using CT-BERT model and obtained results are summarised in Table 3. According to the results, in majority of experiments, ASE is given a higher F1 than MSE. The other fine-strategies: EI and LM did not improve the results for this data set. As possible reasons for this reduction, having a good knowledge about COVID

tweets by the model itself and insufficiency of data for language modelling can be mentioned.

Additionally, we analysed the impact by different learning rates. For initial experiments a random learning rate of $1e^{-5}$ was picked and for further analysis a less value ($1e^{-6}$) and a high value ($2e^{-5}$) were picked. The value $2e^{-5}$ was used for pretraining and experiments of CT-BERT model (Müller et al., 2020). According to this analysis there is a tendency to have higher F1 with higher learning rates.

5.4 Test Set Evaluation

The test data results of our submissions, task baseline and top-ranked system are summarised in Table 4. Considering the evaluation results on validation data set, as InfoMiner 1 we selected the fine-tuned CT-BERT model with ASE and $2e^{-5}$ learning rate. As InfoMiner 2 same model and parameters with MSE was picked. Among them, the highest F1 we received is for MSE strategy.

Model	P	R	F1
Top-ranked	0.9135	0.9057	0.9096
InfoMiner 1	0.9107	0.8856	0.8980
InfoMiner 2	0.9102	0.8909	0.9004
Task baseline	0.7730	0.7288	0.7503

Table 4: Results of test data predictions

6 Conclusion

We have presented the system by InfoMiner team for WNUT-2020 Task 2. For this task, we have shown that the CT-BERT is the most successful transformer model from several transformer models we experimented. Furthermore, we presented several fine tuning strategies: self-ensemble, entity integration and language modelling that can improve the results. Overall, our approach is simple but can be considered as effective since it achieved 10th place in the leader-board.

As a future direction of this research, we hope to analyse the impact by different classification heads such as LSTM and Convolution Neural Network (CNN) in addition to softmax classifier on performance. Also, we hope to incorporate meta information-based features like number of retweets and likes with currently used textual features to involve social aspect for informative tweet identification.

---

[5]Wandb app is available on `https://app.wandb.ai/`

References

Reem ALRashdi and Simon O'Keefe. 2019. Deep learning and word embeddings for tweet classification for crisis response. *arXiv preprint arXiv:1903.11024*.

Carlos Castillo, Marcelo Mendoza, and Barbara Poblete. 2011. Information credibility on twitter. In *Proceedings of the 20th International Conference on World Wide Web*, WWW '11, page 675–684, New York, NY, USA. Association for Computing Machinery.

Freddy Chua and Sitaram Asur. 2013. Automatic summarization of events from social media.

Kevin Clark, Minh-Thang Luong, Quoc V. Le, and Christopher D. Manning. 2020. ELECTRA: Pretraining text encoders as discriminators rather than generators. In *ICLR*.

Zihang Dai, Zhilin Yang, Yiming Yang, Jaime Carbonell, Quoc Le, and Ruslan Salakhutdinov. 2019. Transformer-XL: Attentive language models beyond a fixed-length context. In *Proceedings of the 57th Annual Meeting of the Association for Computational Linguistics*, pages 2978–2988, Florence, Italy. Association for Computational Linguistics.

Thanh Vu Dat Quoc Nguyen and Anh Tuan Nguyen. 2020. BERTweet: A pre-trained language model for English Tweets. *arXiv preprint*, arXiv:2005.10200.

Jacob Devlin, Ming-Wei Chang, Kenton Lee, and Kristina Toutanova. 2019. BERT: Pre-training of deep bidirectional transformers for language understanding. In *Proceedings of the 2019 Conference of the North American Chapter of the Association for Computational Linguistics: Human Language Technologies, Volume 1 (Long and Short Papers)*, pages 4171–4186, Minneapolis, Minnesota. Association for Computational Linguistics.

Hansi Hettiarachchi and Tharindu Ranasinghe. 2019. Emoji powered capsule network to detect type and target of offensive posts in social media. In *Proceedings of the International Conference on Recent Advances in Natural Language Processing (RANLP 2019)*, pages 474–480.

Hansi Hettiarachchi and Tharindu Ranasinghe. 2020. Brums at semeval-2020 task 3: Contextualised embeddings for predicting the (graded) effect of context in word similarity. In *Proceedings of the 14th International Workshop on Semantic Evaluation*, Barcelona, Spain. Association for Computational Linguistics.

D. Inouye and J. K. Kalita. 2011. Comparing twitter summarization algorithms for multiple post summaries. In *2011 IEEE Third International Conference on Privacy, Security, Risk and Trust and 2011 IEEE Third International Conference on Social Computing*, pages 298–306.

Abhinav Kumar, Jyoti Prakash Singh, Yogesh K. Dwivedi, and Nripendra P. Rana. 2020. A deep multi-modal neural network for informative twitter content classification during emergencies. *Annals of Operations Research*.

Zhenzhong Lan, Mingda Chen, Sebastian Goodman, Kevin Gimpel, Piyush Sharma, and Radu Soricut. 2020. Albert: A lite bert for self-supervised learning of language representations. In *International Conference on Learning Representations*.

Chen Liang, Yue Yu, Haoming Jiang, Siawpeng Er, Ruijia Wang, Tuo Zhao, and Chao Zhang. 2020. Bond: Bert-assisted open-domain named entity recognition with distant supervision. In *Proceedings of the 26th ACM SIGKDD International Conference on Knowledge Discovery and Data Mining*, KDD '20, page 1054–1064, New York, NY, USA. Association for Computing Machinery.

Yinhan Liu, Myle Ott, Naman Goyal, Jingfei Du, Mandar Joshi, Danqi Chen, Omer Levy, Mike Lewis, Luke Zettlemoyer, and Veselin Stoyanov. 2019. Roberta: A robustly optimized bert pretraining approach. *arXiv preprint arXiv:1907.11692*.

Martin Müller, Marcel Salathé, and Per E Kummervold. 2020. Covid-twitter-bert: A natural language processing model to analyse covid-19 content on twitter. *arXiv preprint arXiv:2005.07503*.

Dat Quoc Nguyen, Thanh Vu, Afshin Rahimi, Mai Hoang Dao, Linh The Nguyen, and Long Doan. 2020. WNUT-2020 Task 2: Identification of Informative COVID-19 English Tweets. In *Proceedings of the 6th Workshop on Noisy User-generated Text*.

Tharindu Ranasinghe and Hansi Hettiarachchi. 2020. BRUMS at SemEval-2020 task 12 : Transformer based multilingual offensive language identification in social media. In *Proceedings of the 14th International Workshop on Semantic Evaluation*, Barcelona, Spain. Association for Computational Linguistics.

Tharindu Ranasinghe and Marcos Zampieri. 2020. Multilingual offensive language identification with cross-lingual embeddings. In *Proceedings of the 2020 Conference on Empirical Methods in Natural Language Processing*.

Tharindu Ranasinghe, Marcos Zampieri, and Hansi Hettiarachchi. 2019. BRUMS at HASOC 2019: Deep learning models for multilingual hate speech and offensive language identification. *In Proceedings of the 11th annual meeting of the Forum for Information Retrieval Evaluation (December 2019)*.

Jagan Sankaranarayanan, Hanan Samet, Benjamin E. Teitler, Michael D. Lieberman, and Jon Sperling. 2009. Twitterstand: News in tweets. In *Proceedings of the 17th ACM SIGSPATIAL International Conference on Advances in Geographic Information Systems*, GIS '09, page 42–51, New York, NY, USA. Association for Computing Machinery.

Chi Sun, Xipeng Qiu, Yige Xu, and Xuanjing Huang. 2019. How to fine-tune bert for text classification? In *Chinese Computational Linguistics*, pages 194–206, Cham. Springer International Publishing.

Benigno Uria, Marc-Alexandre Côté, Karol Gregor, Iain Murray, and Hugo Larochelle. 2016. Neural autoregressive distribution estimation. *J. Mach. Learn. Res.*, 17(1):7184–7220.

Yige Xu, Xipeng Qiu, Ligao Zhou, and Xuanjing Huang. 2020. Improving bert fine-tuning via self-ensemble and self-distillation. *arXiv preprint arXiv:2002.10345*.

Wei Yang, Yuqing Xie, Aileen Lin, Xingyu Li, Luchen Tan, Kun Xiong, Ming Li, and Jimmy Lin. 2019a. End-to-end open-domain question answering with BERTserini. In *Proceedings of the 2019 Conference of the North American Chapter of the Association for Computational Linguistics (Demonstrations)*, pages 72–77, Minneapolis, Minnesota. Association for Computational Linguistics.

Zhilin Yang, Zihang Dai, Yiming Yang, Jaime Carbonell, Russ R Salakhutdinov, and Quoc V Le. 2019b. Xlnet: Generalized autoregressive pretraining for language understanding. In *Advances in neural information processing systems*, pages 5753–5763.

Zi Yang, Keke Cai, Jie Tang, Li Zhang, Zhong Su, and Juanzi Li. 2011. Social context summarization. In *Proceedings of the 34th International ACM SIGIR Conference on Research and Development in Information Retrieval*, SIGIR '11, page 255–264, New York, NY, USA. Association for Computing Machinery.

Atıf Emre Yüksel, Yaşar Alim Türkmen, Arzucan Özgür, and Berna Altınel. 2019. Turkish tweet classification with transformer encoder. In *Proceedings of the International Conference on Recent Advances in Natural Language Processing (RANLP 2019)*, pages 1380–1387.

BANANA at WNUT-2020 Task 2: Identifying COVID-19 Information on Twitter by Combining Deep Learning and Transfer Learning Models

Tin Van Huynh
University of Information Technology
VNU-HCM, Vietnam
`16521827@gm.uit.edu.vn`

Luan Thanh Nguyen
University of Information Technology
VNU-HCM, Vietnam
`17520721@gm.uit.edu.vn`

Son T. Luu
University of Information Technology
VNU-HCM, Vietnam
`sonlt@uit.edu.vn`

Abstract

The outbreak COVID-19 virus caused a significant impact on the health of people all over the world. Therefore, it is essential to have a piece of constant and accurate information about the disease with everyone. This paper describes our prediction system for WNUT-2020 Task 2: Identification of Informative COVID-19 English Tweets. The dataset for this task contains size 10,000 tweets in English labeled by humans. The ensemble model from our three transformer and deep learning models is used for the final prediction. The experimental result indicates that we have achieved F1 for the INFORMATIVE label on our systems at 88.81% on the test set.

1 Introduction

The rapid spread of the coronavirus (COVID-19) has caused a global health crisis. This virus is hazardous to people's health and causes a big panic all over the world. Statistics show that each day there are 4 million tweets related to COVID-19 on Twitter (Lamsal, 2020). Therefore, it is essential to keep track of the information associated with this disease. Along with the development of many social networking platforms such as Twitter and Facebook. This is the primary way that helps people capture information about COVID-19 regularly. However, there is much content appearing daily on these social media platforms. Most of them do not have information about the status of COVID-19, such as the number of suspected cases or cases near the user's area.

In this article, we present our approach at WNUT-2020 Task 2 (Nguyen et al., 2020) to identify Tweets containing information about COVID-19 on the social networking platform Twitter or not. A Tweet is believed to have information if it includes information such as recovered, suspected, confirmed, and death cases and location or travel

Tweet	Label
A New Rochelle rabbi and a White Plains doctor are among the 18 confirmed coronavirus cases in Westchester. HTTPURL	0
Day 5: On a family bike ride to pick up dinner at @USER Broadway, we encountered our pre-COVID-19 Land Park happy hour crew keeping up the tradition at an appropriate #SocialDistance.HTTPURL	1

Table 1: Several examples in the WNUT-2020 Task 2 dataset. 0 and 1 stand for INFORMATIVE and UNINFORMATIVE, respectively.

history of the patients. Specifically, we described the problem as follows.

- **Input**: Given English Tweets on the social networking platform.

- **Output**: One of two labels (INFORMATIVE and UNINFORMATIVE) predicted by our system.

Several examples are shown in Table 1

In this paper, we have two main contributions as follows.

- Firstly, we implemented four different models based on neural networks and transformers such as Bi-GRU-CNN, BERT, RoBERTa, XLNet to solve the WNUT-2020 Task 2: Identification of informative COVID-19 English Tweets.

- Secondly, we propose a simple ensemble model by combining multiple deep learning and transformer models. This model gives the highest performance compared with the single

Proceedings of the 2020 EMNLP Workshop W-NUT: The Sixth Workshop on Noisy User-generated Text, pages 366–370
Online, Nov 19, 2020. ©2020 Association for Computational Linguistics

models with F1 on the test set is 88.81% and on the development set is 90.65%.

2 Related work

During the happening of the COVID-19 pandemic, the information about the number of infected cases, the number of patients is vital for governments. Dong et al. (2020) constructed a real-time database for tracking the COVID-19 around the world. This dataset is collected by experts from the World Health Organization (WHO), US CDC, and other medical agencies worldwide and is operated by John Hopkins University. Also, there are many other COVID-19 datasets such as multilingual data collected on Twitter from January 2020 (Chen et al., 2020) or Real World Worry Dataset (RWWD) (Kleinberg et al., 2020).

Besides, on social media, the spreading of COVID-19 information is extremely fast and enormous and sometimes leads to misinformation. Shahi et al. (2020) conducted a pilot study about detecting misinformation about COVID-19 on Twitter by analyzing tweets using standard social media analytics techniques. From the researching results, the authors want to help authorities and social media users counter misinformation. Moreover, the rumors and conspiracy theories within the emergence times of COVID-19 spreading had made communities feel fearmongering and panicky, which lead to racism about COVID-19 patients and citizens from infected countries, and mass purchase of face masks as well as the shortage of necessaries, according to (Depoux et al., 2020). Thus it is necessary to identify the right information from the social media text.

3 Dataset

The dataset provided by Nguyen et al. (2020) contains 10,000 English Tweets about COVID-19, which is used to automatically identify whether a tweet contains useful information about the COVID-19 (informative) or not (uninformative). There are 4,719 INFORMATIVE tweets and 5,281 UNINFORMATIVE tweets in the dataset, and three different annotators annotate each tweet. The inter-annotator agreement calculated by Fleiss' Kappa score of the dataset is 81.80%. Also, the dataset is split into the training, development, and test sets with proportion 7-1-2. Table 2 shows the overview information about the dataset.

	INFORMATIVE	UNINFORMATIVE
Training	3,303	3,697
Development	472	528
Test	944	1,056

Table 2: Overview of the WNUT-2020 Task 2 dataset.

4 Methodologies

In this paper, we propose an ensemble method that combines the deep learning models with the transfer learning models to identify information about COVID-19 from users' tweets.

4.1 Deep neural model

We implement the Bi-GRU-CNN model, which was used for salary prediction by Wang et al. (2019) and Job prediction by Van Huynh et al. (2020), with the GloVe-300d word embedding (Pennington et al., 2014). This model consists of three main layers: the word representation layers (word embedding), the 1D Convolutional layers (CONV-1D), and the bidirectional GRU layer (Bi-GRU). This model also achieved high performances on previous study works(Wang et al., 2019; Van Huynh et al., 2019, 2020). Fig 1 illustrates the Bi-GRU-CNN model.

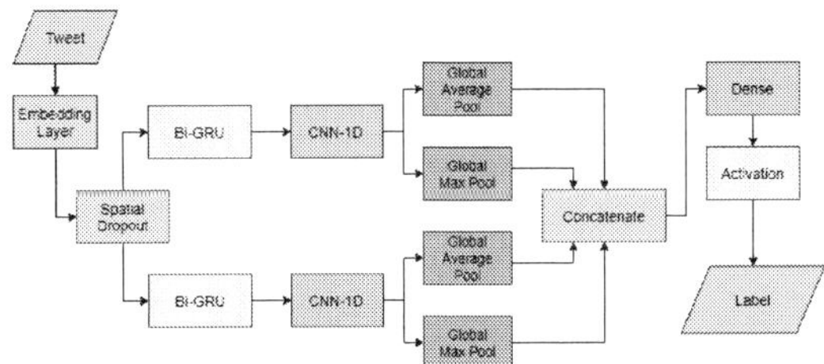

Figure 1: Overview architecture of Bi-GRU-CNN model.

4.2 Transfer learning model

Inspired by transfer learning success on many NLP tasks such as text classification (Do and Ng, 2006; Rizoiu et al., 2019) and machine reading comprehension (Devlin et al., 2019; Van Nguyen et al., 2020). In this paper, we used the SOTA transfer learning models, such as BERT (Devlin et al., 2019), RoBERTa (Liu et al., 2019), and XLNet (Yang et al., 2019) with fine-tuning techniques for the problem of identifying informative tweet about COVID-19. In our experiment, we used the pre-trained language model, as described in Table 3. All of these pre-trained models are constructed on English texts.

Transfer model	Pre-trained model
BERT	*bert_en_uncased*
RoBERTa	*roberta-base*
XLNet	*xlnet-large-cased*

Table 3: List of transformer models used in our experiment.

4.3 Ensemble method

As the success of the ensemble models of previous tasks (Van Huynh et al., 2020; Nguyen et al., 2019), we propose a simple yet effective ensemble approach with the majority voting between the outputs of four different models, including Bi-GRU-CNN, BERT, RoBERTa, and XLNet for classifying whether a tweet contains information about COVID-19 or not. Fig 2 describes our ensemble model.

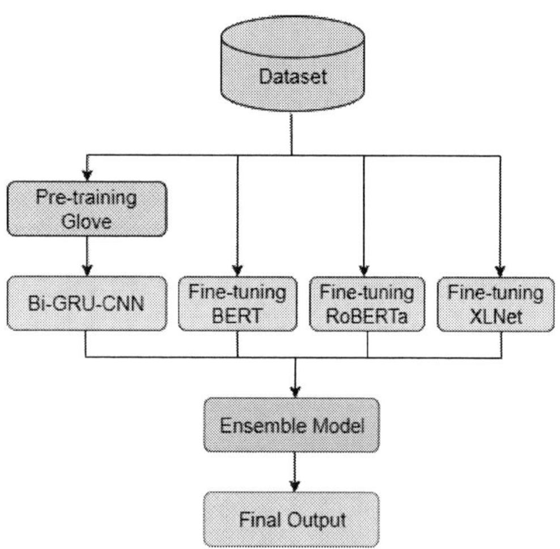

Figure 2: Overview architecture of our ensemble approach.

5 Experiment

5.1 Experimental settings

In this study, we experimented with datasets provided by WNUT-2020 Task 2. Training, development, and testing sets are divided as described in Section 3. To evaluate our models, we use four metrics include accuracy, precision, recall, and F1.

To prepare data for the model training and model evaluation phases, we perform the simple and effective pre-processing of input data as follows:

- Step 1: Converting the tweet into the lower-case strings.

- Step 2: Removing the user names in the tweets.

- Step 3: Deleting all URLs in the tweets.

- Step 4: Representing words into vectors with pre-trained word embedding sets for deep neural network models.

According to analyzing the length of the tweets in the data, we set max_length of the models to be 512 and epochs to be 15 for two models Bi-GRU-CNN and XLNet, and 3 for model BERT and RoBERTa. After searching for extensive hyper-parameter, we set learning_rate equal to 1e-3 and dropout equal to 0.2 for the Bi-GRU-CNN model and learning_rate equal to 1e-5 and dropout equal to 0.1 for three models BERT, RoBERTa, and XLNet.

5.2 Experimental results

Experimental results of the single model and the ensemble model on the development set are presented in Table 4. Specifically, in the single models, the Bi-GRU-CNN model gives the lowest performance with 85.66% by F1 and 86.10% by accuracy. The single model with the highest efficiency is XLNet, which attained 89.86% by F1 and 90.30% by accuracy. In addition, the BERT model gives the highest Precision with 89.53%, and the RoBERTa model achieved the highest Recall result with 90.74%. In particular, our recommend ensemble model gives the best performance when combining the power of single models together, which accomplished 90.65%, 91.00%, and 92.37% by F1, Accuracy, and Recall respectively, according to Table 4. Specifically, our model improved 0.79% by F1 and 0.70% by Accuracy over the most extensive single model (XLNet), and 0.63% by Recall over the RoBERTa model.

Model	Accuracy	Precision	Recall	F1
Bi-GRU-CNN	86.10	83.50	87.92	85.66
BERT	89.79	**89.53**	88.77	89.15
RoBERTa	89.90	87.47	**91.74**	89.56
XLNet	**90.30**	88.66	91.10	**89.86**
Ensemble	**91.00**	88.98	92.37	90.65

Table 4: Model performances on the development set of the COVID-19 dataset

After the system evaluation of WNUT-2020 Task 2, Table 5 displays our ensemble model results on the testing set. This result is compared with the top 5 highest teams' results and the baseline model

(BASELINE - FASTTEXT). Our model with F1 is 88.81%, 2.15% lower than the first rank team, and 13.78% higher than the baseline model. As for the results of accuracy, we get 89.40%, 2.10% lower than the first rank team, and 12.10% higher than the baseline model.

Team Name	Accuracy	Precision	Recall	F1
NutCracker	91.50	91.35	90.57	90.96
NLP_North	91.40	90.29	91.63	90.96
SupportNUTMachine	91.40	90.46	91.42	90.94
#GCDH	91.25	89.19	92.69	90.91
Loner	91.20	89.18	92.58	90.85
BASELINE - FASTTEXT	77.30	72.88	77.10	75.03
BANANA	**89.40**	**88.53**	**89.09**	**88.81**

Table 5: Comparison with our model's performance with that of other teams.

5.3 Result analysis

Fig. 3 describes the confusion matrix of the ensemble methods when predicting informative tweets about COVID-19. It can be inferred from Fig. 3 that the ability of prediction correct label on the INFORMATIVE label is higher than the UNINFORMATIVE label.

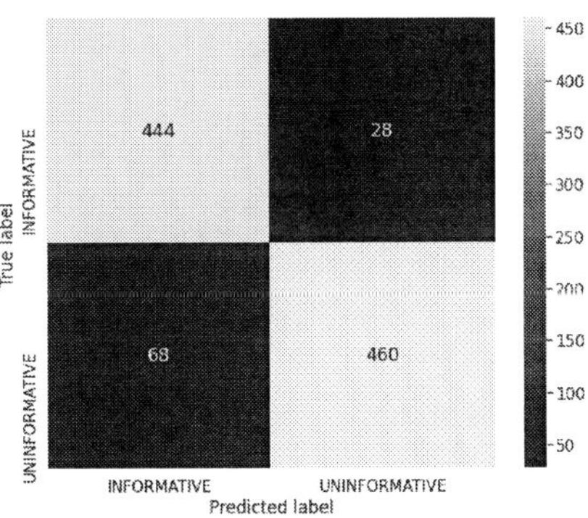

Figure 3: Confusion matrix of our ensemble model on the COVID English Tweet dataset.

In addition, Table 6 displays some error prediction examples from the dataset. Most of the wrong predictions occurred because of the appearance of special characters such as hashtag, the **HTTPURL** phrases, which stand for the URL links in the tweets. For the INFORMATION tweets, the appearance of the **HTTPURL** phrase and the hashtag **#coronavirus** make the classification model predict the wrong label. This mistake is the same for the UNINFORMATION tweets, where the appearance of **HTTPURL** phrase and the hashtags related to the Coronavirus affected the results of the prediction model.

Tweet	PL	TL
NATIONAL NEWS: Coronavirus: Linda Lusardi says COVID-19 made her want to die and turned her vomit blue HTTPURL	UN	IN
Oh, he was sick before getting on the flight back to Australia. So Vail, Denver and possibly LA (if the layover was long enough) are suspect. I bet the LA airport is where he got it :(#coronavirus	UN	IN
20/03/20 PRESS RELEASE Council Urges Consumers to be Considerate Fears about a positive coronavirus (COVID-19) case led shoppers in Fiji to begin stocking up on supplies to fill pantries. HTTPURL	UN	IN

(a) Misclassified INFORMATION examples.

Tweet	PL	TL
Vegetable market Peshawar KP.! People here are least worried about #COVID19 .! 1 infected Asymptomatic person and he would be transmitting it to complete city inside and outside ! HTTPURL	IN	UN
FYI, the state's #COVID19 stats show 395 people have been tested via state lab. But doesn't show a total for all labs. HTTPURL	IN	UN
New post (Mike Pence Celebrates Story of Great Great Grandmother Recovering from Coronavirus) has been published on Randy Salars News And Comment - HTTPURL HTTPURL	IN	UN

(b) Misclassified UNINFORMATION examples.

Table 6: Misclassified examples. PL: predicted label, TL: true label

6   Conclusion and future work

This paper has addressed our work on the WNUT-2020 Task 2: Identifying COVID-19 Information on Twitter. We proposed our ensemble model combining the deep learning models and the transfer learning models for detecting information about COVID-19 from users' tweets. Our ensemble model achieved 91.00% by accuracy and 90.65% by F1 on the development set, and achieved 89.04% by accuracy and 88.81% by F1 on the public test set, which ranked #25 in the competition.

In the future, we will improve our model's performance by exploring different features of the users' tweets and transfer learning models with fine-tuning techniques. Finally, we hope our study can be applied in practice for detecting COVID-19 from social networks to support the COVID-19 battle all over the world.

References

Emily Chen, Kristina Lerman, and Emilio Ferrara. 2020. Tracking social media discourse about the covid-19 pandemic: Development of a public coronavirus twitter data set. *JMIR Public Health and Surveillance*, 6(2):e19273.

Anneliese Depoux, Sam Martin, Emilie Karafillakis, Raman Preet, Annelies Wilder-Smith, and Heidi Larson. 2020. The pandemic of social media panic travels faster than the COVID-19 outbreak. *Journal of Travel Medicine*, 27(3). Taaa031.

Jacob Devlin, Ming-Wei Chang, Kenton Lee, and Kristina Toutanova. 2019. BERT: Pre-training of deep bidirectional transformers for language understanding. In *Proceedings of the 2019 Conference of the North American Chapter of the Association for Computational Linguistics: Human Language Technologies, Volume 1 (Long and Short Papers)*, pages 4171–4186, Minneapolis, Minnesota. Association for Computational Linguistics.

Chuong B Do and Andrew Y Ng. 2006. Transfer learning for text classification. In *Advances in Neural Information Processing Systems*, pages 299–306.

Ensheng Dong, Hongru Du, and Lauren Gardner. 2020. An interactive web-based dashboard to track covid-19 in real time. *The Lancet Infectious Diseases*, 20.

Bennett Kleinberg, Isabelle van der Vegt, and Maximilian Mozes. 2020. Measuring emotions in the covid-19 real world worry dataset. *arXiv preprint arXiv:2004.04225*.

Rabindra Lamsal. 2020. Coronavirus (covid-19) tweets dataset.

Yinhan Liu, Myle Ott, Naman Goyal, Jingfei Du, Mandar Joshi, Danqi Chen, Omer Levy, Mike Lewis, Luke Zettlemoyer, and Veselin Stoyanov. 2019. Roberta: A robustly optimized bert pretraining approach.

Dat Quoc Nguyen, Thanh Vu, Afshin Rahimi, Mai Hoang Dao, Linh The Nguyen, and Long Doan. 2020. WNUT-2020 Task 2: Identification of Informative COVID-19 English Tweets. In *Proceedings of the 6th Workshop on Noisy User-generated Text*.

Duc-Vu Nguyen, Kiet Van Nguyen, and Ngan Luu-Thuy Nguyen. 2019. Nlp@uit at vlsp 2019: A simple ensemble model for vietnamese dependency parsing. *The Sixth International Workshop on Vietnamese Language and Speech Processing VLSP 2019*.

Jeffrey Pennington, Richard Socher, and Christopher D. Manning. 2014. Glove: Global vectors for word representation. In *Empirical Methods in Natural Language Processing (EMNLP)*, pages 1532–1543.

Marian-Andrei Rizoiu, Tianyu Wang, Gabriela Ferraro, and Hanna Suominen. 2019. Transfer learning for hate speech detection in social media. *arXiv preprint arXiv:1906.03829*.

Gautam Kishore Shahi, Anne Dirkson, and Tim A. Majchrzak. 2020. An exploratory study of covid-19 misinformation on twitter.

Tin Van Huynh, Vu Duc Nguyen, Kiet Van Nguyen, Ngan Luu-Thuy Nguyen, and Anh Gia-Tuan Nguyen. 2019. Hate speech detection on vietnamese social media text using the bi-gru-lstm-cnn model. *arXiv preprint arXiv:1911.03644*.

Tin Van Huynh, Kiet Van Nguyen, Ngan Luu-Thuy Nguyen, and Anh Gia-Tuan Nguyen. 2020. Job prediction: From deep neural network models to applications. In *2020 RIVF International Conference on Computing and Communication Technologies (RIVF)*, pages 1–6. IEEE.

Kiet Van Nguyen, Duc-Vu Nguyen, Anh Gia-Tuan Nguyen, and Ngan Luu-Thuy Nguyen. 2020. New vietnamese corpus for machine reading comprehension of health news articles. *arXiv preprint arXiv:2006.11138*.

Zhongsheng Wang, Shinsuke Sugaya, and Dat PT Nguyen. 2019. Salary prediction using bidirectional-gru-cnn model. *Assoc. Nat. Lang. Process.*

Zhilin Yang, Zihang Dai, Yiming Yang, Jaime Carbonell, Russ R Salakhutdinov, and Quoc V Le. 2019. Xlnet: Generalized autoregressive pretraining for language understanding. In *Advances in Neural Information Processing Systems 32*, pages 5753–5763. Curran Associates, Inc.

DATAMAFIA at WNUT-2020 Task 2: A Study of Pre-trained Language Models along with Regularization Techniques for Downstream Tasks

Ayan Sengupta
Noida, India
ayan.sengupta007@gmail.com

Abstract

This document describes the system description developed by team *datamafia* at WNUT-2020 Task 2: Identification of informative COVID-19 English Tweets. This paper contains a thorough study of pre-trained language models on downstream binary classification task over noisy user generated Twitter data. The solution submitted to final test leaderboard is a fine tuned RoBERTa model which achieves F1 score of 90.8% and 89.4% on the dev and test data respectively. In the later part, we explore several techniques for injecting regularization explicitly into language models to generalize predictions over noisy data. Our experiments show that adding regularizations to RoBERTa pre-trained model can be very robust to data and annotation noises and can improve overall performance by more than 1.2%.

1 Introduction

The recent outbreak of Coronavirus disease (COVID-19) has turned the world topsy-turvy with more than 25M+ infected people so far and 800K+ deaths across the globe[1]. Government officials, researchers, health workers and fear trapped common people are largely relying on online information to monitor, tackle and overcome the situation. Social media platforms, particularly - Twitter and Facebook, have become an easily accessible source of information related to the current affairs. Very recently, few researchers (Drias and Drias, 2020; Samuel et al., 2020) have conducted large scale analysis on Twitter data in the context of COVID-19. However, as mentioned by Nguyen et al. 2020b, a huge majority of the information shared on Twitter are not informative and can pose an additional burden to those who are relying on social media to monitor the pandemic. For example - a tweet like *"Half of Uruguay's COVID-19 cases can be traced*

to a single fashion designer" can be speculative and possibly does not contain any insightful information. On the other hand, a tweet like *"Currently 32000+ deaths and their talking spreading it far and wide...BBC News - Coronavirus: Trump unveils plan to reopen states in phases"* can be very useful to a larger population.

To overcome this situation, shared task 2 of WNUT 2020 by Nguyen et al. 2020b allows to automatically identify whether a Tweet is informative in the context of COVID-19 or not. The task dataset contains 10K tweets (written mostly in English) and the associated label - INFORMATIVE and, UNINFORMATIVE labelled by human annotators.

In this task, we use a fine-tuned pre-trained $RoBERTa_{base}$ model (Liu et al., 2019) to learn the contextual representation of texts. We discover further that the last 4 layers of RoBERTa contain semantically rich hidden representation and are diverse, which, when used together can lead to better performance. In our final submitted model, as described in section 2.1, we use the concatenated hidden states of all the tokens from the last 4 layers of $RoBERTa_{base}$. Upon further investigation, we realize that the overparameterized large transformer models can be prone to overfitting when fine-tuned on noisy data and ambiguous annotations. In the later part of our study (section 2.3), we explore various different techniques to inject regularization externally to pre-trained language models to improve generalization capabilities. Although, ensembling diverse set of classifiers (Opitz and Maclin, 1999) is known to be an effective technique for improving generalization, in real-life applications, large ensemble systems aren't much effective for drawing inferences on low-resource devices. Further, interpreting model predictions are also difficult for complex ensemble systems. Due to these operational challenges, we refrain ourselves from using ensem-

---

[1] https://covid19.who.int/

Proceedings of the 2020 EMNLP Workshop W-NUT: The Sixth Workshop on Noisy User-generated Text, pages 371–377
Online, Nov 19, 2020. ©2020 Association for Computational Linguistics

bles and rather focus on single-model systems in our work. We have open-sourced our system and the experiments at Github[2].

2 System Description

In this shared task we use the original train, dev and test datasets provided in the challenge[3]. Dev dataset is used for only validation and evaluating our models. We omit the description of the datasets in this paper due to page constraint, and it can be found in the task description by Nguyen et al. 2020b.

2.1 System Model

After the introduction of self-attention based transformer architecture (Vaswani et al., 2017), several large auto-regressive and auto-encoder based language models (Devlin et al., 2018; Liu et al., 2019; Yang et al., 2019) and their variants have been developed and have showed great results on various NLP downstream tasks including - text classification, Named entity recognition (NER), Natural Language Inference (NLI) etc. Very recently, Nguyen et al. 2020a has developed pre-trained model particularly for English tweets. We use the RoBERTa$_{base}$ (Liu et al., 2019) as our base language model to learn the hidden representation from the text data. Clark et al. 2019; Kovaleva et al. 2019; Hao et al. 2019 showed that different attention heads from different layers of BERT learn different features from text data. Keeping this in mind, we evaluate all the 12 layers of RoBERTa$_{base}$ and figured out that the last 4 layers learn diverse set of hidden representations and can influence the final output the most. Although, original BERT and RoBERTa uses only [*CLS*] token embedding for classification task, our experiment shows that using all the token hidden states can lead to better generalization. Architecture of our submitted model ($Model_{system}$) is shown in Figure 1.

2.2 Other Baselines

Apart from our original submission, we explore other language models and their variants in great details. Each of these models are used to learn the overall representation of the text which is followed by a logistic dense layer to calculate the probability of a text being INFORMATIVE.

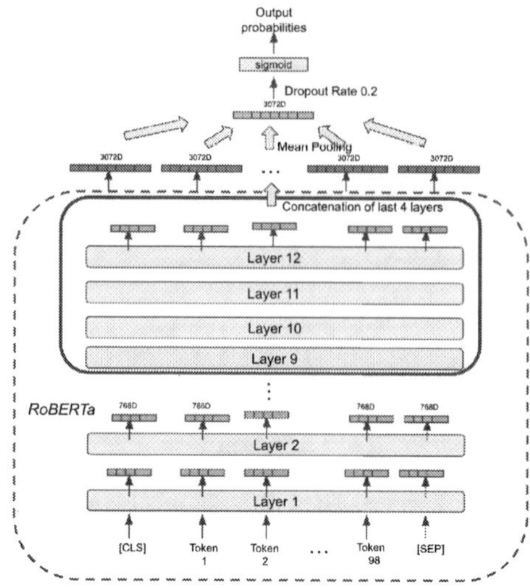

Figure 1: Model architecture by team *datamafia*

- [*CLS*] representation of language models - BERT$_{base}$ (Devlin et al., 2018), RoBERTa$_{base}$, ALBERT$_{base}$(Lan et al., 2020), BERTweet (Nguyen et al., 2020a)

- Mean/Max pooling of all token hidden states from last/all (concatenated) layers from RoBERTa$_{base}$

- RoBERTa$_{base}$ + CNN - We use architecture similar to the one explored by Ma 2019b. We use Wavenet (van den Oord et al., 2016) instead of ordinary convolution layer.

In all these models, we use a dropout of 0.2 before applying the final logistic activation.

2.3 Techniques for Injecting Regularizations into Language Models

Although being an highly over-parameterized models, BERT and its variants are robust to overfitting while fine-tuning (Hao et al., 2019), empirical results from Lee et al. 2020 show that the instability when it is fine-tuned on small and noisy data. Unlike BookCorpus (Zhu et al., 2015) or English Wikipedia data, as used by most of the language models for pretraining, Twitter data is very noisy, unstructured and lacks many linguistic characteristics. To tackle the noisy nature of the dataset, we explore various strategies for regularizing base language model to make it robust to text noises.

- **Transformer Hidden Dropout** - Dropout (Srivastava et al., 2014) is an effective technique to reduce overfitting. Original BERT

---

and RoBERTa language models use hidden dropout rate of 0.1 in the FFN layers. We experiment with various dropout rates $dropout(p) \in [0.0, 0.3]$.

- **Regularization** - As explored by Schwarz et al. 2018, Kirkpatrick et al. 2017, we add an additional L2 regularization penalty term to final loss. We use λ as regularization coefficient to control the effect of penalty term on the overall loss.

- **Mixout** - Mixout is a technique recently proposed by Lee et al. 2020, and shows strong performance improvement when used with BERT on downstream finetuning tasks. We use the parameter $mixout(\mathbf{w}_{pre})$ to tune the effect of mixout in our model.

- **Multi-Sample Dropout** - Inoue 2019 proposed multi-sample dropout to accelerate training as well as, better generalization. Multi-Sample dropout uses an average of multiple dropouts for a single sample.

- **Text Augmentation** - We inject artificial noise to training data by randomly masking a certain % of all tokens and replacing them with contextually similar word predicted by BERT. For text augmentation we use nlpaug package (Ma, 2019a). For augmentation we use parameter $aug_p \in [0.0, 0.3]$ to denote the proportion of the tokens to be masked for each text.

To our best knowledge, next to the work by Lee et al. 2020, our work is the first large-scale empirical study to show the effectiveness of different regularization techniques on pre-trained language models over noisy text data.

2.4 Hyperparamater Settings

In this work, for training, validation and testing, we use the raw data only, without using any further pre-processing. All the pre-trained language models are kept with default configurations. For the base language models, we use Huggingface's transformer library (Wolf et al., 2019). We use the default BytePairEncoding (BPE) for each of the language models to tokenize raw texts with max sequence length of 100. Shorter texts are padded with [PAD] token id. For all the models, we use Adam optimizer (Kingma and Ba, 2014) with an initial

Dataset	F1	Precision	Recall
Test	89.40	88.57	90.25
Dev	90.84	86.56	95.55

Table 1: Performance of $Model_{system}$ on test & dev datasets

learning rate of $2e - 5$, $\beta_1 = 0.9, \beta_2 = 0.999$ and weight decay rate of 0.01. We run each of the experiments for max 15 epochs with an early-stopping criteria based on validation F1 score with a patience of 5. We use a batch size of 32 for both training as well as, validation. Models are checkpointed at each epoch where validation F1 increases from the previous best. We conduct all our experiments on 1 Tesla T4 GPU. All the conducted experiments are logged with Wandb[4,5] (Biewald, 2020).

3 Results

We evaluate the performances of all the models using F1, Precision and Recall scores.

3.1 System and Baseline Results

Table 1 shows system model's performance on the test and dev dataset. In Table 2, we have demonstrated the performance of all the baseline methods on dev dataset. RoBERTa shows the most stable performance among all the language models. Even with just [CLS] token representation, RoBERTa works pretty well.

We can also observe that using more than one layer of RoBERTa usually works better than using only the last layer.

3.2 Performance of Different Reg. Methods

Table 3 shows the performance of regularization techniques described in section 2.3 on the dev data. We observe that RoBERTa language model with any sort of regularization works better than the one without any regularization added. Figure 2 shows the effect of each regularization method on $Model_{system}$ model. Among all the methods, multi-sample dropout and using augmented data show most stability w.r.t all the evaluation metrics. Individual dropout layers in $Model_{multi}$ act differently on each sample and show high variability among each other with, avg. correlation being

[4] https://app.wandb.ai/victor7246/wnut-task2
[5] https://app.wandb.ai/victor7246/wnut-task2-regularization

Model Identifier	Model Description	F1	Precision	Recall
$Model_{system}$	*Our submitted model*	90.84	86.56	**95.55**
$BERT_{CLS}$	BERT$_{base}$ with [CLS]	88.20	**89.35**	87.08
$RoBERTa_{CLS}$	RoBERTa$_{base}$ with [CLS]	**90.87**	87.16	94.91
$ALBERT_{CLS}$	ALBERT$_{base}$ with [CLS]	89.21	88.20	90.25
$BERTweet_{CLS}$	BERTweet with [CLS]	89.96	88.84	91.10
$RoBERTa_{mean12}$	RoBERTa$_{base}$ mean of all tokens (layer 12)	89.61	86.27	93.22
$RoBERTa_{max12}$	RoBERTa$_{base}$ max of all tokens (layer 12)	89.53	84.56	95.12
$RoBERTa_{meanall}$	RoBERTa$_{base}$ mean of all tokens (all layers concat)	90.76	87.13	94.70
$RoBERTa_{maxall}$	RoBERTa$_{base}$ max of all tokens (all layers concat)	90.65	88.02	93.43
$RoBERTa_{CNN}$	RoBERTa$_{base}$ + CNN	90.57	87.70	94.49

Table 2: Performance of all baseline models on dev. Best scores are highlighted in **bold**.

Model Identifier	Model Description	F1	Precision	Recall
$Model_{noreg}$	No Regularization	90.10	87.75	92.58
$Model_{dropout}$	$dropout(p) = 0.1$	91.19	89.25	93.22
$Model_{l2}$	$\lambda = 0.02$	91.08	**92.37**	89.38
$Model_{multi}$	7-Sample Dropout with $dropout(p) = 0.1$	91.22	87.09	**95.76**
$Model_{aug}$	$aug_p = 0.1$ with $dropout(p) = 0.1$	**92.04**	88.78	95.55
$Model_{mixout}$	$mixout(\mathbf{w}_{pre}) = 0.6$	90.40	87.20	93.86

Table 3: Performance of different regularization techniques with $Model_{system}$ on dev data

-0.004. This diversity works like an ensemble and helps the model classifying ambiguous examples correctly. On the other hand, by randomly replacing word tokens in the augmented texts, language models learn the overall context better without depending too much on any particular phrase.

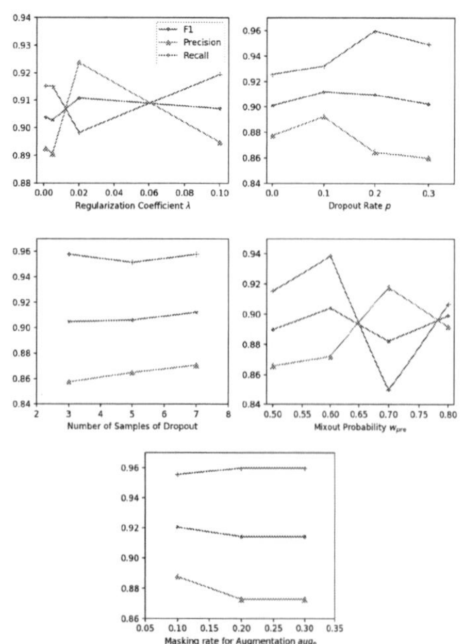

Figure 2: Effect of Regularization Parameters on Classification Performance

4 Result Analysis

In this section, we inspect the language models and explain their predictive capabilities. In exploratory data analysis (EDA), we plot top words present in the corpus, conditioned on the INFORMATIVE and UNINFORMATIVE classes and figure out that "case", "covid", "death", "virus" etc. remains top words for both the classes of documents.

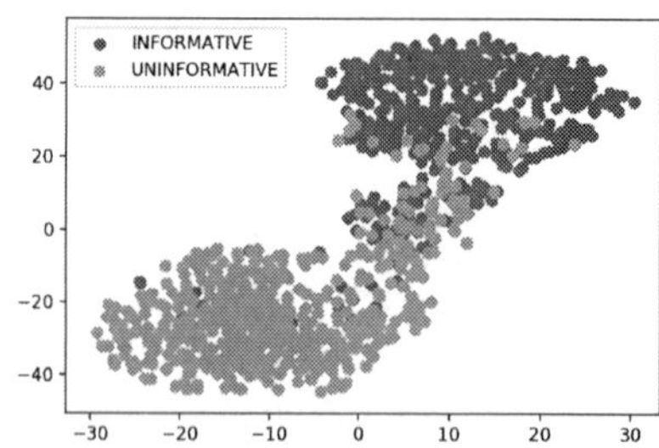

Figure 3: t-SNE plot of text representations extracted by $Model_{system}$

We observe that any language model in just 2-3 epochs of fine-tuning can achieve a F1 score of more than 89%, however, due to the inherent noise of the tweets, around 10% of the examples are ambiguous and difficult to be classified correctly for almost all the standalone models. Figure 3 shows the two different clusters of text representations extracted by system model (embedded onto a lower dimensional space) on the dev dataset, with several misclassified ambiguous examples. From Table 2

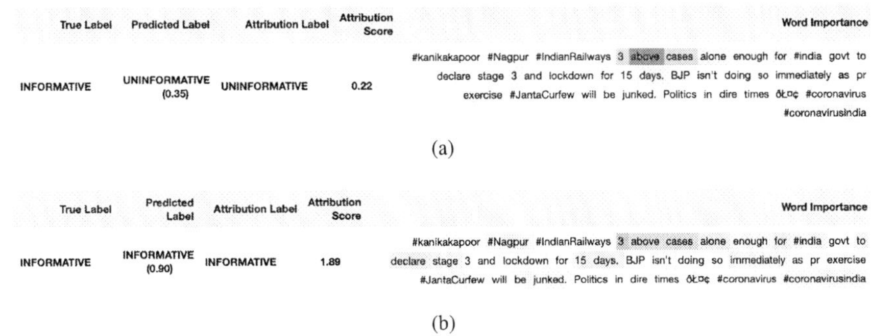

(a)

(b)

Figure 4: Explanations for an INFORMATIVE tweet predicted by $Model_{system}$ (a) and $Model_{aug}$ (b). Tokens with high(low) attribute scores are highlighted in green(red).

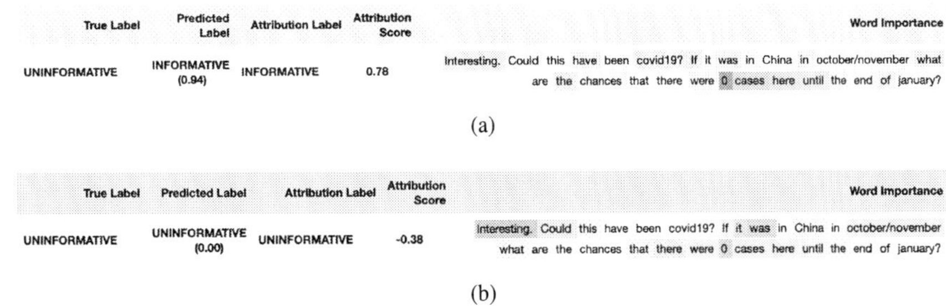

(a)

(b)

Figure 5: Explanations for an UNINFORMATIVE tweet predicted by $Model_{system}$ (a) and $Model_{aug}$ (b)

we can understand that all the models have an inductive bias towards the positive class, which lead to relatively poor precision but high recall. There are 89 examples in the validation set which are wrongly classified by $Model_{system}$. However, 47 of them are correctly predicted by either of the regularized models (models described in Table 3), and 70% of those examples are originally UNINFORMATIVE. We closely inspect the predictions using model interpretation tool Captum (Kokhlikyan et al., 2019), which uses a gradient based attribution method in explaining the predictions. A token with high positive attribution score are assigned more importance by the model and correlates positively with the overall prediction. Similarly, a word with high negative attribution score affects the final outcome adversely. In Figure 4, we explain predictions by $Model_{system}$ and the $Model_{aug}$ on an INFORMATIVE tweet, and found that the system model fails to capture the overall semantics correctly, whereas, $Model_{aug}$ looks at contextually more important words like "declare", "lockdown", "immediately" etc. and predicts the tweet to be INFORMATIVE. Similar observations are found in Figure 5, where, $Model_{system}$ assigns more importance towards frequently occurring words like "cases" and predicts wrongly. On the contrary, $Model_{aug}$ understands the subtle sarcastic tone of the tweet by looking at the phrases "interesting", "was in China" and classifies correctly with high confidence.

5 Conclusion

In this paper, we present a large-scale empirical study of language models with explicit regularizations. We conclude that using hidden states from multiple layers from a language model helps in understanding the context better and further using an additional regularization, we can improve the stability and generalization capabilities of large pre-trained models. In future, we wish to use the insights captured by this work in building a custom and robust language model particularly for noisy user generated texts that are found in social media. Another interesting extension would be to prove the theoretical justifications and calculating the generalization bounds for each of the explored regularization methods. We strongly believe that our study will help the research community in using language models on real-life applications more effectively.

References

Lukas Biewald. 2020. Experiment tracking with weights and biases. Software available from wandb.com.

Kevin Clark, Urvashi Khandelwal, Omer Levy, and Christopher D. Manning. 2019. What does bert look at? an analysis of bert's attention. In *BlackBoxNLP@ACL*.

Jacob Devlin, Ming - Wei Chang, Kenton Lee, and Kristina Toutanova. 2018. BERT: pre-training of deep bidirectional transformers for language understanding. *CoRR*, abs / 1810.04805.

Habiba H. Drias and Yassine Drias. 2020. Mining twitter data on covid-19 for sentiment analysis and frequent patterns discovery. *medRxiv*.

Yaru Hao, Li Dong, Furu Wei, and Ke Xu. 2019. Visualizing and understanding the effectiveness of BERT. In *Proceedings of the 2019 Conference on Empirical Methods in Natural Language Processing and the 9th International Joint Conference on Natural Language Processing (EMNLP-IJCNLP)*, pages 4143–4152, Hong Kong, China. Association for Computational Linguistics.

Hiroshi Inoue. 2019. Multi-sample dropout for accelerated training and better generalization. *CoRR*, abs / 1905.09788.

Diederik P. Kingma and Jimmy Ba. 2014. Adam: A method for stochastic optimization.

James Kirkpatrick, Razvan Pascanu, Neil Rabinowitz, Joel Veness, Guillaume Desjardins, Andrei A. Rusu, Kieran Milan, John Quan, Tiago Ramalho, Agnieszka Grabska-Barwinska, Demis Hassabis, Claudia Clopath, Dharshan Kumaran, and Raia Hadsell. 2017. Overcoming catastrophic forgetting in neural networks. *Proceedings of the National Academy of Sciences*, 114(13):3521–3526.

Narine Kokhlikyan, Vivek Miglani, Miguel Martin, Edward Wang, Jonathan Reynolds, Alexander Melnikov, Natalia Lunova, and Orion Reblitz-Richardson. 2019. Pytorch captum. https://github.com/pytorch/captum.

Olga Kovaleva, Alexey Romanov, Anna Rogers, and Anna Rumshisky. 2019. Revealing the dark secrets of BERT. In *Proceedings of the 2019 Conference on Empirical Methods in Natural Language Processing and the 9th International Joint Conference on Natural Language Processing (EMNLP-IJCNLP)*, pages 4365–4374, Hong Kong, China. Association for Computational Linguistics.

Zhenzhong Lan, Mingda Chen, Sebastian Goodman, Kevin Gimpel, Piyush Sharma, and Radu Soricut. 2020. Albert: A lite bert for self-supervised learning of language representations. In *International Conference on Learning Representations*.

Cheolhyoung Lee, Kyunghyun Cho, and Wanmo Kang. 2020. Mixout: Effective regularization to finetune large-scale pretrained language models. In *International Conference on Learning Representations*.

Yinhan Liu, Myle Ott, Naman Goyal, Jingfei you, Mandar Joshi, Danqi Chen, Omer Levy, Mike Lewis, Luke Zettlemoyer, and Veselin Stoyanov. 2019. Roberta: A robustly optimized BERT pretraining approach. *CoRR*, abs / 1907.11692.

Edward Ma. 2019a. Nlp augmentation. https://github.com/makcedward/nlpaug.

Guoqin Ma. 2019b. Tweets classification with bert in the field of disaster management. In *StudentReport@Stanford.edu*.

Dat Quoc Nguyen, Thanh Vu, and Anh Tuan Nguyen. 2020a. Bertweet: A pre-trained language model for english tweets.

Dat Quoc Nguyen, Thanh Vu, Afshin Rahimi, Mai Hoang Dao, Linh The Nguyen, and Long Doan. 2020b. WNUT-2020 Task 2: Identification of Informative COVID-19 English Tweets. In *Proceedings of the 6th Workshop on Noisy User-generated Text*.

Aaron van den Oord, Sander Dieleman, Heiga Zen, Karen Simonyan, Oriol Vinyals, Alex Graves, Nal Kalchbrenner, Andrew Senior, and Koray Kavukcuoglu. 2016. Wavenet: A generative model for raw audio.

D. Opitz and R. Maclin. 1999. Popular ensemble methods: An empirical study. *jair*.

Jim Samuel, G. G. Md. Nawaz Ali, Md. Mokhlesur Rahman, Ek Esawi, and Yana Samuel. 2020. Covid-19 public sentiment insights and machine learning for tweets classification. *mdpi*.

Jonathan Schwarz, Wojciech Czarnecki, Jelena Luketina, Agnieszka Grabska-Barwinska, Yee Whye Teh, Razvan Pascanu, and Raia Hadsell. 2018. Progress & compress: A scalable framework for continual learning. In *Proceedings of Machine Learning Research*, volume 80 of *Proceedings of Machine Learning Research*, pages 4528–4537, Stockholmsmässan, Stockholm Sweden. PMLR.

Nitish Srivastava, Geoffrey Hinton, Alex Krizhevsky, Ilya Sutskever, and Ruslan Salakhutdinov. 2014. Dropout: A simple way to prevent neural networks from overfitting. *Journal of Machine Learning Research*, 15(56):1929–1958.

Ashish Vaswani, Noam Shazeer, Niki Parmar, Jakob Uszkoreit, Llion Jones, Aidan N Gomez, Ł ukasz Kaiser, and Illia Polosukhin. 2017. Attention is all you need. In I. Guyon, U. V. Luxburg, S. Bengio, H. Wallach, R. Fergus, S. Vishwanathan, and R. Garnett, editors, *Advances in Neural Information Processing Systems 30*, pages 5998–6008. Curran Associates, Inc.

Thomas Wolf, Lysandre Debut, Victor Sanh, Julien Chaumond, Clement Delangue, Anthony Moi, Pierric Cistac, Tim Rault, Rémi Louf, Morgan Funtowicz, Joe Davison, Sam Shleifer, Patrick von Platen, Clara Ma, Yacine Jernite, Julien Plu, Canwen Xu, Teven Le Scao, Sylvain Gugger, Mariama Drame, Quentin Lhoest, and Alexander M. Rush. 2019. Huggingface's transformers: State-of-the-art natural language processing. *ArXiv*, abs/1910.03771.

Zhilin Yang, Zihang Dai, Yiming Yang, Jaime Carbonell, Russ R Salakhutdinov, and Quoc V Le. 2019. Xlnet: Generalized autoregressive pretraining for language understanding. In H. Wallach, H. Larochelle, A. Beygelzimer, F. dÁlché-Buc, E. Fox, and R. Garnett, editors, *Advances in Neural Information Processing Systems 32*, pages 5753–5763. Curran Associates, Inc.

Yukun Zhu, Ryan Kiros, Rich Zemel, Ruslan Salakhutdinov, Raquel Urtasun, Antonio Torralba, and Sanja Fidler. 2015. Aligning books and movies: Towards story-like visual explanations by watching movies and reading books. In *Proceedings of the IEEE International Conference on Computer Vision (ICCV)*.

UPennHLP at WNUT-2020 Task 2 : Transformer models for classification of COVID19 posts on Twitter

Arjun Magge*
Perelman School of Medicine,
University of Pennsylvania,
Philadelphia, PA, USA
Arjun.Magge@pennmedicine.upenn.edu

Varad Pimpalkhute*
Electronics and Communication Engineering,
Indian Institute of Information Technology,
Nagpur, MH, India

Divya Rallapalli
Barrett Honors College,
Arizona State University,
Tempe, AZ, USA

David Siguenza
Great Valley High School,
Malvern, PA, USA

Graciela Gonzalez-Hernandez
DBEI, Perelman School of Medicine,
University of Pennsylvania,
Philadelphia, PA, USA
gragon@pennmedicine.upenn.edu

Abstract

Increasing usage of social media presents new non-traditional avenues for monitoring disease outbreaks, virus transmissions and disease progressions through user posts describing test results or disease symptoms. However, the discussions on the topic of infectious diseases that are informative in nature also span various topics such as news, politics and humor which makes the data mining challenging. We present a system to identify tweets about the COVID19 disease outbreak that are deemed to be informative on Twitter for use in downstream applications. The system scored a F1-score of 0.8941, Precision of 0.9028, Recall of 0.8856 and Accuracy of 0.9010. In the shared task organized as part of the 6th Workshop of Noisy User-generated Text (WNUT), the system was ranked 18th by F1-score and 13th by Accuracy.

1 Introduction

The COVID19 pandemic caused by the coronavirus (nCOV) has presented a unique challenge to the public health research community in the areas of tracking localized and community level transmissions for enforcing effective mobility restrictions and interventions to curb further virus spread. While traditional sources of infection numbers and fatalities include testing facilities and healthcare providers, many new non-traditional sources of information such as social media, wastewater analysis and mobility statistics that may serve as biomarkers for presence of infections in the community. In this work, we focus on using natural language processing (NLP) for mining social media posts for tweets that mention that can be used for public health monitoring purposes or dissemination of information. We accomplish this by introducing a classifier that can be used as a component of an information processing pipeline to detect informative tweets from posts that mention keywords related to discussions around coronavirus.

The system presented in this work was developed as part of the W-NUT 2020 shared task 2 (Nguyen et al., 2020b) where the objective of the task was to classify a given post as informative or uninformative. The rest of the document is structured as follows: we briefly discuss previous related work on COVID19 surveillance on Twitter in the Background section. We describe the annotated dataset and system implementation in the Materials and Methods section followed by preliminary and final evaluation results in the Results section. Finally, we discuss error analysis, limitations and future directions in the Discussion section.

2 Background

Researchers working on noisy user texts such as posts on social media mining have proposed various methods and systems for monitoring infectious disease transmissions and natural disasters

Proceedings of the 2020 EMNLP Workshop W-NUT: The Sixth Workshop on Noisy User-generated Text, pages 378–382
Online, Nov 19, 2020. ©2020 Association for Computational Linguistics

Corpus	Informative	Uninformative
Training Set	3303	3697
Validation Set	472	528
Test Set	944	1056

Table 1: Dataset description for identifying informative tweets on Twitter

such as hurricanes (Paul and Dredze, 2017). Most work on COVID19 monitoring have focused on presenting keywords for data collection related to COVID19 (Chen et al., 2020; Rashed et al., 2020; Wei et al., 2020; Santosh et al., 2020), datasets for classification of tweets into categories for downstream applications(Klein et al., 2020; Golder et al.; Delizo et al., 2020; Liu et al., 2020; Karisani and Karisani, 2020; Müller et al., 2020; Jelodar et al., 2020; Lwowski and Najafirad, 2020; Mackey et al., 2020), and in some cases advanced tasks such as event detection (Zong et al., 2020), detection of symptoms experienced by users who tested positive for the disease (Al-Garadi et al., 2020) and review articles on the topic (Arafat, 2020; Moore et al., 2020).

The classification categories themselves have varied from sentiments expressed in posts (Delizo et al., 2020) and relatedness to the disease (Liu et al., 2020; Karisani and Karisani, 2020) to misinformation detection (Hossain et al., 2020) and personal reports of exposures or test results (Klein et al., 2020). Each dataset contains tweets and annotations that can be processed by information processing pipelines using NLP and machine learning based classification techniques for possible applications in public health using epidemiological analysis.

3 Materials and Methods

The dataset annotated for the task consists of 10,000 tweets that mentioned terms related to COVID19. This included a total of 4719 tweets labeled as *Informative* and 5281 tweets labeled as *Uninformative*. Each tweet was annotated by 3 independent annotators with an inter-annotator agreement score of Fleiss' Kappa of 0.818. The dataset was split into training set (70%), validation set (10%) and test set (20%) for the purposes of development and evaluation of the classification model. We tabulate further details of the splits in Table 1.

Architecture	Prec	Recall	F1	Acc
LR	0.85	0.80	0.82	0.83
Feedforward	0.82	0.80	0.80	0.79
CNN	0.86	0.88	0.84	0.85
BERT	0.83	**0.96**	0.89	0.89
GPT	0.84	0.89	0.86	0.87
XLNET	0.82	0.92	0.90	0.90
RoBERTa	0.86	0.93	0.89	0.89
DistilBERT	0.83	0.93	0.88	0.88
BERTweet	0.88	0.90	0.89	0.90
BERT-Epi	**0.91**	0.93	**0.92**	**0.92**

Table 2: Performance of the experimentation systems on the validation set. Precision, recall and F1-score was calculated for the *Informative* class. We used the above scores to determine the final model used for making the official submission.

3.1 Pre-processing

We pre-processed each tweet to normalize usernames and urls into reserved keywords. Further, we de-emojized the tweets using the emoji package to add descriptive lexical features that convey emotions associated with the tweet. Finally, we expanded contractions for normalizing the text for detecting negations.

3.2 Classification models

We experimented with various machine learning models such as logistic regression with bag-of-word features, convolutional neural networks (CNN) with filter sizes upto 5, fully connected (feed-forward) network, and transformer models using the scikit-learn [1], TensorFlow (Abadi et al., 2016), ktrain (Maiya, 2020) and Flair (Akbik et al., 2018) frameworks.

3.2.1 Non-transformer models

In order to setup baselines, we used the scikit-learn framework to convert the tweet into count vectors based on the individual tokens in the tokenized sentences. For fast inference, we setup the logistic regression (LR) baseline using the count vectors as features. We did not perform elaborate experiments such as employing various word embeddings, n-gram features and feature engineering in favor of building models with better classification performance. We used the same feature set for training a fully connected Feedforward classifier using Tensorflow keras API with 20 neurons and a sigmoid

---

[1] https://scikit-learn.org/

379

layer as an output layer. Lastly we built a CNN text classification model with filter sizes upto five using the same input features discussed above.

3.2.2 Transformer models

We also experimented with various transformer language models such as BERT (Devlin et al., 2019), DistilBERT (Sanh et al., 2019), GPT (Radford et al.), XLNET (Yang et al., 2019) and RoBERTa (Liu et al., 2019) among others that were specifically trained on COVID19 related datasets such as BERT-Epi(Müller et al., 2020), and BERTweet (Nguyen et al., 2020a). We used the Flair framework for training the classifier model where all layers of the model were fine-tuned during the training. The performance was measured across the standard classification metrics of precision, recall and F1-score with the final determining metric identified as the F1-score for the *Informative* class.

We trained each of these models with Adam optimizer and a softmax layer with weighted losses such that *Informative* class loss was weighted 2 times relative to the loss of the *Uninformative* class. The full comparison of the performance of these models has been shown in Table 2. We found that various ensembles of best combinations did not result in better models and hence we chose the final transformer model that was an uncased BERT model trained on COVID19 related tweets (Müller et al., 2020) trained using the Flair framework (Akbik et al., 2018). After hyperparameter tuning the model, we determined the best parameters to be a learning rate of 0.00003 and loss weights of 2 in favor of *Informative* class and the usage of Adam optimizer. For the final model we trained the model on all available tweets combining training and validation sets for 10 epochs. All training experiments including development of the final submission model was performed on Google Colaboratory [2].

4 Results

The final detailed results of the task on the validation and test sets are shown in Table 3. Observing the results of the validation and test set, we find that the performance of the final model deteriorated on the test set. The drop in recall on the test set was significant even though the splits between the classes remained the same. The final model was ranked 18th by the F1-score and 13th by accuracy. The final standings relative the proposed system is

[2]https://colab.research.google.com/

Corpus	Prec	Recall	F1	Acc
Validation	0.894	0.936	0.914	0.918
Test	0.902	0.885	0.894	0.901

Table 3: Performance of the system on the validation and test set for identifying informative tweets on Twitter.

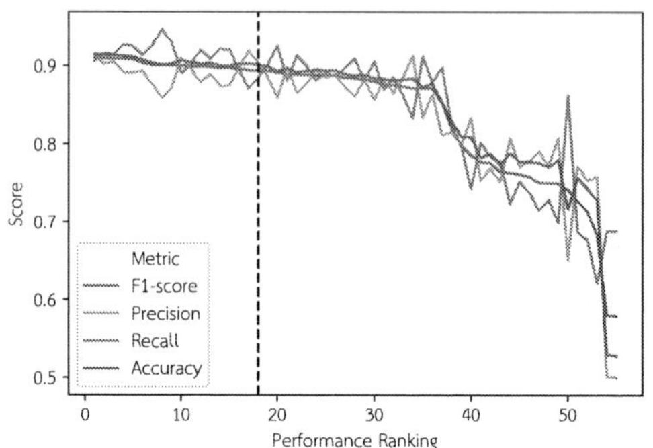

Figure 1: Performance of the systems submitted as part of the shared task across the metrics of F1-score, Precision, Recall and Accuracy compared to the system presented in our work indicated by the dotted line.

shown in Figure 1. We find that the performance of most of the top models (ranks 1-20) including the proposed system were determined to have F1-scores within a narrow margin of 0.89 and 0.91 which shows that the shared task was very competitive.

5 Discussion

On closer analysis of initial errors on the Validation set we found that many tweets were difficult to determine as being in either classes. On performing an 8-fold cross validation, we found that fold 1 which the default split of training and validation set had the lowest F1-scores at 0.92 whereas folds 2-8 had F1-scores in the ranges of 0.94-0.96. On closer analysis of fold 1, we found that many tweets may have been annotated incorrectly in the validation set which may have introduced errors in the final model and hence may require further analyses of the annotations for development of better models.

Overall, transformer models performed significantly better than non-transformer models that we trained on. However, we note that the non-transformer models could be improved by using word-embeddings and attention features in layers among Feedforward and CNN architectures.

The current system proposes a simple classification method which may be useful in removing tweets that are deemed *Uninformative* for use in downstream epidemiological analyses. Further research is required to assess the utility of the tweets obtained from such collections of *Informative* tweets for disease tracking and analyses of symptoms.

5.1 Limitations

Some of the common drawbacks for performing demographic analyses include the problem of selection bias in Twitter users where most of the users tend to live in cities and possess smartphones which may not be representative of the overall population of countries or individual administrative regions. Another drawback noticed among systems trained on social media data is that the model performance seems to decline over time as new terms are introduced into the vocabulary and newer topics are mentioned in conversations around the disease. Although, tweets publicly published on Twitter are available for viewing by users and non-users of Twitter, development of automated methods to determine posts that may determine infections/diagnoses which may be personal in nature may raise valid privacy concerns due to possible adverse social impacts on such individuals. Such information-sharing policies may warrant constant review with changing times and national policies. In this paper, we do not include direct text content of tweets during error analysis for aforementioned reasons.

6 Conclusion

Social media mining offers a non-traditional avenue to extract epidemiological and population level statistics from discussions around a topic. Such noisy information domains presents an NLP challenge for extracting meaningful information for use in downstream applications. In this work, we present a system to identify *Informative* tweets on English language Twitter posts on the topic of COVID19 pandemic for use in downstream tasks such as public health monitoring and epidemiological studies. We use a classification approach to identifying such tweets and the final system scored a F1-score of 0.8941, Precision of 0.9028, Recall of 0.8856 and Accuracy of 0.9010. In the shared task organized as part of the 6th Workshop of Noisy User-generated Text (WNUT), the system was ranked 18th by F1-score and 13th by Accuracy.

References

Martín Abadi, Paul Barham, Jianmin Chen, Zhifeng Chen, Andy Davis, Jeffrey Dean, Matthieu Devin, Sanjay Ghemawat, Geoffrey Irving, Michael Isard, et al. 2016. Tensorflow: A system for large-scale machine learning. In *12th {USENIX} symposium on operating systems design and implementation ({OSDI} 16)*, pages 265–283.

Alan Akbik, Duncan Blythe, and Roland Vollgraf. 2018. Contextual string embeddings for sequence labeling. In *COLING 2018, 27th International Conference on Computational Linguistics*, pages 1638–1649.

Mohammed Ali Al-Garadi, Yuan-Chi Yang, Sahithi Lakamana, and Abeed Sarker. 2020. A text classification approach for the automatic detection of twitter posts containing self-reported covid-19 symptoms.

Mahmoud Arafat. 2020. A review of models for hydrating large-scale twitter data of covid-19-related tweets for transportation research.

Emily Chen, Kristina Lerman, and Emilio Ferrara. 2020. Tracking social media discourse about the covid-19 pandemic: Development of a public coronavirus twitter data set. *JMIR Public Health and Surveillance*, 6(2):e19273.

John Pierre D Delizo, Mideth B Abisado, and Ma Ian P De Los Trinos. 2020. Philippine twitter sentiments during covid-19 pandemic using multinomial naïve-bayes. *International Journal*, 9(1.3).

Jacob Devlin, Ming-Wei Chang, Kenton Lee, and Kristina Toutanova. 2019. Bert: Pre-training of deep bidirectional transformers for language understanding. In *Proceedings of the 2019 Conference of the North American Chapter of the Association for Computational Linguistics: Human Language Technologies, Volume 1 (Long and Short Papers)*, pages 4171–4186.

Su Golder, Ari Z Klein, Arjun Magge, Karen O'Connor, Haitao Cai, Davy Weissenbacher, and Graciela Gonzalez-Hernandez. Extending a chronological and geographical analysis of personal reports of covid-19 on twitter to england, uk. *medRxiv*.

Tamanna Hossain, Robert L Logan IV, Arjuna Ugarte, Yoshitomo Matsubara, Sameer Singh, and Sean Young. 2020. Detecting covid-19 misinformation on social media.

Hamed Jelodar, Yongli Wang, Rita Orji, and Hucheng Huang. 2020. Deep sentiment classification and topic discovery on novel coronavirus or covid-19 online discussions: Nlp using lstm recurrent neural network approach. *arXiv preprint arXiv:2004.11695*.

Negin Karisani and Payam Karisani. 2020. Mining coronavirus (covid-19) posts in social media. *ArXiv*.

Ari Klein, Arjun Magge, Karen O'Connor, Haitao Cai, Davy Weissenbacher, and Graciela Gonzalez-Hernandez. 2020. A chronological and geographical analysis of personal reports of covid-19 on twitter. *medRxiv*.

Junhua Liu, Trisha Singhal, Lucienne Blessing, Kristin L. Wood, and Kwan Hui Lim. 2020. Crisisbert: a robust transformer for crisis classification and contextual crisis embedding. *ArXiv*, abs/2005.06627.

Yinhan Liu, Myle Ott, Naman Goyal, Jingfei Du, Mandar Joshi, Danqi Chen, Omer Levy, Mike Lewis, Luke Zettlemoyer, and Veselin Stoyanov. 2019. Roberta: A robustly optimized bert pretraining approach. *arXiv preprint arXiv:1907.11692*.

Brandon Lwowski and Peyman Najafirad. 2020. Covid-19 surveillance through twitter using self-supervised learning and few shot learning.

Tim Mackey, Vidya Purushothaman, Jiawei Li, Neal Shah, Matthew Nali, Cortni Bardier, Bryan Liang, Mingxiang Cai, and Raphael Cuomo. 2020. Machine learning to detect self-reporting of symptoms, testing access, and recovery associated with covid-19 on twitter: Retrospective big data infoveillance study. *JMIR Public Health and Surveillance*, 6(2):e19509.

Arun S. Maiya. 2020. ktrain: A low-code library for augmented machine learning. *arXiv*, arXiv:2004.10703 [cs.LG].

Jason H Moore, Ian Barnett, Mary Regina Boland, Yong Chen, George Demiris, Graciela Gonzalez-Hernandez, Daniel S Herman, Blanca E Himes, Rebecca A Hubbard, Dokyoon Kim, et al. 2020. Ideas for how informaticians can get involved with covid-19 research.

Martin Müller, Marcel Salathé, and Per E Kummervold. 2020. Covid-twitter-bert: A natural language processing model to analyse covid-19 content on twitter. *arXiv preprint arXiv:2005.07503*.

Dat Quoc Nguyen, Thanh Vu, and Anh Tuan Nguyen. 2020a. Bertweet: A pre-trained language model for english tweets. *arXiv preprint arXiv:2005.10200*.

Dat Quoc Nguyen, Thanh Vu, Afshin Rahimi, Mai Hoang Dao, Linh The Nguyen, and Long Doan. 2020b. WNUT-2020 Task 2: Identification of Informative COVID-19 English Tweets. In *Proceedings of the 6th Workshop on Noisy User-generated Text*.

Michael J Paul and Mark Dredze. 2017. Social monitoring for public health. *Synthesis Lectures on Information Concepts, Retrieval, and Services*, 9(5):1–183.

Alec Radford, Jeffrey Wu, Rewon Child, David Luan, Dario Amodei, and Ilya Sutskever. Language models are unsupervised multitask learners.

Salma Rashed, Johan Frid, and Sonja Aits. 2020. English dictionaries, gold and silver standard corpora for biomedical natural language processing related to sars-cov-2 and covid-19.

Victor Sanh, Lysandre Debut, Julien Chaumond, and Thomas Wolf. 2019. Distilbert, a distilled version of bert: smaller, faster, cheaper and lighter. *arXiv preprint arXiv:1910.01108*.

Roshan Santosh, Sharath Chandra Guntuku, H Schwartz, Lyle Ungar, et al. 2020. Detecting symptoms using context-based twitter embeddings during covid-19.

Jerry Wei, Chengyu Huang, Soroush Vosoughi, and Jason Wei. 2020. What are people asking about covid-19? a question classification dataset. *arXiv preprint arXiv:2005.12522*.

Zhilin Yang, Zihang Dai, Yiming Yang, Jaime Carbonell, Russ R Salakhutdinov, and Quoc V Le. 2019. Xlnet: Generalized autoregressive pretraining for language understanding. In *Advances in neural information processing systems*, pages 5753–5763.

Shi Zong, Ashutosh Baheti, Wei Xu, and Alan Ritter. 2020. Extracting covid-19 events from twitter. *arXiv preprint arXiv:2006.02567*.

UIT-HSE at WNUT-2020 Task 2: Exploiting CT-BERT for Identifying COVID-19 Information on the Twitter Social Network

Khiem Vinh Tran [*]
University of Information Technology
VNU-HCM, Vietnam
`17520634@gm.uit.edu.vn`

Hao Phu Phan [*]
National Research University HSE,
Russia
`ffan@edu.hse.ru`

Kiet Van Nguyen
University of Information Technology
VNU-HCM, Vietnam
`kietnv@uit.edu.vn`

Ngan Luu-Thuy Nguyen
University of Information Technology
VNU-HCM, Vietnam
`ngannlt@uit.edu.vn`

Abstract

Recently, COVID-19 has affected a variety of real-life aspects of the world and has led to dreadful consequences. More and more tweets about COVID-19 has been shared publicly on Twitter. However, the plurality of those Tweets are uninformative, which is challenging to build automatic systems to detect the informative ones for useful AI applications. In this paper, we present our results at the W-NUT 2020 Shared Task 2: Identification of Informative COVID-19 English Tweets. In particular, we propose our simple but effective approach using the transformer-based models based on COVID-Twitter-BERT (CT-BERT) with different fine-tuning techniques. As a result, we achieve the F1-Score of 90.94% with the third place on the leaderboard of this task which attracted 56 submitted teams in total.

1 Introduction

In the mid of April 2020, the COVID-19 pandemic has caused 23M affected and more than 800,000 deaths almost over the world[1], and the number of people affected and death increase day by day. The world faces many challenges from many sides. One of the biggest problems is how to prevent the spread of COVID-19 before the vaccine is ready. Additionally, how to provide people information about COVID-19 with the fastest and most timely is one of the most issues. Traditionally, the information will provide some official sources as WHO or news on TV, but with the incredible speed of virus spreading, this cannot be real-time update. The social network is the channel that can solve this problem, and Twitter is one of the popular social networks with a massive amount of data. The

number of tweets related to COVID-19 on Twitter is up to 4 million daily (Lamsal, 2020), and most of these tweets are uninformative. Because of that reason, detecting which tweet is informative or not is necessary. Thus, the W-NUT 2020 Shared Task 2: Identification of Informative COVID-19 English Tweets (Nguyen et al., 2020b) attracted about 120 different teams coming from 20 countries. We present our solution for this task which is also our main contribution in this paper.

In recent years, transfer learning models such as BERT (Devlin et al., 2018), ALBERT (Lan et al., 2019), BERTweet (Nguyen et al., 2020a), XLM-R (Conneau et al., 2019), XLNet (Yang et al., 2019), COVID-Twitter-BERT (Müller et al., 2020) have achieved the best performances on a variety of NLP tasks, e.g., text classification (Sun et al., 2019), machine reading comprehension (Van Nguyen et al., 2020). Fine-tuning pre-trained language models (Dodge et al., 2020) also have proved the effectiveness of exploring solutions for new tasks. In addition, ensemble approaches were also very effective in previous studies (Araque et al., 2017; Nguyen et al., 2019; Van Huynh et al., 2020). Inspired by these research works, we propose our simple but effective ensemble strategy using different models based on CT-BERT with different fine-tunings, achieving the F1-score of 90.94% on the final test set. This result reaches the third rank on the leaderboard of this competition.

The rest of this paper is structured as follows. Section 2 is task definition. Section 3 introduces information about the dataset .Section 4 describes our approach. Section 5 shows experiments and results on the dataset. Finally, Section 6 concludes the paper and discusses future work.

---

[1] https://www.worldometers.info/coronavirus/. (The COVID-19 information is updated on September 6, 2020)

[0] * These authors contributed equally to this work.

Proceedings of the 2020 EMNLP Workshop W-NUT: The Sixth Workshop on Noisy User-generated Text, pages 383–387
Online, Nov 19, 2020. ©2020 Association for Computational Linguistics

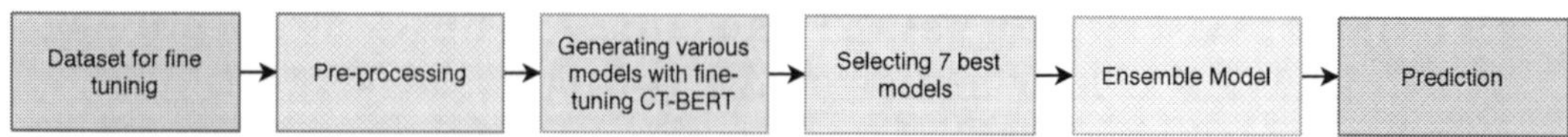

Figure 1: Our simple but effective approach for identifying COVID-19 information.

2 Task Definition

In this section, we summarize the W-NUT-2020 Shared Task 2 (Nguyen et al., 2020b). The objective of this task is to detect whether a COVID-19 text on Twitter is informative or not. Such informative Tweet provides information about recovered, suspected, confirmed, and death cases as well as the location and history of each case. Formally, the task is described as follows.

- **Input**: Given English Tweets on the social networking site Twitter.

- **Output**: One of two different labels (INFORMATIVE and UNINFORMATIVE) predicted by classifiers.

Several examples extracted from the dataset are presented in Table 1.

Tweet	Label
Oklahoma's first confirmed case of coronavirus is in Tulsa County HTTPURL #SmartNews	1
Ladies and gentlemen, put your hands together for... Johnny Covid and the Underlying Comorbidities!	0

Table 1: Example of sentence and label on dataset. 0 and 1 stand for UNINFORMATIVE and INFORMATIVE, respectively.

3 Dataset

We use the dataset about COVID-19 English Tweets (Nguyen et al., 2020b) for our experiment. This corpus consists of nearly 10,000 COVID Tweets, including 4,719 Tweets annotated as informative and 5,281 Tweets annotated as uninformative. Each tweet on this dataset is annotated by three independent annotators with an inter-annotator agreement score of Fleiss' Kappa at 81.80%. This dataset is divided into training/validation/test sets with a 70/10/20 rate. Table 2 shows overview statistics of the dataset.

	Informative	Uninformative
Training	3,303	3,697
Validation	472	528
Test	944	1,056

Table 2: Overview statistics of the dataset of WNUT-2020 Task 2.

4 Our Approach

In this section, we present our simple yet effective approach for this task. Instead of leveraging multiple supper models, we only focus on the CT-BERT model for generating a variety of best-performance models by fine-turning techniques. Figure 1 shows the overview of the approach using three important components which are pre-processing techniques (see Subsection 4.1), the core method CT-BERT (see Subsection 4.2), and the ensemble learning (see Subsection 4.3).

4.1 Pre-processing Techniques

Pre-processing is an essential part of the running model because it can increase the performance of the model. In this part, we try to programmatically apply some pre-processing techniques as follows:

- **Step 1**: Converting Tweets into lower texts.

- **Step 2**: Removing or replacing special characters (emojis including) with ASCII alternatives.

- **Step 3**: Normalizing punctuation.

- **Step 4**: BERT-tokenizer tokenizes each sentence into a list of tokens. Some kinds of contractions may be ignored because they are not listed in vocab. Thus, we use the Pycontractions tool[2] with pre-trained model "glove-twitter-100" to expand the contractions.

- **Step 5**: Expanding some common abbreviations.

- **Step 6**: Segmenting each hashtag into words. If we feed a raw hashtag into the tokenizer,

---

[2]https://pypi.org/project/pycontractions/

usually it will be ignored because the pre-trained model's vocab does not contain any word like this whole hashtag. A hashtag usually contains useful information because it may mark the tweet as a newsletter. Because of that, we segment them, and their words will be less overlooked at the phase of tokenization. Segmenter tool ekphrasis (Baziotis et al., 2017) with twitter corpus are used for this task.

4.2 CT-BERT

The task is defined as the binary-classification task to detect a COVID-19 text on Twitter is informative or not. In this paper, we experiment with COVID-Twitter-BERT (CT-BERT) (Müller et al., 2020) as our default transformer-based model. CT-BERT is based on the BERT-LARGE and is optimized to be used on the COVID-19 domain from social media.

Following the fine-tuning pre-trained language models (Dodge et al., 2020), we fine-tune with different parameters and random seeds. These parameters and random seeds of each model are random. With each change of parameters and random seeds, we obtain an individual model based on CT-BERT.

4.3 Ensemble Learning

From a range of the individual models, we choose seven models with the best F1-score performances. Finally, we implement the ensemble approach using hard or soft voting to predict a final output from outputs of the seven best-performance models.

5 Experiments

In this section, we introduce our simple but effective ensemble model on the dataset. Our systems are evaluated using accuracy, precision (P), recall (R) and F1-score (Nguyen et al., 2020b). Note that P, R and F1-score are calculated on the INFORMATIVE class.

5.1 Data Preparation

Because the original training set is unbalanced, we re-split this training set with a ratio of 50:50, which means that the number of informative labels and uninformative labels is approximately equal, which is more effective in the training phase.

5.2 Experiment Setting

We conduct various experiments on Google Colab Pro (CPU: Intel(R) Xeon(R) CPU @ 2.20GHz; RAM: 25.51 GB; GPU: Tesla P100-PCIE-16GB

with CUDA 10.1). We fine-tuning CT-BERT with different parameters as batch size, learning rate, epoch, random seed. In general, we set batch size to 16 for all models. About learning rate, we set the value is 2.00E-05 for first six models and 3.00E-05 for the 7th model. The difference between each model is the epoch and random seed. As our resources are constrained, we use the method of randomly choosing random seed and try to combine them with other parameters. With the same hyperparameter values, distinct random seeds can lead to substantially different results (Dodge et al., 2020). After many times combine these parameters, we choose seven models with the best F1-score performances. As a result, Table 3 shows the parameters of the seven models.

Model	Batch Size	Learning Rate	Epochs	Random Seed
1	16	2.00E-05	1	96
2	16	2.00E-05	2	144
3	16	2.00E-05	2	380,343
4	16	2.00E-05	3	1
5	16	2.00E-05	3	25
6	16	2.00E-05	4	747
7	16	3.00E-05	2	380,343

Table 3: The parameters of the seven individual models.

5.3 Experimental Results

Table 4 shows our experimental results. Comparing the experimental results of each model with different parameters such as epoch and random seed, we can see that Model 3 with epoch is 2 and random seed is 380,343 achieves the best accuracy of 92.41% with F1 on validation sets. Additionally, the best precision is Model 5 with 92.36%, and the best recall is Model 4 with 94.07%.

Model	P	R	F1	Acc
1	0.9179	0.9237	0.9208	0.9250
2	0.9059	0.9386	0.9220	0.9250
3	0.9202	0.9280	0.9241	0.9280
4	0.9043	0.9407	0.9221	0.9250
5	0.9236	0.9216	0.9226	0.9270
6	0.9076	0.9364	0.9218	0.9250
7	0.9216	0.9216	0.9216	0.9260
Ensemble (SV)	0.9174	0.9407	0.9289	0.9320
Ensemble (HV)	**0.9213**	**0.9428**	**0.9319**	**0.9350**

Table 4: Model performances of our proposed approach on the validation set. HV, SV, P, R, F1, and Acc stand for Hard Voting, Soft Voting, Precision, Recall, F1-score and Accuracy, respectively.

However, Model 4 has the best recall, but the precision of this model is the lowest. It is a challenge for us to choose this model because precision and recall are unbalanced. The two most balanced models are Model 7 with the same precision and recall, and Model 5 with the highest precision and recall is approximately equal to the precision. Because of these challenges, we determine to use the ensemble approach with the hope of getting a better model. On this task, we use both Soft Voting (SV) and Hard Voting (HV) to ensemble these models together. As shown in Table 4, HV has better performance than SV when we ensemble these models together. In particular, we reach 0.9319 in F1-score on the validation set. And we achieve 0.9094 on the test set, which was ranked the third place of the leaderboard of this task.

Rank	Team Name	P	R	F1	Acc
1	NutCracker	0.9135	0.9057	0.9096	0.9150
2	NLP_North	0.9029	0.9163	0.9096	0.9140
3	**UIT-HSE**	**0.9046**	**0.9142**	**0.9094**	**0.9140**
4	#GCDH	0.8919	0.9269	0.9091	0.9125
5	Loner	0.8918	0.9258	0.9085	0.9120
48	Baseline	0.7730	0.7288	0.7503	0.7710

Table 5: Performance of our system on the final scoreboard of the W-NUT-2020 Task 2. P, R, F1, and Acc stand for Precision, Recall, F1-score and Accuracy, respectively.

Table 5 illustrates the result of the top 5 highest teams on this shared task. As you can see from the Table 5, with the F1 Score, our model performance is 90.94% and just lower than the first rank team (NutCracker) and the second rank team (NLP_North) is 0.02% and much higher than the baseline and over 50 submitted teams.

5.4 Error Analysis

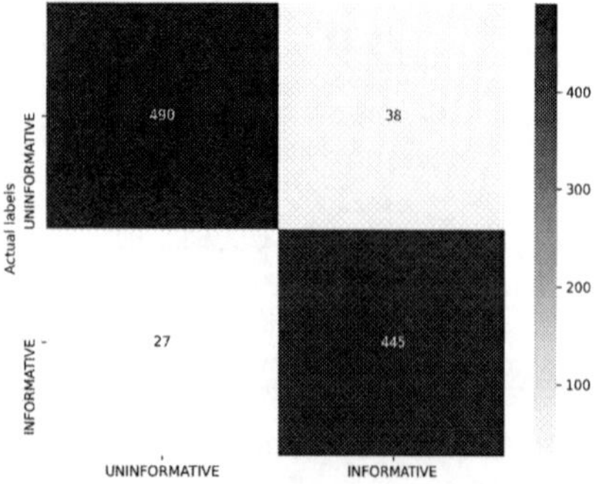

Figure 2: Confusion matrix of our best-performance model for identifying COVID-19 information.

Error analysis is carried out to analyze the errors that we encountered in our system by quantitative

No.	Tweet
1	Anyone wanna tell little Amy Mexico has like 1000 Covid-19 cases to our zillions?
2	if anyone in Austin has a place to stay for just one night pls lmk I tested negative for flu, they didn't even see the need to test me for covid19. I don't feel safe going back to my apartment til I can get management involved, since my roommate owns a Glock & ran from police

Table 6: Examples of the sentences with actual labels are uninformative, but their predictions are informative.

analysis using the confusion matrix of our best-performance model. Fig. 2 shows the confusion matrix of our best model when predicting informative tweets about COVID-19 on the validation set. It can be inferred from Fig. 2 that the ability of prediction of our system on the INFORMATIVE label is better than the UNINFORMATIVE label. As our experiment, we figure out that our wrong predicted cases are the sentences containing informative factors, but they are condition sentences or interrogative sentences. For example, Table 6 shows the sentences with actual labels are uninformative, but their predictions are informative.

6 Conclusion and Future Work

In this paper, we propose the simple but effective ensemble approach to achieve better performance on a new dataset about COVID-19 based on tweets on Twitter and perform experiments to compare CT-BERT performances with different random seed and epoch. The experimental results showed that our proposed ensemble method with combination of data clean is effective for this dataset. Our best performance reaches 93.19% in F1 on the validation set and 90.94% on the test set. Although our model performance achieves rank the third place, there is just a little gap between our model and the best model (a really small difference of 0.02%).

In the future, we plan to combine more strong transfer learning models (Conneau et al., 2019; Yang et al., 2019) with different parameters to obtain higher performances. As our experiment, our ensemble model still does not reach the highest performance, so if we try with other different parameters, it will make different results. In addition, because we use max sequence length of CT-BERT is 96 tokens to fit with pre-trained data of CT-BERT, a small number of sentences that are not short enough will be truncated. We will try to analyze and handle these cases.

References

Oscar Araque, Ignacio Corcuera-Platas, J Fernando Sánchez-Rada, and Carlos A Iglesias. 2017. Enhancing deep learning sentiment analysis with ensemble techniques in social applications. *Expert Systems with Applications*, 77:236–246.

Christos Baziotis, Nikos Pelekis, and Christos Doulkeridis. 2017. Datastories at semeval-2017 task 4: Deep lstm with attention for message-level and topic-based sentiment analysis. In *Proceedings of the 11th International Workshop on Semantic Evaluation (SemEval-2017)*, pages 747–754, Vancouver, Canada. Association for Computational Linguistics.

Alexis Conneau, Kartikay Khandelwal, Naman Goyal, Vishrav Chaudhary, Guillaume Wenzek, Francisco Guzmán, Edouard Grave, Myle Ott, Luke Zettlemoyer, and Veselin Stoyanov. 2019. Unsupervised cross-lingual representation learning at scale. *arXiv preprint arXiv:1911.02116*.

Jacob Devlin, Ming-Wei Chang, Kenton Lee, and Kristina Toutanova. 2018. Bert: Pre-training of deep bidirectional transformers for language understanding. *arXiv preprint arXiv:1810.04805*.

Jesse Dodge, Gabriel Ilharco, Roy Schwartz, Ali Farhadi, Hannaneh Hajishirzi, and Noah Smith. 2020. Fine-tuning pretrained language models: Weight initializations, data orders, and early stopping. *arXiv preprint arXiv:2002.06305*.

Rabindra Lamsal. 2020. Coronavirus (covid-19) tweets dataset.

Zhenzhong Lan, Mingda Chen, Sebastian Goodman, Kevin Gimpel, Piyush Sharma, and Radu Soricut. 2019. Albert: A lite bert for self-supervised learning of language representations. *arXiv preprint arXiv:1909.11942*.

Martin Müller, Marcel Salathé, and Per E Kummervold. 2020. Covid-twitter-bert: A natural language processing model to analyse covid-19 content on twitter. *arXiv preprint arXiv:2005.07503*.

Dat Quoc Nguyen, Thanh Vu, and Anh Tuan Nguyen. 2020a. Bertweet: A pre-trained language model for english tweets. *arXiv preprint arXiv:2005.10200*.

Dat Quoc Nguyen, Thanh Vu, Afshin Rahimi, Mai Hoang Dao, Linh The Nguyen, and Long Doan. 2020b. WNUT-2020 Task 2: Identification of Informative COVID-19 English Tweets. In *Proceedings of the 6th Workshop on Noisy User-generated Text*.

Duc-Vu Nguyen, Kiet Van Nguyen, and Ngan Luu-Thuy Nguyen. 2019. Nlp@uit at vlsp 2019: A simple ensemble model for vietnamese dependency parsing. *The Sixth International Workshop on Vietnamese Language and Speech Processing VLSP 2019*.

Chi Sun, Xipeng Qiu, Yige Xu, and Xuanjing Huang. 2019. How to fine-tune BERT for text classification? In *China National Conference on Chinese Computational Linguistics*, pages 194–206. Springer.

Tin Van Huynh, Kiet Van Nguyen, Ngan Luu-Thuy Nguyen, and Anh Gia-Tuan Nguyen. 2020. Job prediction: From deep neural network models to applications. In *2020 RIVF International Conference on Computing and Communication Technologies (RIVF)*, pages 1–6. IEEE.

Kiet Van Nguyen, Duc-Vu Nguyen, Anh Gia-Tuan Nguyen, and Ngan Luu-Thuy Nguyen. 2020. New vietnamese corpus for machine reading comprehension of health news articles. *arXiv preprint arXiv:2006.11138*.

Zhilin Yang, Zihang Dai, Yiming Yang, Jaime Carbonell, Russ R Salakhutdinov, and Quoc V Le. 2019. Xlnet: Generalized autoregressive pretraining for language understanding. In *Advances in neural information processing systems*, pages 5753–5763.

Emory at WNUT-2020 Task 2: Combining Pretrained Deep Learning Models and Feature Enrichment for Informative Tweet Identification

Yuting Guo
Computer Science
Emory University
Atlanta GA 30322, USA
`yuting.guo@emory.edu`

Mohammed Al-Garadi
Biomedical Informatics
Emory University
Atlanta GA 30322, USA
`maalgar@emory.edu`

Abeed Sarker
Biomedical Informatics
Emory University
Atlanta GA 30322, USA
`abeed@dbmi.emory.edu`

Abstract

This paper describes the system developed by the Emory team for the WNUT-2020 Task 2: "Identification of Informative COVID-19 English Tweet". Our system explores three recent Transformer-based deep learning models pretrained on large-scale data to encode documents. Moreover, we developed two feature enrichment methods to enhance document embeddings by integrating emoji embeddings and syntactic features into deep learning models. Our system achieved F_1-score of 0.897 and accuracy of 90.1% on the test set, and ranked in the top-third of all 55 teams.

1 Introduction

Until August 31, 2020, the COVID-19 outbreak has caused nearly 25 million confirmed cases worldwide, including about 800K deaths (WHO, 2020). Recently, much attention has been paid to building monitoring systems to track the development of COVID-19 by aggregating related data from different sources (*e.g.*, the Johns Hopkins Coronavirus Dashboard[1] and the WHO Coronavirus Disease Dashboard[2]). One potentially important source of information is social media, such as Twitter and Reddit, which provides real-time updates of the COVID-19 outbreak. To deal with the massive amount of social media data, several systems have been developed to detect and extract COVID-19 related information from Twitter (Chen et al., 2020; Banda et al., 2020; Sarker et al., 2020). However, only a minority of the data collections contain relevant information (*e.g.*, the recovered, suspected, confirmed and death cases as well as location or travel history of the cases) that are useful for monitoring systems, and it is costly to manually identify these informative data. To help address the problem, WNUT-2020 Task 2 (Nguyen et al., 2020) focuses on attracting research efforts to create text classification systems that can identify whether a COVID-19 English Tweet is informative or not. This could lead to automated information extraction systems for COVID-19, as well as benefit the development of relevant monitoring systems.

This paper describes the system developed by the Emory team for this task. Our solution explores three recent transformer-based models, which are pretrained on large-scale data and achieve great success on different NLP tasks. The pretrained models convert the input document into a embedding matrix, and the first token (*i.e.*, `[CLS]`) embedding is regarded as the document embedding. We also propose two methods to integrate pretrained deep learning models and empirical features by enriching document embeddings with emoji embeddings and syntactic features. The document embedding is fed into a normalization layer and an output layer, which are fine-tuned with the encoder during the training phase. The output is a probability value from 0 to 1, and the class with the highest probability is chosen. The highest F_1-score of our system is 0.897, ranking 14 of all 55 teams in the leaderboard[3].

2 Related Work

Recently, deep learning models pretrained on large-scale data, such as BERT (Devlin et al., 2019), RoBERTa (Liu et al., 2019), and SpanBERT (Joshi et al., 2020), have improved the performance of many downstream NLP tasks such as named entity recognition, semantic role labeling, emotion detection, and question answering. Although these models are trained on open domain data such as news

---

[1]`https://coronavirus.jhu.edu/map.html`
[2]`https://covid19.who.int/`

[3]`https://competitions.codalab.org/competitions/25845#results`

Proceedings of the 2020 EMNLP Workshop W-NUT: The Sixth Workshop on Noisy User-generated Text, pages 388–393
Online, Nov 19, 2020. ©2020 Association for Computational Linguistics

articles and English Wikipedia, several approaches have been investigated to apply pretrained deep learning models to medical domain tasks. Matero et al. (2019) proposed a dual-context neural model that combines lexical features and personality factors with BERT embeddings for suicide risk assessment. Lee et al. (2019) combined BERT embeddings and BiLSTM (Bidirectional Long Short-Term Memory) to improve the performance of medical text inferences. Roitero et al. (2020) applied machine learning models and BERT to identify medical domain tweets and reported that BERT significantly outperforms some traditional machine learning models such as logistic regression and support vector machines for their task. Encouraged by this considerable progress, our work uses recent pretrained deep learning models as document encoders and fine-tunes the classification model on the dataset provided by the task organizers. Moreover, we develop two feature enrichment methods to enhance the document embeddings generated by pretrained deep learning models.

3 System Description

Figure 1 shows the overall framework of our model for the classification task. In this framework, we use three Transformer-based models described in Section 3.1 as encoders to generate the document embedding e_d, which is the first token (i.e., [CLS]) embedding in our model. The document embedding is normalized by layer normalization and is fed into an output layer with Softmax activation. Also, we implement two feature enrichment methods to enhance document embeddings by integrating emoji embeddings and syntactic features (described in Section 3.2).

3.1 Document Encoder

RoBERTa: Devlin et al. (2019) developed a Transformer-based model named BERT that has achieved great success in several NLP tasks. Recently, Liu et al. (2019) has released a new pretrained model named RoBERTa that is trained with the same model architecture of BERT but on different datasets and pretraining tasks. We use RoBERTa-large as the encoder which outperforms BERT-large on different NLP tasks.

XLNet: Yang et al. (2019) implemented XLNet, a generalized autoregressive method that incorporates the autoregressive model into pretraining and optimizes the language model objective using a permutation method that can overcome the limitation of the masked language model in BERT. We use XLNet-base as the encoder which has been reported to outperform BERT and RoBERTa on some NLP tasks.

ALBERT: Lan et al. (2020) proposed a variant of BERT named ALBERT that applies parameter reduction techniques to reduce memory consumption and to accelerate the training process. ALBERT improves the training efficiency of BERT by factorizing embedding parameters and sharing cross-layer parameters. We use ALBERT-xxlarge as the encoder, which has also achieved state-of-the-art results on several NLP tasks.

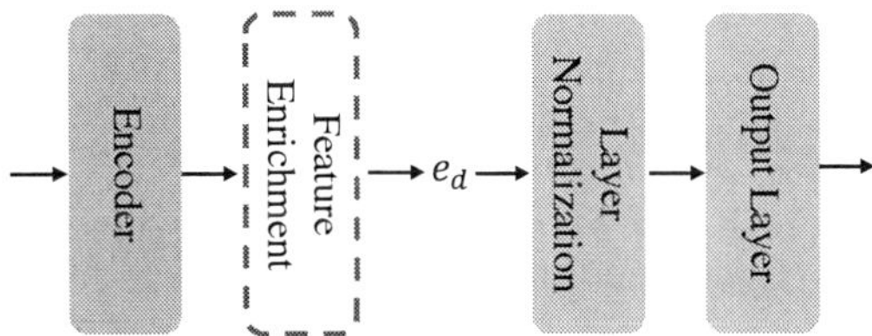

Figure 1: The overall framework of our model.

3.2 Feature Enrichment

Emoji Embedding: Emojis can succinctly represent emotional expressions and have become popular in social media. Recently, several studies have revealed that incorporating emoji information into deep learning models can benefit the performance of tweet classification tasks (Singh et al., 2019; Rangwani et al., 2018). Inspired by that, we employ a pretrained emoji encoder named emoji2vec[4] (Eisner et al., 2016) to convert emojis into emoji embeddings. The emoji embeddings are fed into a fully connection layer with $Tanh$ activation, and the output is concatenated to the [CLS] token embedding as the document embedding. If multiple emojis appear in one tweet, the emoji embeddings will be concatenated into one fixed-length vector.

Syntactic Feature: Syntactic features have been previously used on many NLP tasks (van der Lee and van den Bosch, 2017; Kurtz et al., 2019; Jabreel and Moreno, 2017), and syntactic dependencies often entail key information relevant to sentence topics. In order to utilize syntactic features, we collected a set of COVID-19 related keywords and extracted their governors (also known as heads) that

---

[4]https://github.com/uclnlp/emoji2vec

hold grammatical relations with the COVID-19 related keywords using the Stanford Parser (Chen and Manning, 2014), which can indicate what aspects of the keywords are discussed in tweets. The governor embedding and the [CLS] token embedding are then fed into a self-attention layer (Vaswani et al., 2017), and at the output, the new [CLS] token embedding is regarded as the document embedding.

3.3 Ensemble Model

To improve the robustness of our final system, we apply ensemble techniques to combine the results of different models. For each individual model, we take the class with highest output probability as the inference result during the testing phase. The inference results of all models are combined using a majority vote strategy, which is to return the class predicted by most models.

4 Experiments

4.1 Data Preprocessing

The dataset contains 10K COVID-19 English tweets of which 4719 are labeled as informative and 5218 are labeled as uninformative. To clean tweets data, we used the open source tool `preprocess-twitter`[5] including steps of lowercasing and normalizing numbers, hashtags, capital words and repeated letters. The dataset had been split into training, validation, and test sets with pre-specified sizes. Because the test set is not available when developing our system, we re-split the training set into a new training set and a new validation set with a 90/10 rate, and used the released validation set as the test set. The statistics for the data split are shown in Table 1.

	TRN	DEV	TST	ALL
INFORMATIVE	2928	345	472	3745
UNINFORMATIVE	3310	353	528	4191

Table 1: The statistics of the data split. TRN: the new training set; DEV: the new validation set; TST: The released validation set.

4.2 Training

Our system is implemented in PyTorch and Python 3. We develop five classification models of which three models use different encoders to generate document embeddings, and two models apply emoji

---

[5]`https://nlp.stanford.edu/projects/ glove/preprocess-twitter.rb`

embeddings and syntactic features to enrich document embeddings encoded by RoBERTa [6]. Among these models, the batch size of ALBERT is 16, and that of other models is 32. For the model applying emoji embeddings, the dimension of emoji embeddings is 300, and the max number of emojis in one tweet is 3. For the model applying syntactic features, only the governor of the first keyword is considered in order to control model complexity. Other hyperparameters are the same for all models listed in Table 2. Each model is trained separately on the training set and evaluated on the validation set during the training phase. Each experiment runs 3 times with different random initialization, and the model that achieves the highest accuracy on the validation set is selected for the testing phase.

Hyperparameter	Value
Learning rate	4e-5
Adam epsilon	1e-8
Max sequence length	128
Warmup ratio	0.06
Number of epochs	3

Table 2: Hyperparameter configurations of all models.

5 Results and Analysis

5.1 Task Results

We use F_1-score as the primary metric and also report accuracy of each model. Table 3 describes the results of each individual model and the ensemble model on the released validation set.

Model	Precision	Recall	F1	Acc
RoBERTa	86.7	93.3	89.9	90.1
RoBERTa+Emo	86.7	93.6	90.1	90.2
RoBERTa+Syn	87.2	91.7	89.4	89.7
XLNet	85.8	92.4	89.	89.2
ALBERT	88.8	90.3	89.6	90.1
Ensemble	**88.8**	**94.1**	**91.4**	**91.6**

Table 3: The precision, recall, F_1-score and accuracy of each model on the released validation set. RoBERTa+Emo: the model using RoBERTa as the encoder and applying emoji embeddings. RoBERTa+Syn: the model using RoBERTa as the encoder and applying syntactic features.

As we can observe, the F_1-score and accuracy of the ensemble model is marginally higher than any of the individual models. It indicates that the

---

[6]Due to the limited time and computational resources, we only experimented on adopting emoji embeddings and syntactic features for RoBERTa, and not for XLNet and ALBERT.

Albert Uderzo died in his sleep at his home in **Neuilly**, after a heart attack that was not linked to the coronavirus, his son-in-law **Bernard de Choisy** told the AFP news agency' #asterix
The Indian Express: **New York Zoo** tiger tests positive for coronavirus: Are cats at particular risk?. HTTPURL A group of humans knows everything about this virus. Others don't know anything about it.
Facsism kills in many subtle ways. **Trump** got away with **3,000** deaths in Puerto Rico. He's going to try it again with coronavirus. Time for all members of the media to ovary up and start reporting on the dangerous lies of this regime.

Table 4: Samples of false positives from the released validation set.

document embeddings generated by the individual models can encode information from different perspectives and complement each other.

5.2 Error Analysis

In order to investigate how our system can be improved, we conducted an error analysis on the released validation set. We found that 56 out of 84 error instances were false positives, (*i.e.*, uninformative tweets misclassified as informative), and the remaining 28 instances are false negatives (*i.e.*, informative tweets misclassified as uninformative). We observe that most of the false positives include numbers, locations, and personal names, which can be indicators of informative tweets such as the samples presented in Table 4. These indicators can be the noise that may confuse the model and lead to misclassification of negative instances. It suggests that we still need to improve the ability of our system to understand the context of indicative components in tweets.

5.3 Ablation Study

Given multiple models developed here, we conduct ablation study on each model to see how each individual model can affect the ensemble model. The performance of ensemble models that respectively remove one of the individual models from five models are shown in Table 5. As we can see, removing any of the individual models can increase the precision and decrease the recall of the ensemble model. It indicates that ensemble modeling can better identify negative instances than positive instances. Another notable result is that the recall drops more than other models when removing RoBERTa. Combined with the classification results in Table 3, RoBERTa might contribute most to the high recall of the ensemble model. It is interesting to note that RoBERTa+Emo is the best in the individual models but the least contributed to the ensemble model. The possible reason can be that only 9% of the training data contains emojis so that the emoji features are insufficiently learned during training, which may cause the document

embedding of RoBERTa+Emo not much different from that of RoBERTa.

Model	Precision	Recall	F1	Acc
Ensemble	88.8	**94.1**	**91.4**	**91.6**
w/o ALBERT	89.4	92.6	90.9	91.3
w/o RoBERTa	89.3	91.7	90.5	90.9
w/o RoBERTa+Emo	89.5	92.6	91.0	91.4
w/o RoBERTa+Syn	**89.7**	92.2	90.9	91.3
w/o XLNet	89.5	92.4	90.9	91.3

Table 5: The ablation study of removing each individual model from the ensemble model.

6 Conclusion

This paper describes the system developed by the Emory team for the WNUT-2020 Task 2: "Identification of Informative COVID-19 English Tweets", including system design, implementation, evaluation, and analysis. We explored three pretrained deep learning models to encode documents, and developed two feature enrichment methods to enhance document embeddings by integrating emoji embeddings and syntactic features. For future work, we will continue to develop our system by exploiting other feature enrichment methods, utilizing external knowledge bases, and investigating other pretrained deep learning models.

References

Juan M. Banda, Ramya Tekumalla, Guanyu Wang, Jingyuan Yu, Tuo Liu, Yuning Ding, Katya Artemova, Elena Tutubalina, and Gerardo Chowell. 2020. A large-scale COVID-19 Twitter chatter dataset for open scientific research - an international collaboration. This dataset will be updated bi-weekly at least with additional tweets, look at the github repo for these updates. Release: We have standardized the name of the resource to match our preprint manuscript and to not have to update it every week.

Danqi Chen and Christopher Manning. 2014. A Fast and Accurate Dependency Parser using Neural Networks. In *Proceedings of the 2014 Conference on Empirical Methods in Natural Language Processing (EMNLP)*, pages 740–750, Doha, Qatar. Association for Computational Linguistics.

Emily Chen, Kristina Lerman, and Emilio Ferrara. 2020. Tracking Social Media Discourse About the COVID-19 Pandemic: Development of a Public Coronavirus Twitter Data Set. *JMIR Public Health Surveill*, 6(2):e19273.

Jacob Devlin, Ming-Wei Chang, Kenton Lee, and Kristina Toutanova. 2019. BERT: Pre-training of Deep Bidirectional Transformers for Language Understanding. In *Proceedings of the 2019 North American Chapter of the Association for Computational Linguistics: Human Language Technologies*.

Ben Eisner, Tim Rocktäschel, Isabelle Augenstein, Matko Bošnjak, and Sebastian Riedel. 2016. emoji2vec: Learning Emoji Representations from their Description. In *Proceedings of The Fourth International Workshop on Natural Language Processing for Social Media*, pages 48–54, Austin, TX, USA. Association for Computational Linguistics.

Mohammed Jabreel and Antonio Moreno. 2017. SiTAKA at SemEval-2017 Task 4: Sentiment Analysis in Twitter Based on a Rich Set of Features. In *Proceedings of the 11th International Workshop on Semantic Evaluation (SemEval-2017)*, pages 694–699, Vancouver, Canada. Association for Computational Linguistics.

Mandar Joshi, Danqi Chen, Yinhan Liu, Daniel S. Weld, Luke Zettlemoyer, and Omer Levy. 2020. SpanBERT: Improving Pre-training by Representing and Predicting Spans. *Transactions of the Association for Computational Linguistics 2020*.

Robin Kurtz, Daniel Roxbo, and Marco Kuhlmann. 2019. Improving Semantic Dependency Parsing with Syntactic Features. In *Proceedings of the First NLPL Workshop on Deep Learning for Natural Language Processing*, pages 12–21, Turku, Finland. Linköping University Electronic Press.

Zhenzhong Lan, Mingda Chen, Sebastian Goodman, Kevin Gimpel, Piyush Sharma, and Radu Soricut. 2020. ALBERT: A Lite BERT for Self-supervised Learning of Language Representations. In *International Conference on Learning Representations*.

Chris van der Lee and Antal van den Bosch. 2017. Exploring Lexical and Syntactic Features for Language Variety Identification. In *Proceedings of the Fourth Workshop on NLP for Similar Languages, Varieties and Dialects (VarDial)*, pages 190–199, Valencia, Spain. Association for Computational Linguistics.

Lung-Hao Lee, Yi Lu, Po-Han Chen, Po-Lei Lee, and Kuo-Kai Shyu. 2019. NCUEE at MEDIQA 2019: Medical Text Inference Using Ensemble BERT-BiLSTM-Attention Model. In *Proceedings of the 18th BioNLP Workshop and Shared Task*, pages 528–532, Florence, Italy. Association for Computational Linguistics.

Yinhan Liu, Myle Ott, Naman Goyal, Jingfei Du, Mandar Joshi, Danqi Chen, Omer Levy, Mike Lewis, Luke Zettlemoyer, and Veselin Stoyanov. 2019. RoBERTa: A Robustly Optimized BERT Pretraining Approach. *arXiv preprint arXiv:1907.11692*.

Matthew Matero, Akash Idnani, Youngseo Son, Salvatore Giorgi, Huy Vu, Mohammad Zamani, Parth Limbachiya, Sharath Chandra Guntuku, and H. Andrew Schwartz. 2019. Suicide Risk Assessment with Multi-level Dual-Context Language and BERT. In *Proceedings of the Sixth Workshop on Computational Linguistics and Clinical Psychology*, pages 39–44, Minneapolis, Minnesota. Association for Computational Linguistics.

Dat Quoc Nguyen, Thanh Vu, Afshin Rahimi, Mai Hoang Dao, Linh The Nguyen, and Long Doan. 2020. WNUT-2020 Task 2: Identification of Informative COVID-19 English Tweets. In *Proceedings of the 6th Workshop on Noisy User-generated Text*.

Harsh Rangwani, Devang Kulshreshtha, and Anil Kumar Singh. 2018. NLPRL-IITBHU at SemEval-2018 Task 3: Combining Linguistic Features and Emoji pre-trained CNN for Irony Detection in Tweets. In *Proceedings of The 12th International Workshop on Semantic Evaluation*, pages 638–642, New Orleans, Louisiana. Association for Computational Linguistics.

Kevin Roitero, VDMSM Cristian Bozzato, and G Serra. 2020. Twitter goes to the Doctor: Detecting Medical Tweets using Machine Learning and BERT. In *Proceedings of the International Workshop on Semantic Indexing and Information Retrieval for Health from heterogeneous content types and languages (SIIRH 2020)*.

Abeed Sarker, Sahithi Lakamana, Whitney Hogg-Bremer, Angel Xie, Mohammed Ali Al-Garadi, and Yuan-Chi Yang. 2020. Self-reported COVID-19 symptoms on Twitter: An analysis and a research resource. *medRxiv*.

Abhishek Singh, Eduardo Blanco, and Wei Jin. 2019. Incorporating Emoji Descriptions Improves Tweet Classification. In *Proceedings of the 2019 Conference of the North American Chapter of the Association for Computational Linguistics: Human Language Technologies, Volume 1 (Long and Short Papers)*, pages 2096–2101, Minneapolis, Minnesota. Association for Computational Linguistics.

Ashish Vaswani, Noam Shazeer, Niki Parmar, Jakob Uszkoreit, Llion Jones, Aidan N Gomez, Ł ukasz Kaiser, and Illia Polosukhin. 2017. Attention is All you Need. In I. Guyon, U. V. Luxburg, S. Bengio, H. Wallach, R. Fergus, S. Vishwanathan, and R. Garnett, editors, *Advances in Neural Information Processing Systems 30*, pages 5998–6008. Curran Associates, Inc.

WHO. 2020. Coronavirus disease (COVID-19) Weekly Epidemiological Update. `https://www.who.int/docs/default-source/coronaviruse/situation-reports/`

`20200831-weekly-epi-update-3.pdf?sfvrsn=d7032a2a_4`, Last accessed on 2020-09-04.

Zhilin Yang, Zihang Dai, Yiming Yang, Jaime Carbonell, Russ R Salakhutdinov, and Quoc V Le. 2019. XLNet: Generalized Autoregressive Pretraining for Language Understanding. In H. Wallach, H. Larochelle, A. Beygelzimer, F. dAlché-Buc, E. Fox, and R. Garnett, editors, *Advances in Neural Information Processing Systems 32*, pages 5753–5763. Curran Associates, Inc.

CSECU-DSG at WNUT-2020 Task 2: Exploiting Ensemble of Transfer Learning and Hand-crafted Features for Identification of Informative COVID-19 English Tweets

Fareen Tasneem, Jannatun Naim, Radiathun Tasnia,
Tashin Hossain, and Abu Nowshed Chy
Department of Computer Science & Engineering
University of Chittagong, Chattogram-4331, Bangladesh
{fareen.tasneem,jannatun.naim.cu,radia.tasnia.cu,
tashin.hossain.cu}@gmail.com and nowshed@cu.ac.bd

Abstract

COVID-19 pandemic has become the trending topic on twitter and people are interested in sharing diverse information ranging from new cases, healthcare guidelines, medicine, and vaccine news. Such information assists the people to be updated about the situation as well as beneficial for public safety personnel for decision making. However, the informal nature of twitter makes it challenging to refine the informative tweets from the huge tweet streams. To address these challenges WNUT-2020 introduced a shared task focusing on COVID-19 related informative tweet identification. In this paper, we describe our participation in this task. We propose a neural model that adopts the strength of transfer learning and hand-crafted features in a unified architecture. To extract the transfer learning features, we utilize the state-of-the-art pre-trained sentence embedding model BERT, RoBERTa, and InferSent, whereas various twitter characteristics are exploited to extract the hand-crafted features. Next, various feature combinations are utilized to train a set of multilayer perceptron (MLP) as the base-classifier. Finally, a majority voting based fusion approach is employed to determine the informative tweets. Our approach achieved competitive performance and outperformed the baseline by 7% (approx.).

1 Introduction

Twitter is one of the most prominent microblogging platforms that provides a convenient way of sharing opinions and broadcasting news and information briefly among the mass community. People often prefer using twitter due to its real-time feature because compared to others, it contains most of the notable or official information. Hence, information shared on this platform is very helpful during emergency situations. That is why, in the ongoing COVID-19 pandemic, people are interested

in seeking informative tweets related to COVID-19. An informative tweet may contain the updated information of COVID-19, new cases or death information, medicine or vaccine news, and updated guidelines from diverse sources.

Tweet#1: BREAKING: 21 people on Grand Princess cruise ship docked off the California coast tested positive for coronavirus ...   **Label:** INFORMATIVE
Tweet#2: The WHO is being haunted by an old tweet saying that China found no human transmission .....   **Label:** UNINFORMATIVE

Table 1: Example of sample tweets with labels.

For instance, in Table 1 Tweet#1 is an informative tweet since it contains the updated news of coronavirus affected people on a cruise ship. Besides, Tweet#2 doesn't contain any valuable news or information, instead it provokes annoyance among the people who are keen to know the updates of the COVID-19 situation. Therefore, refining the informative tweets from the real-time tweet stream is a formidable task.

Classifying informative tweets on COVID-19 is an emerging concept. Nevertheless, there are some prior works on identifying informative tweets during crises or disasters. For example, a CNN based approach proposed by (Caragea et al., 2016) for informative tweets identification in disaster. Later, (Fadaei et al., 2018) and (Neppalli et al., 2018) employed CNN with GloVe and Word2Vec features, respectively in the same context. More recently, a work regarding misinformation detection on COVID-19 tweets (Hossain et al., 2020) has also been done.

In this paper, we present our proposed systems submitted to the W-NUT 2020 shared task 2 (Nguyen et al., 2020). The primary goal of the task is to identify informative tweets related to

---

The first four authors have equal contributions.

Proceedings of the 2020 EMNLP Workshop W-NUT: The Sixth Workshop on Noisy User-generated Text, pages 394–398
Online, Nov 19, 2020. ©2020 Association for Computational Linguistics

COVID-19. We exploit the transfer learning features from BERT, RoBERTa, and InferSent along with the n-gram and other hand-crafted features in a unified neural model.

The rest of the contents are structured as follows: we describe our proposed framework in Section 2 whereas Section 3 includes the experimental details and performance analysis. We concluded this paper with plausible future notions in Section 4.

2 Proposed Framework

In this section, we describe our proposed framework. Our target is to identify the informative tweet based on its context. The overview of our proposed framework is presented in Figure 1.

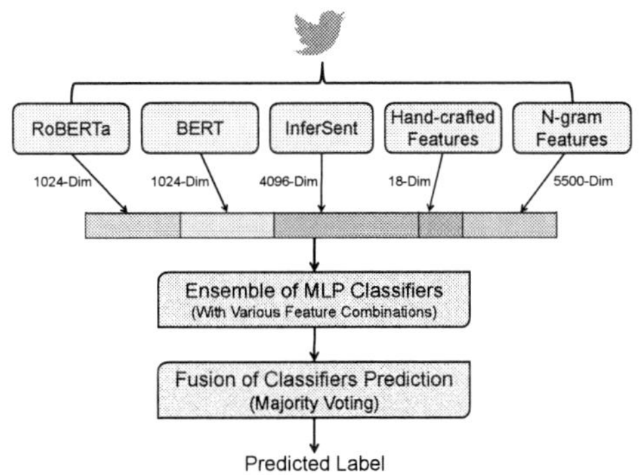

Figure 1: Proposed Framework.

Given a tweet, we explore various techniques to encode the tweet into effective feature vectors. We utilize three pre-trained embedding models including RoBERTa, BERT, and InferSent to extract the effective transfer learning features. Besides, we extract the n-gram and other hand-crafted features. The concatenated features are then passed to a multilayer perceptron (MLP) network for the training. We explore different feature combinations to train and extract the prediction from multiple MLP classifiers. Finally, a majority voting based fusion scheme exploits all the predicted labels and determine the final one.

2.1 Tweet Encoding

BERT: BERT (Devlin et al., 2019) stands for bidirectional encoder representations from transformers, which is a new method of pre-training sentence representations. It captures the context for every existence of given tweets. We employ the BERT-Large, Uncased model to encode each tweet into a 1024-dimensional feature vector included with 24 layers, 16 heads, and 340M parameters.

RoBERTa: RoBERTa (Liu et al., 2019) is considered as an extended version of BERT which is called a robustly optimized BERT pretraining approach. It emphasis on the key hyper-parameters choices and ignoring the next sentence prediction (NSP) objective. It also uses a larger mini-batches and learning rates while training the model. We conduct the RoBERTa-Large pre-trained model based on BERT-Large architecture for encoding each tweet into a 1024-dimensional feature vector.

InferSent: InferSent (Conneau et al., 2017) indicates a sentence encoding approach that is based on natural language interference data for semantically highlighting the sentence through vectorized representations. We exploit the InferSent pre-trained sentence encoding model which is trained with fastText and embedded each tweet into a 4096-dimensional feature vector.

N-gram Bag-of-Words (Bow) Features: The bag-of-words (BoW) representation models a tweet based on its word occurrence statistics. To extract the n-gram features, we utilize maximum features length into a 5500-dimensional feature vector based on word occurrence and use the n-gram range of (1, 8) for capturing the diverse types of features.

To extract the effective n-gram features, we employ the data preprocessing that reduces the effect of noise. We perform the stemming using the Snowball stemmer and remove the accented and special characters from tweets. The tweets may contain some non-standard words (e.g. 2day, suspct). To normalize such noisy words we follow a similar approach used by (Chy et al., 2017), where they utilized two lexical normalization dictionaries (2012; 2012) to address this problem. Besides hashtags may contain important information and segmenting the hashtag (e.g. #CovidPandemic to covid pandemic) might be beneficial to distill the content of the tweets. We utilize a tool provided by Baziotis et al. (2017) to segment the hashtag. Besides, we also demojize (emoji to text) the emoji using a tool[2], expand the contradictions of words, and convert the number into words using PyPi inflection[3].

Other Hand-crafted Features: We extract a set of 18 handcrafted features that comprise of textual features, tweet-specific features, emoticon-based features, POS features, sentiment-based features, and COVID-19 related features. A COVID-19 related informative tweet may contain the news

---

[2]https://github.com/NeelShah18/emot/
[3]https://pypi.org/project/inflection/

Sl.	Feature Definition
F1	*Average Word Length:* Average of characters per word in a tweet.
F2	*Tokenized Words Count:* Number of tokenized words in a tweet (Wang et al., 2019).
F3	*Symbol Count:* Number of symbols present in a tweet (Wang et al., 2019).
F4	*Capital Word Ratio:* The ratio of capital words to total words in a tweet (Wang et al., 2019).
F5	*Digit Ratio:* The ratio of digits to total characters in a tweet (Wang et al., 2019).
F6	*Digits Count:* Number of digits in a tweet (Wang et al., 2019).
F7	*URL Count:* Number of URLs present in a tweet (Pamungkas and Patti, 2018).
F8	*Retweet Count:* Number of retweets present in a tweet (Siddiqua et al., 2016).
F9	*Hashtag Count:* Number of hashtags present in a tweet (Pamungkas and Patti, 2018).
F10	*Number of Emoticons:* Number of emoticons in a tweet (Hogenboom et al., 2015).
F11	*Presence of Emoticon:* Checks if a tweet contains emoticons (Hogenboom et al., 2015).
F12	*Adverb Count:* Number of adverbs in a tweet (Siddiqua et al., 2016).
F13	*Polarity Score:* Determines the sentiment of the tweet (Swanberg et al., 2018) using TextBlob (2014).
F14	*Positive Sentiment Presence:* Checks if a tweet contains positive sentiment using SentiStrength (2012).
F15	*Slang Word Presence:* Checks if slang words are present in a tweet or not using slang word lexicon (2012).
F16	*Special Verb Count:* Number of special verbs (i.e. related to COVID context) in a tweet.
F17	*COVID Cases Presence:* Checks if a tweet contains number of COVID cases or deaths.
F18	*Keywords Count:* Number of COVID related keywords(e.g. tested, quarantine, etc.) in a tweet.
Total	18 Features

Table 2: List of other hand-crafted features used in this work.

about new cases, deaths, and recoveries. We exploit these characteristics and extract the COVID cases presence feature, where we check the presence of numerical value along with some specific keywords (e.g. deaths, affected cases). We have also inspected the presence of some COVID-19 specific keywords and verbs that are more frequent in informative tweets. We built two lexicons and extract the special verb count and keywords count features, accordingly. The features definitions are presented in Table 2.

2.2 Multilayer Perceptron (MLP)

Multilayer Perceptron (MLP) (Windeatt, 2006) is a supervised learning method where backpropagation is used for training. It can be separated from the linear perceptron because of its multi-layer structure and non-linear process. MLP classifier includes various constructive parameters including input layer, hidden layers, output layer, iterations, learning rates, and activation functions. We utilize our MLP classifier with two hidden layers with 500 and 2000 neurons, relu activation function, and set alpha as 0.003. Besides, we use the maximum iterations of 1000 with a random state 1 and a tolerance rate of 0.0001 in our proposed system.

2.3 Fusion of Classifiers Predictions

We empirically exploit various feature combinations in our classifier settings and obtain the prediction from N-number of classification systems. The intuition behind this process is to distill dif-ferent types of contextual information in different settings. Next, we use the majority voting count based scheme to obtain the final prediction label. The core idea behind this type of classification is that the final output class is selected based on the highest number of votes (2010). In prior research, this classification scheme was used to overcome the limitations of a single classifier (2016).

3 Experiments and Evaluations

3.1 Dataset Description

For evaluating our informative tweet identification system, we made use of the COVID-19 Tweet dataset (2020) having 10K COVID-19 related English Tweets. The training set and valid set consists of 7K and 1K tweets with the valance portion of Informative and Uninformative tweets. Along with that, the test dataset consists of 944 Informative and 1056 Uninformative tweets. The detailed statistics were presented in Table 3.

Category	#Train	#Dev	#Test	#Total
Informative	3303	472	944	4719
Uninformative	3697	528	1056	5281
Total	7000	1000	2000	10000

Table 3: The statistics of the dataset.

Following the benchmark of WNUT-2020 Task 2 (2020), we used the accuracy, precision, recall, and F1 score as the evaluation measures, where the F1 score is considered as the primary metric.

3.2 Experimental Setup and Results Analysis

We now describe the settings of our submitted system to the WNUT-2020 Task 2 and analyze the informative tweet identification performances. In our CSECU-DSG#1 system, we have exploited various feature combinations to obtain the predictions from N=7 different classification systems. The feature settings are described in Table 4. Based on the prediction from these 7 systems, a majority voting based method is employed to determine the final label. Besides, we utilize the feature settings $S2$ in Table 4 and the corresponding classifier settings in our CSECU-DSG#2 system.

Sl.	Various Feature Settings Used in CSECU-DSG#1
S1	BERT, N-gram, Other HCF (F9,F7,F8,F10,F16)
S2	RoBERTa ,BERT, N-gram, Other HCF (F9,F7,F8,F11,F10,F16,F12,F14,F15,F18)
S3	RoBERTa ,BERT, N-gram, Other HCF (F1,F3)
S4	RoBERTa ,BERT, N-gram, Other HCF (F7,F8,F9,F10,F16)
S5	InferSent, RoBERTa, BERT, N-gram, Other HCF (F7,F8,F9,F10,F16)
S6	RoBERTa, BERT, N-gram, Other HCF (F14)
S7	RoBERTa, BERT, N-gram, Other HCF (F2,F4,F5,F6,F13,F16,F17,F18)

Table 4: Feature settings of various classifiers.

Now, we compare the performance of our submitted systems against the other participants' systems and the baseline. The organizers used the FastText classifier as the baseline system. The comparative performance are presented in Table 5.

Team_Name	F1 score	Precision	Recall	Accuracy
NutCracker	0.9096	0.9135	0.9057	0.9150
Husky	0.8992	0.8959	0.9025	0.9045
CSECU-DSG#1	0.8198	0.8155	0.8242	0.8290
CSECU-DSG#2	0.8156	0.8134	0.8177	0.8255
IIITBH	0.7979	0.7991	0.7966	0.8095
NLPRL	0.7854	0.8335	0.7426	0.8085
Baseline	0.7503	0.7730	0.7288	0.7710

Table 5: Comparative performance analysis (2020).

It shows that both of our systems achieved competitive performances and obtained nearly similar kinds of performances. This deduces that the classifiers ensemble (CSECU-DSG#1) based on different feature combinations (change mostly hand-crafted features) might not fit for the task since it did not achieve the substantial performance improvement over the single classifier (CSECU-DSG#2) on the test set. Besides, combining a rich set of features without employing effective feature selection techniques and learning models hampered the performance of our model. However, our CSECU-DSG#1 system lacks by $\approx 9\%$ from the top-performing system NutCracker but surpassed the FastText baseline by $\approx 7\%$.

3.3 Discussion

We conduct the feature ablation study to evaluate the effectiveness of different types of features including pre-trained embedding features, n-gram features, and other hand-crafted features. To do this, we utilized our proposed CSECU-DSG#2 based on the validation set. The results are shown in Table 6.

Method	F1 score	Precision	Recall	Accuracy
CSECU-DSG#2	0.8598	0.8553	0.8644	0.8670
Feature Ablation Study				
−RoBERTa	0.8145	0.7587	0.8792	0.8110
−BERT	0.8237	0.8253	0.8962	0.8190
−N-gram	0.8245	0.7828	0.8707	0.8250
−Other HCF	0.8474	0.8253	0.8708	0.8520

Table 6: Feature ablation study on the validation set.

It showed that RoBERTa has the highest impact on the system's performance and the primary metric F1 score decreased by 4.53% while removing this feature. Besides, the F1 score decreased by 3.61%, 3.53%, and 1.24% when ablating the BERT, N-gram, and other hand-crafted features, respectively. This deduced the contribution of these features for informative tweet identification.

4 Conclusion and Future Directions

In this paper, we have explored various transfer learning features along with a rich set of hand-crafted features in an MLP based unified neural framework to identify the COVID-19 related informative tweets. We analyzed the effect of each feature type on the classification performances. Our systems achieved competitive performances among the participants' systems.

In the future, we have a plan to exploit the vast amount of COVID-19 related informative tweets to train and downstream fine-tune the various transfer learning models for extracting effective tweet representations. We also aim to inspect more proficient hand-crafted features for identifying COVID-19 related informative tweets.

References

Christos Baziotis, Nikos Pelekis, and Christos Doulkeridis. 2017. Datastories at semeval-2017 task 4: Deep lstm with attention for message-level and topic-based sentiment analysis. In *Proceedings of the 11th International Workshop on Semantic Evaluation (SemEval-2017)*, pages 747–754.

Cornelia Caragea, Adrian Silvescu, and Andrea H Tapia. 2016. Identifying informative messages in disaster events using convolutional neural networks. In *International Conference on Information Systems for Crisis Response and Management*, pages 137–147.

Abu Nowshed Chy, Md Zia Ullah, and Masaki Aono. 2017. Microblog retrieval using ensemble of feature sets through supervised feature selection. *IEICE TRANSACTIONS on Information and Systems*, 100(4):793–806.

Alexis Conneau, Douwe Kiela, Holger Schwenk, Loic Barrault, and Antoine Bordes. 2017. Supervised learning of universal sentence representations from natural language inference data. *arXiv preprint arXiv:1705.02364*.

Jacob Devlin, Ming-Wei Chang, Kenton Lee, and Kristina Toutanova. 2019. Bert: Pre-training of deep bidirectional transformers for language understanding. In *Proceedings of the 2019 Conference of the North American Chapter of the Association for Computational Linguistics: Human Language Technologies (NAACL:HLT)*, pages 4171–4186.

Noushin Fadaei, Chanjong Im, Sandip Modha, and Thomas Mandl. 2018. Daiict-hildesheim@ information retrieval from microblogs during disasters (irmidis 2018). In *Forum for Information Retrieval Evaluation (FIRE) (Working Notes)*, pages 15–17.

Bo Han, Paul Cook, and Timothy Baldwin. 2012. Automatically constructing a normalisation dictionary for microblogs. In *Proceedings of the 2012 Joint Conference on Empirical Methods in Natural Language Processing and Computational Natural Language Learning (EMNLP-CoNLL)*, pages 421–432. Association for Computational Linguistics (ACL).

Alexander Hogenboom, Danella Bal, Flavius Frasincar, Malissa Bal, Franciska De Jong, and Uzay Kaymak. 2015. Exploiting emoticons in polarity classification of text. *Journal of Web Engineering*, 14(1-2):22–40.

Tamanna Hossain, Robert L Logan IV, Arjuna Ugarte, Yoshitomo Matsubara, Sameer Singh, and Sean Young. 2020. Detecting covid-19 misinformation on social media. In *ACL 2020 Workshop on Natural Language Processing for COVID-19 (NLP-COVID)*.

Fei Liu, Fuliang Weng, and Xiao Jiang. 2012. A broad-coverage normalization system for social media language. In *Proceedings of the 50th Annual Meeting of the Association for Computational Linguistics (ACL): Long Papers-Volume 1*, pages 1035–1044. Association for Computational Linguistics (ACL).

Yinhan Liu, Myle Ott, Naman Goyal, Jingfei Du, Mandar Joshi, Danqi Chen, Omer Levy, Mike Lewis, Luke Zettlemoyer, and Veselin Stoyanov. 2019. Roberta: A robustly optimized bert pretraining approach. *arXiv preprint arXiv:1907.11692*.

Steven Loria, P Keen, M Honnibal, R Yankovsky, D Karesh, E Dempsey, et al. 2014. Textblob: simplified text processing. *Secondary TextBlob: simplified text processing*, 3.

Venkata Kishore Neppalli, Cornelia Caragea, and Doina Caragea. 2018. Deep neural networks versus naive bayes classifiers for identifying informative tweets during disasters. In *ISCRAM*.

Dat Quoc Nguyen, Thanh Vu, Afshin Rahimi, Mai Hoang Dao, Linh The Nguyen, and Long Doan. 2020. WNUT-2020 Task 2: Identification of Informative COVID-19 English Tweets. In *Proceedings of the 6th Workshop on Noisy User-generated Text*.

Endang Wahyu Pamungkas and Viviana Patti. 2018. # nondicevosulserio at semeval-2018 task 3: Exploiting emojis and affective content for irony detection in english tweets. In *Proceedings of The 12th International Workshop on Semantic Evaluation*, pages 649–654.

Lior Rokach. 2010. Ensemble-based classifiers. *Artificial Intelligence Review*, 33(1-2):1–39.

Umme Aymun Siddiqua, Tanveer Ahsan, and Abu Nowshed Chy. 2016. Combining a rule-based classifier with ensemble of feature sets and machine learning techniques for sentiment analysis on microblog. In *2016 19th International Conference on Computer and Information Technology (ICCIT)*, pages 304–309. IEEE.

Kevin Swanberg, Madiha Mirza, Ted Pedersen, and Zhenduo Wang. 2018. Alanis at semeval-2018 task 3: A feature engineering approach to irony detection in english tweets. In *Proceedings of The 12th International Workshop on Semantic Evaluation*, pages 507–511.

Mike Thelwall, Kevan Buckley, and Georgios Paltoglou. 2012. Sentiment strength detection for the social web. *Journal of the American Society for Information Science and Technology (JASIST)*, 63(1):163–173.

Junpei Zhou Xinyu Wang, Po-yao Huang, and Alexander Hauptmann. 2019. Cmu-informedia at trec 2019 incident streams track. In *Proceedings of the 28th Text REtrieval Conference (TREC)*. NIST.

Terry Windeatt. 2006. Accuracy/diversity and ensemble mlp classifier design. *IEEE Transactions on Neural Networks*, 17(5):1194–1211.

IRLab@IITBHU at WNUT-2020 Task 2: Identification of informative COVID-19 English Tweets using BERT

Supriya Chanda
IIT BHU
INDIA
supriyachanda.rs.cse18
@itbhu.ac.in

Eshita Nandy
Gauhati University
INDIA
nandyeshita4
@gmail.com

Sukomal Pal
IIT BHU
INDIA
spal.cse
@itbhu.ac.in

Abstract

This paper reports our submission to the shared Task 2: Identification of informative COVID-19 English tweets at W-NUT 2020. We attempted a few techniques, and we briefly explain here two models that showed promising results in tweet classification tasks: DistilBERT and FastText. DistilBERT achieves a F_1 score of 0.7508 on the test set, which is the best of our submissions.

1 Introduction

The WWW and then Web 2.0 enabled people to express their views and opinions through blog posts, online forums, product review websites, and social media. Millions of people use social network sites like Facebook, Twitter, LinkedIn, and Google Plus to express their emotions, opinions, and share views on different issues that matter in their lives. The present pandemic situation has severely reduced physical interaction and forced us to use virtual platforms where people inform and influence others. Social media generates a large volume of sentiment-rich data every day through tweets, status updates, blog posts, comments, reviews and so on. We often depend upon such user-generated content online to a great extent for decision making.

As the pandemic is spreading worldwide, online media is flooded with uncontrolled user-generated content, lot of which are not at all moderated or quality-checked. It, therefore, becomes more important to understand this spread, get aware of the differences between informative and uninformative news, and act upon it wisely.

Coronavirus causes illness, which can vary from common cold and cough to sometimes more severe disease. SARS-CoV-2 (n-coronavirus) is the new virus of this family, which has led to more than 1 million deaths worldwide[1].

Regularly, we find thousands of tweets by users worldwide, expressing their sentiments on COVID-19. Although these tweets often carry valuable information, they are unstructured and, are, therefore, challenging to process. So, analyzing these tweets is quite essential to understand whether they are informative ones or not.

We used a few machine learning approaches to classify test tweets as either informative or non-informative. Before the classification, we cleaned the tweets, constructed a representation of tweets with different word embedding techniques, and then built the classification model.

2 System Description

2.1 Datasets

The W-NUT shared task[2] organizers provided a dataset (Nguyen et al., 2020) that consists of 10K COVID-19 English tweets[3], that included 4719 tweets labeled as informative and 5281 tweets, labeled as uninformative. The statistics of training, development, and test data corpus collection and class distribution are shown in Table 1. Here, each tweet is annotated by three independent annotators, and an inter-annotator agreement score of Fleiss' Kappa at 0.818 is obtained. Some tweet examples from the training dataset are shown in Table 2.

2.2 Data Pre-processing

The Twitter dataset used in this work is already labeled into two classes: informative and uninformative. Before feeding them into classifier, tweets were pre-processed using the following steps:

---

[1] https://www.worldometers.info/coronavirus/
[2] http://noisy-text.github.io/2020/covid19tweet-task.html
[3] https://github.com/VinAIResearch/COVID19Tweet

Proceedings of the 2020 EMNLP Workshop W-NUT: The Sixth Workshop on Noisy User-generated Text, pages 399–403
Online, Nov 19, 2020. ©2020 Association for Computational Linguistics

Data	INF	UNI	TOTAL
Training	3303	3697	7000
Validation	472	528	1000
Test	944	1056	2000

Table 1: Training, Validation and Test Data set Collection and Class Distribution (informative as INF and uninformative as UNI)

- removal of the hashtag symbol (#) and all the user mentions (@USER)

- removal of stopwords using NLTK[4] library

- removal of Non-ASCII characters

- removal of all the emoticons, symbols, numbers, special characters.

2.3 Word Embedding

Word embedding is arguably the most widely known technique in the recent history of NLP. It captures semantic property of a word. We have used 200-dimension pre-trained GloVe[5] (Pennington et al., 2014) model, Word2Vec (Mikolov et al., 2013), and 300-dimension pre-trained FastText[6] (Mikolov et al., 2018) model for computing the word embedding. Also we have used `bert-base-uncased` and `distilbert-base-uncased` pre-trained models[7] to get a vector as an embedding for the sentence that we can use for classification.

- **Word2Vec:** Training tweets are used to train the model. Each word in the input text is characterized using N-dimensional vector. The dimension of the vector can be configured depending on the complexity of the text data. We used 200 dimensions. Tokens of each tweet are converted into a numerical vector of 200-dimensions before passing them to the model.

- **Glove:** GloVe (Global Vectors for Word Representation) is an extension to word2vec for efficiently learning word vectors. Unlike Word2vec, Glove does not depend on local

statistics, i.e. local context information of words, but contain global statistics like word co-occurrences.

- **FastText:** FastText, developed by Facebook, combines certain concepts introduced by the NLP and ML communities, representing sentences with a bag-of-words and n-grams using subword information and sharing them across classes through a hidden representation.

- **BERT:** Bidirectional Encoder Representations from Transformers (BERT) (Devlin et al., 2019) is a technique for NLP pre-training developed by Google. BERT is pre-trained on a large corpus of unlabelled text, including the entire Wikipedia (that is 2,500 million words!) and Book Corpus (800 million words). BERT-Base uncased have 12 layers (transformer blocks), 12 attention heads, and 110 million parameters.

- **DistilBERT:** DistilBERT (Sanh et al., 2019) is a smaller version of BERT developed and open-sourced by the team at HuggingFace. It is a lighter and faster version of BERT that roughly matches its performance. DistilBERT also compares surprisingly well to BERT on downstream tasks while having respectively about half and one third the number of parameters.

2.4 Classifiers

After pre-processing our data and transforming all the tweets into proper representation form, we implement our classification algorithms and construct our training models. We tried a few hand-picked algorithms, for instance, Logistic Regression, Support Vector Machine, XGBoost, Bidirectional Long Short-Term Memory (Bi-LSTM), and Gated recurrent units (GRU).

- **Support Vector Machine:** SVM, initially designed for binary classification, gives an excellent result for text categorization tasks such as sentiment analysis. Here we consider binary SVM for simplicity. SVM performs classification by finding an optimal hyper-plane that separates two classes. The optimal hyper-plane has a maximum margin (the distance between the nearest data point and hyperplane is called a margin). The datapoint that lies nearest to the hyper-plane is called the support vector.

---

[4] `https://www.nltk.org`

[5] `http://nlp.stanford.edu/data/glove.6B.zip`

[6] `https://fasttext.cc/docs/en/english-vectors.html`

[7] `https://huggingface.co/transformers/pretrained_models.html`

Sample tweets from dataset	Label
Democrats somehow managed to fight ebola without calling it "the African virus." A cluster of COVID-19 cases has emerged in New York CIty's Hassidic neighborhood, so it's only a matter of time before the local Trump Klux Klan starts talking about "the Jew virus."	UNINFORMATIVE
@USER @USER 1 week ago today (March 14), there were only 115 cases of CoVid in FL. Today, last count was at 763... that is a 563% increase in 1 week due to your "slave to Trump" incompetence. Imagine next Saturday if there is another 563% increase-we will be at 9300+. Resign	INFORMATIVE

Table 2: Example tweets from the COVID dataset for both labels

- **Gradient Boosting:** XGBoost is a scalable machine learning approach that has proved to be successful in a lot of data mining and machine learning challenges.

- **Bidirectional Long-Short Term Memory:** BiLSTM combines bidirectional recurrent neural network models and LSTM units to capture the context information. The BiLSTM model treats all inputs equally. For the task of sentiment analysis, the sentiment polarity of the text largely depends on the words with sentiment information. Firstly, the weighted word vectors are used as inputs of the BiLSTM model. Then outputs of the BiLSTM model are used as the representations of the comment texts.

- **Gated Recurrent Unit:** The Gated Recurrent Units (GRU) is the newer generation of Recurrent Neural networks, similar to LSTM. GRU does not have any cell state and used the hidden state to transfer information. It has only two gates, a reset gate and an update gate. GRU is preferred over LSTM because it performs well in terms of time consumption and memory utilization. In this model, we have obtained better accuracy with the GRU layer.

- **Logistic Regression:** Logistic Regression is a classification algorithm, particularly suitable for binary classification, as it provides us a baseline model. In our case, it produces a high-accuracy result.

2.5 Hyper-parameter Settings

We did stopword removal for all the models except DistilBERT and BERT. For Glove+GRU model, the dimension of word embeddings was 300, the hidden units of GRU was 128, `Optimizer` = adam, `loss function` = binary cross entropy, `Dropout` = 0.5, `activation function` = sigmoid. For

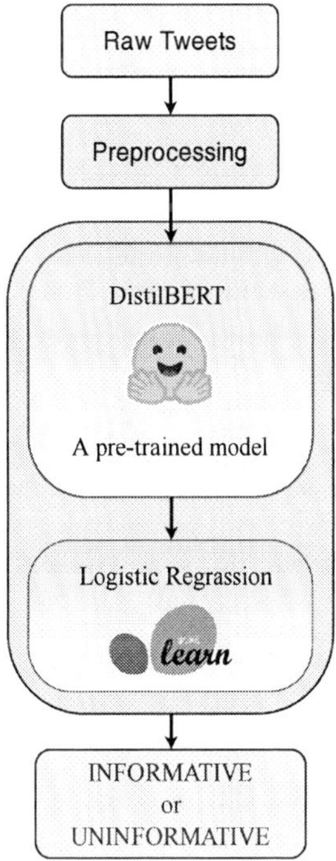

Figure 1: System 2 architecture

Glove+BiLSTM model, the dimension of word embeddings was 300, 3 dense layer `Optimizer` = adam, `loss function` = binary cross entropy, `Dropout` = 0.2, for the first two dense layer the was `activation function` relu and last dense layer it was sigmoid. For Fast-Text+BiLSTM model, the dimension of word embeddings was 300, 3 dense layer `Optimizer` = adam, `loss function` = binary cross entropy, `Dropout` = 0.2, for the first two dense layer the was `activation function` relu and last dense layer it was sigmoid.

3 Results and Analysis

We have used `scikit-learn`[8] machine learning package for the implementation. Table 4 reports our results on validation dataset for both classes

---

[8]`http://scikit-learn.org`

(INFORMATIVE and UNINFORMATIVE). We have selected two models that performed the best F_1 score during the validation phase and submitted it for the final prediction on the test dataset.

We have observed that DistilBERT and LR (Fig 1) gave better F_1 score than others as shown in Table 3. As mentioned in the organizer's evaluation criteria, the three evaluation matrices are calculated only for the INFORMATIVE class on test data. On validation data, we have calculated all matrices for both of the classes and put it on Table 4. That is why the evaluation results shown in Table 4 on validation data are slightly deviating from the evaluation result shown in Table 3 on test data provided by organizers. In the training data, there are some ambiguous keywords like *HTTPURL, coronavirus*. These words were present in both classes, so the models learned on this ambiguous data and got confused on validation data.

System(#)	F_1	Pre	Rec	Acc
FastText + GRU (1)	.7361	.7908	.6886	.7670
DistilBERT + LR (2)	.7508	.7904	.7150	.7760

Table 3: Evaluation results on test set

The experimental results show that DistilBERT outperforms on this task over BERT and others embedding techniques. We compare two network architectures, BiLSTM and GRU. The results show that the GRU model performs better than the BiLSTM model on this task. FastText outperforms over word2vec and Glove because FastText treats each word as a composed of character n-grams. If words are rare their character n grams are still shared with other words - hence the embeddings can still be good. where word2vec and Glove both treat words as the smallest unit to train on.

4 Conclusion

This study reports our system for shared task 2: Identification of informative COVID-19 English tweets in W-NUT 2020. We performed a comparative analysis of Machine learning models: Logistic Regression (LR), Support Vector Machine (SVM), and XG-Boost (XGB), Deep learning models: BiLSTM, GRU with few embedding techniques: Word2Vec, GloVe, FastText, BERT, and DistilBERT. Based on a series of experiments, we find that DistilBERT outperforms on this task. However, there is room for improvement. In the fu-

ture, we plan to use other pre-trained models with some fine-tuning.

References

Jacob Devlin, Ming-Wei Chang, Kenton Lee, and Kristina Toutanova. 2019. BERT: Pre-training of Deep Bidirectional Transformers for Language Understanding. In *Proceedings of the 2019 Conference of the North American Chapter of the Association for Computational Linguistics: Human Language Technologies, Volume 1 (Long and Short Papers)*, pages 4171–4186, Minneapolis, Minnesota. Association for Computational Linguistics.

Tomas Mikolov, Edouard Grave, Piotr Bojanowski, Christian Puhrsch, and Armand Joulin. 2018. Advances in pre-training distributed word representations. In *Proceedings of the International Conference on Language Resources and Evaluation (LREC 2018)*.

Tomas Mikolov, Ilya Sutskever, Kai Chen, Greg S Corrado, and Jeff Dean. 2013. Distributed Representations of Words and Phrases and their Compositionality. In C. J. C. Burges, L. Bottou, M. Welling, Z. Ghahramani, and K. Q. Weinberger, editors, *Advances in Neural Information Processing Systems 26*, pages 3111–3119. Curran Associates, Inc.

Dat Quoc Nguyen, Thanh Vu, Afshin Rahimi, Mai Hoang Dao, Linh The Nguyen, and Long Doan. 2020. WNUT-2020 Task 2: Identification of Informative COVID-19 English Tweets. In *Proceedings of the 6th Workshop on Noisy User-generated Text*.

Jeffrey Pennington, Richard Socher, and Christopher Manning. 2014. GloVe: Global Vectors for Word Representation. In *Proceedings of the 2014 Conference on Empirical Methods in Natural Language Processing (EMNLP)*, pages 1532–1543, Doha, Qatar. Association for Computational Linguistics.

Victor Sanh, Lysandre Debut, Julien Chaumond, and Thomas Wolf. 2019. DistilBERT, a distilled version of BERT: smaller, faster, cheaper and lighter.

	Word2Vec + SVM				Word2Vec + XGB			
	Precision	Recall	F_1-score	support	Precision	Recall	F_1-score	support
UNINFORMATIVE	0.78	0.85	0.81	528	0.76	0.84	0.80	528
INFORMATIVE	0.81	0.83	0.77	472	0.80	0.70	0.74	472
macro avg	0.79	0.79	0.79	1000	0.78	0.77	0.77	1000
weighted avg	0.79	0.79	0.79	1000	0.78	0.77	0.77	1000
Accuracy	0.79				0.77			
	Glove + Bi-LSTM				Glove + GRU			
UNINFORMATIVE	0.79	0.86	0.82	528	0.87	0.73	0.79	528
INFORMATIVE	0.82	0.74	0.78	472	0.75	0.88	0.81	472
macro avg	0.80	0.80	0.80	1000	0.81	0.81	0.80	1000
weighted avg	0.80	0.80	0.80	1000	0.81	0.80	0.80	1000
Accuracy	0.80				0.80			
	FastText + Bi-LSTM				FastText + GRU			
UNINFORMATIVE	0.80	0.84	0.82	528	0.84	0.78	0.81	528
INFORMATIVE	0.81	0.76	0.78	472	0.77	0.83	0.80	472
macro avg	0.80	0.80	0.80	1000	0.81	0.81	0.80	1000
weighted avg	0.80	0.80	0.80	1000	0.81	0.81	**0.81**	1000
Accuracy	0.80				0.81			
	DistilBERT + LR				DistilBERT + XGB			
UNINFORMATIVE	0.80	0.85	0.83	528	0.75	0.82	0.78	528
INFORMATIVE	0.82	0.77	0.79	472	0.77	0.69	0.73	472
macro avg	0.81	0.81	0.81	1000	0.76	0.75	0.76	1000
weighted avg	0.81	0.81	**0.81**	1000	0.76	0.76	0.76	1000
Accuracy	0.81				0.76			
	BERT + LR				BERT + XGB			
UNINFORMATIVE	0.77	0.82	0.79	528	0.75	0.79	0.76	528
INFORMATIVE	0.78	0.72	0.75	472	0.74	0.70	0.72	472
macro avg	0.77	0.77	0.77	1000	0.74	0.74	0.74	1000
weighted avg	0.77	0.77	0.77	1000	0.74	0.74	0.74	1000
Accuracy	0.77				0.74			

Table 4: Precision, recall, F_1-scores, and support for all experiments on validation dataset

NutCracker at WNUT-2020 Task 2: Robustly Identifying Informative COVID-19 Tweets using Ensembling and Adversarial Training

Priyanshu Kumar and Aadarsh Singh

Indian Institute of Technology (Indian School of Mines) Dhanbad, India
{kpriyanshu256, aadarshsingh191198 }@gmail.com

Abstract

We experiment with COVID-Twitter-BERT and RoBERTa models to identify informative COVID-19 tweets. We further experiment with adversarial training to make our models robust. The ensemble of COVID-Twitter-BERT and RoBERTa obtains a F1-score of 0.9096 (on the positive class) on the test data of WNUT-2020 Task 2 and ranks 1st on the leaderboard. The ensemble of the models trained using adversarial training also produces similar result.

1 Introduction

Since 2006, Twitter has been a popular social network where people express their thoughts and opinions on various topics. The enforcement of lockdown in various parts of the world, due to COVID-19, led to an increased usage of social media. Thus, the world has witnessed a plethora of tweets since the beginning of COVID-19. People have tweeted about many issues regarding the pandemic, mostly about the increasing infection rate, carelessness and incapability of governance and authorities to handle the increasing rate of cases. In addition, various preventive measures have also been conveyed through tweets.

Although there have been more than 600 million English tweets on COVID-19 (Lamsal, 2020) , only a few of them are informative enough to be used by various monitoring systems to update their databases. Manual identification of these informative tweets can be tedious and erroneous. Hence, there is a dire need to develop systems in the form of machine learning models that can help us in filtering informative tweets.

In this paper, we present our approaches for the shared task "Identification of informative COVID-19 English Tweets" organized under the Workshop on Noisy User-generated Text (W-NUT). Our

method makes use of ensembles consisting of Bidirectional Encoder Representations from Transformers (BERT) (Devlin et al., 2018) pretrained on COVID-19 tweets (Müller et al., 2020) and Robustly Optimized BERT Pretraining Approach (RoBERTa) (Liu et al., 2019). We also experiment with adversarial training so as to create models that generalise well and are robust.

The rest of the paper is organized as follows: Related work has been discussed in Section 2, followed by a brief description of the data used in Section 3. The proposed methods and experimental settings [1] have been elaborated in Section 4, 5 and 6. Section 7 and 8 contains the results and error analysis respectively. Section 9 concludes the paper and also includes possible future work.

2 Related Work

There has been much research to identify informative tweets during times of emergency and disaster. Neppalli et al. (2018) explored the performance of traditional machine learning algorithms and deep learning approaches for identifying informative tweets during disaster. They created manual features using the content of tweets for machine learning approaches and also tried out features obtained from Convolutional and Recurrent networks for deep learning approaches. A multi-modal approach for classifying informative tweets during disaster was proposed by Madichetty and Sridevi (2020). They combined the features obtained from text by a Convolutional Neural Network and the VGG-16 features obtained from the image accompanying the tweet, using late fusion for better performance than models using only text or only image.

---

[1] Source code available at https://github.com/kpriyanshu256/WNUT-2020-Task-2

Proceedings of the 2020 EMNLP Workshop W-NUT: The Sixth Workshop on Noisy User-generated Text, pages 404–408
Online, Nov 19, 2020. ©2020 Association for Computational Linguistics

Roy et al. (2020) proposed a classification and summarisation approach to identify informative tweets during the Fani cyclone (which occurred in 2019, affecting large parts of South-East Asia). They trained a Support Vector Machine (SVM) on linguistic features and Parts of Speech (POS) tags from tweets to identify informative tweets. To summarise the informative tweets, they experimented with Latent Semantic Analysis (LSA) and Luhn summarisation techniques. Zahera et al. (2019) experimented with the transformer based architecture BERT to classify disaster related tweets into multi-label information types. They preprocessed the tweets of TREC-IS dataset before feeding them into BERT to produce significantly better results than the median score. In addition, they also experimented with Focal loss instead of binary cross-entropy loss.

A new dataset for identifying informative tweet was released by Aggarwal (2019). The results of various machine learning algorithms using GloVe (Pennington et al., 2014) word embeddings, syntactic information in the form of tf-idf vectors and BERT embeddings were also presented in the work.

Due to the abundance of tweets related to COVID-19, many works have been done to analyze the content, intent and effect of such tweets. Singh et al. (2020) presented an analysis of COVID-19 tweets on the grounds of location, content and misinformation spread. A comprehensive study about the content of misinformative COVID-19 tweets and other aspects associated with them have been done by Shahi et al. (2020).

3   Dataset

The dataset (Nguyen et al., 2020) provided to the participants of the shared task contains 10,000 English COVID-19 tweets, out of which 4719 are labeled as INFORMATIVE and 5281 are labeled as UNINFORMATIVE. The tweets were annotated by 3 independent annotators and an inter-annotator agreement score of Fleiss' Kappa at 0.818 was obtained. The dataset contains the tweet ID, the tweet and the corresponding label.

4   Data Preprocessing

Twitter data contains a lot of noise. Therefore, preprocessing on Twitter data will help the pretrained models in better performance. We perform the following data preprocessing steps, most of which have been inspired from Müller et al. (2020) :

1. Unescape HTML tags

2. Remove unnecessary spaces, tabs and newlines

3. Replacing the the mentioned hyperlinks in the tweets (depicted as HTTPURL), with URL. A simple explanation for this could be that "URL" is a more commonly used expression of hyperlinks than HTTPURL.

4. Using the Python emoji [2] library to demojise the emojis i.e. replace them with a short textual description.

The user handles were already replaced by @USER in the tweets, hence no processing was required.

5   Models

We experiment with the following models and techniques:

1. **COVID-Twitter-BERT**: BERT is based on the Transformer architecture (Vaswani et al., 2017). It consists of multi-attention heads which apply a sequence-to-sequence transformation on the input text sequence. For its training, BERT makes use of the following objectives: (a) learn to predict a masked token using the left and right context of the text sequence (Masked Language Model) (b) learn to predict whether two sentences occur in continuation or not (Next Sentence Prediction)

   Müller et al. (2020) pretrain the large version of BERT (BERT-Large) on COVID-19 related tweets posted by users between January 12 and April 16, 2020. This version of BERT has a better understanding of the given data as compared to BERT-large, which is pretrained on texts from Wikipedia. Hence, COVID-Twitter-BERT will be even more beneficial for the task when fine tuned.

2. **RoBERTa Large**: RoBERTa has the same architecture as BERT, but is different from BERT on the grounds of pretraining, which helps in better optimisation and performance. RoBERTa is pretrained on a larger dataset as compared to BERT, uses a larger batch size and replaces the Next Sentence Prediction objective. It also uses dynamic masking pattern

---

[2] https://pypi.org/project/emoji/

as a better alternative to the static masking pattern used in BERT, i.e. RoBERTa duplicates the data and masks those differently each time, whereas BERT will mask the data only once.

3. **Adversarial Training**: With time, adversarial training is gaining popularity in Natural Language Processing (NLP) as well. In the field of Computer Vision, adversarial training is done by perturbing the input images slightly and minimising the adversarial loss. In NLP, the nature of input being discrete, small perturbations are done on the word embeddings. Adversarial training not only increases the robustness of models but also helps in better generalisation. Both properties are beneficial and desirable for identification of informative tweets.

Although many approaches for adversarial training in NLP have been developed, we experiment with the approach proposed by Miyato et al. (2016) with a slight modification. In their approach, first the word embeddings are normalized. The gradients are then computed using the data and the required perturbations are created using the obtained gradients.

Let the sequence of (normalized) word embedding vectors of a text be t. The model parameters are represented by θ. The probability of the text belonging to class y is given by $p(y|t; \theta)$. The adversarial perturbations z_{adv} are computed as follows:

$$g = \nabla_t \, log \, p(y|t; \theta)$$

$$z_{adv} = -\epsilon g / \| g \|_2$$

where ϵ is a hyper-parameter controlling the size of the perturbations. The adversarial loss is defined as :

$$L_{adv}(\theta) = -\frac{1}{N} \sum_{n=1}^{N} log \, p(y_n | t_n + z_{adv,n}; \theta)$$

By using the gradients calculated from the above loss, the weights of the model are updated (the non-perturbed word embeddings of the model are updated). The slight modification in our experiments is that we do not normalize our pretrained word embedding of the model, since it might change the semantic meaning of the pretrained word embeddings. We perform adversarial training on both COVID-Twitter-BERT and RoBERTa Large models using $\epsilon = 1$.

4. **Ensembling**: The ensembling of the predictions for our submissions is done at two levels-

    (a) Fold level i.e. the predictions obtained by the models trained using the different folds (during cross validation) are averaged.

    (b) Model level i.e. the fold level averaged predictions of the two different models are ensembled using averaging.

6   Experimental Settings

We concatenate the training and the validation data and perform a 5-fold stratified cross validation to train our models. Each fold is trained for 5 epochs using early stopping with patience of 3 and tolerance of 1e-3. The models are optimised using AdamW (Loshchilov and Hutter, 2017) with a learning rate of 2e-5 and a batch size of 16. The models have been implemented using Pytorch (Paszke et al., 2019) and Huggingface's Transformers (Wolf et al., 2019) library.

7   Results

We evaluate the performance of the models and their ensemble using cross-validation (CV). We also tabulate the models' performance on the test set as evaluated by the F1 score on the positive class.

The ensembling done at two levels increases the robustness of the results. The out-of-folds predictions were used to find the optimal threshold of the submissions, 0.498 for the ensemble without adversarial training and 0.487 for the ensemble with adversarial training. We also compare our results with the fastText-baseline (Joulin et al., 2016) by the organizers. Table 1 shows the results of our experiments.

The ensemble of COVID-Twitter-BERT and RoBERTa Large performs the best on the test data and also obtains the 1st rank on the leaderboard. Owing to its pretraining, COVID-Twitter-BERT performs better than RoBERTa Large. The adversarial training of the models is also found to boost the scores. The ensemble of adversarial models produces results similar to the ensemble of models trained without adversarial training.

Model	CV	Test
Baseline - fastText	-	0.7503
COVID-Twitter-BERT	0.9622	-
RoBERTa Large	0.9560	-
COVID-Twitter-BERT Adv.	0.9632	-
RoBERTa Large Adv.	0.9578	-
COVID-Twitter-BERT + RoBERTa Large	0.9636	**0.9096**
COVID-Twitter-BERT Adv. + RoBERTa Large Adv.	**0.9655**	0.9082

Table 1: Comparison of results.

8 Analysis

We perform our analysis on the out-of-folds predictions from our two ensembles - without adversarial training and with adversarial training.

We calculate the binary cross entropy loss for all samples and then examine some of the top common mis-classifications by both the ensembles (Table 2).

We observe that there are instances where our models are mistaken. A possible reason might be the variance in gold-labels of samples from annotator-to-annotator. This acts as noise in the labels of the data which is used to train the normal ensemble models. On the other hand, adversarial training adds some noise to the samples. Hence, the models in the adversarial ensemble have been trained on data which has a combination of existing noise and externally added noise. We believe that because of this difference in noise, the models in the two ensembles must be behaving in different ways. To inspect this, we examine the number of samples which have been inferred incorrectly by one ensemble and correctly by the other.

We observe that the normal ensemble misclassified a total of 277 samples whereas, only 260 samples were misclassified by the adversarial ensemble. Moreover, out of the 277 examples that were misclassified by the normal ensemble, 102 were correctly predicted by the adversarial ensemble. On the other hand, only 85 out of the 260 samples misclassified by the adversarial ensemble, were correctly predicted by the normal ensemble. Thus, it is evident that the models in both the ensembles have learnt different patterns from the data.

9 Conclusion

We explored the performance of COVID-Twitter-BERT and RoBERTa-Large at identifying COVID-19 English tweets that are informative in nature. Their ensemble achieves the state-of-the-art performance. Adversarial training is found to improve our model further. For future work, we can pre-train other Transformer-based models on COVID-19 tweets. Data augmentation techniques can help us generate more data for training models. We can also experiment with combining models trained with and without adversarial training.

Tweet	Label
Election Judge Hospitalized After Primary Dies Of Coronavirus #RIP #SemperFi fought for his life while @USER got her hair done #LetThatSinkIn "face of Chicago" thinks she's more important than Chicagoans welfare #LightfootLiedPeopleDied HTTPURL	UNINFORMATIVE
Austin area nursing home residents who test positive for COVID-19 but do not need to be in the hospital will soon be moving to one of two new "isolation facilities," one in Travis County, one in Williamson County: HTTPURL @USER	INFORMATIVE
LOCAL NEWS SHOUTOUT: Have a family member or close friend with a Michigan connection who has died from COVID-19 and would like to share their story with @USER Please contact Georgea Kovanis at gkovanis@USER	INFORMATIVE
BREAKING: Southern AB #coronavirus case rumored to be Steve Busey, the younger brother of movie star @USER According to our sources, Steve works in the oil & gas industry and is a huge @USER fan. #COVID19 HTTPURL	UNINFORMATIVE

Table 2: Some common highly misclassified samples.

Acknowledgments

We thank Google Colab for providing free GPU services for experimentation purposes.

References

Piush Aggarwal. 2019. Classification approaches to identify informative tweets. In *Proceedings of the Student Research Workshop Associated with RANLP 2019*, pages 7–15.

Jacob Devlin, Ming-Wei Chang, Kenton Lee, and Kristina Toutanova. 2018. Bert: Pre-training of deep bidirectional transformers for language understanding. *arXiv preprint arXiv:1810.04805*.

Armand Joulin, Edouard Grave, Piotr Bojanowski, and Tomas Mikolov. 2016. Bag of tricks for efficient text classification. *arXiv preprint arXiv:1607.01759*.

R Lamsal. 2020. Corona virus (covid-19) tweets dataset. *IEEE Dataport*.

Yinhan Liu, Myle Ott, Naman Goyal, Jingfei Du, Mandar Joshi, Danqi Chen, Omer Levy, Mike Lewis, Luke Zettlemoyer, and Veselin Stoyanov. 2019. Roberta: A robustly optimized bert pretraining approach. *arXiv preprint arXiv:1907.11692*.

Ilya Loshchilov and Frank Hutter. 2017. Fixing weight decay regularization in adam. *CoRR*, abs/1711.05101.

Sreenivasulu Madichetty and M Sridevi. 2020. Classifying informative and non-informative tweets from the twitter by adapting image features during disaster. *Multimedia Tools and Applications*, pages 1–23.

Takeru Miyato, Andrew M Dai, and Ian Goodfellow. 2016. Adversarial training methods for semi-supervised text classification. *arXiv preprint arXiv:1605.07725*.

Martin Müller, Marcel Salathé, and Per E Kummervold. 2020. Covid-twitter-bert: A natural language processing model to analyse covid-19 content on twitter. *arXiv preprint arXiv:2005.07503*.

Venkata Kishore Neppalli, Cornelia Caragea, and Doina Caragea. 2018. Deep neural networks versus naive bayes classifiers for identifying informative tweets during disasters. In *ISCRAM*.

Dat Quoc Nguyen, Thanh Vu, Afshin Rahimi, Mai Hoang Dao, Linh The Nguyen, and Long Doan. 2020. WNUT-2020 Task 2: Identification of Informative COVID-19 English Tweets. In *Proceedings of the 6th Workshop on Noisy User-generated Text*.

Adam Paszke, Sam Gross, Francisco Massa, Adam Lerer, James Bradbury, Gregory Chanan, Trevor Killeen, Zeming Lin, Natalia Gimelshein, Luca Antiga, et al. 2019. Pytorch: An imperative style, high-performance deep learning library. In *Advances in neural information processing systems*, pages 8026–8037.

Jeffrey Pennington, Richard Socher, and Christopher D Manning. 2014. Glove: Global vectors for word representation. In *Proceedings of the 2014 conference on empirical methods in natural language processing (EMNLP)*, pages 1532–1543.

Sujoy Roy, Sumit Mishra, and Rakesh Matam. 2020. Classification and summarization for informative tweets. In *2020 IEEE International Students' Conference on Electrical, Electronics and Computer Science (SCEECS)*, pages 1–4. IEEE.

Gautam Kishore Shahi, Anne Dirkson, and Tim A Majchrzak. 2020. An exploratory study of covid-19 misinformation on twitter. *arXiv preprint arXiv:2005.05710*.

Lisa Singh, Shweta Bansal, Leticia Bode, Ceren Budak, Guangqing Chi, Kornraphop Kawintiranon, Colton Padden, Rebecca Vanarsdall, Emily Vraga, and Yanchen Wang. 2020. A first look at covid-19 information and misinformation sharing on twitter. *arXiv preprint arXiv:2003.13907*.

Ashish Vaswani, Noam Shazeer, Niki Parmar, Jakob Uszkoreit, Llion Jones, Aidan N Gomez, Łukasz Kaiser, and Illia Polosukhin. 2017. Attention is all you need. In *Advances in neural information processing systems*, pages 5998–6008.

Thomas Wolf, Lysandre Debut, Victor Sanh, Julien Chaumond, Clement Delangue, Anthony Moi, Pierric Cistac, Tim Rault, Rémi Louf, Morgan Funtowicz, et al. 2019. Transformers: State-of-the-art natural language processing. *arXiv preprint arXiv:1910.03771*.

Hamada M Zahera, Ibrahim A Elgendy, Rricha Jalota, and Mohamed Ahmed Sherif. 2019. Fine-tuned bert model for multi-label tweets classification. In *TREC*.

DSC-IIT ISM at WNUT-2020 Task 2: Detection of COVID-19 informative tweets using RoBERTa

Sirigireddy Dhanalaxmi, Rohit Agarwal* and Aman Sinha*

Indian Institute of Technology (Indian School of Mines) Dhanbad, India
{sirigireddydhanalaxmi, agarwal.102497, amansinha091}@gmail.com

Abstract

Social media such as Twitter is a hotspot of user-generated information. In this ongoing Covid-19 pandemic, there has been an abundance of data on social media which can be classified as informative and uninformative content. In this paper, we present our work to detect informative Covid-19 English tweets using RoBERTa model as a part of the W-NUT workshop 2020. We show the efficacy of our model on a public dataset with an F1-score of 0.89 on the validation dataset and 0.87 on the leaderboard.

1 Introduction

Text analysis of social media data gives broader insights into various topics discussed among people. Twitter is a social media platform where people interact through short texts. This paper constitutes our work for the Shared Task 2 of the 6th Workshop on Noisy User-generated Text (W-NUT) (Nguyen et al., 2020) where we need to classify the Covid-19 English tweets as informative or uninformative. In the context of this shared task, a tweet is considered informative if it is about recovered, suspected, confirmed, and death cases and location or travel history of the cases, and all the other tweets fall into the category of uninformative class. Figure 1 shows an example of both informative and uninformative tweets.

We applied various machine learning models such as logistic regression, Naive Bayes, random forest classifier, support vector machine (SVM), and multi-layer perceptron (MLP). We have also used several state-of-the-art architectures like BERT, DistilBERT, RoBERTa, and ALBERT for detecting informative tweets. We provide a comparative study of all these models and found the RoBERTa model to perform best among all the models.

Informative:

Tweet Id: 1241132432402849793
Text: Latest Updates March 20 ⚠ 5274 new cases and 38 new deaths in the United States Illinois: Governo Pritzker issues "stay at home" order for all residents New York: Governor Cuomo orders 100% of all non-essential workers to stay home Penns...Source (/coronavirus/country/us/)

Uninformative:

Tweet Id: 1239673817552879619
Text: OKLAHOMA CITY — The State Department of Education announced Monday the closure of all K-12 public schools statewide until at least April 6 as the number of COVID-19 cases climb and the risk of community spread grows. HTTPURL

Figure 1: An example of informative and uninformative tweet.

This paper's outline is as follows: Section 2 discusses the previous works related to our paper. Section 3 describes the dataset and the data preprocessing steps. Section 4 describes our methods and section 5 discusses the implementation details of our approaches. Section 6 contains the analysis of the results, which is followed by the conclusion in section 7.

2 Related Work

Detection of useful-crisis-related content has been pivoting around Twitter due to its interactive media via microtexts (Martinez-Rojas et al., 2018). Continuous Bag-of-Words (CBoW) based approach has been used for text classification (Sriram et al., 2010). Castillo et al. (2011) proposes the use of different user-based features representing messages and tweet propagation for classifying tweet credibility.

---

* Equal contribution.

Proceedings of the 2020 EMNLP Workshop W-NUT: The Sixth Workshop on Noisy User-generated Text, pages 409–413
Online, Nov 19, 2020. ©2020 Association for Computational Linguistics

The figure and table at the top of the page:

Informative:

<u>Tweet Id</u>: 1241132432402849793
<u>Text</u>: latest updates march 20 warning selector 5274 new cases and 38 new deaths in the united states illinois governo pritzker issues stay at home order for all residents new york governor cuomo orders 100 of all non essential workers to stay home penns source coronavirus country us

Uninformative:

<u>Tweet Id</u>: 1239673817552879619
<u>Text</u>: oklahoma city the state department of education announced monday the closure of all k 12 public schools statewide until at least april 6 as the number of covid 19 cases climb and the risk of community spread grows

Figure 2: Preprocessed data of the examples shown in fig.1.

	Train	Validation
Number of samples in each class		
Informative	3303	472
Uninformative	3697	528
Word count - before preprocessing		
Maximum	76	62
Minimum	8	11
Average	35.87	37.052
Word count - after preprocessing		
Maximum	217	69
Minimum	7	10
Average	36.301	37.215

Table 1: Dataset statistics - number of samples in each classes, and word count before and after preprocessing data

Some works proposed use of SVM (Malmasi and Zampieri, 2018), logistic regression (Davidson et al., 2017), random forest classifier (Burnap and Williams, 2015) and word embedding based method (Badjatiya et al., 2017) for classification of tweet contents. Liu et al. (2017) provided the use of unsupervised methods to cluster news topics from tweets.

The capability of dependency learning and semantic information extraction enables us to learn complex decision boundaries. The evolution around capturing the semantic relationships between words lead to the widely used Transformer (Vaswani et al., 2017) architecture.

Such models have outperformed conventional methods over natural language processing (NLP) tasks. They have been widely used for various real-world applications such as language modeling (Wang et al., 2019), sarcasm detection (Kumar Jena et al., 2020), summarization (Egonmwan and Chali, 2019), and other language tasks.

3 Dataset

The training and validation data consists of 7000 and 1000 samples, respectively. The test dataset consists of 12000 tweets, out of which 2000 tweets were selected by the organizers for final evaluation. The actual labels of the test dataset was not revealed by the shared task, hence the accuracy metric is only reported for the validation dataset in this paper. The number of samples in each class is presented in Table 1. The maximum, minimum, and average word count of the train and validation data is also shown in Table 1.

Preprocessing data All the texts are converted to lower-case, and the emojis are replaced by their corresponding textual description. Further, contractions in the texts are fixed, and URLs and non-ascii characters are removed. It can be seen from Table 1 that the range of word count has increased after preprocessing for both the train and validation data. The word count increased due to emojis' conversion to text and decreased due to the removal of non-ascii characters. An example of a preprocessed tweet for both the informative and uninformative class is shown in Figure 2.

4 Methods

We have applied various conventional machine learning and transformer-based approaches.

4.1 Conventional approaches

We used traditional ways of word representation such as Bag-of-Words (BoW) and TF-IDF for detecting informative tweets using classifiers such as logistic regression, SVM, Naive Bayes, random forest classifier, and 2-layer MLP.

4.2 Transformer based approaches

Transformer is a way of improving the performance of NLP models. It is an encoder-decoder-type architecture that observes the whole of the input sequence at once. Unlike the recurrent sequential method, it uses an attention mechanism to detect long term dependencies. In this paper, we focus on experimenting with transformer-based architectures like BERT, DistilBERT, RoBERTa, and AL-BERT.

Classifier	Bag-of-Words	TF-IDF Vectors
Logistic Regression	0.78318	0.78331
SVM	0.78054	0.78472
Naive Bayes	0.76371	0.74449
Random Forest	0.55489	0.56447
MLP	0.78695	**0.79912**

Table 2: F1 score of conventional approaches.

BERT Devlin et al. (2018) presents a bi-directional transformer-based language model, pre-trained on deep bidirectional representations from unlabeled text. It is jointly conditioned on both left and right context in all layers, and it is known for outperforming several state-of-the-art systems for various NLP tasks. We have used BERT-base-uncased pre-trained model to perform the informative tweet classification.

DistilBERT Sanh et al. (2019) proposes an approximate version of BERT using half the number of parameters. It improves the inference time while retaining 97% of the performance of BERT. The pre-trained model we used is DistilBERT-base-uncased to analyze the comparative classification with respect to the BERT model.

RoBERTa Liu et al. (2019) adopts the training mechanism used by BERT with a significantly longer training time over longer sequences. It differs from BERT as it uses a dynamic masking pattern compared to static in prior. We have used RoBERTa-base pre-trained model. It is trained with a significantly large dataset and outperforms BERT, DistilBERT, and other variants for various downstream tasks.

ALBERT Lan et al. (2019) introduces another light version of BERT, with low memory consumption and high training speed by which it outperforms the state-of-the-art models for various benchmark datasets. In our experiment, we used the pre-trained ALBERT-base-v1 model.

We have used all these pretrained models with the same parameters (discussed in section 5.2) except for RoBERTa and DistilBERT, which required small changes. In RoBERTa, before tokenizing the sentences, prefix space has to be set true, along with the addition of special tokens. In DistilBERT, the token type id's are not considered.

5 Implementation

5.1 Conventional approach

The BoW and TF-IDF vectors are obtained after the given training, and validation sets undergo pre-processing procedure. The liblinear solver is used in the logistic regression. The maximum depth of the decision tree in random forest classifier is set as 8. In the MLP classifier, lbfgs solver is used with alpha value set as 1e-5, the number of hidden layers is 2 with 5 and 2 neurons in the first and second layers, respectively. Other parameters concerning the conventional methods use default values.

5.2 Transformer-based approach

The sentences after undergoing the cleaning process are tokenized using the pre-trained model's tokenizer. Special tokens are added to detect the start and end of a sentence, and each token is mapped with an id. Next, the padding layer is added with value 0 and truncated to a maximum length of 100 to maintain equal lengths of the embeddings. Attention masks are used to detect padded tokens and actual words. Mask is set to 0 if the token id is 0, else it is set to 1.

The actual training set is further split into two parts (9:1 ratio), i.e., train and dev set to check which learning rate the model performs better. The input arguments are passed to evaluate our validation dataset. Finally, the F1 score is calculated between predicted and actual labels of the validation set.

Reproducibility We have considered batch size as 32, the learning rate of the optimizer as 2e-5, and its epsilon value is set as 1e-8. We trained our model for 4 epochs as determined by optimising on the dev set. To get the reproducible results, we set the seed value for all the Python packages. The torch seed, manual seed, and NumPy seed are set as 0. Further, while using CuDNN backend, we set deterministic as true and benchmark as false.

6 Results

The F1 scores on the validation dataset obtained for conventional methods and transformer-based methods are presented in Table 2 and Table 3 respectively.

It is observed that the TF-IDF vectorizer gives better results when compared to BoW in almost all the conventional approaches. Among all the conventional approaches, MLP gives the best result.

The transformer-based methods performed better compared to all the conventional approaches. BERT and RoBERTa showed competitive performance. However, RoBERTa has shown better results compared to other transformers based methods.

Classifier	F1 score
BERT	0.88634
ALBERT	0.87786
DistilBERT	0.88061
RoBERTa	**0.88991**

Table 3: F1 score of transformer-based approaches.

7 Conclusion

Classifying Twitter texts has been at the forefront of various NLP applications. Here, in this paper we have worked on one such task of classifying a tweet as informative or uninformative in the context of Covid-19. We have extensively compared the performance of various methods for this task. We applied conventional approaches and the latest state-of-the-art transformer-based methods. The results shows that the RoBERTa gives superior result on this task.

Since Twitter is primarily a microblogging media, short text classification using topic modeling (Zhang et al., 2013; Blei and Lafferty, 2009), and topic-enhanced embedding-based approach. (Li et al., 2016) can also be useful for tweet classification. In future work, we wish to apply topic modeling to produce enhanced word embeddings for this task.

References

Pinkesh Badjatiya, Shashank Gupta, Manish Gupta, and Vasudeva Varma. 2017. Deep learning for hate speech detection in tweets. *CoRR*, abs/1706.00188.

David M Blei and John D Lafferty. 2009. Topic models. *Text mining: classification, clustering, and applications*, 10(71):34.

Pete Burnap and Matthew Williams. 2015. Cyber hate speech on twitter: An application of machine classification and statistical modeling for policy and decision making: Machine classification of cyber hate speech. *Policy Internet*, 7.

Carlos Castillo, Marcelo Mendoza, and Barbara Poblete. 2011. Information credibility on twitter. In *Proceedings of the 20th International Conference on World Wide Web*, WWW '11, page 675–684, New York, NY, USA. Association for Computing Machinery.

Thomas Davidson, Dana Warmsley, Michael Macy, and Ingmar Weber. 2017. Automated hate speech detection and the problem of offensive language.

Jacob Devlin, Ming-Wei Chang, Kenton Lee, and Kristina Toutanova. 2018. Bert: Pre-training of deep bidirectional transformers for language understanding. *arXiv preprint arXiv:1810.04805*.

Elozino Egonmwan and Yllias Chali. 2019. Transformer-based model for single documents neural summarization. In *Proceedings of the 3rd Workshop on Neural Generation and Translation*, pages 70–79, Hong Kong. Association for Computational Linguistics.

Amit Kumar Jena, Aman Sinha, and Rohit Agarwal. 2020. C-net: Contextual network for sarcasm detection. In *Proceedings of the Second Workshop on Figurative Language Processing*, pages 61–66, Online. Association for Computational Linguistics.

Zhenzhong Lan, Mingda Chen, Sebastian Goodman, Kevin Gimpel, Piyush Sharma, and Radu Soricut. 2019. Albert: A lite bert for self-supervised learning of language representations. *arXiv preprint arXiv:1909.11942*.

Quanzhi Li, Sameena Shah, Xiaomo Liu, Armineh Nourbakhsh, and Rui Fang. 2016. Tweetsift: Tweet topic classification based on entity knowledge base and topic enhanced word embedding. In *Proceedings of the 25th ACM International on Conference on Information and Knowledge Management*, pages 2429–2432.

X. Liu, A. Nourbakhsh, Q. Li, S. Shah, R. Martin, and J. Duprey. 2017. Reuters tracer: Toward automated news production using large scale social media data. In *2017 IEEE International Conference on Big Data (Big Data)*, pages 1483–1493.

Yinhan Liu, Myle Ott, Naman Goyal, Jingfei Du, Mandar Joshi, Danqi Chen, Omer Levy, Mike Lewis, Luke Zettlemoyer, and Veselin Stoyanov. 2019. Roberta: A robustly optimized bert pretraining approach. *arXiv preprint arXiv:1907.11692*.

Shervin Malmasi and Marcos Zampieri. 2018. Challenges in discriminating profanity from hate speech. *CoRR*, abs/1803.05495.

Maria Martinez-Rojas, Maria del Carmen Pardo-Ferreira, and Juan Carlos Rubio-Romero. 2018. Twitter as a tool for the management and analysis of emergency situations: A systematic literature review. *International Journal of Information Management*, 43:196–208.

Dat Quoc Nguyen, Thanh Vu, Afshin Rahimi, Mai Hoang Dao, Linh The Nguyen, and Long Doan. 2020. WNUT-2020 Task 2: Identification of Informative COVID-19 English Tweets. In *Proceedings of the 6th Workshop on Noisy User-generated Text*.

Victor Sanh, Lysandre Debut, Julien Chaumond, and Thomas Wolf. 2019. Distilbert, a distilled version of bert: smaller, faster, cheaper and lighter. *arXiv preprint arXiv:1910.01108*.

Bharath Sriram, Dave Fuhry, Engin Demir, Hakan Ferhatosmanoglu, and Murat Demirbas. 2010. Short text classification in twitter to improve information filtering. In *Proceedings of the 33rd international ACM SIGIR conference on Research and development in information retrieval*, pages 841–842.

Ashish Vaswani, Noam Shazeer, Niki Parmar, Jakob Uszkoreit, Llion Jones, Aidan N Gomez, Łukasz Kaiser, and Illia Polosukhin. 2017. Attention is all you need. In *Advances in neural information processing systems*, pages 5998–6008.

Chenguang Wang, Mu Li, and Alexander J. Smola. 2019. Language models with transformers. *CoRR*, abs/1904.09408.

Zhifei Zhang, Duoqian Miao, and Can Gao. 2013. Short text classification using latent dirichlet allocation. *Jisuanji Yingyong/ Journal of Computer Applications*, 33(6):1587–1590.

Linguist Geeks on WNUT-2020 Task 2: COVID-19 Informative Tweet Identification using Progressive Trained Language Models and Data Augmentation

Vasudev Awatramani[1]   **Anupam Kumar[1]**
[1]Maharaja Agrasen Institute of Technology
vasudev.w13@gmail.com, anupamkumar@mait.ac.in

Abstract

Since the outbreak of COVID-19, there has been a surge of digital content on social media. The content ranges from news articles, academic reports, tweets, videos, and even memes. Among such an overabundance of data, it is crucial to distinguish which information is actually informative or merely sensational, redundant or false. This work focuses on developing such a language system that can differentiate between Informative or Uninformative tweets associated with COVID-19 for WNUT-2020 Shared Task 2. For this purpose, we employ deep transfer learning models such as BERT along other techniques such as Noisy Data Augmentation and Progress Training. The approach achieves a competitive F1-score of 0.8715 on the final testing dataset.

1   Introduction

The aim of WNUT 2020 Task 2 (Nguyen et. al., 2020), is to produce methods that automatically classify whether an English Tweet associated with the novel coronavirus or COVID-19 is informative or not. An informative tweet may report information regarding recovered, suspected, confirmed and death cases or may include the knowledge of location or travel history of such occurrences. To accomplish such a system, we are provided with a dataset of 10,000 tweets, consisting of 7000 tweets for training, 1000 tweets for a validation set and 2000 tweets for the evaluation phase.

Our solution employed an ensemble of pre-trained models such as BERT (Devlin et. al., 2019), fine-tuned earlier on the task dataset, see Section 2. We also investigated text augmentation techniques such as replacing tokens with synonyms, random removal and swapping of tokens, see Section 3. The work also explored Progressive Training of a given model see Section 4. Certain aspects of these methodologies seemed to perform well and are discussed in detail.

2   Related Work

Sequence Labelling or Text Classification is one of the primary tasks in Computational Linguists. In general, the task contains different levels of scope such as Document Level, Paragraph Level, Sentence Level and Sub-sentence Level (words or groups of words). Typical pipeline for Sequence Labelling consists of feature extraction, followed by dimensionality reduction and a classification technique. Initial approaches for feature extraction involved techniques such as Term Frequency-Inverse Document Frequency (TF-IDF) (Salton et. al., 1998), Word2Vec (Goldberg et. al., 2014) or Global Vectors for Word Representation (GloVe) (Pennington et. al., 2014). Dimensionality reduction can help in reducing time and memory complexity if datasets contain a large vocabulary of unique words. Therefore, this step is sometimes left out nonetheless, prevalent methods for feature extraction include Principal Component Analysis (PCA), Linear Discriminant Analysis (LDA) or t-distributed stochastic neighbor embeddings (t-SNE). Early models for classification such as Naive Bayes, and Support Vector Machines have now been superseded by deep learning models. Such models incorporate sequential processing ability through architectures such as Recurrent Neural Networks which can be worked with a varied length of text sequences as well.

Lately, transfer learning has taken over these pipelines, producing high-quality textual representation by employing enormous corpora used in pre-training. Deep Learning methods have produced dominant performances in many

Proceedings of the 2020 EMNLP Workshop W-NUT: The Sixth Workshop on Noisy User-generated Text, pages 414–418
Online, Nov 19, 2020. ©2020 Association for Computational Linguistics

domains delivering state-of-the-art results. Transfer Learning is one such technique that has dominated this trend with models such as BERT (Devlin et. al., 2019) and RoBERTa (Liu et al., 2019) producing high performance on NLP benchmarks such as GLUE ().

3 Transfer Learning Ensemble

In our approach, we apply models like BERT that have already been pre-trained on data related to COVID-19. For this purpose, we used huggingface's transformers package (Wolf et. al.,2019).

Model	Acc.	F1-Score
CT-BERT	90.2	0.893
mrm8488/bioclinicalBERT-finetuned-covid-papers[1]	88.4	0.872
deepset/covid_bert_base[2]	87.0	0.860

Table 1. Various Models and their performance

Majority of the models that were tested are some variations of BERT. They vary in terms of data that have been fine-tuned on or number of parameters such as BERT-base or BERT-large (model architecture variants for BERT). For instance, deepset/covid_bert_base[2] is fine-tuned on CORD-19 dataset whereas CT-BERT (Müller et al.,2020) is trained on Crowbreaks Dataset(Müller et al.,2019).

In our system, we fine-tuned these models to the data in Shared Task 2 of WNUT 2020. Table 1 describes their performance in terms of accuracy and f1-score. There are slight variations in the training of these networks such as the optimiser used or number of epochs, however for the major part of the system we employed the following:

1. Weighted Adam or AdamW (Loshchilov et al.,2017) as the optimizer as opposed to Adam. The models seemed to converge with the learning rate of 3×10^{-5} and 1×10^{-8} as the epsilon value. We tried LAMB (You et. al.,2019) as well. Both of these optimisers, had similar effect on performance.

2. Dropout Layers with 0.5 dropout probability to counter overfitting.

3. The epochs varied between 3 to 5, corresponding to the model.

4. Some of the models were trained on TPU and rest of GPUs due to computational constraints. Batch size of 128 on TPU proved more benefitting in terms of performance over smaller batch-sizes for the same model.

Ensemble inference is a very popular trick in machine learning competitions. We employed an averaging ensemble of the models, to get an improved f1-score and accuracy on the validation set of 0.897 and 90.6 respectively. Though marginal, we employed the ensemble strategy for our final submission as well.

4 Data Augmentation

Another typical trick to enhance the performance of neural networks is to employ more training data. To this purpose, we applied Data Augmentation techniques that are loosely inspired by those used in computer vision. Moreover, we wanted to add some noise to the input text, in order to produce more robust models, particular because the tweets are ordinarily noisy due to use of emoticons, social media lingos, short forms and symbols such as #, @ or URLs in them. For a given sentence in the training set, performed one of the following procedures with respect to a random probability:

1. **Replacing tokens with Synonym:**
   Randomly choose n words from the sentence and replace each of these words with one of its WordNet synonyms.
   Original Tweet:
   *This week in podcast heaven: Roman Mars singing that one obscure song Reply All "covered" in a recent Super Tech Support **segment** to time his hand washing This **week** in podcast **hell**: Ira Glass **self** quarantining because he shook hands with someone who **tested** positive for COVID-19*
   Augmented Tweet:
   *This week in podcast heaven: Roman Mars singing that one obscure song Reply All " covered " in a recent Super Tech Support **section** to time his hand washing*

---

[1] https://huggingface.co/mrm8488/bioclinicalBERT-finetuned-covid-papers.
[2] https://huggingface.co/deepset/covid_bert_base
[3] https://github.com/makcedward/nlpaug.

2. **Random Swapping:**
Find a pair of random words in the sentence and rearrange their positions in the sentence.
Original Tweet:
*President Trump revealed a grim projection in the **coronavirus pandemic** on Tuesday: Even with the **social distancing** the US is doing now, 100k to 200,000 Americans will likely die as a result of **the ongoing** outbreak. "When you see 100,000 people, that's a minimum number" Trump said*
Augmented Text:
*President Trump revealed a grim projection in the **pandemic coronavirus** on Tuesday Even: with the **distancing social** the US is doing now, 100k to 200, 000 will Americans likely die as a result of **ongoing the** outbreak. you "When see 100, **people 000**, that' s a minimum number" Trump said*

3. **Removing Tokens Randomly:**
Randomly removing words in the sentence.
Original Tweet:
*Hawaii **has** its first case of #Coronavirus. @USER has been devoting more than an hour. Hawaii currently has capacity to only test 1600. **Officials** trying to retrace steps of 2 **tourists** from cruise ship who disembarked in Hilo & tested positive for virus. We are now affected too.*
Augmented Text:
Hawaii its first case. @USER has been devoting more than an hour. Hawaii currently has capacity to test 1600. trying retrace steps of 2 from cruise ship who disembarked in Hilo & tested positive for virus. now. We are now affected too.

For implementing such augmentations, we used Edward Ma's nlpaug package[3], however, we note that such techniques have been studied most recently in the paper EDA (Jason et. al.,2019).

Model	Acc.	F1-Score
Synonym Insertion	90.4	0.901
Random Removal	89.1	0.887
Random Swapping	90.1	0.893
Combination of all 3 Augmentations	90.7	0.902

Table 2. Effect of Augmentations

Table 2. compares the performance of CT-BERT (Müller et al.,2020) trained using augmentation training data, over original validation set.

Other augmentation techniques that we tried but did not use were Antonym Replacement and Sentence Augmentation with models such as GPT-2 (Radford et al.,2019). For instance, replacing with antonyms seemed to distort the meaning of the text unless, the random selection of words somehow resulted in some form of double negation.
Original Tweet:
*Frey says Minneapolis has 131 **known** positive cases of Covid19. So far the city has declined to give **regular** updates on this beyond Friday meetings. Would be nice to get some ward/neighborhood breakdowns, even if known positives don't paint the whole picture.*
Augmented Text with Antonym Replacement:
*Frey says Minneapolis has 131 **ignored** positive cases of Covid19. So far the city has accepted to give **irregular** updates on this beyond Friday meetings. Would be nice to get some ward/ neighborhood breakdowns, even if known positives don' t paint the whole picture.*

Similarly, with GPT-2 augmentations produced were distorting in cases we observed, such as unwarranted repetition of input sentence in the augmented text.

5 Progressive Training of Model

Progressive Training is one of the highly recommended techniques among deep learning practitioners, especially for its practical utility. This may involve training the model first on a smaller segment of the problem such that it training on a smaller sample of data, or priorly training on a smaller number of classes as opposed to all classes. A popular variation in Image Classification has been popularised by Jeremy Howard's FastAi lectures and library (Howard et al.,2020), that involves first training an image classification network on smaller sized images and then gradually increasing the dimensions. Similar intuition was extended for training of Generative Adversarial Networks by the ProGANS (Karras et al.,2017) study.

Inspired by the concept, we developed a similar method by performing the following steps:

1. Assume, the model consisting of two parts:
    a. Transformer Head: Consisting of a BERT architecture
    b. Classifier Network: Usually consists of Dense or Linear Layers.
2. Initially, the entire model is trained on smaller sized encoded vectors of the tweets, having length 128.
3. This is followed by fitting the same transformer head over encoded vectors having length 192, with an uninitialized classifier network
4. The above steps can be iterated up till the encode input length is 256.

Tokenized Vector Length	Acc.	F1-Score
128	90.2	0.893
192	91.13	0.905
256	91.63	0.913

Table 3. Comparison of Progressive Training

In our work, we followed the above described method gaining a marginal improvement as shown in Table 3.

6 Results

We made 2 submissions on the test set involving the following:

a. Ensemble of various BERT models trained over original inputs.
b. Progressively trained Digital Epidemiology Lab's CT-BERT model over augmented inputs.

From the results on the leaderboard, submission b. scored better with an f1-score of 0.8715.

7 Conclusion

We have outlined the motivation, design, and results of the WNUT Shared task 2 on detection of informative tweets pertaining to COVID-19 pandemic. We employed techniques such as Transfer Learning, Ensemble Learning, Data Augmentation and Progressive Training. However, we hope to study the task and come up with new findings in the future. One of the major aspects, we would like to analyze is the timestamp of the tweets. COVID-19 has had a very dynamic impact on social media, with varying trends concerning the number of cases, information regarding vaccine trials or new developments in social distancing guidelines. Therefore, in further work, we would like to include a temporal factor associated with these tweets for more reliable prediction on their informativeness. Furthermore, cross-lingual research and applications such as XLM-Roberta (Conneau et. al, 2020) have been rising in NLP studies. Therefore, data augmentations from multi-lingual or code-mixed tweets and microblogs sources about COVID-19 can comprehensively contribute to robust of the system such as ours. Lastly, to further increase the robustness of the model, we would like to explore techniques such as Knowledge Distillation.

References

Dat Quoc Nguyen, Thanh Vu, Afshin Rahimi, Mai Hoang Dao, Linh The Nguyen and Long Doan. 2020 WNUT-2020 Task 2: Identification of Informative COVID-19 *English Tweets*. In Proceedings of the 6th Workshop on Noisy User-generated Text.

Jacob Devlin, Ming-Wei Chang, Kenton Lee, and Kristina Toutanova. 2019. BERT: Pre-training of Deep Bidirectional Transformers for language understanding. Proceedings of the Annual Conference of the North American Chapter of the Association for Computational Linguistics: Human Language Technologies (NAACL-HLT), pages 4171–4186.

Liu, Y., Ott, M., Goyal, N., Du, J., Joshi, M., Chen, D., Levy, O., Lewis, M., Zettlemoyer, L., and Stoyanov, V. (2019c). Roberta: A robustly optimized bert pretraining approach.

Gerard Salton and Chris Buckley. (1998). Term-weighting approaches in automatic text retrieval. Inf. Process. Manag. 1988, 24, 513–523.

Yoav Goldberg. and Omer Levy. (2014). "word2vec Explained: deriving Mikolov et al.'s negative-sampling word-embedding method."

Pennington, J.; Socher, R.; Manning, C.D. Glove: Global Vectors for Word Representation. In Proceedings of the 2014 Conference on Empirical Methods in Natural Language Processing (EMNLP), Doha, Qatar, 25–29 October 2014; Volume 14, pp. 1532–1543

Wolf, T., Debut, L., Sanh, V., Chaumond, J., Delangue, C., Moi, A., Cistac, P., Rault, T., Louf, R., Funtowicz, M., and Brew, J. (2019). Huggingface's transformers: State-of-the-art natural language processing.

Ilya Loshchilov and Frank Hutter (2017), Decoupled Weight Decay Regularization.

Yang You, Jing Li, Sashank Reddi, Jonathan Hseu, Sanjiv Kumar, Srinadh Bhojanapalli, Xiaodan Song, James Demmel, Kurt Keutzer and Cho-Jui Hsieh (2019), Large Batch Optimization for Deep Learning: Training BERT in 76 minutes

Jason Wei and Kai Zou (2019), EDA: Easy Data Augmentation Techniques for Boosting Performance on Text Classification Tasks. Proceedings of the 2019 Conference on Empirical Methods in Natural Language Processing and the 9th International Joint Conference on Natural Language Processing (EMNLP-IJCNLP)

Martin Müller, Marcel Salathé and Per E Kummervold (2020), COVID-Twitter-BERT: A Natural Language Processing Model to Analyse COVID-19 Content on Twitter

Radford, Alec and Wu, Jeff and Child, Rewon and Luan, David and Amodei, Dario and Sutskever, Ilya (2019). Language Models are Unsupervised Multitask Learners

Martin M Müller and Marcel Salathé (2019). Crowdbreaks: Tracking health trends using public social media data and crowdsourcing. Frontiers in public health, 7, 2019.

Jeremy Howard and Sylvain Gugger (2020). fastai: A Layered API for Deep Learning

Tero Karras, Timo Aila, Samuli Laine and Jaakko Lehtinen (2017) Progressive Growing of GANs for Improved Quality, Stability, and Variation

Alexis Conneau, Kartikay Khandelwal, Naman Goyal, Vishrav Chaudhary, Guillaume Wenzek, Francisco Guzmán, Edouard Grave, Myle Ott, Luke Zettlemoyer, Veselin Stoyanov (2020). Unsupervised Cross-lingual Representation Learning at Scale

NLPRL at WNUT-2020 Task 2: ELMo-based System for Identification of COVID-19 Tweets

Rajesh Kumar Mundotiya, Rupjyoti Baruah, Bhavana Srivastava, Anil Kumar Singh
Department of Computer Science and Engineering
Indian Institute of Technology (BHU), India
Varanasi
{rajeshkm.rs.cse16, rupjyotibaruah.rs.cse18}@iitbhu.ac.in
{bhavanasrivastava.rs.cse17, aksingh.cse}@iitbhu.ac.in

Abstract

The Coronavirus pandemic has been a dominating news on social media for the last many months. Efforts are being made to reduce its spread and reduce the casualties as well as new infections. For this purpose, the information about the infected people and their related symptoms, as available on social media, such as Twitter, can help in prevention and taking precautions. This is an example of using noisy text processing for disaster management. This paper discusses the NLPRL results in Shared Task-2 of WNUT-2020 workshop. We have considered this problem as a binary classification problem and have used a pre-trained ELMo embedding with GRU units. This approach helps classify the tweets with accuracy as 80.85% and 78.54% as F1-score on the provided test dataset. The experimental code is available online[1].

1 Introduction

The Coronavirus disease (officially named COVID-19 by the World Health Organization or WHO on February 11, 2020) is still spreading worldwide, although the numbers in some countries have decreased. In mid-June 2020, there was fear and panic all around the world related to the COVID-19 outbreak. Twitter has been used for gathering information about crisis communications (Cho et al., 2013). There have been a massive number of tweets about the pandemic. One estimate puts the number at about four million COVID-19 English tweets daily (Lamsal, 2020).

For our task, the tweets can be classified in two categories: informative and uninformative. Informative tweets contain some useful information about the pandemic and the affected people and they can help in managing the spread of the pandemic. The rest can be treated as uninformative tweets. The informative tweets provide information about recovered, suspected, confirmed, and deceased cases, and possibly also about a person's location or travel history. The majority of tweets are uninformative. This kind of classification is an example of text classification, which is a core task in many areas of Natural Language Processing (NLP).

2 Related work

Continuous availability of vital number of Twitter posts has been useful for developing more accurate and reliable classification methods for noisy text. Conventional NLP techniques and machine learning-based classification methods do not seem to perform well with Twitter data. Jiang et al. (2018) described a work on identifying health-related Personal Experience Tweets (PET) by combining word embedding and an LSTM neural network that demonstrated significant improvement (with $p < 0.01$) in performance measures of accuracy, precision, recall, F1-score, and ROC/AUC over the conventional methods in identifying PETs.

In the past few months, many researchers have tried out several mathematical and statistical models to predict novel Coronavirus transmission (Zhao et al., 2020; Shim et al., 2020; Benvenuto et al., 2020). Since the COVID-19 dataset is of a time series nature, it is natural to use sequential networks to extract the patterns from it. Some studies have used LSTM networks to forecast the spread of infectious diseases such as the current COVID-19 epidemic (Chimmula and Zhang (2020); Bandyopadhyay and Dutta (2020); Huang et al. (2020); Tomar and Gupta (2020); Pal et al. (2020)).

Dubey (2020), who analyzed the country-wise sentiment analysis of tweets and emotions of the

---

[1]https://github.com/Rajesh-NLP/
Identification_of_informative_COVID-19_
English_Tweets-WNUT-20

Proceedings of the 2020 EMNLP Workshop W-NUT: The Sixth Workshop on Noisy User-generated Text, pages 419–422
Online, Nov 19, 2020. ©2020 Association for Computational Linguistics

people from 12 countries (11th March 2020 to 31st March 2020) revealed that countries like Australia, Belgium, and India were tweeting about COVID-19 with a positive sentiment and people in China had negative sentiments about the same.

Arora et al. (2020) proposed deep learning models to predict the number of COVID-19 positive cases in 32 states of India and its Union Territories. Using RNN based LSTM cells and its variants such as deep LSTM, convolutional LSTM, and bi-directional LSTM as predictive models led to the conclusion that at present Bi-directional LSTM gives the best results, and convolutional LSTM gives the lowest results based on prediction errors.

Contextual embeddings are known to provide better results on the basic NLP problems such as Sentiment analysis (Wang et al., 2020; Müller et al., 2020; Kruspe et al., 2020; Akbik et al., 2018). In this paper, we made an effort to automatically identify whether a COVID-19 English tweet is informative or not, using a model based on a contextual embedding called ELMo (Peters et al., 2018). The dataset of 10K COVID-19 English tweets was provided by the organizers of the shared task.

3   Problem Statement

The goal of WNUT-2020 Task 2, named as the "Identification of informative COVID-19 English tweets", is to classify COVID-19 tweets into informative and uninformative categories. This is a binary classification task to learn $F : X \rightarrow Y$ where $X = \{X_1, X_2, X_3 \ldots, X_m\}$ is a tweet of length m and $Y \in \{informative, uninformative\}$.

4   System Description

Word embeddings or distributed representations of words use dense, real-valued vectors to represent vocabulary words. Word embeddings have a much smaller dimension than the size of the vocabulary and carry syntactic and semantic information about the words, unlike one-hot vectors. In this paper, we use ELMo (Embeddings from Language Models) method proposed by Peters et al. (2018) for word embeddings. The dimensionality of each word vector is 2048.

The Bi-GRU model is a variation of RNN (Hermans and Schrauwen, 2013) that simultaneously models the word representation with its preceding and following information. The output of the word embedding is fed to the GRU(Cho et al., 2014) unit. This GRU unit is then passed to a linear layer for predicting the classes.

5   System Training

The provided dataset (Nguyen et al., 2020) contains 10000 tweets, out of which 4719 tweets are informative, whereas the rest are labeled as uninformative. The dataset is divided into three sub-parts, each used to train, tune and test the model, respectively. The statistics for these sub-parts of the dataset, according to the class, are mentioned in Table 1.

Dataset	Informative	Uninformative
Train	3303	3697
Development	472	528
Test	944	1056

Table 1: Number of tweets in the dataset partitions used for the experiment

We have used pre-trained ELMo embedding with the size of 2048, with 512 GRU hidden units, and 0.5 as the dropout to perform our experiments. The model was trained by using the flair library (Akbik et al., 2019) at a batch size of 32 for 30 epochs, and with a learning rate of 0.1. To prevent overfitting of the model training, we have used the early-stoppage and the patience value of 3.

6   Results

ELMo and contextual string embeddings (Akbik et al., 2018) (released in the Flair framework[2]) are prominent embedding techniques that consider contextual information while generating the word embedding. We tried both an ELMo-based model and a Flair-based model. The embedding used for the Flair-based model was the Flair embedding (not the Pooled Flair embedding). The pre-trained models of these techniques are trained on the news domain for English. In our experiments on the development data, ELMo gave better results. Hence, for the submitted system for test dataset, we have used the ELMo-based model. Using the provided dataset, we obtained the 78.54% as weighted F1-score on the test dataset, whereas 84.79% by ELMo-based model and 83.60% by Flair-based model on the development dataset. The evaluation of the test and development dataset with the usual metrics are outlined in Table 2.

---

[2]`https://github.com/flairNLP/flair/blob/master/resources/docs/embeddings/FLAIR_EMBEDDINGS.md`

Dataset	P	R	F1	Accuracy
Test$_{ELMo}$	83.35	74.26	78.54	80.85
Dev$_{ELMo}$	84.80	84.80	84.79	84.80
Dev$_{Flair}$	84.11	83.10	83.60	84.10

Table 2: Classification results obtained from various evaluation metrics (**P**recision, **R**ecall, weighted **F1**-score and Accuracy) on the Test and Development (Dev) dataset

The *informative* class F1-score obtained on the development dataset (83.69% with ELMo-based model and 83.96% with Flair-based model) are given in Table 3.

Model	Precision	Recall	F1-score
ELMo	84.78	82.63	83.69
Flair	85.34	82.63	83.96

Table 3: Classification results on the *informative* class obtained from various evaluation metrics on the development dataset for the two methods

7 Conclusion

This system description paper reports a simple method that leverages the ELMo embedding features to train a COVID-19 informative tweet identification system. We obtained 78.54% F1-score on the test dataset with ELMo-based approach. For future work, we will use this model with adverse regularization, in order to make it more robust. Further, the self-learning algorithm can be applied an available large monolingual corpus gathered from Twitter.

Acknowledgments

The support and the resources provided by Param Shivay facility under the National Supercomputing Mission, Government of India at the Indian Institute of Technology, Varanasi are gratefully acknowledged.

References

Alan Akbik, Tanja Bergmann, Duncan Blythe, Kashif Rasul, Stefan Schweter, and Roland Vollgraf. 2019. FLAIR: An easy-to-use framework for state-of-the-art NLP. In *Proceedings of the 2019 Conference of the North American Chapter of the Association for Computational Linguistics (Demonstrations)*, pages 54–59, Minneapolis, Minnesota. Association for Computational Linguistics.

Alan Akbik, Duncan Blythe, and Roland Vollgraf. 2018. Contextual string embeddings for sequence labeling. In *Proceedings of the 27th International Conference on Computational Linguistics*, pages 1638–1649, Santa Fe, New Mexico, USA. Association for Computational Linguistics.

Parul Arora, Himanshu Kumar, and Bijaya Ketan Panigrahi. 2020. Prediction and analysis of covid-19 positive cases using deep learning models: A descriptive case study of india. *Chaos, Solitons & Fractals*, 139:110017.

Samir Kumar Bandyopadhyay and Shawni Dutta. 2020. Machine learning approach for confirmation of covid-19 cases: Positive, negative, death and release. *medRxiv*.

Domenico Benvenuto, Marta Giovanetti, Lazzaro Vassallo, Silvia Angeletti, and Massimo Ciccozzi. 2020. Application of the arima model on the covid-2019 epidemic dataset. *Data in brief*, page 105340.

Vinay Kumar Reddy Chimmula and Lei Zhang. 2020. Time series forecasting of covid-19 transmission in canada using lstm networks. *Chaos, Solitons & Fractals*, page 109864.

Kyunghyun Cho, Bart Van Merriënboer, Dzmitry Bahdanau, and Yoshua Bengio. 2014. On the properties of neural machine translation: Encoder-decoder approaches. *arXiv preprint arXiv:1409.1259*.

Seong Eun Cho, Kyujin Jung, and Han Woo Park. 2013. Social media use during japan's 2011 earthquake: how twitter transforms the locus of crisis communication. *Media International Australia*, 149(1):28–40.

Akash Dutt Dubey. 2020. Twitter sentiment analysis during covid19 outbreak. *Available at SSRN 3572023*.

Michiel Hermans and Benjamin Schrauwen. 2013. Training and analysing deep recurrent neural networks. In C. J. C. Burges, L. Bottou, M. Welling, Z. Ghahramani, and K. Q. Weinberger, editors, *Advances in Neural Information Processing Systems 26*, pages 190–198. Curran Associates, Inc.

Chiou-Jye Huang, Yung-Hsiang Chen, Yuxuan Ma, and Ping-Huan Kuo. 2020. Multiple-input deep convolutional neural network model for covid-19 forecasting in china. *medRxiv*.

Keyuan Jiang, Shichao Feng, Qunhao Song, Ricardo A Calix, Matrika Gupta, and Gordon R Bernard. 2018. Identifying tweets of personal health experience through word embedding and lstm neural network. *BMC bioinformatics*, 19(8):210.

Anna Kruspe, Matthias Häberle, Iona Kuhn, and Xiao Xiang Zhu. 2020. Cross-language sentiment analysis of european twitter messages duringthe covid-19 pandemic. *arXiv preprint arXiv:2008.12172*.

Rabindra Lamsal. 2020. Coronavirus (covid-19) tweets dataset.

Martin Müller, Marcel Salathé, and Per E Kummervold. 2020. Covid-twitter-bert: A natural language processing model to analyse covid-19 content on twitter. *arXiv preprint arXiv:2005.07503*.

Dat Quoc Nguyen, Thanh Vu, Afshin Rahimi, Mai Hoang Dao, Linh The Nguyen, and Long Doan. 2020. WNUT-2020 Task 2: Identification of Informative COVID-19 English Tweets. In *Proceedings of the 6th Workshop on Noisy User-generated Text*.

Ratnabali Pal, Arif Ahmed Sekh, Samarjit Kar, and Dilip K Prasad. 2020. Neural network based country wise risk prediction of covid-19. *arXiv preprint arXiv:2004.00959*.

Matthew E Peters, Mark Neumann, Mohit Iyyer, Matt Gardner, Christopher Clark, Kenton Lee, and Luke Zettlemoyer. 2018. Deep contextualized word representations. *arXiv preprint arXiv:1802.05365*.

Eunha Shim, Amna Tariq, Wongyeong Choi, Yiseul Lee, and Gerardo Chowell. 2020. Transmission potential and severity of covid-19 in south korea. *International Journal of Infectious Diseases*.

Anuradha Tomar and Neeraj Gupta. 2020. Prediction for the spread of covid-19 in india and effectiveness of preventive measures. *Science of The Total Environment*, page 138762.

T. Wang, K. Lu, K. P. Chow, and Q. Zhu. 2020. Covid-19 sensing: Negative sentiment analysis on social media in china via bert model. *IEEE Access*, 8:138162–138169.

Shi Zhao, Qianyin Lin, Jinjun Ran, Salihu S Musa, Guangpu Yang, Weiming Wang, Yijun Lou, Daozhou Gao, Lin Yang, Daihai He, et al. 2020. Preliminary estimation of the basic reproduction number of novel coronavirus (2019-ncov) in china, from 2019 to 2020: A data-driven analysis in the early phase of the outbreak. *International journal of infectious diseases*, 92:214–217.

SU-NLP at W-NUT 2020 Task 2: Ensemble Models for Informative Tweet Classification

Kenan Fayoumi
Sabancı University
Istanbul, Turkey
`kenanf@sabanciuniv.edu`

Reyyan Yeniterzi
Sabancı University
Istanbul, Turkey
`reyyan@sabanciuniv.edu`

Abstract

In this paper, we address the problem of identifying informative tweets related to COVID-19 in the form of a binary classification task as part of our submission for W-NUT 2020 Task 2. Specifically, we focus on ensembling methods to boost the classification performance of classification models such as BERT and CNN. We show that ensembling can reduce the variance in performance, specifically for BERT base models.

1 Introduction

After the recent virus outbreak, social media platforms, like Twitter, have been flooded with COVID-19 related content. Some of those content contain useful and valuable information such as the current status of the outbreak in particular locations. However, like any other topic being discussed in social media, the majority of the content is unrelated, subjective, or uninformative. Finding informative content would require extensive manual search, which is not scalable due to the size of the content. Therefore, automatically identifying both relevant and informative content has become an important task. In this paper, we study this specific problem as part of the W-NUT 2020 shared-task on identification of informative COVID-19 English tweets, and report our findings.

We specifically focused on transformer based neural network architectures and also simple but still effective CNN models. We also experiment with ensembling different models as we attempt to reduce the performance variance introduced from a model and combine strength of models in order to improve the final classification performance. Code to our classification and ensemble methods are available at our Github repository [1] .

[1] `https://github.com/SU-NLP/`
`W-NUT2020-Task-2`

2 Data and Task Description

Twitter, which is full of noisy user-generated content, was specifically chosen by the organizers and 10K COVID-19 related tweets were collected and labeled (Nguyen et al., 2020). Collected tweets were labeled as either informative or not. Informative tweets are tweets that provide information about recovered, suspected, confirmed and death cases as well as location or travel history of the cases. Within the collected 10K tweets, 4719 of them were labeled as informative, while the rest 5281 as uninformative. The dataset was split into 70/10/20 for training/validation/test. The test set has not been released publicly, therefore most of our experimental results are over the validation set. Informative class F1 score was used as the official evaluation metric for this task.

3 Classification Models

We approached the problem by first training different classification models, and then combining their strengths. As our first model, we chose a simple yet effective CNN text classification model. As for the rest, three pre-trained transformer-based models were adapted for our particular task. In this section, we discuss these models and their performances.

3.1 CNN

As our baseline experiment, we chose a very common CNN architecture by Kim (2014). CNN has previously proven successful in NLP tasks and we believe it's a strong baseline for text classification tasks. In this article, Kim (2014) showed the useful effects of pre-trained word embeddings on several text classification tasks. Similarly, given that our data is from Twitter, we used two pre-trained embeddings which had been trained on tweets. These are the Glove Twitter 200-dimensional embeddings

Proceedings of the 2020 EMNLP Workshop W-NUT: The Sixth Workshop on Noisy User-generated Text, pages 423–427
Online, Nov 19, 2020. ©2020 Association for Computational Linguistics

trained with 2 billion tweets [2], and the Word2Vec embeddings [3] which had been trained on 400 million tweets and has 400 dimensions.

After hyper-parameter tuning, the optimum setting for the CNN-based models has been found as the following: filter windows of 2, 3, 4, 5 with 300 feature map in each, Rectified Linear Unit (ReLu) activation function, a dropout rate of 20%. Using Adam optimizer for training with a learning rate of 0.001, and 16 as the batch size. All tweets are tokenized by white-spaces and then padded or cropped to a length of 128 tokens.

3.2 BERT

As our stronger baseline, we chose Bidirectional Encoder Representations (BERT) (Devlin et al., 2018). BERT models had been pre-trained over large document collections (Wikipedia and books) in unsupervised manner. Later on, they can be fine-tuned for a particular task by using labeled data of that corresponding task. Similarly we fine-tuned the base BERT model (12 layers, 12 attention heads, and 110 million parameters) for our classification task.

HuggingFace implementation of BERT [4] was used with the following optimized hyper-parameters: learning rate is 1e-5, training batch size is 8, and all tweets are cropped or padded to 128 tokens.

3.3 ALBERT

We also used A Lite BERT for Self-supervised Learning of Language Representations (ALBERT) (Lan et al., 2019). ALBERT had been trained on the same corpus as BERT. It is not only lighter, but it also surpassed BERT in many NLP tasks.

We used the HuggingFace implementation for ALBERT base model [5] and the same hyper-parameters used with BERT.

3.4 CT-BERT

Recent work, like BIOBERT (Lee et al., 2019) and SCIBERT (Beltagy et al., 2019), have shown that pre-training transformer models with specialized corporas can boost performances for domain-specific tasks. Similarly, CT-BERT, (Müller et al.,

2020) which had been pre-trained on a corpus of 22.5 million tweets related to COVID-19, falls into the same domain of our task of tweets about Covid-19, and therefore was explored.

Pre-trained model weights are provided in the authors Github page [6]. Same hyper-parameter setting used in BERT and ALBERT, was also used in this setting.

3.5 Experiments

All classification models' performances on the validation set is reported in Table 1 .

Model	F1 Score
CNN Glove	0.8320
CNN W2V	0.8355
BERT	0.8848
ALBERT	0.8954
CT-BERT	0.9049

Table 1: The performances of the individual classification models on the validation set

According to Table 1, two CNN models with different pre-trained embeddings returned similar performances, but overall performed poorly compared to the BERT model. Even though BERT pre-training data did not contain either tweets or COVID-19 related content, it performed much better due to its better learning capacity.

Similar to the prior literature on text classification, ALBERT, which had been trained on the same corpora as BERT, outperformed BERT in this task as well. CT-BERT which had been trained over a much smaller but more domain-specific dataset (COVID-19 related tweets) has outperformed both BERT and ALBERT in this classification task. Once again, this shows the useful effects of using more specific data collections even in unsupervised pre-training.

3.6 Further Analysis

In order to see whether these models make the same mistakes or not, models' predictions on validation set instances were analyzed. Figure 1 contains examples from the validation set which were misclassified by any one of the models. In the figure, each row represents one instance, black signifies the Informative class examples and pink for the

[2]http://nlp.stanford.edu/data/
wordvecs/glove.twitter.27B.zip
[3]https://github.com/FredericGodin/
TwitterEmbeddings
[4]https://huggingface.co/
bert-base-uncased
[5]https://huggingface.co/albert-base-v2
[6]https://github.com/
digitalepidemiologylab/
COVID-twitter-bert

Uninformative examples. Gold column is the true labels and other columns represents the individual classification models.

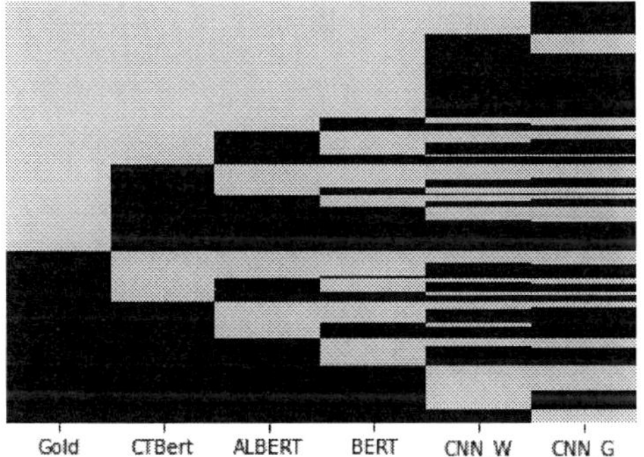

Figure 1: This figure contains all examples from the validation set that were misclassified by any of the listed models.

In Figure 1, one can see the similarity between the predictions made by BERT-based models: BERT, CT-BERT and ALBERT. CNN-based models (Word2Vec and Glove) also made similar mistakes which none of the BERT-based models did. We can also observe that CNN models, BERT and ALBERT have made the correct classification on some examples where our best model CT-BERT has failed. Combining strengths of these different models can improve the decision on these misclassified examples.

We also analyzed the possible performance variance in these models. BERT-base models which are fine-tuned on small data collections suffer from variance in performance. This is due to the randomly initialized weights in the final prediction layer built on top of BERT. Changing the random seed or slightly modifying the input can have an observable effect on the performance. To analyze this effect we trained 5 models with identical hyperparameters and different initial random seeds for all our BERT-based models. Performances of each model and each run on the validation set are reported in Table 2. We can see the difference between the best performing ALBERT model and the worst ALBERT model is more than 0.02 points. Slightly less but similar variance also exists for different BERT and CT-BERT models.

This variance between different versions of the same model, and different architectures having different strengths let us towards ensembling models.

	BERT	ALBERT	CT-BERT
	0.8833	0.8953	0.9115
	0.8789	0.8884	0.9083
	0.8742	0.8879	0.9070
	0.8722	0.8806	0.9050
	0.8669	0.8750	0.8990
Mean	0.8751	0.8854	0.9061

Table 2: The F1 Scores of 5 different randomly initialized BERT, ALBERT and CT-BERT models on the validation set.

4 Ensemble Methods

In this section we describe our two approaches to address the issue of variance in model performances and improve the overall classification accuracy. Our approaches focus on ensembling the probabilities of multiple classification models while making predictions.

4.1 SUM Ensemble

According to Figure 1, each individual model is predicting wrong labels for some instances, in which the other models are doing right. Even our best model CT-BERT is missing some cases which are correctly classified by other models. In order to decrease the amount of these easy and model specific misclassifications, we applied an ensemble approach to combine these different models.

In this ensembling strategy, each model is trained separately. When it is time for prediction, each model's prediction class probabilities are summed up. Then the final prediction label is chosen based on these combined scores. Such an ensemble strategy is especially useful for cases where some models are not certain of their predictions (probabilities around 0.5). In these cases other more certain models step up to make a more confident and hopefully correct prediction.

For this ensembling approach, in order to keep results more balanced 2 CNN-based models and 2 BERT-based models were used. BERT, which is the worst performing BERT-based model, was kept out in this ensembling, and only CT-BERT, ALBERT, CNN W2V and CNN GLOVE models were used.

4.2 SUM CT-BERT Ensemble

The motivation behind this approach is to reduce the variance in performance as shown in Table 2. As reported in Xu et al. (2020), fine-tuning multiple BERT models with different random seeds and ensembling their probability outputs can reduce variance in the overall classification performance. Our work here is a replication of the same work of Xu et al. (2020).

Our best performing model, CT-BERT, was used for this ensembling. 5 CT-BERT models trained with the same hyper-parameters but initialized with different random seeds were used. The individual performances of these models were already reported in Table 2. Similar to our SUM Ensemble approach, individual prediction probabilities were retrieved from each model, and then summed up. The final prediction was obtained from this total score.

4.3 Experiments

These two ensemble models' outputs were used as our system submissions. In Table 3, we report the performances of ensemble models on the validation and test sets.

Model	Val Score	Test Score
SUM Ensemble	0.9087	0.8790
SUM CT-BERT Ens	0.9106	0.8880

Table 3: The F1 Scores of ensemble models on validation and test set

Both ensemble models outperformed the best classifier model (CT-BERT) on validation set, and SUM CT-BERT Ensemble performed slightly better than SUM Ensemble on both validation and test set. In order to understand the specific errors these models made, Figure 1 was replicated, but this time including the two ensembles.

In Figure 2, we can clearly observe that SUM Ensemble is slightly better than CT-BERT. Considering the ensemble strategy, one conclusion we can arrive is that CT-BERT is probably making very confident predictions (probabilities close to 1 or 0) which makes it hard for the other three models to change CT-BERT's predicted label. This overconfidence of CT-BERT was helpful in some cases, but not all the times. This is something we will explore more in the future.

In the case of SUM CT-BERT, we see that ensembling multiple CT-BERT models has better performance than 4 out of the 5 CT-BERT models used in the ensembling process (reported in Table 2). The ensemble score is also better than the mean F1 score of these models (0.9062). Thus, reduc-

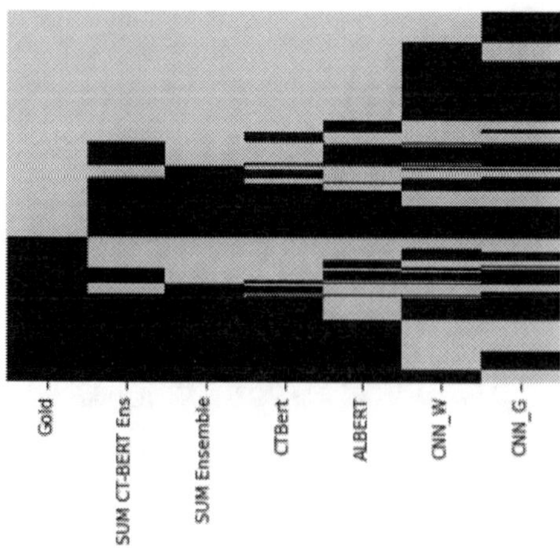

Figure 2: This figure contains all examples from the validation set that were misclassified by any of the listed models and ensembles.

ing the variance caused by random initialization is generally useful.

One thing we would like to note is that all of our models were trained using the official training dataset (70% of the data) only. We did not use validation data (10% of the data) for training when submitting our predictions for the test set. This was an oversight on our part. We believe that training all models on validation set in addition to the original training set, would have yielded better results.

5 Conclusion

In this paper, we presented our work for W-NUT 2020 Task 2: Identification of Informative COVID-19 English Tweets. We experimented with BERT-based models and CNNs as our classification models. After analyzing the classification performance of these different models, we decided to use two different ensembling methods. Both of these ensemble strategies outperformed the individual models. More specifically, the ensemble strategy which addressed the variance in model performance caused by the random initialization, returned the best performance.

References

Iz Beltagy, Kyle Lo, and Arman Cohan. 2019. Scibert: A pretrained language model for scientific text.

Jacob Devlin, Ming-Wei Chang, Kenton Lee, and Kristina Toutanova. 2018. Bert: Pre-training of deep bidirectional transformers for language understanding.

Yoon Kim. 2014. Convolutional neural networks for sentence classification.

Zhenzhong Lan, Mingda Chen, Sebastian Goodman, Kevin Gimpel, Piyush Sharma, and Radu Soricut. 2019. Albert: A lite bert for self-supervised learning of language representations.

Jinhyuk Lee, Wonjin Yoon, Sungdong Kim, Donghyeon Kim, Sunkyu Kim, Chan Ho So, and Jaewoo Kang. 2019. Biobert: a pre-trained biomedical language representation model for biomedical text mining. *Bioinformatics*.

Martin Müller, Marcel Salathé, and Per E Kummervold. 2020. Covid-twitter-bert: A natural language processing model to analyse covid-19 content on twitter.

Dat Quoc Nguyen, Thanh Vu, Afshin Rahimi, Mai Hoang Dao, Linh The Nguyen, and Long Doan. 2020. WNUT-2020 Task 2: Identification of Informative COVID-19 English Tweets. In *Proceedings of the 6th Workshop on Noisy User-generated Text*.

Yige Xu, Xipeng Qiu, Ligao Zhou, and Xuanjing Huang. 2020. Improving bert fine-tuning via self-ensemble and self-distillation.

IDSOU at WNUT-2020 Task 2:
Identification of Informative COVID-19 English Tweets

Sora Ohashi [†]   Tomoyuki Kajiwara [‡]   Chenhui Chu [‡]
Noriko Takemura [‡]   Yuta Nakashima [‡]   Hajime Nagahara [‡]

[†] Graduate School of Information Science and Technology, Osaka University
[‡] Institute for Datability Science, Osaka University

ohashi.sora@ist.osaka-u.ac.jp
{kajiwara, chu, takemura, n-yuta, nagahara}@ids.osaka-u.ac.jp

Abstract

We introduce the IDSOU[1] submission for the WNUT-2020 task 2: identification of informative COVID-19 English Tweets. Our system is an ensemble of pre-trained language models such as BERT. We ranked 16th in the F1 score.

1 Introduction

The spread of the COVID-19 is causing fear and panic to people around the world. To monitor the COVID-19 outbreaks in real-time, SNS analysis such as Twitter is attracting much attention. Although there are 4 million COVID-19 English Tweets posted daily on Twitter (Lamsal, 2020), most of them are uninformative. Against this background, WNUT-2020 held a shared task[2] (Nguyen et al., 2020) to automatically identify whether a COVID-19 English Tweet is informative or not.

Our system employs an ensemble approach based on pre-trained language models. Such pre-trained language models (Devlin et al., 2019; Yang et al., 2019; Liu et al., 2019; Lan et al., 2020; Conneau et al., 2020; Lewis et al., 2020) have achieved high performance in various text classification tasks (Wang et al., 2019). In addition, we employ domain-specific pre-trained language models (Lee et al., 2019; Alsentzer et al., 2019; Müller et al., 2020) to build models suitable for COVID-19 and Twitter domains. Each model is optimized for three types of loss functions, cross-entropy, negative supervision (Ohashi et al., 2020), and Dice similarity coefficient (Li et al., 2020), which are useful for various text classification tasks. Finally, we ensemble 48 classifiers based on 16 pre-trained language models and 3 loss functions with a random forest classifier (Breiman, 2001).

	Train	Dev	Test
Informative	3,303	472	944
Uninformative	3,697	528	1,056
Total	7,000	1,000	2,000

Table 1: Statistics of the dataset.

2 WNUT-2020 Shared Task 2

In the shared task (Nguyen et al., 2020), systems are required to classify whether a COVID-19 English Tweet is informative or not. Such informative Tweets provide information about recovered, suspected, confirmed and death cases as well as location or travel history of the cases. The 10,000 COVID-19 English Tweets[3] shown in Table 1 have been released for the shared task.

The baseline system is based on fastText (Bojanowski et al., 2017). Systems are evaluated by accuracy, precision, recall and F1 score, and are ranked by F1 score, which is the main metric. Note that the latter three metrics are calculated for the informative class only.

3 IDSOU System

We first introduce each base model in Section 3.1 and each loss function in Section 3.2. We then introduce the ensemble model in Section 3.3. Finally, Section 3.4 describes the implementation details.

3.1 Base Models

Recently, the fine-tuning approach for pre-trained language models (Devlin et al., 2019) has achieved the highest performance for many text classification tasks (Wang et al., 2019). We employ the following pre-trained language models of six types of architecture for the shared task.

---

[1] Institute for Datability Science, Osaka University
[2] http://noisy-text.github.io/2020/
[3] https://github.com/VinAIResearch/COVID19Tweet

Proceedings of the 2020 EMNLP Workshop W-NUT: The Sixth Workshop on Noisy User-generated Text, pages 428–433
Online, Nov 19, 2020. ©2020 Association for Computational Linguistics

BERT (Devlin et al., 2019) The transformer encoder pre-trained by multitask learning of masked language modeling and next sentence prediction. We employ three types of pre-trained models, BERT-base,[4] BERT-large,[5] and BERT-large-wwm.[6] BERT-base consists of 12 transformer layers, 12 self-attention heads per layer, and a hidden size of 768. BERT-large and BERT-large-wwm consist of 24 transformer layers, 16 self-attention heads per layer, and a hidden size of 1,024.

XLNet (Yang et al., 2019) The transformer encoder pre-trained by permutation language modeling. We employ two types of pre-trained models, XLNet-base[7] and XLNet-large.[8] The parameters of XLNet-base and XLNet-large are the same as BERT-base and BERT-large, respectively.

RoBERTa (Liu et al., 2019) The transformer encoder pre-trained by masked language modeling. RoBERTa has the same architecture as BERT, but pre-trains more steps on larger data with larger batch sizes. We employ two types of pre-trained models, RoBERTa-base[9] and RoBERTa-large.[10]

XLM-RoBERTa (Conneau et al., 2020) The multilingual transformer encoder pre-trained by masked language modeling. We employ a pre-trained model of XLM-RoBERTa-base.[11] XLM-RoBERTa-base consists of 12 transformer layers, 8 self-attention heads per layer, and a hidden size of 3,072.

ALBERT (Lan et al., 2020) The transformer encoder pre-trained by multitask learning of masked language modeling and sentence order prediction. ALBERT has significantly fewer parameters than the traditional BERT architecture due to two parameter reduction techniques, factorized embedding parameterization and cross-layer parameter sharing. We employ two types of pre-trained models, ALBERT-base[12] and ALBERT-large.[13] ALBERT-base and ALBERT-large have the same number of layers, attention heads, and hidden size as BERT-base and BERT-large, respectively, but the embedded size is 128.

BART (Lewis et al., 2020) The denoising autoencoder based on a bidirectional transformer encoder and a left-to-right transformer decoder. We employ two types of pre-trained models, BART-base[14] and BART-large.[15] BART-base consists of 12 transformer layers, 16 self-attention heads per layer, and a hidden size of 768. BART-large consists of 24 transformer layers, 16 self-attention heads per layer, and a hidden size of 1,024.

The language models mentioned above are pre-trained on corpora in the general domain such as the BookCorpus (Zhu et al., 2015) and English Wikipedia. Recent studies (Lee and Hsiang, 2019; Beltagy et al., 2019) have revealed that language models pre-trained on a domain-specific corpus achieve better performance in that domain. We employ the following three types of BERT models pre-trained on large-scale corpora of the medical domain and Twitter domain to build a classifier suitable for COVID-19 English Tweets.

BioBERT (Lee et al., 2019) The BERT encoder pre-trained on corpora in the biomedical domain such as PubMed abstracts (PubMed)[16] and PubMed Central full-text articles (PMC).[17] We employ two types of pre-trained models, BioBERT-base[18] and BioBERT-large.[19]

ClinicalBERT (Alsentzer et al., 2019) The BERT encoder pre-trained on corpora in both biomedical and clinical domains such as PubMed, PMC, and the MIMIC-III v1.4 database (Johnson et al., 2016). We employ a pre-trained ClinicalBERT[20] model with the same architecture as BERT-base.

---

[4]https://huggingface.co/bert-base-uncased
[5]https://huggingface.co/bert-large-uncased
[6]https://huggingface.co/bert-large-uncased-whole-word-masking
[7]https://huggingface.co/xlnet-base-cased
[8]https://huggingface.co/xlnet-large-cased
[9]https://huggingface.co/roberta-base
[10]https://huggingface.co/roberta-large
[11]https://huggingface.co/xlm-roberta-base

[12]https://huggingface.co/albert-base-v2
[13]https://huggingface.co/albert-large-v2
[14]https://huggingface.co/facebook/bart-base
[15]https://huggingface.co/facebook/bart-large
[16]https://www.ncbi.nlm.nih.gov/pubmed/
[17]https://www.ncbi.nlm.nih.gov/pmc/
[18]https://huggingface.co/dmis-lab/biobert-v1.1
[19]https://huggingface.co/trisongz/biobert_large_cased
[20]https://huggingface.co/emilyalsentzer/Bio_ClinicalBERT

	XE	NS	DS
BERT-base	0.899	**0.904**	0.890
BERT-large	0.898	**0.899**	0.879
BERT-large-wwm	0.901	**0.910**	0.902
XLNet-base	0.898	**0.909**	0.885
XLNet-large	**0.911**	0.907	0.892
RoBERTa-base	0.906	**0.909**	0.896
RoBERTa-large	**0.916**	0.908	0.887
XLM-RoBERTa	**0.891**	0.879	0.856

	XE	NS	DS
ALBERT-base	**0.907**	0.893	0.883
ALBERT-large	**0.900**	0.897	0.867
BART-base	**0.886**	0.885	0.880
BART-large	**0.908**	0.905	0.855
BioBERT-base	**0.893**	0.889	0.873
BioBERT-large	0.896	**0.897**	0.859
ClinicalBERT	**0.879**	0.877	0.878
COVID-Twitter-BERT	0.922	0.923	**0.926**

Table 2: F1 scores of each loss function on the development set.

COVID-Twitter-BERT (Müller et al., 2020)

The BERT encoder pre-trained on the COVID-19 English Tweets. These are 160M Tweets collected between January 12 and April 16, 2020 containing at least one of the keywords "wuhan", "ncov", "coronavirus", "covid", or "sars-cov-2". We employ a pre-trained COVID-Twitter-BERT[21] model with the same architecture as BERT-large.

3.2 Loss Functions

We train classifiers based on pre-trained language models with the following three loss functions.

XE: Cross Entropy

We employ the following cross-entropy loss commonly used in text classification tasks.

$$L_{\text{XE}} = \frac{1}{N} \sum_{i=1}^{N} \log P_i \tag{1}$$

where $P_i := P(y_i|X_i)$, y_i is the gold label, and X_i is the input text.

NS: Negative Supervision (Ohashi et al., 2020)

This loss function separates the representation of Tweets with different labels.

$$L_{\text{NS}} = L_{\text{XE}} + \frac{1}{NM} \sum_{i=i}^{N} \sum_{n=1}^{M} \cos(\boldsymbol{v}_i, \boldsymbol{v}_n) \tag{2}$$

where $\boldsymbol{v}_i$ is the representation of i-th text and $\boldsymbol{v}_n$ is that of negative examples, *i.e.* text representations that has different labels. We set the number of negative examples $M = 2$.

[21]https://huggingface.co/digitalepidemiologylab/covid-twitter-bert

	Loss	F1
BERT-large	XE	0.898
COVID-Twitter-BERT	XE	0.922
Ensemble: 16 models	XE	0.929
Ensemble: 48 models	XE+NS+DS	**0.933**

Table 3: Performance comparison of single model and ensemble model on the development set.

DS: Dice Similarity Coefficient (Li et al., 2020)

The loss function based on Dice-coefficient. The gap between maximizing F1 score and minimizing DS loss is less than that of minimizing XE loss.

$$L_{\text{DS}} = \frac{1}{N} \sum_{i=1}^{N} \left[1 - \frac{2(1 - P_i)P_i y_i + \gamma}{(1 - P_i)P_i + y_i + \gamma} \right] \tag{3}$$

For smoothing purpose, we simply set $\gamma = 1$ following Li et al. (2020).

3.3 Ensemble Model

We ensemble 48 classifiers (16 pre-trained language models for each 3 loss functions) described above to make prediction stable. The Random Forest Classifier (Breiman, 2001) is trained using k-fold cross-validation on the development with the probabilities of the informative class estimated by each base model as the features.

3.4 Implementation Details

We implemented all models based on the Hugging Face's Transformers (Wolf et al., 2019) with Adam optimizer (Kingma and Ba, 2015). Hyperparameters of each base model were determined from the following combinations based on the F1 score in the development set.

Rank	Team	F1	Precision	Recall	Accuracy
1	NutCracker	0.9096	0.9135	0.9057	0.9150
2	NLP_North	0.9096	0.9029	0.9163	0.9140
3	SupportNUTMachine	0.9094	0.9046	0.9142	0.9140
4	#GCDH	0.9091	0.8919	0.9269	0.9125
5	Loner	0.9085	0.8918	0.9258	0.9120
⋮					
11	Husky	0.8992	0.8959	0.9025	0.9045
12	Hanoi001	0.8991	0.8787	0.9206	0.9025
13	UET	0.8989	0.8891	0.9089	0.9035
14	Emory	0.8974	0.8744	0.9216	0.9005
15	NJU ConvAI	0.8973	0.8751	0.9206	0.9005
16	**IDSOU**	**0.8964**	**0.8988**	**0.8941**	**0.9025**
17	ComplexDataLab	0.8945	0.9195	0.8708	0.9030
18	UPennHLP	0.8941	0.9028	0.8856	0.9010
19	datamafia	0.8940	0.8857	0.9025	0.8990
20	NIT_COVID-19	0.8914	0.8594	0.9258	0.8935
21	NHK_STRL	0.8898	0.8985	0.8814	0.8970
⋮					
48	BASELINE	0.7503	0.7730	0.7288	0.7710
⋮					
55	TMU-COVID19	0.5789	0.5000	0.6875	0.5280

Table 4: Official results in descending order of the F1 score.

- Batch size: [16, 32]
- Learning rate: [1e-5, 3e-5, 5e-5]
- Early stopping: [5]

We implemented the ensemble model based on the scikit-learn (Pedregosa et al., 2011). Hyperparameters of the random forest classifier were determined through 5-fold cross-validation from the following combinations in the development set.

- `n_estimators`: [50, 100, 150]
- `max_depth`: [2, 4, 8]
- `min_samples_split`: [2, 8, 32]
- `max_samples`: [0.2, 0.5, 0.8, 1.0]

We followed the default data split provided by the task organizers. No external data has been used.

4   Results

Table 2 shows the F1 scores of each base model on the development set. The COVID-Twitter-BERT pre-trained with the in-domain corpus achieved the highest performance as expected. Since non-expert posts make up the majority of SNS, models pre-trained in the biomedical and clinical domains did not outperform that of the general domain.

Regarding the loss function, XE loss showed stable performance. NS loss is effective for 6 out of 16 models and seems to be compatible with BERT. DS loss achieved the best performance in combination with COVID-Twitter-BERT, although overall performance is not high.

Table 3 shows the effect of our ensemble method. These results reveal the effectiveness of the ensemble of both different pre-trained language models and different loss functions.

Table 4 shows the official results. We ranked 16th out of 55 teams in the F1 score.

5   Conclusions

We describe the IDSOU submission for the WNUT-2020 task 2. Our system is an ensemble model based on 16 pre-trained language models and 3 loss functions with a random forest classifier. In the official result, we ranked 16th out of 55 teams.

Acknowledgments

This work was supported by Innovation Platform for Society 5.0 from Japan Ministry of Education, Culture, Sports, Science and Technology.

References

Emily Alsentzer, John Murphy, William Boag, Wei-Hung Weng, Di Jindi, Tristan Naumann, and Matthew McDermott. 2019. Publicly Available Clinical BERT Embeddings. In *Proceedings of the 2nd Clinical Natural Language Processing Workshop*, pages 72–78.

Iz Beltagy, Kyle Lo, and Arman Cohan. 2019. SciB-ERT: A Pretrained Language Model for Scientific Text. In *Proceedings of the 2019 Conference on Empirical Methods in Natural Language Processing and the 9th International Joint Conference on Natural Language Processing*, pages 3615–3620.

Piotr Bojanowski, Edouard Grave, Armand Joulin, and Tomas Mikolov. 2017. Enriching Word Vectors with Subword Information. *Transactions of the Association for Computational Linguistics*, 5:135–146.

Leo Breiman. 2001. Random Forests. *Machine Learning*, 45:5–32.

Alexis Conneau, Kartikay Khandelwal, Naman Goyal, Vishrav Chaudhary, Guillaume Wenzek, Francisco Guzmán, Edouard Grave, Myle Ott, Luke Zettlemoyer, and Veselin Stoyanov. 2020. Unsupervised Cross-lingual Representation Learning at Scale. In *Proceedings of the 58th Annual Meeting of the Association for Computational Linguistics*, pages 8440–8451.

Jacob Devlin, Ming-Wei Chang, Kenton Lee, and Kristina Toutanova. 2019. BERT: Pre-training of Deep Bidirectional Transformers for Language Understanding. In *Proceedings of the 2019 Conference of the North American Chapter of the Association for Computational Linguistics: Human Language Technologies*, pages 4171–4186.

Alistair E.W. Johnson, Tom J. Pollard, Lu Shen, Li wei H. Lehman, Mengling Feng, Mohammad Ghassemi, Benjamin Moody, Peter Szolovits, Leo Anthony Celi, and Roger G. Mark. 2016. MIMIC-III, a Freely Accessible Critical Care Database. *Scientific Data*, 3(160035).

Diederik P. Kingma and Jimmy Ba. 2015. Adam: A Method for Stochastic Optimization. In *Proceedings of the 3rd International Conference on Learning Representations*.

Rabindra Lamsal. 2020. Coronavirus (COVID-19) Tweets Dataset.

Zhenzhong Lan, Mingda Chen, Sebastian Goodman, Kevin Gimpel, Piyush Sharma, and Radu Soricut. 2020. ALBERT: A Lite BERT for Self-supervised Learning of Language Representations. In *Proceedings of the Eighth International Conference on Learning Representations*.

Jieh-Sheng Lee and Jieh Hsiang. 2019. PatentBERT: Patent Classification with Fine-Tuning a pre-trained BERT Model. *arXiv:1906.02124*.

Jinhyuk Lee, Wonjin Yoon, Sungdong Kim, Donghyeon Kim, Sunkyu Kim, Chan Ho So, and Jaewoo Kang. 2019. BioBERT: A Pre-trained Biomedical Language Representation Model for Biomedical Text Mining. *Bioinformatics*, pages 1234–1240.

Mike Lewis, Yinhan Liu, Naman Goyal, Marjan Ghazvininejad, Abdelrahman Mohamed, Omer Levy, Veselin Stoyanov, and Luke Zettlemoyer. 2020. BART: Denoising Sequence-to-Sequence Pre-training for Natural Language Generation, Translation, and Comprehension. In *Proceedings of the 58th Annual Meeting of the Association for Computational Linguistics*, pages 7871–7880.

Xiaoya Li, Xiaofei Sun, Yuxian Meng, Junjun Liang, Fei Wu, and Jiwei Li. 2020. Dice Loss for Data-imbalanced NLP Tasks. In *Proceedings of the 58th Annual Meeting of the Association for Computational Linguistics*, pages 465–476.

Yinhan Liu, Myle Ott, Naman Goyal, Jingfei Du, Mandar Joshi, Danqi Chen, Omer Levy, Mike Lewis, Luke Zettlemoyer, and Veselin Stoyanov. 2019. RoBERTa: A Robustly Optimized BERT Pretraining Approach. *arXiv:1907.11692*.

Martin Müller, Marcel Salathé, and Per E Kummervold. 2020. COVID-Twitter-BERT: A Natural Language Processing Model to Analyse COVID-19 Content on Twitter. *arXiv:2005.07503*.

Dat Quoc Nguyen, Thanh Vu, Afshin Rahimi, Mai Hoang Dao, Linh The Nguyen, and Long Doan. 2020. WNUT-2020 Task 2: Identification of Informative COVID-19 English Tweets. In *Proceedings of the 6th Workshop on Noisy User-generated Text*.

Sora Ohashi, Junya Takayama, Tomoyuki Kajiwara, Chenhui Chu, and Yuki Arase. 2020. Text Classification with Negative Supervision. In *Proceedings of the 58th Annual Meeting of the Association for Computational Linguistics*, pages 351–357.

Fabian Pedregosa, Gaël Varoquaux, Alexandre Gramfort, Vincent Michel, Bertrand Thirion, Olivier Grisel, Mathieu Blondel, Peter Prettenhofer, Ron Weiss, Vincent Dubourg, Jake Vanderplas, Alexandre Passos, David Cournapeau, Matthieu Brucher, Matthieu Perrot, and Édouard Duchesnay. 2011. Scikit-learn: Machine Learning in Python. *Journal of Machine Learning Research*, 12(85):2825–2830.

Alex Wang, Amanpreet Singh, Julian Michael, Felix Hill, Omer Levy, and Samuel R. Bowman. 2019. GLUE: A Multi-Task Benchmark and Analysis Platform for Natural Language Understanding. In *Proceedings of the 7th International Conference on Learning Representations*.

Thomas Wolf, Lysandre Debut, Victor Sanh, Julien Chaumond, Clement Delangue, Anthony Moi, Pierric Cistac, Tim Rault, R'emi Louf, Morgan Funtowicz, and Jamie Brew. 2019. HuggingFace's Transformers: State-of-the-art Natural Language Processing. *arXiv:1910.03771*.

Zhilin Yang, Zihang Dai, Yiming Yang, Jaime Carbonell, Russ R. Salakhutdinov, and Quoc V. Le. 2019. XLNet: Generalized Autoregressive Pretraining for Language Understanding. In *Proceedings of the 33rd Conference on Neural Information Processing Systems*, pages 5753–5763.

Yukun Zhu, Ryan Kiros, Richard Zemel, Ruslan Salakhutdinov, Raquel Urtasun, Antonio Torralba, and Sanja Fidler. 2015. Aligning Books and Movies: Towards Story-like Visual Explanations by Watching Movies and Reading Books. *arXiv:1506.06724*.

ComplexDataLab at WNUT-2020 Task 2: Detecting Informative COVID-19 Tweets by Attending over Linked Documents

Kellin Pelrine, Jacob Danovitch, Albert Orozco Camacho, Reihaneh Rabbany
School of Computer Science, McGill University
Mila - Quebec AI Institute
{kellin.pelrine, jacob.danovitch, alorozco53, reihaneh.rabbany}@mila.quebec

Abstract

Given the global scale of COVID-19 and the flood of social media content related to it, how can we find informative discussions? We present GAPFORMER, which effectively classifies content as informative or not. It reformulates the problem as graph classification, drawing on not only the tweet but connected web pages and entities. We leverage a pre-trained language model as well as the connections between nodes to learn a pooled representation for each document network. We show it outperforms several competitive baselines and present ablation studies supporting the benefit of the linked information. Code is available on GitHub[1].

1 Introduction

COVID-19 is a critical public health crisis, with over 25 million cases and 840 thousand deaths worldwide and counting (WHO, 2020). One important way to fight the pandemic is through understanding and leveraging the vast amount of information humans produce related to it on social media. Success here can facilitate individual and overall case detections, contact tracing, case predictions, effective information dissemination, and more (Li et al., 2020; Qin et al., 2020). However, the data is far too big - for example, hundreds of millions of tweets (Qazi et al., 2020) - to extract all the useful information by hand. There is also a huge amount of useless and even outright false information (Alam et al., 2020; Cui and Lee, 2020). Therefore, algorithms that extract useful information effectively are crucial.

WNUT-2020 Task 2 (Nguyen et al., 2020) is to build such a system on a particular twitter dataset, and predict which tweets are informative "about

recovered, suspected, confirmed and death cases as well as location or travel history of the cases." We present here GAPFORMER, which combines multiple sources of information - the tweet, content of linked web pages, and information about named entities related to the tweet - to improve detection of informative content.

Our experiments show GAPFORMER outperforms 7 baselines. It also performs best when incorporating all three types of data, showing the efficacy of using the proposed graph structure. We believe this method can also be applied in other related settings, such as misinformation detection, and have work in progress to investigate possible extensions.

2 Background and Related Work

Before COVID-19, mining information from tweets about disaster events has been considered in several contexts. The CrisisNLP (Imran et al., 2016) collection has twitter datasets from 19 crises, including diseases Ebola and MERS. There are also works analyzing particular events (Takahashi et al., 2015; Kankanamge et al., 2020; Chen et al., 2020) and methods (Kumar et al., 2011; To et al., 2017; Singh et al., 2019; Aggarwal, 2019).

However, COVID-19 is unprecedented in its global scale and impact. While there is also a historic amount of research taking place to counter it (Brainard, 2020), more is needed - there are still lives to be saved. In addition, while people have tackled related COVID-19 twitter data tasks (Boulos and Geraghty, 2020; Alam et al., 2020; Cui and Lee, 2020), to our knowledge this particular task formulation has not been thoroughly investigated prior to this shared task competition.

With the success of transformer-based models (Vaswani et al., 2017; Devlin et al., 2018), it is natural to consider applying them here. BERTweet

---

[1]https://github.com/ComplexData-MILA/gapformer

434

Proceedings of the 2020 EMNLP Workshop W-NUT: The Sixth Workshop on Noisy User-generated Text, pages 434–439
Online, Nov 19, 2020. ©2020 Association for Computational Linguistics

(Dat Quoc Nguyen and Nguyen, 2020) and covid-twitter-bert (Müller et al., 2020), BERT language models fine-tuned on twitter data (and the latter on tweets related to COVID-19 specifically), are particularly relevant. However, pure language models struggle to consider additional contextual information beyond the raw content of the tweet. As our experiments show, this is an important limitation.

Because this limitation applies to many other applications as well, a rapidly growing area of research is embedding additional contextual knowledge into language models, especially with the use of graph structures (Rosset et al., 2020; Zhang, 2020; Cui et al., 2020). This is often done at the language modelling level, such as how (Lu et al., 2020) uses normalized mutual information to inject global information into each layer of BERT. That said, other work has focused on injecting knowledge into an existing pre-trained language model. In particular, `Transformer-XH` (Zhao et al., 2020) proposes a way to leverage the network structure of documents alongside a pre-trained model for a classification task. GAPFORMER builds on this line of work by proposing a simple yet effective architecture which contextualizes each node before pooling the graph into a single fixed embedding.

3 Proposed Method

Symbols	Definitions
$\mathcal{G} = \{\mathcal{V}, \mathcal{E}\}$	A graph and its vertex/edge sets
$\mathbf{A}$	Adjacency matrix of $\mathcal{G}$
$\mathbf{D}$	Degree vector of $\mathcal{V}$
LM	Pre-trained language model
$\mathbf{W}, \mathbf{b}$	Weight matrix, bias vector
t	A tweet
$A_t = \{a_i\}$	Articles linked to by t
$E_t = \{e_j\}$	Entities mentioned by t

Table 1: Symbols and Definitions

Our work presents **GrAph Pooling Transformer** (GAPFORMER), which combines powerful semantic representations from pretrained language models with structured information from graph neural networks by incorporating additional context from entities and web documents within each tweet. We reformulate the task as graph classification, where each instance is a single graph comprised of one tweet as well as the extracted entities and docu-ments.

3.1 Graph Construction

For each instance, we construct a graph $\mathcal{G} = \{\mathcal{V}, \mathcal{E}\}$ with the documents and entities in each tweet t as nodes and t itself as a supernode. We describe the construction process below.

3.1.1 Node Selection

We extract each entity mentioned in a given tweet t, and link them to their respective Wikipedia entries. We then represent the entities with their associated Wikipedia documents. The full set of entities extracted from t forms E_t. We use the Python packages `FLAIR` (Akbik et al., 2019) for named entity recognition and `BLINK` (Wu et al., 2019) for entity linking.

We also retrieve the content of any news articles linked to by the tweet, with the intuition that tweets which cite their sources are more likely to be informative, and that the content of said sources is likely to provide a useful signal as well. We use the `newspaper3k` Python package (Lucas Ou-Yang, 2013) to retrieve the summaries for each article, as full articles tend to be particularly long and may contain superfluous information. This set of articles forms A_t.

Finally, to form the vertex set, we take $\mathcal{V} = A_t \cup E_t \cup \{t\}$.

3.1.2 Edge Selection

To begin, we draw an edge between t and each node $n \in \mathcal{V}$ to embed t with additional information (including t itself, forming a self-loop). To better contextualize this information, we also draw edges for pairs of entities, as the intent of an entity mention may vary between different contexts. However, we must also be wary of simply adding as many connections as possible, which would decrease efficiency. We select which entity pairs to connect by calculating the normalized pointwise mutual information (NPMI) (Lu et al., 2020) between each pair. Using NPMI as the selection criterion allows us to connect nodes which frequently co-occur (mentioned in the same tweet) throughout the dataset, suggesting a more meaningful relationship. Empirically, we observed 0.15 to be a sensible threshold.

For entities e_i and e_j:

$$\text{pmi}(e_i, e_j) = \frac{p(e_i, e_j)}{p(e_i)p(e_j)} \qquad (1)$$

$$\text{npmi}(e_i, e_j) = \frac{\text{pmi}(e_i, e_j)}{-\log p(x, y)} \qquad (2)$$

The full algorithm for edge selection is described in algorithm 1.

Data: Vertex set $\mathcal{V} = A_t \cup E_t \cup \{t\}$
Result: Edge set $\mathcal{E}$
1   $\mathcal{E} = \{\}$;
2   **for** n *in* $\mathcal{V}$ **do**
3   add (n, t) to $\mathcal{E}$
4   **end**
5   **for** e_i *in* E_t **do**
6   **for** e_j *in* E_t **do**
7   **if** $\text{npmi}(e_i, e_j) > 0.15$ **then**
8   add (e_i, e_j) to $\mathcal{E}$
9   **end**
10   **end**
11 **end**

Algorithm 1: Edge selection algorithm

3.2 GAPFORMER

For each instance in the dataset, we construct a graph $\mathcal{G}$ as described above. Each node $n_i \in \mathcal{G}$ is represented by a text document (either a tweet, entity description, or article). We tokenize each node and obtain word embeddings using a pre-trained transformer language model. We pool the word embeddings by selecting the embedding for the `[CLS]` tokens from the final output layer, forming the graph's node embeddings.

After embedding each node with the pretrained language model, we apply k layers of mean-pooling `GraphSAGE` convolutions (Hamilton et al., 2017) to contextualize each node with respect to their neighbors. We then aggregate the graph to a single embedding using max pooling, attention, or another pooling mechanism. Empirically, we find max pooling to be most effective on this dataset. Finally, we use a linear layer to predict output logits.

The full algorithm is presented in algorithm 2. The model is trained end-to-end using cross entropy loss, and optimized with `AdamW` (Loshchilov and Hutter, 2017). Full implementation details are available in our GitHub repository.

Data: Vertices $\mathcal{V}$; Adjacency matrix $\mathbf{A}$;
       Degree vector $\mathbf{D}$
Result: Prediction logits $\hat{\mathbf{y}}$
1   $\mathbf{x} = \text{LM}(\mathcal{V})$;
2   **for** i *in* $1..k$ **do**
3     $\mathbf{h} = \mathbf{D}^{-1} \cdot \mathbf{A}\mathbf{x}$;
4     $\mathbf{x} = \sigma\left(\mathbf{W}_i \cdot \text{concat}(\mathbf{x}, \mathbf{h}) + \mathbf{b}_i\right)$;
5   **end**
6   $\mathbf{x} = \text{pooling}(\mathbf{x})$;
7   $\hat{\mathbf{y}} = \sigma(\mathbf{W}_\ell \mathbf{x} + \mathbf{b})$

Algorithm 2: GAPFORMER algorithm

4 Experiments

4.1 Data

The dataset provided for this task (Nguyen et al., 2020) consists of ten thousand tweets, labeled "informative" and "uninformative." A default split into train, validate, and test sets is also given, with details shown in table 2.

	Informative	Uninformative	Total
Train	3303	3697	7000
Validate	472	528	1000
Test	944	1056	2000

Table 2: Dataset Information

Since we do not have access to the actual test set for this task (it will only be published after camera-ready deadline for this paper), we treat the validation set provided as the test test in our reported results. We also randomly split 1000 tweets from the train set as the validation set used for hyper-parameter tuning of the deep learning based models, i.e. early stopping, to avoid corrupting the actual validation set (our test set).

4.2 Baselines

We compare our model with several baselines:

- Naive Bayes (**NB**).

- Logistic Regression (**LR**).

- Support Vector Machine (**SVM**).

- GloVe + **LSTM**. This applies an LSTM to word embeddings generated from the tweets using 200-dimensional GloVe Twitter word embeddings (Pennington et al., 2014).

- Base **BERT**. This is the original BERT model with a classification head. The entire model is fine-tuned during training. It is implemented using Huggingface Transformers and trained using Pytorch-Lightning. (Wolf et al., 2019; Falcon, 2019).

- **BERTweet** (Dat Quoc Nguyen and Nguyen, 2020). This is a BERT model fine-tuned on twitter data. Our implementation fine-tuned the weights provided by the authors with training identical to Base BERT.

- COVID-Twitter-BERT (**CTBERT**) (Müller et al., 2020). This is BERT but fine-tuned on COVID-19 twitter data. It was also trained identically to Base BERT.

The first 3 all use term frequency-inverse document frequency (TF-IDF) as features and the default Scikit-learn (Pedregosa et al., 2011) implementation. The last 3 (BERT-based models), as well as GAPFORMER, all use the AdamW optimizer (Loshchilov and Hutter, 2017) with a linear scheduler with warmup, set to learning rate 7e-6, and are trained using an NVIDIA RTX8000 GPU. For GAPFORMER, we find **CTBERT** to be the most effective pre-trained language model, and use it in all experiments. We train it for 8 epochs with batch size 2 and accumulating 8 batches for gradient calculations, because CTBert is too big to fit a bigger batch in GPU memory. We also use precision 16, max sequence length 128, .5 dropout for the graph stage, and max pooling.

4.3 Results

	F1	Precision	Recall	Accuracy
NB	.743	.770	.718	.766
LR	.791	.840	.748	.814
SVM	.803	.858	.754	.825
LSTM	.823	.830	.816	.834
BERT	.894	.879	.909	.898
BERTweet	.903	.862	**.949**	.904
CTBERT	.913	.903	.924	.917
GAPFORMER	**.927**	**.915**	.939	**.930**

Table 3: Results

As shown in table 3, GAPFORMER outperforms the baselines in all categories except recall. The strength in precision matches with our results in the shared task competition (on the test set, rather than the withheld validation set used above), where we were #1 in that metric, as shown in table 4.

Metric	Value	Rank
Accuracy	.903	10
Precision	.920	1
Recall	.871	23
F-1	.895	17

Table 4: Shared task competition results. 122 teams total, of which 55 submitted results.

4.4 Effect of Articles and Entities

To examine the effectiveness of each component of our graph, we conduct an ablation study. We compare the full GAPFORMER using tweets, entities, and articles linked in the tweet (including other tweets if a URL points to them), denoted here **T + E + A**, with tweets only (**T**), tweets plus entities only (**T + E**), and tweets plus articles only (**T + A**) Results are shown in table 5.

	F1	Precision	Recall	Accuracy
T	.899	.826	**.985**	.895
T + E	.919	.891	.949	.921
T + A	.917	**.923**	.911	.922
T + E + A	**.927**	.915	.939	**.930**

Table 5: Ablation Results

From this table, we can see that using all three information sources performs best in terms of overall accuracy and F1 score. Although just using the tweet gives particularly high recall, the overall performance is significantly worse than the others, about 3% lower in accuracy and F1 compared with using all three. This shows strongly that GAPFORMER is leveraging the articles and entities effectively to achieve better accuracy.

5 Conclusions

We presented GAPFORMER, which detects informative Covid-19 tweets, using a graph classification system that leverages articles and entities. This is done by first building graphs using normalized pointwise mutual information to determine related nodes, and then combining pre-trained language models with `GraphSAGE` convolutions and a pooling mechanism to classify them.

As shown in the experiments, this way of incorporating additional data is effective. It enables this system to outperform all seven baselines tested.

In future work, we plan to extend and upgrade this system in several ways:

- Enable broader input data, e.g. tweet replies

and user information. This will include heterogeneous data rather than only text.

- Improve performance by collecting and using more labeled data.

- Adapt it to other tasks. For example, we believe GAPFORMER can be used to effectively detect Covid-19 misinformation.

We are also looking at real-world applications of this tool. Since accuracy and other metrics are already above 90%, we believe it can have practical value, especially with the improvements above. We aim therefore to find direct ways to use GAPFORMER to help mitigate the Covid-19 pandemic.

References

Piush Aggarwal. 2019. Classification approaches to identify informative tweets. In *Proceedings of the Student Research Workshop Associated with RANLP 2019*, pages 7–15. 1

Alan Akbik, Tanja Bergmann, Duncan Blythe, Kashif Rasul, Stefan Schweter, and Roland Vollgraf. 2019. Flair: An easy-to-use framework for state-of-the-art nlp. In *Proceedings of the 2019 Conference of the North American Chapter of the Association for Computational Linguistics (Demonstrations)*, pages 54–59. 2

Firoj Alam, Fahim Dalvi, Shaden Shaar, Nadir Durrani, Hamdy Mubarak, Alex Nikolov, Giovanni Da San Martino, Ahmed Abdelali, Hassan Sajjad, Kareem Darwish, and Preslav Nakov. 2020. Fighting the covid-19 infodemic in social media: A holistic perspective and a call to arms. 1

Maged N Kamel Boulos and Estella M Geraghty. 2020. Geographical tracking and mapping of coronavirus disease covid-19/severe acute respiratory syndrome coronavirus 2 (sars-cov-2) epidemic and associated events around the world: how 21st century gis technologies are supporting the global fight against outbreaks and epidemics. 1

Jeffrey Brainard. 2020. Scientists are drowning in covid-19 papers. can new tools keep them afloat. *Science*. 1

Sijing Chen, Jin Mao, Gang Li, Chao Ma, and Yujie Cao. 2020. Uncovering sentiment and retweet patterns of disaster-related tweets from a spatiotemporal perspective–a case study of hurricane harvey. *Telematics and Informatics*, 47:101326. 1

Limeng Cui and Dongwon Lee. 2020. Coaid: Covid-19 healthcare misinformation dataset. 1

Limeng Cui, Haeseung Seo, Maryam Tabar, Fenglong Ma, Suhang Wang, and Dongwon Lee. 2020. Deterrent: Knowledge guided graph attention network for detecting healthcare misinformation. In *Proceedings of the 26th ACM SIGKDD International Conference on Knowledge Discovery & Data Mining*, pages 492–502. 2

Thanh Vu Dat Quoc Nguyen and Anh Tuan Nguyen. 2020. BERTweet: A pre-trained language model for English Tweets. *arXiv preprint*, arXiv:2005.10200. 2, 4

Jacob Devlin, Ming-Wei Chang, Kenton Lee, and Kristina Toutanova. 2018. BERT: pre-training of deep bidirectional transformers for language understanding. *CoRR*, abs/1810.04805. 1

WA Falcon. 2019. Pytorch lightning. *GitHub. Note: https://github.com/PyTorchLightning/pytorch-lightning Cited by*, 3. 4

Will Hamilton, Zhitao Ying, and Jure Leskovec. 2017. Inductive representation learning on large graphs. In *Advances in neural information processing systems*, pages 1024–1034. 3

Muhammad Imran, Prasenjit Mitra, and Carlos Castillo. 2016. Twitter as a lifeline: Human-annotated twitter corpora for nlp of crisis-related messages. In *Proceedings of the Tenth International Conference on Language Resources and Evaluation (LREC 2016)*, Paris, France. European Language Resources Association (ELRA). 1

Nayomi Kankanamge, Tan Yigitcanlar, Ashantha Goonetilleke, and Md Kamruzzaman. 2020. Determining disaster severity through social media analysis: Testing the methodology with south east queensland flood tweets. *International journal of disaster risk reduction*, 42:101360. 1

Shamanth Kumar, Geoffrey Barbier, Mohammad Ali Abbasi, and Huan Liu. 2011. Tweettracker: An analysis tool for humanitarian and disaster relief. *ICwSM*, 11:78–82. 1

L. Li, Q. Zhang, X. Wang, J. Zhang, T. Wang, T. Gao, W. Duan, K. K. Tsoi, and F. Wang. 2020. Characterizing the propagation of situational information in social media during covid-19 epidemic: A case study on weibo. *IEEE Transactions on Computational Social Systems*, 7(2):556–562. 1

Ilya Loshchilov and Frank Hutter. 2017. Decoupled weight decay regularization. 3, 4

Zhibin Lu, Pan Du, and Jian-Yun Nie. 2020. Vgcn-bert: Augmenting bert with graph embedding for text classification. In *European Conference on Information Retrieval*, pages 369–382. Springer. 2

Lucas Ou-Yang. 2013. Newspaper3k. 2

Martin Müller, Marcel Salathé, and Per E Kummervold. 2020. Covid-twitter-bert: A natural language processing model to analyse covid-19 content on twitter. *arXiv preprint*, arXiv:2005.07503. 2, 4

Dat Quoc Nguyen, Thanh Vu, Afshin Rahimi, Mai Hoang Dao, Linh The Nguyen, and Long Doan. 2020. WNUT-2020 Task 2: Identification of Informative COVID-19 English Tweets. In *Proceedings of the 6th Workshop on Noisy User-generated Text*. 1, 3

F. Pedregosa, G. Varoquaux, A. Gramfort, V. Michel, B. Thirion, O. Grisel, M. Blondel, P. Prettenhofer, R. Weiss, V. Dubourg, J. Vanderplas, A. Passos, D. Cournapeau, M. Brucher, M. Perrot, and E. Duchesnay. 2011. Scikit-learn: Machine learning in Python. *Journal of Machine Learning Research*, 12:2825–2830. 4

Jeffrey Pennington, Richard Socher, and Christopher D. Manning. 2014. Glove: Global vectors for word representation. In *Empirical Methods in Natural Language Processing (EMNLP)*, pages 1532–1543. 3

Umair Qazi, Muhammad Imran, and Ferda Ofli. 2020. Geocov19: a dataset of hundreds of millions of multilingual covid-19 tweets with location information. *SIGSPATIAL Special*, 12(1):6–15. 1

Lei Qin, Qiang Sun, Yidan Wang, Ke-Fei Wu, Mingchih Chen, Ben-Chang Shia, and Szu-Yuan Wu. 2020. Prediction of number of cases of 2019 novel coronavirus (covid-19) using social media search index. *International Journal of Environmental Research and Public Health*, 17(7):2365. 1

Corby Rosset, Chenyan Xiong, Minh Q. Phan, Xia Song, Paul. Bennett, and Saurabh Tiwary. 2020. Knowledge-aware language model pretraining. *ArXiv*, abs/2007.00655. 2

Jyoti Prakash Singh, Yogesh K Dwivedi, Nripendra P Rana, Abhinav Kumar, and Kawaljeet Kaur Kapoor. 2019. Event classification and location prediction from tweets during disasters. *Annals of Operations Research*, 283(1):737–757. 1

Bruno Takahashi, Edson C Tandoc Jr, and Christine Carmichael. 2015. Communicating on twitter during a disaster: An analysis of tweets during typhoon haiyan in the philippines. *Computers in human behavior*, 50:392–398. 1

Hien To, Sumeet Agrawal, Seon Ho Kim, and Cyrus Shahabi. 2017. On identifying disaster-related tweets: Matching-based or learning-based? In *2017 IEEE Third International Conference on Multimedia Big Data (BigMM)*, pages 330–337. IEEE. 1

Ashish Vaswani, Noam Shazeer, Niki Parmar, Jakob Uszkoreit, Llion Jones, Aidan N Gomez, Łukasz Kaiser, and Illia Polosukhin. 2017. Attention is all you need. In *Advances in neural information processing systems*, pages 5998–6008. 1

WHO. 2020. World Health Organization coronavirus disease (covid-19) dashboard. `WHOCoronavirusDisease(COVID-19) Dashboard`. Accessed: 2020-09-02. 1

Thomas Wolf, Lysandre Debut, Victor Sanh, Julien Chaumond, Clement Delangue, Anthony Moi, Pierric Cistac, Tim Rault, R'emi Louf, Morgan Funtowicz, and Jamie Brew. 2019. Huggingface's transformers: State-of-the-art natural language processing. *ArXiv*, abs/1910.03771. 4

Ledell Wu, Fabio Petroni, Martin Josifoski, Sebastian Riedel, and Luke Zettlemoyer. 2019. Zeroshot entity linking with dense entity retrieval. In *arXiv:1911.03814*. 2

Jiawei Zhang. 2020. G5: A universal graph-bert for graph-to-graph transfer and apocalypse learning. *arXiv preprint arXiv:2006.06183*. 2

Chen Zhao, Chenyan Xiong, Corby Rosset, Xia Song, Paul N. Bennett, and Saurabh Tiwary. 2020. Transformer-xh: Multi-evidence reasoning with extra hop attention. In *8th International Conference on Learning Representations, ICLR 2020, Addis Ababa, Ethiopia, April 26-30, 2020*. OpenReview.net. 2

NEU at WNUT-2020 Task 2: Data Augmentation To Tell BERT That Death Is Not Necessarily Informative

Kumud Chauhan
Northeastern University
`chauhan.ku@northeastern.edu`

Abstract

Millions of people around the world are sharing COVID-19 related information on social media platforms. Since not all the information shared on the social media is useful, a machine learning system to identify informative posts can help users in finding relevant information. In this paper, we present a BERT classifier system for W-NUT2020 Shared Task 2: Identification of Informative COVID-19 English Tweets. Further, we show that BERT exploits some easy signals to identify informative tweets, and adding simple patterns to uninformative tweets drastically degrades BERT performance. In particular, simply adding "10 deaths" to tweets in dev set, reduces BERT F1-score from 92.63 to 7.28. We also propose a simple data augmentation technique that helps in improving the robustness and generalization ability of the BERT classifier.

1 Introduction

COVID-19 pandemic as well as COVID-19 related information both are spreading across the world rapidly. Easy access to the internet made the consumption and sharing of information much faster. Millions of people are sharing COVID-19 related information using social media channels such as Facebook, Twitter. Social media is divided over several issues related to masks, social distancing, COVID-19 testing, etc. Unfortunately, the response to the coronavirus has been often determined by people's ideology instead of health officials' guidelines. One challenge with massive information available on social media is to separate useful COVID-19 related information from the noise. As a testimony, the director of WHO in Munich Security conference said "We're not just fighting an epidemic; we're fighting an infodemic"[1].

---

[1] `https://www.who.int/dg/speeches/detail/munich-security-conference`

NLP community have taken multiple initiatives to fight this infodemic including misinformation identification (Shahi et al., 2020), finding answers to COVID related questions (Esteva et al., 2020).

In this paper, we present our system in the W-NUT 2020 Shared Task 2: Identification of Informative COVID-19 English Tweets (Nguyen et al., 2020). We use transformer (Vaswani et al., 2017) based models such as BERT (Devlin et al., 2018) to classify COVID-19 tweets into informative and uninformative category. We observe that BERT heavily relies on death-related information to identify informative tweets, and can be easily fooled by adding a simple death count information to any uninformative tweet. Further, to improve robustness of the model, we propose a targeted data augmentation technique. Our contributions are as follows:

- We show that while BERT based models perform well on the shared task dataset, their performance falls drastically if we add death-related information to uninformative tweets.

- We propose a simple data augmentation method that aims at replacing the most discriminative words with other words to reduce the model's heavy reliance on specific words.

2 Task Description

The goal of the shared task 2 is to classify English tweets into INFORMATIVE or UNINFORMATIVE category. INFORMATIVE tweets provide information about recovered, suspected, confirmed, and death cases as well as location or travel history of the cases. The dataset consists of 10,000 COVID English Tweets, including 4719 Tweets labeled as INFORMATIVE and 5281 Tweets labeled as UNINFORMATIVE. Table 1 shows the descriptive statistics of the train, dev, and test partition of the dataset.

Proceedings of the 2020 EMNLP Workshop W-NUT: The Sixth Workshop on Noisy User-generated Text, pages 440–443
Online, Nov 19, 2020. ©2020 Association for Computational Linguistics

Split	Informative	Uninformative
Train	3303	3697
Dev	472	528
Test	944	1056

Table 1: Train, Dev and Testset statistics

3 Method

The task is formulated as a binary classification task. Since transformers based models provide state of the art performance on the text classification task, we use a pre-trained BERT as a classifier.

3.1 Classifiers

For the classification task, we consider two different variants of the BERT model. Our first model is pre-trained *bert-large-uncased* BERT model (Devlin et al., 2018). The second model is COVID-Twitter-BERT (CT-BERT) which is a transformer-based model pre-trained on a large corpus of Twitter messages on the topic of COVID-19. (Müller et al., 2020). Note that both models are similar in size and use the same base architecture. The only difference is in terms of the data used for pre-training. While *bert-large-uncased* is trained on Wikipedia and Books corpus, CT-BERT is trained on 22.5M tweets corpus.

3.2 BERT Exploits Easy Clues For Classification

Machine Learning systems can perform well by relying on heuristics that are effective for frequent example types but break down in more challenging cases. (McCoy et al., 2019; Niven and Kao, 2019). In our exploratory experiments, we found that the BERT classifier heavily relies on some easy clues such as the presence of reported deaths related terms such as "deaths", "died" to identify INFORMATIVE tweets. For example, BERT model classify the following uninformative tweet from validation set (1248314498747895813) as informative.

Data from National Records of Scotland shows that in the last full week, registered deaths from all causes across Scotland was 60% higher than the five-year average at 1,741 deaths compared with the average of 1,098." Most of that will be #COVID19? HTTPURL

The above tweet contains death count related information, model fails to recognize it as uninformative tweet. This leads us to experiment with adding such signals to UNINFORMATIVE tweets, to our surprise, it results in a huge drop in classification performance. For example, simply adding "10 deaths" to all tweets in the dev set, reduces BERT F1-score from 92.63 to 7.28.

Since such models can break for any uninformative tweet which contains variants of reported deaths, it raises questions about models' robustness and usefulness in a real-world application. In this paper, we explore data augmentation as a method to improve the robustness of such models.

3.3 Data Augmentation To Improve Robustness And Generalization

---

Algorithm 1: Data Augmentation

Input : 1. Training Dataset D_{train}
       2. BERT model

1   Find top N most important unigrams $Replacement\_set$ using chi-square test.

2   $D_{aug} \leftarrow \{\}$

3   **foreach** $\{x_i, y_i\} \in D_{train}$ **do**

4   Replace all word $w \in Replacement\_set$ in x_i with $MASK$ token

5   Generate a new example $\hat{x}_i$ by replacing word $\hat{w}$ using BERT Model such that $\hat{w} \notin Replacement\_set$

6      $D_{aug} \leftarrow D_{aug} \cup \{\hat{x}_i, y_i\}$

7   **end**

Data Augmentation have been extensively used to improve classification performance in low-data regime (Wu et al., 2019; Kumar et al., 2019; Wei and Zou, 2019; Kumar et al., 2020). In our early experiments, we found that pre-trained model-based data augmentation does not improve BERT classification performance in full data regime which is consistent with previous work (Kumar et al., 2019). Instead, we use targeted data augmentation, as described in algorithm 1 to improve the robustness of the BERT classifier.

Our data augmentation algorithm is motivated by the fact that BERT relies on the presence of simple markers to distinguish between INFORMATIVE vs UNINFORMATIVE classes. We propose to replace such markers with other words so that model does not rely too much on such markers. We hypothesize that such markers should have high discriminative power since the model relies on these words to distinguish between two categories. In our

Model	Mean Dev F1
Bert	90.46 (0.29)
CT-BERT	92.72 (0.18)
CT-BERT$_{\text{Aug}}$	**92.84** (0.26)

Table 2: Mean F1 with (STD) on Dev partition of the data. Mean and STD are computed over 5 runs.

Top 20 unigrams
breaking, bringing, case, cases, confirmed, confirms, county, deaths, department, died, employee, help, new, old, positive, recovered, reported, tested, total, user

Table 3: Top 20 unigram features identified using chi-squared test statistics

Model	Dev F1
CT-BERT	7.28
CT-BERT$_{\text{Aug}}$	34.68

Table 4: F1 score on Dev set where "10 deaths" is prepended to all tweets in devset

experiments, we use chi-squared stats to find unigrams which have the most discriminative power and use them as markers. Then, we replace such words with $MASK$ token and use BERT to find the replacement of such words. We generate one example for every example in the training set which doubles the size of our training set. We use CT-BERT$_{\text{Aug}}$ to refer to the CT-BERT model trained using augmented data.

4 Experiments

For our experiments, we use Huggingface's transformers package (Wolf et al., 2019). We use AdamW optimizer with a learning rate of $4e - 5$, batch size of 32, and 70 as the max sequence length. We use the pooled representation of the hidden state of the first special token([CLS]) as the sentence embedding. A dropout probability of 0.1 is applied to the sentence embedding before passing it to the 1-layer Softmax classifier. All models are trained for 7 epochs and the best model is selected on the basis of dev set performance.

For the model robustness experiment, we create a modified dev set where we add "10 deaths" to the beginning of all tweets in the dev set and test model performance against that. Since the main purpose of this paper is not to identify such universal adversarial triggers (Wallace et al., 2019), but to highlight the lack of robustness, our modified dev set provides a proxy for robustness experiment.

5 Results

We use train set to train BERT and CT-BERT model and report performance on dev set. Table 2 shows the mean F1 performance with STD on dev set. All experiments are repeated 5 times. Since, our task is a tweets classification task, as expected CT-BERT which is pre-trained on tweets data, performs better than the *bert-large-uncased* BERT model. Given that both models have the same number of parameters and have been trained with the same hyperparameters, the better performance of CT-BERT can be attributed to CT-BERT model pre-training. We submitted CT-BERT predictions on the test set for the final submission, and obtained 89.92 F1 score on the testset[2].

Data Augmentation further improves CT-BERT's classification performance from 92.72 to 92.84. Table 3 represents the top 20 unigrams identified using chi-squared statistics [3] (Liu and Setiono, 1995). Most of these words appear more frequently in one category over another and that's why these are ranked higher in chi-squared test.

As shown in Table 4, we observe a sharp drop in CT-BERT performance on dev set when we add "10 deaths" to all tweets. This sharp drop comes from that fact that model classified most of the uninformative tweets as informative tweets because of the presence of death count information. While data augmentation helps in improving the robustness, CT-BERT$_{\text{Aug}}$ still struggles in adversarial setting.

6 Discussion

Pre-trained language models provide state of the art performance on most of the NLP benchmark datasets. Unsurprisingly, CT-BERT does well on the shared task dataset. While these models can be further improved using ensemble techniques, improved fine-tuning (?), a more important research direction is to assess the applicability of such models to identify informative information in real-world applications.

We show the fragile nature of such classifiers using a simple adversarial task where the model

---

[2]For final submission, we submitted a CT-BERT model predictions based on dev set accuracy.

[3]`https://scikit-learn.org/stable/modules/generated/sklearn.feature_selection.chi2.html`

fails to classify an uninformative tweet if we add "10 deaths" to it. While not reported in the paper, we observe similar results for any "N deaths" pattern. On a social media platform such as Twitter, fake news or uninformative tweets might contain a similar pattern, and state of the art classifiers might not be able to correctly identify them. It raises serious concerns about the robustness of such systems. While our proposed data augmentation helps in improving the model robustness, it still falls short from what is expected from a trustworthy system.

7 Conclusion

In this paper, we introduce BERT based classifiers to identify informative tweets. We show that while such classifiers performs well on standard test benchmarks, they exploits easy clues for classification and their performance degrades drastically in the presence of simple adversarial triggers. We show that targeted data augmentation can help in improving the robustness and classification performance of such classifiers. In future, we will explore universal adversarial triggers (Song et al., 2020) to create a more challenging adversarial dataset and will also explore other techniques such as stability training (Zheng et al., 2016) to improve model robustness.

References

Jacob Devlin, Ming-Wei Chang, Kenton Lee, and Kristina Toutanova. 2018. Bert: Pre-training of deep bidirectional transformers for language understanding. *arXiv preprint arXiv:1810.04805*.

Andre Esteva, Anuprit Kale, Romain Paulus, Kazuma Hashimoto, Wenpeng Yin, Dragomir Radev, and Richard Socher. 2020. Co-search: Covid-19 information retrieval with semantic search, question answering, and abstractive summarization. *arXiv preprint arXiv:2006.09595*.

Varun Kumar, Ashutosh Choudhary, and Eunah Cho. 2020. Data augmentation using pre-trained transformer models. *arXiv preprint arXiv:2003.02245*.

Varun Kumar, Hadrien Glaude, Cyprien de Lichy, and William Campbell. 2019. A closer look at feature space data augmentation for few-shot intent classification. *arXiv preprint arXiv:1910.04176*.

Huan Liu and Rudy Setiono. 1995. Chi2: Feature selection and discretization of numeric attributes. In *Proceedings of 7th IEEE International Conference on Tools with Artificial Intelligence*, pages 388–391. IEEE.

R Thomas McCoy, Ellie Pavlick, and Tal Linzen. 2019. Right for the wrong reasons: Diagnosing syntactic heuristics in natural language inference. *arXiv preprint arXiv:1902.01007*.

Martin Müller, Marcel Salathé, and Per E Kummervold. 2020. Covid-twitter-bert: A natural language processing model to analyse covid-19 content on twitter. *arXiv preprint arXiv:2005.07503*.

Dat Quoc Nguyen, Thanh Vu, Afshin Rahimi, Mai Hoang Dao, Linh The Nguyen, and Long Doan. 2020. WNUT-2020 Task 2: Identification of Informative COVID-19 English Tweets. In *Proceedings of the 6th Workshop on Noisy User-generated Text*.

Timothy Niven and Hung-Yu Kao. 2019. Probing neural network comprehension of natural language arguments. *arXiv preprint arXiv:1907.07355*.

Gautam Kishore Shahi, Anne Dirkson, and Tim A Majchrzak. 2020. An exploratory study of covid-19 misinformation on twitter. *arXiv preprint arXiv:2005.05710*.

Liwei Song, Xinwei Yu, Hsuan-Tung Peng, and Karthik Narasimhan. 2020. Universal adversarial attacks with natural triggers for text classification. *arXiv preprint arXiv:2005.00174*.

Ashish Vaswani, Noam Shazeer, Niki Parmar, Jakob Uszkoreit, Llion Jones, Aidan N Gomez, Łukasz Kaiser, and Illia Polosukhin. 2017. Attention is all you need. In *Advances in neural information processing systems*, pages 5998–6008.

Eric Wallace, Shi Feng, Nikhil Kandpal, Matt Gardner, and Sameer Singh. 2019. Universal adversarial triggers for attacking and analyzing nlp. *arXiv preprint arXiv:1908.07125*.

Jason Wei and Kai Zou. 2019. Eda: Easy data augmentation techniques for boosting performance on text classification tasks. *arXiv preprint arXiv:1901.11196*.

Thomas Wolf, Lysandre Debut, Victor Sanh, Julien Chaumond, Clement Delangue, Anthony Moi, Pierric Cistac, Tim Rault, Rémi Louf, Morgan Funtowicz, et al. 2019. Huggingface's transformers: State-of-the-art natural language processing. *ArXiv*, pages arXiv–1910.

Xing Wu, Shangwen Lv, Liangjun Zang, Jizhong Han, and Songlin Hu. 2019. Conditional bert contextual augmentation. In *International Conference on Computational Science*, pages 84–95. Springer.

Stephan Zheng, Yang Song, Thomas Leung, and Ian Goodfellow. 2016. Improving the robustness of deep neural networks via stability training. In *Proceedings of the ieee conference on computer vision and pattern recognition*, pages 4480–4488.

LynyrdSkynyrd at WNUT-2020 Task 2: Semi-Supervised Learning for Identification of Informative COVID-19 English Tweets

Abhilasha Sancheti[*]
University of Maryland
College Park, USA
sancheti@cs.umd.edu

Kushal Chawla[*]
University of Southern California
Los Angeles, USA
kchawla@usc.edu

Gaurav Verma
Adobe Research
Bangalore, India
gaverma@adobe.com

Abstract

In this work, we describe our system for WNUT-2020 shared task on the identification of informative COVID-19 English tweets. Our system is an ensemble of various machine learning methods, leveraging both traditional feature-based classifiers as well as recent advances in pre-trained language models that help in capturing the syntactic, semantic, and contextual features from the tweets. We further employ pseudo-labelling to incorporate the unlabelled Twitter data released on the pandemic. Our best performing model achieves an F1-score of 0.9179 on the provided validation set and 0.8805 on the blind test-set.

1 Introduction

As of October 8, 2020, the novel coronavirus, SARS CoV-2, has infected 35.8 million people and led to over 1 million deaths [1]. With several stay-at-home orders and lockdowns in place, people have spent considerably more time than usual in disseminating and consuming information through social media. A subset of this publicly shared information relates to COVID-19, and ranges from information about new cases and deaths, lapses in policies made by local and state agencies, denied access to testing, etc. Since well-designed tools that monitor such information can help in quick identification and response from concerned agencies, recent research has focused on automatically detecting information and events related to COVID-19. For instance, Zong et al. (2020) aim to identify events on Twitter that relate to a new reported case or death, lapses in testing facilities, and information about cure and prevention, Lopez et al. (2020) analyze tweets to understand the perceptions of COVID-19 policies and how they change over time.

In the same vein as above, the 2020 edition of Workshop on Noisy User-generated Text (W-NUT 2020) hosted a shared task on 'Identification of Informative COVID-19 English Tweets'. The task involves automatically identifying whether an English Tweet related to COVID-19 is 'informative' or not. For a tweet to be considered informative in this context, it should provide information about recovered, suspected, confirmed, and death cases as well as location or travel history of the cases. The goal for developing such an automated system is to help track the development of the COVID-19 outbreak and to provide users the information related to the virus, e.g. any new suspicious/confirmed cases near/in the users' regions.

Aligned with the goals of this shared task, our paper details the use of state-of-the-art natural language processing techniques for identifying informative COVID-19 tweets. We experiment with a variety of methods, ranging from feature-based classifiers to leveraging recent advances in pre-trained neural architectures (Section 3). To further improve performance, we incorporate unlabelled tweets released on COVID-19 via masked language modelling and pseudo-labelling techniques. Our best performing model is an ensemble that uses Logistic Regression to combine the output probabilities of several base classifiers (Section 4). We further analyze the impact of pre-processing and semi-supervision through ablation studies. Through our qualitative adversarial analysis, we show how the predictions of BERT model are sensitive towards specific tokens such as 'confirmed case' or even locations and numerals, which also guides our data pre-processing steps.

2 Data Preprocessing

We conduct classification experiments on the COVID-19 Tweets dataset (Nguyen et al., 2020)

---

[*] Denotes equal contribution.
[1] https://covid19.who.int

Proceedings of the 2020 EMNLP Workshop W-NUT: The Sixth Workshop on Noisy User-generated Text, pages 444–449
Online, Nov 19, 2020. ©2020 Association for Computational Linguistics

provided for the shared task. The data split consists of 7000 tweets for training, 1000 in the validation set and 2000 in the blind test-set.

We start by lowercasing all the tweets, and replacing all urls with 'httpurl' and all usernames with '@user'. We then normalize all characters and pictograms. Additionally, we remove bad symbols (e.g. from a different language), any html tags, duplicated symbols or characters (like dots, question marks, special symbols, dashes or exclamations), and unnecessary underscores in the tokens. We also isolate punctuations, expand contractions (e.g. there'll to there will), and replace leet alphabets with their correct English versions using leet vocabulary[2]. We convert emojis into their text form [3] and finally normalize the different ways in which 'COVID-19' is written (e.g., covid-19, covid2019, covid19, or covid 2019) by replacing each occurrence with 'covid19'. These steps help to limit the vocabulary for better learning. On top of the above steps, we create different versions of the dataset as described below.

Cleaned: No further processing is done.

NUM-replaced: All the numerals in the dataset (except 19 in 'covid19') are replaced by NUM followed by the number of digits in the number.

LOC-replaced: We use the Python Spacy library[4] to get the named entity tags for each token in a tweet and replace the token having a 'GPE' (geopolitical entities i.e. countries, states, or cities) tag with 'LOC', so that the informativeness of a tweet is agnostic of a particular location.

NUM-LOC-replaced: We replace both numerals and tokens with 'GPE' tags in this version.

The motivation behind different versions of the dataset comes from our analysis (presented in Section 4) of the model trained on the **Cleaned** version of the dataset. We show how the model predictions are sensitive towards locations and numerals in a tweet, as a result of the patterns in the dataset. Hence, using NUM and LOC helps mitigate these issues. Following this pre-processing, we train a variety of machine learning models to classify tweets into two classes: informative and uninformative. We use the data split provided by the task organizers throughout to ensure consistency.

3 System Description

The system submitted for the shared-task is an ensemble of a variety of machine learning models which we discuss below in detail.

3.1 Fine-tuning pre-trained models

Motivated by their state-of-the-art performance on several downstream natural language processing tasks, we use pre-trained models like BERT (Devlin et al., 2018) for our classification task. BERT model learns a contextual representation of an input text which helps in representing the semantic information contained in an input. Borrowing notations from Sun et al. (2019), we leverage the pre-trained model in the following ways.

BERT-FiT: Following the standard fine-tuning pipeline (Devlin et al., 2018), the model is initialized with a pre-trained architecture and is further **Fine-T**uned on the provided labelled dataset.

BERT-ITPT-FiT: Inspired by the improvements using with**In T**ask **P**re-**T**raining (Sun et al., 2019), we further train the out-of-the-box pre-trained model on our training dataset using the masked language modeling (MLM) objective for 3 epochs. Thereafter, the model is fine-tuned for classification using the associated ground-truth labels.

BERT-IDPT-FiT: Extending the above approach, we extract a total of 27,388 tweets related to the pandemic using the Twitter API[5] for **In-D**omain **P**re-**T**raining. We use the tweet IDs released with the Covid-19 tweets dataset (Lamsal, 2020) and the WNUT shared task on Event Extraction[6]. The extracted tweets are pre-processed in the same manner as described in Section 2 and augmented with the training set to further train the pre-trained model on the MLM loss for 5 epochs. Once trained, we then fine-tune the model on the classification task using the provided labelled training set. As we show later (Table 1), leveraging additional in-domain tweets further helps in improving the performance on our task.

---

[2]https://en.wikipedia.org/wiki/Leet
[3]We use pre-processing script available at https://www.kaggle.com/kyakovlev/preprocessing-bert-public/
[4]Spacy's en_core_web_sm module.

[5]https://developer.twitter.com/en/docs/labs/tweets-and-users/quick-start/get-tweets
[6]http://noisy-text.github.io/2020/extract_covid19_event-shared_task.html

We primarily use 'bert-base-uncased' architecture for all our experiments and train separate models[7] for each version of the dataset as well as each variant of the BERT model. All the models are fine-tuned for 20 epochs with the maximum input length set to 100, batch size to 8, and dropout to 0.3. The model having best F1-score for the 'Informative' class on the validation dataset is used for evaluation.

We also experimented with other pre-trained models: BERT-Large (Devlin et al., 2018), RoBERTa (Liu et al., 2019), XLNet (Yang et al., 2019), and Covid-BERT (Müller et al., 2020) but did not find any visible difference in performance. Hence, we restricted our experiments to BERT-base owing to its smaller size and consequently, lesser consumption of computational resources.

3.2 Classification using fastText (fastText)

Joulin et al. (2017) proposed fastText – a simple and efficient baseline for text classification that uses bag of n-gram features to capture partial information about the local word order. We use the fastText library to train a classifier for our task. We train the model for 10 epochs with a learning rate initialized at 0.1 and the maximum length of n-grams is set to 3.

3.3 Most-frequent N-gram features (ngram)

We also build our own implementation of n-gram features. Using the **NUM-LOC-replaced** version of the dataset, we extract the most frequent 5000 unigrams, bigrams, and trigrams for each class and use the presence or absence of these n-grams in a given tweet, as features. These features are used as input to a feed-forward neural network, with two hidden layers of size 64, dropout of 0.1, and activation as ReLU. Although the feature vector is highly sparse, we find this approach to perform reasonably well on our task.

3.4 Leveraging the Universal Sentence Encoder (USE)

We leverage the Universal Sentence Encoder (Cer et al., 2018) to get sentence embeddings of the tweets. These 512-dimensional embeddings are used as input features to a feed-forward neural network identical to the one described above for n-gram features. Sentence embedding based classifiers also take into account the contextual (short-range as well as long-range) information of each word as well as ordering of the words, unlike the n-gram based models, performing well in practice.

3.5 Hand-crafted features (HCF)

Next, leveraging the advances in affective computing, we build a total of 150 hand-crafted features, comprising both syntactic and affect features. Syntactic features include statistics from the tweet based on the counts of punctuation marks along with NER and POS tags. We also include text readability metrics from the textstat toolkit[8]. On the other hand, affect features are based on existing lexicons in the literature. Specifically, we use Warriner VAD wordlists (Warriner et al., 2013), formality word-lists (Brooke et al., 2010), PERMA model (Seligman, 2012), Temporal word lists (Park et al., 2015), EmoLex (Mohammad et al., 2013), and lastly, LIWC (Pennebaker et al., 2001). All the features are concatenated to form a feature vector for each tweet which is used as an input to the feed-forward network described previously.

3.6 Employing Pseudo-Labelling (PL)

In order to leverage the unlabelled data for feature-based methods, we resort to pseudo-labelling. The models are trained for at most 50 epochs in the following manner: After every 10 epochs, we select the checkpoint with the best F1-score for the 'Informative' class saved till now and use it to predict labels on the collected unlabelled tweets (same as described in Section 3.1). We randomly pick 1000 tweets on which the prediction confidence is above 0.99 and consider the predicted labels for these tweets as pseudo ground-truth labels. Hence, these 1000 tweets are removed from the set of unlabelled data and instead added to the training dataset for future epochs. The training continues from the best checkpoint found till now.

In Section 4, we show improvements due to the use of pseudo-labelling across all the methods based on fixed feature vectors. We also tried pseudo labelling with BERT. However, using MLM to incorporate unlabelled tweets (**BERT-IDPT-FiT**), performs better than pseudo-labelling in that case.

---

[7]We use huggingface library available at `https://github.com/huggingface/transformers` for fine-tuning of pre-trained models.

[8]`https://pypi.org/project/textstat/`

Model	Accuracy↑	Precision↑	Recall↑	F1-score↑
Majority	0.5280	0.0000	0.0000	0.0000
HCF-PL	0.7460	0.7410	0.7104	0.7252
USE-PL	0.7756	0.7196	0.8601	0.7834
fastText	0.8083	0.8372	0.7373	0.7840
ngram-PL	0.8090	0.7932	0.8072	0.7997
BERT-FiT	0.9010	0.8768	0.9201	0.8977
BERT-ITPT-FiT	0.9010	0.8716	0.9272	0.8984
BERT-IDPT-FiT	0.9070	0.8736	**0.9392**	0.9050
Ensemble	**0.9209**	**0.9034**	0.9322	0.9176
Ensemble-TT	**0.9209**	0.9002	0.9364	**0.9179**

Table 1: Performance of various models on Precision, Recall and F1-score for Informative class and model accuracy on the validation dataset. The numbers are averaged over 3 runs. BERT-based and fastText models were trained on different pre-processed versions of the dataset. We report the scores for the corresponding best performing configuration above.

3.7 Ensemble Model

Our final model is an ensemble of the base classifiers described above. To build an ensemble, we train a logistic regression model using the output probabilities from a subset of the base classifiers, as features. Further, we tune the threshold above which the model would output the class as 'Informative', and otherwise output 'Uninformative'. The ensemble model without any threshold tuning is referred to as **Ensemble**. The model with threshold tuning is referred to as **Ensemble-TT**, that uses a threshold value of 0.5168 instead of 0.5.

4 Results and Analysis

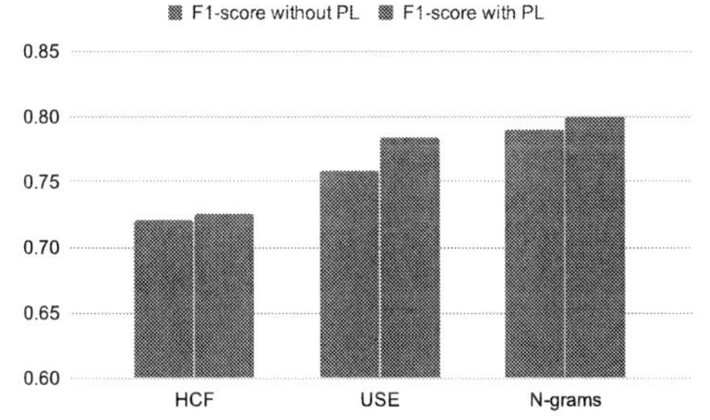

Figure 1: Effect of pseudo-labelling on F1-score for the Informative class. Pseudo-labelling improves the performance for all three methods.

The primary evaluation metric for the shared task is F1-score for the 'Informative' class. The other metrics used are the Precision and Recall for Informative class and the overall accuracy of the model.

We first illustrate the benefit of employing

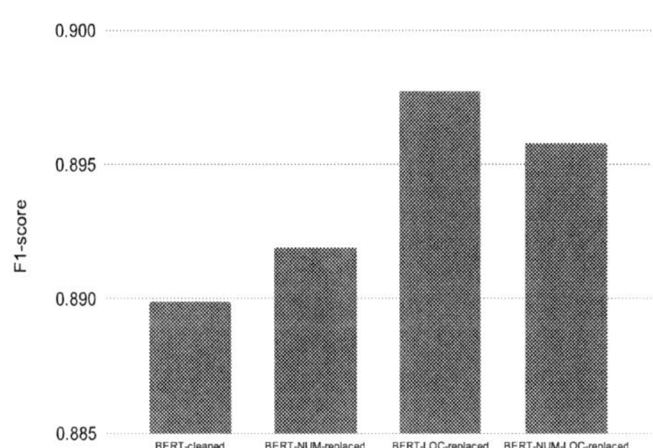

Figure 2: Impact of different ways of data pre-processing on F1-score using the **BERT-FiT** model.

pseudo-labelling in Figure 1. All three methods, namely **HCF**, **USE** and **ngrams** achieve better F1-scores by leveraging the unlabelled data, along with the provided training dataset. Hence, we next compare these models with other baselines and BERT-based pre-trained methods in Table 1. All models easily beat the majority baseline, attesting that the models are learning useful patterns from the data. While feature-based methods perform reasonably well with **ngram-PL** achieving an F1-score close to 0.8, they are outperformed by BERT-based methods with approximately a 10% gain. High performance of **BERT-IDPT-FiT** shows that incorporating additional in-domain data using the MLM objective improves the performance. Finally, an ensemble using logistic regression achieves the best precision, resulting from a reduction in the number of false positives, while still maintaining the same recall. Our best performing model, **Ensemble-TT** achieves an F1-score of 0.9179 on the validation dataset and 0.8805 on the blind test-set.

Input: the taslee palm city estate in maitama , abuja , has alerted ...	Prediction
... its residents.	0
... its residents of a case .	1
... its residents of a confirmed case .	1
... its residents of coronavirus.	0
... its residents of a case of coronavirus .	1
... its residents of a confirmed case of coronavirus .	1
... its residents of malaria.	0
... its residents of a case of malaria .	1
... its residents of a confirmed case of malaria .	1

Table 2: **BERT-FiT** predictions on artificially-created examples, inspired from an instance in the validation dataset. 0 (1) refers to Uninformative (Informative) class.

Qualitative Adversarial Analysis: In Table 2, we show the sensitivity of **BERT-FiT** model towards specific tokens such as 'confirmed' and 'case' in

Input	Prediction
his family members got infected in santa clara .	1
his family members got infected in rohini .	0
5 family members got infected in rohini .	1
5 family members are healthy in rohini .	1

Table 3: **BERT-FiT** predictions on artificially-created examples, depicting bias towards numerals and locations. 0 (1) refers to Uninformative (Informative) class.

the tweets. Using these tokens governs the output predictions, regardless of whether the tweet is talking about covid-19 or an arbitrarily chosen disease, malaria. This is justified since the dataset mostly contains the tweets related to the pandemic, but suggests to exercise caution while using such models for downstream monitoring applications. Further, in Table 3, we show sensitivity towards numeric and location tokens in the tweets. Mere change of location to a less frequent one in the dataset or use of numerals inverts the model predictions, regardless of whether the tweet is actually informative or not. This observation infact inspires our data-pre-processing stages, where we mask the numeric and location tokens from the dataset. We investigate this further in Figure 2, which establishes that effective pre-processing can help mitigate these biases, while keeping the performance at-par or better on our classification task.

5 Conclusion

In this paper, we describe our system to identify informative COVID-19 English tweets. We find that an ensemble model which uses a logistic regression to combine the predictions of a variety of feature-based to neural methods achieves the best performance on the shared task. Our analysis shows that incorporating unlabelled tweets results in consistent performance gains. We show how the trained model can be sensitive to specific tokens in the tweets, and hence, advice for exercising caution while deploying machine learning models for downstream monitoring applications.

References

Julian Brooke, Tong Wang, and Graeme Hirst. 2010. Automatic acquisition of lexical formality. In *Proceedings of the 23rd International Conference on Computational Linguistics: Posters*. Association for Computational Linguistics.

Daniel Cer, Yinfei Yang, Sheng-yi Kong, Nan Hua, Nicole Limtiaco, Rhomni St John, Noah Constant, Mario Guajardo-Cespedes, Steve Yuan, Chris Tar, et al. 2018. Universal sentence encoder. *arXiv preprint arXiv:1803.11175*.

Jacob Devlin, Ming-Wei Chang, Kenton Lee, and Kristina Toutanova. 2018. Bert: Pre-training of deep bidirectional transformers for language understanding. *arXiv preprint arXiv:1810.04805*.

Armand Joulin, Édouard Grave, Piotr Bojanowski, and Tomáš Mikolov. 2017. Bag of tricks for efficient text classification. In *Proceedings of the 15th Conference of the European Chapter of the Association for Computational Linguistics: Volume 2, Short Papers*.

Rabindra Lamsal. 2020. Coronavirus (covid-19) tweets dataset.

Yinhan Liu, Myle Ott, Naman Goyal, Jingfei Du, Mandar Joshi, Danqi Chen, Omer Levy, Mike Lewis, Luke Zettlemoyer, and Veselin Stoyanov. 2019. Roberta: A robustly optimized bert pretraining approach. *arXiv preprint arXiv:1907.11692*.

Christian E Lopez, Malolan Vasu, and Caleb Gallemore. 2020. Understanding the perception of covid-19 policies by mining a multilanguage twitter dataset. *arXiv preprint arXiv:2003.10359*.

Saif Mohammad, Svetlana Kiritchenko, and Xiaodan Zhu. 2013. Nrc-canada: Building the state-of-the-art in sentiment analysis of tweets. In *Second Joint Conference on Lexical and Computational Semantics (* SEM), Volume 2: Proceedings of the Seventh International Workshop on Semantic Evaluation (SemEval 2013)*.

Martin Müller, Marcel Salathé, and Per E Kummervold. 2020. Covid-twitter-bert: A natural language processing model to analyse covid-19 content on twitter. *arXiv preprint arXiv:2005.07503*.

Dat Quoc Nguyen, Thanh Vu, Afshin Rahimi, Mai Hoang Dao, Linh The Nguyen, and Long Doan. 2020. WNUT-2020 Task 2: Identification of Informative COVID-19 English Tweets. In *Proceedings of the 6th Workshop on Noisy User-generated Text*.

Gregory Park, H Andrew Schwartz, Maarten Sap, Margaret L Kern, Evan Weingarten, Johannes C Eichstaedt, Jonah Berger, David J Stillwell, Michal Kosinski, Lyle H Ungar, et al. 2015. Living in the past, present, and future: Measuring temporal orientation with language. *Journal of personality*.

James W Pennebaker, Martha E Francis, and Roger J Booth. 2001. Linguistic inquiry and word count: Liwc 2001. *Mahway: Lawrence Erlbaum Associates*.

Martin EP Seligman. 2012. *Flourish: A visionary new understanding of happiness and well-being*. Simon and Schuster.

Chi Sun, Xipeng Qiu, Yige Xu, and Xuanjing Huang.
2019. How to fine-tune bert for text classification?
In *China National Conference on Chinese Computational Linguistics*. Springer.

Amy Beth Warriner, Victor Kuperman, and Marc Brysbaert. 2013. Norms of valence, arousal, and dominance for 13,915 english lemmas. *Behavior research methods*.

Zhilin Yang, Zihang Dai, Yiming Yang, Jaime Carbonell, Russ R Salakhutdinov, and Quoc V Le. 2019.
Xlnet: Generalized autoregressive pretraining for
language understanding. In *Advances in neural information processing systems*.

Shi Zong, Ashutosh Baheti, Wei Xu, and Alan Ritter. 2020. Extracting covid-19 events from twitter.
arXiv preprint arXiv:2006.02567.

NIT_COVID-19 at WNUT-2020 Task 2: Deep Learning Model RoBERTa for Identify Informative COVID-19 English Tweets

Jagadeesh M S, Alphonse P J A
Department of Computer Applications
National Institute of Technology
Tiruchirapalli,TamilNadu, India
malla.sree@gmail.com[1],
alphonse@nitt.edu[2]

Abstract

This paper presents the model submitted by NIT_COVID-19 team for identified informative COVID-19 English tweets at WNUT-2020 Task2. This shared task addresses the problem of automatically identifying whether an English tweet related to informative (novel coronavirus) or not. These informative tweets provide information about recovered, confirmed, suspected, and death cases as well as location or travel history of the cases. The proposed approach includes pre-processing techniques and pre-trained RoBERTa with suitable hyper-parameters for English coronavirus tweet classification. The performance achieved by the proposed model for shared task WNUT 2020 Task2 is 89.14% in the F1-score metric.

1 Introduction

Present the world is suffering from a novel coronavirus (Linton et al., 2020) from December-2019 to till date. It spreads all the continents and almost all countries in the world. Now a days many online tools or resources (Xu et al., 2020) provide coronavirus information to people in the world, but these resources are not continuously up to date. They are updating in a particular time interval. The world's major trusted resources like WHO (World Health Organization) (Chakraborty and Maity, 2020) also update this COVID-19 related information once a day. This pandemic COVID-19 has been spreading rapidly(Shao et al., 2020). In this situation world is looking for an automatic monitoring system for identifying useful information about COVID-19.

One of the most popular and trusted online social network platform (Karampelas, 2013) is TWITTER, an alternative source for updating the present pandemic information. Twitter is getting nearly 4 million COVID-19 tweets daily (Lopez et al., 2020), but only a few of them are informative. Twitter API provides tweet information openly to the research community. This is very useful to identify automatically informative COVID-19 tweets.

In this WNUT-2020 shared task-2, we proposed a model for automatically identifying COVID-19 informative tweets, which describes information about confirmed, recovered, and suspected and death cases as well as location or travel history of the COVID-19 affected patients. We have used pre-trained deep learning "RoBERTa" (Liu et al., 2019) with word-level embedding along with some pre-processing techniques. We also experimented with CNN (Moriya and Shibata, 2018) and pre-trained BERT (Devlin et al., 2018)– encoded sentences as input. The proposed deep learning Model gives a high F1- score compares to the above approaches. After discussed the related work in section 2, section 3 discussed the methodology and the data in detail and discusses the results in section 4. We analyze the results and error analysis in section 5 and section 6 concludes the paper.

2 Realated Work

Informative tweet identification has been of interest for researchers in recent years. Early work in the related fields include detection of online media (ALRashdi and O'Keefe, 2019), racism (Kabir and Madria, 2019), and disaster (Sreenivasulu and Sridevi, 2020). Papers published in recent years include (Madichetty and Sridevi, 2019), which introduces the tweet classification detection dataset and experiments with different machine learning models, such as naıve Bayes, logistic regression, random forests, and linear SVMs to investigate hate speech and disrespectful language, which experiments further on the same dataset using SVMs with n-grams and skip-grams features, and (Gambäck and Sikdar, 2017) and (Bohra et al., 2018), both exploring the performance of neural networks and comparing them with other machine learning ap-

450

Proceedings of the 2020 EMNLP Workshop W-NUT: The Sixth Workshop on Noisy User-generated Text, pages 450–454
Online, Nov 19, 2020. ©2020 Association for Computational Linguistics

proaches. Also, there has been published a couple of surveys covering various work addressing the identification of abusive, toxic, and offensive language, hate speech, etc., and their methodology including (Schmidt and Wiegand, 2017) and (Fortuna and Nunes, 2018). Additionally, there were several workshops and shared tasks on offensive language identification and related problems, including TA-COS2, Abusive Language Online3, and TRAC4 and GermEval (Wiegand et al., 2018), which shows the significance of the problem.

3 Methodology

The methodology used for WNUT-2020 Task 2, consists of a preprocessing phase and a deep learning model implementation phase.

3.1 Pre-processing

This phase consists of

1. Tokenization: In this step, the entire sentence (Pitsilis et al., 2018)is split into words (Tokens). Python "nltk" package helps to split the tweet into the tokens.

2. Convert Tokens to lower cases: The tokens from tokenization are may in lower or upper cases. In this step convert all tokens convert into the same case(here lower case).

3. Filter out punctuation: Remove all punctuation's (Gupta and Joshi, 2017) from the tokens.

4. Filter out stop words(and pipeline): Remove commonly used English words (Munková et al., 2013)(English stop words)

5. Stem words: Simply convert tokens into their genitive singular form (Grefenstette, 1996). For example, the wait is a stem word for waiting and waited.

3.2 Deep Learning Model

The goal of this WNUT-2020 task 2 is to identify a given COVID-19 tweet that is INFORMATIVE or UNINFORMATIVE. In this task, we have used a pre-trained deep learning model RoBERTa (Robustly Optimized BERT Approach), which is an optimized model for BERT (Jawahar et al., 2019). RoBERTa has features like

1. Train the data up to 160 GB.

2. Increase the number of iterations up to 500k.

3. Train the model with batch size 8k.

4. Larger byte-level BPE vocabulary with 50k sub word units.

5. Dynamically changing the masking pattern applied to the training data.

We trained the RoBERTa model with different combinations of hyperparameters for the given dataset, which was provided by WNUT-2020. Finally, we have gotten better metrics for hyper parametric values.

- Used 'roberta-base'

- Maximum learning rate is equal to 1e-5.

- We used batch size is equal to 16.

- Maximum sequence length of tweet in the dataset is 143.

- Avoid over-fitting we set hidden dropout is equal to 0.05.

- Hidden size for 'roberta-base' is equal to 768.

- An 'adam' is used for optimizer.

- Trained for 50 epochs.

3.3 Baseline Methods

we used three baseline methods:

- An Random Forest (Bhagat and Patil, 2015) with maximum depth of 26 and no of estimators 500.

- An SVM (Penagarikano et al., 2011) with 1- to 3-gram word TFIDF character count feature vectors as input.

- An CNN (Zhang et al., 2018) with embedding layer output size of 128 and fully connected. "adam" is used as an optimizer.

The CNN was trained for 25 epochs with stochastic gradient descent. Using Scikit-learn (Pedregosa et al., 2011), the baseline methods were implemented.

Data Set	INFORMATIVE	UNINFORMATIVE
Training	3303	3697
Validation	472	528
Test	944	1056

Table 1: COVID-19 English Tweets Data Set Details

4 Data

The main dataset used to train our model is COVID-19 INFORMATIVE English tweets identification (COVID-19 tweet dataset)(Nguyen et al., 2020), which was provided by WNUT-2020 at Task 2. This dataset consists of training, validation, and testing phases with 7000, 1000, and 12000 tweet records respectively. Training and validation tweet records have fields name with Id, Text, and Label. The tweet classification was done, based on the tweet information, which includes recovered, suspected, confirmed death cases, as well as location or travel history of the cases that come under IN-FORMATIVE tweets and other non-informative COVID-19 tweets, comes under UNINFORMA-TIVE.

The 'COVID-19 English Tweets' dataset provides 3303 INFORMATIVE tweets and 3697 UN-INFORMATIVE tweets from the training dataset, 472 INFORMATIVE, and 528 UNINFORMA-TIVE tweets from the validation dataset. The test dataset is a large set of 12k tweets and the actual 2k test tweets test the model in the form of an F1-Score metric. This test set consists of 944 INFOR-MATIVE and 1056 UNINFORMATIVE unlabeled tweets as shown in table 1.

5 Results and Error Analysis

Finally, We done experiment on the baseline models in 3.3 and the model described in section 3.2 using the COVID-19 English tweets data sets.The task organizers did not provide any baseline scores for this task. For better results on the validation data set, RoBERTa model trained on training data set, tested on validation data set and obtained results shown in the table 2. Models of deep learning need a large amount of data for training. So for better results on the test data set, RoBERTa model trained on both training data set as well as validation data set and tested on test data set and obtained results shown in the table 3. The best results are noted in bold. This data comprises tweets with INFORMATIVE and UNINFORMATIVE labels in binary classification. RoBERTa gives best per-

Model	F1-score	Accuracy
Random Forest	81.5894	82.0688
SVM	82.7105	82.0488
CNN	83.7370	83.0691
BERT	88.9787	89.1006
RoBERTa	**89.1864**	**89.5000**

Table 2: Results obtained on the Validation Set.

Model	F1-score	Accuracy	Recall	precision
RoBERTa	**89.14**	**89.35**	**92.58**	**85.94**

Table 3: Results obtained on the Test Data Set.

formance on validation data by a margin of more than 0.2 with the best baseline performance(BERT) (Karisani and Karisani, 2020). From the confusing matrix as shown in Figure 1 we observe that the performance of RoBERTa on INFORMATIVE is quite good, but not on UNINFORMATIVE. we can observe the detailed results of RoBERTa in table 4.

We have submitted results of our model on test data as part of WNUT-2020 Task 2 for recognising COVID-19 English informative tweets. The organizers released unlabeled test data for the final evaluation phase. This is a large set of 12K tweets, and the actual 2K test tweets by which our model has evaluated are hidden in this large set. Our model output metric values on test data are F1-score is 89.14, precision is 85.94, recall is 92.35, and accuracy value is 89.35 as shown in table 3.

RoBERTa outperformed well,compare with BERT, by 0.20 % F1-score. The baseline model results, however,worse than the RoBERTa and , probably due the fact that the RoBERTa model requires fine-tuning for more task specific representations. The majority of RoBERTa errors are in INFORMATIVE class.

6 Conclusion and Future Work

In this (WNUT-2020 shared Task2) competition, We introduced the NIT_COVID-19 team's ap-

Label	F1-score	Accuracy
INFORMATIVE	89.89	90.23
UNINFORMATIVE	88.16	88.32

Table 4: Detailed RoBERTa Model Metric values on validation data set

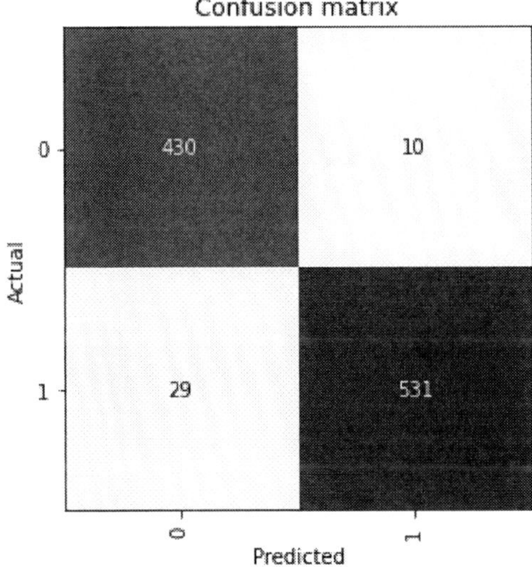

0 - Represents INFORMATIVE
1 - Represents UNINFORMATIVE

Figure 1: Confusion Matrix for validation set

proach to the issue of informative tweet recognition and automatic categorization from the COVID-19 tweet master dataset of informative tweets. The pre-trained deep learning RoBERTa model outperformed the remaining models, including Random Forest, SVM,CNN and BERT. Furthermore, the analysis of the results indicates the some of INFORMATIVE tweets are not identified by the model. Such deficiencies demand larger training corpa and need a prominent features for training. In future work we will concentrate on latest pre-trained deep learning models and other issues for better results.

References

Reem ALRashdi and Simon O'Keefe. 2019. Deep learning and word embeddings for tweet classification for crisis response. *arXiv preprint arXiv:1903.11024*.

Reshma C Bhagat and Sachin S Patil. 2015. Enhanced smote algorithm for classification of imbalanced bigdata using random forest. In *2015 IEEE International Advance Computing Conference (IACC)*, pages 403–408. IEEE.

Aditya Bohra, Deepanshu Vijay, Vinay Singh, Syed Sarfaraz Akhtar, and Manish Shrivastava. 2018. A dataset of hindi-english code-mixed social media text for hate speech detection. In *Proceedings of the second workshop on computational modeling of people's opinions, personality, and emotions in social media*, pages 36–41.

Indranil Chakraborty and Prasenjit Maity. 2020. Covid-19 outbreak: Migration, effects on society, global environment and prevention. *Science of the Total Environment*, page 138882.

Jacob Devlin, Ming-Wei Chang, Kenton Lee, and Kristina Toutanova. 2018. Bert: Pre-training of deep bidirectional transformers for language understanding. *arXiv preprint arXiv:1810.04805*.

Paula Fortuna and Sérgio Nunes. 2018. A survey on automatic detection of hate speech in text. *ACM Computing Surveys (CSUR)*, 51(4):1–30.

Björn Gambäck and Utpal Kumar Sikdar. 2017. Using convolutional neural networks to classify hate-speech. In *Proceedings of the first workshop on abusive language online*, pages 85–90.

David A Hull Gregory Grefenstette. 1996. A detailed analysis of english stemming algorithms. *Rank Xerox Research Centre*, 6:1–16.

Itisha Gupta and Nisheeth Joshi. 2017. Tweet normalization: A knowledge based approach. In *2017 International Conference on Infocom Technologies and Unmanned Systems (Trends and Future Directions)(ICTUS)*, pages 157–162. IEEE.

Ganesh Jawahar, Benoît Sagot, and Djamé Seddah. 2019. What does bert learn about the structure of language?

Md Yasin Kabir and Sanjay Madria. 2019. A deep learning approach for tweet classification and rescue scheduling for effective disaster management. In *Proceedings of the 27th ACM SIGSPATIAL International Conference on Advances in Geographic Information Systems*, pages 269–278.

Panagiotis Karampelas. 2013. *Techniques and tools for designing an online social network platform*. Springer.

Negin Karisani and Payam Karisani. 2020. Mining coronavirus (covid-19) posts in social media. *arXiv preprint arXiv:2004.06778*.

Natalie M Linton, Tetsuro Kobayashi, Yichi Yang, Katsuma Hayashi, Andrei R Akhmetzhanov, Sung-mok Jung, Baoyin Yuan, Ryo Kinoshita, and Hiroshi Nishiura. 2020. Incubation period and other epidemiological characteristics of 2019 novel coronavirus infections with right truncation: a statistical analysis of publicly available case data. *Journal of clinical medicine*, 9(2):538.

Yinhan Liu, Myle Ott, Naman Goyal, Jingfei Du, Mandar Joshi, Danqi Chen, Omer Levy, Mike Lewis, Luke Zettlemoyer, and Veselin Stoyanov. 2019. Roberta: A robustly optimized bert pretraining approach. *arXiv preprint arXiv:1907.11692*.

Christian E Lopez, Malolan Vasu, and Caleb Gallemore. 2020. Understanding the perception of covid-19 policies by mining a multilanguage twitter dataset. *arXiv preprint arXiv:2003.10359*.

Sreenivasulu Madichetty and M Sridevi. 2019. Detecting informative tweets during disaster using deep neural networks. In *2019 11th International Conference on Communication Systems & Networks (COMSNETS)*, pages 709–713. IEEE.

Shun Moriya and Chihiro Shibata. 2018. Transfer learning method for very deep cnn for text classification and methods for its evaluation. In *2018 IEEE 42nd Annual Computer Software and Applications Conference (COMPSAC)*, volume 2, pages 153–158. IEEE.

Daša Munková, Michal Munk, and Martin Vozár. 2013. Influence of stop-words removal on sequence patterns identification within comparable corpora. In *International Conference on ICT Innovations*, pages 67–76. Springer.

Dat Quoc Nguyen, Thanh Vu, Afshin Rahimi, Mai Hoang Dao, Linh The Nguyen, and Long Doan. 2020. WNUT-2020 Task 2: Identification of Informative COVID-19 English Tweets. In *Proceedings of the 6th Workshop on Noisy User-generated Text*.

F. Pedregosa, G. Varoquaux, A. Gramfort, V. Michel, B. Thirion, O. Grisel, M. Blondel, P. Prettenhofer, R. Weiss, V. Dubourg, J. Vanderplas, A. Passos, D. Cournapeau, M. Brucher, M. Perrot, and E. Duchesnay. 2011. Scikit-learn: Machine learning in Python. *Journal of Machine Learning Research*, 12:2825–2830.

Mikel Penagarikano, Amparo Varona, Luis Javier Rodriguez-Fuentes, and German Bordel. 2011. Dimensionality reduction for using high-order n-grams in svm-based phonotactic language recognition. In *Twelfth Annual Conference of the International Speech Communication Association*.

Georgios K Pitsilis, Heri Ramampiaro, and Helge Langseth. 2018. Detecting offensive language in tweets using deep learning. *arXiv preprint arXiv:1801.04433*.

Anna Schmidt and Michael Wiegand. 2017. A survey on hate speech detection using natural language processing. In *Proceedings of the Fifth International workshop on natural language processing for social media*, pages 1–10.

Nian Shao, Yu Chen, Jin Cheng, and Wen Bin Chen. 2020. Some novel statistical time delay dynamic model by statistics data from ccdc on novel coronavirus pneumonia. *Kongzhi Lilun Yu Yingyong/Control Theory and Applications*, 37(4).

Madichetty Sreenivasulu and M Sridevi. 2020. Comparative study of statistical features to detect the target event during disaster. *Big Data Mining and Analytics*, 3(2):121–130.

Michael Wiegand, Melanie Siegel, and Josef Ruppenhofer. 2018. Overview of the germeval 2018 shared task on the identification of offensive language.

Bo Xu, Moritz UG Kraemer, Bernardo Gutierrez, Sumiko Mekaru, Kara Sewalk, Alyssa Loskill, Lin Wang, Emily Cohn, Sarah Hill, Alexander Zarebski, et al. 2020. Open access epidemiological data from the covid-19 outbreak. *The Lancet Infectious Diseases*, 20(5):534.

Jiarui Zhang, Yingxiang Li, Juan Tian, and Tongyan Li. 2018. Lstm-cnn hybrid model for text classification. In *2018 IEEE 3rd Advanced Information Technology, Electronic and Automation Control Conference (IAEAC)*, pages 1675–1680. IEEE.

EdinburghNLP at WNUT-2020 Task 2: Leveraging Transformers with Generalized Augmentation for Identifying Informativeness in COVID-19 Tweets

Nickil Maveli

ILCC, School of Informatics

University of Edinburgh

`n.maveli@sms.ed.ac.uk`

Abstract

Twitter has become an important communication channel in times of emergency. The ubiquitousness of smartphones enables people to announce an emergency they're observing in real-time. Because of this, more agencies are interested in programatically monitoring Twitter (disaster relief organizations and news agencies) and therefore recognizing the informativeness of a tweet can help filter noise from large volumes of data. In this paper, we present our submission for *WNUT-2020 Task 2: Identification of informative COVID-19 English Tweets*. Our most successful model is an ensemble of transformers including *RoBERTa*, *XLNet*, and *BERTweet* trained in a Semi-Supervised Learning (SSL) setting. The proposed system achieves a F1 score of **0.9011** on the test set (ranking **7**[th] on the leaderboard), and shows significant gains in performance compared to a baseline system using fasttext embeddings.

1 Introduction

In late December 2019, the outbreak of a novel coronavirus causing COVID-19 was reported[1]. Due to the rapid spread of the virus, the World Health Organization declared a state of emergency. Social media platforms such as Twitter provides a powerful lens for identifying people's behavior, decision-making, and information sources before, during, and after wide-scope events, such as natural disasters (Becker et al., 2010). Identifying relevant information in tweets is challenging due to the low signal-to-noise ratio.

The basic goal of WNUT-2020 Task 2 (Nguyen et al., 2020) is to automatically identify whether a COVID-19 English Tweet is Informative or not. Such Informative Tweets provide information about recovered, suspected, confirmed and death cases as well as location or travel history of the cases. About 4M COVID-19 English Tweets are daily being posted on twitter, the majority of which being not informative. In many instances, it's not always clear whether a person's words are actually announcing a disaster response. Consider an example of an UNINFORMATIVE tweet from the dataset as shown in Table 1:

Text	Label
1) Some thoughts on China's 1Q macro numbers. China's economy was the first to suffer the consequences of fighting the novel coronavirus and is the first on the road to recovery. After an initial cover-up and more than 3,000 deaths, China appears to have brought COVID-19	0

Table 1: A hard to classify tweet.

However, this observation is hard to decipher examining only the vocabulary used; the tweet contains a variety of top frequent informative words (*"coronavirus"*, *"covid-19"*, *"deaths"*). This example hints that in order to reach meaningful results, we may have to examine contextual linguistic features, model the annotator's bias, introduce adversarial examples, etc (Geva et al., 2019; Goodfellow et al., 2015).

In this paper, we build an ensemble of Transformer (Vaswani et al., 2017) models to leverage its strength in capturing contextual information. The data used to train these models is an augmented version carefully prepared to alleviate confirmation bias and thereby improve generalization. The final inference result is the majority voting of the class from all constituent models through optimal thresholding as a post-processing step. Our best model (ensemble) achieves F1 scores of **0.9248**

---

[1]`https://www.ncbi.nlm.nih.gov/pmc/articles/PMC7159299/`

Proceedings of the 2020 EMNLP Workshop W-NUT: The Sixth Workshop on Noisy User-generated Text, pages 455–461
Online, Nov 19, 2020. ©2020 Association for Computational Linguistics

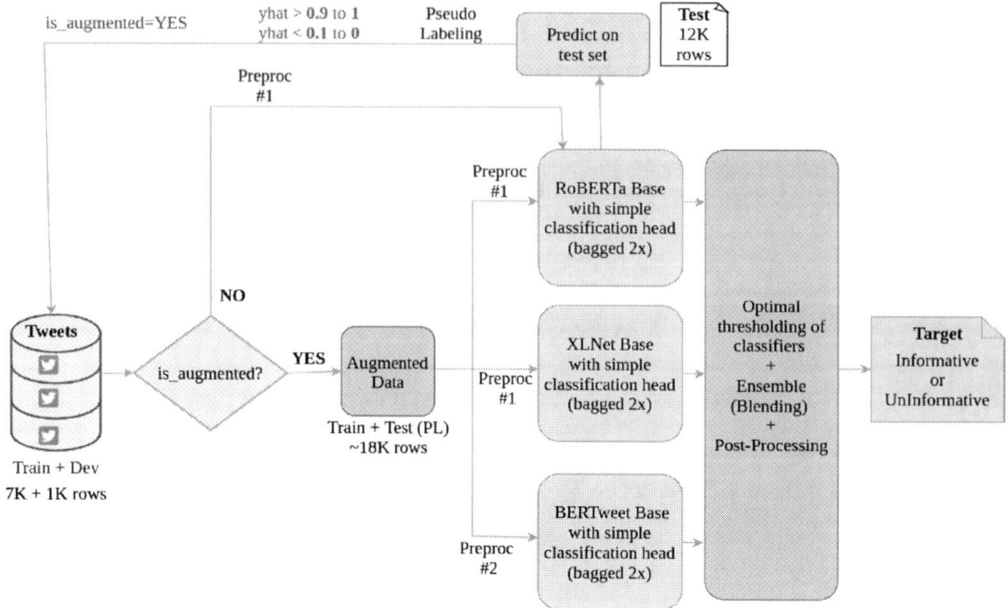

Figure 1: Our proposed model architecture. A RoBERTa model does the classification on the 12K test-set, while being trained using 7K train-set. Later, 11K most confident predictions are appended to the train-set. The new concatenated data is fed to the ensemble models leading to better generalization and improved model performance.

and **0.9011** on the dev and test set respectively.

2 Related Work

Recently, research has started to investigate the use of deep learning in the area of disaster response. For example, Caragea et al. (2016) used CNN to identify informative messages in data from flooding disasters and reported significant improvements in performance over SVM and fully connected ANN. Nguyen et al. (2017) used CNNs on situational awareness crisis data and noted improvements over traditional algorithms. Lazreg et al. (2016) used LSTM network to learn a model from crisis tweets and used this model to generate snippets of information summarizing the tweets. Wang and Lillis (2019) classified actionable tweets using ELMo contextual word embeddings, whereas Ma (2019) used a monolingual BERT-based model for disaster-related tweet classification.

Text classification generally consists of two processes: an encoder that converts texts to numerical representations and a classifier that estimates hidden relations between the representations and class labels. The text representations are generated using N-gram statistics (Wang and Manning, 2012), word embeddings (Joulin et al., 2017; Wang et al., 2018). More recently, powerful pre-trained models for text representations, e.g. BERT (Devlin et al., 2018),

have shown state of-the-art performance on text classification tasks using only the simple classifier of a fully connected layer.

3 System Description

We formulated this task as a binary text classification problem with INFORMATIVE and UNINFORMATIVE as the class names. As shown in Figure 1, the framework of our Informativeness classification model consists of three modules: *Transformer* and *BERTweet* ensemble learning, generalized augmentation via pseudo-labeling, optimal thresholding via post-processing to adjust distribution of class labels in target.

3.1 Data Preprocessing

The preprocessing pipeline consists of the following two strategies.

- **Preproc #1:** Texts are lowercased. Non-ascii letters, urls, @RT:[NAME], @[NAME] are removed. Break apart common single tokens; Eg: *RoBERTa* makes a single token for "...", so convert all single [...] tokens into three [.][.][.] tokens. Similarly, split "! ! !". All *Transformer* models use this preprocessing strategy.

456

- **Preproc #2:** Texts are normalized using `TweetTokenizer`[2]. Some of the normalization steps are - Expand text contractions(*"can't"* to *"cannot"*, *"M"* to *"million"*, etc), text normalization (*"p . m ."* to *"p.m."*, etc). All *BERTweet* models use this preprocessing strategy.

3.2 Model

We trained 6 models: 2 each of *RoBERTa-base*, *XLNet-base-cased*, and *BERTweet-base* respectively on a 5-fold setup to find the optimal epoch and it's performance was evaluated on the validation set after every epoch. Later, it was trained on the complete dataset.

3.2.1 RoBERTa

The meaning of words can vary subtly from one context to another, and *RoBERTa* generates contextualized word representations to capture the context-sensitive semantics of words (Liu et al., 2019). The use of word representations from *RoBERTa* has resulted in state-of-the-art performance in a variety of language understanding tasks. Given a sentence s consisting of n words $\{w_1, \ldots, w_n\}$, *RoBERTa* model generates their contextualized representations $\{\mathbf{v}^c_{s,w_1}, \ldots, \mathbf{v}^c_{s,w_n}\}$.

3.2.2 XLNet

XLNet is an auto-regressive language model which outputs the joint probability of a sequence of tokens based on the transformer architecture with recurrence (Yang et al., 2019). It's training objective calculates the probability of a word token conditioned on all permutations of word tokens in a sentence, as opposed to just those to the left or just those to the right of the target token.

3.2.3 BERTweet

It is the first public large-scale language model pre-trained for English Tweets that is trained using a 80GB corpus of 850M English Tweets (Dat Quoc Nguyen and Nguyen, 2020). It uses the same architecture as *BERT-base*, which is trained with a masked language modeling objective (Devlin et al., 2018). *BERTweet-base* model claims to do better than *RoBERTa-base* and outperforms previous SOTA models on three downstream Tweet NLP tasks of POS tagging, NER and text classification.

[2]`https://github.com/VinAIResearch/`
`BERTweet/blob/master/TweetNormalizer.py`

Parameter	Version 1	Version 2
Max Sequence Length	128	192
Epochs	4	4
Batch Size	16	16
Learning Rate	2e-5	3e-5
Optimizer	Adam	AdamW (0.01)
FGM	no	yes

Table 2: Training Hyperparameters. To perform bagging, Version 1 and Version 2 were used.

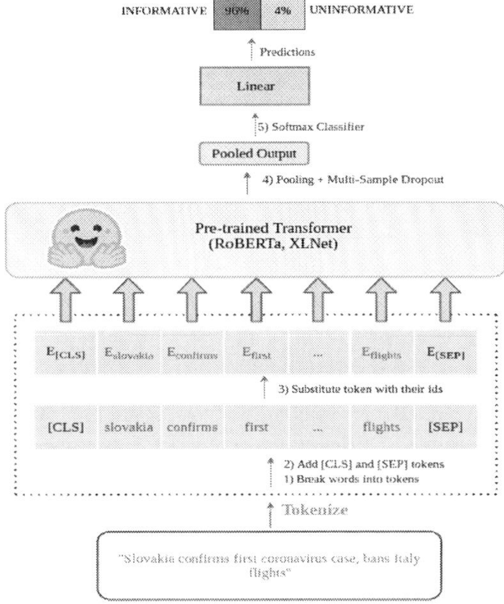

Figure 2: Pre-trained Transformer model architecture for informativeness classification.

3.2.4 Loss

Training Loss, Binary Cross Entropy Loss is defined as follows:

$$BCE = \begin{cases} -log(f(s_1)) & if \quad t_1 = 1 \\ -log(1 - f(s_1)) & if \quad t_1 = 0 \end{cases}$$

where $f()$ is the *sigmoid* function and s_1 and t_1 are the score and the ground truth label for the class C_1, which is also the class C_i in C.

4 Experimentation

We use only the dataset provided by the organizers to perform our experiments. Overall, there are a total of 10K Tweets split in the ratio of 70/10/20 into train/dev/test set respectively. However, for the final evaluation, 12K unlabeled noisy Tweets were provided, out of which 2K test Tweets were the actual ones the models were evaluated upon.

Model	Without Augmentation			With Augmentation		
	Precision	Recall	F1	Precision	Recall	F1
RoBERTa$_{\text{BASE_1}}$	0.8652	0.9386	0.9004	0.9619	0.8833	0.9209
RoBERTa$_{\text{BASE_2}}$	0.8760	0.9280	0.9012	**0.9640**	0.8818	0.9211
XLNet$_{\text{BASE_1}}$	0.8583	0.9364	0.8956	0.9619	0.8798	0.9190
XLNet$_{\text{BASE_2}}$	0.8580	0.9343	0.8945	0.9619	0.8731	0.9153
BERTweet$_{\text{BASE_1}}$	0.8630	0.9343	0.8973	0.9534	0.8858	0.9184
BERTweet$_{\text{BASE_2}}$	0.8483	**0.9597**	0.9006	0.9449	0.8974	0.9206
Ensemble	0.8790	0.9386	0.9078	0.9513	0.8998	**0.9248**

Table 3: Results on Dev Data.

Model	P	R	F1
Baseline FASTTEXT	0.7730	0.7288	0.7503
RoBERTa-XLNet-BERTweet-Ensemble	0.8768	0.9269	0.9011

Table 4: Results on Test set.

4.1 Setup

We installed the Python `transformers` library developed by huggingface (Wolf et al., 2019). Pretrained *RoBERTa-base* and *XLNet-base-cased* models with a single linear layer which is simply a feed-forward network that acts as a classification head were used. Figure 2 shows a high-level overview of the architecture.

To speed up training, sequence bucketing by removing unnecessary padding was employed (Khomenko et al., 2017). To improve the robustness of neural networks, and improving resistance to adversarial attacks, Fast Gradient Method (FGM) was used (Miyato et al., 2017) at the end of *Transformer* models. Multi-Sample Dropout (Inoue, 2019) was used when using dropout before the last layer with $p = 0.5$, seemed to converge loss faster. Output of each dropout layer was then passed to a shared weight *fc* layer. Next, we took the average of the outputs from *fc* layer as the final output. Table 2 lists the chosen parameters while model training.

For the *BERTweet-base* model, tweets were normalized and tokenized[3] with a *CNN-Dropout* layer for the inference. Through a bunch of hyperparameters experimented from a finite sample space, we set the *batch_size* = 16, *epochs* = 5, *max_seq_len* = 128, *learning_rate* = $3e - 6$, along with Learning Rate Schedulers (Loshchilov and Hutter, 2017).

---

[3]`https://www.kaggle.com/christofhenkel/setup-tokenizer`

4.2 Augmentation

Data is carefully augmented with the help of pseudo labeling which is the process of adding confident predicted test data to the training data. Inorder to make the Cross Validation (CV) less over-optimistic, we exclude the pseudo labels from validation folds. In other words, get the labels, run the kfold on only the original data points with real labels, and add the labels to train exactly at training time. That way the CV isn't biased by easy and artificially noiseless targets.

$$\hat{y_{new}} = \begin{cases} 1 & if \quad \hat{y_r} \geq 0.9 \\ 0 & if \quad \hat{y_r} < 0.1 \end{cases}$$

where $\hat{y_r}$ is the meta-prediction on the 12K test-set using *RoBERTa-base* and $\hat{y_{new}}$ is the new label associated with it. These are then concatenated back to the train set, making an augmented data of 18915 rows to develop the final model. In other words, 11915 out of 12K rows in the test-set were identified as confident predictions after pseduo labeling. The thresholds were decided based on several optimization ranges so as to maximize the F-score on holdout dev set.

4.3 Post-Processing

The idea here is to make the distribution of labels in dev/test set to match corresponding distribution of labels in train set so as to maintain the class ratio. Hence, probabilities from all the 6 models were added and a majority voting cutoff value of **4** was found out by fine-tuning that maximized the F-score on holdout dev set.

$$p = \sum_{i=1}^{6} \vec{p_i}$$

$$p_{out} = \begin{cases} 1 & if \quad p \geq 4 \\ 0 & if \quad p < 4 \end{cases}$$

where $\vec{p_i}$ is the probability vector calculated by the 6 models $i \in \{1, \ldots, 6\}$. p is the ensemble output, whereas p_{out} is the final prediction.

5 Results and Error Analysis

Ablation analysis was performed to compare the performance of our model variants. We can evaluate the effect of contextual features by comparing our model with and without augmentation. Table 3 summarizes the performance on Dev Data.

Without augmentation, we notice a situation of high recall, low precision. Our classifier thinks a lot of tweets belong to INFORMATIVE class. This likely leads to a higher number of false positive measurements, and a lower overall accuracy. For the $BERTweet_{BASE\_2}$ model that gives the highest recall, 81 false positive and 19 false negative cases were identified. Whereas with augmentation, a situation of low recall, high precision was observed. This makes sense as the model has access to more positive training samples and is able to make better decisions. Our classifier is very picky, and does not think many tweets are INFORMATIVE. For the $RoBERTa_{BASE\_2}$ model that gives the highest precision, 61 false positive and 17 false negative cases were identified. Ideally, in the real-world scenario, the high recall case would be more favourable as we want the model to label everything that could potentially be an INFORMATIVE Tweet, because a human personnel will most likely then interpret these results.

Understandably, the fine-tuned *RoBERTa* model outperformed every other experimented models. Bagging the models also lead to lower variance and robust predictions. Table 4 shows the final results wherein our model improves the organizer's baseline by 20%. The effect of augmentation in the final ensemble was drastic as the F-score increased by about 1.87%. Moreover, the idea of summing the probabilities of single models while ensembling worked better in comparison to choosing the most common label after finding different cutoff points that maximized F-score of individual models.

The confusion matrix of our best model is as shown in Figure 3. We look through the examples where our model made misclassification, and summarize the patterns of these error examples along with their attention visualization (Vig, 2019).

- Inaccurate interpretation of contexts. In the sentence, *"Writing 101: don't put 2 numbers side by side. The punctuation is easy to miss.*

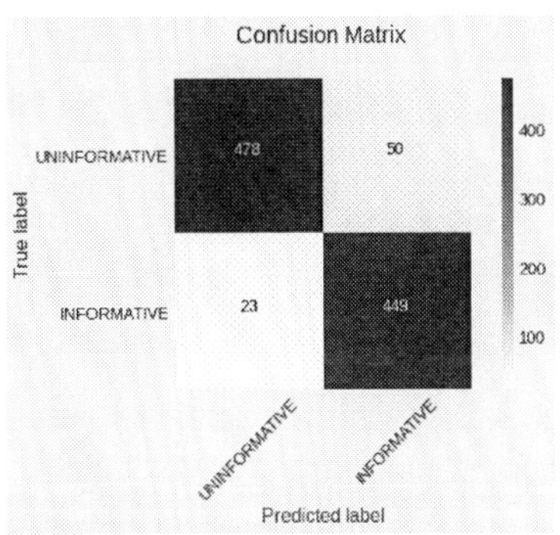

Figure 3: Confusion Matrix.

I first read this as being 51,385 people have died in Ontario from Covid.", much of the attention weights are focused on the latter part. Our model may not capture this shift correctly given the long-distance dependency, which results in a false positive prediction. See Figure 4 (Appendix A) for attention visualization.

- Misinformation due to ambiguity and subjectivity. In the sentence, *"I just remember this news recently China keeping two sets of coronavirus pandemic numbers? "Leaked" infection numbers over 154,000; deaths approach 25,000"*, it could be well evident that some events may not really happen as the source of the news lacked credibility. This could have prompted inter-annotator disagreement. See Figure 5 (Appendix A) for attention visualization.

6 Conclusion

We adopted an ensemble approach to reduce the variance of predictions and improve the model performance. The empirical results showed the effectiveness of our model. We also performed an error analysis to gain insights into the model behavior. In future, we would like to combine user-related tweet features (followers, friends, favorite counts, etc) and tweet-related meta features (retweets, creation_date, sentiment, etc) along with contextual representation. Moreover, extending to multilingual tweets (Chowdhury et al., 2020) is a potential future direction to pursue.

Acknowledgements

We would like to thank the anonymous reviewers for their time and comments which have helped make this paper and its contribution better.

References

Hila Becker, Mor Naaman, and Luis Gravano. 2010. Learning similarity metrics for event identification in social media. In *WSDM*, pages 291–300. ACM.

Cornelia Caragea, A. Silvescu, and A. Tapia. 2016. Identifying informative messages in disaster events using convolutional neural networks. In *ICIS 2016*.

Jishnu Ray Chowdhury, Cornelia Caragea, and Doina Caragea. 2020. Cross-lingual disaster-related multi-label tweet classification with manifold mixup. In *ACL (student)*, pages 292–298. Association for Computational Linguistics.

Thanh Vu Dat Quoc Nguyen and Anh Tuan Nguyen. 2020. BERTweet: A pre-trained language model for English Tweets. *arXiv preprint*, arXiv:2005.10200.

Jacob Devlin, Ming-Wei Chang, Kenton Lee, and Kristina Toutanova. 2018. BERT: pre-training of deep bidirectional transformers for language understanding. *CoRR*, abs/1810.04805.

Mor Geva, Yoav Goldberg, and Jonathan Berant. 2019. Are we modeling the task or the annotator? an investigation of annotator bias in natural language understanding datasets. In *EMNLP/IJCNLP (1)*, pages 1161–1166. Association for Computational Linguistics.

Ian J. Goodfellow, Jonathon Shlens, and Christian Szegedy. 2015. Explaining and harnessing adversarial examples. In *ICLR (Poster)*.

Hiroshi Inoue. 2019. Multi-sample dropout for accelerated training and better generalization. *CoRR*, abs/1905.09788.

Armand Joulin, Edouard Grave, Piotr Bojanowski, and Tomas Mikolov. 2017. Bag of tricks for efficient text classification. In *EACL (2)*, pages 427–431. Association for Computational Linguistics.

Viacheslav Khomenko, Oleg Shyshkov, Olga Radyvonenko, and Kostiantyn Bokhan. 2017. Accelerating recurrent neural network training using sequence bucketing and multi-gpu data parallelization. *CoRR*, abs/1708.05604.

Mehdi Ben Lazreg, Morten Goodwin, and Ole-Christoffer Granmo. 2016. Information abstraction from crises related tweets using recurrent neural network. In *AIAI*, volume 475 of *IFIP Advances in Information and Communication Technology*, pages 441–452. Springer.

Yinhan Liu, Myle Ott, Naman Goyal, Jingfei Du, Mandar Joshi, Danqi Chen, Omer Levy, Mike Lewis, Luke Zettlemoyer, and Veselin Stoyanov. 2019. Roberta: A robustly optimized BERT pretraining approach. *CoRR*, abs/1907.11692.

Ilya Loshchilov and Frank Hutter. 2017. SGDR: stochastic gradient descent with warm restarts. In *ICLR (Poster)*. OpenReview.net.

Guoqin Ma. 2019. Tweets classification with bert in the field of disaster management.

Takeru Miyato, Andrew M. Dai, and Ian J. Goodfellow. 2017. Adversarial training methods for semi-supervised text classification. In *ICLR (Poster)*. OpenReview.net.

Dat Quoc Nguyen, Thanh Vu, Afshin Rahimi, Mai Hoang Dao, Linh The Nguyen, and Long Doan. 2020. WNUT-2020 Task 2: Identification of Informative COVID-19 English Tweets. In *Proceedings of the 6th Workshop on Noisy User-generated Text*.

Dat Tien Nguyen, Kamla Al-Mannai, Shafiq R. Joty, Hassan Sajjad, Muhammad Imran, and Prasenjit Mitra. 2017. Robust classification of crisis-related data on social networks using convolutional neural networks. In *ICWSM*, pages 632–635. AAAI Press.

Ashish Vaswani, Noam Shazeer, Niki Parmar, Jakob Uszkoreit, Llion Jones, Aidan N. Gomez, Lukasz Kaiser, and Illia Polosukhin. 2017. Attention is all you need. In *NIPS*, pages 5998–6008.

Jesse Vig. 2019. A multiscale visualization of attention in the transformer model. In *ACL (3)*, pages 37–42. Association for Computational Linguistics.

Congcong Wang and David Lillis. 2019. Classification for crisis-related tweets leveraging word embeddings and data augmentation. In *TREC*, volume 1250 of *NIST Special Publication*. National Institute of Standards and Technology (NIST).

Guoyin Wang, Chunyuan Li, Wenlin Wang, Yizhe Zhang, Dinghan Shen, Xinyuan Zhang, Ricardo Henao, and Lawrence Carin. 2018. Joint embedding of words and labels for text classification. In *ACL (1)*, pages 2321–2331. Association for Computational Linguistics.

Sida I. Wang and Christopher D. Manning. 2012. Baselines and bigrams: Simple, good sentiment and topic classification. In *ACL (2)*, pages 90–94. The Association for Computer Linguistics.

Thomas Wolf, Lysandre Debut, Victor Sanh, Julien Chaumond, Clement Delangue, Anthony Moi, Pierric Cistac, Tim Rault, Rémi Louf, Morgan Funtowicz, and Jamie Brew. 2019. Huggingface's transformers: State-of-the-art natural language processing. *CoRR*, abs/1910.03771.

Zhilin Yang, Zihang Dai, Yiming Yang, Jaime G. Carbonell, Ruslan Salakhutdinov, and Quoc V. Le. 2019. Xlnet: Generalized autoregressive pretraining for language understanding. In *NeurIPS*, pages 5754–5764.

A Appendix

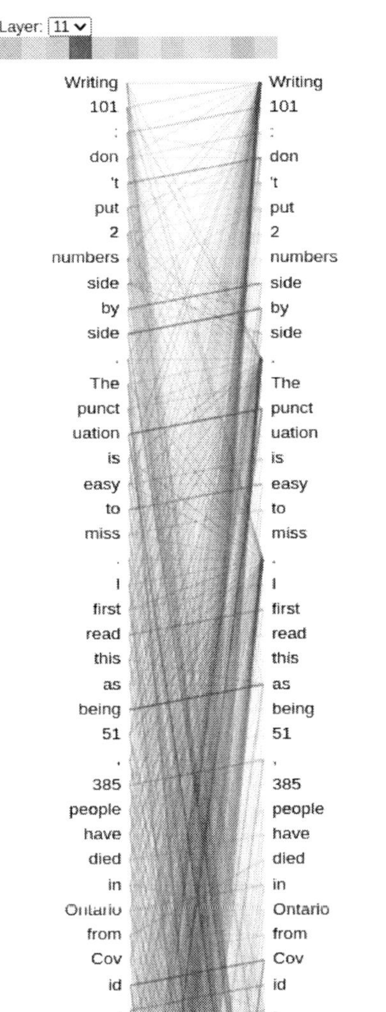

Figure 4: Attention-head view for the last layer of *RoBERTa-base* showing attention to other words predictive of word. In this pattern, attention seems to be directed to other words that are predictive of the source word, excluding the source word itself. In the example below, most of the attention from "id" is directed to "Cov", whereas most of the attention from "Cov" is not focused on "id".

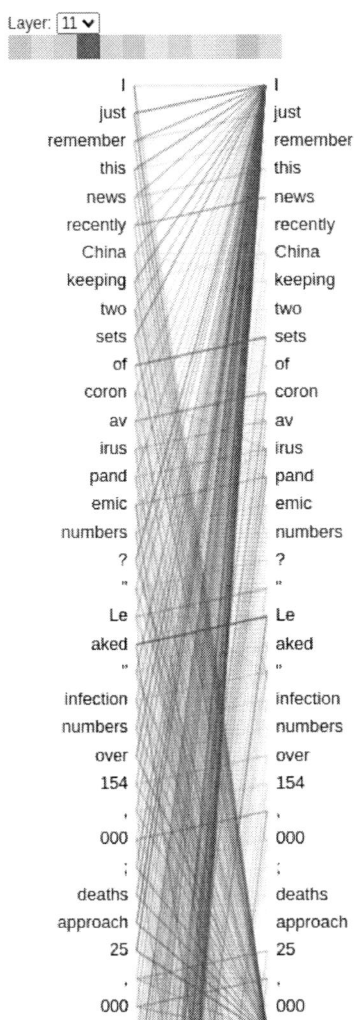

Figure 5: Attention-head view for the last layer of *RoBERTa-base* showing attention to either the previous or the next token in the sentence. For instance, most of the attention for "China" is directed to the previous word "I". Considering a different example, most of the attention for "coron" is directed to the next word "irus" skipping "av" in between.

#GCDH at WNUT-2020 Task 2: BERT-Based Models for the Detection of Informativeness in English COVID-19 Related Tweets

Hanna Varachkina
University of Göttingen
GCDH[*]
Papendiek 16
37073 Göttingen
Germany
hanna.varachkina@
stud.uni-goettingen.de

Stefan Ziehe
University of Göttingen
Institute of Computer Science
Goldschmidtstraße 7
37077 Göttingen
Germany
stefan.ziehe@
cs.uni-goettingen.de

Tillmann Dönicke
University of Göttingen
GCDH[*]
Papendiek 16
37073 Göttingen
Germany
tillmann.doenicke@
uni-goettingen.de

Franziska Pannach
University of Göttingen
GCDH[*]
Papendiek 16
37073 Göttingen
Germany
franziska.pannach@
stud.uni-goettingen.de

Abstract

In this system paper, we present a transformer-based approach to the detection of informativeness in English tweets on the topic of the current COVID-19 pandemic. Our models distinguish informative tweets, i.e. tweets containing statistics on recovery, suspected and confirmed cases and COVID-19 related deaths, from uninformative tweets. We present two transformer-based approaches as well as a Naive Bayes classifier and a support vector machine as baseline systems. The transformer models outperform the baselines by more than 0.1 in F1-score, with F1-scores of 0.9091 and 0.9036. Our models were submitted to the shared task *Identification of informative COVID-19 English tweets (WNUT-2020 Task 2)*.

1 Introduction

As of the end of August 2020, the outbreak of the COVID-19 pandemic has lead to 24.5 million cases world-wide and affected individuals, communities and nations in all parts of the world[1]. In order to receive reliable data on cases in their area, users rely on information systems, such as the Coronavirus Resource Center introduced by the Johns Hopkins University.[2] However, those systems mainly utilize statistics provided by official health institutes, such as the World Health Organisation or the Robert Koch Institute. In order to confirm the numbers of COVID-19 related confirmed cases, recoveries or deaths, those official information channels release data once a day.

Alternative sources, e.g. social media outlets such as Twitter, publish a vast amount of data in real-time. Therefore, the WNUT-2020 Shared Task 2 (Nguyen et al., 2020) called for systems that can distinguish informative Twitter messages, so-called tweets, from uninformative data. A sophisticated informativeness detection system can be used to update COVID-19 information systems for users world-wide on a real-time basis.

In this paper, we present different machine-learning approaches on the identification of informative tweets. We first evaluate Naive Bayes and support-vector-machine approaches with hand-crafted features. Subsequently, we employ transformer-based models, such as COVID-Twitter-BERT (Müller et al., 2020), which provide the best results.

This paper is structured as follows: Section 2 explains the task and the data provided by the hosts of the shared task, Section 3 explains different approaches on the machine-learning systems, Sections 4 and 5 present and discuss results. We finish this paper with a conclusion in Section 6 and an outview on future work in Section 7.

Our source code is available at `https://gitlab.gwdg.de/tillmann.doenicke/wnut-2020`.

2 Data

The organizers of the shared task provided raw data of a tweet ID, tweet text and the label "informative" or "uninformative". Participants were free to make use of additional data (Nguyen et al., 2020). We used the suggested split of the dataset with 7,000 tweets for training and 1,000 for validation.

3 Models

3.1 Baselines

For our baseline models, we tokenized the tweets with NLTK's tweetTokenizer[3], lowercased all tokens except all-capitals tokens and optionally

---

[*]Göttingen Centre for Digital Humanities
[1]`https://coronavirus.jhu.edu/map.html`
[2]`https://coronavirus.jhu.edu/`
[3]`https://www.nltk.org/api/nltk.tokenize.html`

Proceedings of the 2020 EMNLP Workshop W-NUT: The Sixth Workshop on Noisy User-generated Text, pages 462–465
Online, Nov 19, 2020. ©2020 Association for Computational Linguistics

masked all numbers except "19" (as in "COVID-19"). (Masking numbers means replacing them with a special token "#NUMBER#".) We then extracted token n-grams with $n \in \{1, \ldots, 5\}$ to use them as features.

Our first baseline model is a Naive Bayes classifier (NBC) with binary features (n-gram in tweet or not), implemented with NLTK's NaiveBayesClassifier[4].

The second baseline model is a support vector machine (SVM), implemented with scikit-learn's SVM module[5]. We tested binary features, count features (frequency of n-gram in tweet) and tf·idf features. To reduce computation time, we only considered n-grams which occurred at least 10 times in the training corpus.

We also tested a wide range of additional features for the SVM: a tweet's sentiment analysis scores, its Gunning fog index, the number of medical terms (we extracted the most informative terms from the CORD-19 dataset[6], a collection of scholarly articles about COVID-19), most of the content features[7] from Wang et al. (2015), and Boolean features which capture whether a tweet ends with an URL (to capture posts with a link to a source, e.g. a newspaper article), starts with a USER (to capture retweets), or contains an opinion expression from a hand-crafted list such as "I think" or "my point of view".

Suspecting that informativeness is expressed through statements with neutral sentiment, we extracted sentiment using the NLTK sentiment analysis module VADER[8]. However, we assume that the majority of the raw data provided in the task was already pre-filtered for neutral sentiment, as illustrated in Figure 1: The smallest score for neutral sentiment observed in the raw training data set was 0.335 (1 tweet), with 998 tweets that showed a perfect neutral sentiment score of 1.

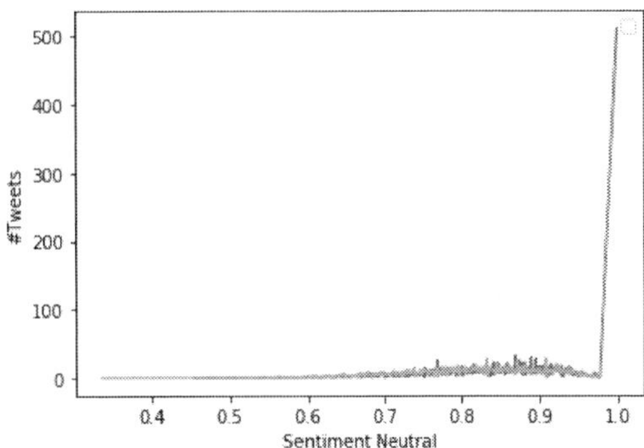

Figure 1: Distribution of neutral sentiment in informative (orange) and uninformative (blue) tweets, 1 being perfectly neutral

3.2 BERT-Based Models

Our other models rely on BERT (Devlin et al., 2018), a language model based on the transformer architecture that can be adapted to text classification tasks. For these models the data was preprocessed using the code provided by Müller et al. (2020). Retweet tags were removed, user names and URLs were replaced by a corresponding text token ("twitteruser" or "httpurl") and all unicode emoticons were substituted by textual ASCII representations. These preprocessing steps converted 64 tweets into empty strings, which were subsequently removed from the training set. We further moved the last 24 tweets from the training set (now 6,912 tweets) to the validation set (now 1,024 tweets). This allows for using a constant batch size of 32 during training.

The first model is based on the uncased BERT-large model. We fine-tuned it for two epochs on the training data for the given classification task. The second one is based on COVID-Twitter-BERT (CT-BERT) (Müller et al., 2020), a version of the uncased BERT-large model that was fine-tuned on 22.5M COVID-19 related tweets (0.6B words). CT-BERT was our choice because it is also based on BERT-large and is specifically fine-tuned for tweets related to COVID-19. We further fine-tuned it for three epochs on the training set. All the training was done on Tensor Processing Units (TPUs) provided in Google Colaboratory[9], which allowed us to use a sequence length of 96, a training batch size of 32 and an evaluation batch size of 1024. We used the Adam optimizer (Kingma and Ba, 2015) with a base learning rate of 2e-5. Additionally, we

---

[4]http://www.nltk.org/api/nltk.classify.html#module-nltk.classify.naivebayes

[5]https://scikit-learn.org/stable/modules/generated/sklearn.svm.SVC.html

[6]https://www.kaggle.com/allen-institute-for-ai/CORD-19-research-challenge

[7]Number of words, number of characters, number of capitalization words, number of capitalization words per word, maximum word length, mean word length, number of exclamation marks, number of question marks, number of URL links, number of URL links per word, number of hashtags, number of hashtags per word, number of mentions, number of mentions per word.

[8]https://www.nltk.org/_modules/nltk/sentiment/vader.html

[9]https://colab.research.google.com/

used smaller learning rates for earlier BERT layers by decaying them with a decay factor of $\xi = 0.95$ as described in Sun et al. (2019).

4 Results

Table 1 shows the results for all models. The NBC achieves its highest F1-score of 0.8012 when using only uni- and bigrams as features and not masking numbers. The SVM achieves its highest F1-score of 0.8009 when using uni- and bigrams as binary features and masking numbers. None of the additional features did help improving the performance of the SVM.

BERT-based models perform better than baseline models. The best result was achieved using the CT-BERT model trained on the domain-specific Twitter data on the topic of COVID-19 ("CT-BERT-1" in Table 1). It reached an F1-score of 0.9231 on the validation set. In comparison, the BERT-large model only achieved an F1-score of 0.8928.

Model	F1	Prec.	Rec.	Acc.
NBC	0.8012	0.7721	0.8326	0.8050
SVM	0.8009	0.8380	0.7669	0.8200
BERT	0.8928	0.8965	0.8891	0.8984
CT-BERT-1	0.9231	0.8988	0.9487	0.9248

Table 1: F1-score, Precision, Recall and Accuracy on the validation set

We submitted predictions made by CT-BERT to the shared task, both after training only on the training set (CT-BERT-1) for three epochs and after additionally training on the validation set (CT-BERT-2) for two epochs. We achieved similar results in both cases. A larger number of training examples (7,936 compared to 6,912) could not improve the model's performance on the final test set (Table 2), although it led to a higher precision (Table 3).

Model	Training data	F1
CT-BERT-1	6,912 tweets	0.9091
CT-BERT-2	7,936 tweets	0.9036

Table 2: Model overview and F1-score on the final evaluation set

Note that the final test set of about 2,000 tweets was hidden in a larger test set of about 12,000 tweets for the system evaluation (Nguyen et al., 2020). Numbers reported in Tables 2 and 3 are provided by the shared task organizers.

Model	Prec.	Rec.	Acc.
CT-BERT-1	0.8919	0.9269	0.9125
CT-BERT-2	0.9036	0.9036	0.9090

Table 3: Precision, Recall and Accuracy on the final evaluation set

5 Discussion

Due to the fact that the transformer-based models were pre-trained on much larger, external datasets (Devlin et al., 2018; Müller et al., 2020), it is unsurprising that they outperform our baseline models, which were solely trained on the shared task's dataset.

Our transformer-based models predict informative tweets slightly better than uninformative tweets. On the validation set, the BERT model delivers 115 falsely classified tweets, 28 of which were wrongly classified as uninformative and 87 which were classified as informative. The CT-BERT-1 model falsely predicted 25 tweets as uninformative and 52 as informative. Therefore, the main difference lies in the prediction of uninformative tweets, for which CT-BERT-1 yields better results. This leads to a better recall of the CT-BERT-1 model compared to the BERT model.

Upon manual inspections, the falsely classified tweets fall into different categories, such as tweets that show statistics but also a personal opinion, personal stories and events, or political statements and protective measures against COVID (e.g. "amazon and facebook ask seattle employees to work from home after coronavirus cases httpurl" annotated as informative). We cannot determine a pattern for the cases in which CT-BERT-1 yields better predictions than BERT.

Without the guidelines on how tweets were annotated for the dataset, it is hard to assess why certain tweets were initially labelled as informative or uninformative in the data provided. Therefore, we were not able to identify the reason why certain predictions were incorrect.

6 Conclusion

We show in our paper how a transformer-based approach can yield good results with relatively little fine-tuning.

Our best-performing model, the CT-BERT-1 model, predicted informativeness with an F1-score of 0.9091 in the final W-NUT Task 2 evaluation.

Detecting informativeness of a small text unit, such as a tweet, is one of the many steps that are required in order to build trustworthy real-time news applications.

7 Future Work

The task of identifying informativeness in small text units, such as Twitter messages, is an important step towards building real-time news applications. In order to build systems that can be trusted, the next step needs to address the validation of claims. Verifying how factual a statement is, requires additional knowledge bases and ultimately, a common, indisputable understanding of what "the truth" is.

Furthermore, such a system needs to consider that a piece of information might be correct only at a certain point in time. A Twitter message might be both informative and factual, but provide information that is outdated, such as yesterday's number of new COVID-19 cases, which ultimately has little value in terms of real-time news feeds.

Solving the binary classification task of distinguishing informative tweets from uninformative tweets does not yet determine whether a tweet contains relevant information.

Lastly, the common goal of researchers in the field of informativeness and factuality detection should be to create resources that are general enough to be used without a large amount of event related data or human annotations. Only then we are able to provide systems that can be employed immediately for new arising crisis situations, such as natural disasters.

References

Jacob Devlin, Ming-Wei Chang, Kenton Lee, and Kristina Toutanova. 2018. BERT: Pre-training of deep bidirectional transformers for language understanding. *arXiv preprint arXiv:1810.04805*.

Diederik P. Kingma and Jimmy Ba. 2015. Adam: A method for stochastic optimization. *arXiv preprint arXiv:1412.6980*.

Martin Müller, Marcel Salathé, and Per E. Kummervold. 2020. COVID-Twitter-BERT: A natural language processing model to analyse COVID-19 content on Twitter. *arXiv preprint arXiv:2005.07503*.

Dat Quoc Nguyen, Thanh Vu, Afshin Rahimi, Mai Hoang Dao, Linh The Nguyen, and Long Doan. 2020. WNUT-2020 Task 2: Identification of Informative COVID-19 English Tweets. In *Proceedings of the 6th Workshop on Noisy User-generated Text*.

Chi Sun, Xipeng Qiu, Yige Xu, and Xuanjing Huang. 2019. How to fine-tune BERT for text classification? In *Chinese Computational Linguistics*, pages 194–206. Springer International Publishing.

Bo Wang, Arkaitz Zubiaga, Maria Liakata, and Rob Procter. 2015. Making the most of tweet-inherent features for social spam detection on Twitter. *arXiv preprint arXiv:1503.07405*.

Not-NUTs at W-NUT 2020 Task 2: A BERT-based System in Identifying Informative COVID-19 English Tweets

Thai Hoang
University of Washington
qthai912@cs.washington.edu

Phuong Vu *
University of Rochester
pvu3@u.rochester.edu

Abstract

As of 2020 when the COVID-19 pandemic is full-blown on a global scale, people's need to have access to legitimate information regarding COVID-19 is more urgent than ever, especially via online media where the abundance of irrelevant information overshadows the more informative ones. In response to such, we proposed a model that, given an English tweet, automatically identifies whether that tweet bears informative content regarding COVID-19 or not. By ensembling different BERTweet model configurations, we have achieved competitive results that are only shy of those by top performing teams by roughly 1% in terms of F1 score on the informative class. In the post-competition period, we have also experimented with various other approaches that potentially boost generalization to a new dataset. Our repository can be found in the following link:
https://github.com/quocthai9120/
W-NUT-2020-Shared-Task-2

1 Introduction

Following the rise of smart technology and an increasingly wide coverage of Internet, social network websites are becoming ubiquitous these days. Besides serving as a platform for various types of entertainment, social media is particularly helpful in spreading information, and such can be leveraged to keep the majority of its users well-informed amidst a natural disaster or a pandemic like COVID-19. One major advantage of sourcing information via social media is that all information is updated in real-time. Any person with a social media account can post or share information instantly at the moment he/she witness a noteworthy event. This is a much faster way to obtain information compared to reading newspaper, watching the news on TV, or viewing other official source

of information since most tend to be updated only at mid-day or at the end of day. Nevertheless, information on social media platforms is mostly not verified, heavily opinionated towards the person who posted it, and at worst, completely inaccurate. This highlights the need for a system that can automatically identify legitimate information from the huge pool of information.

In order to address the aforementioned need for such a system, in this paper we attempt to tackle the WNUT 2020 Task 2: Identification of Informative COVID-19 English Tweets (Nguyen et al., 2020b). As stated in the task's description paper, this task requires its participants to build and refine systems that, given an English Tweet carrying COVID-19-related content, automatically classify whether it is informative or not. In the context of this shared task, being informative is defined as bearing information regarding suspected, confirmed, recovered or death cases related to COVID-19 as well as location or travel history of these cases.

2 Related work

Text classification is a simple but practical task in the field of natural language processing. Early models such as Naive Bayes, Logistic Regression, and Support Vector Machine are widely known and used as a headstart for experimenting classification tasks due to their simplicity and fast training time while still able to achieve a reasonable performance.

The rise of modern neural network brings deep learning to the classification tasks within the language processing field as it helps induce features for learning. Further development of recurrent networks gives us the ability to deal with sequences of varied lengths, which improves the performance of text classification to a great extent.

While classifying texts, it is essential to make the machine understand deeply the characteristics of input sequences. Because of that, having a well-

---

*Equal contribution with the first author

Proceedings of the 2020 EMNLP Workshop W-NUT: The Sixth Workshop on Noisy User-generated Text, pages 466–470
Online, Nov 19, 2020. ©2020 Association for Computational Linguistics

performing system that embed text sequences is an important prerequisite in building a good model for text classification.

Recently, pre-trained language models let us achieve high quality text embeddings, which then can be used for further downstream tasks. For language processing, the most famous pre-trained contextual language models recently are BERT (Devlin et al., 2018), ELMOs (Peters et al., 2018), and XL-NET (Yang et al., 2019).

3 System Description

We use the pre-trained language model BERTweet (Nguyen et al., 2020a), an English Tweet domain-specific model inspired by the original BERT model (Devlin et al., 2018), as the core for our system (more details will be discussed later). To accomplish the task of identifying informativeness of COVID-19 English Tweets, we attach a classification block on top of our BERTweet block, which is a combination of one or more linear layers. Figure 1 indicates the high level detail of our system.

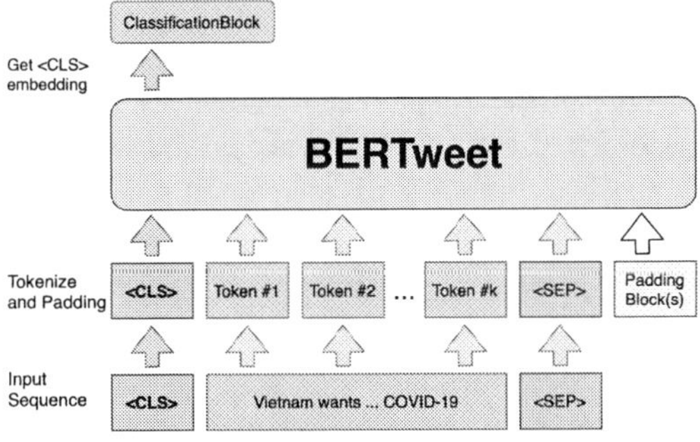

Figure 1: An overview of our model for identify Informative COVID-19 English Tweets

3.1 BERTweet

BERTweet (Nguyen et al., 2020a) is a large-scale language model pre-trained for English Tweets. Because of its nature of being a domain-specific model, BERTweet has achieved state-of-the-art performances on many downstream Tweet NLP tasks such as part-of-speech tagging, named entity recognition, and text classification, outperformed top models such as RoBERTa-base (Liu et al., 2019) and XLM-R-base (Conneau et al., 2019). Trained on 845M Tweets streamed from 01/2012 to 08/2019 and 5M Tweets related the COVID-19 pandemic as pre-training resources, BERTweet has

an advantage compares to other models for classifying COVID-19 related English Tweets.

3.1.1 Input Processing

Before feeding into the BERTweet model, we first tokenize input sequences with BPE Tokenizer (Sennrich et al., 2015), then pad the input sequences with the [CLS] and [SEP] tokens at their beginning and ending positions. To ensure all sequences have uniform length, we also add padding blocks at the end of the input sequences. The tokenized and padded input sequences are then fed directly into the Transformer block to retrieve contextualized sequence embeddings.

3.1.2 Embedding Extraction

Each Transformer layer within BERTweet model learns different information. We experiment different ways of extracting the pooled token from our BERTweet model, which corresponds to the encoded [CLS] token in our implementation, to analyze the performance on this downstream task. More detail would be discussed in the "Experiments" section.

3.1.3 Global Local BERTweet

By a close manual inspection of the dataset provided for the task, we realize that many Tweets have noteworthy information at some particular parts. Follow that reasoning, paying special attention to smaller parts of the Tweets is also important. Inspired by that idea, we propose a method to train 3 BERTweet models simultaneously: one for getting contextualized embeddings over the whole input sequences, one for getting embeddings over the first part of the Tweets, and one for getting embeddings over the remaining part. The pooled token from each model would then be extracted and concatenated together for the system to learn both global and local information of the Tweets. Please refer to Figure 2 for a visualization of the model.

3.2 Classification Block

The classification block contains one or more linear layers stacked on top of each other. The final layer is then used to classify whether a Tweet is informative or not.

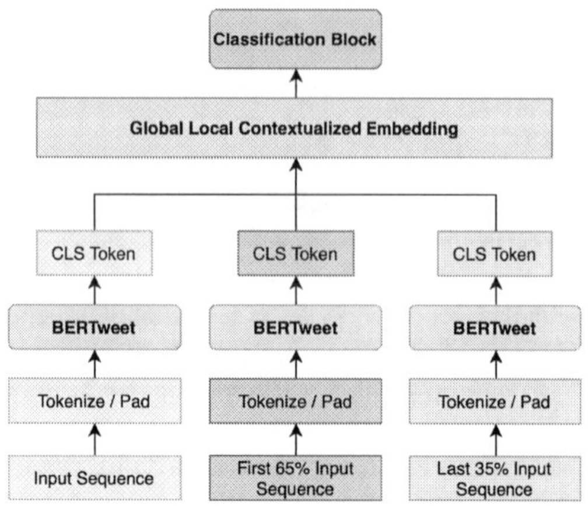

Figure 2: Global Local BERTweet Model

4 Experiments

4.1 Dataset

We use the dataset released by the competition organizer, consisting of 10,000 COVID-19 English Tweet. Each Tweet in the dataset is annotated by 3 annotators independently, and the overall inter-annotator agreement score of Fleiss' Kappa is 0.818. The dataset is then divided into 3 distinct set for training, validation, and testing, with the ratio of 70/10/20, respectively. Table 1 shows the division of the dataset.

	Informative	Uninformative
Training Set	3303	3697
Validation Set	472	528
Test Set	944	1056

Table 1: Number of Tweets of each category in the original dataset

4.1.1 Re-splitting Data

During the final evaluation phrase, we re-split the dataset by combining training and validation sets then dividing randomly with the ratio of 90/10. The test set is not modified.

4.2 Implementation

4.2.1 Main Library and Framework

We mainly rely on the `transformers` library (Wolf et al., 2019) with `PyTorch` framework (Paszke et al., 2017) to run our code.

4.2.2 Two-Phrase Training

We divide the training process into two phrases. In the first phrase, we freeze all the BERTweet paramaters to train the classification block. In the second phrase, we then unfreeze all parameters in our end-to-end model for finetuning.

4.2.3 Optimizer

For all models belonging to the scope of our project, we utilized the AdamW optimizer as implemented in the `transformers` library. This is a third-party implementation of the algorithm originally proposed in the paper named Decoupled Weight Decay Regularization (Loshchilov and Hutter, 2019)

4.2.4 Hyperparameters Configuration

The max length for padding input sequences before feeding into the BERTweet model is set to be 256. We trained our models on 1 NVIDIA Tesla V100 and 1 NVIDIA GeForce RTX 2080 Ti using batch size of 16 and 32 alternatively. We use an initial learning rate of $5e - 4$ in 12 epochs for the first phrase and $4e - 5$ in 6 epochs for the second phrase of training along with linear learning rate decay then choose the best checkpoint.

4.3 Model Performance

4.3.1 Baselines

We pre-process input data by tokenizing the data, record the count of occurrences of each token in a matrix then transform such count matrix into a tf-idf representation. To do so, we use CountVectorizer() and TfidfTransformer() as implemented in `sklearn` (Pedregosa et al., 2011). We then use 3 different classifiers, namely SVM, Naive Bayes and Logistic Regression, to get results on the original validation set. We acknowledge that the performance of these baselines are relatively poor; nevertheless, it is a trade-off between accuracy and efficiency since follow a non-deep learning approach which does not require much time regarding training and finetuning.

Models	F1 Score
Logistic Regression	**0.7827**
Naive Bayes	0.7486
Support Vector Machine	0.7678

Table 2: Baseline model performances on original validation set

4.3.2 BERTweet Embedding Extraction

As mentioned above, we experiment different ways to extract embeddings after feeding Tweets into

BERTweet model. Table 3 shows the results of these implementations on original validation set.

BERTweet Embedding	F1 Score
Last Layer	0.8912
All 12 Layers (concat)	0.9006
Last 4 Layers (concat)	0.8934
Last 2 Layers (concat)	0.9001
Last 2 + First 2 (concat)	0.9013
Last + First (concat)	**0.9045**
Last 2 + Mid 2 (concat)	0.9012
Last + Mid (concat)	0.8836

Table 3: Different BERTweet configurations

4.3.3 Global Local BERTweet

Besides experimenting ways to extract BERTweet embeddings, we also experiment different configurations for our Global Local BERTweet model. Table 4 shows the result of these implementations on original validation set.

Global	Head	Tail	F1
last	last	last	0.9021
last 4 (concat)	last	last	0.9028
last 4 (concat)	last + first (concat)	first	**0.9075**
last 4 (average)	last + first (concat)	first	0.8963
last 2 + first 2 (concat)	last + first 2 (concat)	last + first 2 (concat)	0.9067

Table 4: Different BERTweet configuration

4.3.4 Ensembling

Define $\mathbf{p}_i$ (dimension (1×2)) to be the predicted softmax vector of model i-th for each Tweet, c to be the classes (namely Informative/Uninformative), and N to be the number of models. Let $\mathbf{C}$ be a function that takes a softmax vector as an input and returns the corresponding binary classification result as output.

The output o_{mv} of majority voting is calculated as follows:

$$o_{mv} = \underset{c}{\text{argmax}} \sum_{i=1}^{N} \mathbf{C}(p_i) \qquad (1)$$

The output o_a of averaging is calculated as follows:

$$o_a = \underset{c}{\text{argmax}} \frac{1}{N} \sum_{i=1}^{N} p_i \qquad (2)$$

We ensemble all the models shown in Table 3 and Table 4 by doing majority voting and averaging softmax vectors. The results on original validation set are summarized in Table 5.

Ensembling Method	F1
Majority Voting	**0.9130**
Averaging	0.9111

Table 5: Ensembling performance

4.3.5 Final Evaluation

During final evaluation phrase, we used the Majority votted prediction of our BERTweet models after training on the re-splitted training set and got the F1 Score of 0.8991 on the hidden test set, which ranked 12 over 56 participated teams. The first team got the corresponding score of 0.9096.

4.4 Additional Works

To investigate our assumption that Tweet length does affect classification result, we analyze the Tweets in the given dataset and come up with an idea to choose the best models for ensembling while dealing with Tweets within a particular length. In particular, we divide the Tweets sequence into 3 categories: short Tweets ($0 - 22$ words), medium Tweets ($23 - 44$ words), long Tweets (> 44 words). For each category, we choose 7 models that have the most correct predictions on our training set and use these models for predictions. With this, we gain 0.9182 F1-Score on the original validation set. Indeed, the reported result shows that the selective ensembling of BERTweet models based tailor-trained for a certain range of input Tweet length does boost classification performance.

5 Conclusion

In this paper, we proposed a system that carries out the automatic identification of informative versus uninformative tweets. While this system is simple, it has leveraged recent advances and state-of-the-art results in natural language processing and deep learning, namely BERT-based models. For our future work, we will augment this system so that it can work for various forms of information circulating on social media such as Facebook status, Reddit post, Instagram caption, etc.

References

Alexis Conneau, Kartikay Khandelwal, Naman Goyal, Vishrav Chaudhary, Guillaume Wenzek, Francisco Guzmán, Edouard Grave, Myle Ott, Luke Zettlemoyer, and Veselin Stoyanov. 2019. Unsupervised cross-lingual representation learning at scale.

Jacob Devlin, Ming-Wei Chang, Kenton Lee, and Kristina Toutanova. 2018. Bert: Pre-training of deep bidirectional transformers for language understanding.

Yinhan Liu, Myle Ott, Naman Goyal, Jingfei Du, Mandar Joshi, Danqi Chen, Omer Levy, Mike Lewis, Luke Zettlemoyer, and Veselin Stoyanov. 2019. Roberta: A robustly optimized bert pretraining approach.

Ilya Loshchilov and Frank Hutter. 2019. Decoupled weight decay regularization. In *International Conference on Learning Representations*.

Dat Quoc Nguyen, Thanh Vu, and Anh Tuan Nguyen. 2020a. BERTweet: A pre-trained language model for English Tweets. *arXiv preprint*, arXiv:2005.10200.

Dat Quoc Nguyen, Thanh Vu, Afshin Rahimi, Mai Hoang Dao, Linh The Nguyen, and Long Doan. 2020b. WNUT-2020 Task 2: Identification of Informative COVID-19 English Tweets. In *Proceedings of the 6th Workshop on Noisy User-generated Text*.

Adam Paszke, Sam Gross, Soumith Chintala, Gregory Chanan, Edward Yang, Zachary DeVito, Zeming Lin, Alban Desmaison, Luca Antiga, and Adam Lerer. 2017. Automatic differentiation in pytorch.

F. Pedregosa, G. Varoquaux, A. Gramfort, V. Michel, B. Thirion, O. Grisel, M. Blondel, P. Prettenhofer, R. Weiss, V. Dubourg, J. Vanderplas, A. Passos, D. Cournapeau, M. Brucher, M. Perrot, and E. Duchesnay. 2011. Scikit-learn: Machine learning in Python. *Journal of Machine Learning Research*, 12:2825–2830.

Matthew E. Peters, Mark Neumann, Mohit Iyyer, Matt Gardner, Christopher Clark, Kenton Lee, and Luke Zettlemoyer. 2018. Deep contextualized word representations.

Rico Sennrich, Barry Haddow, and Alexandra Birch. 2015. Neural machine translation of rare words with subword units.

Thomas Wolf, Lysandre Debut, Victor Sanh, Julien Chaumond, Clement Delangue, Anthony Moi, Pierric Cistac, Tim Rault, Rémi Louf, Morgan Funtowicz, Joe Davison, Sam Shleifer, Patrick von Platen, Clara Ma, Yacine Jernite, Julien Plu, Canwen Xu, Teven Le Scao, Sylvain Gugger, Mariama Drame, Quentin Lhoest, and Alexander M. Rush. 2019. Huggingface's transformers: State-of-the-art natural language processing.

Zhilin Yang, Zihang Dai, Yiming Yang, Jaime Carbonell, Ruslan Salakhutdinov, and Quoc V. Le. 2019. Xlnet: Generalized autoregressive pretraining for language understanding.

CIA_NITT at WNUT-2020 Task 2: Classification of COVID-19 Tweets Using Pre-trained Language Models

Yandrapati Prakash Babu
Department of Computer Applications
NIT Trichy, India
prakash.babu23@gmail.com

Rajagopal Eswari
Department Computer Applications
NIT Trichy, India
eswari@nitt.edu

Abstract

This paper presents our models for WNUT 2020 shared task2. The shared task2 involves identification of COVID-19 related informative tweets. We treat this as binary text classification problem and experiment with pre-trained language models. Our first model which is based on CT-BERT achieves F1-score of 88.7% and second model which is an ensemble of CT-BERT, RoBERTa and SVM achieves F1-score of 88.52%.

1 Introduction

As of September 07,2020 COVID-19 Coronavirus infected 27.3M people and caused 887K deaths[1]. Real time updates regarding the number of infected cases and death cases is given in dashboards. These dashboards make use of information from social networking sites like twitter. As majority of the tweets posted online are uninformative, it is necessary identify the informative tweets which include useful information related to recovered, suspected, confirmed and death cases as well as location or travel history of the cases.

The WNUT 2020 shared task2 involves identification of informative tweets. We treat this as binary text classification problem. Prior to 2018, most of the text classification models are based on Convolutional Neural Network (CNN) or Recurrent Neural Network(RNN). These models are shallow in nature and cannot learn more informative features from the input. Moreover as these models are to trained from scratch, they require more number of training instances (Kalyan and Sangeetha, 2020a,b).

Recently pre-trained language models like BERT (Devlin et al., 2019), RoBERTa (Liu et al., 2019) achieved significant improvements in many of the natural language processing tasks (Qiu et al., 2020).

BERT is a transformer encoder based language model trained using 16 GB text corpus using language modeling and next sentence prediction objectives. The 16GB text corpus includes 3.5B words from Wikipedia articles and 0.8B words from Books. BERT model is available in two versions namely BERT-base (consists of 12 transformer encoder layers with 768 hidden vector size) and BERT-large (consists of 24 transformer encoder layers with 1024 hidden vector size). As BERT models are trained using generic less noisy text corpus, these may not be effective for noisy text like tweets. Moreover,these models don't include any domain specific information. A common strategy is to adapt BERT model to a specific domain is to further pre-train the model or train the model from scratch using domain specific text.

In this paper, we propose two models to identify informative COVID-19 tweets. First model is based on Covid-Twitter-BERT (CT-BERT) which is a BERT-Large based model which is further trained on 160M Corona virus related tweets (Müller et al., 2020). Second model is ensemble of CT-BERT, RoBERTa and SVM (Islam et al., 2017). As CT-BERT is initialized from BERT-large weights and further pre-trained on COVID tweets, it has two advantages compared to BERT-large which is pre-trained on generic less noisy texts. First advantage is, CT-BERT includes domain as well as specific information and second advantage is, CT-BERT can better handle noisy texts like tweets. Our CT-BERT based model achieves F1-score of 88.87% and ensemble model achieves F1-score of 88.52%

2 Related work

Text classification is one of the core NLP tasks. It involves assigning labels to text sequences like phrases, sentences or documents. It has applica-

---

[1] https://www.worldometers.info/coronavirus/

Proceedings of the 2020 EMNLP Workshop W-NUT: The Sixth Workshop on Noisy User-generated Text, pages 471–474
Online, Nov 19, 2020. ©2020 Association for Computational Linguistics

Label	Training	Validation	Test
INFORMATIVE	3303	472	944
UNINFORMATIVE	3697	528	1056

Table 1: Original Split of Dataset

Label	Training	Validation
INFORMATIVE	3024	751
UNINFORMATIVE	3376	849

Table 2: After Splitting the Dataset

tions in various NLP tasks like sentiment analysis, spam classification, abusive text detection etc (Minaee et al., 2020). The use of deep learning models for text classification started with using models like Convolutional Neural Network or Recurrent Neural Network (Kim, 2014; Nowak et al., 2017). These models are used on the top of word embeddings. To over the issue of Out of Vocabulary (OOV) words, char level CNN or RNN are used (Zhang et al., 2015). As these models are shallow in nature and need to be trained from scratch, it requires more number of training instances to train these models. Recently, with the introduction of deep pre-trained language models like BERT, RoBERTa , there is no need to train the downstream model from scratch. To adapt the model to downstream task, it is enough to add task specific layers and fine-tune the model for few epochs (Devlin et al., 2019; Liu et al., 2019).

3 Methodology

3.1 Dataset and Pre-Processing

The dataset contains 20K tweets each of which is labeled as 0 (uninformative tweet) or 1 (informative tweet) (Nguyen et al., 2020). The dataset is divided into train, validation and test sets(Actual 2k test tweets mixed with the 10K tweets), total test set size 12K. The statistics of the original dataset is reported in Table 1 and the dataset splitted into 80% and 20% reported in Table 2.

As tweets are noisy in nature, we do the following pre-processing steps

- remove unnecessary punctuation and non-ASCII characters.

- standardize words with repeating characters (e.g. coooool → cool)

- replace emoji characters with their text descriptions[2]

- replace interjection words with their meanings (e.g. oww → pain)

- replace contraction with full form (e.g., I'm → I am)

- replace twitter slang words with related words (e.g., 2morrow → tomorrow

3.2 Model Description

We treat the problem of identification of informative tweets as binary text classification. Following the recent trend of using pre-trained language models in NLP, we propose models based on BERT and RoBERTa.

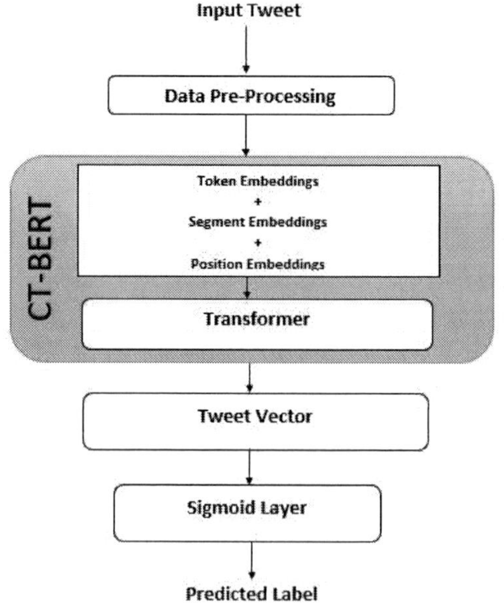

Figure 1: Overview of Model-1

Model-1 This model is based on COVID-Twitter-BERT (CT-BERT). CT-BERT is initialized from BERT-Large weights and further pre-trained on 160M Corona virus related tweets. As it is binary classification, a fully connected sigmoid layer is included on the top of CT-BERT. The entire model (CT-BERT + fully connected sigmoid layer) is then fine-tuned using the training dataset. The original tweet is added with the special tokens [CLS] and [SEP] and then tokenized using word-piece tokenizer. The embedding of each token is obtained by the summation of word-piece, position

<hr>

[2]We gather list of emojis and corresponding descriptions from https://emojipedia.org/

472

and segment embeddings. A sequence of 24 transformer encoder layers is applied on these token embeddings to get the final hidden state vectors. Following , we treat $e_t \in R^h$ the final hidden vector of [CLS] token as the representation of tweet. Then, e_t is passed through fully connected sigmoid layer to get the required label $\hat{p} \in [0, 1]$(as shown in figure 1).

$$e_t = CTBERT(tweet) \quad (1)$$

$$\hat{p} = Sigmoid(W^T e_t + b) \quad (2)$$

Model-2 This model is ensemble of CT-BERT, RoBERTa and TF-IDF with SVM. In this model we used base model of Roberta and TF-IDF is used for to extract the features from the tweets which were used in the SVM. Each model is individually trained using the training set. In case of CT-BERT and RoBERTa, task-specific classifier layer having fully connected sigmoid layer is added and the entire model is fine-tuned. In case of SVM, the model is trained using the tf-idf vectors of training tweets and we use kernel as sigmoid. The final prediction is obtained from the average of predictions of all these models(as shown in figure 2).

Model	F1 Score	Precision	Recall
CT-BERT	96.03	93.8	98.26
RoBERTa	93.85	92.16	95.60
TFIDF+SVM	82.90	87.90	79.09
CT-BERT+ RoBERTa	95.64	96.35	94.94
CT-BERT+ (TFIDF+SVM)	85.62	97.12	76.56
RoBERTa+ (TFIDF+SVM)	84.94	95.66	76.43
CT-BERT+ RoBERTa+ (TFIDF+SVM)	95.68	93.96	97.47

Table 3: F1-score, Precision, and Recall on Validation data

Model	F1 Score	Precision	Recall
CT-BERT	95.17	92.14	98.40
CT-BERT+ RoBERTa+ (TFIDF+SVM)	95.31	94.50	96.13

Table 4: F1-score, Precision, and Recall of proposed models on Validation data without using pre-processing steps

3.3 Evaluation Metrics

The model is officially evaluated using precision, recall and F1-score metrics.

$$Precision = \frac{T_{positive}}{T_{positive} + F_{positive}}$$

$$Recall = \frac{T_{positive}}{T_{positive} + F_{negative}}$$

$$F1 - Score = 2X \frac{Precision * Recall}{Precision + Recall}$$

3.4 Implementation Details

Task organizers provided training and validation sets with labels . We merged both training and validation set and split into 80% train and validation sets with 80% and 20% of instances. We set batch size = 32, learning rate = 3e-5 and epochs=3 after doing random search over the hyperparameter space. All our models are implemented using tranformers library in PyTorch (Wolf et al., 2019).

4 Results

To identify informative tweets related to Corona virus, we experimented with two models. First

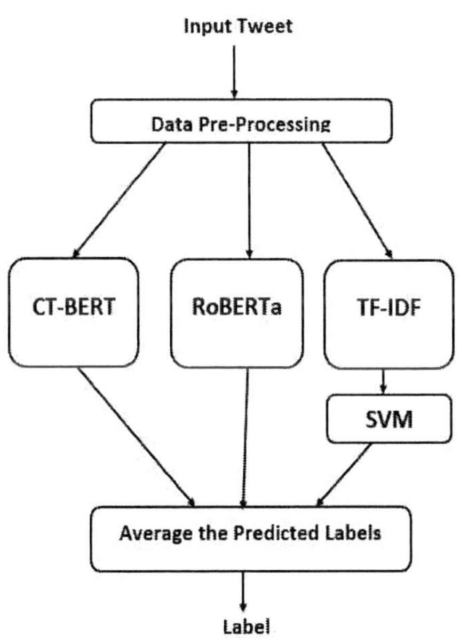

Figure 2: Overview of Model-2

Model	F1 Score	Precision	Recall
CT-BERT	88.87	87.72	90.04
CT-BERT+ RoBERTa+ (TFIDF+SVM)	88.52	89.24	87.82

Table 5: F1-score, Precision, and Recall of proposed models on Test data

model is based on CT-BERT and second model is an ensemble of CT-BERT, RoBERTa and SVM with TF-IDF. The pre-processing steps improved the results. The performance on the validation set using pre-processing steps is reported in Table 3, the performance on the validation set without using pre-processing steps is reported in Table 4 and on test set is reported in Table 5. As reported in Table 3, a) SVM with TF-IDF features performed poorly. This is because as text is noisy, TF-IDF based features are less informative. b) CT-BERT outperformed RoBERTa as CT-BERT is trained on COVID- 19 related tweets. As reported in Table 5, CT-BERT based model achieved F1-score of 88.87% and ensemble model achieved F1-score of 88.52%. From the Table 5, it is clear that CT-BERT based model achieved slightly better results compared to ensemble model.

5   Conclusion

In this work, we present our models to identify COVID-19 related informative tweets. We treat this as binary text classification problem. We propose two models based on pre-trained language models for this task. Our model based on CT-BERT achieved F1-score of 88.87%.

References

Jacob Devlin, Ming-Wei Chang, Kenton Lee, and Kristina Toutanova. 2019. Bert: Pre-training of deep bidirectional transformers for language understanding. In *Proceedings of the 2019 Conference of the North American Chapter of the Association for Computational Linguistics: Human Language Technologies, Volume 1 (Long and Short Papers)*, pages 4171–4186.

M. S. Islam, F. E. M. Jubayer, and S. I. Ahmed. 2017. A support vector machine mixed with tf-idf algorithm to categorize bengali document. In *2017 International Conference on Electrical, Computer and Communication Engineering (ECCE)*, pages 191–196.

Katikapalli Subramanyam Kalyan and S Sangeetha. 2020a. Bertmcn: Mapping colloquial phrases to standard medical concepts using bert and highway network. Technical report, EasyChair.

Katikapalli Subramanyam Kalyan and S Sangeetha. 2020b. Secnlp: A survey of embeddings in clinical natural language processing. *Journal of biomedical informatics*, 101:103323.

Yoon Kim. 2014. Convolutional neural networks for sentence classification. In *Proceedings of the 2014 Conference on Empirical Methods in Natural Language Processing (EMNLP)*, pages 1746–1751, Doha, Qatar. Association for Computational Linguistics.

Yinhan Liu, Myle Ott, Naman Goyal, Jingfei Du, Mandar Joshi, Danqi Chen, Omer Levy, Mike Lewis, Luke Zettlemoyer, and Veselin Stoyanov. 2019. Roberta: A robustly optimized bert pretraining approach. *arXiv preprint arXiv:1907.11692*.

Shervin Minaee, Nal Kalchbrenner, Erik Cambria, Narjes Nikzad, Meysam Chenaghlu, and Jianfeng Gao. 2020. Deep learning based text classification: A comprehensive review. *arXiv preprint arXiv:2004.03705*.

Martin Müller, Marcel Salathé, and Per E Kummervold. 2020. Covid-twitter-bert: A natural language processing model to analyse covid-19 content on twitter. *arXiv preprint arXiv:2005.07503*.

Dat Quoc Nguyen, Thanh Vu, Afshin Rahimi, Mai Hoang Dao, Linh The Nguyen, and Long Doan. 2020. WNUT-2020 Task 2: Identification of Informative COVID-19 English Tweets. In *Proceedings of the 6th Workshop on Noisy User-generated Text*.

Jakub Nowak, Ahmet Taspinar, and Rafał Scherer. 2017. Lstm recurrent neural networks for short text and sentiment classification. In *International Conference on Artificial Intelligence and Soft Computing*, pages 553–562. Springer.

Xipeng Qiu, Tianxiang Sun, Yige Xu, Yunfan Shao, Ning Dai, and Xuanjing Huang. 2020. Pre-trained models for natural language processing: A survey. *arXiv preprint arXiv:2003.08271*.

Thomas Wolf, Lysandre Debut, Victor Sanh, Julien Chaumond, Clement Delangue, Anthony Moi, Pierric Cistac, Tim Rault, Rémi Louf, Morgan Funtowicz, et al. 2019. Transformers: State-of-the-art natural language processing. *arXiv preprint arXiv:1910.03771*.

Xiang Zhang, Junbo Zhao, and Yann LeCun. 2015. Character-level convolutional networks for text classification. In *Advances in neural information processing systems*, pages 649–657.

UET at WNUT-2020 Task 2: A Study of Combining Transfer Learning Methods for Text Classification with RoBERTa

Huy Quang Dao
University of Engineering and Technology
Vietnam National University, Ha Noi
huydao98.uet@gmail.com

Tam Minh Nguyen
Sun Asterisk Inc.
nguyen.minh.tamb
@sun-asterisk.com

Abstract

This paper reports our approach and the results of our experiments for W-NUT task 2: Identification of Informative COVID-19 English Tweets. In this paper, we test out the effectiveness of transfer learning method with state of the art language models as RoBERTa on this text classification task. Moreover, we examine the benefit of applying additional fine-tuning and training techniques including fine-tuning discrimination, gradual unfreezing as well as our custom head for the classifier. Our best model results in a high F1-score of 89.89 on the task's test dataset and that of 90.96 on the public validation set without ensembling multiple models and additional data.

1 Introduction

Identification of Informative COVID-19 English Tweets (Nguyen et al., 2020) is the task of "providing users the information related to the virus". It is meaningful in the sense that with an increasing amount of tweets about the virus, many among them are uninformative and even harmful to the viewers. Manually identifying uninformative tweets is costly. Therefore, a system which can perform the task automatically would be tremendously helpful.

With the rise of deep learning, particularly transfer learning for solving text classification problem, we would like to propose an approach that leads to high performance (represents by a high F1-score of 89.89) on the task's test dataset. This approach uses pre-training method with state-of-the-art pre-trained language model RoBERTa (Liu et al., 2019), combines with many existing fine-tuning techniques including one-cycle-policy learning rate(Smith, 2018),fine-tuning discrimination, gradual unfreezing (Howard and Ruder, 2018), label smoothing (Pereyra et al., 2017), and our custom-head model.

Other than using pre-training with a state-of-the-art pre-trained language model, there is no clear winning factor for our success as all fine-tuning techniques need to incorporate to form our best model. Our main contributions are:

• We perform numerous experiments to support our hypothesis. Which is fine-tuning state-of-the-art pre-trained language models such as RoBERTa is more beneficial to the Identification of Informative COVID-19 English Tweets task than several training-from-scratch models.

• We combine many fine-tuning techniques to form our best model and experiments with the effect of each technique by gradually stacking them onto our base model then observe their effects.

2 Related work

2.1 Language model pre-training

Universal feature representation function, through pre-training language model on large amount of unlabeled data, namely ELMo (Peters et al., 2018), GPT (Radford, 2018), BERT (Devlin et al., 2018) and XLNet (Yang et al., 2019) has brought tremendous gains in performance for many NLP tasks. The rise of those models has been most beneficial to transfer learning for downstream tasks such as text classification, Question Answering, Text Summarization. Different from learning fixed feature vectors of words without regard to its context such as Word2Vec (Mikolov et al., 2013) or Glove (Pennington et al., 2014), those above self-training method learn context-dependent word representation, results in high quality features learning for text (Jawahar et al., 2019).

2.2 Tranfering training techniques

ULMfit (Howard and Ruder, 2018) introduced a novel fine-tuning method which is task-adaptive pre-training which boosts upmost NLP downstream

Proceedings of the 2020 EMNLP Workshop W-NUT: The Sixth Workshop on Noisy User-generated Text, pages 475–479
Online, Nov 19, 2020. ©2020 Association for Computational Linguistics

task's performance. The authors fine-tune the pre-trained language model in order to adapt the weights to a new task distribution. Moreover, the authors experiment with a combination of several training techniques, that they suggest, to bring a gain in performance for many common transfer learning settings, such as Learning Rate Discrimination, Gradual Unfreezing, and Slanted Triangular Learning Rate. Our work has been mostly inspired by this paper.

Don't stop pre-training (Gururangan et al., 2020) sheds light on the effectiveness of domain-adaptive pre-training and task-adaptive pretraining in 4 different domains with 8 downstream tasks, 2 tasks each domain, including tasks with limited and redundant labeled data. The paper points out that task – adaptive pre-training results in better performance compared to only fine-tuning weights on downstream tasks. Unfortunately, we did not experiment with this technique for WNUT-2020 Task 2: Identification of informative COVID-19 English Tweets competition.

2.3 RoBERTa

RoBERTa (Liu et al., 2019) was built based on BERT's language masking strategy. However, RoBERTa model modifies several key hyperparameters in BERT including removing BERT's next-sentence pretraining objective and training with much larger mini-batches as well as learning rates. It outperforms BERT on a variety of NLP tasks and archives comparable performance with the SOTA model XLNET (Yang et al., 2019). Likewise BERT, RoBERTa has two different settings, RoBERTa Base which uses 12 layers of Transformer Encoder and 24 Transformers Encoder Layers with RoBERTa Large. We experiment with both RoBERTa Base and RoBERTa Large as out base model and show a comparison in performance between them.

3 System description

3.1 Pretraining and backbone mode:

Fine-tuning the downstream task's model in Natural Language Processing using pre-trained language models, such as BERT, has been experimentally shown to be effective, both in terms of convergence time and performance (Gururangan et al., 2020). However, the choice of the pre-trained model affects the result of the downstream task. Since RoBERTa Base and RoBERTa Large have

achieved significant gain in performance in many common fine-tuning settings, we experiment using both models as the backbone for our task's base model.

Our base model is simply designed to test out the effectiveness of our choice of backbone, custom head, and training techniques. We use both RoBERTa Base and RoBERTa Large (Liu et al., 2019) as our backbone in all model settings to compare the effectiveness of each backbone.

Our base model includes a backbone extracting all information of an input sequence into the [CLS] token's features of the last backbone's layer. Those features are then linearly projected onto 2D, followed by a Softmax activation to predict the probability of the label being "Informative" or "Uninformative" given the input. Notice that we use cyclical learning rate and label smoothing to all model's settings in our experiment including the base model's settings.

More complex model settings use a more complex custom head and are gradually added advanced training techniques.

In order to emphasize the significant contribution of the pre-training method using the SOTA language model, we also train used-to-be state of the art models in text classification including Hierarchical Attention Networks (Yang et al., 2016) combined with Weight-Dropped GRU (Merity et al., 2017), Bidirectional Long Short-Term Memory Networks with Two Dimensional Convolutional Neural Network (Zhou et al., 2016) and Non-Static Convolutional Neural Network (Kim, 2014). As expected, the results of training those models from scratch have been around 8.0 lower F1-score than our base model. The detailed result is demonstrated in the Experiment Results section.

3.2 Custom head design

The higher layer in RoBERTa model captures higher-level features and semantic meaning (Jawahar et al., 2019) . We would like to incorporate more types of features by using not only [CLS] token's features of the last backbone's layers but those of 4 last backbone layers. We concatenate all those features, subsequently linearly project them on lower-dimensional space. We refer to the output of this process as features of branch one. Note that with each linear layer except the last one, we always stack one Batch Normalization (Ioffe and Szegedy, 2015) layer following ReLU activation.

We suspect that it is burdening to use only [CLS] token's features as the only source of information for the prediction of the model. To resolve this, we also utilize features of the rest of the tokens of the last backbone layers in our custom head. We put the rest tokens' features through a Bidirectional LSTM (Hochreiter and Schmidhuber, 1997), 1D Convolutional Neural Network, and Max Pooling Over Time to extract and summarize useful information. The output of this process is referred to as feature branch two. We then aggregate 2 branches' features through concatenation. Finally, we apply a linear classifier on top of those combined features. The choice of 4 layers are the only heuristic, not thoroughly scientific, this choice can be further examined in our future works.

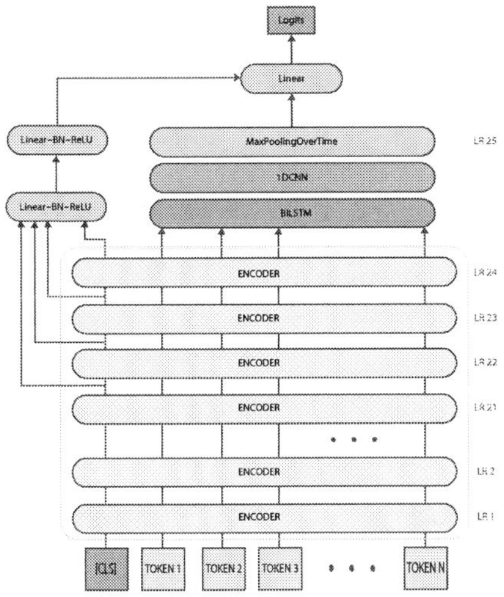

Figure 1: Architecture of the best proposed model.

Figure 1 describes our best architecture which has RoBERTa Large as the backbone, and our custom head on top of it. We refer to section 3 as the source of more details.

3.3 Transfer learning techniques

Learning rate discrimination: Intermediate layers in BERT model learn a "rich hierarchy of linguistic information, starting with surface features at the bottom, syntactic features in the middle followed by semantic features at the top" (Jawahar et al., 2019). We expect the same behavior for its variants which is RoBERTa (Liu et al., 2019). Therefore, when adapting to a new domain or a new task, it would be more appropriate to strongly adapt the layer that captures the semantic meaning and slowly, slightly adapts the weights of lower layers which contain most general knowledge (Yosinski et al., 2014). We achieve that by setting the learning rate differently for each layer, the lower layer has a small learning rate while higher ones update their weights at a higher rate.

Cyclical learning rate: The cyclical learning rate has been empirically shown to improve neural network performance. The learning rate should neither be set to be too large nor too small but first to get warm up by a gradual increase, followed by a gradual decrease. By doing that, learning would less likely to over-fit (due to small learning rate) or diverse (due to large learning rate). For more specifications, we refer to the experiment section.

Gradual unfreezing: ULMfit (Howard and Ruder, 2018) pointed out the risk of catastrophic forgetting appears as the result of fine-tuning all layers of the backbone model simultaneously. To avoid that, the paper suggests to apply multi-phase training, each unfreezes one layer, from top to bottom gradually. In the experiments section, we show that incorporating these techniques results in better overall models' performance

4 Experimental Results

4.1 Data preparation

Data description: The original dataset contains 7000 samples for training and 1000 ones for validating, and an additional public validation set. It is an almost balanced dataset with 3303 samples being labeled INFORMATIVE and 3697 are UN-INFORMATIVE tweets. The average length of the sample in each class is 40 tokens.

Data preprocessing: We first exclude all emoji in the dataset. Our justification is that: we observe the same fraction of sequences containing emoji in both INFORMATIVE and UNINFORMATIVE data, indicating that information from emoji is unlikely to be useful for this classification task.

For the tweet domain, there are typical elements such as hashtags, URL-links, mentions that needed to be handled. However, the given dataset has already replaced URL-links and mentions with special tokens @USER and @HTTPURL respectively. We choose to discard all other non-English languages in the dataset and keep hashtags elements.

4.2 Model's hyper-parameters settings and system configuration

In order to test out the effect of all model's settings in our experiments, we prefix hyper-parameters

Model	Precision	Recall	F1	Accuracy
BiLSTM + 2DCNN (*)	77.89	83.31	80.51	80.90
Non Static CNN (*)	81.63	80.38	81.00	82.18
HAN + WD-GRU (*)	82.65	82.08	82.36	83.40
RoBERTa Base	87.60	92.97	90.21	90.46
RoBERTa Large	**88.40**	**92.84**	**90.57**	**90.86**

Table 1: Comparing pretraining using RoberTa and training from scratch with previous SOTA models on text classification. (*) denotes for our implementation.

Model	Precision	Recall	F1	Accuracy
RoBERTa Base	87.60	92.97	90.21	90.46
RoBERTa Base + DLr	87.84	93.09	90.39	90.64
RoBERTa Base + DLr + Head	88.66	92.33	90.46	90.80
RoBERTa Base + DLr + Head + GU	88.40	93.22	90.75	91.02
RoBERTa Large	88.40	92.84	90.57	90.86
RoBERTa Large + DLr	87.84	93.74	90.69	90.90
RoBERTa Large + DLr + Head	**88.75**	92.84	90.75	91.06
RoBERTa Large + DLr + Head + GU	88.15	**93.96**	**90.96**	**91.14**

Table 2: Comparing models using RoBERTa Base and RoBERTa Large as backbone. DLr denotes Discrimination Learning Rate, Head denotes Custom Head and GU denotes Gradual Unfreezing.

across all settings except for the number of mini-batch sizes and the number of training epochs. Due to the limits of GPU memory, each model uses RoBERTa Base has a minibatch of size 50 whereas those of model using RoBERTa Large are 10. We train with the number of epochs which equals the number of encoder layers plus 1 and 10 epochs for the model using and not-using Gradual unfreezing, the final result is averaged results of 10 times training with different random seeds. In a different setting, we set LSTM's hidden size is the same as RoBERTa hidden size, the kernel size of 1D CNN is 3. The maximum learning rate using in the one-cycle policy is 1e-5. Our choice of optimizer is AdamW (Loshchilov and Hutter, 2017). All out models were trained using only one GPU Tesla T4 with 16GB memory.

4.3 Evaluation metrics

We report our results with Accuracy, F1-score, Recall, and Precision metrics on the validation set. However, most of our analysis focuses on F1-score since it is the harmonic mean of Precision and Recall and it is a better representative of performance than Accuracy when the data is not perfectly balanced.

4.4 Results and analysis

Table 1 compared the performance of several architectures training from scratch and pre-training method using RoBERTa in our base settings. These traditional architecture are Hierarchical Attention Networks (Yang et al., 2016) combined with Weight-Dropped GRU (Merity et al., 2017) (HAN + WD-GRU), Bidirectional Long Short-Term Memory Networks with Two Dimensional Convolutional Neural Network (BiLSTM + 2DCNN) (Zhou et al., 2016) and Non Static Convolutional Neural Network (Kim, 2014) (Non-static CNN) . As far as we expect, the pre-training method significantly out-performs training from scratch with traditional architecture results in a gain of around 8.0 F1-score.

Table 2 compared the performance of 4 models using RoBERTa Base and 4 models using RoBERTa Large as the backbone. Each backbone is tested out with a base setting (the only backbone with a linear classifier, details are described in section 3), then that base setting is gradually added with fine-tuning techniques (DLr is discriminative learning rate; GU is gradual Unfreezing) and our custom head.

There are two standing out observations in table 2. Firstly, RoBERTa Large outperforms RoBERTa Base in all model settings. Which meets our expectations.

Secondly, gradually adding up training technique and custom head leads to a gradual increase in F1-score. This emphasizes the positive effect of all techniques and custom heads on this task's performance. Overall, our winning model results in an 89.89 F1-score.

5 Conclusion

In this paper, we experiment with the effectiveness of transfer learning using state-of-the-art language pre-trained model RoBERTa with the incorporation of several fine-tuning and training techniques for the informative tweet identifying the task. Our best model results in high F1-scores in both public and test dataset.

For future work, we would like to explore the effectiveness of different text augmentation strategies and task-adaptive pre-training instead of only fine-tuning the classification task.

References

Jacob Devlin, Ming-Wei Chang, Kenton Lee, and Kristina Toutanova. 2018. Bert: Pre-training of deep bidirectional transformers for language understanding.

Suchin Gururangan, Ana Marasović, Swabha Swayamdipta, Kyle Lo, Iz Beltagy, Doug Downey, and Noah A. Smith. 2020. Don't stop pretraining: Adapt language models to domains and tasks.

Sepp Hochreiter and Jürgen Schmidhuber. 1997. Long short-term memory. *Neural computation*, 9(8):1735–1780.

Jeremy Howard and Sebastian Ruder. 2018. Universal language model fine-tuning for text classification.

Sergey Ioffe and Christian Szegedy. 2015. Batch normalization: Accelerating deep network training by reducing internal covariate shift.

Ganesh Jawahar, Benoît Sagot, and Djamé Seddah. 2019. What does BERT learn about the structure of language? In *ACL 2019 - 57th Annual Meeting of the Association for Computational Linguistics*, Florence, Italy.

Yoon Kim. 2014. Convolutional neural networks for sentence classification.

Yinhan Liu, Myle Ott, Naman Goyal, Jingfei Du, Mandar Joshi, Danqi Chen, Omer Levy, Mike Lewis, Luke Zettlemoyer, and Veselin Stoyanov. 2019. Roberta: A robustly optimized bert pretraining approach.

Ilya Loshchilov and Frank Hutter. 2017. Decoupled weight decay regularization.

Stephen Merity, Nitish Shirish Keskar, and Richard Socher. 2017. Regularizing and optimizing lstm language models.

Tomas Mikolov, Kai Chen, Greg Corrado, and Jeffrey Dean. 2013. Efficient estimation of word representations in vector space.

Dat Quoc Nguyen, Thanh Vu, Afshin Rahimi, Mai Hoang Dao, Linh The Nguyen, and Long Doan. 2020. WNUT-2020 Task 2: Identification of Informative COVID-19 English Tweets. In *Proceedings of the 6th Workshop on Noisy User-generated Text*.

Jeffrey Pennington, Richard Socher, and Christopher Manning. 2014. GloVe: Global vectors for word representation. In *Proceedings of the 2014 Conference on Empirical Methods in Natural Language Processing (EMNLP)*, pages 1532–1543, Doha, Qatar. Association for Computational Linguistics.

Gabriel Pereyra, George Tucker, Jan Chorowski, Łukasz Kaiser, and Geoffrey Hinton. 2017. Regularizing neural networks by penalizing confident output distributions.

Matthew E. Peters, Mark Neumann, Mohit Iyyer, Matt Gardner, Christopher Clark, Kenton Lee, and Luke Zettlemoyer. 2018. Deep contextualized word representations.

A. Radford. 2018. Improving language understanding by generative pre-training.

Leslie N. Smith. 2018. A disciplined approach to neural network hyper-parameters: Part 1 – learning rate, batch size, momentum, and weight decay.

Zhilin Yang, Zihang Dai, Yiming Yang, Jaime Carbonell, Ruslan Salakhutdinov, and Quoc V. Le. 2019. Xlnet: Generalized autoregressive pretraining for language understanding.

Zichao Yang, Diyi Yang, Chris Dyer, Xiaodong He, Alex Smola, and Eduard Hovy. 2016. Hierarchical attention networks for document classification. In *Proceedings of the 2016 Conference of the North American Chapter of the Association for Computational Linguistics: Human Language Technologies*, pages 1480–1489, San Diego, California. Association for Computational Linguistics.

Jason Yosinski, Jeff Clune, Yoshua Bengio, and Hod Lipson. 2014. How transferable are features in deep neural networks? In Z. Ghahramani, M. Welling, C. Cortes, N. D. Lawrence, and K. Q. Weinberger, editors, *Advances in Neural Information Processing Systems 27*, pages 3320–3328. Curran Associates, Inc.

Peng Zhou, Zhenyu Qi, Suncong Zheng, Jiaming Xu, Hongyun Bao, and Bo Xu. 2016. Text classification improved by integrating bidirectional lstm with two-dimensional max pooling.

Dartmouth CS at WNUT-2020 Task 2: Informative COVID-19 Tweet Classification Using BERT

Dylan Whang
Dartmouth College
Hanover, NH
dylanmwhang@gmail.com

Soroush Vosoughi
Dartmouth College
Hanover, NH
soroush@dartmouth.edu

Abstract

We describe the systems developed for the WNUT-2020 shared task 2, identification of informative COVID-19 English Tweets. BERT is a highly performant model for Natural Language Processing tasks. We increased BERT's performance in this classification task by fine-tuning BERT and concatenating its embeddings with Tweet-specific features and training a Support Vector Machine (SVM) for classification (henceforth called BERT+). We compared its performance to a suite of machine learning models. We used a Twitter specific data cleaning pipeline and word-level TF-IDF to extract features for the non-BERT models. BERT+ was the top performing model with an F1-score of 0.8713.

1 Introduction

In an effort to aid automated the development of COVID-19 related monitoring systems, the WNUT-2020 shared task 2: Identification of informative COVID-19 English Tweets tasked participants with developing systems to automatically classify Tweets as INFORMATIVE or UNINFORMATIVE. The WNUT task organizers have constructed and provided a data set of 10,000 Tweets related to Covid-19 for this task. (Nguyen et al., 2020b).

For this language processing task, we used Google's Bidirectional Encoder Representations from Transformers (BERT) to achieve performant results. BERT uses the now ubiquitous Transformer neural network architecture as explained in depth in the article, "Attention is All You Need," (Vaswani et al., 2017) and garnered acclaim for obtaining new state-of-the-art results on eleven natural language processing tasks, including pushing the GLUE score to 80.5%. (Devlin et al., 2019)

To optimize BERT for this task, we fine-tuned the BERT-large-uncased pretrained language model on the WNUT-2020 shared task 2 data set. We then further improved performance by concatenating the fine-tuned BERT embedding vectors with Tweet-specific features and using a Support Vector Machine (SVM) for classification (BERT+).

To benchmark the performance of the BERT+ model, we compared its performance to five traditional classifiers. We also developed a preprocessing pipeline for data cleaning and used Text Frequency Inverse Document Frequency (TF-IDF) to extract features for the traditional classifiers.

1.1 Pretrained BERT model

We used the BERT-large-uncased pretrained language model. This BERT model contains an encoder with 24 Transformer blocks, 16 self-attention heads, with the hidden size of 1024.

BERT generates its pretrained word and sentence level embeddings by using two objectives: Masked Language Modeling (MLM) and Next Sentence Prediction (NSP).

During pretraining, BERT utilizes MLM by first selecting 15% of the inputted tokens for potential masking. Our of this 15%, 80% are replaced with the [MASK] Token, 10% are replaced by a randomly selected word, and the remaining 10% are not manipulated. The MLM Objective is a cross-entropy loss on predicting the masked tokens.

BERT also uses NSP in its pretraining. The NSP objective is a binary classification loss for predicting if two sequences follow each other. NSP uses an equal proportion of consecutive sentences for the text corpus as positive examples and randomly paired sentences as negative examples. (Liu et al., 2020)

The "BERT for sequence classification" model utilizes the special [CLS] classifier token as the first token in every sequence. This token contains the classification embedding of the sequence. BERT uses the final hidden state of the [CLS] to-

Proceedings of the 2020 EMNLP Workshop W-NUT: The Sixth Workshop on Noisy User-generated Text, pages 480–484
Online, Nov 19, 2020. ©2020 Association for Computational Linguistics

ken as the aggregated sequence representation for classification tasks. (Devlin et al., 2019)

2 Data

The data set provided consists of 10,000 English Tweets related to COVID-19. Each Tweet is labeled either INFORMATIVE or UNINFORMATIVE. The Tweets were annotated by three independent annotators with an inter-annotator agreement score of Fleiss' Kappa at .818. The dataset is partitioned into training, validation, and test sets at a ratio of 7:1:2. The training set contains 3,303 INFORMATIVE and 3,697 UNINFORMATIVE Tweets. The validation set contains 472 INFORMATIVE and 528 UNINFORMATIVE Tweets. The unlabeled Test set contains 944 INFORMATIVE, 1,056 UNINFORMATIVE, and 10,000 unlabeled Tweets as noise.

3 Preprocessing

To clean the raw Tweets we created a data processing pipeline to: 1) remove non-alphanumeric characters, 2) remove stop-words, 3) convert words to their lemmas, and 4) convert words to lower case. We used the Natural Language Toolkit (NLTK) Python package (Bird and Loper, 2004) for these methods.

To handle the unique lexicon of Twitter, we implemented additional preprocessing methods to: 1) remove @USER tokens, 2) remove HTTPURL tokens, 3) remove the "#" character, 4) compress repeated characters, and 5) represent emojis as words.

The data set provided replaced URLs and in-Tweet mentions of other users with the HTTPURL and @USER tokens respectively. Our data-cleaning pipeline removes these tokens when cleaning the data to avoid the models over-fitting to these tokens that do not reflect their original usage within the Tweet. Similarly, we removed the # character from Tweets.

We converted emojis into word tokens so that the models would interpret the emojis as words. When using BERT, this allowed the BERT model to generate word embeddings for these emojis

Tweets occasionally contain repeated characters with the purpose of emphasizing a word. For example, "yesssss" instead of "yes". In order to consistently capture this kind of emphasis as a separate feature from the original word, we compressed the repetition of a single character into two

repetitions of that character.

4 Methods

4.1 Traditional ML models

Using the Sklearn Python package, we generated two separate feature vectors from the preprocessed Tweets. The first method generated feature vectors based on the raw counts of word level unigrams in each Tweet. The second method used TF-IDF to extract word-level unigrams, bigrams, and trigrams features. TF-IDF is a numerical statistic that captures the frequency of a term against the frequency of the documents it appears in. TF-IDF reduces the weight of common words and increases the weight of less frequent words. (Ramos, 1999)

We used the Sklearn to implement five traditional machine learning models using the features described above: Logistic Regression, Multinomial Naïve-Bayes, Decision Tree, Random Forest, and K-Neighbors (Pedregosa et al., 2011), using the default hyper-parameters.

4.2 Fine-tuned BERT model

We first partitioned each Tweet into an array of word tokens. The BERT model requires that each document is the same length, so we padded each array with the embedding 0 so that the length of each entry was 128 tokens. The length of 128 tokens was selected, because the maximum number of words a Tweet could contain within the 255 characters limit is 128 words. We added the '[SEP]' token to the end of each array to denote the end of a sequence. Because we used BERTForSequenceClassification, we also added the special '[CLS]' classifier token to the beginning of the array. (Devlin et al., 2019)

For our fine-tuning optimizer, we utilized the Adam algorithm with weight decay (AdamW) as introduced in "Decoupled Weight Decay Regularization." (Loshchilov and Hutter, 2019) We used the default parameters $\beta_1 = 0.9$, $\beta_2 = 0.999$, and epsilon $= .1e - 8$. We chose a learning weight of 2e-5 as it offered the lowest training and validation loss when compared to other learning rates between 1e-5 and 1e-4. As fine-tuning BERT required extensive computational resources, we used a Google Colab Research notebook for implementation as it allowed for high-RAM GPU processing. This fine-tuning approach follows the original BERT paper. (Devlin et al., 2019)

4.3 Fine-tuned BERT+ model

In an attempt to capture additional differences in the language of `INFORMATIVE` and `UNINFORMATIVE` Tweets that would not be observed by BERT, we extracted 1024 dimensional embeddings from the the last, non-softmax layer of our fine-tuned BERT and concatenated those with seven Twitter-specific features. We then trained a SVM classifier on these concatenated feature vectors using `Sklearn`'s SVM implementation with default hyper-parameters.

The Twitter-specific features for each Tweet were: 1) Count of the following in the Tweet: `HTTPURL` token, #, `@USER` token, and emoji 2) word count, 3) syllable count, and 4) a Boolean specifying whether the Tweet contains profanity. To generate some of these features, we used `PyPI`'s `profanity-check`, `syllables`, and `emojis` packages (https://pypi.org/).

5   Results

The results reported in subsections 5.1 and 5.2 were generated using 8-fold cross validation on the combined train and validation data sets.

5.1   Preprocessing experiments

Our best performing combination of data-cleaning methods, called the Optimal Preprocessor (OP), utilized the Twitter lexicon specific methods we created: 1) `@USER` token removal, 2) `HTTPURL` token removal, 3) `"#"` character removal, 4) repeated character compression, and 5) word representation of emojis. The performance of the OP combined with other preprocessing methods can be seen in Table 1.

To compare the performances of the `TfidfVectorizer` and `CountVectorizer` for feature extraction, we used the OP for data cleaning and Logistic Regression model for predictions. The `TfidfVectorizer` consistently outperformed the `CountVectorizer` with the average F1-scores of .8422 and .8279 respectively.

5.2   Traditional ML models

Using data processed through our OP with features extracted with TF-IDF, we achieved the F1-scores seen in Table 2 for our suite of machine learning models. Logistic Regression consistently outperformed the other methods. Table 3 displays selected features with the highest and lowest weights from the Logistic Regression model.

Preprocessing Pipeline	F1-score
Optimal Preprocessor (OP)	**.8424**
OP with Stop-word removal	.8320
OP with Alpha Numeric filter	.8384
OP with forced lowercase	.8351
OP with word lemma conversion	.8337
No preprocessing of data	.8339

Table 1:   Average F1-score from 8-fold cross validation using Logistic Regression model with TF-IDF.

Model/Classifier	F1-score
Logistic Regression	**.8422**
Multinomial Naïve-Bayes	.8356
Random Forest	.8201
K-Neighbors	.8201
Decision Tree	.7313
Baseline Stratified Dummy	.4723

Table 2:   Averaged F1-score across K-fold cross validation (k=8) with TF-IDF.

5.3   BERT models

To generate the results for our BERT models, we fit each BERT model with the train data set and evaluate on the validation data set. The pretrained BERT model yielded a F-1 score of .8312, our fine-tuned BERT model yielded a F-1 score of .8701, and the BERT+ model yielded a further improved F1-score of .8713 (see Table 4).

6   Discussion

6.1   Preprocessing and feature extraction

The method to compress repeated characters in our final data preprocessor might have improved the performance of our model by generating a common word level feature between features that would have been interpreted differently. For example, if one user Tweet, "good," and another user Tweeted, "gooood," these different words would now represent the same feature.

While stop-word removal and word lemma conversion are commonly in the field of NLP, the presence of the stop words and the complexity of words pre-lemma conversion appeared to help our machine learning models detect stylometric features and improved the performance of our machine learning models.

For feature extraction, TF-IDF outperformed the word count vectorizer. As TF-IDF decreases the weight of terms that occur frequently across all doc-

Feature (n-gram with n=[1,2,3])	weight
cases	5.9113
positive	5.4668
deaths	4.9618
died	4.7764
confirmed	4.5300
tested	4.5110
in	3.9934
positive for	3.7167
has	3.6581
tested positive	3.4429

Table 3: Top 10 Features with weights of the greatest magnitude from the highest performing model (Logistic Regression).

BERT Model	F1-Score
Fine-tuned BERT+	**.8713**
Fine-tuned BERT	.8701
Pre-trained BERT	.8312

Table 4: BERT models trained on the train data set and evaluated on the validation data set.

uments and increases the weight of less common terms, (Ramos, 1999) it is unsurprising that it outperforms the simple word count feature extraction.

6.2 Traditional ML models

With optimized data cleaning and feature extraction, our highest performing traditional models out performed the base pretrained BERT model. This high performance demonstrates the efficacy of fine tuning the preprocessing steps to achieve competitive performances with these models.

The features in Table 3 depict the features that strongly impact the classification of Tweets in the Logistic Regression model. Based on the description from the WNUT-2020 shared task 2 description of INFORMATIVE Tweets as Tweets that, "provide information about recovered, suspected, confirmed and death cases as well as location or travel history of the cases," (Nguyen et al., 2020b) it is unsurprising that word-level features concerning cases, test results, and deaths have large weights.

6.3 BERT

Somewhat surprisingly the pre-trained BERT model was outperformed by our logistic regression model for this task. This shows that even for large-scale pre-trained language models such as BERT, task-specific fine-tuning is of utmost importance.

Though both the fined-tuned BERT and BERT+ models both outperformed the logistic regression model, the difference in performance was not large. (around 3% boost in performance when using the BERT+ model compared to the logistic regression). We believe this is because BERT is not ideal for classifying noisy Twitter data as it has been trained on well-formed English sentences. This is why several Twitter-specific models have been proposed to deal with noisy Twitter data (Vosoughi et al., 2016; Nguyen et al., 2020a).

7 Conclusion & Future Work

In this paper, we have described multiple techniques for automatically identifying and classifying informative COVID-19 Tweets. We have demonstrated the applicability of Logistic Regression with an optimized data cleaning pipeline and TF-IDF for feature extraction for the task of Tweet classification. We have also displayed the higher performance of the BERT+ model. Automated classification of real time data feeds will be important as the COVID-19 pandemic continues to impact the world around us.

For future work, we would to like pre-train a BERT model on a large corpus of Tweets as Twitter's lexicon and grammatical styling differ from normal usage of the English language. We also want to compare the performance of our fine-tuned BERT model to the performances of other state of-the-art, pretrained NLP models such as fast.ai's ULMFIT (Howard and Ruder, 2018) and OpenAI's GPT2 (Radford et al., 2018) on this task. We would also like to train a Convolutional Neural Network for Tweet classification. Moreover, as (Kim, 2014) has demonstrated, Convolutional Neural Network (CNN) trained on top of pre-trained word vectors can achieve state-of-the-art performance for sequence classification. We would like to develop a similar method of utilizing a CNN for the task of Tweet classification.

References

Steven Bird and Edward Loper. 2004. NLTK: The natural language toolkit. In *Proceedings of the ACL Interactive Poster and Demonstration Sessions*, pages 214–217, Barcelona, Spain. Association for Computational Linguistics.

Jacob Devlin, Ming-Wei Chang, Kenton Lee, and Kristina Toutanova. 2019. BERT: Pre-training of deep bidirectional transformers for language understanding. In *Proceedings of the 2019 Conference of the North American Chapter of the Association for Computational Linguistics: Human Language Technologies, Volume 1 (Long and Short Papers)*, pages 4171–4186, Minneapolis, Minnesota. Association for Computational Linguistics.

Jeremy Howard and Sebastian Ruder. 2018. Universal language model fine-tuning for text classification. In *ACL*. Association for Computational Linguistics.

Yoon Kim. 2014. Convolutional neural networks for sentence classification. In *Proceedings of the 2014 Conference on Empirical Methods in Natural Language Processing, EMNLP 2014, October 25-29, 2014, Doha, Qatar, A meeting of SIGDAT, a Special Interest Group of the ACL*, pages 1746–1751.

Yinhan Liu, Myle Ott, Naman Goyal, Jingfei Du, Mandar Joshi, Danqi Chen, Omer Levy, Mike Lewis, Luke Zettlemoyer, and Veselin Stoyanov. 2020. Ro{bert}a: A robustly optimized {bert} pretraining approach.

Ilya Loshchilov and Frank Hutter. 2019. Decoupled weight decay regularization. In *International Conference on Learning Representations*.

Dat Quoc Nguyen, Thanh Vu, and Anh Tuan Nguyen. 2020a. Bertweet: A pre-trained language model for english tweets. *arXiv preprint arXiv:2005.10200*.

Dat Quoc Nguyen, Thanh Vu, Afshin Rahimi, Mai Hoang Dao, Linh The Nguyen, and Long Doan. 2020b. WNUT-2020 Task 2: Identification of Informative COVID-19 English Tweets. In *Proceedings of the 6th Workshop on Noisy User-generated Text*.

F. Pedregosa, G. Varoquaux, A. Gramfort, V. Michel, B. Thirion, O. Grisel, M. Blondel, P. Prettenhofer, R. Weiss, V. Dubourg, J. Vanderplas, A. Passos, D. Cournapeau, M. Brucher, M. Perrot, and E. Duchesnay. 2011. Scikit-learn: Machine learning in Python. *Journal of Machine Learning Research*, 12:2825–2830.

Alec Radford, Jeffrey Wu, Rewon Child, David Luan, Dario Amodei, and Ilya Sutskever. 2018. Language models are unsupervised multitask learners.

Juan Ramos. 1999. Using tf-idf to determine word relevance in document queries.

Ashish Vaswani, Noam Shazeer, Niki Parmar, Jakob Uszkoreit, Llion Jones, Aidan N. Gomez, Lukasz Kaiser, and Illia Polosukhin. 2017. Attention is all you need.

Soroush Vosoughi, Prashanth Vijayaraghavan, and Deb Roy. 2016. Tweet2vec: Learning tweet embeddings using character-level cnn-lstm encoder-decoder. In *Proceedings of the 39th International ACM SIGIR conference on Research and Development in Information Retrieval*, pages 1041–1044.

SunBear at WNUT-2020 Task 2: Improving RoBERTa-Based Noisy Text Classification with Knowledge of the Data domain

Linh Bao Doan
Sun Asterisk Inc.
`doan.bao.linh`
`@sun-asterisk.com`

Viet-Anh Nguyen
Sun Asterisk Inc.
`nguyen.viet.anh`
`@sun-asterisk.com`

Quang Pham Huu
Sun Asterisk Inc.
`pham.huu.quang`
`@sun-asterisk.com`

Abstract

This paper proposes an improved custom model for WNUT task 2: Identification of Informative COVID-19 English Tweet. We improve experiment with the effectiveness of fine-tuning methodologies for state-of-the-art language model RoBERTa (Liu et al., 2019). We make a preliminary instantiation of this formal model for the text classification approaches. With appropriate training techniques, our model is able to achieve 0.9218 F1-score on public validation set and the ensemble version settles at top 9 F1-score (0.9005) and top 2 Recall (0.9301) on private test set.

1 Introduction

Since the outbreak of COVID-19 pandemic, frequently updated information becomes a huge problem of concern. Social media platforms consequently become real-time sources for news about flare-up data. In any case, the flare-up has been spreading quickly, we observe a monstrous amount of information on social networks, for example around 4 million COVID-19 English Tweets every day on Twitter, in which most of these Tweets are uninformative. Therefore, it is crucial to collect the informative ones (for example Corona Virus Tweets identified with new cases or dubious cases) for downstream applications. In any case, manual ways to deal with recognizing useful Tweets require critical human endeavors, and hence are expensive.

Based on the dataset provided in WNUT-2020 Task 2: Identification of informative COVID-19 English Tweets (Nguyen et al., 2020), we propose a fine-tuning strategy to adopt the universal language model RoBERTa as an backbone model for text classification purposes. We also conduct several experiments in varied fine-tuning architectures on the pre-trained RoBERTa. Our best model results in a high F1-score of 0.9005 on the task's private test

dataset and that of 0.9218 on the public validation set with Multilayer Perceptron Head.

2 Related work

One of the most important parts in text classification problems is input representation. Traditional methods construct context-independent embeddings for words. *Mikolov et al.* (Mikolov et al., 2013) introduce an open-source *Word2Vec*, which consists of two models: Continuous Bag of Words (CBOW) and Skip-gram model. The models were trained on 1.6 billion words to learn linguistic contexts of words. While Word2Vec is a self-supervised algorithm, GloVe (Pennington et al., 2014) is trained unsupervised to form word embeddings. GloVe factorizes co-occurrence matrix of words, resulting in dense word vectors. However, both GloVe and Word2Vec fail representing rare or out-of-vocabulary words. FastText (Mikolov et al., 2018) mitigates this problem by decomposing words as a sum of character n-grams. This handles unseen words very well because these character n-grams may still occur in other words. In contrast to context-independent embeddings, modern language models encode word semantics within contexts. Word vectors obtained from these methods achieve better results on downstream tasks because a word in different contexts expresses different meanings. Bidirectional Encoder Representations from Transformers (Devlin et al., 2018), or BERT for short, outperforms the previous best result with GLUE score of 80.4%, which is 7.6% improvement. There are two variants of BERT: base and large; the large model is a stack of 24 Transformers' encoders for a total of 340M parameters while the base one has only 12 encoders. GPT-2 (Radford et al., 2019) by OpenAI is a gigantic model with 1.5 billion parameters and 48 layers, setting new state-of-the-art results on 7 out of 8 datasets. Face-

Proceedings of the 2020 EMNLP Workshop W-NUT: The Sixth Workshop on Noisy User-generated Text, pages 485–490
Online, Nov 19, 2020. ©2020 Association for Computational Linguistics

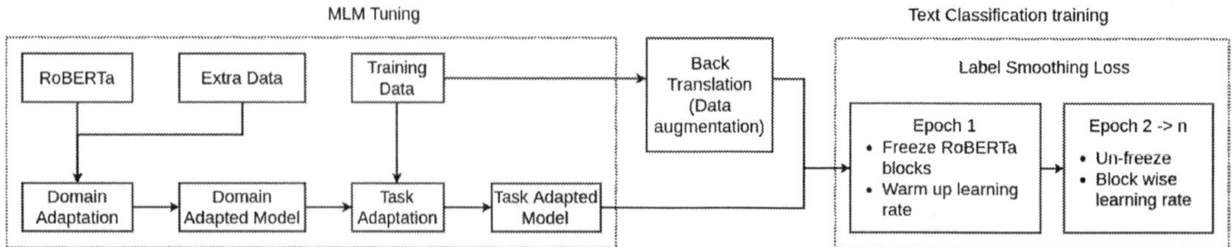

Figure 1: Our overall pipeline for hierarchical MLM tuning and main task training.

book Research team improves training procedures for BERT, introducing RoBERTa (Liu et al., 2019). The improvements include extended training time on a ten-times bigger dataset, increased batch size, using byte-level encoding with larger vocabulary, excluding next sentence predicting task, and dynamic masking pattern modifying.

3 Proposed method

Figure 1 illustrates our process. For MLM tuning we propose hierarchical tuning process that consists of two steps: Domain adaptation using extra COVID data and Task adaptation using the given training data. After MLM Tuning, we utilize different training techniques for text classification such as back translation, warm-up learning rate, layer freezing and layer-wise learning rates. This section provides details of this pipeline.

3.1 RoBERTa network for Text Classification Task

Taking advantage of RoBERTa as a backbone, we propose a customized network with appreciably modifications. Figure 2 illustrates our proposed architecture. The "base" version of RoBERTa is used. It has 12 Transformer blocks, each block outputs a 768-D vector for each token. Since the output of different Transformer blocks represent different semantic levels for the inputs, in our experiments we combine outputs of those Transformer blocks by concatenation. This combination is fed to a classification head. We propose two types of the head:

- **MLP Head:** A simple feed forward network with one hidden layer. This head takes the last token embedding as its input.

- **BiLSTM Head:** A recurrent neural network with one Bidirectional LSTM layer. This network takes embeddings of all tokens.

The hyperparameters are shown in Section 4.

3.2 Fine-tuning Masked Language Model (MLM)

3.2.1 Direct tuning on task data

RoBERTa apparently is an excellent language model since it was trained on a huge dataset in a broad domain. However, the general domain is also a drawback when it comes to downstream tasks with completely different domains such as classifying users' tweets on Twitter. Therefore, in order to produce high-quality outputs from the model, there is a need of fine-tuning MLM task on the task dataset for RoBERTa. This adapts the universal language model into our narrow domain, giving it prior knowledge for later classification training.

Choosing learning rate is the key factor for the convergence. If learning rate is too small, the model may converge too slow causing harder to fit to new data distribution. On the other hand, large learning rate can lead to the problem of useful feature forgetting. Hence, we employ warm-up learning rate scheduler (Howard and Ruder, 2018) to help the model converge faster while preserving its good initialization.

3.2.2 Hierarchical tuning with extra data

We assume fine-tuning only on the dataset might cause overfitting on the chosen dataset only. Hence, we propose a hierarchical fine-tuning strategy for RoBERTa: the first phase we train with custom domain COVID Tweets dataset for ***domain adaptation***, then the second phase is a fine-tuning process with WNUT Task 2 dataset for ***task adaptation***. Our custom COVID Tweets dataset is gathered from Twitter platform, including unlabeled 1 million posts in general COVID domain, which has the hashtag of **#Covid, #Covid19**, and **#Coronavirus**. We expect this model to generalize better on different distributed dataset in the same field of COVID Tweets.

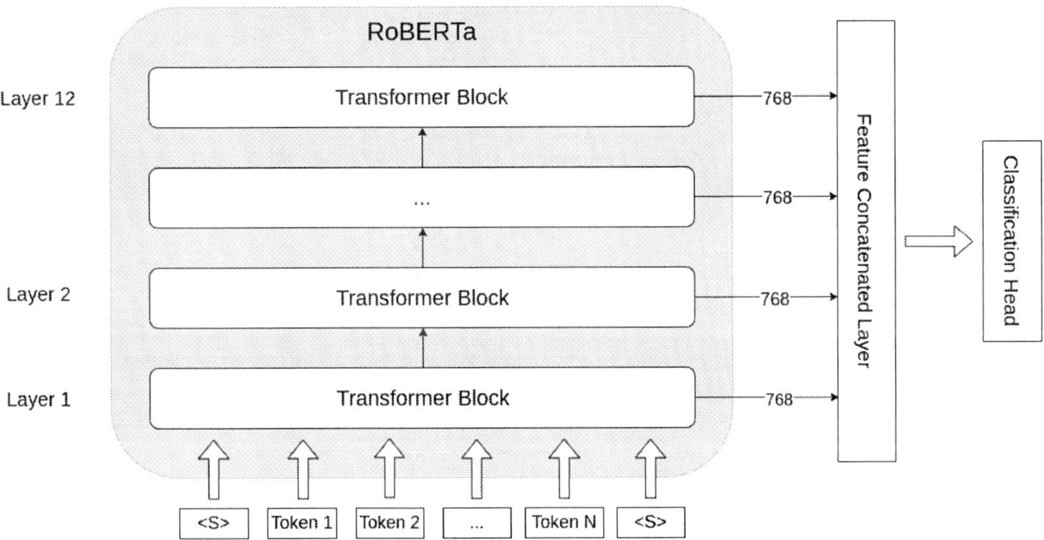

Figure 2: The architecture of the proposed model. The input is tokenized into a sequence of BPE tokens. RoBERTa, the "base" version, takes this sequence and propagates it through 12 Transformer layers. By concatenating outputs from these 12 layers, we form a long sentence representation for the follow-up classification head, which is a simple Multi-layer Perceptron/Long Short-Term Memory network.

3.3 Text classification training

3.3.1 Back Translation

Recently research (Xie et al., 2019; Edunov et al., 2018) have shown that back-translating monolingual data can be used as a potential form of data augmentation in Text Classification. The idea behind back translation is to translate a sentence from the original language (English) to another selected language and then translate back to the original language. This utilizes the power of current well-developed translation engines. In our experiment, 25% of the data samples is back-translated into Vietnamese, the same amount goes for Italian and French, and the rest 25% is kept unchanged. This assures the languages contribute equally to the overall dataset. Totally, the dataset size is increased by 75%.

3.3.2 Model freezing with layer-wise learning rates

Layer freezing helps preserving useful knowledge that a pre-trained neural network has learned. Since RoBERTa has been trained on a huge dataset, we would not want the model to derive too far from its pre-train weights. The training procedure is divided into 2 steps:

- **Step 1:** We freeze RoBERTa to train the classification head for the first epoch. Warm-up learning rate (Section 3.2.1) is also applied.

Because RoBERTa's weights are already well trained, this step helps escape from narrow local optimum.

- **Step 2:** RoBERTa is unfrozen, a whole network is trained. In RoBERTa, upper layers produce embeddings with more context-specific than lower layers. This motivates us to further apply layer-wise learning rate: set a small learning rate for the shallowest layer, increase the learning rate as the layer goes deeper.

3.3.3 Label Smoothing

When training a huge neural network on a relatively small dataset, overconfidence is a problem leading to bad behaviours of the model. This phenomenon occurs when the model gives predictions with confidence higher than its accuracy. While there have been a lot of studies for overfitting reduction, overconfidence problem attracts less attention from researchers. In this study, we employ label smoothing (Szegedy et al., 2015) to prevent model from being too certain about its predictions. Instead of assigning "hard" one-hot encoded ground truth, label smoothing adds a small perturbation into the label by a smoothing parameter α.

Model	Precision	Recall	F1	Accuracy
RoBERTa + MLP Head	0.9407	0.8740	0.9061	0.9080
RoBERTa + BiLSTM Head	0.9322	0.8853	0.9082	0.9110
Direct tuning + MLP Head + Label smoothing	**0.9492**	0.8960	**0.9218**	**0.9240**
Direct tuning + BiLSTM Head + Label smoothing	0.9364	**0.8983**	0.9170	0.9200
Direct tuning + MLP Head + Back translation + Label smoothing	0.9343	0.8909	0.9121	0.9150
Hierarchical tuning + MLP Head + Back translation + Label smoothing	0.9449	0.8745	0.9084	0.9100

Table 1: Comparison of different tuning and training techniques on the public validation set.

$$y'_k = y_k(1 - \alpha) + \alpha/K$$

, where y_k is output probabilities of K classes.

Moreover, label smoothing also helps stabilize the training process. When using cross-entropy loss, one-hot encoded labels cause numerical instabilities if the prediction is close to one-hot form. In that case, the loss will become $1 \log 0 = -\infty$. By setting $\alpha \neq 0$, this problem can be solved.

4 Experiments and Results

4.1 Experiment setup

Our set-up is proceeded as following instruction. We trained our networks with PyTorch framework on GPU GeForce GTX 2080Ti with batch size 32 for 20 epochs. We used AdamW (Loshchilov and Hutter, 2017) for the optimization and a learning rate of $3e - 5$, decayed 0.01 except for LayerNorm layers. Label smoothing hyperparameter α was empirically experimented with multiple values of 0, 0.1, 0.15, 0.2 and the last value possessed promising results. The numbers of hidden units of MLP Head and BiLSTM Head to 768 and 256 respectively.

4.2 Evaluation metrics

Evaluation metrics for assessing are Accuracy, F1-score, Recall and Precision metrics on public validation set. Accuracy can be used when the class distribution is similar while F1-score is a better choice of metric when there are imbalanced classes.

$$precision = \frac{TP}{TP + FP}$$

$$recall = \frac{TP}{TP + FN}$$

$$F_1 = \frac{2}{precision^{-1} + recall^{-1}}$$

, where TP: True Positive, FP: False Positive, FN: False Negative

4.3 Results

Table 1 compares the performance of multiple trial architectures training with pre-trained method using RoBERTa in our base settings. The original RoBERTa with MLP Head shows the better result than LSTM head, but the difference is not really noticeable (0.9082 vs. 0.9061). When applying direct tuning MLM and label smoothing, the gap has been widened, specifically, 0.9218 for MLP Head and 0.9170 for LSTM Head.

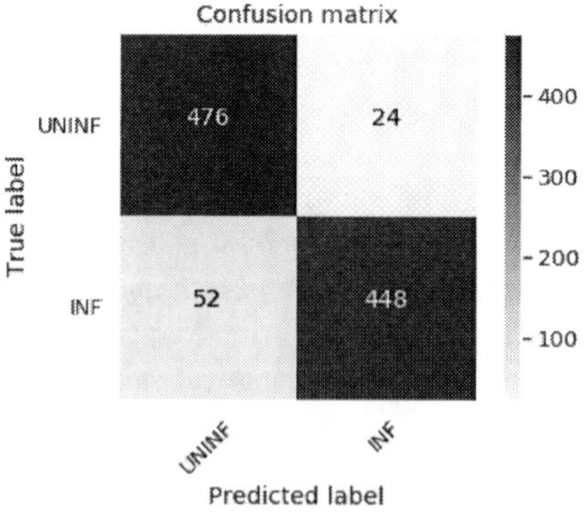

Figure 3: Confusion matrix on the public validation set

In the table, hierarchical tuning and back translation method did not yield better results than direct tuning without back translation one. Nevertheless, we expect this method can generalize well on many different distributed datasets and thus, we ensembled the two versions with voting and submitted to the private test benchmark. We ended up at top 9 on the leaderboard with 0.9005 F1-score and

Table 2: Some failures of our system.

Text	Model prediction	Truth label
Some people metaphorically shake their walking sticks at the TV like Grandpa Simpson & rage "flu has already killed thousands in USA", "but guns have already killed over 6,000 in USA this year" - all true. But Coronavirus is In Addition to those deaths. HTTPURL	INFORMATIVE	UNINFORMATIVE
2/26 PCR test 2/27 Negative result 2/28 X-ray shows n.p. Discharge. Stay near Haneda airport 2/29 Akita airport Return 3/6 Follow up: Visit B in Akita. Fever & cough - B consults with designated outpatient service(C) And PCR + covid19 HTTPURL	INFORMATIVE	UNINFORMATIVE
Amazon and Facebook ask Seattle employees to work from home after coronavirus cases HTTPURL	UNINFORMATIVE	INFORMATIVE
Third of Sacramento coronavirus cases linked to church events - Los Angeles Times. Pathetic! HTTPURL	UNINFORMATIVE	INFORMATIVE

0.9301 Recall, in which our Recall score reached the second place.

4.4 Error Analysis

A question that as important as designing a subtle method is "what make the model fail". By answering this question we can gain an insight into our model performance and further improve it. The method used for analyzing is the bottom row in Table 1. Firstly, we plot confusion matrix (Figure 3), observe that both True Positive and True Negative are evenly distributed with a small proportion of False Negative and False Positive, indicating our model did not bias towards any classes. Secondly, we randomly sample some failures the model made (Table 2). It seems like sentences containing more numbers are usually (mis)classified as INFORMATIVE while the ones containing less numbers are classified as UNINFORMATIVE. This can be explained that INFORMATIVE tweets provide information about recovered, suspected, confirmed and death cases. Therefore, numbers appearance is inevitable.

5 Conclusion

In this paper, we have explored and proposed our pipeline to solve the Identification of Informative COVID-19 English Tweet task by using a pre-trained universal language model. By conducting a lot of experiments, we have demonstrated that the use of RoBERTa and our fine-tuning strategy is highly effective in text classification tasks. With our proposed methods, we have achieved prominent results on the WNUT Task 2.

For future work, we will design more complex classification head architectures to improve model's performance as well as solving problems indicated in Section 4.4. Furthermore, we would like to employ our model and pipeline in different languages such as Vietnamese to see how they adapt to new languages.

References

Jacob Devlin, Ming-Wei Chang, Kenton Lee, and Kristina Toutanova. 2018. Bert: Pre-training of deep bidirectional transformers for language understanding.

Sergey Edunov, Myle Ott, Michael Auli, and David Grangier. 2018. Understanding back-translation at scale.

Jeremy Howard and Sebastian Ruder. 2018. Universal language model fine-tuning for text classification.

Yinhan Liu, Myle Ott, Naman Goyal, Jingfei Du, Mandar Joshi, Danqi Chen, Omer Levy, Mike Lewis, Luke Zettlemoyer, and Veselin Stoyanov. 2019. Roberta: A robustly optimized bert pretraining approach.

Ilya Loshchilov and Frank Hutter. 2017. Decoupled weight decay regularization.

Tomas Mikolov, Kai Chen, Greg Corrado, and Jeffrey Dean. 2013. Efficient estimation of word representations in vector space.

Tomas Mikolov, Edouard Grave, Piotr Bojanowski, Christian Puhrsch, and Armand Joulin. 2018. Advances in pre-training distributed word representations. In *Proceedings of the International Conference on Language Resources and Evaluation (LREC 2018)*.

Dat Quoc Nguyen, Thanh Vu, Afshin Rahimi, Mai Hoang Dao, Linh The Nguyen, and Long Doan. 2020. WNUT-2020 Task 2: Identification of Informative COVID-19 English Tweets. In *Proceedings of the 6th Workshop on Noisy User-generated Text*.

Jeffrey Pennington, Richard Socher, and Christopher Manning. 2014. GloVe: Global vectors for word representation. In *Proceedings of the 2014 Conference on Empirical Methods in Natural Language Processing (EMNLP)*, pages 1532–1543, Doha, Qatar. Association for Computational Linguistics.

A. Radford, Jeffrey Wu, R. Child, David Luan, Dario Amodei, and Ilya Sutskever. 2019. Language models are unsupervised multitask learners.

Christian Szegedy, Vincent Vanhoucke, Sergey Ioffe, Jonathon Shlens, and Zbigniew Wojna. 2015. Rethinking the inception architecture for computer vision.

Qizhe Xie, Zihang Dai, Eduard Hovy, Minh-Thang Luong, and Quoc V. Le. 2019. Unsupervised data augmentation for consistency training.

ISWARA at WNUT-2020 Task 2: Identification of Informative COVID-19 English Tweets using BERT and FastText Embeddings

Wava Carissa Putri[*1], **Rani Aulia Hidayat**[*1],
Isnaini Nurul Khasanah[*1], **Rahmad Mahendra**[2]
Faculty of Computer Science, Universitas Indonesia
[1]{wava.carissa01, rani.auila,isnaini.nurul91}@ui.ac.id
[2]rahmad.mahendra@cs.ui.ac.id

Abstract

This paper presents Iswara's participation in the WNUT-2020 Task 2 "Identification of Informative COVID-19 English Tweets using BERT and FastText Embeddings", which tries to classify whether a certain tweet is considered informative or not. We proposed a method that utilizes word embeddings and using word occurrence related to the topic for this task. We compare several models to get the best performance. Results show that pairing BERT with word occurrences outperforms fastText with F1-Score, precision, recall, and accuracy on test data of 76%, 81%, 72%, and 79%, respectively.

1 Introduction

Twitter is known for being one of the major platforms during disasters (Ashktorab et al., 2014) since it is accessible for everyone and could give real-time information about the disaster (Vieweg, 2010). The outbreak of COVID-19 causes a large flow of information about the pandemic within the site. The increase in the number of tweets raised concern about the relevancy of the tweets to the COVID-19 itself. Identifying relevant tweets manually form Twitter is costly and needs significant human efforts (Nguyen et al., 2020).

WNUT-2020 has organized a shared task which focuses on identifying whether an English tweet related to COVID-19 is informative or not. Tweets containing information about recovered, suspected, confirmed, and death cases of COVID-19 is defined as an informative tweet. This paper aims to present the approaches we developed as part of our participation in WNUT-2020 Task 2. In this research, we proposed two approaches to identify informative COVID-19 tweets. The first approach is based on the BERT model, whereas the second approach is based on the FastText model. The first approach is experimented on two classification models such as Logistic Regression (LR) and Support Vector Machine (SVM). Word occurrence also used as an additional feature during the experiment. The second approach uses a built-in classifier from the FastText library.

The rest of the paper is organized as follows. In section 2, we explain the methodology we developed. Section 3 describes the results analysis about the experiments. Finally, section 4 concludes the paper and lists the future works.

2 Methodology

We first analyze the training data provided by the task organizers. It consisted of 7,000 tweets, with 3,697 tweets labeled as uninformative and 3,303 tweets as informative. The validation data consisted of 1000 tweets, with 528 uninformative tweets and 472 informative tweets. Most of the tweets were written in English. However, we found that there are several words that were written in non-ASCII characters.

The rise of word embedding led us to use pre-trained word embedding models such as BERT and fastText in our experiments. To process with the pre-trained model, we had to preprocess the tweets beforehand. We tried to remove URLs, Non-ASCII characters, tokens such as 'RT', '@', '&','<', '>' and extra space. All of the tweets were changed into lowercase letters.

---

[*] These authors contributed equally to this work

Proceedings of the 2020 EMNLP Workshop W-NUT: The Sixth Workshop on Noisy User-generated Text, pages 491–494
Online, Nov 19, 2020. ©2020 Association for Computational Linguistics

In this experiment, we used pre-trained word embedding models to generate a word embedding representation of each tweet. Each representation is fed into a classifier to identify which class the tweet belongs to. BERT (Devlin et al., 2018) is used to create a representation of the tweets. Meanwhile, fastText (Joulin et al.,2017) is used directly for the tweet classification after modifying the label by adding the term "__label__" followed by the actual label.

Prior research found that BERT (Müller et al., 2020; Roitero et al., 2020) and fastText (Stein et al., 2019; Jha and Mamidi, 2017; Alessa et al., 2018) are useful for tweet classification tasks. There are a variety of pre-trained models available for BERT. However, we decided to use DistilBERT (Sanh et al., 2019) since it has a similar performance with other pre-trained models, but it has a much smaller representation model.

In addition, we also used word occurrences and number existence of the preprocessed tweets as the features that we used to classify the tweets. We combined the word occurrences with the word embedding representation. The occurrences of words 'corona' and 'covid' are being used as features to represent that a tweet is related to COVID-19. As Nguyen et al. (2020) stated, a tweet is considered as informative if it contains any information about recovered, suspected, confirmed, and death cases. Hence, the occurrences of words 'recover', 'suspect', 'confirm', 'death', and 'case' are used. Moreover, the number of cases is sometimes mentioned in the tweets. We covered this by using the existence of numerical value as the feature. The number existence feature will be true if a tweet contains a numerical value, and false if there is no numerical value in the tweet.

There are several classifiers that we used in this study to identify the informative tweets. Those classifiers are Logistic Regression, Support Vector Machine, and Multinomial Logistic Regression (built-in classifier in fastText library). Furthermore, we compared the performance of each classifier to get the best model.

Logistic Regression (LR) is a machine learning method that calculates the result by considering each feature's weight. It has been applied to classify tweets into certain topics (S.T. et al., 2016). After tuning the parameters, we decided to train our LR model with a value of 5.263252631578947 for C and a maximum iteration of 10,000.

Support Vector Machine has been proven to give acceptable performance for tweets classification (Kurniawan et al., 2016). This classifier is well known for its ability to map nonlinear data into a higher dimensional space using the kernel trick. In this study, we focused on implementing the RBF kernel. Parameters C and gamma have a significant role in SVM with RBF kernels. The value of parameters C and gamma that we used to train the SVM model are 10 and 0.01, respectively. Those parameters are obtained after the tuning process.

Joulin et al. (2017) showed that fastText gives on par accuracy compared to deep learning classifiers but with faster training and validation process. As mentioned earlier, we labeled each tweet with the text "__label__" followed by the actual label (informative or uninformative). Then, we train the model on the preprocessed train data using the fastText library. This library will extract fastText embeddings and process it with the built-in classifier, Multinomial Logistic Regression (MLR). To find the best hyperparameters, we tried automatic and manual hyperparameter optimization. Based on the evaluation score on the validation data, we find better results using hyperparameters that we find manually. The value of hyperparameters learning rate, maximum length of word n-gram, epoch, minimum number of word occurrences, number of buckets, and loss function used in this study are 0.075, 2, 150, 6, 200000, and 'hs', respectively.

3   Results and Analysis

There are several scenarios of features in this study. The first scenario is using BERT as the feature. In the second scenario, we combined word occurrences (WO) with BERT as the features. We employed the first and second scenarios to LR and SVM with parameters we defined in the previous section. In the next scenario, we used the preprocessed tweets as the feature for fastText to generate fastText embbedings (FT).

Since the task is focused on informative tweets' performance, the evaluation metrics we compare in our study are F1-Score, precision, recall, and accuracy of the informative labeled tweets. Before submitting the final model to be evaluated using test data on WNUT-2020 system, we evaluated the model by the validation data. Figure 1 shows all experiments that have been done in this study.

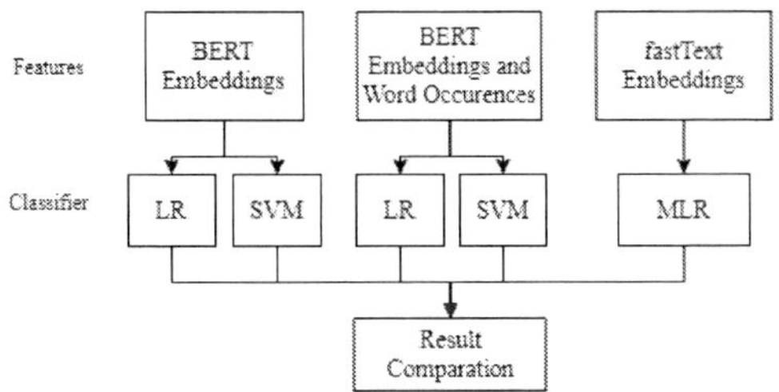

Figure 1. Experiment Scenarios

Table 1 shows the result of each experiment evaluated on validation data. The best F1-score is 0.81 and it was obtained by two models. The first model used preprocessed tweets with fastText, which resulted in precision, recall, and accuracy of 0.85, 0.77, and 0.83, respectively. The next model used BERT and word occurrences as features with SVM as classifier with precision, recall, and accuracy of 0.83, 0.78, and 0.82, respectively.

Features	Classifier	F1-Score	Precision	Recall	Accuracy
FT	MLR	0.81	0.85	0.77	0.83
BERT	LR	0.79	0.81	0.77	0.81
BERT	SVM	0.79	0.82	0.76	0.81
BERT & WO	LR	0.79	0.82	0.77	0.81
BERT & WO	SVM	0.81	0.83	0.78	0.82

Table 1. Result on Validation Data

From the experiments we conducted, the performance of BERT increased when combined with word occurrences as the additional features whether it is employed to LR or SVM. It is shown that using COVID-19 related word occurrences as features successfully manages the model to identify informative tweets better.

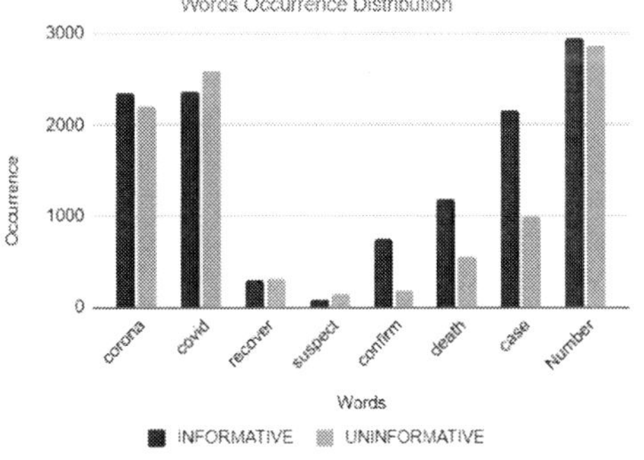

Figure 2. Word Occurrences Distribution

Figure 2 shows that there is not much difference in the occurrence of words 'corona', 'covid', 'recover' and numerical value in informative and uninformative tweets. Meanwhile, there is a high difference in the occurrence of words 'confirm', 'death', and 'case' between informative and uninformative tweets. It means that the word occurrences help the model to classify the tweets.

Because of the limited number of submissions on WNUT-20202 system on Task 2, we chose the best two models based on the experiments result. These two models were officially evaluated on test data in the system provided by WNUT-2020.

Table 2 presents the performance of each model. It is shown that the performance of the model, which used BERT and word occurrences with SVM, outperforms the model that used fastText with MLR. The best model achieved an F1-Score of 0.763, precision of 0.807, recall of 0.723, and accuracy of 0.788.

Features	Classifier	F1-Score	Precision	Recall	Accuracy
BERT & WO	SVM	0.763	0.807	0.724	0.788
FT	MLR	0.757	0.791	0.725	0.780

Table 2. Result of Test Data on WNUT-2020 System.

We found that fastText performs better when evaluated on the validation data. However, the combination BERT and word occurrences shows better results when evaluated on the test data. One reason may be that since BERT created subwords rather than n-grams in their approach, it could help the model to handle out of vocabulary words in the test data better.

4 Conclusion

This paper presents our approach for WNUT-2020 Task 2 to identify whether a tweet related to COVID-19 is informative or not. The proposed method for this shared task is combining word embedding with word occurrences as features. We compared several scenarios of features with different classifiers such as Logistic Regression (LR), Support Vector Machine (SVM), and Multinomial Logistic Regression (MLR), built-in classifier in fastText library, on validation data.

The validation data result showed that there are two models that give the highest F1-Score of 0.81. The first model used the fastText embeddings with built-in MLR has precision, recall, and accuracy of 0.85, 0.77, and 0.83, respectively. The second model used the BERT embeddings and word occurrences as features with SVM as the classifier has precision, recall, and accuracy of 0.83, 0.78, and 0.82, respectively. These two models are evaluated on the WNUT-2020 system with test data. On the test data, the model that used BERT embeddings and word occurrences with SVM outperforms the model which used fastText embeddings with MLR. It achieved an F1-Score of 0.763, precision of 0.807, recall of 0.723, and accuracy of 0.788.

The use of richer features such as Named Entity Recognition to identify location mentioned in a tweet and the use of Part of Speech Tagging can be done as the future works. Moreover, the implementation of advanced algorithms such as deep learning might also increase the performance of the model to identify informative tweets.

References

Ashktorab, Z., Brown, C., Nandi, M., & Culotta, A. 2014 . Tweedr: Mining twitter to inform disaster response. In *Information Systems for Crisis Response and Management (ISCRAM)*, pages 269-272.

Vieweg, S. 2010. Microblogged contributions to the emergency arena: Discovery, interpretation and implications. *Computer Supported Collaborative Work*, pages 515-516.

Dat Quoc Nguyen, Thanh Vu, Afshin Rahimi, Mai Hoang Dao, Linh The Nguyen, and Long Doan. 2020. WNUT-2020 Task 2: Identification of Informative COVID-19 English Tweets. In *Proceedings of the 6th Workshop Noisy User-generated Text*.

Jacob Devlin, Ming-Wei Chang, Kenton Lee, and Kristina Toutanova. 2018. *BERT: Pre-training of Deep Bidirectional Transformers for Language Understanding*. arXiv preprint arXiv:1810.04805.

Armand Joulin, Edouard Grave, Piotr Bojanowski, and Tomas Mikolov. 2017. Bag of Tricks for Efficient Text Classification. In *Proceedings of the 15th Conference of the European Chapter of the Association for Computational Linguistics* (Volume 2: Short Papers). Association for Computational Linguistics, pages 427-431.

Martin Müller, Marcel Salathé, and Per E Kummervold. 2020. *COVID-Twitter-BERT: A Natural Language Processing Model to Analyse COVID-19 Content on Twitter*. arXiv preprint arXiv:2005.07503.

Roger Alan Stein, Patricia A. Jaques, and João Francisco Valiati. 2019. *An analysis of hierarchical text classification using word embeddings*. Information Sciences, 471, pages 216-232.

Aksitha Jha, and Radhika Mamidi. 2017. When does a compliment become sexist? analysis and classification of ambivalent sexism using twitter data. In *Proceedings of the second workshop on NLP and computational social science*. Association for Computational Linguistics, pages 7-16.

Victor Sanh, Lysandre Debut, Julien Chaumond, and Thomas Wolf. 2019. *DistilBERT, a distilled version of BERT: smaller, faster, cheaper and lighter*. arXiv preprint arXiv:1910.01108.

Indra S.T., Liza Wikarsa, and Rinaldo Turang. 2016. Using Logistic Regression Method to Classify Tweets into the Selected Topics. *2016 International Conference on Advanced Computer Science and Information Systems (ICACSIS)*, pages 385-390.

Dwi Aji Kurniawan, Sunu Wibrama, and Nur Akhmad Setiawan. 2016. Real-time Traffic Classification with Twitter Data Mining. *2016 8th International Conference on Information Technology and Electrical Engineering (ICITEE)*, pages 1-5.

Kevin Roitero, Cristian Bozzato, Vincenzo Della Mea, Steffano Mizzaro, and Giuseppe Serra. 2020. Twitter goes to the Doctor: Detecting Medical Tweets using Machine Learning and BERT. In *Proceedings of the International Workshop on Semantic Indexing and Information Retrieval for Health from heterogeneous content types and languages (SIIRH) 2020*.

Ali Alessa, Miad Faezipour, and Zakhriya Alhassan. 2018. Text classification of flu-related tweets using fasttext with sentiment and keyword features. *2018 IEEE International Conference on Healthcare Informatics (ICHI)*, pages 366-367.

COVCOR20 at WNUT-2020 Task 2: An Attempt to Combine Deep Learning and Expert rules

Ali Hürriyetoğlu
Koç University
ahurriyetoglu@ku.edu.tr

Ali Safaya
Koç University
asafaya@ku.edu.tr

Osman Mutlu
Koç University
omutlu@ku.edu.tr

Nelleke Oostdijk
Radboud University
n.oostdijk@let.ru.nl

Erdem Yörük
Koç University
eryoruk@ku.edu.tr

Abstract

In the scope of WNUT-2020 Task 2, we developed various text classification systems, using deep learning models and one using linguistically informed rules. While both of the deep learning systems outperformed the system using the linguistically informed rules, we found that through the integration of (the output of) the three systems a better performance could be achieved than the standalone performance of each approach in a cross-validation setting. However, on the test data the performance of the integration was slightly lower than our best performing deep learning model. These results hardly indicate any progress in line of integrating machine learning and expert rules driven systems. We expect that the release of the annotation manuals and gold labels of the test data after this workshop will shed light on these perplexing results.

1 Introduction

The COVID-19 pandemic urged various science disciplines to do their best so as to contribute to understanding and relieving its impact. Thus, scholars and practitioners working on information sciences have been dedicating significant effort to help. Collecting and analyzing data published on social media platforms have become the focus in this respect. We joined the community that aims at organizing data collected from social media (in this use case: Twitter), as informative and uninformative. The WNUT-2020 Task 2 considers tweets about recovered, suspected, confirmed and death cases as well as location or travel history of the cases as informative. All other tweets are considered to be uninformative. The organizers did not share an annotation manual nor was a baseline system made available, presumably to prevent use of any other manually annotated data and to encourage broad participation respectively (Nguyen et al., 2020b).[1]

The effort was managed in terms of a shared task, in which the organizers share a dataset that consists of annotated tweets and conduct the evaluation of the submissions. The task requires the participating teams to develop short-text classification systems that facilitate the training and development data to generalize to the test set they release. Although the gold labels of the training and development data were available to the participants, neither the gold labels of the test data nor the annotation guidelines for any part of the data were shared with the participants. Moreover, the test instances were unknown to the participating teams. They were hidden in a larger dataset. Each team was allowed to submit only two outputs of the systems they developed for classifying tweets on the Codalab page of the task.[2] The highest score in terms of F1 positive class of each team was used to rank them in the leaderboard.

Integrating automatically created machine learning based (ML) models with manually formulated rules to tackle a text classification task promises the best of both worlds. We pursued this goal by integrating the output of two deep learning models and a rule-based system under the team name COVCOR20. Although the integration slightly improves the total performance on the training and development sets in a cross-validation setting, the overall performance on the test data turned out to be slightly worse than our best ML system. Our best submission was ranked 22nd among 55 teams. The integration of our systems would be ranked 27th if its score were used as the final score for our team.

[1]http://noisy-text.github.io/2020/ covid19tweet-task.html, accessed on September 4, 2020.

[2]https://competitions.codalab.org/ competitions/25845, accessed on September 4, 2020.

Proceedings of the 2020 EMNLP Workshop W-NUT: The Sixth Workshop on Noisy User-generated Text, pages 495–498
Online, Nov 19, 2020. ©2020 Association for Computational Linguistics

The deep learning models and the rule-based system are introduced in Sections 2 and 3 respectively. Next, the Section 4 describes how we integrate the output of these systems. Then Section 5 provide the results and their discussion. Finally, we conclude this report and share our future plans continuing in this line of research in Section 6.

2 Deep learning models

We created various deep learning models by merging the training and development data released by the organizers. We applied k-fold cross-validation by splitting the data into five parts. The average performance in terms of F1 of five optimization and test iterations is used to compare these models. The hyper-parameter optimization is focused on F1 of the positive class. Table 1 provides performances of the models we tested. CNNText, BiLSTM, and BERT-CNN were borrowed from Safaya et al. (2020), BERT is the standard model from Devlin et al. (2019), and BERTweet is the model created by Nguyen et al. (2020a).

We developed a novel model that we call Fused-1 and Fused-2 that has a modified version of CharRNN[3] is a character language model that consists of two LSTM layers and is pretrained on 112 thousand tweets related to COVID19 which we collected. In Fused-1 CharRNN is applied in parallel with BERT, while in Fused-2 it is used in parallel with BERTweet. Just as in BERT-CNN, we feed the output of the last hidden layer of CharRNN to a Convolutional Neural Network (CNN). We also have another CNN that takes BERT or BERTweet output as its input. Upon this, we concatenate the output of these two CNNs (the first one using BERT or BERTweet as embedder and the latter using CharRNN as embedder), and we feed it to a fully connected layer to get the final output[4].

We used Fused-2 as it is the best performing model in the aforementioned cross-validation setting. Moreover, we observed that the average number of the sentences in wrongly predicted instances is larger than the correctly predicted cases using the best performing deep learning model. Therefore, we generated a second output for each tweet by

---

[3]https://github.com/alisafaya/char-rnn.pytorch, acccessed on September 6, 2020.

[4]All details of the models and the optimization can be found on the repository https://github.com/emerging-welfare/covid19-tweet, which we have created for this shared task

Model	F1	Std
CNNText	.8543	.0116
BiLSTM	.8595	.0089
BERT	.9432	.0066
BERT-CNN	.9478	.0060
BERTweet	.9499	.0029
Fused-1	.9552	.0022
Fused-2	.9560	.0024

Table 1: Model performances in terms of F1 and Standard Deviation (Std).

predicting each sentence separately. If at least one sentence in a tweet is predicted as informative, the prediction for the whole tweet becomes positive, i.e. informative. The precision decreased, the recall increased, and the F1 slightly decreased in this setting.

3 Rule-based system

The rule-based system uses a set of handcrafted rules constructed by an expert for the task at hand and a task-specific lexicon. The system is designed to identify only instances of the positive class, which for this particular task are the tweets that are considered to be informative. The rules describe, in terms of linguistic patterns, the salient part(s) of these tweets. Whenever a rule fires, the tweet will be labelled as informative; tweets for which no rule is found to apply are considered noninformative by default. A similar rule-based approach has been used successfully in other shared tasks (e.g. Hürriyetoğlu and Oostdijk (2017); Oostdijk and Hürriyetoğlu (2017); Oostdijk and van Halteren (2019)). There, the approach has been shown to yield consistently high precision across different datasets, while recall generally falls short of that yielded by ML approaches.

In this case the lexicon we compiled has 779 entries. Entries here are of the form: word type – semantic/syntactic word class – (optionally) label, e.g.

case N informative	death N informative
first NUMord	covid19 Ncorona
new ADJ	confirmed ADJ

In order to have maximum control over the strings matched, in most cases entries are delimited by word boundary markers (\b), indicating the beginning and the end of a word or multi-word expression. An exception was made with the entries referring to the virus (including for example, covid19, covid-19, coronavirus) where not including the initial word boundary marker allows for the matching of instances where the word is part of a hashtag.

The rules set comprises 409 rules. They describe how the lexical entries can combine to form larger strings, the length of which in the present case varies between 2 to 7 words. Example rules are[5]

    NUMord *N
    ADJ Ncorona *N
    NUMord ADJ *N

which account for instances like *first case, first confirmed death*, and *new covid19 deaths*. One of the strengths of the rule-based approach is that the rules generalize beyond the instances observed in the training set, provided that the individual words appear in the lexicon.

The performance achieved with the rule-based system was as follows: on the training set precision was .845, recall .893 and F1 86.9; on the validation set precision was .77, recall .852 and F1 .809. We are able increase the precision at the expense of decreasing recall by requiring the number of detected spans to be equal or more than a certain threshold. For instance, the precision and recall become .91 and .53 in average if we set this threshold to be 2.

4   Integrating outputs

We have shown that ML and rule-based approaches yield complementary output for text classification tasks in various settings in our previous work (Hürriyetoğlu and Oostdijk, 2017; Oostdijk and Hürriyetoğlu, 2017; Oostdijk and van Halteren, 2019). Therefore, we continued to work along this line by focusing on integrating the outputs of these systems in the scope of this shared task. However, voting and applying OR and AND operations on the predictions did not outperform the best deep learning model Fused-2. The only integration that perform slightly better was giving precedence to the rule-based system in case the two output versions of Fused-2 conflict and the rule-based system predicts a tweet as uninformative. In case the rule-based system predicts it informative, we used prediction of the best system, which is Fused-2 on all text of a tweet. This adjustment increased F1 from .9560 to .9581 in our cross-validation setting.

5   Results

We submitted the best performing deep learning model, which is Fused-2 using all text of a tweet and the best performing integration. The deep learning model yielded .8887 and the integration yielded 0.8856 F1. Our team ranked 22 with these scores.[6] The best overall F1 score in the shared task was .9096.

The decrease of the scores from around .9560 on development set to .8887 on the test set shows that rule-based system could have had a chance by itself. However, the restriction of the submission count to be 2 did not allow us to evaluate this.

6   Conclusion and future work

We have presented our effort in the scope of a shared task that aims at pushing the state of the art for classifying short-texts (i.e. tweets in the reported use case), as informative or uninformative.

We could extend the training set with cluster mining using Relevancer (Hürriyetoğlu et al., 2016), use the rule-based system to extend the training set (Hürriyetoğlu, 2019), or use the rule-based system to generate fine-grained data that can be used in a multi-task setting.

Acknowledgements

The authors from Koç University are funded by the European Research Council (ERC) Starting Grant 714868 awarded to Dr. Erdem Yörük for his project Emerging Welfare.

References

Jacob Devlin, Ming-Wei Chang, Kenton Lee, and Kristina Toutanova. 2019. BERT: Pre-training of deep bidirectional transformers for language understanding. In *Proceedings of the 2019 Conference of the North American Chapter of the Association for Computational Linguistics: Human Language Technologies, Volume 1 (Long and Short Papers)*, pages 4171–4186, Minneapolis, Minnesota. Association for Computational Linguistics.

Ali Hürriyetoğlu. 2019. *Extracting Actionable Information from Microtexts*. Ph.D. thesis, Radboud University Nijmegen.

Ali Hürriyetoğlu, Christian Gudehus, Nelleke Oostdijk, and Antal van den Bosch. 2016. *Relevancer: Finding and Labeling Relevant Information in Tweet Col-*

---

[5]The asterisk indicates the element from which the string inherits its label.

[6]All results of the competition are on: `https://competitions.codalab.org/competitions/25845#results`

lections, pages 210–224. Springer International Publishing, Cham.

Ali Hürriyetoğlu and Nelleke Oostdijk. 2017. Extracting Humanitarian Information from Tweets. In *Proceedings of the First International Workshop on Exploitation of Social Media for Emergency Relief and Preparedness*, Aberdeen, United Kingdom.

Dat Quoc Nguyen, Thanh Vu, and Anh Tuan Nguyen. 2020a. BERTweet: A pre-trained language model for English Tweets. *arXiv preprint*, arXiv:2005.10200.

Dat Quoc Nguyen, Thanh Vu, Afshin Rahimi, Mai Hoang Dao, Linh The Nguyen, and Long Doan. 2020b. WNUT-2020 Task 2: Identification of Informative COVID-19 English Tweets. In *Proceedings of the 6th Workshop on Noisy User-generated Text*.

Nelleke Oostdijk and Hans van Halteren. 2019. Team taurus at semeval-2019 task 9: Expert-informed pattern recognition for suggestion mining. In *Proceedings of the 13th International Workshop on Semantic Evaluation*, pages 1247–1253.

Nelleke Oostdijk and Ali Hürriyetoğlu. 2017. Detecting the need for resources and their availability. In *Majumder, P.; Mitra, M.; Mehta, P.(ed.), FIRE 2017 Working Notes. Working notes of FIRE 2017–Forum for Information Retrieval Evaluation*, pages 34–37. Bangalore, India:[Sn].

Ali Safaya, Moutasem Abdullatif, and Deniz Yuret. 2020. Kuisail at semeval-2020 task 12: Bert-cnn for offensive speech identification in social media.

TEST_POSITIVE at W-NUT 2020 Shared Task-3:
Joint Event Multi-task Learning for Slot Filling in Noisy Text

Chacha Chen [1]
Penn State
chachachen@psu.edu

Chieh-Yang Huang
Penn State
chiehyang@psu.edu

Yaqi Hou
UNC at Chapel Hill
yaqi.hou@unc.edu

Yang Shi
NC State
yshi26@ncsu.edu

Enyan Dai
Penn State
emd5759@psu.edu

Jiaqi Wang[*]
Penn State
jqwang@psu.edu

Abstract

The competition of extracting COVID-19 events from Twitter is to develop systems that can automatically extract related events from tweets. The built system should identify different pre-defined slots for each event, in order to answer important questions (e.g., *Who is tested positive? What is the age of the person? Where is he/she?*). To tackle these challenges, we propose the Joint Event Multi-task Learning (JOELIN) model. Through a unified global learning framework, we make use of all the training data across different events to learn and fine-tune the language model. Moreover, we implement a type-aware post-processing procedure using named entity recognition (NER) to further filter the predictions. JOELIN outperforms the BERT baseline by 17.2% in micro F1.[1]

1   Introduction

In this work, we report the system architecture and results of the team TEST_POSITIVE in the competition of W-NUT 2020 sharred Task-3: extracting COVID-19 event from Twitter.

Since February 2020, the pandemic COVID-19 has been spreading all over the world, posing a significant threat to mankind in every aspect. The information sharing about a pandemic has been critical in stopping virus spreading. With the recent advance of social networks and machine learning, we are able to automatically detect potential events of COVID cases, and identify key information to prepare ahead.

We are interested in COVID-19 related event extraction from tweets. With the prevalence of coronavirus, Twitter has been a valuable source of news and information. Twitter users share COVID-19 related topics about personal narratives and news on social media (Müller et al., 2020). The information

could be helpful for doctors, epidemiologists, and policymakers in controlling the pandemic. However, manual extracting useful information from tremendous amount of tweets is impossible. Hence, we aim to develop a system to automatically extract structured knowledge from Twitter.

Extracting COVID-19 related events from Twitter is non-trivial due to the following challenges:

(1) **How to deal with limited annotations in heterogeneous events and subtasks?**. The creation of the annotated data relies completely on human labors, and thus only a limited amount of data can be obtained in each event categories. There are a variety types of events and subtasks. Many existing works solve these low resource problem by different approaches, inlcuding crowdsourcing (Müller et al., 2020; Finin et al., 2010; Potthast et al., 2018), unsupervised training (Xie et al., 2019; Hsu et al., 2017), or multi-task learning (Zhang and Yang, 2017; Pentyala et al., 2019). Here we adopt multi-task training paradigm to benefit from the inter-event and intra-event (subtasks) information sharing. In this way, JOELIN learns a shared embedding network globally from all events data. In this way, we implicitly augment the dataset by global training and fine-tuning the language model.

(2) **How to make type-aware predictions?** Existing work (Zong et al., 2020) did not encode the information of different subtask types into the model, while it could be useful in suggesting the candidate slot entity type. In order to make type-aware predictions, we propose a NER-based post-processing procedure in the end of JOELIN pipeline. We use NER to automatically tag the candidate slots and remove the candidate whose entity type does not match the corresponding subtask type. For example, as shown in Figure 1, in subtask "Who", "my wife's grandmother" is a valid candidate slot, while "old persons home", tagged as location entity, would be replaced with "Not Specified" during the

---

[1]https://github.com/Chacha-Chen/JOELIN

Proceedings of the 2020 EMNLP Workshop W-NUT: The Sixth Workshop on Noisy User-generated Text, pages 499–504
Online, Nov 19, 2020. ©2020 Association for Computational Linguistics

post-processing.

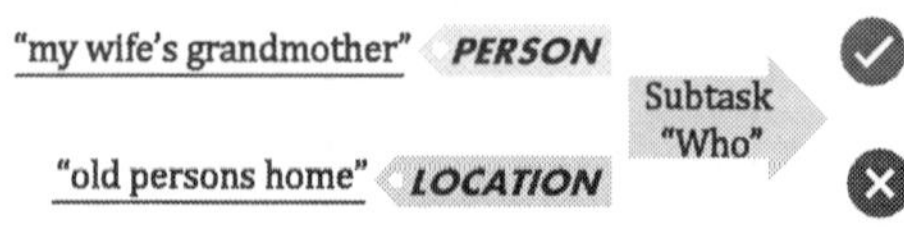

Figure 1: Illustration of NER-based post-processing.

In summary, JOELIN is enabled by the following technical contributions:

- **A joint event multi-task learning framework for different events and subtasks.** With the unified global training framework, we train and fine-tune the language model across all events and make predictions based on multi-task learning to learn from limited data.

- **A NER-based type-aware post-processing approach.** We leverage NER tagging on the model predictions and filter out wrong predictions based on subtask types. In this way, JOELIN benefits from subtask type prior knowledge and further boosts the performance.

2   Related Work

Event Extraction from Twitter   Impressive efforts have been made to detect events from Twitter. Existing works include domain specific event extraction and open domain event extraction. For domain specific extraction, approaches mainly focus on extracting a particular type of events, including natural disasters (Sakaki et al., 2010), traffic events (Dabiri and Heaslip, 2019), user mobility behaviors (Yuan et al., 2013), and etc. The open domain scenario is more challenging and usually relies on unsupervised approaches. Existing works usually create clusters with event-related keywords (Parikh and Karlapalem, 2013), or named entities (McMinn and Jose, 2015; Edouard et al., 2017). Additionally, Ritter et al. (2012) and Zhou et al. (2015) design general pipelines to extract and categorize events in supervised and unsupervised manner respectively.

Different from previous works, we deal with COVID-19 related event extraction in particular. Zong et al. (2020) provide a BERT baseline for the same task. But we create a unified framework to learn simultaneously for different categories of events and subtasks.

Type-aware Slot Filling   Yang et al. (2016) formulate entity type constraints and use integer linear programming to combine them with relation classification. Adel and Schütze (2019) propose to in-

tegrate entity and relation classes in convolutional neural networks and learn the correlation from data. We propose a NER-based post-processing technique for type-aware slot filling. By filtering out entity mis-matched predictions, JOELIN can efficiently boost the performance with minimum hand-crafted rules.

COVID-19 Twitter Analysis   With the quarantine situation, people can share thoughts and make comments about COVID-19 on Twitter. It has become a research source for researchers to explore and study. Singh et al. (2020) show that Twitter conversations indicate a spatio-temporal relationship between information flow and new cases of COVID-19. There is some work about COVID-19 datasets. Banda et al. (2020) provide a large-scale curated dataset of over 152 million tweets. Chen et al. (2020) collect tweets and forms a multilingual COVID-19 Twitter dataset. Based on the collected data, Jahanbin and Rahmanian (2020) propose a model to predict COVID-19 breakout by monitoring and tracking information on Twitter. Though there are some works about COVID-19 tweets analyisis (Müller et al., 2020; Jimenez-Sotomayor et al., 2020; Lopez et al., 2020), the work about automatically extracting structured knowledge of COVID-19 events from tweets is still limited.

3   Method

In this section, we introduce our approach JOELIN and its data pre-processing and post-processing steps in detail. First, we pre-process the noisy Twitter data following the data cleaning procedures in Müller et al. (2020). Second, we train JOELIN and fine-tune the pre-trained language model end-to-end. Specifically, we design the JOELIN classifier in a joint event multi-task learning framework. Moreover, we provide four options of embedding types and ensemble the outputs with the highest validation score. Finally, we further utilize NER techniques to post-process our results with minimum hand-crafted rules.

3.1   Data Pre-processing

Prior to training, the original tweets are cleaned following Müller et al. (2020). The punctuations are standardized and unicode emoticons are expanded into textual ASCII representations[2]. All Twitter usernames are replaced with a special token <USER> for pseudonymisation, URLs with

---

[2]https://pypi.org/project/emoji/

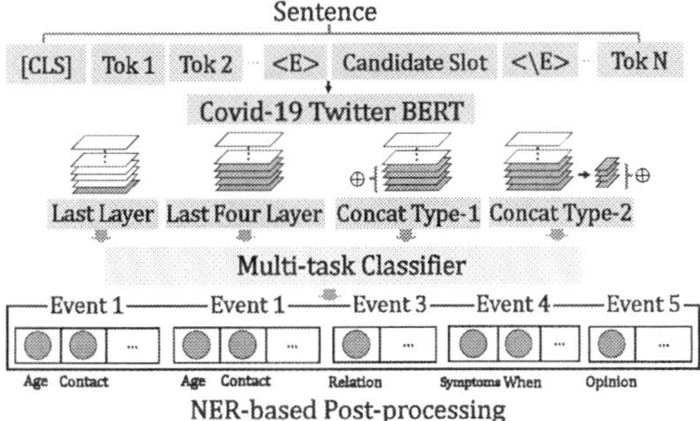

Figure 2: Our approach comprises of 2 main components: (1) global language model across events and subtasks; (2) multi-task learning classifier.

<URL>, and COVID-19 related tags, such as #COVID19, #coronavirus, #COVID etc., with <COVID_TAG>. Note that the data cleaning step is designed as a hyper-parameter and can be on or off during the experiments.

We construct the training instance as follows. The annotated data is a collection of tweets. Each tweet is accompanied by hand-labeled candidate chunks. Each candidate chunk is extracted and sandwiched by a pair of tokens <E> and </E>. The masked text, together with the annotated label, will then serve as one instance of the input.

3.2 The JOELIN Model

JOELIN consists of four modules as shown in Figure 2: the pre-trained COVID Twitter BERT (CT-BERT) (Müller et al., 2020), four different embedding layers, joint event multi-task learning framework with global parameter sharing, and the output ensemble module.

COVID Twitter BERT   It has been a common practice that pre-trained language models, e.g., BERT (Devlin et al., 2018) and RoBERTa (Liu et al., 2019), are used for a supervised fine-tuning for specific downstream tasks. In this work, we use CT-BERT as JOELIN pre-trained language model. The CT-BERT is trained on a corpus of 160M tweets related to COVID-19. CT-BERT shows great improvement compared to BERT-LARGE and RoBERTa. We further fine-tune CT-BERT with the provided dataset.

Feature Extraction   With the hidden representation of token <E> given by CT-BERT, we further apply various choices of different feature extraction methods to choose the more useful features. Inspired by Devlin et al. (2018), we implemented

the following four feature extraction methods:

1. *Last hidden layer*: we directly use the last hidden layer of CT-BERT as our classifier input.

2. *Summation of last four*: we sum the last four hidden layer outputs as the classifier input.

3. *Concatenation of last four (type-1)*: we directly concatenate the last four layers, and flatten the vector before feeding it to the classifier.

4. *Concatenation of last four (type-2)*: Each of last four layers is passed through a fully-connected layer and reduced to a quarter of its original hidden size. We flatten the vectors before passing through the classifier.

Joint Event Multi-task Learning   To tackle the challenge of limited annotated data, we apply a global parameter sharing model across all events. Specifically, we jointly learn and fine-tune the language embedding across different events and apply a multi-task classifier for prediction. As shown in Figure 2, the language embedding as well as the feature extraction mechanism are jointly learned and fine-tuned globally. We then apply a fully-connected layer as our classifier for all the subtasks in different categories of events. In this way, JOELIN benefits from using data of all the events and their subtasks. Compared with training separate models for each event, joint training across different tasks significantly boosts the performance.

Model Ensemble   It has long been observed that ensembles of models boost overall performance. Hence, in this work, we train multiple models with different feature extraction approaches, and we select the top 5 models with best performance and ensemble them by majority voting. Note that we choose the best model for each subtask in validation. In testing, we use the average of the top 5.

3.3 NER-based Post-processing

We further filter our prediction based on NER for post-processing. Specifically, we use spaCy's NER model[3] to tag the predicted candidate slots. We collect all the tags of each word in candidate slots. Then we compare the entity tags with the subtask. If one of the candidate tags does not match the subtask type, we invalidate the prediction by replacing it with *"NOT SPECIFIED"*. For example, if the subtask is "who", we nullify those candidate slots whose tags are not related to persons, as shown in Figure 1.

---

[3]https://spacy.io/

4 Experiments and Analysis

4.1 Dataset

The dataset[4] is composed of annotated tweets sampled from January 15, 2020 to April 26, 2020. It contains 7,500 tweets for the following 5 events: (1) tested positive, (2) tested negative, (3) can not test, (4) death, and (5) cure and prevention. Each event contains several slot subtasks.

4.2 Implementation Details

We randomly split the dataset into training and validation in a 80:20 ratio. The model is trained with the AdamW optimizer (Loshchilov and Hutter, 2017) toward minimizing the binary cross entropy loss with batch size of 32 and learning rate of $2e$-5. To deal with the class imbalance issue, we apply class weighting on the loss function. With grid-search, the best weight is 10 and 1 for positive and negative samples respectively.

4.3 Results and Discussion

We evaluate JOELIN with BERT and CT-BERT baselines. We measure the performance of different models with F1 score and micro F1 score, in consideration of imbalanced sample sizes. The overall results are shown in Table 1. Compared with the performance of BERT (Zong et al., 2020) and CT-BERT (Müller et al., 2020), JOELIN significantly outperforms the best baseline CT-BERT by 7.6% in micro F1. In terms of performance on subtasks, JOELIN outperforms the best baseline CT-BERT by up to 44.9% in recent travel of event TESTED POSITIVE. The performance gains of JOELIN are attributed to the well-designed joint event multi-task learning framework and the type-aware NER-based post-processing.

4.4 Ablation Study

We conduct an ablation study to understand the contribution of type-aware post-processing in JOELIN. We remove the post-processing step as a reduced model (JOELIN-P) and compare the micro F1 scores. As shown in Table 2, JOELIN has better micro F1 score in comparison with the reduced model JOELIN-P. It supports the claim that our proposed type-aware post processing with NER can significantly boost the performance.

5 Conclusion

In this work, we build JOELIN upon a joint event multi-task learning framework. We use NER-based

---

[4] https://github.com/viczong/extract_COVID19_events_from_Twitter

Sub-task	BERT	CT-BERT	JOELIN
TESTED POSITIVE			
age	0.519	0.571	0.769
close_contact	0.262	0.333	0.420
employer	0.394	0.391	0.453
gender_male	0.664	0.669	0.711
gender_female	0.635	0.698	0.779
name	0.740	0.774	0.807
recent_travel	0.227	0.391	0.567
relation	0.476	0.621	0.769
when	0.571	0.571	0.741
where	0.560	0.631	0.660
TESTED NEGATIVE			
age	0.000	0.750	0.750
close_contact	0.000	0.133	0.133
gender_male	0.479	0.660	0.706
gender_female	0.214	0.649	0.766
how_long	0.000	0.400	0.800
name	0.519	0.646	0.675
relation	0.449	0.720	0.784
when	0.000	0.471	0.471
where	0.372	0.578	0.651
CAN NOT TEST			
relation	0.516	0.608	0.771
symptoms	0.517	0.704	0.757
name	0.382	0.545	0.550
when	0.000	0.000	0.000
where	0.509	0.500	0.638
DEATH			
age	0.727	0.722	0.789
name	0.642	0.715	0.774
relation	0.378	0.646	0.680
symptoms	0.000	0.000	0.444
when	0.633	0.605	0.690
where	0.483	0.613	0.628
CURE AND PREVENTION			
opinion	0.520	0.573	0.627
what_cure	0.583	0.671	0.671
who_cure	0.389	0.515	0.545
micro avg. F1	0.576	0.647	**0.696**

Table 1: Overall performance of JOELIN compared with BERT and CT-BERT on validation data. The results are reported with F1 score. For JOELIN, we report the best of all subtask results.

Model	Micro F1
JOELIN-P	0.488
JOELIN	**0.511**

Table 2: Ablation model comparison on test data.

post-processing to generate type-aware predictions. The results show JOELIN significantly boosts the performance of extracting COVID-19 events from noisy tweets over BERT and CT-BERT baselines. In the future, we would like to extend JOELIN to open domain event extraction tasks, which is more challenging and requires a more general pipeline.

References

Heike Adel and Hinrich Schütze. 2019. Type-aware convolutional neural networks for slot filling. *Journal of Artificial Intelligence Research*, 66:297–339.

Juan M Banda, Ramya Tekumalla, Guanyu Wang, Jingyuan Yu, Tuo Liu, Yuning Ding, and Gerardo Chowell. 2020. A large-scale covid-19 twitter chatter dataset for open scientific research–an international collaboration. *arXiv preprint arXiv:2004.03688*.

Emily Chen, Kristina Lerman, and Emilio Ferrara. 2020. Covid-19: The first public coronavirus twitter dataset. *arXiv preprint arXiv:2003.07372*.

Sina Dabiri and Kevin Heaslip. 2019. Developing a twitter-based traffic event detection model using deep learning architectures. *Expert systems with applications*, 118:425–439.

Jacob Devlin, Ming-Wei Chang, Kenton Lee, and Kristina Toutanova. 2018. Bert: Pre-training of deep bidirectional transformers for language understanding. *arXiv preprint arXiv:1810.04805*.

Amosse Edouard, Elena Cabrio, Sara Tonelli, and Nhan Le Thanh. 2017. Graph-based event extraction from twitter.

Tim Finin, William Murnane, Anand Karandikar, Nicholas Keller, Justin Martineau, and Mark Dredze. 2010. Annotating named entities in twitter data with crowdsourcing. In *Proceedings of the NAACL HLT 2010 Workshop on Creating Speech and Language Data with Amazon's Mechanical Turk*, pages 80–88.

Wei-Ning Hsu, Yu Zhang, and James Glass. 2017. Unsupervised domain adaptation for robust speech recognition via variational autoencoder-based data augmentation. In *2017 IEEE Automatic Speech Recognition and Understanding Workshop (ASRU)*, pages 16–23. IEEE.

Kia Jahanbin and Vahid Rahmanian. 2020. Using twitter and web news mining to predict covid-19 outbreak. *Asian Pacific Journal of Tropical Medicine*, 13.

Maria Renee Jimenez-Sotomayor, Carolina Gomez-Moreno, and Enrique Soto-Perez-de Celis. 2020. Coronavirus, ageism, and twitter: An evaluation of tweets about older adults and covid-19. *Journal of the American Geriatrics Society*.

Yinhan Liu, Myle Ott, Naman Goyal, Jingfei Du, Mandar Joshi, Danqi Chen, Omer Levy, Mike Lewis, Luke Zettlemoyer, and Veselin Stoyanov. 2019. Roberta: A robustly optimized bert pretraining approach. *arXiv preprint arXiv:1907.11692*.

Christian E Lopez, Malolan Vasu, and Caleb Gallemore. 2020. Understanding the perception of covid-19 policies by mining a multilanguage twitter dataset. *arXiv preprint arXiv:2003.10359*.

Ilya Loshchilov and Frank Hutter. 2017. Decoupled weight decay regularization. *arXiv preprint arXiv:1711.05101*.

Andrew J McMinn and Joemon M Jose. 2015. Real-time entity-based event detection for twitter. In *International conference of the cross-language evaluation forum for european languages*, pages 65–77. Springer.

Martin Müller, Marcel Salathé, and Per E Kummervold. 2020. Covid-twitter-bert: A natural language processing model to analyse covid-19 content on twitter. *arXiv preprint arXiv:2005.07503*.

Ruchi Parikh and Kamalakar Karlapalem. 2013. Et: events from tweets. In *Proceedings of the 22nd international conference on world wide web*, pages 613–620.

Shiva Pentyala, Mengwen Liu, and Markus Dreyer. 2019. Multi-task networks with universe, group, and task feature learning. *arXiv preprint arXiv:1907.01791*.

Martin Potthast, Tim Gollub, Kristof Komlossy, Sebastian Schuster, Matti Wiegmann, Erika Patricia Garces Fernandez, Matthias Hagen, and Benno Stein. 2018. Crowdsourcing a large corpus of clickbait on twitter. In *Proceedings of the 27th international conference on computational linguistics*, pages 1498–1507.

Alan Ritter, Oren Etzioni, and Sam Clark. 2012. Open domain event extraction from twitter. In *Proceedings of the 18th ACM SIGKDD international conference on Knowledge discovery and data mining*, pages 1104–1112.

Takeshi Sakaki, Makoto Okazaki, and Yutaka Matsuo. 2010. Earthquake shakes twitter users: real-time event detection by social sensors. In *Proceedings of the 19th international conference on World wide web*, pages 851–860.

Lisa Singh, Shweta Bansal, Leticia Bode, Ceren Budak, Guangqing Chi, Kornraphop Kawintiranon, Colton Padden, Rebecca Vanarsdall, Emily Vraga, and Yanchen Wang. 2020. A first look at covid-19 information and misinformation sharing on twitter. *arXiv preprint arXiv:2003.13907*.

Qizhe Xie, Zihang Dai, Eduard Hovy, Minh-Thang Luong, and Quoc V Le. 2019. Unsupervised data augmentation for consistency training. *arXiv preprint arXiv:1904.12848*.

Bishan Yang, Ndapandula Nakashole, Bryan Kisiel, Emmanouil A Platanios, Abulhair Saparov, Shashank Srivastava, Derry Wijaya, and Tom M Mitchell. 2016. Cmuml micro-reader system for kbp 2016 cold start slot filling, event nugget detection, and event argument linking. In *TAC*.

Quan Yuan, Gao Cong, Zongyang Ma, Aixin Sun, and Nadia Magnenat Thalmann. 2013. Who, where, when and what: discover spatio-temporal topics for twitter users. In *Proceedings of the 19th ACM SIGKDD international conference on Knowledge discovery and data mining*, pages 605–613.

Yu Zhang and Qiang Yang. 2017. A survey on multi-task learning. *arXiv preprint arXiv:1707.08114*.

Deyu Zhou, Liangyu Chen, and Yulan He. 2015. An unsupervised framework of exploring events on twitter: Filtering, extraction and categorization. In *Twenty-ninth aaai conference on artificial intelligence*.

Shi Zong, Ashutosh Baheti, Wei Xu, and Alan Ritter. 2020. Extracting covid-19 events from twitter.

imec-ETRO-VUB at W-NUT 2020 Shared Task-3: A Multilabel BERT-based system for predicting COVID-19 events

Xiangyu Yang   **Giannis Bekoulis**   **Nikos Deligiannis**

ETRO, Vrije Universiteit Brussel, 1050 Brussels, Belgium

imec, Kapeldreef 75, 3001 Leuven, Belgium

{xyanga,gbekouli,ndeligia}@etrovub.be

Abstract

In this paper, we present our system designed to address the W-NUT 2020 shared task for COVID-19 Event Extraction from Twitter. To mitigate the noisy nature of the Twitter stream, our system makes use of the COVID-Twitter-BERT (CT-BERT), which is a language model pre-trained on a large corpus of COVID-19 related Twitter messages. Our system is trained on the COVID-19 Twitter Event Corpus and is able to identify relevant text spans that answer pre-defined questions (i.e., slot types) for five COVID-19 related events (i.e., TESTED POSITIVE, TESTED NEGATIVE, CAN-NOT-TEST, DEATH and CURE & PREVENTION). We have experimented with different architectures; our best performing model relies on a multilabel classifier on top of the CT-BERT model that jointly trains all the slot types for a single event. Our experimental results indicate that our Multilabel-CT-BERT system outperforms the baseline methods by 7 percentage points in terms of micro average F_1 score. Our model ranked as 4th in the shared task leaderboard.

1 Introduction

COVID-19, a highly infectious disease, has dramatically influenced the world. According to official COVID-19 related data from World Health Organization (WHO), the number of confirmed cases has surpassed 29 million, and the death toll rises to 922,252 as of 15 September 2020[1]. Many countries have taken necessary measures, such as social distancing and mask wearing to prevent the spreading of the virus. Because of these measures, the communication among people has been changed. As a result, people tend to share their opinions on social media while also obtaining useful information from other users. Twitter, a popular social media

[1] https://www.who.int/emergencies/diseases/novel-coronavirus-2019

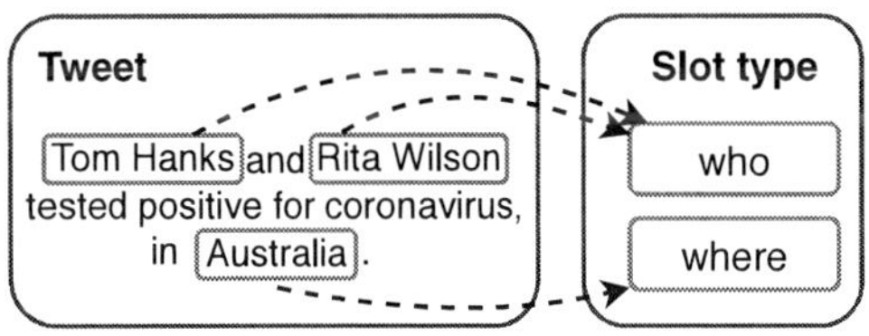

Figure 1: An example of an annotated tweet. That tweet reports a TESTED POSITIVE case. The goal of the task is to identify that the text spans "Tom Hanks" and "Rita Wilson" are slots of type "who", and "Australia" is a slot of type "where".

platform, allows its users to share views through short Twitter messages (tweets). With a large number of COVID-19 related tweets shared in a daily basis, Twitter is a valuable source for one to find relevant information about COVID-19.

The "W-NUT 2020 shared task 3: COVID-19 event extraction from Twitter" is the task of finding useful information from COVID-19 related tweets. In this work, we focus on the provided dataset COVID-19 Twitter Event Corpus to build a system that can identify text spans (slots) that answer predefined questions related to COVID-19 events (e.g., "Who is tested positive (negative)?"). This task (i.e., identifying text spans that answer pre-defined questions) has been framed as a slot filling problem by the organizers of the competition and a detailed description of that is available on the work of Zong et al. (2020). Figure 1 illustrates an example of an annotated tweet. That tweet reports a TESTED POSITIVE case. The goal of the task is to identify that the text spans "Tom Hanks" and "Rita Wilson" are slots of type "who", and "Australia" is a slot of type "where".

The rest of the paper is organized as follows. Section 2 introduces the related work on slot filling tasks. Section 3 describes the dataset we used to build our system along with the tweet pre-processing technique. Section 4 presents our pro-

505

Proceedings of the 2020 EMNLP Workshop W-NUT: The Sixth Workshop on Noisy User-generated Text, pages 505–513

Online, Nov 19, 2020. ©2020 Association for Computational Linguistics

posed Multilabel-CT-BERT system as well as the underlying techniques. Section 5 presents the baseline and other methods that have been tested in the context of this competition. Section 6 shows our experimental setup and results for the proposed systems and the baseline model. Section 7 summarizes our findings and concludes our work on this W-NUT shared task.

2   Related Work

The slot filling task is the problem where the goal is to identify fine-grained information (related to specific events of interest) from an input sequence. Specifically, given a text sequence, the aim is to find relevant text spans for certain types of slots (Benson et al., 2011), where in our case are the different slot types (e.g., "who", "where") for different event types (e.g., TESTED POSITIVE, TESTED NEGATIVE).

For the slot filling task, several approaches have been proposed in the literature. In particular, convolutional neural networks (CNNs) and recurrent neural networks (RNNs) have been exploited in the works of Peng et al. (2015); Kurata et al. (2016); Vu (2016). More recently, Chen et al. (2019) developed a BERT-based joint intent classification and slot filling model. Their system relies on the pre-trained BERT model to encode the input sequences, and jointly trains the intent classification and slot filling tasks by maximizing the conditional probability between the two tasks. In another work, Coope et al. (2020) introduced a slot filling model called Span-ConveRT that is based on the ConveRT language model (Henderson et al., 2019) to extract text spans from dialogs. In this work, we focus on developing a system that can extract COVID-19 related information from Twitter messages. To do so, we make use of a language model that is optimized for COVID-19 related tweets, and we fine-tune the system by jointly training the different slots.

3   Dataset

We use the dataset provided by the shared task for our proposed system. The name of the dataset is COVID-19 Twitter Event Corpus (Zong et al., 2020).

3.1   COVID-19 Twitter Event Corpus

This corpus contains five COVID-19 related event types: TESTED POSITIVE, TESTED

Event Type	# of Annotated Tweets	# of Collected Tweets	# of Slots
TESTED POSITIVE	2,500	2,400	9
TESTED NEGATIVE	1,200	1,146	8
CAN NOT TEST	1,200	1,127	5
DEATH	1,300	1,231	6
CURE & PREVENTION	1,300	1,245	3
TOTAL	7,500	7,149	31

Table 1: Statistics of the COVID-19 Twitter Event Corpus and the number of tweets for the collected corpus.

NEGATIVE, CAN-NOT-TEST, DEATH and CURE & PREVENTION. These event types are used to study the information that people are sharing on social media during the COVID-19 era. Table 1 shows the statistics of the COVID-19 Twitter Event Corpus. The number of overall annotated tweets is 7,500. However, due to the Twitter policy, the redistribution of Twitter content is restricted. Since the distributed corpus only includes the tweet IDs, we collected the tweet text from the Twitter server. The total number of the collected annotated tweets is 7,149, and the reason is that some of the tweets are deleted by the users or the Twitter server. The models in Section 4 and Section 5 are evaluated on the collected dataset.

3.2   Pre-processing

The COVID-19 Twitter Event Corpus provides candidate chunks along with annotations for each tweet text. To prepare instances for our system, we first replace the URLs in the tweets by a special [URL] token, and then enclose the current candidate chunk within special entity start and end tags: <E> and </E>, respectively (as in the work of Zong et al. (2020)). Table 2 shows an example of a processed tweet with an enclosed candidate chunk. In the example, the current candidate chunk is the word "Australia". To process the tweet, we enclose it inside the <E> and </E> tags. The processed result is "Tom Hanks and Rita Wilson tested positive for coronavirus, in <E> Australia </E>.".

4   Proposed System

In this section, we first introduce the underlying methods (BERT and CT-BERT) of our system. Then, we describe the proposed Multilabel-CT-BERT system in detail.

4.1   BERT

BERT (Bidirectional Encoder Representations from Transformers) (Devlin et al., 2019) is a language representation model based on Transformers (Vaswani et al., 2017). The BERT model is

tweet text	"Tom Hanks and Rita Wilson tested positive for coronavirus, in Australia."
candidate chunk	"Australia"
processed tweet text	"Tom Hanks and Rita Wilson tested positive for coronavirus, in <E> Australia </E>."

Table 2: An example of a pre-processed tweet. Given the text of a tweet and the current candidate chunk, we enclose the candidate chunk inside <E> and </E> tags within the tweet text. In this example, the candidate chunk Australia is enclosed in the aforementioned tags and placed back to the original tweet.

pre-trained on large unlabeled corpora (by using a bidirectional strategy) either in the masked language model task or in the next sentence prediction task. By applying appropriate inputs and outputs to the pre-trained BERT model, it can be easily fine-tuned end-to-end on a specific NLP (Natural Language Processing) task, such as sentence classification, sentence tagging, and question answering.

BERT is basically a stack of multiple transformer encoders. The encoder consists of a self-attention layer that helps the encoder to pay attention to other tokens of the input sequence while encoding a specific token, and a feed forward neural network that processes the output encoding from the attention layer. The BERT input representation is the sum of three embeddings: (i) token, (ii) segment and (iii) position embeddings. For the token embeddings, a special `[CLS]` token is added at the beginning of the input sequence, and a special `[SEP]` token is added at the end of each input sequence. The segment embeddings can inform the BERT model about the sequence that the current token belongs to. The position embeddings indicate the positions of the input tokens inside the sequence. The outputs of the BERT model are high-level representations of the input tokens. The hidden states of the `[CLS]` token can be used to perform various NLP tasks (e.g., text classification). There are two model architectures for BERT: BERT-BASE and BERT-LARGE. The BERT-LARGE model has more model parameters (e.g., hidden dimensions) than the BERT-BASE model.

4.2 CT-BERT

COVID-Twitter-BERT (CT-BERT) (Müller et al., 2020) is a transformer-based language model that is pre-trained on a large number of COVID-19 related tweets, while the BERT model is pre-trained on textual data from Wikipedia and book corpora. Therefore, the main drawback of the BERT model in the context of this competition is that the pre-trained BERT model does not contain relevant information about COVID-19, while it mainly includes formal language. In this competition, the dataset consists of user-generated noisy text from social media like Twitter, which contains informal language. To overcome the aforementioned shortcomings of the BERT model, the CT-BERT is proposed to better represent the COVID-19 related text.

The CT-BERT is based on the BERT-LARGE model and uses the same pre-training techniques as BERT, but the pre-training step of the CT-BERT starts with the trained weights from the BERT-LARGE model. The pre-trained CT-BERT can then be used for a wide variety of NLP tasks, such as classification and question answering.

4.3 Multilabel-CT-BERT

The idea of our multilabel system is motivated by the following observation: for one event type, we observed that some slot types are semantically related to each other, so we can use a multilabel classifier to jointly train all the slot types within one event type. In addition, the use of the CT-BERT pre-trained model mitigates the noisy nature of the tweets.

Figure 2 illustrates the architecture of our proposed Multilabel-CT-BERT system. The system is based on the pre-trained CT-BERT model. It takes a processed tweet with an enclosed candidate chunk as an input to the pretrained CT-BERT model. The model produces hidden states for each input token. Then the hidden representation of the special entity tag <E> is used as input to the multilabel classifier on top of the CT-BERT to predict the labels for the current chunk. Our system aims to minimize the binary cross-entropy with logits loss (BCEWithLogitsLoss), which is implemented in PyTorch (Paszke et al., 2017).

5 Other systems

In this section, we describe several other systems including the baseline model, the Multilabel-BERT system, the NLI (Natural Language Inference) system and the Pairwise system.

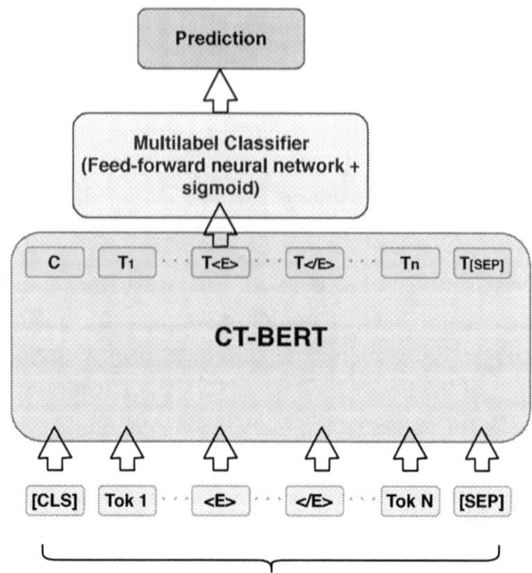

Figure 2: Multilabel-CT-BERT system architecture. This system consists of a pre-trained CT-BERT model in blue rectangle, and a multilabel classifier on top of the CT-BERT model in the grey rectangle. The small yellow and green rectangles represent the input sequence and the hidden representations, respectively. C is the hidden state of the [CLS] token. T_x is the corresponding hidden state of the input token X. The red rectangle is the prediction of the current enclosed chunk. The input to this system is a tweet text with an enclosed candidate chunk, and the hidden state of the entity tag <E> is used by the multilabel classifier for making predictions.

5.1 Baseline

Multitask-BERT-BASE (Zong et al., 2020) is a fine-tuned model that relies on BERT-BASE and has been proposed by the task organizers. For this model, each slot filling task is transformed into a binary classification problem: given a tweet T and a candidate slot S, the model predicts whether the slot S answers the pre-defined question (Zong et al., 2020). To leverage the semantically related slot types such as the "gender" slot with the "who" slot, this model jointly trains the slot types by sharing the same parameters for these slot type classifiers. The input to this model is the text of the tweet with the candidate chunk enclosed inside the special start <E> and end </E> tags. The final BERT hidden representation of the <E> tag is passed to a fully connected layer with a *softmax* activation function in order to validate or not the candidate chunk (i.e., binary prediction). More-

over, the BERT-LARGE model was exploited and is referred to as **Multitask-BERT-LARGE**.

5.2 Multilabel-BERT System

Multilabel-BERT-BASE is the variant of the Multilabel-CT-BERT that instead of using the CT-BERT pre-trained model, this model relies on BERT-BASE. Equivalently, the **Multilabel-BERT-LARGE** model is based on BERT-LARGE.

5.3 NLI System

NLI, which stands for Natural Language Inference, is the task of determining whether a "hypothesis" sentence is correct or not given a "premise" sentence. For the NLI system that we used in this work, the "premise" sentence is the slot filling question that used to annotate the COVID-19 Twitter Event Corpus, and the "hypothesis" sentence is the pre-processed tweet with an enclosed candidate chunk. A multiclass classifier, which consists of a feed-forward neural network and a *softmax* layer, is added on top of the BERT-BASE model. The number of classes is determined by the slot types in an event type, since one event type can have several slot types. The input to this system is a pair of one "premise" sentence and one "hypothesis" sentence. The output of this system is the predicted class, which is determined by the highest prediction score from all the classes. There are two variants of this system: **NLI-CLS** and **NLI-E**. The input to the multiclass classifier in the NLI-CLS is the hidden state of the [CLS] token while in the NLI-E is the hidden state of the <E> token. This system aims to minimize the cross entropy loss between the different classes. Figure 3 shows the NLI system architecture.

5.4 Pairwise System

Figure 4 shows the architecture of the pairwise system. The pairwise system contains two parts: the BERT-BASE model and on top of that a binary classifier. The binary classifier has a feed-forward neural network with a *tanh* activation layer. This system focuses on each slot type for a single event type and treats each slot filling task as a binary prediction problem. One sentence for this system is defined as a tweet text with an enclosed candidate chunk like the processed tweet text shown in Table 2. For each candidate chunk, we generate such a sentence. In total, the number of all the sentences is the number of all the candidate chunks in the provided corpus.

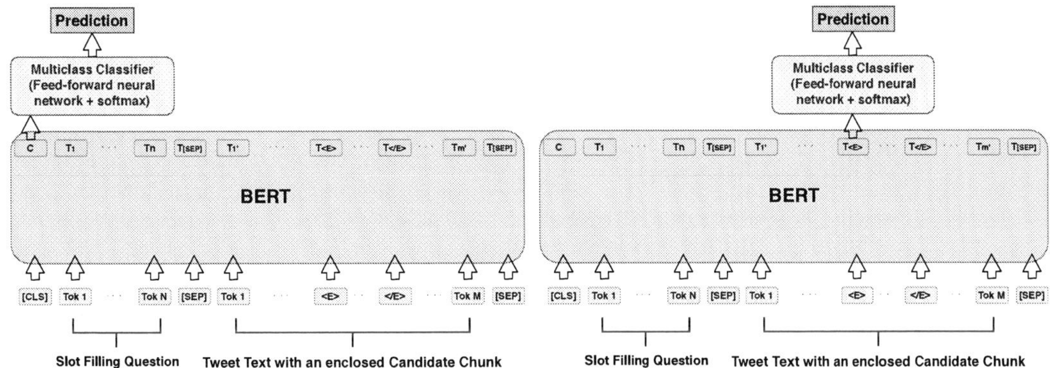

Figure 3: NLI system architecture. The left part is the NLI-CLS model and the right part is the NLI-E model. These two models have a similar structure. Both have two components, a pre-trained BERT model in the blue rectangle and a multiclass classifier in the grey rectangle. The small yellow rectangles represent the system input. The green rectangles are the hidden states for the input tokens. C is the hidden state of the [CLS] token. T_x is the corresponding hidden state of the input token X. The input to these models is a slot filling question and a tweet text. These two models differ in the way they use the hidden state as the input to the multiclass classifier.

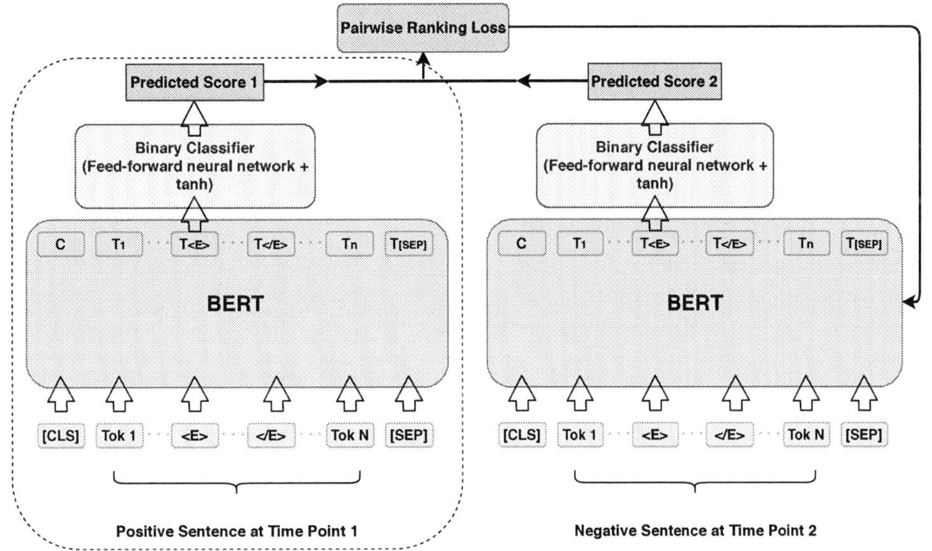

Figure 4: Pairwise system architecture. The left and right parts represent the same model structure but at different time points. The blue part is the pre-trained BERT model, the yellow part is the input tokens, the green part is the hidden states, the grey part is the binary classifier. C is the hidden state of the [CLS] token. T_x is the corresponding hidden state of the input token X. During the training step, the system first takes as input a "positive" sentence at time point 1 and produces a predicted score for the "positive" sentence. Then the system processes a "negative" sentence at time point 2 to generate a predicted score for the "negative" sentence. The two predicted scores are used to calculate the pairwise ranking loss to update the model parameters. For the prediction step, only the part in the dotted rectangle is used, and the input is one sentence that we would like to know the slot type of the enclosed candidate chunk within that sentence. By thresholding the predicted score for that sentence, we can get the corresponding label for the enclosed candidate chunk.

There are two steps for this system, the training and the prediction step. During training, the input to this system is a pair of one "positive" sentence and one "negative" sentence. The "positive" sentence is the sentence that the inner enclosed candidate chunk answers the current slot filling question. The "negative" sentence is determined by the "positive" sentence: for each "positive" sentence, all the remaining sentences are considered as "negative" sentences. This system aims at minimizing the pairwise ranking loss using PyTorch (Paszke et al., 2017), which is calculated as:

$$\text{loss}(x, y) = \max(0, -y \times (x_1 - x_2) + \text{margin}) \tag{4}$$

where x_1 and x_2 are input pairs (i.e., a "positive" and a "negative" sentence), $y = 1$ or -1. If $y = 1$ then the first input x_1 ranks higher than the second input x_2, and vice-versa for $y = -1$.

During prediction, the input is one sentence with the unknown slot type of the enclosed candidate chunk, and the output is the predicted label for the enclosed chunk. The output is determined by using a threshold value for the predicted scores of the binary classifier.

6   Experiments and Results

We compare our Multilabel-CT-BERT system with other systems (i.e., NLI, pairwise and baseline) to demonstrate the effectiveness of the proposed architecture. Our code is available on GitHub[2].

6.1   Experimental Setup

Since each slot filling task in Multitask-BERT-BASE (Zong et al., 2020) is modeled as a binary classification problem, the non-binary "gender" slot is split into "gender male" and "gender female" slots. The Multitask-BERT-BASE uses a 60/15/20 split ratio to split the collected dataset into train/dev/test sets and is optimized using the Adam algorithm (Kingma and Ba, 2015) with 2×10^{-5} as a learning rate. In order to compare with the Multitask-BERT-BASE, the same parameters are used for the rest of the models.

For the pairwise system, the number of training instances (pairs of sentences) could be too large so that the pairwise model becomes difficult to train. Thus we used a downsampling strategy to reduce the number of the sentence pairs. For every positive sentence, we randomly select a specific number of negative sentences. The ratio of the number of negative sentences with respect to the number of positive sentences is denoted as r. Two models are built for this system: **Pairwise-r50** (r = 50) and **Pairwise-r100** (r = 100).

For the Multitask-BERT-BASE, the Multilabel-BERT-BASE, the NLI-CLS, the NLI-E, the Pairwise-r50, and the Pairwise-r100, the batch size

and epochs are set to 32 and 8, respectively. For the Multitask-BERT-LARGE, Multilabel-BERT-LARGE, and Multilabel-CT-BERT, the batch size and epochs are set to 64 and 15, respectively. For all the models, except for the NLI-CLS and the NLI-E, the best threshold for each slot filling task is determined by performing a grid search on the corresponding dev set. For grid search, the candidate thresholds for all the models, except for the NLI-CLS, the NLI-E, the Pairwise-r50, and the Pairwise-r100, are $\{0.1, 0.2, ..., 0.9\}$. The candidate thresholds for the Pairwise-r50 and the Pairwise-r100 are $\{-0.9, -0.8, ..., -0.1, 0, 0.1, ..., 0.9\}$. For each model, the evaluation is performed on the test set.

Model	micro avg F_1	macro avg F_1
Multitask-BERT-BASE	0.5826	0.5498
Multitask-BERT-LARGE	0.5827	0.5539
NLI-E	0.5567	0.4984
NLI-CLS	0.5694	0.4913
Pairwise-r50	0.5458	0.4978
Pairwise-r100	0.5580	0.5064
Multilabel-BERT-BASE	0.6005	0.5717
Multilabel-BERT-LARGE	0.6206	0.5928
Multilabel-CT-BERT	**0.6585**	**0.6132**

Table 3: The aggregated results in terms of micro avg F_1 and macro avg F_1 scores. Micro avg F_1 combines the predictions (TP, FP, FN) from all the slot types and macro avg F_1 is the mean of all the F_1 scores for all the slot types.

6.2   Results

Table 3 shows the results[3] of the Multitask-BERT-BASE, Multitask-BERT-LARGE, NLI-E, NLI-CLS, Pairwise-r50, Pairwise-r100, Multilabel-BERT-BASE, Multilabel-BERT-LARGE, and Multilabel-CT-BERT in terms of micro avg F_1 (combining the predictions from all the slot types) and macro avg F_1 (the mean of all the F_1 scores of all the slot types) scores. We observe that our proposed Multilabel-CT-BERT is the best system among the compared systems on this shared task. The NLI and pairwise models are not performing better with respect to the

---

[3]For the W-NUT shared task 3, the organizers initially released an original dataset and then replaced it with a newer version of the dataset. Before the release of the new dataset, our experiments were performed on the original dataset and we observed that the NLI and pairwise systems failed to outperform the other systems. Therefore, we only evaluated the performance of the other systems on the new dataset. As a result, the reported results on the NLI and pairwise systems are based on the original dataset while the results of the rest of the systems (Multilabel-CT-BERT, Multilabel-BERT system and the baseline system) are based on the new dataset.

---

[2]https://github.com/Glovesme/covid19-event-extraction

Positive slot	#	Multitask-BERT-BASE			Multitask-BERT-LARGE			Multilabel-BERT-BASE			Multilabel-BERT-LARGE			Multilabel-CT-BERT		
		P	R	F_1	P	R	F_1	P	R	F_1	P	R	F_1	P	R	F_1
who	471	0.75	0.72	0.73	0.71	0.78	0.75	0.76	0.78	0.77	0.78	0.74	0.76	0.83	0.74	0.78
c.contact	39	0.29	0.27	0.28	0.46	0.5	0.37	0.56	0.24	0.33	0.59	0.3	0.4	0.61	0.43	0.5
relation	12	0.4	0.31	0.35	0.4	0.67	0.5	0.35	0.67	0.46	0.39	0.69	0.5	0.47	0.69	0.56
employer	77	0.58	0.36	0.45	0.37	0.69	0.49	0.53	0.47	0.5	0.5	0.54	0.52	0.6	0.41	0.49
recent .v	34	0.44	0.33	0.38	0.47	0.33	0.38	0.67	0.41	0.51	0.48	0.41	0.44	0.43	0.46	0.44
age	15	0.71	0.67	0.69	0.76	0.72	0.74	0.76	0.72	0.74	0.81	0.72	0.76	0.86	0.67	0.75
where	150	0.58	0.59	0.58	0.57	0.68	0.62	0.55	0.66	0.6	0.58	0.63	0.6	0.65	0.66	0.65
gender_m	126	0.64	0.71	0.67	0.68	0.66	0.67	0.64	0.72	0.68	0.67	0.65	0.66	0.64	0.7	0.67
gender_f	47	0.76	0.54	0.63	0.67	0.63	0.65	0.64	0.65	0.65	0.68	0.54	0.6	0.64	0.7	0.67
when	13	0.29	0.43	0.35	0.48	0.43	0.45	0.37	0.39	0.39	0.4	0.61	0.48	0.67	0.5	0.57
micro F_1		0.6193			0.6508			0.6452			0.6497			**0.6834**		
macro F_1		0.511			0.562			0.563			0.5726			**0.608**		

Negative slot	#	Multitask-BERT-BASE			Multitask-BERT-LARGE			Multilabel-BERT-BASE			Multilabel-BERT-LARGE			Multilabel-CT-BERT		
		P	R	F_1	P	R	F_1	P	R	F_1	P	R	F_1	P	R	F_1
who	140	0.6	0.58	0.59	0.59	0.58	0.59	0.67	0.58	0.63	0.64	0.6	0.62	0.72	0.64	0.68
relation	25	0.6	0.63	0.61	0.57	0.67	0.62	0.73	0.67	0.7	0.63	0.71	0.67	0.78	0.58	0.67
where	22	0.44	0.52	0.48	0.48	0.48	0.48	0.34	0.45	0.39	0.44	0.73	0.55	0.58	0.64	0.61
gender_m	48	0.65	0.59	0.62	0.54	0.75	0.62	0.6	0.65	0.62	0.65	0.65	0.65	0.67	0.61	0.64
gender_f	20	0.61	0.52	0.56	0.45	0.48	0.47	0.63	0.57	0.6	0.59	0.62	0.6	0.67	0.67	0.67
micro F_1		0.586			0.5785			0.6095			0.6213			**0.6614**		
macro F_1		0.572			0.556			0.588			0.618			**0.654**		

CAN NOT TEST slot	#	Multitask-BERT-BASE			Multitask-BERT-LARGE			Multilabel-BERT-BASE			Multilabel-BERT-LARGE			Multilabel-CT-BERT		
		P	R	F_1	P	R	F_1	P	R	F_1	P	R	F_1	P	R	F_1
who	108	0.56	0.51	0.53	0.55	0.56	0.55	0.52	0.52	0.52	0.65	0.56	0.6	0.71	0.57	0.63
relation	44	0.71	0.45	0.56	0.54	0.47	0.51	0.58	0.57	0.57	0.8	0.45	0.58	0.61	0.57	0.59
where	23	0.68	0.39	0.5	0.61	0.45	0.52	0.59	0.42	0.49	0.62	0.68	0.65	0.7	0.61	0.65
symptoms	54	0.6	0.46	0.53	0.56	0.55	0.56	0.57	0.52	0.54	0.64	0.57	0.6	0.58	0.59	0.58
micro F_1		0.5297			0.5409			0.5304			0.6069			**0.6157**		
macro F_1		0.53			0.535			0.53			0.6075			**0.6125**		

DEATH slot	#	Multitask-BERT-BASE			Multitask-BERT-LARGE			Multilabel-BERT-BASE			Multilabel-BERT-LARGE			Multilabel-CT-BERT		
		P	R	F_1	P	R	F_1	P	R	F_1	P	R	F_1	P	R	F_1
who	141	0.67	0.68	0.67	0.66	0.6	0.63	0.7	0.73	0.71	0.66	0.74	0.7	0.56	0.84	0.67
relation	26	0.7	0.27	0.39	0.64	0.35	0.45	0.68	0.58	0.62	0.55	0.62	0.58	0.63	0.38	0.48
when	23	0.66	0.63	0.64	0.68	0.5	0.58	0.64	0.46	0.53	0.68	0.74	0.71	0.62	0.78	0.69
where	54	0.74	0.53	0.62	0.78	0.53	0.63	0.55	0.79	0.65	0.61	0.72	0.66	0.46	0.79	0.59
age	33	0.68	0.87	0.76	0.72	0.93	0.81	0.58	0.77	0.66	0.7	0.77	0.73	0.69	0.83	0.76
micro F_1		0.6516			0.6318			0.6613			**0.6866**			0.6527		
macro F_1		0.616			0.62			0.634			**0.676**			0.638		

CURE&PREV slot	#	Multitask-BERT-BASE			Multitask-BERT-LARGE			Multilabel-BERT-BASE			Multilabel-BERT-LARGE			Multilabel-CT-BERT		
		P	R	F_1	P	R	F_1	P	R	F_1	P	R	F_1	P	R	F_1
opinion	62	0.5	0.56	0.53	0.33	0.61	0.43	0.39	0.71	0.5	0.41	0.34	0.37	0.68	0.58	0.63
what	148	0.56	0.61	0.58	0.7	0.57	0.63	0.65	0.62	0.64	0.61	0.69	0.65	0.59	0.76	0.66
who	61	0.49	0.41	0.45	0.45	0.41	0.43	0.46	0.53	0.49	0.51	0.41	0.45	0.52	0.53	0.52
micro F_1		0.532			0.5113			0.5559			0.5387			**0.6125**		
macro F_1		0.52			0.4967			0.5433			0.49			**0.6033**		
micro avg F_1		0.5826			0.5827			0.6005			0.6206			**0.6585**		
macro avg F_1		0.5498			0.5539			0.5717			0.5928			**0.6132**		

Table 4: The results of Multitask-BERT-BASE, Multitask-BERT-LARGE, Multilabel-BERT-BASE, Multilabel-BERT-LARGE, and Multilabel-CT-BERT. # indicates the number of golden slots in the test set. Positive is the TESTED POSITIVE event. Negative is the TESTED NEGATIVE event. c.contact is the close contact slot type. recent.v is the recent travel slot type. gender_m is the gender male slot type while the gender_f is the gender female slot type.

baseline models. The reasons for this performance difference are that the NLI system uses formal language while the tweets contains informal language and the pairwise models use only part of the training data. Since these two systems are not performing well on this shared task, the detailed results for these two models are included only in the Appendix (see A.1 and A.2). As we can observe from the results, the multilabel BERT-based models also perform better than the baseline models. This is because that these systems not only train the slots jointly, but also share the same parameters for them by using a feed-forward neural network on top of the underlying model (BERT or COVID-Twitter-BERT). Multilabel-CT-BERT outperforms the multilabel BERT-based models because the CT-BERT-based model is optimized on COVID-19 related tweets.

Table 4 shows the detailed results of Multitask-BERT-BASE, Multitask-BERT-LARGE, Multilabel-BERT-BASE, Multilabel-BERT-LARGE, and Multilabel-CT-BERT. The results are based on the test set. For each model, the precision (P), recall (R) and F_1 (F_1) scores are reported for each slot type of each event type. In addition, the micro F_1 and macro F_1 are reported for each event type, and the micro avg F_1 and macro avg F_1 are reported for all the event types.

From these detailed results of Table 4 (i.e., micro avg F_1 and macro avg F_1), we can observe that the multilabel-based systems (Multilabel-BERT-BASE, Multilabel-BERT-LARGE and Multilabel-CT-BERT) outperform the multitask-based systems (Multitask-BERT-BASE and Multitask-BERT-LARGE). We also notice that systems using BERT-LARGE perform better than those using BERT-BASE. Except for the slightly worse performance in terms of micro F_1 and macro F_1 on the DEATH event type compared to other multilabel systems, the Multilabel-CT-BERT substantially improves the system performance on the rest of the event types. Compared to the baseline model, the Multilabel-CT-BERT achieves a micro avg F_1 of 65.85% (7.59 percentage points absolute improvement) and macro avg F_1 of 61.32% (6.34 percentage points absolute improvement).

To conclude, the Multilabel-CT-BERT system is the best performing system among the compared systems on the COVID-19 Twitter Event Corpus, and it achieves a performance of 61.6% in terms of F_1 score in the test data[4] of the shared task.

7 Conclusion

In this paper, a COVID-Twitter-BERT based Multilabel-CT-BERT system is proposed in the context of the W-NUT shared task to deal with the slot filling problem of the recently introduced COVID-19 Twitter Event Corpus. Our experimental results illustrate that the proposed Multilabel-CT-BERT system outperforms the baseline and other proposed models in terms of micro avg F_1 and macro avg F_1 scores.

References

Edward Benson, Aria Haghighi, and Regina Barzilay. 2011. Event discovery in social media feeds. In *Proceedings of the 49th Annual Meeting of the Association for Computational Linguistics: Human Language Technologies*, pages 389–398.

Qian Chen, Zhu Zhuo, and Wen Wang. 2019. Bert for joint intent classification and slot filling. *arXiv preprint arXiv:1902.10909*.

Sam Coope, Tyler Farghly, Daniela Gerz, Ivan Vulić, and Matthew Henderson. 2020. Span-convert: Few-shot span extraction for dialog with pretrained conversational representations. *arXiv preprint arXiv:2005.08866*.

Jacob Devlin, Ming-Wei Chang, Kenton Lee, and Kristina Toutanova. 2019. Bert: Pre-training of deep bidirectional transformers for language understanding. In *Proceedings of the 2019 Conference of the North American Chapter of the Association for Computational Linguistics: Human Language Technologies, Volume 1 (Long and Short Papers)*, pages 4171–4186.

Matthew Henderson, Iñigo Casanueva, Nikola Mrkšić, Pei-Hao Su, Ivan Vulić, et al. 2019. Convert: Efficient and accurate conversational representations from transformers. *arXiv preprint arXiv:1911.03688*.

Diederik Kingma and Jimmy Ba. 2015. Adam: A method for stochastic optimization. In *International Conference on Learning Representations*, San Diego, USA.

Gakuto Kurata, Bing Xiang, Bowen Zhou, and Mo Yu. 2016. Leveraging sentence-level information with encoder lstm for semantic slot filling. In *Proceedings of the 2016 Conference on Empirical Methods in Natural Language Processing*, pages 2077–2083.

Martin Müller, Marcel Salathé, and Per E Kummervold. 2020. Covid-twitter-bert: A natural language processing model to analyse covid-19 content on twitter. *arXiv preprint arXiv:2005.07503*.

Adam Paszke, Sam Gross, Soumith Chintala, Gregory Chanan, Edward Yang, Zachary DeVito, Zeming Lin, Alban Desmaison, Luca Antiga, and Adam Lerer. 2017. Automatic differentiation in PyTorch. In *Proceedings of the NIPS 2017 Autodiff Workshop*.

Baolin Peng, Kaisheng Yao, Li Jing, and Kam-Fai Wong. 2015. Recurrent neural networks with external memory for spoken language understanding. In *Natural Language Processing and Chinese Computing*, pages 25–35. Springer.

Ashish Vaswani, Noam Shazeer, Niki Parmar, Jakob Uszkoreit, Llion Jones, Aidan N Gomez, Łukasz Kaiser, and Illia Polosukhin. 2017. Attention is all you need. In *Advances in Neural Information Processing Systems*, pages 5998–6008.

Ngoc Thang Vu. 2016. Sequential convolutional neural networks for slot filling in spoken language understanding. In *Proceedings of Interspeech 2016*, pages 3250–3254.

Shi Zong, Ashutosh Baheti, Wei Xu, and Alan Ritter. 2020. Extracting covid-19 events from twitter. *arXiv preprint arXiv:2006.02567*.

---

[4]This test data is provided by the task organizers, and it contains 500 tweets for each event type.

A   Appendices

A.1   NLI System Results

Table 5 shows the detailed results of the NLI models: NLI-CLS and NLI-E.

A.2   Pairwise System Results

Table 6 shows the detailed results of the pairwise models: Pairwise-r50 and Pairwise-r100.

Positive slot	#	NLI-E			NLI-CLS		
		P	R	F_1	P	R	F_1
who	471	0.74	0.73	0.73	0.75	0.75	0.75
c.contact	39	0.39	0.44	0.41	0.3	0.33	0.31
relation	12	0.44	0.33	0.38	0.41	0.58	0.48
employer	77	0.37	0.39	0.38	0.5	0.22	0.31
recent .v	34	0.53	0.26	0.35	0.38	0.18	0.24
age	15	0.58	0.73	0.65	0.57	0.87	0.68
where	150	0.49	0.59	0.53	0.46	0.69	0.55
gender_m	126	0.7	0.51	0.59	0.7	0.58	0.63
gender_f	47	0.7	0.66	0.68	0.78	0.62	0.69
when	13	0.37	0.77	0.5	0.2	0.62	0.3
micro F_1		0.6194			**0.6245**		
macro F_1		**0.52**			0.494		
Negative slot	#	NLI-E			NLI-CLS		
		P	R	F_1	P	R	F_1
who	140	0.55	0.66	0.6	0.61	0.62	0.62
relation	25	0.29	0.2	0.24	0.78	0.28	0.41
where	22	0.28	0.32	0.3	0	0	0
gender_m	48	0.59	0.56	0.57	0.57	0.54	0.55
gender_f	20	0.6	0.45	0.51	0.67	0.5	0.57
micro F_1		0.5323			**0.5567**		
macro F_1		**0.44**			0.43		
CAN NOT TEST slot	#	NLI-E			NLI-CLS		
		P	R	F_1	P	R	F_1
who	108	0.72	0.44	0.55	0.56	0.54	0.55
relation	44	0.7	0.36	0.48	0.53	0.43	0.48
where	23	0.48	0.65	0.56	0.4	0.61	0.48
symptoms	54	0.75	0.39	0.51	0.58	0.35	0.44
micro F_1		**0.5305**			0.5023		
macro F_1		**0.525**			0.4875		
DEATH slot	#	NLI-E			NLI-CLS		
		P	R	F_1	P	R	F_1
who	141	0.72	0.44	0.55	0.64	0.76	0.69
relation	26	0.7	0.36	0.48	0.63	0.46	0.53
when	23	0.48	0.65	0.56	0.51	0.51	0.51
where	54	0.75	0.39	0.51	0.81	0.25	0.38
age	33	0.55	0.88	0.67	0.66	0.76	0.7
micro F_1		0.5803			**0.6197**		
macro F_1		0.554			**0.562**		
CURE&PREV slot	#	NLI-E			NLI-CLS		
		P	R	F_1	P	R	F_1
opinion	62	0.49	0.42	0.45	0.53	0.55	0.54
what	148	0.63	0.62	0.63	0.6	0.56	0.58
who	61	0.39	0.21	0.28	0.46	0.26	0.33
micro F_1		0.5209			**0.5439**		
macro F_1		0.453			**0.4833**		
micro avg F_1		0.5567			**0.5694**		
macro avg F_1		**0.4984**			0.4913		

Table 5: The detailed results of NLI-E and NLI-CLS.

Positive slot	#	Pairwise-r50			Pairwise-r100		
		P	R	F_1	P	R	F_1
who	471	0.74	0.75	0.74	0.78	0.7	0.74
c.contact	39	0.23	0.38	0.29	0.24	0.31	0.27
relation	12	0.28	0.58	0.38	0.5	0.08	0.14
employer	77	0.44	0.4	0.42	0.44	0.44	0.44
recent .v	34	0.53	0.26	0.35	0.41	0.65	0.5
age	15	0.42	0.53	0.47	0.5	0.87	0.63
where	150	0.54	0.58	0.56	0.47	0.67	0.55
gender_m	126	0.61	0.61	0.61	0.69	0.61	0.65
gender_f	47	0.51	0.59	0.55	0.65	0.55	0.6
when	13	0.44	0.62	0.52	0.22	0.77	0.34
micro F_1		0.6085			**0.6177**		
macro F_1		**0.489**			0.486		
Negative slot	#	Pairwise-r50			Pairwise-r100		
		P	R	F_1	P	R	F_1
who	140	0.53	0.69	0.6	0.6	0.56	0.58
relation	25	0.39	0.48	0.43	0.37	0.64	0.47
where	22	0.32	0.68	0.43	0.32	0.55	0.41
gender_m	48	0.38	0.27	0.32	0.54	0.46	0.5
gender_f	20	0.61	0.55	0.58	0.36	0.75	0.48
micro F_1		0.5202			**0.5245**		
macro F_1		0.472			**0.4879**		
CAN NOT TEST slot	#	Pairwise-r50			Pairwise-r100		
		P	R	F_1	P	R	F_1
who	108	0.5	0.55	0.52	0.52	0.57	0.54
relation	44	0.52	0.55	0.53	0.5	0.52	0.51
where	23	0.3	0.61	0.41	0.28	0.61	0.38
symptoms	54	0.34	0.65	0.45	0.45	0.41	0.43
micro F_1		0.487			**0.4899**		
macro F_1		**0.4775**			0.465		
DEATH slot	#	Pairwise-r50			Pairwise-r100		
		P	R	F_1	P	R	F_1
who	141	0.63	0.77	0.69	0.69	0.63	0.66
relation	26	0.32	0.73	0.45	0.33	0.69	0.45
when	23	0.47	0.92	0.62	0.48	0.78	0.6
where	54	0.46	0.6	0.52	0.57	0.55	0.56
age	33	0.58	0.85	0.69	0.61	0.82	0.7
micro F_1		**0.6227**			0.6221		
macro F_1		0.594			**0.594**		
CURE&PREV slot	#	Pairwise-r50			Pairwise-r100		
		P	R	F_1	P	R	F_1
opinion	62	0.29	0.76	0.42	0.45	0.5	0.47
what	148	0.52	0.68	0.59	0.6	0.63	0.62
who	61	0.32	0.39	0.36	0.34	0.43	0.38
micro F_1		0.4907			**0.5357**		
macro F_1		0.4566			**0.49**		
micro avg F_1		0.5458			**0.558**		
macro avg F_1		0.4978			**0.5046**		

Table 6: The detailed results of Pairwise-r50 and Pairwise-r100.

UCD-CS at W-NUT 2020 Shared Task-3: A Text to Text Approach for COVID-19 Event Extraction on Social Media

Congcong Wang
School of Computer Science
University College Dublin
Dublin, Ireland
congcong.wang@ucdconnect.ie

David Lillis
School of Computer Science
University College Dublin
Dublin, Ireland
david.lillis@ucd.ie

Abstract

In this paper, we describe our approach in the shared task: *COVID-19 event extraction from Twitter*. The objective of this task is to extract answers from COVID-related tweets to a set of predefined slot-filling questions. Our approach treats the event extraction task as a question answering task by leveraging the transformer-based T5 text-to-text model.

According to the official evaluation scores returned, namely F1, our submitted run achieves competitive performance compared to other participating runs (Top 3). However, we argue that this evaluation may underestimate the actual performance of runs based on text-generation. Although some such runs may answer the slot questions well, they may not be an exact string match for the gold standard answers. To measure the extent of this underestimation, we adopt a simple exact-answer transformation method aiming at converting the well-answered predictions to exactly-matched predictions. The results show that after this transformation our run overall reaches the same level of performance as the best participating run and state-of-the-art F1 scores in three of five COVID-related events. Our code is publicly available to aid reproducibility[1].

1 Introduction

Since the outbreak of COVID-19, a wide variety of research has been conducted to mine insights or gain rapid access to information in relation to the crisis. For example, the TREC-COVID challenge seeks advanced techniques for finding useful information from the CORD-19 corpus comprising hundreds of thousands of COVID-related academic articles (Wang et al., 2020; Roberts et al., 2020). Related research focuses on mining valuable information from social media (Müller et al.,

2020; Dimitrov et al., 2020). This is largely inspired by the fact that social media motivates people to share information or express their opinions quickly. However, this user-generated content is usually noisy and enormous during crises, and thus needs to be condensed and filtered before further processing and analysis.

Motivated by this, the ACL Workshop on Noisy User-generated Text 2020 proposed a shared task (W-NUT Task-3) of *extracting COVID-19 related events from Twitter* (Zong et al., 2020). The major objective of this task is to seek computational linguistic techniques for extracting text spans from a corpus of raw tweets to answer a set of predefined slot questions. The corpus used in the task can be described in two parts. First, the corpus consists of approximately 7,500 tweets categorised into five broad event types: (1) TESTED POSITIVE, (2) TESTED NEGATIVE, (3) CAN NOT TEST, (4) DEATH and (5) CURE AND PREVENTION. As the names indicate, these tweets are a summary of people's primary concerns about COVID-19 that they likely post about on social media. Secondly, for the tweets in each event, a set of questions or slot-filling types are defined to help gather more fine-grained information about the tweets. The human annotations, (i.e., ground truths) of the corpus are simply the answers to the predefined questions. Figure 1 illustrates an example from this corpus. This example represents a TESTED POSITIVE or TESTED NEGATIVE event, and the associated slot-filling questions relate to the "who" and the "duration" slots, asking who has tested positive or negative and how long it takes to know the test result. The annotation process in part 2 is conducted by annotators who select answers from a drop-down list of candidate choices[2]. This ex-

---

[1] https://github.com/wangcongcong123/ttt/tree/master/covid_event

[2] The choices are automatically-extracted text spans obtained through a Twitter tagging tool (Ritter et al., 2011) or predefined choices such as "not specified", "yes", "no", etc.

Proceedings of the 2020 EMNLP Workshop W-NUT: The Sixth Workshop on Noisy User-generated Text, pages 514–521
Online, Nov 19, 2020. ©2020 Association for Computational Linguistics

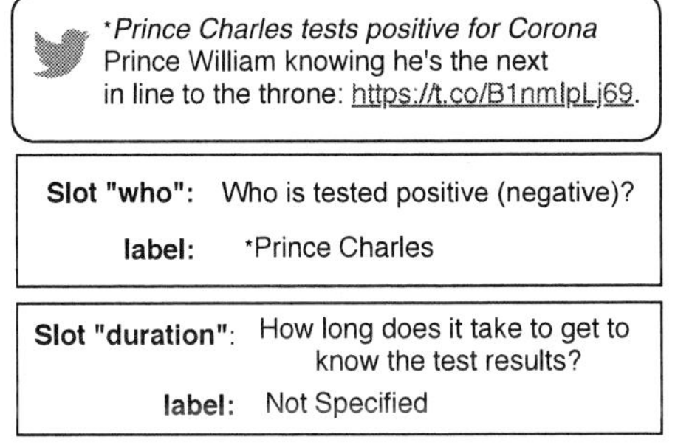

Figure 1: An example of the event extraction task: this shows a tweet represents a TESTED POSITIVE or TESTED NEGATIVE event. The objective is to extract answers to the slot questions concerning the event.

plains why the label for slot "who" in Figure 1 has the symbol $*$ at the beginning.

Using this corpus, we leverage a text-to-text model for generating answers to the slot questions. Given that recent years have witnessed the success of transformers (Vaswani et al., 2017; Devlin et al., 2019; Raffel et al., 2020) in natural language processing (NLP) via transfer learning, we adopt the T5 (Raffel et al., 2020) model architecture and its pre-trained weights. The method is straightforward but effective, easy to adapt to domain-similar tasks, and efficient in data input without needing additional pre-processing and part-of-speech features. In this paper, we report its performance as compared to other participating runs. Our run achieves competitive performance as indicated by F1. However, evaluation is based on exact matches, and thus a prediction is deemed a true positive only when it is a character-by-character match with the ground truth from the candidate answers. Since our method treats the task as a text-generation-based question answering task instead of categorising labels from a fixed list of candidate labels, it potentially generates well-answered predictions that do not exactly match the ground truth answers. Having observed some of these mismatches in our experiment we subsequently transformed these to exact-matched answers using a simple approach based on Levenshtein string edit distance (Levenshtein, 1966). After this transformation, our best run reaches the same level of F1 performance as the best participating run.

For more details, see (Zong et al., 2020).

2   Related Work

The literature has seen much work on processing crisis-related messages on social media. For example, the TREC Incident Streams (McCreadie et al., 2020) track is a research initiative for seeking computational linguistic techniques for finding actionable information from Twitter during crises. With similar motivations to this initiative, many techniques have been applied for crisis messages categorisation and analysis in recent years. For instance, Miyazaki et al. (2019) apply label embedding for crisis tweet classification adopting a bi-directional LSTM model. Wang and Lillis (2020) leverage contextual ELMO embeddings (Peters et al., 2018) and data augmentation. CrisisBERT is proposed for crisis event detection (Liu et al., 2020) through fine-tuning the pre-trained BERT (Devlin et al., 2019).

More recently, the COVID-19 pandemic has motivated research on insights mining, information extraction and classification on social media. Since the pandemic is characterised by being long-lived, unlike more short-term crises such as earthquakes or shootings, the messages on social media are studied to gain a better understanding of the pandemic from multiple perspectives. For example, TweetsCOV19 (Dimitrov et al., 2020) is a corpus of semantically annotated tweets about COVID-19 that can potentially be used to explore public opinion and perception on the pandemic. Müller et al. (2020) introduce COVID-Twitter-BERT, which pre-trains a BERT model on hundreds of millions of COVID-related tweets and then fine-tunes the model to downstream tasks including vaccine sentiment analysis and vaccine stance classification.

Although most recent work involves fine-tuning transformer-based models for COVID-related short message processing, we have chosen to take an alternative approach for this task. Inspired by the text-to-text T5 model, our approach formulates the W-NUT Task 3 as a question-answering problem. The principal idea is that its unified source and target structure can be easily adapted to other domain-similar tasks such as informativeness classification or vaccine sentiment for COVID-related tweets. Regarding fine-tuning T5 for COVID-related language tasks, probably the most relevant work is that Tang et al. (2020) fine-tuned T5 for COVID-related question answering from scientific articles. However, they con-

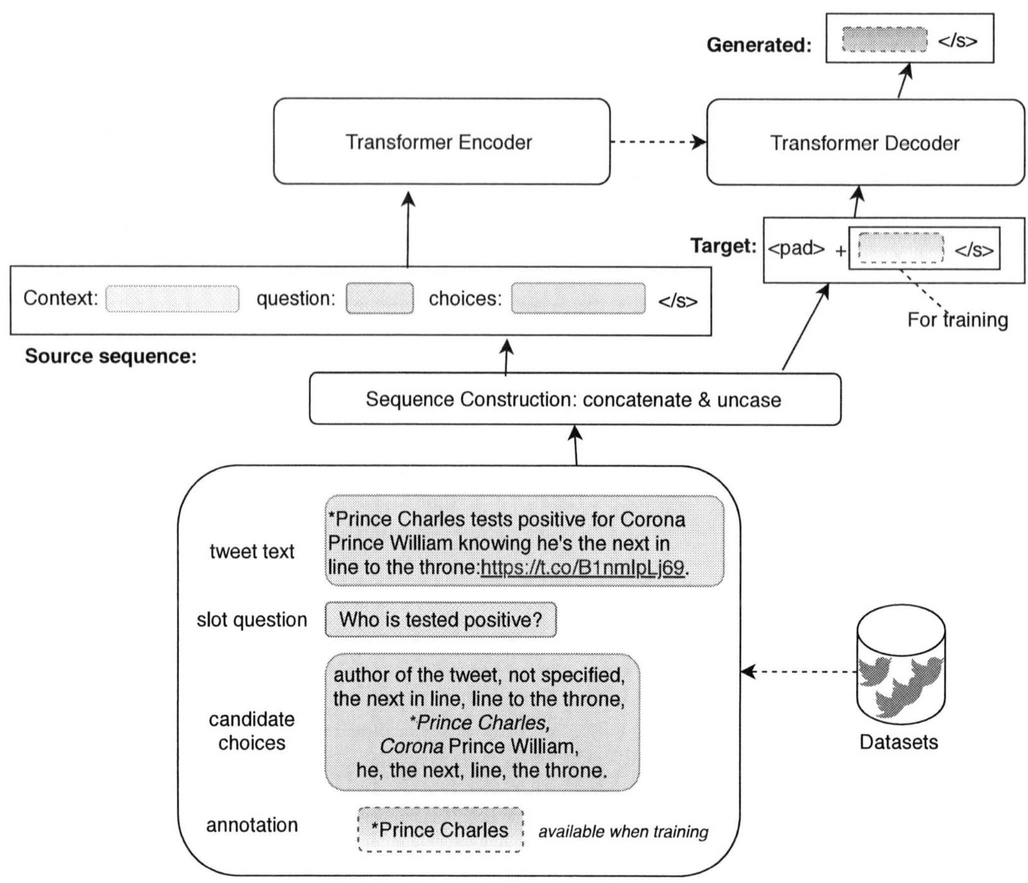

Figure 2: The system architecture of our approach

structed the source sequence by concatenating a document and a query, and the target sequence is a generated token indicating the document's relevance to the query. Our approach is characterised by being capable of unifying various text classification tasks to a general question answering task. In our approach, the source sequence takes the raw text as the context, a classification description as the question and the classification's labels as the candidate choices. The target sequence is simply the generated answers that are exact text spans from the source sequence, indicating which label(s) the text belongs to.

3 Method

In this section, we detail our approach in W-NUT Task-3. We firstly describe how a general transformer encoder-decoder model work in a sequence-to-sequence way and then introduce our approach adapting it to the event extraction task. Basically, given a source sequence $X : \{x_1, x_2, ..., x_n\}$, the transformer encoder uses it as the input to output its contextualised encoding sequence $\overline{X} : \{\overline{x}_1, \overline{x}_2, ..., \overline{x}_n\}$. The encoding process can be represented by a mapping function f with learnable parameters θ_e, as follows.

$$f_{\theta_e} : \mathbf{X}_{1:n} \rightarrow \overline{\mathbf{X}}_{1:n}.$$

The encoded source sequence then is used as the input to the transformer decoder that defines the conditional probability distribution of a target sequence $Y : \{y_1, y_2, ..., y_m\}$ given $\overline{X}_{1:n}$:

$$p_{\theta_d}(\mathbf{Y}_{1:m}|\overline{\mathbf{X}}_{1:n}) = \prod_{i=1}^{m} p_{\theta_d}(\mathbf{y}_i|\mathbf{Y}_{0:i-1}, \overline{\mathbf{X}}_{1:n}).$$

Where p with learnable parameters θ_d is the function to learn the conditional probability distribution by the decoder. The target token y_i is generated conditional on both the source context $\overline{X}_{1:n}$ and its previous $i - 1$ already-generated tokens in an auto-regressive way. The powerful part of the transformer-based decoder is that it applies a single directional attention mechanism, i.e., masked multi-head attention as proposed by Vaswani et al. (2017) to learn the relations between the target token and its previous tokens. Meanwhile, it applies a bi-directional attention mechanism, i.e., multi-head attention, to learn the relations between the target token and the source context, which is also used in the encoder to learn the relations (self-attentions) between the source tokens.

Inspired by the feature of target generation given a source in a transformer encoder-decoder model, we leverage it for the shared task. Figure 2 presents the system architecture of our approach. The core component of the system is the sequence construction, which converts each tweet in the dataset into a source sequence and target sequence that well fits to train the transformer encoder-decoder model in a text-to-text fashion. As introduced, each tweet in the dataset is annotated in two parts, 1), labels indicating the event types, 2), answers to the slot questions. Our approach uses both parts of the annotations to construct the source and target sequences as follows:

- **Source**: This sequence is constructed from the raw tweets through mapping their major four attributes, i.e., as outlined in Figure 2, the tweet text is mapped to "context", event type question (part 1) or slot question (part 2)[3] to "question", and the candidate choices to "choices". The leads to the final source sequence concatenating all these fields in the form: "context: {tweet text} question: {slot/event question} choices: {candidates}".

- **Target**: The target sequence needs both part 1 and part 2 annotations in training. They are simply mapped from the event labels for part 1 ("yes" or "no" indicating if the tweet falls into the event as specified in the question field of the source sequence) and annotation answers for part 2. Where the annotations are not available in inference, the source sequence and the target sequence with the start decoder token <pad> are fed as input to the model for generating the answers directly.

Although the aforementioned only details the

sequence construction process using the event extraction corpus as an example, it follows similar steps when adapting to similar tasks. For example, for a binary informativeness classification task, the question field can be replaced by something like "Is the tweet informative of COVID-19?" and choices can be "yes" or "no" implying INFORMATIVENESS or UNINFORMATIVENESS. We leave this generalisation capability to future work and here continue to focus on the event extraction task.

After the source and target sequences are constructed, the next step is to train a transformer encoder-decoder model. As evidenced in the literature, sequence-to-sequence transformers such as BART (Lewis et al., 2019) or T5 (Raffel et al., 2020) has demonstrated great success in various downstream language tasks via transfer learning. Since T5 has different pre-trained weights available where in particular its small version is easy to handle in the pilot study, we set up the encoder-decoder model following the T5 (Raffel et al., 2020) architecture and train it on this task via fine-tuning its pre-trained weights.

4   Experiments

This section describes the details of experimental process and results.

4.1   Data Preparation

Because the original dataset is released with only Tweets IDs, some tweets had become invalid prior to our retrieval time and consequently 7,149 valid tweets were used in our experiments. Since each training tweet is assigned one event type label and multiple slot annotations, there a total of 34,464 examples used in our experiments after source and target sequence construction. Among these, we sample 10% as the validation set and the rest as the training set.

4.2   Training

Batch size	16
Epoch	12
Learning rate (LR)	5e-05
LR scheduler	Warmup linear decay
Warmup ratio	0.10
Optimizer	Adam

Table 1: Hyper-parameters of model training

In our experiments, we chose t5-small, t5-base, and t5-large for fine-tuning. Ta-

---

[3]The event type questions are manually constructed: taking DEATH as an example: *Does this tweet report death from coronavirus?*

ble 1 shows the hyper-parameter configuration in our experiments. The batch size is selected from the options of $\{8, 16, 32\}$, based on evaluation on the validation set and the other hyper-parameters are determined with reference to the literature in a similar domain (Liu et al., 2020). We fine-tune each model with 12 epochs as we observe no further improvements after this. The maximum source and target sequence lengths were set to be 473 and 78 respectively since no examples exceeded these. The training was accelerated by a TPU3-8, taking around 4 hours to complete the t5-large fine-tuning. After the model is fine-tuned, we use greedy decoding during inference. This is because the generated texts are usually short answers in our problem and thus top-k or top-p sampling (Holtzman et al., 2019) would give similar results as greedy decoding.

	F1	P	R	Params
small-2	0.5308	0.4308	0.6913	1.0x
base-2	0.6225	0.5449	0.7258	3.7x
large-2	0.6392	0.5800	0.7118	12.8x

(a) Evaluation results of different sizes of models where **large-2** is the officially submitted **run-2** and Params refers to the model's parameters relative to t5-small that has around 60M parameters.

team name	F1	P	R
winners	0.6598⋆	0.7272	0.6039
HLTRI	0.6476	0.7532⋆	0.5679
Our (run-2)	0.6392	0.5800	0.7118⋆
VUB	0.6160	0.6875	0.5580
UPennHLP	0.5237	0.6754	0.4277
Test_Positive	0.5114	0.5377	0.4875

(b) Evaluation results of submitted runs ranked by F1. **Our (run-2)** is named **UCD_CS** officially.

Ours	F1	P	R
run-1	0.6429⋆	0.5815	0.7188 ⋆
run-2	0.6392	0.5800	0.7118
run-3	0.6367	0.5920⋆	0.6887

(c) Evaluation results of our t5-large runs at different epochs.

Ours	F1	P	R
post-run-1	0.6571⋆	0.5956	0.7327⋆
post-run-2	0.6517	0.5921	0.7247
post-run-3	0.6495	0.6050⋆	0.7012

(d) Evaluation results of our t5-large runs after post-processing.

Table 2: F1, precision (P) and recall (R) scores averaged over the five COVID-19 events where ⋆ refers to the highest in each column.

4.3 Results and Discussion

We saved the last three checkpoints of the final fine-tuned T5 models ready for evaluation at epochs 10, 11, and 12 (denoted as **run-3**, **run-2**, and **run-1** for t5-large respectively). The evaluation was conducted on a test set of 2,500 tweets (500 per event) for part-2 only. Since this shared task only allows one submission from each team and we found trivial difference between **run-2** and **run-1** based on the validation evaluation, we submitted **run-2** for the official evaluation. Table 2b reports the F1, recall (R) and precision (P) scores of the submitted runs. Additionally, we put the evaluation results of all our three t5-large runs in Table 2c as well as of different sizes of T5 models in Table 2a for reference[4] (discussed in Section 4.3.2).

4.3.1 Performance

First, Table 2a indicates that the larger the model is, the better overall performance it can achieve. Interestingly, as compared to small-2, large-2's advantage over base-2 seems not significant (F1: 0.6392 versus 0.6225) given its 12.8x larger size versus base-2's 3.7x larger size. Hence, our base-2 can achieve competitive performance with a decent number of parameters. Here we continue to focus on the large runs since we want to explore the limit of our approach's performance.

Table 2b presents the evaluation results of our t5-large based runs at different epochs. It shows that our submitted run (i.e., run-2) achieved competitive performance as compared to other participating runs (F1: our 0.6392 versus the highest 0.6598). Particularly, our run exhibited a significant advantage in recall over other runs (0.7118 versus the second-highest of 0.6039). However, this advantage is combined with a trade-off in terms of precision. This reveals that our run was somewhat "active" at finding the answers to the slot questions. This is consistent with its performance at event type level as well. Table 4 shows the evaluation results of our run-2 at event type level (we will discuss post-run-2 in Section 4.3.2). We find that our run achieves the best recall in every event type but quite behind in precision, especially for can_not_test, death and cure. To further analyse the cause of low precision, we

---

[4]The small-2 and base-2 corresponds to t5-small and t5-base respectively that are fine-tuned with the same experimental setup as **run-2**

Example 1	Tweet text	only precautionary steps can protect and prevent us from corona virus. sanitation, mask, alertness, yoga and healthy food.
	Slot question (where)	**what is the cure for coronavirus mentioned by the author of the tweet?**
	Our raw prediction	mask, alertness, yoga and healthy food
	Post-processed prediction	virus. sanitation, mask, alertness, yoga and healthy food
	Ground truth	virus. sanitation, mask, alertness, yoga and healthy food
Example 2	Tweet text	@bbhuttozardari what is your sindh government doing? stop playing politics at this time and take measures to prevent spread of corona. provide healthcare facilities. sometimes doing something is better than barking tweets.
	Slot question (what)	**what is the cure for coronavirus mentioned by the author of the tweet?**
	Our raw prediction	provide healthcare facilities
	Post-processed prediction	. provide healthcare facilities
	Ground truth	. provide healthcare facilities
Example 3	Tweet text	@realdonaldtrump they're drinking bleach to cure covid-19?.
	Slot question (what)	**what is the cure for coronavirus mentioned by the author of the tweet?**
	Our raw prediction	bleach
	Post-processed prediction	@realdonaldtrump they're drinking bleach
	Ground truth	@realdonaldtrump they're drinking bleach
Example 4	Tweet text	@joshua4congress my sister is a vet with an active-duty husband and a 6wk old baby. she has a fever and symptoms but can't get tested bc she lives in a military base in texas. they require exposure to a confirmed positive. she had to give birth without family the day after our grandma died.
	Slot question (where)	**where is the can't-be-tested situation reported?**
	Our raw prediction	a military base in texas
	Post-processed prediction	a military base
	Ground truth	texas
Example 5	Tweet text	so in a few weeks time 4 year olds will be expected to be back in school but can't get tested. doesn't make sense. #covid19 #dailybriefings
	Slot question (who)	**who can not get a test?**
	Our raw prediction	4 year olds
	Post-processed prediction	year olds
	Ground truth	a few weeks time 4 year olds

Table 3: Examples of mismatches (uncased), i.e., predictions that are self-evidently correct answers, but do not exactly match the ground truths in violet text. The orange text refers to the original submitted predictions generated by our approach and the blue text refers to the transformed predictions from the raw predictions based on their edit distances to candidate answers.

rethink the metrics used to evaluate runs with a similar approach to ours.

4.3.2 Post Processing

It is worth noting that, the part 2 annotations were originally labeled by providing a fixed list of candidate choices. For example, the candidate choices in Figure 2 are either pre-defined (author of the tweet, not specified) or text spans extracted from the raw tweet via the named entity tagging tool (Ritter et al., 2011). This makes it easy to treat the task as a classification-based slot filling task, i.e, binary categorising if a candidate choice answers a given slot type (Zong et al., 2020). In this sense, the F1, P and R are good metrics for evaluating the performance of a system in this task. However, our approach is based on answer-generation and thus it is likely to generate some correct predictions that are not exact character matches. In situations where a mismatch occurs this is doubly penalised by the metrics. The

prediction made by our system will be considered to be a false positive, because it does not match a label from the gold standard. Simultaneously the presence of a gold standard label that our system does not return results in a false negative being counted also. We argue this can result in the metrics underestimating the effective performance of such systems as it has an adverse effect on precision, recall and F1 score.

Table 2d presents a list of examples from **run-1** where this occurs. In these examples, the raw generated predictions are good answers to the corresponding slot questions, although they do not exactly match the ground truth from the candidate options. In particular, in example 2, the answer "provide healthcare facilities" is taken as a false positive as it misses the dot character at the beginning. In examples 3 and 5, our raw prediction is arguable a better answer than the ground truth. Example 1 is especially interesting in that our raw prediction omits one important word ("sani-

	F1			P			R		
	best	run-2	post-run-2	best	run-2	post-run-2	best	run-2	post-run-2
positive	0.6973	0.6778	**0.6989**	0.8569	0.7380	0.7620	0.6267	0.6267	**0.6454**
negative	0.7030	0.7030	**0.7047**	0.7107	0.6873	0.6890	0.7194	0.7194	**0.7212**
can_not_test	0.6523	0.5660	0.5667	0.6863	0.4646	0.4656	0.7240	0.7240	0.7240
death	0.6942	0.6048	0.6191	0.7240	0.4917	0.5041	0.7855	0.7855	**0.8020**
cure	0.6205	0.6078	**0.6236**	0.8405	0.4961	0.6236	0.7843	0.7843	**0.8028**

Table 4: The evaluation results of our run-2 and post-run-2 at event type level where best represents the highest score across all participating runs. These in bold stand for new state-of-the-art scores in W-NUT task-3 after applying **TransM**.

tation") whereas the ground truth includes an additional word that is not part of the most appropriate question answer ("virus"). To alleviate this effect, we apply a simple post-processing method to transform the raw predictions to these that can best be exactly matched with the ground truth labels. The transformation method (which we name "TransM") is described as follows.

TransM: Given the raw prediction r for an example x and its candidate choices c : $[c_1, c_2, ..c_i·, c_n]$ where n is the number of candidates, r is converted to the final prediction t that is the one selected from c with the shortest edit distance to p. The edit distance is simply calculated by the Levenshtein (Levenshtein, 1966) distance divided by the length of c_i.

After this post-processing, we can now see from Table 2d that most of the post-processed predictions have been transformed to exactly-matched predictions. As a result, we re-evaluate our T5 large runs with the transformed predictions and present the results in Table 2d and report run-2 performance at event type level after applying TransM, i.e., post-run-2 in Table 4. First, Table 2d shows that our three runs can achieve higher scores overall as compared to the original predictions-based runs. Also, our best run post-run-1 can actually reach the same level of performance as the best participating run (F1: 0.6571 versus 0.6598). Referring to Table 4, it presents that not only does our post-run-2 achieve noticeable improvements across F1, P, and R in almost every event as compared to run-2 but it hits new state-of-the-art F1 scores in the `positive`, `negative` and `cure` events. Notably, for `positive` and `cure`, our run-2 was around 2 points behind the best participating runs in F1 but it reached the new state-of-the-art F1 scores after applying TransM (0.6989 and 0.6236). This reveals that the exact-matched metrics were exerting stronger underestimation in measuring our system's performance for

answering tested-positive and cure-and-prevention related questions than other types of questions.

Although the post-processing alleviates the underestimation of performance, our run is not the best in precision. Arguably, the last two rows (example 4-5) in Table 2d are good examples showing that in some cases that our raw predictions contain the ground truths but are taken as false positives despite the post-processing: i.e., TransM helps alleviate the underestimation but not completely eliminate it. We present a complete list of unmatched predictions generated by run-2 or post-run-2 to enable the community to examine the system's performance openly and critically[5].

5 Conclusion

This paper presents our text-to-text based approach at W-NUT 2020 shared task 3. We show that the principal idea behind the approach is adaptability to other domain-similar tasks such as informativeness classification of COVID-19 tweets. We expect to conduct more work on this adaptability in the future. It is even more interesting to test the idea in zero-shot learning. For example, how well it performs if transferring the model that is trained on the event extraction corpus to do inference in the informativeness task directly without further training. In addition, we empirically present that our system is effective, achieving competitive performance and arguably the state-of-the-art F1 scores in three of five COVID-events in the shared task. Despite the effectiveness, one concern of our approach is the model size. Our best performed model is fine-tuned using the large version of T5 with around 770M parameters (Li et al., 2020). This makes it important to compress the model efficiently in the future.

---

[5] https://github.com/wangcongcong123/ttt/tree/master/covid_event

Acknowledgments

We would like to thank Google's TensorFlow Research Cloud (TFRC) team who provided TPUs credits to support this research.

References

Jacob Devlin, Ming-Wei Chang, Kenton Lee, and Kristina Toutanova. 2019. BERT: Pre-training of deep bidirectional transformers for language understanding. In *Proceedings of the 2019 Conference of the North American Chapter of the Association for Computational Linguistics: Human Language Technologies, Volume 1 (Long and Short Papers)*, pages 4171–4186, Minneapolis, Minnesota. Association for Computational Linguistics.

Dimitar Dimitrov, Erdal Baran, Pavlos Fafalios, Ran Yu, Xiaofei Zhu, Matthäus Zloch, and Stefan Dietze. 2020. TweetsCOV19 – A Knowledge Base of Semantically Annotated Tweets about the COVID-19 Pandemic. *arXiv preprint arXiv:2006.14492*.

Ari Holtzman, Jan Buys, Li Du, Maxwell Forbes, and Yejin Choi. 2019. The curious case of neural text degeneration. In *International Conference on Learning Representations*.

Vladimir I Levenshtein. 1966. Binary codes capable of correcting deletions, insertions, and reversals. In *Soviet physics doklady*, volume 10, pages 707–710.

Mike Lewis, Yinhan Liu, Naman Goyal, Marjan Ghazvininejad, Abdelrahman Mohamed, Omer Levy, Ves Stoyanov, and Luke Zettlemoyer. 2019. Bart: Denoising sequence-to-sequence pre-training for natural language generation, translation, and comprehension. *arXiv preprint arXiv:1910.13461*.

Zhuohan Li, Eric Wallace, Sheng Shen, Kevin Lin, Kurt Keutzer, Dan Klein, and Joseph E. Gonzalez. 2020. Train large, then compress: Rethinking model size for efficient training and inference of transformers.

Junhua Liu, Trisha Singhal Lucienne Blessing, Kristin L Wood, and Kwan Hui Lim. 2020. CrisisBERT: Robust Transformer for Crisis Classification and Contextual Crisis Embedding. *arXiv preprint arXiv:2005.06627*.

Richard McCreadie, Cody Buntain, and Ian Soboroff. 2020. Incident Streams 2019: Actionable Insights and How to Find Them. *Proceedings of the International ISCRAM Conference*, 2020-May(May).

Taro Miyazaki, Kiminobu Makino, Yuka Takei, Hiroki Okamoto, and Jun Goto. 2019. Label embedding using hierarchical structure of labels for twitter classification. In *Proceedings of the 2019 Conference on Empirical Methods in Natural Language Processing and the 9th International Joint Conference on Natural Language Processing (EMNLP-IJCNLP)*, pages 6318–6323.

Martin Müller, Marcel Salathé, and Per E Kummervold. 2020. COVID-Twitter-BERT: A Natural Language Processing Model to Analyse COVID-19 Content on Twitter. *arXiv preprint arXiv:2005.07503*.

Matthew Peters, Mark Neumann, Mohit Iyyer, Matt Gardner, Christopher Clark, Kenton Lee, and Luke Zettlemoyer. 2018. Deep contextualized word representations. *Proceedings of the 2018 Conference of the North American Chapter of the Association for Computational Linguistics: Human Language Technologies, Volume 1 (Long Papers)*.

Colin Raffel, Noam Shazeer, Adam Roberts, Katherine Lee, Sharan Narang, Michael Matena, Yanqi Zhou, Wei Li, and Peter J Liu. 2020. Exploring the limits of transfer learning with a unified text-to-text transformer. *Journal of Machine Learning Research*, 21(140):1–67.

Alan Ritter, Sam Clark, Oren Etzioni, et al. 2011. Named entity recognition in tweets: an experimental study. In *Proceedings of the 2011 conference on empirical methods in natural language processing*, pages 1524–1534.

Kirk Roberts, Tasmeer Alam, Steven Bedrick, Dina Demner-Fushman, Kyle Lo, Ian Soboroff, Ellen Voorhees, Lucy Lu Wang, and William R Hersh. 2020. TREC-COVID: rationale and structure of an information retrieval shared task for COVID-19. *Journal of the American Medical Informatics Association*. Ocaa091.

Raphael Tang, Rodrigo Nogueira, Edwin Zhang, Nikhil Gupta, Phuong Cam, Kyunghyun Cho, and Jimmy Lin. 2020. Rapidly bootstrapping a question answering dataset for covid-19. *arXiv preprint arXiv:2004.11339*.

Ashish Vaswani, Noam Shazeer, Niki Parmar, Jakob Uszkoreit, Llion Jones, Aidan N Gomez, Łukasz Kaiser, and Illia Polosukhin. 2017. Attention is all you need. In *Advances in neural information processing systems*, pages 5998–6008.

Congcong Wang and David Lillis. 2020. Classification for Crisis-Related Tweets Leveraging Word Embeddings and Data Augmentation. In *Proceedings of the Twenty-Eighth Text REtrieval Conference (TREC 2019)*, Gaithersburg, MD.

Lucy Lu Wang, Kyle Lo, Yoganand Chandrasekhar, Russell Reas, Jiangjiang Yang, Doug Burdick, Darrin Eide, Kathryn Funk, Yannis Katsis, Rodney Kinney, Yunyao Li, Ziyang Liu, William Merrill, Paul Mooney, Dewey Murdick, Devvret Rishi, Jerry Sheehan, Zhihong Shen, Brandon Stilson, Alex Wade, Kuansan Wang, Nancy Xin Ru Wang, Chris Wilhelm, Boya Xie, Douglas Raymond, Daniel S. Weld, Oren Etzioni, and Sebastian Kohlmeier. 2020. CORD-19: The COVID-19 Open Research Dataset.

Shi Zong, Ashutosh Baheti, Wei Xu, and Alan Ritter. 2020. Extracting COVID-19 Events from Twitter.

Winners at W-NUT 2020 Shared Task-3: Leveraging Event Specific and Chunk Span features to Extract COVID Events from tweets

Ayush Kaushal and **Tejas Vaidhya**

Indian Institute of Technology, Kharagpur

`ayushk4@gmail.com, iamtejasvaidhya@gmail.com`

Abstract

Twitter has acted as an important source of information during disasters and pandemic, especially during the times of COVID-19. In this paper, we describe our system entry for *WNUT 2020 Shared Task-3*. The task was aimed at automating the extraction of a variety of COVID-19 related events from Twitter, such as individuals who recently contracted the virus, someone with symptoms who were denied testing and believed remedies against the infection. The system consists of separate multi-task models for slot-filling subtasks and sentence-classification subtasks while leveraging the useful sentence-level information for the corresponding event. The system uses COVID-Twitter-Bert with attention-weighted pooling of candidate slot-chunk features to capture the useful information chunks. The system **ranks 1st** at the leader-board with **F1 of 0.6598**, without using any ensembles or additional datasets. The code and trained models are available at this https url[1].

1 Introduction

The World Health Organization declared COVID-19, a global pandemic on March 11, 2020. As of 2020/09/21, there are over 30 million cases[2] and 900,000 deaths due to the infection. With the imposed lockdown, work from home and physical distancing, social media like twitter saw an increased usage. A large part of the use was posting and consuming information on the novel infection. These information include potential reasons for contraction of the disease, such as via exposure to a family member who tested positive, or someone who is showing COVID symptoms but was denied testing. Accompanying to the pandemic was an infodemic of misinformation about COVID-19, including fake

remedies, treatments and prevention-suggestions in social media (Alam et al., 2020).

Zong et al. (2020) show the possibility to automatically extract structured knowledge on COVID-19 events from Twitter and released a dataset of COVID related tweets across 5 event types. We used this dataset in our experiments for the shared-task. These tweets are annotated for whether they belong to an event (we refer to this as the **event-prediction** task in this paper) and their event-specific questions (factual or opinion). We identify these event-specific questions into two types of subtasks, **slot-filling** and **sentence classification**.

Our system consists of separate multi-task models for slot-filling subtasks and sentence-classification subtasks. Our contribution comprises improvement upon the baseline (mentioned in section 2) in three ways:

- We incorporate the event-prediction task as auxiliary subtask and fuse its features for all the event-specific subtasks.

- We perform an attention-weighted pooling over the candidate chunk span enabling the model to attend to subtask specific cues.

- We use the domain-specific Bert of Covid-Twitter Bert (Müller et al., 2020).

2 Related Works

Sentence classification tasks (such as opinion or sentiment mining) as well as slot-filling tasks have greatly progressed with deep learning advancements such as LSTM (Hochreiter and Schmidhuber, 1997), Tree-LSTM (Tai et al., 2015) and transfer learning over pre-trained models (Peters et al., 2018; Howard and Ruder, 2018; Devlin et al., 2019). Among these, CT-Bert outperforms others on COVID related twitter tasks (Müller et al., 2020). Taking inspiration from the same, we use

---

[1]https://github.com/Ayushk4/extract_covid_entity
[2]https://coronavirus.jhu.edu/map.html

Proceedings of the 2020 EMNLP Workshop W-NUT: The Sixth Workshop on Noisy User-generated Text, pages 522–529
Online, Nov 19, 2020. ©2020 Association for Computational Linguistics

CT-Bert as part of our architecture. A variety of slot-filling approaches have been built on top of these deep learning advancements (Kurata et al., 2016; Qin et al., 2019). The proposed baseline for our task (Zong et al., 2020) modifies Bert model for slot-filling problem inspired by Baldini Soares et al. (2019). Due to the excellent performance offered by Bert (Devlin et al., 2019) and Baldini Soares et al. (2019), we build upon this baseline approach.

Extraction of structured knowledge from tweets pertaining of events (Benson et al., 2011) has been studied for disaster and crises management (Abhik and Toshniwal, 2013; Rudra et al., 2018) and in pandemic scenarios (Al-Garadi et al., 2016). Extracting such entities can be useful for epidemiologists, deciding policies and preventing spread (Al-Garadi et al., 2016; Zong et al., 2020).

Due to the fast-spreading nature of the infection, it is also difficult to manually trace the spread of the pandemic. However, with twitter event-specific entity extraction and Geo-location, one could potentially build a real-time pandemic surveillance system (Lwowski and Najafirad, 2020; Al-Garadi et al., 2020). Bal et al. (2020) show that health-issues related misinformation is prevalent in social media, while Alam et al. (2020) talks about covid-specific misinformation. Such systems for extracting structured knowledge over the tweets talking about potential cures for COVID will help study how users perceive the COVID misinformation.

In §3, we describe the dataset and the problem statement. Then in §4, we discuss the details of our two multi-task models followed by experiments, results and conclusion.

3 Dataset and Problem statement

Now, we will briefly go over the dataset. The reader may refer (Zong et al., 2020) for full details. Each of the 7500 tweets in the dataset belongs to one of the 5 event types: tested-positive, tested-negative, can-not-test, death, and cure. The first four events aimed at extracting structured reports of coronavirus related events, such as self-reported cases or news stories about public figures who were exposed to the virus. Each tweet was first annotated for whether it belongs to its respective event (e.g. Is the tweet belonging to the tested-positive event talking about someone who tested positive?). Throughout this paper, we refer to this as the **Event-Prediction** task. The tweets that correspond to its event were then annotated for event-specific questions or **sub-**

Event	# Tweets
Tested positive	2397
Tested negative	1144
Can Not Test	1128
Death	1231
Cure/Prevention	1244
Total	7144

Table 1: Dataset statistics, scraped during early July.

Tweet	*Sigh of relief. My wife 's COVID-19 test came back negative today . The Lord has been gracious. One of my favorite pics I took of her. #thankful.[URL]*
Slot Filling	{Who}: My wife's, {Where}: Not Specified, {When}: today, {CloseContact}: Not Specified, {Age}: Not specified, {Duration}: Not Specified
Sentence Classify	{Relation}: Yes, {Gender}: Female
Corresponding Event	{Did someone test negative?} Yes

Figure 1: An example tweet from tested negative event.

tasks about factual information and user's opinions. All annotations are done by multiple Amazon Mechanical Turks with inter-annotation agreement. The event-specific questions or subtasks (e.g. name, age, gender of the person tested positive) varies depending on the event. These subtasks are of two categories: **slot-filling** (e.g., Who tested positive/negative?, Where are they located?, Who is in close contact with person contracting the disease?) and **sentence classification** (e.g. Is author related to infected person?, Does the author experience any symptoms?, Does the author believe a cure method is effective?).

The dataset released tweet IDs and their annotations. We obtain our text corresponding to tweets using the official Twitter API[3]. Table 1 shows the statistics for the dataset we scrapped in early July.[4] Figure 1 shows an annotated example from the dataset. We identify the event-specific subtasks into two categories shown in Table 2.

We now formally describe the two types of event-specific subtasks:

Slot-filling subtasks: Assume n slot-filling subtasks $\{S_1, S_2...S_n\}$. We set up each slot-filling subtask S_i as a supervised binary classification problem. Given the tweet t and the candidate slot s, the model $f(t, s) \rightarrow \{0, 1\}$ predicts whether s answers its designated question. We extract a list of

---

[3] https://developer.twitter.com/

[4] We get about 350 fewer tweets than the corpus. Some tweets are not obtainable over time as the accounts/tweets get deleted, renamed, banned, or change-visibility etc.

Event	Sentence Classification	Slot-Filling task
Tested positive	gender, relation	who,age,recent-visit,when,where,employer,c.-contact
Tested negative	gender, relation	who,age,when,where,duration,close-contact
Can Not Test	relation, symptoms	who,when,where
Death	relation, symptoms	who,age,when,where
Cure	opinion	what is the cure, who is promoting cure

Table 2: The proposed event-specific subtasks split into two subtask types: slot-filling and sentence classification

candidate slot of all noun chunks and name entities in each of the tweets by using a Twitter tagging tool (Ritter et al., 2011) same as the baseline.

Sentence classification subtasks: Assume m sentence classification subtasks $\{C_1, C_2...C_m, \}$. Given a sentence classification subtask C_i aims to learn a model $g(t) \rightarrow \{l_1, l_2...l_k\}$, where t is a tweet and l_j is a label. Here the number of labels can vary depending on the subtask, for example, gender is labelled with {Male, Female, Others/Not Specified}, Relation with {Yes, No}, Opinion with {effective, no cure, not effective, no opinion} and so on. All these subtasks are 'supervised' classification problems.

The dataset is also annotated with whether a tweet corresponds to its respective event or not. We treat this as an additional **Event-Prediction task**. This is a binary classification task that aims to learn a model $h(t) \rightarrow 0, 1$ where t is a tweet.

4 Approach

In the following subsections §4.1 and §4.2, we describe our multi-task model for slot-filling and sentence-classification respectively.

4.1 Slot-filling

We improve upon the baseline (Zong et al., 2020) by using domain-specific Bert, using attention-weighted pooling over the candidate chunk feature sequence, incorporating auxiliary Event-Prediction task and utilizing its logits for all the slot-filling subtasks. Before describing the approach, we first describe the Bert baseline. Our slot-filling model can be seen in figure 2.

The baseline consists of Bert based classifier. It takes a tweet t as input and encloses the candidate slot s, within the tweet, inside special entity start $< E >$ and end $< /E >$ markers. The Bert hidden representation of token $< E >$ is then processed through a fully connected layer with softmax activation to make the binary prediction for a task (Baldini Soares et al., 2019). Since many slot-filling

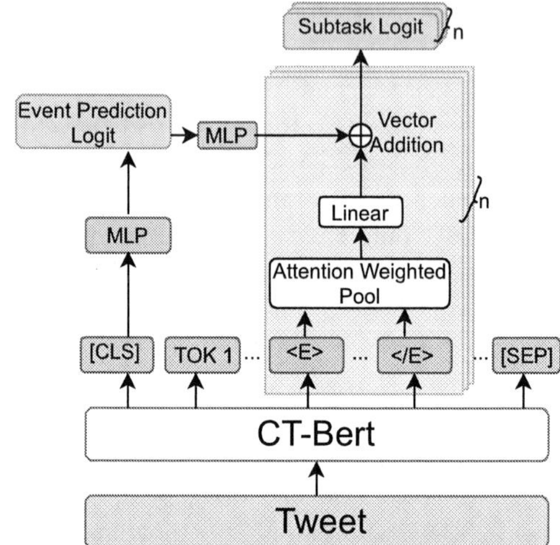

Figure 2: Slot-Filling Model, described in Section §4.1. Here n is the number of slot-filling subtasks.

tasks within an event are semantically related to each other, they jointly trained the final softmax layers of all the subtasks S_i in an event by sharing their Bert model parameters.

COVID Twitter Bert (CT-Bert) is a Bert-Large model pretrained on Twitter Corpus on COVID-19 topics, leading to marginal improvements from Bert on tasks based on Twitter datasets(Müller et al., 2020). This motivates us to use CT-Bert instead of Bert from the baseline model.

The baseline, uses the Bert hidden representation of token $< E >$ for classification. Here, however, we use attention-weighted pool of the CT-Bert hidden representation of tokens between $< E >$ and $< /E >$ (both inclusive). Formally, let $\{x_0, ...x_p, ...x_q, ...x_n\}$ be the output vectors from the hidden representation of CT-Bert where p and q are indices of $< E >$ and $< /E >$ respectively, then for any of the slot-filling subtask S_j, we get its pooled vector as follows:

$$\widetilde{x}^{S_j} = \sum_{i=p}^{q} \alpha_i^{S_j} x_i \qquad (1)$$

$$\alpha_i^{S_j} = Softmax_{p\ to\ q}(x_i^T a^{S_j})$$

where x_i^T denotes the transpose of x_i, a^{S_j} is a trainable vector. The motivation for attention weighted pooling is that depending on the task, model can attend to different portions of the candidate slot chunk. Next we obtain the binary classification score vector:

$$h^{S_j} = W^{S_j} \widetilde{x}^{S_j} + b^{S_j} \qquad (2)$$

Here W^{S_j} and b^{S_j} are trainable parameters.

We treat the Event-Prediction task as an auxiliary task and then fuse its logits to each of the other slot-filling subtasks. The motivation is that a task-specific entity shall be present in a tweet only if the tweet belongs to its respective event.

To predict the label for Event-Prediction task, we take the CT-Bert features of $[CLS]$ token and pass it through a MultiLayer Perceptron (MLP) to get logits h_{ces}.

We fuse h_{ces} prediction over each subtasks S_j by adding it to h^{S_j} (from (2)) to get the logits $h_f^{S_j}$:

$$h_f^{S_j} = h^{S_j} + MLP^{S_j}(h_{ces}) \qquad (3)$$

In practice, we share the parameters of the MLP^{S_j} across all the slot-filling subtasks S_j.

Given a tweet t and slot s, our loss for slot-filling model over n slot-filling subtasks $\{S_1, S_2...S_n\}$ and Event-Prediction task looks like:

$$Loss(t, s, y_{ces}, (y_1, y_2...y_n))$$

$$= \lambda_1 CE_{Loss}(h_{ces}, y_{ces}) + \sum_{k=1}^{n} CE_{Loss}(h_f^{S_k}, y_k)$$
$$(4)$$

where CE_{loss} is softmax cross entropy loss, y_{ces} is ground truth label for Event-Prediction task and $(y_1, y_2...y_n)$ are the labels for the candidate slot s of tweet t for the subtasks $\{S_1, S_2...S_n\}$. We keep $\lambda_1 = 1$.

Our preprocessing for this is same as baseline.

4.2 Sentence classification

Our Sentence classification model is shown in figure 3. We use a Bert based sentence classifier and improve it by using CT-Bert, incorporating the auxiliary Event-Prediction task and attention-weighted pooling over the entire sequence.

This model uses CT-Bert instead of Bert and the auxiliary Event-Prediction task for same reason as the slot-filling model.

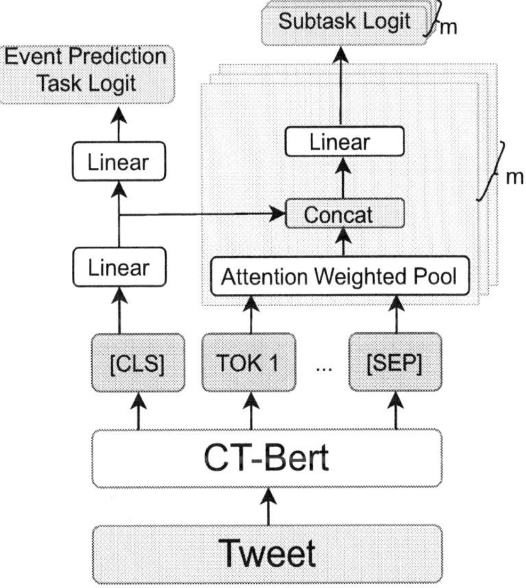

Figure 3: Sentence Classification model, described in section. §4.2. Here m is the number of Sentence Classification subtasks.

An attention-weighted pooling is done over the feature sequences from CT-Bert to extract the most relevant information. Formally, let $\{x_0, x_1, ...x_n\}$ be the output vectors from CT-Bert (here 0 and n are indices of $[CLS]$ and $[SEP]$ respectively). Then for any of the sentence classification subtask C_j, we get its pooled vector $\widetilde{x}^{C_j}$ as follows:

$$\widetilde{x}^{C_j} = \sum_{i=0}^{n} \beta_i^{C_j} x_i \qquad (5)$$

$$\beta_i^{C_j} = Softmax_i(x_i^T a^{C_j} + c^{C_j})$$

where a^{C_j}, c^{C_j} are trainable vector and scalar respectively.

For the Event-Prediction task, we take the CT-Bert vector representation of $[CLS]$ token and pass it through a MLP. Assume the MLP's final and hidden states to be v_{ces} and h'_{ces}.

Next, we incorporate information from Event-Prediction task into sentence classification subtask C_j. Since the sentence classification subtasks aren't binary classification, so, unlike the slot-filling model, we cannot merely add the Event-Prediction logits to all tasks. Additionally, we desire sentence-level event specific features for each of the sentence level predictions. Hence, we concatenate the hidden state features from the MLP of Event-Prediction task h'_{ces} to pooled vector $\widetilde{x}^{C_j}$

from 5 to get the logits $h_f^{C_j}$ for each subtask C_j, as follows:

$$h_f^{C_j} = [\widetilde{x}^{C_j}; h'_{ces}]^T W^{C_j} + b^{C_j} \qquad (6)$$

Here ^{T} denotes transpose, $[;]$ denotes vector concatenation. W^{C_j} and b^{C_j} are trainable.

Given a tweet t, our loss for sentence classification model over m sentence classification subtasks $\{C_1, C_2...C_m\}$ and Event-Prediction task is:

$$Loss(t, y_{ces}, (y_1, y_2...y_m))$$

$$= \lambda_2 CE_{Loss}(v_{ces}, y_{ces}) + \sum_{k=1}^{m} CE_{Loss}(h_f^{C_k}, y_k) \qquad (7)$$

where CE_{Loss} is softmax cross entropy loss, y_{ces} is ground truth label for Event-Prediction task and $(y_1, y_2...y_m)$ are the labels for tweet t for the subtasks $\{C_1, C_2...C_m\}$. We keep $\lambda_2 = 1$.

Preprocessing for sentence classification is done using ekphrasis library (Baziotis et al., 2017). We remove Emoji, URL, Email, punctuation and normalize text by word segmenting, lower-casing and word decontraction.

5   Experiments

All the experiments were performed using PyTorch (Paszke et al., 2019) and Hugging Face's transformers (Wolf et al., 2019). We use git and wandb (Biewald, 2020) for experiment tracking. Optimization is done using Adam (Kingma and Ba, 2014) with a learning rate of 2e-5. Slot-filling models are trained for 8 epochs and sentence classification model for 10 epochs. Average training time per epoch on Tesla P100 is ≈ 4 minutes for slot-filling, and ≈ 30 second for sentence classification.

We use a 70-30 split for train-valid set. The valid set is used to obtain the best threshold for each of the slot classification tasks over the grid $\{0.1, 0.2, ..., 0.9\}$. We exclude labels with "No consensus" from our data.[5]

All the MLP have 1 hidden layer and 0.1 dropout. MLP_{S_j} has 4 hidden size, LeakyReLU activation (Maas et al., 2013) with 0.1 negative slope, rest of the MLP have 50 hidden size and Tanh activation.

---

[5]As per the submission guidelines, some subtasks like opinion had their label classes merged. We incorporate these changes in our model.

Event	F1	P	R
Tested Positive	.68	.80	.58
Tested Negative	.66	.66	.67
Can Not Test	.65	.67	.64
Death	.69	.72	.67
Cure/Prevention	.63	.75	.53
Overall	**.66**	**.73**	**.60**

Table 3: Micro averaged scores on the held out test set for our final submission.

6   Results

Our performance on the held-out test set is shown in Table 3. Our system **ranks 1st position** in the W-NUT 2020 Shared Task-3 (Zong et al., 2020). We also independently rank 1st for 3 of the 5 events: 'Can Not Test', 'Death', and 'Cure'.

Now we discuss our various experiments.

Slot-filling: We experimented with a variety of architectures for slot-filling model. **Our (SF)** is our Slot-Filling Model from §4.1. **Our (SF) w/o pool** is our slot-filling model that uses the CT-Bert hidden representation of token $< E >$ to classify instead of doing an attention-weighted pooling. **Our (SF) w/o CES** is our slot-filling model without Event-Prediction task. **CT-Bert** and **Bert-large** are baseline models using CT-Bert and Bert-large instead of Bert-base.

Table 4 shows the performance of these models. There is a considerable performance difference by using CT-Bert instead of Bert, demonstrate the benefits of domain specific pre-training. *Our (SF) w/o pool* and *Our (SF) w/o CES* outperform CT-Bert demonstrating the importance of Event-Prediction task and attention-weighted pooling over slot-chunk respectively. *Our (SF)* using CT-Bert with Event-Prediction and attention-weighted pooling performs the best among these models.

Sentence level tasks: We experimented with various architectures for sentence level tasks. **Our (SC)** is our Sentence Classification architecture from §4.2. **Our (SC) w/o CES** is our Sentence Classification without Event-Prediction task. **Bert multitask** model predicts using the $[CLS]$ representation from Bert (Devlin et al., 2019). We also build an LSTM model (Hochreiter and Schmidhuber, 1997) with GloVe embedding (Pennington et al., 2014), and twitter-tokenization using Word-

Model	Micro F1	Macro F1
Our (SF)	**.684**	**.558**
Our (SF) w/o pool	.678	.557
Our (SF) w/o CES	.665	.552
CT-Bert	.662	.551
Bert (large)	.610	.529
Bert (baseline)	.612	.528

Table 4: Results of slot-filling models on our 70-30 split. We report results on the valid set across *all slot filling subtasks* across the 5 events.

Model	Micro F1	Macro F1
Our (SC)	**.788**	**.767**
Our (SC) w/o CES	.777	.731
CT-Bert multitask	.760	.717
Bert multitask	.715	.612
LSTM multitask	.614	.543

Table 5: Results sentence classification models on our 70-30 split. We report results on the valid set across *all sentence classification subtasks* across the 5 events.

Tokenizers package (Kaushal et al., 2020).

Table 5 shows the performance of these architectures. Our (SC) outperforms others on macro F1 and micro F1, followed by Our (SC) w/o CES. The performance difference between these two, shows the benefits of including the Event-Prediction task. While the performance difference between CT-Bert multitask and Our (SC) w/o CES shows the gains from attention weighted pooling. CT-Bert also outperforms Bert multitask, showing its usefulness in our proposed system over using Bert. Lastly, Bert multitask, and all the models using Bert/CT-Bert outperform LSTM by a very large margin demonstrating the superiority of these pretrained language models.

Separate Sentence classification and slot filling models: Consider **Bert separate**, a simple system treating the two categories of tasks separately. It has the Bert baseline as its slot filling model and a simple Bert sentence classifier using features from $[CLS]$ for sentence prediction. Bert separate does not have the event-prediction auxilliary task or any attention weighted pooling. Table 6 shows the performance of *Bert separate* against the baseline. *Bert separate* outperforms the Bert baseline by a considerable margin, thus showing the importance of treating the two subtasks differently.

Model	Micro F1	Macro F1
Bert Separate	**.631**	**.545**
Bert Baseline	.608	.512

Table 6: Results comparing the systems treating the sentence classification and slot-filling subtasks separately vs those treating it similarly. We report results on the valid set across *all the subtasks* of both categories across the 5 events.

7 Conclusion and Future Work

In this paper, we presented our system that bagged 1st position in the WNUT-2020 Shared Task-3 on Extracting COVID Entities from Twitter. We divided the event-specific subtasks into slot-filling and sentence classification subtasks, building separate architectures for the two. For both architectures, we used COVID-Twitter Bert, weighted-attention pooling over chunk-spans/sentence and fused logits and features from auxiliary Event-Prediction task. Our ablation studies demonstrated the usefulness of each component in our system.

There is a lot of scope of improvement for subtasks with few positive labels. Pretraining on relevant data (such as COVID-misinformation datasets for event cure) is a promising direction.

Another direction would be to reduce the training and inference time of slot-filling model by *not* enclosing the candidate chunk within special start $< E >$ and special end $< /E >$ tokens. We can instead use the attention-weighted pooling over candidate slot chunks. This will reduce the number of Bert forward passes from $O(k)$ to $O(1)$, where k is the number of candidate chunks in a tweet.

Acknowledgments

We are very grateful for the invaluable suggestions given by Nikhil Shah, Dibya Prakash Das and Sayan Sinha. We also thank the organizers of the Shared Task-3 at WNUT, EMNLP-2020.

References

Dhekar Abhik and Durga Toshniwal. 2013. Sub-event detection during natural hazards using features of social media data. In *Proceedings of the 22nd International Conference on World Wide Web*, pages 783–788.

Mohammed Al-Garadi, Muhammad Khan, Kasturi Varathan, Ghulam Mujtaba, and Abdelkodose Abdulla. 2016. Using online social networks to track a pandemic: A systematic review. *Journal of Biomedical Informatics*, 62.

Mohammed Ali Al-Garadi, Yuan-Chi Yang, Sahithi Lakamana, and Abeed Sarker. 2020. Text classification approach for the automatic detection of twitter posts containing self-reported covid-19 symptoms.

Firoj Alam, Fahim Dalvi, Shaden Shaar, Nadir Durrani, Hamdy Mubarak, Alex Nikolov, Giovanni Da San Martino, Ahmed Abdelali, Hassan Sajjad, Kareem Darwish, and Preslav Nakov. 2020. Fighting the covid-19 infodemic in social media: A holistic perspective and a call to arms.

Rakesh Bal, Sayan Sinha, Swastika Dutta, Risabh Joshi, Sayan Ghosh, and Ritam Dutt. 2020. Analysing the extent of misinformation in cancer related tweets. *Proceedings of the International AAAI Conference on Web and Social Media*, 14(1):924–928.

Livio Baldini Soares, Nicholas FitzGerald, Jeffrey Ling, and Tom Kwiatkowski. 2019. Matching the blanks: Distributional similarity for relation learning. In *Proceedings of the 57th Annual Meeting of the Association for Computational Linguistics*, pages 2895–2905, Florence, Italy. Association for Computational Linguistics.

Christos Baziotis, Nikos Pelekis, and Christos Doulkeridis. 2017. DataStories at SemEval-2017 task 4: Deep LSTM with attention for message-level and topic-based sentiment analysis. In *Proceedings of the 11th International Workshop on Semantic Evaluation (SemEval-2017)*, pages 747–754, Vancouver, Canada. Association for Computational Linguistics.

Edward Benson, Aria Haghighi, and Regina Barzilay. 2011. Event discovery in social media feeds. In *Proceedings of the 49th Annual Meeting of the Association for Computational Linguistics: Human Language Technologies*, pages 389–398, Portland, Oregon, USA. Association for Computational Linguistics.

Lukas Biewald. 2020. Experiment tracking with weights and biases. Software available from wandb.com.

Jacob Devlin, Ming-Wei Chang, Kenton Lee, and Kristina Toutanova. 2019. BERT: Pre-training of deep bidirectional transformers for language understanding. In *Proceedings of the 2019 Conference of the North American Chapter of the Association for Computational Linguistics: Human Language Technologies, Volume 1 (Long and Short Papers)*, pages 4171–4186, Minneapolis, Minnesota. Association for Computational Linguistics.

Sepp Hochreiter and Jürgen Schmidhuber. 1997. Long short-term memory. *Neural Comput.*, 9(8):1735–1780.

Jeremy Howard and Sebastian Ruder. 2018. Universal language model fine-tuning for text classification. In *Proceedings of the 56th Annual Meeting of the Association for Computational Linguistics (Volume 1: Long Papers)*, pages 328–339, Melbourne, Australia. Association for Computational Linguistics.

Ayush Kaushal, Lyndon White, Mike Innes, and Rohit Kumar. 2020. Wordtokenizers.jl: Basic tools for tokenizing natural language in julia. *Journal of Open Source Software*, 5(46):1956.

Diederik P Kingma and Jimmy Ba. 2014. Adam: A method for stochastic optimization. *arXiv preprint arXiv:1412.6980*.

Gakuto Kurata, Bing Xiang, Bowen Zhou, and Mo Yu. 2016. Leveraging sentence-level information with encoder LSTM for semantic slot filling. In *Proceedings of the 2016 Conference on Empirical Methods in Natural Language Processing*, pages 2077–2083, Austin, Texas. Association for Computational Linguistics.

Brandon Lwowski and Peyman Najafirad. 2020. Covid-19 surveillance through twitter using self-supervised learning and few shot learning.

Andrew L. Maas, Awni Y. Hannun, and Andrew Y. Ng. 2013. Rectifier nonlinearities improve neural network acoustic models. In *in ICML Workshop on Deep Learning for Audio, Speech and Language Processing*.

Martin Müller, Marcel Salathé, and Per E Kummervold. 2020. Covid-twitter-bert: A natural language processing model to analyse covid-19 content on twitter.

Adam Paszke, Sam Gross, Francisco Massa, Adam Lerer, James Bradbury, Gregory Chanan, Trevor Killeen, Zeming Lin, Natalia Gimelshein, Luca Antiga, Alban Desmaison, Andreas Kopf, Edward Yang, Zachary DeVito, Martin Raison, Alykhan Tejani, Sasank Chilamkurthy, Benoit Steiner, Lu Fang, Junjie Bai, and Soumith Chintala. 2019. Pytorch: An imperative style, high-performance deep learning library. In *Advances in Neural Information Processing Systems 32*, pages 8026–8037. Curran Associates, Inc.

Jeffrey Pennington, Richard Socher, and Christopher Manning. 2014. GloVe: Global vectors for word representation. In *Proceedings of the 2014 Conference on Empirical Methods in Natural Language Processing (EMNLP)*, pages 1532–1543, Doha, Qatar. Association for Computational Linguistics.

Matthew Peters, Mark Neumann, Mohit Iyyer, Matt Gardner, Christopher Clark, Kenton Lee, and Luke Zettlemoyer. 2018. Deep contextualized word representations. In *Proceedings of the 2018 Conference of the North American Chapter of the Association for Computational Linguistics: Human Language Technologies, Volume 1 (Long Papers)*, pages

2227–2237, New Orleans, Louisiana. Association for Computational Linguistics.

Libo Qin, Wanxiang Che, Yangming Li, Haoyang Wen, and Ting Liu. 2019. A stack-propagation framework with token-level intent detection for spoken language understanding. In *Proceedings of the 2019 Conference on Empirical Methods in Natural Language Processing and the 9th International Joint Conference on Natural Language Processing (EMNLP-IJCNLP)*, pages 2078–2087, Hong Kong, China. Association for Computational Linguistics.

Alan Ritter, Sam Clark, Mausam, and Oren Etzioni. 2011. Named entity recognition in tweets: An experimental study. In *Proceedings of the 2011 Conference on Empirical Methods in Natural Language Processing*, pages 1524–1534, Edinburgh, Scotland, UK. Association for Computational Linguistics.

Koustav Rudra, Pawan Goyal, Niloy Ganguly, Prasenjit Mitra, and Muhammad Imran. 2018. Identifying sub-events and summarizing disaster-related information from microblogs. In *The 41st International ACM SIGIR Conference on Research and Development in Information Retrieval*, SIGIR '18, page 265–274, New York, NY, USA. Association for Computing Machinery.

Kai Sheng Tai, Richard Socher, and Christopher D. Manning. 2015. Improved semantic representations from tree-structured long short-term memory networks. In *Proceedings of the 53rd Annual Meeting of the Association for Computational Linguistics and the 7th International Joint Conference on Natural Language Processing (Volume 1: Long Papers)*, pages 1556–1566, Beijing, China. Association for Computational Linguistics.

Thomas Wolf, Lysandre Debut, Victor Sanh, Julien Chaumond, Clement Delangue, Anthony Moi, Pierric Cistac, Tim Rault, Rémi Louf, Morgan Funtowicz, Joe Davison, Sam Shleifer, Patrick von Platen, Clara Ma, Yacine Jernite, Julien Plu, Canwen Xu, Teven Le Scao, Sylvain Gugger, Mariama Drame, Quentin Lhoest, and Alexander M. Rush. 2019. Huggingface's transformers: State-of-the-art natural language processing. *ArXiv*, abs/1910.03771.

Shi Zong, Ashutosh Baheti, Wei Xu, and Alan Ritter. 2020. Extracting covid-19 events from twitter.

HLTRI at W-NUT 2020 Shared Task-3: COVID-19 Event Extraction from Twitter Using Multi-Task Hopfield Pooling

Maxwell Weinzierl
Human Language Technology
Research Institute,
University of Texas at Dallas
maw150130@utdallas.edu

Sanda Harabagiu
Human Language Technology
Research Institute,
University of Texas at Dallas
sanda@utdallas.edu

Abstract

Extracting structured knowledge involving self-reported events related to the COVID-19 pandemic from Twitter has the potential to inform surveillance systems that play a critical role in public health. The event extraction challenge presented by the W-NUT 2020 Shared Task 3 focused on the identification of five types of events relevant to the COVID-19 pandemic and their respective set of pre-defined slots encoding demographic, epidemiological, clinical as well as spatial, temporal or subjective knowledge. Our participation in the challenge led to the design of a neural architecture for jointly identifying all Event Slots expressed in a tweet relevant to an event of interest. This architecture uses COVID-Twitter-BERT as the pre-trained language model. In addition, to learn *text span embeddings* for each Event Slot, we relied on a special case of Hopfield Networks, namely Hopfield pooling. The results of the shared task evaluation indicate that our system performs best when it is trained on a larger dataset, while it remains competitive when training on smaller datasets.

1 Introduction

With the outbreak of the COVID-19 pandemic, people turned to social media platforms, such as Twitter, to read and to share timely information about their experiences with testing, treatment and deaths caused by the virus. Extracting information about these types of events has the potential to inform COVID-19 surveillance systems, which play a critical role in the public health mission of agencies at the international, national and local level.

The shared task organized by the 6-th Workshop on Noisy User-generated Text (W-NUT) in 2020 focused on extracting COVID-19 events from Twitter by targeting five types of events of interest, which are illustrated in Table 1, and further detailed in Zong et al. (2020). These five types of self-reported

Event Type	Event Slots
TESTED POSITIVE	*age, close_contact, employer, gender, name, recent_travel, relation, when, where*
TESTED NEGATIVE	*age, close_contact, gender, name, relation, when, where*
CAN NOT TEST	*name, relation, symptoms, when, where*
DEATH	*age, name, relation, when, where*
CURE	*opinion, what_cure, who_cure*

Table 1: The Event Types and their corresponding Event Slots defined in the W-NUT 2020 Shared Task on COVID-19 Event Extraction.

events are typically expressed in Twitter postings of people that indicate when they might be at increased risk of COVID-19 due to a coworker or other close contact testing positive for the virus, or when they have symptoms but were denied access to testing. Moreover, for each Event Type of interest, a set of pre-defined slots were provided, to account for information that may answer important questions involving the events (e.g., *Who tested positive? Where did they recently travel? Who is their employer?*). The complete list of Event Slots associated with each Event Type is illustrated in Table 1.

Interestingly, events of type TESTED POSITIVE, TESTED NEGATIVE, CAN NOT TEST and DEATH have slots answering questions about *when* and *where*, which help ground the events temporally and spatially, potentially informing systems that try to capture automatically trends of testing results for the COVID-19 virus. Some slots for events of type TESTED POSITIVE, TESTED NEGATIVE, also encode answers about demographic information, e.g. *age, gender* as well as epidemiological information, e.g. *close_contact* or *relation*. Only events of the type TESTED POSITIVE have a slot for *employer*. Some clinical information is available through the

Proceedings of the 2020 EMNLP Workshop W-NUT: The Sixth Workshop on Noisy User-generated Text, pages 530–538
Online, Nov 19, 2020. ©2020 Association for Computational Linguistics

slot *symptoms* of events of type CAN NOT TEST or the slots *what_cure* and *who_cure* of the events of type CURE. For the CURE type of events, a slot capturing the opinion of the tweet reporter was also annotated, providing a means for analyzing the change in opinions throughout time.

The organizers of the W-NUT Shared Task 3 provided participants with a set of $7,500$ annotated tweets, $7,013$ of which we were able to download. The tweets are categorized by the type of event they mention. In each category of tweets, every tweet was annotated with (1) the text spans that can be mapped in any of the slots corresponding to the Event Type, as well as (2) the corresponding Event Slot category. Moreover, in each tweet, text spans that were not mapped to any Event Slot were also provided. The training data we have used contains $3,794$ Event Type mentions and $10,778$ Event Slot instances. This timely and richly-annotated twitter dataset allowed participants to design and train their event extraction systems, expecting to be tested on a different set of tweets, which were labeled with the Event Type, probably a byproduct of tweet retrieval using keywords proven to return relevant posting for the events of interest. In the test set, the tweet text spans are also provided.

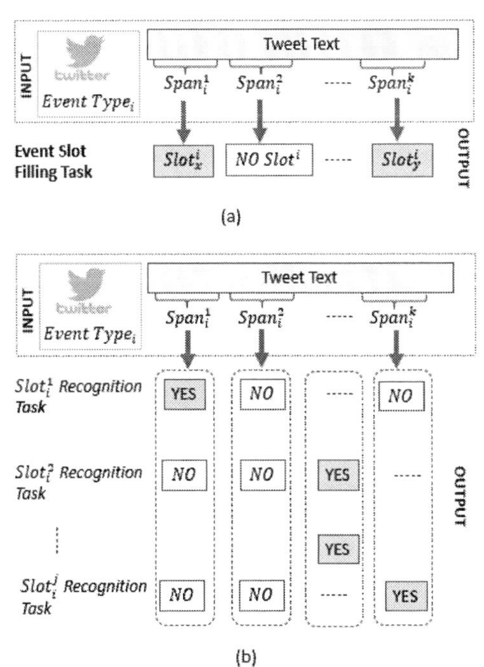

Figure 1: (a) The Task of Event Slot Filling; (b) Multi-Task Binary Classification of Tweet Text Spans.

The challenge of event extraction from Twitter texts was defined as an Event Slot filling task, as illustrated in Figure 1(a). Each tweet text is associated with one of the five *Event Type_i* listed in Table 1 and its defined Event Slots $ES_i = (ES_1^i, ES_2^i, , , ES_{n(i)}^i)$. In addition, a set of text spans from the tweet, $(Span_i^1, Span_i^2, ...Span_i^k)$ are provided. Filling the slots of the mention(s) of an event of *Event Type_i* is made possible by assigning to each tweet text span either to one of the Event Slots ES_j^i for the *Event Type_i* or to none of these Event Slots. To be noted that this is a many-to-many assignment, as (1) the same $Span_i^1$ may be assigned to more than one Event Slot from ES_i and (2) more than one text span can be assigned to the same Event Slot from ES_i. This is because, the notion of *event mention* is avoided, thus when multiple mentions of the same Event Type are expressed in the same tweet, some of the Event Slots that are filled for one of the mention, whereas other are filled for different mentions.

Casting the Event Slot filling as a binary classification problem, as suggested in Zong et al. (2020), is illustrated in Figure 1(b), where we show how a separate recognition task is considered for each of the Event Slots from ES_i. In this case, for each tweet text span, the recognition task of Event Slot ES_j^i is identifying whether any of the provided text spans can fill that slot or not. In this way, the Event Slot filling task is cast as a Multi-Task binary classification problem. As before, the same text span may fill different Event Slots, pertaining to different event mentions.

Because event extraction in this challenge is based on a mapping operation from tweet text spans to Event Slots, we contemplated methods of representing these spans that could take into account more than deep contextual information. We hypothesized that the representation of the tweet text spans should be specific to each of the Event Slot recognition tasks depicted in Figure 1(b). While contextual span representations based on the widely used BERT model (Devlin et al., 2019) have been successful in many applications, e.g. end-to-end relation extraction (Eberts and Ulges, 2020) or coreference resolution (Joshi et al., 2020), we believe that representing tweet text spans could be improved when considering modern Hopfield Networks in which the update rule is the attention mechanism used in the transformer and BERT, an idea recently advocated in Ramsauer et al. (2020). These ideas led the design of our Multi-Task, Event-specific Ex-

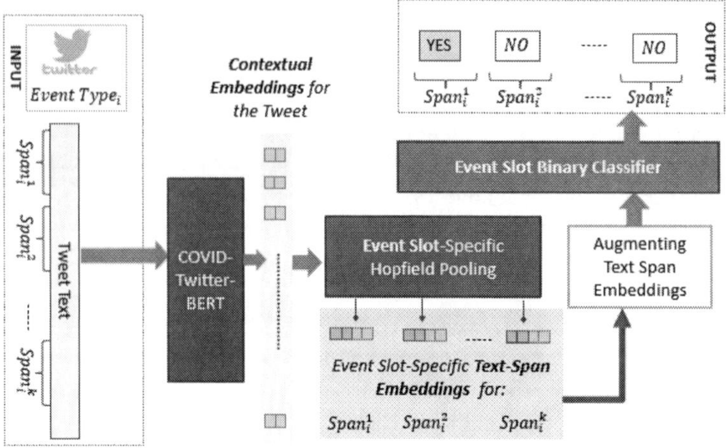

Figure 2: The Multi-Task Event-specific Extraction system using BERT and Hopfield Pooling (MT-EsE.BHP).

traction system using BERT and Hopfield Pooling (MT-EsE.BHP).

2   Related Work

Zong et al. (2020) introduced the collection of tweets used for training in this shared-task along with the annotation schema and provided two baselines: a logistic regression model and a multi-task BERT model. Their multi-task BERT model utilized the contextual embedding for the token <E> as their span embedding, while we expand on this span embedding representation with width embeddings and a slot-specific Hopfield pooling embedding. We also make use of COVID-Twitter-BERT, as opposed to BERT-base used by Zong et al. (2020).

Mackey et al. (2020) utilized an unsupervised approach to cluster tweets in which users discuss experiences associated with possible COVID-19 symptoms. They used the biterm topic model (BTM) (Yan et al., 2013) to identify tweet topic clusters, and then manually annotated tweets which fell within relevant topic clusters. In contrast, we made use of the annotated tweets which discuss relevant COVID-19 events, as provided by the W-NUT 2020 Shared Task-3, designing a supervised approach capable to extract events and their slots, not only symptom discussions.

Zhang et al. (2020) manually identified twitter users which appeared depressed and retrieved historical tweets from these users. They attempted to identify whether a twitter user may be depressed based on their public tweet history using the language model XLNet (Yang et al., 2019) and they

perform user-level classification using a Support Vector Machine (SVM). They apply this system to detect and monitor trends of depression during the COVID-19 pandemic. We differ from this system by utilizing a domain-specific language model with COVID-Twitter-BERT is trained to extract several types of events and their corresponding slots from tweets related to COVID-19.

3   The Approach

3.1   The MT-EsE.BHP

The overall architecture of the MT-EsE.BHP is illustrated in Figure 2. Given a tweet in which events of type *Event Type$_i$* are discussed, along with the text spans that can be potentially mapped into any of the events slots from ES_i, the pre-trained domain-specific language model COVID-Twitter-BERT (Müller et al., 2020) is used to produce for each word-piece token in the tweet a contextual embedding. COVID-Twitter-BERT was pre-trained on a large corpus of Tweets related to COVID-19, and it also contains learned embeddings for URLs (<url>) and @ mentioned Twitter users (@<user>) which are used in place of URLs and usernames.

The contextual embeddings are used to learn embedding representations for each text span from the tweet that can be potentially mapped to any of the Event Slots of the events of *Event Type$_i$* discussed in the tweet. In the MT-EsE.BHP a separate *text-span embedding* is learned for each Event Slot from ES_i. A special case of a Hopfield Network, namely Hopfield Pooling is used for learning each

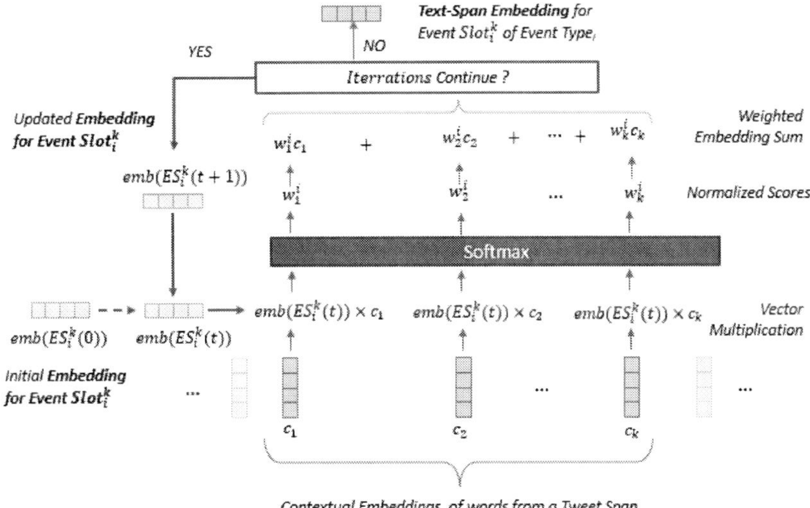

Figure 3: Hopfield Pooling for an Event Slot ES_i^k of any *Event Type$_i$*.

Event Slot-specific text-span embedding. Details of how Hopfield Pooling works are provided in Section 3.2. As Figure 2 shows, because the text-span embeddings have the same dimension, regardless of the width of the text span, the text-span embeddings were augmented by concatenating an embedding corresponding to the width information for each text span. The augmented text-span embeddings are used by each Event Slot Binary classifier, which decides the mapping of each text span from the tweet to any of the Event Slots from ES_i. The binary classifier is implemented as a single-layer Softmax classifier.

3.2 Hopfield Pooling

Continuous Hopfield Networks have recently been shown to be equivalent to iterative attention (Ramsauer et al., 2020), where current attention systems are equivalent to a Hopfield Network with no update steps. Hopfield pooling is a special case of a Hopfield Network, where the query for the network is a single vector. Hopfield pooling provides a way to summarize k embeddings into a single fixed-length embedding in an iterative way. Additionally, the single query vector can be a learned embedding, and this embedding can be different for different tasks in a multi-task system, which is useful when the semantics for each task are different. For each Event Slot ES_i^j from the set of Event Slots ES_i defined for *Event Type$_i$* (with $i = 1, ..., 5$ corresponding to the Event Types and their slots

listed in Table 1), Hopfield pooling enables the MT-EsE.BHP to learn text-span embeddings. For example, when learning the text-span embedding for the span *"my sister"* while considering the Event Slot *gender*, the pooling will likely entirely focus on the contextual embedding for *"sister"*, while when considering the *relation* Event Slot, the pooling will likely focus equally on both contextual embeddings for the words *"my"* and *"sister*, as they are both relevant to identify that the author of the tweet has a relationship with someone mentioned in that tweet text span.

Figure 3 illustrates the process of performing Hopfield pooling for an Event Slot ES_i^k of any *Event Type$_i$*, resulting in the text-span embedding for a tweet span. This process is based on the learning of an *embedding* for the Event Slot ES_i^k of *Event Type$_i$*, denoted as $emb(ES_i^k)$. As shown in Figure 3, $emb(ES_i^k)$ is randomly initialized. At each iteration, a vector multiplication between the contextual embeddings of the words from the tweet text span and the current Event Slot embedding $emb(ES_i^k(t))$ takes place. The vector product is producing unnormalized scores, which we normalize into $w_1^i, w_2^i, \ldots, w_k^i$ with the Softmax operation. These scores are then multiplied by their respective contextualized embeddings $c_1, c_2, \ldots, c_k$ and point-wise added together to produce a new single embedding. If we have not yet performed the required number of Hopfield update iterations, then the new embedding becomes $emb(ES_i^k(t+1))$ and

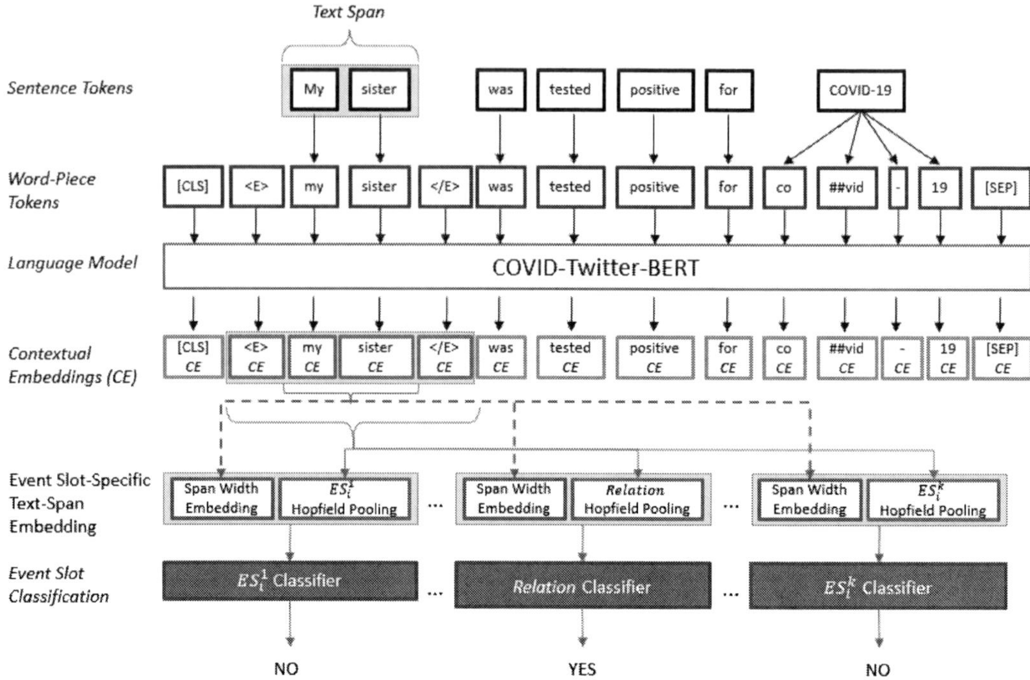

Figure 4: Example of Event Extraction for the *relation* Event Slot of the TESTED POSITIVE Event Type.

we repeat the whole process again. Otherwise, the update iterations are finished, which results in the final Event Slot-specific Hopfield span embedding.

3.3 A Detailed Example

Figure 4 provides a detailed description of how the MT-EsE.BHP operates on a sentence from a tweet categorized under the TESTED POSITIVE Event Type, when mapping the text span "*My sister*" into the *relation* Event Slot. First, the text span is surrounded by special tokens (<E> ... </E>). These tokens provide the language model contextual information as to where the text span is located in the sentence. Next, the sentence is word-piece tokenized (Devlin et al., 2019) and provided as an input to the COVID-Twitter-BERT language model. The language model generates a contextualized embedding for each word-piece token, which provides a representation of the word-piece token with respect to the whole sentence. Next, we perform Event Slot-specific Hopfield pooling for every Event Slot associated with the TESTED POSITIVE Event Type to produce the embedding of the text span, in the same manner as detailed in Section 3.2 and illustrated in Figure 3. As we have discussed Section 3.2, Hopfield pooling also learns an embedding for each Event Slot of TESTED POSITIVE.

In Figure 4 the embedding of the Event Slot *relation* is illustrated, as well as embeddings learned for other Event Slots, e.g. ES_i^1 or ES_i^k. These embeddings are concatenating together a learned *width embedding* which represents the width of the text span that may be potentially mapped into the Event Slots. The width embedding provides information to each Event Slot classifier as to the width of the text span, since this information is lost when performing Hopfield pooling. Finally, a binary Event Slot Classifier for every Event Slot of TESTED POSITIVE decides whether the text span can be mapped in its corresponding Event Slot. Figure 4 shows the illustrated text span is mapped in the *relation* Event Slot.

4 Results

We trained five separate models, for each of the five Event Types, and they all share the same training schedule and settings: We use an initial learning rate of $2e^{-5}$, warmed up to from 0 over the first epoch and then decayed to 0 linearly for the 9 remaining epochs, with the ADAM optimizer (Kingma and Ba, 2015). We train with gradient accumulation, where we accumulate the gradients for a batch size of 32 with 4 batches of size 8. We initialize the span width embeddings with a nor-

Overall	Precision	Recall	F_1
Best	75.32	71.18	65.98
Median	68.14	56.30	62.76
Worst	53.77	42.77	51.14
MT-EsE.BHP	75.32	56.79	64.76
TESTED POSITIVE	**Precision**	**Recall**	**F_1**
Best	85.69	62.67	69.73
Median	78.32	57.54	67.67
Worst	44.32	44.71	44.52
MT-EsE.BHP	82.98	60.13	69.73
TESTED NEGATIVE	**Precision**	**Recall**	**F_1**
Best	71.07	71.94	70.30
Median	66.14	64.30	63.98
Worst	53.91	40.83	50.56
MT-EsE.BHP	71.07	61.87	66.15
CAN NOT TEST	**Precision**	**Recall**	**F_1**
Best	68.63	72.40	65.23
Median	64.13	52.11	55.79
Worst	46.46	43.51	45.19
MT-EsE.BHP	68.63	56.82	62.17
DEATH	**Precision**	**Recall**	**F_1**
Best	72.40	78.55	69.42
Median	57.42	64.36	61.16
Worst	49.17	52.15	52.12
MT-EsE.BHP	61.64	62.05	61.84
CURE	**Precision**	**Recall**	**F_1**
Best	84.05	78.43	62.05
Median	76.96	46.61	59.76
Worst	49.61	34.82	45.11
MT-EsE.BHP	83.52	45.30	58.74

Table 2: Overall results and results from each Event Type for the MT-EsE.BHP in the official shared-task evaluation.

mal distribution, an embedding size of 25, and 100 embeddings for widths $0 - 99$, where spans above width 99 are represented by the width 99 embedding. We apply a dropout rate of 0.10 to the output of the Slot-specific Hopfield span embedding, and we found best development performance when the number of update steps for Hopfield pooling was 2 with only 1 attention head. We split the provided collection of tweets into train (60%), dev (15%), and test (25%) sets for model development and assessment. We select threshold values for each binary slot classifier based on maximum F_1-score[1] performance on the dev set. We selected this training schedule and these hyper-parameters based on initial experiments of our system on the TESTED POSITIVE collection of tweets. We discuss the impact of this decision further in Section 5.

---

[1] F_1-score is defined as $F_1 = 2 \times Precision \times Recall/(Precision + Recall)$

Performance on the shared-task was determined based on micro F_1 score for the mapping of text spans into Event Slots, computed for each Event Type and overall, on an unseen evaluation set of 2500 tweets with 500 tweets per Event Type. Participating teams were provided the evaluation tweets 5 days in advance of the run submission deadline, and only one submission was allowed per team. Our team name and single submission were titled "HLTRI" and utilized the MT-EsE.BHP described in this paper. Our system produced an overall F_1 score of 64.76% for mapping Event Slots across all Event Types, which accounts for the 2nd-best overall results in the official shared-task evaluation. Our system obtained the best results for mapping tweets text spans in the Event Slots of the TESTED POSITIVE Event Type, and 3rd-best for the TESTED NEGATIVE Event Type, 2nd-best for the CAN NOT TEST Event Type, 3rd-best for the DEATH Event Type, and 4th for CURE Event Type. Overall the precision, recall, and F_1 scores for the mapping of text spans into Event Slots in the official shared-task evaluation are provided in Table 2. In the Table, we also show the best, median, and worst precision, recall, and F_1 scores across all team submissions. We believe that our system performed best on the mapping into Event Slots for the TESTED POSITIVE Event Type, because in the training data, we were provided with the most annotated tweets for this Event Type. We also performed well on mapping into the Event Slots of the CAN NOT TEST Event Type, out-performing the median F_1 score by 6.38%. Our system was competitive on all but the CURE Event Type, scoring above the median F_1 scores and coming close to the best F_1 scores on all other Event Types.

Detailed results are provided in Table 3 for each mapping of a text span into an Event Slot when using the official shared-task evaluation script. As seen, with the exclusion of the CURE Event Type, we largely score well on mapping into Event Slots for which more training examples were provided, and even score well for mapping into Event Slots for which much less training data was available, due to our multi-task learning framework setting for learning how to map jointly text spans into Event Slots. We explain our poor performance for mapping into the Event Slots pertaining to the CURE Event Type because our system obtained poor recall across all three Event Slots, but particularly in the *who_cure* Event Slot.

TESTED POS.	Precision	Recall	F_1	#
age	66.67	40.00	50.00	5
close_contact	71.43	32.79	44.94	61
employer	75.93	33.88	46.86	121
gender	91.23	51.49	65.82	101
name	86.93	81.60	84.18	375
recent_travel	62.50	18.52	28.57	27
relation	50.00	55.00	52.38	20
when	60.00	40.91	48.65	22
where	84.03	56.82	67.80	176
TESTED NEG.	**Precision**	**Recall**	**F_1**	**#**
age	100.00	55.56	71.43	9
close_contact	20.00	14.81	17.02	27
gender	75.53	60.17	66.98	118
name	76.01	75.18	75.60	274
relation	75.00	51.92	61.36	52
when	40.00	29.63	34.04	27
where	60.53	46.94	52.87	49
CAN NOT TEST	**Precision**	**Recall**	**F_1**	**#**
relation	90.62	46.77	61.70	62
symptoms	71.79	60.87	65.88	46
name	65.38	66.67	66.02	153
when	66.67	11.76	20.00	17
where	56.00	46.67	50.91	30
DEATH	**Precision**	**Recall**	**F_1**	**#**
age	83.33	90.91	86.96	33
name	57.93	60.43	59.15	139
relation	100.00	30.30	46.51	33
when	57.14	72.73	64.00	33
where	55.56	61.54	58.39	65
CURE	**Precision**	**Recall**	**F_1**	**#**
opinion	83.70	50.66	63.11	152
what_cure	84.85	53.44	65.57	262
who_cure	81.05	32.77	46.67	235

Table 3: Detailed results produced by the MT-EsE.BHP.

5 Discussion

The event organizers released the annotated evaluation tweets at the same time they released evaluation results, therefore we were able to analyze Event Slot-specific performance and perform a qualitative error analysis on specific tweets and Event Slots which were incorrectly classified.

We found that our system performed best on mapping text spans into Event Slots for the largest Event Type: TESTED POSITIVE, and within that Event Type also performed better on average on Event Slots which had more examples in the training data. While this is partially due to the fact that the TESTED POSITIVE Event Type has the largest collection of annotated tweets, approximately double that of all other Event Types, this is also likely due to the fact that most of the training hyper-parameters, listed in Section 4, were selected based on initial experimental performance on the training TESTED POSITIVE collection. This hyper-parameter selection decision likely biased our overall architecture towards improved performance on mapping of a text span into an Event Slot for the TESTED POSITIVE Event Type at the cost of reducing performance in other Event Types. This hypothesis is supported by our shared-task evaluation ranking, where we came in 1st in TESTED POSITIVE but placed lower in all other Event Types.

Table 3 provides detailed performance for each Event Slot along with the number of examples in the evaluation dataset. We see that our multi-task learning framework maintains performance for some Event Slots that were provided with a small set of examples, such as *age*, while other for Event Slots, provided also with a small set of examples, such as *when*, there is clearly room for improvement. We believe that sharing a learned language model informed by COVID-Twitter-BERT contributes to this baseline level of performance, while the slot-specific span representation using Hopfield pooling improves performance upwards when performing mapping into Event Slots that were provided with a larger set if examples. Hopfield pooling provides the system a mechanism by which to learn how to best merge the shared contextual representation produced by COVID-Twitter-BERT into a slot-specific representation useful for slot-specific classification. We also see that mapping text spans into Event Slots for the CURE Event Type had high precision, but very poor recall even with a relatively large number of provided examples, leading to our poor F_1 scores for this Event Type. More specifically, we see that the recall of the *who_cure* slot is extremely poor, therefore we investigate this further in our error analysis.

Table 4 lists tweets in which our system was incorrect. Example 1 demonstrates the failure of the MT-EsE.BHP to identify that *"Vice President Mike Pence"* is an *employer* who's staff member tested positive for coronavirus. This is likely due to the fact that, in the collection of tweets, it is atypical to list a single person as an employer as opposed to the organization they employ the employee through. More tweets which follow this pattern would likely be necessary to learn this use of *employer*. A typical mistake made by the MT-EsE.BHP on the *close_contact* slot is visible in Example 2, where the system fails to recognize the implication that *"the mother"* was not a close

Event Type	Tweet with Text Span	MT-EsE.BHP	Annotation
TESTED POS.	"Staffer for [*Vice President Mike Pence*] tests positive for coronavirus <url>"	×	*employer*
TESTED NEG.	"Reports coming out that the infant child of [*the mother*] who died of Covid-19 tested negative for Covid-19. The Sars-COV-2 is mysterious."	*close_contact*	×
CAN NOT TEST	"[*@LouisianaGov*] @LADeptHealth Still can't get tested though."	×	*where*
DEATH	"@FALLOFTHECABAL [*I*] personally know 3 1ST respknders and 2 nurses who have died from complications of COVID-19. i have no horse in this race so to speak."	×	*relation*
CURE	"At @WhiteHouse briefing today, a so-called reporter said that [*Biden*] recommends flying our flag at half-staff. Well,, That sure must be the cure for #COVID19. My suggestion: Wait till AFTER the PANDEMIC is OVER, then, in honor of those who died, fly the mast at half-staff."	*who_cure*	×
CURE	"@DonaldJTrumpJr [*You*] advocate drinking bleach to cure covid-19. We are all aware of how much you understand disease."	×	*who_cure*

Table 4: Tweets and text spans where the MT-EsE.BHP incorrectly classifies an Event Slot.

contact, since she had COVID-19 and died from it, but the "*infant child*" was a close contact due to the implied closeness of a mother to her infant child. Example 3 shows the difficulty of noticing that an author tweeting "*@LouisianaGov*" due to their inability to get tested likely lives in the location of Louisiana. Typos are prevalent in user-generated text, and Example 4 demonstrates a typo with "*1st respknders*" which likely causes the language model to miss the contextual clues that the author of the tweet has some *relation* with first responders and nurses who have contracted and died from complications due to COVID-19. Example 4 and 5 demonstrate one of the primary reasons we believe our system performs poorly on the CURE Event Type, and specifically the *who_cure* Event Slot. We see sarcasm demonstrated in Example 4, where the author of the tweet is sarcastically stating that Biden's recommendation of flying a flag at half-staff is an actual potential cure for COVID-19. Tay et al. (2018) discuss the "sophisticated speech act" of sarcasm in the context of social communities such as Twitter and Reddit, and they note that sarcasm can severely disrupt opinion mining systems. Sarcasm can be very difficult to identify (Joshi et al., 2017), and many of the tweets discussing COVID-19 cures contain sarcastic content which can be difficult to distinguish. Our system mistakenly identified Biden as *who_cure*, while the annotator picked up on the sarcasm and did not annotate this instance. Example 5 demonstrates a debatable instance of sarcasm on the other side, where the annotation states that "*You*", being Donald Trump Jr., advocates for drinking bleach as a cure for COVID-19. Our system does not identify that Donald Trump Jr. advocates for the cure of drinking bleach, but the annotator agrees that, in this instance, the author of the tweet is legitimately making the claim that Donald Trump Jr. advocates for this cure.

6 Conclusion

In this paper we described the Multi-Task Event-specific Extraction system using BERT and Hopfield Pooling (MT-EsE.BHP) that was developed for the W-NUT 2020 Shared Task 3. Our system learned how to take advantage of contextual embeddings such that embeddings for text spans can be learned, while also learning embeddings for each Event Slot of each Event Type. This was made possible by using Hopfield Pooling. The text span embeddings informed binary classifiers (one for each Event Slot) that decided whether tweet text spans can be mapped into an Event Slot or not. Separate such binary classifiers were trained for each Event Type. The results that we obtained are promising. These results could be further used to learn how to associate Event Slots for each mention of an Event Type in tweets, instead of producing only a bag of filled Event Slots. This would be a requirement for knowledge extraction from COVID-relevant tweets useful for Public Health applications.

References

Jacob Devlin, Ming-Wei Chang, Kenton Lee, and Kristina Toutanova. 2019. BERT: Pre-training of deep bidirectional transformers for language understanding. In *Proceedings of the 2019 Conference of the North American Chapter of the Association for Computational Linguistics: Human Language Technologies, Volume 1 (Long and Short Papers)*, pages 4171–4186. Association for Computational Linguistics.

Markus Eberts and Adrian Ulges. 2020. Span-based joint entity and relation extraction with transformer pre-training. In *European Conference on Artificial Intelligence*.

Aditya Joshi, Pushpak Bhattacharyya, and Mark J. Carman. 2017. Automatic sarcasm detection: A survey. *ACM Comput. Surv.*, 50(5).

Mandar Joshi, Danqi Chen, Yinhan Liu, Daniel S. Weld, Luke Zettlemoyer, and Omer Levy. 2020. Spanbert: Improving pre-training by representing and predicting spans. *Transactions of the Association for Computational Linguistics*, 8:64–77.

Diederik P. Kingma and Jimmy Ba. 2015. Adam: A method for stochastic optimization. In *3rd International Conference on Learning Representations, ICLR 2015, San Diego, CA, USA, May 7-9, 2015, Conference Track Proceedings*.

Tim Mackey, Vidya Purushothaman, Jiawei Li, Neal Shah, Matthew Nali, Cortni Bardier, Bryan Liang, Mingxiang Cai, and Raphael Cuomo. 2020. Machine learning to detect self-reporting of symptoms, testing access, and recovery associated with covid-19 on twitter: Retrospective big data infoveillance study. *JMIR Public Health Surveill*, 6(2):e19509.

Martin Müller, Marcel Salathé, and Per E Kummervold. 2020. Covid-twitter-bert: A natural language processing model to analyse covid-19 content on twitter. *https://arxiv.org/abs/2005.07503*.

Hubert Ramsauer, Bernhard Schäfl, Johannes Lehner, Philipp Seidl, Michael Widrich, Lukas Gruber, Markus Holzleitner, Milena Pavlović, Geir Kjetil Sandve, Victor Greiff, David Kreil, Michael Kopp, Günter Klambauer, Johannes Brandstetter, and Sepp Hochreiter. 2020. Hopfield networks is all you need. *https://arxiv.org/abs/2006.02567*.

Yi Tay, Anh Tuan Luu, Siu Cheung Hui, and Jian Su. 2018. Reasoning with sarcasm by reading in-between. In *Proceedings of the 56th Annual Meeting of the Association for Computational Linguistics (Volume 1: Long Papers)*, pages 1010–1020, Melbourne, Australia. Association for Computational Linguistics.

Xiaohui Yan, Jiafeng Guo, Yanyan Lan, and Xueqi Cheng. 2013. A biterm topic model for short texts. pages 1445–1456.

Zhilin Yang, Zihang Dai, Yiming Yang, Jaime Carbonell, Russ R Salakhutdinov, and Quoc V Le. 2019. Xlnet: Generalized autoregressive pretraining for language understanding. In H. Wallach, H. Larochelle, A. Beygelzimer, F. dAlché-Buc, E. Fox, and R. Garnett, editors, *Advances in Neural Information Processing Systems 32*, pages 5753–5763. Curran Associates, Inc.

Yipeng Zhang, Hanjia Lyu, Yubao Liu, Xiyang Zhang, Yu Wang, and Jiebo Luo. 2020. Monitoring depression trend on twitter during the covid-19 pandemic. *https://arxiv.org/abs/2007.00228*.

Shi Zong, Ashutosh Baheti, Wei Xu, and Alan Ritter. 2020. Extracting covid-19 events from twitter.

Association for Computational Linguistics
209 N. Eighth Street
Stroudsburg, Pennsylvania 18360